PISA 2012 Results: Excellence Through Equity

GIVING EVERY STUDENT
THE CHANCE TO SUCCEED
(VOLUME II)

OECD

BETTER POLICIES FOR BETTER LIVES

This work is published on the responsibility of the Secretary-General of the OECD. The opinions expressed and arguments employed herein do not necessarily reflect the official views of the Organisation or of the governments of its member countries.

This document and any map included herein are without prejudice to the status of or sovereignty over any territory, to the delimitation of international frontiers and boundaries and to the name of any territory, city or area.

Please cite this publication as:

OECD (2013), *PISA 2012 Results: Excellence Through Equity: Giving Every Student the Chance to Succeed (Volume II)*, PISA, OECD Publishing.
http://dx.doi.org/10.1787/9789264201132-en

ISBN 978-92-64-20112-5 (print)
ISBN 978-92-64-20113-2 (PDF)

Note by Turkey: The information in this document with reference to "Cyprus" relates to the southern part of the Island. There is no single authority representing both Turkish and Greek Cypriot people on the Island. Turkey recognises the Turkish Republic of Northern Cyprus (TRNC). Until a lasting and equitable solution is found within the context of the United Nations, Turkey shall preserve its position concerning the "Cyprus issue".

Note by all the European Union Member States of the OECD and the European Union: The Republic of Cyprus is recognised by all members of the United Nations with the exception of Turkey. The information in this document relates to the area under the effective control of the Government of the Republic of Cyprus.

The statistical data for Israel are supplied by and under the responsibility of the relevant Israeli authorities. The use of such data by the OECD is without prejudice to the status of the Golan Heights, East Jerusalem and Israeli settlements in the West Bank under the terms of international law.

Photo credits:
© Flying Colours Ltd/Getty Images
© Jacobs Stock Photography/Kzenon
© khoa vu/Flickr/Getty Images
© Mel Curtis/Corbis
© Shutterstock/Kzenon
© Simon Jarratt/Corbis

Corrigenda to OECD publications may be found on line at: *www.oecd.org/publishing/corrigenda*.
© OECD 2013

Foreword

Equipping citizens with the skills necessary to achieve their full potential, participate in an increasingly interconnected global economy, and ultimately convert better jobs into better lives is a central preoccupation of policy makers around the world. Results from the OECD's recent Survey of Adult Skills show that highly skilled adults are twice as likely to be employed and almost three times more likely to earn an above-median salary than poorly skilled adults. In other words, poor skills severely limit people's access to better-paying and more rewarding jobs. Highly skilled people are also more likely to volunteer, see themselves as actors rather than as objects of political processes, and are more likely to trust others. Fairness, integrity and inclusiveness in public policy thus all hinge on the skills of citizens.

The ongoing economic crisis has only increased the urgency of investing in the acquisition and development of citizens' skills – both through the education system and in the workplace. At a time when public budgets are tight and there is little room for further monetary and fiscal stimulus, investing in structural reforms to boost productivity, such as education and skills development, is key to future growth. Indeed, investment in these areas is essential to support the recovery, as well as to address long-standing issues such as youth unemployment and gender inequality.

In this context, more and more countries are looking beyond their own borders for evidence of the most successful and efficient policies and practices. Indeed, in a global economy, success is no longer measured against national standards alone, but against the best-performing and most rapidly improving education systems. Over the past decade, the OECD Programme for International Student Assessment, PISA, has become the world's premier yardstick for evaluating the quality, equity and efficiency of school systems. But the evidence base that PISA has produced goes well beyond statistical benchmarking. By identifying the characteristics of high-performing education systems PISA allows governments and educators to identify effective policies that they can then adapt to their local contexts.

The results from the PISA 2012 assessment, which was conducted at a time when many of the 65 participating countries and economies were grappling with the effects of the crisis, reveal wide differences in education outcomes, both within and across countries. Using the data collected in previous PISA rounds, we have been able to track the evolution of student performance over time and across subjects. Of the 64 countries and economies with comparable data, 40 improved their average performance in at least one subject. Top performers such as Shanghai in China or Singapore were able to further extend their lead, while countries like Brazil, Mexico, Tunisia and Turkey achieved major improvements from previously low levels of performance.

Some education systems have demonstrated that it is possible to secure strong and equitable learning outcomes at the same time as achieving rapid improvements. Of the 13 countries and economies that significantly improved their mathematics performance between 2003 and 2012, three also show improvements in equity in education during the same period, and another nine improved their performance while maintaining an already high level of equity – proving that countries do not have to sacrifice high performance to achieve equity in education opportunities.

Nonetheless, PISA 2012 results show wide differences between countries in mathematics performance. The equivalent of almost six years of schooling, 245 score points, separates the highest and lowest average performances of the countries that took part in the PISA 2012 mathematics assessment. The difference in mathematics performances within countries is even greater, with over 300 points – the equivalent of more than seven years of schooling – often separating the highest- and the lowest-achieving students in a country. Clearly, all countries and economies have excellent students, but few have enabled all students to excel.

The report also reveals worrying gender differences in students' attitudes towards mathematics: even when girls perform as well as boys in mathematics, they report less perseverance, less motivation to learn mathematics, less belief in their own mathematics skills, and higher levels of anxiety about mathematics. While the average girl underperforms in mathematics compared with the average boy, the gender gap in favour of boys is even wider among the highest achieving students. These findings have serious implications not only for higher education, where young women are already under-represented in the science, technology, engineering and mathematics fields of study, but also later on, when these young women enter the labour market. This confirms the findings of the OECD Gender Strategy, which identifies some of the factors that create – and widen – the gender gap in education, labour and entrepreneurship. Supporting girls' positive attitudes towards and investment in learning mathematics will go a long way towards narrowing this gap.

PISA 2012 also finds that the highest-performing school systems are those that allocate educational resources more equitably among advantaged and disadvantaged schools and that grant more autonomy over curricula and assessments to individual schools. A belief that all students can achieve at a high level and a willingness to engage all stakeholders in education – including students, through such channels as seeking student feedback on teaching practices – are hallmarks of successful school systems.

PISA is not only an accurate indicator of students' abilities to participate fully in society after compulsory school, but also a powerful tool that countries and economies can use to fine-tune their education policies. There is no single combination of policies and practices that will work for everyone, everywhere. Every country has room for improvement, even the top performers. That's why the OECD produces this triennial report on the state of education across the globe: to share evidence of the best policies and practices and to offer our timely and targeted support to help countries provide the best education possible for all of their students. With high levels of youth unemployment, rising inequality, a significant gender gap, and an urgent need to boost growth in many countries, we have no time to lose. The OECD stands ready to support policy makers in this challenging and crucial endeavour.

Angel Gurría
OECD Secretary-General

Acknowledgements

This report is the product of a collaborative effort between the countries participating in PISA, the experts and institutions working within the framework of the PISA Consortium, and the OECD Secretariat. The report was drafted by Andreas Schleicher, Francesco Avvisati, Francesca Borgonovi, Miyako Ikeda, Hiromichi Katayama, Flore-Anne Messy, Chiara Monticone, Guillermo Montt, Sophie Vayssettes and Pablo Zoido of the OECD Directorate for Education and Skills and the Directorate for Financial Affairs, with statistical support from Simone Bloem and Giannina Rech and editorial oversight by Marilyn Achiron. Additional analytical and editorial support was provided by Adele Atkinson, Jonas Bertling, Marika Boiron, Célia Braga-Schich, Tracey Burns, Michael Davidson, Cassandra Davis, Elizabeth Del Bourgo, John A. Dossey, Joachim Funke, Samuel Greiff, Tue Halgreen, Ben Jensen, Eckhard Klieme, André Laboul, Henry Levin, Juliette Mendelovits, Tadakazu Miki, Christian Monseur, Simon Normandeau, Mathilde Overduin, Elodie Pools, Dara Ramalingam, William H. Schmidt (whose work was supported by the Thomas J. Alexander fellowship programme), Kaye Stacey, Lazar Stankov, Ross Turner, Elisabeth Villoutreix and Allan Wigfield. The system-level data collection was conducted by the OECD NESLI (INES Network for the Collection and Adjudication of System-Level Descriptive Information on Educational Structures, Policies and Practices) team: Bonifacio Agapin, Estelle Herbaut and Jean Yip. Volume II also draws on the analytic work undertaken by Jaap Scheerens and Douglas Willms in the context of PISA 2000. Administrative support was provided by Claire Chetcuti, Juliet Evans, Jennah Huxley and Diana Tramontano.

The OECD contracted the Australian Council for Educational Research (ACER) to manage the development of the mathematics, problem solving and financial literacy frameworks for PISA 2012. Achieve was also contracted by the OECD to develop the mathematics framework with ACER. The expert group that guided the preparation of the mathematics assessment framework and instruments was chaired by Kaye Stacey; Joachim Funke chaired the expert group that guided the preparation of the problem-solving assessment framework and instruments; and Annamaria Lusardi led the expert group that guided the preparation of the financial literacy assessment framework and instruments. The PISA assessment instruments and the data underlying the report were prepared by the PISA Consortium, under the direction of Raymond Adams at ACER.

The development of the report was steered by the PISA Governing Board, which is chaired by Lorna Bertrand (United Kingdom), with Benő Csapó (Hungary), Daniel McGrath (United States) and Ryo Watanabe (Japan) as vice chairs. Annex C of the volumes lists the members of the various PISA bodies, as well as the individual experts and consultants who have contributed to this report and to PISA in general.

Table of Contents

BOXES

FIGURES

TABLES

This book has...

StatLinkS
A service that delivers Excel® files
from the printed page!

Look for the *StatLinks* at the bottom left-hand corner of the tables or graphs in this book.
To download the matching Excel® spreadsheet, just type the link into your Internet browser,
starting with the *http://dx.doi.org* prefix.
If you're reading the PDF e-book edition, and your PC is connected to the Internet, simply
click on the link. You'll find *StatLinks* appearing in more OECD books.

Executive Summary

PISA defines equity in education as providing all students, regardless of gender, family background or socio-economic status, with opportunities to benefit from education. Defined in this way, equity does not imply that everyone should have the same results. It does mean, however, that students' socio-economic status or the fact that they have an immigrant background has little or no impact on their performance, and that all students, regardless of their background, are offered access to quality educational resources and opportunities to learn.

Of the 39 countries and economies that participated in both PISA 2003 and 2012, Mexico, Turkey and Germany improved both their mathematics performance and their levels of equity in education during the period.

These three countries improved both equity and performance either by reducing the extent to which students' socio-economic background predicts their mathematics performance or by reducing the average difference in performance between advantaged and disadvantaged students. Ten additional countries and economies improved their average performance between 2003 and 2012 while maintaining their equity levels.

Australia, Canada, Estonia, Finland, Hong Kong-China, Japan, Korea, Liechtenstein, Macao-China and the Netherlands and achieve high levels of performance and equity in education opportunities as assessed in PISA 2012.

Equity in education opportunities is average in 10 countries and economies and below average in 3 of the 23 countries and economies that perform above the OECD average in mathematics. In all countries and economies that participated in PISA 2012, a student's socio-economic status has a strong impact on his or her performance. Across OECD countries, 15% of the variation in student performance in mathematics is attributed to differences in students' socio-economic status. Among high-performing countries, this proportion ranges from 3% in Macao-China to 20% in Belgium. In contrast, in Bulgaria, Chile, France, Hungary, Peru, the Slovak Republic and Uruguay more than 20% of the difference in student performance can be attributed to students' socio-economic status.

Across OECD countries, a more socio-economically advantaged student scores 39 points higher in mathematics – the equivalent of nearly one year of schooling – than a less-advantaged student.

Among the 23 highest-performing countries and economies, performance differences related to socio-economic status are narrower-than-average in Canada, Estonia, Finland, Hong Kong-China, Macao-China and Viet Nam, about average in 12 countries and economies, and wider-than-average in 5. Striking performance differences are also observed between students in advantaged schools and those in disadvantaged schools: students attending socio-economically advantaged schools outscore those in disadvantaged schools by more than 104 points in mathematics, on average across OECD countries.

Across OECD countries 6% of the entire student population are "resilient", meaning that they beat the socio-economic odds against them and exceed expectations, when compared with students in other countries.

In Hong Kong-China, Macao-China, Shanghai-China, Singapore and Viet Nam 13% or more of the overall student population are resilient and perform among the top 25% across all participating countries after taking socio-economic status into account. Between 2003 and 2012, the share of resilient students increased in Germany, Italy, Mexico, Poland, Tunisia and Turkey.

The share of immigrant students in OECD countries increased from 9% in 2003 to 12% in 2012 while the difference in mathematics performance between immigrant and non-immigrant students shrank by 10 score points during the same period.

Immigrant students tend to be socio-economically disadvantaged in comparison to non-immigrant students, yet even when comparing students of similar socio-economic status, immigrant students perform worse in mathematics than non-immigrant students. In 2012, they scored an average of 37 points lower in mathematics than non-immigrant students before accounting for socio-economic status, and an average of 23 points lower after accounting for socio-economic status. In Canada, Ireland, Israel, New Zealand and the United Kingdom, however, immigrant and non-immigrant students perform equally well.

The concentration of immigrant students in a school is not, in itself, associated with poor performance.

In general, immigrant students and those who do not speak the language of assessment at home tend to be concentrated in disadvantaged schools. In the United States, for example, 40% of students in disadvantaged schools are immigrants, whereas 13% of students in advantaged schools are. Across OECD countries, students who attend schools where more than one in four students are immigrants tend to perform worse than those in schools with no immigrant students. However, the 19 score-point difference between the two groups is more than halved – to 7 points – after the socio-economic status of the students and schools is taken into account. Belgium, Estonia, Greece, Mexico and Portugal are the only countries where there are performance differences of 20 score points or more between the two groups, after accounting for socio-economic status.

Across OECD countries, students who reported that they had attended pre-primary school for more than one year score 53 points higher in mathematics – the equivalent of more than one year of schooling – than students who had not attended pre-primary education.

In all but two countries with available data, students who had attended pre-primary education for more than one year outperformed students who had not, before taking socio-economic status into account. This finding remains unchanged even after socio-economic status is accounted for, except in Croatia, Estonia, Ireland, Korea, Latvia, Slovenia and the United States.

OECD countries allocate at least an equal, if not a larger, number of mathematics teachers to socio-economically disadvantaged schools as to advantaged schools; but disadvantaged schools tend to have great difficulty in attracting qualified teachers.

In the Netherlands, the proportion of qualified teachers in advantaged schools (52%) is three times larger than the proportion of qualified teachers in disadvantaged schools (14%), while the student-teacher ratio is 28% higher in advantaged schools than it is in disadvantaged schools (18 students compared with 14 students per teacher, respectively).

■ Table II.A [1/2] ■
SNAPSHOT OF EQUITY IN EDUCATION IN PISA 2012 AND CHANGE SINCE PISA 2003

Countries/economies with mean mathematics performance above the OECD average
Countries/economies where the strength of the relationship between mathematics performance and socio-economic status is below the OECD average
Countries/economies where performance differences across socio-economic groups are below the OECD average

Countries/economies with mean mathematics performance not statistically different from the OECD average
Countries/economies where the strength of the relationship between mathematics performance and socio-economic status is not statistically different from the OECD average
Countries/economies where performance differences across socio-economic spectrum are not statistically different from the OECD average

Countries/economies with mean mathematics performance below the OECD average
Countries/economies where the strength of the relationship between mathematics performance and socio-economic status is above the OECD average
Countries/economies where performance differences across socio-economic spectrum are above the OECD average

	Mean performance in mathematics	Strength of the relationship between mathematics performance and socio-economic status	Performance difference across socio-economic groups	Percentage of resilient students
	Mean score	Percentage of explained variance in mathematics performance	Score-point difference in mathematics associated with a one-unit increase in ESCS[1]	Percentage of disadvantaged students who perform among the top 25% of students across all participating countries and economies, after accounting for ESCS[1]
OECD average	494	14.8	39	6.4
Macao-China	538	2.6	17	16.9
Hong Kong-China	561	7.5	27	18.1
Liechtenstein	535	7.6	28	10.1
Estonia	521	8.6	29	9.5
Finland	519	9.4	33	8.1
Canada	518	9.4	31	8.3
Japan	536	9.8	41	11.3
Korea	554	10.1	42	12.7
Netherlands	523	11.5	40	8.6
Australia	504	12.3	42	6.3
Switzerland	531	12.8	38	9.9
Singapore	573	14.4	44	15.1
Ireland	501	14.6	38	6.3
Viet Nam	511	14.6	29	16.9
Shanghai-China	613	15.1	41	19.2
Slovenia	501	15.6	42	5.9
Austria	506	15.8	43	6.1
Denmark	500	16.5	39	4.9
Poland	518	16.6	41	8.4
Germany	514	16.9	43	7.5
Chinese Taipei	560	17.9	58	12.3
New Zealand	500	18.4	52	5.3
Belgium	515	19.6	49	7.1
Norway	489	7.4	32	5.3
Iceland	493	7.7	31	5.2
United Kingdom	494	12.5	41	5.8
Latvia	491	14.7	35	6.4
Czech Republic	499	16.2	51	5.9
Portugal	487	19.6	35	7.7
France	495	22.5	57	5.4
Qatar	376	5.6	27	0.4
Kazakhstan	432	8.0	27	2.1
Jordan	386	8.4	22	0.9
Indonesia	375	9.6	20	2.5
United Arab Emirates	434	9.8	33	1.2
Thailand	427	9.9	22	6.3
Italy	485	10.1	30	6.4
Mexico	413	10.4	19	3.9
Sweden	478	10.6	36	4.3
Russian Federation	482	11.4	38	5.2
Serbia	449	11.7	34	3.6
Croatia	471	12.0	36	5.1
Tunisia	388	12.4	22	2.9
Montenegro	410	12.7	33	1.3
Malaysia	421	13.4	30	2.7
Lithuania	479	13.8	36	5.6
Cyprus*	440	14.1	38	1.9
Turkey	448	14.5	32	7.2
United States	481	14.8	35	5.2
Argentina	388	15.1	26	1.1
Colombia	376	15.4	25	1.5
Greece	453	15.5	34	3.2
Brazil	391	15.7	26	1.7
Spain	484	15.8	34	6.4
Israel	466	17.2	51	3.1
Luxembourg	490	18.3	37	6.1
Costa Rica	407	18.9	24	1.9
Romania	445	19.3	38	2.8
Bulgaria	439	22.3	42	2.1
Uruguay	409	22.8	37	2.1
Hungary	477	23.1	47	4.1
Chile	423	23.1	34	1.7
Peru	368	23.4	33	0.5
Slovak Republic	482	24.6	54	3.9

Note: Countries/economies in which the change between PISA 2003 and PISA 2012 (2012 - 2003) is statistically significant are marked in bold.
1. ESCS refers to the *PISA index of economic, social and cultural status*.
Countries and economies are presented in three groups: those whose mean performance is above the OECD average, those whose mean performance is not statistically different from the OECD average, and those whose mean performance is below the OECD average. Within each group, countries and economies are ranked in ascending order of the strength of the relationship between performance and socio-economic status observed in PISA 2012.
* See notes in the Reader's Guide.
Source: OECD, PISA 2012 Database, Tables II.2.1, II.2.7a, II.2.7b, II.2.8b and II.2.9b.
StatLink ᵃᵐˢᵖ http://dx.doi.org/10.1787/888932964889

■ Table II.A [2/2] ■
SNAPSHOT OF EQUITY IN EDUCATION IN PISA 2012 AND CHANGE SINCE PISA 2003

	Countries/economies with mean mathematics performance above the OECD average
	Countries/economies where the strength of the relationship between mathematics performance and socio-economic status is below the OECD average
	Countries/economies where performance differences across socio-economic groups are below the OECD average
	Countries/economies with mean mathematics performance not statistically different from the OECD average
	Countries/economies where the strength of the relationship between mathematics performance and socio-economic status is not statistically different from the OECD average
	Countries/economies where performance differences across socio-economic spectrum are not statistically different from the OECD average
	Countries/economies with mean mathematics performance below the OECD average
	Countries/economies where the strength of the relationship between mathematics performance and socio-economic status is above the OECD average
	Countries/economies where performance differences across socio-economic spectrum are above the OECD average

	Trends in mathematics performance	Trends in the strength of the relationship between mathematics performance and socio-economic status	Trends in the slope of the socio-economic gradient for mathematics	Trends in the percentage of resilient students
	Change between PISA 2003 and PISA 2012 in mathematics mean score (2012 - 2003)	Change between PISA 2003 and PISA 2012 in the percentage of variance in mathematics performance explained by students' ESCS[1] (2012 - 2003)	Change between PISA 2003 and PISA 2012 in the score-point difference in mathematics performance associated with a one-unit increase on ESCS[1] (2012 - 2003)	Change between PISA 2003 and PISA 2012 in the percentage of resilient students (2012 - 2003)
OECD average	**-3**	**-2.0**	**0**	**-0.3**
Macao-China	**11**	0.8	5	**-2.5**
Hong Kong-China	**11**	-0.4	-3	1.1
Liechtenstein	-1	**-14.9**	**-19**	c
Estonia	m	m	m	m
Finland	**-26**	-1.1	**5**	**-3.3**
Canada	**-14**	-0.8	1	**-1.6**
Japan	2	-2.0	-2	0.5
Korea	**12**	-4.4	5	0.6
Netherlands	**-15**	**-6.8**	0	-1.7
Australia	**-20**	-1.6	2	**-1.9**
Switzerland	4	**-5.2**	-3	0.8
Singapore	m	m	m	m
Ireland	-1	-1.1	2	-0.2
Viet Nam	m	m	m	m
Shanghai-China	m	m	m	m
Slovenia	m	m	m	m
Austria	0	0.8	2	-0.6
Denmark	**-14**	-0.8	1	**-1.7**
Poland	**27**	0.2	1	**2.5**
Germany	**11**	**-6.9**	-1	**1.3**
Chinese Taipei	m	m	m	m
New Zealand	**-24**	1.8	**8**	**-2.9**
Belgium	**-15**	**-3.4**	-2	**-1.2**
Norway	-6	**-4.7**	**-8**	1.1
Iceland	**-22**	0.6	5	**-1.7**
United Kingdom	m	m	m	m
Latvia	7	2.8	1	0.4
Czech Republic	**-17**	-2.3	5	-0.7
Portugal	**21**	1.1	**7**	-0.1
France	**-16**	2.2	**14**	**-2.5**
Qatar	m	m	m	m
Kazakhstan	m	m	m	m
Jordan	m	m	m	m
Indonesia	**15**	2.4	-1	0.7
United Arab Emirates	m	m	m	m
Thailand	**10**	-1.5	-1	-1.5
Italy	**20**	-2.2	-1	**1.8**
Mexico	**28**	**-6.8**	**-11**	2.3
Sweden	**-31**	**-3.7**	-1	**-2.9**
Russian Federation	**14**	0.8	7	-1.4
Serbia	m	m	m	m
Croatia	m	m	m	m
Tunisia	**29**	-1.4	-3	1.3
Montenegro	m	m	m	m
Malaysia	m	m	m	m
Lithuania	m	m	m	m
Cyprus*	m	m	m	m
Turkey	**25**	**-10.4**	**-18**	4.4
United States	-2	**-4.2**	**-7**	0.5
Argentina	m	m	m	m
Colombia	m	m	m	m
Greece	8	-0.5	-2	0.4
Brazil	**35**	0.7	-5	-0.1
Spain	-1	**3.2**	**6**	-2.1
Israel	m	m	m	m
Luxembourg	-3	1.7	2	-0.1
Costa Rica	m	m	m	m
Romania	m	m	m	m
Bulgaria	m	m	m	m
Uruguay	**-13**	**6.9**	3	-1.1
Hungary	**-13**	-2.6	-3	0.1
Chile	m	m	m	m
Peru	m	m	m	m
Slovak Republic	**-17**	1.0	6	-0.1

Note: Countries/economies in which the change between PISA 2003 and PISA 2012 (2012 - 2003) is statistically significant are marked in bold.
1. ESCS refers to the *PISA index of economic, social and cultural status.*
Countries and economies are presented in three groups: those whose mean performance is above the OECD average, those whose mean performance is not statistically different from the OECD average, and those whose mean performance is below the OECD average. Within each group, countries and economies are ranked in ascending order of the strength of the relationship between performance and socio-economic status observed in PISA 2012.
* See notes in the Reader's Guide.
Source: OECD, PISA 2012 Database, Tables II.2.1, II.2.7a, II.2.7b, II.2.8b and II.2.9b.
StatLink http://dx.doi.org/10.1787/888932964889

Reader's Guide

Data underlying the figures

The data referred to in this volume are presented in Annex B and, in greater detail, including some additional tables, on the PISA website (*www.pisa.oecd.org*).

Four symbols are used to denote missing data:

a   The category does not apply in the country concerned. Data are therefore missing.

c   There are too few observations or no observation to provide reliable estimates (i.e. there are fewer than 30 students or fewer than 5 schools with valid data).

m   Data are not available. These data were not submitted by the country or were collected but subsequently removed from the publication for technical reasons.

w   Data have been withdrawn or have not been collected at the request of the country concerned.

Country coverage

This publication features data on 65 countries and economies, including all 34 OECD countries and 31 partner countries and economies (see map in the section *What is PISA?*).

The statistical data for Israel are supplied by and under the responsibility of the relevant Israeli authorities. The use of such data by the OECD is without prejudice to the status of the Golan Heights, East Jerusalem and Israeli settlements in the West Bank under the terms of international law.

Two notes were added to the statistical data related to Cyprus:

1. Note by Turkey: The information in this document with reference to "Cyprus" relates to the southern part of the Island. There is no single authority representing both Turkish and Greek Cypriot people on the Island. Turkey recognises the Turkish Republic of Northern Cyprus (TRNC). Until a lasting and equitable solution is found within the context of the United Nations, Turkey shall preserve its position concerning the "Cyprus issue".

2. Note by all the European Union Member States of the OECD and the European Union: The Republic of Cyprus is recognised by all members of the United Nations with the exception of Turkey. The information in this document relates to the area under the effective control of the Government of the Republic of Cyprus.

Calculating international averages

An OECD average corresponding to the arithmetic mean of the respective country estimates was calculated for most indicators presented in this report. The OECD average is used to compare performance across school systems. In the case of some countries, data may not be available for specific indicators, or specific categories may not apply. Readers should, therefore, keep in mind that the term "OECD average" refers to the OECD countries included in the respective comparisons.

Rounding figures

Because of rounding, some figures in tables may not exactly add up to the totals. Totals, differences and averages are always calculated on the basis of exact numbers and are rounded only after calculation.

All standard errors in this publication have been rounded to one or two decimal places. Where the value 0.0 or 0.00 is shown, this does not imply that the standard error is zero, but that it is smaller than 0.05 or 0.005, respectively.

Reporting student data

The report uses "15-year-olds" as shorthand for the PISA target population. PISA covers students who are aged between 15 years 3 months and 16 years 2 months at the time of assessment and who are enrolled in school and have completed at least 6 years of formal schooling, regardless of the type of institution in which they are enrolled and of whether they are in full-time or part-time education, of whether they attend academic or vocational programmes, and of whether they attend public or private schools or foreign schools within the country.

Reporting school data

The principals of the schools in which students were assessed provided information on their schools' characteristics by completing a school questionnaire. Where responses from school principals are presented in this publication, they are weighted so that they are proportionate to the number of 15-year-olds enrolled in the school.

Focusing on statistically significant differences

This volume discusses only statistically significant differences or changes. These are denoted in darker colours in figures and in bold font in tables. See Annex A3 for further information.

Abbreviations used in this report

ESCS	PISA index of economic, social and cultural status	PPP	Purchasing power parity
GDP	Gross domestic product	S.D.	Standard deviation
ISCED	International Standard Classification of Education	S.E.	Standard error
ISCO	International Standard Classification of Occupations	STEM	Science, Technology, Engineering and Mathematics

Further documentation

For further information on the PISA assessment instruments and the methods used in PISA, see the *PISA 2012 Technical Report* (OECD, forthcoming). The reader should note that there are gaps in the numbering of tables because some tables appear on line only and are not included in this publication. To consult the set of web-only data tables, visit the PISA website (*www.pisa.oecd.org*).

This report uses the OECD StatLinks service. Below each table and chart is a url leading to a corresponding Excel™ workbook containing the underlying data. These urls are stable and will remain unchanged over time. In addition, readers of the e-books will be able to click directly on these links and the workbook will open in a separate window, if their internet browser is open and running.

What is PISA?

"What is important for citizens to know and be able to do?" That is the question that underlies the triennial survey of 15-year-old students around the world known as the Programme for International Student Assessment (PISA). PISA assesses the extent to which students near the end of compulsory education have acquired key knowledge and skills that are essential for full participation in modern societies. The assessment, which focuses on reading, mathematics, science and problem solving, does not just ascertain whether students can reproduce knowledge; it also examines how well students can extrapolate from what they have learned and apply that knowledge in unfamiliar settings, both in and outside of school. This approach reflects the fact that modern economies reward individuals not for what they know, but for what they can do with what they know.

PISA is an ongoing programme that offers insights for education policy and practice, and that helps monitor trends in students' acquisition of knowledge and skills across countries and economies and in different demographic subgroups within each country. PISA results reveal what is possible in education by showing what students in the highest-performing and most rapidly improving school systems can do. The findings allow policy makers around the world to gauge the knowledge and skills of students in their own countries in comparison with those in other countries, set policy targets against measurable goals achieved by other school systems, and learn from policies and practices applied elsewhere. While PISA cannot identify cause-and-effect relationships between policies/practices and student outcomes, it can show educators, policy makers and the interested public how education systems are similar and different – and what that means for students.

A test the whole world can take

PISA is now used as an assessment tool in many regions around the world. It was implemented in 43 countries and economies in the first assessment (32 in 2000 and 11 in 2002), 41 in the second assessment (2003), 57 in the third assessment (2006) and 75 in the fourth assessment (65 in 2009 and 10 in 2010). So far, 65 countries and economies have participated in PISA 2012.

In addition to OECD member countries, the survey has been or is being conducted in:

East, South and Southeast Asia: Himachal Pradesh-India, Hong Kong-China, Indonesia, Macao-China, Malaysia, Shanghai-China, Singapore, Chinese Taipei, Tamil Nadu-India, Thailand and Viet Nam.

Central, Mediterranean and Eastern Europe, and Central Asia: Albania, Azerbaijan, Bulgaria, Croatia, Georgia, Kazakhstan, Kyrgyzstan, Latvia, Liechtenstein, Lithuania, the former Yugoslav Republic of Macedonia, Malta, Moldova, Montenegro, Romania, the Russian Federation and Serbia.

The Middle East: Jordan, Qatar and the United Arab Emirates.

Central and South America: Argentina, Brazil, Colombia, Costa Rica, Netherlands-Antilles, Panama, Peru, Trinidad and Tobago, Uruguay and Miranda-Venezuela.

Africa: Mauritius and Tunisia.

Decisions about the scope and nature of the PISA assessments and the background information to be collected are made by participating countries based on recommendations from leading experts. Considerable efforts and resources are devoted to achieving cultural and linguistic breadth and balance in assessment materials. Since the design and translation of the test, as well as sampling and data collection, are subject to strict quality controls, PISA findings are considered to be highly valid and reliable.

...

Map of PISA countries and economies

OECD countries

Australia	Japan
Austria	Korea
Belgium	Luxembourg
Canada	Mexico
Chile	Netherlands
Czech Republic	New Zealand
Denmark	Norway
Estonia	Poland
Finland	Portugal
France	Slovak Republic
Germany	Slovenia
Greece	Spain
Hungary	Sweden
Iceland	Switzerland
Ireland	Turkey
Israel	United Kingdom
Italy	United States

Partner countries and economies in PISA 2012

Albania	Montenegro
Argentina	Peru
Brazil	Qatar
Bulgaria	Romania
Colombia	Russian Federation
Costa Rica	Serbia
Croatia	Shanghai-China
Cyprus[1,2]	Singapore
Hong Kong-China	Chinese Taipei
Indonesia	Thailand
Jordan	Tunisia
Kazakhstan	United Arab Emirates
Latvia	Uruguay
Liechtenstein	Viet Nam
Lithuania	
Macao-China	
Malaysia	

Partner countries and economies in previous cycles

Azerbaijan
Georgia
Himachal Pradesh-India
Kyrgyzstan
Former Yugoslav Republic of Macedonia
Malta
Mauritius
Miranda-Venezuela
Moldova
Panama
Tamil Nadu-India
Trinidad and Tobago

1. Note by Turkey: The information in this document with reference to "Cyprus" relates to the southern part of the Island. There is no single authority representing both Turkish and Greek Cypriot people on the Island. Turkey recognises the Turkish Republic of Northern Cyprus (TRNC). Until a lasting and equitable solution is found within the context of the United Nations, Turkey shall preserve its position concerning the "Cyprus issue".

2. Note by all the European Union Member States of the OECD and the European Union: The Republic of Cyprus is recognised by all members of the United Nations with the exception of Turkey. The information in this document relates to the area under the effective control of the Government of the Republic of Cyprus.

PISA's unique features include its:

- policy orientation, which links data on student learning outcomes with data on students' backgrounds and attitudes towards learning and on key factors that shape their learning, in and outside of school, in order to highlight differences in performance and identify the characteristics of students, schools and school systems that perform well;

- innovative concept of "literacy", which refers to students' capacity to apply knowledge and skills in key subjects, and to analyse, reason and communicate effectively as they identify, interpret and solve problems in a variety of situations;

- relevance to lifelong learning, as PISA asks students to report on their motivation to learn, their beliefs about themselves, and their learning strategies;

- regularity, which enables countries and economies to monitor their progress in meeting key learning objectives; and

- breadth of coverage, which, in PISA 2012, encompasses the 34 OECD member countries and 31 partner countries and economies.

Key features of PISA 2012

The content

- The PISA 2012 survey focused on mathematics, with reading, science and problem solving as minor areas of assessment. For the first time, PISA 2012 also included an assessment of the financial literacy of young people, which was optional for countries and economies.

- PISA assesses not only whether students can reproduce knowledge, but also whether they can extrapolate from what they have learned and apply their knowledge in new situations. It emphasises the mastery of processes, the understanding of concepts, and the ability to function in various types of situations.

The students

- Around 510 000 students completed the assessment in 2012, representing about 28 million 15-year-olds in the schools of the 65 participating countries and economies.

The assessment

- Paper-based tests were used, with assessments lasting a total of two hours for each student. In a range of countries and economies, an additional 40 minutes were devoted to the computer-based assessment of mathematics, reading and problem solving.

- Test items were a mixture of multiple-choice items and questions requiring students to construct their own responses. The items were organised in groups based on a passage setting out a real-life situation. A total of about 390 minutes of test items were covered, with different students taking different combinations of test items.

- Students answered a background questionnaire, which took 30 minutes to complete, that sought information about themselves, their homes and their school and learning experiences. School principals were given a questionnaire, to complete in 30 minutes, that covered the school system and the learning environment. In some countries and economies, optional questionnaires were distributed to parents, who were asked to provide information on their perceptions of and involvement in their child's school, their support for learning in the home, and their child's career expectations, particularly in mathematics. Countries and economies could choose two other optional questionnaires for students: one asked students about their familiarity with and use of information and communication technologies, and the second sought information about their education to date, including any interruptions in their schooling and whether and how they are preparing for a future career.

WHO ARE THE PISA STUDENTS?

Differences between countries in the nature and extent of pre-primary education and care, in the age of entry into formal schooling, in the structure of the school system, and in the prevalence of grade repetition mean that school grade levels are often not good indicators of where students are in their cognitive development. To better compare student performance internationally, PISA targets a specific age of students. PISA students are aged between 15 years 3 months and 16 years 2 months at the time of the assessment, and have completed at least 6 years of formal schooling. They can be enrolled in any type of institution, participate in full-time or part-time education, in academic or vocational programmes, and attend public or private schools or foreign schools within the country or economy. (For an operational definition of this target population, see Annex A2.) Using this age across countries and over time allows PISA to compare consistently the knowledge and skills of individuals born in the same year who are still in school at age 15, despite the diversity of their education histories in and outside of school.

The population of participating students is defined by strict technical standards, as are the students who are excluded from participating (see Annex A2). The overall exclusion rate within a country was required to be below 5% to ensure that, under reasonable assumptions, any distortions in national mean scores would remain within plus or minus 5 score points, i.e. typically within the order of magnitude of 2 standard errors of sampling. Exclusion could take place either through the schools that participated or the students who participated within schools (see Annex A2, Tables A2.1 and A2.2).

There are several reasons why a school or a student could be excluded from PISA. Schools might be excluded because they are situated in remote regions and are inaccessible, because they are very small, or because of organisational or operational factors that precluded participation. Students might be excluded because of intellectual disability or limited proficiency in the language of the assessment.

In 28 out of the 65 countries and economies participating in PISA 2012, the percentage of school-level exclusions amounted to less than 1%; it was less than 4% in all countries and economies. When the exclusion of students who met the internationally established exclusion criteria is also taken into account, the exclusion rates increase slightly. However, the overall exclusion rate remains below 2% in 30 participating countries and economies, below 5% in 57 participating countries and economies, and below 7% in all countries except Luxembourg (8.4%). In 11 out of the 34 OECD countries, the percentage of school-level exclusions amounted to less than 1% and was less than 3% in 31 OECD countries. When student exclusions within schools were also taken into account, there were 11 OECD countries below 2% and 26 OECD countries below 5%.

(For more detailed information about the restrictions on the level of exclusions in PISA 2012, see Annex A2.)

WHAT KINDS OF RESULTS DOES THE TEST PROVIDE?

The PISA assessment provides three main types of outcomes:

- basic indicators that provide a baseline profile of students' knowledge and skills;

- indicators that show how skills relate to important demographic, social, economic and educational variables; and

- indicators on trends that show changes in student performance and in the relationships between student-level and school-level variables and outcomes.

Although indicators can highlight important issues, they do not provide direct answers to policy questions. To respond to this, PISA also developed a policy-oriented analysis plan that uses the indicators as a basis for policy discussion.

WHERE CAN YOU FIND THE RESULTS?

This is the second of six volumes that present the results from PISA 2012. It begins by defining equity in education and discusses how PISA measures equity. Chapter 2 focuses on the relationship between socio-economic status and student performance in mathematics; Chapter 3 examines various aspects of students' background that have an impact on education outcomes, such as family structure and immigrant background; and Chapter 4 explores the close relationship among educational resources, such as opportunities to learn, teacher quality and quantity, and the school's disciplinary climate, and socio-economic status and performance in mathematics. Whenever comparable data are available, trends between 2003 and 2012 are highlighted, and case studies, examining the policy reforms adopted by countries that have improved in PISA, are presented throughout. The concluding chapter discusses the policy implications of the PISA results.

The other five volumes cover the following issues:

Volume I, *What Students Know and Can Do: Student Performance in Mathematics, Reading and Science,* summarises the performance of students in PISA 2012. It describes how performance is defined, measured and reported, and then provides results from the assessment, showing what students are able to do in mathematics. After a summary of mathematics performance, it examines the ways in which this performance varies on subscales representing different aspects of mathematics literacy. Given that any comparison of the outcomes of education systems needs to take into consideration countries' social and economic circumstances, and the resources they devote to education, the volume also presents the results within countries' economic and social contexts. In addition, the volume examines the relationship between the frequency and intensity of students' exposure to subject content in school, what is known as "opportunity to learn", and student performance. The volume concludes with a description of student results in reading and science. Trends in student performance in mathematics between 2003 and 2012, in reading between 2000 and 2012, and in science between 2006 and 2012 are examined when comparable data are available. Throughout the volume, case studies examine in greater detail the policy reforms adopted by countries that have improved in PISA.

Volume III, *Ready to Learn: Students' Engagement, Drive and Self-Beliefs,* explores students' engagement with and at school, their drive and motivation to succeed, and the beliefs they hold about themselves as mathematics learners. The volume identifies the students who are at particular risk of having low levels of engagement in, and holding negative dispositions towards, school in general and mathematics in particular, and how engagement, drive, motivation and self-beliefs are related to mathematics performance. The volume identifies the roles schools can play in shaping the well-being of students and the role parents can play in promoting their children's engagement with and dispositions towards learning. Changes in students' engagement, drive, motivation and self-beliefs between 2003 and 2012, and how those dispositions have changed during the period among particular subgroups of students, notably socio-economically advantaged and disadvantaged students, boys and girls, and students at different levels of mathematics proficiency, are examined when comparable data are available. Throughout the volume, case studies examine in greater detail the policy reforms adopted by countries that have improved in PISA.

Volume IV, *What Makes Schools Successful? Resources, Policies and Practices,* examines how student performance is associated with various characteristics of individual schools and of concerned school systems. It discusses how 15-year-old students are selected and grouped into different schools, programmes, and education levels, and how human, financial, educational and time resources are allocated to different schools. The volume also examines how school systems balance autonomy with collaboration, and how the learning environment in school shapes student performance. Trends in these variables between 2003 and 2012 are examined when comparable data are available, and case studies, examining the policy reforms adopted by countries that have improved in PISA, are presented throughout the volume.

Volume V, *Skills for Life: Student Performance in Problem Solving,* presents student performance in the PISA 2012 assessment of problem solving, which measures students' capacity to respond to non-routine situations in order to achieve their potential as constructive and reflective citizens. It provides the rationale for assessing problem-solving skills and describes performance within and across countries and economies. In addition, the volume highlights the relative strengths and weaknesses of each school system and examines how they are related to individual student characteristics, such as gender, immigrant background and socio-economic status. The volume also explores the role of education in fostering problem-solving skills.

Volume VI, *Students and Money: Financial Literacy Skills for the 21st Century,* examines 15-year-old students' performance in financial literacy in the 18 countries and economies that participated in this optional assessment. It also discusses the relationship of financial literacy to students' and their families' background and to students' mathematics and reading skills. The volume also explores students' access to money and their experience with financial matters. In addition, it provides an overview of the current status of financial education in schools and highlights relevant case studies.

The frameworks for assessing mathematics, reading and science in 2012 are described in *PISA 2012 Assessment and Analytical Framework: Mathematics, Reading, Science, Problem Solving and Financial Literacy* (OECD, 2013). They are also summarised in this volume.

Technical annexes at the end of this report describe how questionnaire indices were constructed and discuss sampling issues, quality-assurance procedures, the reliability of coding, and the process followed for developing the assessment instruments. Many of the issues covered in the technical annexes are elaborated in greater detail in the *PISA 2012 Technical Report* (OECD, forthcoming).

All data tables referred to in the analysis are included at the end of the respective volume in Annex B1, and a set of additional data tables is available on line (*www.pisa.oecd.org*). A Reader's Guide is also provided in each volume to aid in interpreting the tables and figures that accompany the report. Data from regions within the participating countries are included in Annex B2.

References

OECD (forthcoming), *PISA 2012 Technical Report*, PISA, OECD Publishing.

OECD (2013), *PISA 2012 Assessment and Analytical Framework: Mathematics, Reading, Science, Problem Solving and Financial Literacy*, PISA, OECD Publishing.
http://dx.doi.org/10.1787/9789264190511-en

1

Defining and Measuring Equity in Education

This chapter discusses how PISA defines and measures equity in education and identifies some of the groups of students across all PISA-participating countries and economies, who are most at risk when education systems do not give all students the same chances to succeed.

By measuring the knowledge and skills of 15-year-olds, PISA offers insights into how participating countries and economies are beginning to develop their future talent pools. Indeed, the new Survey of Adult Skills (PIAAC), finds a close correlation between countries' performance in the different cycles of PISA and the proficiency of the corresponding age groups in literacy and numeracy in the OECD Skills Outlook 2013 (OECD, 2013). In analysing results of the PISA assessment in the context of various social characteristics of students and schools, such as socio-economic status, gender and immigrant background, PISA also shows how equitably participating countries and economies are providing education opportunities and realising education outcomes – an indication of the level of equity in the society, as a whole.

What the data tell us

- Of the 39 countries and economies that participated in both PISA 2003 and 2012, Mexico, Turkey and Germany improved both their mathematics performance and their levels of equity in education during the period.

- Australia, Canada, Estonia, Finland, Hong Kong-China, Japan, Korea, Liechtenstein and Macao-China achieve high levels of performance and equity in education outcomes as assessed in PISA 2012.

What people know and what they can do with what they know has a major impact on their life chances (Figure II.1.1). The Survey of Adult Skills (PIAAC) shows, for example, that individuals scoring at the highest levels in literacy are almost three times as likely to enjoy higher wages than those scoring at the lowest levels, and those with low literacy skills are also more than twice as likely to be unemployed (OECD, 2013).

How skills are distributed across the population also has significant implications on how economic and social outcomes are distributed within society. The skills survey shows, for example, that higher levels of inequality in literacy and numeracy skills are associated with greater inequality in the distribution of income. If large proportions of adults have low reading and numeracy skills, the introduction and wider diffusion of productivity-improving technologies and work organisation practices can be hampered and that, in turn, will stall improvements in living standards. In other words, today's education is tomorrow's economy.

■ Figure II.1.1 ■

Likelihood of positive social and economic outcomes among highly literate adults

Increased likelihood (odds ratio) of adults scoring at Level 4/5 in literacy on the Survey of Adult Skills (PIAAC) reporting high earnings, high levels of trust and political efficacy, good health, participating in volunteer activities and being employed, compared with adults scoring at or below Level 1 in literacy (adjusted)

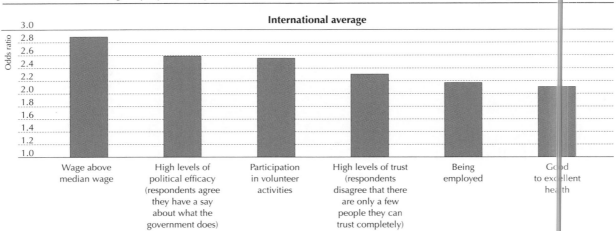

Notes: Odds ratios are adjusted for age, gender, educational attainment and immigrant and language background.
High wages are defined as workers' hourly earnings that are above the country's median.
Source: Based on data from the Survey of Adult Skills (PIAAC) 2012.
StatLink ᶜⁱˢᴸ http://dx.doi.org/10.1787/888932964794

And the impact of skills goes far beyond earnings, employment, economic growth and prosperity: in all countries, individuals with lower literacy proficiency are more likely than those with better literacy skills to report poor health, believe that they have little impact on political processes, and are less likely to trust others. Inequity in the distribution of skills across societies is thus reflected in broader social inequities.

PISA defines equity in education[1] as providing all students, regardless of gender, family background or socio-economic status, with similar opportunities to benefit from education. For example, the stronger the impact of a student's socio-economic status on his or her performance, the less equitable the school system. Equity, defined in this way, does not imply that everyone should have the same results, nor does it imply teaching the same material or providing the same resources to all students.

■ Figure II.1.2 ■
Student performance and equity

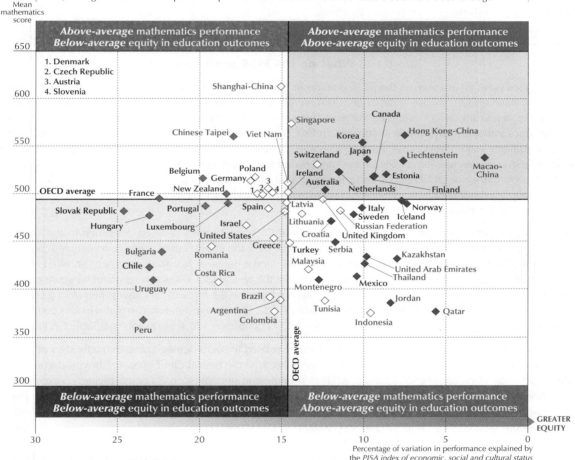

Source: OECD, PISA 2012 Database, Table II.2.1.
StatLink ⬛⬛⬛ http://dx.doi.org/10.1787/888932964794

PISA consistently finds that high performance and greater equity in education opportunities and outcomes are not mutually exclusive: one does not have to be sacrificed to achieve the other. In 20 of the 23 countries and economies that scored above the OECD average in mathematics in PISA 2012, the strength of the relationship between student performance and socio-economic status (the proportion of the variation in performance described by the variation in socio-economic status) is at or below the OECD average. School systems in Australia, Canada, Estonia, Finland,

Hong Kong-China, Japan, Korea, Liechtenstein, Macao-China and the Netherlands achieve high mathematics performance[2] while the relationship between student performance and socio-economic status is weaker than average. School systems in Austria, Denmark, Germany, Ireland, Poland, Slovenia, Shanghai-China, Singapore, Switzerland and Viet Nam achieve high mathematics performance without introducing greater inequities in education outcomes (Figure II.1.2).

Even more encouraging, trend data from 2003 to 2012 show that, of the 39 countries and economies that participated in both PISA assessments, 13 improved their average mathematics performance. Of these improving countries and economies, Mexico, Turkey and Germany also improved their equity levels, either by reducing the extent to which students' socio-economic background predicts their mathematics performance or by reducing the average difference in performance between advantaged and disadvantaged students. Ten additional countries and economies improved their average performance between PISA 2003 and PISA 2012 while maintaining their equity levels.

Performance differences between socio-economically advantaged and disadvantaged students, immigrant and non-immigrant students, or between those attending rural and urban schools indicate the degree to which an education system is equitable. They often reveal how various student characteristics, or the environment in which students learn, are related to performance. Box II.1.1 provides details on how to interpret performance differences in PISA. Tracking the evolution of these disparities over time can help school systems monitor whether and how inequities in education opportunities and outcomes are growing or shrinking.

Box II.1.1. **What do the PISA scores mean?**

Mathematics was first assessed as the main domain in PISA in 2003. At that time, the mathematics performance scale was standardised to have a mean of 500 score points and a standard deviation of 100 score points. This means that across all OECD countries that participated in PISA 2003, the typical student scored 500 points in mathematics and about two-thirds of students in OECD countries scored between 400 and 600 points. Almost 40% of students scored between 450 and 550 points. A performance gap of 100 points thus represents a large difference in performance. Test results are best understood when compared against a specific standard, such as the average performance of OECD countries or the described proficiency levels on each of the PISA scales. There is neither a top/maximum nor bottom/minimum score in PISA; an individual student, school or school system cannot "pass" or "fail" the PISA test.

An entire proficiency level in mathematics spans about 70 score points – a large difference in the skills and knowledge students at that level possess. Such a gap represents the equivalent of about two years of schooling in the typical OECD country. The average performance difference between two students, each enrolled in one of two consecutive grades (for example, Grades 9 and 10) in the typical OECD country, is about 41 score points. As reported in Volume I, the difference in mean performance between the highest- and lowest-performing country in mathematics in PISA 2012 is 245 score points (see Table II.2.1). The average difference in mathematics performance between the top and bottom quarters of students in OECD countries is 128 score points (see Table I.2.3a).

However, most differences in mathematics performance related to socio-demographic characteristics of students or schools are much smaller than an entire proficiency level. In the typical OECD country, boys outscore girls in mathematics by 11 points (see Table I.2.3a), while non-immigrant students score 34 points higher, on average, than their peers with an immigrant background (see Table II.3.4a). Socio-economically advantaged students (in the top quarter of socio-economic status in their country) score an average of 90 points higher than their disadvantaged peers (bottom quarter) (see Table II.2.4a), and students in city schools score about 31 points higher than students in rural schools, on average (see Table II.3.3a).

HOW PISA EXAMINES EQUITY IN EDUCATION OPPORTUNITIES

The quantity and quality of educational resources

Education systems that are successful, both in quality and equity, attract the highest-quality resources to where these resources can make the most difference. PISA provides information on how school systems allocate their resources for education and whether that allocation is related to student or school characteristics, such as socio-economic status, immigrant background or school location.

PISA distributes questionnaires to students and school principals to collect information about the quantity and quality of educational resources available to them. For example, schools are asked about the quality of school infrastructure and the availability of qualified teachers. Students are asked about how much class time is devoted to the subjects they learn and the extent of their after-school learning activities.

PISA measures equity in resource allocation across school systems by analysing the responses to the questionnaires and comparing those responses with performance results. This volume provides a glimpse of some school policies and practices, including resource allocation. Volume IV explores in detail some of the school- and system-based policies and practices, including allocation of educational resources, related to student and school performance and how they reflect the level of equity in a system.

Instructional content and practices

The quantity and quality of educational resources will have no effect on learning if students are not exposed to the course content that they need to master to be able to participate fully in society. For this reason, PISA measures the kinds of mathematics tasks 15-year-olds have encountered in their mathematics classes and their relative familiarity with those tasks, as developed over their school lives. This volume explores how exposure to and familiarity with mathematics concepts and processes, also known as "opportunity to learn" mathematics, varies by student, school and school system, and how that variation affects equity in education outcomes.

PISA also monitors equity in education by exploring the learning environment at school. Data on such issues as teacher-student relations, teacher morale and classroom discipline, all gathered through the questionnaires distributed among students and school authorities, are correlated among themselves and with student performance. Large disparities in the quality of the learning environment within and between schools could indicate inequities in education opportunities.

Combining better performance with greater equity

The countries and economies participating in PISA demonstrate that excellence and equity are attainable under a wide variety of conditions.

National income

High income is neither a prerequisite for nor a guarantee of high performance and equity. As discussed in Volume I, a country's per capita GDP explains about 12% of the between-country variation in average performance among OECD countries, and 21% of the variation among partner countries and economies (see Figure I.2.1).[3] Countries and economies of similar wealth show very different mean performance in PISA. For example, Canada and Poland score 518 points on the mathematics assessment, yet per capita GDP in Poland is half that of Canada. Per capita GDP in Japan and France is around the OECD average of USD 35 000, yet mathematics performance in these countries ranges from well above the OECD average in Japan (536 points) to around the OECD average in France. Furthermore, countries with very different per capita GDP show similar performance: Latvia and Luxembourg both perform slightly below the OECD average, but per capita GDP in Latvia is under USD 17 000 while it is more than USD 84 000 in Luxembourg (see Table I.2.27).

Countries and economies such as Estonia, Hong Kong-China, Poland, Shanghai-China, Singapore, Slovenia, Chinese Taipei and Viet Nam show that the notion of a world neatly divided between highly developed, educated countries and emerging, low-educated countries is no longer valid. Some emerging economies, particularly in East Asia, are rapidly raising the level and quality of their population's education. As discussed in Volume IV, at first glance it may appear that high-income countries and economies (defined here as those with a per capita GDP above USD 20 000) – and those that can and do spend more on education – show better student performance in PISA. Indeed, high-income countries and economies have an average mathematics performance almost 70 score points higher than that of countries whose per capita GDP is below the USD 20 000 threshold. However, while the relationship between higher income and better performance is marked among those countries below the threshold, among high-income countries, there is no significant relationship between higher income and better performance.

A similar pattern is observed for equity in education. Across all participating countries and economies, per capita GDP is only weakly related with equity in education. There appears to be no relationship between per capita GDP and the strength of the relationship between performance and socio-economic status. Among countries whose per capita

GDP is below the USD 20 000 threshold, higher per capita GDP is positively associated with larger differences in performance between socio-economically advantaged and disadvantaged students and school – in other words, less equity in education outcomes. This relationship is no longer apparent, however, among high-income countries.

As explored in Volume IV, there is no overall relationship between spending on education and average performance. PISA results show that once a certain level of spending is reached, more resources no longer predict higher achievement (see Figure IV.1.8). Expenditure of up to about USD 50 000 per student from the age of 6 to 15 is positively related to higher mean performance but also to disparities in performance between students of different socio-economic status. This finding highlights the importance for countries that are boosting public spending on education from relatively low levels to adopt effective policies on equity.

How countries spend their limited resources matters as much as, if not more than, the amount they are spending. As explored in Volume IV, differences in the allocation of educational resources are generally related to better performance (see Table IV.1.20). In particular, greater equity in the distribution of educational resources is associated with higher mathematics performance. As shown in Figure IV.1.11, even after accounting for per capita GDP, 30% of the variation in mathematics performance across OECD countries can be explained by differences in how educational resources are allocated between advantaged and disadvantaged schools.

Socio-economic heterogeneity

Socio-economic diversity in student populations can coexist with high performance and equity. Of the 23 countries with mean performance above the OECD average, Hong Kong-China and Macao-China have above-average equity and greater socio-economic diversity than average (as measured by the range of socio-economic status between the 5th and 95th percentiles, see Figure II.5.1a) and in Finland socio-economic diversity is average. Among those countries/economies with high performance and average levels of equity (as measured by the strength of the relationship between performance and socio-economic status), Shanghai-China and Singapore both show above-average socio-economic diversity, while the Netherlands, Switzerland, Denmark and Germany have average socio-economic diversity.

Similarly, the proportion of low performers relative to top performers, the range of performance between the top and bottom 25% of students, or simply the variation in performance, is either weakly or not at all related to equity in education. Higher-performing countries and economies tend to show greater variation in performance (see Figure I.2.24), but those differences are only weakly related to socio-economic disparities. For example, in Shanghai-China, Singapore and Chinese Taipei, average performance is high and so is overall variation in student performance (see Table II.2.8a).

Immigrant students

Canada, Hong Kong-China and Macao-China combine high levels of achievement and above-average equity – and more than 30% of students in these countries and economies are immigrants. In fact, performance differences between immigrant and non-immigrant students are relatively small in Canada and Hong Kong-China. By contrast, Spain and Greece show relatively large differences in performance between immigrant and non-immigrant students despite having smaller, although still significant, populations of immigrant students (see Table II.3.4a).

EXAMINING EQUITY THROUGHOUT THIS REPORT

Chapter 2 of this volume analyses equity in education outcomes, particularly the relationship between performance and socio-economic status, at both the student and school levels. Chapter 3 examines an array of student and school characteristics and their relationship with performance. It focuses on family structure, immigrant background, language spoken at home and school location and explores what, if any, impact these characteristics have on student performance. Chapter 4 describes how exposure and familiarity with formal mathematics, opportunity to learn, and resources are distributed across different groups of students. Chapter 5 concludes with a discussion of policy options and implications countries can draw on from the evidence and analysis presented in this volume.

This is not the only volume of the *PISA 2012 Results* publication that covers the issue of equity in education. Volume I introduces gender as an important equity issue. It addresses the myth that girls are systematically worse at mathematics than boys and discusses the complexity of the issue. It also proposes that since mathematics skills are critical for both boys and girls as they pursue further education or a career, inequities related to gender are not only unfair, but also ultimately damaging to the wider society and economy.

Volume III looks at differences in attitudes, behaviour and approaches to learning across gender, socio-economic status, family characteristics and school location. These, too, are associated with inequities in the acquisition of knowledge and skills.

Volume IV examines how the policies and practices adopted in schools and school systems are related to performance and equity. While some of these policies are introduced in this volume, Volume IV discusses them in greater depth.

Notes

1. This definition builds previous PISA cycles and the educational equity framework published in *Education at a Glance 2011: OECD Indicators* (OECD, 2011). In particular, the conceptual framework for this chapter draws heavily from Levin (2010).

2. The focus in this volume is on mathematics performance. Most of the analyses presented in this volume can be replicated for each of the domains assessed in PISA 2012. For the most part, the results are likely to be similar, regardless of the domain, but there may be substantial differences in some areas.

3. Here the measure of per capita GDP used is in PPP terms, that is, in equivalent units or as typically known in purchasing power parity.

References

Levin, H. (2010), "A Guiding Framework for Measuring Educational Equity", INES Network for the Collection and the Adjudication of System-Level Descriptive Information on Educational Structures, Policies and Practices, EDU/EDPC/INES/NESLI(2010)6, March 2010.

OECD (2013), *OECD Skills Outlook 2013: First Results from the Survey of Adult Skills*, OECD Publishing.
http://dx.doi.org/10.1787/9789264204256-en

OECD (2011), *Education at a Glance 2011: OECD Indicators*, OECD Publishing.
http://dx.doi.org/10.1787/eag-2011-en

2

Equity in Outcomes

This chapter focuses on the relationship between student performance in mathematics and socio-economic status. It examines cross-country differences in this relationship and discusses trends between 2003 and 2012 in equity in education related to socio-economic status, highlighting those countries and economies that have improved both their performance and the level of equity in their education systems.

Across OECD countries, 14.8% of differences in performance among students are explained by disparities in students' socio-economic status, whether the focus is on mathematics, reading or science[1] (Table II.2.1). In countries and economies where this relationship is strong, students from disadvantaged families are less likely to achieve high levels of performance. Some 39 score points – the equivalent of one year of formal schooling – separate the mathematics performance – and the difference is very similar for reading and science – of those students who are considered socio-economically advantaged and those whose socio-economic status is close to the OECD average (Table II.2.1).[2]

In OECD countries, parents of socio-economically advantaged students (those in the top quarter of the socio-economic distribution in their country, or one standard deviation above the average on the *PISA index of economic, social and cultural status*) are highly educated (95% have attained a tertiary education) and work in skilled occupations (97%). In contrast, the parents of socio-economically disadvantaged students (those in the bottom quarter of the socio-economic distribution in their country, or one standard deviation below the average on the *PISA index of economic, social and cultural status*), have much lower educational attainment, and very few (6%) work in skilled occupations. Advantaged students also report having many more books at home than their disadvantaged peers (282 compared with 69 on average), as well as works of art, classical literature and books of poetry (Table II.2.2). While disadvantaged students have fewer books, cultural possessions and some educational resources at home, a large majority has access to a desk, a quiet place to study, a dictionary, a computer and an Internet connection at home (Table II.2.2). For a more detailed definition of socio-economic advantage and disadvantage, as measured by PISA, see Box II.2.1 below.

Large differences in performance associated with the background of students and schools – whether socio-economic status, immigrant or language background – signal that learning opportunities are not equitably distributed throughout a school system or that not all students have access to the high-quality instruction and material, financial and human resources that could help them succeed in school and beyond.

What the data tell us

- Some 6% of students across OECD countries – nearly one million students – are "resilient", meaning that they beat the socio-economic odds against them and exceed expectations, when compared with students in other countries. In Korea, Hong Kong-China, Macao-China, Shanghai-China, Singapore and Viet Nam, 13% of students or more are resilient and perform among the top 25% of students across all participating countries and economies.

- Across OECD countries, a more socio-economically advantaged student scores 39 points higher in mathematics – the equivalent of nearly one year of schooling – than a less-advantaged student.

PISA measures performance only among 15-year-olds who are enrolled in education, and has no way to estimate the performance of 15-year-olds who are not enrolled in any educational programme. In most OECD countries, there are very few 15-year-olds who do not attend school, but the situation is different in some partner countries. In these countries, the impact of social background on learning outcomes of 15-year-olds is likely to be underestimated.

This chapter examines how variation in student performance is related to socio-economic status and how this relationship is shaped by the way performance and socio-economic status vary within countries.[3] Equity in education opportunities is analysed in the context of mean performance in mathematics.

PERFORMANCE AND SOCIO-ECONOMIC STATUS ACROSS SCHOOL SYSTEMS

While many socio-economically disadvantaged students succeed at school, and many achieve at high levels on the PISA assessment, socio-economic status is still a strong predictor of performance in many countries, and is associated with large differences in performance in most countries and economies that participate in PISA. Socio-economically advantaged students and schools tend to outscore their disadvantaged peers by larger margins than between any other two groups of students.

Still, socio-economic status is not destiny: many countries and economies that have seen improvements in their mean performance on PISA have also managed to weaken the link between socio-economic status and performance.

Sometimes, this results in a narrowing of the gap in performance between advantaged and disadvantaged students. Figure II.2.1 shows the socio-economic gradient, a depiction of the relationship between socio-economic status and performance. This report focuses on the strength of this relationship – PISA's main measure of equity in education outcomes. If this relationship is weak, then a student's socio-economic status does not predict his or her performance. While a single measure cannot capture the many complexities of equity in education, it can provide a useful benchmark against which to compare school systems.

■ Figure II.2.1 ■
Students' socio-economic status and performance, OECD countries

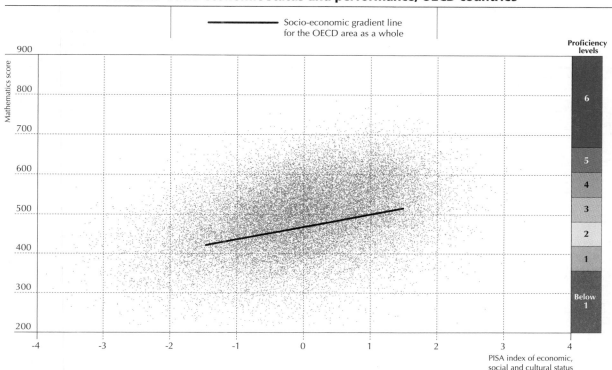

Note: Each dot represents an OECD student picked at random out of ten OECD students.
Source: OECD, PISA 2012 Database.
StatLink ⌗ http://dx.doi.org/10.1787/888932964813

How to read this figure

Every dot in Figure II.2.1 represents a student, chosen at random, from an OECD country (10% of all students in OECD countries are represented in the figure). The horizontal axis represents the student's socio-economic status (as measured by the *PISA index of economic, social and cultural status*). The student's mathematics score in PISA 2012 is shown on the vertical axis. The dark line that appears among the dots represents the relationship between student performance and socio-economic status, what is known as the **socio-economic gradient**. The line depicts the typical performance of a student given his or her socio-economic status. The **strength of the socio-economic gradient** refers to how well socio-economic status predicts performance. When the dots are very close to the dark line, the student's performance in mathematics is the same as would be predicted given his or her socio-economic status, so the socio-economic gradient is considered strong. If the dots are far away from the line, the student's actual performance is not the same as would be predicted by his or her socio-economic status, so the socio-economic gradient is considered weak. The strength of the socio-economic gradient is measured by the proportion of the variation in performance that is explained by differences in socio-economic status.

The **slope of the socio-economic gradient** refers to the impact of socio-economic status on performance, or the average difference in performance between two students whose socio-economic status differs by one unit on the *PISA index of economic, social and cultural status*. As such, it is a summary measure of the differences in performance observed across socio-economic groups. A flat line, parallel to the horizontal axis, implies that there are only small differences in performance related to socio-economic status; in other words, advantaged and disadvantaged students perform equally well. A steep line, however, signals large performance differences related to socio-economic status.

Chapter 5 of this volume presents the socio-economic gradient for all countries and economies that participated in PISA 2012. Most countries show either steep, strong socio-economic gradients or flat, weak gradients. But, as Figure II.2.2 shows, two other combinations are also possible. Australia is the only country where performance differences related to socio-economic status are relatively large (above the OECD average), but the strength of the relationship between performance and socio-economic status is relatively weak (below the OECD average); thus the country shows a steep, weak socio-economic gradient. In Portugal, Chile, Costa Rica and Peru, the relationship between performance and socio-economic status is strong, but performance differences related to socio-economic status are small; thus these countries show flat, strong socio-economic gradients.

■ Figure II.2.2 ■

Comparing countries' and economies' performance in mathematics and equity in education outcomes

Countries/economies with mean mathematics performance **above** the OECD average
Countries/economies where the strength of the relationship between mathematics performance and socio-economic status is **below** the OECD average
Countries/economies where performance differences across socio-economic groups are **below** the OECD average

Countries/economies with mean mathematics performance not statistically different from the OECD average
Countries/economies where the strength of the relationship between mathematics performance and socio-economic status is not statistically different from the OECD average
Countries/economies where performance differences across socio-economic spectrum are not statistically different from the OECD average

Countries/economies with mean mathematics performance **below** the OECD average
Countries/economies where the strength of the relationship between mathematics performance and socio-economic status is **above** the OECD average
Countries/economies where performance differences across socio-economic spectrum are **above** the OECD average

	Mean performance in mathematics	Strength of the relationship between mathematics performance and socio-economic status	Performance differences across socio-economic groups
	Mean score	Percentage of explained variance in mathematics performance	Score-point difference in mathematics associated with a one-unit increase in the PISA index of economic, social and cultural status
OECD average	494	14.8	39
Macao-China	538	2.6	17
Hong Kong-China	561	7.5	27
Liechtenstein	535	7.6	28
Estonia	521	8.6	29
Finland	519	9.4	33
Canada	518	9.4	31
Japan	536	9.8	41
Korea	554	10.1	42
Netherlands	523	11.5	40
Australia	504	12.3	42
Switzerland	531	12.8	38
Singapore	573	14.4	44
Ireland	501	14.6	38
Viet Nam	511	14.6	29
Shanghai-China	613	15.1	41
Slovenia	501	15.6	42
Austria	506	15.8	43
Denmark	500	16.5	39
Poland	518	16.6	41
Germany	514	16.9	43
Chinese Taipei	560	17.9	58
New Zealand	500	18.4	52
Belgium	515	19.6	49
Norway	489	7.4	32
Iceland	493	7.7	31
United Kingdom	494	12.5	41
Latvia	491	14.7	35
Czech Republic	499	16.2	51
Portugal	487	19.6	35
France	495	22.5	57
Qatar	376	5.6	27
Kazakhstan	432	8.0	27
Jordan	386	8.4	22
Indonesia	375	9.6	20
United Arab Emirates	434	9.8	33
Thailand	427	9.9	22
Italy	485	10.1	30
Mexico	413	10.4	19
Sweden	478	10.6	36
Russian Federation	482	11.4	38
Serbia	449	11.7	34
Croatia	471	12.0	36
Tunisia	388	12.4	22
Montenegro	410	12.7	33
Malaysia	421	13.4	30
Lithuania	479	13.8	36
Turkey	448	14.5	32
United States	481	14.8	35
Argentina	388	15.1	26
Colombia	376	15.4	25
Greece	453	15.5	34
Brazil	391	15.7	26
Spain	484	15.8	34
Israel	466	17.2	51
Luxembourg	490	18.3	37
Costa Rica	407	18.9	24
Romania	445	19.3	38
Bulgaria	439	22.3	42
Uruguay	409	22.8	37
Hungary	477	23.1	47
Chile	423	23.1	34
Peru	368	23.4	33
Slovak Republic	482	24.6	54

Note: Countries and economies are presented in three groups: those whose mean performance is above the OECD average, those whose mean performance is not statistically different from the OECD average, and those whose mean performance is below the OECD average. Within each group, countries and economies are ranked in descending order of the strength of the relationship between performance and socio-economic status.
Source: OECD, PISA 2012 Database, Table II.2.1.
StatLink ⬛🔗 http://dx.doi.org/10.1787/888932964813

Success in education can be defined as a combination of high levels of achievement and high levels of equity in education outcomes. As Figure II.2.2 shows, of the 23 systems that perform above the OECD average in PISA 2012, the strength of the relationship between performance and socio-economic status is weaker than average in 10 countries and economies: Australia, Canada, Estonia, Finland, Hong Kong-China, Japan, Korea, Liechtenstein, Macao-China and the Netherlands.[4] In 10 of the 23 countries and economies (Austria, Denmark, Germany, Ireland, Poland, Shanghai-China, Singapore, Slovenia, Switzerland and Viet Nam), the strength of this relationship is about average. Only in two high-performing countries and one high-performing economy – Belgium, New Zealand and Chinese Taipei – is the relationship between performance and socio-economic status stronger than average (Figure II.2.2).

As discussed below, since 2003, Turkey, Mexico and Germany saw both an improvement in overall mathematics performance and greater equity in education outcomes. Moreover, among the other countries and economies that show improvement since PISA 2003, all but one either maintained or improved their equity levels, showing how improvements in mathematics performance need not come at the expense of equity in the school system. Box II.2.4 provides more details on Mexico's improvement in PISA, including the education policies and programmes the country implemented over the past decade. Similarly, Box II.3.2 outlines the path to Germany's improvement, and Box I.2.5 (in Volume I of this series) focuses on Turkey's improvement in PISA.[5]

Box II.2.1. **What is socio-economic status and how is it measured?**

Socio-economic status is a broad concept that summarises many different aspects of a student, school or system. A student's socio-economic status is estimated by an index, the *PISA index of social, cultural and economic status*, which is based on such indicators as parental education and occupation, the number and type of home possessions that are considered proxies for wealth, and the educational resources available at home. The index is built to be internationally comparable (see the *PISA 2012 Technical Report* [OECD, forthcoming]). Students are considered socio-economically advantaged if they are among the 25% of students with the highest *PISA index of social, economic and cultural status* in their country or economy; socio-economically disadvantaged students are those among the 25% of students with the lowest *PISA index of social, economic and cultural status*.

PISA consistently finds that socio-economic status is associated with performance at the system, school and student levels. These patterns reflect, in part, the inherent advantages in resources that relatively high socio-economic status provides. However, they also reflect other characteristics that are associated with socio-economic status but that have not been measured by the PISA index. For example, at the system level, high socio-economic status is related to greater wealth and higher spending on education. At the school level, higher socio-economic status is associated with a range of characteristics of a community that might be related to student performance, such as a safe environment, and the availability of quality educational resources, such as public libraries or museums. At the individual level, socio-economic status may be related to parental attitudes towards education, in general, and to their involvement in their child's education, in particular.

In the typical OECD country, a majority of parents (52%) have a tertiary education (ISCED 5 and 6), a small proportion attained secondary education (ISCED 2) as their highest level of education (12%), and the rest (36%) attained other post-secondary qualifications (ISCED 3 and 4). On average, 4% of parents work in elementary occupations (within ISCO major group 9), 16% in semi-skilled blue-collar occupations (within ISCO major groups 6, 7 and 8), 26% in semi-skilled white-collar occupations (within ISCO major groups 4 and 5), and 54% in skilled occupations (within ISCO major groups 1, 2 and 3).[6] On average, more than 90% of students enjoy a desk, a quiet place to study, a dictionary, an Internet connection and a DVD player at home. Books of poetry are one of the least common household possessions: fewer than 50% of students reported reporting having them at home. Classical literature and educational software are also relatively uncommon, followed by technical reference books and works of art. The average household has over 155 books (Table II.2.3). This general profile differs widely across countries. For example, in Iceland, parents have spent an average of more than 16 years in education, while parents in Turkey have spent an average of less than nine years in education. On average, students in Hungary, Korea and Luxembourg reported having more than 220 books at home, while those in Brazil, Colombia and Tunisia reported having fewer than 45 books at home (Table II.2.3).

...

In OECD countries, parents of socio-economically advantaged students are highly educated: the majority (95%) has attained tertiary education and nearly all (97%) work in a skilled occupation. One of the home possessions that most clearly distinguishes advantaged students from their peers is the quantity of books at home. Socio-economically advantaged students reported having 282 books at home, on average – compared to an average of 69 books reported by their disadvantaged peers. Other cultural possessions, such as works of art, classical literature and books of poetry, also characterise advantaged students: at least seven out of ten advantaged students reported having these at home. Advantaged students more than disadvantaged students also reported having technical references books, educational software and a dishwasher at home (Table II.2.2).

In contrast, the parents of socio-economically disadvantaged students have much lower educational attainment. Across OECD countries, most parents of disadvantaged students (almost 55%) attained some post-secondary education, 35% attained secondary education (or less) as their highest level of formal schooling, and only 10% attained tertiary education. Very few disadvantaged students have a parent working in a skilled occupation (6%); most parents of these students work in white-collar semi-skilled occupations (41%). Some 39% work in elementary occupations and 13% work in blue-collar semi-skilled occupations. While disadvantaged students have fewer books, cultural possessions and educational resources at home, at least 84% of them have access to a desk, a quiet place to study, a dictionary, a computer and an Internet connection at home. Most (73%) reported having textbooks at home (Table II.2.2).

Some other material measures of wealth, such as the number of televisions and cell phones in a household, are similar among both advantaged and disadvantaged students; but differences in the number of computers, cars, and rooms with a bath or shower are marked. For example, disadvantaged students have fewer than two computers at home while advantaged students have more than three (Table II.2.2).

The OECD average, however, hides significant variations across countries in each of these elements. For illustrative purposes, this volume looks into some of the components at different points, but caution is advised when analysing differences across individual elements, as they are inevitably only part of a complex story (Table II.2.2).

Disparities in performance related to socio-economic status

On average, the performance difference between advantaged (the top quarter of socio-economic status) and disadvantaged (the bottom quarter of socio-economic status) students is 90 score points, or the equivalent of more than two years of schooling and more than one PISA proficiency level. Disadvantaged students are, on average, more than twice as likely as students who are not considered disadvantaged to score in the bottom quarter of the performance distribution (Table II.2.4a).

OECD countries with greater equity in education outcomes, as measured by the strength of the relationship between performance and socio-economic status, show smaller performance differences between students from different socio-economic groups, as measured by the slope of the socio-economic gradient. The correlation between the slope and the strength of the socio-economic gradient is 0.62 across OECD countries and 0.58 across all participating countries and economies. Canada, Estonia, Finland, Hong Kong-China and Macao-China combine high performance, a weak relationship between performance and socio-economic status, and relatively narrow performance differences across socio-economic groups. Among high-performing countries, Belgium, New Zealand and Chinese Taipei are the only two school systems where performance differences are above average and so is the strength of the relationship between socio-economic status and performance. Among countries that perform at or below the OECD average, the same pattern is observed in France, Hungary and the Slovak Republic. Australia is the only country where differences in mathematics performance between advantaged and disadvantaged students are large, but the strength of the relationship between performance and socio-economic status is weaker than average. Chile, Costa Rica, Peru and Portugal are the only countries with relatively narrow performance gaps, despite a strong relationship between socio-economic status and performance (Figure II.2.2).

The element of socio-economic status that plays a bigger role in explaining these differences varies across countries. For example, across OECD countries, students with highly educated parents outscore students with low-educated parents by 77 score points – equivalent to an entire proficiency level.[7] A similar gap (85 score points) is observed among students whose parents work in elementary occupations and those whose parents work in skilled occupations.

■ Figure II.2.3 ■
Proportion of the variation in mathematics performance explained by elements of socio-economic status

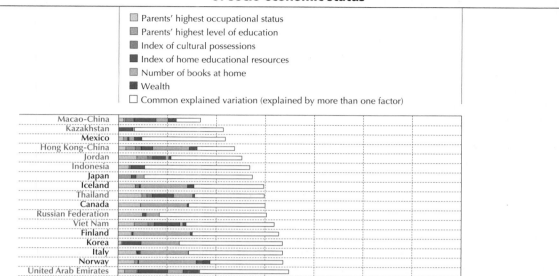

Legend:
- ☐ Parents' highest occupational status
- ☐ Parents' highest level of education
- ☐ Index of cultural possessions
- ■ Index of home educational resources
- ☐ Number of books at home
- ■ Wealth
- ☐ Common explained variation (explained by more than one factor)

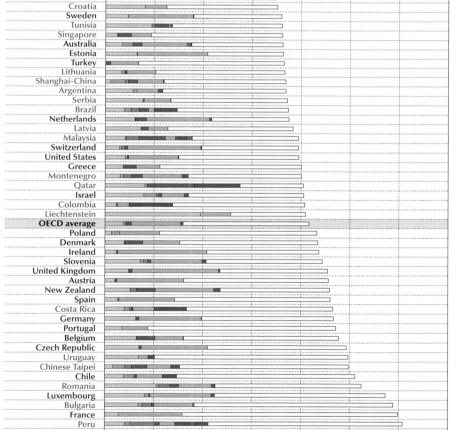

Countries and economies are ranked in ascending order of the sum of total explained variation in mathematics performance by elements of socio-economic status.

Source: OECD, PISA 2012 Database, Table II.2.6.

StatLink ᵃᵖᵃ http://dx.doi.org/10.1787/888932964813

In Estonia, the performance gaps associated with parental education and occupation are not as wide, between 53 and 56 score points. However, in Italy and Spain, the performance gaps observed between students whose parents work in different occupations (around 82 score points) are wider than those observed between students whose parents have different levels of education (around 48 and 57 score points, respectively) (Table II.2.5).

Figure II.2.3 summarises, for each country, the degree to which various components of socio-economic status are associated with mathematics performance. Since these components tend to be associated with each other – for example, a student whose parents are better educated is also likely to have parents in higher-status occupations – the graph displays the influence of these features together, and shows the variance in student performance explained by each feature once the influence of the others has been accounted for. The final segment shows the variance explained jointly by all factors (Table II.2.6).

Resilient students

Many socio-economically disadvantaged students, schools and systems still achieve high performance in PISA 2012 by international standards. As Volume IV explains, the amount a country or economy spends on education and its per capita GDP are only weakly related to performance in PISA. Beyond a certain threshold, both of these measures of wealth account for only a limited proportion of the cross-country variation in mean mathematics performance.

Across OECD countries, 6.4% of the entire student population – or nearly one million students – beat the socio-economic odds against them when compared with similar students in other countries. In Hong Kong-China, Korea, Macao-China, Shanghai-China, Singapore and Viet Nam, more than half of disadvantaged students (those in the bottom quarter of the socio-economic scale within a country or economy) or 12.5% of the overall student population perform among the top 25% of students across all participating countries, after taking their socio-economic status into account. Not only do they beat the odds when compared to similar students in other countries, many of these students perform at the highest levels on the PISA scales. PISA refers to these students as "resilient" because they manage to overcome difficult socio-economic circumstances and succeed in school.[8] Figure II.2.4 shows the percentage of resilient students – as a proportion of the overall student population – across countries and economies and the widely different profiles across school systems (Table II.2.7a).

The share of resilient students increased significantly in Turkey, Mexico, Poland, Italy, Tunisia and Germany, meaning that these countries provided more chances for their disadvantaged students to perform at high levels in 2012 than they did in 2003 (see below for a discussion of trends in equity, and particularly in student resiliency).

Mean performance, after taking account of socio-economic status

Comparing countries' performance after accounting for socio-economic status allows for comparisons of different education systems based on the performance of students with similar socio-economic status. A simple hypothetical exercise is to analyse the performance of students with an average socio-economic status across OECD countries (that is, at the mean of the index, or zero) and use this as the basis for analysing the performance of the system. The question addressed is: What would be the average performance of this system if all students had the OECD-average socio-economic status?

Most education systems perform similarly before and after accounting for socio-economic status, but there are exceptions.[9] Figure II.2.5 shows that Portugal would perform above the OECD average if socio-economic status were taken into account. Turkey's performance would also improve from below average to average. Among the partner economies, Viet Nam would markedly improve its rankings if socio-economic status were taken into account using this simple hypothetical exercise (Table II.2.4a). In relative terms, these are the only three countries that would climb more than 10 positions in their performance rankings if socio-economic status were taken into account.

Education systems can also be compared according to the performance of socio-economically advantaged and disadvantaged students (those in the top and bottom quarters of socio-economic status within the country). As Figure II.2.6 shows, in OECD systems that combine high equity in education outcomes and high mean performance, such as Canada, Estonia, Japan and Korea, disadvantaged students rank very highly internationally and so do their advantaged peers.

Among countries and economies with above-OECD-average performance, disadvantaged students in Canada, Denmark, Estonia, Finland, Ireland and Macao-China rank higher than their advantaged peers by more than five positions. Among systems whose mean performance is around the OECD average, the difference is equally marked in Latvia, Norway and Iceland. Among countries and economies with below-OECD-average performance, disadvantaged students in Italy, the Russian Federation and Sweden rank higher than their advantaged peers by more than five positions.

■ Figure II.2.4 ■
Percentage of resilient students

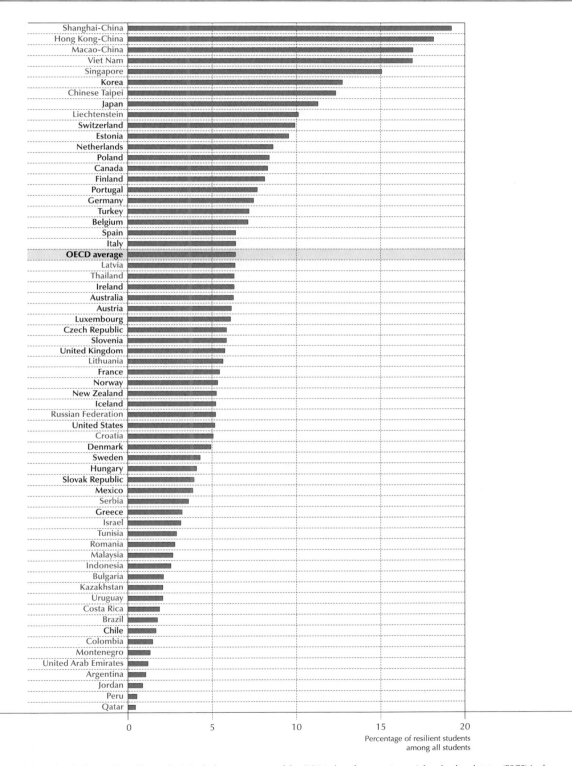

Percentage of resilient students
among all students

Note: A student is classified as resilient if he or she is in the bottom quarter of the *PISA index of economic, social and cultural status* (ESCS) in the country of assessment and performs in the top quarter of students among all countries, after accounting for socio-economic status.
Countries and economies are ranked in descending order of the percentage of resilient students.
Source: OECD, PISA 2012 Database, Table II.2.7a.
StatLink ⌨ http://dx.doi.org/10.1787/888932964813

■ Figure II.2.5 ■

Mean mathematics performance, before and after accounting for countries'/economies' socio-economic profile

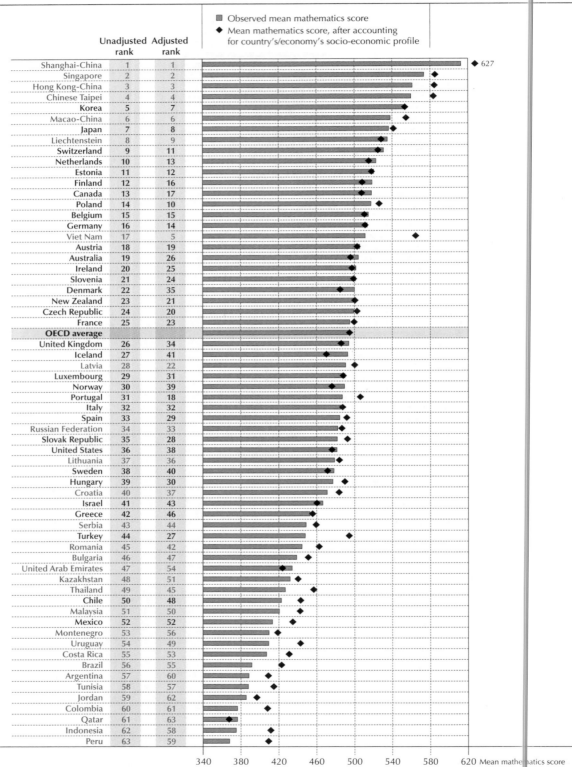

■ Observed mean mathematics score

◆ Mean mathematics score, after accounting for country's/economy's socio-economic profile

	Unadjusted rank	Adjusted rank
Shanghai-China	1	1
Singapore	2	2
Hong Kong-China	3	3
Chinese Taipei	4	4
Korea	5	7
Macao-China	6	6
Japan	7	8
Liechtenstein	8	9
Switzerland	9	11
Netherlands	10	13
Estonia	11	12
Finland	12	16
Canada	13	17
Poland	14	10
Belgium	15	15
Germany	16	14
Viet Nam	17	5
Austria	18	19
Australia	19	26
Ireland	20	25
Slovenia	21	24
Denmark	22	35
New Zealand	23	21
Czech Republic	24	20
France	25	23
OECD average		
United Kingdom	26	34
Iceland	27	41
Latvia	28	22
Luxembourg	29	31
Norway	30	39
Portugal	31	18
Italy	32	32
Spain	33	29
Russian Federation	34	33
Slovak Republic	35	28
United States	36	38
Lithuania	37	36
Sweden	38	40
Hungary	39	30
Croatia	40	37
Israel	41	43
Greece	42	46
Serbia	43	44
Turkey	44	27
Romania	45	42
Bulgaria	46	47
United Arab Emirates	47	54
Kazakhstan	48	51
Thailand	49	45
Chile	50	48
Malaysia	51	50
Mexico	52	52
Montenegro	53	56
Uruguay	54	49
Costa Rica	55	53
Brazil	56	55
Argentina	57	60
Tunisia	58	57
Jordan	59	62
Colombia	60	61
Qatar	61	63
Indonesia	62	58
Peru	63	59

340   380   420   460   500   540   580   620 Mean mathematics score

Countries and economies are ranked in descending order of the observed mean mathematics score.
Source: OECD, PISA 2012 Database, Table II.2.1.

StatLink ᕫᕮᕲ http://dx.doi.org/10.1787/888932964813

EXCELLENCE THROUGH EQUITY: GIVING EVERY STUDENT THE CHANCE TO SUCCEED – VOLUME II

■ Figure II.2.6 ■
Mean mathematics performance, by national quarter of socio-economic status

▶ Top quarter (value indicates position in the ranking)
● Third quarter
◇ Second quarter
▬ Bottom quarter (value indicates position in the ranking)

Country	Range of students' socio-economic status (difference between top and bottom quarter)	Bottom quarter rank	Top quarter rank
Shanghai-China	2.46	1	1
Hong Kong-China	2.50	2	4
Singapore	2.34	3	2
Macao-China	2.20	4	16
Korea	1.90	5	5
Japan	1.84	6	7
Chinese Taipei	2.15	7	3
Estonia	2.07	8	15
Liechtenstein	2.31	9	12
Switzerland	2.29	10	6
Finland	1.96	11	19
Canada	2.19	12	17
Netherlands	1.97	13	11
Poland	2.30	14	9
Viet Nam	2.82	15	18
Germany	2.40	16	10
Iceland	2.05	17	34
Australia	2.01	18	23
Ireland	2.17	19	26
Denmark	2.14	20	29
Belgium	2.31	21	8
Norway	1.91	22	37
Slovenia	2.24	23	22
United Kingdom	2.04	24	27
Austria	2.16	25	21
Latvia	2.28	26	33
OECD average	**2.30**		
Czech Republic	1.92	27	20
Italy	2.53	28	36
Russian Federation	1.92	29	39
New Zealand	2.08	30	14
Spain	2.66	32	31
Sweden	2.06	31	40
France	2.04	33	13
United States	2.49	34	32
Portugal	3.07	35	24
Lithuania	2.34	36	38
Luxembourg	2.83	37	25
Croatia	2.19	38	41
Hungary	2.47	39	30
Slovak Republic	2.31	40	28
Serbia	2.32	41	46
Greece	2.57	42	42
Turkey	2.81	43	45
Israel	2.11	44	35
Romania	2.35	45	43
Thailand	2.99	46	49
Kazakhstan	1.91	47	52
United Arab Emirates	2.07	48	50
Malaysia	2.53	49	51
Mexico	3.28	50	55
Bulgaria	2.65	51	44
Chile	2.92	52	47
Montenegro	2.29	53	53
Costa Rica	3.22	54	54
Uruguay	2.92	55	48
Tunisia	3.28	56	58
Jordan	2.55	57	60
Brazil	3.04	58	56
Indonesia	2.81	59	62
Argentina	2.88	60	57
Colombia	3.06	61	61
Qatar	2.18	62	63
Peru	3.20	63	59

300   400   500   600   700 Mean mathematics score

Countries and economies are ranked in descending order of the mean performance of students in the bottom quarter of the PISA index of economic, social and cultural status (ESCS).
Source: OECD, PISA 2012 Database, Table II.2.4a.
StatLink ᐃᒪᒉ http://dx.doi.org/10.1787/888932964813

By contrast, among countries with above-OECD-average performance, advantaged students in Belgium, Germany, New Zealand and Poland rank higher than their disadvantaged peers by more than five positions. The same is observed in the Czech Republic, France and Portugal, among systems that perform around the OECD average, and in Bulgaria, Hungary, Israel, Luxembourg, the Slovak Republic and Uruguay, among those that perform below the OECD average (Figure II.2.6).

Many factors related to socio-economic disadvantage are not directly affected by education policy, at least not in the short term. To what extent can schools and school policies moderate the impact of socio-economic disadvantage on student performance? The overall relationship between socio-economic background and student performance indicates the capacity of education systems to provide equitable learning opportunities. However, from a policy perspective, this relationship is even more important, as it indicates how equity is interrelated with systemic aspects of education. Better schools for disadvantaged students can help reduce socio-economic disparities in performance; but countries also need to consider other policies that affect families, such as those to reduce poverty, malnutrition, and inadequate housing, those to improve parents' education, and other social policies that can also improve student learning.

Between-school variation in performance

Ensuring consistently high standards across schools is a formidable challenge for any school system. Some performance differences between schools may be related to the socio-economic composition of the school's student population or other characteristics of the student body. School location may also explain differences between schools. For example, urban and rural schools often do not provide the same opportunities or have access to the same quantity and quality of resources. In some countries and economies, there is also a large degree of residential segregation based on income or on cultural or ethnic background. In decentralised school systems, performance differences between schools may also be related to differences in the level of government authority responsible for education. Box II.2.2 examines the variation in student performance among the countries that collected regional/state data through PISA.

Box II.2.2. **Geographic location, regions and variation in student performance**

Australia, Belgium, Canada, Italy, Mexico, Spain, the United Kingdom and the partner countries Brazil, Colombia and the United Arab Emirates collected enough data at the sub-national level to allow for a detailed analysis of how student performance varies across different regions and geographical locations. Annex B2 of each Volume of the *PISA 2012 Results* provides in-depth results for those countries that provided results at the sub-national level. Figure II.2.a shows the range of performance across regions compared with mean performance across countries.

For each of the countries listed above, this box describes how much of the variation in students' mathematics performance is observed among students within schools and regions; among schools within regions; and across regions. It also analyses how much of this variation can be described by variations in socio-economic status across students, schools and regions. Table B2.II.25 presents the variation at each level as a proportion of the total variation in performance observed across OECD countries.

Differences in mean mathematics performance across OECD countries account for 10% of the variation in student performance – meaning that performance differences among countries are relatively small compared with performance differences among individual students (see Figure IV.1.2 in Volume IV). In most countries, performance variations across regions account for less than 3% of the variation observed across OECD countries. In Italy, however, performance variations across regions account for almost 8% of the total variation in student performance across OECD countries. In the United Kingdom, there are practically no aggregate performance differences across England, Northern Ireland, Wales and Scotland; however, there are performance differences across schools within regions.

Performance differences among schools within the same region are particularly large in Belgium (they represent 59% of the total variation in student performance across OECD countries) and Italy (45%) compared with the OECD average of 36%. Variations in the performance of students who attend the same school are relatively large in Australia (representing 68% of the total variation in student performance in OECD countries), the United Kingdom (65%), Canada (64%) and Spain (64%), compared with the OECD average of 54% (Table B2.II.25).

...

■ Figure II.2.a ■

Mean mathematics performance in countries and regions

■ Country's/economy's mean mathematics score
○ Regions

Shanghai-China		Shanghai-China
Singapore		Singapore
Hong Kong-China		Hong Kong-China
Chinese Taipei		Chinese Taipei
Korea		Korea
Macao-China		Macao-China
Japan		Japan
Liechtenstein		Liechtenstein
Switzerland		Switzerland
Netherlands		Netherlands
Estonia		Estonia
Finland		Finland
Canada		Canada
Poland		Poland
Belgium		Belgium
Germany		Germany
Viet Nam		Viet Nam
Austria		Austria
Australia		Australia
Ireland		Ireland
Slovenia		Slovenia
Denmark		Denmark
New Zealand		New Zealand
Czech Republic		Czech Republic
France		France
OECD average		**OECD average**
United Kingdom		United Kingdom
Iceland		Iceland
Latvia		Latvia
Luxembourg		Luxembourg
Norway		Norway
Portugal		Portugal
Italy		Italy
Spain		Spain
Russian Federation		Russian Federation
Slovak Republic		Slovak Republic
United States		United States
Lithuania		Lithuania
Sweden		Sweden
Hungary		Hungary
Croatia		Croatia
Israel		Israel
Greece		Greece
Serbia		Serbia
Turkey		Turkey
Romania		Romania
Bulgaria		Bulgaria
United Arab Emirates		United Arab Emirates
Kazakhstan		Kazakhstan
Thailand		Thailand
Chile		Chile
Malaysia		Malaysia
Mexico		Mexico
Montenegro		Montenegro
Uruguay		Uruguay
Costa Rica		Costa Rica
Albania		Albania
Brazil		Brazil
Argentina		Argentina
Tunisia		Tunisia
Jordan		Jordan
Colombia		Colombia
Qatar		Qatar
Indonesia		Indonesia
Peru		Peru

340   390   440   490   540   590   640   Mean mathematics score

Note: Annex B2 provides a list of all of the regions included and their average mathematics performance.
Countries and economies are ranked in descending order of mean mathematics performance.
Source: OECD, PISA 2012 Database, Tables I.2.3a and B2.I.3.

StatLink ᵐˢᵖ http://dx.doi.org/10.1787/888932964813

...

Disparities in socio-economic status explain a relative large share of the difference in performance among regions, particularly in some countries, such as Spain and the United Arab Emirates, where differences in socio-economic status among students, schools and regions explain more than 85% of the performance differences observed among regions. The proportion of variation in performance explained in this way is also high in Colombia (70%), Belgium (70%) and Mexico (58%). By contrast, socio-economic differences explain only 16% of performance differences among regions in Canada and 26% in Australia. In Italy, socio-economic status explains 47% of performance differences across regions. In Belgium and the United Kingdom, differences in performance among schools within regions are closely related to socio-economic status. In the United Kingdom, socio-economic status explains 62% of performance differences among schools within the same region, while in Belgium, socio-economic status explains 73% of performance differences among schools located in the same region. By contrast, in Canada, Mexico and the United Arab Emirates, socio-economic status explains less than 50% of the differences among schools located in the same region (across OECD countries, an average of 48% of the performance differences among schools in the same region is so explained). In most countries, socio-economic disparities among students in the same school account for only 3% of the performance differences observed within schools. In Spain, however, 9% of the performances differences observed within schools are so explained (Table B2.II.25).

Between-school differences in performance may also be related to the quality of the school or staff or to the education policies implemented in some schools and not in others. System-level policies may also help to explain why student performance varies between schools. Systems with small between-school variations in performance are those that, in general, are comprehensive, meaning that they do not differentiate by programme, school or student ability. Other systems try to meet the needs of each student by creating different tracks or pathways through education and inviting students to choose among them at an earlier or later age. Volume IV of this publication examines how both school policies and practices and system-level policies vary and relate to performance differences between students and schools.

Figure II.2.7 shows the variation in performance within each country. The length of the bar represents the total variation in that country as a proportion of the OECD average level of variation in performance. The dark part of the bar represents the proportion of those differences that is observed between schools, the light bar represents the proportion of those differences that is observed within schools.

Across OECD countries, 37% of the overall performance differences are observed between schools and 63% within schools. The extent of between-school differences in performance varies widely across school systems.[10] For example, between-school differences account for less than 15% of the OECD average total variation in performance in Estonia, Denmark, Norway, Sweden, Iceland, Finland and Albania. Because Denmark, Estonia and Finland also manage to achieve higher-than-average mean performance, in these countries and economies parents and students can expect that, no matter what school they attend, they are likely to achieve at high levels. In contrast, in Chinese Taipei, the Netherlands, Liechtenstein, Belgium, Hungary and Turkey differences between schools account for more than 60% of the OECD average variation. The overall level of variation in these countries tends to be larger than average, particularly in Chinese Taipei and Belgium (Figure II.2.7 and Table II.2.8a).

Performance differences across schools and socio-economic disparities

More than half of the performance differences observed across students in different schools can be accounted for by socio-economic disparities across students and schools, on average across OECD countries (Figure II.2.8). A student's study programme, identified through the PISA student questionnaire and other sources, also plays a significant role in explaining performance differences across schools in many countries, accounting for 40% of the differences. The programme is identified by education level (e.g. upper or lower secondary), orientation of the curriculum (e.g. general or vocational), and intent (e.g. providing general access to other education levels or direct access to the labour market). Across OECD countries, 71% of the performance differences across students in different schools is accounted for by a combination of socio-economic status and the student's study programme (Table II.2.9a).

■ Figure II.2.7 ■
Total variation in mathematics performance and variation between and within schools
Expressed as a percentage of the variation in student performance across OECD countries

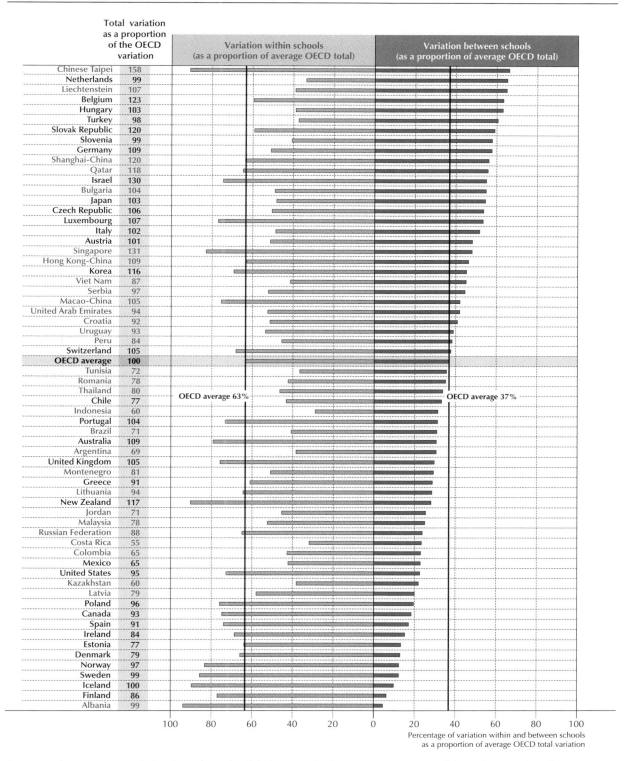

	Total variation as a proportion of the OECD variation
Chinese Taipei	158
Netherlands	99
Liechtenstein	107
Belgium	123
Hungary	103
Turkey	98
Slovak Republic	120
Slovenia	99
Germany	109
Shanghai-China	120
Qatar	118
Israel	130
Bulgaria	104
Japan	103
Czech Republic	106
Luxembourg	107
Italy	102
Austria	101
Singapore	131
Hong Kong-China	109
Korea	116
Viet Nam	87
Serbia	97
Macao-China	105
United Arab Emirates	94
Croatia	92
Uruguay	93
Peru	84
Switzerland	105
OECD average	**100**
Tunisia	72
Romania	78
Thailand	80
Chile	77
Indonesia	60
Portugal	104
Brazil	71
Australia	109
Argentina	69
United Kingdom	105
Montenegro	81
Greece	91
Lithuania	94
New Zealand	117
Jordan	71
Malaysia	78
Russian Federation	88
Costa Rica	55
Colombia	65
Mexico	65
United States	95
Kazakhstan	60
Latvia	79
Poland	96
Canada	93
Spain	91
Ireland	84
Estonia	77
Denmark	79
Norway	97
Sweden	99
Iceland	100
Finland	86
Albania	99

Variation within schools (as a proportion of average OECD total)
Variation between schools (as a proportion of average OECD total)

OECD average 63%   OECD average 37%

Percentage of variation within and between schools
as a proportion of average OECD total variation

Countries and economies are ranked in descending order of the between-school variation as a proportion of the total variation in performance across OECD countries.

Source: OECD, PISA 2012 Database, Table II.2.8a.

StatLink ⟲ http://dx.doi.org/10.1787/888932964813

■ Figure II.2.8 ■

Performance differences between and within schools explained by students' and schools' socio-economic status

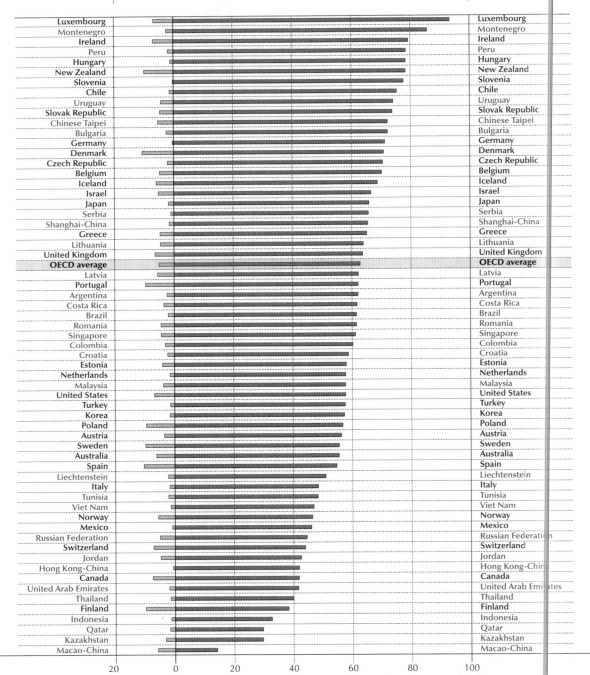

Countries and economies are ranked in descending order of the percentage of variation in mathematics performance between schools explained by the PISA index of economic, social and cultural status *of students and schools.*

Source: OECD, PISA 2012 Database, Table II.2.9a.

StatLink ⟨ﬁﬁ⟩ http://dx.doi.org/10.1787/888932964813

EXCELLENCE THROUGH EQUITY: GIVING EVERY STUDENT THE CHANCE TO SUCCEED – VOLUME II

Equity between schools is greater in countries with greater equity in outcomes in general, as measured by the strength of the relationship between performance and socio-economic status, including school systems with high average mathematics performance, such as Canada, Finland and Hong Kong-China. In all three, less than 45% of between-school differences in performance is explained by socio-economic disparities. Socio-economic disparities between schools are closely associated with performance differences in Luxembourg, where 93% of the between-school variation in performance is explained by the socio-economic status of students and schools. In Chile, Hungary, Ireland, New Zealand, Peru and Slovenia, more than 75% of the performance differences between schools is explained by the socio-economic status of students and schools.

Students' study programmes are strongly related to performance differences between schools in Germany, Luxembourg and the Netherlands, where more than 80% of the performance variation is explained by the programme in which a student is enrolled. After taking the socio-economic status of students and schools into account, in Belgium, Germany, Luxembourg, the Netherlands, Portugal and Shanghai-China, 85% or more of between-school performance differences is explained by students' study programmes and their socio-economic status, and schools' socio-economic profiles (Table II.2.9a).

Across OECD countries, the socio-economic status of students and schools and students' study programmes are more weakly associated with the differences in performance observed between students who attend the same school (within-school variation).[11] In Denmark, Finland, New Zealand, Poland, Portugal, Spain and Sweden, between 9% and 10% of the performance difference within schools can be explained by differences in students' socio-economic status. In Luxembourg, Macao-China, Malaysia, the Netherlands and Portugal, socio-economic status and study programmes explain between 20% and 38% of performance differences within schools (Table II.2.9a).

Box II.2.3. **What are the main characteristics of students attending socio-economically advantaged and disadvantaged schools?**

Advantaged (disadvantaged) schools are those where the typical student in the school, or the socio-economic profile of the school, is above (below) the socio-economic status of the typical student in the country, and the country's/economy's mean socio-economic status. In each school, a random sample of 35 students participate in PISA (for more details, see the *PISA 2012 Technical Report* [OECD, forthcoming]). Since the socio-economic profile of the school is calculated using the information provided by these students, the precision of the estimate depends on the number of students in the school who take the test and the diversity of their answers. This was taken into account when classifying schools as advantaged, disadvantaged or average. If the difference between the school's socio-economic profile and the socio-economic status of the typical student in the country (the mean socio-economic status at the country level) was not statistically significant, the school was classified as a socio-economically average school. If the school profile was statistically significantly above the country mean, the school is classified as an advantaged school. If the profile was below the country mean, the school is classified as a disadvantaged school. Schools in which only a few students participated in PISA are therefore more likely to be categorised as socio-economically average schools.

Across OECD countries, 73% of students attending advantaged schools have at least one parent with a tertiary education (ISCED levels 5 and 6) compared with 33% of students in disadvantaged schools. While 77% of students in advantaged schools have parents who work in skilled occupations (ISCO major groups 1, 2 and 3), only 32% of students in disadvantaged schools have parents who work in those occupations. Some 61% of students in advantaged schools have poetry books at home, while 36% of students in disadvantaged schools do. However, there are wide variations in the averages across countries. For example, among OECD countries, in Canada, Finland and Sweden more than 80% of students in advantaged schools and more than 50% of students in disadvantaged schools have tertiary-educated parents. In contrast, in Israel, Japan, Korea and the United States, while more than 80% of students in advantaged schools have highly educated parents, fewer than 40% of students in disadvantaged schools do. There is also wide variation across school systems in the proportions of students in advantaged and disadvantages schools whose parents work in high-status occupations (Table II.2.10).

■ Figure II.2.9 ■

Performance differences within and between schools across socio-economic groups

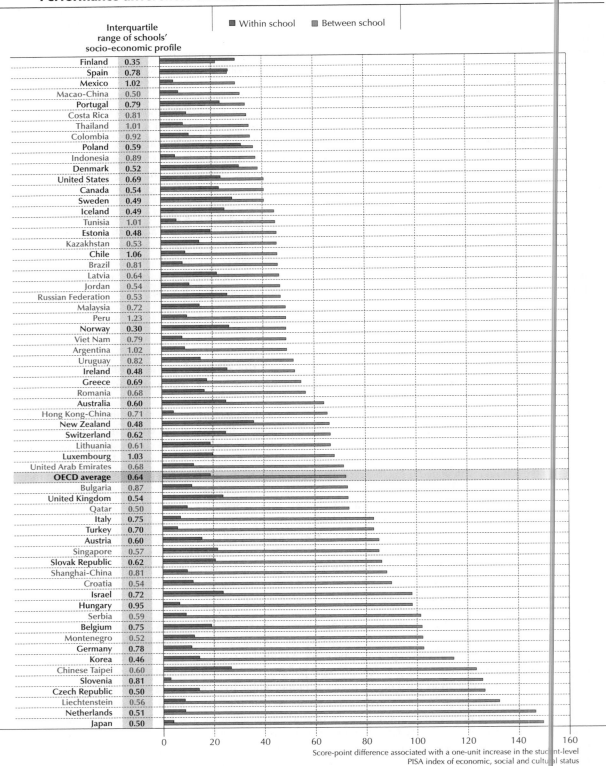

Countries and economies are ranked in ascending order of the between-schools score-point difference associated with a one-unit increase in the student-level PISA index of economic, social and cultural status.

Source: OECD, PISA 2012 Database, Tables II.2.9a and II.2.13a.

StatLink ⟨⟩ http://dx.doi.org/10.1787/888932964813

■ Figure II.2.10 ■

Mathematics performance of students in socio-economically advantaged, average and disadvantaged schools

► Socio-economically advantaged schools (value indicates position in the ranking)
▪ Socio-economically average schools (value indicates position in the ranking)
— Socio-economically disadvantaged schools (value indicates position in the ranking)

Average socio-economic status			Country	Rank (disadvantaged)	Rank (average)	Rank (advantaged)
Socio-economically disadvantaged schools[1]	Socio-economically average schools[1]	Socio-economically advantaged schools[1]				
-1.06	-0.35	0.25	Shanghai-China	1	1	1
-1.22	-0.89	-0.32	Macao-China	2	7	16
-0.71	-0.33	0.45	Singapore	3	3	2
-1.33	-0.84	0.05	Hong Kong-China	4	2	4
-0.04	0.36	0.77	Finland	5	10	29
-0.40	0.06	0.66	Estonia	6	14	20
-0.28	0.11	0.73	Switzerland	7	12	7
-0.46	0.03	0.48	Korea	8	5	5
-0.12	0.38	0.90	Canada	9	17	21
-0.86	-0.44	0.15	Chinese Taipei	10	4	3
-0.74	-0.22	0.47	Poland	11	15	13
-0.49	-0.08	0.37	Japan	12	6	6
-2.46	-1.85	-0.78	Viet Nam	13	11	14
0.03	0.42	0.91	Norway	14	30	35
-0.08	0.39	0.97	Denmark	15	22	28
0.27	0.74	1.16	Iceland	16	27	39
-0.30	0.24	0.77	Australia	17	19	17
-0.17	0.22	0.74	Sweden	18	35	42
-0.95	-0.32	0.32	Latvia	19	32	32
-0.62	-0.16	0.39	Russian Federation	20	36	37
-0.79	-0.23	0.52	Spain	21	31	38
-0.23	0.26	0.79	United Kingdom	22	26	23
-0.44	0.19	0.82	Germany	23	13	10
-0.41	0.07	0.68	Austria	24	9	19
-0.56	-0.02	0.60	**OECD average**			
-0.45	0.17	0.71	Luxembourg	25	20	25
-0.51	0.02	0.58	New Zealand	26	21	18
-1.15	-0.49	0.61	Portugal	27	23	26
-0.26	0.23	0.68	Netherlands	28	8	8
-0.51	0.09	0.63	Ireland	29	18	30
-0.46	0.12	0.68	Belgium	30	16	11
-0.47	0.03	0.66	Slovenia	31	24	12
-0.48	0.17	0.78	United States	32	28	40
-0.55	-0.09	0.51	Czech Republic	33	25	9
-0.76	-0.13	0.45	Lithuania	34	34	31
-0.79	-0.35	0.32	Croatia	35	39	24
-0.65	-0.08	0.55	Italy	36	29	27
-0.86	-0.17	0.50	Slovak Republic	37	33	15
-0.81	-0.37	0.12	Kazakhstan	38	46	51
-0.95	-0.27	0.42	Hungary	39	38	22
-2.04	-1.37	-0.40	Thailand	40	47	49
-1.07	-0.51	0.22	Romania	41	43	43
-2.05	-1.49	-0.63	Turkey	42	42	33
-0.74	-0.33	0.36	Serbia	43	41	36
-0.39	0.18	0.67	Israel	44	37	34
-0.77	-0.07	0.61	Greece	45	40	44
-0.26	0.29	0.80	United Arab Emirates	46	44	47
-1.29	-0.66	0.36	Chile	47	51	46
-1.36	-0.76	-0.04	Malaysia	48	52	48
-1.99	-1.12	-0.10	Mexico	49	50	54
-0.97	-0.29	0.46	Bulgaria	50	45	41
-1.88	-0.99	0.16	Costa Rica	51	53	50
-1.51	-0.89	0.26	Uruguay	52	48	45
-0.63	-0.30	0.17	Montenegro	53	49	52
-1.87	-1.23	-0.11	Brazil	54	56	53
-1.02	-0.46	0.30	Jordan	55	57	56
-2.38	-1.88	-0.85	Indonesia	56	60	60
-2.04	-1.22	-0.22	Tunisia	57	55	55
-0.03	0.42	0.81	Qatar	58	61	61
-1.43	-0.75	0.05	Argentina	59	54	57
-2.12	-1.28	-0.40	Colombia	60	58	59
-2.13	-1.25	-0.28	Peru	61	59	58

300   400   500   600   700
Mean mathematics score

1. A socio-economically disadvantaged school is one whose students' mean socio-economic status is statistically significantly below the mean socio-economic status of the country/economy; an average school is one where there is no difference between the school's and the country's/economy's mean socio-economic status; and an advantaged school is one whose students' mean socio-economic status is statistically significantly above the country/economy mean.
Countries and economies are ranked in descending order of the mean performance of students in disadvantaged schools.
Source: OECD, PISA 2012 Database, Table II.4.2.
StatLink ⟐ http://dx.doi.org/10.1787/888932964813

■ Figure II.2.11 ■

Distribution of students across school performance and socio-economic profile[1]

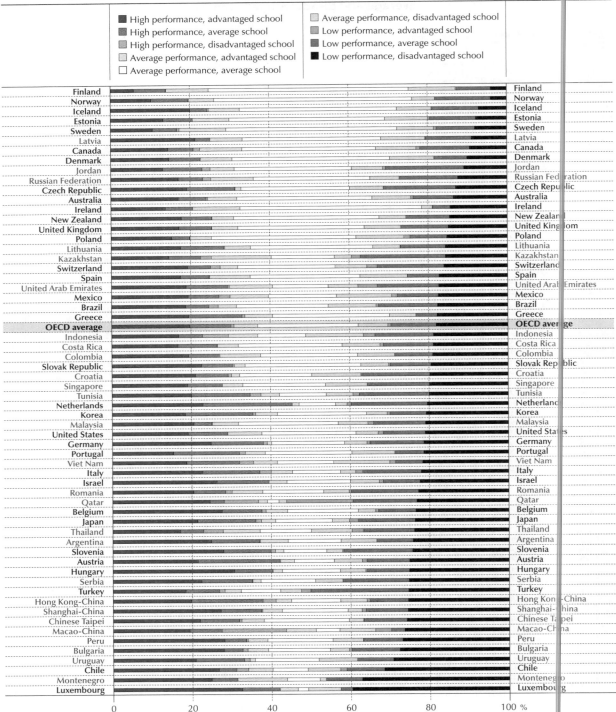

1. A socio-economically disadvantaged school is one whose students' mean socio-economic status is statistically significantly below the mean socio-economic status of the country/economy; an average school is one where there is no difference between schools' and the country's/economy's mean socio-economic status; and an advantaged school is one whose students' mean socio-economic status is statistically significantly above the country/economy mean. A low-performing school is one in which average school performance is statistically significantly below the mean performance in the country/economy; an average-performing school is one in which there is no difference between the two; and a high-performing school is one in which average school performance is statistically significantly above the country/economy mean. Small schools are more likely to be classified as average schools.
Countries and economies are ranked in ascending order of the proportion of students in low-performing schools that are also disadvantaged schools.
Source: OECD, PISA 2012 Database, Table II.2.11.
StatLink ⟨msl⟩ http://dx.doi.org/10.1787/888932964813

On average across OECD countries, students attending more socio-economically advantaged schools score 72 points higher in mathematics than students attending a less advantaged school. Within schools, more advantaged students score 19 points higher in mathematics than less advantaged students attending that same school.[12] Figure II.2.9 shows the average performance differences among students attending different schools and among students within the same school, by socio-economic status (Table II.2.9a). Between-school differences in student performance across socio-economic status are relatively small – less than 30 score points – in Finland, Mexico and Spain (41 score points is the equivalent of about one year of formal schooling). However, these differences exceed 140 score points in Japan and the Netherlands.

Students in advantaged schools perform better than those in disadvantaged schools, but they may not perform particularly well when compared against an international standard. Box II.2.3 explains how PISA classifies schools as socio-economically advantaged, average and disadvantaged and describes the main characteristics of these schools. Figure II.2.10 shows the performance of students in advantaged and disadvantaged schools across countries. Across OECD countries, 104 score points separate students in advantaged and disadvantaged schools. While in Finland and Macao-China the differences are relatively small (less than 40 score points; although still large, the difference is smaller than the OECD average), in the Czech Republic, the Netherlands, the Slovak Republic and Chinese Taipei, the gap exceeds 150 score points.

Figure II.2.10 also shows the average socio-economic status of students attending advantaged, average and disadvantaged schools. Some students who attend schools with a relatively disadvantaged student population manage to achieve high levels of performance. For example, students attending disadvantaged schools in Hong Kong-China, Macao-China, Shanghai-China and Singapore score higher than 500 points, on average, in mathematics. Yet the average socio-economic status of these students is well below average, particularly in Hong Kong-China, Macao-China and Shanghai-China, where it is more than one unit below the OECD average (Table II.4.2).

In general, poor performance and socio-economic disadvantage are closely associated at the school level, but some school systems are better than others at weakening that relationship. Across OECD countries, 18% of students attend disadvantaged, low-performing schools and 20% attend advantaged, high-performing schools.[13] As Figure II.2.11 shows, however, these averages vary widely across countries. In Finland, for example, 4% of students attend disadvantaged, low-performing schools and 6% attend advantaged, high-performing schools. In Norway, Estonia, Canada and Sweden, fewer than 10% of students attend disadvantaged, low-performing schools and fewer than 15% attend advantaged, high-performing schools (Table II.2.11).

PROVIDING ACCESS TO SCHOOLING TO ALL 15-YEAR-OLDS

Access to schooling is a precondition to inclusion and equity in education. Across most OECD countries, all students have access to school throughout compulsory education. Regardless of performance or even equity, any system where a large proportion of 15-year-olds is not enrolled in school cannot be considered a high-quality and equitable education system. Almost all OECD countries achieved universal access to schooling more than a decade ago and enrolment rates in primary and lower secondary education are very close to 100%. Some of the countries that joined the OECD recently and some partner countries have achieved this goal more recently or are moving towards its fulfilment.

Between PISA 2003 and PISA 2012, Indonesia and Brazil added more than 485 000 and 425 000 students, respectively, to the total population of 15-year-olds enrolled in Grade 7 or above, an increase of 16% and 18%, respectively, during the period. Adding these new students has been a formidable achievement since in both countries increased enrolment has not led to a decline in learning outcomes. Among OECD countries, Turkey and Mexico also saw an increase in the absolute numbers of students added and in the percentage of enrolled students over the same period. All these countries provided access to schooling to more students – even as the population of 15-year-olds was shrinking, which means that rising enrolment has implied improved capacity to retain students as they progress through higher grades. In the case of Brazil, these achievements are the result of policy measures to minimise grade repetition and dropout (Table II.2.12).

In most countries and economies that participate in PISA, the proportion of 15-year-olds who are not enrolled in school is very small; thus including proxy results for them would have limited impact on an education system's mean performance. For example, one could assume that students outside the education system would score at the lowest level of performance identified in PISA (the lower end of Level 1 in the mathematics performance scale, or 358 score points) and weight these students by their proportion in the population of 15-year-olds. As Table II.2.12 shows, most countries would show no or very small changes in average performance after taking into account the performance of those outside the school system. Of the six countries and economies where the changes in performance are largest (more than 15 score points; Hong Kong-China, Macao-China, Mexico, Shanghai-China, Turkey and Viet Nam), only Viet Nam would drop a significant number of places in its relative rank (up to 24 places in the ranking, followed by Macao-China, with a loss of up to 10 places).

Box II.2.4. **Improving in PISA: Mexico**

Enrolment in Mexico increased ten-fold between 1950 and 2007, from about 3 million to more than 30 million students. In 2003, 58% of 15-year-olds were enrolled in Grade 7 or above. Still, despite continuing increases in enrolment, in 2012, fewer than 70% of the country's 15-year-olds were enrolled in school. In addition to low participation rates, Mexico also faces substantial challenges in providing quality education to its students. In 2012, more than half of Mexican students performed below the baseline level of proficiency in mathematics and fewer than 1% of students were considered top performers in PISA. Average performance still lags well behind the OECD average, to the point that the average Mexican 15-year-old student performs the equivalent of nearly two years below the OECD average.

Yet Mexico has improved its performance over the past decade. Between 2003 and 2012, student performance in reading and mathematics improved. In 2003, the average 15-year-old scored 385 points on the PISA mathematics assessment; in 2012, he or she scored 413 points – an average increase of 3.1 score points per year, which is the third highest increase among OECD countries, but a rate of progress that would still require a quarter of a century for Mexico to catch up with the OECD average. Improvements in performance are largest among the lowest-achieving students: they improved by more than 40 score points – the equivalent of one year of formal schooling – between 2003 and 2012. At the same time, the proportion of 15-year-olds who scored below Level 2 in mathematics dropped 11 percentage points during the period. Although an improvement of more than 20 score points in mathematics in PISA is observed among the highest-achieving students (those in the 90th percentile of mathematics performance), the percentage of students who perform at proficiency Level 5 or above in mathematics remained unchanged between 2003 and 2012.

Reducing the impact of socio-economic status on performance

Mexico was also able to moderate the impact of social background on learning outcomes between 2003 and 2012. The difference in mathematics performance between advantaged and disadvantaged students decreased from around 60 score points in 2003 to around 40 points in 2012. In conjunction with this, the relationship between socio-economic status and performance weakened: in 2003, 17% of the variation in mathematics performance was explained by socio-economic status; in 2012, 10% of the variation was so explained. This means that 15-year-olds' chances of becoming high- or low-achieving students in 2012 were less related to their socio-economic status than they were in 2003. In fact, Mexico's improvement in both mathematics performance and equity since PISA 2003 is largely the result of improvements among disadvantaged and low-performing schools, such that performance differences in PISA between schools have narrowed over the period.

Mexican students' experiences in school also changed between 2003 and 2012. While 30% of 15-year-old students in 2003 reported that they had repeated a grade at least once in their schooling, only 15% reported so in 2012. Students in 2012 spent around 15 minutes more per week in mathematics lessons but around 35 minutes less per week doing homework, on average, than students in 2003 did. Students in 2012 also reported better disciplinary climates in their classrooms and better student-teacher relations than students in 2003 did. In addition, the proportion of teachers hired on an hour-by-hour basis increased from 33% in 2000 to 38% in 2011 (SEP, 2013). These changes in grade repetition, learning time and learning environment, can be considered improvements only if they have led to improved teaching, learning and better student performance. This would not be the case if, for example, students had been promoted automatically at the end of the school year, more learning time had not reduced students' exposure to other equally relevant subjects, and if teachers hired on an hourly basis had to teach in poorer working conditions.

Offering targeted funding and support and independent assessment

During the past decade, Mexico has developed some programmes to promote enrolment in pre-primary education, support schools in need, and generate incentives for students to stay in school. Other, more recent

...

reforms shed light on the policy direction currently taken by Mexico. These reforms include curricular reform and the introduction of assessment and evaluation mechanisms through an independent entity. As these are relatively recent and complex reforms, further studies are needed to assess the extent to which the changes in evaluation, assessment and curriculum explain Mexico's improvement in PISA.

As part of these reforms, pre-primary education was made compulsory in 2002 (the effect of this policy on student performance later on will only be observed in PISA 2015). Work continues on improving the quality of urban care centres for children of low-income and working parents, establishing a national system of day-care centres, and disseminating a framework syllabus to help pre-primary institutions develop curricula that are adapted to their needs.

Education in Mexico, including initial and in-service teacher training, is managed at the state level, but there are mechanisms through which the Ministry implements policies throughout the country. Several targeted funding schemes and support programmes were implemented to promote a more equitable distribution of support and financing, particularly among disadvantaged schools and states. The *Programa Escuelas de Calidad* (PEC, Quality Schools), which was launched in 2001, allocates grants to finance school-improvement plans. It grants autonomy to schools and encourages shared decision making among directors, teachers, parents, union representatives, former students and community members through School Participation Councils. Nearly half of all schools in Mexico have an affiliated Council. The *Plan Estratégico de Transformación Escolar* (PETE) helps stakeholders to develop an annual work plan for which a five-year grant is awarded. Some 70% of the grant for the first four years and 50% of the funds for the fifth year are allocated for supplies, infrastructure and other material resources. Also, between 2009 and 2012, the *Estrategia para la Mejora del Logro Educativo* (EIMLE, Strategy for the Improvement of Educational Achievement) has reached more than 7 000 of the lowest-achieving schools, training networks of teachers and building capacity within the schools through mentorships. The *Programa Escuelas de Tiempo Completo* (PETC, Full-time Schools) aims to lengthen the school day by four hours. It mainly focuses on marginalised urban populations, or populations with large proportions of indigenous, migrant, or other low-performing students. Three years after it was created in 2007, PETC had reached over 2 000 schools across 30 states. Meanwhile, *ConstruyeT*, a programme that focuses on teacher training and practice, reaches one-third of Mexico's schools and enjoys the support of UNICEF, PNUD, UNESCO and 29 NGOs; and the *Better Schools Programme* has refurbished 19 000 pre-primary to lower-secondary schools most in need of repair. Although these programmes mostly target disadvantaged schools and states, the nature of PISA data cannot establish the extent to which, if at all, these programmes have promoted Mexico's performance in PISA (OECD, 2012a).

Other programmes provide incentives for students to stay in school. *Oportunidades* is a cash-transfer programme targeting health and education for families living below the poverty line. The programme began in 2002 and reached more than five million families in 2012, helping to improve enrolment rates in secondary education, particularly among girls. The *Programa de Becas de Media Superior*, another cash-transfer programme, aims to reduce dropout rates at the upper secondary level. These programmes may have contributed to the reduction of dropout rates, but other factors may have contributed as well, inasmuch as dropout rates were declining even before these programmes were implemented (SEP, 2013).

In 2002, the government announced the creation of the *Instituto Nacional para la Evaluación de la Educación* (INEE) charged with measuring and evaluating the education system's quality and performance. The institute was granted complete autonomy from the Ministry of Education in 2013. In line with the idea of creating an information system that would enable stakeholders to follow schools' performance, in 2006, the federal government introduced the National Assessment of Academic Achievement in Schools (ENLACE) to measure student performance across the country. It was applied in each grade after and including Grade 3 for Spanish and mathematics. As ENLACE evolved, however, results from the assessment began to be used for multiple, and sometimes conflicting, purposes, and the stakes, for teachers and schools, associated with performance in ENLACE grew. These pressures, and the increasing incentives to "teach to the test", have prompted calls for modifications to be made to the assessment and/or its use (Santiago et al., 2012; OECD, 2013).

In 2012, the government introduced a profound reform of the curriculum, the Comprehensive Reform of Basic Education (RIEB) that places students at the centre of learning. The reform emphasises concepts such as assessment for learning, expected learning outcomes, collaborative learning, project-based work, student self-assessment

...

and peer assessment, and criterion-referenced marking. It also calls for greater co-ordination across the different primary grades and improves continuity with both pre-primary and lower secondary education. The reform faces the challenge of ensuring the proposed changes eventually enter the classroom and alter what and how students are taught. In conjunction with the curricular reform, the RIEB, also continues initiatives begun in the mid 2000s that have extended the school year from 180 to 200 days and made progress towards ensuring a full-day schedule for all schools. In addition, upper secondary education was made compulsory in 2012 with the goal of attaining universal coverage by 2022. Other ongoing policy efforts include professionalising teaching and establishing a teacher-evaluation system.

Sources:

OECD (2013), *Education Policy Outlook: Mexico*, OECD Publishing.

OECD (2012a), *Avances en las Reformas de la Educación Básica en México: Una Perspectiva de la OCDE (versión preliminar)*, OECD Publishing, *www.sep.gob.mx/work/models/sep1/Resource/3048/2/images/Avances_en_las_reformas_de_la_educacion_basica.pdf*

Santiago, P., et al. (2012), *OECD Reviews of Evaluation and Assessment in Education: Mexico 2012*, OECD Reviews of Evaluation and Assessment in Education, OECD Publishing. *http://dx.doi.org/10.1787/9789264172647-en*

Subsecretaría de Educación Pública (SEP) (2013), *Reporte de Indicadores Educativos*, SEP, Distrito Federal, Mexico.

Zorrilla, M. and B. Barba (2008), "Reforma Educativa en México: Descentralización y Nuevos Actores", *Sinéctica*, 30.

TRENDS IN EQUITY BETWEEN PISA 2003 AND PISA 2012

By analysing data across different PISA assessments, it is possible to identify those countries and economies that have moved towards a more equitable school system. In 2003, and on average across OECD countries with comparable data for 2012, the slope of the socio-economic gradient was 39 points, meaning that a disadvantaged students (one with value of -1 on the *PISA index of economic, social and cultural status* [ESCS]) scored 39 points lower in the PISA mathematics assessment than a student with average socio-economic status (one with an ESCS value of 0). Box II.2.5 describes how ESCS can be compared over time). Advantaged students (those with a value of 1 on the ESCS index) were expected to score, on average, 39 points higher than a student with average socio-economic status, and 78 points higher than a disadvantaged student. That year, 17% of the variation in students' mathematics performance, on average across OECD countries, could be explained by students' socio-economic status (OECD, 2004 and Table II.2.5b).

Box II.2.5. **Comparing indices in PISA 2003 and PISA 2012**

PISA indices, like the *PISA index of economic, social and cultural status*, are based on information gathered from the student questionnaire. In PISA 2012, each index is scaled so that a value of 0 indicates the OECD average and a value of 1 indicates the average standard deviation across OECD countries (see Annex A1 for details on how each index is constructed). Similarly, in PISA 2003, each index was scaled so that a value of 0 indicated the OECD average and a value of 1 indicated the average standard deviation across OECD countries. To compare the evolution of these indices over time, the PISA 2012 scale was used and all index values for PISA 2003 were rescaled accordingly. As a result, the values of the indices for 2003 presented in this report differ from those produced in *Learning for Tomorrow's World: First Results from PISA 2003* (OECD, 2004).

Calculating the percentage of resilient students also needs to be adapted to be comparable across time. A resilient student is identified by comparing certain students to the rest of the students who participated in the PISA assessment in any given year. Because more countries and economies participated in PISA 2012 than did in PISA 2003, in order to compare resilience over time, the pooled sample to calculate resilience in 2012 must be based on the same countries and economies that were used to estimate resilience in PISA 2003. As a result, the estimates for resilience for PISA 2012 that are comparable over time differ from those presented for the overall PISA 2012 sample of countries and economies.

By 2012, the OECD average impact of socio-economic status on performance (the slope of the socio-economic gradient; for those OECD countries that have comparable data from PISA 2003 and PISA 2012) remained at 39 score points in mathematics, but the degree to which students' socio-economic status predicted performance in mathematics (the strength of the socio-economic gradient) decreased from 17% to 15%. In other words, by 2012 it was relatively easier than it was in 2003 for students to confound predictions about their performance based on their socio-economic status.

Turkey and Mexico moved towards greater equity by reducing both the slope and the strength of the socio-economic gradient, all the while improving performance. In both Mexico and Turkey the general improvement in mathematics performance also meant that it was easier for students in 2012 than for students in 2003 to confound expectations about performance, given their socio-economic status, and that the average difference in performance between advantaged and disadvantaged students shrank. While in Germany the performance gap between socio-economically advantaged and disadvantaged students remained unchanged, more students were able to overcome that relationship, as measured by the weakening of the strength of the socio-economic gradient. Most importantly, in these three countries, the improvement in equity was combined with an improvement in mathematics performance. Other countries and economies that improved mathematics performance (Brazil, Greece, Hong Kong-China, Italy, Macao-China, Poland and Tunisia) maintained their equity levels; only in Portugal were improvements in performance accompanied by a reduction in equity, mainly in the strength of the socio-economic gradient. These results highlight how, for most countries and economies, improvements in performance need not come at the expense of equity (Figures II.2.12 and II.2.13).

■ Figure II.2.12 ■

Change between 2003 and 2012 in the strength of the socio-economic gradient and annualised mathematics performance

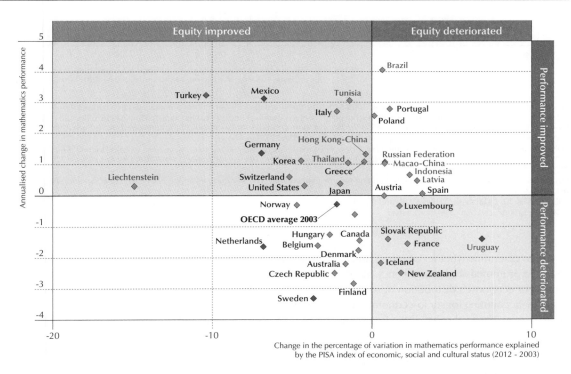

Notes: Changes in both equity and performance between 2003 and 2012 that are statistically significant are indicated in a darker tone.
The annualised change is the average annual change in PISA score points from a country's/economy's earliest participation in PISA to PISA 2012. It is calculated taking into account all of a country's/economy's participation in PISA. For more details on the calculation of the annualised change, see Annex A5.
Only countries and economies with comparable data from PISA 2003 and PISA 2012 are shown.
For comparability over time, PISA 2003 values on the *PISA index of economic, social and cultural status* have been rescaled to the PISA 2012 scale of the index. PISA 2003 results reported in this table may thus differ from those presented in *Learning for Tomorrow's World: First Results from PISA 2003* (OECD, 2004) (see Annex A5 for more details).
OECD average 2003 considers only those countries with comparable mathematics scores and values on the *PISA index for economic, social and cultural status* since PISA 2003.
Source: OECD, PISA 2012 Database, Tables I.2.3b and II.2.9b.
StatLink ᴍꜱᴾ http://dx.doi.org/10.1787/888932964813

■ Figure II.2.13 ■

Change between 2003 and 2012 in the slope of the socio-economic gradient and annualised mathematics performance

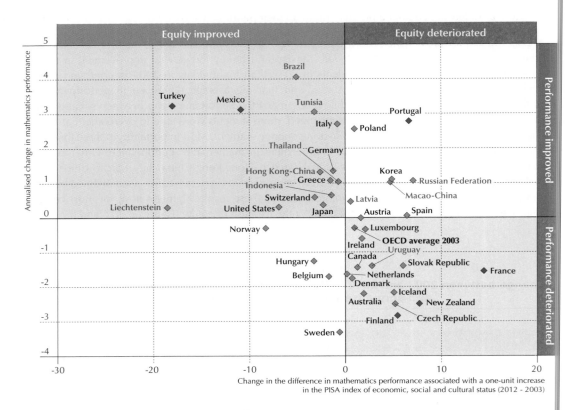

Notes: Changes in both equity and performance between 2003 and 2012 that are statistically significant are indicated in a darker tone.
The annualised change is the average annual change in PISA score points from a country's/economy's earliest participation in PISA to PISA 2012. It is calculated taking into account all of a country's/economy's participation in PISA. For more details on the calculation of the annualised change, see Annex A5.
Only countries and economies with comparable data from PISA 2003 and PISA 2012 are shown.
For comparability over time, PISA 2003 values on the *PISA index of economic, social and cultural status* have been rescaled to the PISA 2012 scale of the index. PISA 2003 results reported in this table may thus differ from those presented in *Learning for Tomorrow's World: First Results from PISA 2003* (OECD, 2004) (see Annex A5 for more details).
OECD average 2003 considers only those countries with comparable mathematics scores and values on the *PISA index for economic, social and cultural status* since PISA 2003.
Source: OECD, PISA 2012 Database, Tables I.2.3b and II.2.9b.
StatLink ⟐ http://dx.doi.org/10.1787/888932964813

Another way to determine whether countries and economies are moving towards more equitable school systems is to see how they have promoted student resiliency. Resilient students are disadvantaged students (those in the bottom quarter of a country's or economy's distribution of socio-economic status) who perform in the top quarter of performance in all countries, after accounting for socio-economic status. Countries and economies in which the proportion of students who are resilient is growing are those that are improving the chances for disadvantaged students to become high achievers.

In PISA 2003, 6.4% of students in OECD countries were resilient; by 2012, this share had decreased slightly to 6.1%. Only in Germany, Italy, Mexico, Poland, Tunisia and Turkey did the share of resilient students increase by more than one percentage point. In 11 countries and economies, the share of resilient students shrank – meaning that in these countries/economies it is less likely that disadvantaged students will perform at a high level (Figure II.2.14) (see Box II.2.5 for a description of how resilience is calculated for comparison across PISA assessments).

Consistent with the improvements in student resiliency since 2003, students in the bottom quarter of socio-economic status in Brazil, Italy, Mexico, Poland, Tunisia and Turkey improved their mathematics performance the most between PISA 2003 and PISA 2012. In these countries, for example, a student who, in 2012, was in the bottom quarter of the *PISA index of economic, social and cultural status* scored more than 25 points higher in the PISA mathematics assessment than a student who was in the bottom quarter of this index in 2003; in Germany, Hong Kong-China, Korea, Portugal and Switzerland students in the bottom quarter of the *PISA index of economic, social and cultural status* improved their performance by at least 15 score points. In Italy, Poland, Portugal and Tunisia, the improvement among disadvantaged students was part of a general improvement in mathematics performance among all students, while in Brazil, Hong Kong-China, Germany, Korea, Mexico, Switzerland and Turkey, the improvement observed among disadvantaged students is considerably larger than the improvement observed – if any – among advantaged students (Table II.2.7b).

■ Figure II.2.14 ■

Change between 2003 and 2012 in student resiliency to socio-economic status

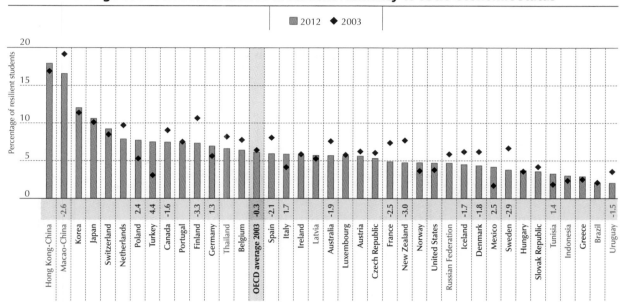

Notes: Only countries and economies with comparable data from PISA 2003 and PISA 2012 are shown.
Resiliency values for 2012 may differ from those shown in Figure II.2.4 as the pooled reference population for resilient students used in this figure is restricted to those countries and economies with comparable data in PISA 2003 and PISA 2012.
The percentage-point difference in the share of resilient students in PISA 2003 and PISA 2012 (2012 - 2003) is shown above the country/economy name. Only statistically significant differences are shown.
OECD average 2003 compares only OECD countries with comparable mathematics scores since 2003.
Countries and economies are ranked in descending order of the percentage of resilient students in 2012.
Source: OECD, PISA 2012 Database, Table II.2.7b.
StatLink ꜟ꜠ꜰ http://dx.doi.org/10.1787/888932964813

Trends in the profile and distribution of students in schools

Given that a student's peers can be a great source of inspiration and motivation for learning, and given the stigma associated with disadvantaged and low-performing schools, countries and economies striving to provide more equitable learning opportunities generally also aim to attain higher levels of social inclusion. Education policy can play a decisive role in fostering both (OECD, 2012b).

Social inclusion is the degree to which students with different socio-economic status attend the same school or the degree to which different schools have different socio-economic profiles. Increasing social inclusion in a school system – thus reducing socio-economic segregation – has been suggested as the most effective policy to improve equity in both the short and long term, far more effective than creating magnet schools or offering school choice (Eaton, 2001; Wells and Crain, 1997). In 2003, and on average across OECD countries, 76% of the variation in students' socio-economic status was observed within schools. Social inclusion was greatest, at more than 85%, which signals the greatest socio-economic diversity, within schools in Finland, Iceland, Norway and Sweden. The lowest levels of social inclusion (less than 65%) were observed in Brazil, Hungary, Mexico, Thailand and Turkey. In the former group of countries, the socio-economic composition of each school is relatively close to the socio-economic composition of the country/economy; in the latter group of countries/economies, advantaged students are less likely to attend the same school as disadvantaged students, and vice versa.

The degree of social inclusion did not change between 2003 and 2012, on average across OECD countries with comparable data. It decreased in Hong Kong-China, Latvia and New Zealand, but improved in Italy, Japan, Korea, Switzerland and Turkey, meaning that the schools in these countries, there was a greater mix of students from different socio-economic backgrounds in 2012 than in 2003. Mathematics performance in Italy and Turkey also improved during the period, indicating that greater academic inclusion can coincide with improvements in socio-economic inclusion (Figure II.2.15). Korea's trend towards greater social inclusion is combined with similar levels of academic inclusion (Figure II.2.15 and Table II.2.1b).[14] This means that schools in Korea may have remained as selective in admitting academically proficient students, but that socio-economic status is less a factor in admission to these schools. In Korea, students were more likely to attend schools with students from different socio-economic backgrounds, and were equally likely to attend the same school as students with different academic abilities.

■ Figure II.2.15 ■
Change between 2003 and 2012 in social inclusion

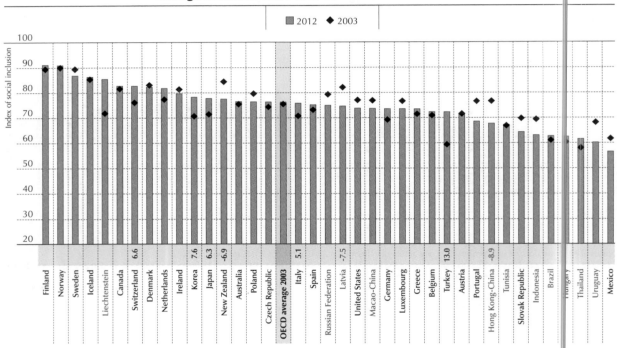

Notes: Only countries and economies with comparable data from PISA 2003 and PISA 2012 are shown.
The *index of social inclusion* is the percentage of the total variation of student socio-economic status found within schools.
The percentage-point difference in the *index of social inclusion* is shown above the country/economy name. Only statistically significant differences are shown.
OECD average 2003 compares only OECD countries with comparable mathematics scores since 2003.
For comparability over time, PISA 2003 values on the *PISA index of economic, social and cultural status* have been rescaled to the PISA 2012 scale of the index. PISA 2003 results reported in this table may thus differ from those presented in *Learning for Tomorrow's World: First Results from PISA 2003* (OECD, 2004) (see Annex A5 for more details).
Countries and economies are ranked in descending order of the index of social inclusion *in PISA 2012.*
Source: OECD, PISA 2012 Database, Table II.2.13b.
StatLink ⟦᠍᠍⟧ http://dx.doi.org/10.1787/888932964813

The above discussion looks only at equity in education as it relates to socio-economic status, yet equity refers more broadly to others sources of disadvantage for students. Chapter 3 of this volume explores other potential sources of disadvantage for students, such as where they live, the type of family they come from, including whether they have an immigrant background, and the degree to which different countries and economies are able to limit how these disadvantages influence students' mathematics performance. Chapter 3 also identifies the countries and economies that have succeeded in reducing the impact of these characteristics on students' performance.

Notes

1. Throughout the rest of this volume, the focus is on mathematics performance. While there may be significant differences across the domains assessed in PISA, those differences are outside of the scope of this volume. Therefore, whenever student performance is mentioned it refers to mathematics performance. The percentage of the variance in student performance that can be explained by differences in socio-economic status across students is 14.8%. This statistic corresponds to the r-squared of a simple regression of performance on socio-economic status.

2. That is, those separated by one unit on the *PISA index of social, economic and cultural status*. The index is standardised to have a mean of zero a standard deviation of one across students in OECD countries.

3. Here, variation in student performance is measured by the statistical variance of the student-performance measures, such as the score on the PISA mathematics scale.

4. Here, the focus is on the strength of the relationship between student performance and socio-economic status as measured by the explained variance or r-squared of a simple correlation of performance on socio-economic status.

5. Other volumes of this report highlight other countries' improvements in PISA and outline their recent policy reforms (e.g. Germany in Chapter 3 of this volume, Brazil, Turkey, Korea and Estonia in Volume I, Japan and Portugal in Volume III, and Colombia, Israel, Poland and Tunisia in Volume IV).

6. ISCO major group 0 (armed forces was divided into two categories and either added to skilled (ISCO 01) or semi-skilled blue-collar occupations (ISCO 03). Students, housewives and vague occupations were coded as missing.

7. Here, highly educated means one or both parents attained tertiary education (ISCED level 5 and 6); low educated means one or both parents attained secondary education (ISCED level 2) as their highest level of education.

8. This measure of resiliency in PISA is a useful one for comparisons among countries. However, it cannot take account of more refined information. For example, a student may have a good or poor testing day or a good or poor learning year or may be shown to be resilient in some subjects and not in others. Furthermore, socio-economic status is a general measure and may not reflect unmeasured differences among and within countries and cultures that would result in a different mode of identification of resilience. Because the identification of resilient students rely on the extremes of the distribution, the measure is less precise.

9. This comparison is based on an international measure of socio-economic status, but disregards the fact that the families of these students may hold very different positions in their own societies. For example, in country where the mean socio-economic status is well below the OECD average, a student with the socio-economic status of the average OECD student may be advantaged when compared with his or her peers. In some countries, the OECD average socio-economic status represents an advantaged status, while in others it does not. Despite these assumptions and the limitations they impose on this exercise, the exercise yields some useful insights.

10. Note that these results also depend on how schools are defined and organised within countries and by the units that were chosen for sampling purposes. For example, in some countries, some of the schools in the PISA sample were defined as administrative units (even if they spanned several geographically separate institutions, as in Italy; in others they were defined as those parts of larger educational institutions that serve 15-year-olds; in still others they were defined as physical school buildings; and in others they were defined from a management perspective (e.g. entities having a principal). The *PISA 2012 Technical Report* (OECD, forthcoming) provides an overview of how schools were defined. Note also that, because of the manner in which students were sampled, the within-school variation includes variation between classes as well as between students. In Slovenia, the primary sampling unit is defined as a group of students who follow the same study programme within a school (an educational track within a school). So in this particular case the between-school variance is actually the within-school, between-track difference.

11. Given the design of PISA, with samples of 35 students per school, and the difficulties in measuring socio-economic status for each student with high precision, this is to be expected. For further details see Hauser (2009), "On "Quality and Equity in the Performance of Students and Schools", mimeo available at:

https://edsurveys.rti.org/PISA/documents/HauserQuality-Equity_in_PISA_rmh_053009a.pdf

12. The performance gap is larger across schools because it is associated with many school characteristics, such as policies and practices, school location and others that cannot be measured in PISA, that are not included in this analysis. In addition, the analysis of differences within schools draws on less information and on data that are necessarily less precise because it relies only on the information provided by one individual – the student – whereas the school data aggregate information from all the students taking part in the assessment in that school.

13. The definition of high-, average- and low-performing schools is similar to that used for identifying socio-economically disadvantaged, average and advantaged schools. Average school performance is compared with average performance at the system level and schools are classified as high-/low-performing if their average performance is statistically significantly above/below the system's average performance. Both the variance in student performance and the number of observations in a school contribute to the standard error of the estimated average performance at the school level, and therefore to the classification of schools as high-, average- or low-performing.

14. Academic inclusion is the degree to which students with different academic abilities and needs share the same school, or the degree to which schools have different average performance levels. It is also a measure of the likelihood that a country or economy's low- and high-achieving students attend the same school. PISA measures academic inclusion as the percentage of the variation in mathematics performance that occurs within schools; it can also be interpreted as the degree to which students in a school resemble the academic distribution in the country/economy as a whole. The *index of academic inclusion* ranges from 0 to 100 with values closer to 100 indicating greater inclusion.

References

Eaton, S.E. (2001), *The Other Boston Busing Story: What's Won and Lost across the Boundary Line*, Yale University Press, New Haven.

OECD (forthcoming), *PISA 2012 Technical Report*, PISA, OECD Publishing.

OECD (2013), *Education Policy Outlook: Mexico*, OECD Publishing.
http://www.oecd.org/edu/EDUCATION%20POLICY%20OUTLOOK%20MEXICO_EN.pdf

OECD (2012a), *Avances en las Reformas de la Educación Básica en México: Una Perspectiva de la OCDE (preliminary version)*, OECD Publishing.
www.sep.gob.mx/work/models/sep1/Resource/3048/2/images/Avances_en_las_reformas_de_la_educacion_basica.pdf

OECD (2012b), *Equity and Quality in Education: Supporting Disadvantaged Students and Schools*, OECD Publishing.
http://dx.doi.org/10.1787/9789264130852-en

OECD (2004), *Learning for Tomorrow's World: First Results from PISA 2003*, PISA, OECD Publishing.
http://dx.doi.org/10.1787/9789264006416-en

Santiago, P., et al. (2012), *OECD Reviews of Evaluation and Assessment in Education: Mexico 2012*, OECD Reviews of Evaluation and Assessment in Education, OECD Publishing.
http://dx.doi.org/10.1787/9789264172647-en

Subsecretaría de Educación Pública (SEP) (2013), *Reporte de Indicadores Educativos*, SEP, Distrito Federal, Mexico.

Wells, A.S. and **R.L. Crain** (1997), *Stepping over the Color Line: African-American Students in White Suburban Schools*, Yale University Press, New Haven.

Zorrilla, M. and **B. Barba** (2008), "Reforma Educativa en México: Descentralización y Nuevos Actores", *Sinéctica, 30.*

3

The Challenge
of Diversity

This chapter examines various aspects of students' and schools' characteristics that have an impact on education outcomes, including family structure, parents' job status, school location, immigrant background and language spoken at home. It also discusses trends in immigrant students' mathematics performance up to 2012.

Socio-economic status is only one aspect of a student's background that is related to mathematics performance. Other factors include family structure, school location, immigrant background and language spoken at home (as compared with the language of assessment in PISA). All of these factors have an impact on the work of schools and teachers, and the way in which schools and teachers address them has an impact on education outcomes. They are also in many cases closely related to the socio-economic status of students and schools. This chapter discusses the relationship between student performance and these factors.

Across OECD countries, around 14% of 15-year-old students come from single-parent families (Table II.3.1); more than 10% from families where the father or mother does not work (Table II.3.2); 11% have an immigrant background (Table II.3.4a); 6% are immigrant students who usually speak a language at home that is different from the one in which they are taught at school (Table II.3.5); and 9% attend schools in small rural communities (Table II.3.3a). This chapter explores equity in education across groups of students who share some of these individual and school characteristics. Analysing equity across different groups of students can help policy makers target or adjust education and social policy to the needs of an increasingly diverse student population.

What the data tell us

- The share of immigrant students in OECD countries increased from 9% in 2003 to 11% in 2012 while the performance disadvantage of immigrant students as compared to students without an immigrant background but with similar socio-economic status shrank by 11 score points during the same period.

- Across OECD countries, students who attend schools where more than one in four students are immigrants tend to perform worse than those in schools with no immigrant students; but after accounting for the socio-economic background of students and schools, the 19-point difference in mathematics scores is more than halved, to 7 score points.

FAMILY STRUCTURE AND STUDENT PERFORMANCE

The family is usually the first place where students can be encouraged to learn. Parents may read to their young children, assist them with homework, and/or participate in school activities (OECD, 2012a). For every student, supportive parents can offer encouragement and meet with teachers or school administrators to keep track of their child's progress in school.[1]

Among OECD countries, around 14% of the 15-year-old students who participated in PISA 2012 were from single-parent families. Many of them also come from socio-economically disadvantaged backgrounds. On average across OECD countries, students from single-parent families are disadvantaged when compared with students from other types of families generally because their parents have lower educational attainment or work in occupations of lower status, or the family has fewer home possessions as reported by the students themselves (Table II.3.1).

Figure II.3.1 depicts the average mathematics performance of students who live in a single-parent household compared to students in other types of families,[2] before and after accounting for socio-economic status. Across OECD countries, the performance gap between students from single-parent families and those from other types of families is 15 score points – or the equivalent of almost half a year of schooling – before taking socio-economic status into account.

Students from single-parent families are 1.23 times more likely to score in the bottom quarter of mathematics performance in their country than students from other types of families; this is known as the "relative risk" for students from single-parent households compared with that for students from other types of families (Table II.3.1). Box II.3.3 presents another way of evaluating the relevance of risk factors, such as family structure or immigrant background, in the entire student population.

In general, accounting for socio-economic status reduces, and in some cases eliminates, the performance gap observed between students from single-parent families and those from other types of families. While family structure is related to socio-economic status, analysis of PISA data cannot disentangle the separate impact of each of these variables on student performance. That performance differences remain marked even after accounting for students' socio-economic status suggests that there is an independent relationship between family structure and education opportunities.

■ Figure II.3.1 ■

Difference in mathematics performance, by type of family

Differences in performance before and after accounting for socio-economic status

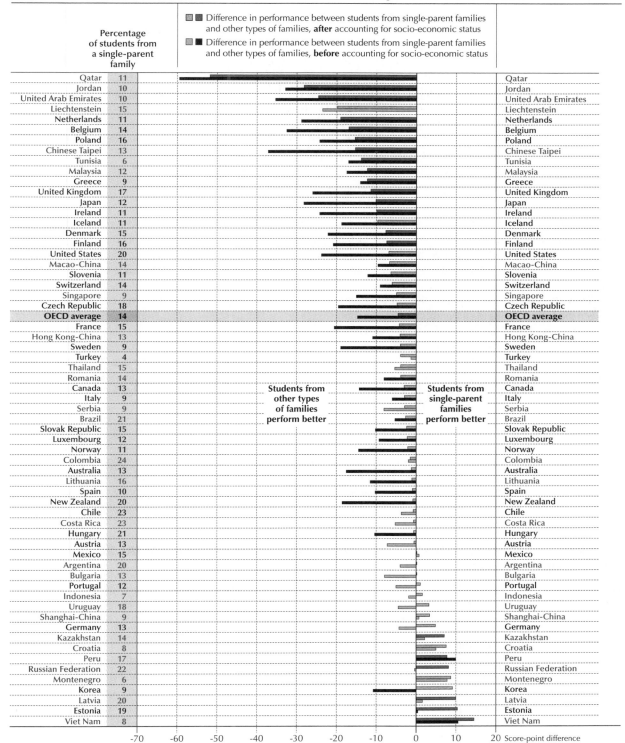

Note: Score-point differences that are statistically significant are marked in a darker tone.

Countries and economies are ranked in ascending order of the score-point difference between students from single-parent families and other types of families, after accounting for socio-economic status.

Source: OECD, PISA 2012 Database, Table II.3.1.

StatLink ᵐᵖ http://dx.doi.org/10.1787/888932964832

Box II.3.1. **Population relevance or attributable risk**

One way of measuring the importance of risk factors is through "population relevance". Population relevance expresses the proportion of the total outcome, such as low mathematics scores, that is associated with membership in a potentially vulnerable population. In the context of single-parent families, the population relevance would measure the extent to which the incidence of poor performance in mathematics among the entire student population would be reduced if the risk of low performance among students from single-parent households were the same as that among students from other types of families. Analysis suggests that if public policy were able to reduce the risk of low performance among students from single-parent families to the same as that among students from other types of families, then the proportion of low-performing students would be reduced by 3% (Table II.3.1). While the relative risk of low performance simply suggests the degree of vulnerability to poor performance a student from particular population is, population relevance provides an absolute measure of how prevalent this source of vulnerability is for the entire student population. The population relevance depends on the relative risk associated with membership in the vulnerable group and on the relative size of the vulnerable group.

On average, after accounting for socio-economic status, students from single-parent families score five points lower in mathematics than students from other types of families. More than 20% of students in Brazil, Chile, Colombia, Costa Rica, Hungary and the United States come from single-parent families and they perform at the same level as their peers from other types of families, after accounting for socio-economic status (before the adjustment, however the performance is lower in the United States, Hungary and Brazil). In Latvia and the Russian Federation, they also constitute more than 20% of the student population and perform better than their peers. As Figure II.3.1 shows, however the gap between these two groups of students is particularly large in Qatar, Jordan, the United Arab Emirates and the Netherlands where, after accounting for socio-economic status, the difference is 19 score points or more. In Poland, Chinese Taipei, Tunisia, Malaysia, Greece, the United Kingdom and Japan, the difference is greater than 10 score points (Table II.3.1). In Qatar, Poland, the United States, Jordan, Denmark, the United Arab Emirates and Finland the population relevance is higher than 6%; that means that the proportion of low-performing students would decrease by more than 6% if the risk of low performance among students from single-parent households were as low as that of students from other types of families (population relevance) (Table II.3.1).

While the evidence that students from single-parent families perform relatively poorly is discouraging, the variation in performance differences across countries suggests that the relationship is not inevitable. Public policy, in general, and education policies, in particular, can narrow the gaps by making it easier for single parents to support and foster their children's education (Pong, Dronkers and Hampden-Thompson, 2004). School systems and individual schools can consider, for example, how and what kinds of parental engagement are to be encouraged among single parents who have limited time to devote to school activities. Education policies need to be examined in conjunction with other policies, such as those related to welfare and childcare.

PARENTS' JOB STATUS: TARGETING EDUCATION POLICIES THROUGH SOCIAL POLICY FOR THE UNEMPLOYED

Education and other social policies play an important role in improving student learning at school. Differences across countries and economies in the impact of parents' unemployment on student performance suggest that some countries/economies manage to mitigate the potentially negative effects that unemployment has on education outcomes.

On average, 11% of 15-year-old students across OECD countries reported that their fathers' current job status is "other than working" (full or part time). They reported that their fathers are either currently unemployed (not working but looking for a job) or they hold another job status (home duties, retired, etc.). Some 28% of 15-year-olds reported similar job status for their mother. Parents' job status is closely linked to socio-economic status, with large gaps in performance between students whose parents are working and those whose parents are not. However, even after accounting for socio-economic status, students in OECD countries who reported that their fathers are not working score six points lower than those who reported that their fathers are working. Students who reported that their mothers are not working score eight points lower than those who reported that their mothers are working. The relative risk of low performance among students with one parent who isn't working, regardless of which parent it is, is more than 1.4 times greater than for other students. The population relevance is almost 5% when a student's father is not working and more than 9% when a student's mother is not working (Table II.3.2).

■ Figure II.3.2 [Part 1/2] ■

Difference in mathematics performance, by parents' work status

Differences in performance before and after accounting for socio-economic status

Difference in performance between students whose **fathers** are and are not working:

▣ ■ **after** accounting for socio-economic status
▣ ■ **before** accounting for socio-economic status

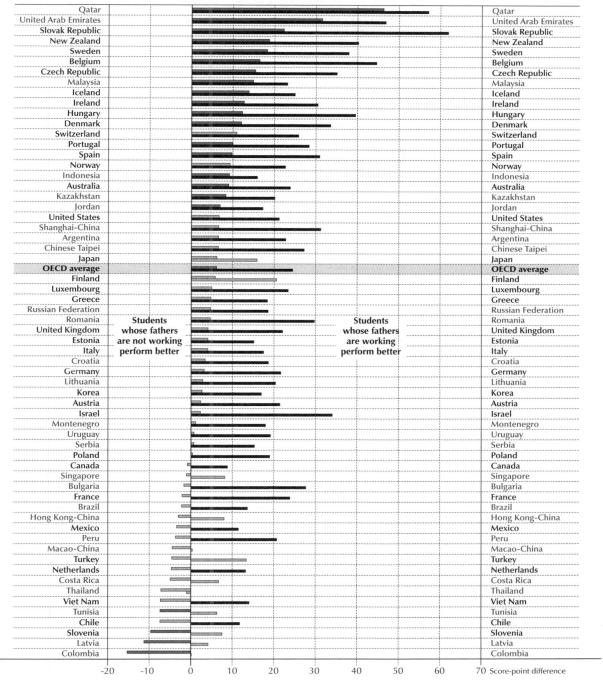

Note: Score-point differences that are statistically significant are marked in a darker tone.
Countries and economies are ranked in descending order of the score-point differences between students whose fathers/mothers are/are not working, after accounting for socio-economic status.
Source: OECD, PISA 2012 Database, Table II.3.2.
StatLink ⟲ http://dx.doi.org/10.1787/888932964832

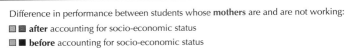

■ Figure II.3.2 [Part 2/2] ■

Difference in mathematics performance, by parents' work status

Differences in performance before and after accounting for socio-economic status

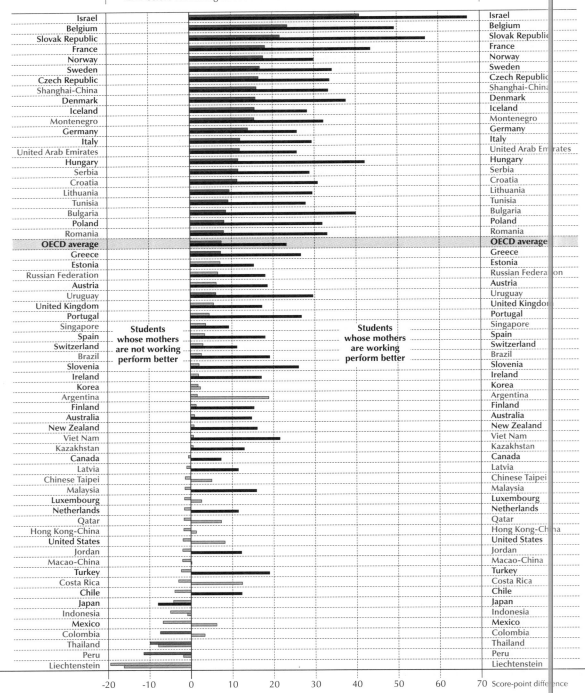

Note: Score-point differences that are statistically significant are marked in a darker tone.
Countries and economies are ranked in descending order of the score-point differences between students whose fathers/mothers are/are not working, after accounting for socio-economic status.
Source: OECD, PISA 2012 Database, Table II.3.2.

StatLink ⟨ᴹˢᴾⁱ⟩ http://dx.doi.org/10.1787/888932964832

In the Slovak Republic, Sweden, Belgium, the Czech Republic, Iceland, Hungary and Denmark, parents' job status (of both the father and the mother) is associated with performance gaps ranging from 12 score points in Denmark when students' fathers are not working to 24 and 22 score points in Belgium and the Slovak Republic when students' mothers are not working, after accounting for socio-economic status (Figure II.3.2). In Norway, Germany, France, as well as in Croatia, Montenegro, Serbia and Shanghai-China large differences are observed only in relation to mothers' job status. Israel shows the largest performance gap related to mothers' job status (41 score points), but there is no gap related to fathers' job status. Population relevance is highest in the Slovak Republic, Romania, the United Arab Emirates, Hungary, where the proportion of low-performing students would shrink by more than 10% if the risk of low performance among students whose fathers are not working were as low as that of students whose fathers are working; and in Israel, Montenegro, the Slovak Republic, the United Arab Emirates, where the proportion of low-performing students would shrink by more than 20% if the risk of low performance among students whose mothers are not working were as low as that of students whose mothers are working (Table II.3.2).

SCHOOL LOCATION AND VARIATION IN PERFORMANCE ACROSS GEOGRAPHICAL AREAS

In some countries, student performance and the socio-economic or organisational profile of school systems vary considerably according to where schools are located. To capture variation in student performance among school systems and regions within countries, some countries have collected information from PISA at regional levels. Results from these regions are presented in Annex B2 of this volume. Box II.2.2 describes how much of the variation in performance takes place between regions for those countries that collected this information in PISA.

Another way to analyse variation in performance related to geographical characteristics is by school location. Countries vary widely in the densities, characteristics and distributions of populations across different types of communities (Table II.3.3a), and these differences need to be borne in mind when interpreting how students in these different communities perform. Large cities or densely populated areas tend to offer important advantages for schools, such as a richer cultural environment, a more attractive workplace for teachers, more school choice, and better job prospects that can help to motivate students. At the same time, they often pose greater socio-economic challenges. In addition, not all students can enjoy the advantages that large urban centres offer. They may, for example, come from socio-economically disadvantaged backgrounds, speak a different language at home than the one spoken at school, or have only one parent to turn to for support and assistance.

On average across OECD countries, students in schools located in towns (3 000 to about 100 000 inhabitants) outperform students in rural schools (fewer than 3 000 inhabitants) by 11 score points, after taking socio-economic status into account. Students in city schools (more than 100 000 inhabitants) outperform students in town schools by 4 score points, after taking socio-economic status into account (Table II.3.3a).

As Figure II.3.3 shows, after accounting for socio-economic status, students in all schools, regardless of their location, perform above the OECD average in Shanghai-China, Singapore, Hong Kong-China, Chinese Taipei, Viet Nam, Macao-China, Korea, Japan, Liechtenstein, Poland, Switzerland, Estonia, Germany, the Netherlands, Finland, Canada, Austria, and the Czech Republic. In all of these countries except Viet Nam, Japan and Poland, the difference in performance between students in rural schools and those in schools located in large cities is less than 10 score points (Table II.3.3a).

In general, students who attend schools in rural areas tend to score lower than students in schools in other types of locations. The difference is particularly large when performance is compared to that of students in city schools, although differences are observed between students in rural schools and those in schools located in towns. For example, in Slovenia students in city schools outperform those in rural schools by 74 score points, after accounting for differences in students' socio-economic status; but most of that performance gap (65 score points) is already apparent between students in towns and rural areas. Comparing students of similar socio-economic status, the largest performance gaps between students in rural and city schools are observed in Bulgaria, Hungary, Peru, Qatar and Slovenia (above 41 score points or the equivalent of one year of schooling). Students who attend urban schools are, on average, more socio-economically advantaged than those who attend schools in towns. In Belgium, Denmark, Ireland and Turkey, students in town schools perform better than students in city schools, before taking socio-economic status into account; but the differences are not marked. On average in the United States, students in urban schools underperform when compared to those in rural schools, even when they are more socio-economically advantaged (Table II.3.3a).

■ Figure II.3.3 ■

Mean mathematics performance, by school location, after accounting for socio-economic status

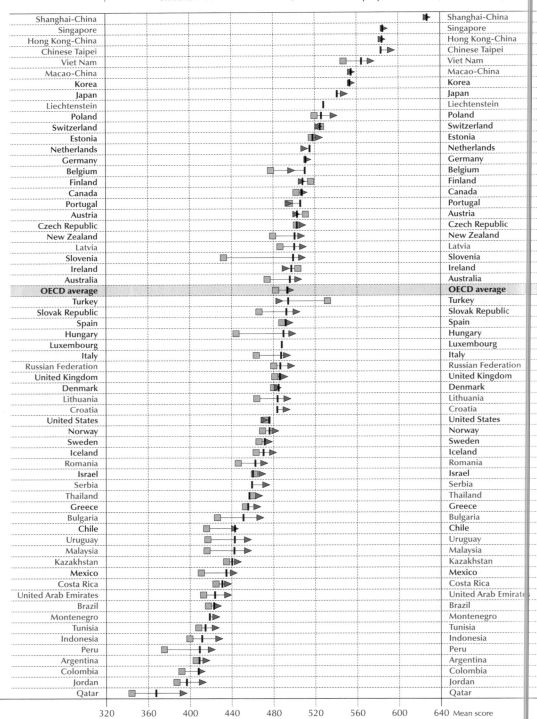

	All students
	Students in schools in cities (100 000 people or more)
	Students in schools in rural areas (fewer than 3 000 people)

Countries and economies are ranked in descending order of the mean performance of all students, after accounting for socio-economic status.
Source: OECD, PISA 2012 Database, Tables II.2.1 and II.3.3a.
StatLink ⟨ᵐˢᵖ⟩ http://dx.doi.org/10.1787/888932964832

Figure II.3.3 also compares the performance of students in large cities across countries, after accounting for socio-economic status. Shanghai-China, Chinese Taipei, Singapore, Hong Kong-China, Viet Nam, Macao-China, Korea, and Japan show the highest mathematics performance – 548 or more score points, on average, among students in city schools, at least one year of schooling above the OECD average.

The difference in socio-economic status between rural and city schools varies considerably across countries. The differences are greatest in Mexico, Bulgaria, Peru, Chile, Colombia, Viet Nam, Thailand, Brazil, Portugal, Hungary, Tunisia and Costa Rica, where the difference is than larger than one unit on the *PISA index of economic, social and cultural status* (Table II.3.3a).

Differences in performance partly reflect differences in the socio-economic status of students who attend schools in urban and rural areas and/or other factors that may be associated with socio-economic disparities that have an impact on student performance. Comparing performance before and after accounting for socio-economic status shows the extent to which differences in student performance related to school location are associated with disparities in socio-economic status among school locations within countries. A large difference in performance both before and after accounting for socio-economic status indicates a significant difference in the socio-economic profiles of urban and rural areas. For example, across OECD countries on average, the performance gap between students who attend schools in rural areas and those who attend schools in towns is 20 score points, but the gap is reduced to 11 score points when students of similar socio-economic status are compared. The difference is greater between rural and city schools, where the estimated difference shrinks from 31 to 13 score points after accounting for socio-economic status (Table II.3.3a).

In PISA 2003 and among the OECD countries that participated in the PISA 2012 assessment, students in rural schools scored an average of 472 points in mathematics, students in schools located in towns scored 497 points, and students in schools located in cities scored 513 points. By 2012, the mathematics performance of students in rural and town schools had not changed, but that of students in city schools had declined by seven points. Across the countries and economies with comparable data for 2003 and 2012 and that show improvements in mathematics performance during this period, the observed improvement is spread across all types of communities. The only exception is Turkey, where much of the improvement observed in mathematics is concentrated among students in town schools who improved their mathematics scores by 59 points between PISA 2003 and PISA 2012, after taking socio-economic differences into account (Table II.3.3b).

EQUITY IN OUTCOMES FOR IMMIGRANT STUDENTS

Migration is not a new phenomenon; but with ageing populations and the looming threat of labour and skill shortages in many OECD countries, the issue has climbed to the top of the policy agenda. Both within and across countries, students with an immigrant background constitute a heterogeneous group. They differ in their country of origin, language and culture, and bring a wide range of skills, knowledge and motivations to their schools. Although a significant subgroup of migrants is highly skilled, that is not true for many others who are socio-economically disadvantaged. Such disadvantage, along with cultural and ethnic differences, can create divisions and inequities between the host society and newcomers. These problems go well beyond how migration flows can be channelled and managed; they require consideration of how immigrants can be integrated into host societies in ways that are acceptable to both the immigrants and the populations in the receiving countries.

Integrating immigrant students into schools is a challenge for most countries; yet a country's success in integrating immigrants' children into society is a key indication of the efficacy of social policy in general and education policy in particular. The variation in performance differences between immigrant and non-immigrant students across countries, even after accounting for socio-economic status, suggests that policy has an important role to play in eliminating those differences. But given the diversity of immigrant student populations across countries, designing education policies to address those students' specific needs – particularly that of language instruction – is not an easy task.

Education policy alone is unlikely to address all the issues related to differences in performance between immigrant and non-immigrant students. For example, immigrant students' performance in PISA is more strongly (and negatively) associated with the concentration of socio-economic disadvantage in schools than with the concentration of immigrants *per se* or the concentration of students who speak a different language at home than the one in which they are taught at school. Reducing the concentration of disadvantage in schools may require changes in other social policy, such as housing or welfare, to encourage a more balanced social mix in schools.

The impact of other social policies on the profile of immigrant students

When interpreting performance gaps between non-immigrants students and those with an immigrant background, it is important to consider the differences in the socio-economic, education and linguistic backgrounds of countries' immigrant populations. The composition of immigrant populations is shaped by immigration policies and practices, and the criteria used to decide who will be admitted into a country vary considerably across countries. While some countries receive relatively large numbers of immigrants each year, often with relatively little selectivity, other countries have much smaller or more selective migrant inflows. In addition, the extent to which the social, educational and occupational status of potential immigrants is taken into account in immigration and naturalisation decisions differs across countries. The composition of past migration flows tends to persist because established networks facilitate migration from the same countries of origin. In addition, some migration flows may not be easily restricted because of international treaties (i.e. free circulation agreements and the Convention relating to the Status of Refugees) or because of generally recognised human rights (i.e. the right of immigrants or citizens to live with their families). As a result, immigrant populations are more skilled or socio-economically advantaged in some countries than in others. Among OECD countries:

- Australia, Canada and New Zealand are countries with immigration policies that favour the better qualified.
- The United States has a migration system that tends to favour family migration, both of the immediate family, as in other countries, and also of parents, siblings and adult children.
- In the 1960s and 1970s, Austria, Denmark, Germany, Luxembourg, Norway, Sweden and Switzerland recruited temporary immigrant workers, many of whom then settled permanently. Immigration increased again over the past ten years, except in Germany. In Austria, Germany and Switzerland, and to a lesser extent in Sweden, immigrants are less likely to have an upper secondary education and more likely to have a tertiary degree. As a result, migrants tend to be of two types – the low-skilled and the highly qualified.
- France and the United Kingdom draw many immigrants from former colonies who have often already mastered the language of the host country.
- Finland, Greece, Ireland, Italy, Portugal and Spain, among other countries, experienced a sharp growth in migration inflows in the early 2000s.

High levels of performance across a diverse student population

PISA distinguishes between three types of student immigrant status: non-immigrant students (those without an immigrant background, sometimes referred to as native students, who were born in the country where they were assessed by PISA or who had at least one parent born in that country);[3] second-generation students (who were born in the country of assessment but whose parents are foreign-born); and first-generation students (foreign-born students whose parents are also foreign-born).[4] This chapter focuses first on immigrant students as a whole (first- and second-generation immigrant students) and then analyses equity in outcomes for first- and second-generation students separately.

Across OECD countries, 11% of the students assessed by PISA 2012 have an immigrant background. These immigrant students tend to be socio-economically disadvantaged in comparison to non-immigrant students. They also score an average of 34 points lower in the PISA mathematics assessment than non-immigrant students, and an average of 21 points lower after accounting for socio-economic differences. In fact, immigrant students are 1.70 times more likely than non-immigrant students to perform in the bottom quarter of the performance distribution. If education policy reduced their vulnerability to poor performance to the levels observed among non-immigrant students, the proportion of low-performing students in the entire population would shrink by 7% (Table II.3.4a).

In Canada, New Zealand and Australia the size of the immigrant student population is well above the OECD average (29%, 26% and 23%), and both immigrant and non-immigrant students perform, on average, well above the OECD mean (more than 500 score points). In Australia immigrant students outperform non-immigrants by 29 score points, even after accounting for socio-economic differences. In Canada and New Zealand, both groups perform equally well. The same is true in Ireland, but the proportion of immigrant students (10%) in the country is closer to the OECD average (11%). Among partner countries and economies, Macao-China, Hong Kong-China, Liechtenstein and Singapore also have large proportions of immigrant students and enjoy high levels of average performance among immigrant and non-immigrant students. In Macao-China and Hong Kong-China, immigrant students perform better than non-immigrant students after accounting for socio-economic status; in Singapore the two groups perform equally well; and in Liechtenstein immigrant students score 40 points lower in mathematics, on average, than non-immigrant students (Table II.3.4a).

■ Figure II.3.4 ■

Difference in mathematics performance between immigrant and non-immigrant students

Before and after accounting for socio-economic status

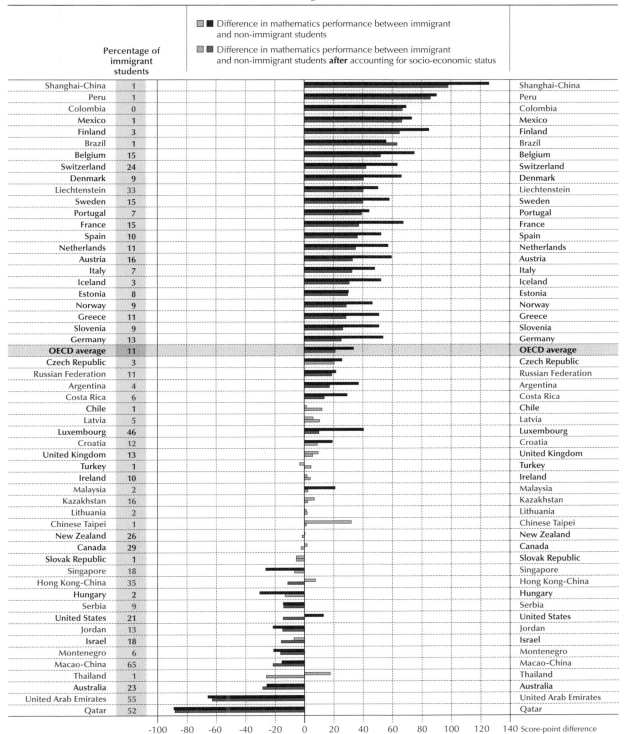

Note: Score-point differences that are statistically significant are marked in a darker tone.
Countries and economies are ranked in descending order of the score-point difference between immigrant and non-immigrant students, after accounting for socio-economic status.
Source: OECD, PISA 2012 Database, Table II.3.4a.
StatLink ᵐˢ⁴ http://dx.doi.org/10.1787/888932964832

Among OECD countries, immigrant and non-immigrant students perform equally well in Canada, New Zealand, Israel, the United Kingdom and Ireland (also in the Slovak Republic, Turkey and Chile, but the size of the immigrant student populations in these countries is less than 1%). In Belgium, France, Switzerland, Austria, Sweden, Spain, Luxembourg, Norway, the Netherlands and Denmark, immigrant students account for 9% or more of the student populations, and they are between 2.0 and 2.4 times more likely than non-immigrant students to score in the bottom quarter of the performance distribution. The same pattern is seen in Colombia, Peru, Finland and Mexico, but in both cases the proportion of students who are immigrants is relatively small – 1% and 3%, respectively. Among partner economies, this pattern is observed in Shanghai-China and Brazil, but the proportion of students who are immigrants is negligible. In Luxembourg, if the risk of low performance among immigrant students were the same as that among non-immigrant students, the proportion of low-performing students in the country would shrink by 31%; in Switzerland, it would shrink by 24%. The proportion of low performers in Belgium, France, Austria, Sweden, Denmark and Germany would also be significantly reduced under that scenario. Only in Liechtenstein, among partner countries and economies, is the population relevance for immigrant students similarly high (Table II.3.4a).

Higher levels of performance among an increasingly diverse student population

In PISA 2003, 9% of students across OECD countries had an immigrant background. They scored 47 points lower in mathematics than their non-immigrant peers; when students with similar socio-economic status were compared, the performance difference was smaller – 33 points – but still present. By 2012, the share of immigrant students across OECD countries with comparable data for 2003 and 2012 increased to 11%, and the difference in mathematics performance in favour of non-immigrant students decreased by around 10 score points. The narrowing of the immigrant student performance gap in mathematics is observed (at 10 score points) even after comparing immigrant and non-immigrant students of similar socio-economic background. Furthermore, the socio-economic status profile of immigrant students in 2012 was slightly more advantaged than that of immigrant students in 2003 (the socio-economic status of non-immigrant students also rose during the period). These results point to the fact that in 2012, and on average across OECD countries, immigrant students face less socio-economic and performance disadvantage when compared to immigrant students in 2003 Despite these changes and the improvements, however, in 2012, immigrant students still faced a significant disadvantage in mathematics performance compared with their non-immigrant peers, albeit to a lesser degree than they did in 2003 (Figure II.3.5).

Among those countries and economies where at least 5% of the student population were immigrants in both 2003 and 2012, in Belgium, Germany, New Zealand, Switzerland and the United States the difference in mathematics performance between students with an immigrant background and those without narrowed between 2003 and 2012 (Figure II.3.5). In Belgium, Germany and Switzerland, the narrowing is the result of greater performance improvements among students with an immigrant background than among students without an immigrant background. In Germany, the performance disadvantage among immigrant students shrank: in 2003, non-immigrant students outscored students with an immigrant background by 81 points in mathematics; by 2012 this difference had decreased to 54 score points (Box II.3.2 outlines Germany's improvement in PISA and their recent policy trajectory). In fact, in Belgium and Switzerland, the reduction is still observed even when comparing students with similar socio-economic status. In the United States, among students with similar socio-economic status, the difference in performance between students with an immigrant and background and those without shrank by 23 points in the period. In Australia, there was no difference in mathematics performance between immigrant and non-immigrant students in 2003; in 2012, immigrant students outperformed non-immigrant students. Only in France and Italy did the performance disadvantage of immigrant students increase between 2003 and 2012. While in Italy this increase is largely explained by the drop in the socio-economic status of immigrant students, in France the increase in the performance disadvantage is observed after comparing students with a similar socio-economic status (Figure II.3.5).

A rapid increase in the proportion of students with an immigrant background – especially in countries and economies that had predominantly non-immigrant populations – poses challenges to education systems. Students with an immigrant background may have different educational needs, particularly if their native language is different from that of the host country; but they also may have different strengths and talents, and school systems needs to be aware of both these needs and these strengths if immigrant students are to flourish. Between 2003 and 2012, the share of students with an immigrant background grew by five percentage points or more in Canada, Ireland, Italy, Spain and the United States, and grew by more than ten percentage points in Luxembourg and Liechtenstein. In 2003, the school systems in Ireland, Italy and Spain were predominantly composed of non-immigrant students, but by 2012 the share of immigrant students nearly tripled (Figure II.3.6). In Ireland, the increase in the share of immigrant students is mostly unrelated to changes in their academic disadvantage (Figure II.3.5).

■ Figure II.3.5 ■

Change between 2003 and 2012 in immigrant students' mathematics performance

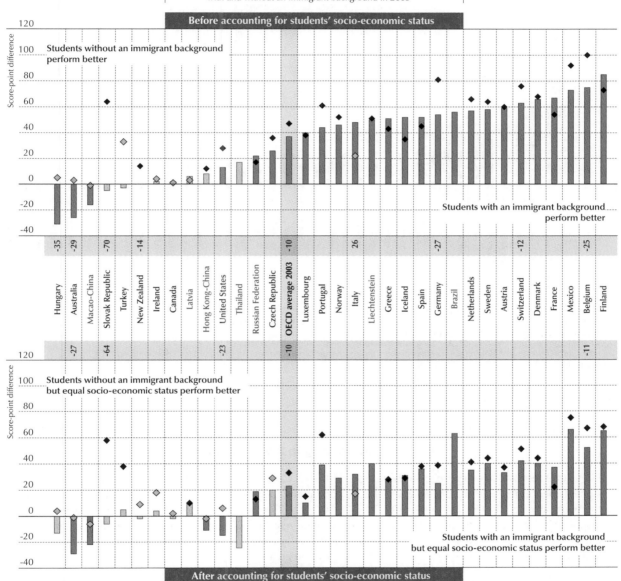

■ ■ Difference in mathematics performance between students with and without an immigrant background in 2012

◆ ◆ Difference in mathematics performance between students with and without an immigrant background in 2003

Notes: Differences in mathematics performance between students without and with an immigrant background in 2003 and 2012 that are statistically significant are marked in a darker tone.

Only countries and economies with comparable data from PISA 2003 and PISA 2012 are shown.

The change in the score-point difference in mathematics between students without and with an immigrant background before accounting for students' socio-economic status between 2012 and 2003 is shown above the country/economy name, and the difference after accounting for students' socio-economic status is shown below the country/economy name. Only statistically significant differences are shown.

OECD average 2003 compares only OECD countries with comparable mathematics scores since 2003.

For comparability over time, PISA 2003 values on the *PISA index of economic, social and cultural status* have been rescaled to the PISA 2012 scale of the index. PISA 2003 results reported in this table may thus differ from those presented in *Learning for Tomorrow's World: First Results from PISA 2003* (OECD, 2004) (see Annex A5 for more details).

Countries and economies are ranked in ascending order of the score-point difference between students with and without an immigrant background before accounting for socio-economic status in 2012.

Source: OECD, PISA 2012 Database, Table II.3.4b.

StatLink ⟐⟐⟐ http://dx.doi.org/10.1787/888932964832

■ Figure II.3.6 ■

Change between 2003 and 2012 in the share of students with an immigrant background

Percentage of students with an immigrant background

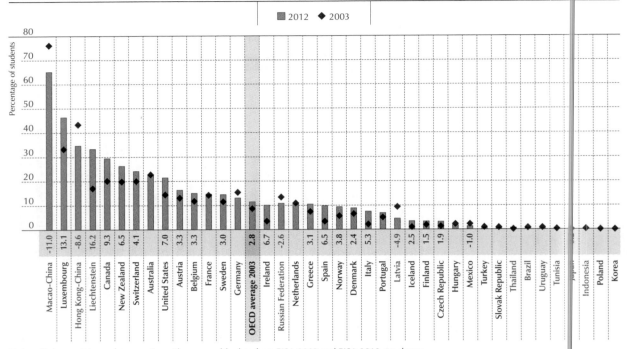

Notes: Only countries and economies with comparable data from PISA 2003 and PISA 2012 are shown.
The percentage-point difference between 2003 and 2012 in the share of students with an immigrant background is shown above the country/economy name. Only statistically significant differences are shown.
OECD 2003 average compares only OECD countries with comparable data since PISA 2003.
Countries and economies are ranked in descending order of the percentage of students with an immigrant background in 2012.
Source: OECD, PISA 2012 Database, Table II.3.4b.
StatLink ▄▆▊▙ http://dx.doi.org/10.1787/888932964832

Box II.3.2. **Improving in PISA: Germany**

PISA 2000 results placed German students close to the OECD average, highlighting that more than one in five students performed below proficiency Level 2 in reading and that social equity levels in education were among the worst among all OECD countries (OECD, 2010a). Since Germany is a federal country where each *Land* is responsible for its own education system, broad education reform could only occur as the result of a concerted effort among the individual *Länder*. The "PISA shock" that followed publication of the PISA 2000 results was a jolt that spurred reform measures to promote higher quality and greater equity in the school system.

Over the past decade Germany has consistently improved its reading and mathematics performance while improving overall equity in education, as well. Average mathematics scores have improved at an average rate of 1.4 score points per year, from 503 score points in 2003 to 514 points in 2012, with the result that Germany moved from OECD average performance in mathematics in 2003 to significantly above the OECD average in 2012. Performance in reading improved by 1.8 score points per year, from 484 score points in 2000 to 508 points in 2012. Improvements in both subjects are largely the result of better performance among low-achieving and disadvantaged students. In PISA 2012, poor-performing students (the 10% of students with the lowest scores) scored over 20 points higher in mathematics than their counterparts in 2003 did. Similar improvements were observed in reading: in 2012, poor-performing students scored nearly 50 points higher than their counterparts did in 2000.

Because low-achieving students are more likely to come from disadvantaged backgrounds, the observed improvement in mathematics, driven by low-achieving students, also reflects greater equity in the education system.

...

While disadvantaged students (those in the bottom quarter of the *PISA index of economic, social and cultural status*) improved their mathematics performance by 20 score points, no such improvement was observed among students in the second, third or top quarter of the socio-economic scale. As a result, students' socio-economic status is less predictive of their mathematics performance in PISA 2012 than it was in PISA 2003. In 2003, 24% of the variation in mathematics performance was explained by students' socio-economic status; by 2012, 17% of the variation was so explained. During that period, Germany moved from being a country with below-OECD-average equity in education to one with an average degree of equity. Improvements in equity are also evident among students with an immigrant background: in 2003 immigrant students scored an average of 81 points below non-immigrant students in mathematics; by 2012, this disadvantage had narrowed to 53 score points.

Reforms prompted by PISA results

Following the PISA 2000 results, the Standing Conference of Ministers of Education and Cultural Affairs (KMK) defined seven areas of action to improve the quality of the education system. Although these and other education-related recommendations from the KMK that followed were non-binding, most programmes were adopted by most states. To promote the achievement, particularly among disadvantaged children and those with an immigrant background, as well as to promote education opportunities through both in- and out-of-school activities for all students, the national government began to subsidise all-day schools (*Ganzagsschule*). In 2002, one in ten schools was an all-day school; by 2012, more than half of all schools were. Although attendance in all-day programmes is only compulsory in only some schools so far, schools remain open all day, offering lunch and extracurricular activities, supplementary education and instruction in the afternoon for those students who need or want it. One in three students takes part in full-day schools (KMK, 2013).

Another key recommendation from the KMK was to develop binding standards and outcome-oriented evaluations. Following the KMK's recommendation, education standards were introduced in 2003 and 2004 for Grades 4, 9 and 10 in German and mathematics. Standards for foreign language instruction (English/French), as well as biology, chemistry and physics were also introduced for Grades 9 and 10. Since 2004, each state's curriculum is based on these standards. In addition, assessments were created to measure progress against the standards at both the state and national levels. They are conducted across the 16 federal states, monitoring the performance of individual schools and the school system as a whole. Evaluations at Grades 3 and 8 are conducted in every school. Reflecting these changes, students who took part in PISA 2012 were 22 percentage points more likely to attend schools where assessments are used to compare the school against national or regional benchmarks, and 13 percentage points more likely to attend schools where assessments are used to monitor school progress from year to year. Also, students are more likely to attend schools where student assessments are used to evaluate whether students/classes have reached the expected level of achievement and to identify aspects of the curriculum that could be improved. The national results from these assessments are compiled in the *Bildung in Deutschland*, a biennial report on the state of education at all levels.

In 2001, the KMK signalled the need to improve teacher professionalism, particularly regarding skills in diagnosing students and in teaching methods. Changes in these areas are reflected in students' and principals' reports in PISA. Students in 2012 were almost 20 percentage points more likely than students in 2003 were to attend schools where teacher practice is monitored through peer reviews, and 10 percentage points more likely to attend schools where teacher practice is monitored through student achievement. In the past decade, reforms have aimed to strengthen pedagogical training by focusing on new teachers' pedagogical and psychological competencies. In-service teacher training is promoted, with the objective of having all teachers participate in the near future.

In most states, the school system is structured around four years of primary school followed by a three-track school system (*Hauptschule, Realschule* and *Gymnasium*) with specific education pathways related to each track. While the *Hauptschule* leads to a vocational and terminal secondary qualification, the *Realschule* is intended for vocational- and academic-track students who want to continue on to vocational/technical or academic tertiary programmes. Many states have begun merging the two vocational tracks into one, motivated by changes in labour market demands that have increased the demand for skills, and demographic changes that have reduced the population of the catchment areas of rural schools.

Concurrent with these reform efforts, social and demographic changes have shifted the profile of Germany's student population. In PISA 2012, socio-economically disadvantaged students and students with an immigrant background had higher levels of the *PISA index of social, economic and cultural status* than disadvantaged

...

students and students with an immigrant background in 2003, and the overall proportion of students that are first- or second-generation immigrants decreased. Also, in 2003, a German student in the bottom quarter of the socio-economic distribution was situated at -1.34 on the ESCS, but a student in the bottom quarter of that index in 2012 was situated at -0.99 (no such change was observed among students in the top quarter of the socio-economic distribution). Similarly, the socio-economic status of students with an immigrant background also improved between PISA 2003 and PISA 2012 (Tables II.2.3b and II.3.4b).

Essentially, these changes mean that the differences in socio-economic status between disadvantaged and advantaged students and between students with an immigrant background and those without have narrowed between PISA 2003 and PISA 2012. These results suggest that Germany's observed improvement in PISA over time may be due to the shifting social and demographic profile of students in parallel to the contribution of any particular policy or programme (Tables I.2.4, I.4.4 and I.5.4).

Sources:

KMK (Sekretariat der Ständigen Konferenz der Kultusminister der Länder in der Bundesrepublik Deutschland) (2013), *Allgemein bildende Schulen in Ganztagsform in den Ländern in der Bundesrepublik Deutschland, Statistik 2007 bis 2011*, Bonn.

OECD (2011), *Lessons from PISA for the United States*, Strong Performers and Successful Reformers in Education, OECD Publishing. *http://dx.doi.org/10.1787/9789264096660-en*

OECD (2010a), *PISA 2009 Results: Learning Trends: Changes in Student Performance Since 2000 (Volume V)*, PISA, OECD Publishing. *http://dx.doi.org/10.1787/9789264091580-en*

Box II.3.3. **Language minorities among non-immigrant students**

Only 4% of 15-year-old students across OECD countries are non-immigrants who do not speak the language of assessment at home. But this proportion varies considerably among countries: in Luxembourg they represent 53% of students; in Belgium and Spain, 14% of students; in Italy, 10%; in the Slovak Republic, 7%; in Turkey, 6%; and in Estonia, Switzerland and Canada, between 3% and 4%. In all countries but Canada, these students are socio-economically disadvantaged when compared with other non-immigrant students. The difference in socio-economic status is widest in the Slovak Republic and Turkey and it is relatively narrow in Switzerland, Estonia and Luxembourg. The difference in mathematics performance between non-immigrant students who do not speak the language of assessment at home and those who do is particularly pronounced in the Slovak Republic where, even after accounting for socio-economic status, 50 score points separate the two groups. In Italy and Switzerland, around 23 score points separate the two groups, and in Estonia, the difference is 14 score points. In Canada and Luxembourg, all non-immigrant students perform at the same level, regardless of the language they speak at home; in Belgium and Spain, they do so after accounting for socio-economic status (Table II.3.8).

In 15 partner countries and economies, non-immigrant students who do not speak the language of assessment at home are a sizable proportion of the student population, and the differences across countries and economies are even greater. These students constitute more than 40% of the student population in Indonesia, Thailand, Malaysia, and Singapore, between 10% and 17% in Chinese Taipei, Qatar and Bulgaria, and between 3% and 10% in Kazakhstan, Lithuania, Latvia, the United Arab Emirates, the Russian Federation, Macao-China, Peru, Jordan and Serbia. In Bulgaria, Peru, Singapore, Thailand, Indonesia, Chinese Taipei, Latvia, the Russian Federation, Serbia, Lithuania and Hong Kong-China these students are socio-economically disadvantaged, compared with other non-immigrant students. In the United Arab Emirates, Qatar, Hong Kong-China, Macao-China, Jordan, Malaysia, and Kazakhstan, they are advantaged compared with other non-immigrant students. Performance gaps in favour of those non-immigrant students who do not speak the language of assessment at home are particularly marked (15 or more score points) in Qatar, Malaysia and the United Arab Emirates. In Singapore, Chinese Taipei, Lithuania, Bulgaria, Peru and Liechtenstein non-immigrant students who speak the language of assessment at home outperform non-immigrant students who do not speak the assessment language at home by more than 10 score points (Table II.3.5).

Language minorities among immigrant students

The most obvious challenge for many students with immigrant parents is adapting to a new language and a new learning environment. The most vulnerable immigrant students are those who arrive at a late age, unable to speak the language of the host country, and from a country where education standards are not as high as those in the host country. Such students would benefit from policies and programmes that take these multiple disadvantages into account. Not all immigrant students face the same challenges; some may be in host countries whose languages and cultures are similar to those in their countries of origin. Ignoring such specific problems may result in the marginalisation of immigrant students at a critical age and with poor prospects for integration (OECD, 2012b).

On average across OECD countries, 6% of 15-year-olds are immigrant students who speak a language at home that is different from the language of assessment. About a third of students in Luxembourg fall into this category as do about 12% of students in Canada, New Zealand, Switzerland and the United States. In Australia, Austria, Belgium, Denmark, France, Germany, Greece, Ireland, Israel, Italy, the Netherlands, Norway, Slovenia, Spain, Sweden and the United Kingdom more than 3% of students are immigrant students who speak a language at home that is different from the language of assessment.

■ Figure II.3.7 ■

Difference in mathematics performance, by immigrant and language background

Before and after accounting for socio-economic status

Percentage of immigrant students who do not speak the language of assessment at home

■ Performance difference between immigrant students who do not speak the language of assessment at home and non-immigrant students who speak the language of assessment at home, **after** accounting for socio-economic status

■ Performance difference between immigrant students who do not speak the language of assessment at home and non-immigrant students who speak the language of assessment at home, **before** accounting for socio-economic status

Country	Percentage
Mexico	0
Finland	3
Belgium	7
Russian Federation	2
Switzerland	12
Estonia	2
Italy	4
Sweden	8
Spain	5
Greece	4
France	5
Luxembourg	32
Argentina	1
Austria	10
Germany	5
Hong Kong-China	4
Slovenia	5
Iceland	3
Netherlands	5
Denmark	4
Norway	6
OECD average	6
Portugal	2
Latvia	1
Czech Republic	2
New Zealand	13
Kazakhstan	1
Ireland	4
Singapore	14
Jordan	1
United States	12
United Kingdom	6
Macao-China	7
Canada	14
Israel	8
Serbia	1
Australia	7
United Arab Emirates	25
Qatar	26

-120 -100 -80 -60 -40 -20 0 20 40 60 80 100 Score-point difference

Note: Score-point differences that are statistically significant are marked in a darker tone.
Countries and economies are ranked in descending order of the score-point difference between immigrant students who do not speak the language of assessment at home and non-immigrant students who do.
Source: OECD, PISA 2012 Database, Table II.3.5.
StatLink ᴹˢᴾ http://dx.doi.org/10.1787/888932964832

Among partner countries and economies, about 25% of students in Qatar and the United Arab Emirates fall into this category, as do 14% in Singapore, 11% in Liechtenstein, 7% in Macao-China and 4% in Hong Kong-China. In some countries, non-immigrant students who do not speak the language of assessment at home are also a significant proportion of the overall population. Box II.3.3 describes PISA results for this group of students (Table II.3.5).

In Austria, Belgium, France, New Zealand, Sweden and Switzerland the attributable risk or population relevance (a measure of the extent of the population affected by a particular characteristic that puts students at risk of low performance) of immigrant students who do not speak the language of assessment at home was 6% or more; in Luxembourg, it reached 29%. In these countries, the risk of being in bottom quarter of the performance distribution is more than double among immigrant students than among any other students. Among these countries, in Austria, Belgium, Luxembourg, New Zealand and Sweden, the difference in performance between non-immigrant students who speak the language of assessment at home and non-immigrant students who do not is between 30 and 53 score points, after accounting for socio-economic status; in Switzerland, 45 score points separate these two groups; and in Belgium, the difference is 53 score points (Table II.3.5 and Figure II.3.7).

Not understanding the language of the country of residence upon arrival is a disadvantage; but so is insufficient exposure to that language outside of school. Policies aimed at supporting immigrant students who do not speak the language of assessment at home should focus on both school and home. An often-discussed possibility is to provide language lessons to parents and encourage them to become engaged in their child's education, if they aren't already. That can help students to improve their language skills, which, in turn, will improve their performance in school and make integration into the host society easier (for a list of policies implemented in different OECD countries in this area, see the OECD review of migrant education [OECD, 2010b]).

First- and second-generation students

The term "immigrant students" used here includes students whose two parents were born abroad but who, themselves, were born in the country of assessment (second generation) or in another country (first generation). Comparing the performance of first- and second-generation students can provide information about the characteristics of different immigrant cohorts, while comparing these two groups with non-immigrant students can provide an idea of the extent to which school systems manage to integrate immigrant students into schools and the role played by immigration policy.

Some 5% of students across OECD countries, on average, are first-generation immigrant students; 6% are second-generation. In general, there are no significant differences in socio-economic status between the two groups. By contrast, second-generation students score 10 points higher, on average, on the PISA mathematics assessment than first-generation students. Across OECD countries, an average of more than 45 score points separates non-immigrant and first-generation students, while the performance difference between non-immigrant and second-generation students is 31 score points. Accounting for socio-economic status, however, narrows the gaps to 29 and 18 score points, respectively, as immigrant students are generally disadvantaged in comparison to non-immigrant students. On average across OECD countries, if the risk of low performance among first- and second-generation students were as low as that among non-immigrant students, the proportion of low-performing students in the country would decrease by about 4% (Table II.3.6a).

In Australia, Canada, and Ireland, first-generation, second-generation and non-immigrant students perform, on average, at or above the OECD average in mathematics. Except for second-generation students in Ireland, each of these three groups represents at least 8% of the total student population in these countries. In New Zealand, first-generation students perform around or above average, but second-generation students do not. In Hungary, first-generation students perform above the OECD average, but they represent only around 1% of the overall student population. As Figure II.3.8 shows, these differences translate into higher or lower proportions of first- and second-generation students achieving above Level 3 in the mathematics performance compared with non-immigrant students.

The "late-arrival penalty"

In general, the older an immigrant student is when he or she arrives in the host country, the lower his or her score on the PISA mathematics assessment (Table II.3.8). This "late-arrival penalty" appears to be associated with a lack of mastery of the assessment language (OECD, 2012b). More generally, any difficulty in adapting to a different culture and school system, or cross-national differences in education standards, may also contribute to poorer performance among immigrant students.

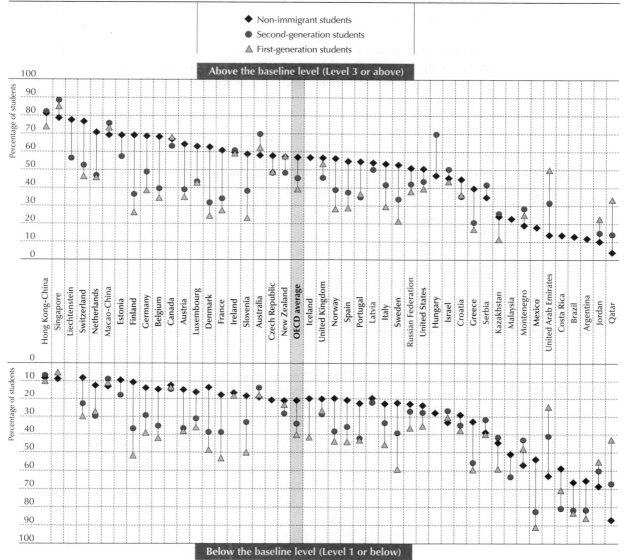

■ Figure II.3.8 ■

Percentage of students with mathematics performance below and above the baseline level (Level 2), by immigrant background

◆ Non-immigrant students
● Second-generation students
△ First-generation students

Note: This figure shows only countries/economies where data are available for at least one category of immigrant students (first- or second-generation).
Countries and economies are ranked in descending order of the percentage of non-immigrant students scoring at Level 3 or above.
Source: OECD, PISA 2012 Database, Table II.3.7.
StatLink http://dx.doi.org/10.1787/888932964832

First-generation students who arrived when they were of lower secondary-school age from less-developed countries where the home language was different from language of assessment in the host country constitute a particularly vulnerable group. These students have to both quickly acquire knowledge of the language of assessment and try to catch up to the performance of their peers in the host country, all while coping with the problems of adjusting to a new school and social environment.

In some cases, students' late arrival is the result of immigration policy. Most countries require that immigrants have adequate lodgings and income before family reunification is allowed. Although such requirements are well-intentioned, the result may be that children have to wait years before they can immigrate, thus making it more difficult for them to integrate into school and into the society of the host country (Heath and Kilpi-Jakonen, 2012). Providing language instruction to older immigrant students is essential.

CONCENTRATION OF DISADVANTAGE

Underperformance among immigrant students can be partly linked to the fact that these students tend to be concentrated in disadvantaged schools (OECD, 2012b). Immigrants tend to settle in neighbourhoods with other immigrants, often of their own origin and socio-economic status, when they move to a new country. By doing so, they build a network of relatives and friends who share their culture and can also help newly arrived immigrants make their way through administrative procedures and perhaps even find work. In addition, early selection or tracking policies in the school system may wind up grouping students of similar origin in the same institution, regardless of where they live. Studies of this phenomenon have shown that the concentration of immigrant students, in itself, need not have adverse effects, provided that there is access to social and public services of a quality comparable to those found elsewhere, and provided that ethnic agglomerations do not become permanent enclaves with little possibility of outward – and upward – mobility (Damm and Rosholm, 2010; Edin, Fredriksson and Aslund, 2004).

This section examines the extent to which the concentration of immigrant or language-minority students is associated with less-favourable education outcomes. The concentration of immigrant students or those who do not speak the language of assessment at home is measured as the proportion of students with such characteristics in each school.[5]

PISA 2012 results suggest that students who attend schools where the proportion of immigrant students is large perform as well as those who attend schools where the proportion of immigrant students is small, after the socio-economic profiles of the students and the school are taken into account. Across OECD countries, students who attend schools where the concentration of immigrants is high (i.e. where more than a quarter of students are immigrants) tend to perform worse than those in schools with no immigrant students. The observed difference between these two groups is 18 score points, but after accounting for the socio-economic status of the students and schools, the difference is more than halved, to five score points. In fact, Greece and Belgium are the only countries with large immigrant student populations (more than 10%), where there is a large performance difference after accounting for socio-economic status (40 and 30 score points, respectively) (Table II.3.9).

In Estonia, Portugal and Hungary there are also large differences after accounting for socio-economic status, but the size of the immigrant population is smaller. In the Netherlands, Germany and Ireland large performance differences between these two types of schools are observed before accounting for socio-economic status; but most of these differences are strongly related to socio-economic disparities, as they are no longer observed after taking socio-economic status into account. A similar pattern is observed in Slovenia, Italy, Argentina and Finland, but in these countries/economies the immigrant population is smaller (less than 10%). In 14 out of 35 countries with comparable data, students in schools with high concentrations of immigrant students underperform before accounting for socio-economic disparities. After taking socio-economic status into account, the number of countries/economies drops to 7; and in most, the performance gaps are so reduced, or even halved, that they are practically insignificant (Table II.3.9).

A similar pattern is observed when considering the concentration of students who do not speak the language of assessment at home, although differences in performance are larger (Table II.3.10). Across OECD countries, before accounting for students' and schools' socio-economic profile, the difference in mathematics performance between students in schools with high concentrations of students who do not speak the language of assessment at home and those in schools where all students speak the assessment language at home is almost 30 score points, but that difference disappears after taking socio-economic status into account. However, in 16 of the 42 countries with available data, large differences in mathematics performance are observed across these schools; but in all but six of them, those differences are no longer observed after taking socio-economic status into account. Before taking socio-economic status into account, the largest differences are observed in the Netherlands, Bulgaria, Italy, the Slovak Republic, Slovenia, Thailand, Turkey, Mexico and Lithuania. After accounting for socio-economic status, the largest differences in mathematics performances are observed in Hong Kong-China, Switzerland, Indonesia, Greece and Peru.

In general, immigrant students and those who do not speak the language of assessment at home tend to be concentrated in disadvantaged schools (Figure II. 3.9). For example, in the United States, 40% of students in disadvantaged schools are immigrant students, whereas they account for 13% of the student population in advantaged schools (Table II.4.2). In Hong Kong-China, Macao-China and Luxembourg, the gap in the proportion of immigrant students attending advantaged and disadvantaged is larger than 20 percentage points. A similar pattern is observed among immigrant students who do not speak the language of assessment at home.

■ Figure II.3.9 ■

Proportion of immigrant students in socio-economically disadvantaged, average and advantaged schools[1]

	Percentage of immigrant students in the total population		

■ Socio-economically disadvantaged schools
Ɩ Socio-economically average schools
▶ Socio-economically advantaged schools

Country	%		Country
Korea	0		Korea
Viet Nam	0		Viet Nam
Poland	0		Poland
Indonesia	0		Indonesia
Romania	0		Romania
Uruguay	0		Uruguay
Tunisia	0		Tunisia
Bulgaria	1		Bulgaria
Chinese Taipei	1		Chinese Taipei
Chile	1		Chile
Brazil	1		Brazil
Colombia	0		Colombia
Japan	0		Japan
Hungary	2		Hungary
Slovak Republic	1		Slovak Republic
Peru	1		Peru
Turkey	1		Turkey
Lithuania	2		Lithuania
Thailand	1		Thailand
Malaysia	2		Malaysia
Mexico	1		Mexico
Shanghai-China	1		Shanghai-China
Czech Republic	3		Czech Republic
Latvia	5		Latvia
Montenegro	6		Montenegro
Finland	3		Finland
Argentina	4		Argentina
Portugal	7		Portugal
Iceland	3		Iceland
Costa Rica	6		Costa Rica
Jordan	13		Jordan
Estonia	8		Estonia
Serbia	9		Serbia
Italy	7		Italy
Russian Federation	11		Russian Federation
Slovenia	9		Slovenia
Ireland	10		Ireland
Spain	10		Spain
Croatia	12		Croatia
Singapore	18		Singapore
OECD average	**11**		**OECD average**
Israel	18		Israel
Denmark	9		Denmark
Netherlands	11		Netherlands
Greece	11		Greece
Germany	13		Germany
United Kingdom	13		United Kingdom
Norway	9		Norway
Australia	23		Australia
Sweden	15		Sweden
Austria	16		Austria
Belgium	15		Belgium
Kazakhstan	16		Kazakhstan
Switzerland	24		Switzerland
New Zealand	26		New Zealand
Canada	29		Canada
United States	21		United States
United Arab Emirates	55		United Arab Emirates
Hong Kong-China	35		Hong Kong-China
Qatar	52		Qatar
Luxembourg	46		Luxembourg
Macao-China	65		Macao-China

0   10   20   30   40   50   60   70   80   Percentage of immigrant students

How to read this chart: On average across countries and economies, immigrant students represent 11% of the total student population; however, they represent 16% of students attending socio-economically disadvantaged schools, 5% of those attending average schools, and 9% of those attending socio-economically advantaged schools.

1. A socio-economically disadvantaged school is one whose students' mean socio-economic status is statistically significantly below the mean socio-economic status of the country/economy; an average school is one where there is no difference between the schools' and the country's/economy's mean socio-economic status; and an advantaged school is one whose students' mean socio-economic status is statistically significantly above the country's/economy's mean socio-economic status.
Countries and economies are ranked in ascending order of the proportion of immigrant students in socio-economically disadvantaged schools.
Source: OECD, PISA 2012 Database, Tables II.3.4a and II.4.2.
StatLink ᵃᵐˢᵖ http://dx.doi.org/10.1787/888932964832

PERFORMANCE, IMMIGRANT STATUS AND COUNTRY OF ORIGIN

With increasing inflows of immigrants comes greater diversity in backgrounds – and in education outcomes. Some PISA-participating countries collect information about immigrant students' country of birth and that of their parents, which allows for developing deeper insights into these students' performance and the extent to which host countries are meeting immigrant students' needs. Results from these countries show that immigrant students from the same country and of similar socio-economic status perform very differently across school systems.

Performance differences are large among immigrant students who were born in partner countries. For example, immigrant students from the Russian Federation who are living in Germany outperform those who are living in Greece by more than 75 score points, after taking into account their socio-economic status. Students of Turkish origin living in Belgium outperform Turkish immigrant students of similar socio-economic status, but who are living in Finland by almost 55 score points. On average across host countries with comparable PISA data, immigrant students from Viet Nam score well in mathematics regardless of their country of destination. Those living in Australia attain a mean score of 548 points while those living in the Czech Republic score 524 points.

Among immigrant students from OECD countries, performance differences across host countries are equally large. For example, immigrant students from France who are living in Switzerland outperform French immigrant students living in Israel by more than 60 score points after accounting for socio-economic status. Students of Portuguese origin living in Switzerland outperform those of the same origin and with similar socio-economic status who live in Luxembourg by 58 score points. Immigrant students from Germany living in Austria outperform those living in Switzerland by 37 score points (Table II.3.11).

The wide performance differences between students of similar socio-economic status and a common country of origin suggest that schools and education policy in the host countries influence these students' performance. While immigration policies, similarities between the immigrants' and the host culture, and other social policies also explain some of these differences in performance, some education systems appear to facilitate the integration of immigrant students better than others.

Some groups of immigrant students achieve high levels of performance regardless of the country to which they immigrated. For example, immigrant students from China living in Australia and New Zealand are all among the top ten highest-performing groups of immigrant students of all host countries, as are immigrant students from Korea living in New Zealand, and immigrant students from India and Viet Nam living in Australia. Students of German origin in Austria and Luxembourg are the only immigrant students not from Asian countries who are among these top-performing groups.

The mean mathematics performance among all these groups is 548 score points or higher (Table II.3.11), the equivalent of more than one full year of schooling above the OECD average. These students show that it is possible to succeed at school even when confronted with the challenges of adapting to a new country, a new school system and, in many cases, a new culture and language.

Countries that are just beginning to receive increasing numbers of immigrant students from diverse backgrounds can learn from the experience of those systems that have been confronted with this challenge for longer and have succeeded in integrating these students into their school systems. The fact that immigrant students from the same country of origin, cultural backgrounds and socio-economic status perform so differently across host countries indicates that education and social policy can have an impact not only on these students' performance but also on how prepared they are to make the most of available opportunities in their host countries.

Notes

1. The literature on the relationship between family structure and performance is vast, and parental engagement is only one of the aspects analysed in this literature. The literature has focused on the economic situation and, particularly, the stress levels of the family stemming from the transition from one type of family to another and from precarious economic situations. See, for example, Buchmann and Hannum (2001) for a cross-national look at this relationship; McLanahan and Sandefur (1994) for the consequences for students; Raley, Frisco and Wildsmith (2005) for a study of status and stress by comparing single-parent households to cohabitation; and Jeynes (2005) for a discussion about parental involvement in single-parent households. For classic studies on the differences in the use of language by social class, including parent-child interactions and language quality and richness, see Brice Heath (1983). Also, see Volume IV of this report for differences in the types and level of parental involvement in schools across selected PISA countries.

2. Students reported on who usually lives at home with them: a) Mother (including stepmother or foster mother); b) Father (including stepfather or foster father); c) Brother(s) (including stepbrothers); d) Sister(s) (including stepsisters); e) Grandparent(s); Others (e.g. cousin). Students from single-parent families are those who responded "No" and "Yes" to a) and b), or "Yes" and "No" to a) and b). That is, they reported that they live with one parent but not the other. Any other response is categorised as "other", unless the student did not respond to this question at all.

3. This implies that students who were born abroad but who had at least one parent born in the country of assessment are also classified as students without an immigrant background.

4. If information on only one of the parents is missing, it is assumed that the other parent has the same immigrant background as the one whose information is missing. If the information on the country of birth of the student is missing, the variable is coded as missing.

5. Robustness checks were conducted to exclude schools with few observations, but the results did not change in any significant way.

References

Brice Heath, S. (1983), *Ways with Words: Language, Life, and Work in Communities and Classrooms*, Cambridge University Press, New York and Cambridge.

Buchmann, C. and **E. Hannum** (2001), "Stratification in Developing Countries: A Review of Theories and Research", *Annual Review of Sociology*, Vol. 27, pp. 77-102.

Damm, A. and **M. Rosholm** (2010), "Employment Effects of Spatial Dispersal of Refugees," *Review of Economics of the Household*, Springer, Vol. 8(1), pp. 105-146.

Edin, P., P. Fredriksson and **O. Åslund** (2004), "Settlement Policies and the Economic Success of Immigrants," *Journal of Population Economics*, Springer, Vol. 17(1), pp. 133-155.

Heath, A. and **E. Kilpi-Jakonen** (2012), "Immigrant Children's Age at Arrival and Assessment Results", *OECD Education Working Papers*, No. 75, OECD Publishing.
http://dx.doi.org/10.1787/5k993zsz6g7h-en

Jeynes, W.H. (2005), "A Meta-Analysis of the Relation of Parental Involvement to Urban Elementary School Student Academic Achievement", *Urban Education,* Vol. 40, No. 3, pp. 237-269.

Sekretariat der Ständigen Konferenz der Kultusminister der Länder in der Bundesrepublik Deutschland (KMK) (2013), *Allgemein bildende Schulen in Ganztagsform in den Ländern in der Bundesrepublik Deutschland, Statistik 2007 bis 2011*, Bonn.

McLanahan, S. and **G.D. Sandefur** (1994), *Growing Up with a Single Parent: What Hurts, What Helps,* Harvard University Press, Cambridge, Massachusetts.

OECD (2012a), *Let's Read Them a Story! The Parent Factor in Education*, PISA, OECD Publishing.
http://dx.doi.org/10.1787/9789264176232-en

OECD (2012b), *Untapped Skills: Realising the Potential of Immigrant Students*, PISA, OECD Publishing.
http://dx.doi.org/10.1787/9789264172470-en

OECD (2011), *Lessons from PISA for the United States*, Strong Performers and Successful Reformers in Education, OECD Publishing.
http://dx.doi.org/10.1787/9789264096660-en

OECD (2010a), *PISA 2009 Results: Learning Trends: Changes in Student Performance Since 2000 (Volume V)*, PISA, OECD Publishing.
http://dx.doi.org/10.1787/9789264091580-en

OECD (2010b), *Closing the Gap for Immigrant Students: Policies, Practice and Performance*, OECD Reviews of Migrant Education, OECD Publishing.
http://dx.doi.org/10.1787/9789264075788-en

Pong, S., J. Dronkers and **G. Hampden-Thompson** (2004), "Family Policies and Children's School Achievement in Single- Versus Two-Parent Families", *Journal of Marriage and Family*, Vol. 65, Issue 3, pp. 681-699.

Raley, R.K., M.L. Frisco and **E. Wildsmith** (2005), "Maternal Cohabitation and Educational Success", *Sociology of Education,* April 2005, Vol. 78, No. 2, pp. 144-164.

4

Equity in Opportunities to Learn and in Resources

This chapter explores the concept of equity as it relates to the frequency with which students are exposed to certain mathematics problems in class, teacher quality and quantity, the school's disciplinary climate, and students' participation in pre-primary education. It examines the close relationship among these resources, socio-economic status and performance in mathematics.

Previous research has shown a relationship between students' exposure to subject content in school, what is known as "opportunity to learn", and student performance (Schmidt et al., 2001). Building on previous measures of opportunity to learn (Carroll, 1963; Wiley and Harnischfeger, 1974; Sykes, Schneider and Planck, 2009; Schmidt et al., 2001), the PISA 2012 assessment included questions to students about the mathematics theories, concepts and content to which they might have been exposed in school, and the amount of class time they spent studying these various subjects. As reported in Volume I, there are widely different experiences across systems, schools and students. When these differences are related to student or school characteristics, such as the socio-economic status of students or schools, the proportion of immigrant or minority-language students, or the size of the community in which a school is located, inequities can arise.[1]

What the data tell us

- Opportunities to learn formal mathematical problems at school and familiarity with fundamental concepts of algebra and geometry have a stronger impact on performance when the entire student population benefits from them.

- Disparities in exposure to formal mathematics are more marked in school systems that separate students into different schools based on their performance – and, given the strong relationship between performance and socio-economic status, in systems where the unintended result of separation by performance is separation by socio-economic status.

- Across OECD countries, students who reported that they had attended pre-primary school for more than one year score 53 points higher in mathematics – the equivalent of more than one years of schooling – than students who had not attended pre-primary education.

- OECD countries allocate at least an equal, if not a larger, number of teachers to socio-economically disadvantaged schools as to advantaged schools; but disadvantaged schools tend to have great difficulty in attracting qualified teachers.

Volume I of this publication defines and describes a series of indices of exposure and familiarity to formal mathematics based on students' reports. Students were asked about their familiarity with different mathematical concepts. They also reported on how often they had encountered different mathematics problems at school, some focusing on formal mathematics, others on more applied mathematics. These indices provide a measure of the kinds of opportunities to learn mathematics students are exposed to in compulsory education. They reflect what 15-year-old students experience at school but also what they had been exposed to before taking part in PISA. While student self-reports, by definition, give the students' perspective on the types and frequency of mathematics problems to which they are exposed, they may also reflect other student perceptions, such as students' level of comfort with or mastery of these types of problems. Volume I examines how these answers are related to student performance across countries. This section focuses on familiarity with basic concepts of algebra and geometry (such as "quadratic function", "linear equation", "polygon" or "cosine") and exposure to formal mathematics problems in school lessons (such as, "Solve: $2x+3=7$" or "Find the volume of a box with sides 3m, 4m and 5m").

Figure II.4.1 shows the main measures of equity in exposure to formal mathematics and how they relate to mean performance, and the main measures of equity in outcomes. It contains the key data and results discussed in this chapter.

Differences across schools in students' exposure to basic concepts of formal mathematics in algebra and geometry are closely related to performance differences between students attending socio-economically advantaged and disadvantaged schools.[2] While differences in exposure do not account for all performance differences between these two groups of students, they do account for much of them. Figure II.4.2 shows the relationship among these disparities.

In countries with high mean scores in mathematics and high levels of equity in education outcomes, differences between students in advantaged and disadvantaged schools are smaller, both in terms of mathematics performance and exposure to formal mathematics (Figure II.4.1). For example, Estonia, Finland, and Canada, all in the bottom-left quadrant of Figure II.4.2, show narrow performance gaps between students who attend socio-economically advantaged and disadvantaged schools. Among schools systems with high average mathematics achievement and high equity in education outcomes (as measured by the strength of the relationship between performance and socio-economic status) (Figure II.4.1), only Japan and Korea show large differences in student performance and average disparities in opportunities to learn between advantaged and disadvantaged schools (top-right quadrant of Figure II.4.2).

■ Figure II.4.1 ■
Summary of PISA measures of equity in exposure to formal mathematics

Higher quality or equity than the OECD average
Not statistically different from the OECD average
Lower quality or equity than the OECD average

	Average student performance in mathematics	Strength of the relationship between student performance and socio-economic status[1] — Percentage of explained variation in student performance	Performance differences across socio-economic status: Slope of the socio-economic gradient[1] — Score-point difference associated with a one-unit increase in socio-economic status	Mean index of exposure to formal mathematics	Variation of the index of exposure to formal mathematics	Within-school variation of the index of exposure to formal mathematics as a proportion of the sum of the within- and between-school variation	Within-school variation in socio-economic status as a proportion of the sum of the within- and between-school variation	Within-school variation of student performance as a proportion of the sum of the within- and between-school variation
OECD average	494	14.8	39	1.70	0.37	80.4	75.6	64.1
Shanghai-China	613	15.1	41	2.30	0.21	82.8	66.8	53.1
Singapore	573	14.4	44	2.23	0.41	83.5	76.4	63.3
Hong Kong-China	561	7.5	27	1.83	0.40	92.8	67.7	57.6
Chinese Taipei	560	17.9	58	1.98	0.33	81.9	76.7	57.9
Korea	554	10.1	42	2.07	0.27	73.6	78.3	60.4
Macao-China	538	2.6	17	2.20	0.32	86.1	73.7	58.2
Japan	536	9.8	41	2.05	0.22	71.6	77.8	47.0
Liechtenstein	535	7.6	28	1.55	0.57	53.7	85.5	37.5
Switzerland	531	12.8	38	1.41	0.50	59.6	82.7	64.4
Netherlands	523	11.5	40	1.50	0.45	68.2	81.8	34.1
Estonia	521	8.6	29	2.00	0.21	92.0	81.5	82.7
Finland	519	9.4	33	1.72	0.35	87.9	91.1	92.5
Canada	518	9.4	31	1.98	0.37	89.0	82.8	80.2
Poland	518	16.6	41	1.83	0.30	92.5	76.4	79.5
Belgium	515	19.6	49	1.83	0.52	72.1	72.4	48.6
Germany	514	16.9	43	1.66	0.43	66.7	73.6	47.0
Viet Nam	511	14.6	29	1.96	0.22	83.3	58.3	47.9
Austria	506	15.8	43	1.54	0.47	57.3	71.2	51.6
Australia	504	12.3	42	1.69	0.49	80.1	76.5	72.1
Ireland	501	14.6	38	1.47	0.37	90.9	79.7	81.8
Slovenia	501	15.6	42	1.93	0.32	78.7	74.6	41.3
Denmark	500	16.5	39	1.62	0.36	87.7	82.3	83.5
New Zealand	500	18.4	52	1.51	0.51	82.7	77.5	76.2
Czech Republic	499	16.2	51	1.80	0.29	71.2	76.4	48.5
France	495	22.5	57	1.87	0.32	w	w	w
United Kingdom	494	12.5	41	1.63	0.43	82.2	79.4	71.8
Iceland	493	7.7	31	1.14	0.39	95.8	86.4	90.1
Latvia	491	14.7	35	2.03	0.22	88.9	74.7	74.4
Luxembourg	490	18.3	37	1.45	0.51	85.8	73.6	59.0
Norway	489	7.4	32	m	m	m	91.0	87.1
Portugal	487	19.6	35	1.73	0.37	89.5	68.6	70.1
Italy	485	10.1	30	1.83	0.39	68.0	75.9	48.5
Spain	484	15.8	34	1.87	0.44	88.0	75.2	81.2
Russian Federation	482	11.4	38	2.10	0.16	94.7	75.0	73.2
Slovak Republic	482	24.6	54	1.70	0.32	67.2	64.4	50.1
United States	481	14.8	35	2.00	0.41	89.5	73.8	76.3
Lithuania	479	13.8	36	1.65	0.27	91.8	78.7	69.3
Sweden	478	10.6	36	0.77	0.31	92.5	86.9	87.5
Hungary	477	23.1	47	1.96	0.29	72.4	62.6	38.1
Croatia	471	12.0	36	2.07	0.32	87.7	75.9	55.7
Israel	466	17.2	51	1.81	0.41	80.0	74.6	57.6
Greece	453	15.5	34	1.91	0.34	93.1	73.5	67.9
Serbia	449	11.7	34	2.04	0.29	89.1	78.0	54.0
Turkey	448	14.5	32	1.92	0.30	85.1	72.3	38.2
Romania	445	19.3	38	2.02	0.40	78.0	64.4	54.6
Bulgaria	439	22.3	42	1.96	0.45	82.0	59.6	47.2
United Arab Emirates	434	9.8	33	2.13	0.50	80.3	73.9	55.6
Kazakhstan	432	8.0	27	1.97	0.32	90.5	76.8	63.5
Thailand	427	9.9	22	1.70	0.29	85.2	61.6	57.9
Chile	423	23.1	34	1.70	0.34	75.2	47.2	56.6
Malaysia	421	13.4	30	1.59	0.36	88.1	71.5	67.6
Mexico	413	10.4	19	1.78	0.43	82.3	56.5	64.8
Montenegro	410	12.7	33	1.90	0.40	92.8	80.6	63.5
Uruguay	409	22.8	37	1.64	0.47	76.3	60.2	58.0
Costa Rica	407	18.9	24	1.53	0.52	79.4	61.8	57.6
Albania	394	m	m	2.09	0.42	93.1	0.0	95.4
Brazil	391	15.7	26	1.43	0.51	72.4	62.8	56.9
Argentina	388	15.1	26	1.35	0.48	74.7	66.5	55.6
Tunisia	388	12.4	22	1.23	0.36	94.4	67.2	50.7
Jordan	386	8.4	22	2.15	0.57	84.8	79.6	64.0
Colombia	376	15.4	25	1.76	0.51	83.6	63.2	64.9
Qatar	376	5.6	27	1.72	0.67	76.1	75.5	53.8
Indonesia	375	9.6	20	1.60	0.33	81.9	63.1	48.0
Peru	368	23.4	33	1.79	0.51	79.8	54.2	54.4

1. Single-level bivariate regression of mathematics performance on the *PISA index of economic, social and cultural status* (ESCS); the slope is the regression coefficient for the ESCS, and the strength corresponds to the r-squared*100.
Countries and economies are ranked in descending order of mean mathematics performance.
Source: OECD, PISA 2012 Database, Tables II.2.1, II.2.8a, II.2.13a and II.4.1.
StatLink ᐧᐧᐧᐧᐧ http://dx.doi.org/10.1787/888932964851

■ Figure II.4.2 ■

Magnitude of performance differences related to students' exposure to formal mathematics, by schools' socio-economic profile

Between students in advantaged schools and those in disadvantaged schools

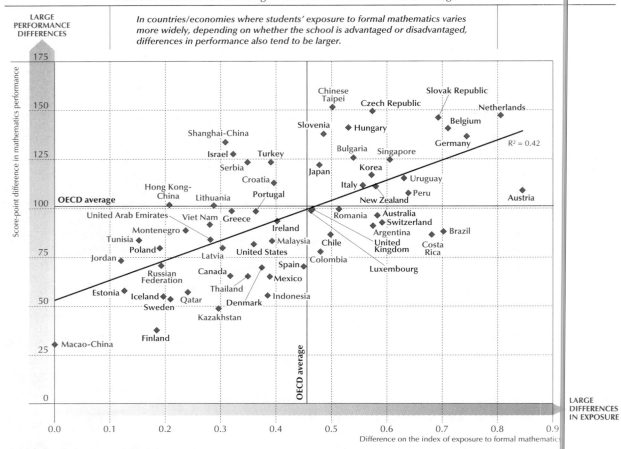

Note: Depending on the organisation of schooling (comprehensive vs. institutional differentiation according to performance) differences across schools are to be expected for certain aspects of learning opportunities to meet students' needs.
Source: OECD, PISA 2012 Database, Tables II.4.2 and II.4.3.
StatLink http://dx.doi.org/10.1787/888932964851

Figure II.4.2 also shows that, on average across OECD countries, there is a very strong relationship between the differences between advantaged and disadvantaged schools in mathematics performance and in exposure to formal mathematics (the correlation between these two measures is 0.65). On average across OECD countries, the difference in mathematics performance amounts to 104 score points. The difference in exposure to mathematics across school's socio-economic profile is also large (more than 0.45 in the index of exposure of formal mathematics or three quarters of a standard deviation on the index, 0.60). On average, students in advantaged schools reported that they had "often heard of" the more advanced topics of mathematics related to algebra and geometry and had also had "frequent" encounters with problems dealing with formal mathematics, more generally, in class. Students in disadvantaged schools reported that they had heard of these topics somewhere between "once or twice" and "a few times" in class.

DISPARITIES IN EXPOSURE TO FORMAL MATHEMATICS, SOCIO-ECONOMIC STATUS AND PERFORMANCE

Students who are not exposed to mathematics concepts and processes in school cannot be expected to learn (on their own), much less excel at, that material. Allocating more and better resources to education will only go so far; what is taught in the classroom – and how it is taught – ultimately determines whether those resources serve the school system's primary objective: providing high-quality, equitable education to all. Breadth and depth of instructional content and delivery is critical for student learning, particularly in mathematics.

Opportunities to learn may differ across students and schools for many reasons. If the school system tracks students into different schools that distinguish, for example, between academic and vocational pathways, students' exposure to mathematics may vary accordingly, depending on the schools they attend. Exposure to different mathematical concepts and experience with mathematical problems may also differ among students within a particular school, especially when students are grouped by ability and taught different material. Instructional content and delivery may also differ within a school if 15-year-old students are enrolled in different grades within the same school or if students choose different programme strands.

Disparities within countries

On average across OECD countries, 15-year-old students reported that they had heard of mathematical concepts in algebra and geometry "a few times" but had "frequent" encounters with problems involving formal mathematics. While there are significant differences across school systems, there are even larger differences between schools within a country and among students within schools.[3] Most of the differences are observed among students who attend the same school (65%); differences between schools within countries account for 17% of the overall differences and differences across countries and economies account for the remaining 18% of the differences.[4]

School systems that combine high average performance and equity tend to offer all their students frequent exposure to formal mathematics concepts (as measured by higher-than-average means on the *index of exposure to formal mathematics* and lower than average overall and between-school variations in the same index). Of the nine countries with high performance and equity, Liechtenstein is the only where mean exposure to formal mathematics is below average. Of this group, only in Australia, Hong Kong-China and Liechtenstein the variation in exposure to formal mathematics is above average. Liechtenstein is the only system where the variation is large and between school differences are above average. Japan and Korea are the only two countries on this group where differences between schools in exposure to formal mathematics are above average (Figure II.4.1).

Differences in exposure to mathematics and average mathematics performance across school systems

Fewer disparities in exposure to mathematics concepts are associated with higher mean performance, particularly in those school systems where the frequency of exposure to and familiarity with formal mathematical concepts is greater than the OECD average. Exposure to formal mathematics problems at school and familiarity with fundamental concepts of algebra and geometry have a stronger impact on average performance when the entire student population has benefited from them. As Figure II.4.3 shows, the countries that achieve high levels of performance tend to show smaller disparities in exposure to formal mathematics.

Figure II.4.3 also shows that when school systems provide frequent exposure to formal mathematics concepts and practices, there is a strong relationship between differences in exposure to formal mathematics and average performance. Estonia, Japan and Korea, for example, all perform well above the OECD average; in addition, exposure to formal mathematics in these countries is also well above the OECD average and differences in opportunities are below average. These patterns are also seen across partner countries and economies, with Shanghai-China achieving particularly high average performance associated with frequent exposure to formal mathematics problems and familiarity with fundamental mathematics concepts in geometry and algebra, and markedly small variations in those opportunities.

When exposure to formal mathematics is below the OECD average, disparities are not strongly related to mean performance (as represented in the left hand side of Figure II.4.3). There are countries that provide less frequent exposure to formal mathematics, have less variation in those opportunities, and show poorer average performance, such as Costa Rica, Luxembourg, and Uruguay; but there are also countries, such as Austria, Germany, the Netherlands, New Zealand and Switzerland, that provide less frequent exposure to mathematics, show large disparities in exposure and also show above-average performance (Figure II.4.3).

Between-school differences in opportunity to learn, socio-economic status and performance

In most school systems where there is some kind of selection of students, students tend to be selected into schools on the basis of their performance. As explored in Chapter 2, performance tends to be closely related to socio-economic status; so often the unintended result of separating students by performance is the separation of students by socio-economic status as well. Results from PISA 2012 show that disparities in exposure to formal mathematics are more marked in systems that separate students into different schools based on their performance – and, given the relationship between performance and socio-economic status, in systems where the unintended result of separation by performance is separation by socio-economic status. Large between-school differences in opportunities to learn, socio-economic status and performance are associated with systems that show lower levels of equity in education outcomes and, in some cases, lower average performance.

■ Figure II.4.3 ■

Relationship between mathematics performance and variation in students' exposure to formal mathematics

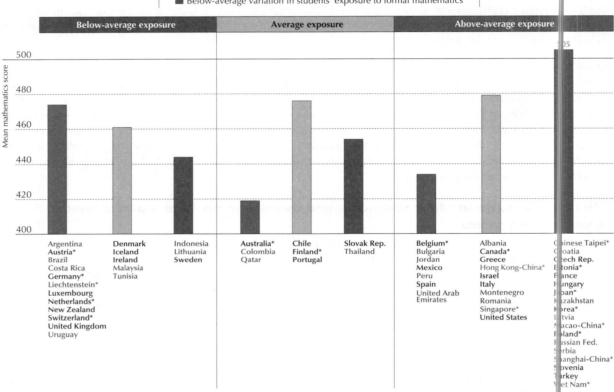

Notes: Depending on the organisation of schooling (comprehensive vs. institutional differentiation according to performance), differences across schools are to be expected for certain learning opportunities to meet students' needs.
Countries with mean mathematics performance above the OECD average are marked with an asterisk.
Source: OECD, PISA 2012 Database, Tables I.2.3a and II.4.1.
StatLink ᠍᠍᠍ http://dx.doi.org/10.1787/888932964851

As Figure II.4.1 shows, Canada, Denmark, Estonia, Finland, Iceland and Sweden all show below-average between-school differences in performance, socio-economic status and exposure to formal mathematics. These systems not only succeed in minimising differences between schools across these three indicators, they all show greater-than-average equity in education outcomes, as measured by the strength of the relationship between socio-economic status and performance, except Denmark, where equity is average. Canada, Denmark, Estonia and Finland perform above average, Iceland shows average performance, and only Sweden performs below average.

By contrast, Argentina, Brazil, Chile, Hungary and the Slovak Republic all show large between-school differences in performance, socio-economic status and exposure to formal mathematics. Average performance is below the OECD average in all these school systems. Chile, Hungary and the Slovak Republic also show below-average equity in education outcomes, while equity in Argentina and Brazil is at the OECD average, as measured by the strength of the relationship between socio-economic status and performance.

■ Figure II.4.4 ■

Between-school differences in exposure to formal mathematics, socio-economic status and performance

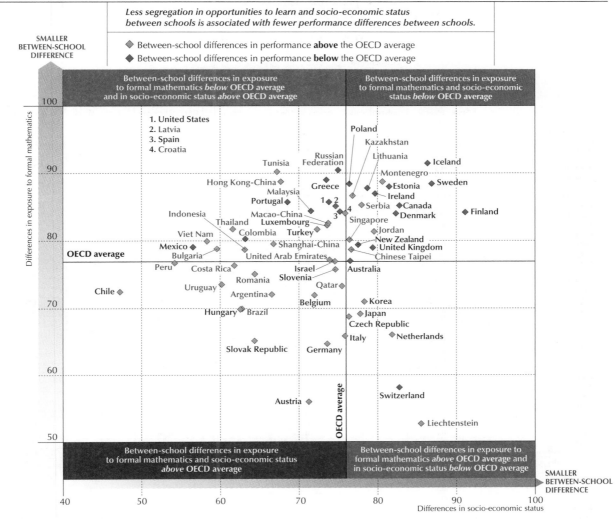

Less segregation in opportunities to learn and socio-economic status between schools is associated with fewer performance differences between schools.

◆ Between-school differences in performance **above** the OECD average
◆ Between-school differences in performance **below** the OECD average

Note: Depending on the organisation of schooling (comprehensive vs. institutional differentiation according to performance), differences across schools are to be expected for certain learning opportunities to meet students' needs.
Source: OECD, PISA 2012 Database, Tables II.2.8a, II.2.13a and II.4.1.
StatLink ◫◫◱ http://dx.doi.org/10.1787/888932964851

Between-school differences and the overall variation in exposure to formal mathematics are above average in Austria, Belgium, Germany, Liechtenstein, the Netherlands and Switzerland (with above-average performance) and Argentina, Brazil and Italy (with below-average performance). In all of these countries, except Switzerland, between-school differences in performance are below average. Socio-economic differences between schools are above average in Argentina and Brazil, average in Austria, Belgium, Germany and Italy, and below average in Liechtenstein, the Netherlands and Switzerland. None of these countries, except Italy and Liechtenstein, achieves above-average equity in education outcomes, as measured by the strength of the relationship between socio-economic status and performance.

EQUITY IN EDUCATIONAL RESOURCES

A potential source of inequity in learning outcomes and opportunities lies in the distribution of resources across students and schools. A positive relationship between the socio-economic profile of schools and the quantity or quality of resources means that advantaged schools benefit from more or better resources; a negative relationship implies that more or better resources are devoted to disadvantaged schools. No relationship between the two implies that schools attended by disadvantaged students are as likely to have access to better or more resources as schools attended by advantaged students.

■ Figure II.4.5 ■

Summary of PISA measures of equity in educational resources

Disadvantaged schools are more likely to have more or better resources; correlation is stronger than 0.25
Advantaged schools are more likely to have more or better resources; correlation is stronger than 0.25

	Simple correlation between the school mean socio-economic profile and:							
	Student-teacher ratio[1]	Composition and qualifications of mathematics teaching staff (proportion of teachers with university-level qualifications)	Student-related factors affecting school climate	Proportion of students who leave school without a certificate	Parental pressure to achieve	Attendance at after-school lessons		Hours spent on homework or other study set by teachers
OECD average	0.16	0.14	0.30	-0.28	0.31	0.10		0.18
Australia	-0.05	0.02	0.52	-0.31	0.36	0.14		0.25
Austria	-0.11	0.60	0.23	-0.22	0.25	0.12		0.23
Belgium	0.59	0.61	0.56	-0.36	0.30	0.17		0.31
Canada	0.20	0.02	0.36	-0.31	0.41	0.10		0.18
Chile	-0.03	0.19	0.45	-0.34	0.44	0.08		0.16
Czech Republic	0.05	0.28	0.31	-0.18	0.28	0.02		0.14
Denmark	0.20	0.09	0.35	-0.30	0.35	0.00		0.05
Estonia	0.45	0.00	0.09	-0.12	0.13	0.02		0.04
Finland	0.36	0.01	0.01	0.02	0.14	0.05		0.05
France	w	w	w	w	w	w		w
Germany	0.19	0.00	0.29	-0.18	0.13	0.08		0.14
Greece	0.18	0.19	0.14	-0.37	0.35	0.21		0.20
Hungary	-0.04	0.16	0.47	-0.43	0.49	0.20		0.32
Iceland	0.42	0.18	-0.01	-0.07	0.24	0.05		0.11
Ireland	0.32	-0.08	0.42	-0.33	0.56	0.10		0.15
Israel	-0.03	0.21	0.14	-0.20	0.37	-0.06		0.07
Italy	0.40	0.30	0.41	-0.35	0.30	0.24		0.38
Japan	0.30	0.18	0.34	-0.39	0.44	0.31		0.33
Korea	0.27	0.02	0.25	-0.24	0.42	0.36		0.28
Luxembourg	0.17	0.46	0.47	-0.38	-0.06	0.06		0.16
Mexico	0.02	0.01	0.12	-0.02	0.10	0.09		0.16
Netherlands	0.43	0.51	0.21	-0.34	0.39	0.12		0.22
New Zealand	0.15	0.21	0.53	-0.80	0.44	0.14		0.24
Norway	0.27	0.00	0.28	c	0.47	0.09		0.12
Poland	0.07	-0.07	0.04	-0.05	0.07	0.01		0.03
Portugal	0.41	-0.15	0.17	0.08	0.38	0.12		0.17
Slovak Republic	0.04	-0.15	0.25	-0.28	0.30	-0.01		0.16
Slovenia	0.25	0.43	0.27	-0.23	0.27	0.04		0.16
Spain	0.17	-0.04	0.45	-0.31	0.27	0.04		0.08
Sweden	0.26	0.12	0.43	-0.49	0.40	0.11		0.17
Switzerland	-0.07	0.18	0.08	c	-0.10	0.06		0.12
Turkey	-0.37	0.04	0.31	-0.19	0.21	0.05		0.04
United Kingdom	-0.18	0.00	0.35	-0.29	0.48	0.16		0.31
United States	0.02	-0.02	0.42	-0.31	0.47	0.14		0.25
Albania	m	m	m	m	m	m		m
Argentina	0.05	0.17	0.33	-0.24	0.15	0.04		0.10
Brazil	-0.21	-0.01	0.38	-0.21	0.31	0.05		0.13
Bulgaria	-0.02	0.00	0.23	-0.39	0.40	0.17		0.33
Chinese Taipei	-0.01	0.02	0.36	-0.20	0.29	0.29		0.36
Colombia	-0.07	-0.04	0.25	-0.06	0.07	0.12		0.18
Costa Rica	0.18	0.15	0.43	-0.41	0.22	0.13		0.22
Croatia	0.22	0.42	0.20	-0.22	0.19	0.10		0.24
Hong Kong-China	0.04	0.04	0.21	0.02	-0.07	0.20		0.14
Indonesia	-0.11	0.20	0.17	-0.19	-0.06	0.14		0.16
Jordan	-0.07	-0.01	0.06	-0.18	0.19	-0.03		0.04
Kazakhstan	0.22	0.21	-0.04	-0.04	0.20	0.08		0.13
Latvia	0.37	0.16	0.01	-0.14	0.13	0.11		0.17
Liechtenstein	0.50	0.46	0.45	c	-0.56	0.01		0.12
Lithuania	0.05	0.05	0.24	-0.17	0.15	0.04		0.16
Macao-China	-0.05	-0.09	0.26	-0.23	0.16	0.15		0.16
Malaysia	0.08	-0.10	0.41	-0.23	0.30	0.11		0.18
Montenegro	0.40	0.27	0.20	-0.25	-0.07	0.05		0.16
Peru	0.20	-0.05	0.29	-0.14	0.18	0.08		0.13
Qatar	0.07	-0.09	-0.02	-0.06	0.19	-0.03		0.13
Romania	-0.19	0.24	0.27	-0.24	0.06	0.16		0.25
Russian Federation	0.35	0.27	0.21	-0.07	0.26	0.06		0.09
Serbia	0.29	0.07	0.24	-0.21	0.31	0.03		0.10
Shanghai-China	-0.26	0.26	0.17	-0.35	0.19	0.24		0.35
Singapore	0.11	0.36	0.47	-0.17	0.38	0.13		0.18
Thailand	0.11	0.03	0.12	-0.28	0.30	0.22		0.24
Tunisia	0.05	0.03	-0.08	-0.19	0.23	0.03		0.07
United Arab Emirates	-0.05	-0.05	0.11	-0.22	0.26	-0.03		0.11
Uruguay	-0.08	0.23	0.54	-0.35	0.25	0.09		0.10
Viet Nam	0.12	0.10	0.20	-0.26	0.24	0.21		0.20

Note: The data are indicated in bold if within-country/economy correlation is significantly different from the OECD average.
1. Negative correlations indicate more favourable characteristics for advantaged students.
Source: OECD, PISA 2012 Database, Table II.4.6.
StatLink ᵃᵐˢᵖ http://dx.doi.org/10.1787/888932964851

Figure II.4.5 shows the relationship between the socio-economic profile of schools – the average *PISA index of economic, social and cultural status* of the students in the school – and various school characteristics, such as the student-teacher ratio, the proportion of full-time teachers, the *index of teacher shortage,* and the *index of quality of educational resources* (see Volume IV for more analysis and details about these indices). Relationships involving disadvantaged schools whose principal reported more and/or better-quality resources are coloured light blue; relationships involving disadvantaged schools whose principals reported less and/or lower-quality resources are coloured medium blue. If the relationship in a school system, overall, is stronger than the OECD average, the correlation appears in bold; for those school systems where there is no apparent relationship, the cell in the table is coloured blue.

More is not always better

For students attending disadvantaged schools, quantity of resources does not necessarily translate into quality of resources. In general, more disadvantaged students attend schools with lower student-teacher ratios, but more advantaged students attend schools that have a higher proportion of teachers who have a university degree.

Findings from PISA suggest that many students face the double liability of coming from a disadvantaged background and attending a school with lower-quality teaching resources. Taking into account the size of the student population in schools, OECD countries allocate at least an equal, if not a larger, number of mathematics teachers to disadvantaged schools as to advantaged schools. As Figure II.4.6 shows, however, disadvantaged schools tend to have great difficulty in attracting qualified teachers. For example, in the Netherlands the proportion of qualified teachers in socio-economically advantaged schools is three times higher than the proportion of qualified teachers in disadvantaged schools (52% versus 14%), while the student-teacher ratio is 28% higher in socio-economically advantaged than in disadvantaged schools (18 versus 14 students per teacher, respectively). A similar situation is observed in Belgium, Croatia, Greece, Iceland, Italy, Kazakhstan, Luxembourg, Montenegro, the Russian Federation and Slovenia. In Austria, the student-teacher ratio in socio-economically advantaged schools is smaller and the proportion of university-educated teachers is higher than in disadvantaged schools. That is, disadvantaged schools have fewer teachers per student and those teachers tend to have had less education. A similar situation is observed in Romania, Shanghai-China and Uruguay.

Ensuring an equitable distribution of resources is still a major challenge for many countries, if not in terms of the quantity of resources, then in terms of their quality. As Figure II.4.7 shows, student socio-economic status and school socio-economic profile explain a significant proportion of the variation in teacher quality across schools. Between 17% and 27% of the variation in teacher quality across schools in Croatia, Liechtenstein, Luxembourg, the Netherlands and Slovenia is so explained, as is more than 35% of that variation in Austria and Belgium. Volume IV takes this analysis further by examining the inter-relationship between socio-economic status and resources, policies and practices in greater detail.

Challenging school environments

Disadvantaged schools often have poor disciplinary climates. As Figure II.4.8 shows, the differences in disciplinary climate between advantaged and disadvantaged schools are particularly marked in Croatia, Hungary, Shanghai-China and Slovenia, with a difference of more than half a unit on the *index of disciplinary climate,* while in Estonia, Jordan, Latvia, Norway, Peru and Thailand there are no apparent differences in disciplinary climate across schools related to the schools' socio-economic profile. As Figure II.4.9 shows, in some systems socio-economic status is strongly related to disciplinary climate while in others the relationship is much weaker. The variation across school systems in the strength of this relationship suggests that system- and school-level policies play a role in increasing or mitigating these differences.

While all these factors may be more or less related to student performance, it is clear that they do not constitute the kind of supportive learning environments that disadvantaged students need. If schools are to compensate for resources and support that students are lacking at home, it is hard to imagine how these environments can enable disadvantaged students to reach their potential.

Learning opportunities outside school and parents' expectations of schools

Parents play a key role in their children's education in various ways, including by providing additional learning opportunities through after-school programmes or private tutoring to enhance or support learning at school, setting high expectations for their children and the school they attend, demanding that those expectations are met, and putting pressure on schools to achieve higher academic standards. In all of these areas, socio-economic status and resources at home are closely related.

■ Figure II.4.6 ■

Teacher quantity and quality, by schools' socio-economic profile

Proportion of teachers with university degrees		Student/teacher ratio			Resources in disadvantaged school as a proportion of resources in advantaged schools
Advantaged schools	Disadvantaged schools	Advantaged schools	Disadvantaged schools		
53.0	70.1	10.4	7.8	Portugal	
78.1	83.1	20.1	17.0	Peru	
91.1	95.7	9.7	8.7	Poland	
87.4	90.9	11.4	9.2	Finland	
89.3	92.6	12.0	12.0	United Arab Emirates	
87.5	90.4	13.7	13.3	Malaysia	
82.1	84.4	15.0	16.7	Jordan	
90.1	92.2	25.4	26.0	Colombia	
92.0	93.3	15.2	16.4	Macao-China	
94.4	95.3	14.7	11.6	Spain	
87.1	87.9	22.9	31.3	Brazil	
97.0	97.8	16.0	12.5	Qatar	
92.1	92.3	14.2	20.7	Turkey	
99.2	99.4	15.0	12.6	Ireland	
96.3	96.5	16.9	14.7	Canada	
96.5	96.6	13.8	14.5	United Kingdom	
100.0	100.0	11.6	10.7	Norway	
100.0	99.8	13.0	10.0	Japan	
100.0	99.8	16.6	14.0	Korea	
99.6	99.4	21.1	19.8	Thailand	
87.9	87.5	30.5	27.3	Mexico	
98.8	98.3	18.5	16.8	United States	
98.1	97.5	15.1	14.5	Hong Kong-China	
97.2	95.9	12.4	12.7	Australia	
99.9	98.5	12.6	13.4	Hungary	
91.7	90.1	11.6	11.2	Lithuania	
92.0	89.8	14.1	11.4	Tunisia	
91.8	89.1	18.0	18.0	Chinese Taipei	
92.4	89.2	13.1	12.8	Slovak Republic	
97.0	93.5	15.9	14.0	Singapore	
96.6	91.9	10.5	14.7	Shanghai-China	
98.3	92.5	15.0	18.1	Romania	
94.3	88.6	13.4	11.1	Denmark	
95.9	89.3	15.5	14.1	New Zealand	
90.1	83.6	19.2	18.0	Viet Nam	
95.0	88.0	22.4	21.4	Chile	
88.8	81.4	13.8	12.5	**OECD average**	
97.3	88.6	9.3	9.0	Luxembourg	
93.4	85.1	15.5	12.2	Russian Federation	
94.8	86.2	16.8	14.6	Montenegro	
93.9	85.3	9.3	7.7	Greece	
99.2	89.2	14.0	12.2	Croatia	
91.3	81.8	10.8	11.1	Israel	
95.3	84.8	12.5	12.6	Czech Republic	
95.7	84.3	12.3	8.7	Italy	
89.3	77.7	16.7	17.9	Indonesia	
83.3	72.3	25.3	16.5	Costa Rica	
91.1	79.0	11.0	9.2	Kazakhstan	
87.6	74.9	14.0	11.4	Sweden	
55.8	47.5	10.4	8.1	Latvia	
96.8	80.4	12.0	9.5	Slovenia	
6.2	4.9	13.3	10.5	Serbia	
89.9	68.9	11.7	9.8	Iceland	
77.8	58.2	11.6	12.1	Switzerland	
23.8	15.4	11.3	9.6	Argentina	
12.0	7.5	13.2	15.5	Uruguay	
51.2	25.3	11.5	6.9	Belgium	
51.6	14.3	18.1	14.1	Netherlands	
83.3	18.3	10.0	12.8	Austria	

Chart annotations:

Advantaged schools have more students per teacher and a lower proportion of qualified teachers than disadvantaged schools

Advantaged schools have fewer students per teacher and a higher proportion of qualified teachers than disadvantaged schools

Horizontal axis: -80 -60 -40 -20 0 20 40 60 80 100 %

Note: Differences in resources between students in advantaged and disadvantaged schools that are statistically significant are marked in a darker tone.
Countries and economies are ranked in ascending order of the proportion of qualified teachers in advantaged schools relative to the proportion of qualified teachers in disadvantaged schools.
Source: OECD, PISA 2012 Database, Tables II.4.8 and II.4.9.
StatLink ᵐˢ http://dx.doi.org/10.1787/888932964851

■ Figure II.4.7 ■

Differences in teacher quality explained by students' and schools' socio-economic profile

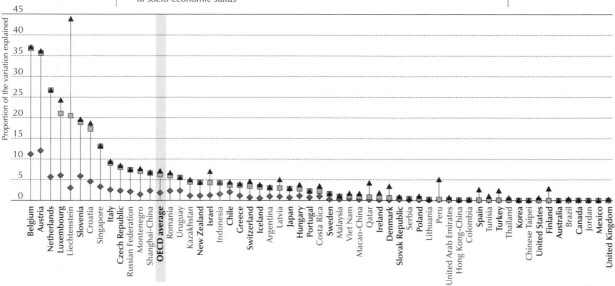

Countries and economies are ranked in descending order of the variation in the percentage of university-trained teachers explained by students' and schools' socio-economic status.
Source: OECD, PISA 2012 Database, Table II.4.9.
StatLink ⌗⌗ http://dx.doi.org/10.1787/888932964851

■ Figure II.4.8 ■

Differences in disciplinary climate, by schools' socio-economic profile

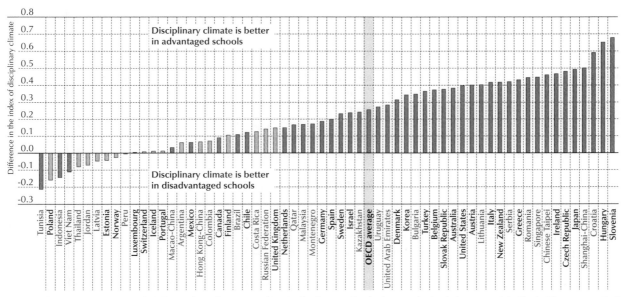

Note: Differences in the *index of disciplinary climate* between students in disadvantaged and advantaged schools that are statistically significant are marked in a darker tone.
Countries and economies are ranked in ascending order of the difference between disadvantaged and advantaged schools.
Source: OECD, PISA 2012 Database, Table II.4.10.
StatLink ⌗⌗ http://dx.doi.org/10.1787/888932964851

■ Figure II.4.9 ■

Differences in disciplinary climate explained by students' and schools' socio-economic profile

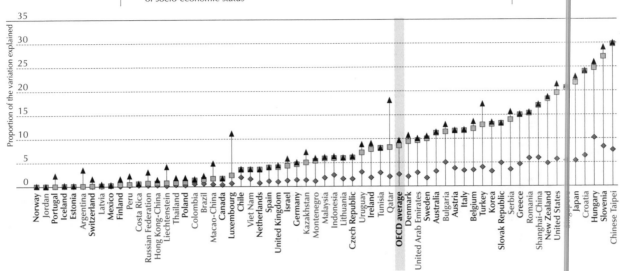

Countries and economies are ranked in descending order of the variation in the index of disciplinary climate *explained by students' and schools' socio-economic status.*
Source: OECD, PISA 2012 Database, Table II.4.10.
StatLink http://dx.doi.org/10.1787/888932964851

In all countries/economies that participated in PISA 2012, socio-economically advantaged students tend to spend more hours after school doing homework or other study required by their teachers. The relationship between a student's socio-economic status and the time spent on homework (on all subjects) is relatively strong (a correlation above 0.3) in Belgium, Bulgaria, Hungary, Italy, Japan, Shanghai-China, Chinese Taipei and the United Kingdom. Socio-economically advantaged students tend to spend more time than disadvantaged students attending after-school classes organised by a commercial company and paid for by their parents and the relationship is particularly strong (with a correlation above 0.3) in Japan and Korea (Figure II.4.5).

Parents' aspirations for their child's education are also strongly related to socio-economic status. The parents of advantaged students have higher aspirations for their child's education than parents of disadvantaged students do. Advantaged parents also put greater pressure on schools to meet high academic standards. In all countries and economies (except Hong Kong-China, Indonesia, Liechtenstein, Luxembourg, Montenegro and Switzerland), more advantaged students attend schools whose principals reported that "there is constant pressure from many parents who expect our school to set very high academic standards and to have our students achieve them" (Figure II.4.5).

OPPORTUNITIES, RESOURCES, PERFORMANCE AND SOCIO-ECONOMIC STATUS

Student performance is related to socio-economic status, at both the school and the student levels, and to the resources and opportunities available to students and schools. Across OECD countries, 49% of the performance differences among students who attend different schools is accounted for by differences in access to opportunities and resources. The average difference in mathematics performance between more advantaged and less advantaged schools drops from 69 score points to 35 score points after taking these differences into account. Differences in opportunities and resources also account for 39% of the performance differences observed among students who attend the same school. Differences in disciplinary climate account for 17% of performance differences, and the quality of teachers accounts for 8% of performance differences (Table II.4.9). Figure II.4.10 shows the between-school difference in performance, before and after accounting for differences in opportunities to learn and educational resources across both students and schools for those countries with available data.[5]

■ Figure II.4.10 ■

Performance differences related to differences in exposure to formal mathematics to learn and resources[1]

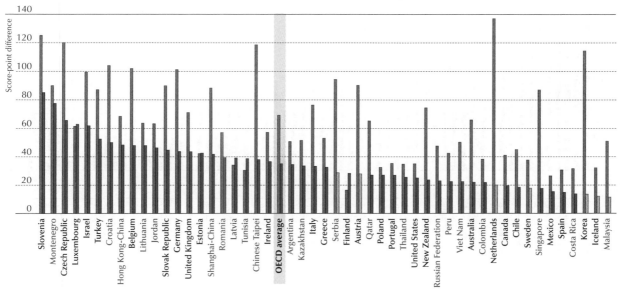

Note: Score-point differences that are statistically significant are marked in a darker tone.
1. Score-point differences between schools that differ by one unit on the *PISA index of economic, social and cultural status*.
Countries and economies are ranked in descending order of the score-point difference between two students attending schools that differ by one unit on the PISA index of economic, social and cultural status *after accounting for differences in opportunity to learn and resources.*
Source: OECD, PISA 2012 Database, Table II.4.11.
StatLink http://dx.doi.org/10.1787/888932964851

PARTICIPATION IN PRE-PRIMARY EDUCATION

Many of the inequities that exist within school systems are already present when students enter formal schooling and persist as students progress through school (Alexander, Entwisle and Olson, 1997; Downey, von Hippel and Broh, 2004). Because these inequities tend to grow when school is out of session, earlier entrance into the school system may help to reduce them. With earlier entrance into pre-primary education, students are better prepared to enter and succeed in formal schooling.

Figure II.4.11 shows the advantage in mathematics performance among students who reported having attended pre-primary education for more than one year over those who reported that they had not, both before and after accounting for students' socio-economic status. In all countries with available data, except Estonia and Latvia, students who had attended pre-primary education for more than one year outperformed students who had not. This finding remains unchanged after socio-economic status is accounted for in all countries with available data (except Estonia and Latvia). On average across OECD countries, the advantage amounts to more than 53 score points before accounting for socio-economic status, and to 31 points after accounting for socio-economic status. The difference between the two suggests that attendance in pre-primary education for more than one year is somewhat related to socio-economic status; still, there is a strong, independent relationship between having attended pre-primary school and performance at age 15. Those who did not participate in pre-primary education are 1.84 times more likely to score at the bottom of the performance distribution.

In France and the Slovak Republic, students who reported having attended pre-primary school for more than one year score at least 100 points higher in mathematics than students who had not attended pre-primary education. In France, only 2% of students had not participated in any pre-primary education, while 92% had attended for more than one year.

■ Figure II.4.11 ■

Differences in mathematics performance, by attendance at pre-primary school

Between students who attended pre-primary school for more than one year and those who had not attended

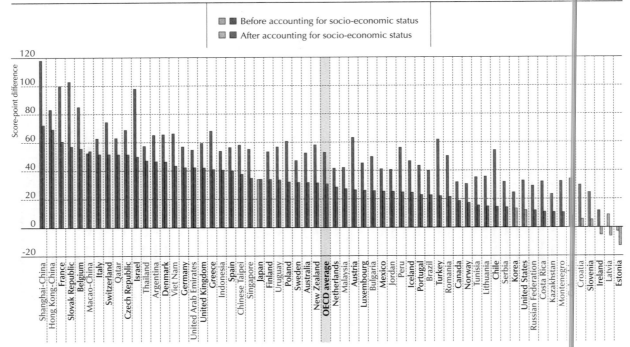

Note: Score-point differences that are statistically significant are marked in a darker tone.

Countries and economies are ranked in descending order of the score-point difference in mathematics performance between students who reported that they had attended pre-primary school (ISCED 0) for more than one year and those who had not attended pre-primary school, after accounting for socio-economic status.

Source: OECD, PISA 2012 Database, Table II.4.12.

StatLink ᕦ᠊᠊ᔑ᠊ http://dx.doi.org/10.1787/888932964851

Those who had not participated are largely those from disadvantaged families. However, even after students' socio-economic status is accounted for, the strong relationship between attendance in pre-primary school and performance persists, although differences in performance are halved. The situation is similar in Shanghai-China, where the performance difference before accounting for socio-economic status is 118 score points but 72 points after taking socio-economic status into account. After accounting for socio-economic status, the score differences between students who had not attended pre-primary education and those who had attended for more than one year are largest (i.e. at least 50 score points) in Belgium, the Czech Republic, France, Hong Kong-China, Italy, Macao-China, Qatar, Shanghai-China, the Slovak Republic and Switzerland. However, among this group of countries, the population relevance is less than 5% (the OECD average population relevance) in all countries except Shanghai-China (7%), the Slovak Republic (11%) and Qatar (17%) (Table II.4.12).

Figure II.4.12 highlights those countries where the participation rates are relatively low (the proportion of students who did not attend pre-primary school is high) and the relative risk of low performance for those who did not attend is particularly high. Indonesia and Turkey show high relative risk and very low participation rates. Croatia, Lithuania, Montenegro, Qatar and Tunisia also show low participation rates and relative risks that are relevant even if they are below the OECD average. In contrast, in France, Israel, Shanghai-China and the Slovak Republic, the relative risk is very high but few students are vulnerable to this type of risk.

In practically all countries, there is no significant difference in performance observed between advantaged and disadvantaged students when considering the relationship between pre-primary attendance and mathematics performance at age 15 (Table II.4.13). In 32 OECD countries and 22 partner countries and economies, disadvantaged and advantaged students benefit equally from pre-primary attendance. Across OECD countries, immigrant students who had attended pre-primary school score as well as immigrant students who had not attended, except in Canada and Estonia (Table II.4.14).

Many other factors, apart from participation in pre-primary education, have an impact on 15-year-olds' performance in school, and the estimates provided here are limited because they do not take many of these other factors into account. Volume IV of this report explores these issues further and examines how they have evolved since PISA 2003. The trends show that equity issues related to pre-primary education are on the rise in many countries, and that disadvantaged students, those who would benefit most from pre-primary education, are still under-represented in pre-primary enrolments.

■ Figure II.4.12 ■

Pre-primary school, mathematics performance and students' socio-economic status

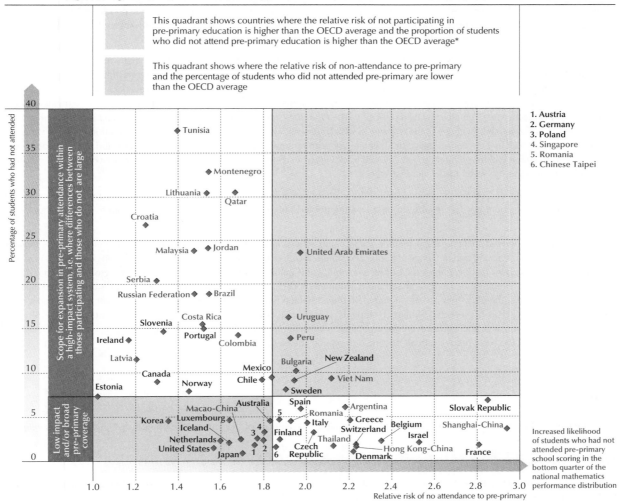

*Turkey and Indonesia have a large percentage of students who did not attend pre-primary (70% and 46%, respectively) and high relative risk, and Kazakhstan also has a high non-attendance rate (65%) but a lower-than-average relative risk. They are not included in this figure to make differences among other countries more visible.

Source: OECD, PISA 2012 Database, Tables II.4.12.

StatLink ᵃᵐˢᴸ᭸ http://dx.doi.org/10.1787/888932964851

Notes

1. For a more in-depth analysis of opportunity to learn in PISA 2012, see Schmidt et al. (2013).

2. Advantaged (disadvantaged) schools are those where the typical student in the school, or the socio-economic profile of the school, is above (below) the socio-economic status of the typical student in the country, the country mean socio-economic status. In each school, a random sample of 35 students are to take part in PISA (for more details see the *PISA 2012 Technical Report* [OECD, forthcoming]). The socio-economic profile of the school is calculated using the information provided by these students. Therefore, the precision of the estimate depends on the number of students that actually take the test in the school and the diversity of their answers. This precision was taken into account when classifying schools as advantaged, disadvantaged or average. If the difference between the school socio-economic profile and the socio-economic status of the typical student in the country (the mean socio-economic status at the country level) was not statistically significant, the school was classified as a school with an average socio-economic profile. If the school profile was statistically significantly above the country mean, the school is classified as a socio-economically advantaged school. If the profile was below the country mean, the school is classified as a socio-economically disadvantaged school.

3. These results also depend on how schools are defined and organised within countries, and by the units that were chosen for sampling purposes. For example, in some countries, some of the schools in the PISA sample were defined as administrative units (even if they spanned several geographically separate institutions, as in Italy); in others, they were defined as those parts of larger educational institutions that serve 15-year-olds; in others they were defined as physical school buildings; and in yet others they were defined from a management perspective (e.g., entities having a principal). The *PISA 2012 Technical Report* (OECD, forthcoming) provides an overview of how schools were defined. Because of the manner in which students were sampled, the within-school variation includes variation between classes as well as between students. In Slovenia, the primary sampling unit is defined as a group of students who follow the same study programme within a school (an educational track within a school). So in this particular case, the between-school variation is actually the difference between tracks within a school.

4. These are the results of a simple decomposition of the variation on a three-level model, with students nested within schools, and schools nested within countries. The results are based on the pooled sample of all the countries and economies that participated in PISA 2012.

5. All the models presented in Table II.4.9 include student and school level socio-economic status, then individual characteristics (gender, immigrant background and language at home) and school location are included. All of these variables are kept for every single model. School and student level variables measuring availability and quality of resources are introduced one group at a time. At the end, all variables are combined in a single model: the "combined model". Some students, schools and countries do not have data for some of these variables, therefore they are not included on the combined model. Then a baseline model, only with student and school level socio-economic status is presented, where all students, schools and countries without data have been omitted, which allows a more direct comparison with the estimates in the combined model. Figure II.4.10 presents the results of these last two models, the combined model and the basic model with all missing observations deleted.

References

Alexander, K.L., D.R. Entwisle and L.S. Olson (2007), "Lasting Consequences of the Summer Learning Gap", *American Sociological Review*, Vol. 72, pp. 167-80.

Carroll, J.B. (1963), "A model of School Learning", *Teachers College Record*, Vol. 64, No. 8, pp. 723-733.

Downey D. B., P.T. von Hippel and B.A. Broh (2004), "Are Schools the Great Equalizer? Cognitive Inequality during the Summer Months and the School Year", *American Sociological Review*, October 2004 Vol. 69, No. 5, pp. 613-35.

OECD (forthcoming), *PISA 2012 Technical Report*, PISA, OECD Publishing.

Schmidt, W.H., L.S. Cogan and P. Zoido (2013), "Schooling Matters: Opportunity to Learn in PISA 2012", *OECD Education Working Papers*, No. 95, OECD Publishing.
http://dx.doi.org/10.1787/5k3v0hldmchl-en

Schmidt, W.H., et al. (2001), *Why Schools Matter: A Cross-National Comparison of Curriculum and Learning*, Jossey-Bass, San Francisco.

Sykes, G., B. Schneider and D.N. Plank (2009), *Handbook of Education Policy Research*, Routledge, New York.

Wiley, D.E. and A. Harnischfeger (1974), "Explosion of a Myth: Quantity of Schooling and Exposure to Instruction, Major Educational Vehicles", *Educational Researcher*, Vol. 3, No. 4, pp. 7-12.

5

Policy Implications of Equity in Education

This chapter analyses the different measures of equity in education produced by PISA and considers various policy options for improving performance and equity in education outcomes and opportunities for all students.

Home background influences success in education, and schooling often reinforces that influence. Although poor performance in school does not automatically stem from socio-economic disadvantage, the socio-economic status of students and schools does appear to have a powerful influence on learning outcomes. Because advantaged families are better able to reinforce and enhance the effect of schools, because students from advantaged families attend higher-quality schools, or because schools are simply better-equipped to nurture and develop young people from advantaged backgrounds, in many countries schools tend to reproduce existing patterns of socio-economic advantage, rather than create a more equitable distribution of learning opportunities and outcomes.

Other characteristics of students, besides their socio-economic status, are closely related to performance in PISA. Family structure, parents' job status, immigrant background and the language spoken at home are not only associated with performance differences, they are also interlinked. For example, children of low-educated parents, who also tend to be disadvantaged, are likely to be among those students whose parents are not working. In some countries, adult immigrants may find it hard to find an occupation that matches their education and skills; thus they may end up in low-status occupations, which, in turn, will be translated into a more disadvantaged socio-economic status among immigrant students.

In short, socio-economic disadvantage is closely interconnected with many of the student and school characteristics that are associated with performance. It is often difficult to disentangle the impact of socio-economic status on performance from that of other factors. In drawing conclusions for education policy and practice from the results presented here, it is crucial to understand the interplay between all these factors.

In general, the results that emerge from this volume show large differences between countries in the extent to which socio-economic status influences learning outcomes, which suggests that it is indeed possible to attain high levels of equity in education even among high-performing countries and economies. Differences across countries in the extent to which student- and school-level factors are associated with performance and socio-economic status show that system- and school-level policies and practices have an impact on both equity and performance outcomes.

This volume highlights the importance of taking socio-economic status into account when analysing performance differences. For example, students from single-parent families tend to underperform when compared with students from other types of families; however in many countries and economies, the performance difference disappears once students' socio-economic status is taken into account. Another finding shows that schools with large populations of immigrant students tend to underperform. Yet once the socio-economic status of students and, crucially, the socio-economic profile of the schools themselves – a measure of the concentration of socio-economic disadvantage at the school level – is taken into account much, if not all, of the underperformance of these schools can be linked to the disadvantaged socio-economic status of their students, both immigrant and non-immigrant.

The allocation of resources across schools is also associated with equity in outcomes and opportunities. With some notable exceptions, OECD countries try to allocate at least an equal, if not a larger, number of teachers per student in disadvantaged schools as they do in advantaged schools. This said, disadvantaged schools still report great difficulties in attracting qualified teachers. In other words, in disadvantaged schools, more resources do not necessarily translate into better-quality resources. This finding suggests that many students face the double drawback of coming from a disadvantaged background and attending a school with lower-quality resources. Many countries also show a strong relationship between the socio-economic status of students and their success at school. In some of these countries, these disparities are magnified by large variations in the socio-economic profile of schools' student populations.

This volume also presents evidence of the close relationship between education opportunities, as measured by students' reports on their exposure to and familiarity with formal mathematics, and students' socio-economic status and performance. Some education systems tend to separate students, either across classes or schools, according to their performance. Evidence from PISA shows that school systems that segregate students across schools according to their performance also tend to be those where students are segregated by socio-economic status and exposure to formal mathematics. That in some school systems disadvantaged students have less exposure to and familiarity with basic mathematic concepts suggests that these systems need to do more to address the academic needs of these students before they reach the end of compulsory education.

In Finland, early detection mechanisms, such as periodic individualised assessments of students by several groups of teachers, and special education opportunities enable educators to identify specific subject areas that students struggle to learn. Struggling students are then offered the necessary support early on in their schooling, before they become stuck and cannot continue their education at the same pace as their peers. By contrast, in other systems, students are retained and keep receiving the same inadequate opportunities to learn until the system can no longer keep them behind. Israel (see Box IV.1.4) and Germany (Box II.3.2) have designed programmes that offer more learning opportunities to immigrant and minority students by providing a longer school day (Germany) or encouraging students to participate in smaller study groups (Israel).

The analyses pertaining to school effectiveness presented in this report are based on data describing school offerings at the late-primary or secondary levels. However, an assessment such as PISA provides an indication of students' cumulative learning such that a country's results in PISA, or in any assessment for that matter, depend on the quality of care and stimulation provided to children during infancy and their pre-school years, as well as on the opportunities children have to learn, both in school and at home, during their elementary and secondary school years.

Improving quality and equity thus requires a long-term view and a broad perspective. For some countries, this may mean safeguarding the healthy development of young children or improving early childhood education. For others, it may mean socio-economic reforms that enable families to provide better care for their children. And in many countries, it may mean greater efforts to increase socio-economic inclusion and improve school offerings.

PATTERNS IN THE RELATIONSHIP BETWEEN PERFORMANCE AND SOCIO-ECONOMIC STATUS

Australia, Canada, Estonia, Finland, Hong Kong-China, Japan, Korea, Liechtenstein and Macao-China show above-OECD-average mean performance and a weak relationship between socio-economic status and student performance (the strength of the socio-economic gradient). In Viet Nam, the strength of this relationship is around average while performance differences associated with socio-economic disparities (the slope of the socio-economic gradient) are below average (Figure II.5.1a). These countries combine high average performance with equity, demonstrating that the two are not mutually exclusive.

While the focus here is on socio-economic context, many of these countries also achieve greater levels of equity in other respects. Socio-economic disadvantage is, in many cases, a proxy for other sources of disadvantage. But this is not always the case. For example, in Finland, where differences in performance between advantaged and disadvantaged students are small, immigrant students underperform when compared to other students – and by a relatively large margin – even after accounting for socio-economic status. In Poland, rural schools perform well below urban schools, regardless of the schools' socio-economic profile.

Low performing students – those who do not reach a baseline level of performance (Level 2 in the PISA mathematics scale) – are at risk of later failing to integrate successfully into the labour market and into society more generally. Equity cannot be achieved where significant proportions of students fall behind. The same applies where a large proportion of 15-year-olds are not in school.

How can the impact of social background be moderated so that all students can realise their potential? The relationships between home background and performance described in this volume are manifested in very different patterns across different countries; thus, strategies for improvement need to be tailored accordingly. Figures II.5.1a and b show the key characteristics of the relationship between students' and schools' socio-economic profile and performance across education systems.

Figures II.5.2 to II.5.13 show the average performance and the socio-economic composition of the student population for each school in the countries/economies that participated in PISA 2012. As elsewhere in this volume, the socio-economic composition of a school is measured by the mean *PISA index of economic, social and cultural status* of the students who attend the school. Each circle in these figures represents one school, with the size of the circle proportional to the number of 15-year-olds enrolled in that school. The patterns show the extent to which students are segregated across schools according to their performance or socio-economic status. The figures show the overall performance differences across socio-economic groups, or the gradient between performance and socio-economic status, represented by the thin black line. The figures also present the average performance differences among schools with different socio-economic profiles – the between-school gradient, represented by the grey line, and the average within-school gradient, represented by the blue line. Schools above the between-school gradient (grey line) perform better than predicted by the socio-economic status of their students; schools below the between-school gradient perform worse than predicted by the socio-economic status of their students.

■ Figure II.5.1a ■

Summary of PISA measures of equity in education

Higher quality or equity than the OECD average
Not statistically different from the OECD average
Lower quality or equity than the OECD average

	Average student performance	Percentage of students performing below Level 2	Strength of the relationship between student performance and socio-economic status — Percentage of explained variation in student performance	Performance differences across socio-economic status: slope of the socio-economic gradient — Score-point difference associated with a one-unit increase in socio-economic status	Length of the projection of the gradient line — Difference between 95th and 5th percentile of socio-economic status
OECD average	494	23.1	14.8	39	2.83
Shanghai-China	613	3.8	15.1	41	3.00
Singapore	573	8.3	14.4	44	2.98
Hong Kong-China	561	8.6	7.5	27	3.10
Chinese Taipei	560	12.9	17.9	58	2.69
Korea	554	9.2	10.1	42	2.38
Macao-China	538	10.9	2.6	17	2.94
Japan	536	11.2	9.8	41	2.22
Liechtenstein	535	14.1	7.6	28	3.02
Switzerland	531	12.5	12.8	38	2.85
Netherlands	523	14.9	11.5	40	2.41
Estonia	521	10.6	8.6	29	2.48
Finland	519	12.3	9.4	33	2.39
Canada	518	13.9	9.4	31	2.71
Poland	518	14.5	16.6	41	2.74
Belgium	515	19.1	19.6	49	2.75
Germany	514	17.8	16.9	43	2.91
Viet Nam	511	14.3	14.6	29	2.84
Austria	506	18.8	15.8	43	2.72
Australia	504	19.8	12.3	42	2.48
Ireland	501	17.0	14.6	38	2.65
Slovenia	501	20.3	15.6	42	2.69
Denmark	500	17.0	16.5	39	2.57
New Zealand	500	22.8	18.4	52	2.58
Czech Republic	499	21.2	16.2	51	2.37
France	495	22.5	22.5	57	2.54
United Kingdom	494	21.9	12.5	41	2.53
Iceland	493	21.6	7.7	31	2.55
Latvia	491	20.1	14.7	35	2.77
Luxembourg	490	24.5	18.3	37	2.48
Norway	489	22.5	7.4	32	2.36
Portugal	487	25.0	19.6	35	2.74
Italy	485	24.8	10.1	30	2.13
Spain	484	23.7	15.8	34	2.26
Russian Federation	482	24.1	11.4	38	2.34
Slovak Republic	482	27.6	24.6	54	2.89
United States	481	26.0	14.8	35	2.12
Lithuania	479	26.2	13.8	36	2.75
Sweden	478	27.2	10.6	36	2.47
Hungary	477	28.2	23.1	47	2.02
Croatia	471	30.0	12.0	36	2.76
Israel	466	33.7	17.2	51	2.56
Greece	453	35.8	15.5	34	2.12
Serbia	449	39.1	11.7	34	2.87
Turkey	448	42.2	14.5	32	2.64
Romania	445	41.0	19.3	38	2.01
Bulgaria	439	43.9	22.3	42	2.23
United Arab Emirates	434	46.5	9.8	33	2.79
Kazakhstan	432	45.5	8.0	27	2.34
Thailand	427	50.0	9.9	22	2.79
Chile	423	51.7	23.1	34	2.66
Malaysia	421	52.0	13.4	30	2.24
Mexico	413	54.9	10.4	19	2.10
Montenegro	410	56.9	12.7	33	2.82
Uruguay	409	56.0	22.8	37	2.67
Costa Rica	407	60.1	18.9	24	2.93
Albania	394	60.8	m	m	m
Brazil	391	67.3	15.7	26	3.80
Argentina	388	66.7	15.1	26	3.60
Tunisia	388	67.9	12.4	22	3.11
Jordan	386	68.7	8.4	22	3.16
Colombia	376	74.0	15.4	25	3.83
Qatar	376	69.7	5.6	27	2.93
Indonesia	375	75.9	9.6	20	3.60
Peru	368	74.7	23.4	33	4.14

Countries and economies are ranked in descending order of mean mathematics performance.
Source: OECD, PISA 2012 Database, Tables II.2.1, II.2.8a, II.2.9a, II.2.13a and II.3.7.
StatLink ⟐ http://dx.doi.org/10.1787/888932964870

■ Figure II.5.1b ■
Summary of PISA measures of equity in education (continued)

	Higher quality or equity than the OECD average
	Not statistically different from the OECD average
	Lower quality or equity than the OECD average

	Average student performance	Within-school effects of socio-economic status[1] Student-level score-point difference associated with a one-unit increase in student-level socio-economic status	Between-school effects of socio-economic status[2] School-level score-point difference associated with a one-unit increase in the school mean socio-economic profile	Within-school strength of the relationship between student performance and socio-economic status[1] Percentage of the overall variation in mathematics performance explained by students' and schools' ESCS	Between-school strength of the relationship between student performance and socio-economic status[2] Percentage of the overall variation in mathematics performance explained by students' and schools' ESCS	School variation in the distribution of socio-economic status[3] Interquartile range of the distribution of school mean socio-economic profile	Within-school variation in socio-economic status as a proportion of the sum of the within- and between-school variation[4]	Within-school variation in student performance as a proportion of the sum of the within- and between-school variation[5]
OECD average	494	19	72	5.2	62.8	0.64	76	64
Shanghai-China	613	10	88	1.6	65.4	0.81	67	53
Singapore	573	22	85	4.4	61.2	0.57	76	63
Hong Kong-China	561	4	65	0.7	41.9	0.71	68	58
Chinese Taipei	560	27	123	5.3	72.2	0.60	77	58
Korea	554	14	114	1.5	57.3	0.46	78	60
Macao-China	538	7	31	5.8	14.2	0.50	74	58
Japan	536	4	150	1.8	65.9	0.50	78	47
Liechtenstein	535	8	132	2.2	51.0	0.56	86	37
Switzerland	531	25	66	7.2	44.0	0.62	83	64
Netherlands	523	9	147	1.5	57.8	0.51	82	34
Estonia	521	19	45	4.0	58.0	0.48	81	83
Finland	519	29	22	9.8	38.3	0.35	91	92
Canada	518	23	41	7.5	41.8	0.54	83	80
Poland	518	32	36	9.5	56.8	0.59	76	79
Belgium	515	19	102	4.8	70.1	0.75	72	49
Germany	514	11	103	0.4	71.3	0.78	74	47
Viet Nam	511	8	49	1.4	46.9	0.79	58	48
Austria	506	15	85	3.5	56.3	0.60	71	52
Australia	504	25	64	6.1	55.5	0.60	77	72
Ireland	501	26	52	6.9	79.3	0.48	80	82
Slovenia	501	3	126	0.1	77.7	0.81	75	41
Denmark	500	31	38	10.6	70.9	0.52	82	84
New Zealand	500	36	66	9.9	78.4	0.48	78	76
Czech Republic	499	14	127	2.1	70.5	0.50	76	49
France	495	22	113	w	w	w	w	w
United Kingdom	494	24	73	6.4	63.6	0.54	79	72
Iceland	493	25	45	5.9	68.8	0.49	86	90
Latvia	491	22	46	5.5	62.2	0.64	75	74
Luxembourg	490	20	68	6.7	93.3	1.03	74	59
Norway	489	27	49	5.6	46.4	0.30	91	87
Portugal	487	23	33	9.6	62.1	0.79	69	70
Italy	485	7	83	1.7	48.4	0.75	76	49
Spain	484	27	26	10.4	54.7	0.78	75	81
Russian Federation	482	26	47	5.0	44.5	0.53	75	73
Slovak Republic	482	21	86	4.6	73.8	0.62	64	50
United States	481	24	41	6.8	57.8	0.69	74	76
Lithuania	479	19	66	4.5	63.9	0.61	79	69
Sweden	478	28	41	9.8	55.5	0.49	87	87
Hungary	477	6	98	1.1	78.4	0.95	63	38
Croatia	471	12	90	2.3	58.8	0.54	76	56
Israel	466	24	98	5.2	66.5	0.72	75	58
Greece	453	18	55	4.7	65.1	0.69	73	68
Serbia	449	9	101	1.0	65.6	0.59	78	54
Turkey	448	6	83	1.4	57.6	0.70	72	38
Romania	445	17	57	4.5	61.5	0.68	64	55
Bulgaria	439	12	73	2.5	72.2	0.87	60	47
United Arab Emirates	434	12	71	1.9	41.6	0.68	74	56
Kazakhstan	432	15	45	3.1	29.7	0.53	77	63
Thailand	427	9	35	1.5	40.0	1.01	62	58
Chile	423	9	46	1.4	75.4	1.06	47	57
Malaysia	421	15	49	3.8	57.8	0.72	72	68
Mexico	413	5	29	0.9	46.1	1.02	57	65
Montenegro	410	12	102	2.4	85.7	0.52	81	64
Uruguay	409	15	52	4.3	74.1	0.82	60	58
Costa Rica	407	10	34	3.5	61.7	0.81	62	58
Albania	394	m	m	m	m	m	m	95
Brazil	391	8	46	2.0	61.5	0.81	63	57
Argentina	388	9	49	2.4	62.1	1.02	67	56
Tunisia	388	6	45	2.1	48.3	1.01	67	51
Jordan	386	11	47	4.8	42.6	0.54	80	64
Colombia	376	11	35	3.0	60.3	0.92	63	65
Qatar	376	10	73	1.7	29.7	0.50	75	54
Indonesia	375	6	37	1.3	32.7	0.89	63	48
Peru	368	10	49	1.9	78.4	1.23	54	54

1. Two-level regression of mathematics performance on student-level *PISA index of economic, social and cultural status* (ESCS) and school mean ESCS; within-school slope for ESCS and student-level variation explained by the model.
2. Two-level regression of mathematics performance on student ESCS and school mean ESCS; between-school slope of ESCS and school-level variation explained by the model.
3. Difference between the top and bottom quartiles calculated at the school level.
4. Also referred to as the *index of social inclusion* is calculated as 100*(1-rho), where rho stands for the intra-class correlation of socio-economic status, i.e. the variation in the *PISA index of social, economic and cultural status* of students between schools, divided by the sum of the variation in students' socio-economic status between schools and the variance in students' socio-economic status within schools.
5. Also referred to as the *index of academic inclusion*, which is calculated as 100*(1-rho), where rho stands for the intra-class correlation of performance, i.e. the variation in student performance between schools, divided by the sum of the variation in student performance between schools and the variation in student performance within schools.
Countries and economies are ranked in descending order of the average mathematics performance.
Source: OECD, PISA 2012 Database, Tables I.2.3a, II.2.1, II.2.8a, II.2.9a, II.2.13a and II.3.7.
StatLink ᔫᕹ http://dx.doi.org/10.1787/888932964870

The figures summarise the three levels at which the relationship between student background and performance manifests itself. One is the strength of the relationship between student performance and socio-economic status in a given country, as measured by how much of the variation in student performance can be attributed to variations in socio-economic status. The second shows the degree to which the variation in average performance among schools can be attributed to the variation in the average socio-economic status of the schools' student populations. The third reflects the relationship between student performance and socio-economic status within a given school: how much of the variation in student performance within a given school can be attributed to variations in socio-economic status within that particular school. The amount of socio-economic variation and the overall performance differences within a country are also relevant. While these figures do not capture all of the inequities that may be observed within countries, they can provide a reliable indication of equity in education opportunities, particularly from an international perspective.

Analysing these patterns can help policy makers in designing policies to improve equity in education opportunities (Willms, 2006). Some options, which can be considered in combination, include:

- **Targeting low performance, regardless of students' background, either by targeting low-performing schools or low-performing students within schools, depending on the extent to which low performance is concentrated by school.** Where between-school differences in performance are relatively large, interventions may be targeted at low-performing schools; where they are relatively small, interventions can be directed at low-performing students in each school. Such policies often tend to provide a specialised curriculum or additional instructional resources for particular students based on their level of academic achievement. For example, some school systems provide early-prevention programmes that target children who are deemed to be at risk of failure at school when they enter early childhood programmes or schools, while other systems provide late-prevention or recovery programmes for children who fail to progress at a normal rate during the first few years of primary school. Some performance-targeted programmes aim to provide a modified curriculum for high-achieving students, such as programmes for gifted students. Grade repetition is also sometimes considered a performance-targeted policy, because the decision to have a student repeat a grade is usually based on school performance. However, in many cases, grade repetition does not entail a modified curriculum or additional instructional resources; therefore, it does not fit the definition of a performance-targeted policy used here. In fact, as Volume IV of this report shows, grade repetition is a costly option that is rarely advisable when designing policies for higher performance and greater equity. The focus of performance-targeted policies tends to be at the lower end of the performance scale, regardless of the students' socio-economic status, and their objective is to bring low-performing students up to par with their peers. This volume and Volume IV of this report describe how countries such as Colombia (Box IV.4.3), Mexico (Box II.2.4) and Poland (Box IV.2.1), for example, have improved the information infrastructure of their education systems so that they can better identify and support struggling students and schools.

- **Targeting disadvantaged children through a specialised curriculum, additional instructional resources or economic assistance for these students.** A relatively strong social gradient, which accounts for a substantial proportion of performance variation, can indicate the relevance of such policies. Again, policies can be designed either at the school or individual level, depending on the strength of the inter-school social gradient and the extent to which schools are segregated by socio-economic status. Some approaches select students on the basis of a risk factor other than socio-economic status, such as whether the students are recent immigrants, members of an ethnic minority, or living in a rural or low-income community. The important distinction is that these programmes select students based on the families' socio-economic status rather than on the students' cognitive ability. As mentioned in Boxes II.3.2 and IV.1.4, countries such as Germany and Israel are indeed targeting students with an immigrant background or schools in small and rural communities. While not tackling socio-economic disadvantage per se, because of the close interconnection among different sources of disadvantage, these policies address inequities in a broad sense. While policies targeting disadvantaged children can aim at improving these students' performance in school, they can also be used to provide additional economic resources to these students. The emphasis here is on improving the economic circumstances of students from poor families, rather than offering specialised curricula or additional educational resources. Good examples of these kinds of policies are conditional cash transfers, as implemented in Brazil, Colombia and Mexico, through which parents receive funds if their children attend school. Providing free transportation and free lunch programmes for students from poor families is an example. More generally, providing transfer payments to poor families is one of the primary policy levers at the national level. The distinction between these kinds of compensatory policies and socio-economically targeted policies is not always clear-cut. For example, some jurisdictions have compensatory funding formulas that allocate funds for education to schools based on their students' socio-economic profile. In some sense this is a compensatory policy, but it could also be considered a socio-economically targeted policy since the intention is to provide additional educational resources to students from disadvantaged backgrounds.

As described in the different volumes of this report, countries such as Brazil (see Box I.2.4), Germany (Box II.3.2), Israel (see Box IV.1.4), Mexico (Box II.2.4) and Turkey (see Box I.2.5) and have already implemented targeted policies to improve the performance of low-achieving schools or students, or have distributed more resources to those regions and schools that need them most.

- **Applying more universal policies to raise standards for all students**. These types of policies are likely to be most relevant in countries with weaker gradients and less variation in student performance. They can involve altering the content and pace of the curriculum, improving instructional techniques, introducing full-day schooling, changing the age of entry into school, or increasing the time spent in classes. Some countries, such as Denmark and Germany, responded to PISA 2000 results by introducing major school and curricular reforms that included some of these changes. There have also been efforts to increase parents' engagement, including by encouraging greater involvement at home and more participation in school governance. Many universal policies are directed at changing teacher practices, or they aim to increase the accountability of schools and school systems by assessing student performance. As described in this and other volumes of this report, some countries have introduced system-wide reforms that are aimed at moving towards more comprehensive schooling (Poland) or less tracking (Germany). These reforms simultaneously address various sources of inequity, such as a socio-economically disadvantaged background, immigrant status or a challenging family structure. Some countries are focusing on improving the overall quality of educational resources – including by recruiting and hiring high-quality teachers – and making them available to all schools, particularly disadvantaged schools. Countries that have improved their performance in PISA, like Brazil (see Box I.2.4), Colombia (see Box IV.4.3), Estonia (see Box I.5.1), Israel (see Box IV.1.4), Japan (see Box III.3.1) and Poland (see Box IV.2.1), for example, have established policies to improve the quality of their teaching staff by adding to the requirements to earn a teaching license, providing incentives for high-achieving students to enter the profession, increasing salaries to make the profession more attractive and to retain more teachers, or by offering incentives for teachers to engage in in-service teacher-training programmes.

- **Including marginalised students in mainstream schools and classrooms**. Inclusive practices often concentrate on including students with disabilities in regular classrooms, rather than segregating them in special classes or schools. This volume considers inclusive policies as those that aim to include students who may be segregated, for example by socio-economic disadvantage. Some inclusive policies try to reduce between-school socio-economic segregation by redrawing school-catchment boundaries, amalgamating schools, or by creating magnet schools in low-income areas. As discussed in Volume IV of this report, many school systems are highly stratified. In these systems, there may be more incentives for schools to select the best students, and fewer incentives to work with difficult students if there is an option of transferring them to other schools. Some of the school systems that have improved in performance and equity in recent years are becoming more inclusive. For example, Poland (see Box IV.2.1) reformed its education system by delaying the age of selection into different programmes; and schools in Germany (Box II.3.2) are also moving towards reducing the levels of stratification across education programmes.

The rest of this chapter describes various policy options available to countries, depending on how student performance is related to the social context of students and schools. If the proportion of low-performing students is large, then policy interventions should target these students. Box II.5.1 offers guidance on designing policies to improve performance and equity in other cases. For example, universal policies are most beneficial for countries shown in the top-left quadrant. Policies that target socio-economic disadvantage may be more effective for the countries shown in the right quadrants, while policies that target low performance may be more effective for countries shown in the bottom quadrants.

Box II.5.1. **A framework of policies to improve performance and equity in education**

This volume identifies two main measures of equity in education outcomes: the strength of the relationship between performance and socio-economic status (the strength of the socio-economic gradient) and the size of performance differences across socio-economic groups (the slope of the socio-economic gradient). The following typology describes countries based on their mean performance and depending on whether they score above or below the OECD average in these measures.

...

	Performance differences across socio-economic groups (slope of the socio-economic gradient)		
	Below OECD average: *Flat* **socio-economic gradient**	**Average**	**Above OECD average** *Steep* **socio-economic gradient**
Below OECD average: *Weak* **socio-economic gradient**	**Canada** **Estonia** **Finland** **Hong Kong-China** Iceland *Italy* *Jordan* *Kazakhstan* **Macao-China** *Mexico* *Montenegro* Norway *Qatar* *Serbia* *Thailand* *United Arab Emirates*	*Croatia* **Japan** **Korea** **Netherlands** **Liechtenstein** *Sweden*	**Australia**
Average	*Argentina* *Brazil* *Colombia* *Costa Rica* *Greece* *Indonesia* *Malaysia* *Spain* *Tunisia* *Turkey* *United States* **Viet Nam**	**Austria** **Denmark** **Germany** **Ireland** Latvia *Lithuania* **Poland** *Romania* *Russian Federation* **Shanghai-China** **Slovenia** **Switzerland** United Kingdom	Czech Republic *Israel* **Singapore**
Above OECD average: *Strong* **socio-economic gradient**	*Chile* *Luxembourg* *Peru* Portugal	*Bulgaria* *Uruguay*	**Belgium** France *Hungary* **New Zealand** *Slovak Republic* **Chinese Taipei**

Notes: Countries and economies with mean mathematics performance above the OECD average are shown in **bold**.
Countries and economies with mean mathematics performance below the OECD average are shown in *italics*.

Considering these two dimensions of equity in education and the policy options described above can help policy makers map a way forward to raise quality and improve equity.

	Performance differences across the socio-economic spectrum are:	
	Small: Flat gradient	**Large: Steep gradient**
Impact of socio-economic status on performance is weak	When performance differences across the socio-economic spectrum are small and students often perform better (or worse) than expected, given their socio-economic status, one of the main policy goals is to improve performance across the board. In these cases, universal policies tend to be most effective. These types of policies include changing curricula or instructional systems and/or improving the quality of the teaching staff, e.g. by requiring more qualifications to earn a teaching license, providing incentives for high-achieving students to enter the profession, increasing salaries to make the profession more attractive and to retain more teachers, and/or offering incentives for teachers to engage in in-service teacher-training programmes.	When performance differences across the socio-economic spectrum are large and students often perform better (or worse) than expected given their socio-economic status, one of the main policy goals is to improve performance among the lowest performers, regardless of their socio-economic status. If these cases, targeting disadvantaged students only would provide extra support to some students who are already performing relatively well, while it would leave out some students who are not necessarily disadvantaged but who perform poorly. Policies can be targeted to low-performing students if these students can be easily identified, or to low-performing schools, particularly if low performance is concentrated in particular schools. Examples of such policies involve evaluation, feedback and appraisals for students, teachers and schools, or establishing early-warning mechanisms and providing a modified curriculum or additional instructional support for struggling students.
Impact of socio-economic status on performance is strong	When performance differences across the socio-economic spectrum are small but students perform as expected, given their socio-economic status, one of the main policy goals is to dismantle the barriers to high performance associated with socio-economic disadvantage. In these cases, effective compensatory policies target disadvantaged students or schools, providing them with additional support, resources or assistance. Free lunch programmes or free textbooks for disadvantaged families are other examples.	When performance differences across the socio-economic spectrum are large and students perform as would be expected, given their socio-economic status, one of the main policy goals is to reduce performance differences and improve performance particularly among disadvantaged students. A combination of policies targeting low performance and socio-economic disadvantage tend to be most effective in these cases, since universal policies may be less effective in improving both equity and performance simultaneously.

...

Another important aspect to consider is whether these policies target students or schools. In many cases, it may not be cost-effective to target individual students who are struggling in a particular subject area or who are facing a particularly challenging situation in or outside of school. The evidence collected in PISA can provide some indication as to when school- or student-level interventions would prove more effective. Two indicators offer guidance in this respect: the extent of between-school differences in socio-economic profiles, and the relationship between a school's socio-economic profile and its mean performance.

Where few differences are observed across schools, targeting students within schools is an option. By contrast, if large performance or socio-economic differences are observed between schools, then targeting specific schools – for example, low-performing or socio-economically disadvantaged schools – becomes a possibility. Targeting socio-economically disadvantaged schools may prove effective where there are large performance differences across schools related to socio-economic status.

A DISPROPORTIONATE NUMBER OF LOW-PERFORMING STUDENTS

Where many students score below the baseline level of proficiency, policies that target low-performing students may be more effective, regardless of those countries'/economies' level of equity in education. The proportion of students who score below proficiency Level 2 in mathematics is particularly large – more than 40% – in Albania, Argentina, Brazil, Bulgaria, Chile, Colombia, Costa Rica, Indonesia, Jordan, Kazakhstan, Malaysia, Mexico, Montenegro, Peru, Qatar, Romania, Thailand, Tunisia, Turkey, the United Arab Emirates and Uruguay (Figure II.5.1). In these countries, socio-economic status is not strongly related to performance (except in Bulgaria, Chile, Costa Rica, Peru and Uruguay), and performance differences across socio-economic groups are below the OECD average (except in Bulgaria, Romania and Uruguay, where they are at the OECD average). Performance is generally poor and there is little variation in performance among students, even though differences in socio-economic status may be considerable. In all these countries, the range of socio-economic status (the difference in socio-economic status between the top and bottom 5% of students) is above the OECD average (except in Kazakhstan, where it is below average, and Montenegro and the United Arab Emirates, where it is average). In addition, in many of these countries, there are many 15-year-olds who are not enrolled in school and who did not participate in the PISA assessment. Because this population is likely to be socio-economically disadvantaged, the students in these countries and economies appear as a more homogeneous population than the entire group of 15-year-olds. In some of these countries, the PISA measures of socio-economic status may not discriminate sufficiently among levels of disadvantage. Figure II.5.2 contrasts the profiles of some of these countries.

Some countries in this group, like Brazil, Colombia and Mexico, have implemented policies targeting socio-economically disadvantaged students. The fairly small proportion of variation in student performance that is explained by socio-economic status suggests that poor performance deserves as much attention as socio-economic disadvantage.

DIFFERENT SLOPES AND STRENGTHS OF SOCIO-ECONOMIC GRADIENTS

School administrators often wonder whether efforts to improve student performance should be targeted mainly at those students who perform poorly or those from socio-economically disadvantaged backgrounds. Performance differences across the socio-economic spectrum, together with the proportion of performance variation explained by socio-economic status, are useful indicators for answering this question. There is an important distinction between the slope of the social gradient, which refers to the average size of the performance gap associated with a given difference in socio-economic status, and its strength, which is associated with how closely students conform to predictions of performance based on their socio-economic status.

In countries with relatively flat gradients, i.e. where performance differences related to socio-economic status are small, policies that specifically target students from disadvantaged backgrounds would not, by themselves, address the needs of many of the country's low-performing students.

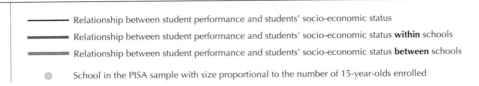

■ Figure II.5.2 ■

Relationship between school performance and schools' socio-economic profile in countries that have large proportions of students performing below Level 2: Indonesia, Kazakhstan, Peru and Tunisia

—— Relationship between student performance and students' socio-economic status

—— Relationship between student performance and students' socio-economic status **within** schools

—— Relationship between student performance and students' socio-economic status **between** schools

○ School in the PISA sample with size proportional to the number of 15-year-olds enrolled

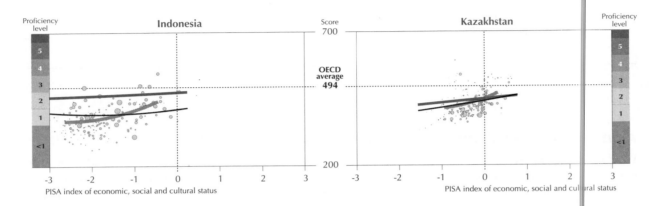

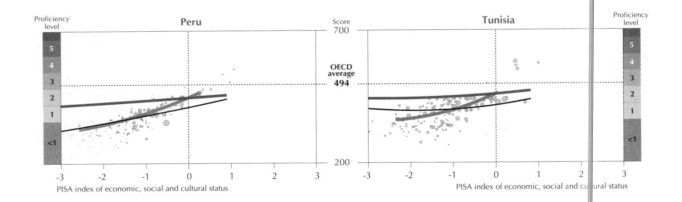

Source: OECD, PISA 2012 Database.

StatLink ᵃₛᵖ http://dx.doi.org/10.1787/888932964984

Universal policies for countries where performance differences are small and there is a weak relationship between performance and socio-economic status

Canada, Estonia, Finland, Hong Kong-China and Macao-China are the only school systems that participated in PISA 2012 that share above-average performance and above-average equity, whether measured by the strength of the relationship between socio-economic status and performance or the size of the performance differences across socio-economic groups (Figure II.5.1a). Within this group, even large differences in students' socio-economic status (such as those observed in Hong Kong-China and Macao-China, where the length of the gradient is above the OECD average) are, on average, not associated with large performance differences among students. In general, universal policies that reach all students are more likely to help these countries improve their performance and maintain above-average levels of equity in education outcomes. Japan, Korea and Liechtenstein also share above-average performance and a weak relationship between socio-economic status and performance, but performance differences across socio-economic status are around average. Beyond universal policies, these countries may consider policies targeted to low performers who may not necessarily be defined by their socio-economic status (for example, immigrant students in Finland), or to poor-performing schools, when differences between schools are very large. In no high-performing country is the socio-economic gradient flat and strong.

■ Figure II.5.3 ■

Relationship between school performance and schools' socio-economic profile in countries with high performance and flat and weak gradients: Canada and Viet Nam

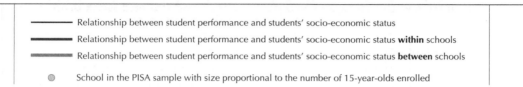

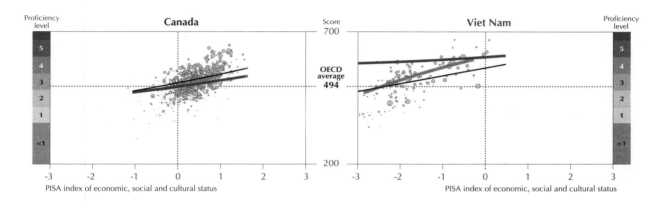

Source: OECD, PISA 2012 Database.
StatLink ᴍ⥩ http://dx.doi.org/10.1787/888932965003

Among countries whose mean performance is below or around the OECD average, greater equity in outcomes implies that all students perform equally well – or poorly – regardless of their background or that there are small differences in performance between advantaged and disadvantaged students. Iceland and Norway show average performance and high equity. Among OECD countries, Italy and Mexico show below-OECD-average performance and high equity; however some 25% of students in Italy and 55% of students in Mexico are low performers. Among the partner countries, Jordan, Kazakhstan, Montenegro, Qatar, Thailand and the United Arab Emirates all share high levels of equity and large proportions of students who perform below the baseline level of performance. In Greece, Spain, the United States and Viet Nam, performance differences related to socio-economic status (the slope of the gradient) are also below average, but the relationship between socio-economic status and performance (the strength of the gradient) is close to the OECD average. While Argentina, Brazil, Colombia, Indonesia, Malaysia, Tunisia and Turkey share this profile, in all of these countries more than 40% of students are low performers.

These data suggest that in many of these countries, a relatively smaller proportion of low-performing students come from disadvantaged backgrounds, and the relationship between performance and socio-economic status is weak. Thus, by themselves, policies that specifically target students from disadvantaged backgrounds would not address the needs of many of the country's lower-performing students. As is true in high-performing countries, in these countries, universal policies that reach all students and schools are likely to have more of an impact in improving performance while maintaining high levels of equity.

By contrast, targeting low achievers may prove more effective than targeting disadvantaged students. For example, if the goal is to ensure that most students achieve a minimum level of performance, policies that target disadvantaged students would be providing services to a sizeable proportion of students who already perform well. Where large proportions of students perform below the baseline level, policies targeting these students may be needed in order to ensure they are not left behind. Among countries that perform below the OECD average, the proportion of students who score below the baseline level differs widely. In some countries, like Italy, the proportion is close to the OECD average, while in others, such as Argentina, Brazil, Colombia, Indonesia, Malaysia, Tunisia and Turkey, the proportion of students below the baseline level ranges from 42% in Turkey to 76% in Indonesia. Where the proportion of students who score below the baseline level is large, it is necessary to target these students and the schools they attend.

■ Figure II.5.4 ■

Relationship between school performance and schools' socio-economic profile in countries with average or low performance and flat and weak gradients: Brazil, Italy, Mexico and the United States

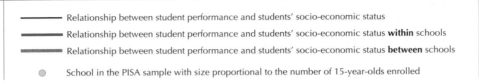

——— Relationship between student performance and students' socio-economic status

——— Relationship between student performance and students' socio-economic status **within** schools

——— Relationship between student performance and students' socio-economic status **between** schools

⬤ School in the PISA sample with size proportional to the number of 15-year-olds enrolled

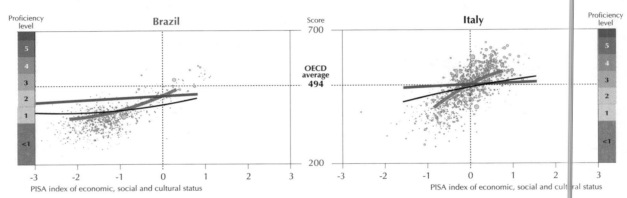

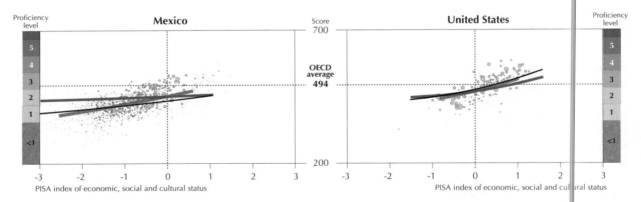

Source: OECD, PISA 2012 Database.
StatLink ⬛⬛⬛ http://dx.doi.org/10.1787/888932965022

Policies that target socio-economic disadvantage for those countries where there are small performance differences and a strong relationship between performance and socio-economic status

When the socio-economic gradient is flat but strong, meaning that performance differences related to socio-economic status are small, but there is a close relationship between socio-economic status and performance, a combination of universal policies and policies targeting disadvantaged students and schools may be most effective. One way of addressing the strong relationship between socio-economic status and performance is to add more flexibility to education systems, such as by offering pathways across programmes in tracked systems; another is to provide more and better resources and opportunities to disadvantaged students. Certain universal policies, such as increasing the amount or quality of the time students spend at school, can also improve equity because they are likely to have a larger impact on disadvantaged students. Chile, Costa Rica, Peru and Portugal are the only countries where the socio-economic gradient is flat and strong. More than 40% of students in all of these countries, except Portugal, perform below the baseline proficiency level in mathematics. Policies that target low-performing students and schools, as well as universal policies to improve performance across the board, may be most effective in these countries.

■ Figure II.5.5 ■

Relationship between school performance and schools' socio-economic profile with average or low performance and flat and strong gradients: Chile, Greece, Malaysia and Turkey

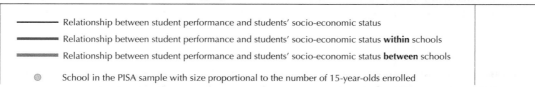

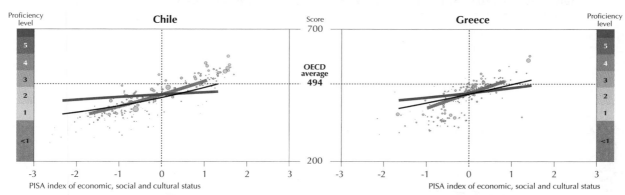

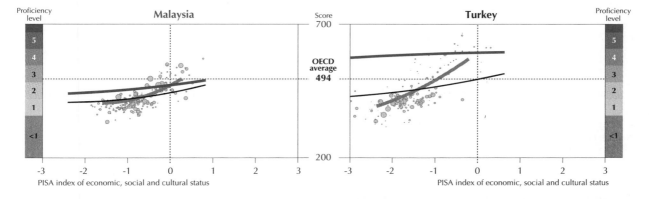

Source: OECD, PISA 2012 Database.
StatLink ⌗ http://dx.doi.org/10.1787/888932965041

Policies that target both performance and socio-economic disadvantage for countries where there are large performance differences and a strong relationship between performance and socio-economic status

In countries where performance differences across socio-economic groups are very large (a steep gradient), policies that target disadvantaged students are likely to be more effective, particularly if the strength of the relationship between performance and socio-economic status is also above average.

New Zealand and Chinese Taipei are the only two high-performing countries/economies with below-average levels of equity in education outcomes. Targeting low-performing and/or disadvantaged students is a policy option for both of these countries, as the steepness of the gradient suggests that low-performing students could rapidly improve their performance if their socio-economic status also improved. The stronger-than-average relationship between socio-economic status and performance, however, suggests that in these countries very few students overcome the barriers to high performance that are linked with socio-economic status. Therefore, these countries also need to provide greater opportunities for socio-economically disadvantaged students to achieve higher performance. A combination of policies to improve equity while maintaining high levels of performance at the system level appears to be the most advisable course of action for these countries.

Austria, Belgium and Singapore also share high performance and large performance differences across socio-economic groups, but the strength of the relationship between performance and socio-economic status is only average. To address those large differences, these countries can focus on compensatory policies that support disadvantaged students and schools so that they are given as many opportunities and resources as their more advantaged peers.

■ Figure II.5.6 ■

Relationship between school performance and schools' socio-economic profile in countries with high performance and steep and strong gradients: Germany and New Zealand

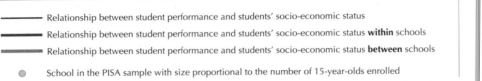

——— Relationship between student performance and students' socio-economic status

——— Relationship between student performance and students' socio-economic status **within** schools

——— Relationship between student performance and students' socio-economic status **between** schools

● School in the PISA sample with size proportional to the number of 15-year-olds enrolled

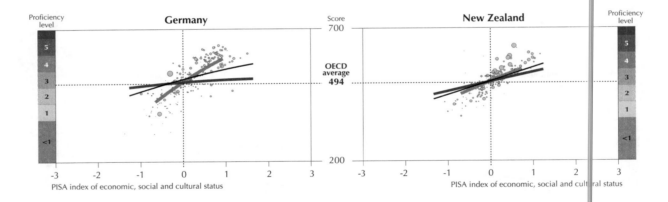

Source: OECD, PISA 2012 Database.
StatLink http://dx.doi.org/10.1787/888932965060

Where both poor performance and low equity are observed, such as in Hungary and the Slovak Republic, policies that target both performance and socio-economic disadvantage may prove effective in reaching those who need support the most – who, in these cases, are often the same students. The steep slope suggests that performance improves quickly as socio-economic status improves. However, the strong relationship between socio-economic status and performance suggests that few students perform better than what can be expected given their socio-economic status. Reforms that add flexibility to school systems, so that disadvantaged and poor-performing students have access to better resources and/or more and better opportunities to learn, can also help. Bulgaria, Luxembourg and Uruguay share this profile, although differences in performance related to socio-economic status are average, which suggests that universal policies aimed at improving the performance of all students may also be effective.

For countries where the impact of socio-economic status on performance is high (a steep slope), but only part of the variation in performance is explained by socio-economic status (a weak socio-economic gradient), policies that target disadvantaged students may not be as effective. In these countries, there tends to be a sizeable group of poor-performing students who are not disadvantaged. Among the high-performing countries, Australia is the only country participating in PISA 2012 with a weak relationship between socio-status and above-average performance differences across socio-economic groups.

■ Figure II.5.7 ■
Relationship between school performance and schools' socio-economic profile in countries with low performance and steep and strong gradients: Hungary, Israel, Singapore and the Slovak Republic

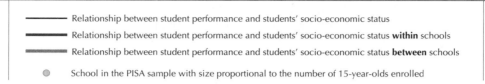

——— Relationship between student performance and students' socio-economic status

——— Relationship between student performance and students' socio-economic status **within** schools

——— Relationship between student performance and students' socio-economic status **between** schools

● School in the PISA sample with size proportional to the number of 15-year-olds enrolled

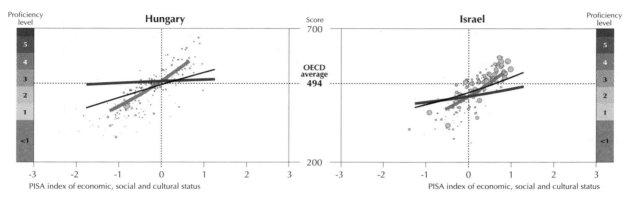

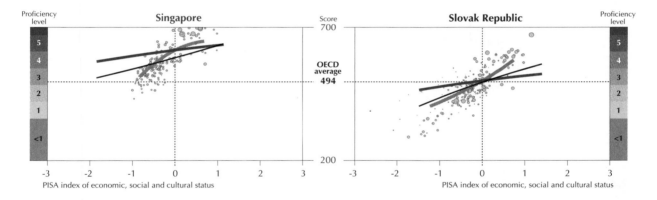

Source: OECD, PISA 2012 Database.
StatLink http://dx.doi.org/10.1787/888932965079

These large differences suggest that targeting disadvantaged students and schools may help Austria improve equity while maintaining high performance. Viet Nam is the only high-performing country where there are small performance differences related to socio-economic status and where the strength of the relationship between performance and socio-economic status is around average. In this case, policies that target low-performing students and schools may help improve equity while maintaining high levels of performance.

LARGE SOCIO-ECONOMIC DISPARITIES

It is equally important to understand the degree of socio-economic disparity within a country when interpreting the relationship between performance and socio-economic status. For example, Bulgaria, Japan, Korea, Luxembourg, Sweden and Uruguay have socio-economic gradients with similar slopes (a performance difference of between 36 and 42 score points related to socio-economic status); but the range of values on the *PISA index of economic, social and cultural status* (the length of the gradient) between the 5th and 95th percentile of students spans at least 3.2 units on the index (more than three times the average difference in socio-economic status between two students randomly chosen across OECD countries) in Bulgaria, Luxembourg and Uruguay, but less than 2.5 units in Japan, Korea and Sweden.

In other words, the populations of 15-year-old students in Bulgaria, Luxembourg and Uruguay are far more socio-economically diverse than the student populations in Japan, Korea and Sweden. This difference partly explains why, in Sweden, for example, socio-economic status accounts for less-than-average variation in performance, while in Uruguay socio-economic status has a stronger-than-average impact on performance. Socio-economic diversity, measured in this way, is greatest in Chile, Mexico, Portugal and Turkey, among OECD countries; but many partner countries and economies also show greater-than-OECD-average socio-economic diversity, particularly Brazil, Colombia, Costa Rica, Peru, Thailand, Tunisia, Uruguay and Viet Nam. In all of these countries and economies, compensatory policies that target disadvantaged students and schools can help improve performance and equity in education.

■ Figure II.5.8 ■

**Relationship between school performance and schools' socio-economic profile
in countries with marked socio-economic disparities and average equity in outcomes:
Bulgaria, Colombia, Costa Rica and Ireland**

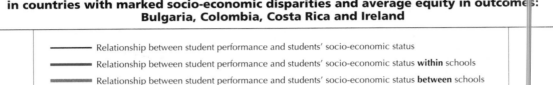

———— Relationship between student performance and students' socio-economic status

———— Relationship between student performance and students' socio-economic status **within** schools

———— Relationship between student performance and students' socio-economic status **between** schools

⬤ School in the PISA sample with size proportional to the number of 15-year-olds enrolled

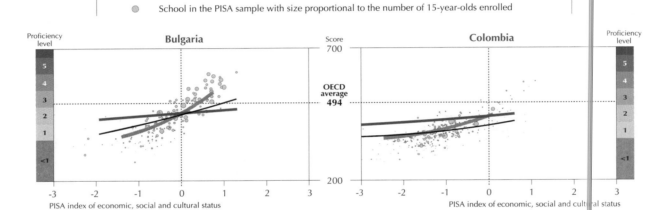

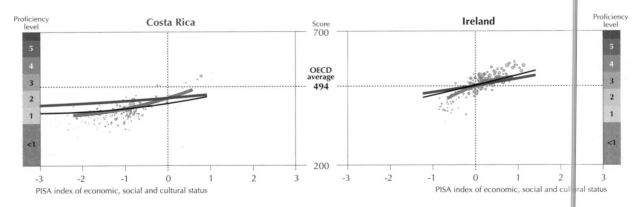

Source: OECD, PISA 2012 Database.
StatLink http://dx.doi.org/10.1787/888932965098

In countries with large disparities and a weak relationship between socio-economic status and performance, such as Mexico and Thailand, compensatory policies to help the most disadvantaged students would be effective. By contrast, where socio-economic disparities are smaller and have a weaker effect on performance, for example in the Czech Republic, Finland, Japan, Korea and Norway, policies targeting social reform are unlikely to be the most effective way of improving student performance because they are not likely to reach many students.

■ Figure II.5.9 ■

Relationship between school performance and schools' socio-economic profile in countries with high equity but marked socio-economic disparities: Hong Kong-China, Jordan, Qatar and Thailand

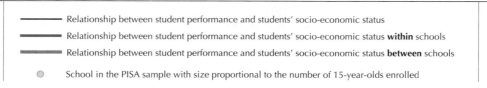

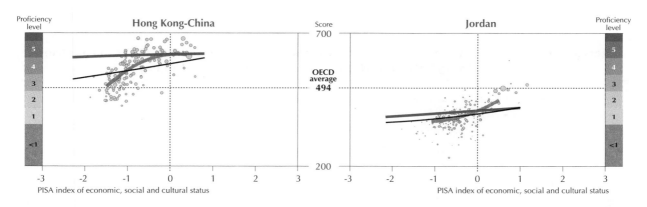

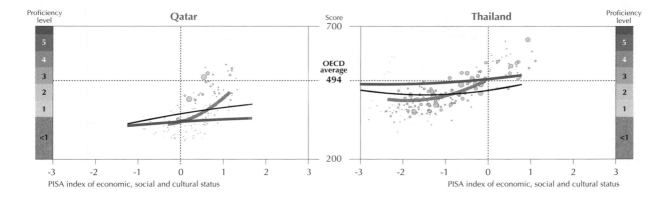

Source: OECD, PISA 2012 Database.

StatLink ⌗ http://dx.doi.org/10.1787/888932965117

TARGETING LOW-PERFORMING AND SOCIO-ECONOMICALLY DISADVANTAGED SCHOOLS

When performance or socio-economic disparities between schools are large, policies that target schools rather than students may be more effective, particularly when there is a strong and marked relationship between a school's socio-economic profile and average performance.

The relationship between a school's socio-economic profile and student performance can be described in several ways. One way is to focus on how much better a student who goes to a school with a more advantaged student population can be expected to perform in mathematics. A second is how closely the performance of individual students actually follows this prediction, or the strength of the relationship.[1] These factors are all important in countries where students' opportunities to learn are strongly affected by differences in schools' socio-economic profile. In countries where large differences are observed, policies that target disadvantaged schools are more likely to succeed in improving performance and equity.

As Figure II.5.1b shows, in Uruguay, 74% of the difference in student performance across schools is related to socio-economic factors, that is, schools tend to fall into two categories: higher-performing schools with a more advantaged socio-economic profile, and schools with lower performance and more disadvantaged student populations. Most important, the variation in the socio-economic profile of schools is great, meaning that there is a large difference in socio-economic status between advantaged and disadvantaged schools. In Iceland, while performance disparities related to schools' socio-economic profile are comparatively large as well (69%), the overall differences in the socio-economic profiles of schools are much smaller. That explains why Iceland has, overall, one of the more equitable education systems while Uruguay has one of the least equitable systems. In countries in which most of the variation is accounted for by between-school socio-economic factors, policies aimed at reducing social segregation should be a priority, as such disparities among schools tend to reinforce the inequities of the system.

■ Figure II.5.10 ■

Relationship between school performance and schools' socio-economic profiles in countries with strong between-school gradients: Iceland and Uruguay

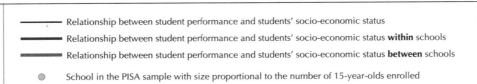

———— Relationship between student performance and students' socio-economic status

———— Relationship between student performance and students' socio-economic status **within** schools

———— Relationship between student performance and students' socio-economic status **between** schools

○ School in the PISA sample with size proportional to the number of 15-year-olds enrolled

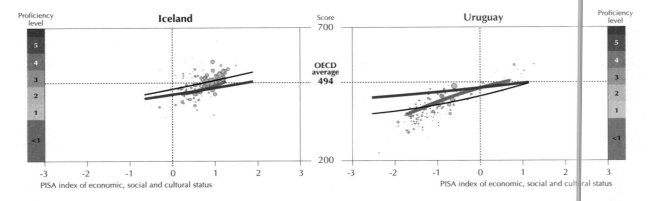

Source: OECD, PISA 2012 Database.
StatLink http://dx.doi.org/10.1787/888932965136

A similar contrast can be observed among countries where performance differences across socio-economic status are relatively small. For example, in Norway and Portugal, the between-school differences in mathematics performance are relatively small, around 49 and 33 score points, respectively (compared to an OECD average of more than 70 score points). However, schools vary considerably in their socio-economic profile. A school's socio-economic profile is a much better predictor of performance in Portugal, where 62% of the variation in performance is explained by the schools' socio-economic profile, than in Norway, where 46% of the variation in performance is so explained. That is, while many schools in Norway perform differently than what would have been predicted based on their socio-economic profile, in Portugal, socio-economic status is closely associated with a school's performance. Policies that target disadvantaged schools are thus more likely to be effective in Portugal. In Norway, these policies will not help low-performing schools that are not necessarily disadvantaged.

Targeting disadvantaged schools may be a viable option in those countries where differences in socio-economic profiles are large (i.e. the between-school socio-economic differences account for a large proportion of the variation in socio-economic status). Such policies may prove particularly effective where the relationship between performance and socio-economic status at the school level is marked, either because there are large performance differences across schools with different socio-economic profiles or because there is a strong relationship between the socio-economic profile of a school and mean student performance at the school.

■ Figure II.5.11 ■

Relationship between school performance and schools' socio-economic profile in countries with weak between-school gradients: Norway and Portugal

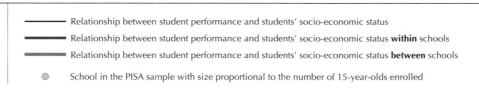

———— Relationship between student performance and students' socio-economic status

———— Relationship between student performance and students' socio-economic status **within** schools

———— Relationship between student performance and students' socio-economic status **between** schools

○ School in the PISA sample with size proportional to the number of 15-year-olds enrolled

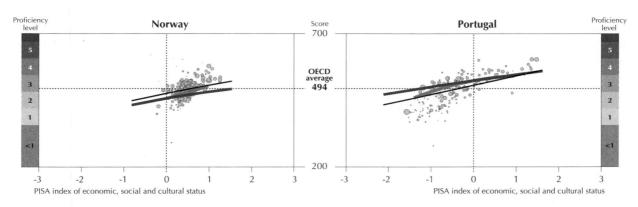

Source: OECD, PISA 2012 Database.
StatLink http://dx.doi.org/10.1787/888932965155

Targeting disadvantaged schools may be important in Hungary, Shanghai-China and the Slovak Republic, where socio-economic differences between schools are large – they account for a larger-than-average proportion of the variation in socio-economic status (37%, 33% and 36%, respectively, compared with the OECD average of 24%, [Figure II.5.1b] – and where between-school performance differences across socio-economic groups (98 score points, 88 points and 86 points, respectively) are above the OECD average (72 score points). In all three countries, schools' socio-economic profiles are strongly related to school mean performance, explaining between 65% of the variation in mean school performance in Shanghai-China and 78% in Hungary (compared with an OECD average of 63%). Argentina, Brazil, Bulgaria, Chile, Colombia, Costa Rica, Peru, Portugal, Romania and Uruguay also show large between-school differences in socio-economic profiles and a strong relationship between performance and socio-economic status. In all of these countries, performance differences across schools related to the schools' socio-economic profiles are below average (except in Bulgaria, where they are average); but the strength of the relationship between schools' mean performance and their socio-economic profiles are at or above average. The proportion of the performance differences explained by the variation in socio-economic profiles ranges from 60% in Colombia to 78% in Peru. Hong Kong-China is the only economy where differences between schools in socio-economic profiles are at the OECD average, but the strength of the relationship between schools' socio-economic profiles and performance is below average.

Targeting low-performing schools may also be an option, particularly when the school's socio-economic status is strongly related to performance differences. The evidence in PISA suggests that policies targeting low-performing schools may be particularly effective for Belgium, the Czech Republic, Germany, Hungary, the Slovak Republic and Slovenia. In all of these countries, between-school differences account for at least half of the variation in performance. The school systems of these countries tend to track students into different schools according to their performance, so it is not surprising that there are many between-school performance differences across these countries. The average impact of schools' socio-economic profile on performance (the between-school socio-economic gradient) ranges from 86 score points in the Slovak Republic to 127 points in the Czech Republic, compared with the OECD average difference of 72 score points. In all these countries, more than 70% of the differences in performance are explained by students' and schools' socio-economic status, compared with the OECD average of 63% (Figure II.5.1b). Socio-economic disparities across schools account for more than 35% of the variation in socio-economic status in Hungary and the Slovak Republic. Within-school differences in performance across socio-economic groups are above average only in the Slovak Republic.

TARGETING STUDENTS WITHIN SCHOOLS

To some extent, school systems that separate students into different schools, based on ability, can expect to have narrower differences in student performance within each school, both overall and relative to socio-economic status. The other side of the coin is that the social disparities between schools account for more of the performance differences among these countries than social disparities within schools. Thus, even Korea, one of the most unequal countries in terms of between-school gradients, and Viet Nam, one of the most equal, show similar results when analysed according to within-school gradients (Figure II.5.12). In no country do within-school social differences account for more than 11% of variation in student performance.

In Denmark, Finland, New Zealand, Poland, Portugal, Spain and Sweden, 9% or more of the performance differences within schools are explained by differences in socio-economic status – a stronger-than-average relationship between performance and socio-economic status within schools. In all these countries, school-level policies, in addition to system-level policies, would prove more effective.

Figure II.5.13 shows the relationship between school performance and schools' socio-economic profile for all OECD countries and partner countries and economies that are not used as examples in previous chapters.

■ Figure II.5.12 ■

Relationship between school performance and schools' socio-economic profile in countries with marked performance differences within schools: Denmark, Finland, Spain and Switzerland

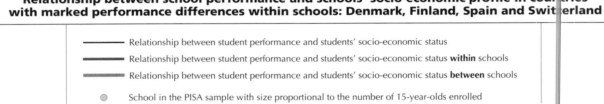

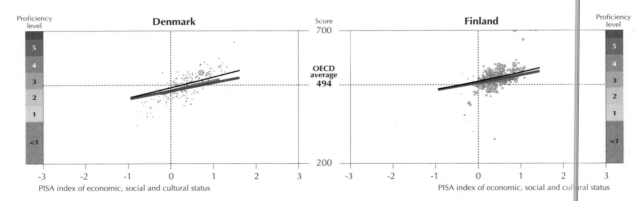

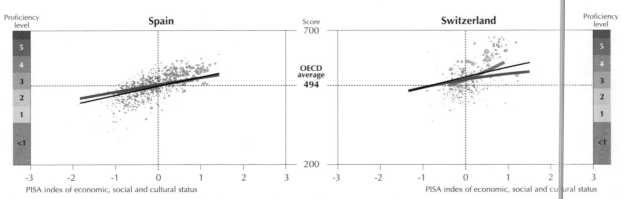

Source: OECD, PISA 2012 Database.
StatLink http://dx.doi.org/10.1787/888932965174

■ Figure II.5.13 [Part 1/5] ■

Relationship between school performance and schools' socio-economic profile for all other countries and economies

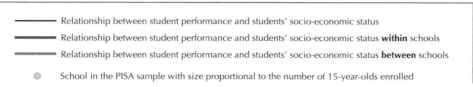

——— Relationship between student performance and students' socio-economic status

——— Relationship between student performance and students' socio-economic status **within** schools

——— Relationship between student performance and students' socio-economic status **between** schools

○ School in the PISA sample with size proportional to the number of 15-year-olds enrolled

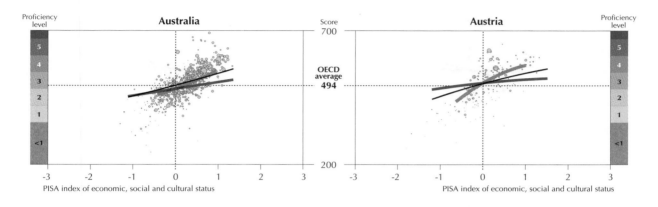

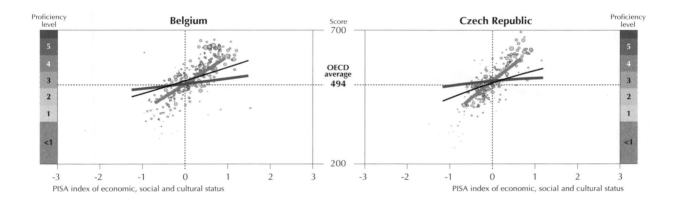

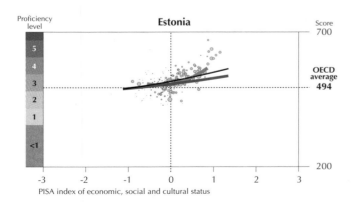

Source: OECD, PISA 2012 Database.
StatLink ⟐ http://dx.doi.org/10.1787/888932965193
StatLink ⟐ http://dx.doi.org/10.1787/888932965212

■ Figure II.5.13 [Part 2/5] ■

Relationship between school performance and schools' socio-economic profile for all other countries and economies

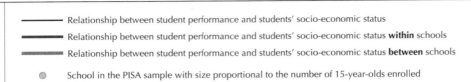

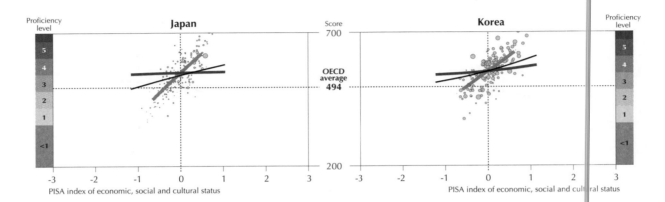

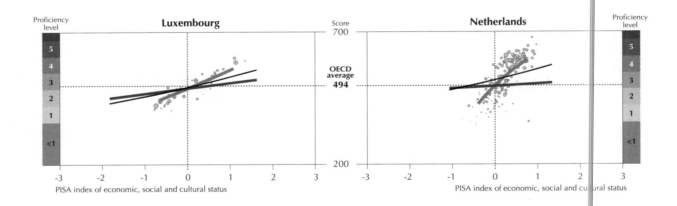

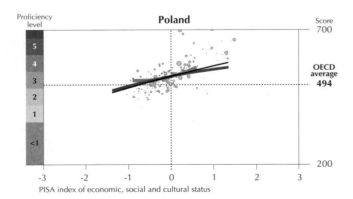

Source: OECD, PISA 2012 Database.
StatLink ᴍ� http://dx.doi.org/10.1787/888932965193
StatLink ᴍᴍsᴸ http://dx.doi.org/10.1787/888932965212

■ Figure II.5.13 [Part 3/5] ■

Relationship between school performance and schools' socio-economic profile for all other countries and economies

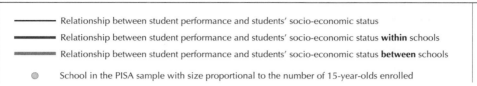

—— Relationship between student performance and students' socio-economic status

—— Relationship between student performance and students' socio-economic status **within** schools

—— Relationship between student performance and students' socio-economic status **between** schools

◉ School in the PISA sample with size proportional to the number of 15-year-olds enrolled

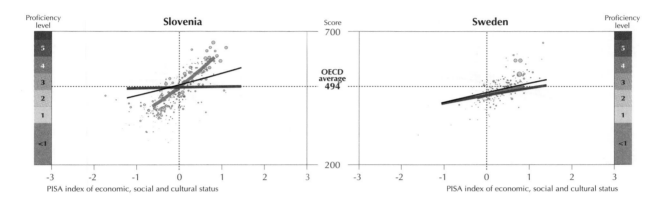

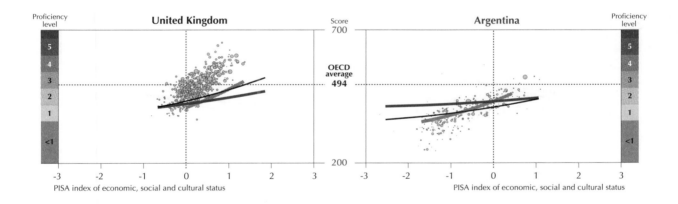

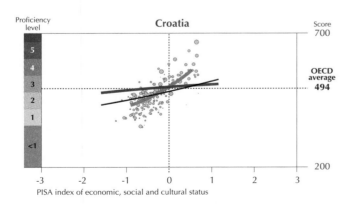

Source: OECD, PISA 2012 Database.
StatLink ⟐⟐⟐ http://dx.doi.org/10.1787/888932965193
StatLink ⟐⟐⟐ http://dx.doi.org/10.1787/888932965212

■ Figure II.5.13 [Part 4/5] ■

Relationship between school performance and schools' socio-economic profile for all other countries and economies

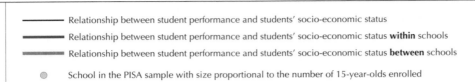

—— Relationship between student performance and students' socio-economic status

—— Relationship between student performance and students' socio-economic status **within** schools

—— Relationship between student performance and students' socio-economic status **between** schools

○ School in the PISA sample with size proportional to the number of 15-year-olds enrolled

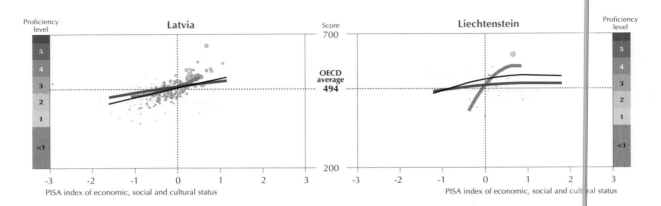

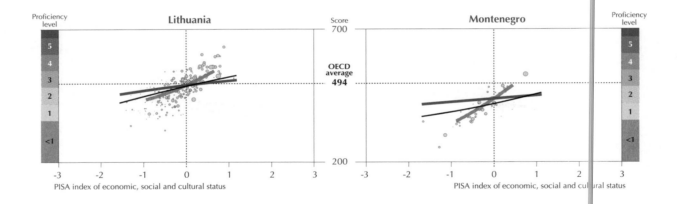

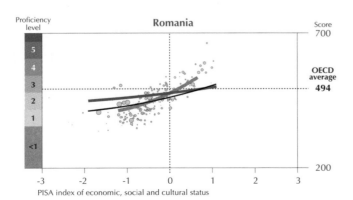

Source: OECD, PISA 2012 Database.

StatLink http://dx.doi.org/10.1787/888932965193

StatLink http://dx.doi.org/10.1787/888932965212

■ Figure II.5.13 [Part 5/5] ■

Relationship between school performance and schools' socio-economic profile for all other countries and economies

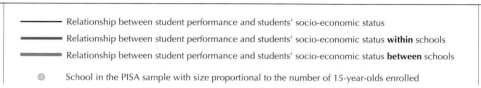

Relationship between student performance and students' socio-economic status

Relationship between student performance and students' socio-economic status **within** schools

Relationship between student performance and students' socio-economic status **between** schools

School in the PISA sample with size proportional to the number of 15-year-olds enrolled

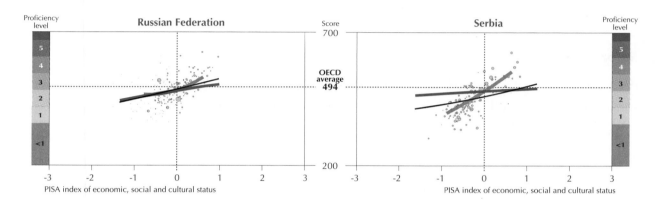

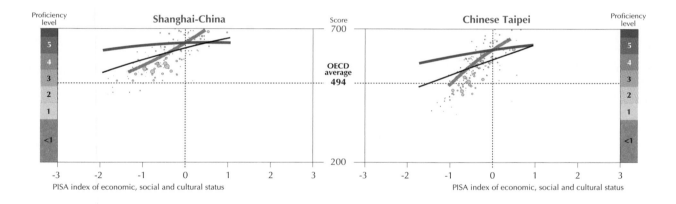

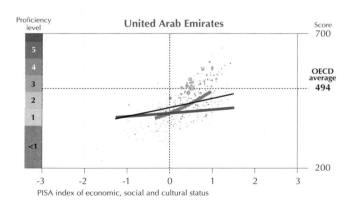

Source: OECD, PISA 2012 Database.
StatLink http://dx.doi.org/10.1787/888932965193
StatLink http://dx.doi.org/10.1787/888932965212

Note

1. Note that these results also depend on how schools are defined and organised within countries/economies and by the units that were chosen for sampling purposes. For example, in some countries, some of the schools in the PISA sample were defined as administrative units (even if they spanned several geographically separate institutions, as in Italy; in others, they were defined as those parts of larger educational institutions that serve 15-year-olds; in still others, they were defined as physical school buildings; and in others they were defined from a management perspective (e.g. entities having a principal). The *PISA 2012 Technical Report* (OECD, forthcoming) provides an overview of how schools were defined. Because of the manner in which students were sampled, the within-school variation includes variation between classes as well as between students. In Slovenia, the primary sampling unit is defined as a group of students who follow the same study programme within a school (an educational track within a school). So in this particular case, the between-school variance is actually the difference between tracks within the schools.

References

OECD (forthcoming), *PISA 2012 Technical Report*, PISA, OECD Publishing.

Willms, J.D. (2006), *Learning Divides: Ten Policy Questions About the Performance and Equity of Schools and Schooling Systems*, UNESCO Institute for Statistics, Montreal.

Annex A

PISA 2012 TECHNICAL BACKGROUND

All figures and tables in Annex A are available on line

Annex A1: Construction of mathematics scales and indices from
the student, school and parent context questionnaires
http://dx.doi.org/10.1787/888932937073

Annex A2: The PISA target population, the PISA samples
and the definition of schools
http://dx.doi.org/10.1787/888932937092

Annex A3: Technical notes on analyses in this volume

Annex A4: Quality assurance

Annex A5: Technical details of trends analyses
http://dx.doi.org/10.1787/888932937054

ANNEX A1

CONSTRUCTION OF MATHEMATICS SCALES AND INDICES FROM THE STUDENT, SCHOOL AND PARENT CONTEXT QUESTIONNAIRES

How the PISA 2012 mathematics assessments were designed, analysed and scaled

The development of the PISA 2012 mathematics tasks was co-ordinated by an international consortium of educational research institutions contracted by the OECD, under the guidance of a group of mathematics experts from participating countries. Participating countries contributed stimulus material and questions, which were reviewed, tried out and refined iteratively over the three years leading up to the administration of the assessment in 2012. The development process involved provisions for several rounds of commentary from participating countries and economies, as well as small-scale piloting and a formal field trial in which samples of 15-year-olds (about 1 000 students) from participating countries and economies took part. The mathematics expert group recommended the final selection of tasks, which included material submitted by participating countries and economies. The selection was made with regard to both their technical quality, assessed on the basis of their performance in the field trial, and their cultural appropriateness and interest level for 15-year-olds, as judged by the participating countries. Another essential criterion for selecting the set of material as a whole was its fit to the framework described in Volume 1, in order to maintain the balance across various categories of context, content and process. Finally, it was carefully ensured that the set of questions covered a range of difficulty, allowing good measurement and description of the mathematics literacy of all 15-year-old students, from the least proficient to the highly able.

More than 110 print mathematics questions were used in PISA 2012, but each student in the sample only saw a fraction of the total pool because different sets of questions were given to different students. The mathematics questions selected for inclusion in PISA 2012 were organised into half-hour clusters. These, along with clusters of reading and science questions, were assembled into booklets containing four clusters each. Each participating student was then given a two-hour assessment. As mathematics was the focus of the PISA 2012 assessment, every booklet included at least one cluster of mathematics material. The clusters were rotated so that each cluster appeared in each of the four possible positions in the booklets, and each pair of clusters appeared in at least one of the 13 booklets that were used.

This design, similar to those used in previous PISA assessments, makes it possible to construct a single scale of mathematics proficiency, in which each question is associated with a particular point on the scale that indicates its difficulty, whereby each student's performance is associated with a particular point on the same scale that indicates his or her estimated proficiency. A description of the modelling technique used to construct this scale can be found in the *PISA 2012 Technical Report* (OECD, forthcoming).

The relative difficulty of tasks in a test is estimated by considering the proportion of test takers who answer each question correctly. The relative proficiency of students taking a particular test can be estimated by considering the proportion of test questions they answer correctly. A single continuous scale shows the relationship between the difficulty of questions and the proficiency of students. By constructing a scale that shows the difficulty of each question, it is possible to locate the level of mathematics literacy that the question represents. By showing the proficiency of each student on the same scale, it is possible to describe the level of mathematics literacy that the student possesses.

The location of student proficiency on this scale is set in relation to the particular group of questions used in the assessment. However, just as the sample of students taking PISA in 2012 is drawn to represent all the 15-year-olds in the participating countries and economies, so the individual questions used in the assessment are designed to represent the definition of mathematics literacy adequately. Estimates of student proficiency reflect the kinds of tasks they would be expected to perform successfully. This means that students are likely to be able to complete questions successfully at or below the difficulty level associated with their own position on the scale (but they may not always do so). Conversely, they are unlikely to be able to successfully complete questions above the difficulty level associated with their position on the scale (but they may sometimes do so).

The further a student's proficiency is located above a given question, the more likely he or she is to successfully complete the question (and other questions of similar difficulty); the further the student's proficiency is located below a given question, the lower the probability that the student will be able to successfully complete the question, and other questions of similar difficulty.

How mathematics proficiency levels are defined in PISA 2012

PISA 2012 provides an overall mathematics literacy scale, drawing on all the questions in the mathematics assessment, as well as scales for three process and four content categories. The metric for the overall mathematics scale is based on a mean for OECD countries set at 500 in PISA 2003, with a standard deviation of 100. To help interpret what students' scores mean in substantive terms, the scale is divided into levels, based on a set of statistical principles, and then descriptions are generated, based on the tasks that are located within each level, to describe the kinds of skills and knowledge needed to successfully complete those tasks.

For PISA 2012, the range of difficulty of tasks allows for the description of six levels of mathematics proficiency: Level 1 is the lowest described level, then Level 2, Level 3 and so on up to Level 6.

Students with a proficiency within the range of Level 1 are likely to be able to successfully complete Level 1 tasks (and others like them), but are unlikely to be able to complete tasks at higher levels. Level 6 reflects tasks that present the greatest challenge in terms of mathematics skills and knowledge. Students with scores in this range are likely to be able to complete mathematics tasks located at that level successfully, as well as all the other mathematics tasks in PISA.

PISA applies a standard methodology for constructing proficiency scales. Based on a student's performance on the tasks in the test, his or her score is generated and located in a specific part of the scale, thus allowing the score to be associated with a defined proficiency level. The level at which the student's score is located is the highest level for which he or she would be expected to answer correctly most of a random selection of questions within the same level. Thus, for example, in an assessment composed of tasks spread uniformly across Level 3, students with a score located within Level 3 would be expected to complete at least 50% of the tasks successfully. Because a level covers a range of difficulty and proficiency, success rates across the band vary. Students near the bottom of the level would be likely to succeed on just over 50% of the tasks spread uniformly across the level, while students at the top of the level would be likely to succeed on well over 70% of the same tasks.

Figure I.2.21 in Volume I provides details of the nature of mathematics skills, knowledge and understanding required at each level of the mathematics scale.

Context questionnaire indices

This section explains the indices derived from the student and school context questionnaires used in PISA 2012.

Several PISA measures reflect indices that summarise responses from students, their parents or school representatives (typically principals) to a series of related questions. The questions were selected from a larger pool of questions on the basis of theoretical considerations and previous research. The *PISA 2012 Assessment and Analytical Framework* (OECD, 2013) provides an in-depth description of this conceptual framework. Structural equation modelling was used to confirm the theoretically expected behaviour of the indices and to validate their comparability across countries and economies. For this purpose, a model was estimated separately for each country and collectively for all OECD countries. For a detailed description of other PISA indices and details on the methods, see the *PISA 2012 Technical Report* (OECD, forthcoming).

There are two types of indices: simple indices and scale indices.

Simple indices are the variables that are constructed through the arithmetic transformation or recoding of one or more items, in exactly the same way across assessments. Here, item responses are used to calculate meaningful variables, such as the recoding of the four-digit ISCO-08 codes into "Highest parents' socio-economic index (HISEI)" or, teacher-student ratio based on information from the school questionnaire.

Scale indices are the variables constructed through the scaling of multiple items. Unless otherwise indicated, the index was scaled using a weighted likelihood estimate (WLE) (Warm, 1989), using a one-parameter item response model (a partial credit model was used in the case of items with more than two categories). For details on how each scale index was constructed see the *PISA 2012 Technical Report* (OECD, forthcoming). In general, the scaling was done in three stages:

- The item parameters were estimated from equal-sized subsamples of students from all participating countries and economies.
- The estimates were computed for all students and all schools by anchoring the item parameters obtained in the preceding step.
- The indices were then standardised so that the mean of the index value for the OECD student population was zero and the standard deviation was one (countries being given equal weight in the standardisation process).

Sequential codes were assigned to the different response categories of the questions in the sequence in which the latter appeared in the student, school or parent questionnaires. Where indicated in this section, these codes were inverted for the purpose of constructing indices or scales. Negative values for an index do not necessarily imply that students responded negatively to the underlying questions. A negative value merely indicates that the respondents answered less positively than all respondents did on average across OECD countries. Likewise, a positive value on an index indicates that the respondents answered more favourably, or more positively, than respondents did, on average, across OECD countries. Terms enclosed in brackets < > in the following descriptions were replaced in the national versions of the student, school and parent questionnaires by the appropriate national equivalent. For example, the term <qualification at ISCED level 5A> was translated in the United States into "Bachelor's degree, post-graduate certificate program, Master's degree program or first professional degree program". Similarly the term <classes in the language of assessment> in Luxembourg was translated into "German classes" or "French classes" depending on whether students received the German or French version of the assessment instruments.

In addition to simple and scaled indices described in this annex, there are a number of variables from the questionnaires that correspond to single items not used to construct indices. These non-recoded variables have prefix of "ST" for the questionnaire items in the student questionnaire, "SC" for the items in the school questionnaire, and "PA" for the items in the parent questionnaire. All the context questionnaires as well as the PISA international database, including all variables, are available through *www.pisa.oecd.org*.

Scaling of questionnaire indices for trend analyses

In PISA, to gather information about students' and schools' characteristics, both students and schools complete a background questionnaire. In PISA 2003 and PISA 2012 several questions were kept untouched, enabling the comparison of responses to these questions over time. In this report, only questions that maintained an exact wording are used for trends analyses. Questions with subtle word changes or questions with major word changes were not compared across time because it is impossible to discern whether observed changes in the response are due to changes in the construct they are measuring or to changes in the way the construct is being measured.

Also, in PISA, as described in this Annex, questionnaire items are used to construct indices. Whenever the questions used in the construction of indices remains intact in PISA 2003 and PISA 2012, the corresponding indices are compared. Two types of indices are used in PISA: simple indices and scale indices.

Simple indices recode a set of responses to questionnaire items. For trends analyses, the values observed in PISA 2003 are compared directly to PISA 2012, just as simple responses to questionnaire items are. This is the case of indices like student-teacher ratio and ability grouping in mathematics.

Scale indices, on the other hand, imply WLE estimates which require rescaling in order to be comparable across PISA cycles. Scale indices, like the *PISA index of economic, social and cultural status*, the *index of sense of belonging*, the *index of attitudes towards school*, the *index of intrinsic motivation to learn mathematics*, the *index of instrumental motivation to learn mathematics*, the *index of mathematics self-efficacy*, the *index of mathematics self-concept*, the *index of anxiety towards mathematics*, the *index of teacher shortage*, the *index of quality of physical infrastructure*, the *index of quality of educational resources*, the *index of disciplinary climate*, the *index of teacher-student relations*, the *index of teacher morale*, the *index of student-related factors affecting school climate* and the *index of teacher-related factors affecting school climate*, were scaled, in PISA 2012 to have an OECD average of 0 and a standard deviation of 1, on average, across OECD countries. These same scales were scaled, in PISA 2003, to have an OECD average of 0 and a standard deviation of 1. Because they are on different scales, values reported in *Learning for Tomorrow's World: First Results from PISA 2003* (OECD, 2004) cannot be compared with those reported in this volume. To make these scale indices comparable, values for 2003 have been rescaled to the 2012 scale, using the PISA 2012 parameter estimates.

These re-scaled indices are available at *www.pisa.oecd.org*. They can be merged to the corresponding PISA 2003 dataset using the country names, school and student-level identifiers. The rescaled *PISA index of economic, social and cultural status* is also available to be merged with the PISA 2000, PISA 2006 and PISA 2009 dataset.

Student-level simple indices

Age

The variable AGE is calculated as the difference between the middle month and the year in which students were assessed and their month and year of birth, expressed in years and months.

Study programme

In PISA 2012, study programmes available to 15-year-old students in each country were collected both through the student tracking form and the student questionnaire (ST02). All study programmes were classified using ISCED (OECD, 1999). In the PISA international database, all national programmes are indicated in a variable (PROGN) where the first six digits refer to the national centre code and the last two digits to the national study programme code.

The following internationally comparable indices were derived from the data on study programmes:

- Programme level (ISCEDL) indicates whether students are (1) primary education level (ISCED 1); (2) lower-secondary education level; or (3) upper secondary education level.

- Programme designation (ISCEDD) indicates the designation of the study programme: (1) "A" (general programmes designed to give access to the next programme level); (2) "B" (programmes designed to give access to vocational studies at the next programme level); (3) "C" (programmes designed to give direct access to the labour market); or (4) "M" (modular programmes that combine any or all of these characteristics).

- Programme orientation (ISCEDO) indicates whether the programme's curricular content is (1) general; (2) pre-vocational; (3) vocational; or (4) modular programmes that combine any or all of these characteristics.

Occupational status of parents

Occupational data for both a student's father and a student's mother were obtained by asking open-ended questions in the student questionnaire (ST12, ST16). The responses were coded to four-digit ISCO codes (ILO, 1990) and then mapped to the SEI index of Ganzeboom et al. (1992). Higher scores of SEI indicate higher levels of occupational status. The following three indices are obtained:

- Mother's occupational status (OCOD1).

- Father's occupational status (OCOD2).

- The highest occupational level of parents (HISEI) corresponds to the higher SEI score of either parent or to the only available parent's SEI score.

[Part 1/1]

Table A1.1 **Levels of parental education converted into years of schooling**

	Completed ISCED level 1 (primary education)	Completed ISCED level 2 (lower secondary education)	Completed ISCED levels 3B or 3C (upper secondary education providing direct access to the labour market or to ISCED 5B programmes)	Completed ISCED level 3A (upper secondary education providing access to ISCED 5A and 5B programmes) and/ or ISCED level 4 (non-tertiary post-secondary)	Completed ISCED level 5A (university level tertiary education) or ISCED level 6 (advanced research programmes)	Completed ISCED level 5B (non-university tertiary education)
OECD						
Australia	6.0	10.0	11.0	12.0	15.0	14.0
Austria	4.0	9.0	12.0	12.5	17.0	15.0
Belgium[1]	6.0	9.0	12.0	12.0	17.0	15.0
Canada	6.0	9.0	12.0	12.0	17.0	15.0
Chile	6.0	8.0	12.0	12.0	17.0	16.0
Czech Republic	5.0	9.0	11.0	13.0	16.0	16.0
Denmark	7.0	10.0	13.0	13.0	18.0	16.0
Estonia	6.0	9.0	12.0	12.0	16.0	15.0
Finland	6.0	9.0	12.0	12.0	16.5	14.5
France	5.0	9.0	12.0	12.0	15.0	14.0
Germany	4.0	10.0	13.0	13.0	18.0	15.0
Greece	6.0	9.0	11.5	12.0	17.0	15.0
Hungary	4.0	8.0	10.5	12.0	16.5	13.5
Iceland	7.0	10.0	13.0	14.0	18.0	16.0
Ireland	6.0	9.0	12.0	12.0	16.0	14.0
Israel	6.0	9.0	12.0	12.0	15.0	15.0
Italy	5.0	8.0	12.0	13.0	17.0	16.0
Japan	6.0	9.0	12.0	12.0	16.0	14.0
Korea	6.0	9.0	12.0	12.0	16.0	14.0
Luxembourg	6.0	9.0	12.0	13.0	17.0	16.0
Mexico	6.0	9.0	12.0	12.0	16.0	14.0
Netherlands	6.0	10.0	13.0	12.0	16.0	15.0
New Zealand	5.5	10.0	11.0	12.0	15.0	14.0
Norway	6.0	9.0	12.0	12.0	16.0	14.0
Poland	a	8.0	11.0	12.0	16.0	15.0
Portugal	6.0	9.0	12.0	12.0	17.0	15.0
Slovak Republic[2]	4.0	9.0	12.0	13.0	18.0	16.0
Slovenia	4.0	8.0	11.0	12.0	16.0	15.0
Spain	5.0	8.0	10.0	12.0	16.5	13.0
Sweden	6.0	9.0	11.5	12.0	16.0	14.0
Switzerland	6.0	9.0	12.5	12.5	17.5	14.5
Turkey	5.0	8.0	11.0	11.0	15.0	13.0
United Kingdom (exclud. Scotland)	6.0	9.0	12.0	13.0	16.0	15.0
United Kingdom (Scotland)	7.0	9.0	11.0	13.0	17.0	15.0
United States	6.0	9.0	a	12.0	16.0	14.0
Partners						
Albania	6.0	9.0	12.0	12.0	16.0	16.0
Argentina	6.0	10.0	12.0	12.0	17.0	14.5
Azerbaijan	4.0	9.0	11.0	11.0	17.0	14.0
Brazil	4.0	8.0	11.0	11.0	16.0	14.5
Bulgaria	4.0	8.0	10.0	12.0	17.5	15.0
Colombia	5.0	9.0	11.0	11.0	15.5	14.0
Costa Rica	6.0	9.0	11.0	12.0	14.0	16.0
Croatia	4.0	8.0	11.0	12.0	17.0	15.0
Hong Kong-China	6.0	9.0	11.0	13.0	16.0	14.0
Indonesia	6.0	9.0	12.0	12.0	15.0	14.0
Jordan	6.0	10.0	12.0	12.0	16.0	14.5
Kazakhstan	4.0	9.0	11.5	12.5	15.0	14.0
Latvia	4.0	8.0	11.0	11.0	16.0	14.0
Liechtenstein	5.0	9.0	11.0	13.0	17.0	14.0
Lithuania	3.0	8.0	11.0	11.0	16.0	15.0
Macao-China	6.0	9.0	11.0	12.0	16.0	15.0
Malaysia	6.0	9.0	11.0	13.0	15.0	16.0
Montenegro	4.0	8.0	11.0	12.0	16.0	15.0
Peru	6.0	9.0	11.0	11.0	17.0	14.0
Qatar	6.0	9.0	12.0	12.0	16.0	15.0
Romania	4.0	8.0	11.5	12.5	16.0	14.0
Russian Federation	4.0	9.0	11.5	12.0	15.0	a
Serbia	4.0	8.0	11.0	12.0	17.0	14.5
Shanghai-China	6.0	9.0	12.0	12.0	16.0	15.0
Singapore	6.0	8.0	10.0	11.0	16.0	13.0
Chinese Taipei	6.0	9.0	12.0	12.0	16.0	14.0
Thailand	6.0	9.0	12.0	12.0	16.0	14.0
Tunisia	6.0	9.0	12.0	13.0	17.0	16.0
United Arab Emirates	5.0	9.0	12.0	12.0	16.0	15.0
Uruguay	6.0	9.0	12.0	12.0	17.0	15.0
Viet Nam	5.0	9.0	12.0	12.0	17.0	a

1. In Belgium the distinction between universities and other tertiary schools doesn't match the distinction between ISCED 5A and ISCED 5B.

2. In the Slovak Republic, university education (ISCED 5A) usually lasts five years and doctoral studies (ISCED 6) lasts three more years. Therefore, university graduates will have completed 18 years of study and graduates of doctoral programmes will have completed 21 years of study.

Source: OECD, PISA 2012 Database.

StatLink ⟐ http://dx.doi.org/10.1787/888932937073

Some of the analyses distinguish between four different categories of occupations by the major groups identified by the ISCO coding of the highest parental occupation: Elementary (ISCO 9), semi-skilled blue-collar (ISCO 6, 7 and 8), semi-skilled white-collar (ISCO 4 and 5), skilled (ISCO 1, 2 and 3). This classification follows the same methodology used in other OECD publications such as *Education at a Glance* (OECD, 2013b) and the *OECD Skills Outlook* (OECD, 2013c).[1]

Educational level of parents

The educational level of parents is classified using ISCED (OECD, 1999) based on students' responses in the student questionnaire (ST13, ST14, ST17 and ST18).

As in PISA 2000, 2003, 2006 and 2009, indices were constructed by selecting the highest level for each parent and then assigning them to the following categories: (0) None, (1) ISCED 1 (primary education), (2) ISCED 2 (lower secondary), (3) ISCED level 3B or 3C (vocational/pre-vocational upper secondary), (4) ISCED 3A (upper secondary) and/or ISCED 4 (non-tertiary post-secondary), (5) ISCED 5B (vocational tertiary), (6) ISCED 5A, 6 (theoretically oriented tertiary and post-graduate). The following three indices with these categories are developed:

- Mother's educational level (MISCED).
- Father's educational level (FISCED).
- Highest educational level of parents (HISCED) corresponds to the higher ISCED level of either parent.

Highest educational level of parents was also converted into the number of years of schooling (PARED). For the conversion of level of education into years of schooling, see Table A1.1.

Immigration and language background

Information on the country of birth of students and their parents is collected in a similar manner as in PISA 2000, PISA 2003, PISA 2006 and PISA 2009 by using nationally specific ISO coded variables. The ISO codes of the country of birth for students and their parents are available in the PISA international database (COBN_S, COBN_M, and COBN_F).

The *index on immigrant background* (IMMIG) has the following categories: (1) non-immigrant students (those students born in the country of assessment, or those with at least one parent born in that country; students who were born abroad with at least one parent born in the country of assessment are also classified as non-immigrant students), (2) second-generation students (those born in the country of assessment but whose parents were born in another country) and (3) first-generation students (those born outside the country of assessment and whose parents were also born in another country). Students with missing responses for either the student or for both parents, or for all three questions have been given missing values for this variable.

Students indicate the language they usually speak at home. The data are captured in nationally-specific language codes, which were recoded into variable LANGN with the following two values: (1) language at home is the same as the language of assessment, and (2) language at home is a different language than the language of assessment.

Relative grade

Data on the student's grade are obtained both from the student questionnaire (ST01) and from the student tracking form. As with all variables that are on both the tracking form and the questionnaire, inconsistencies between the two sources are reviewed and resolved during data-cleaning. In order to capture between-country variation, the relative grade index (GRADE) indicates whether students are at the modal grade in a country (value of 0), or whether they are below or above the modal grade level (+ x grades, - x grades).

The relationship between the grade and student performance was estimated through a multilevel model accounting for the following background variables: *i)* the *PISA index of economic, social and cultural status*; *ii)* the *PISA index of economic, social and cultural status* squared; *iii)* the school mean of the *PISA index of economic, social and cultural status*; *iv)* an indicator as to whether students were foreign-born first-generation students; *v)* the percentage of first-generation students in the school; and *vi)* students' gender.

Table A1.2 presents the results of the multilevel model. Column 1 in Table A1.2 estimates the score-point difference that is associated with one grade level (or school year). This difference can be estimated for the 32 OECD countries in which a sizeable number of 15-year-olds in the PISA samples were enrolled in at least two different grades. Since 15-year-olds cannot be assumed to be distributed at random across the grade levels, adjustments had to be made for the above-mentioned contextual factors that may relate to the assignment of students to the different grade levels. These adjustments are documented in Columns 2 to 7 of the table. While it is possible to estimate the typical performance difference among students in two adjacent grades net of the effects of selection and contextual factors, this difference cannot automatically be equated with the progress that students have made over the last school year but should be interpreted as a lower boundary of the progress achieved. This is not only because different students were assessed but also because the content of the PISA assessment was not expressly designed to match what students had learned in the preceding school year but more broadly to assess the cumulative outcome of learning in school up to age 15. For example, if the curriculum of the grades in which 15-year-olds are enrolled mainly includes material other than that assessed by PISA (which, in turn, may have been included in earlier school years) then the observed performance difference will underestimate student progress.

[Part 1/1]

Table A1.2 **A multilevel model to estimate grade effects in mathematics accounting for some background variables**

Multilevel model to estimate grade effects in mathematics performance[1], accounting for:

	grade		PISA index of economic, social and cultural status		PISA index of economic, social and cultural status squared		school mean of the PISA index of economic, social and cultural status		first-generation students		percentage of first-generation students at the school level		student is a female		intercept	
	Coeff	S.E.	Coeff	S.E.	Coeff	S.E.	Coeff	S.E.	Coeff	S.E.	Coeff	S.E.	Coeff	S.E.	Coeff	S.E.
OECD																
Australia	35	(2.3)	20	(1.4)	1	(1.1)	68	(7.1)	6	(3.9)	0	(0.2)	-12	(2.9)	481	(4.1)
Austria	36	(2.7)	11	(1.8)	-2	(1.6)	62	(8.2)	-9	(6.5)	0	(0.3)	-28	(3.3)	526	(5.8)
Belgium	43	(2.4)	4	(1.4)	1	(0.9)	83	(14.6)	-3	(4.7)	0	(0.6)	-15	(2.0)	528	(8.0)
Canada	44	(2.5)	19	(1.5)	3	(1.1)	29	(6.8)	6	(3.7)	0	(0.1)	-13	(1.9)	506	(4.0)
Chile	33	(1.8)	9	(1.5)	1	(0.7)	37	(3.6)	-2	(10.2)	-1	(1.1)	-29	(2.1)	469	(4.7)
Czech Republic	47	(3.5)	13	(2.0)	-3	(2.0)	111	(9.3)	1	(9.1)	-2	(0.9)	-24	(2.9)	502	(4.2)
Denmark	34	(3.9)	26	(2.2)	2	(1.6)	44	(8.0)	-34	(5.3)	0	(0.5)	-18	(2.2)	483	(5.4)
Estonia	41	(2.7)	16	(2.0)	2	(2.3)	25	(6.7)	-20	(17.0)	-4	(0.6)	-7	(2.5)	530	(3.3)
Finland	52	(4.4)	22	(2.1)	6	(1.9)	38	(13.2)	-38	(8.7)	-1	(0.8)	1	(3.1)	501	(7.7)
France	49	(4.8)	16	(2.3)	2	(1.7)	60	(9.5)	-6	(5.8)	0	(0.4)	-18	(2.7)	509	(6.3)
Germany	41	(2.1)	5	(1.5)	1	(1.4)	108	(8.3)	-20	(7.9)	-2	(0.7)	-28	(2.6)	487	(5.6)
Greece	41	(6.3)	17	(1.7)	1	(1.2)	29	(6.8)	8	(6.3)	0	(0.2)	-15	(2.6)	458	(4.5)
Hungary	32	(3.0)	7	(1.8)	3	(1.2)	64	(8.6)	42	(23.9)	-1	(0.5)	-27	(2.5)	494	(5.6)
Iceland	c	c	19	(3.2)	3	(1.9)	24	(9.4)	-31	(11.0)	-1	(0.5)	7	(3.5)	454	(8.4)
Ireland	18	(1.8)	24	(1.7)	1	(1.8)	60	(6.1)	10	(4.8)	0	(0.3)	-15	(3.0)	491	(4.4)
Israel	35	(4.2)	21	(2.6)	3	(1.5)	91	(14.8)	-12	(7.7)	1	(0.8)	-11	(4.2)	446	(9.7)
Italy	35	(1.9)	3	(0.9)	-1	(0.7)	54	(5.5)	-13	(3.4)	0	(0.1)	-23	(1.7)	495	(3.1)
Japan	c	c	3	(2.1)	1	(2.2)	156	(13.3)	c	c	c	c	-14	(3.2)	548	(5.5)
Korea	40	(14.6)	25	(4.7)	5	(3.0)	75	(20.8)	c	c	c	c	-10	(5.8)	555	(6.2)
Luxembourg	50	(2.3)	12	(1.8)	0	(0.8)	55	(5.4)	-7	(4.3)	0	(0.1)	-23	(2.7)	481	(4.7)
Mexico	26	(1.8)	8	(1.1)	2	(0.4)	17	(2.0)	-44	(6.0)	-1	(0.5)	-14	(1.5)	451	(3.1)
Netherlands	35	(2.6)	6	(1.6)	0	(1.1)	108	(22.6)	-14	(9.4)	-1	(1.1)	-19	(2.1)	480	(8.1)
New Zealand	35	(5.6)	31	(2.5)	-1	(1.8)	60	(8.4)	-1	(4.4)	0	(0.4)	-10	(3.2)	502	(9.6)
Norway	36	(17.8)	24	(2.5)	-2	(1.7)	29	(29.3)	-21	(7.8)	-1	(0.8)	3	(4.0)	474	(18.0)
Poland	80	(7.0)	26	(2.1)	-2	(1.8)	37	(6.9)	c	c	c	c	-5	(3.7)	539	(4.5)
Portugal	51	(2.9)	17	(1.5)	2	(0.9)	27	(4.0)	10	(7.1)	0	(0.5)	-17	(2.2)	540	(4.3)
Slovak Republic	42	(3.8)	21	(2.2)	-1	(1.4)	39	(7.5)	c	c	c	c	-20	(3.0)	530	(4.4)
Slovenia	24	(6.2)	1	(1.7)	4	(1.5)	72	(12.9)	-34	(6.7)	0	(0.8)	-25	(2.9)	484	(5.2)
Spain	64	(1.5)	14	(0.9)	2	(0.7)	21	(3.0)	-16	(3.0)	0	(0.2)	-24	(1.5)	531	(2.4)
Sweden	67	(6.7)	27	(2.1)	2	(1.4)	29	(7.8)	-21	(8.0)	0	(0.2)	3	(3.0)	461	(4.6)
Switzerland	52	(3.0)	20	(1.8)	-2	(1.2)	20	(7.9)	-29	(4.5)	-1	(0.3)	-20	(2.4)	528	(4.3)
Turkey	29	(2.9)	1	(2.4)	-1	(1.0)	47	(9.1)	c	c	c	c	-22	(2.7)	553	(17.0)
United Kingdom	23	(5.4)	20	(2.3)	3	(1.8)	88	(8.2)	4	(6.2)	0	(0.3)	-9	(3.2)	465	(4.9)
United States	41	(3.3)	21	(1.8)	7	(1.5)	51	(9.4)	9	(8.0)	1	(0.4)	-12	(3.5)	457	(6.5)
OECD average	41	(1.0)	16	(0.4)	1	(0.3)	56	(1.9)	-10	(1.6)	0	(0.1)	-15	(0.5)	498	(1.2)
Partners																
Albania	6	(3.9)	m	m	m	m	m	m	c	c	c	c	0	(4.1)	395	(4.0)
Argentina	31	(1.7)	9	(1.7)	2	(0.9)	38	(7.1)	1	(12.1)	-2	(1.0)	-18	(2.3)	446	(5.3)
Brazil	31	(1.2)	5	(2.1)	0	(0.7)	26	(4.3)	-49	(19.1)	0	(1.4)	-25	(1.8)	432	(7.3)
Bulgaria	30	(4.2)	12	(1.6)	1	(1.1)	25	(12.6)	c	c	c	c	-10	(2.6)	429	(8.0)
Colombia	25	(1.3)	7	(2.4)	1	(0.7)	26	(4.1)	c	c	c	c	-30	(2.0)	444	(5.7)
Costa Rica	26	(1.3)	8	(1.6)	1	(0.6)	25	(4.2)	-7	(8.0)	0	(0.8)	-29	(2.3)	447	(7.5)
Croatia	21	(2.8)	9	(1.9)	-1	(1.3)	71	(13.7)	-10	(7.6)	-1	(0.9)	-24	(2.9)	504	(8.1)
Cyprus*	39	(6.0)	18	(1.8)	2	(1.1)	61	(8.7)	-5	(5.5)	0	(0.2)	-14	(2.4)	439	(5.3)
Hong Kong-China	36	(2.2)	4	(2.6)	1	(1.2)	48	(14.5)	26	(4.3)	0	(1.0)	-22	(3.3)	613	(18.1)
Indonesia	17	(2.7)	6	(2.3)	1	(0.6)	27	(5.6)	c	c	c	c	-6	(1.9)	438	(10.9)
Jordan	37	(5.3)	12	(2.1)	2	(0.8)	22	(14.9)	6	(6.6)	2	(1.0)	9	(11.7)	393	(11.4)
Kazakhstan	16	(2.5)	14	(2.4)	0	(1.5)	36	(10.3)	-5	(5.0)	0	(0.3)	-4	(2.2)	459	(5.2)
Latvia	53	(4.0)	18	(1.9)	2	(1.8)	25	(5.9)	c	c	c	c	-7	(3.0)	510	(3.8)
Liechtenstein	40	(8.9)	8	(4.1)	-5	(2.7)	107	(25.4)	-10	(9.3)	-2	(1.0)	-27	(5.2)	543	(20.9)
Lithuania	32	(3.4)	17	(1.8)	-2	(1.5)	47	(6.9)	c	c	c	c	-7	(2.6)	483	(4.1)
Macao-China	50	(1.7)	7	(2.9)	2	(1.4)	8	(12.2)	24	(3.0)	-1	(0.5)	-26	(2.3)	544	(14.2)
Malaysia	79	(7.0)	15	(2.3)	2	(0.9)	53	(7.2)	c	c	c	c	2	(2.1)	466	(6.5)
Montenegro	9	(3.1)	13	(1.9)	1	(1.0)	76	(15.6)	16	(7.0)	-2	(1.1)	-11	(3.2)	437	(8.6)
Peru	25	(1.3)	8	(2.1)	1	(0.6)	36	(3.8)	c	c	c	c	-28	(2.5)	434	(6.4)
Qatar	28	(2.2)	6	(1.4)	1	(0.7)	26	(7.9)	32	(3.3)	1	(0.1)	2	(4.1)	310	(5.4)
Romania	-5	(5.6)	20	(2.3)	5	(1.0)	51	(9.6)	c	c	c	c	-7	(2.8)	475	(7.4)
Russian Federation	34	(2.5)	22	(2.2)	-1	(1.5)	21	(9.6)	-16	(6.4)	-1	(0.5)	-2	(2.6)	487	(4.7)
Serbia	33	(10.4)	8	(2.1)	-1	(1.7)	81	(11.8)	-11	(11.5)	0	(0.9)	-26	(3.9)	480	(8.0)
Shanghai-China	43	(5.5)	6	(2.4)	-3	(1.4)	52	(6.5)	-27	(16.1)	-1	(1.0)	-14	(2.6)	674	(7.6)
Singapore	44	(3.3)	21	(2.2)	0	(1.2)	81	(12.6)	29	(4.8)	-1	(0.3)	-1	(2.7)	608	(9.4)
Chinese Taipei	47	(13.2)	21	(3.8)	-6	(2.1)	114	(9.6)	c	c	c	c	3	(4.1)	638	(9.8)
Thailand	16	(3.9)	13	(3.0)	3	(1.1)	-22	(10.8)	c	c	c	c	2	(3.5)	418	(17.5)
Tunisia	36	(1.7)	7	(2.0)	2	(0.7)	12	(7.0)	c	c	c	c	-26	(1.7)	429	(11.5)
United Arab Emirates	33	(1.5)	9	(1.3)	3	(0.8)	23	(7.4)	31	(2.1)	1	(0.1)	-2	(4.7)	387	(4.1)
Uruguay	39	(2.1)	15	(2.0)	3	(0.9)	35	(4.3)	c	c	c	c	-19	(2.3)	480	(4.7)
Viet Nam	36	(4.8)	12	(4.1)	3	(1.1)	26	(15.1)	c	c	c	c	-22	(4.4)	550	(32.4)

Note: Values that are statistically significant are indicated in bold (see Annex A3).
1. Multilevel regression model (student and school levels): Mathematics performance is regressed on the variables of school policies and practices presented in this table.
* See notes at the beginning of this Annex.
StatLink ⟐⟐⟐ http://dx.doi.org/10.1787/888932937073

Learning time

Learning time in test language (LMINS) was computed by multiplying students' responses on the number of minutes on average in the test language class by number of test language class periods per week (ST69 and ST70). Comparable indices were computed for mathematics (MMINS) and science (SMINS).

Student-level scale indices

Instrumental motivation to learn mathematics

The *index of instrumental motivation to learn mathematics* (INSTMOT) was constructed using student responses over the extent they strongly agreed, agreed, disagreed or strongly disagreed to a series of statements in question (ST29) when asked to think about their views on mathematics: Making an effort in mathematics is worth because it will help me in the work that I want to do later on; Learning mathematics is worthwhile for me because it will improve my career <prospects, chances>; Mathematics is an important subject for me because I need it for what I want to study later on; I will learn many things in mathematics that will help me get a job.

For trends analyses, the PISA 2003 values of the *index of instrumental motivation to learn mathematics* were rescaled to be comparable to those in PISA 2012. As a result, values for the *index of instrumental motivation to learn mathematics* for PISA 2003 reported in this volume may differ from those reported in *Learning for Tomorrow's World: First Results from PISA 2003* (OECD, 2004).

Disciplinary climate

The *index of disciplinary climate* (DISCLIMA) was derived from students' reports on how often the followings happened in their lessons of the language of instruction (ST81): *i)* students don't listen to what the teacher says; *ii)* there is noise and disorder; *iii)* the teacher has to wait a long time for the students to <quieten down>; *iv)* students cannot work well; and *v)* students don't start working for a long time after the lesson begins. In this index higher values indicate a better disciplinary climate.

For trends analyses, the PISA 2003 values of the *index of disciplinary climate* were rescaled to be comparable to those in PISA 2012. As a result, values for the *index of disciplinary climate* for PISA 2003 reported in this volume may differ from those reported in *Learning for Tomorrow's World: First Results from PISA 2003* (OECD, 2004).

Teacher-student relations

The *index of teacher-student relations* (STUDREL) was derived from students' level of agreement with the following statements. The question asked (ST86) stated "Thinking about the teachers at your school: to what extent do you agree with the following statements": *i)* Students get along well with most of my teachers; *ii)* Most teachers are interested in students' well-being; *iii)* Most of my teachers really listen to what I have to say; *iv)* if I need extra help, I will receive it from my teachers; and *v)* Most of my teachers treat me fairly. Higher values on this index indicate positive teacher-student relations.

For trends analyses, the PISA 2003 values of the *index of student-teacher relations* were rescaled to be comparable to those in PISA 2012. As a result, values for the *index of student-teacher relations* for PISA 2003 reported in this volume may differ from those reported in *Learning for Tomorrow's World: First Results from PISA 2003* (OECD, 2004).

Economic, social and cultural status

The *PISA index of economic, social and cultural status* (ESCS) was derived from the following three indices: *highest occupational status of parents* (HISEI), *highest educational level of parents* in years of education according to ISCED (PARED), and *home possessions* (HOMEPOS). The *index of home possessions* (HOMEPOS) comprises all items on the indices of WEALTH, CULTPOSS and HEDRES, as well as books in the home recoded into a four-level categorical variable (0-10 books, 11-25 or 26-100 books, 101-200 or 201-500 books, more than 500 books).

The *PISA index of economic, social and cultural status* (ESCS) was derived from a principal component analysis of standardised variables (each variable has an OECD mean of zero and a standard deviation of one), taking the factor scores for the first principal component as measures of the *PISA index of economic, social and cultural status*.

Principal component analysis was also performed for each participating country or economy to determine to what extent the components of the index operate in similar ways across countries or economy. The analysis revealed that patterns of factor loading were very similar across countries, with all three components contributing to a similar extent to the index (for details on reliability and factor loadings, see the *PISA 2012 Technical Report* (OECD, forthcoming).

The imputation of components for students with missing data on one component was done on the basis of a regression on the other two variables, with an additional random error component. The final values on the *PISA index of economic, social and cultural status* (ESCS) for 2012 have an OECD mean of 0 and a standard deviation of one.

ESCS was computed for all students in the five cycles, and ESCS indices for trends analyses were obtained by applying the parameters used to derive standardised values in 2012 to the ESCS components for previous cycles. These values will therefore not be directly comparable to ESCS values in the databases for previous cycles, though the differences are not large for the 2006 and 2009 cycles. ESCS values in earlier cycles were computed using different algorithms, so for 2000 and 2003 the differences are larger.

Changes to the computation of socio-economic status for PISA 2012

While the computation of socio-economic status followed what had been done in previous cycles, PISA 2012 undertook an important upgrade with respect to the coding of parental occupation. Prior to PISA 2012, the 1988 International Standard Classification of Occupations (ISCO-88) was used for the coding of parental occupation. By 2012, however, ISCO-88 was almost 25 years old and it was no longer tenable to maintain its use as an occupational coding scheme.[2] It was therefore decided to use its replacement, ISCO-08, for occupational coding in PISA 2012.

The change from ISCO-88 to ISCO-08 required an update of the International Socio-Economic Index (ISEI) of occupation codes. PISA 2012 therefore used a modified quantification scheme for ISCO-08 (referred to as ISEI-08), as developed by Harry Ganzeboom (2010). ISEI-08 was constructed using a database of 198 500 men and women with valid education, occupation and (personal) incomes derived from the combined 2002-07 datasets of the International Social Survey Programme (ISSP) (Ganzeboom, 2010). The methodology used for this purpose was similar to the one employed in the construction of ISEI for ISCO-68 and ISCO-88 described in different publications (Ganzeboom, de Graff and Treiman, 1992; Ganzeboom and Treiman,1996; Ganzeboom and Treiman, 2003).[3]

The main differences with regard to the previous ISEI construction are the following:

- A new database was used which is more recent, larger and cross-nationally more diverse than the one used earlier.
- The new ISEI was constructed using data for women and men, while previously only men were used to estimate the scale. The data on income were corrected for hours worked to adjust the different prevalence of part-time work between men and women in many countries.

A range of validation activities accompanied the transition from ISCO-88/ISEI-88 to ISCO-08/ISEI-08, including a comparison of *i)* the distributions of ISEI-88 with ISEI-08 in terms of range, mean and standard deviations for both mothers' and fathers' occupations and *ii)* correlations between the two ISEI indicators and performance, again separately undertaken for mothers' and fathers' occupations.

For this cycle, in order to obtain trends for all cycles from 2000 to 2012, the computation of the indices WEALTH, HEDRES, CULTPOSS and HOMEPOS was based on data from all cycles from 2000 to 2012. HOMEPOS is of particular importance as it is used in the computation of ESCS. These were then standardised on 2012 so that the OECD mean is 0 and the standard deviation is 1. This means that the indices calculated on the previous cycle will be on the 2012 scale and thus not directly comparable to the indices in the database for the previously released cycles. To estimate item parameters for scaling, a calibration sample from all cycles was used, consisting of 500 students from all countries in the previous cycles, and 750 from 2012, as any particular student questionnaire item only occurs in two-thirds of the questionnaires in 2012.

The items used in the computation of the indices has changed to some extent from cycle to cycle, though cycles they have remained much the same from 2006 to 2012. The earlier cycles were are in general missing a few items that are present in the later cycles, but it was felt leaving out items only present in the later cycles would give too much weight to the earlier cycles. So a superset of all items (except country specific items) in the five cycles was used, and international item parameters were derived from this set.

The second step was to estimate WLEs for the indices, anchoring parameters on the international item set while estimating the country specific item parameters. This is the same procedure used in previous cycles.

Family wealth

The *index of family wealth* (WEALTH) is based on students' responses on whether they had the following at home: a room of their own, a link to the Internet, a dishwasher (treated as a country-specific item), a DVD player, and three other country-specific items (some items in ST26); and their responses on the number of cellular phones, televisions, computers, cars and the number of rooms with a bath or shower (ST27).

Home educational resources

The *index of home educational resources* (HEDRES) is based on the items measuring the existence of educational resources at home including a desk and a quiet place to study, a computer that students can use for schoolwork, educational software, books to help with students' school work, technical reference books and a dictionary (some items in ST26).

Cultural possessions

The *index of cultural possessions* (CULTPOSS) is based on students' responses to whether they had the following at home: classic literature, books of poetry and works of art (some items in ST26).

The rotated design of the student questionnaire

A major innovation in PISA 2012 is the rotated design of the student questionnaire. One of the main reasons for a rotated design, which had previously been implemented for the cognitive assessment, was to extend the content coverage of the student questionnaire. Table A1.3 provides an overview of the rotation design and content of questionnaire forms for the main survey.

Table A1.3 Student questionnaire rotation design

Form A	Common Question Set (all forms)	Question Set 1 – Mathematics Attitudes/ Problem Solving	Question Set 3 – Opportunity to Learn/ Learning Strategies
Form B	Common Question Set (all forms)	Question Set 2 – School Climate/Attitudes towards School/Anxiety	Question Set 1 – Mathematics Attitudes/ Problem Solving
Form C	Common Question Set (all forms)	Question Set 3 – Opportunity to Learn/ Learning Strategies	Question Set 2 – School Climate/Attitudes towards School/Anxiety

Note: For details regarding the questions in each question set, please refer to the *PISA 2012 Technical Report* (OECD, forthcoming).

The *PISA 2012 Technical Report* (OECD, forthcoming) provides all details regarding the rotated design of the student questionnaire in PISA 2012, including its implications in terms of *i)* proficiency estimates, *ii)* international reports and trends, *iii)* further analyses, *iv)* structure and documentation of the international database, and *v)* logistics. The rotated design has negligible implications for proficiency estimates and correlations of proficiency estimates with context constructs. The international database (available at *www.pisa.oecd.org*) includes all background variables for each student. The variables based on the questions that students answered reflect their responses; those that are based on questions that were not administered show a distinctive missing code. Rotation allows the estimation of a full co-variance matrix which means that all variables can be correlated with all other variables. It does not affect conclusions in terms of whether or not an effect would be considered significant in multilevel models.

School-level simple indices

School and class size

The *index of school size* (SCHSIZE) was derived by summing up the number of girls and boys at a school (SC07).

Student-teacher ratio

The *student-teacher ratio* (STRATIO) was obtained by dividing the school size by the total number of teachers (SC09). The number of part-time teachers was weighted by 0.5 and the number of full-time teachers was weighted by 1.0 in the computation of this index.

The *student-mathematics teacher ratio* (SMRATIO) was obtained by dividing the school size by the total number of mathematics teachers (SC10Q11 and SC10Q12). The number of part-time mathematics teachers was weighted by 0.5 and the number of full time mathematics teachers was weighted by 1.0 in the computation of this index.

School type

Schools are classified as either public or private, according to whether a private entity or a public agency has the ultimate power to make decisions concerning its affairs (SC01). This information is combined with SC02 which provides information on the percentage of total funding which comes from government sources to create the *index of school type* (SCHLTYPE). This index has three categories: (1) government-independent private schools controlled by a non-government organisation or with a governing board not selected by a government agency that receive less than 50% of their core funding from government agencies, (2) government-dependent private schools controlled by a non-government organisation or with a governing board not selected by a government agency that receive more than 50% of their core funding from government agencies, and (3) public schools controlled and managed by a public education authority or agency.

Availability of computers

The *index of computer availability* (RATCMP15) was derived from dividing the number of computers available for educational purposes available to students in the modal grade for 15-year-olds (SC11Q02) by the number of students in the modal grade for 15-year-olds (SC11Q01). The wording of the questions asking about computer availability changed between 2006 and 2009. Comparisons involving availability of computers are possible for 2012 data with 2009 data, but not with 2006 or earlier.

The *index of computers connected to the Internet* (COMPWEB) was derived from dividing the number of computers for educational purposes available to students in the modal grade for 15-year-olds that are connected to the web (SC11Q03) by the number of computers for educational purposes available to students in the modal grade for 15-year-olds (SC11Q02).

Quantity of teaching staff at school

The *proportion of fully certified teachers* (PROPCERT) was computed by dividing the number of fully certified teachers (SC09Q21 plus 0.5*SC09Q22) by the total number of teachers (SC09Q11 plus 0.5*SC09Q12). The proportion of teachers who have an ISCED 5A qualification (PROPQUAL) was calculated by dividing the number of these kind of teachers (SC09Q31 plus 0.5*SC09Q32) by the total number of teachers (SC09Q11 plus 0.5*SC09Q12). The proportion of mathematics teachers (PROPMATH) was computed by dividing the number of mathematics teachers (SC10Q11 plus 0.5*SC10Q12) by the total number of teachers (SC09Q11 plus 0.5*SC09Q12).

The proportion of mathematics teachers who have an ISCED 5A qualification (PROPMA5A) was computed by dividing the number of mathematics teachers who have an ISCED 5A qualification (SC10Q21 plus 0.5*SC10Q22) by the number of mathematics teachers (SC10Q11 plus 0.5*SC10Q12).

Although both PISA 2003 and PISA 2012 asked school principals about the school's teaching staff, the wording of the questions on the proportion of teachers with an ISCED 5A qualification changed, rendering comparisons impossible.

Academic selectivity

The *index of academic selectivity* (SCHSEL) was derived from school principals' responses on how frequently consideration was given to the following two factors when students were admitted to the school, based on a scale with response categories "never", "sometimes" and "always" (SC32Q02 and SC32Q03): students' record of academic performance (including placement tests); and recommendation of feeder schools. This index has the following three categories: (1) schools where these two factors are "never" considered for admission, (2) schools considering at least one of these two factors "sometimes" but neither factor "always", and (3) schools where at least one of these two factors is "always" considered for admission.

Although both PISA 2003 and PISA 2012 asked school principals about the school's criteria for admitting students, the wording of the questions changed, rendering comparisons impossible.

Ability grouping

The *index of ability grouping in mathematics classes* (ABGMATH) was derived from the two items of school principals' reports on whether their school organises mathematics instruction differently for student with different abilities "for all classes", "for some classes", or "not for any classes" (SC15Q01 for mathematics classes study similar content but at different levels and SC15Q02 for different classes study different content or sets of mathematics topics that have different levels of difficulty). This index has the following three categories: (1) no mathematic classes study different levels of difficulty or different content (i.e. "not for any classes" for both SC15Q01 and SC15Q02); (2) some mathematics classes study different levels of difficulty or different content (i.e. "for some classes" for either SC15Q01 or SC15Q02); (3) all mathematics classes study different levels of difficulty or different content (i.e. "for all classes" for either SC15Q01 or SC15Q02).

Extracurricular activities offered by school

The *index of mathematics extracurricular activities at school* (MACTIV) was derived from school principals' reports on whether their schools offered the following activities to students in the national modal grade for 15-year-olds in the academic year of the PISA assessment (SC16 and SC21 for the last one): *i)* mathematics club, ii) mathematics competition, *iii)* club with a focus on computers/Information, Communication Technology, and *iv)* additional mathematics lessons. This index was developed by summing up the number of activities that a school offers. For "additional mathematics lessons" (SC21), it is counted as one when school principals responded "enrichment mathematics only", "remedial mathematics only" or "without differentiation depending on the prior achievement level of the students"; and it is counted as two when school principals responded "both enrichment and remedial mathematics".

The *index of creative extracurricular activities at school* (CREACTIV) was derived from school principals' reports on whether their schools offered the following activities to students in the national modal grade for 15-year-olds in the academic year of the PISA assessment (SC16): *i)* band, orchestra or choir, *ii)* school play or school musical, and *iii)* art club or art activities. This index was developed by adding up the number of activities that a school offers.

Use of assessment

School principals were asked to report whether students' assessments are used for the following purposes (SC18): *i)* to inform parents about their child's progress; *ii)* to make decisions about students' retention or promotion; *iii)* to group students for instructional purposes; *iv)* to compare the school to district or national performance; *v)* to monitor the school's progress from year to year; *vi)* to make judgements about teachers' effectiveness; *vii)* to identify aspects of instruction or the curriculum that could be improved; and *viii)* to compare the school with other schools. The *index of use of assessment* (ASSESS) was derived from these eight items by adding up the number of "yes" in principals' responses to these questions.

School responsibility for resource allocation

School principals were asked to report whether "principals", "teachers", "school governing board", "regional or local education authority" or "national education authority" have a considerable responsibility for the following tasks (SC33): *i)* selecting teachers for hire; *ii)* firing teachers; *iii)* establishing teachers' starting salaries; *iv)* determining teachers' salary increases; *v)* formulating the school budget; and *vi)* deciding on budget allocations within the school. *The index of school responsibility for resource allocation* (RESPRES) was derived from these six items. The ratio of the number of responsibilities that "principals" and/or "teachers" have for these six items to the number of responsibilities that "regional or local education authority" and/or "national education authority" have for these six items was computed. Positive values on this index indicate relatively more responsibility for schools than local, regional or national education authority. This index has an OECD mean of 0 and a standard deviation of 1.

Although both PISA 2003 and PISA 2012 asked school principals about the school's responsibility for resource allocation, the wording of the questions changed, rendering comparisons impossible.

School responsibility for curriculum and assessment

School principals were asked to report whether "principals", "teachers", "school governing board", "regional or local education authority", or "national education authority" have a considerable responsibility for the following tasks (SC33): *i)* establishing student assessment policies; *ii)* choosing which textbooks are used; *iii)* determining course content; and *iv)* deciding which courses are offered. The *index of the school responsibility for curriculum and assessment* (RESPCUR) was derived from these four items. The ratio of the number of responsibilities that "principals" and/or "teachers" have for these four items to the number of responsibilities that "regional or local education authority" and/or "national education authority" have for these four items was computed. Positive values of this index indicate relatively more responsibility for schools than local, regional or national education authority. This index has an OECD mean of 0 and a standard deviation of 1.

Although both PISA 2003 and PISA 2012 asked school principals about the school's responsibility for admission and instruction policies, the wording of the questions changed, rendering comparisons impossible.

School-level scale indices

School principals' leadership

The *index of school management: framing and communicating the school's goals and curricular development* (LEADCOM) was derived from school principals' responses about the frequency with which they were involved in the following school affairs in the previous school year (SC34): *i)* use student performance results to develop the school's educational goals; *ii)* make sure that the professional development activities of teachers are in accordance with the teaching goals of the school; *iii)* ensure that teachers work according to the school's educational goals; and *iv)* discuss the school's academic goals with teachers at faculty meetings. The *index of school management: instructional leadership* (LEADINST) was derived from school principals' responses about the frequency with which they were involved in the following school affairs in the previous school year (SC34) *i)* promote teaching practices based on recent educational research, *ii)* praise teachers whose students are actively participating in learning, and *iii)* draw teachers' attention to the importance of pupils' development of critical can social capacities. The *index of school management: promoting instructional improvements and professional development* (LEADPD) was derived from school principals' responses about the frequency with which they were involved in the following school affairs in the previous school year (SC34): *i)* take the initiative to discuss matters, when a teacher has problems in his/her classroom; *ii)* pay attention to disruptive behaviour in classrooms; and *iii)* solve a problem together with a teacher, when the teacher brings up a classroom problem. The *index of school management: teacher participation* (LEADTCH) was derived from school principals' responses about the frequency with which they were involved in the following school affairs in the previous school year (SC34): *i)* provide staff with opportunities to participate in school decision-making; *ii)* engage teachers to help build a school culture of continuous improvement; and *iii)* ask teachers to participate in reviewing management practices. Higher values on these indices indicate greater involvement of school principals in school affairs.

Teacher shortage

The *index of teacher shortage* (TCSHORT) was derived from four items measuring school principals' perceptions of potential factors hindering instruction at their school (SC14). These factors are a lack of: *i)* qualified science teachers; *ii)* qualified mathematics teachers; *iii)* qualified <test language> teachers; and *iv)* qualified teachers of other subjects. Higher values on this index indicate school principals' reports of higher teacher shortage at a school.

For trends analyses, the PISA 2003 values of the *index of teacher shortage* were rescaled to be comparable to those in PISA 2012. As a result, values for the *index of teacher shortage* for PISA 2003 reported in this volume may differ from those reported in *Learning for Tomorrow's World: First Results from PISA 2003* (OECD, 2004).

Quality of school's educational resources

The *index of quality of school educational resources* (SCMATEDU) was derived from six items measuring school principals' perceptions of potential factors hindering instruction at their school (SC14). These factors are: *i)* shortage or inadequacy of science laboratory equipment; *ii)* shortage or inadequacy of instructional materials; *iii)* shortage or inadequacy of computers for instruction; *iv)* lack or inadequacy of Internet connectivity; *v)* shortage or inadequacy of computer software for instruction; and *vi)* shortage or inadequacy of library materials. As all items were inverted for scaling, higher values on this index indicate better quality of educational resources.

For trends analyses, the PISA 2003 values of the *index of quality of educational resources* were rescaled to be comparable to those in PISA 2012. As a result, values for the *index of quality educational resources* for PISA 2003 reported in this volume may differ from those reported in *Learning for Tomorrow's World: First Results from PISA 2003* (OECD, 2004). One of the questions included to compute the *index of quality of educational resources* in PISA 2012 ("lack or inadequacy of internet connection") was not included in the PISA 2003 questionnaire. Estimation of the PISA 2003 index treats this question as missing and, under the assumption that the relationship between the items remains unchanged with the inclusion of the new questions, the PISA 2003 and PISA 2012 values of the *index of quality of educational resources* are comparable after the rescaling.

Quality of schools' physical infrastructure

The *index of quality of physicals' infrastructure* (SCMATBUI) was derived from three items measuring school principals' perceptions of potential factors hindering instruction at their school (SC14). These factors are: *i)* shortage or inadequacy of school buildings and grounds; *ii)* shortage or inadequacy of heating/cooling and lighting systems; and *iii)* shortage or inadequacy of instructional space (e.g. classrooms). As all items were inverted for scaling, higher values on this index indicate better quality of physical infrastructure.

For trends analyses, the PISA 2003 values of the *index of quality of physical infrastructure* were rescaled to be comparable to those in PISA 2012. As a result, values for the *index of quality of physical infrastructure* for PISA 2003 reported in this volume may differ from those reported in *Learning for Tomorrow's World: First Results from PISA 2003* (OECD, 2004).

Teacher behaviour

The *index on teacher-related factors affecting school climate* (TEACCLIM) was derived from school principals' reports on the extent to which the learning of students was hindered by the following factors in their schools (SC22): *i)* students not being encouraged to achieve their full potential; *ii)* poor student-teacher relations; *iii)* teachers having to teach students of heterogeneous ability levels within the same class; *iv)* teachers having to teach students of diverse ethnic backgrounds (i.e. language, culture) within the same class; *v)* teachers' low expectations of students; *vi)* teachers not meeting individual students' needs; *vii)* teacher absenteeism; *viii)* staff resisting change; *ix)* teachers being too strict with students; *x)* teachers being late for classes; and *xi)* teachers not being well prepared for classes. As all items were inverted for scaling, higher values on this index indicate a positive teacher behaviour.

For trends analyses, the PISA 2003 values of the *index of teacher-related factors affecting school climate* were rescaled to be comparable to those in PISA 2012. As a result, values for the *index of teacher-related factors affecting school climate* for PISA 2003 reported in this volume may differ from those reported in *Learning for Tomorrow's World: First Results from PISA 2003* (OECD, 2004). Four of the questions included to compute the *index of teacher-related factors affecting school climate* in PISA 2012 ("teachers having to teach students of heterogeneous ability levels within the same class," "teachers having to teach students of diverse ethnic backgrounds (i.e. language, culture) within the same class," "teachers being late for classes," and "teachers not being well prepared for classes") were not included in the PISA 2003 questionnaire. Estimation of the PISA 2003 index treats these indices as missing and, under the assumption that the relationship between the items remains unchanged with the inclusion of the new questions, the PISA 2003 and PISA 2012 values on the *index of teacher-related factors affecting school climate* are comparable after the rescaling.

Student behaviour

The *index of student-related factors affecting school climate* (STUDCLIM) was derived from school principals' reports on the extent to which the learning of students was hindered by the following factors in their schools (SC22): *i)* student truancy; *ii)* students skipping classes; *iii)* students arriving late for school; *iv)* students not attending compulsory school events (e.g. sports day) or excursions, *v)* students lacking respect for teachers; *vi)* disruption of classes by students; *vii)* student use of alcohol or illegal drugs; and *viii)* students intimidating or bullying other students. As all items were inverted for scaling, higher values on this index indicate a positive student behaviour.

For trends analyses, the PISA 2003 values of the *index of student-related factors affecting school climate* were rescaled to be comparable to those in PISA 2012. As a result, values for the *index of student-related factors affecting school climate* for PISA 2003 reported in this volume may differ from those reported in *Learning for Tomorrow's World: First Results from PISA 2003* (OECD, 2004). Two of the questions included to compute the *index of student-related factors affecting school climate* in PISA 2012 ("students arriving late for school," and "students not attending compulsory school events (e.g. sports day) or excursions") were not included in the PISA 2003 questionnaire. Estimation of the PISA 2003 index treats these questions as missing and, under the assumption that the relationship between the items remains unchanged with the inclusion of the new questions, the PISA 2003 and PISA 2012 values on the *index of student-related factors affecting school climate* are comparable after the rescaling.

Teacher morale

The *index of teacher morale* (TCMORALE) was derived from school principals' reports on the extent to which they agree with the following statements considering teachers in their schools (SC26): *i)* the morale of teachers in this school is high; *ii)* teachers work with enthusiasm; *iii)* teachers take pride in this school; and *iv)* teachers value academic achievement. As all items were inverted for scaling, higher values on this index indicate more positive teacher morale.

For trends analyses, the PISA 2003 values of the *index of teacher morale* were rescaled to be comparable to those in PISA 2012. As a result, values for the *index of teacher morale* for PISA 2003 reported in this volume may differ from those reported in *Learning for Tomorrow's World: First Results from PISA 2003* (OECD, 2004).

Questions used for the construction of the three opportunity to learn indices

Six questions were used from the Student Questionnaire to cover both the content and the time aspects of the opportunity to learn. These questions are shown below.

Question 1

How often have you encountered the following types of mathematics tasks during your time at school?

(Please tick only one box on each row.)

		Frequently	Sometimes	Rarely	Never
a)	Working out from a <train timetable> how long it would take to get from one place to another.	☐1	☐2	☐3	☐4
b)	Calculating how much more expensive a computer would be after adding tax.	☐1	☐2	☐3	☐4
c)	Calculating how many square metres of tiles you need to cover a floor.	☐1	☐2	☐3	☐4
d)	Understanding scientific tables presented in an article.	☐1	☐2	☐3	☐4
e)	Solving an equation like: $6x^2 + 5 = 29$	☐1	☐2	☐3	☐4
f)	Finding the actual distance between two places on a map with a 1:10 000 scale.	☐1	☐2	☐3	☐4
g)	Solving an equation like $2(x + 3) = (x + 3)(x - 3)$	☐1	☐2	☐3	☐4
h)	Calculating the power consumption of an electronic appliance per week.	☐1	☐2	☐3	☐4
i)	Solving an equation like: $3x + 5 = 17$	☐1	☐2	☐3	☐4

Question 2

Thinking about mathematical concepts: how familiar are you with the following terms?

(Please tick only one box in each row.)

		Never heard of it	Heard of it once or twice	Heard of it a few times	Heard of it often	Know it well, understand the concept
a)	Exponential Function	☐1	☐2	☐3	☐4	☐5
b)	Divisor	☐1	☐2	☐3	☐4	☐5
c)	Quadratic Function	☐1	☐2	☐3	☐4	☐5
d)	Linear Equation	☐1	☐2	☐3	☐4	☐5
e)	Vectors	☐1	☐2	☐3	☐4	☐5
f)	Complex Number	☐1	☐2	☐3	☐4	☐5
g)	Rational Number	☐1	☐2	☐3	☐4	☐5
h)	Radicals	☐1	☐2	☐3	☐4	☐5
i)	Polygon	☐1	☐2	☐3	☐4	☐5
j)	Congruent Figure	☐1	☐2	☐3	☐4	☐5
k)	Cosine	☐1	☐2	☐3	☐4	☐5
l)	Arithmetic Mean	☐1	☐2	☐3	☐4	☐5
m)	Probability	☐1	☐2	☐3	☐4	☐5

The next four questions are about students' experience with different kinds of mathematics problems at school. They include some descriptions of problems and dark blue-coloured boxes, each containing a mathematics problem. The students had to read each problem but did not have to solve it.

Question 3

In the box is a series of problems. Each requires you to understand a problem written in text and perform the appropriate calculations. Usually the problem talks about practical situations, but the numbers and people and places mentioned are made up. All the information you need is given. Here are two examples:

> 1. <Ann> is two years older than <Betty> and <Betty> is four times as old as <Sam>. When <Betty> is 30, how old is <Sam>?
> 2. Mr <Smith> bought a television and a bed. The television cost <$625> but he got a 10% discount. The bed cost <$200>. He paid <$20> for delivery. How much money did Mr <Smith> spend?

We want to know about your experience with these types of word problems at school. Do not solve them!

(Please tick only one box in each row.)

		Frequently	Sometimes	Rarely	Never
a)	How often have you encountered these types of problems in your **mathematics lessons**?	☐1	☐2	☐3	☐4
b)	How often have you encountered these types of problems in the **tests you have taken at school**?	☐1	☐2	☐3	☐4

Question 4

Below are examples of another set of mathematical skills.

1) Solve 2x + 3 = 7.
2) Find the volume of a box with sides 3m, 4m and 5m.

We want to know about your experience with these types of problems at school. Do not solve them!

(Please tick only one box in each row.)

		Frequently	Sometimes	Rarely	Never
a)	How often have you encountered these types of problems in your **mathematics lessons**?	☐1	☐2	☐3	☐4
b)	How often have you encountered these types of problems in the **tests you have taken at school?**	☐1	☐2	☐3	☐4

Question 5

In the next type of problem, you have to use mathematical knowledge and draw conclusions. There is no practical application provided. Here are two examples.

1) Here you need to use geometrical theorems:

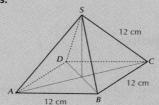

Determine the height of the pyramid.

2) Here you have to know what a prime number is:

If n is any number: can (n+1)² be a prime number?

We want to know about your experience with these types of problems at school. Do not solve them!

(Please tick only one box in each row.)

		Frequently	Sometimes	Rarely	Never
a)	How often have you encountered these types of problems in your **mathematics lessons**?	☐1	☐2	☐3	☐4
b)	How often have you encountered these types of problems in the **tests you have taken at school?**	☐1	☐2	☐3	☐4

Question 6

In this type of problem, you have to apply suitable mathematical knowledge to find a useful answer to a problem that arises in everyday life or work. The data and information are about real situations. Here are two examples.

Example 1

A TV reporter says "This graph shows that there is a huge increase in the number of robberies from 1998 to 1999."

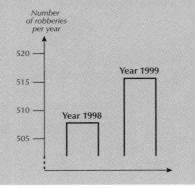

...

Example 2

For years the relationship between a person's recommended maximum heart rate and the person's age was described by the following formula:

Recommended maximum heart rate = 220 – age

Recent research showed that this formula should be modified slightly. The new formula is as follows:

Recommended maximum heart rate = 208 – (0.7 × age)

From which age onwards does the recommended maximum heart rate increase as a result of the introduction of the new formula? Show your work.

We want to know about your experience with these types of problems at school. Do not solve them!

(Please check only one box in each row.)

		Frequently	Sometimes	Rarely		Never
a)	How often have you encountered these types of problems in your **mathematics lessons**?	☐1	☐2	☐3		☐4
b)	How often have you encountered these types of problems in the **tests you have taken at school?**	☐1	☐2	☐3		☐4

The three opportunity to learn indices

From these questions, three indices were constructed:

- **The index of exposure to word problems**
  This index was coded using the frequency choices for the word-problem type of task (Question 3) as follows: frequently = 3, sometimes and rarely = 1, and never = 0.

- **The index of exposure to applied mathematics**
  This index was constructed as the mean of the applied tasks involving both the mathematics contexts (Question 5) and the real-world contexts (Question 6). Each was separately scaled as: frequently = 3, sometimes = 2, rarely =1, and never = 0.

- **The index of exposure to formal mathematics**
  This index was created as the average of three scales.

  - Two separate scales were constructed using the item asking for the degree of the student's familiarity with 7 of the 13 mathematics content areas (Question 2). The five response categories reflecting the degree to which they had heard of the topic were scaled 0 to 4 with 0 representing "never heard of it" 4 representing they "knew it well". The frequency codes for the three topics – exponential functions, quadratic functions, and linear equations – were averaged to define familiarity with algebra. Similarly, the average of four topics defined a geometry scale, including vectors, polygons, congruent figures, and cosines.

  - The third scale was derived from the item where students indicated how often they had been confronted with problems defined as formal mathematics (Question 4). The frequency categories were coded as "frequently", "sometimes", and "rarely" equalling 1 and "never" equal to 0, resulting in a dichotomous variable. The algebra, geometry and formal mathematics tasks were averaged to form the index "formal mathematics", which ranged in values from 0 to 3, similar to the other three indices.

Notes

1. Note that for ISCO coding 0 "Arm forces", the following recoding was followed: "Officers" were coded as "Managers" (ISCO 1), and "Other armed forces occupations" (drivers, gunners, seaman, generic armed forces) as "Plant and Machine operators" (ISCO 8). In addition, all answers starting with "97" (housewives, students, and "vague occupations") were coded into missing.

2. The update from ISCO-88 to ISCO-08 mainly involved *i)* more adequate categories for IT-related occupations, *ii)* distinction of military ranks and *iii)* a revision of the categories classifying different managers.

3. Information on ISCO08 and ISEI08 is included from *http://www.ilo.org/public/english/bureau/stat/isco/index.htm* and *http://home.fsw.vu.nl/hbg.ganzeboom/isco08*.

References

Ganzeboom, H.B.G. (2010), "A new international socio-economic index [ISEI] of occupational status for the International Standard Classification of Occupation 2008 [ISCO-08] constructed with data from the ISSP 2002-2007; with an analysis of quality of occupational measurement in ISSP ", paper presented at Annual Conference of International Social Survey Programme, Lisbon, 1 May 2010.

Ganzeboom, H.B.G. and **D.J. Treiman** (2003), "Three Internationally Standardised Measures for Comparative Research on Occupational Status ", in Jürgen H.P. Hoffmeyer-Zlotnik and Christof Wolf (eds.), *Advances in Cross-National Comparison: A European Working Book for Demographic and Socio-Economic Variables,* Kluwer Academic Press, New York.

Ganzeboom, H.B.G. and **D.J. Treiman** (1996), "Internationally Comparable Measures of Occupational Status for the 1988 International Standard Classification of Occupations", *Social Science Research*, Vol. 25, pp. 201-39.

Ganzeboom, H.B.G., P. de Graaf and **D.J. Treiman** (1992), "A Standard International Socio-Economic Index of Occupational Status", *Social Science Research,* Vol. 21, Issue 1, pp. 1-56.

Ganzeboom, H.B.G., R. Luijkx and **D.J. Treiman** (1989), "InterGenerational Class Mobility in Comparative Perspective", *Research in Social Stratification and Mobility*, Vol. 8, pp. 3-79.

ILO (1990), *ISCO-88: International Standard Classification of Occupations,* International Labour Office, Geneva.

OECD (forthcoming), *PISA 2012 Technical Report,* OECD Publishing.

OECD (2013a), *PISA 2012 Assessment and Analytical Framework: Mathematics, Reading, Science, Problem Solving and Financial Literacy,* PISA, OECD Publishing.
http://dx.doi.org/10.1787/9789264190511-en

OECD (2013b), *Education at a Glance 2013: OECD Indicators,* OECD Publishing.
http://dx.doi.org/10.1787/eag-2013-en

OECD (2013c), *OECD Skills Outlook 2013: First Results from the Survey of Adult Skills,* OECD Publishing.
http://dx.doi.org/10.1787/9789264204256-en

OECD (2004), *Learning for Tomorrow's World: First Results from PISA 2003*, PISA, OECD Publishing.
http://dx.doi.org/10.1787/9789264006416-en

OECD (1999), *Classifying Educational Programmes: Manual for ISCED-97 Implemention in OECD Countries*, OECD Publishing.
www.oecd.org/education/skills-beyond-school/1962350.pdf

Warm, T.A. (1989), "Weighted likelihood estimation of ability in item response theory", Psychometrika, Volume 54, Issue 3, pp. 427-450.
http://dx.doi.org/10.1007/BF02294627

ANNEX A2

THE PISA TARGET POPULATION, THE PISA SAMPLES AND THE DEFINITION OF SCHOOLS

Definition of the PISA target population

PISA 2012 provides an assessment of the cumulative yield of education and learning at a point at which most young adults are still enrolled in initial education.

A major challenge for an international survey is to ensure that international comparability of national target populations is guaranteed in such a venture.

Differences between countries in the nature and extent of pre-primary education and care, the age of entry into formal schooling and the institutional structure of education systems do not allow the definition of internationally comparable grade levels of schooling. Consequently, international comparisons of education performance typically define their populations with reference to a target age group. Some previous international assessments have defined their target population on the basis of the grade level that provides maximum coverage of a particular age cohort. A disadvantage of this approach is that slight variations in the age distribution of students across grade levels often lead to the selection of different target grades in different countries, or between education systems within countries, raising serious questions about the comparability of results across, and at times within, countries. In addition, because not all students of the desired age are usually represented in grade-based samples, there may be a more serious potential bias in the results if the unrepresented students are typically enrolled in the next higher grade in some countries and the next lower grade in others. This would exclude students with potentially higher levels of performance in the former countries and students with potentially lower levels of performance in the latter.

In order to address this problem, PISA uses an age-based definition for its target population, i.e. a definition that is not tied to the institutional structures of national education systems. PISA assesses students who were aged between 15 years and 3 (complete) months and 16 years and 2 (complete) months at the beginning of the assessment period, plus or minus a 1 month allowable variation, and who were enrolled in an educational institution with Grade 7 or higher, regardless of the grade levels or type of institution in which they were enrolled, and regardless of whether they were in full-time or part-time education. Educational institutions are generally referred to as schools in this publication, although some educational institutions (in particular, some types of vocational education establishments) may not be termed schools in certain countries. As expected from this definition, the average age of students across OECD countries was 15 years and 9 months. The range in country means was 2 months and 5 days (0.18 years), from the minimum country mean of 15 years and 8 months to the maximum country mean of 15 years and 10 months.

Given this definition of population, PISA makes statements about the knowledge and skills of a group of individuals who were born within a comparable reference period, but who may have undergone different educational experiences both in and outside of schools. In PISA, these knowledge and skills are referred to as the yield of education at an age that is common across countries. Depending on countries' policies on school entry, selection and promotion, these students may be distributed over a narrower or a wider range of grades across different education systems, tracks or streams. It is important to consider these differences when comparing PISA results across countries, as observed differences between students at age 15 may no longer appear as students' educational experiences converge later on.

If a country's scale scores in reading, scientific or mathematical literacy are significantly higher than those in another country, it cannot automatically be inferred that the schools or particular parts of the education system in the first country are more effective than those in the second. However, one can legitimately conclude that the cumulative impact of learning experiences in the first country, starting in early childhood and up to the age of 15, and embracing experiences both in school, home and beyond, have resulted in higher outcomes in the literacy domains that PISA measures.

The PISA target population did not include residents attending schools in a foreign country. It does, however, include foreign nationals attending schools in the country of assessment.

To accommodate countries that desired grade-based results for the purpose of national analyses, PISA 2012 provided a sampling option to supplement age-based sampling with grade-based sampling.

Population coverage

All countries attempted to maximise the coverage of 15-year-olds enrolled in education in their national samples, including students enrolled in special educational institutions. As a result, PISA 2012 reached standards of population coverage that are unprecedented in international surveys of this kind.

The sampling standards used in PISA permitted countries to exclude up to a total of 5% of the relevant population either by excluding schools or by excluding students within schools. All but eight countries, Luxembourg (8.40%), Canada (6.38%), Denmark (6.18%), Norway (6.11%), Estonia (5.80%), Sweden (5.44%), the United Kingdom (5.43%) and the United States (5.35%), achieved this standard, and in 30 countries and economies, the overall exclusion rate was less than 2%. When language exclusions were accounted for (i.e. removed from the overall exclusion rate), Norway, Sweden, the United Kingdom and the United States no longer had an exclusion rate greater than 5%. For details, see *www.pisa.oecd.org*.

Exclusions within the above limits include:

- At the school level: *i)* schools that were geographically inaccessible or where the administration of the PISA assessment was not considered feasible; and *ii)* schools that provided teaching only for students in the categories defined under "within-school exclusions", such as schools for the blind. The percentage of 15-year-olds enrolled in such schools had to be less than 2.5% of the nationally desired target population [0.5% maximum for *i)* and 2% maximum for *ii)*]. The magnitude, nature and justification of school-level exclusions are documented in the *PISA 2012 Technical Report* (OECD, forthcoming).

- At the student level: *i)* students with an intellectual disability; *ii)* students with a functional disability; *iii)* students with limited assessment language proficiency; *iv)* other – a category defined by the national centres and approved by the international centre; and *v)* students taught in a language of instruction for the main domain for which no materials were available. Students could not be excluded solely because of low proficiency or common discipline problems. The percentage of 15-year-olds excluded within schools had to be less than 2.5% of the nationally desired target population.

Table A2.1 describes the target population of the countries participating in PISA 2012. Further information on the target population and the implementation of PISA sampling standards can be found in the *PISA 2012 Technical Report* (OECD, forthcoming).

- **Column 1** shows the *total number of 15-year-olds* according to the most recent available information, which in most countries meant the year 2011 as the year before the assessment.

- **Column 2** shows the number of 15-year-olds enrolled in schools in Grade 7 or above (as defined above), which is referred to as the *eligible population*.

- **Column 3** shows the *national desired target population*. Countries were allowed to exclude up to 0.5% of students a priori from the eligible population, essentially for practical reasons. The following a priori exclusions exceed this limit but were agreed with the PISA Consortium: Belgium excluded 0.23% of its population for a particular type of student educated while working; Canada excluded 1.14% of its population from Territories and Aboriginal reserves; Chile excluded 0.04% of its students who live in Easter Island, Juan Fernandez Archipelago and Antarctica; Indonesia excluded 1.55% of its students from two provinces because of operational reasons; Ireland excluded 0.05% of its students in three island schools off the west coast; Latvia excluded 0.08% of its students in distance learning schools; and Serbia excluded 2.11% of its students taught in Serbian in Kosovo.

- **Column 4** shows the *number of students enrolled in schools that were excluded from the national desired target population* either from the sampling frame or later in the field during data collection.

- **Column 5** shows the *size of the national desired target population after subtracting the students enrolled in excluded schools*. This is obtained by subtracting Column 4 from Column 3.

- **Column 6** shows the *percentage of students enrolled in excluded schools*. This is obtained by dividing Column 4 by Column 3 and multiplying by 100.

- **Column 7** shows the *number of students participating in PISA 2012*. Note that in some cases this number does not account for 15-year-olds assessed as part of additional national options.

- **Column 8** shows the *weighted number of participating students*, i.e. the number of students in the nationally defined target population that the PISA sample represents.

- Each country attempted to maximise the coverage of the PISA target population within the sampled schools. In the case of each sampled school, all eligible students, namely those 15 years of age, regardless of grade, were first listed. Sampled students who were to be excluded had still to be included in the sampling documentation, and a list drawn up stating the reason for their exclusion. **Column 9** indicates the *total number of excluded students*, which is further described and classified into specific categories in Table A2.2.

- **Column 10** indicates the *weighted number of excluded students*, i.e. the overall number of students in the nationally defined target population represented by the number of students excluded from the sample, which is also described and classified by exclusion categories in Table A2.2. Excluded students were excluded based on five categories: *i)* students with an intellectual disability – the student has a mental or emotional disability and is cognitively delayed such that he/she cannot perform in the PISA testing situation; *ii)* students with a functional disability – the student has a moderate to severe permanent physical disability such that he/she cannot perform in the PISA testing situation; *iii)* students with a limited assessment language proficiency – the student is unable to read or speak any of the languages of the assessment in the country and would be unable to overcome the language barrier in the testing situation (typically a student who has received less than one year of instruction in the languages of the assessment may be excluded); *iv)* other – a category defined by the national centres and approved by the international centre; and *v)* students taught in a language of instruction for the main domain for which no materials were available.

- **Column 11** shows the *percentage of students excluded within schools*. This is calculated as the weighted number of excluded students (Column 10), divided by the weighted number of excluded and participating students (Column 8 plus Column 10), then multiplied by 100.

- **Column 12** shows the *overall exclusion rate*, which represents the weighted percentage of the national desired target population excluded from PISA either through school-level exclusions or through the exclusion of students within schools. It is calculated as the school-level exclusion rate (Column 6 divided by 100) plus within-school exclusion rate (Column 11 divided by 100) multiplied by 1 minus the school-level exclusion rate (Column 6 divided by 100). This result is then multiplied by 100.

[Part 1/2]

Table A2.1 **PISA target populations and samples**

	Population and sample information							
	Total population of 15-year-olds	Total enrolled population of 15-year-olds at Grade 7 or above	Total in national desired target population	Total school-level exclusions	Total in national desired target population after all school exclusions and before within-school exclusions	School-level exclusion rate (%)	Number of participating students	Weighted number of participating students
	(1)	(2)	(3)	(4)	(5)	(6)	(7)	(8)
Australia	291 967	288 159	288 159	5 702	282 457	1.98	17 774	250 779
Austria	93 537	89 073	89 073	106	88 967	0.12	4 756	82 242
Belgium	123 469	121 493	121 209	1 324	119 885	1.09	9 690	117 912
Canada	417 873	409 453	404 767	2 936	401 831	0.73	21 548	348 070
Chile	274 803	252 733	252 625	2 687	249 938	1.06	6 857	229 199
Czech Republic	96 946	93 214	93 214	1 577	91 637	1.69	6 535	82 101
Denmark	72 310	70 854	70 854	1 965	68 889	2.77	7 481	65 642
Estonia	12 649	12 438	12 438	442	11 996	3.55	5 867	11 634
Finland	62 523	62 195	62 195	523	61 672	0.84	8 829	60 047
France	792 983	755 447	755 447	27 403	728 044	3.63	5 682	701 399
Germany	798 136	798 136	798 136	10 914	787 222	1.37	5 001	756 907
Greece	110 521	105 096	105 096	1 364	103 732	1.30	5 125	96 640
Hungary	111 761	108 816	108 816	1 725	107 091	1.59	4 810	91 179
Iceland	4 505	4 491	4 491	10	4 481	0.22	3 508	4 169
Ireland	59 296	57 979	57 952	0	57 952	0.00	5 016	54 010
Israel	118 953	113 278	113 278	2 784	110 494	2.46	6 061	107 745
Italy	605 490	566 973	566 973	8 498	558 475	1.50	38 142	521 288
Japan	1 241 786	1 214 756	1 214 756	26 099	1 188 657	2.15	6 351	128 179
Korea	687 104	672 101	672 101	3 053	669 048	0.45	5 033	603 632
Luxembourg	6 187	6 082	6 082	151	5 931	2.48	5 260	5 523
Mexico	2 114 745	1 472 875	1 472 875	7 307	1 465 568	0.50	33 806	326 025
Netherlands	194 000	193 190	193 190	7 546	185 644	3.91	4 460	196 262
New Zealand	60 940	59 118	59 118	579	58 539	0.98	5 248	53 414
Norway	64 917	64 777	64 777	750	64 027	1.16	4 686	59 432
Poland	425 597	410 700	410 700	6 900	403 800	1.68	5 662	379 275
Portugal	108 728	127 537	127 537	0	127 537	0.00	5 722	96 034
Slovak Republic	59 723	59 367	59 367	1 480	57 887	2.49	5 737	54 486
Slovenia	19 471	18 935	18 935	115	18 820	0.61	7 229	18 303
Spain	423 444	404 374	404 374	2 031	402 343	0.50	25 335	374 266
Sweden	102 087	102 027	102 027	1 705	100 322	1.67	4 739	94 988
Switzerland	87 200	85 239	85 239	2 479	82 760	2.91	11 234	79 679
Turkey	1 266 638	965 736	965 736	10 387	955 349	1.08	4 848	866 681
United Kingdom	738 066	745 581	745 581	19 820	725 761	2.66	12 659	688 236
United States	3 985 714	4 074 457	4 074 457	41 142	4 033 315	1.01	6 111	3 536 153
Albania	76 910	50 157	50 157	56	50 101	0.11	4 743	42 466
Argentina	684 879	637 603	637 603	3 995	633 608	0.63	5 908	545 942
Brazil	3 574 928	2 786 064	2 786 064	34 932	2 751 132	1.25	20 091	2 470 804
Bulgaria	70 188	59 684	59 684	1 437	58 247	2.41	5 282	54 255
Colombia	889 729	620 422	620 422	4	620 418	0.00	11 173	560 805
Costa Rica	81 489	64 326	64 326	0	64 326	0.00	4 602	40 384
Croatia	48 155	46 550	46 550	417	46 133	0.90	6 153	45 502
Cyprus*	9 956	9 956	9 955	128	9 827	1.29	5 078	9 650
Hong Kong-China	84 200	77 864	77 864	813	77 051	1.04	4 670	70 636
Indonesia	4 174 217	3 599 844	3 544 028	8 039	3 535 989	0.23	5 622	2 645 155
Jordan	129 492	125 333	125 333	141	125 192	0.11	7 038	111 098
Kazakhstan	258 716	247 048	247 048	7 374	239 674	2.98	5 808	208 411
Latvia	18 789	18 389	18 375	655	17 720	3.56	5 276	16 054
Liechtenstein	417	383	383	1	382	0.26	293	314
Lithuania	38 524	35 567	35 567	526	35 041	1.48	4 618	33 042
Macao-China	6 600	5 416	5 416	6	5 410	0.11	5 335	5 366
Malaysia	544 302	457 999	457 999	225	457 774	0.05	5 197	432 080
Montenegro	8 600	8 600	8 600	18	8 582	0.21	4 744	7 714
Peru	584 294	508 969	508 969	263	508 706	0.05	6 035	419 945
Qatar	11 667	11 532	11 532	202	11 330	1.75	10 966	11 003
Romania	146 243	146 243	146 243	5 091	141 152	3.48	5 074	140 915
Russian Federation	1 272 632	1 268 814	1 268 814	17 800	1 251 014	1.40	6 418	1 172 539
Serbia	80 089	75 870	74 212	1 987	72 285	2.67	4 684	67 934
Shanghai-China	108 056	90 796	90 796	1 252	89 544	1.38	6 374	85 127
Singapore	53 637	52 163	52 163	293	51 870	0.56	5 546	51 088
Chinese Taipei	328 356	328 336	328 336	1 747	326 589	0.53	6 046	292 542
Thailand	982 080	784 897	784 897	9 123	775 774	1.16	6 606	703 012
Tunisia	132 313	132 313	132 313	169	132 144	0.13	4 407	120 784
United Arab Emirates	48 824	48 446	48 446	971	47 475	2.00	11 500	40 612
Uruguay	54 638	46 442	46 442	14	46 428	0.03	5 315	39 771
Viet Nam	1 717 996	1 091 462	1 091 462	7 729	1 083 733	0.71	4 959	956 517

Notes: For a full explanation of the details in this table please refer to the *PISA 2012 Technical Report* (OECD, forthcoming). The figure for total national population of 15-year-olds enrolled in Column 2 may occasionally be larger than the total number of 15-year-olds in Column 1 due to differing data sources.
Information for the adjudicated regions is available on line.
* See notes at the beginning of this Annex.
StatLink ᴍˢᴾ http://dx.doi.org/10.1787/888932937092

[Part 2/2]
Table A2.1 **PISA target populations and samples**

		Population and sample information			Coverage indices		
		Number of excluded students	Weighted number of excluded students	Within-school exclusion rate (%)	Overall exclusion rate (%)	Coverage index 1: Coverage of national desired population	Coverage index 2: Coverage of national enrolled population	Coverage index 3: Coverage of 15-year-old population
		(9)	(10)	(11)	(12)	(13)	(14)	(15)
OECD	Australia	505	5 282	2.06	4.00	0.960	0.960	0.859
	Austria	46	1 011	1.21	1.33	0.987	0.987	0.879
	Belgium	39	367	0.31	1.40	0.986	0.984	0.955
	Canada	1 796	21 013	5.69	6.38	0.936	0.926	0.833
	Chile	18	548	0.24	1.30	0.987	0.987	0.834
	Czech Republic	15	118	0.14	1.83	0.982	0.982	0.847
	Denmark	368	2 381	3.50	6.18	0.938	0.938	0.908
	Estonia	143	277	2.33	5.80	0.942	0.942	0.920
	Finland	225	653	1.08	1.91	0.981	0.981	0.960
	France	52	5 828	0.82	4.42	0.956	0.956	0.885
	Germany	8	1 302	0.17	1.54	0.985	0.985	0.948
	Greece	136	2 304	2.33	3.60	0.964	0.964	0.874
	Hungary	27	928	1.01	2.58	0.974	0.974	0.816
	Iceland	155	156	3.60	3.81	0.962	0.962	0.925
	Ireland	271	2 524	4.47	4.47	0.955	0.955	0.911
	Israel	114	1 884	1.72	4.13	0.959	0.959	0.906
	Italy	741	9 855	1.86	3.33	0.967	0.967	0.861
	Japan	0	0	0.00	2.15	0.979	0.979	0.909
	Korea	17	2 238	0.37	0.82	0.992	0.992	0.879
	Luxembourg	357	357	6.07	8.40	0.872	0.916	0.893
	Mexico	58	3 247	0.24	0.74	0.993	0.993	0.627
	Netherlands	27	1 056	0.54	4.42	0.956	0.956	1.012
	New Zealand	255	2 030	3.66	4.61	0.954	0.954	0.876
	Norway	278	3 133	5.01	6.11	0.939	0.939	0.916
	Poland	212	11 566	2.96	4.59	0.954	0.954	0.891
	Portugal	124	1 560	1.60	1.60	0.984	0.984	0.883
	Slovak Republic	29	246	0.45	2.93	0.971	0.971	0.912
	Slovenia	84	181	0.98	1.58	0.984	0.984	0.940
	Spain	959	14 931	3.84	4.32	0.957	0.957	0.884
	Sweden	201	3 789	3.84	5.44	0.946	0.946	0.930
	Switzerland	256	1 093	1.35	4.22	0.958	0.958	0.914
	Turkey	21	3 684	0.42	1.49	0.985	0.985	0.684
	United Kingdom	486	20 173	2.85	5.43	0.946	0.946	0.932
	United States	319	162 194	4.39	5.35	0.946	0.946	0.887
Partners	Albania	1	10	0.02	0.14	0.999	0.999	0.552
	Argentina	12	641	0.12	0.74	0.993	0.993	0.797
	Brazil	44	4 900	0.20	1.45	0.986	0.986	0.691
	Bulgaria	6	80	0.15	2.55	0.974	0.974	0.773
	Colombia	23	789	0.14	0.14	0.999	0.999	0.630
	Costa Rica	2	12	0.03	0.03	1.000	1.000	0.496
	Croatia	91	627	1.36	2.24	0.978	0.978	0.945
	Cyprus*	157	200	2.03	3.29	0.967	0.967	0.969
	Hong Kong-China	38	518	0.73	1.76	0.982	0.982	0.839
	Indonesia	2	860	0.03	0.26	0.997	0.982	0.634
	Jordan	19	304	0.27	0.39	0.996	0.996	0.858
	Kazakhstan	25	951	0.45	3.43	0.966	0.966	0.806
	Latvia	14	76	0.47	4.02	0.960	0.959	0.854
	Liechtenstein	13	13	3.97	4.22	0.958	0.958	0.753
	Lithuania	130	867	2.56	4.00	0.960	0.960	0.858
	Macao-China	3	3	0.06	0.17	0.998	0.998	0.813
	Malaysia	7	554	0.13	0.18	0.998	0.998	0.794
	Montenegro	4	8	0.10	0.31	0.997	0.997	0.897
	Peru	8	549	0.13	0.18	0.998	0.998	0.719
	Qatar	85	85	0.77	2.51	0.975	0.975	0.943
	Romania	0	0	0.00	3.48	0.965	0.965	0.964
	Russian Federation	69	11 940	1.01	2.40	0.976	0.976	0.921
	Serbia	10	136	0.20	2.87	0.971	0.951	0.848
	Shanghai-China	8	107	0.13	1.50	0.985	0.985	0.788
	Singapore	33	315	0.61	1.17	0.988	0.988	0.952
	Chinese Taipei	44	2 029	0.69	1.22	0.988	0.988	0.891
	Thailand	12	1 144	0.16	1.32	0.987	0.987	0.716
	Tunisia	5	130	0.11	0.24	0.998	0.998	0.913
	United Arab Emirates	11	37	0.09	2.09	0.979	0.979	0.832
	Uruguay	15	99	0.25	0.28	0.997	0.997	0.728
	Viet Nam	1	198	0.02	0.73	0.993	0.993	0.557

Notes: For a full explanation of the details in this table please refer to the *PISA 2012 Technical Report* (OECD, forthcoming). The figure for total national population of 15-year-olds enrolled in Column 2 may occasionally be larger than the total number of 15-year-olds in Column 1 due to differing data sources.
Information for the adjudicated regions is available on line.
* See notes at the beginning of this Annex.
StatLink ᵐˢᵖ http://dx.doi.org/10.1787/888932937092

[Part 1/1]
Table A2.2 **Exclusions**

	Student exclusions (unweighted)						Student exclusions (weighted)					
	Number of excluded students with functional disability (Code 1)	Number of excluded students with intellectual disability (Code 2)	Number of excluded students because of language (Code 3)	Number of excluded students for other reasons (Code 4)	Number of excluded students because of no materials available in the language of instruction (Code 5)	Total number of excluded students	Weighted number of excluded students with functional disability (Code 1)	Weighted number of excluded students with intellectual disability (Code 2)	Weighted number of excluded students because of language (Code 3)	Weighted number of excluded students for other reasons (Code 4)	Weighted number of excluded students because of no materials available in the language of instruction (Code 5)	Total weighted number of excluded students
	(1)	(2)	(3)	(4)	(5)	(6)	(7)	(8)	(9)	(10)	(11)	(12)
OECD												
Australia	39	395	71	0	0	505	471	3 925	886	0	0	5 282
Austria	11	24	11	0	0	46	332	438	241	0	0	1 011
Belgium	5	22	12	0	0	39	24	154	189	0	0	367
Canada	82	1 593	121	0	0	1 796	981	18 682	1 350	0	0	21 013
Chile	3	15	0	0	0	18	74	474	0	0	0	548
Czech Republic	1	8	6	0	0	15	1	84	34	0	0	118
Denmark	10	204	112	42	0	368	44	1 469	559	310	0	2 381
Estonia	7	134	2	0	0	143	14	260	3	0	0	277
Finland	5	80	101	15	24	225	43	363	166	47	35	653
France	52	0	0	0	0	52	5 828	0	0	0	0	5 828
Germany	0	4	4	0	0	8	0	705	597	0	0	1 302
Greece	3	18	4	111	0	136	49	348	91	1 816	0	2 304
Hungary	1	15	2	9	0	27	36	568	27	296	0	928
Iceland	5	105	27	18	0	155	5	105	27	18	0	156
Ireland	13	159	33	66	0	271	121	1 521	283	599	0	2 524
Israel	9	91	14	0	0	114	133	1 492	260	0	0	1 884
Italy	64	566	111	0	0	741	596	7 899	1 361	0	0	9 855
Japan	0	0	0	0	0	0	0	0	0	0	0	0
Luxembourg	6	261	90	0	0	357	6	261	90	0	0	357
Mexico	21	36	1	0	0	58	812	2 390	45	0	0	3 247
Netherlands	5	21	1	0	0	27	188	819	50	0	0	1 056
New Zealand	27	118	99	0	11	255	235	926	813	0	57	2 030
Norway	11	192	75	0	0	278	120	2 180	832	0	0	3 133
Poland	23	89	6	88	6	212	1 470	5 187	177	4 644	89	11 566
Portugal	69	48	7	0	0	124	860	605	94	0	0	1 560
Korea	2	15	0	0	0	17	223	2 015	0	0	0	2 238
Slovak Republic	2	14	0	13	0	29	22	135	0	89	0	246
Slovenia	13	27	44	0	0	84	23	76	81	0	0	181
Spain	56	679	224	0	0	959	618	11 330	2 984	0	0	14 931
Sweden	120	0	81	0	0	201	2 218	0	1 571	0	0	3 789
Switzerland	7	99	150	0	0	256	41	346	706	0	0	1 093
Turkey	5	14	2	0	0	21	757	2 556	371	0	0	3 684
United Kingdom	40	405	41	0	0	486	1 468	15 514	3 191	0	0	20 173
United States	37	219	63	0	0	319	18 399	113 965	29 830	0	0	162 194
Partners												
Albania	0	0	1	0	0	1	0	0	10	0	0	10
Argentina	1	11	0	0	0	12	84	557	0	0	0	641
Brazil	17	27	0	0	0	44	1 792	3 108	0	0	0	4 900
Bulgaria	6	0	0	0	0	6	80	0	0	0	0	80
Colombia	12	10	1	0	0	23	397	378	14	0	0	789
Costa Rica	0	2	0	0	0	2	0	12	0	0	0	12
Croatia	10	78	3	0	0	91	69	539	19	0	0	627
Cyprus*	8	54	60	35	0	157	9	64	72	55	0	200
Hong Kong-China	4	33	1	0	0	38	57	446	15	0	0	518
Indonesia	1	0	1	0	0	2	426	0	434	0	0	860
Jordan	8	6	5	0	0	19	109	72	122	0	0	304
Kazakhstan	9	16	0	0	0	25	317	634	0	0	0	951
Latvia	3	7	4	0	0	14	8	45	24	0	0	76
Liechtenstein	1	7	5	0	0	13	1	7	5	0	0	13
Lithuania	10	120	0	0	0	130	66	801	0	0	0	867
Macao-China	0	1	2	0	0	3	0	1	2	0	0	3
Malaysia	3	4	0	0	0	7	274	279	0	0	0	554
Montenegro	3	1	0	0	0	4	7	1	0	0	0	8
Peru	3	5	0	0	0	8	269	280	0	0	0	549
Qatar	23	43	19	0	0	85	23	43	19	0	0	85
Romania	0	0	0	0	0	0	0	0	0	0	0	0
Russian Federation	25	40	4	0	0	69	4 345	6 934	660	0	0	11 940
Serbia	4	4	2	0	0	10	53	55	28	0	0	136
Shanghai-China	1	6	1	0	0	8	14	80	14	0	0	107
Singapore	5	17	11	0	0	33	50	157	109	0	0	315
Chinese Taipei	6	36	2	0	0	44	296	1 664	70	0	0	2 029
Thailand	2	10	0	0	0	12	13	1 131	0	0	0	1 144
Tunisia	4	1	0	0	0	5	104	26	0	0	0	130
United Arab Emirates	3	7	1	0	0	11	26	9	2	0	0	37
Uruguay	9	6	0	0	0	15	66	33	0	0	0	99
Viet Nam	0	1	0	0	0	1	0	198	0	0	0	198

Exclusion codes:
Code 1 Functional disability – student has a moderate to severe permanent physical disability.
Code 2 Intellectual disability – student has a mental or emotional disability and has either been tested as cognitively delayed or is considered in the professional opinion of qualified staff to be cognitively delayed.
Code 3 Limited assessment language proficiency – student is not a native speaker of any of the languages of the assessment in the country and has been resident in the country for less than one year.
Code 4 Other reasons defined by the national centres and approved by the international centre.
Code 5 No materials available in the language of instruction.
Note: For a full explanation of the details in this table please refer to the *PISA 2012 Technical Report* (OECD, forthcoming).
Information for the adjudicated regions is available on line.
* See notes at the beginning of this Annex.
StatLink ⟲ http://dx.doi.org/10.1787/888932937092

- **Column 13** presents an *index of the extent to which the national desired target population is covered by the PISA sample*. Canada, Denmark, Estonia, Luxembourg, Norway, Sweden, the United Kingdom and the United States were the only countries where the coverage is below 95%.

- **Column 14** presents an *index of the extent to which 15-year-olds enrolled in schools are covered by the PISA sample*. The index measures the overall proportion of the national enrolled population that is covered by the non-excluded portion of the student sample. The index takes into account both school-level and student-level exclusions. Values close to 100 indicate that the PISA sample represents the entire education system as defined for PISA 2012. The index is the weighted number of participating students (Column 8) divided by the weighted number of participating and excluded students (Column 8 plus Column 10), times the nationally defined target population (Column 5) divided by the eligible population (Column 2).

- **Column 15** presents an *index of the coverage of the 15-year-old population*. This index is the weighted number of participating students (Column 8) divided by the total population of 15-year-old students (Column 1).

This high level of coverage contributes to the comparability of the assessment results. For example, even assuming that the excluded students would have systematically scored worse than those who participated, and that this relationship is moderately strong, an exclusion rate in the order of 5% would likely lead to an overestimation of national mean scores of less than 5 score points (on a scale with an international mean of 500 score points and a standard deviation of 100 score points). This assessment is based on the following calculations: if the correlation between the propensity of exclusions and student performance is 0.3, resulting mean scores would likely be overestimated by 1 score point if the exclusion rate is 1%, by 3 score points if the exclusion rate is 5%, and by 6 score points if the exclusion rate is 10%. If the correlation between the propensity of exclusions and student performance is 0.5, resulting mean scores would be overestimated by 1 score point if the exclusion rate is 1%, by 5 score points if the exclusion rate is 5%, and by 10 score points if the exclusion rate is 10%. For this calculation, a model was employed that assumes a bivariate normal distribution for performance and the propensity to participate. For details, see the *PISA 2012 Technical Report* (OECD, forthcoming).

Sampling procedures and response rates

The accuracy of any survey results depends on the quality of the information on which national samples are based as well as on the sampling procedures. Quality standards, procedures, instruments and verification mechanisms were developed for PISA that ensured that national samples yielded comparable data and that the results could be compared with confidence.

Most PISA samples were designed as two-stage stratified samples (where countries applied different sampling designs, these are documented in the *PISA 2012 Technical Report* [OECD, forthcoming]). The first stage consisted of sampling individual schools in which 15-year-old students could be enrolled. Schools were sampled systematically with probabilities proportional to size, the measure of size being a function of the estimated number of eligible (15-year-old) students enrolled. A minimum of 150 schools were selected in each country (where this number existed), although the requirements for national analyses often required a somewhat larger sample. As the schools were sampled, replacement schools were simultaneously identified, in case a sampled school chose not to participate in PISA 2012.

In the case of Iceland, Liechtenstein, Luxembourg, Macao-China and Qatar, all schools and all eligible students within schools were included in the sample.

Experts from the PISA Consortium performed the sample selection process for most participating countries and monitored it closely in those countries that selected their own samples. The second stage of the selection process sampled students within sampled schools. Once schools were selected, a list of each sampled school's 15-year-old students was prepared. From this list, 35 students were then selected with equal probability (all 15-year-old students were selected if fewer than 35 were enrolled). The number of students to be sampled per school could deviate from 35, but could not be less than 20.

Data-quality standards in PISA required minimum participation rates for schools as well as for students. These standards were established to minimise the potential for response biases. In the case of countries meeting these standards, it was likely that any bias resulting from non-response would be negligible, i.e. typically smaller than the sampling error.

A minimum response rate of 85% was required for the schools initially selected. Where the initial response rate of schools was between 65% and 85%, however, an acceptable school response rate could still be achieved through the use of replacement schools. This procedure brought with it a risk of increased response bias. Participating countries were, therefore, encouraged to persuade as many of the schools in the original sample as possible to participate. Schools with a student participation rate between 25% and 50% were not regarded as participating schools, but data from these schools were included in the database and contributed to the various estimations. Data from schools with a student participation rate of less than 25% were excluded from the database.

PISA 2012 also required a minimum participation rate of 80% of students within participating schools. This minimum participation rate had to be met at the national level, not necessarily by each participating school. Follow-up sessions were required in schools in which too few students had participated in the original assessment sessions. Student participation rates were calculated over all original schools, and also over all schools, whether original sample or replacement schools, and from the participation of students in both the original assessment and any follow-up sessions. A student who participated in the original or follow-up cognitive sessions was regarded as a participant. Those who attended only the questionnaire session were included in the international database and contributed to the statistics presented in this publication if they provided at least a description of their father's or mother's occupation.

[Part 1/2]

Table A2.3 **Response rates**

	Initial sample – before school replacement					Final sample – after school replacement		
	Weighted school participation rate before replacement (%)	Weighted number of responding schools (weighted also by enrolment)	Weighted number of schools sampled (responding and non-responding) (weighted also by enrolment)	Number of responding schools (unweighted)	Number of responding and non-responding schools (unweighted)	Weighted school participation rate after replacement (%)	Weighted number of responding schools (weighted also by enrolment)	Weighted number of schools sampled (responding and non-responding) (weighted also by enrolment)
	(1)	(2)	(3)	(4)	(5)	(6)	(7)	(8)
OECD								
Australia	98	268 631	274 432	757	790	98	268 631	274 432
Austria	100	88 967	88 967	191	191	100	88 967	88 967
Belgium	84	100 482	119 019	246	294	97	115 004	119 006
Canada	91	362 178	396 757	828	907	93	368 600	396 757
Chile	92	220 009	239 429	200	224	99	236 576	239 370
Czech Republic	98	87 238	88 884	292	297	100	88 447	88 797
Denmark	87	61 749	71 015	311	366	96	67 709	70 892
Estonia	100	12 046	12 046	206	206	100	12 046	12 046
Finland	99	59 740	60 323	310	313	99	59 912	60 323
France	97	703 458	728 401	223	231	97	703 458	728 401
Germany	98	735 944	753 179	227	233	98	737 778	753 179
Greece	93	95 107	102 087	176	192	99	100 892	102 053
Hungary	98	99 317	101 751	198	208	99	101 187	101 751
Iceland	99	4 395	4 424	133	140	99	4 395	4 424
Ireland	99	56 962	57 711	182	185	99	57 316	57 711
Israel	91	99 543	109 326	166	186	94	103 075	109 895
Italy	89	478 317	536 921	1 104	1 232	97	522 686	536 821
Japan	86	1 015 198	1 175 794	173	200	96	1 123 211	175 794
Korea	100	661 575	662 510	156	157	100	661 575	662 510
Luxembourg	100	5 931	5 931	42	42	100	5 931	5 931
Mexico	92	1 323 816	1 442 242	1 431	1 562	95	1 374 615	442 234
Netherlands	75	139 709	185 468	148	199	89	165 635	185 320
New Zealand	81	47 441	58 676	156	197	89	52 360	58 616
Norway	85	54 201	63 653	177	208	95	60 270	63 642
Poland	85	343 344	402 116	159	188	98	393 872	402 116
Portugal	95	122 238	128 129	186	195	96	122 713	128 050
Slovak Republic	87	50 182	57 353	202	236	99	57 599	58 201
Slovenia	98	18 329	18 680	335	353	98	18 329	18 680
Spain	100	402 604	403 999	902	904	100	402 604	403 999
Sweden	99	98 645	99 726	207	211	100	99 536	99 767
Switzerland	94	78 825	83 450	397	422	98	82 032	83 424
Turkey	97	921 643	945 357	165	170	100	944 807	945 357
United Kingdom	80	564 438	705 011	477	550	89	624 499	699 839
United States	67	2 647 253	3 945 575	139	207	77	3 040 661	3 938 077
Partners								
Albania	100	49 632	49 632	204	204	100	49 632	49 632
Argentina	95	578 723	606 069	218	229	96	580 989	606 069
Brazil	93	2 545 863	2 745 045	803	886	95	2 622 293	2 747 688
Bulgaria	99	57 101	57 574	186	188	100	57 464	57 574
Colombia	87	530 553	612 605	323	363	97	596 557	612 261
Costa Rica	99	64 235	64 920	191	193	99	64 235	64 920
Croatia	99	45 037	45 636	161	164	100	45 608	45 636
Cyprus*	97	9 485	9 821	117	131	97	9 485	9 821
Hong Kong-China	79	60 277	76 589	123	156	94	72 064	76 567
Indonesia	95	2 799 943	2 950 696	199	210	98	2 892 365	2 951 028
Jordan	100	119 147	119 147	233	233	100	119 147	119 147
Kazakhstan	100	239 767	239 767	218	218	100	239 767	239 767
Latvia	88	15 371	17 488	186	213	100	17 428	17 448
Liechtenstein	100	382	382	12	12	100	382	382
Lithuania	98	33 989	34 614	211	216	100	34 604	34 604
Macao-China	100	5 410	5 410	45	45	100	5 410	5 410
Malaysia	100	455 543	455 543	164	164	100	455 543	455 543
Montenegro	100	8 540	8 540	51	51	100	8 540	8 540
Peru	98	503 915	514 574	238	243	99	507 602	514 574
Qatar	100	11 333	11 340	157	164	100	11 333	11 340
Romania	100	139 597	139 597	178	178	100	139 597	139 597
Russian Federation	100	1 243 564	1 243 564	227	227	100	1 243 564	1 243 564
Serbia	90	65 537	72 819	143	160	95	69 433	72 752
Shanghai-China	100	89 832	89 832	155	155	100	89 832	89 832
Singapore	98	50 415	51 687	170	176	98	50 945	51 896
Chinese Taipei	100	324 667	324 667	163	163	100	324 667	324 667
Thailand	98	757 516	772 654	235	240	100	772 452	772 654
Tunisia	99	129 229	130 141	152	153	99	129 229	130 141
United Arab Emirates	99	46 469	46 748	453	460	99	46 469	46 748
Uruguay	99	45 736	46 009	179	180	100	46 009	46 009
Viet Nam	100	1 068 462	1 068 462	162	162	100	1 068 462	1 068 462

Information for the adjudicated regions is available on line.
* See notes at the beginning of this Annex.
StatLink ⟦⟧ http://dx.doi.org/10.1787/888932937092

[Part 2/2]
Table A2.3   **Response rates**

		Final sample – after school replacement		Final sample – students within schools after school replacement				
		Number of responding schools (unweighted)	Number of responding and non-responding schools (unweighted)	Weighted student participation rate after replacement (%)	Number of students assessed (weighted)	Number of students sampled (assessed and absent) (weighted)	Number of students assessed (unweighted)	Number of students sampled (assessed and absent) (unweighted)
		(9)	(10)	(11)	(12)	(13)	(14)	(15)
OECD	Australia	757	790	87	213 495	246 012	17 491	20 799
	Austria	191	191	92	75 393	82 242	4 756	5 318
	Belgium	282	294	91	103 914	114 360	9 649	10 595
	Canada	840	907	81	261 928	324 328	20 994	25 835
	Chile	221	224	95	214 558	226 689	6 857	7 246
	Czech Republic	295	297	90	73 536	81 642	6 528	7 222
	Denmark	339	366	89	56 096	62 988	7 463	8 496
	Estonia	206	206	93	10 807	11 634	5 867	6 316
	Finland	311	313	91	54 126	59 653	8 829	9 789
	France	223	231	89	605 371	676 730	5 641	6 308
	Germany	228	233	93	692 226	742 416	4 990	5 355
	Greece	188	192	97	92 444	95 580	5 125	5 301
	Hungary	204	208	93	84 032	90 652	4 810	5 184
	Iceland	133	140	85	3 503	4 135	3 503	4 135
	Ireland	183	185	84	45 115	53 644	5 016	5 977
	Israel	172	186	90	91 181	101 288	6 061	6 727
	Italy	1 186	1 232	93	473 104	510 005	38 084	41 003
	Japan	191	200	96	1 034 803	1 076 786	6 351	6 609
	Korea	156	157	99	595 461	603 004	5 033	5 101
	Luxembourg	42	42	95	5 260	5 523	5 260	5 523
	Mexico	1 468	1 562	94	1 193 866	1 271 639	33 786	35 972
	Netherlands	177	199	85	148 432	174 697	4 434	5 215
	New Zealand	177	197	85	40 397	47 703	5 248	6 206
	Norway	197	208	91	51 155	56 286	4 686	5 156
	Poland	182	188	88	325 389	371 434	5 629	6 452
	Portugal	187	195	87	80 719	92 395	5 608	6 426
	Slovak Republic	231	236	94	50 544	53 912	5 737	6 106
	Slovenia	335	353	90	16 146	17 849	7 211	7 921
	Spain	902	904	90	334 382	372 042	26 443	29 027
	Sweden	209	211	92	87 359	94 784	4 739	5 141
	Switzerland	410	422	92	72 116	78 424	11 218	12 138
	Turkey	169	170	98	850 830	866 269	4 847	4 939
	United Kingdom	505	550	86	528 231	613 736	12 638	14 649
	United States	161	207	89	2 429 718	2 734 268	6 094	6 848
Partners	Albania	204	204	92	39 275	42 466	4 743	5 102
	Argentina	219	229	88	457 294	519 733	5 804	6 680
	Brazil	837	886	90	2 133 035	2 368 438	19 877	22 326
	Bulgaria	187	188	96	51 819	54 145	5 280	5 508
	Colombia	352	363	93	507 178	544 862	11 164	12 045
	Costa Rica	191	193	89	35 525	39 930	4 582	5 187
	Croatia	163	164	92	41 912	45 473	6 153	6 675
	Cyprus*	117	131	93	8 719	9 344	5 078	5 458
	Hong Kong-China	147	156	93	62 059	66 665	4 659	5 004
	Indonesia	206	210	95	2 478 961	2 605 254	5 579	5 885
	Jordan	233	233	95	105 493	111 098	7 038	7 402
	Kazakhstan	218	218	99	206 053	208 411	5 808	5 874
	Latvia	211	213	91	14 579	16 039	5 276	5 785
	Liechtenstein	12	12	93	293	314	293	314
	Lithuania	216	216	92	30 429	33 042	4 618	5 018
	Macao-China	45	45	99	5 335	5 366	5 335	5 366
	Malaysia	164	164	94	405 983	432 080	5 197	5 529
	Montenegro	51	51	94	7 233	7 714	4 799	5 117
	Peru	240	243	96	398 193	414 728	6 035	6 291
	Qatar	157	164	100	10 966	10 996	10 966	10 996
	Romania	178	178	98	137 860	140 915	5 074	5 188
	Russian Federation	227	227	97	1 141 317	1 172 539	6 418	6 602
	Serbia	152	160	93	60 366	64 658	4 681	5 017
	Shanghai-China	155	155	98	83 821	85 127	6 374	6 467
	Singapore	172	176	94	47 465	50 330	5 546	5 887
	Chinese Taipei	163	163	96	281 799	292 542	6 046	6 279
	Thailand	239	240	99	695 088	702 818	6 606	6 681
	Tunisia	152	153	90	108 342	119 917	4 391	4 857
	United Arab Emirates	453	460	95	38 228	40 384	11 460	12 148
	Uruguay	180	180	90	35 800	39 771	5 315	5 904
	Viet Nam	162	162	100	955 222	956 517	4 959	4 966

Information for the adjudicated regions is available on line.
* See notes at the beginning of this Annex.
StatLink ⟲ http://dx.doi.org/10.1787/888932937092

Table A2.3 shows the response rates for students and schools, before and after replacement.

- **Column 1** shows the *weighted participation rate of schools before replacement*. This is obtained by dividing Column 2 by Column 3, multiply by 100.

- **Column 2** shows the *weighted number of responding schools before school replacement* (weighted by student enrolment).

- **Column 3** shows the *weighted number of sampled schools before school replacement* (including both responding and non-responding schools, weighted by student enrolment).

- **Column 4** shows the *unweighted number of responding schools before school replacement*.

- **Column 5** shows the *unweighted number of responding and non-responding schools before school replacement*.

- **Column 6** shows the *weighted participation rate of schools after replacement*. This is obtained by dividing Column 7 by Column 8, multiply by 100.

- **Column 7** shows the *weighted number of responding schools after school replacement (weighted by student enrolment)*.

- **Column 8** shows the *weighted number of schools sampled after school replacement* (including both responding and non-responding schools, weighted by student enrolment).

- **Column 9** shows the *unweighted number of responding schools after school replacement*.

- **Column 10** shows the *unweighted number of responding and non-responding schools after school replacement*.

- **Column 11** shows the *weighted student participation rate after replacement*. This is obtained by dividing Column 12 by Column 13, multiply by 100.

- **Column 12** shows the *weighted number of students assessed*.

- **Column 13** shows the *weighted number of students sampled* (including both students who were assessed and students who were absent on the day of the assessment).

- **Column 14** shows the *unweighted number of students assessed*. Note that any students in schools with student-response rates less than 50% were not included in these rates (both weighted and unweighted).

- **Column 15** shows the *unweighted number of students sampled* (including both students that were assessed and students who were absent on the day of the assessment). Note that any students in schools where fewer than half of the eligible students were assessed were not included in these rates (neither weighted nor unweighted).

Definition of schools

In some countries, sub-units within schools were sampled instead of schools and this may affect the estimation of the between-school variance components. In Austria, the Czech Republic, Germany, Hungary, Japan, Romania and Slovenia, schools with more than one study programme were split into the units delivering these programmes. In the Netherlands, for schools with both lower and upper secondary programmes, schools were split into units delivering each programme level. In the Flemish Community of Belgium, in the case of multi-campus schools, implantations (campuses) were sampled, whereas in the French Community, in the case of multi-campus schools, the larger administrative units were sampled. In Australia, for schools with more than one campus, the individual campuses were listed for sampling. In Argentina, Croatia and Dubai (United Arab Emirates), schools that had more than one campus had the locations listed for sampling. In Spain, the schools in the Basque region with multi-linguistic models were split into linguistic models for sampling.

Grade levels

Students assessed in PISA 2012 are at various grade levels. The percentage of students at each grade level is presented by country and economy in Table A2.4a and by gender within each country and economy in Table A2.4b.

[Part 1/1]

Table A2.4a **Percentage of students at each grade level**

	All students											
	7th grade		8th grade		9th grade		10th grade		11th grade		12th grade and above	
	%	S.E.	%	S.E.	%	S.E.	%	S.E.	%	S.E.	%	S.E.
Australia	0.0	(0.0)	0.1	(0.0)	10.8	(0.5)	70.0	(0.6)	19.1	(0.4)	0.0	(0.0)
Austria	0.3	(0.1)	5.4	(0.7)	43.3	(0.9)	51.0	(1.0)	0.1	(0.0)	0.0	c
Belgium	0.9	(0.1)	6.4	(0.5)	30.9	(0.6)	60.8	(0.6)	1.0	(0.1)	0.0	(0.0)
Canada	0.1	(0.0)	1.1	(0.1)	13.2	(0.6)	84.6	(0.6)	1.0	(0.1)	0.1	(0.0)
Chile	1.4	(0.3)	4.1	(0.6)	21.7	(0.8)	66.1	(1.2)	6.7	(0.3)	0.0	c
Czech Republic	0.4	(0.1)	4.5	(0.4)	51.1	(1.2)	44.1	(1.3)	0.0	c	0.0	c
Denmark	0.1	(0.0)	18.2	(0.8)	80.6	(0.8)	1.0	(0.2)	0.0	c	0.0	c
Estonia	0.6	(0.2)	22.1	(0.7)	75.4	(0.7)	1.9	(0.3)	0.0	c	0.0	c
Finland	0.7	(0.2)	14.2	(0.4)	85.0	(0.4)	0.0	c	0.1	(0.1)	0.0	c
France	0.0	(0.0)	1.9	(0.3)	27.9	(0.7)	66.6	(0.7)	3.5	(0.3)	0.1	(0.1)
Germany	0.6	(0.1)	10.0	(0.6)	51.9	(0.8)	36.7	(0.9)	0.8	(0.4)	0.0	c
Greece	0.3	(0.1)	1.2	(0.3)	4.0	(0.7)	94.5	(1.0)	0.0	c	0.0	c
Hungary	2.8	(0.5)	8.7	(0.9)	67.8	(0.9)	20.6	(0.6)	0.0	c	0.0	c
Iceland	0.0	c	0.0	c	0.0	c	100.0	c	0.0	c	0.0	c
Ireland	0.0	(0.0)	1.9	(0.2)	60.5	(0.8)	24.3	(1.2)	13.3	(1.0)	0.0	c
Israel	0.0	(0.0)	0.3	(0.1)	17.1	(0.9)	81.7	(0.9)	0.8	(0.3)	0.0	c
Italy	0.4	(0.1)	1.7	(0.2)	16.8	(0.6)	78.5	(0.7)	2.6	(0.2)	0.0	(0.0)
Japan	0.0	c	0.0	c	0.0	c	100.0	c	0.0	c	0.0	c
Korea	0.0	c	0.0	c	5.9	(0.8)	93.8	(0.8)	0.2	(0.1)	0.0	c
Luxembourg	0.7	(0.1)	10.2	(0.2)	50.7	(0.1)	38.0	(0.1)	0.5	(0.1)	0.0	c
Mexico	1.1	(0.1)	5.2	(0.3)	30.8	(1.0)	60.8	(1.1)	2.1	(0.3)	0.1	(0.0)
Netherlands	0.0	c	3.6	(0.4)	46.7	(1.0)	49.2	(1.1)	0.5	(0.1)	0.0	c
New Zealand	0.0	c	0.0	c	0.1	(0.1)	6.2	(0.4)	88.3	(0.5)	5.4	(0.4)
Norway	0.0	c	0.0	c	0.4	(0.1)	99.4	(0.1)	0.2	(0.0)	0.0	c
Poland	0.5	(0.1)	4.1	(0.4)	94.9	(0.4)	0.5	(0.2)	0.0	c	0.0	c
Portugal	2.4	(0.3)	8.2	(0.7)	28.6	(1.6)	60.5	(2.1)	0.3	(0.1)	0.0	c
Slovak Republic	1.7	(0.3)	4.5	(0.5)	39.5	(1.5)	52.7	(1.4)	1.6	(0.5)	0.0	c
Slovenia	0.0	c	0.3	(0.2)	5.1	(0.8)	90.7	(0.8)	3.9	(0.2)	0.0	c
Spain	0.1	(0.0)	9.8	(0.5)	24.1	(0.4)	66.0	(0.6)	0.0	(0.0)	0.0	c
Sweden	0.0	(0.0)	3.7	(0.3)	94.0	(0.6)	2.2	(0.5)	0.0	c	0.0	c
Switzerland	0.6	(0.1)	12.9	(0.8)	60.6	(1.0)	25.6	(1.0)	0.2	(0.1)	0.0	c
Turkey	0.5	(0.2)	2.2	(0.3)	27.6	(1.2)	65.5	(1.2)	4.0	(0.3)	0.3	(0.1)
United Kingdom	0.0	c	0.0	c	0.0	(0.0)	1.3	(0.3)	95.0	(0.3)	3.6	(0.1)
United States	0.0	c	0.3	(0.1)	11.7	(1.1)	71.2	(1.1)	16.6	(0.8)	0.2	(0.1)
OECD average	0.5	(0.0)	4.9	(0.1)	34.7	(0.1)	51.9	(0.2)	7.7	(0.1)	0.3	(0.0)
Albania	0.1	(0.1)	2.2	(0.3)	39.4	(2.4)	58.0	(2.5)	0.3	(0.1)	0.0	c
Argentina	2.0	(0.5)	12.0	(1.2)	22.6	(1.4)	59.4	(2.1)	2.8	(0.6)	1.1	(0.7)
Brazil	0.0	c	6.9	(0.5)	13.5	(0.7)	34.9	(1.0)	42.0	(1.0)	2.6	(0.2)
Bulgaria	0.9	(0.2)	4.6	(0.5)	89.5	(0.7)	4.9	(0.4)	0.0	(0.0)	0.0	c
Colombia	5.5	(0.6)	12.1	(0.7)	21.5	(0.8)	40.2	(0.9)	20.7	(1.0)	0.0	c
Costa Rica	7.4	(0.9)	13.7	(0.9)	39.6	(1.3)	39.1	(1.8)	0.2	(0.1)	0.0	c
Croatia	0.0	c	0.0	c	79.8	(0.4)	20.2	(0.4)	0.0	c	0.0	c
Cyprus*	0.0	(0.0)	0.5	(0.1)	4.5	(0.1)	94.3	(0.1)	0.7	(0.1)	0.0	(0.0)
Hong Kong-China	1.1	(0.1)	6.5	(0.4)	25.9	(0.7)	65.0	(0.9)	1.5	(1.4)	0.0	c
Indonesia	1.9	(0.4)	8.3	(0.8)	37.7	(2.6)	47.7	(3.0)	3.9	(0.6)	0.6	(0.6)
Jordan	0.1	(0.0)	1.1	(0.1)	6.0	(0.4)	92.9	(0.4)	0.0	c	0.0	c
Kazakhstan	0.2	(0.1)	4.9	(0.5)	67.2	(1.9)	27.4	(2.0)	0.2	(0.1)	0.1	(0.1)
Latvia	2.1	(0.4)	14.8	(0.7)	80.0	(0.8)	3.0	(0.4)	0.0	(0.0)	0.0	c
Liechtenstein	4.9	(0.7)	14.2	(1.5)	66.3	(1.3)	14.6	(0.2)	0.0	c	0.0	c
Lithuania	0.2	(0.1)	6.2	(0.6)	81.2	(0.7)	12.4	(0.7)	0.0	(0.0)	0.0	c
Macao-China	5.4	(0.1)	16.4	(0.2)	33.2	(0.2)	44.6	(0.1)	0.4	(0.1)	0.0	(0.0)
Malaysia	0.0	c	0.1	(0.0)	4.0	(0.5)	96.0	(0.5)	0.0	(0.0)	0.0	c
Montenegro	0.0	c	0.1	(0.0)	79.5	(0.1)	20.4	(0.1)	0.0	c	0.0	c
Peru	2.7	(0.4)	7.8	(0.5)	18.1	(0.7)	47.7	(0.9)	23.7	(0.8)	0.0	c
Qatar	0.9	(0.0)	3.1	(0.1)	13.8	(0.1)	64.8	(0.1)	17.1	(0.1)	0.3	(0.0)
Romania	0.2	(0.1)	7.4	(0.5)	87.2	(0.6)	5.1	(0.4)	0.0	c	0.0	c
Russian Federation	0.6	(0.1)	8.1	(0.5)	73.8	(1.6)	17.4	(1.8)	0.1	(0.1)	0.0	c
Serbia	0.1	(0.1)	1.5	(0.7)	96.7	(0.1)	1.7	(0.2)	0.0	c	0.0	c
Shanghai-China	1.1	(0.2)	4.5	(0.6)	39.6	(1.5)	54.2	(1.3)	0.6	(0.1)	0.1	(0.1)
Singapore	0.4	(0.1)	2.0	(0.2)	8.0	(0.3)	89.6	(0.3)	0.1	(0.1)	0.0	c
Chinese Taipei	0.0	c	0.2	(0.1)	36.2	(0.7)	63.6	(0.7)	0.0	c	0.0	c
Thailand	0.1	(0.0)	0.3	(0.1)	20.7	(1.0)	76.0	(1.1)	2.9	(0.5)	0.0	c
Tunisia	5.0	(0.6)	11.8	(1.3)	20.6	(1.4)	56.7	(2.7)	5.9	(0.5)	0.0	c
United Arab Emirates	0.9	(0.2)	2.8	(0.2)	11.3	(0.8)	61.9	(1.0)	22.2	(0.7)	0.9	(0.2)
Uruguay	6.9	(0.8)	12.2	(0.6)	22.4	(1.0)	57.3	(1.5)	1.3	(0.2)	0.0	c
Viet Nam	0.4	(0.2)	2.7	(0.7)	8.3	(1.7)	88.6	(2.3)	0.0	c	0.0	c

Information for the adjudicated regions is available on line.
* See notes at the beginning of this Annex.
StatLink ᴤ http://dx.doi.org/10.1787/888932937092

[Part 1/2]

Table A2.4b **Percentage of students at each grade level, by gender**

	Boys											
	7th grade		8th grade		9th grade		10th grade		11th grade		12th grade and above	
	%	S.E.	%	S.E.	%	S.E.	%	S.E.	%	S.E.	%	S.E.
Australia	0.0	c	0.1	(0.0)	13.1	(0.9)	69.2	(0.9)	17.5	(0.6)	0.0	(0.0)
Austria	0.3	(0.1)	6.0	(0.9)	44.8	(1.4)	48.9	(1.5)	0.0	c	0.0	c
Belgium	1.0	(0.1)	7.1	(0.6)	33.8	(0.9)	57.1	(1.0)	1.0	(0.2)	0.0	(0.0)
Canada	0.1	(0.1)	1.3	(0.2)	14.8	(0.8)	82.7	(0.8)	0.9	(0.1)	0.1	(0.1)
Chile	1.4	(0.4)	5.0	(0.9)	24.2	(1.0)	63.1	(1.6)	6.4	(0.4)	0.0	c
Czech Republic	0.7	(0.2)	5.5	(0.6)	54.9	(2.0)	39.0	(2.1)	0.0	c	0.0	c
Denmark	0.1	(0.0)	23.4	(1.0)	75.7	(1.0)	0.8	(0.3)	0.0	c	0.0	c
Estonia	0.8	(0.3)	25.7	(1.0)	71.7	(1.1)	1.7	(0.4)	0.0	c	0.0	c
Finland	0.9	(0.4)	16.2	(0.6)	82.8	(0.7)	0.0	c	0.1	(0.1)	0.0	c
France	0.1	(0.1)	2.3	(0.4)	30.8	(0.9)	63.5	(1.0)	3.2	(0.5)	0.1	(0.1)
Germany	0.9	(0.2)	11.6	(0.7)	53.6	(1.1)	33.2	(1.2)	0.7	(0.3)	0.0	c
Greece	0.4	(0.2)	1.8	(0.6)	4.8	(1.0)	93.0	(1.4)	0.0	c	0.0	c
Hungary	3.9	(0.6)	12.1	(1.5)	67.1	(1.3)	17.0	(0.8)	0.0	c	0.0	c
Iceland	0.0	c	0.0	c	0.0	c	100.0	c	0.0	c	0.0	c
Ireland	0.0	c	2.4	(0.3)	63.6	(1.0)	21.1	(1.4)	13.0	(1.3)	0.0	c
Israel	0.1	(0.1)	0.3	(0.1)	18.9	(1.3)	79.6	(1.3)	1.2	(0.5)	0.0	c
Italy	0.5	(0.2)	2.1	(0.3)	19.3	(0.7)	75.8	(0.7)	2.3	(0.2)	0.0	c
Japan	0.0	c	0.0	c	0.0	c	100.0	c	0.0	c	0.0	c
Korea	0.0	c	0.0	c	6.4	(1.2)	93.4	(1.2)	0.2	(0.1)	0.0	c
Luxembourg	0.7	(0.1)	10.7	(0.2)	51.1	(0.2)	37.0	(0.2)	0.6	(0.1)	0.0	c
Mexico	1.3	(0.2)	6.3	(0.3)	33.0	(1.1)	57.2	(1.2)	2.1	(0.5)	0.0	(0.0)
Netherlands	0.0	c	4.4	(0.6)	49.5	(1.1)	45.7	(1.2)	0.4	(0.1)	0.0	c
New Zealand	0.0	c	0.0	c	0.2	(0.1)	7.0	(0.5)	88.0	(0.7)	4.8	(0.5)
Norway	0.0	c	0.0	c	0.6	(0.1)	99.1	(0.1)	0.3	(0.0)	0.0	c
Poland	0.9	(0.2)	5.7	(0.6)	93.0	(0.6)	0.4	(0.2)	0.0	c	0.0	c
Portugal	2.6	(0.5)	9.9	(0.9)	30.1	(1.7)	57.0	(2.2)	0.4	(0.2)	0.0	c
Slovak Republic	1.5	(0.3)	5.4	(0.8)	40.1	(2.0)	51.5	(2.1)	1.5	(0.5)	0.0	c
Slovenia	0.0	c	0.4	(0.3)	6.3	(1.0)	90.2	(1.0)	3.1	(0.4)	0.0	c
Spain	0.1	(0.1)	11.8	(0.6)	25.8	(0.6)	62.2	(0.7)	0.1	(0.1)	0.0	c
Sweden	0.1	(0.1)	4.6	(0.5)	93.7	(0.8)	1.7	(0.6)	0.0	c	0.0	c
Switzerland	0.5	(0.1)	13.9	(0.9)	60.6	(1.7)	24.7	(2.0)	0.2	(0.1)	0.0	c
Turkey	0.3	(0.1)	2.6	(0.5)	33.2	(1.5)	60.3	(1.5)	3.2	(0.4)	0.3	(0.1)
United Kingdom	0.0	c	0.0	c	0.0	(0.0)	1.7	(0.4)	94.7	(0.4)	3.7	(0.2)
United States	0.0	c	0.4	(0.2)	14.6	(1.1)	69.8	(1.1)	14.9	(0.9)	0.3	(0.2)
OECD average	0.6	(0.1)	5.9	(0.1)	35.6	(0.2)	50.1	(0.2)	7.5	(0.1)	0.3	(0.1)
Albania	0.1	(0.1)	2.9	(0.4)	42.9	(2.7)	53.8	(2.8)	0.2	(0.1)	0.0	c
Argentina	2.8	(0.3)	15.0	(1.7)	25.8	(1.9)	52.6	(2.6)	3.0	(0.9)	0.8	(0.5)
Brazil	0.0	c	9.0	(0.6)	15.8	(0.8)	36.1	(1.1)	37.2	(1.0)	1.9	(0.2)
Bulgaria	1.3	(0.3)	5.8	(0.7)	88.2	(1.0)	4.6	(0.4)	0.0	c	0.0	c
Colombia	7.4	(0.8)	13.5	(1.0)	22.1	(1.0)	38.8	(1.4)	18.2	(1.2)	0.0	c
Costa Rica	9.3	(1.3)	16.4	(1.2)	38.5	(1.5)	35.7	(2.0)	0.0	(0.0)	0.0	c
Croatia	0.0	c	0.0	c	82.0	(0.6)	18.0	(0.6)	0.0	c	0.0	c
Cyprus*	0.0	(0.0)	0.5	(0.1)	4.7	(0.1)	94.0	(0.2)	0.7	(0.1)	0.0	c
Hong Kong-China	1.2	(0.2)	6.9	(0.5)	27.5	(0.7)	63.0	(1.0)	1.4	(1.3)	0.0	c
Indonesia	2.3	(0.4)	10.0	(1.1)	38.5	(3.0)	45.5	(3.7)	3.1	(0.6)	0.7	(0.6)
Jordan	0.1	(0.1)	0.8	(0.2)	5.7	(0.6)	93.4	(0.6)	0.0	c	0.0	c
Kazakhstan	0.3	(0.1)	5.5	(0.6)	68.4	(2.4)	25.4	(2.6)	0.2	(0.1)	0.2	(0.2)
Latvia	3.6	(0.8)	18.0	(0.9)	76.4	(1.3)	2.0	(0.3)	0.0	(0.0)	0.0	c
Liechtenstein	4.5	(1.2)	16.5	(2.1)	69.4	(2.2)	9.6	(0.6)	0.0	c	0.0	c
Lithuania	0.2	(0.1)	7.3	(0.6)	82.2	(0.9)	10.4	(0.8)	0.0	(0.0)	0.0	c
Macao-China	7.1	(0.2)	19.3	(0.2)	33.3	(0.2)	40.0	(0.2)	0.2	(0.1)	0.0	(0.0)
Malaysia	0.0	c	0.1	(0.1)	5.1	(0.7)	94.7	(0.7)	0.0	c	0.0	c
Montenegro	0.0	c	0.1	(0.1)	82.0	(0.3)	17.9	(0.3)	0.0	c	0.0	c
Peru	3.1	(0.5)	9.1	(0.8)	19.5	(0.7)	46.2	(1.0)	22.1	(0.9)	0.0	c
Qatar	1.2	(0.1)	3.6	(0.1)	14.0	(0.1)	64.6	(0.2)	16.1	(0.2)	0.0	(0.0)
Romania	0.3	(0.2)	6.5	(0.6)	88.7	(0.7)	4.5	(0.4)	0.0	c	0.0	c
Russian Federation	0.7	(0.2)	8.9	(0.7)	73.7	(1.5)	16.7	(1.8)	0.1	(0.1)	0.0	c
Serbia	0.1	(0.1)	1.9	(0.9)	96.7	(1.0)	1.4	(0.2)	0.0	c	0.0	c
Shanghai-China	1.3	(0.3)	5.3	(0.8)	41.6	(1.6)	51.2	(1.4)	0.6	(0.1)	0.0	(0.0)
Singapore	0.4	(0.1)	2.0	(0.3)	8.3	(0.4)	89.3	(0.5)	0.0	(0.0)	0.0	c
Chinese Taipei	0.0	c	0.2	(0.2)	37.4	(1.5)	62.4	(1.5)	0.0	c	0.0	c
Thailand	0.1	(0.1)	0.4	(0.2)	22.9	(1.3)	74.1	(1.5)	2.5	(0.5)	0.0	c
Tunisia	6.3	(0.8)	14.6	(1.6)	21.9	(1.6)	52.3	(3.0)	4.9	(0.5)	0.0	c
United Arab Emirates	1.3	(0.3)	3.1	(0.3)	12.9	(0.9)	60.3	(1.2)	21.8	(1.0)	0.0	(0.1)
Uruguay	9.4	(1.3)	13.1	(0.8)	24.0	(1.1)	52.4	(1.9)	1.2	(0.2)	0.0	c
Viet Nam	0.7	(0.3)	3.5	(0.8)	10.5	(2.2)	85.3	(2.8)	0.0	c	0.0	c

Information for the adjudicated regions is available on line.
* See notes at the beginning of this Annex.
StatLink ⫘⫘ http://dx.doi.org/10.1787/888932937092

[Part 2/2]

Table A2.4b **Percentage of students at each grade level, by gender**

		Girls										
		7th grade		8th grade		9th grade		10th grade		11th grade		12th grade and above	
		%	S.E.	%	S.E.	%	S.E.	%	S.E.	%	S.E.	%	S.E.
OECD	Australia	0.0	(0.0)	0.2	(0.1)	8.3	(0.3)	70.8	(0.6)	20.7	(0.6)	0.0	(0.0)
	Austria	0.3	(0.1)	4.7	(0.7)	41.8	(1.3)	53.1	(1.4)	0.1	(0.1)	0.0	c
	Belgium	0.9	(0.1)	5.7	(0.5)	28.0	(0.7)	64.4	(0.8)	1.0	(0.2)	0.0	c
	Canada	0.1	(0.0)	0.9	(0.1)	11.5	(0.5)	86.4	(0.5)	1.2	(0.1)	0.0	(0.0)
	Chile	1.3	(0.3)	3.3	(0.6)	19.3	(1.0)	69.0	(1.2)	7.1	(0.4)	0.0	c
	Czech Republic	0.1	(0.1)	3.5	(0.5)	47.1	(2.0)	49.4	(2.1)	0.0	c	0.0	c
	Denmark	0.1	(0.0)	13.0	(0.9)	85.6	(0.9)	1.3	(0.3)	0.0	c	0.0	c
	Estonia	0.3	(0.1)	18.6	(0.8)	79.0	(0.9)	2.2	(0.4)	0.0	c	0.0	c
	Finland	0.5	(0.1)	12.0	(0.4)	87.3	(0.4)	0.0	c	0.2	(0.1)	0.0	c
	France	0.0	c	1.6	(0.3)	25.1	(1.1)	69.4	(1.1)	3.8	(0.4)	0.1	(0.1)
	Germany	0.3	(0.1)	8.2	(0.6)	50.2	(1.0)	40.4	(1.1)	0.8	(0.4)	0.0	c
	Greece	0.3	(0.1)	0.5	(0.1)	3.1	(0.7)	96.1	(0.8)	0.0	c	0.0	c
	Hungary	1.8	(0.7)	5.7	(0.8)	68.4	(1.1)	24.1	(0.8)	0.0	c	0.0	c
	Iceland	0.0	c	0.0	c	0.0	c	100.0	c	0.0	c	0.0	c
	Ireland	0.1	(0.1)	1.4	(0.2)	57.3	(1.0)	27.6	(1.4)	13.7	(1.2)	0.0	c
	Israel	0.0	(0.0)	0.2	(0.1)	15.5	(1.0)	83.8	(1.0)	0.4	(0.1)	0.0	c
	Italy	0.3	(0.1)	1.2	(0.2)	14.0	(0.6)	81.5	(0.8)	3.0	(0.3)	0.0	(0.0)
	Japan	0.0	c	0.0	c	0.0	c	100.0	c	0.0	c	0.0	c
	Korea	0.0	c	0.0	c	5.4	(1.1)	94.4	(1.1)	0.2	(0.1)	0.0	c
	Luxembourg	0.7	(0.1)	9.7	(0.2)	50.2	(0.2)	39.0	(0.2)	0.4	(0.1)	0.0	c
	Mexico	0.8	(0.1)	4.1	(0.3)	28.7	(1.0)	64.2	(1.1)	2.1	(0.3)	0.1	(0.1)
	Netherlands	0.0	c	2.7	(0.4)	43.8	(1.1)	53.0	(1.1)	0.5	(0.2)	0.0	c
	New Zealand	0.0	c	0.0	c	0.1	(0.1)	5.3	(0.4)	88.6	(0.6)	5.9	(0.6)
	Norway	0.0	c	0.0	c	0.2	(0.1)	99.8	(0.1)	0.0	c	0.0	c
	Poland	0.2	(0.1)	2.6	(0.3)	96.7	(0.4)	0.6	(0.2)	0.0	c	0.0	c
	Portugal	2.2	(0.3)	6.6	(0.7)	27.2	(1.6)	63.8	(2.2)	0.2	(0.1)	0.0	c
	Slovak Republic	1.9	(0.5)	3.5	(0.5)	38.8	(1.9)	54.0	(1.9)	1.8	(0.5)	0.0	c
	Slovenia	0.0	c	0.2	(0.2)	3.8	(0.9)	91.2	(1.0)	4.7	(0.5)	0.0	c
	Spain	0.1	(0.0)	7.8	(0.5)	22.3	(0.7)	69.9	(0.8)	0.0	(0.0)	0.0	c
	Sweden	0.0	c	2.8	(0.3)	94.4	(0.6)	2.8	(0.6)	0.0	c	0.0	c
	Switzerland	0.6	(0.2)	11.9	(1.0)	60.7	(1.7)	26.6	(1.8)	0.2	(0.1)	0.0	c
	Turkey	0.7	(0.3)	1.7	(0.3)	21.9	(1.2)	70.8	(1.1)	4.8	(0.4)	0.2	(0.1)
	United Kingdom	0.0	c	0.0	c	0.0	(0.0)	1.0	(0.3)	95.4	(0.3)	3.6	(0.2)
	United States	0.0	c	0.1	(0.1)	8.8	(1.2)	72.7	(1.3)	18.3	(0.9)	0.2	(0.1)
	OECD average	0.4	(0.0)	3.9	(0.1)	33.7	(0.2)	53.8	(0.2)	7.9	(0.1)	0.3	(0.1)
Partners	Albania	0.1	(0.1)	1.4	(0.4)	35.7	(2.6)	62.5	(2.6)	0.3	(0.1)	0.0	c
	Argentina	1.2	(0.3)	9.1	(0.9)	19.7	(1.3)	65.8	(1.9)	2.7	(0.4)	1.4	(0.8)
	Brazil	0.0	c	5.0	(0.4)	11.5	(0.7)	33.8	(1.0)	46.4	(1.1)	3.3	(0.2)
	Bulgaria	0.5	(0.2)	3.3	(0.5)	90.9	(0.7)	5.2	(0.5)	0.0	(0.0)	0.0	c
	Colombia	3.9	(0.6)	10.8	(0.7)	21.0	(0.9)	41.4	(1.1)	22.9	(1.1)	0.0	c
	Costa Rica	5.7	(0.8)	11.3	(0.8)	40.5	(1.3)	42.1	(1.7)	0.4	(0.2)	0.0	c
	Croatia	0.0	c	0.0	c	77.5	(0.6)	22.5	(0.6)	0.0	c	0.0	c
	Cyprus*	0.0	c	0.5	(0.1)	4.2	(0.2)	94.6	(0.2)	0.7	(0.1)	0.0	(0.0)
	Hong Kong-China	0.9	(0.2)	6.0	(0.6)	24.2	(0.8)	67.3	(1.0)	1.6	(1.5)	0.0	c
	Indonesia	1.5	(0.4)	6.4	(0.8)	36.8	(2.9)	50.0	(3.0)	4.7	(0.8)	0.5	(0.5)
	Jordan	0.0	(0.0)	1.3	(0.2)	6.3	(0.5)	92.4	(0.6)	0.0	c	0.0	c
	Kazakhstan	0.1	(0.1)	4.4	(0.5)	65.9	(1.9)	29.3	(2.1)	0.2	(0.1)	0.0	c
	Latvia	0.6	(0.2)	11.6	(0.8)	83.7	(1.1)	4.1	(0.7)	0.0	c	0.0	c
	Liechtenstein	5.3	(1.3)	11.5	(1.9)	62.8	(1.9)	20.4	(0.8)	0.0	c	0.0	c
	Lithuania	0.1	(0.1)	5.2	(0.6)	80.2	(0.9)	14.4	(0.8)	0.0	(0.0)	0.0	c
	Macao-China	3.5	(0.1)	13.3	(0.2)	33.1	(0.3)	49.5	(0.3)	0.7	(0.2)	0.0	c
	Malaysia	0.0	c	0.0	c	2.9	(0.4)	97.1	(0.4)	0.0	(0.1)	0.0	c
	Montenegro	0.0	c	0.0	c	77.1	(0.3)	22.9	(0.3)	0.0	c	0.0	c
	Peru	2.3	(0.5)	6.6	(0.6)	16.8	(1.0)	49.1	(1.2)	25.3	(1.0)	0.0	c
	Qatar	0.5	(0.1)	2.7	(0.1)	13.6	(0.1)	64.9	(0.2)	18.2	(0.1)	0.2	(0.0)
	Romania	0.1	(0.1)	8.3	(0.6)	85.9	(0.9)	5.7	(0.6)	0.0	c	0.0	c
	Russian Federation	0.6	(0.2)	7.3	(0.5)	73.9	(2.0)	18.1	(2.0)	0.1	(0.1)	0.0	c
	Serbia	0.1	(0.1)	1.0	(0.6)	96.8	(0.7)	2.0	(0.3)	0.0	c	0.0	c
	Shanghai-China	0.8	(0.2)	3.8	(0.5)	37.6	(1.8)	57.0	(1.8)	0.6	(0.1)	0.1	(0.1)
	Singapore	0.4	(0.1)	2.1	(0.2)	7.6	(0.4)	89.8	(0.4)	0.2	(0.1)	0.0	c
	Chinese Taipei	0.0	c	0.1	(0.1)	35.0	(1.5)	64.9	(1.4)	0.0	c	0.0	c
	Thailand	0.0	(0.0)	0.2	(0.1)	19.0	(1.2)	77.5	(1.2)	3.3	(0.5)	0.0	c
	Tunisia	3.9	(0.5)	9.3	(1.1)	19.4	(1.5)	60.6	(2.5)	6.7	(0.6)	0.0	c
	United Arab Emirates	0.6	(0.1)	2.6	(0.4)	9.7	(1.1)	63.4	(1.7)	22.6	(1.3)	1.2	(0.3)
	Uruguay	4.6	(0.6)	11.4	(0.8)	21.0	(1.1)	61.7	(1.5)	1.4	(0.2)	0.0	c
	Viet Nam	0.1	(0.1)	2.1	(0.6)	6.4	(1.5)	91.4	(1.9)	0.0	c	0.0	c

Information for the adjudicated regions is available on line.
* See notes at the beginning of this Annex.
StatLink http://dx.doi.org/10.1787/888932937092

ANNEX A3

TECHNICAL NOTES ON ANALYSES IN THIS VOLUME

Methods and definitions

Relative risk or increased likelihood

The relative risk is a measure of the association between an antecedent factor and an outcome factor. The relative risk is simply the ratio of two risks, i.e. the risk of observing the outcome when the antecedent is present and the risk of observing the outcome when the antecedent is not present. Figure A3.1 presents the notation that is used in the following.

■ Figure A3.1 ■

Labels used in a two-way table

p_{11}	p_{12}	$p_{1.}$
p_{21}	p_{22}	$p_{2.}$
$p_{.1}$	$p_{.2}$	$p_{..}$

$p_{..}$ is equal to $\frac{n_{..}}{n_{..}}$, with $n_{..}$ the total number of students and $p_{..}$ is therefore equal to 1, $P_{i.}$, $P_{.j}$ respectively represent the marginal probabilities for each row and for each column. The marginal probabilities are equal to the marginal frequencies divided by the total number of students. Finally, the P_{ij} represents the probabilities for each cell and are equal to the number of observations in a particular cell divided by the total number of observations.

In PISA, the rows represent the antecedent factor, with the first row for "having the antecedent" and the second row for "not having the antecedent". The columns represent the outcome: the first column for "having the outcome" and the second column for "not having the outcome". The relative risk is then equal to:

$$RR = \frac{(p_{11}/p_{1.})}{(p_{21}/p_{2.})}$$

Attributable risk or population relevance

The attributable risk, also referred to as population relevance in the text and tables of this volume, is interpreted as follows: if the risk factor could be eliminated, then the rate of occurrence of the outcome characteristic in the population would be reduced by this coefficient. The attributable risk is equal to (see Figure A3.1 for the notation that is used in the following formula):

$$AR = \frac{(p_{11}\,p_{22}) - (p_{12}\,p_{21})}{(p_{.1}\,p_{2.})}$$

The coefficients are multiplied by 100 to express the result as a percentage.

Statistics based on multilevel models

Statistics based on multi level models include variance components (between- and within-school variance), the index of inclusion derived from these components, and regression coefficients where this has been indicated. Multilevel models are generally specified as two-level regression models (the student and school levels), with normally distributed residuals, and estimated with maximum likelihood estimation. Where the dependent variable is mathematics performance, the estimation uses five plausible values for each student's performance on the mathematics scale. Models were estimated using Mplus® software.

In multilevel models, weights are used at both the student and school levels. The purpose of these weights is to account for differences in the probabilities of students being selected in the sample. Since PISA applies a two-stage sampling procedure, these differences are due to factors at both the school and the student levels. For the multilevel models, student final weights (W_FSTUWT) were used. Within-school-weights correspond to student final weights, rescaled to sum up within each school to the school sample size. Between-school weights correspond to the sum of student final weights (W_FSTUWT) within each school. The definition of between-school weights has changed with respect to PISA 2009.

The index of inclusion is defined and estimated as:

$$100 * \frac{\sigma_w^2}{\sigma_w^2 + \sigma_b^2}$$

where σ_w^2 and σ_b^2, respectively, represent the within- and between-variance estimates.

The results in multilevel models, and the between-school variance estimate in particular, depend on how schools are defined and organised within countries and by the units that were chosen for sampling purposes. For example, in some countries, some of the schools in the PISA sample were defined as administrative units (even if they spanned several geographically separate institutions, as in Italy); in others they were defined as those parts of larger educational institutions that serve 15-year-olds; in still others they were defined as physical school buildings; and in others they were defined from a management perspective (e.g. entities having a principal). The *PISA 2012 Technical Report* (OECD, forthcoming) and Annex A2 provide an overview of how schools were defined. In Slovenia, the primary sampling unit is defined as a group of students who follow the same study programme within a school (an educational track within a school). So in this particular case the between-school variance is actually the within-school, between-track variation. The use of stratification variables in the selection of schools may also affect the estimate of the between-school variance, particularly if stratification variables are associated with between-school differences.

Because of the manner in which students were sampled, the within-school variation includes variation between classes as well as between students.

Multiple imputation replaces each missing value with a set of plausible values that represent the uncertainty about the right value to impute. The multiple imputed data sets are then analysed by using standard procedures for complete data and by combining results from these analyses. Five imputed values are computed for each missing value. Different methods can be used according to the pattern of missing values. For arbitrary missing data patterns, the MCMC (Monte Carlo Markov Chain) approach can be used.

This approach is used with the SAS procedure MI for the multilevel analyses in this volume. Multiple imputation is conducted separately for each model and each country, except for the model with all variables (Tables IV.1.12a, IV.1.12b and IV.1.12c) in which the data were constructed from imputed data for the individual models, such as the model for learning environment, model for selecting and grouping students, etc. Where continuous values are generated for missing discrete variables, these are rounded to the nearest discrete value of the variable. Each of the five plausible value of mathematics performance is analysed by Mplus® software using one of the five imputed data sets, which were combined taking account of the between imputation variance.

Standard errors and significance tests

The statistics in this report represent estimates of national performance based on samples of students, rather than values that could be calculated if every student in every country had answered every question. Consequently, it is important to measure the degree of uncertainty of the estimates. In PISA, each estimate has an associated degree of uncertainty, which is expressed through a standard error. The use of confidence intervals provides a way to make inferences about the population means and proportions in a manner that reflects the uncertainty associated with the sample estimates. From an observed sample statistic and assuming a normal distribution, it can be inferred that the corresponding population result would lie within the confidence interval in 95 out of 100 replications of the measurement on different samples drawn from the same population.

In many cases, readers are primarily interested in whether a given value in a particular country is different from a second value in the same or another country, e.g. whether girls in a country perform better than boys in the same country. In the tables and charts used in this report, differences are labelled as statistically significant when a difference of that size, smaller or larger, would be observed less than 5% of the time, if there were actually no difference in corresponding population values. Similarly, the risk of reporting a correlation as significant if there is, in fact, no correlation between two measures, is contained at 5%.

Throughout the report, significance tests were undertaken to assess the statistical significance of the comparisons made.

Gender differences and differences between subgroup means

Gender differences in student performance or other indices were tested for statistical significance. Positive differences indicate higher scores for boys while negative differences indicate higher scores for girls. Generally, differences marked in bold in the tables in this volume are statistically significant at the 95% confidence level.

Similarly, differences between other groups of students (e.g. native students and students with an immigrant background) were tested for statistical significance. The definitions of the subgroups can in general be found in the tables and the text accompanying the analysis. All differences marked in bold in the tables presented in Annex B of this report are statistically significant at the 95% level.

Differences between subgroup means, after accounting for other variables

For many tables, subgroup comparisons were performed both on the observed difference ("before accounting for other variables") and after accounting for other variables, such as the *PISA index of economic, social and cultural status of students* (ESCS). The adjusted differences were estimated using linear regression and tested for significance at the 95% confidence level. Significant differences are marked in bold.

Performance differences between the top and bottom quartiles of PISA indices and scales

Differences in average performance between the top and bottom quarters of the PISA indices and scales were tested for statistical significance. Figures marked in bold indicate that performance between the top and bottom quarters of students on the respective index is statistically significantly different at the 95% confidence level.

Differences between subgroups of schools

In this Volume, schools are compared across several aspects, such as resource allocation or performance. For this purpose, schools are grouped in categories by socio-economic status of students and schools, public-private status, lower and upper secondary education and school location. The differences between subgroups of schools are tested for statistical significance in the following way:

- *Socio-economic status of students*: Students in the top quarter of ESCS are compared to students in the bottom quarter of ESCS. If the difference is statistically significant at the 95% confidence levels, both figures are marked in bold. The second and third quarters do not enter the comparison.

- *Socio-economic status of schools*: advantaged schools are compared to disadvantaged schools. If the difference is statistically significant at the 95% confidence levels, both figures are marked in bold. Average schools do not enter the comparison.

- *Public and private schools:* Government-dependent and government-independent private schools are jointly considered as private schools. Figures in bold in data tables presented in Annex B of this report indicate statistically significant differences, at the 95% confidence level, between public and private schools.

- *Education levels*: Students at the upper secondary education are compared to students at the lower secondary education. If the difference is statistically significant at the 95% confidence levels, both figures are marked in bold.

- *School location*: For the purpose of significance tests, "schools located in a small town" and "schools located in a town" are jointly considered to form a single group. Figures for "schools located in a city or large city" are marked in bold in data tables presented in Annex B of this report if the difference with this middle category ("schools located in a small town" and "schools located in a town") is significant at the 95% confidence levels. In turn, figures for "schools located in a village, hamlet, or rural area" are marked in bold if the difference with this middle category is significant. Differences between the extreme categories were not tested for significance.

Change in the performance per unit of the index

For many tables, the difference in student performance per unit of the index shown was calculated. Figures in bold indicate that the differences are statistically significantly different from zero at the 95% confidence level.

Relative risk or increased likelihood

Figures in bold in the data tables presented in Annex B of this report indicate that the relative risk is statistically significantly different from 1 at the 95% confidence level. To compute statistical significance around the value of 1 (the null hypothesis), the relative-risk statistic is assumed to follow a log-normal distribution, rather than a normal distribution, under the null hypothesis.

Attributable risk or population relevance

Figures in bold in the data tables presented in Annex B of this report indicate that the attributable risk is statistically significantly different from 0 at the 95% confidence level.

Standard errors in statistics estimated from multilevel models

For statistics based on multilevel models (such as the estimates of variance components and regression coefficients from two-level regression models) the standard errors are not estimated with the usual replication method which accounts for stratification and sampling rates from finite populations. Instead, standard errors are "model-based": their computation assumes that schools, and students within schools, are sampled at random (with sampling probabilities reflected in school and student weights) from a theoretical, infinite population of schools and students which complies with the model's parametric assumptions.

The standard error for the estimated index of inclusion is calculated by deriving an approximate distribution for it from the (model-based) standard errors for the variance components, using the delta-method.

Standard errors in trend analyses of performance: Link error

Standard errors for performance trend estimates had to be adjusted because the equating procedure that allows scores in different PISA assessments to be compared introduces a form of random error that is related to performance changes on the link items. These more conservative standard errors (larger than standard errors that were estimated before the introduction of the link error) reflect not only the measurement precision and sampling variation as for the usual PISA results, but also the link error (see Annex A5 for a technical discussion of the link error).

Link items represent only a subset of all items used to derive PISA scores. If different items were chosen to equate PISA scores over time, the comparison of performance for a group of students across time could vary. As a result, standard errors for the estimates of the change over time in mathematics, reading or science performance of a particular group (e.g. a country or economy, a region, boys, girls, students with an immigrant background, students without an immigrant background, socio-economically advantaged students, students in public schools, etc.) include the link error in addition to the sampling and imputation error commonly added to estimates in performance for a particular year. Because the equating procedure adds uncertainty to the position in the distribution (a change in the intercept) but does not result in any change in the variance of a distribution, standard errors for location-invariant estimates do not include the link error. Location-invariant estimates include, for example, estimates for variances, regression coefficients for student- or school-level covariates, and correlation coefficients.

Figures in bold in the data tables for trends in performance presented in Annex B of this report indicate that the the change in performance for that particular group is statistically significantly different from 0 at the 95% confidence level. The standard errors used to calculate the statistical significance of the reported trend include the link error.

ANNEX A4
QUALITY ASSURANCE

Quality assurance procedures were implemented in all parts of PISA 2012, as was done for all previous PISA surveys.

The consistent quality and linguistic equivalence of the PISA 2012 assessment instruments were facilitated by providing countries with equivalent source versions of the assessment instruments in English and French and requiring countries (other than those assessing students in English and French) to prepare and consolidate two independent translations using both source versions. Precise translation and adaptation guidelines were supplied, also including instructions for selecting and training the translators. For each country, the translation and format of the assessment instruments (including test materials, marking guides, questionnaires and manuals) were verified by expert translators appointed by the PISA Consortium before they were used in the PISA 2012 Field Trial and Main Study. These translators' mother tongue was the language of instruction in the country concerned and they were knowledgeable about education systems. For further information on the PISA translation procedures, see the *PISA 2012 Technical Report* (OECD, forthcoming).

The survey was implemented through standardised procedures. The PISA Consortium provided comprehensive manuals that explained the implementation of the survey, including precise instructions for the work of School Co-ordinators and scripts for Test Administrators to use during the assessment sessions. Proposed adaptations to survey procedures, or proposed modifications to the assessment session script, were submitted to the PISA Consortium for approval prior to verification. The PISA Consortium then verified the national translation and adaptation of these manuals.

To establish the credibility of PISA as valid and unbiased and to encourage uniformity in administering the assessment sessions, Test Administrators in participating countries were selected using the following criteria: it was required that the Test Administrator not be the reading, mathematics or science instructor of any students in the sessions he or she would administer for PISA; it was recommended that the Test Administrator not be a member of the staff of any school where he or she would administer for PISA; and it was considered preferable that the Test Administrator not be a member of the staff of any school in the PISA sample. Participating countries organised an in-person training session for Test Administrators.

Participating countries and economies were required to ensure that: Test Administrators worked with the School Co-ordinator to prepare the assessment session, including updating student tracking forms and identifying excluded students; no extra time was given for the cognitive items (while it was permissible to give extra time for the student questionnaire); no instrument was administered before the two one-hour parts of the cognitive session; Test Administrators recorded the student participation status on the student tracking forms and filled in a Session Report Form; no cognitive instrument was permitted to be photocopied; no cognitive instrument could be viewed by school staff before the assessment session; and Test Administrators returned the material to the national centre immediately after the assessment sessions.

National Project Managers were encouraged to organise a follow-up session when more than 15% of the PISA sample was not able to attend the original assessment session.

National Quality Monitors from the PISA Consortium visited all national centres to review data-collection procedures. Finally, School Quality Monitors from the PISA Consortium visited a sample of seven schools during the assessment. For further information on the field operations, see the *PISA 2012 Technical Report* (OECD, forthcoming).

Marking procedures were designed to ensure consistent and accurate application of the marking guides outlined in the PISA Operations Manuals. National Project Managers were required to submit proposed modifications to these procedures to the Consortium for approval. Reliability studies to analyse the consistency of marking were implemented.

Software specially designed for PISA facilitated data entry, detected common errors during data entry, and facilitated the process of data cleaning. Training sessions familiarised National Project Managers with these procedures.

For a description of the quality assurance procedures applied in PISA and in the results, see the *PISA 2012 Technical Report* (OECD, forthcoming).

The results of adjudication showed that the PISA Technical Standards were fully met in all countries and economies that participated in PISA 2012, with the exception of Albania. Albania submitted parental occupation data that was incomplete and appeared inaccurate, since there was over-use of a narrow range of occupations. It was not possible to resolve these issues during the course of data cleaning, and as a result neither parental occupation data nor any indices which depend on this data are included in the international dataset. Results for Albania are omitted from any analyses which depend on these indices.

ANNEX A5

TECHNICAL DETAILS OF TRENDS ANALYSES

Comparing mathematics, reading and science performance across PISA cycles

The PISA 2003, 2006, 2009 and 2012 assessments use the same mathematics performance scale, which means that score points on this scale are directly comparable over time. The same is true for the reading performance scale used since PISA 2000 and the science performance scale used since PISA 2006. The comparability of scores across time is possible because of the use of link items that are common across assessments and can be used in the equating procedure to align performance scales. The items that are common across assessments are a subset of the total items that make up the assessment because PISA progressively renews its pool of items. As a result, out of a total of 110 items in the PISA 2012 mathematics assessment, 84 are linked to 2003 items, 48 to 2006 items and 35 to 2009 items. The number of PISA 2012 items linked to the PISA 2003 assessment is larger than the number linked to the PISA 2006 or the PISA 2009 assessments because mathematics was a major domain in PISA 2003 and PISA 2012. In PISA 2006 and PISA 2009, mathematics was a minor domain and all the mathematics items included in these assessments were link items. The *PISA 2012 Technical Report* (OECD, forthcoming) provides the technical details on equating the PISA 2012 mathematics scale for trends purposes.

Link error

Standard errors for performance trend estimates had to be adjusted because the equating procedure that allows scores in different PISA assessments to be compared introduces a form of random error that is related to performance changes on the link items. These more conservative standard errors (larger than standard errors that were estimated before the introduction of the link error) reflect not only the measurement precision and sampling variation as for the usual PISA results, but also the link error provided in Table A5.1.

Link items represent only a subset of all items used to derive PISA scores. If different items were chosen to equate PISA scores over time, the comparison of performance for a group of students across time could vary. As a result, standard errors for the estimates of the change over time in mathematics, reading or science performance of a particular group (e.g. a country or economy, a region, boys, girls, students with an immigrant background, students without an immigrant background, socio-economically advantaged students, students in public schools, etc.) include the link error in addition to the sampling and imputation error commonly added to estimates in performance for a particular year. Because the equating procedure adds uncertainty to the position in the distribution (a change in the intercept) but does not result in any change in the variance of a distribution, standard errors for location-invariant estimates do not include the link error. Location-invariant estimates include, for example, estimates for variances, regression coefficients for student- or school-level covariates, and correlation coefficients.

Link error for scores between two PISA assessments

The following equations describe how link errors between two PISA assessments are calculated. Suppose we have L score points in K units. Use i to index items in a unit and j to index units so that $\hat{\mu}_{ij}^{y}$ is the estimated difficulty of item i in unit j for year y, and let for example to compare PISA 2006 and PISA 2003:

$$c_{ij} = \hat{\mu}_{ij}^{2006} - \hat{\mu}_{ij}^{2003}$$

The size (total number of score points) of unit j is m_j so that:

$$\sum_{j=1}^{K} m_j = L$$

and

$$\bar{m} = \frac{1}{K} \sum_{j=1}^{K} m_j$$

Further let:

$$c_{.j} = \frac{1}{m_j} \sum_{j=1}^{m_j} c_{ij}$$

and

$$\bar{c} = \frac{1}{N} \sum_{j=1}^{K} \sum_{i=1}^{m_j} c_{ij}$$

then the link error, taking clustering into account, is as follows:

$$error_{2006,2003} = \sqrt{\frac{\sum_{j=1}^{K} m_j^2 (c_{.j} - \bar{c})^2}{K(K-1)\bar{m}^2}}$$

This approach for estimating the link errors was used in PISA 2006, PISA 2009 and PISA 2012. The link errors for comparisons of PISA 2012 results with previous assessments are shown in Table A5.1.

[Part 1/1]

Table A5.1   **Link error for comparisons of performance between PISA 2012 and previous assessments**

Comparison	Mathematics	Reading	Science
PISA 2000 to PISA 2012		5.923	
PISA 2003 to PISA 2012	1.931	5.604	
PISA 2006 to PISA 2012	2.084	5.580	3.512
PISA 2009 to PISA 2012	2.294	2.602	2.006

Note: Comparisons between PISA 2012 scores and previous assessments can only be made to when the subject first became a major domain. As a result, comparisons in mathematics performance between PISA 2012 and PISA 2000 are not possible, nor are comparisons in science performance between PISA 2012 and PISA 2000 or 2003.
StatLink http://dx.doi.org/10.1787/888932937054

Link error for other types of comparisons of student performance

The link error for other comparisons of performance does not have a straightforward theoretical solution as does the link error for comparison between two PISA assessments. The link error between two PISA assessments, described above, can be used, however, to empirically estimate the magnitude of the link error for the comparison of the percentage of students in a particular proficiency level or the magnitude of the link error associated with the estimation of the annualised and curvilinear change.

The empirical estimation of these link errors uses the assumption that the magnitude of the link error follows a normal distribution with mean 0 and a standard deviation equal to the link error shown in Table A5.1. From this distribution, 500 errors are drawn and added to the first plausible value for each assessment prior to 2012. The estimate of interest (change in the percentage of students in a particular proficiency level or the annualised change) is calculated for each of the 500 replicates. The standard deviation of these 500 estimates is then used as the link error for the annualised change, the quadratic change, and the change in the percentage of students scoring in a particular proficiency level. The values used to adjust standard errors in the calculation of the change in the percentage of students in each proficiency Level group are shown in Table A5.2 and those used for the adjustment of the linear and quadratic terms in the regressions models used to estimate the annualised change and the curvilinear change are shown in Table A5.3.

Comparisons of performance: Difference between two assessments and annualised change

To evaluate the evolution of performance, analyses report the change in performance between two cycles. Comparisons between two assessments (e.g. a country's/economy's change in performance between PISA 2003 and PISA 2012 or the change in performance of a subgroup) are calculated as:

$$\Delta_{2012-t} = PISA_{2012} - PISA_t$$

where Δ_{2012-t} is the difference in performance between PISA 2012 and a previous PISA assessment, where t can take any of the following values: 2000, 2003, 2006 or 2009. $PISA_{2012}$ is the mathematics, reading or science score observed in PISA 2012, and $PISA_t$ is the mathematics, reading or science score observed in a previous assessment (2000, 2003, 2006 or 2009). The standard error of the change in performance $\sigma(\Delta_{2012-t})$ is:

$$\sigma(\Delta_{2012-t}) = \sqrt{\sigma_{2012}^2 + \sigma_t^2 + error_{2012,t}^2}$$

where σ_{2012} is the standard error observed for $PISA_{2012}$, σ_t is the standard error observed for $PISA_t$ and $error_{2012,t}$ is the link error for comparisons of mathematics, reading or science performance between the PISA 2012 assessment and a previous (t) assessment. The value for $error_{2012,t}$ is shown in Table A5.1.

A second set of analyses reported in PISA relate to annualised changes in performance. The annualised change is the average annual rate of change observed through a country's/economy's participation in PISA. The annualised change is the average rate of change for a country's/economy's average mathematics, reading and science scores throughout their participation in PISA assessments. Thus, a positive annualised change of x points indicates that the country/economy has improved in performance by x points per year since its earliest comparable PISA results participated in PISA. For countries and economies that have participated in only two assessments, the annualised change is equal to the difference between the two assessments, divided by the number of years that passed between the assessments.

The annualised change in performance is calculated through an individual-level OLS regression of the form:

$$PISA_i = \beta_0 + \beta_1 year_i + \varepsilon_i$$

where $PISA_i$ is student i's mathematics, reading or science score, $year_i$ is the year student i took the PISA assessment and ε_i is an error term indicating student i's difference from the group mean. Under this specification, the estimate for β_1 indicates the annualised rate of change. Just as a link error is added when drawing comparisons between two PISA assessments, the standard errors for β_1 also include a link error:

$$\sigma_{link}(\beta_1) = \sqrt{\sigma^2(\beta_1) + error_{annual}^2}$$

where $error_{annual}$ is the link error associated to the linear term in a regression model. It is presented in Table A5.3.

[Part 1/3]

Table A5.2 Link error for comparisons of proficiency levels between PISA 2012 and previous assessments

		Mathematics comparison between PISA 2012 and...									
		PISA 2003						PISA 2006		PISA 2009	
		Below Level 2			Level 5 or above			Below Level 2	Level 5 or above	Below Level 2	Level 5 or above
		All	Boys	Girls	All	Boys	Girls	All	All	All	All
OECD	Australia	0.534	0.462	0.612	0.435	0.477	0.393	0.588	0.464	0.634	0.498
	Austria	0.566	0.567	0.579	0.501	0.537	0.470	0.610	0.530	m	m
	Belgium	0.484	0.476	0.495	0.556	0.572	0.543	0.521	0.596	0.556	0.637
	Canada	0.457	0.385	0.530	0.539	0.583	0.498	0.484	0.577	0.518	0.615
	Chile	m	m	m	m	m	m	0.934	0.094	0.995	0.099
	Czech Republic	0.532	0.410	0.670	0.437	0.429	0.456	0.582	0.455	0.630	0.486
	Denmark	0.601	0.554	0.657	0.379	0.400	0.359	0.653	0.402	0.703	0.430
	Estonia	m	m	m	m	m	m	0.457	0.538	0.490	0.577
	Finland	0.400	0.452	0.348	0.445	0.435	0.465	0.429	0.485	0.462	0.520
	France	0.541	0.568	0.519	0.471	0.487	0.462	0.587	0.497	0.631	0.528
	Germany	0.445	0.404	0.494	0.518	0.554	0.482	0.482	0.543	0.517	0.586
	Greece	1.029	0.927	1.133	0.192	0.240	0.149	1.099	0.206	1.163	0.221
	Hungary	0.640	0.586	0.699	0.374	0.387	0.370	0.680	0.397	0.723	0.428
	Iceland	0.560	0.567	0.555	0.419	0.370	0.477	0.594	0.447	0.640	0.481
	Ireland	0.542	0.440	0.655	0.426	0.509	0.353	0.584	0.459	0.627	0.491
	Israel	m	m	m	m	m	m	0.785	0.376	0.836	0.399
	Italy	0.635	0.562	0.714	0.350	0.427	0.270	0.683	0.375	0.735	0.402
	Japan	0.421	0.365	0.487	0.740	0.787	0.694	0.448	0.788	0.479	0.843
	Korea	0.326	0.300	0.365	0.660	0.618	0.714	0.355	0.727	0.383	0.774
	Luxembourg	0.555	0.607	0.509	0.377	0.445	0.312	0.603	0.397	0.652	0.426
	Mexico	0.998	0.998	0.999	0.062	0.088	0.038	1.079	0.064	1.154	0.067
	Netherlands	0.473	0.446	0.504	0.622	0.720	0.522	0.507	0.659	0.541	0.698
	New Zealand	0.657	0.691	0.632	0.420	0.497	0.344	0.706	0.451	0.759	0.478
	Norway	0.600	0.524	0.683	0.329	0.283	0.385	0.642	0.347	0.683	0.374
	Poland	0.537	0.602	0.486	0.574	0.639	0.515	0.572	0.624	0.615	0.669
	Portugal	0.516	0.483	0.556	0.458	0.531	0.387	0.566	0.482	0.608	0.508
	Slovak Republic	0.691	0.698	0.694	0.286	0.331	0.243	0.721	0.319	0.771	0.343
	Slovenia	m	m	m	m	m	m	0.711	0.491	0.767	0.520
	Spain	0.619	0.543	0.699	0.377	0.464	0.290	0.671	0.402	0.714	0.431
	Sweden	0.696	0.661	0.735	0.296	0.297	0.302	0.757	0.324	0.814	0.346
	Switzerland	0.414	0.278	0.555	0.636	0.672	0.606	0.446	0.682	0.478	0.730
	Turkey	1.008	0.911	1.111	0.220	0.289	0.154	1.085	0.235	1.158	0.253
	United Kingdom	m	m	m	m	m	m	0.575	0.317	0.628	0.348
	United States	0.735	0.697	0.777	0.382	0.409	0.358	0.787	0.404	0.836	0.430
Partners	Albania	m	m	m	m	m	m	m	m	0.810	0.033
	Argentina	m	m	m	m	m	m	0.906	0.019	0.970	0.021
	Brazil	0.900	1.042	0.773	0.068	0.081	0.059	0.968	0.072	1.031	0.075
	Bulgaria	m	m	m	m	m	m	0.777	0.230	0.830	0.245
	Colombia	m	m	m	m	m	m	0.778	0.022	0.829	0.024
	Costa Rica	m	m	m	m	m	m	m	m	1.179	0.043
	Croatia	m	m	m	m	m	m	0.804	0.248	0.859	0.263
	Dubai (UAE)	m	m	m	m	m	m	m	m	0.731	0.390
	Hong Kong-China	0.250	0.224	0.287	0.805	0.695	0.940	0.277	0.864	0.295	0.917
	Indonesia	0.715	0.662	0.776	0.025	0.021	0.036	0.758	0.025	0.812	0.026
	Jordan	m	m	m	m	m	m	1.017	0.052	1.081	0.053
	Kazakhstan	m	m	m	m	m	m	m	m	1.216	0.060
	Latvia	0.638	0.725	0.557	0.439	0.412	0.469	0.677	0.455	0.725	0.484
	Liechtenstein	0.552	0.680	0.479	1.055	1.440	0.697	0.579	1.065	0.610	1.147
	Lithuania	m	m	m	m	m	m	0.863	0.337	0.927	0.364
	Macao-China	0.343	0.309	0.383	0.697	0.754	0.643	0.369	0.755	0.395	0.806
	Malaysia	m	m	m	m	m	m	m	m	0.984	0.091
	Montenegro	m	m	m	m	m	m	0.840	0.064	0.891	0.069
	Peru	m	m	m	m	m	m	m	m	0.760	0.055
	Qatar	m	m	m	m	m	m	0.577	0.082	0.616	0.089
	Romania	m	m	m	m	m	m	1.101	0.164	1.169	0.176
	Russian Federation	0.804	0.890	0.723	0.344	0.321	0.375	0.871	0.363	0.933	0.392
	Serbia	m	m	m	m	m	m	0.939	0.157	1.011	0.168
	Shanghai-China	m	m	m	m	m	m	m	m	0.194	0.776
	Singapore	m	m	m	m	m	m	m	m	0.293	0.894
	Chinese Taipei	m	m	m	m	m	m	0.327	0.625	0.354	0.673
	Thailand	0.911	1.048	0.810	0.085	0.063	0.108	0.974	0.093	1.039	0.104
	Tunisia	0.804	0.643	0.955	0.056	0.040	0.074	0.857	0.059	0.911	0.062
	United Arab Emirates*	m	m	m	m	m	m	m	m	0.942	0.112
	Uruguay	0.817	0.793	0.846	0.065	0.105	0.035	0.881	0.069	0.944	0.075

Note: The link error is calculated empirically by adding a random error component from a normal distribution with mean equal to zero and standard deviation equal to those shown in Table A5.1 to each student's scores in PISA 2000, PISA 2003, PISA 2006 or PISA 2009. Each country's percentage of students in each proficiency level band are then calculated for each of 500 replications. The standard deviation in the observed coefficients is the result of the added error and is the reported link error.
* United Arab Emirates excluding Dubai.
StatLink ▭▭▭ http://dx.doi.org/10.1787/888932937054

[Part 2/3]

Table A5.2 Link error for comparisons of proficiency levels between PISA 2012 and previous assessments

		Reading comparison between PISA 2012 and...											
		PISA 2000						PISA 2003		PISA 2006		PISA 2009	
		Below Level 2			Level 5 or above			Below Level 2	Level 5 or above	Below Level 2	Level 5 or above	Below Level 2	Level 5 or above
		All	Boys	Girls	All	Boys	Girls	All	All	All	All	All	All
OECD	Australia	1.294	1.569	1.008	1.293	1.033	1.570	1.289	1.282	1.246	1.254	0.601	0.599
	Austria	1.488	1.772	1.216	0.968	0.691	1.248	1.482	0.959	1.431	0.943	m	m
	Belgium	1.177	1.243	1.114	1.392	1.162	1.627	1.182	1.380	1.143	1.350	0.551	0.656
	Canada	1.057	1.269	0.847	1.457	1.175	1.741	1.058	1.449	1.016	1.410	0.525	0.676
	Chile	2.510	2.601	2.427	0.121	0.067	0.174	m	m	2.423	0.118	1.200	0.051
	Czech Republic	1.615	1.871	1.355	0.919	0.591	1.269	1.609	0.914	1.568	0.901	0.737	0.429
	Denmark	1.375	1.721	1.031	0.854	0.584	1.131	1.372	0.846	1.320	0.827	0.603	0.419
	Estonia	m	m	m	m	m	m	m	m	1.011	1.194	0.391	0.602
	Finland	1.197	1.858	0.502	1.601	1.038	2.199	1.200	1.588	1.161	1.551	0.510	0.730
	France	1.119	1.282	0.968	1.326	1.121	1.526	1.115	1.321	1.077	1.288	0.485	0.603
	Germany	1.269	1.487	1.046	1.375	1.026	1.741	1.271	1.353	1.232	1.334	0.594	0.648
	Greece	1.527	1.937	1.130	0.784	0.603	0.964	1.524	0.776	1.478	0.765	0.729	0.375
	Hungary	1.353	1.619	1.109	0.955	0.774	1.136	1.352	0.947	1.314	0.933	0.574	0.439
	Iceland	1.588	1.826	1.348	0.889	0.603	1.210	1.576	0.882	1.537	0.865	0.755	0.466
	Ireland	1.213	1.474	0.947	1.510	1.184	1.851	1.220	1.511	1.177	1.466	0.569	0.766
	Israel	1.355	1.274	1.447	1.145	0.950	1.338	m	m	1.316	1.111	0.619	0.568
	Italy	1.468	1.630	1.295	1.040	0.816	1.281	1.463	1.032	1.418	1.011	0.678	0.482
	Japan	0.831	0.876	0.794	1.743	1.572	1.937	0.834	1.734	0.799	1.692	0.391	0.828
	Korea	0.845	1.006	0.668	1.832	1.657	2.037	0.838	1.822	0.812	1.785	0.414	0.904
	Luxembourg	m	m	m	m	m	m	1.460	1.130	1.415	1.112	0.663	0.543
	Mexico	2.844	2.892	2.802	0.097	0.076	0.117	2.836	0.036	2.751	0.093	1.308	0.052
	Netherlands	m	m	m	m	m	m	1.350	1.404	1.312	1.370	0.66	0.661
	New Zealand	1.323	1.581	1.061	1.367	1.300	1.443	1.322	1.360	1.280	1.328	0.654	0.618
	Norway	1.259	1.569	0.945	1.236	0.840	1.658	1.254	1.231	1.210	1.204	0.514	0.526
	Poland	1.040	1.370	0.729	1.223	0.902	1.532	1.038	1.212	0.996	1.187	0.48	0.544
	Portugal	1.410	1.671	1.147	1.064	0.746	1.391	1.408	1.059	1.353	1.036	0.66	0.506
	Slovak Republic	m	m	m	m	m	m	1.775	0.717	1.714	0.706	0.80	0.343
	Slovenia	m	m	m	m	m	m	m	m	1.790	0.647	0.85	0.259
	Spain	1.539	1.682	1.400	0.824	0.641	1.016	1.532	0.815	1.483	0.803	0.66	0.380
	Sweden	1.509	1.831	1.186	1.023	0.719	1.339	1.502	1.018	1.455	0.995	0.72	0.510
	Switzerland	1.401	1.744	1.062	1.265	0.835	1.702	1.406	1.255	1.359	1.222	0.66	0.548
	Turkey	m	m	m	m	m	m	2.157	0.589	2.082	0.581	1.03	0.248
	United Kingdom	m	m	m	m	m	m	m	m	1.251	1.008	0.57	0.463
	United States	1.448	1.836	1.053	1.017	0.804	1.241	1.441	1.008	m	m	0.62	0.455
Partners	Albania	2.316	2.059	2.609	0.197	0.191	0.211	m	m	m	m	1.10	0.080
	Argentina	2.544	2.469	2.624	0.139	0.113	0.175	m	m	2.471	0.136	1.22	0.062
	Brazil	2.716	2.627	2.800	0.124	0.068	0.178	2.707	0.123	2.633	0.121	1.28	0.063
	Bulgaria	1.542	1.600	1.486	0.556	0.250	0.891	m	m	1.505	0.539	0.68	0.275
	Colombia	m	m	m	m	m	m	m	m	2.731	0.079	1.31	0.032
	Costa Rica	m	m	m	m	m	m	m	m	m	m	1.23	0.065
	Croatia	m	m	m	m	m	m	m	m	1.625	0.739	0.73	0.340
	Dubai (UAE)	m	m	m	m	m	m	m	m	m	m	0.98	0.295
	Hong Kong-China	0.758	0.837	0.673	2.017	1.723	2.366	0.762	1.996	0.734	1.961	0.36	0.886
	Indonesia	3.255	2.874	3.652	c	c	c	3.230	0.023	3.151	0.023	1.55	0.008
	Jordan	m	m	m	m	m	m	m	m	2.626	0.094	1.28	0.054
	Kazakhstan	m	m	m	m	m	m	m	m	m	m	1.35	0.002
	Latvia	1.591	2.138	1.043	0.689	0.327	1.066	1.585	0.681	1.532	0.664	0.74	0.302
	Liechtenstein	1.187	1.124	1.373	1.712	1.318	2.214	1.170	1.709	1.132	1.676	0.75	0.900
	Lithuania	m	m	m	m	m	m	m	m	1.708	0.602	0.80	0.324
	Macao-China	m	m	m	m	m	m	1.382	1.157	1.346	1.130	0.65	0.526
	Malaysia	m	m	m	m	m	m	m	m	m	m	1.30	0.015
	Montenegro	m	m	m	m	m	m	m	m	2.567	0.215	1.26	0.075
	Peru	2.488	2.406	2.571	0.132	c	0.175	m	m	m	m	1.10	0.058
	Qatar	m	m	m	m	m	m	m	m	1.958	0.256	0.94	0.125
	Romania	2.498	2.587	2.417	0.330	0.230	0.431	m	m	2.411	0.325	1.15	0.177
	Russian Federation	2.090	2.393	1.791	0.666	0.447	0.895	2.088	0.659	2.031	0.643	1.00	0.314
	Serbia	m	m	m	m	m	m	m	m	2.254	0.431	1.00	0.221
	Shanghai-China	m	m	m	m	m	m	m	m	m	m	0.20	1.133
	Singapore	m	m	m	m	m	m	m	m	m	m	0.37	0.985
	Chinese Taipei	m	m	m	m	m	m	m	m	1.034	1.575	0.54	0.744
	Thailand	2.755	3.240	2.379	0.138	0.038	0.218	2.754	0.135	2.671	0.136	1.29	0.054
	Tunisia	m	m	m	m	m	m	2.586	0.057	2.513	0.056	1.26	0.041
	United Arab Emirates*	m	m	m	m	m	m	m	m	m	m	1.10	0.084
	Uruguay	m	m	m	m	m	m	2.506	0.176	2.431	0.172	1.2	0.097

Note: The link error is calculated empirically by adding a random error component from a normal distribution with mean equal to zero and standard deviation equal to those shown in Table A5.1 to each student's scores in PISA 2000, PISA 2003, PISA 2006 or PISA 2009. Each country's percentage of students in each proficiency level band are then calculated for each of 500 replications. The standard deviation in the observed coefficients is the result of the added error and is the reported link error.

* United Arab Emirates excluding Dubai.

StatLink ⟨⟩ http://dx.doi.org/10.1787/888932937054

[Part 3/3]
Table A5.2   **Link error for comparisons of proficiency levels between PISA 2012 and previous assessments**

		Science comparison between PISA 2012 and...							
		PISA 2006						PISA 2009	
		Below Level 2			Level 5 or above			Below Level 2	Level 5 or above
		All	Boys	Girls	All	Boys	Girls	All	All
OECD	Australia	0.702	0.699	0.708	0.816	0.779	0.855	0.419	0.486
	Austria	0.935	0.912	0.963	0.704	0.742	0.669	m	m
	Belgium	0.805	0.748	0.867	0.767	0.764	0.772	0.451	0.433
	Canada	0.584	0.585	0.584	0.856	0.933	0.783	0.338	0.478
	Chile	1.563	1.488	1.639	0.143	0.207	0.087	0.888	0.079
	Czech Republic	0.836	0.719	0.970	0.605	0.444	0.786	0.456	0.361
	Denmark	0.922	0.872	0.975	0.519	0.573	0.478	0.540	0.277
	Estonia	0.506	0.560	0.456	0.933	0.929	0.941	0.310	0.518
	Finland	0.457	0.518	0.398	1.040	0.864	1.236	0.259	0.585
	France	0.830	0.761	0.899	0.634	0.718	0.562	0.489	0.326
	Germany	0.717	0.676	0.768	0.892	0.970	0.814	0.430	0.501
	Greece	1.222	1.308	1.146	0.279	0.342	0.224	0.722	0.165
	Hungary	1.073	1.186	0.971	0.606	0.677	0.542	0.639	0.365
	Iceland	0.940	0.930	0.957	0.484	0.496	0.476	0.486	0.288
	Ireland	0.748	0.826	0.680	0.677	0.691	0.668	0.425	0.401
	Israel	0.957	0.877	1.038	0.557	0.736	0.388	0.537	0.337
	Italy	1.014	0.959	1.075	0.516	0.566	0.465	0.607	0.303
	Japan	0.499	0.521	0.478	1.093	1.285	0.888	0.313	0.612
	Korea	0.499	0.586	0.404	0.976	1.129	0.809	0.293	0.584
	Luxembourg	0.947	0.751	1.156	0.650	0.603	0.705	0.548	0.386
	Mexico	2.072	1.952	2.190	0.022	0.028	0.017	1.195	0.014
	Netherlands	0.879	0.668	1.106	0.911	0.968	0.856	0.541	0.548
	New Zealand	0.796	0.677	0.923	0.803	0.900	0.707	0.433	0.451
	Norway	0.864	0.812	0.921	0.551	0.521	0.585	0.486	0.298
	Poland	0.620	0.708	0.545	0.813	0.795	0.835	0.334	0.484
	Portugal	0.953	0.928	0.982	0.422	0.442	0.407	0.522	0.221
	Slovak Republic	1.013	1.100	0.924	0.424	0.463	0.386	0.566	0.253
	Slovenia	0.918	1.222	0.600	0.758	0.832	0.685	0.542	0.414
	Spain	0.884	0.840	0.932	0.501	0.591	0.411	0.517	0.286
	Sweden	0.973	0.918	1.033	0.454	0.447	0.466	0.560	0.254
	Switzerland	0.740	0.725	0.760	0.712	0.665	0.765	0.443	0.389
	Turkey	1.492	1.514	1.480	0.246	0.296	0.203	0.870	0.130
	United Kingdom	0.718	0.648	0.790	0.808	0.862	0.768	0.411	0.452
	United States	0.938	0.946	0.938	0.507	0.546	0.476	0.527	0.288
Partners	Albania	m	m	m	m	m	m	0.808	0.051
	Argentina	1.800	1.660	1.941	0.053	0.066	0.047	1.025	0.027
	Brazil	1.755	1.616	1.882	0.038	0.049	0.034	1.019	0.017
	Bulgaria	1.207	1.248	1.169	0.264	0.249	0.286	0.723	0.149
	Colombia	1.891	2.043	1.768	0.012	0.022	0.004	1.111	0.005
	Costa Rica	m	m	m	m	m	m	1.026	0.036
	Croatia	0.965	1.036	0.895	0.456	0.465	0.452	0.572	0.284
	Dubai (UAE)	m	m	m	m	m	m	0.720	0.182
	Hong Kong-China	0.299	0.304	0.296	1.454	1.556	1.341	0.167	0.873
	Indonesia	1.740	1.763	1.728	c	c	c	0.932	c
	Jordan	1.669	1.530	1.808	0.051	0.057	0.053	0.936	0.028
	Kazakhstan	m	m	m	m	m	m	1.048	0.025
	Latvia	0.953	1.016	0.898	0.460	0.470	0.457	0.566	0.288
	Liechtenstein	0.597	0.867	0.380	0.728	0.928	0.584	0.269	0.423
	Lithuania	0.869	0.924	0.819	0.501	0.382	0.628	0.489	0.320
	Macao-China	0.685	0.640	0.742	0.656	0.820	0.494	0.434	0.383
	Malaysia	m	m	m	m	m	m	1.058	0.026
	Montenegro	1.689	1.595	1.793	0.067	0.071	0.070	1.035	0.042
	Peru	m	m	m	m	m	m	0.822	0.000
	Qatar	1.126	0.940	1.328	0.132	0.124	0.143	0.657	0.071
	Romania	1.861	1.923	1.810	0.129	0.129	0.130	1.122	0.094
	Russian Federation	1.298	1.333	1.267	0.398	0.390	0.407	0.801	0.230
	Serbia	1.482	1.599	1.369	0.117	0.115	0.125	0.844	0.061
	Shanghai-China	m	m	m	m	m	m	0.150	1.006
	Singapore	m	m	m	m	m	m	0.307	0.650
	Chinese Taipei	0.751	0.742	0.763	0.764	0.788	0.747	0.480	0.426
	Thailand	1.781	1.899	1.696	0.135	0.092	0.172	1.060	0.078
	Tunisia	1.794	1.703	1.877	0.022	0.033	0.021	1.049	0.014
	United Arab Emirates*	m	m	m	m	m	m	0.758	0.075
	Uruguay	1.352	1.225	1.468	0.096	0.157	0.049	0.760	0.052

Note: The link error is calculated empirically by adding a random error component from a normal distribution with mean equal to zero and standard deviation equal to those shown in Table A5.1 to each student's scores in PISA 2000, PISA 2003, PISA 2006 or PISA 2009. Each country's percentage of students in each proficiency level band are then calculated for each of 500 replications. The standard deviation in the observed coefficients is the result of the added error and is the reported link error.
* United Arab Emirates excluding Dubai.
StatLink ⟮⟯ http://dx.doi.org/10.1787/888932937054

[Part 1/1]

Link error for comparisons of annualised and curvilinear change between PISA 2012 and previous assessments

Table A5.3

		Comparisons between PISA 2012 and all previous comparable assessments in...					
		Mathematics		Reading		Science	
		Linear term	Quadratic term	Linear term	Quadratic term	Linear term	Quadratic term
		Error	Error	Error	Error	Error	Error
OECD	Australia	0.192	0.092	0.194	0.149	0.595	0.168
	Austria	0.195	0.091	0.193	0.148	0.594	0.168
	Belgium	0.191	0.091	0.194	0.147	0.597	0.168
	Canada	0.199	0.092	0.187	0.148	0.592	0.168
	Chile	0.305	0.185	0.292	0.169	0.605	0.168
	Czech Republic	0.183	0.088	0.237	0.147	0.609	0.168
	Denmark	0.205	0.094	0.187	0.149	0.588	0.168
	Estonia	0.297	0.185	0.481	0.459	0.610	0.168
	Finland	0.195	0.092	0.193	0.148	0.593	0.168
	France	0.189	0.090	0.206	0.148	0.599	0.168
	Germany	0.189	0.084	0.305	0.145	0.635	0.168
	Greece	0.195	0.091	0.209	0.150	0.592	0.168
	Hungary	0.194	0.092	0.193	0.149	0.594	0.168
	Iceland	0.196	0.092	0.188	0.147	0.595	0.168
	Ireland	0.196	0.091	0.191	0.149	0.593	0.168
	Israel	0.330	0.185	0.235	0.172	0.593	0.168
	Italy	0.191	0.091	0.200	0.148	0.597	0.168
	Japan	0.194	0.092	0.202	0.150	0.592	0.168
	Korea	0.199	0.094	0.187	0.149	0.590	0.168
	Luxembourg	0.203	0.094	0.184	0.148	0.590	0.168
	Mexico	0.202	0.094	0.186	0.149	0.589	0.168
	Netherlands	0.194	0.091	0.189	0.148	0.594	0.168
	New Zealand	0.191	0.092	0.193	0.148	0.596	0.168
	Norway	0.199	0.092	0.186	0.147	0.593	0.168
	Poland	0.185	0.088	0.231	0.148	0.606	0.168
	Portugal	0.203	0.093	0.187	0.150	0.587	0.168
	Slovak Republic	0.184	0.089	0.320	0.223	0.607	0.168
	Slovenia	0.306	0.185	0.460	0.459	0.605	0.168
	Spain	0.194	0.092	0.198	0.148	0.595	0.168
	Sweden	0.191	0.090	0.191	0.146	0.599	0.168
	Switzerland	0.186	0.089	0.203	0.147	0.603	0.168
	Turkey	0.216	0.096	0.287	0.219	0.586	0.168
	United Kingdom	0.194	0.091	0.190	0.148	0.595	0.168
	United States	0.198	0.092	0.188	0.147	0.593	0.168
Partners	Albania	0.748	m	0.238	0.205	0.678	m
	Argentina	0.340	0.185	0.228	0.171	0.590	0.168
	Brazil	0.205	0.094	0.199	0.151	0.586	0.168
	Bulgaria	0.318	0.185	0.281	0.168	0.599	0.168
	Colombia	0.326	0.185	0.428	0.459	0.595	0.168
	Costa Rica	0.748	m	0.848	m	0.678	m
	Croatia	0.317	0.185	0.440	0.459	0.599	0.168
	Dubai (UAE)	0.748	m	0.848	m	0.678	m
	Hong Kong-China	0.195	0.092	0.201	0.177	0.593	0.168
	Indonesia	0.234	0.095	0.262	0.176	0.581	0.168
	Jordan	0.346	0.185	0.413	0.459	0.588	0.168
	Kazakhstan	0.748	m	0.848	m	0.678	m
	Latvia	0.184	0.086	0.255	0.148	0.614	0.168
	Liechtenstein	0.239	0.095	0.239	0.150	0.579	0.168
	Lithuania	0.310	0.185	0.451	0.459	0.602	0.168
	Macao-China	0.189	0.090	0.292	0.222	0.598	0.168
	Malaysia	0.748	m	0.848	m	0.678	m
	Montenegro	0.336	0.185	0.419	0.459	0.591	0.168
	Peru	0.748	m	0.245	0.205	0.678	m
	Qatar	0.358	0.185	0.411	0.459	0.584	0.168
	Romania	0.308	0.185	0.287	0.207	0.604	0.168
	Russian Federation	0.186	0.084	0.284	0.148	0.620	0.168
	Serbia	0.329	0.185	0.424	0.459	0.594	0.168
	Shanghai-China	0.748	m	0.848	m	0.678	m
	Singapore	0.748	m	0.848	m	0.678	m
	Chinese Taipei	0.336	0.185	0.419	0.459	0.591	0.168
	Thailand	0.199	0.093	0.208	0.176	0.590	0.168
	Tunisia	0.191	0.091	0.288	0.221	0.595	0.168
	United Arab Emirates*	1.122	m	1.273	m	1.017	m
	Uruguay	0.205	0.092	0.274	0.220	0.589	0.168

Note: The link error is calculated empirically by adding a random error component from a normal distribution with mean equal to zero and standard deviation equal to those shown in Table A5.1 to each student's scores in PISA 2000, PISA 2003, PISA 2006 or PISA 2009. The linear and quadratic terms of a regression model are then calculated for each of 500 replications. The standard deviation in the observed coefficients is the result of the added error and is the reported link error.

* United Arab Emirates excluding Dubai.

StatLink ᴹˢᴾ http://dx.doi.org/10.1787/888932937054

The annualised change is a more robust measure of a country's/economy's progress in education outcomes as it is based on information available from all assessments. It is thus less sensitive to abnormal measurements that may alter a country's/economy's PISA trends if results are compared only between two assessments. The annualised change is calculated as the best-fitting line throughout a country's/economy's participation in PISA. The year that individual students participated in PISA is regressed on their PISA scores, yielding the annualised change. The annualised change also takes into account the fact that, for some countries and economies, the period between PISA assessments is less than three years. This is the case for those countries and economies that participated in PISA 2000 or PISA 2009 as part of PISA+: they conducted the assessment in 2001, 2002 or 2010 instead of 2000 or 2009. Figure A5.1 compares the value of the annualised change in mathematics with the difference in mathematics performance observed in PISA 2012 and PISA 2003.

■ Figure A5.1 ■

Annualised change in mathematics performance since PISA 2003 and observed differences in performance between PISA 2012 and PISA 2003

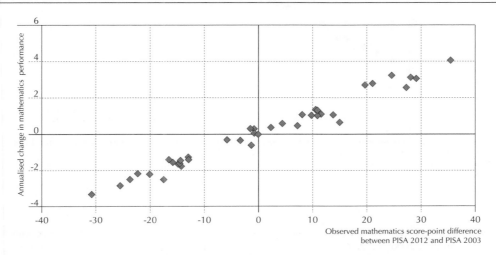

Notes: The annualised change is the average annual change in PISA score points from a country's/economy's earliest participation in PISA to PISA 2012. It is calculated taking into account all of the country's/economy's participation in PISA.
Source: OECD, PISA 2012 Database, Table I.2.3b.
StatLink ⟦⟧ http://dx.doi.org/10.1787/888932937054

■ Figure A5.2 ■

Annualised change in reading performance since PISA 2000 and observed differences in performance between PISA 2012 and PISA 2000

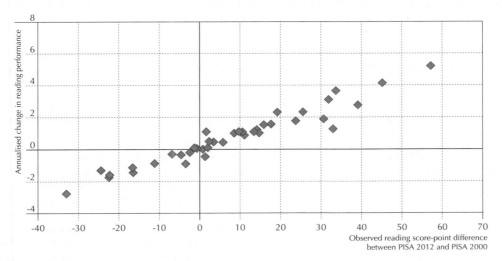

Notes: The annualised change is the average annual change in PISA score points from a country's/economy's earliest participation in PISA to PISA 2012. It is calculated taking into account all of the country's/economy's participation in PISA.
Source: OECD, PISA 2012 Database, Table I.4.3b.
StatLink ⟦⟧ http://dx.doi.org/10.1787/888932937054

■ Figure A5.3 ■

**Annualised change in science performance since PISA 2006 and observed differences
in performance between PISA 2012 and PISA 2006**

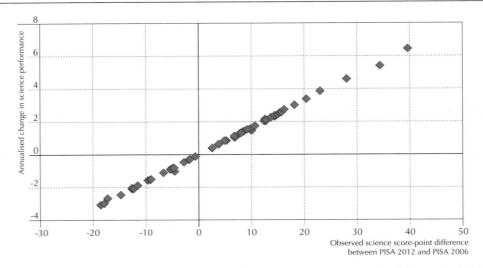

Notes: The annualised change is the average annual change in PISA score points from a country's/economy's earliest participation in PISA to PISA 2012.
It is calculated taking into account all of the country's/economy's participation in PISA.
Source: OECD, PISA 2012 Database, Table I.5.3b.
StatLink 🔗 http://dx.doi.org/10.1787/888932937054

Figures A5.2 and A5.3 do the same for reading and science: they compare the annualised change in performance with the difference between PISA 2012 and PISA 2000 and PISA 2006, respectively. In general, and especially in the comparison between science in PISA 2006 and PISA 2012, the annualised change provides a result similar to the difference in performance between two assessments. As more assessments are taken into account, the annualised change begins to differ from the observed trend, providing a more complete picture of a country's/economy's progress in PISA.

Comparing items and non-performance scales across PISA cycles

To gather information about students' and schools' characteristics, PISA asks both students and schools to complete a background questionnaire. In PISA 2003 and PISA 2012 several questions were left untouched, allowing for a comparison of responses to these questions over time. In this report, only questions that retained the same wording were used for trends analyses. Questions with subtle word changes or questions with major word changes were not compared across time because it is impossible to discern whether observed changes in the response are due to changes in the construct they are measuring or to changes in the way the construct is being measured.

Also, as described in Annex A1, questionnaire items in PISA are used to construct indices. Whenever the questions used in the construction of indices remains intact in PISA 2003 and PISA 2012, the corresponding indices are compared. Two types of indices are used in PISA: simple indices and scale indices.

Simple indices recode a set of responses to questionnaire items. For trends analyses, the values observed in PISA 2003 are compared directly to PISA 2012, just as simple responses to questionnaire items are. This is the case of indices like student-teacher ratio and ability grouping in mathematics.

Scale indices, on the other hand, imply WLE estimates which require rescaling in order to be comparable across PISA cycles. Scale indices, like the *PISA index of economic, social and cultural status*, the *index of sense of belonging*, the *index of attitudes towards school*, the *index of intrinsic motivation to learn mathematics*, the *index of instrumental motivation to learn mathematics*, the *index of mathematics self-efficacy*, the *index of mathematics self-concept*, the *index of anxiety towards mathematics*, the *index of teacher shortage*, the *index of quality of physical infrastructure*, the *index of quality of educational resources*, the *index of disciplinary climate*, the *index of student-teacher relations*, the *index of teacher morale*, the *index of student-related factors affecting school climate*, and the *index of teacher-related factors affecting school climate*, were scaled in PISA 2012 to have an OECD mean of 0 and a standard deviation of 1. In PISA 2003 these same scales were scaled to have an OECD average of 0 and a standard deviation of 1. Because they are on different scales, values reported in *Learning for Tomorrow's World: First Results from PISA 2003* (OECD, 2004) cannot be compared with those reported in this volume. To make these scale indices comparable, values for 2003 have been rescaled to the 2012 scale, using the PISA 2012 parameter estimates.

To evaluate change in these items and scales, analyses report the change in the estimate between two assessments, usually PISA 2003 and PISA 2012. Comparisons between two assessments (e.g. a country's/economy's change in the *index of anxiety towards mathematics* between PISA 2003 and PISA 2012 or the change in this index for a subgroup) is calculated as:

$$\Delta_{2012,t} = PISA_{2012} - PISA_t$$

where $\Delta_{2012,t}$ is the difference in the index between PISA 2012 and a previous assessment, $PISA_{2012}$ is the index value observed in PISA 2012, and $PISA_t$ is the index value observed in a previous assessment (2000, 2003, 2006 or 2009). The standard error of the change in performance $\sigma(\Delta_{2012-t})$ is:

$$\sigma(\Delta_{2012-t}) = \sqrt{\sigma_{2012}^2 + \sigma_t^2}$$

where σ_{2012} is the standard error observed for $PISA_{2012}$ and σ_t is the standard error observed for $PISA_t$. These comparisons are based on an identical set of items; there is no uncertainty related to the choice of items for equating purposes, so no link error is needed.

Although only scale indices that use the same items in PISA 2003 and PISA 2012 are valid for trend comparisons, this does not imply that PISA 2012 indices that include exactly the same items as 2003 as well as new questionnaire items cannot be compared with PISA 2003 indices that included a smaller pool of items. In such cases, for example the *index of sense of belonging,* trend analyses were conducted by treating as missing in PISA 2003 items that were asked in the context of PISA 2012 but not in the PISA 2003 student questionnaire. This means that while the full set of information was used to scale the sense of belonging index in 2012, the PISA 2003 sense of belonging index was scaled under the assumption that if the 2012 items that were missing in 2003 had been asked in 2003, the overall index and index variation would have remained the same as those that were observed on common 2003 items. This is a tenable assumption inasmuch as in both PISA 2003 and PISA 2012 the questionnaire items used to construct the scale hold as an underlying factor in the construction of the scale.

OECD average

Throughout this report, the OECD average is used as a benchmark. It is calculated as the average across OECD countries, weighting each country equally. Some OECD countries did not participate in certain assessments, other OECD countries do not have comparable results for some assessments, others did not include certain questions in their questionnaires or changed them substantially from assessment to assessment. For this reason in trends tables and figures, the OECD average is reported as assessment-specific, that is, it includes only those countries for which there is comparable information in that particular assessment. This way, the 2003 OECD average includes only those OECD countries that have comparable information from the 2003 assessment, even if the results it refers to the PISA 2012 assessment and more countries have comparable information. This restriction allows for valid comparisons of the OECD average over time.

References

OECD (forthcoming), *PISA 2012 Technical Report, PISA,* OECD Publishing.

OECD (2004), *Learning for Tomorrow's World: First Results from PISA 2003*, PISA, OECD Publishing.
http://dx.doi.org/10.1787/9789264006416-en

Annex B

PISA 2012 DATA

All tables in Annex B are available on line

Annex B1: Results for countries and economies
http://dx.doi.org/10.1787/888932964908
http://dx.doi.org/10.1787/888932964927
http://dx.doi.org/10.1787/888932964946

Annex B2: Results for regions within countries
http://dx.doi.org/10.1787/888932964965

Annex B3: List of tables available on line

The reader should note that there are gaps
in the numbering of tables because some tables
appear on line only and are not included in this publication.

ANNEX B1

RESULTS FOR COUNTRIES AND ECONOMIES

[Part 1/2]
Relationship between performance in mathematics, reading and science, and socio-economic status

Table II.2.1 — *Results based on students' self-reports*

	Unadjusted mathematics mean score		Mathematics performance accounted for the mean ESCS[1]		Strength of the relationship between mathematics performance and ESCS[2] — Percentage of explained variance in mathematics performance		Slope of the socio-economic gradient for mathematics[2] — Score-point difference in mathematics associated with one-unit increase in ESCS		Length of the projection of the gradient line[3] — 5th percentile of ESCS		95th percentile of ESCS		Difference between 95th and 5th percentile of ESCS	
	Mean score	S.E.	Mean score	S.E.		S.E.		S.E.	Index	S.E.	Index	S.E.	Diff	S.E.
OECD														
Australia	504	(1.6)	496	(1.6)	**12.3**	(0.8)	42	(1.3)	-1.11	(0.02)	1.36	(0.01)	2.47	(0.02)
Austria	506	(2.7)	503	(2.5)	**15.8**	(1.5)	43	(2.2)	-1.21	(0.04)	1.51	(0.03)	2.72	(0.05)
Belgium	515	(2.1)	510	(1.8)	**19.6**	(1.4)	49	(1.7)	-1.26	(0.04)	1.49	(0.03)	2.75	(0.04)
Canada	518	(1.8)	508	(1.6)	**9.4**	(0.7)	31	(1.2)	-1.06	(0.03)	1.65	(0.02)	2.71	(0.03)
Chile	423	(3.1)	443	(2.7)	**23.1**	(1.9)	34	(1.6)	-2.34	(0.06)	1.32	(0.02)	3.66	(0.06)
Czech Republic	499	(2.9)	503	(2.5)	**16.2**	(1.5)	51	(2.7)	-1.17	(0.03)	1.20	(0.02)	2.37	(0.03)
Denmark	500	(2.3)	485	(1.7)	**16.5**	(1.4)	39	(1.7)	-0.95	(0.03)	1.62	(0.02)	2.57	(0.03)
Estonia	521	(2.0)	518	(1.9)	**8.6**	(0.9)	29	(1.7)	-1.13	(0.02)	1.36	(0.01)	2.49	(0.02)
Finland	519	(1.9)	508	(1.9)	**9.4**	(0.9)	33	(1.8)	-0.93	(0.02)	1.45	(0.02)	2.38	(0.03)
France	495	(2.5)	500	(2.2)	**22.5**	(1.3)	57	(2.2)	-1.36	(0.03)	1.17	(0.01)	2.53	(0.03)
Germany	514	(2.9)	511	(2.6)	**16.9**	(1.4)	43	(2.0)	-1.25	(0.04)	1.65	(0.02)	2.90	(0.04)
Greece	453	(2.5)	456	(1.9)	**15.5**	(1.5)	34	(1.8)	-1.67	(0.05)	1.46	(0.04)	3.13	(0.05)
Hungary	477	(3.2)	490	(2.8)	**23.1**	(2.3)	47	(2.8)	-1.76	(0.04)	1.26	(0.03)	3.02	(0.04)
Iceland	493	(1.7)	470	(2.1)	**7.7**	(1.0)	31	(2.1)	-0.65	(0.03)	1.90	(0.02)	2.55	(0.04)
Ireland	501	(2.2)	497	(2.0)	**14.6**	(1.2)	38	(1.8)	-1.23	(0.02)	1.42	(0.01)	2.65	(0.02)
Israel	466	(4.7)	460	(3.8)	**17.2**	(1.5)	51	(2.6)	-1.27	(0.05)	1.30	(0.01)	2.57	(0.05)
Italy	485	(2.0)	487	(1.8)	**10.1**	(0.6)	30	(1.2)	-1.58	(0.01)	1.56	(0.02)	3.14	(0.03)
Japan	536	(3.6)	541	(3.3)	**9.8**	(1.6)	41	(3.9)	-1.17	(0.02)	1.05	(0.01)	2.22	(0.03)
Korea	554	(4.6)	553	(3.9)	**10.1**	(1.4)	42	(3.3)	-1.23	(0.03)	1.15	(0.02)	2.38	(0.03)
Luxembourg	490	(1.1)	488	(1.3)	**18.3**	(1.1)	37	(1.2)	-1.85	(0.03)	1.64	(0.02)	3.48	(0.05)
Mexico	413	(1.4)	435	(1.4)	**10.4**	(0.8)	19	(0.8)	-3.03	(0.04)	1.08	(0.03)	4.10	(0.05)
Netherlands	523	(3.5)	515	(3.2)	**11.5**	(1.7)	40	(3.1)	-1.06	(0.03)	1.35	(0.02)	2.41	(0.04)
New Zealand	500	(2.2)	500	(2.2)	**18.4**	(1.3)	52	(1.9)	-1.33	(0.03)	1.25	(0.04)	2.58	(0.05)
Norway	489	(2.7)	476	(2.8)	**7.4**	(1.0)	32	(2.4)	-0.81	(0.02)	1.55	(0.01)	2.36	(0.02)
Poland	518	(3.6)	526	(3.2)	**16.6**	(1.7)	41	(2.4)	-1.39	(0.02)	1.35	(0.02)	2.74	(0.02)
Portugal	487	(3.8)	506	(2.6)	**19.6**	(1.8)	35	(1.6)	-2.13	(0.03)	1.62	(0.02)	3.74	(0.03)
Slovak Republic	482	(3.4)	492	(2.6)	**24.6**	(2.1)	54	(2.9)	-1.48	(0.06)	1.42	(0.03)	2.90	(0.07)
Slovenia	501	(1.2)	499	(1.3)	**15.6**	(1.0)	42	(1.5)	-1.23	(0.02)	1.46	(0.02)	2.69	(0.03)
Spain	484	(1.9)	492	(1.6)	**15.8**	(1.0)	34	(1.1)	-1.82	(0.02)	1.43	(0.02)	3.26	(0.03)
Sweden	478	(2.3)	471	(1.9)	**10.6**	(1.1)	36	(1.9)	-1.05	(0.02)	1.42	(0.04)	2.47	(0.04)
Switzerland	531	(3.0)	525	(2.7)	**12.8**	(1.2)	38	(1.8)	-1.34	(0.03)	1.51	(0.01)	2.85	(0.03)
Turkey	448	(4.8)	494	(6.6)	**14.5**	(1.8)	32	(2.4)	-3.01	(0.04)	0.63	(0.07)	3.64	(0.07)
United Kingdom	494	(3.3)	486	(2.6)	**12.5**	(1.2)	41	(2.4)	-1.04	(0.02)	1.49	(0.03)	2.52	(0.04)
United States	481	(3.6)	476	(2.7)	**14.8**	(1.3)	35	(1.7)	-1.52	(0.05)	1.61	(0.04)	3.12	(0.06)
OECD average	494	(0.5)	495	(0.5)	**14.8**	(0.2)	39	(0.4)	-1.42	(0.01)	1.40	(0.00)	2.83	(0.01)
Partners														
Albania	m	m	m	m	m	m	m	m	m	m	m	m	m	m
Argentina	388	(3.5)	409	(3.0)	**15.1**	(1.5)	26	(1.7)	-2.54	(0.07)	1.06	(0.03)	3.60	(0.07)
Brazil	391	(2.1)	423	(3.2)	**15.7**	(1.6)	26	(1.7)	-2.98	(0.02)	0.81	(0.04)	3.80	(0.05)
Bulgaria	439	(4.0)	451	(3.2)	**22.3**	(2.3)	42	(2.7)	-1.92	(0.10)	1.30	(0.02)	3.23	(0.09)
Colombia	376	(2.9)	408	(3.6)	**15.4**	(1.8)	25	(1.7)	-3.21	(0.04)	0.62	(0.04)	3.83	(0.06)
Costa Rica	407	(3.0)	431	(3.1)	**18.9**	(2.1)	24	(1.6)	-3.00	(0.07)	0.92	(0.03)	3.93	(0.07)
Croatia	471	(3.5)	484	(3.7)	**12.0**	(1.4)	36	(2.6)	-1.60	(0.03)	1.16	(0.02)	2.76	(0.04)
Cyprus*	440	(1.1)	438	(1.1)	**14.1**	(1.1)	38	(1.6)	-1.30	(0.04)	1.49	(0.02)	2.79	(0.04)
Hong Kong-China	561	(3.2)	584	(3.1)	**7.5**	(1.5)	27	(2.6)	-2.29	(0.03)	0.82	(0.05)	3.10	(0.05)
Indonesia	375	(4.0)	411	(8.1)	**9.6**	(3.0)	20	(3.4)	-3.35	(0.05)	0.25	(0.08)	3.60	(0.08)
Jordan	386	(3.1)	397	(3.4)	**8.4**	(1.3)	22	(2.2)	-2.15	(0.06)	1.01	(0.03)	3.16	(0.07)
Kazakhstan	432	(3.0)	440	(3.1)	**8.0**	(1.7)	27	(2.8)	-1.56	(0.03)	0.78	(0.02)	2.34	(0.04)
Latvia	491	(2.8)	500	(2.5)	**14.7**	(1.7)	35	(2.1)	-1.62	(0.04)	1.15	(0.03)	2.77	(0.05)
Liechtenstein	535	(4.0)	528	(4.5)	**7.6**	(3.1)	28	(5.8)	-1.22	(0.12)	1.80	(0.17)	3.02	(0.18)
Lithuania	479	(2.6)	484	(2.2)	**13.8**	(1.2)	36	(1.8)	-1.57	(0.02)	1.18	(0.01)	2.75	(0.02)
Macao-China	538	(1.0)	555	(1.6)	**2.6**	(0.4)	17	(1.5)	-2.19	(0.02)	0.74	(0.03)	2.94	(0.04)
Malaysia	421	(3.2)	442	(3.6)	**13.4**	(1.6)	30	(2.1)	-2.41	(0.06)	0.84	(0.03)	3.24	(0.07)
Montenegro	410	(1.1)	419	(1.2)	**12.7**	(0.9)	33	(1.3)	-1.70	(0.04)	1.13	(0.02)	2.82	(0.05)
Peru	368	(3.7)	409	(4.0)	**23.4**	(2.4)	33	(2.0)	-3.23	(0.05)	0.91	(0.07)	4.14	(0.07)
Qatar	376	(0.8)	367	(0.9)	**5.6**	(0.5)	27	(1.2)	-1.24	(0.03)	1.69	(0.03)	2.93	(0.04)
Romania	445	(3.8)	463	(3.5)	**19.3**	(2.4)	38	(2.9)	-1.92	(0.07)	1.09	(0.04)	3.01	(0.07)
Russian Federation	482	(3.0)	487	(3.0)	**11.4**	(1.7)	38	(3.2)	-1.36	(0.04)	0.98	(0.03)	2.34	(0.05)
Serbia	449	(3.4)	459	(3.2)	**11.7**	(1.4)	34	(2.4)	-1.62	(0.04)	1.24	(0.02)	2.87	(0.04)
Shanghai-China	613	(3.3)	627	(2.7)	**15.1**	(1.9)	41	(2.7)	-1.95	(0.07)	1.05	(0.02)	3.00	(0.07)
Singapore	573	(1.3)	585	(1.2)	**14.4**	(0.9)	44	(1.4)	-1.84	(0.03)	1.14	(0.02)	2.98	(0.03)
Chinese Taipei	560	(3.3)	583	(2.5)	**17.9**	(1.4)	58	(2.5)	-1.74	(0.03)	0.95	(0.02)	2.69	(0.03)
Thailand	427	(3.4)	457	(4.9)	**9.9**	(2.2)	22	(2.4)	-2.99	(0.03)	0.80	(0.05)	3.79	(0.06)
Tunisia	388	(3.9)	415	(5.7)	**12.4**	(2.4)	22	(2.6)	-3.28	(0.05)	0.83	(0.06)	4.11	(0.08)
United Arab Emirates	434	(2.4)	424	(2.0)	**9.8**	(1.0)	33	(1.9)	-1.29	(0.06)	1.49	(0.02)	2.79	(0.06)
Uruguay	409	(2.8)	443	(2.8)	**22.8**	(1.9)	37	(1.8)	-2.53	(0.03)	1.14	(0.04)	3.67	(0.05)
Viet Nam	511	(4.8)	565	(6.3)	**14.6**	(2.3)	29	(2.6)	-3.37	(0.04)	0.48	(0.12)	3.84	(0.12)

Note: Values that are statistically significant are indicated in bold (see Annex A3). There are no direct comparisons with the OECD average in these tables.
1. ESCS refers to the *PISA index of economic, social and cultural status*.
2. Single-level bivariate regression of performance on the ESCS, the slope is the regression coefficient for ESCS.
3. Percentiles calculated at the student level.
4. Student-level regression of mathematics performance on the ESCS and the squared term of the ESCS; the index of curvilinearity is the regression coefficient for the squared term.
* See notes at the beginning of this Annex.
StatLink ⟶ http://dx.doi.org/10.1787/888932964908

[Part 2/2]
Relationship between performance in mathematics, reading and science, and socio-economic status

Table II.2.1   *Results based on students' self-reports*

		Index of curvilinearity[4]		Strength of the relationship between reading performance and ESCS[2]		Slope of the socio-economic gradient for reading[2]		Strength of the relationship between science performance and ESCS[2]		Slope of the socio-economic gradient for science[2]	
		Score-point difference in mathematics associated with one-unit increase in ESCS squared	S.E.	Percentage of explained variance in reading performance	S.E.	Score-point difference in reading associated with one-unit increase in ESCS	S.E.	Percentage of explained variance in science performance	S.E.	Score-point difference in science associated with one-unit increase in ESCS	S.E.
OECD	Australia	2.0	(1.1)	12.0	(0.8)	42	(1.3)	11.9	(0.7)	43	(1.3)
	Austria	-4.6	(2.0)	15.3	(1.6)	42	(2.3)	18.3	(1.7)	46	(2.2)
	Belgium	1.7	(1.3)	18.2	(1.4)	47	(1.8)	19.2	(1.4)	48	(1.7)
	Canada	1.7	(1.0)	8.1	(0.7)	30	(1.3)	7.8	(0.7)	29	(1.4)
	Chile	3.3	(0.8)	20.4	(1.8)	31	(1.5)	20.2	(1.9)	32	(1.7)
	Czech Republic	-5.0	(2.9)	14.8	(1.5)	46	(2.7)	14.3	(1.7)	46	(3.1)
	Denmark	1.3	(1.5)	15.3	(1.3)	39	(1.9)	15.7	(1.5)	43	(2.2)
	Estonia	3.7	(2.2)	6.8	(1.0)	26	(1.9)	7.4	(0.9)	27	(1.9)
	Finland	1.6	(1.7)	7.5	(0.9)	33	(2.2)	7.9	(0.9)	33	(2.1)
	France	4.3	(1.5)	18.7	(1.5)	58	(2.9)	21.5	(1.3)	58	(2.4)
	Germany	-4.5	(1.6)	15.0	(1.4)	37	(2.0)	17.1	(1.4)	42	(2.2)
	Greece	1.3	(1.2)	12.0	(1.3)	34	(2.1)	13.7	(1.4)	33	(1.9)
	Hungary	-1.4	(1.8)	20.0	(2.1)	42	(2.3)	22.4	(2.2)	44	(2.3)
	Iceland	1.3	(1.9)	6.3	(1.0)	30	(2.3)	7.5	(0.9)	33	(2.1)
	Ireland	0.5	(1.5)	15.1	(1.2)	39	(1.9)	14.5	(1.2)	41	(2.0)
	Israel	5.5	(1.2)	11.2	(1.4)	44	(2.9)	14.7	(1.4)	48	(2.9)
	Italy	-3.2	(0.7)	9.7	(0.7)	31	(1.1)	9.6	(0.7)	30	(1.1)
	Japan	-2.6	(2.4)	7.9	(1.5)	38	(3.9)	7.3	(1.4)	36	(3.9)
	Korea	6.6	(2.2)	7.9	(1.2)	33	(2.8)	6.7	(1.1)	29	(2.6)
	Luxembourg	2.6	(1.1)	15.6	(1.0)	37	(1.3)	20.0	(1.0)	42	(1.1)
	Mexico	1.3	(0.4)	10.9	(0.9)	21	(0.9)	10.5	(0.8)	18	(0.8)
	Netherlands	3.1	(1.8)	10.8	(1.7)	39	(3.2)	12.5	(1.8)	43	(3.1)
	New Zealand	-0.3	(2.0)	16.5	(1.4)	52	(2.4)	18.2	(1.5)	54	(2.3)
	Norway	-1.6	(1.6)	6.3	(1.0)	33	(2.7)	6.9	(1.0)	34	(2.8)
	Poland	-2.1	(1.7)	13.4	(1.6)	36	(2.2)	14.4	(1.7)	36	(2.4)
	Portugal	0.1	(1.1)	16.5	(1.7)	31	(1.8)	18.7	(1.7)	32	(1.6)
	Slovak Republic	-3.9	(2.0)	24.1	(2.1)	56	(3.3)	26.4	(2.0)	56	(2.9)
	Slovenia	1.7	(1.5)	14.2	(1.1)	40	(1.6)	14.1	(1.0)	39	(1.5)
	Spain	-0.3	(0.7)	12.5	(1.0)	31	(1.3)	13.6	(0.9)	31	(1.1)
	Sweden	-1.1	(1.4)	9.1	(1.1)	38	(2.5)	10.4	(1.2)	38	(2.4)
	Switzerland	-1.5	(1.7)	13.9	(1.0)	38	(1.4)	15.4	(1.0)	40	(1.4)
	Turkey	3.3	(1.2)	14.5	(1.8)	30	(2.1)	11.0	(1.6)	24	(1.8)
	United Kingdom	5.5	(1.5)	11.8	(1.1)	40	(2.3)	13.5	(1.2)	45	(2.3)
	United States	6.5	(1.2)	12.6	(1.3)	33	(1.8)	14.2	(1.4)	36	(1.8)
	OECD average	0.8	(0.3)	13.1	(0.2)	38	(0.4)	14.0	(0.2)	38	(0.4)
Partners	Albania	m	m	m	m	m	m	m	m	m	m
	Argentina	3.1	(1.1)	11.9	(1.5)	29	(2.1)	15.1	(1.8)	29	(2.2)
	Brazil	5.6	(1.1)	11.0	(1.1)	24	(1.3)	13.5	(1.4)	25	(1.5)
	Bulgaria	2.5	(1.6)	21.9	(2.2)	53	(2.9)	23.8	(2.3)	47	(2.8)
	Colombia	3.5	(0.9)	15.6	(1.9)	28	(1.9)	12.7	(1.8)	23	(1.8)
	Costa Rica	4.0	(0.9)	14.7	(2.1)	23	(1.7)	16.3	(2.2)	23	(1.7)
	Croatia	2.6	(1.6)	11.2	(1.4)	34	(2.5)	9.8	(1.2)	31	(2.3)
	Cyprus*	2.3	(1.2)	8.2	(0.8)	35	(1.9)	13.7	(1.0)	39	(1.7)
	Hong Kong-China	0.9	(1.4)	5.2	(1.2)	20	(2.5)	6.0	(1.3)	21	(2.3)
	Indonesia	5.4	(1.9)	6.2	(2.2)	17	(3.1)	8.4	(2.5)	18	(2.7)
	Jordan	3.0	(1.3)	4.8	(1.0)	19	(2.1)	7.0	(1.2)	21	(2.2)
	Kazakhstan	1.6	(1.8)	12.2	(1.4)	34	(2.1)	9.5	(1.4)	30	(2.3)
	Latvia	-1.0	(1.7)	14.0	(2.0)	36	(2.7)	11.9	(1.7)	30	(2.2)
	Liechtenstein	-12.3	(5.1)	7.0	(3.1)	25	(5.6)	9.7	(3.4)	29	(5.2)
	Lithuania	-1.7	(1.4)	11.3	(1.1)	32	(1.7)	11.8	(1.2)	32	(1.9)
	Macao-China	0.8	(1.4)	1.5	(0.4)	11	(1.4)	2.1	(0.6)	13	(1.8)
	Malaysia	6.2	(1.1)	7.7	(1.4)	23	(2.2)	10.3	(1.4)	25	(1.9)
	Montenegro	2.9	(1.4)	10.9	(1.0)	34	(1.5)	11.6	(0.9)	32	(1.4)
	Peru	1.4	(1.2)	23.6	(2.6)	37	(2.3)	21.7	(2.5)	30	(1.8)
	Qatar	-2.7	(0.7)	5.2	(0.5)	29	(1.4)	5.4	(0.5)	28	(1.2)
	Romania	6.0	(1.0)	16.5	(2.0)	38	(2.6)	16.9	(2.1)	34	(2.5)
	Russian Federation	1.0	(2.3)	13.1	(1.6)	43	(3.2)	14.6	(1.9)	43	(3.1)
	Serbia	3.7	(1.6)	8.7	(1.2)	30	(2.3)	8.8	(1.2)	29	(2.2)
	Shanghai-China	-3.9	(1.8)	15.6	(1.8)	33	(2.0)	15.3	(2.0)	33	(2.1)
	Singapore	1.7	(1.4)	15.2	(0.9)	43	(1.4)	16.5	(1.0)	46	(1.6)
	Chinese Taipei	-0.5	(1.8)	15.1	(1.4)	42	(2.2)	16.7	(1.4)	40	(1.8)
	Thailand	7.5	(1.4)	10.0	(1.9)	21	(2.1)	8.2	(1.8)	19	(2.1)
	Tunisia	5.9	(1.4)	9.2	(1.8)	21	(2.2)	8.2	(1.7)	18	(2.0)
	United Arab Emirates	0.8	(1.1)	7.1	(0.9)	30	(1.9)	8.9	(1.0)	33	(2.1)
	Uruguay	4.4	(1.2)	17.5	(1.8)	35	(2.0)	19.8	(1.8)	37	(1.9)
	Viet Nam	-0.1	(1.4)	11.7	(2.1)	23	(2.3)	10.1	(1.8)	22	(2.2)

Note: Values that are statistically significant are indicated in bold (see Annex A3). There are no direct comparisons with the OECD average in these tables.
1. ESCS refers to the *PISA index of economic, social and cultural status*.
2. Single-level bivariate regression of performance on the ESCS, the slope is the regression coefficient for ESCS.
3. Percentiles calculated at the student level.
4. Student-level regression of mathematics performance on the ESCS and the squared term of the ESCS; the index of curvilinearity is the regression coefficient for the squared term.
* See notes at the beginning of this Annex.
StatLink ⟶ http://dx.doi.org/10.1787/888932964908

[Part 1/7]

Elements of socio-economic status, by quarters of socio-economic status within countries

Table II.2.2 — *Results based on students' self-reports*

	Parents' highest level of education: Percentage of students with at least one parent whose highest educational attainment is lower secondary (ISCED 2 or lower)								Parents' highest level of education: Percentage of students with at least one parent whose highest educational attainment is upper secondary or post-secondary non-tertiary (ISCED 3 and 4)							
	Bottom quarter of ESCS[1]		Second quarter of ESCS		Third quarter of ESCS		Top quarter of ESCS		Bottom quarter of ESCS		Second quarter of ESCS		Third quarter of ESCS		Top quarter of ESCS	
	%	S.E.	%	S.E.	%	S.E.	%	S.E.	%	S.E.	%	S.E.	%	S.E.	%	S.E.
Australia	30.5	(0.8)	9.6	(0.6)	1.7	(0.2)	0.0	(0.0)	55.7	(1.0)	50.1	(1.1)	26.6	(0.9)	.3	(0.4)
Austria	17.7	(1.5)	0.8	(0.3)	0.2	(0.1)	0.0	(0.0)	73.7	(1.9)	63.3	(1.9)	44.9	(1.6)	.2	(0.8)
Belgium	19.1	(1.3)	0.6	(0.2)	0.0	(0.0)	0.0	(0.0)	72.0	(1.5)	44.7	(1.3)	11.1	(0.9)	.6	(0.1)
Canada	12.4	(0.9)	0.4	(0.1)	0.0	(0.0)	0.0	(0.0)	61.6	(1.0)	29.3	(0.9)	5.9	(0.5)	.7	(0.1)
Chile	78.0	(1.5)	10.3	(0.9)	1.1	(0.3)	0.0	(0.0)	21.8	(1.4)	86.7	(1.1)	56.5	(1.7)	.6	(0.7)
Czech Republic	4.6	(0.9)	0.3	(0.2)	0.0	(0.0)	0.0	(0.0)	92.4	(1.4)	88.5	(1.1)	65.1	(1.6)	16.6	(1.3)
Denmark	20.4	(1.3)	2.4	(0.5)	0.2	(0.1)	0.0	(0.0)	62.2	(1.6)	34.4	(1.4)	10.3	(1.0)	.5	(0.2)
Estonia	8.5	(1.1)	0.9	(0.3)	0.1	(0.1)	0.0	(0.0)	83.5	(1.4)	52.8	(1.6)	21.8	(1.4)	.9	(0.4)
Finland	11.3	(0.7)	0.3	(0.1)	0.0	(0.0)	0.0	(0.0)	46.4	(1.3)	19.8	(1.1)	4.9	(0.5)	0.2	(0.1)
France	33.5	(1.7)	3.5	(0.6)	0.9	(0.3)	0.0	(0.0)	53.7	(1.6)	50.3	(1.7)	35.5	(1.3)	5.5	(0.7)
Germany	64.9	(1.7)	22.5	(1.4)	3.7	(0.7)	0.0	(0.0)	28.3	(1.7)	42.5	(1.5)	33.1	(1.5)	2.6	(0.5)
Greece	40.1	(1.7)	2.5	(0.5)	0.1	(0.1)	0.0	(0.0)	57.3	(1.7)	64.1	(1.6)	24.5	(1.3)	0.8	(0.2)
Hungary	36.2	(1.9)	2.0	(0.5)	0.0	(0.0)	0.0	(0.0)	63.1	(1.9)	82.2	(1.1)	39.9	(1.6)	2.1	(0.4)
Iceland	26.9	(1.5)	2.0	(0.5)	0.0	(0.0)	0.0	(0.0)	55.7	(1.7)	40.2	(1.9)	9.0	(1.0)	1.5	(0.4)
Ireland	28.7	(1.3)	2.8	(0.4)	0.4	(0.2)	0.0	(0.0)	60.6	(1.6)	56.0	(1.5)	24.6	(1.2)	3.0	(0.5)
Israel	16.8	(1.6)	0.9	(0.3)	0.0	(0.0)	0.0	(0.0)	69.7	(1.6)	50.0	(1.6)	13.3	(1.1)	2.4	(0.4)
Italy	74.3	(0.8)	7.1	(0.4)	0.6	(0.1)	0.0	(0.0)	25.2	(0.8)	75.0	(0.7)	60.9	(0.8)	8.6	(0.5)
Japan	5.7	(0.8)	1.0	(0.2)	0.1	(0.1)	0.0	(0.0)	79.0	(1.2)	41.2	(1.6)	21.6	(1.1)	1.7	(0.4)
Korea	11.9	(1.1)	1.0	(0.3)	0.0	(0.0)	0.0	(0.0)	80.5	(1.1)	61.0	(1.6)	17.6	(1.1)	1.2	(0.3)
Luxembourg	74.6	(1.3)	5.2	(0.4)	0.2	(0.1)	0.0	(0.0)	23.8	(1.2)	63.0	(1.4)	27.4	(1.2)	2.4	(0.4)
Mexico	98.3	(0.2)	77.9	(0.7)	21.9	(0.7)	0.6	(0.2)	1.5	(0.2)	15.9	(0.6)	34.2	(0.7)	6.8	(0.3)
Netherlands	22.4	(1.5)	2.0	(0.5)	0.0	(0.0)	0.0	(0.0)	60.7	(1.8)	45.4	(1.9)	15.8	(1.6)	0.7	(0.2)
New Zealand	23.6	(1.6)	4.5	(0.7)	0.7	(0.3)	0.0	(0.0)	64.9	(1.6)	60.8	(1.8)	29.3	(1.7)	5.4	(0.8)
Norway	11.0	(1.0)	0.4	(0.2)	0.1	(0.1)	0.0	(0.0)	62.7	(1.4)	39.2	(1.4)	12.7	(1.0)	2.4	(0.5)
Poland	11.5	(1.1)	0.7	(0.3)	0.3	(0.2)	0.0	(0.0)	88.5	(1.1)	98.5	(0.4)	87.0	(1.1)	8.4	(1.0)
Portugal	99.5	(0.2)	76.7	(1.4)	18.3	(1.2)	0.4	(0.1)	0.5	(0.2)	22.2	(1.3)	61.9	(1.5)	1.3	(1.1)
Slovak Republic	13.6	(1.9)	0.1	(0.1)	0.0	(0.0)	0.0	(0.0)	85.0	(1.9)	93.6	(0.7)	73.7	(1.5)	3.4	(1.2)
Slovenia	15.9	(1.3)	0.3	(0.1)	0.0	(0.0)	0.0	(0.0)	82.1	(1.3)	85.1	(1.2)	38.7	(1.6)	4.4	(0.6)
Spain	81.3	(0.9)	13.9	(0.8)	2.4	(0.3)	0.0	(0.0)	16.0	(0.9)	54.6	(1.4)	34.7	(0.9)	2.9	(0.5)
Sweden	19.7	(1.2)	1.9	(0.5)	0.1	(0.1)	0.0	(0.0)	52.4	(1.4)	38.7	(1.5)	9.2	(0.9)	1.1	(0.3)
Switzerland	44.5	(1.3)	6.4	(0.6)	0.6	(0.2)	0.0	(0.0)	42.2	(1.2)	49.7	(1.5)	30.6	(1.2)	1.4	(0.3)
Turkey	99.8	(0.1)	92.3	(0.8)	43.6	(1.6)	3.5	(0.6)	0.2	(0.1)	6.2	(0.7)	39.2	(1.5)	9.1	(1.1)
United Kingdom	13.4	(1.1)	1.3	(0.3)	0.0	(0.0)	0.0	(0.0)	66.4	(1.8)	49.2	(1.3)	27.7	(1.4)	4.5	(0.6)
United States	34.7	(2.0)	1.3	(0.4)	0.1	(0.1)	0.0	(0.0)	56.3	(2.0)	54.8	(1.7)	16.2	(1.3)	2.3	(0.4)
OECD average	35.4	(0.2)	10.5	(0.1)	2.9	(0.1)	0.1	(0.0)	54.3	(0.2)	53.2	(0.2)	31.3	(0.2)	4.6	(0.1)
Albania	m	m	m	m	m	m	m	m	m	m	m	m	m	m	m	m
Argentina	90.4	(1.3)	31.1	(1.5)	3.8	(0.7)	0.0	(0.0)	8.6	(1.2)	48.8	(1.5)	26.7	(1.5)	2.0	(0.4)
Brazil	96.8	(0.3)	44.4	(1.0)	7.7	(0.6)	0.3	(0.3)	3.2	(0.3)	54.5	(1.0)	70.9	(1.2)	7.9	(1.0)
Bulgaria	27.6	(2.1)	0.9	(0.2)	0.1	(0.1)	0.0	(0.0)	70.5	(2.1)	80.5	(1.1)	36.6	(1.3)	2.2	(0.4)
Colombia	96.0	(0.7)	48.8	(1.8)	5.0	(0.7)	0.2	(0.1)	3.5	(0.7)	33.9	(1.8)	21.1	(1.4)	3.3	(0.5)
Costa Rica	87.4	(1.3)	21.8	(1.5)	2.8	(0.5)	0.0	(0.0)	8.4	(0.9)	48.9	(2.0)	32.6	(1.6)	4.2	(0.7)
Croatia	18.9	(1.4)	0.1	(0.1)	0.0	(0.0)	0.0	(0.0)	76.1	(1.5)	67.0	(1.6)	45.7	(1.5)	3.8	(0.6)
Cyprus*	19.7	(1.1)	0.3	(0.1)	0.1	(0.1)	0.0	(0.0)	76.0	(1.1)	72.0	(1.3)	19.7	(1.2)	1.4	(0.3)
Hong Kong-China	86.5	(1.0)	24.8	(1.2)	7.6	(0.7)	0.1	(0.1)	13.5	(1.0)	73.8	(1.3)	79.7	(1.2)	26.7	(1.8)
Indonesia	98.3	(0.4)	71.6	(1.5)	20.4	(1.5)	2.0	(0.4)	1.7	(0.4)	26.6	(1.5)	68.7	(1.8)	31.3	(1.9)
Jordan	40.9	(1.6)	6.5	(0.7)	0.6	(0.2)	0.1	(0.1)	51.3	(1.6)	51.9	(1.4)	18.2	(1.0)	1.5	(0.4)
Kazakhstan	5.3	(0.9)	0.2	(0.1)	0.0	(0.0)	0.0	(0.0)	33.7	(1.8)	11.2	(1.2)	2.7	(0.5)	0.3	(0.2)
Latvia	10.6	(1.3)	0.2	(0.1)	0.0	(0.0)	0.0	(0.0)	85.5	(1.5)	65.4	(1.6)	17.8	(1.4)	1.3	(0.5)
Liechtenstein	39.8	(6.5)	2.7	(1.9)	0.0	(0.0)	0.0	(0.0)	45.5	(6.5)	60.0	(5.2)	25.4	(5.4)	0.5	(1.2)
Lithuania	5.5	(0.7)	0.4	(0.2)	0.1	(0.1)	0.0	(0.0)	90.3	(0.9)	37.4	(1.6)	8.8	(0.8)	0.3	(0.2)
Macao-China	95.0	(0.6)	67.4	(1.4)	30.9	(1.3)	3.8	(0.6)	5.0	(0.6)	31.4	(1.4)	60.4	(1.4)	32.5	(1.4)
Malaysia	60.5	(2.1)	9.3	(1.0)	1.9	(0.5)	0.0	(0.0)	38.8	(2.1)	84.1	(1.1)	70.7	(1.4)	19.7	(1.4)
Montenegro	16.0	(1.2)	0.2	(0.1)	0.0	(0.0)	0.0	(0.0)	77.9	(1.2)	54.5	(1.6)	15.2	(1.2)	1.1	(0.3)
Peru	83.3	(1.0)	21.9	(1.4)	1.7	(0.4)	0.0	(0.0)	16.5	(1.0)	71.4	(1.4)	60.0	(1.4)	8.7	(0.8)
Qatar	36.3	(0.9)	2.0	(0.3)	0.2	(0.1)	0.0	(0.0)	41.3	(0.8)	24.1	(1.0)	5.5	(0.4)	3.0	(0.3)
Romania	22.3	(1.8)	0.7	(0.3)	0.2	(0.1)	0.0	(0.0)	64.9	(1.8)	62.5	(1.6)	35.1	(1.7)	7.4	(0.7)
Russian Federation	4.9	(0.9)	0.2	(0.1)	0.0	(0.1)	0.0	(0.0)	27.4	(1.5)	3.4	(0.6)	1.2	(0.3)	0.1	(0.1)
Serbia	18.7	(1.6)	0.5	(0.1)	0.0	(0.0)	0.0	(0.0)	76.0	(1.7)	59.5	(1.5)	24.6	(1.2)	1.2	(0.4)
Shanghai-China	77.5	(1.4)	19.5	(1.2)	2.5	(0.4)	0.1	(0.1)	21.3	(1.5)	64.0	(1.3)	34.3	(1.4)	2.7	(0.5)
Singapore	37.3	(1.2)	2.4	(0.4)	0.1	(0.1)	0.0	(0.0)	59.2	(1.2)	75.7	(1.1)	31.8	(1.3)	2.3	(0.4)
Chinese Taipei	43.5	(1.3)	2.9	(0.5)	0.7	(0.2)	0.1	(0.1)	49.1	(1.2)	60.1	(1.4)	31.5	(1.3)	6.5	(0.8)
Thailand	98.8	(0.3)	77.8	(1.3)	22.7	(1.2)	1.4	(0.3)	1.2	(0.3)	21.9	(1.3)	71.7	(1.3)	28.5	(1.6)
Tunisia	92.0	(1.0)	24.9	(1.4)	2.0	(0.5)	0.1	(0.1)	7.9	(0.9)	70.7	(1.5)	73.6	(1.6)	16.1	(1.3)
United Arab Emirates	34.0	(1.1)	1.4	(0.3)	0.1	(0.1)	0.0	(0.0)	51.7	(1.0)	32.8	(1.3)	6.5	(0.6)	2.5	(0.4)
Uruguay	98.7	(0.4)	70.3	(1.6)	11.3	(0.8)	0.3	(0.2)	1.1	(0.3)	25.5	(1.3)	44.5	(1.5)	6.0	(0.7)
Viet Nam	99.3	(0.2)	86.6	(1.2)	42.0	(1.8)	5.0	(0.6)	0.7	(0.2)	13.0	(1.1)	56.6	(1.8)	51.9	(1.9)

1. ESCS refers to the *PISA index of economic, social and cultural status*.
2. The variable indicating the number of books available at home has been coded as: 0-10 books was coded as 5 books, 11-25 books as 18 books, 26-100 books as 63 books, 101-200 books as 150.5 books, 201-500 books as 350.5 books and more than 500 books as 750.5 books.
* See notes at the beginning of this Annex.

StatLink http://dx.doi.org/10.1787/888932964908

[Part 2/7]
Elements of socio-economic status, by quarters of socio-economic status within countries

Table II.2.2 *Results based on students' self-reports*

		Parents' highest level of education: Percentage of students with at least one parent whose highest educational attainment is tertiary or advanced research (ISCED 5 or 6)								Parents' highest occupation: Percentage of students with at least one parent working in an occupation considered as elementary (ISCO 9)							
		Bottom quarter of ESCS		Second quarter of ESCS		Third quarter of ESCS		Top quarter of ESCS		Bottom quarter of ESCS		Second quarter of ESCS		Third quarter of ESCS		Top quarter of ESCS	
		%	S.E.	%	S.E.	%	S.E.	%	S.E.	%	S.E.	%	S.E.	%	S.E.	%	S.E.
OECD	Australia	13.8	(0.7)	40.3	(1.0)	71.7	(0.9)	95.7	(0.4)	33.7	(1.0)	7.2	(0.5)	0.5	(0.1)	0.1	(0.1)
	Austria	8.6	(1.0)	35.9	(1.9)	54.9	(1.5)	92.8	(0.8)	42.2	(1.8)	21.7	(1.5)	3.1	(0.5)	0.2	(0.1)
	Belgium	8.9	(0.8)	54.7	(1.3)	88.9	(0.9)	99.4	(0.1)	40.3	(1.4)	18.8	(1.2)	1.2	(0.3)	0.0	(0.0)
	Canada	26.0	(1.0)	70.2	(0.9)	94.1	(0.5)	99.3	(0.1)	29.9	(1.1)	9.4	(0.6)	1.0	(0.2)	0.2	(0.1)
	Chile	0.3	(0.2)	3.0	(0.5)	42.4	(1.7)	94.4	(0.7)	41.9	(1.7)	39.2	(1.6)	17.7	(1.2)	0.8	(0.3)
	Czech Republic	3.0	(0.7)	11.3	(1.1)	34.8	(1.6)	81.4	(1.3)	49.2	(1.9)	21.3	(1.5)	4.9	(0.7)	0.3	(0.3)
	Denmark	17.4	(1.4)	63.3	(1.4)	89.5	(1.0)	99.5	(0.2)	26.2	(1.2)	6.7	(0.7)	0.5	(0.3)	0.0	(0.0)
	Estonia	8.0	(0.9)	46.2	(1.6)	78.1	(1.4)	98.1	(0.4)	48.4	(1.8)	24.3	(1.5)	2.8	(0.5)	0.0	(0.0)
	Finland	42.4	(1.2)	79.8	(1.1)	95.0	(0.5)	99.8	(0.1)	31.2	(1.2)	7.6	(0.6)	0.5	(0.2)	0.1	(0.2)
	France	12.8	(1.0)	46.1	(1.6)	63.7	(1.3)	94.5	(0.7)	37.6	(1.8)	12.8	(1.0)	1.0	(0.3)	0.1	(0.1)
	Germany	6.7	(0.8)	35.1	(1.6)	63.0	(1.6)	97.4	(0.5)	36.6	(1.5)	16.4	(1.4)	2.9	(0.6)	0.1	(0.1)
	Greece	2.5	(0.5)	33.4	(1.5)	75.4	(1.3)	99.2	(0.2)	48.0	(1.5)	23.4	(1.5)	3.8	(0.6)	0.3	(0.1)
	Hungary	0.8	(0.3)	15.7	(1.0)	60.0	(1.6)	97.9	(0.4)	55.2	(2.0)	30.1	(1.5)	8.8	(1.0)	0.2	(0.1)
	Iceland	17.4	(1.2)	57.8	(1.9)	91.0	(1.0)	98.5	(0.4)	26.9	(1.6)	8.1	(1.0)	1.0	(0.3)	0.3	(0.2)
	Ireland	10.7	(1.1)	41.1	(1.5)	74.9	(1.2)	97.0	(0.5)	30.5	(1.5)	12.8	(1.0)	2.5	(0.5)	0.0	(0.0)
	Israel	13.5	(0.9)	49.1	(1.7)	86.8	(1.1)	97.6	(0.4)	37.4	(2.1)	7.8	(0.8)	0.3	(0.2)	0.0	(0.0)
	Italy	0.5	(0.1)	17.9	(0.6)	38.6	(0.8)	91.4	(0.5)	53.9	(0.9)	32.2	(0.8)	7.1	(0.5)	0.3	(0.1)
	Japan	15.3	(1.0)	57.9	(1.6)	78.3	(1.1)	98.3	(0.4)	30.8	(1.3)	11.8	(1.0)	1.7	(0.3)	0.1	(0.1)
	Korea	7.6	(0.9)	38.0	(1.5)	82.3	(1.0)	98.8	(0.3)	29.1	(1.4)	5.4	(0.7)	0.7	(0.3)	0.0	(0.0)
	Luxembourg	1.5	(0.3)	31.9	(1.3)	72.3	(1.2)	97.6	(0.4)	53.0	(1.5)	23.8	(1.2)	2.4	(0.4)	0.1	(0.1)
	Mexico	0.2	(0.1)	6.2	(0.4)	44.0	(0.8)	92.5	(0.4)	32.9	(1.0)	38.5	(0.8)	20.3	(0.6)	1.2	(0.2)
	Netherlands	16.8	(1.5)	52.6	(2.0)	84.2	(1.6)	99.3	(0.2)	28.7	(1.8)	4.4	(0.7)	0.2	(0.2)	0.1	(0.1)
	New Zealand	11.4	(0.9)	34.8	(1.6)	70.1	(1.7)	94.6	(0.8)	40.7	(1.6)	11.1	(1.1)	0.3	(0.2)	0.1	(0.1)
	Norway	26.3	(1.5)	60.3	(1.4)	87.2	(1.0)	97.6	(0.5)	20.8	(1.2)	3.4	(0.6)	0.3	(0.2)	0.0	(0.0)
	Poland	0.0	(0.0)	0.9	(0.3)	12.7	(1.2)	91.6	(1.0)	67.8	(1.7)	47.4	(1.6)	7.7	(0.9)	0.0	(0.0)
	Portugal	0.0	(0.0)	1.0	(0.3)	19.8	(1.1)	88.4	(1.1)	52.9	(1.7)	38.7	(1.5)	12.3	(1.2)	0.3	(0.2)
	Slovak Republic	1.4	(0.4)	6.3	(0.7)	26.3	(1.5)	86.7	(1.2)	45.5	(2.1)	36.4	(1.7)	11.8	(1.4)	0.1	(0.1)
	Slovenia	2.0	(0.7)	14.6	(1.2)	61.2	(1.6)	95.5	(0.6)	47.8	(1.6)	16.5	(1.2)	2.3	(0.5)	0.1	(0.0)
	Spain	2.7	(0.4)	31.5	(1.4)	62.9	(0.9)	97.1	(0.5)	48.5	(1.2)	29.6	(0.9)	7.7	(0.6)	0.1	(0.1)
	Sweden	27.9	(1.3)	59.4	(1.6)	90.7	(0.9)	98.9	(0.3)	25.6	(1.4)	8.5	(0.9)	0.4	(0.2)	0.0	(0.0)
	Switzerland	13.3	(0.8)	44.0	(1.5)	68.8	(1.2)	98.6	(0.3)	38.2	(1.3)	8.2	(0.7)	0.7	(0.3)	0.0	(0.0)
	Turkey	0.1	(0.1)	1.5	(0.3)	17.2	(1.1)	77.4	(1.3)	54.6	(2.4)	43.9	(1.8)	29.4	(1.5)	3.2	(0.5)
	United Kingdom	20.2	(1.4)	49.6	(1.4)	72.2	(1.4)	95.5	(0.6)	20.3	(1.2)	6.9	(1.3)	0.5	(0.2)	0.1	(0.1)
	United States	9.0	(0.9)	43.9	(1.6)	83.6	(1.3)	97.7	(0.4)	23.7	(1.3)	7.5	(0.8)	0.9	(0.3)	0.2	(0.1)
	OECD average	**10.3**	**(0.2)**	**36.3**	**(0.2)**	**65.8**	**(0.2)**	**95.3**	**(0.1)**	**39.1**	**(0.3)**	**18.9**	**(0.2)**	**4.7**	**(0.1)**	**0.3**	**(0.0)**
Partners	Albania	m	m	m	m	m	m	m	m	m	m	m	m	m	m	m	m
	Argentina	1.1	(0.4)	20.1	(1.2)	69.5	(1.7)	97.9	(0.4)	51.3	(1.4)	39.8	(1.5)	18.1	(1.5)	0.7	(0.3)
	Brazil	0.0	(0.0)	1.2	(0.2)	21.3	(1.1)	81.8	(1.0)	32.9	(1.2)	29.3	(1.1)	12.4	(0.8)	1.5	(0.3)
	Bulgaria	1.9	(0.4)	18.6	(1.2)	63.3	(1.3)	97.8	(0.4)	53.7	(1.7)	30.1	(1.4)	10.4	(0.9)	0.5	(0.2)
	Colombia	0.5	(0.2)	17.3	(1.4)	73.9	(1.7)	96.5	(0.5)	58.1	(1.6)	46.2	(1.7)	27.1	(1.4)	3.1	(0.5)
	Costa Rica	4.2	(0.9)	29.4	(2.2)	64.5	(1.6)	95.8	(0.7)	31.7	(3.1)	32.6	(1.9)	18.1	(1.3)	0.4	(0.2)
	Croatia	5.1	(0.6)	32.8	(1.6)	54.3	(1.6)	96.2	(0.6)	47.7	(1.6)	27.4	(1.4)	9.2	(0.7)	0.4	(0.2)
	Cyprus*	4.2	(0.5)	27.8	(1.3)	80.2	(1.3)	98.6	(0.3)	44.8	(1.7)	17.6	(1.1)	3.6	(0.5)	0.4	(0.2)
	Hong Kong-China	0.1	(0.1)	1.3	(0.4)	12.7	(1.0)	73.2	(1.9)	30.1	(1.2)	28.6	(1.4)	5.4	(0.8)	0.0	(0.0)
	Indonesia	0.0	(0.0)	1.8	(0.5)	10.9	(1.1)	66.6	(2.1)	53.4	(3.7)	39.4	(2.9)	30.9	(2.4)	4.4	(0.8)
	Jordan	7.9	(0.7)	41.6	(1.3)	81.2	(1.1)	98.5	(0.4)	55.2	(1.7)	21.0	(1.3)	2.1	(0.4)	0.3	(0.2)
	Kazakhstan	61.0	(1.8)	88.6	(1.1)	97.3	(0.5)	99.7	(0.2)	45.6	(2.2)	23.9	(1.4)	2.0	(0.4)	0.0	(0.0)
	Latvia	3.9	(0.8)	34.3	(1.6)	82.3	(1.4)	98.7	(0.5)	38.6	(2.2)	18.7	(1.3)	6.1	(1.0)	0.2	(0.1)
	Liechtenstein	14.4	(4.0)	37.6	(5.0)	74.3	(5.4)	99.7	(0.9)	35.5	(5.7)	0.0	(0.0)	2.8	(2.0)	0.0	(0.0)
	Lithuania	4.2	(0.7)	62.2	(1.6)	91.2	(0.8)	99.7	(0.2)	55.6	(1.4)	30.9	(1.6)	4.2	(0.6)	0.3	(0.2)
	Macao-China	0.0	(0.0)	1.2	(0.3)	8.8	(0.7)	63.7	(1.4)	19.6	(1.0)	13.2	(1.0)	3.0	(0.5)	0.8	(0.2)
	Malaysia	0.7	(0.3)	6.7	(0.8)	27.4	(1.5)	80.2	(1.4)	48.6	(1.8)	39.5	(1.5)	12.8	(1.0)	0.7	(0.3)
	Montenegro	6.2	(0.6)	45.2	(1.6)	84.7	(1.2)	99.0	(0.3)	43.6	(1.7)	22.4	(1.3)	7.3	(0.8)	0.4	(0.2)
	Peru	0.1	(0.1)	6.8	(0.6)	38.2	(1.3)	91.3	(0.8)	23.8	(1.5)	44.4	(1.3)	29.3	(1.0)	4.4	(0.7)
	Qatar	22.4	(0.8)	73.9	(1.0)	94.3	(0.4)	97.0	(0.3)	23.1	(0.9)	4.1	(0.4)	0.7	(0.2)	0.8	(0.2)
	Romania	12.8	(1.1)	36.6	(1.6)	64.8	(1.7)	92.6	(0.7)	54.5	(2.0)	45.6	(1.6)	22.9	(1.4)	0.9	(0.3)
	Russian Federation	67.7	(1.5)	96.4	(0.6)	98.8	(0.3)	99.9	(0.1)	42.8	(1.9)	16.5	(1.1)	1.7	(0.4)	0.0	(0.0)
	Serbia	5.3	(0.7)	40.0	(1.4)	75.4	(1.2)	98.8	(0.4)	26.8	(1.5)	18.1	(1.2)	5.3	(0.7)	0.0	(0.0)
	Shanghai-China	1.2	(0.3)	16.6	(1.0)	63.2	(1.3)	97.2	(0.5)	41.8	(1.9)	14.9	(1.1)	2.8	(0.5)	0.0	(0.0)
	Singapore	3.5	(0.5)	21.8	(1.1)	68.2	(1.4)	97.7	(0.4)	25.7	(1.4)	5.1	(0.8)	0.5	(0.2)	0.0	(0.0)
	Chinese Taipei	7.4	(0.6)	36.9	(1.5)	67.9	(1.2)	93.4	(0.8)	50.8	(1.4)	28.3	(1.3)	6.3	(0.7)	0.5	(0.2)
	Thailand	0.0	(0.0)	0.3	(0.2)	5.6	(0.7)	70.1	(1.7)	66.3	(1.8)	52.5	(1.6)	31.8	(1.5)	4.4	(0.6)
	Tunisia	0.2	(0.1)	4.3	(0.7)	24.3	(1.6)	83.8	(1.3)	20.5	(1.7)	32.4	(1.6)	23.1	(1.4)	1.3	(0.3)
	United Arab Emirates	14.3	(0.9)	65.8	(1.3)	93.3	(0.6)	97.5	(0.4)	13.1	(1.0)	2.9	(0.4)	0.7	(0.2)	0.4	(0.1)
	Uruguay	0.2	(0.2)	4.3	(0.7)	44.2	(1.4)	93.7	(0.7)	29.5	(1.4)	33.2	(1.5)	17.5	(1.1)	1.6	(0.4)
	Viet Nam	0.1	(0.1)	1.5	(0.4)	43.1	(2.0)	90.6	(1.3)	88.0	(1.2)	69.1	(2.0)	16.1	(1.7)		

1. ESCS refers to the *PISA index of economic, social and cultural status*.
2. The variable indicating the number of books available at home has been coded as: 0-10 books was coded as 5 books, 11-25 books as 18 books, 26-100 books as 63 books, 101-200 books as 150.5 books, 201-500 books as 350.5 books and more than 500 books as 750.5 books.
* See notes at the beginning of this Annex.
StatLink http://dx.doi.org/10.1787/888932964908

[Part 3/7]
Elements of socio-economic status, by quarters of socio-economic status within countries

Table II.2.2 — *Results based on students' self-reports*

	Parents' highest occupation: Percentage of students with at least one parent working in an occupation considered as semi-skilled blue-collar (ISCO 6, 7 and 8)								Parents' highest occupation: Percentage of students with at least one parent working in an occupation considered as semi-skilled white-collar (ISCO 4 and 5)							
	Bottom quarter of ESCS		Second quarter of ESCS		Third quarter of ESCS		Top quarter of ESCS		Bottom quarter of ESCS		Second quarter of ESCS		Third quarter of ESCS		Top quarter of ESCS	
	%	S.E.	%	S.E.	%	S.E.	%	S.E.	%	S.E.	%	S.E.	%	S.E.	%	S.E.
Australia	16.0	(0.6)	0.6	(0.2)	0.0	(0.0)	0.0	(0.0)	40.7	(1.0)	25.7	(1.0)	3.7	(0.5)	.5	(0.1)
Austria	9.0	(0.9)	0.8	(0.3)	0.1	(0.1)	0.0	(0.0)	46.1	(1.9)	48.6	(1.6)	22.1	(1.3)	.2	(0.6)
Belgium	16.3	(0.8)	2.0	(0.3)	0.1	(0.1)	0.0	(0.0)	38.6	(1.2)	44.6	(1.1)	12.7	(0.8)	.3	(0.1)
Canada	9.9	(0.7)	1.0	(0.2)	0.0	(0.0)	0.0	(0.0)	46.9	(1.2)	32.6	(1.0)	7.7	(0.5)	.7	(0.2)
Chile	37.4	(1.7)	10.0	(0.8)	1.9	(0.4)	0.0	(0.0)	19.7	(1.5)	44.6	(1.4)	40.2	(1.6)	.8	(0.5)
Czech Republic	4.7	(1.0)	0.7	(0.3)	0.1	(0.1)	0.0	(0.0)	44.0	(1.8)	54.5	(1.9)	32.3	(1.7)	.1	(0.9)
Denmark	10.4	(1.0)	0.7	(0.2)	0.0	(0.0)	0.0	(0.0)	58.6	(1.6)	47.4	(1.6)	5.2	(0.6)	.2	(0.1)
Estonia	6.9	(0.8)	0.6	(0.3)	0.1	(0.1)	0.0	(0.0)	41.7	(1.9)	41.5	(1.4)	10.3	(1.0)	.3	(0.2)
Finland	3.4	(0.4)	0.2	(0.1)	0.0	(0.0)	0.0	(0.0)	54.3	(1.5)	34.3	(1.3)	5.5	(0.6)	.1	(0.1)
France	15.9	(1.1)	0.9	(0.3)	0.0	(0.0)	0.0	(0.0)	42.1	(1.8)	46.1	(1.5)	8.8	(1.0)	.1	(0.1)
Germany	7.3	(0.9)	1.0	(0.4)	0.0	(0.0)	0.0	(0.0)	51.1	(1.6)	46.2	(1.9)	22.6	(1.3)	.1	(0.5)
Greece	17.2	(1.2)	3.0	(0.4)	0.2	(0.1)	0.0	(0.0)	32.8	(1.5)	52.4	(1.3)	24.6	(1.0)	.6	(0.2)
Hungary	12.6	(1.4)	1.7	(0.4)	0.3	(0.2)	0.0	(0.0)	30.3	(1.6)	50.7	(1.6)	30.8	(1.5)	.8	(0.6)
Iceland	9.2	(1.0)	0.6	(0.3)	0.0	(0.0)	0.1	(0.1)	47.7	(1.6)	31.7	(1.5)	4.2	(0.7)	.7	(0.3)
Ireland	11.1	(1.0)	1.0	(0.3)	0.0	(0.0)	0.0	(0.0)	52.0	(1.6)	45.5	(1.4)	12.9	(1.1)	.8	(0.2)
Israel	7.1	(0.8)	0.1	(0.1)	0.0	(0.0)	0.0	(0.0)	42.7	(2.1)	19.7	(1.3)	2.5	(0.5)	.5	(0.2)
Italy	11.2	(0.6)	2.3	(0.2)	0.2	(0.0)	0.0	(0.0)	31.9	(0.8)	51.3	(0.9)	35.6	(0.8)	.4	(0.4)
Japan	12.1	(0.9)	1.9	(0.4)	0.1	(0.1)	0.0	(0.0)	54.0	(1.4)	57.1	(1.5)	27.0	(1.1)	.3	(0.3)
Korea	10.8	(1.0)	0.6	(0.2)	0.0	(0.0)	0.0	(0.0)	50.6	(1.5)	49.3	(1.7)	24.7	(1.3)	.7	(0.4)
Luxembourg	14.6	(1.1)	2.7	(0.5)	0.0	(0.0)	0.0	(0.0)	28.7	(1.4)	53.1	(1.5)	28.0	(1.3)	.0	(0.4)
Mexico	51.3	(1.3)	15.1	(0.6)	4.0	(0.4)	0.1	(0.0)	15.1	(0.7)	40.4	(0.7)	50.2	(0.8)	.2	(0.4)
Netherlands	6.8	(0.9)	0.2	(0.1)	0.0	(0.0)	0.0	(0.0)	51.2	(2.1)	26.6	(1.2)	3.2	(0.6)	.5	(0.3)
New Zealand	12.0	(1.0)	0.1	(0.1)	0.1	(0.1)	0.0	(0.0)	36.7	(1.7)	27.2	(1.3)	5.2	(0.7)	.6	(0.2)
Norway	5.3	(0.6)	0.0	(0.0)	0.1	(0.1)	0.0	(0.0)	59.9	(1.5)	22.0	(1.2)	2.0	(0.4)	.3	(0.3)
Poland	5.8	(0.7)	0.4	(0.2)	0.0	(0.0)	0.0	(0.0)	25.8	(1.6)	45.1	(1.6)	22.6	(1.3)	.8	(0.3)
Portugal	21.1	(1.5)	6.0	(0.7)	1.3	(0.3)	0.0	(0.0)	23.1	(1.3)	44.8	(1.6)	48.8	(1.6)	.6	(0.9)
Slovak Republic	18.1	(1.9)	2.5	(0.6)	0.5	(0.3)	0.0	(0.0)	35.8	(1.8)	56.4	(1.6)	40.8	(1.6)	.7	(0.8)
Slovenia	11.0	(1.1)	0.7	(0.3)	0.0	(0.0)	0.0	(0.0)	36.5	(1.3)	40.8	(1.7)	19.5	(1.3)	.0	(0.3)
Spain	16.3	(0.9)	6.3	(0.5)	1.7	(0.3)	0.0	(0.0)	32.7	(1.2)	49.1	(1.1)	33.2	(1.1)	.8	(0.3)
Sweden	6.3	(0.8)	0.0	(0.0)	0.0	(0.0)	0.0	(0.0)	60.5	(1.4)	38.0	(1.7)	4.8	(0.6)	.3	(0.2)
Switzerland	4.8	(0.6)	0.5	(0.2)	0.1	(0.1)	0.0	(0.0)	47.8	(1.1)	36.4	(1.6)	8.3	(0.9)	.5	(0.1)
Turkey	20.4	(1.6)	11.4	(1.1)	4.4	(0.7)	0.4	(0.2)	24.3	(2.0)	40.4	(1.7)	51.1	(1.9)	1.8	(1.9)
United Kingdom	8.7	(0.8)	0.5	(0.2)	0.0	(0.0)	0.0	(0.0)	58.6	(1.7)	37.4	(1.5)	6.4	(0.6)	.5	(0.5)
United States	21.0	(1.5)	1.6	(0.5)	0.1	(0.1)	0.0	(0.0)	45.2	(1.9)	32.2	(1.5)	8.7	(0.9)	.4	(0.3)
OECD average	13.3	(0.2)	2.3	(0.1)	0.4	(0.0)	0.0	(0.0)	41.4	(0.3)	41.6	(0.2)	19.6	(0.2)	.9	(0.1)
Albania	m	m	m	m	m	m	m	m	m	m	m	m	m	m	m	m
Argentina	21.9	(1.5)	9.0	(1.0)	3.4	(0.6)	0.0	(0.0)	23.9	(1.5)	42.1	(1.7)	44.2	(1.8)	7.2	(0.7)
Brazil	28.8	(1.1)	11.3	(0.7)	3.4	(0.4)	0.1	(0.0)	36.5	(1.1)	50.1	(0.9)	44.8	(1.2)	11.0	(0.7)
Bulgaria	12.4	(1.4)	2.7	(0.6)	0.8	(0.3)	0.1	(0.1)	30.9	(1.6)	45.0	(1.4)	28.5	(1.4)	2.8	(0.5)
Colombia	16.2	(1.3)	9.9	(0.9)	3.8	(0.6)	0.4	(0.2)	24.1	(1.5)	39.4	(1.7)	54.2	(1.6)	19.4	(1.4)
Costa Rica	31.2	(3.0)	13.3	(1.5)	2.9	(0.6)	0.1	(0.1)	34.1	(2.0)	45.6	(1.9)	43.9	(1.9)	4.4	(0.9)
Croatia	5.2	(0.6)	0.9	(0.3)	0.3	(0.2)	0.0	(0.0)	45.4	(1.8)	55.8	(1.4)	37.5	(1.8)	5.3	(0.7)
Cyprus*	8.8	(0.9)	1.0	(0.3)	0.1	(0.1)	0.0	(0.0)	43.1	(1.5)	60.0	(1.4)	43.2	(1.6)	6.2	(0.8)
Hong Kong-China	21.9	(1.2)	5.6	(0.8)	0.4	(0.2)	0.0	(0.0)	44.9	(1.5)	54.0	(1.7)	33.7	(1.5)	3.6	(0.6)
Indonesia	36.5	(3.5)	32.2	(3.0)	16.1	(1.8)	1.5	(0.4)	10.0	(1.3)	26.0	(2.1)	42.5	(2.2)	21.8	(2.3)
Jordan	6.9	(1.0)	0.7	(0.2)	0.0	(0.0)	0.0	(0.0)	26.0	(1.2)	29.3	(1.5)	10.0	(1.0)	0.7	(0.3)
Kazakhstan	11.1	(1.0)	1.5	(0.4)	0.0	(0.0)	0.0	(0.0)	36.0	(2.3)	32.0	(1.6)	4.9	(0.7)	0.7	(0.3)
Latvia	17.6	(1.8)	2.6	(0.6)	0.2	(0.1)	0.0	(0.0)	42.5	(2.1)	49.5	(1.9)	19.5	(1.4)	1.3	(0.3)
Liechtenstein	5.7	(3.2)	0.0	(0.0)	0.0	(0.0)	0.0	(0.0)	30.4	(5.3)	13.3	(3.6)	10.0	(3.2)	0.0	(0.0)
Lithuania	13.5	(1.2)	3.7	(0.5)	0.4	(0.2)	0.0	(0.0)	29.3	(1.3)	41.5	(1.5)	12.7	(1.1)	0.6	(0.2)
Macao-China	15.5	(1.1)	3.9	(0.5)	0.8	(0.2)	0.1	(0.1)	62.3	(1.3)	74.0	(1.2)	65.8	(1.5)	29.8	(1.3)
Malaysia	27.2	(2.0)	13.5	(1.1)	2.1	(0.5)	0.0	(0.0)	21.5	(1.4)	35.8	(1.6)	33.4	(1.5)	5.1	(0.7)
Montenegro	12.7	(1.1)	2.7	(0.6)	0.2	(0.1)	0.0	(0.0)	40.1	(1.7)	49.6	(1.5)	36.7	(2.0)	3.4	(0.7)
Peru	62.0	(1.7)	19.5	(1.1)	4.6	(0.5)	0.6	(0.3)	13.9	(1.0)	34.7	(1.4)	54.8	(1.2)	21.4	(1.2)
Qatar	2.2	(0.3)	0.1	(0.1)	0.0	(0.0)	0.0	(0.0)	34.4	(1.1)	17.0	(0.9)	5.0	(0.4)	3.2	(0.3)
Romania	11.4	(1.3)	3.9	(0.8)	1.4	(0.4)	0.0	(0.0)	31.0	(1.7)	41.9	(1.8)	34.9	(1.6)	3.2	(0.6)
Russian Federation	5.8	(0.7)	0.3	(0.2)	0.1	(0.1)	0.0	(0.0)	46.4	(2.0)	47.7	(1.5)	13.4	(0.9)	1.2	(0.4)
Serbia	10.5	(1.0)	3.2	(0.6)	0.9	(0.3)	0.0	(0.0)	60.0	(1.6)	60.8	(1.5)	40.4	(1.5)	5.9	(0.8)
Shanghai-China	5.5	(0.8)	0.6	(0.2)	0.0	(0.0)	0.0	(0.0)	43.1	(1.7)	44.6	(1.5)	15.9	(1.1)	1.3	(0.3)
Singapore	10.0	(0.8)	0.4	(0.2)	0.0	(0.0)	0.0	(0.0)	49.9	(1.4)	27.1	(1.3)	3.7	(0.5)	0.1	(0.1)
Chinese Taipei	11.5	(0.9)	1.5	(0.4)	0.0	(0.0)	0.1	(0.1)	35.7	(1.5)	52.9	(1.4)	31.8	(1.3)	5.6	(0.9)
Thailand	20.4	(1.4)	16.3	(1.2)	8.5	(0.9)	1.2	(0.3)	12.7	(1.0)	26.5	(1.5)	41.9	(1.4)	20.9	(1.1)
Tunisia	64.4	(1.9)	38.1	(1.6)	9.0	(1.0)	0.5	(0.2)	14.2	(1.2)	23.7	(1.6)	40.3	(1.7)	10.9	(1.1)
United Arab Emirates	2.6	(0.4)	0.0	(0.0)	0.1	(0.1)	0.0	(0.0)	33.6	(1.5)	11.1	(0.9)	3.7	(0.5)	2.1	(0.4)
Uruguay	42.6	(1.6)	16.0	(1.1)	6.9	(0.8)	0.6	(0.2)	26.6	(1.4)	45.4	(1.4)	57.0	(1.3)	12.8	(1.2)
Viet Nam	4.1	(1.1)	3.2	(0.7)	3.3	(0.6)	1.2	(0.3)	5.3	(0.8)	8.5	(0.9)	25.0	(1.7)	32.7	(1.7)

1. ESCS refers to the *PISA index of economic, social and cultural status*.
2. The variable indicating the number of books available at home has been coded as: 0-10 books was coded as 5 books, 11-25 books as 18 books, 26-100 books as 63 books, 101-200 books as 150.5 books, 201-500 books as 350.5 books and more than 500 books as 750.5 books.
* See notes at the beginning of this Annex.
StatLink http://dx.doi.org/10.1787/888932964908

[Part 4/7]
Elements of socio-economic status, by quarters of socio-economic status within countries

Table II.2.2   *Results based on students' self-reports*

| | Parents' highest occupation: Percentage of students with at least one parent working in an occupation considered as skilled (ISCO 1, 2 and 3) | | | | | | | | Cultural possessions: Percentage of students who reported that they have poetry books at home | | | | | | | |
| | Bottom quarter of ESCS | | Second quarter of ESCS | | Third quarter of ESCS | | Top quarter of ESCS | | Bottom quarter of ESCS | | Second quarter of ESCS | | Third quarter of ESCS | | Top quarter of ESCS | |
	%	S.E.	%	S.E.	%	S.E.	%	S.E.	%	S.E.	%	S.E.	%	S.E.	%	S.E.
Australia	9.6	(0.6)	66.4	(1.1)	95.8	(0.4)	99.3	(0.1)	18.9	(0.8)	27.0	(0.9)	35.1	(0.9)	62.5	(1.0)
Austria	2.7	(0.6)	28.9	(1.3)	74.7	(1.4)	96.6	(0.6)	35.5	(1.7)	49.6	(1.7)	59.9	(1.5)	81.2	(1.4)
Belgium	4.9	(0.5)	34.6	(1.2)	86.0	(0.8)	99.6	(0.1)	13.4	(0.8)	23.7	(1.2)	35.0	(1.3)	55.6	(1.2)
Canada	13.3	(0.7)	56.9	(1.0)	91.3	(0.6)	99.0	(0.2)	19.0	(1.0)	27.1	(0.9)	31.7	(1.1)	58.2	(1.1)
Chile	1.0	(0.3)	6.3	(0.6)	40.1	(1.7)	93.5	(0.6)	48.8	(1.4)	52.5	(1.7)	53.8	(1.5)	60.3	(1.5)
Czech Republic	2.2	(0.5)	23.5	(1.7)	62.7	(1.8)	93.6	(1.0)	20.8	(1.8)	36.6	(1.6)	45.5	(1.6)	71.3	(1.5)
Denmark	4.8	(0.6)	45.2	(1.6)	94.3	(0.7)	99.8	(0.1)	11.0	(0.7)	18.0	(1.2)	30.5	(1.7)	59.4	(1.5)
Estonia	3.1	(0.6)	33.6	(1.5)	86.8	(1.1)	99.7	(0.2)	54.2	(1.9)	67.9	(1.7)	75.8	(1.5)	90.2	(1.0)
Finland	11.2	(0.9)	57.8	(1.3)	94.0	(0.6)	99.8	(0.2)	30.5	(1.2)	43.3	(1.3)	54.0	(1.6)	78.6	(1.2)
France	4.4	(0.6)	40.2	(1.5)	90.1	(1.1)	99.8	(0.1)	21.2	(1.5)	31.8	(1.6)	44.6	(1.8)	72.4	(1.4)
Germany	5.0	(0.6)	36.3	(2.0)	74.6	(1.3)	97.8	(0.5)	36.2	(1.5)	51.6	(1.4)	64.4	(1.5)	78.9	(1.2)
Greece	1.9	(0.5)	21.4	(1.1)	71.4	(1.1)	99.1	(0.3)	23.6	(1.5)	35.6	(1.4)	49.4	(1.8)	70.0	(1.5)
Hungary	1.9	(0.5)	17.5	(1.2)	60.1	(1.6)	97.1	(0.6)	37.8	(1.7)	62.1	(1.6)	75.5	(1.3)	90.5	(1.1)
Iceland	16.2	(1.2)	59.6	(1.5)	94.9	(0.7)	99.0	(0.4)	51.6	(1.6)	68.3	(1.7)	75.6	(1.3)	92.7	(0.9)
Ireland	6.4	(0.7)	40.6	(1.5)	84.6	(1.1)	99.2	(0.2)	18.8	(1.3)	27.5	(1.5)	36.8	(1.4)	59.5	(1.5)
Israel	12.8	(1.3)	72.4	(1.4)	97.1	(0.5)	99.5	(0.2)	35.2	(1.5)	42.9	(1.5)	54.2	(1.7)	76.9	(1.3)
Italy	3.0	(0.3)	14.2	(0.6)	57.1	(0.8)	95.3	(0.4)	35.3	(0.7)	48.3	(0.8)	62.9	(0.8)	81.1	(0.8)
Japan	3.1	(0.5)	29.2	(1.3)	71.3	(1.1)	98.6	(0.3)	9.1	(0.8)	19.6	(1.0)	28.3	(1.3)	46.7	(1.3)
Korea	9.4	(0.9)	44.7	(1.6)	74.5	(1.3)	98.4	(0.4)	39.4	(1.4)	57.7	(1.5)	69.9	(1.6)	85.5	(1.1)
Luxembourg	3.8	(0.5)	20.4	(1.4)	69.6	(1.4)	97.9	(0.4)	29.0	(1.2)	42.8	(1.4)	57.3	(1.5)	79.1	(1.1)
Mexico	0.7	(0.2)	5.9	(0.3)	25.5	(0.7)	88.5	(0.5)	31.9	(0.9)	41.9	(0.8)	45.7	(0.8)	58.9	(0.8)
Netherlands	13.3	(1.2)	68.8	(1.3)	96.5	(0.7)	99.3	(0.3)	12.9	(1.2)	18.1	(1.3)	30.7	(1.7)	51.6	(2.1)
New Zealand	10.8	(1.0)	61.4	(1.5)	94.4	(0.7)	99.3	(0.2)	21.4	(1.2)	29.3	(1.5)	37.4	(1.8)	62.3	(1.5)
Norway	14.0	(1.2)	74.7	(1.2)	97.6	(0.4)	99.7	(0.2)	20.9	(1.2)	33.1	(1.4)	49.3	(2.0)	76.7	(1.5)
Poland	0.6	(0.3)	7.2	(0.8)	69.6	(1.5)	99.2	(0.3)	20.8	(1.0)	44.3	(1.5)	52.4	(1.7)	72.4	(1.5)
Portugal	2.9	(0.6)	10.5	(0.7)	37.6	(1.4)	93.1	(0.9)	24.9	(1.2)	41.5	(1.6)	54.7	(1.3)	79.8	(1.2)
Slovak Republic	0.7	(0.3)	4.8	(0.7)	46.8	(1.5)	90.1	(0.9)	37.4	(1.9)	60.5	(1.6)	65.6	(1.6)	78.8	(1.2)
Slovenia	4.7	(0.6)	42.1	(1.6)	78.2	(1.3)	98.9	(0.3)	36.9	(1.5)	55.6	(1.7)	64.5	(1.5)	85.4	(1.2)
Spain	2.5	(0.3)	15.0	(0.8)	57.5	(1.0)	97.1	(0.3)	38.1	(0.9)	48.8	(1.2)	63.1	(1.1)	78.1	(1.0)
Sweden	7.6	(0.7)	53.5	(1.6)	94.8	(0.6)	99.7	(0.2)	15.2	(1.2)	26.0	(1.5)	33.4	(1.6)	64.9	(1.5)
Switzerland	9.2	(0.9)	54.9	(1.5)	91.0	(1.0)	99.5	(0.1)	22.6	(1.3)	29.3	(1.2)	38.1	(1.4)	61.9	(1.4)
Turkey	0.7	(0.3)	4.4	(0.6)	15.1	(1.4)	62.4	(1.9)	37.7	(1.8)	58.2	(1.7)	64.1	(1.6)	78.5	(1.2)
United Kingdom	12.5	(1.1)	55.1	(1.7)	93.1	(0.6)	99.4	(0.2)	18.0	(1.0)	30.4	(1.5)	39.7	(1.5)	66.8	(1.3)
United States	10.0	(1.0)	58.6	(1.5)	90.4	(1.0)	99.3	(0.3)	22.4	(1.5)	30.9	(1.3)	39.3	(1.9)	63.6	(1.5)
OECD average	6.2	(0.1)	37.3	(0.2)	75.3	(0.2)	96.8	(0.1)	28.0	(0.2)	40.6	(0.2)	50.5	(0.3)	71.5	(0.2)
Albania	m	m	m	m	m	m	m	m	m	m	m	m	m	m	m	m
Argentina	2.9	(0.6)	9.0	(1.0)	34.4	(2.0)	92.1	(0.8)	44.1	(1.8)	50.4	(1.8)	55.7	(2.0)	64.0	(1.8)
Brazil	1.9	(0.3)	9.2	(0.6)	39.4	(1.2)	87.5	(0.8)	46.5	(0.9)	50.0	(1.2)	52.4	(1.1)	57.6	(1.0)
Bulgaria	3.0	(0.5)	22.2	(1.0)	60.4	(1.6)	96.6	(0.5)	34.8	(1.7)	59.5	(1.3)	74.2	(1.2)	87.0	(1.1)
Colombia	1.6	(0.4)	4.4	(0.6)	14.9	(1.3)	77.0	(1.5)	42.7	(1.9)	51.8	(1.7)	56.5	(1.6)	68.1	(1.4)
Costa Rica	3.0	(0.5)	8.5	(1.1)	35.1	(2.1)	95.1	(0.9)	20.2	(1.3)	28.1	(1.5)	34.7	(1.5)	51.6	(2.4)
Croatia	1.6	(0.3)	15.9	(1.1)	53.0	(1.8)	94.3	(0.8)	13.1	(1.0)	21.9	(1.2)	38.8	(1.5)	59.0	(1.6)
Cyprus*	3.2	(0.6)	21.4	(1.4)	53.0	(1.6)	93.4	(0.8)	22.5	(1.2)	38.4	(1.4)	47.8	(1.5)	69.7	(1.3)
Hong Kong-China	3.0	(0.6)	12.0	(1.0)	60.2	(1.5)	96.5	(0.6)	27.7	(1.7)	41.8	(1.7)	55.0	(1.6)	74.2	(1.6)
Indonesia	0.2	(0.1)	2.4	(0.5)	10.5	(0.9)	72.3	(2.8)	21.6	(1.6)	36.3	(1.8)	43.2	(1.9)	46.9	(2.3)
Jordan	11.9	(1.0)	49.1	(1.5)	87.8	(1.0)	99.0	(0.3)	23.8	(1.2)	38.5	(1.3)	42.8	(1.6)	62.9	(1.6)
Kazakhstan	7.4	(1.0)	42.5	(1.9)	93.1	(0.9)	99.3	(0.3)	61.1	(2.0)	74.4	(1.7)	74.3	(1.7)	86.3	(1.1)
Latvia	1.4	(0.4)	28.9	(1.9)	74.3	(1.4)	98.6	(0.4)	45.0	(1.9)	61.4	(1.8)	72.4	(1.6)	88.4	(1.0)
Liechtenstein	28.4	(5.5)	86.7	(3.6)	87.2	(3.7)	100.0	(0.0)	30.8	(5.2)	44.8	(5.3)	62.8	(5.5)	76.5	(5.1)
Lithuania	1.6	(0.4)	23.9	(1.4)	82.8	(1.1)	99.1	(0.3)	30.8	(1.3)	45.8	(1.5)	58.1	(1.8)	80.5	(1.3)
Macao-China	2.6	(0.4)	9.0	(0.8)	30.5	(1.5)	69.3	(1.4)	24.9	(1.2)	35.7	(1.4)	45.7	(1.3)	58.7	(1.3)
Malaysia	2.6	(0.5)	11.2	(1.0)	51.8	(1.7)	94.2	(0.7)	35.3	(1.4)	39.6	(1.5)	38.7	(1.5)	49.9	(1.6)
Montenegro	3.6	(0.6)	25.2	(1.5)	55.6	(2.1)	96.4	(0.7)	54.1	(1.4)	70.1	(1.3)	76.4	(1.3)	90.4	(1.0)
Peru	0.2	(0.1)	1.4	(0.3)	11.4	(0.9)	73.6	(1.3)	69.0	(1.4)	73.5	(1.7)	72.2	(1.4)	75.8	(1.5)
Qatar	40.3	(1.0)	78.9	(0.9)	94.3	(0.5)	95.9	(0.3)	42.3	(0.9)	46.3	(1.0)	53.7	(1.1)	79.4	(0.8)
Romania	3.1	(0.6)	8.5	(0.9)	40.8	(1.6)	95.9	(0.6)	67.1	(1.9)	81.9	(1.2)	89.4	(1.0)	94.6	(0.8)
Russian Federation	5.1	(0.7)	35.4	(1.6)	84.8	(0.9)	98.8	(0.4)	55.7	(1.5)	76.2	(1.6)	84.8	(1.0)	93.4	(0.7)
Serbia	2.8	(0.5)	17.8	(1.1)	53.4	(1.6)	94.1	(0.4)	45.7	(1.7)	67.7	(1.4)	76.1	(1.2)	89.8	(0.9)
Shanghai-China	9.8	(0.9)	39.8	(1.5)	81.4	(1.2)	98.7	(0.3)	60.5	(1.5)	72.7	(1.4)	82.2	(1.1)	92.6	(0.7)
Singapore	14.5	(0.9)	67.4	(1.3)	95.8	(0.6)	99.9	(0.1)	16.2	(1.1)	24.2	(1.1)	37.3	(1.4)	55.2	(1.5)
Chinese Taipei	2.1	(0.4)	17.4	(1.1)	62.0	(1.4)	93.8	(0.9)	26.4	(1.4)	47.8	(1.4)	61.6	(1.4)	81.6	(1.0)
Thailand	0.6	(0.3)	4.7	(0.7)	17.8	(1.5)	73.5	(1.3)	38.2	(1.4)	44.4	(1.4)	45.4	(1.4)	48.4	(1.7)
Tunisia	0.9	(0.3)	5.7	(0.8)	27.6	(1.2)	87.3	(1.3)	17.9	(1.4)	27.4	(1.5)	37.0	(1.9)	48.7	(1.7)
United Arab Emirates	50.7	(1.5)	85.9	(1.1)	95.5	(0.5)	97.5	(0.4)	30.6	(1.2)	37.2	(1.2)	44.6	(1.2)	70.8	(1.2)
Uruguay	1.3	(0.3)	5.4	(0.6)	18.7	(1.3)	85.0	(1.2)	28.7	(1.4)	45.2	(1.5)	50.4	(1.9)	63.9	(1.9)
Viet Nam	0.0	(0.0)	0.3	(0.2)	2.5	(0.6)	50.1	(1.9)	26.0	(1.8)	40.3	(1.7)	47.2	(2.1)	49.9	(1.6)

1. ESCS refers to the *PISA index of economic, social and cultural status.*
2. The variable indicating the number of books available at home has been coded as: 0-10 books was coded as 5 books, 11-25 books as 18 books, 26-100 books as 63 books, 101-200 books as 150.5 books, 201-500 books as 350.5 books and more than 500 books as 750.5 books.
* See notes at the beginning of this Annex.
StatLink ⟐ http://dx.doi.org/10.1787/888932964908

[Part 5/7]

Elements of socio-economic status, by quarters of socio-economic status within countries

Table II.2.2 *Results based on students' self-reports*

	Cultural possessions: Percentage of students who reported that they have works of art at home								Cultural possessions: Percentage of students who reported that they have a desk for study at home							
	Bottom quarter of ESCS		Second quarter of ESCS		Third quarter of ESCS		Top quarter of ESCS		Bottom quarter of ESCS		Second quarter of ESCS		Third quarter of ESCS		Top quarter of ESCS	
	%	S.E.	%	S.E.	%	S.E.	%	S.E.	%	S.E.	%	S.E.	%	S.E.	%	S.E.
Australia	58.7	(1.0)	68.7	(0.9)	79.1	(0.8)	90.1	(0.6)	82.7	(0.8)	90.4	(0.5)	94.7	(0.4)	95.9	(0.2)
Austria	55.8	(1.5)	70.7	(1.4)	76.7	(1.3)	87.5	(1.1)	92.4	(0.9)	96.5	(0.6)	98.1	(0.4)	99.4	(0.2)
Belgium	35.4	(1.1)	52.8	(1.3)	60.4	(1.5)	80.7	(0.8)	90.8	(0.7)	96.8	(0.6)	98.5	(0.4)	99.5	(0.1)
Canada	58.4	(1.1)	70.9	(1.0)	76.7	(0.9)	90.9	(0.5)	77.2	(1.0)	83.6	(0.7)	90.7	(0.6)	96.3	(0.4)
Chile	22.1	(1.2)	38.0	(1.4)	56.0	(1.5)	70.9	(1.3)	50.0	(1.7)	69.0	(1.5)	76.9	(1.5)	80.7	(0.6)
Czech Republic	33.8	(1.8)	40.8	(1.8)	53.1	(1.5)	68.7	(1.4)	97.5	(0.6)	98.9	(0.3)	99.8	(0.1)	99.7	(0.2)
Denmark	56.4	(1.7)	71.3	(1.3)	79.2	(1.5)	94.2	(0.6)	80.4	(1.2)	89.7	(0.9)	92.7	(0.8)	98.5	(0.4)
Estonia	45.9	(1.8)	60.7	(1.5)	66.1	(1.5)	81.6	(1.3)	96.4	(0.6)	97.6	(0.5)	97.4	(0.5)	99.3	(0.2)
Finland	61.2	(1.5)	73.3	(1.2)	79.0	(1.1)	90.7	(0.8)	89.7	(0.9)	93.6	(0.6)	95.2	(0.4)	98.6	(0.3)
France	17.6	(1.2)	31.0	(1.6)	41.8	(1.3)	67.0	(1.4)	96.1	(0.6)	98.0	(0.5)	98.9	(0.3)	99.8	(0.1)
Germany	53.6	(1.6)	65.5	(1.7)	76.0	(1.5)	86.9	(0.9)	93.5	(0.8)	96.5	(0.7)	98.3	(0.4)	99.2	(0.4)
Greece	42.4	(1.6)	61.9	(1.6)	73.0	(1.2)	83.8	(1.1)	95.4	(0.8)	98.4	(0.4)	98.1	(0.5)	99.5	(0.2)
Hungary	29.8	(1.6)	45.9	(1.6)	56.9	(1.6)	74.3	(1.3)	94.9	(0.7)	98.2	(0.4)	98.9	(0.4)	99.4	(0.3)
Iceland	77.7	(1.5)	90.0	(1.1)	94.1	(0.8)	98.7	(0.4)	90.3	(1.0)	94.4	(0.9)	95.7	(0.7)	99.6	(0.2)
Ireland	55.3	(1.5)	69.2	(1.2)	77.7	(1.2)	88.3	(1.0)	77.2	(1.3)	89.1	(0.9)	93.3	(0.9)	97.9	(0.4)
Israel	46.8	(1.7)	63.8	(1.4)	75.1	(1.4)	88.7	(0.8)	89.9	(1.1)	95.0	(0.9)	97.6	(0.5)	99.0	(0.4)
Italy	52.8	(0.9)	64.0	(0.7)	75.5	(0.6)	85.0	(0.5)	94.1	(0.4)	97.1	(0.3)	98.3	(0.2)	99.0	(0.1)
Japan	17.9	(1.0)	27.3	(1.4)	36.2	(1.2)	53.8	(1.5)	90.2	(1.2)	95.2	(0.8)	96.8	(0.5)	98.7	(0.3)
Korea	24.0	(1.2)	40.1	(1.4)	55.2	(1.7)	76.4	(1.2)	91.3	(0.8)	96.6	(0.5)	98.0	(0.4)	99.4	(0.2)
Luxembourg	56.2	(1.3)	71.1	(1.4)	80.9	(1.1)	92.0	(0.8)	94.5	(0.6)	96.5	(0.5)	97.8	(0.5)	99.4	(0.2)
Mexico	13.8	(0.6)	25.4	(1.0)	35.5	(0.7)	59.6	(1.0)	61.4	(0.9)	69.6	(0.7)	80.1	(0.7)	90.4	(0.4)
Netherlands	52.6	(1.7)	65.5	(1.2)	73.5	(1.4)	88.6	(1.5)	90.7	(0.9)	95.2	(0.6)	96.7	(0.5)	99.4	(0.2)
New Zealand	51.7	(1.6)	68.6	(1.6)	74.9	(1.3)	90.5	(0.9)	67.6	(1.5)	84.3	(1.1)	90.4	(0.9)	96.2	(0.6)
Norway	70.1	(1.3)	81.0	(1.2)	89.3	(1.1)	96.6	(0.5)	92.2	(0.7)	96.1	(0.6)	98.1	(0.4)	99.8	(0.1)
Poland	31.6	(1.5)	50.3	(1.6)	56.5	(1.6)	69.0	(1.8)	93.8	(0.8)	98.9	(0.4)	98.5	(0.4)	99.0	(0.3)
Portugal	43.5	(1.5)	58.4	(1.4)	69.9	(1.5)	81.3	(1.2)	89.2	(0.9)	95.7	(0.6)	97.4	(0.5)	99.1	(0.3)
Slovak Republic	39.8	(1.8)	59.5	(1.5)	69.1	(1.3)	81.2	(1.3)	74.2	(2.1)	94.7	(0.8)	96.3	(0.6)	98.2	(0.6)
Slovenia	54.6	(1.6)	69.3	(1.5)	75.8	(1.4)	90.8	(1.0)	98.6	(0.4)	99.7	(0.1)	99.7	(0.1)	99.7	(0.2)
Spain	39.3	(0.9)	51.2	(1.2)	67.9	(1.1)	81.7	(1.0)	95.8	(0.5)	97.8	(0.3)	98.8	(0.2)	99.4	(0.1)
Sweden	63.7	(1.8)	75.6	(1.3)	80.9	(1.2)	94.4	(0.7)	81.5	(1.4)	90.2	(0.8)	92.1	(0.8)	97.3	(0.5)
Switzerland	48.8	(1.4)	59.5	(1.1)	70.0	(1.3)	82.3	(1.1)	96.5	(0.4)	97.4	(0.4)	98.2	(0.4)	99.2	(0.2)
Turkey	10.6	(0.9)	22.4	(1.3)	36.6	(1.5)	57.1	(1.8)	61.7	(1.6)	88.3	(1.0)	93.3	(0.8)	98.4	(0.4)
United Kingdom	43.7	(1.6)	56.5	(1.4)	65.9	(1.2)	84.0	(1.0)	72.0	(1.1)	82.6	(1.1)	88.8	(0.9)	97.2	(0.5)
United States	49.3	(2.1)	64.8	(1.5)	75.2	(1.3)	87.6	(0.9)	61.4	(1.4)	74.8	(1.3)	81.0	(1.1)	94.0	(0.7)
OECD average	44.6	(0.2)	58.4	(0.2)	67.9	(0.2)	82.2	(0.2)	85.3	(0.2)	92.2	(0.1)	94.9	(0.1)	98.2	(0.1)
Albania	m	m	m	m	m	m	m	m	m	m	m	m	m	m	m	m
Argentina	17.5	(1.4)	26.3	(1.4)	37.2	(1.6)	57.6	(1.6)	69.1	(1.8)	80.9	(1.6)	87.9	(1.0)	94.2	(0.8)
Brazil	24.6	(1.0)	30.5	(1.2)	41.1	(1.2)	57.6	(1.5)	45.5	(1.1)	57.8	(1.1)	71.3	(0.7)	85.5	(0.8)
Bulgaria	36.5	(1.5)	59.3	(1.5)	67.9	(1.4)	81.4	(1.2)	76.6	(1.9)	94.1	(0.7)	96.2	(0.7)	98.2	(0.4)
Colombia	28.7	(1.6)	43.8	(1.6)	55.8	(1.4)	73.4	(1.5)	43.1	(2.1)	63.0	(1.8)	75.2	(1.6)	90.9	(1.1)
Costa Rica	22.5	(1.4)	33.4	(1.8)	54.9	(1.8)	73.2	(1.5)	60.0	(2.0)	79.1	(1.2)	90.2	(1.0)	95.4	(0.7)
Croatia	35.3	(1.5)	52.1	(1.5)	65.9	(1.4)	80.4	(1.1)	96.4	(0.5)	98.7	(0.3)	98.9	(0.4)	99.3	(0.2)
Cyprus*	47.9	(1.8)	69.4	(1.3)	78.5	(1.3)	88.8	(1.0)	94.8	(0.5)	98.3	(0.4)	98.3	(0.4)	99.6	(0.2)
Hong Kong-China	15.4	(1.2)	25.3	(1.1)	40.3	(1.5)	60.7	(1.7)	83.7	(1.0)	93.3	(0.7)	94.8	(0.7)	98.3	(0.3)
Indonesia	32.5	(1.6)	48.6	(2.0)	62.1	(1.7)	70.3	(1.6)	47.8	(1.9)	68.9	(1.8)	77.2	(1.3)	91.0	(0.9)
Jordan	20.4	(1.1)	34.5	(1.6)	43.0	(1.6)	60.8	(1.5)	34.8	(1.6)	63.9	(1.6)	77.2	(1.1)	92.3	(0.7)
Kazakhstan	45.8	(1.4)	61.8	(2.2)	62.7	(1.8)	77.3	(1.7)	81.1	(1.7)	93.3	(0.9)	96.0	(0.7)	99.4	(0.3)
Latvia	43.7	(2.1)	58.1	(1.5)	62.1	(1.4)	79.3	(1.5)	94.8	(0.9)	98.6	(0.4)	98.9	(0.2)	99.6	(0.2)
Liechtenstein	63.8	(5.8)	69.7	(5.8)	84.4	(4.3)	90.3	(4.0)	98.5	(1.6)	98.7	(1.3)	98.5	(1.5)	100.0	(0.0)
Lithuania	51.7	(1.4)	65.7	(1.4)	72.0	(1.3)	87.5	(1.0)	97.1	(0.5)	99.1	(0.3)	99.1	(0.3)	99.6	(0.2)
Macao-China	14.5	(1.0)	25.1	(1.2)	37.9	(1.3)	57.2	(1.4)	72.8	(1.3)	83.0	(1.0)	90.9	(0.8)	96.2	(0.5)
Malaysia	36.7	(1.3)	45.5	(1.5)	48.4	(1.5)	58.1	(1.4)	74.1	(1.5)	87.0	(1.1)	89.1	(0.8)	94.5	(0.7)
Montenegro	45.6	(1.3)	63.6	(1.7)	74.8	(1.4)	91.9	(0.9)	94.7	(0.5)	97.7	(0.5)	98.4	(0.4)	99.4	(0.2)
Peru	35.3	(1.6)	42.0	(1.5)	48.5	(1.6)	57.7	(2.1)	49.8	(1.5)	74.1	(1.3)	87.1	(1.0)	93.9	(0.6)
Qatar	43.7	(0.9)	57.7	(1.0)	66.0	(0.8)	85.4	(0.8)	58.8	(1.0)	84.0	(0.7)	90.2	(0.6)	97.4	(0.3)
Romania	28.8	(1.2)	49.7	(1.5)	64.0	(1.6)	76.3	(1.6)	86.9	(1.2)	96.7	(0.6)	98.1	(0.4)	99.2	(0.3)
Russian Federation	38.1	(1.7)	57.1	(1.5)	61.6	(1.7)	78.5	(1.8)	97.0	(0.4)	97.9	(0.4)	99.3	(0.2)	99.3	(0.2)
Serbia	37.4	(1.6)	58.8	(1.6)	78.3	(1.4)	85.1	(1.3)	95.5	(0.6)	99.0	(0.3)	99.2	(0.3)	99.6	(0.2)
Shanghai-China	29.3	(1.4)	50.7	(1.6)	64.0	(1.4)	82.0	(1.1)	94.1	(0.7)	98.1	(0.4)	98.6	(0.4)	99.6	(0.2)
Singapore	24.9	(1.2)	38.4	(1.2)	51.3	(1.5)	70.1	(1.4)	80.9	(1.0)	91.9	(0.8)	96.8	(0.5)	98.9	(0.3)
Chinese Taipei	16.8	(1.0)	37.9	(1.3)	51.1	(1.3)	72.0	(1.4)	85.2	(0.9)	95.6	(0.5)	97.1	(0.4)	99.3	(0.2)
Thailand	52.4	(1.6)	66.0	(1.4)	71.1	(1.6)	75.1	(1.2)	68.2	(1.6)	83.7	(1.2)	92.2	(0.9)	95.5	(0.7)
Tunisia	17.1	(1.2)	27.9	(1.3)	39.5	(1.6)	56.5	(2.1)	72.4	(1.8)	88.3	(1.0)	96.3	(0.6)	98.9	(0.3)
United Arab Emirates	33.1	(1.1)	48.9	(1.2)	57.0	(1.3)	79.0	(1.3)	63.8	(1.2)	84.5	(0.9)	92.6	(0.6)	96.5	(0.4)
Uruguay	19.8	(1.2)	34.2	(1.3)	49.9	(1.7)	75.1	(1.4)	62.4	(1.5)	85.1	(1.0)	90.8	(0.9)	97.2	(0.6)
Viet Nam	27.3	(1.6)	43.6	(1.8)	49.4	(1.5)	61.3	(1.9)	87.4	(1.3)	96.9	(0.6)	98.5	(0.4)	99.8	(0.1)

1. ESCS refers to the *PISA index of economic, social and cultural status*.
2. The variable indicating the number of books available at home has been coded as: 0-10 books was coded as 5 books, 11-25 books as 18 books, 26-100 books as 63 books, 101-200 books as 150.5 books, 201-500 books as 350.5 books and more than 500 books as 750.5 books.
* See notes at the beginning of this Annex.

StatLink http://dx.doi.org/10.1787/888932964908

[Part 6/7]
Elements of socio-economic status, by quarters of socio-economic status within countries
Table II.2.2   *Results based on students' self-reports*

| | Educational resources at home: Percentage of students who reported that they have a quiet place to study at home | | | | | | | | Educational resources at home: Percentage of students who reported that they have a dictionary at home | | | | | | | |
| | Bottom quarter of ESCS | | Second quarter of ESCS | | Third quarter of ESCS | | Top quarter of ESCS | | Bottom quarter of ESCS | | Second quarter of ESCS | | Third quarter of ESCS | | Top quarter of ESCS | |
	%	S.E.	%	S.E.	%	S.E.	%	S.E.	%	S.E.	%	S.E.	%	S.E.	%	S.E.
Australia	79.2	(0.9)	87.7	(0.7)	91.5	(0.6)	96.5	(0.4)	91.7	(0.6)	95.2	(0.4)	98.2	(0.3)	99.7	(0.1)
Austria	92.6	(0.8)	97.3	(0.4)	97.9	(0.5)	98.7	(0.3)	96.7	(0.6)	97.8	(0.5)	99.1	(0.4)	99.6	(0.3)
Belgium	87.5	(0.9)	93.5	(0.7)	95.5	(0.5)	98.3	(0.3)	93.9	(0.8)	98.1	(0.3)	99.1	(0.3)	99.4	(0.2)
Canada	87.0	(0.8)	90.2	(0.6)	93.1	(0.6)	97.9	(0.3)	91.1	(0.6)	96.2	(0.4)	97.6	(0.4)	99.5	(0.2)
Chile	70.1	(1.3)	79.9	(1.0)	85.6	(0.9)	91.1	(0.8)	95.6	(0.9)	98.7	(0.3)	99.1	(0.3)	99.3	(0.2)
Czech Republic	87.4	(1.2)	93.5	(1.0)	94.9	(0.7)	97.7	(0.5)	85.5	(1.6)	94.9	(0.8)	98.0	(0.5)	99.1	(0.3)
Denmark	81.5	(1.3)	91.4	(0.8)	92.9	(0.7)	97.0	(0.6)	90.6	(0.9)	96.6	(0.5)	98.4	(0.4)	99.5	(0.2)
Estonia	88.0	(1.2)	93.0	(0.8)	93.9	(0.7)	97.3	(0.4)	85.5	(1.1)	93.7	(0.8)	96.2	(0.6)	98.7	(0.3)
Finland	91.6	(0.8)	95.1	(0.5)	95.9	(0.5)	98.4	(0.3)	78.9	(1.2)	89.6	(0.9)	94.2	(0.7)	98.9	(0.3)
France	90.7	(0.9)	94.8	(0.6)	96.3	(0.7)	98.8	(0.3)	96.5	(0.6)	97.9	(0.5)	99.0	(0.3)	99.9	(0.1)
Germany	93.7	(0.9)	97.0	(0.5)	97.1	(0.5)	98.8	(0.3)	93.4	(1.0)	97.3	(0.5)	98.1	(0.4)	99.5	(0.2)
Greece	77.0	(1.1)	84.8	(1.1)	87.4	(1.1)	92.6	(0.7)	93.6	(0.8)	97.6	(0.5)	97.9	(0.5)	99.5	(0.2)
Hungary	85.6	(1.4)	92.6	(1.0)	93.8	(0.8)	96.4	(0.6)	81.1	(1.6)	94.3	(0.8)	97.9	(0.5)	99.4	(0.2)
Iceland	93.3	(0.8)	95.5	(0.6)	96.5	(0.7)	98.7	(0.3)	90.9	(1.1)	96.0	(0.6)	98.4	(0.4)	99.6	(0.2)
Ireland	81.9	(1.2)	89.5	(0.9)	90.2	(0.8)	96.2	(0.6)	94.6	(0.9)	97.7	(0.5)	99.1	(0.3)	99.6	(0.2)
Israel	87.2	(1.2)	92.4	(0.8)	95.2	(0.7)	98.2	(0.4)	93.4	(0.8)	97.7	(0.6)	98.4	(0.4)	99.7	(0.2)
Italy	88.0	(0.5)	91.2	(0.5)	94.3	(0.4)	95.5	(0.4)	97.8	(0.3)	98.7	(0.2)	99.5	(0.1)	99.5	(0.1)
Japan	80.0	(1.1)	88.0	(0.8)	88.4	(0.9)	93.3	(0.6)	95.3	(0.7)	97.9	(0.3)	99.2	(0.2)	99.4	(0.2)
Korea	68.2	(1.4)	80.3	(1.3)	85.6	(0.9)	93.3	(0.8)	92.4	(0.8)	96.9	(0.5)	98.8	(0.3)	99.9	(0.1)
Luxembourg	89.5	(0.8)	93.3	(0.7)	96.1	(0.5)	97.9	(0.4)	95.8	(0.5)	97.8	(0.4)	98.4	(0.4)	99.8	(0.1)
Mexico	61.0	(0.9)	69.0	(0.8)	73.7	(0.8)	83.7	(0.5)	95.6	(0.4)	97.7	(0.2)	98.0	(0.2)	98.5	(0.2)
Netherlands	94.5	(0.7)	96.4	(0.6)	98.5	(0.6)	98.6	(0.4)	92.4	(1.0)	96.2	(0.6)	98.8	(0.3)	100.0	(0.0)
New Zealand	74.5	(1.7)	87.8	(0.9)	88.2	(1.0)	95.7	(0.6)	87.6	(1.1)	95.3	(0.7)	96.5	(0.7)	99.0	(0.3)
Norway	90.8	(0.9)	93.3	(0.7)	96.1	(0.6)	97.9	(0.5)	84.2	(1.2)	90.7	(0.9)	97.0	(0.5)	98.2	(0.4)
Poland	91.0	(1.0)	97.2	(0.4)	96.5	(0.6)	97.9	(0.5)	96.6	(0.6)	98.7	(0.4)	98.5	(0.4)	99.5	(0.2)
Portugal	91.1	(0.8)	95.4	(0.7)	96.9	(0.5)	97.9	(0.5)	92.1	(0.6)	97.1	(0.5)	98.3	(0.4)	99.4	(0.2)
Slovak Republic	74.9	(1.7)	87.9	(1.0)	90.5	(0.9)	95.5	(0.8)	79.2	(1.6)	95.8	(0.7)	96.8	(0.5)	99.0	(0.3)
Slovenia	88.8	(1.0)	94.5	(0.6)	93.8	(0.8)	98.0	(0.4)	84.9	(1.1)	92.9	(0.8)	95.8	(0.7)	98.7	(0.3)
Spain	88.9	(0.6)	92.6	(0.5)	94.0	(0.5)	96.5	(0.4)	98.1	(0.3)	99.0	(0.3)	99.1	(0.3)	99.7	(0.1)
Sweden	86.7	(1.1)	93.0	(0.7)	93.8	(0.8)	96.9	(0.6)	83.3	(1.2)	89.7	(0.9)	93.8	(0.7)	98.6	(0.3)
Switzerland	93.4	(0.7)	96.6	(0.4)	97.5	(0.4)	98.0	(0.4)	90.3	(0.8)	95.4	(0.6)	97.5	(0.4)	99.3	(0.2)
Turkey	63.7	(1.6)	85.1	(1.2)	88.2	(1.0)	94.9	(0.8)	93.0	(0.7)	97.5	(0.5)	98.2	(0.4)	99.3	(0.2)
United Kingdom	78.4	(1.5)	87.1	(0.9)	90.3	(0.8)	96.3	(0.5)	85.9	(1.0)	93.3	(0.7)	96.3	(0.5)	99.6	(0.1)
United States	80.1	(1.3)	85.4	(1.0)	91.4	(0.8)	97.2	(0.4)	80.9	(1.2)	88.7	(0.9)	95.2	(0.7)	98.5	(0.4)
OECD average	84.1	(0.2)	90.7	(0.1)	92.7	(0.1)	96.4	(0.1)	90.5	(0.2)	95.8	(0.1)	97.8	(0.1)	99.3	(0.0)
Albania	m	m	m	m	m	m	m	m	m	m	m	m	m	m	m	m
Argentina	68.4	(1.6)	72.2	(2.0)	79.2	(1.1)	89.0	(0.9)	94.5	(0.8)	97.6	(0.5)	97.9	(0.8)	99.2	(0.4)
Brazil	70.0	(0.9)	74.1	(0.7)	79.6	(0.7)	88.1	(0.8)	88.3	(0.6)	93.2	(0.5)	95.3	(0.5)	98.1	(0.2)
Bulgaria	61.7	(1.7)	72.2	(1.1)	71.8	(1.3)	78.7	(1.2)	63.4	(2.1)	87.2	(1.1)	94.7	(0.7)	98.1	(0.4)
Colombia	64.1	(1.6)	67.9	(1.3)	75.0	(1.4)	82.9	(1.1)	96.6	(0.5)	98.6	(0.3)	98.5	(0.4)	99.4	(0.3)
Costa Rica	71.7	(1.6)	79.7	(1.4)	87.5	(1.0)	92.4	(0.8)	92.8	(0.9)	96.5	(0.6)	97.6	(0.6)	98.1	(0.5)
Croatia	80.8	(0.9)	84.5	(1.2)	89.7	(0.9)	90.1	(0.9)	93.5	(0.7)	96.8	(0.5)	97.8	(0.4)	99.6	(0.2)
Cyprus*	81.3	(1.1)	88.3	(1.0)	92.5	(0.9)	96.2	(0.6)	91.6	(0.7)	97.2	(0.4)	97.7	(0.5)	99.2	(0.3)
Hong Kong-China	68.2	(1.6)	80.0	(1.3)	86.4	(1.1)	93.2	(0.8)	96.9	(0.5)	98.8	(0.3)	99.1	(0.3)	99.5	(0.2)
Indonesia	36.1	(1.6)	53.3	(1.9)	64.5	(1.4)	77.4	(1.6)	87.3	(1.1)	93.7	(0.7)	96.3	(0.6)	97.6	(0.7)
Jordan	68.7	(1.5)	85.4	(1.2)	87.2	(1.0)	94.6	(0.6)	68.9	(1.5)	86.9	(1.1)	90.0	(1.2)	95.6	(0.6)
Kazakhstan	79.1	(1.2)	89.3	(0.9)	88.4	(1.1)	94.5	(0.7)	75.2	(1.6)	89.6	(1.1)	93.8	(0.8)	97.7	(0.5)
Latvia	86.2	(1.5)	91.8	(1.2)	93.9	(0.8)	96.3	(0.6)	83.0	(1.6)	91.5	(1.3)	97.6	(0.4)	98.6	(0.4)
Liechtenstein	97.2	(2.0)	98.5	(1.5)	98.5	(1.5)	98.7	(1.3)	90.7	(3.4)	97.0	(2.1)	98.7	(1.3)	100.0	(0.0)
Lithuania	87.4	(0.9)	92.9	(0.7)	92.3	(0.8)	96.8	(0.5)	81.7	(1.2)	88.2	(0.9)	93.5	(0.7)	97.6	(0.4)
Macao-China	63.9	(1.4)	75.5	(1.2)	84.3	(0.9)	89.9	(0.9)	96.0	(0.5)	96.7	(0.5)	97.9	(0.4)	99.0	(0.3)
Malaysia	50.3	(1.5)	62.9	(1.4)	71.3	(1.4)	80.0	(1.2)	92.8	(0.8)	96.6	(0.6)	95.6	(0.6)	98.5	(0.3)
Montenegro	86.2	(1.0)	90.2	(1.0)	92.2	(0.8)	95.9	(0.8)	87.1	(1.1)	94.5	(0.7)	96.4	(0.6)	99.4	(0.3)
Peru	69.2	(1.8)	76.6	(1.2)	82.8	(1.0)	88.6	(0.9)	96.5	(0.5)	98.3	(0.4)	99.4	(0.2)	99.8	(0.1)
Qatar	78.6	(0.8)	87.2	(0.6)	92.8	(0.5)	97.9	(0.3)	70.9	(0.8)	87.6	(0.6)	93.7	(0.5)	97.5	(0.3)
Romania	83.6	(1.2)	91.9	(0.9)	96.1	(0.6)	97.2	(0.6)	73.2	(1.6)	85.0	(1.3)	90.6	(1.0)	94.8	(0.7)
Russian Federation	82.5	(1.0)	87.9	(0.9)	87.9	(0.8)	94.9	(0.6)	80.6	(1.6)	92.2	(1.0)	95.8	(0.7)	98.6	(0.3)
Serbia	90.7	(0.8)	96.0	(0.5)	96.4	(0.5)	96.9	(0.6)	81.3	(1.3)	92.7	(0.8)	95.6	(0.7)	99.0	(0.3)
Shanghai-China	80.4	(1.5)	91.9	(0.9)	94.9	(0.6)	97.7	(0.5)	97.5	(0.5)	99.2	(0.2)	99.1	(0.3)	99.6	(0.2)
Singapore	62.4	(1.2)	77.3	(1.1)	85.6	(0.9)	91.2	(0.7)	95.9	(0.4)	98.1	(0.3)	99.0	(0.3)	99.5	(0.3)
Chinese Taipei	64.7	(1.2)	80.4	(1.0)	85.1	(0.9)	90.8	(0.7)	91.7	(0.7)	97.8	(0.3)	99.4	(0.2)	99.3	(0.2)
Thailand	60.5	(1.5)	70.7	(1.4)	78.8	(1.1)	85.8	(1.2)	70.5	(1.6)	80.6	(1.4)	88.9	(1.1)	95.4	(0.8)
Tunisia	60.2	(1.5)	76.1	(1.3)	89.4	(1.0)	92.2	(0.9)	65.1	(1.6)	83.1	(1.3)	92.1	(0.9)	94.9	(0.7)
United Arab Emirates	78.7	(1.1)	86.1	(0.8)	90.3	(0.7)	95.5	(0.5)	81.0	(0.8)	92.5	(0.6)	95.2	(0.6)	99.1	(0.2)
Uruguay	77.4	(1.3)	86.3	(1.1)	89.8	(0.9)	96.2	(0.5)	95.8	(0.6)	98.0	(0.5)	99.3	(0.3)	99.2	(0.3)
Viet Nam	70.4	(2.2)	85.5	(1.4)	86.9	(1.2)	92.0	(0.9)	44.5	(2.0)	66.1	(2.2)	81.6	(1.5)	91.9	(1.3)

1. ESCS refers to the *PISA index of economic, social and cultural status*.
2. The variable indicating the number of books available at home has been coded as: 0-10 books was coded as 5 books, 11-25 books as 18 books, 26-100 books as 63 books, 101-200 books as 150.5 books, 201-500 books as 350.5 books and more than 500 books as 750.5 books.
* See notes at the beginning of this Annex.
StatLink ᵐˢᵖ http://dx.doi.org/10.1787/888932964908

[Part 7/7]
Elements of socio-economic status, by quarters of socio-economic status within countries

Table II.2.2 *Results based on students' self-reports*

| | Average number of books available in students' homes[2] | | | | | | | |
| | Bottom quarter of ESCS | | Second quarter of ESCS | | Third quarter of ESCS | | Top quarter of ESCS | |
	Mean	S.E.	Mean	S.E.	Mean	S.E.	Mean	S.E.
Australia	97	(3.5)	140	(4.1)	189	(3.9)	297	(5.3)
Austria	56	(3.3)	104	(4.8)	171	(6.9)	323	(12.5)
Belgium	61	(3.0)	107	(4.5)	161	(5.5)	275	(7.1)
Canada	88	(3.9)	129	(3.8)	166	(4.0)	287	(5.7)
Chile	26	(2.0)	47	(2.6)	68	(2.9)	139	(4.9)
Czech Republic	80	(5.2)	123	(5.9)	161	(8.0)	280	(8.6)
Denmark	62	(2.9)	100	(3.9)	150	(5.5)	289	(10.1)
Estonia	103	(5.4)	135	(5.4)	172	(6.3)	294	(8.0)
Finland	83	(3.2)	112	(3.9)	155	(4.2)	262	(5.6)
France	55	(3.3)	95	(5.3)	149	(5.7)	276	(8.3)
Germany	85	(4.8)	135	(5.6)	217	(8.1)	346	(10.3)
Greece	66	(4.3)	100	(4.2)	144	(5.0)	271	(9.0)
Hungary	70	(4.4)	161	(5.5)	240	(8.9)	414	(10.1)
Iceland	127	(5.6)	162	(6.1)	229	(7.5)	315	(8.0)
Ireland	66	(3.9)	107	(4.3)	167	(5.7)	283	(7.7)
Israel	92	(6.7)	148	(7.5)	210	(10.3)	287	(13.5)
Italy	57	(1.8)	97	(2.5)	165	(3.2)	289	(6.7)
Japan	100	(4.3)	149	(4.6)	179	(5.0)	251	(6.7)
Korea	107	(4.4)	188	(5.0)	251	(6.8)	369	(10.6)
Luxembourg	83	(4.6)	154	(5.4)	274	(7.5)	423	(6.3)
Mexico	19	(1.0)	25	(1.1)	36	(1.2)	100	(3.6)
Netherlands	58	(4.7)	93	(5.0)	154	(6.3)	271	(11.7)
New Zealand	83	(4.6)	138	(6.4)	175	(7.1)	307	(7.7)
Norway	97	(4.9)	142	(5.6)	209	(7.1)	322	(9.5)
Poland	53	(3.1)	93	(4.3)	136	(7.1)	285	(10.7)
Portugal	33	(2.0)	60	(3.0)	101	(4.3)	252	(8.8)
Slovak Republic	39	(3.4)	85	(4.5)	115	(5.9)	226	(6.4)
Slovenia	50	(4.1)	83	(4.7)	123	(6.4)	230	(8.3)
Spain	69	(2.5)	117	(3.1)	185	(3.9)	312	(5.5)
Sweden	83	(5.5)	144	(5.9)	187	(5.8)	316	(7.3)
Switzerland	56	(2.6)	98	(3.5)	162	(6.4)	287	(5.5)
Turkey	25	(1.6)	46	(2.6)	75	(4.5)	179	(8.6)
United Kingdom	71	(3.8)	110	(4.0)	161	(6.4)	285	(8.2)
United States	43	(2.4)	81	(5.4)	113	(5.3)	228	(7.5)
OECD average	69	(0.7)	112	(0.8)	163	(1.0)	282	(1.4)
Albania	m	m	m	m	m	m	m	m
Argentina	29	(3.2)	44	(3.0)	62	(4.3)	132	(5.5)
Brazil	22	(1.4)	26	(1.4)	36	(1.6)	82	(3.6)
Bulgaria	36	(2.8)	83	(4.7)	117	(5.3)	228	(8.2)
Colombia	17	(1.6)	27	(1.2)	37	(2.0)	80	(4.0)
Costa Rica	12	(0.8)	23	(1.3)	40	(2.6)	105	(6.9)
Croatia	26	(1.5)	51	(2.8)	83	(4.0)	172	(6.2)
Cyprus*	64	(3.6)	109	(4.3)	137	(5.9)	261	(7.8)
Hong Kong-China	37	(1.8)	63	(3.1)	101	(3.5)	217	(9.3)
Indonesia	37	(3.6)	45	(3.2)	67	(3.9)	105	(6.1)
Jordan	33	(2.3)	56	(3.6)	92	(4.5)	157	(6.3)
Kazakhstan	37	(2.5)	71	(3.9)	90	(5.7)	163	(10.5)
Latvia	64	(5.5)	128	(6.8)	161	(7.4)	261	(6.9)
Liechtenstein	61	(12.8)	139	(19.6)	202	(25.9)	331	(35.8)
Lithuania	48	(3.2)	81	(4.1)	121	(5.8)	231	(7.4)
Macao-China	33	(1.9)	46	(2.7)	62	(3.1)	133	(4.6)
Malaysia	47	(2.7)	81	(4.1)	105	(5.2)	176	(6.8)
Montenegro	47	(3.1)	92	(5.4)	143	(6.5)	264	(7.9)
Peru	18	(1.3)	32	(2.1)	49	(2.8)	89	(4.9)
Qatar	61	(2.4)	97	(3.3)	125	(3.9)	239	(4.9)
Romania	37	(3.1)	65	(3.8)	102	(5.1)	222	(9.4)
Russian Federation	58	(4.4)	121	(4.6)	160	(5.5)	253	(8.8)
Serbia	34	(2.6)	57	(3.2)	92	(4.9)	215	(7.7)
Shanghai-China	44	(2.1)	73	(3.4)	113	(4.3)	208	(8.0)
Singapore	54	(2.4)	91	(3.8)	129	(4.3)	234	(5.8)
Chinese Taipei	62	(3.5)	112	(4.6)	157	(5.2)	288	(6.0)
Thailand	29	(1.7)	42	(2.2)	60	(2.9)	118	(5.8)
Tunisia	16	(1.1)	27	(2.8)	45	(3.0)	91	(5.2)
United Arab Emirates	44	(2.2)	74	(3.7)	113	(4.8)	211	(4.8)
Uruguay	19	(1.5)	32	(1.7)	63	(4.1)	145	(8.3)
Viet Nam	31	(2.0)	51	(2.5)	59	(3.0)	83	(4.9)

1. ESCS refers to the *PISA index of economic, social and cultural status.*
2. The variable indicating the number of books available at home has been coded as: 0-10 books was coded as 5 books, 11-25 books as 18 books, 26-100 books as 63 books, 101-200 books as 150.5 books, 201-500 books as 350.5 books and more than 500 books as 750.5 books.
* See notes at the beginning of this Annex.
StatLink ⑤ http://dx.doi.org/10.1787/888932964908

[Part 1/2]
Elements of socio-economic status across countries
Table II.2.3 *Results based on students' self-reports*

	ESCS[1] Mean index	S.E.	Highest parental education, in years Mean years	S.E.	Highest parental education: Percentage of students with at least one parent whose educational attainment is... No post-secondary education (ISCED 2 or less) %	S.E.	Upper secondary or post-secondary education (ISCED 3 and 4) %	S.E.	Tertiary education (ISCED 5 and 6) %	S.E.	Highest parental occupation: Percentage of students with at least one parent working in an occupation considered as... Elementary (ISCO 9) %	S.E.	Semi-skilled blue-collar (ISCO 6, 7 and 8) %	S.E.	Semi-skilled white-collar (ISCO 4 and 5) %	S.E.	Skilled (ISCO 1, 2 and 3) %	S.E.
OECD																		
Australia	0.25	(0.01)	13.2	(0.0)	10.4	(0.3)	34.2	(0.5)	55.4	(0.5)	4.2	(0.2)	10.4	(0.3)	17.7	(0.4)	67.8	(0.6)
Austria	0.08	(0.02)	13.8	(0.1)	4.7	(0.5)	47.3	(1.0)	48.0	(1.0)	2.5	(0.2)	16.8	(0.9)	30.0	(0.7)	50.7	(1.1)
Belgium	0.15	(0.02)	14.5	(0.1)	4.9	(0.4)	32.2	(0.8)	62.9	(0.8)	4.6	(0.3)	15.1	(0.6)	24.1	(0.6)	56.3	(1.0)
Canada	0.41	(0.02)	15.0	(0.0)	3.2	(0.3)	24.4	(0.6)	72.4	(0.7)	2.7	(0.2)	10.1	(0.4)	22.0	(0.5)	65.1	(0.7)
Chile	-0.58	(0.04)	12.6	(0.1)	22.4	(1.4)	42.6	(1.2)	35.0	(1.2)	12.3	(0.8)	24.9	(0.8)	27.6	(0.8)	35.2	(1.2)
Czech Republic	-0.07	(0.02)	13.5	(0.1)	1.2	(0.2)	66.2	(0.9)	32.6	(0.9)	1.4	(0.3)	18.9	(0.8)	34.2	(0.9)	45.5	(1.0)
Denmark	0.43	(0.02)	15.3	(0.0)	5.7	(0.4)	26.9	(0.9)	67.4	(1.0)	2.8	(0.3)	8.4	(0.5)	27.9	(0.9)	61.0	(1.2)
Estonia	0.11	(0.01)	14.0	(0.0)	2.4	(0.3)	40.0	(0.9)	57.6	(0.9)	1.9	(0.2)	18.9	(0.8)	23.4	(0.7)	55.8	(0.9)
Finland	0.36	(0.02)	15.0	(0.0)	2.9	(0.3)	17.8	(0.6)	79.3	(0.6)	0.9	(0.1)	9.9	(0.5)	23.6	(0.6)	65.6	(0.8)
France	-0.04	(0.02)	13.0	(0.0)	9.5	(0.5)	36.3	(0.9)	54.3	(0.9)	4.2	(0.3)	12.9	(0.6)	24.3	(0.7)	58.6	(1.0)
Germany	0.19	(0.02)	14.2	(0.1)	22.8	(0.9)	26.6	(0.7)	50.5	(1.1)	2.1	(0.3)	14.0	(0.6)	30.5	(0.8)	53.4	(1.0)
Greece	-0.06	(0.03)	13.9	(0.1)	10.7	(0.7)	36.7	(0.9)	52.6	(1.1)	5.1	(0.4)	18.9	(1.0)	27.6	(0.8)	48.4	(1.3)
Hungary	-0.25	(0.02)	13.1	(0.1)	9.6	(0.8)	46.9	(1.1)	43.6	(1.3)	3.6	(0.4)	23.6	(0.9)	28.6	(0.8)	44.2	(1.3)
Iceland	0.78	(0.01)	16.1	(0.0)	7.2	(0.4)	26.6	(0.7)	66.1	(0.8)	2.5	(0.3)	9.1	(0.5)	21.1	(0.7)	67.4	(0.7)
Ireland	0.13	(0.02)	13.6	(0.0)	8.0	(0.4)	36.1	(0.9)	55.9	(1.0)	3.0	(0.3)	11.5	(0.6)	27.8	(0.8)	57.7	(0.9)
Israel	0.17	(0.03)	13.6	(0.1)	4.4	(0.5)	33.9	(1.2)	61.7	(1.4)	1.8	(0.2)	11.4	(0.8)	16.4	(0.9)	70.5	(1.3)
Italy	-0.05	(0.02)	13.3	(0.0)	20.5	(0.4)	42.4	(0.4)	37.1	(0.5)	3.4	(0.2)	23.4	(0.5)	30.8	(0.4)	42.4	(0.6)
Japan	-0.07	(0.02)	14.1	(0.0)	1.7	(0.2)	35.9	(1.0)	62.4	(1.0)	3.5	(0.2)	11.1	(0.5)	34.8	(0.7)	50.5	(0.8)
Korea	0.01	(0.03)	14.0	(0.1)	3.2	(0.3)	40.1	(1.5)	56.7	(1.6)	2.9	(0.3)	8.8	(0.6)	31.6	(0.9)	56.7	(1.2)
Luxembourg	0.07	(0.01)	13.6	(0.1)	20.0	(0.6)	29.2	(0.6)	50.8	(0.7)	4.3	(0.3)	19.8	(0.5)	27.9	(0.7)	47.9	(0.7)
Mexico	-1.11	(0.02)	10.8	(0.1)	49.7	(0.8)	14.6	(0.3)	35.7	(0.7)	17.6	(0.6)	23.2	(0.4)	29.0	(0.5)	30.1	(0.7)
Netherlands	0.23	(0.02)	13.9	(0.1)	6.1	(0.4)	30.7	(1.2)	63.2	(1.2)	1.7	(0.2)	8.4	(0.5)	20.4	(0.9)	69.5	(1.0)
New Zealand	0.04	(0.02)	13.0	(0.0)	7.2	(0.5)	40.1	(0.9)	52.7	(1.0)	3.1	(0.3)	13.0	(0.6)	17.4	(0.6)	66.5	(0.9)
Norway	0.46	(0.02)	13.9	(0.0)	2.9	(0.3)	29.3	(0.9)	67.9	(1.0)	1.3	(0.2)	6.1	(0.4)	21.1	(0.7)	71.5	(0.8)
Poland	-0.21	(0.03)	12.7	(0.1)	3.1	(0.3)	70.6	(1.2)	26.3	(1.3)	1.6	(0.2)	30.7	(1.1)	23.6	(0.8)	44.2	(1.4)
Portugal	-0.48	(0.05)	11.0	(0.2)	48.7	(1.7)	24.0	(0.8)	27.3	(1.6)	7.1	(0.6)	26.1	(1.0)	30.8	(1.0)	36.0	(1.8)
Slovak Republic	-0.18	(0.02)	14.1	(0.1)	3.4	(0.5)	66.4	(1.1)	30.1	(1.2)	5.3	(0.6)	23.5	(0.9)	35.7	(0.9)	35.6	(1.2)
Slovenia	0.07	(0.01)	13.1	(0.0)	4.1	(0.3)	52.6	(0.8)	43.3	(0.8)	2.9	(0.3)	16.7	(0.6)	24.5	(0.6)	55.9	(0.8)
Spain	-0.19	(0.03)	12.4	(0.1)	24.4	(0.8)	27.1	(0.6)	48.5	(1.0)	6.1	(0.3)	21.5	(0.8)	29.4	(0.7)	43.0	(1.1)
Sweden	0.28	(0.02)	14.1	(0.1)	5.4	(0.4)	25.4	(0.7)	69.2	(0.7)	1.6	(0.2)	8.6	(0.5)	25.9	(0.8)	63.9	(0.9)
Switzerland	0.17	(0.02)	14.0	(0.1)	12.9	(0.5)	31.0	(0.6)	56.2	(0.8)	1.3	(0.2)	11.8	(0.6)	23.3	(0.9)	63.6	(1.3)
Turkey	-1.46	(0.04)	8.7	(0.1)	59.9	(1.2)	16.1	(0.6)	24.0	(1.0)	9.2	(0.7)	32.8	(1.2)	36.9	(1.2)	21.2	(1.0)
United Kingdom	0.27	(0.02)	14.2	(0.0)	3.7	(0.3)	36.9	(0.8)	59.4	(0.8)	2.3	(0.2)	6.9	(0.5)	25.7	(0.8)	65.0	(1.1)
United States	0.17	(0.04)	13.7	(0.1)	9.0	(0.8)	32.4	(1.1)	58.6	(1.5)	5.7	(0.5)	8.1	(0.5)	21.6	(0.8)	64.6	(1.3)
OECD average	0.00	(0.00)	13.5	(0.0)	12.2	(0.1)	35.9	(0.2)	51.9	(0.2)	4.0	(0.1)	15.7	(0.1)	26.4	(0.1)	53.9	(0.2)
Partners																		
Albania	m	m	12.1	(0.1)	24.4	(0.9)	46.3	(0.8)	29.3	(0.8)	6.0	(0.4)	37.4	(1.1)	19.0	(0.8)	37.7	(1.0)
Argentina	-0.72	(0.04)	12.5	(0.1)	31.3	(1.3)	21.5	(0.7)	47.1	(1.3)	8.6	(0.6)	27.5	(1.1)	29.4	(1.0)	34.6	(1.6)
Brazil	-1.17	(0.02)	10.2	(0.1)	37.3	(0.8)	36.6	(0.7)	26.0	(0.8)	10.9	(0.4)	19.0	(0.6)	35.6	(0.6)	34.5	(0.7)
Bulgaria	-0.28	(0.04)	13.7	(0.1)	7.2	(0.8)	47.5	(1.0)	45.4	(1.2)	4.0	(0.4)	23.7	(1.1)	26.8	(0.8)	45.5	(1.4)
Colombia	-1.26	(0.04)	10.9	(0.1)	37.5	(1.3)	15.4	(0.8)	47.0	(1.5)	7.6	(0.5)	33.7	(1.2)	34.3	(0.9)	24.5	(1.0)
Costa Rica	-0.98	(0.04)	12.1	(0.1)	28.0	(1.1)	23.5	(1.0)	48.5	(1.3)	11.9	(1.0)	20.7	(1.2)	32.0	(1.1)	35.4	(1.4)
Croatia	-0.34	(0.02)	13.7	(0.0)	4.8	(0.4)	48.2	(0.8)	47.1	(0.8)	1.6	(0.2)	21.2	(0.7)	36.0	(0.9)	41.2	(1.1)
Cyprus*	0.09	(0.01)	14.1	(0.1)	5.1	(0.3)	42.2	(0.7)	52.7	(0.7)	2.5	(0.3)	16.6	(0.6)	38.2	(0.9)	42.8	(0.9)
Hong Kong-China	-0.79	(0.05)	11.4	(0.1)	29.7	(1.4)	48.4	(1.1)	21.8	(2.0)	7.0	(0.5)	16.0	(0.8)	34.0	(1.2)	42.9	(2.0)
Indonesia	-1.80	(0.05)	10.1	(0.1)	48.1	(1.7)	32.1	(1.1)	19.8	(1.5)	21.6	(1.9)	32.0	(2.1)	25.1	(1.4)	21.3	(1.7)
Jordan	-0.42	(0.02)	13.6	(0.1)	12.0	(0.6)	30.7	(0.8)	57.3	(1.1)	1.9	(0.2)	19.6	(0.8)	16.5	(0.6)	61.9	(0.9)
Kazakhstan	-0.32	(0.02)	14.2	(0.1)	1.4	(0.2)	12.0	(0.7)	86.6	(0.8)	3.1	(0.3)	17.9	(0.9)	18.4	(0.9)	60.5	(1.3)
Latvia	-0.26	(0.03)	13.3	(0.1)	2.7	(0.4)	42.6	(1.2)	54.7	(1.3)	5.1	(0.5)	15.9	(0.8)	28.1	(1.0)	50.8	(1.3)
Liechtenstein	0.30	(0.05)	13.6	(0.2)	10.9	(2.0)	33.0	(2.4)	56.1	(2.5)	2.1	(0.9)	9.8	(1.6)	13.2	(1.8)	75.0	(2.3)
Lithuania	-0.13	(0.02)	14.0	(0.0)	1.5	(0.2)	34.2	(0.9)	64.3	(0.9)	4.4	(0.4)	22.8	(0.7)	21.0	(0.6)	51.8	(0.9)
Macao-China	-0.89	(0.01)	10.5	(0.0)	49.3	(0.6)	32.3	(0.6)	18.4	(0.5)	5.0	(0.3)	9.2	(0.4)	58.0	(0.7)	27.8	(0.6)
Malaysia	-0.72	(0.03)	12.7	(0.1)	17.9	(0.9)	53.3	(0.9)	28.8	(1.2)	10.7	(0.7)	25.4	(1.0)	24.0	(0.8)	40.0	(1.4)
Montenegro	-0.25	(0.01)	13.7	(0.0)	4.0	(0.3)	37.2	(0.7)	58.8	(0.8)	3.9	(0.3)	18.4	(0.6)	32.5	(0.8)	45.2	(0.8)
Peru	-1.23	(0.05)	11.5	(0.1)	26.7	(1.3)	39.2	(1.0)	34.1	(1.5)	21.7	(1.2)	25.4	(0.8)	31.2	(0.7)	21.7	(1.3)
Qatar	0.44	(0.01)	14.3	(0.0)	9.8	(0.3)	18.6	(0.4)	71.7	(0.4)	0.6	(0.1)	7.1	(0.3)	15.0	(0.4)	77.3	(0.4)
Romania	-0.47	(0.04)	13.6	(0.1)	5.8	(0.6)	42.5	(1.1)	51.7	(1.2)	4.2	(0.5)	31.0	(1.2)	27.8	(1.0)	37.1	(1.6)
Russian Federation	-0.11	(0.02)	13.9	(0.0)	1.3	(0.3)	8.0	(0.5)	90.7	(0.6)	1.6	(0.2)	15.3	(0.8)	27.2	(0.8)	56.0	(1.1)
Serbia	-0.30	(0.02)	13.5	(0.1)	4.8	(0.5)	40.3	(1.0)	54.9	(1.1)	3.6	(0.3)	12.5	(0.6)	41.8	(1.0)	42.0	(1.1)
Shanghai-China	-0.36	(0.04)	12.8	(0.1)	24.9	(1.3)	30.6	(0.8)	44.5	(1.3)	1.5	(0.2)	14.9	(0.8)	26.2	(0.9)	57.4	(1.3)
Singapore	-0.26	(0.01)	12.4	(0.0)	10.0	(0.4)	42.2	(0.7)	47.8	(0.7)	2.6	(0.2)	7.8	(0.5)	20.2	(0.6)	69.4	(0.6)
Chinese Taipei	-0.40	(0.02)	13.0	(0.1)	11.8	(0.6)	36.8	(0.8)	51.4	(1.1)	3.3	(0.3)	21.5	(0.9)	31.5	(0.6)	43.8	(1.2)
Thailand	-1.35	(0.04)	10.1	(0.1)	50.2	(1.4)	30.8	(0.7)	19.0	(1.2)	11.6	(0.7)	38.8	(1.2)	25.5	(0.8)	24.2	(1.2)
Tunisia	-1.19	(0.05)	11.9	(0.1)	29.8	(1.3)	42.1	(1.0)	28.1	(1.2)	28.0	(1.3)	19.4	(0.9)	22.3	(0.9)	30.4	(1.4)
United Arab Emirates	0.32	(0.02)	14.1	(0.1)	8.9	(0.4)	23.4	(0.6)	67.7	(0.9)	0.7	(0.1)	4.3	(0.3)	12.6	(0.6)	82.4	(0.6)
Uruguay	-0.88	(0.03)	11.4	(0.1)	45.1	(1.1)	19.3	(0.6)	35.6	(1.0)	16.5	(0.7)	20.5	(0.6)	35.5	(0.8)	27.6	(1.0)
Viet Nam	-1.81	(0.05)	9.8	(0.1)	58.2	(1.5)	30.5	(1.0)	11.2	(1.0)	2.9	(0.5)	66.0	(1.7)	17.9	(0.9)	13.2	(1.1)

1. ESCS refers to the *PISA index of economic, social and cultural status*.
2. The variable indicating the number of books available at home has been coded as follows: 0-10 books was coded as 5 books, 11-25 books as 18 books, 26-100 books as 63 books, 101-200 books as 150.5 books, 201-500 books as 350.5 books and more than 500 books as 750.5 books.
* See notes at the beginning of this Annex.
StatLink ⟨ISL⟩ http://dx.doi.org/10.1787/888932964908

[Part 2/2]

Table II.2.3 Elements of socio-economic status across countries

Results based on students' self-reports

	Cultural possessions: Percentage of students who reported that they have the following possessions at home						Educational resources at home: Percentage of students who reported that they have the following possessions at home						ICT resources at home: Percentage of students who reported that they have the following at home						Family wealth/possessions at home: Percentage of students who reported that they have the following possessions at home		Average number of books available at student's home[2]	
	Classical literature		Poetry books		Works of art		A desk at which to study		A quiet place to study		A dictionary		A computer to use for school work		Educational software		Internet access		A DVD player			
	%	S.E.	%	S.E.	%	S.E.	%	S.E.	%	S.E.	%	S.E.	%	S.E.	%	S.E.	%	S.E.	%	S.E.	Mean	S.E.
OECD																						
Australia	40.2	(0.6)	35.8	(0.5)	74.1	(0.5)	91.6	(0.3)	88.6	(0.3)	96.1	(0.2)	97.8	(0.1)	77.6	(0.5)	97.2	(0.2)	98.4	(0.2)	80.4	(2.6)
Austria	39.9	(1.2)	56.5	(1.0)	72.7	(0.7)	96.6	(0.3)	96.6	(0.3)	98.3	(0.3)	98.3	(0.3)	47.3	(0.9)	98.8	(0.2)	96.8	(0.3)	63.0	(5.5)
Belgium	38.1	(0.8)	31.8	(0.7)	57.1	(0.7)	96.2	(0.3)	93.6	(0.4)	97.4	(0.2)	96.9	(0.3)	60.8	(0.7)	98.2	(0.2)	98.3	(0.1)	50.4	(3.7)
Canada	36.6	(0.7)	34.0	(0.6)	74.1	(0.5)	86.9	(0.4)	92.0	(0.3)	96.0	(0.2)	97.3	(0.2)	66.7	(0.5)	98.0	(0.2)	98.3	(0.2)	67.2	(3.3)
Chile	39.2	(1.0)	53.9	(0.8)	46.7	(1.0)	71.3	(0.9)	81.7	(0.7)	98.2	(0.3)	85.8	(0.9)	30.7	(0.7)	76.3	(1.2)	90.1	(0.5)	69.7	(2.3)
Czech Republic	67.8	(1.1)	43.5	(1.1)	49.0	(1.0)	98.9	(0.2)	93.4	(0.4)	94.3	(0.5)	97.4	(0.3)	53.6	(0.9)	97.4	(0.3)	96.1	(0.3)	60.7	(4.6)
Denmark	48.8	(0.9)	29.7	(0.9)	75.1	(0.8)	90.3	(0.5)	90.6	(0.5)	96.3	(0.3)	99.2	(0.2)	81.2	(0.8)	99.6	(0.1)	98.9	(0.2)	49.8	(4.0)
Estonia	72.9	(0.7)	72.0	(0.9)	63.7	(0.8)	97.7	(0.2)	93.0	(0.4)	93.5	(0.4)	89.5	(0.6)	73.8	(0.8)	98.9	(0.2)	88.9	(0.5)	76.0	(3.7)
Finland	51.3	(0.9)	51.6	(0.8)	76.0	(0.7)	94.3	(0.3)	95.3	(0.3)	90.4	(0.4)	98.9	(0.2)	36.8	(0.7)	99.6	(0.1)	98.2	(0.2)	53.2	(2.9)
France	64.0	(1.0)	42.2	(1.0)	39.3	(0.9)	98.2	(0.2)	95.0	(0.4)	98.3	(0.2)	96.8	(0.3)	36.5	(0.9)	98.1	(0.2)	97.8	(0.2)	42.8	(4.0)
Germany	44.8	(1.0)	57.8	(0.8)	70.5	(0.9)	96.8	(0.3)	96.6	(0.3)	97.1	(0.3)	98.2	(0.2)	51.4	(0.8)	98.6	(0.2)	97.5	(0.2)	94.4	(5.6)
Greece	50.0	(1.3)	44.6	(1.1)	65.2	(1.0)	97.9	(0.3)	85.4	(0.6)	97.2	(0.3)	91.9	(0.5)	44.5	(1.0)	87.7	(0.7)	95.2	(0.3)	44.7	(4.0)
Hungary	64.1	(1.1)	66.4	(1.0)	51.7	(0.9)	97.8	(0.3)	92.0	(0.6)	93.1	(0.6)	94.0	(0.6)	44.9	(0.8)	93.6	(0.6)	97.1	(0.3)	221.6	(6.0)
Iceland	69.3	(0.9)	72.0	(0.6)	90.1	(0.5)	95.0	(0.4)	96.0	(0.3)	96.2	(0.4)	99.0	(0.2)	77.7	(0.7)	99.6	(0.1)	98.4	(0.2)	208.1	(3.0)
Ireland	34.1	(0.9)	35.6	(0.9)	72.6	(0.7)	89.3	(0.6)	89.3	(0.4)	97.6	(0.3)	95.2	(0.3)	57.6	(0.9)	97.9	(0.2)	99.1	(0.1)	155.5	(4.3)
Israel	53.4	(1.3)	52.2	(1.1)	68.4	(1.0)	95.3	(0.5)	93.2	(0.4)	97.2	(0.3)	94.2	(0.5)	50.2	(1.0)	91.5	(0.8)	88.5	(0.7)	184.1	(8.0)
Italy	62.6	(0.7)	56.9	(0.6)	69.3	(0.5)	97.1	(0.2)	92.2	(0.3)	98.9	(0.1)	96.7	(0.2)	53.4	(0.5)	96.9	(0.2)	97.3	(0.1)	152.2	(3.1)
Japan	50.4	(1.1)	25.8	(0.8)	33.7	(0.8)	95.1	(0.4)	87.3	(0.5)	97.9	(0.2)	70.1	(0.9)	15.2	(0.5)	88.6	(0.7)	94.9	(0.3)	169.9	(3.6)
Korea	80.9	(0.8)	63.1	(1.1)	48.9	(1.1)	96.3	(0.3)	81.8	(0.7)	97.0	(0.3)	94.5	(0.4)	54.9	(1.1)	97.2	(0.3)	53.6	(1.1)	228.6	(6.7)
Luxembourg	41.7	(0.5)	52.1	(0.6)	75.0	(0.6)	97.0	(0.2)	94.1	(0.3)	97.8	(0.2)	96.8	(0.2)	49.5	(0.6)	97.8	(0.2)	97.5	(0.2)	234.0	(3.2)
Mexico	48.0	(0.5)	44.6	(0.5)	33.6	(0.5)	75.4	(0.4)	71.8	(0.5)	97.4	(0.1)	57.3	(0.8)	28.5	(0.5)	47.4	(0.8)	84.3	(0.4)	45.3	(1.3)
Netherlands	28.8	(1.1)	28.3	(1.2)	70.0	(1.1)	95.7	(0.4)	97.0	(0.2)	96.8	(0.4)	98.2	(0.2)	63.4	(1.0)	99.5	(0.1)	98.8	(0.2)	143.5	(5.3)
New Zealand	27.4	(0.9)	37.3	(0.9)	71.0	(0.9)	84.2	(0.6)	86.2	(0.6)	94.4	(0.4)	93.6	(0.4)	62.1	(0.9)	92.6	(0.4)	97.2	(0.3)	174.2	(4.2)
Norway	56.5	(1.1)	45.0	(1.2)	84.1	(0.7)	96.6	(0.3)	94.4	(0.3)	92.5	(0.4)	98.6	(0.2)	67.9	(0.8)	99.4	(0.1)	98.2	(0.2)	192.2	(5.4)
Poland	78.0	(0.9)	47.4	(1.1)	51.8	(1.1)	97.5	(0.3)	95.6	(0.4)	98.3	(0.2)	97.2	(0.3)	71.2	(0.8)	95.3	(0.4)	92.1	(0.5)	141.7	(6.1)
Portugal	55.3	(1.4)	50.1	(1.3)	63.3	(1.0)	95.3	(0.4)	95.3	(0.4)	96.7	(0.3)	96.9	(0.4)	48.1	(0.9)	95.3	(0.4)	93.7	(0.5)	111.5	(5.3)
Slovak Republic	55.0	(1.0)	60.6	(1.1)	62.4	(0.9)	90.8	(0.7)	87.2	(0.7)	92.7	(0.5)	91.9	(0.7)	54.4	(1.1)	92.9	(0.6)	95.0	(0.4)	115.8	(3.4)
Slovenia	59.4	(0.9)	60.5	(0.7)	72.6	(0.7)	99.4	(0.1)	93.7	(0.4)	93.0	(0.4)	98.5	(0.3)	68.2	(0.7)	99.1	(0.2)	94.6	(0.4)	121.4	(3.2)
Spain	65.6	(0.7)	57.0	(0.7)	60.0	(0.7)	98.0	(0.2)	93.0	(0.3)	98.9	(0.1)	96.1	(0.2)	47.1	(0.6)	94.7	(0.3)	97.2	(0.2)	170.8	(3.7)
Sweden	54.4	(0.8)	34.8	(0.8)	78.5	(0.7)	90.3	(0.5)	92.6	(0.4)	91.3	(0.4)	98.6	(0.2)	63.1	(0.9)	99.3	(0.1)	98.5	(0.2)	181.4	(3.9)
Switzerland	31.0	(0.8)	37.9	(0.9)	65.1	(0.7)	97.8	(0.2)	96.4	(0.3)	95.6	(0.3)	97.7	(0.2)	43.8	(0.8)	99.0	(0.1)	96.8	(0.3)	150.7	(3.5)
Turkey	58.1	(1.2)	59.6	(0.9)	31.6	(1.0)	85.3	(0.8)	82.9	(0.7)	97.0	(0.3)	68.0	(1.2)	34.9	(1.1)	57.3	(1.2)	61.2	(1.0)	81.0	(4.1)
United Kingdom	38.7	(1.1)	38.6	(0.9)	62.4	(0.9)	84.9	(0.6)	87.8	(0.7)	93.6	(0.4)	97.1	(0.3)	72.7	(0.8)	98.4	(0.2)	98.7	(0.2)	155.5	(4.2)
United States	35.8	(1.1)	39.1	(1.0)	69.2	(0.9)	77.7	(0.7)	88.5	(0.5)	90.8	(0.5)	91.0	(0.6)	62.2	(1.0)	92.6	(0.6)	97.6	(0.3)	116.2	(4.3)
OECD average	51.2	(0.2)	47.6	(0.2)	63.2	(0.1)	92.6	(0.1)	90.9	(0.1)	95.8	(0.1)	93.2	(0.1)	54.5	(0.1)	93.4	(0.1)	93.7	(0.1)	156.1	(0.7)
Partners																						
Albania	41.6	(0.9)	79.6	(0.8)	54.0	(0.9)	91.9	(0.5)	91.1	(0.6)	77.8	(0.7)	64.8	(0.8)	43.2	(0.9)	54.3	(0.9)	84.1	(0.7)	54.3	(1.7)
Argentina	63.7	(1.4)	53.6	(1.2)	34.5	(1.0)	82.9	(1.0)	77.1	(1.0)	97.3	(0.4)	83.8	(1.4)	46.1	(1.6)	74.4	(1.5)	88.7	(0.6)	66.9	(2.8)
Brazil	41.1	(0.6)	51.6	(0.6)	38.4	(0.9)	65.0	(0.6)	77.9	(0.4)	93.7	(0.3)	71.8	(0.7)	28.4	(0.5)	74.7	(0.7)	92.2	(0.3)	41.6	(1.4)
Bulgaria	67.7	(1.3)	63.8	(1.2)	61.4	(1.0)	91.4	(0.7)	71.1	(0.8)	85.8	(1.0)	93.2	(0.6)	58.6	(1.0)	93.4	(0.6)	84.4	(0.6)	115.8	(4.2)
Colombia	50.5	(1.1)	54.7	(1.0)	50.4	(1.1)	68.0	(1.3)	72.5	(0.8)	98.3	(0.2)	62.9	(1.5)	34.1	(1.1)	53.9	(1.4)	82.4	(0.7)	40.3	(1.8)
Costa Rica	58.4	(1.3)	33.6	(1.1)	45.9	(1.3)	81.1	(0.9)	82.8	(0.7)	96.3	(0.4)	73.7	(1.4)	39.6	(1.1)	66.4	(1.3)	83.6	(0.7)	45.3	(2.5)
Croatia	46.9	(1.0)	33.2	(0.9)	58.4	(0.8)	98.3	(0.2)	86.2	(0.5)	96.9	(0.2)	94.2	(0.4)	57.8	(0.9)	95.6	(0.4)	95.3	(0.3)	82.7	(2.7)
Cyprus*	41.6	(0.7)	44.5	(0.7)	71.1	(0.7)	97.8	(0.2)	89.5	(0.4)	96.4	(0.2)	96.7	(0.3)	56.2	(0.8)	96.4	(0.3)	94.2	(0.3)	142.9	(2.9)
Hong Kong-China	64.5	(1.3)	49.6	(1.3)	35.3	(1.2)	92.5	(0.4)	81.9	(0.9)	98.6	(0.2)	98.8	(0.2)	45.2	(1.1)	99.3	(0.1)	90.7	(0.5)	104.4	(5.3)
Indonesia	22.3	(1.2)	37.0	(1.2)	53.3	(1.2)	71.2	(1.1)	56.4	(1.1)	93.7	(0.5)	25.8	(1.9)	19.3	(1.5)	23.1	(1.9)	76.4	(1.1)	63.4	(2.6)
Jordan	32.7	(0.7)	42.0	(0.8)	39.7	(0.9)	66.9	(1.0)	83.8	(0.6)	85.1	(0.8)	83.3	(0.7)	55.0	(0.9)	65.3	(0.8)	70.3	(0.8)	84.3	(2.3)
Kazakhstan	78.6	(0.9)	74.0	(1.0)	61.9	(1.2)	92.4	(0.8)	87.8	(0.5)	89.1	(0.8)	65.8	(1.4)	54.6	(1.1)	55.1	(1.3)	90.5	(0.5)	90.1	(4.6)
Latvia	66.3	(1.0)	66.8	(1.0)	60.7	(0.9)	97.9	(0.3)	92.0	(0.5)	92.6	(0.5)	93.1	(0.5)	68.8	(0.8)	92.9	(0.6)	85.0	(0.7)	153.7	(3.8)
Liechtenstein	41.9	(2.7)	53.9	(2.9)	76.7	(2.4)	98.9	(0.6)	97.9	(0.8)	96.3	(1.3)	98.9	(0.6)	54.4	(2.7)	98.6	(0.7)	97.9	(0.8)	180.4	(13.1)
Lithuania	49.1	(1.1)	53.8	(0.9)	69.2	(0.8)	98.7	(0.2)	92.3	(0.4)	90.1	(0.5)	95.8	(0.3)	59.2	(0.9)	93.8	(0.4)	88.2	(0.5)	120.4	(3.7)
Macao-China	44.4	(0.6)	41.2	(0.6)	33.6	(0.6)	85.6	(0.5)	78.3	(0.5)	97.4	(0.2)	97.1	(0.2)	58.7	(0.6)	98.4	(0.2)	87.1	(0.5)	68.4	(1.8)
Malaysia	21.5	(0.7)	40.9	(0.9)	47.2	(0.9)	86.2	(0.6)	66.1	(0.9)	95.9	(0.3)	68.4	(1.2)	40.4	(1.1)	62.9	(1.4)	79.9	(0.7)	102.1	(3.4)
Montenegro	63.5	(0.7)	72.8	(0.7)	68.9	(0.6)	97.5	(0.2)	91.1	(0.4)	94.4	(0.4)	91.8	(0.4)	61.1	(0.7)	88.2	(0.4)	96.3	(0.3)	136.4	(2.7)
Peru	73.8	(0.8)	72.6	(0.7)	45.9	(1.0)	76.2	(1.0)	79.0	(0.7)	98.5	(0.2)	52.2	(1.7)	33.8	(1.1)	41.9	(1.8)	84.6	(0.8)	47.3	(2.1)
Qatar	43.5	(0.4)	55.5	(0.5)	63.2	(0.5)	82.4	(0.4)	89.1	(0.3)	87.3	(0.3)	92.0	(0.3)	62.8	(0.5)	92.3	(0.2)	86.9	(0.3)	130.4	(1.9)
Romania	72.0	(1.2)	83.2	(0.9)	54.7	(1.1)	95.2	(0.4)	92.1	(0.5)	85.9	(0.8)	87.2	(0.8)	53.7	(1.2)	81.0	(1.1)	71.1	(1.1)	106.4	(5.1)
Russian Federation	83.1	(0.8)	77.5	(0.8)	58.8	(1.1)	98.4	(0.2)	88.3	(0.4)	91.7	(0.7)	92.9	(0.7)	69.2	(0.8)	92.2	(0.8)	94.1	(0.4)	148.3	(4.5)
Serbia	66.5	(0.9)	69.8	(0.9)	63.8	(0.9)	98.4	(0.2)	94.9	(0.3)	92.1	(0.5)	95.2	(0.4)	58.6	(1.1)	89.5	(0.6)	89.0	(0.5)	99.4	(3.7)
Shanghai-China	81.1	(0.9)	77.0	(0.8)	56.5	(1.1)	97.6	(0.3)	91.2	(0.6)	98.9	(0.2)	83.0	(1.0)	44.2	(1.0)	85.8	(1.0)	87.5	(0.6)	109.5	(3.9)
Singapore	38.8	(0.8)	33.3	(0.7)	46.2	(0.8)	92.1	(0.3)	79.1	(0.5)	98.1	(0.2)	94.9	(0.3)	68.6	(0.6)	97.1	(0.2)	93.4	(0.3)	127.0	(2.4)
Chinese Taipei	52.3	(1.0)	54.4	(1.0)	44.4	(1.0)	94.3	(0.3)	80.2	(0.5)	97.0	(0.3)	90.8	(0.4)	41.6	(0.8)	96.1	(0.3)	92.6	(0.3)	154.9	(4.0)
Thailand	41.5	(0.9)	44.0	(0.8)	66.3	(0.8)	84.9	(0.7)	73.9	(0.7)	83.8	(0.9)	63.3	(1.4)	36.8	(1.3)	49.1	(1.4)	90.3	(0.5)	62.2	(2.6)
Tunisia	36.9	(1.3)	32.7	(1.1)	35.2	(1.1)	88.9	(0.8)	79.5	(0.9)	83.7	(0.9)	57.0	(1.6)	35.9	(1.3)	50.8	(1.5)	66.9	(1.1)	44.5	(2.1)
United Arab Emirates	40.1	(0.7)	45.7	(0.6)	54.4	(0.8)	84.3	(0.5)	87.6	(0.4)	91.9	(0.4)	93.1	(0.3)	59.2	(0.7)	94.0	(0.4)	89.2	(0.4)	110.8	(2.2)
Uruguay	45.8	(1.0)	47.0	(0.9)	44.7	(1.0)	83.8	(0.7)	87.4	(0.6)	98.0	(0.2)	89.0	(0.5)	41.7	(1.0)	82.7	(0.7)	91.1	(0.5)	64.8	(2.9)
Viet Nam	50.6	(1.3)	40.8	(1.2)	45.4	(1.1)	95.6	(0.5)	83.7	(1.0)	71.0	(1.5)	39.6	(1.6)	15.0	(1.0)	29.2	(1.7)	70.3	(1.0)	56.2	(2.1)

1. ESCS refers to the *PISA index of economic, social and cultural status.*
2. The variable indicating the number of books available at home has been coded as follows: 0-10 books was coded as 5 books, 11-25 books as 18 books, 2[illegible]-100 books as 63 books, 101-200 books as 150.5 books, 201-500 books as 350.5 books and more than 500 books as 750.5 books.

* See notes at the beginning of this Annex.

StatLink http://dx.doi.org/10.1787/888932964908

[Part 1/1]

Table II.2.4a Students' socio-economic status and mathematics performance

By national quarters of the PISA index of economic, social and cultural status*; results based on students' self-reports*

		PISA index of economic, social and cultural status (ESCS)										Performance in mathematics, by national quarters of this index								Increased likelihood of students in the bottom quarter of the ESCS index scoring in the bottom quarter of the mathematics performance distribution	
		All students		Bottom quarter		Second quarter		Third quarter		Top quarter		Bottom quarter		Second quarter		Third quarter		Top quarter			
		Mean index	S.E.	Mean index	S.E.	Mean index	S.E.	Mean index	S.E.	Mean index	S.E.	Mean score	S.E.	Mean score	S.E.	Mean score	S.E.	Mean score	S.E.	Ratio	S.E.
OECD	Australia	0.25	(0.01)	-0.84	(0.02)	0.05	(0.02)	0.61	(0.01)	1.18	(0.01)	463	(2.2)	492	(2.0)	521	(2.9)	550	(2.6)	**2.12**	(0.09)
	Austria	0.08	(0.02)	-0.97	(0.03)	-0.25	(0.02)	0.33	(0.03)	1.19	(0.03)	458	(4.2)	495	(4.2)	519	(3.8)	552	(4.2)	**2.34**	(0.16)
	Belgium	0.15	(0.02)	-1.05	(0.03)	-0.19	(0.03)	0.55	(0.02)	1.27	(0.02)	460	(3.7)	497	(3.3)	536	(3.0)	575	(3.3)	**2.43**	(0.14)
	Canada	0.41	(0.02)	-0.75	(0.02)	0.16	(0.02)	0.79	(0.02)	1.44	(0.01)	486	(2.3)	509	(2.5)	529	(2.5)	558	(2.9)	**1.84**	(0.08)
	Chile	-0.58	(0.04)	-1.97	(0.05)	-1.02	(0.04)	-0.27	(0.05)	0.95	(0.03)	378	(4.0)	409	(3.8)	429	(3.6)	477	(5.4)	**2.38**	(0.17)
	Czech Republic	-0.07	(0.02)	-0.98	(0.02)	-0.37	(0.02)	0.16	(0.02)	0.93	(0.02)	450	(4.4)	486	(4.6)	508	(4.3)	552	(4.0)	**2.26**	(0.18)
	Denmark	0.43	(0.02)	-0.70	(0.03)	0.16	(0.04)	0.81	(0.03)	1.44	(0.02)	460	(3.4)	489	(3.5)	513	(2.9)	545	(3.4)	**2.36**	(0.15)
	Estonia	0.11	(0.01)	-0.92	(0.02)	-0.23	(0.02)	0.44	(0.02)	1.16	(0.01)	496	(3.0)	508	(3.2)	523	(3.6)	559	(2.9)	**1.61**	(0.11)
	Finland	0.36	(0.02)	-0.68	(0.02)	0.13	(0.02)	0.73	(0.02)	1.28	(0.01)	488	(3.1)	509	(2.5)	529	(3.2)	555	(2.6)	**1.90**	(0.10)
	France	-0.04	(0.02)	-1.10	(0.02)	-0.30	(0.02)	0.29	(0.02)	0.95	(0.01)	442	(3.5)	476	(3.1)	511	(4.1)	561	(4.0)	**2.56**	(0.16)
	Germany	0.19	(0.02)	-0.99	(0.03)	-0.16	(0.02)	0.52	(0.04)	1.42	(0.02)	467	(5.1)	502	(3.9)	540	(3.8)	569	(4.3)	**2.40**	(0.16)
	Greece	-0.06	(0.03)	-1.34	(0.03)	-0.46	(0.03)	0.32	(0.04)	1.22	(0.02)	413	(4.0)	439	(3.9)	460	(3.5)	502	(3.7)	**2.06**	(0.16)
	Hungary	-0.25	(0.03)	-1.46	(0.04)	-0.65	(0.03)	0.09	(0.04)	1.01	(0.03)	422	(4.8)	464	(3.6)	486	(4.6)	539	(6.6)	**2.75**	(0.21)
	Iceland	0.78	(0.01)	-0.34	(0.02)	0.57	(0.02)	1.19	(0.02)	1.71	(0.01)	464	(2.9)	481	(3.1)	508	(3.2)	526	(3.7)	**1.76**	(0.11)
	Ireland	0.13	(0.02)	-0.97	(0.02)	-0.19	(0.03)	0.48	(0.03)	1.20	(0.02)	462	(4.3)	489	(3.1)	512	(2.9)	545	(3.3)	**2.09**	(0.12)
	Israel	0.17	(0.03)	-0.98	(0.04)	-0.03	(0.04)	0.58	(0.03)	1.12	(0.02)	409	(5.3)	452	(5.6)	490	(6.3)	524	(5.7)	**2.49**	(0.18)
	Italy	-0.05	(0.01)	-1.29	(0.01)	-0.41	(0.02)	0.25	(0.02)	1.24	(0.02)	447	(2.4)	475	(2.7)	498	(2.6)	522	(2.8)	**1.92**	(0.08)
	Japan	-0.07	(0.02)	-0.99	(0.02)	-0.35	(0.02)	0.20	(0.02)	0.85	(0.02)	500	(5.2)	528	(4.1)	551	(4.3)	575	(5.9)	**1.95**	(0.13)
	Korea	0.01	(0.03)	-0.97	(0.03)	-0.23	(0.03)	0.33	(0.03)	0.92	(0.02)	516	(4.9)	538	(4.8)	567	(6.2)	595	(6.6)	**1.77**	(0.12)
	Luxembourg	0.07	(0.01)	-1.42	(0.02)	-0.26	(0.02)	0.57	(0.02)	1.41	(0.01)	438	(2.9)	470	(2.7)	508	(2.5)	546	(2.7)	**2.38**	(0.14)
	Mexico	-1.11	(0.02)	-2.66	(0.02)	-1.65	(0.02)	-0.74	(0.03)	0.61	(0.03)	385	(1.9)	407	(1.9)	417	(1.9)	447	(2.4)	**1.85**	(0.07)
	Netherlands	0.23	(0.02)	-0.82	(0.03)	0.02	(0.03)	0.58	(0.02)	1.15	(0.02)	484	(5.3)	513	(3.8)	537	(4.8)	565	(5.1)	**1.97**	(0.14)
	New Zealand	0.04	(0.02)	-1.05	(0.02)	-0.22	(0.03)	0.39	(0.02)	1.04	(0.02)	444	(3.2)	493	(4.0)	514	(3.9)	559	(3.6)	**2.61**	(0.18)
	Norway	0.46	(0.02)	-0.56	(0.02)	0.27	(0.02)	0.79	(0.02)	1.35	(0.02)	459	(4.2)	479	(3.7)	504	(3.9)	522	(3.6)	**1.83**	(0.13)
	Poland	-0.21	(0.03)	-1.22	(0.02)	-0.69	(0.02)	-0.01	(0.05)	1.08	(0.03)	473	(3.6)	501	(4.2)	526	(5.3)	571	(6.3)	**2.18**	(0.16)
	Portugal	-0.48	(0.05)	-1.85	(0.03)	-1.06	(0.04)	-0.23	(0.07)	1.21	(0.07)	441	(4.5)	474	(5.0)	495	(4.8)	548	(5.2)	**2.31**	(0.14)
	Slovak Republic	-0.18	(0.03)	-1.25	(0.04)	-0.57	(0.02)	0.02	(0.04)	1.06	(0.03)	416	(6.5)	473	(3.7)	496	(4.3)	545	(6.2)	**2.98**	(0.22)
	Slovenia	0.07	(0.01)	-1.03	(0.01)	-0.31	(0.02)	0.39	(0.02)	1.22	(0.02)	458	(2.6)	486	(3.1)	511	(3.1)	552	(3.2)	**2.04**	(0.12)
	Spain	-0.19	(0.03)	-1.50	(0.02)	-0.60	(0.03)	0.17	(0.03)	1.16	(0.03)	442	(2.8)	471	(2.4)	495	(2.8)	533	(2.5)	**2.20**	(0.10)
	Sweden	0.28	(0.02)	-0.82	(0.02)	0.02	(0.02)	0.65	(0.02)	1.25	(0.01)	443	(2.9)	470	(4.0)	495	(3.4)	518	(3.9)	**1.94**	(0.11)
	Switzerland	0.17	(0.02)	-1.00	(0.02)	-0.12	(0.03)	0.52	(0.03)	1.29	(0.02)	488	(4.0)	519	(4.0)	543	(3.9)	576	(4.6)	**2.06**	(0.13)
	Turkey	-1.46	(0.04)	-2.74	(0.03)	-1.96	(0.03)	-1.21	(0.05)	0.07	(0.06)	412	(4.5)	436	(4.2)	447	(6.0)	498	(8.3)	**1.82**	(0.11)
	United Kingdom	0.27	(0.02)	-0.78	(0.02)	0.00	(0.03)	0.61	(0.02)	1.26	(0.02)	458	(4.1)	477	(4.1)	508	(4.1)	545	(4.0)	**1.86**	(0.11)
	United States	0.17	(0.04)	-1.14	(0.05)	-0.11	(0.04)	0.60	(0.04)	1.35	(0.04)	442	(3.9)	462	(4.6)	494	(5.4)	532	(4.6)	**2.04**	(0.16)
	OECD average	0.00	(0.00)	-1.15	(0.00)	-0.32	(0.00)	0.34	(0.01)	1.15	(0.00)	452	(0.7)	482	(0.6)	506	(0.7)	542	(0.8)	**2.15**	(0.02)
Partners	Albania	m	m	m	m	m	m	m	m	m	m	m	m	m	m	m	m	m	m	m	m
	Argentina	-0.72	(0.04)	-2.15	(0.06)	-1.12	(0.04)	-0.33	(0.06)	0.73	(0.04)	355	(4.1)	379	(4.4)	394	(4.6)	433	(4.3)	**2.09**	(0.15)
	Brazil	-1.17	(0.02)	-2.64	(0.02)	-1.61	(0.02)	-0.81	(0.03)	0.39	(0.04)	360	(2.0)	377	(2.1)	395	(2.9)	437	(5.2)	**1.85**	(0.09)
	Bulgaria	-0.28	(0.04)	-1.59	(0.06)	-0.67	(0.03)	0.10	(0.04)	1.06	(0.03)	384	(5.1)	424	(4.1)	449	(6.1)	501	(5.9)	**2.52**	(0.19)
	Colombia	-1.26	(0.04)	-2.82	(0.04)	-1.65	(0.05)	-0.83	(0.04)	0.24	(0.05)	343	(4.1)	365	(3.7)	382	(3.2)	417	(5.2)	**2.07**	(0.18)
	Costa Rica	-0.98	(0.04)	-2.61	(0.05)	-1.41	(0.05)	-0.52	(0.06)	0.62	(0.04)	373	(4.0)	394	(3.7)	412	(3.8)	450	(5.4)	**2.14**	(0.18)
	Croatia	-0.34	(0.02)	-1.35	(0.02)	-0.70	(0.02)	-0.14	(0.03)	0.84	(0.02)	438	(3.5)	459	(3.9)	471	(4.9)	517	(5.9)	**1.78**	(0.13)
	Cyprus*	0.09	(0.01)	-1.06	(0.02)	-0.28	(0.01)	0.43	(0.02)	1.25	(0.02)	398	(2.5)	428	(2.5)	448	(2.8)	492	(2.8)	**2.02**	(0.14)
	Hong Kong-China	-0.79	(0.05)	-2.00	(0.03)	-1.20	(0.05)	-0.46	(0.07)	0.50	(0.06)	532	(4.8)	554	(3.7)	567	(4.4)	600	(5.8)	**1.70**	(0.12)
	Indonesia	-1.80	(0.05)	-3.09	(0.03)	-2.28	(0.05)	-1.54	(0.06)	-0.28	(0.10)	356	(4.3)	363	(3.9)	374	(4.5)	408	(9.7)	**1.44**	(0.10)
	Jordan	-0.42	(0.02)	-1.77	(0.03)	-0.71	(0.03)	0.01	(0.03)	0.78	(0.02)	361	(3.0)	375	(2.9)	395	(3.9)	419	(5.8)	**1.62**	(0.13)
	Kazakhstan	-0.32	(0.02)	-1.31	(0.02)	-0.57	(0.03)	0.02	(0.03)	0.60	(0.02)	405	(4.0)	427	(3.4)	437	(3.7)	458	(5.2)	**1.80**	(0.17)
	Latvia	-0.26	(0.03)	-1.39	(0.03)	-0.64	(0.04)	0.10	(0.04)	0.90	(0.02)	453	(4.5)	472	(3.4)	508	(4.6)	532	(4.8)	**2.05**	(0.18)
	Liechtenstein	0.30	(0.05)	-0.89	(0.08)	0.01	(0.05)	0.66	(0.07)	1.42	(0.06)	490	(9.6)	552	(11.7)	542	(12.0)	564	(11.5)	**2.33**	(0.48)
	Lithuania	-0.13	(0.02)	-1.34	(0.02)	-0.48	(0.03)	0.30	(0.03)	1.00	(0.02)	439	(3.8)	465	(3.6)	491	(4.2)	522	(3.4)	**2.15**	(0.11)
	Macao-China	-0.89	(0.01)	-1.91	(0.01)	-1.23	(0.01)	-0.68	(0.01)	0.28	(0.02)	521	(2.6)	535	(2.6)	543	(2.3)	558	(2.4)	**1.36**	(0.06)
	Malaysia	-0.72	(0.03)	-1.99	(0.04)	-1.07	(0.03)	-0.38	(0.05)	0.54	(0.04)	388	(3.1)	406	(3.7)	425	(4.7)	465	(5.4)	**1.78**	(0.14)
	Montenegro	-0.25	(0.01)	-1.40	(0.02)	-0.57	(0.02)	0.09	(0.02)	0.89	(0.02)	375	(2.0)	401	(2.8)	413	(2.6)	453	(2.8)	**1.96**	(0.10)
	Peru	-1.23	(0.05)	-2.79	(0.04)	-1.68	(0.05)	-0.89	(0.06)	0.41	(0.08)	317	(3.3)	352	(3.8)	382	(5.3)	421	(7.4)	**2.54**	(0.17)
	Qatar	0.44	(0.01)	-0.76	(0.01)	0.29	(0.01)	0.79	(0.01)	1.43	(0.01)	338	(1.8)	377	(1.8)	399	(2.1)	401	(2.2)	**1.69**	(0.10)
	Romania	-0.47	(0.04)	-1.58	(0.05)	-0.80	(0.03)	-0.26	(0.04)	0.76	(0.05)	407	(4.5)	428	(3.9)	444	(4.0)	501	(7.8)	**2.07**	(0.15)
	Russian Federation	-0.11	(0.02)	-1.10	(0.03)	-0.37	(0.03)	0.22	(0.03)	0.82	(0.02)	445	(4.9)	468	(4.3)	496	(3.6)	521	(5.1)	**1.96**	(0.16)
	Serbia	-0.30	(0.02)	-1.37	(0.02)	-0.70	(0.03)	-0.05	(0.03)	0.95	(0.03)	416	(4.4)	436	(3.8)	450	(4.7)	495	(5.0)	**1.74**	(0.13)
	Shanghai-China	-0.36	(0.04)	-1.63	(0.05)	-0.70	(0.04)	0.06	(0.04)	0.83	(0.03)	562	(6.3)	602	(4.8)	627	(3.8)	660	(5.3)	**2.19**	(0.15)
	Singapore	-0.26	(0.01)	-1.46	(0.02)	-0.54	(0.02)	0.09	(0.02)	0.88	(0.02)	523	(2.9)	557	(3.3)	588	(3.2)	627	(2.8)	**2.17**	(0.12)
	Chinese Taipei	-0.40	(0.02)	-1.47	(0.03)	-0.70	(0.03)	-0.11	(0.03)	0.68	(0.03)	497	(5.2)	546	(4.5)	572	(4.0)	626	(5.2)	**2.46**	(0.14)
	Thailand	-1.35	(0.04)	-2.72	(0.03)	-1.89	(0.04)	-1.06	(0.05)	0.27	(0.07)	407	(4.7)	412	(3.0)	421	(3.9)	468	(7.1)	**1.45**	(0.11)
	Tunisia	-1.19	(0.05)	-2.86	(0.05)	-1.59	(0.06)	-0.73	(0.05)	0.42	(0.06)	362	(3.8)	370	(4.7)	393	(4.1)	430	(8.9)	**1.62**	(0.15)
	United Arab Emirates	0.32	(0.02)	-0.81	(0.03)	0.19	(0.02)	0.67	(0.01)	1.26	(0.01)	391	(3.2)	427	(2.4)	454	(3.6)	466	(4.2)	**2.09**	(0.10)
	Uruguay	-0.88	(0.03)	-2.23	(0.02)	-1.40	(0.03)	-0.59	(0.04)	0.69	(0.05)	364	(3.3)	390	(3.8)	414	(4.1)	472	(5.5)	**2.15**	(0.14)
	Viet Nam	-1.81	(0.05)	-3.08	(0.03)	-2.27	(0.03)	-1.63	(0.05)	-0.26	(0.09)	473	(6.1)	499	(4.9)	518	(5.8)	555	(8.2)	**1.99**	(0.16)

Note: Values that are statistically significant are indicated in bold (see Annex A3).

* See notes at the beginning of this Annex.

StatLink http://dx.doi.org/10.1787/888932964908

[Part 1/3]

Change between 2003 and 2012 in students' socio-economic status and mathematics performance

Table II.2.4b   *By national quarters of the PISA index of economic, social and cultural status; results based on students' self-reports*

	PISA 2003																	
	PISA index of economic, social and cultural status (ESCS)										Performance in mathematics, by national quarters of this index							Increased likelihood of students in the bottom quarter of the ESCS index scoring in the bottom quarter of the mathematics performance distribution
	All students		Bottom quarter		Second quarter		Third quarter		Top quarter		Bottom quarter		Second quarter		Third quarter		Top quarter		
	Mean index	S.E.	Mean index	S.E.	Mean index	S.E.	Mean index	S.E.	Mean index	S.E.	Mean score	S.E.	Mean score	S.E.	Mean score	S.E.	Mean score	S.E.	Ratio	S.E.
OECD																				
Australia	0.04	(0.02)	-1.09	(0.02)	-0.28	(0.02)	0.36	(0.02)	1.17	(0.02)	479	(4.0)	511	(2.8)	535	(3.4)	573	(2.9)	2.16	(0.11)
Austria	-0.26	(0.03)	-1.31	(0.03)	-0.59	(0.03)	-0.03	(0.03)	0.89	(0.03)	465	(4.7)	490	(3.9)	519	(4.5)	556	(4.2)	2.10	(0.14)
Belgium	-0.03	(0.02)	-1.33	(0.02)	-0.40	(0.03)	0.36	(0.03)	1.26	(0.02)	465	(4.6)	515	(3.9)	553	(3.7)	598	(2.9)	2.93	(0.17)
Canada	0.21	(0.02)	-0.99	(0.02)	-0.13	(0.02)	0.57	(0.02)	1.41	(0.02)	502	(2.2)	524	(2.2)	545	(2.7)	573	(3.0)	1.90	(0.08)
Czech Republic	-0.05	(0.02)	-1.14	(0.02)	-0.39	(0.03)	0.21	(0.03)	1.10	(0.03)	468	(4.2)	508	(4.3)	539	(4.0)	574	(4.6)	2.63	(0.18)
Denmark	0.08	(0.03)	-1.18	(0.03)	-0.27	(0.04)	0.42	(0.04)	1.34	(0.04)	466	(4.0)	502	(4.0)	527	(3.2)	564	(4.6)	2.34	(0.17)
Finland	0.06	(0.02)	-1.20	(0.02)	-0.30	(0.02)	0.43	(0.03)	1.30	(0.02)	510	(3.1)	535	(2.7)	553	(3.0)	579	(3.0)	1.99	(0.14)
France	-0.32	(0.03)	-1.53	(0.03)	-0.66	(0.03)	-0.01	(0.04)	0.93	(0.04)	461	(4.9)	495	(4.2)	526	(3.5)	565	(3.7)	2.34	(0.14)
Germany	0.01	(0.03)	-1.34	(0.03)	-0.36	(0.03)	0.31	(0.03)	1.43	(0.03)	448	(4.5)	495	(5.9)	531	(4.9)	571	(4.2)	3.10	(0.24)
Greece	-0.30	(0.05)	-1.57	(0.03)	-0.72	(0.04)	-0.03	(0.07)	1.11	(0.07)	402	(4.5)	430	(4.6)	452	(5.8)	497	(6.4)	2.03	(0.16)
Hungary	-0.31	(0.02)	-1.45	(0.02)	-0.72	(0.02)	-0.08	(0.03)	1.01	(0.03)	427	(4.5)	475	(3.8)	505	(4.4)	553	(4.7)	2.90	(0.19)
Iceland	0.55	(0.02)	-0.68	(0.02)	0.26	(0.02)	0.92	(0.02)	1.69	(0.02)	485	(3.0)	510	(3.0)	521	(3.5)	546	(2.6)	1.79	(0.12)
Ireland	-0.26	(0.03)	-1.43	(0.03)	-0.61	(0.03)	0.03	(0.04)	0.96	(0.04)	457	(4.2)	490	(3.7)	519	(3.2)	544	(4.1)	2.37	(0.17)
Italy	-0.29	(0.03)	-1.63	(0.02)	-0.71	(0.03)	0.04	(0.03)	1.16	(0.04)	420	(5.0)	456	(4.1)	482	(3.6)	505	(4.1)	2.11	(0.13)
Japan	-0.42	(0.02)	-1.42	(0.03)	-0.72	(0.03)	-0.18	(0.03)	0.63	(0.03)	487	(6.1)	524	(5.7)	547	(4.4)	579	(6.6)	2.13	(0.14)
Korea	-0.36	(0.03)	-1.55	(0.03)	-0.68	(0.02)	-0.08	(0.03)	0.85	(0.05)	496	(4.3)	534	(4.2)	552	(4.1)	586	(6.8)	2.10	(0.14)
Luxembourg	-0.09	(0.01)	-1.55	(0.02)	-0.37	(0.02)	0.33	(0.02)	1.23	(0.02)	446	(2.5)	475	(3.0)	507	(2.9)	545	(2.8)	2.22	(0.17)
Mexico	-1.32	(0.05)	-2.72	(0.03)	-1.89	(0.05)	-1.01	(0.08)	0.34	(0.06)	341	(5.0)	373	(3.9)	395	(6.1)	433	(5.7)	2.33	(0.22)
Netherlands	-0.08	(0.02)	-1.32	(0.03)	-0.44	(0.03)	0.27	(0.03)	1.15	(0.02)	497	(5.2)	530	(4.6)	548	(3.6)	596	(4.3)	2.30	(0.20)
New Zealand	-0.13	(0.02)	-1.31	(0.03)	-0.40	(0.02)	0.21	(0.02)	0.97	(0.02)	472	(3.8)	511	(3.2)	538	(3.7)	575	(3.4)	2.32	(0.14)
Norway	0.19	(0.03)	-0.85	(0.03)	-0.07	(0.03)	0.50	(0.03)	1.17	(0.02)	451	(3.4)	488	(4.0)	505	(4.0)	538	(3.5)	2.02	(0.14)
Poland	-0.41	(0.02)	-1.46	(0.02)	-0.82	(0.02)	-0.22	(0.03)	0.87	(0.03)	444	(4.4)	475	(2.9)	503	(3.7)	540	(3.3)	2.22	(0.14)
Portugal	-0.91	(0.05)	-2.46	(0.03)	-1.57	(0.05)	-0.58	(0.06)	0.99	(0.07)	423	(4.4)	453	(4.4)	469	(4.3)	521	(4.7)	2.19	(0.16)
Slovak Republic	-0.25	(0.03)	-1.37	(0.04)	-0.64	(0.03)	0.00	(0.03)	1.02	(0.03)	436	(6.1)	484	(4.2)	517	(3.7)	555	(4.4)	2.93	(0.19)
Spain	-0.51	(0.04)	-1.95	(0.03)	-0.97	(0.05)	-0.16	(0.06)	1.04	(0.05)	448	(3.3)	472	(3.5)	494	(5.0)	528	(3.0)	1.98	(0.13)
Sweden	0.08	(0.03)	-1.20	(0.03)	-0.24	(0.03)	0.46	(0.03)	1.32	(0.03)	468	(4.0)	493	(4.2)	519	(3.4)	557	(4.2)	1.94	(0.10)
Switzerland	-0.23	(0.03)	-1.51	(0.03)	-0.58	(0.03)	0.08	(0.04)	1.11	(0.04)	469	(3.7)	518	(4.6)	540	(4.2)	579	(5.7)	2.51	(0.14)
Turkey	-1.15	(0.06)	-2.34	(0.04)	-1.62	(0.05)	-0.95	(0.07)	0.31	(0.11)	374	(4.8)	395	(6.8)	429	(7.9)	496	(15.8)	2.00	(0.20)
United States	0.05	(0.03)	-1.22	(0.04)	-0.28	(0.04)	0.40	(0.03)	1.30	(0.03)	431	(3.7)	465	(3.7)	495	(4.8)	542	(3.9)	2.42	(0.14)
OECD average 2003	-0.22	(0.01)	-1.45	(0.01)	-0.59	(0.01)	0.09	(0.01)	1.07	(0.01)	453	(0.8)	487	(0.8)	513	(0.8)	551	(1.0)	2.29	(0.03)
Partners																				
Brazil	-1.56	(0.05)	-3.10	(0.04)	-2.08	(0.06)	-1.14	(0.05)	0.07	(0.06)	317	(5.9)	344	(6.3)	349	(5.9)	417	(9.2)	1.72	(0.16)
Hong Kong-China	-1.27	(0.04)	-2.39	(0.03)	-1.64	(0.03)	-1.07	(0.04)	0.02	(0.06)	513	(5.8)	545	(4.8)	558	(7.9)	586	(5.3)	1.93	(0.17)
Indonesia	-1.86	(0.04)	-3.08	(0.03)	-2.29	(0.04)	-1.58	(0.04)	-0.51	(0.05)	341	(3.9)	350	(3.5)	355	(4.9)	395	(7.3)	1.28	(0.10)
Latvia	-0.34	(0.03)	-1.43	(0.03)	-0.69	(0.03)	-0.06	(0.04)	0.80	(0.04)	446	(4.5)	472	(4.2)	494	(5.0)	522	(5.2)	2.03	(0.14)
Liechtenstein	-0.31	(0.04)	-1.57	(0.06)	-0.66	(0.06)	-0.01	(0.06)	1.00	(0.07)	478	(10.5)	521	(10.7)	542	(10.2)	603	(9.7)	2.65	(0.47)
Macao-China	-1.60	(0.02)	-2.72	(0.04)	-1.93	(0.03)	-1.36	(0.04)	-0.39	(0.04)	514	(6.4)	523	(7.7)	530	(6.8)	542	(5.7)	1.22	(0.15)
Russian Federation	-0.61	(0.03)	-1.78	(0.03)	-1.03	(0.03)	-0.28	(0.05)	0.67	(0.04)	433	(4.7)	455	(5.4)	474	(5.5)	510	(4.7)	1.83	(0.12)
Thailand	-1.86	(0.04)	-3.17	(0.04)	-2.45	(0.03)	-1.71	(0.05)	-0.13	(0.06)	397	(3.5)	399	(3.6)	410	(4.1)	463	(6.4)	1.30	(0.09)
Tunisia	-1.69	(0.04)	-3.10	(0.03)	-2.24	(0.04)	-1.40	(0.05)	-0.01	(0.07)	332	(3.0)	343	(2.8)	358	(3.3)	403	(7.3)	1.54	(0.13)
Uruguay	-0.76	(0.04)	-2.24	(0.03)	-1.21	(0.04)	-0.35	(0.04)	0.75	(0.04)	379	(5.1)	402	(4.0)	425	(5.3)	483	(5.2)	1.93	(0.15)

Notes: Values that are statistically significant are indicated in bold (see Annex A3).
Only countries and economies with comparable data from PISA 2003 and PISA 2012 are shown.
For comparability over time, PISA 2003 values on the *PISA index of economic, social and cultural status* have been rescaled to the PISA 2012 scale of the index. PISA 2003 results reported in this table may thus differ from those presented in *Learning for Tomorrow's World: First Results from PISA 2003* (OECD, 2004) (see Annex A5 for more details).
StatLink ⟨⟩ http://dx.doi.org/10.1787/888932964908

EXCELLENCE THROUGH EQUITY: GIVING EVERY STUDENT THE CHANCE TO SUCCEED – VOLUME II

[Part 2/3]

Change between 2003 and 2012 in students' socio-economic status and mathematics performance
Table II.2.4b *By national quarters of the PISA index of economic, social and cultural status; results based on students' self-reports*

	PISA 2012													
	PISA index of economic, social and cultural status (ESCS)										Performance in mathematics, by national quarters of this index			Increased likelihood of students in the bottom quarter of the ESCS index scoring in the bottom quarter of the mathematics performance distribution
	All students		Bottom quarter		Second quarter		Third quarter		Top quarter		Bottom quarter	Second quarter	Third quarter	Top quarter	
	Mean index	S.E.	Mean index	S.E.	Mean index	S.E.	Mean index	S.E.	Mean index	S.E.	Mean score S.E.	Mean score S.E.	Mean score S.E.	Mean score S.E.	Ratio	S.E.

OECD

Australia	0.25	(0.01)	-0.84	(0.02)	0.05	(0.02)	0.61	(0.01)	1.18	(0.01)	463 (2.2)	492 (2.0)	521 (2.9)	550 (2.5)	2.14	(0.09)
Austria	0.08	(0.02)	-0.97	(0.03)	-0.25	(0.02)	0.33	(0.03)	1.19	(0.03)	458 (4.2)	495 (4.2)	519 (3.8)	552 (4.1)	2.36	(0.16)
Belgium	0.15	(0.02)	-1.05	(0.03)	-0.19	(0.03)	0.55	(0.02)	1.27	(0.02)	460 (3.6)	497 (3.3)	536 (3.0)	575 (3.3)	2.43	(0.15)
Canada	0.41	(0.02)	-0.75	(0.02)	0.16	(0.02)	0.79	(0.02)	1.44	(0.01)	486 (2.4)	509 (2.4)	529 (2.5)	558 (2.9)	1.86	(0.08)
Czech Republic	-0.07	(0.02)	-0.98	(0.02)	-0.37	(0.02)	0.16	(0.02)	0.93	(0.02)	450 (4.3)	486 (4.4)	508 (4.3)	552 (4.0)	2.27	(0.18)
Denmark	0.43	(0.02)	-0.70	(0.03)	0.16	(0.04)	0.81	(0.03)	1.44	(0.02)	460 (3.5)	489 (3.5)	513 (3.0)	545 (3.4)	2.39	(0.16)
Finland	0.36	(0.02)	-0.68	(0.02)	0.13	(0.02)	0.73	(0.02)	1.28	(0.01)	488 (3.1)	509 (2.5)	529 (3.2)	555 (2.6)	1.89	(0.10)
France	-0.04	(0.02)	-1.10	(0.02)	-0.30	(0.02)	0.29	(0.02)	0.95	(0.01)	442 (3.4)	477 (3.2)	511 (4.1)	561 (3.9)	2.57	(0.16)
Germany	0.19	(0.02)	-0.99	(0.03)	-0.16	(0.03)	0.52	(0.04)	1.42	(0.02)	467 (5.1)	503 (3.9)	540 (3.8)	569 (4.3)	2.41	(0.17)
Greece	-0.06	(0.03)	-1.34	(0.03)	-0.46	(0.03)	0.32	(0.04)	1.22	(0.02)	413 (3.9)	439 (4.0)	459 (3.4)	502 (3.7)	2.05	(0.17)
Hungary	-0.25	(0.03)	-1.46	(0.04)	-0.65	(0.03)	0.09	(0.04)	1.01	(0.03)	422 (4.8)	464 (3.7)	487 (4.6)	539 (6.6)	2.74	(0.21)
Iceland	0.78	(0.01)	-0.34	(0.02)	0.57	(0.02)	1.19	(0.02)	1.71	(0.01)	464 (3.0)	481 (3.2)	508 (3.3)	526 (3.7)	1.75	(0.11)
Ireland	0.13	(0.02)	-0.97	(0.02)	-0.19	(0.02)	0.48	(0.03)	1.20	(0.02)	462 (4.4)	489 (3.2)	513 (2.9)	545 (3.3)	2.11	(0.12)
Italy	-0.05	(0.01)	-1.29	(0.01)	-0.41	(0.02)	0.25	(0.02)	1.24	(0.02)	447 (2.4)	475 (2.7)	498 (2.6)	522 (2.8)	1.91	(0.08)
Japan	-0.07	(0.02)	-0.99	(0.02)	-0.35	(0.02)	0.20	(0.02)	0.85	(0.02)	500 (5.2)	528 (4.1)	551 (4.3)	575 (5.9)	1.97	(0.13)
Korea	0.01	(0.02)	-0.97	(0.03)	-0.23	(0.03)	0.33	(0.03)	0.92	(0.02)	516 (4.9)	538 (4.8)	567 (6.2)	595 (6.6)	1.76	(0.11)
Luxembourg	0.07	(0.01)	-1.42	(0.02)	-0.26	(0.02)	0.57	(0.02)	1.41	(0.01)	439 (2.9)	470 (2.7)	508 (2.6)	547 (2.7)	2.38	(0.13)
Mexico	-1.11	(0.02)	-2.66	(0.02)	-1.65	(0.03)	-0.74	(0.03)	0.61	(0.03)	385 (1.9)	407 (1.9)	417 (1.9)	447 (2.4)	1.84	(0.07)
Netherlands	0.23	(0.02)	-0.82	(0.03)	0.02	(0.03)	0.58	(0.02)	1.15	(0.02)	484 (5.2)	513 (3.7)	537 (4.9)	565 (5.1)	2.02	(0.15)
New Zealand	0.04	(0.02)	-1.05	(0.02)	-0.22	(0.03)	0.39	(0.02)	1.04	(0.02)	445 (3.2)	493 (3.9)	514 (4.0)	559 (3.6)	2.64	(0.19)
Norway	0.46	(0.02)	-0.56	(0.02)	0.27	(0.03)	0.79	(0.02)	1.35	(0.02)	459 (4.2)	479 (3.7)	504 (3.9)	522 (3.7)	1.83	(0.13)
Poland	-0.21	(0.03)	-1.22	(0.02)	-0.69	(0.02)	-0.01	(0.05)	1.08	(0.03)	473 (3.6)	501 (4.1)	526 (5.2)	571 (6.3)	2.17	(0.16)
Portugal	-0.48	(0.05)	-1.85	(0.03)	-1.06	(0.04)	-0.23	(0.07)	1.21	(0.07)	441 (4.5)	474 (4.9)	495 (4.8)	548 (5.2)	2.34	(0.15)
Slovak Republic	-0.18	(0.03)	-1.25	(0.04)	-0.57	(0.02)	0.02	(0.04)	1.06	(0.03)	416 (6.5)	473 (3.7)	496 (4.4)	545 (6.2)	2.99	(0.23)
Spain	-0.19	(0.03)	-1.50	(0.03)	-0.60	(0.03)	0.17	(0.03)	1.16	(0.03)	442 (2.8)	471 (2.4)	495 (2.8)	533 (2.5)	2.19	(0.10)
Sweden	0.28	(0.02)	-0.82	(0.02)	0.02	(0.02)	0.65	(0.02)	1.25	(0.01)	443 (2.9)	470 (3.9)	495 (3.5)	518 (3.9)	1.95	(0.12)
Switzerland	0.17	(0.02)	-1.00	(0.02)	-0.12	(0.03)	0.52	(0.03)	1.29	(0.02)	488 (4.0)	519 (4.1)	543 (3.9)	576 (4.6)	2.06	(0.13)
Turkey	-1.46	(0.04)	-2.74	(0.03)	-1.96	(0.04)	-1.21	(0.05)	0.07	(0.06)	412 (4.5)	435 (4.2)	447 (5.9)	498 (8.3)	1.83	(0.12)
United States	0.17	(0.04)	-1.14	(0.05)	-0.11	(0.04)	0.60	(0.04)	1.35	(0.03)	442 (3.9)	462 (4.6)	493 (5.4)	532 (4.8)	2.06	(0.17)
OECD average 2003	0.00	(0.00)	-1.15	(0.00)	-0.33	(0.01)	0.34	(0.01)	1.15	(0.01)	454 (0.7)	484 (0.7)	509 (0.7)	544 (0.8)	2.17	(0.03)

Partners

Brazil	-1.17	(0.02)	-2.64	(0.02)	-1.61	(0.02)	-0.81	(0.03)	0.39	(0.04)	360 (2.0)	377 (2.1)	395 (2.9)	437 (5.3)	1.84	(0.09)
Hong Kong-China	-0.79	(0.05)	-2.00	(0.03)	-1.20	(0.05)	-0.46	(0.07)	0.50	(0.06)	532 (4.8)	554 (3.8)	567 (4.4)	599 (5.8)	1.71	(0.12)
Indonesia	-1.80	(0.05)	-3.09	(0.03)	-2.28	(0.05)	-1.54	(0.06)	-0.28	(0.10)	356 (4.3)	363 (3.9)	374 (4.5)	408 (9.8)	1.43	(0.09)
Latvia	-0.26	(0.03)	-1.39	(0.03)	-0.64	(0.04)	0.11	(0.04)	0.90	(0.04)	453 (4.5)	472 (3.5)	507 (4.6)	532 (4.8)	2.06	(0.17)
Liechtenstein	0.30	(0.05)	-0.89	(0.08)	0.01	(0.06)	0.66	(0.07)	1.42	(0.06)	490 (9.6)	552 (11.2)	544 (12.3)	561 (11.7)	2.32	(0.45)
Macao-China	-0.89	(0.01)	-1.91	(0.01)	-1.23	(0.01)	-0.68	(0.01)	0.28	(0.02)	521 (2.6)	535 (2.6)	543 (2.3)	558 (2.4)	1.36	(0.06)
Russian Federation	-0.11	(0.02)	-1.10	(0.03)	-0.37	(0.03)	0.22	(0.03)	0.82	(0.02)	445 (4.8)	468 (4.3)	496 (3.6)	521 (5.1)	1.95	(0.16)
Thailand	-1.35	(0.04)	-2.72	(0.03)	-1.89	(0.04)	-1.06	(0.05)	0.27	(0.07)	407 (4.7)	412 (3.0)	421 (3.9)	468 (7.1)	1.43	(0.12)
Tunisia	-1.19	(0.05)	-2.86	(0.05)	-1.59	(0.06)	-0.73	(0.05)	0.42	(0.06)	362 (3.8)	370 (4.8)	393 (4.1)	430 (8.8)	1.61	(0.15)
Uruguay	-0.88	(0.03)	-2.23	(0.02)	-1.40	(0.03)	-0.59	(0.04)	0.69	(0.05)	364 (3.3)	390 (3.7)	414 (4.1)	472 (5.5)	2.15	(0.14)

Notes: Values that are statistically significant are indicated in bold (see Annex A3).
Only countries and economies with comparable data from PISA 2003 and PISA 2012 are shown.
For comparability over time, PISA 2003 values on the *PISA index of economic, social and cultural status* have been rescaled to the PISA 2012 scale of the index. PISA 2003 results reported in this table may thus differ from those presented in *Learning for Tomorrow's World: First Results from PISA 2003* (OECD, 2004) (see Annex A5 for more details).
StatLink ⌧ http://dx.doi.org/10.1787/888932964908

[Part 3/3]
Change between 2003 and 2012 in students' socio-economic status and mathematics performance
Table II.2.4b *By national quarters of the PISA index of economic, social and cultural status; results based on students' self-reports*

		Change between 2003 and 2012 (PISA 2012 - PISA 2003)												
	PISA index of economic, social and cultural status (ESCS)					Performance in mathematics, by national quarters of this index								Increased likelihood of students in the bottom quarter of the ESCS index scoring in the bottom quarter of the mathematics performance distribution
	All students	Bottom quarter	Second quarter	Third quarter	Top quarter	Bottom quarter		Second quarter		Third quarter		Top quarter		
	Dif. S.E.	Dif. S.E.	Dif. S.E.	Dif. S.E.	Dif. S.E.	Score dif. S.E.		Score dif. S.E.		Score dif. S.E.		Score dif. S.E.		Ratio dif S.E.
Australia	**0.21** (0.02)	**0.25** (0.03)	**0.32** (0.03)	**0.25** (0.03)	0.00 (0.02)	**-17** (4.6)		**-19** (3.5)		**-13** (4.5)		**-24** (3.8)		-0.02 (0.14)
Austria	**0.34** (0.04)	**0.34** (0.04)	**0.34** (0.04)	**0.36** (0.04)	**0.30** (0.04)	-7 (6.3)		6 (5.7)		1 (5.9)		-4 (5.9)		0.26 (0.21)
Belgium	**0.17** (0.03)	**0.28** (0.04)	**0.21** (0.04)	**0.19** (0.04)	0.01 (0.03)	-5 (5.9)		**-18** (5.1)		**-18** (4.8)		**-23** (4.4)		-0.50 (0.22)
Canada	**0.20** (0.02)	**0.24** (0.03)	**0.29** (0.03)	**0.23** (0.03)	0.03 (0.02)	**-15** (3.2)		**-15** (3.3)		**-16** (3.7)		**-15** (4.1)		-0.04 (0.11)
Czech Republic	-0.01 (0.03)	**0.16** (0.04)	0.02 (0.03)	-0.05 (0.04)	**-0.17** (0.03)	**-18** (6.0)		**-22** (6.1)		**-31** (5.9)		**-22** (6.1)		-0.37 (0.26)
Denmark	**0.35** (0.04)	**0.47** (0.04)	**0.43** (0.05)	**0.39** (0.05)	**0.09** (0.04)	-6 (5.3)		**-13** (5.3)		**-13** (4.4)		**-20** (5.7)		0.05 (0.23)
Finland	**0.31** (0.03)	**0.52** (0.03)	**0.43** (0.03)	**0.29** (0.03)	-0.01 (0.02)	**-22** (4.4)		**-26** (3.7)		**-24** (4.4)		**-24** (4.0)		-0.10 (0.17)
France	**0.28** (0.03)	**0.43** (0.04)	**0.36** (0.04)	**0.31** (0.04)	0.02 (0.04)	**-19** (6.0)		**-19** (5.3)		**-15** (5.4)		-5 (5.4)		0.22 (0.21)
Germany	**0.19** (0.04)	**0.35** (0.04)	**0.20** (0.04)	**0.21** (0.05)	-0.01 (0.04)	**19** (6.8)		8 (7.1)		9 (5.5)		-3 (6.0)		-0.69 (0.29)
Greece	**0.24** (0.06)	**0.23** (0.05)	**0.25** (0.05)	**0.35** (0.08)	0.12 (0.08)	11 (6.0)		10 (6.0)		8 (6.7)		5 (7.4)		0.02 (0.23)
Hungary	0.06 (0.04)	-0.01 (0.04)	0.07 (0.04)	**0.17** (0.05)	0.01 (0.04)	-5 (6.5)		**-11** (5.4)		**-19** (6.4)		-14 (8.1)		-0.16 (0.28)
Iceland	**0.23** (0.02)	**0.34** (0.03)	**0.30** (0.03)	**0.26** (0.03)	0.02 (0.02)	**-21** (4.2)		**-29** (4.4)		**-13** (4.8)		**-20** (4.5)		-0.03 (0.17)
Ireland	**0.39** (0.04)	**0.45** (0.04)	**0.41** (0.06)	**0.45** (0.05)	**0.23** (0.05)	5 (6.1)		-1 (4.9)		-6 (4.3)		1 (5.3)		-0.26 (0.21)
Italy	**0.23** (0.03)	**0.34** (0.02)	**0.30** (0.03)	**0.21** (0.03)	**0.08** (0.04)	**27** (5.5)		**20** (4.9)		**16** (4.4)		**17** (5.0)		-0.20 (0.15)
Japan	**0.35** (0.03)	**0.43** (0.03)	**0.37** (0.03)	**0.38** (0.03)	**0.22** (0.03)	12 (8.0)		4 (7.0)		4 (6.1)		-4 (8.9)		-0.16 (0.19)
Korea	**0.38** (0.04)	**0.58** (0.04)	**0.45** (0.04)	**0.40** (0.05)	0.07 (0.05)	**19** (6.5)		4 (6.4)		14 (7.4)		9 (9.5)		-0.34 (0.18)
Luxembourg	**0.16** (0.02)	**0.13** (0.03)	**0.11** (0.04)	**0.24** (0.02)	**0.18** (0.02)	-7 (3.8)		-5 (4.1)		1 (3.9)		1 (3.8)		0.16 (0.21)
Mexico	**0.21** (0.06)	0.06 (0.04)	**0.24** (0.05)	**0.27** (0.08)	**0.28** (0.07)	**44** (5.4)		**34** (4.3)		**21** (6.4)		**13** (6.2)		-0.50 (0.23)
Netherlands	**0.32** (0.03)	**0.51** (0.04)	**0.46** (0.04)	**0.31** (0.04)	0.00 (0.03)	-14 (7.4)		**-17** (5.9)		-11 (6.1)		**-32** (6.6)		-0.28 (0.25)
New Zealand	**0.17** (0.03)	**0.27** (0.04)	**0.17** (0.03)	**0.18** (0.03)	**0.07** (0.03)	**-28** (5.0)		**-19** (5.1)		**-24** (5.5)		**-16** (5.0)		0.32 (0.24)
Norway	**0.28** (0.03)	**0.29** (0.03)	**0.34** (0.03)	**0.29** (0.03)	**0.18** (0.03)	8 (5.4)		-9 (5.4)		-1 (5.6)		**-16** (5.1)		-0.19 (0.19)
Poland	**0.20** (0.04)	**0.24** (0.03)	**0.13** (0.03)	**0.21** (0.06)	**0.21** (0.05)	**29** (5.7)		**26** (5.0)		**23** (6.4)		**31** (7.1)		-0.05 (0.21)
Portugal	**0.42** (0.07)	**0.60** (0.04)	**0.51** (0.06)	**0.35** (0.10)	**0.23** (0.10)	**18** (6.3)		**21** (6.6)		**26** (6.5)		**27** (7.1)		0.15 (0.22)
Slovak Republic	0.06 (0.04)	**0.12** (0.06)	0.07 (0.04)	0.02 (0.05)	0.04 (0.05)	**-21** (8.9)		-10 (5.6)		**-22** (5.7)		-11 (7.6)		0.06 (0.29)
Spain	**0.32** (0.05)	**0.46** (0.03)	**0.37** (0.04)	**0.34** (0.07)	0.13 (0.06)	-5 (4.3)		-1 (4.2)		2 (5.8)		5 (3.8)		0.21 (0.17)
Sweden	**0.19** (0.03)	**0.38** (0.04)	**0.26** (0.04)	**0.19** (0.04)	-0.07 (0.03)	**-25** (5.0)		**-24** (5.7)		**-24** (4.9)		**-40** (5.7)		0.01 (0.15)
Switzerland	**0.40** (0.04)	**0.51** (0.04)	**0.46** (0.04)	**0.45** (0.05)	**0.18** (0.05)	**19** (5.5)		1 (6.1)		4 (5.7)		-3 (7.3)		-0.44 (0.19)
Turkey	**-0.31** (0.07)	**-0.40** (0.04)	**-0.33** (0.06)	**-0.26** (0.09)	-0.23 (0.12)	**38** (6.6)		**41** (7.9)		18 (9.9)		2 (17.8)		-0.18 (0.24)
United States	**0.12** (0.05)	0.08 (0.06)	**0.17** (0.05)	**0.20** (0.06)	0.04 (0.05)	11 (5.4)		-3 (5.9)		-2 (7.2)		-9 (6.1)		-0.36 (0.22)
OECD average 2003	**0.22** (0.01)	**0.30** (0.01)	**0.27** (0.01)	**0.25** (0.01)	**0.08** (0.01)	1 (1.1)		**-3** (1.0)		**-4** (1.1)		**-7** (1.3)		-0.12 (0.04)
Brazil	**0.39** (0.05)	**0.46** (0.04)	**0.47** (0.06)	**0.33** (0.06)	**0.32** (0.07)	**43** (6.2)		**33** (6.6)		**45** (6.6)		20 (10.6)		0.11 (0.18)
Hong Kong-China	**0.48** (0.06)	**0.39** (0.04)	**0.44** (0.05)	**0.61** (0.09)	**0.49** (0.09)	19 (7.5)		9 (6.1)		9 (9.1)		13 (7.9)		-0.22 (0.21)
Indonesia	0.06 (0.06)	-0.02 (0.04)	0.00 (0.06)	0.04 (0.08)	**0.23** (0.11)	**15** (5.8)		**13** (5.2)		**19** (6.7)		14 (12.2)		0.14 (0.14)
Latvia	**0.09** (0.04)	0.05 (0.04)	0.04 (0.05)	**0.16** (0.05)	**0.10** (0.04)	7 (6.3)		0 (5.5)		**14** (6.8)		9 (7.0)		0.03 (0.22)
Liechtenstein	**0.61** (0.07)	**0.68** (0.10)	**0.68** (0.08)	**0.67** (0.09)	**0.42** (0.09)	12 (14.2)		**31** (15.5)		3 (16.0)		**-42** (15.2)		-0.34 (0.65)
Macao-China	**0.71** (0.03)	**0.81** (0.04)	**0.70** (0.03)	**0.68** (0.03)	**0.67** (0.05)	7 (6.9)		12 (8.1)		13 (7.2)		**16** (6.2)		0.15 (0.16)
Russian Federation	**0.50** (0.04)	**0.69** (0.04)	**0.66** (0.04)	**0.50** (0.06)	**0.15** (0.04)	11 (6.7)		13 (6.9)		**22** (6.5)		11 (6.9)		0.13 (0.20)
Thailand	**0.52** (0.06)	**0.46** (0.05)	**0.56** (0.05)	**0.65** (0.07)	**0.40** (0.09)	10 (5.9)		**13** (4.7)		**12** (5.6)		5 (9.6)		0.13 (0.15)
Tunisia	**0.50** (0.06)	**0.24** (0.06)	**0.65** (0.07)	**0.67** (0.08)	**0.43** (0.09)	**31** (4.8)		**27** (5.5)		**35** (5.2)		**27** (11.5)		0.07 (0.20)
Uruguay	**-0.12** (0.05)	0.00 (0.04)	**-0.19** (0.05)	**-0.24** (0.06)	-0.07 (0.06)	**-15** (6.1)		**-12** (5.4)		-11 (6.7)		-11 (7.6)		0.21 (0.20)

Notes: Values that are statistically significant are indicated in bold (see Annex A3).
Only countries and economies with comparable data from PISA 2003 and PISA 2012 are shown.
For comparability over time, PISA 2003 values on the *PISA index of economic, social and cultural status* have been rescaled to the PISA 2012 scale of the index. PISA 2003 results reported in this table may thus differ from those presented in *Learning for Tomorrow's World: First Results from PISA 2003* (OECD, 2004) (see Annex A5 for more details).
StatLink http://dx.doi.org/10.1787/888932964908

[Part 1/4]
Performance and selected elements of socio-economic status across countries

Table II.2.5 · *Results based on students' self-reports*

	Parents' highest level of education											
	Percentage low (Low) % (S.E.)	Percentage high (High) % (S.E.)	Mean perf. low (Low) Mean score (S.E.)	Mean perf. high (High) Mean score (S.E.)	Difference Score dif. (S.E.)	Increased likelihood low Ratio (S.E.)	Pop. relevance low % (S.E.)	Increased likelihood high Ratio (S.E.)	Pop. relevance high % (S.E.)	Effect size low (S.E.)	Effect size high (S.E.)
OECD											
Australia	10.4 (0.3)	55.4 (0.5)	461 (2.9)	528 (2.1)	**66** (3.3)	**1.83** (0.08)	8.0 (0.7)	0.55 (0.03)	-32.9 (2.7)	**-0.6** (0.0)	0.5 (0.0)
Austria	4.7 (0.5)	48.0 (1.0)	429 (9.0)	524 (3.3)	**95** (9.5)	**2.43** (0.25)	6.3 (1.1)	0.62 (0.04)	-22.5 (3.2)	**-0.9** (0.1)	0.4 (0.0)
Belgium	4.9 (0.4)	62.9 (0.8)	453 (8.0)	539 (2.6)	**86** (8.4)	**2.00** (0.17)	4.7 (0.9)	0.52 (0.04)	-43.5 (4.5)	**-0.7** (0.1)	0.6 (0.0)
Canada	3.2 (0.3)	72.4 (0.7)	458 (5.6)	530 (2.1)	**72** (5.6)	**2.20** (0.16)	3.7 (0.5)	0.63 (0.03)	-37.1 (4.3)	**-0.7** (0.1)	0.4 (0.0)
Chile	22.4 (1.4)	35.0 (1.2)	377 (3.5)	458 (4.0)	**82** (4.9)	**2.37** (0.16)	23.5 (2.4)	0.46 (0.04)	-23.5 (2.7)	**-0.8** (0.1)	0.7 (0.1)
Czech Republic	1.2 (0.2)	32.6 (0.9)	406 (17.8)	529 (4.2)	**123** (18.1)	**2.70** (0.43)	2.0 (0.7)	0.67 (0.06)	-12.0 (2.6)	**-1.1** (0.2)	0.5 (0.0)
Denmark	5.7 (0.4)	67.4 (1.0)	443 (5.3)	516 (2.2)	**73** (5.7)	**2.28** (0.18)	6.9 (1.0)	0.55 (0.04)	-44.1 (5.3)	**-0.8** (0.1)	0.5 (0.0)
Estonia	2.4 (0.3)	57.6 (0.9)	478 (7.1)	531 (2.6)	**53** (7.4)	**1.89** (0.25)	2.1 (0.6)	0.77 (0.04)	-15.2 (3.5)	**-0.6** (0.1)	0.3 (0.0)
Finland	2.9 (0.2)	79.3 (0.6)	466 (7.6)	528 (1.9)	**62** (7.6)	**2.04** (0.17)	2.9 (0.5)	0.60 (0.03)	-46.3 (5.5)	**-0.7** (0.1)	0.4 (0.0)
France	9.5 (0.5)	54.3 (0.9)	431 (4.7)	524 (3.1)	**93** (5.3)	**2.37** (0.16)	11.5 (1.1)	0.53 (0.04)	-33.8 (3.6)	**-0.9** (0.1)	0.5 (0.0)
Germany	22.8 (0.9)	50.5 (1.1)	481 (4.4)	543 (3.3)	**62** (4.3)	**1.95** (0.13)	17.8 (2.1)	0.60 (0.04)	-25.5 (3.3)	**-0.6** (0.0)	0.4 (0.0)
Greece	10.7 (0.7)	52.6 (1.1)	403 (4.5)	473 (3.1)	**70** (5.7)	**2.11** (0.18)	10.6 (1.6)	0.60 (0.05)	-26.6 (4.2)	**-0.7** (0.1)	0.5 (0.0)
Hungary	9.6 (0.7)	43.6 (1.3)	395 (6.6)	508 (5.0)	**113** (8.6)	**3.01** (0.26)	16.1 (2.0)	0.51 (0.05)	-26.9 (3.7)	**-1.1** (0.1)	0.6 (0.0)
Iceland	7.2 (0.4)	66.1 (0.8)	456 (5.4)	504 (2.3)	**49** (6.0)	**1.67** (0.14)	4.6 (1.0)	0.73 (0.04)	-21.9 (4.6)	**-0.5** (0.1)	0.3 (0.0)
Ireland	8.0 (0.4)	55.9 (1.0)	458 (5.1)	521 (2.2)	**63** (5.1)	**1.77** (0.14)	5.8 (1.0)	0.56 (0.04)	-32.7 (3.7)	**-0.6** (0.1)	0.5 (0.0)
Israel	4.4 (0.5)	61.7 (1.4)	377 (6.4)	499 (4.7)	**122** (7.5)	**2.64** (0.21)	6.7 (1.0)	0.41 (0.03)	-57.5 (6.1)	**-1.0** (0.1)	0.8 (0.0)
Italy	20.5 (0.4)	37.1 (0.5)	450 (2.4)	497 (2.5)	**48** (3.0)	**1.76** (0.06)	13.5 (0.9)	0.80 (0.03)	-7.9 (1.3)	**-0.5** (0.0)	0.2 (0.0)
Japan	1.7 (0.2)	62.4 (1.0)	484 (12.2)	557 (4.2)	**74** (12.6)	**2.01** (0.32)	1.7 (0.6)	0.52 (0.04)	-42.8 (5.3)	**-0.6** (0.1)	0.5 (0.1)
Korea	3.2 (0.3)	56.7 (1.6)	509 (9.7)	574 (5.1)	**65** (9.7)	**1.66** (0.19)	2.1 (0.6)	0.59 (0.04)	-30.7 (4.4)	**-0.5** (0.1)	0.5 (0.1)
Luxembourg	20.0 (0.6)	50.8 (0.7)	440 (3.1)	518 (1.8)	**78** (3.6)	**2.23** (0.15)	19.7 (2.0)	0.52 (0.03)	-32.3 (2.7)	**-0.7** (0.0)	0.6 (0.0)
Mexico	49.7 (0.8)	35.7 (0.7)	397 (1.5)	433 (1.8)	**37** (2.1)	**1.79** (0.06)	28.2 (1.6)	0.60 (0.02)	-16.6 (1.2)	**-0.5** (0.0)	0.4 (0.0)
Netherlands	6.1 (0.4)	63.2 (1.2)	478 (7.9)	537 (3.9)	**59** (7.5)	**1.76** (0.19)	4.4 (1.1)	0.71 (0.06)	-22.1 (6.4)	**-0.6** (0.1)	0.3 (0.0)
New Zealand	7.2 (0.5)	52.7 (1.0)	449 (5.5)	528 (3.1)	**79** (5.4)	**1.90** (0.17)	6.1 (1.0)	0.61 (0.04)	-25.7 (3.5)	**-0.7** (0.1)	0.5 (0.0)
Norway	2.9 (0.3)	67.9 (1.0)	424 (8.5)	502 (2.6)	**78** (8.7)	**2.30** (0.25)	3.6 (0.7)	0.65 (0.04)	-31.6 (5.3)	**-0.8** (0.1)	0.3 (0.0)
Poland	3.1 (0.3)	26.3 (1.3)	439 (8.1)	568 (5.5)	**128** (9.8)	**2.50** (0.24)	4.4 (0.8)	0.33 (0.04)	-21.3 (2.1)	**-1.0** (0.1)	0.8 (0.0)
Portugal	48.7 (1.7)	27.3 (1.6)	461 (4.0)	531 (4.1)	**71** (5.1)	**2.23** (0.16)	37.4 (3.1)	0.47 (0.05)	-16.7 (2.5)	**-0.6** (0.0)	0.6 (0.1)
Slovak Republic	3.4 (0.4)	30.1 (1.2)	345 (11.0)	519 (5.5)	**173** (13.0)	**3.44** (0.28)	7.7 (1.3)	0.63 (0.06)	-12.6 (2.5)	**-1.6** (0.1)	0.5 (0.1)
Slovenia	4.1 (0.3)	43.3 (0.8)	443 (6.8)	530 (2.0)	**87** (7.7)	**1.94** (0.23)	3.7 (0.9)	0.54 (0.04)	-25.1 (2.6)	**-0.7** (0.1)	0.5 (0.0)
Spain	24.4 (0.8)	48.5 (1.0)	450 (2.9)	507 (2.2)	**57** (3.2)	**1.89** (0.09)	17.8 (1.6)	0.56 (0.03)	-27.3 (2.7)	**-0.6** (0.0)	0.5 (0.0)
Sweden	5.4 (0.4)	69.2 (0.7)	429 (6.7)	490 (2.6)	**61** (6.7)	**1.96** (0.18)	5.0 (0.9)	0.76 (0.04)	-19.4 (5.4)	**-0.7** (0.1)	0.3 (0.0)
Switzerland	12.9 (0.5)	56.2 (0.8)	475 (4.0)	549 (3.3)	**74** (4.1)	**2.18** (0.12)	13.2 (1.2)	0.65 (0.04)	-24.9 (3.3)	**-0.7** (0.0)	0.4 (0.0)
Turkey	59.9 (1.4)	24.0 (1.0)	428 (3.7)	488 (7.5)	**59** (6.2)	**1.89** (0.17)	34.6 (3.9)	0.57 (0.06)	-11.5 (1.9)	**-0.6** (0.0)	0.6 (0.1)
United Kingdom	3.7 (0.3)	59.4 (0.8)	450 (7.2)	511 (3.4)	**61** (7.3)	**1.82** (0.19)	2.9 (0.9)	0.77 (0.04)	-15.8 (4.4)	**-0.6** (0.1)	0.3 (0.0)
United States	9.0 (0.8)	58.6 (1.5)	441 (5.2)	501 (4.0)	**61** (5.9)	**1.75** (0.15)	6.4 (1.2)	0.55 (0.04)	-35.4 (4.8)	**-0.6** (0.1)	0.5 (0.0)
OECD average	**12.2** (0.1)	**51.9** (0.2)	**440** (1.2)	**517** (0.6)	**77** (1.3)	**2.13** (0.03)	**10.2** (0.3)	**0.59** (0.01)	**-27.1** (0.7)	**-0.7** (0.0)	**0.5** (0.0)
Partners											
Albania	24.4 (0.9)	29.3 (0.8)	394 (3.4)	395 (3.2)	1 (4.2)	1.01 (0.11)	0.2 (0.7)	0.99 (0.08)	-0.2 (2.5)	0.0 (0.0)	0.0 (0.0)
Argentina	31.3 (1.3)	47.1 (1.3)	362 (3.4)	410 (4.1)	**48** (4.2)	**1.93** (0.17)	22.6 (3.1)	0.53 (0.04)	-28.4 (3.5)	**-0.6** (0.0)	0.5 (0.0)
Brazil	37.3 (0.8)	26.0 (0.8)	366 (1.9)	424 (4.4)	**58** (4.5)	**1.78** (0.09)	22.5 (2.0)	0.61 (0.04)	-11.3 (1.6)	**-0.6** (0.0)	0.5 (0.0)
Bulgaria	7.2 (0.8)	45.4 (1.2)	357 (9.6)	468 (4.3)	**111** (10.4)	**2.68** (0.25)	10.7 (1.6)	0.51 (0.04)	-28.5 (3.6)	**-1.1** (0.1)	0.6 (0.0)
Colombia	37.5 (1.3)	47.0 (1.5)	352 (3.1)	396 (3.6)	**43** (3.8)	**1.90** (0.16)	25.2 (3.5)	0.54 (0.04)	-27.8 (4.2)	**-0.6** (0.0)	0.5 (0.0)
Costa Rica	28.0 (1.1)	48.5 (1.3)	379 (3.3)	423 (3.7)	**43** (4.1)	**1.89** (0.14)	20.0 (2.6)	0.63 (0.05)	-21.9 (3.8)	**-0.6** (0.1)	0.4 (0.1)
Croatia	4.8 (0.4)	47.1 (0.8)	416 (6.1)	482 (4.6)	**65** (7.3)	**2.04** (0.23)	4.7 (1.0)	0.82 (0.05)	-9.0 (2.6)	**-0.7** (0.1)	0.2 (0.0)
Cyprus*	5.1 (0.3)	52.7 (0.7)	389 (6.3)	461 (2.0)	**72** (6.6)	**1.91** (0.18)	4.4 (0.9)	0.63 (0.04)	-24.5 (3.7)	**-0.6** (0.1)	0.5 (0.0)
Hong Kong-China	29.7 (1.4)	21.8 (2.0)	537 (4.1)	601 (5.3)	**64** (6.6)	**1.59** (0.11)	14.9 (2.2)	0.48 (0.07)	-12.9 (2.8)	**-0.4** (0.0)	0.5 (0.1)
Indonesia	48.1 (1.4)	19.8 (1.5)	361 (3.5)	403 (10.3)	**42** (10.4)	**1.37** (0.09)	15.2 (3.1)	0.75 (0.09)	-5.2 (2.9)	**-0.4** (0.1)	0.5 (0.1)
Jordan	12.0 (0.6)	57.3 (1.1)	355 (3.9)	401 (4.1)	**46** (5.0)	**1.69** (0.15)	7.7 (1.6)	0.67 (0.04)	-23.7 (4.0)	**-0.5** (0.1)	0.4 (0.0)
Kazakhstan	1.4 (0.2)	86.6 (0.8)	391 (12.6)	435 (3.2)	**44** (12.6)	**1.99** (0.34)	1.3 (0.4)	0.66 (0.07)	-41.6 (12.9)	**-0.6** (0.2)	0.4 (0.1)
Latvia	2.7 (0.4)	54.7 (1.3)	442 (11.3)	508 (3.7)	**66** (10.7)	**2.08** (0.30)	2.8 (0.9)	0.61 (0.06)	-27.1 (5.6)	**-0.6** (0.1)	0.5 (0.1)
Liechtenstein	10.9 (2.0)	56.1 (2.5)	476 (14.6)	544 (5.9)	**68** (16.4)	**2.14** (0.53)	11.0 (5.2)	0.82 (0.19)	-11.5 (12.8)	**-0.8** (0.2)	0.2 (0.1)
Lithuania	1.5 (0.2)	64.3 (0.9)	413 (13.2)	496 (2.7)	**83** (13.1)	**2.30** (0.29)	1.9 (0.5)	0.50 (0.03)	-46.7 (4.4)	**-0.8** (0.2)	0.5 (0.0)
Macao-China	49.3 (0.6)	18.4 (0.5)	531 (1.6)	554 (3.0)	23 (3.6)	1.27 (0.06)	11.8 (2.2)	0.80 (0.06)	-3.8 (1.1)	-0.2 (0.0)	0.2 (0.0)
Malaysia	17.9 (0.9)	28.8 (1.2)	396 (3.7)	442 (5.1)	**46** (5.8)	**1.47** (0.11)	7.8 (1.7)	0.77 (0.07)	-6.9 (2.3)	**-0.4** (0.1)	0.4 (0.0)
Montenegro	4.0 (0.3)	58.8 (0.8)	349 (5.0)	425 (1.5)	**76** (5.1)	**2.28** (0.23)	4.9 (0.9)	0.60 (0.04)	-30.6 (4.3)	**-0.9** (0.1)	0.4 (0.0)
Peru	26.7 (1.3)	34.1 (1.5)	324 (3.1)	403 (5.5)	**79** (6.2)	**2.24** (0.17)	24.9 (2.3)	0.48 (0.04)	-21.7 (3.0)	**-0.8** (0.1)	0.6 (0.0)
Qatar	9.8 (0.5)	71.7 (0.4)	328 (2.5)	391 (1.1)	**64** (2.7)	**1.63** (0.10)	5.8 (0.9)	0.66 (0.03)	-32.8 (4.1)	**-0.7** (0.0)	0.5 (0.0)
Romania	5.8 (0.6)	51.7 (1.2)	402 (6.5)	458 (4.7)	**56** (7.5)	**1.77** (0.19)	4.3 (1.1)	0.73 (0.06)	-16.3 (4.3)	**-0.6** (0.1)	0.3 (0.1)
Russian Federation	1.3 (0.3)	90.7 (0.6)	416 (13.5)	487 (3.1)	**71** (13.6)	**1.99** (0.42)	1.2 (0.5)	0.60 (0.07)	-56.8 (14.5)	**-0.8** (0.1)	0.5 (0.1)
Serbia	4.8 (0.5)	54.9 (1.1)	397 (8.3)	460 (3.9)	**63** (8.4)	**1.94** (0.21)	4.3 (1.1)	0.78 (0.05)	-13.5 (3.5)	**-0.6** (0.1)	0.3 (0.0)
Shanghai-China	24.9 (1.3)	44.5 (1.3)	564 (5.5)	643 (3.6)	**79** (6.0)	**2.10** (0.25)	21.5 (2.5)	0.50 (0.04)	-28.5 (2.9)	**-0.7** (0.0)	0.6 (0.0)
Singapore	10.0 (0.4)	47.8 (0.7)	525 (3.9)	602 (2.0)	**76** (4.6)	**1.71** (0.11)	6.6 (0.9)	0.50 (0.03)	-31.7 (2.8)	**-0.5** (0.0)	0.6 (0.0)
Chinese Taipei	11.8 (0.6)	51.4 (1.1)	493 (6.0)	591 (3.4)	**99** (6.6)	**2.06** (0.14)	11.2 (1.3)	0.48 (0.03)	-36.5 (3.4)	**-0.7** (0.1)	0.6 (0.0)
Thailand	50.2 (1.4)	19.0 (1.2)	412 (3.2)	474 (6.8)	**61** (6.8)	**1.40** (0.11)	16.6 (3.8)	0.45 (0.06)	-11.6 (1.8)	**-0.4** (0.0)	0.7 (0.1)
Tunisia	29.8 (1.3)	28.1 (1.2)	366 (3.4)	417 (7.6)	**52** (7.7)	**1.56** (0.14)	14.3 (2.9)	0.65 (0.07)	-10.8 (2.6)	**-0.5** (0.1)	0.5 (0.1)
United Arab Emirates	8.9 (0.4)	67.7 (0.9)	384 (3.1)	453 (2.8)	**69** (3.6)	**1.86** (0.11)	7.1 (0.9)	0.68 (0.03)	-54.5 (4.0)	**-0.7** (0.0)	0.7 (0.0)
Uruguay	45.1 (1.1)	35.6 (1.0)	378 (2.9)	444 (4.2)	**65** (4.9)	**2.25** (0.18)	36.1 (3.1)	0.50 (0.04)	-21.6 (2.5)	**-0.7** (0.1)	0.6 (0.1)
Viet Nam	58.2 (1.5)	11.2 (1.0)	492 (4.4)	559 (9.7)	**67** (9.3)	**1.93** (0.19)	35.0 (4.3)	0.47 (0.10)	-6.3 (1.6)	**-0.6** (0.1)	0.6 (0.1)

Note: Values that are statistically significant are indicated in bold (see Annex A3).
* See notes at the beginning of this Annex.
StatLink ⟐ http://dx.doi.org/10.1787/888932964908

[Part 2/4]

Table II.2.5 Performance and selected elements of socio-economic status across countries

Results based on students' self-reports

Parents' highest occupation

	Percentage of students whose parents' highest occupation is low- (elementary) or high- (professional, managerial) skilled: Low		High		Mean performance of students whose parents' highest occupation is low- (elementary) or high- (professional, managerial) skilled: Low		High		Difference in performance between students whose parents work in high- and low-skilled occupations		Increased likelihood of students whose parents work in elementary occupations of scoring in the bottom quarter of the mathematics performance distribution		Population relevance of students whose parents work in elementary occupations scoring in the bottom quarter of the mathematics performance distribution		Increased likelihood of students whose parents work in high-skilled occupations scoring in the bottom quarter of the mathematics performance distribution		Population relevance of students whose parents work in high-skilled occupations scoring in the bottom quarter of the mathematics performance distribution		Effect size in mathematics performance for students whose parents work in elementary occupations		Effect size in mathematics performance for students whose parents work in high-skilled occupations	
	%	S.E.	%	S.E.	Mean score	S.E.	Mean score	S.E.	Score dif.	S.E.	Ratio	S.E.	%	S.E.	Ratio	S.E.	%	S.E.	Effect size	S.E.	Effect size	S.E.
OECD																						
Australia	4.2	(0.2)	67.8	(0.6)	454	(4.5)	523	(1.9)	70	(4.6)	1.98	(0.12)	4.0	(0.5)	0.53	(0.02)	-46.3	(3.1)	-0.6	(0.1)	0.5	(0.0)
Austria	2.5	(0.2)	50.7	(1.1)	440	(10.4)	533	(3.2)	93	(11.2)	2.12	(0.25)	2.7	(0.7)	0.43	(0.04)	-40.9	(4.0)	-0.8	(0.1)	0.6	(0.0)
Belgium	4.6	(0.3)	56.3	(1.0)	441	(6.0)	550	(2.3)	109	(6.7)	2.32	(0.18)	5.7	(0.8)	0.39	(0.02)	-52.5	(3.0)	-0.9	(0.1)	0.7	(0.0)
Canada	2.7	(0.2)	65.1	(0.7)	471	(6.0)	537	(2.0)	66	(6.1)	1.89	(0.18)	2.4	(0.5)	0.56	(0.02)	-39.9	(3.0)	-0.6	(0.1)	0.5	(0.0)
Chile	12.3	(0.8)	35.2	(1.2)	385	(4.1)	463	(4.2)	78	(5.6)	1.85	(0.11)	9.5	(1.3)	0.41	(0.04)	-26.2	(2.6)	-0.6	(0.1)	0.8	(0.1)
Czech Republic	1.4	(0.3)	45.5	(1.0)	399	(15.0)	535	(3.1)	136	(15.5)	3.02	(0.42)	2.7	(0.8)	0.42	(0.05)	-36.0	(4.1)	-1.2	(0.2)	0.7	(0.0)
Denmark	2.8	(0.3)	61.0	(1.2)	447	(7.4)	522	(2.4)	75	(7.4)	1.95	(0.18)	2.6	(0.5)	0.47	(0.04)	-47.8	(5.5)	-0.7	(0.1)	0.6	(0.0)
Estonia	1.9	(0.2)	55.8	(0.9)	484	(9.2)	540	(2.3)	56	(9.5)	1.55	(0.26)	1.0	(0.5)	0.51	(0.03)	-37.9	(3.5)	-0.5	(0.1)	0.5	(0.0)
Finland	0.9	(0.1)	65.6	(0.8)	463	(13.3)	534	(2.1)	70	(13.7)	2.16	(0.42)	1.0	(0.4)	0.56	(0.03)	-40.8	(4.1)	-0.7	(0.2)	0.5	(0.0)
France	4.2	(0.3)	58.6	(1.0)	445	(6.9)	528	(3.0)	83	(7.2)	1.88	(0.15)	3.6	(0.6)	0.39	(0.03)	-56.1	(4.4)	-0.6	(0.1)	0.7	(0.0)
Germany	2.1	(0.3)	53.4	(1.0)	441	(13.1)	550	(3.4)	109	(13.3)	2.22	(0.26)	2.5	(0.6)	0.42	(0.04)	-45.1	(4.6)	-0.9	(0.1)	0.7	(0.0)
Greece	5.1	(0.4)	48.4	(1.3)	395	(6.2)	482	(3.0)	87	(6.8)	2.19	(0.18)	5.7	(0.8)	0.46	(0.04)	-35.9	(3.9)	-0.8	(0.1)	0.6	(0.0)
Hungary	3.6	(0.4)	44.2	(1.3)	411	(9.3)	518	(4.8)	107	(10.7)	2.27	(0.27)	4.4	(1.1)	0.38	(0.03)	-37.9	(3.6)	-0.8	(0.1)	0.8	(0.1)
Iceland	2.5	(0.3)	67.4	(0.7)	428	(9.6)	510	(2.1)	82	(9.8)	2.36	(0.29)	3.3	(0.7)	0.59	(0.04)	-38.3	(4.7)	-0.8	(0.1)	0.4	(0.0)
Ireland	3.0	(0.3)	57.7	(0.9)	438	(8.1)	522	(1.9)	84	(8.0)	2.40	(0.23)	4.1	(0.7)	0.52	(0.03)	-37.8	(3.6)	-0.9	(0.1)	0.5	(0.0)
Israel	1.8	(0.2)	70.5	(1.3)	387	(13.0)	497	(5.0)	110	(13.7)	2.41	(0.27)	2.5	(0.6)	0.41	(0.03)	-71.1	(7.8)	-0.9	(0.1)	0.8	(0.1)
Italy	3.4	(0.2)	42.4	(0.6)	433	(4.1)	515	(2.4)	82	(4.2)	1.93	(0.11)	3.1	(0.3)	0.49	(0.02)	-27.6	(1.6)	-0.6	(0.0)	0.5	(0.0)
Japan	3.5	(0.2)	50.5	(0.8)	513	(7.2)	557	(4.4)	44	(7.8)	1.34	(0.18)	1.2	(0.6)	0.65	(0.04)	-21.2	(3.3)	-0.3	(0.1)	0.4	(0.0)
Korea	2.9	(0.3)	56.7	(1.2)	503	(9.3)	570	(5.2)	67	(9.5)	1.93	(0.24)	2.6	(0.6)	0.65	(0.04)	-24.7	(3.5)	-0.6	(0.1)	0.4	(0.0)
Luxembourg	4.3	(0.3)	47.9	(0.7)	430	(6.5)	531	(1.8)	100	(6.8)	2.07	(0.18)	4.4	(0.8)	0.32	(0.02)	-47.9	(2.7)	-0.7	(0.1)	0.9	(0.0)
Mexico	17.6	(0.6)	30.1	(0.7)	388	(2.2)	441	(1.7)	53	(2.7)	1.67	(0.07)	10.6	(1.1)	0.52	(0.03)	-16.9	(1.3)	-0.5	(0.0)	0.5	(0.0)
Netherlands	1.7	(0.2)	69.5	(1.0)	448	(12.5)	543	(3.3)	95	(12.7)	2.46	(0.33)	2.5	(0.6)	0.51	(0.03)	-52.3	(5.2)	-0.9	(0.2)	0.6	(0.0)
New Zealand	3.1	(0.3)	66.5	(0.9)	422	(8.0)	528	(2.8)	106	(8.1)	2.51	(0.20)	4.4	(0.7)	0.43	(0.03)	-61.8	(5.7)	-1.0	(0.1)	0.7	(0.0)
Norway	1.3	(0.2)	71.5	(0.8)	444	(12.1)	503	(2.6)	59	(12.3)	1.81	(0.29)	1.1	(0.4)	0.58	(0.04)	-42.3	(5.7)	-0.6	(0.1)	0.4	(0.0)
Poland	1.6	(0.2)	44.2	(1.4)	476	(14.3)	552	(5.0)	76	(14.5)	1.70	(0.30)	1.1	(0.5)	0.40	(0.04)	-36.1	(3.7)	-0.5	(0.2)	0.7	(0.0)
Portugal	7.1	(0.6)	36.0	(1.8)	428	(5.6)	532	(3.6)	103	(5.9)	2.34	(0.18)	8.7	(1.0)	0.36	(0.04)	-30.2	(3.4)	-0.8	(0.1)	0.7	(0.0)
Slovak Republic	5.3	(0.6)	35.6	(1.2)	404	(9.7)	535	(4.7)	131	(10.8)	2.52	(0.25)	7.4	(1.2)	0.35	(0.03)	-30.2	(2.6)	-0.9	(0.1)	0.8	(0.0)
Slovenia	2.9	(0.3)	55.9	(0.8)	452	(8.7)	527	(1.9)	75	(8.6)	1.96	(0.26)	2.7	(0.9)	0.46	(0.03)	-42.8	(3.5)	-0.6	(0.1)	0.6	(0.0)
Spain	6.1	(0.3)	43.0	(1.1)	434	(3.7)	516	(2.0)	82	(3.6)	1.95	(0.13)	5.5	(0.7)	0.41	(0.02)	-34.3	(2.4)	-0.6	(0.0)	0.6	(0.0)
Sweden	1.6	(0.2)	63.9	(0.9)	425	(9.7)	501	(2.3)	76	(9.8)	1.84	(0.24)	1.3	(0.4)	0.51	(0.03)	-45.4	(4.5)	-0.7	(0.1)	0.6	(0.0)
Switzerland	1.3	(0.2)	63.6	(1.3)	449	(10.9)	552	(3.2)	103	(10.7)	2.48	(0.29)	1.9	(0.4)	0.49	(0.03)	-48.7	(4.7)	-0.9	(0.1)	0.6	(0.0)
Turkey	9.2	(0.7)	21.2	(1.0)	422	(4.5)	492	(7.9)	70	(8.2)	1.43	(0.12)	3.8	(1.1)	0.56	(0.07)	-10.4	(1.9)	-0.4	(0.1)	0.6	(0.1)
United Kingdom	2.3	(0.2)	65.0	(1.1)	447	(11.4)	517	(3.1)	70	(11.2)	1.83	(0.26)	1.9	(0.6)	0.54	(0.04)	-42.7	(5.2)	-0.6	(0.1)	0.6	(0.0)
United States	5.7	(0.5)	64.6	(1.3)	428	(5.3)	503	(3.6)	75	(5.8)	2.07	(0.21)	5.8	(1.0)	0.50	(0.04)	-47.4	(6.0)	-0.7	(0.1)	0.6	(0.0)
OECD average	4.0	(0.1)	53.9	(0.2)	437	(1.6)	522	(0.6)	85	(1.6)	2.07	(0.04)	3.7	(0.1)	0.48	(0.01)	-39.8	(0.7)	-0.7	(0.0)	0.6	(0.0)
Partners																						
Albania	6.0	(0.4)	37.7	(1.0)	373	(6.9)	391	(3.8)	18	(7.4)	1.18	(0.15)	1.0	(0.9)	1.01	(0.09)	0.5	(3.3)	-0.2	(0.1)	0.0	(0.0)
Argentina	8.6	(0.6)	34.6	(1.6)	364	(7.1)	424	(3.1)	60	(6.6)	1.59	(0.16)	4.8	(1.3)	0.43	(0.04)	-24.5	(3.1)	-0.4	(0.1)	0.6	(0.0)
Brazil	10.9	(0.4)	34.5	(0.7)	360	(2.9)	426	(4.1)	66	(4.8)	1.67	(0.10)	6.8	(0.9)	0.50	(0.03)	-21.0	(1.9)	-0.5	(0.0)	0.6	(0.0)
Bulgaria	4.0	(0.4)	45.5	(1.4)	369	(8.9)	484	(4.5)	114	(10.5)	2.34	(0.22)	5.1	(0.9)	0.34	(0.03)	-43.0	(4.1)	-0.9	(0.1)	0.8	(0.1)
Colombia	7.6	(0.5)	24.5	(1.0)	346	(4.1)	411	(4.9)	65	(6.2)	1.60	(0.14)	4.4	(1.0)	0.43	(0.06)	-16.1	(2.2)	-0.5	[illegible]	0.6	(0.1)
Costa Rica	11.9	(1.0)	35.4	(1.4)	379	(4.1)	438	(3.9)	60	(5.3)	1.70	(0.16)	7.7	(1.6)	0.41	(0.05)	-26.3	(3.2)	-0.5	[illegible]	0.7	(0.1)
Croatia	1.6	(0.2)	41.2	(1.1)	432	(9.6)	507	(5.1)	74	(10.8)	1.83	(0.23)	1.3	(0.4)	0.45	(0.04)	-29.2	(2.9)	-0.5	[illegible]	0.7	(0.0)
Cyprus*	2.5	(0.3)	42.8	(0.8)	396	(8.2)	478	(2.1)	82	(8.6)	1.77	(0.21)	1.9	(0.5)	0.45	(0.05)	-30.8	(3.4)	-0.6	[illegible]	0.7	(0.0)
Hong Kong-China	7.0	(0.5)	42.9	(2.0)	528	(8.1)	586	(3.9)	58	(9.0)	1.62	(0.17)	4.2	(1.1)	0.60	(0.06)	-20.9	(3.9)	-0.4	[illegible]	0.4	(0.1)
Indonesia	21.6	(1.9)	21.3	(1.7)	356	(5.1)	407	(7.8)	51	(9.0)	1.46	(0.18)	9.0	(3.6)	0.56	(0.06)	-10.5	(2.0)	-0.4	[illegible]	0.5	(0.1)
Jordan	1.9	(0.2)	61.9	(0.9)	368	(6.5)	410	(3.7)	41	(7.4)	1.46	(0.22)	0.9	(0.4)	0.62	(0.04)	-30.8	(4.5)	-0.4	[illegible]	0.5	(0.0)
Kazakhstan	3.1	(0.3)	60.5	(1.3)	410	(8.1)	442	(3.6)	32	(8.4)	1.51	(0.23)	1.6	(0.7)	0.67	(0.05)	-25.0	(5.0)	-0.3	[illegible]	0.3	(0.1)
Latvia	5.1	(0.5)	50.8	(1.3)	435	(7.6)	520	(3.4)	85	(8.2)	2.30	(0.32)	6.3	(1.6)	0.39	(0.04)	-44.5	(4.8)	-0.8	[illegible]	0.7	(0.0)
Liechtenstein	2.1	(0.9)	75.0	(2.3)	c	c	557	(5.2)	c	c	c	c	c	c	0.36	(0.07)	-92.0	(25.4)	c	c	0.9	(0.1)
Lithuania	4.4	(0.4)	51.8	(0.9)	434	(6.8)	507	(2.7)	73	(6.9)	1.99	(0.19)	4.2	(0.8)	0.46	(0.03)	-38.9	(3.3)	-0.6	[illegible]	0.6	(0.0)
Macao-China	5.0	(0.3)	27.8	(0.6)	517	(5.5)	556	(2.3)	40	(5.7)	1.35	(0.13)	1.7	(0.7)	0.77	(0.05)	-6.9	(1.5)	-0.3	[illegible]	0.2	(0.0)
Malaysia	10.7	(0.7)	40.0	(1.4)	389	(3.6)	452	(4.3)	63	(5.1)	1.60	(0.12)	6.0	(1.1)	0.53	(0.04)	-22.9	(3.2)	-0.5	[illegible]	0.6	(0.0)
Montenegro	3.9	(0.3)	45.2	(0.8)	374	(5.8)	444	(2.1)	70	(6.0)	1.97	(0.19)	3.6	(0.7)	0.46	(0.03)	-32.6	(2.9)	-0.6	[illegible]	0.6	(0.0)
Peru	21.7	(1.2)	21.7	(1.3)	320	(3.4)	419	(6.8)	100	(7.3)	2.40	(0.19)	23.3	(2.3)	0.32	(0.04)	-17.4	(2.2)	-0.8	[illegible]	0.8	(0.1)
Qatar	0.6	(0.1)	77.3	(0.4)	316	(9.1)	406	(1.1)	90	(9.1)	2.33	(0.38)	0.8	(0.2)	0.47	(0.02)	-69.2	(3.6)	-0.9	[illegible]	0.7	(0.0)
Romania	4.2	(0.5)	37.1	(1.6)	404	(8.1)	488	(5.4)	85	(8.8)	1.87	(0.21)	3.5	(0.8)	0.36	(0.04)	-30.8	(3.2)	-0.6	[illegible]	0.8	(0.1)
Russian Federation	1.6	(0.2)	56.0	(1.1)	424	(8.3)	504	(3.6)	80	(9.0)	1.93	(0.25)	1.4	(0.4)	0.53	(0.04)	-36.0	(4.3)	-0.8	[illegible]	0.6	(0.1)
Serbia	3.6	(0.3)	42.0	(1.1)	409	(7.4)	484	(4.2)	75	(8.2)	1.73	(0.19)	2.6	(0.7)	0.42	(0.03)	-32.0	(3.0)	-0.5	[illegible]	0.7	(0.0)
Shanghai-China	1.5	(0.2)	57.4	(1.3)	535	(14.3)	635	(3.5)	100	(14.2)	2.27	(0.29)	1.9	(0.6)	0.53	(0.04)	-36.9	(4.2)	-0.8	[illegible]	0.5	(0.0)
Singapore	2.6	(0.2)	69.4	(0.6)	498	(8.0)	594	(1.7)	96	(7.8)	2.25	(0.18)	3.2	(0.5)	0.49	(0.02)	-54.2	(4.0)	-0.8	[illegible]	0.6	(0.0)
Chinese Taipei	3.3	(0.3)	43.8	(1.2)	477	(8.4)	605	(3.7)	128	(8.7)	2.30	(0.21)	4.1	(0.7)	0.40	(0.03)	-35.8	(3.2)	-0.8	[illegible]	0.7	(0.0)
Thailand	11.6	(0.7)	24.2	(1.2)	398	(5.5)	466	(5.4)	68	(7.4)	1.68	(0.13)	7.3	(1.4)	0.52	(0.05)	-13.2	(2.0)	-0.5	[illegible]	0.6	(0.0)
Tunisia	28.0	(1.3)	30.4	(1.4)	361	(3.7)	430	(7.0)	70	(7.6)	1.77	(0.18)	17.6	(3.4)	0.40	(0.06)	-22.4	(3.1)	-0.6	[illegible]	0.7	(0.1)
United Arab Emirates	0.7	(0.1)	82.4	(0.6)	375	(12.9)	453	(2.6)	78	(12.5)	2.07	(0.34)	0.7	(0.3)	0.52	(0.03)	-65.9	(6.0)	-0.9	[illegible]	0.6	(0.0)
Uruguay	16.5	(0.7)	27.6	(1.0)	365	(4.6)	468	(4.4)	103	(6.1)	1.97	(0.14)	13.8	(1.7)	0.26	(0.03)	-25.6	(2.0)	-0.7	[illegible]	0.9	(0.1)
Viet Nam	2.9	(0.5)	13.2	(1.1)	489	(14.5)	567	(8.9)	78	(16.3)	1.42	(0.31)	1.2	(1.0)	0.30	(0.06)	-10.2	(1.6)	-0.3	(0.2)	0.8	(0.1)

Note: Values that are statistically significant are indicated in bold (see Annex A3).

* See notes at the beginning of this Annex.

StatLink http://dx.doi.org/10.1787/888932964908

[Part 3/4]
Performance and selected elements of socio-economic status across countries
Table II.2.5   *Results based on students' self-reports*

| | Percentage of students who reported that they have books of poetry at home | | Mean performance of students who reported that they have books of poetry at home and of those who do not | | | | Difference in performance between students who reported that they have books of poetry at home and those who do not | | Increased likelihood of students without poetry books at home scoring in the bottom quarter of the mathematics performance distribution | | Population relevance of students without poetry books at home scoring in the bottom quarter of the mathematics performance distribution | | Effect size on mathematics performance for students without poetry books at home | |
| | | | Yes | | No | | | | | | | | | |
	%	S.E.	Mean score	S.E.	Mean score	S.E.	Score dif.	S.E.	Ratio	S.E.	%	S.E.	Effect size	S.E.
Australia	35.8	(0.5)	525	(2.4)	498	(1.6)	27	(2.4)	1.36	0.07	18.8	(2.9)	-0.3	(0.0)
Austria	56.5	(1.0)	520	(2.8)	492	(3.4)	28	(3.5)	1.47	0.10	17.0	(3.2)	-0.3	(0.0)
Belgium	31.8	(0.7)	546	(3.1)	506	(2.2)	40	(3.2)	1.71	0.12	32.6	(3.6)	-0.4	(0.0)
Canada	34.0	(0.6)	534	(2.5)	514	(1.8)	20	(2.0)	1.38	0.06	20.0	(2.7)	-0.2	(0.0)
Chile	53.9	(0.8)	426	(3.1)	420	(3.5)	6	(2.3)	1.05	0.07	2.2	(2.9)	-0.1	(0.0)
Czech Republic	43.5	(1.1)	526	(3.2)	482	(3.2)	44	(4.0)	1.84	0.16	32.1	(4.2)	-0.5	(0.0)
Denmark	29.7	(0.9)	527	(2.9)	491	(2.4)	36	(3.2)	1.83	0.16	36.7	(4.6)	-0.5	(0.0)
Estonia	72.0	(0.9)	529	(2.2)	502	(2.7)	27	(2.7)	1.50	0.11	12.4	(2.3)	-0.3	(0.0)
Finland	51.6	(0.8)	537	(2.1)	505	(2.1)	32	(2.3)	1.68	0.10	24.8	(2.8)	-0.4	(0.0)
France	42.2	(1.0)	532	(3.2)	472	(2.8)	60	(3.7)	2.42	0.25	45.0	(4.0)	-0.6	(0.0)
Germany	57.8	(0.8)	532	(3.4)	506	(3.7)	26	(3.8)	1.45	0.11	16.1	(3.2)	-0.3	(0.0)
Greece	44.6	(1.1)	469	(2.9)	444	(2.7)	24	(3.2)	1.38	0.09	17.5	(3.5)	-0.3	(0.0)
Hungary	66.4	(1.0)	501	(3.9)	437	(3.5)	63	(4.7)	2.53	0.21	33.9	(3.3)	-0.7	(0.0)
Iceland	72.0	(0.6)	506	(2.1)	466	(2.8)	40	(3.5)	1.69	0.10	16.2	(2.0)	-0.4	(0.0)
Ireland	35.6	(0.9)	519	(2.5)	497	(2.5)	22	(2.9)	1.44	0.10	22.0	(3.8)	-0.3	(0.0)
Israel	52.2	(1.1)	478	(5.4)	463	(4.5)	15	(4.6)	1.13	0.09	5.6	(3.6)	-0.1	(0.0)
Italy	56.9	(0.6)	499	(2.2)	469	(2.1)	30	(1.9)	1.56	0.06	19.4	(1.6)	-0.3	(0.0)
Japan	25.8	(0.8)	563	(4.7)	529	(3.6)	34	(4.3)	1.69	0.15	33.7	(4.8)	-0.4	(0.0)
Korea	63.1	(1.1)	572	(4.8)	529	(4.3)	42	(3.6)	1.75	0.11	21.7	(2.4)	-0.4	(0.0)
Luxembourg	52.1	(0.6)	509	(1.6)	472	(1.6)	37	(2.4)	1.57	0.07	21.5	(2.1)	-0.4	(0.0)
Mexico	44.6	(0.5)	418	(1.7)	413	(1.3)	6	(1.4)	1.05	0.04	2.4	(2.1)	-0.1	(0.0)
Netherlands	28.3	(1.2)	544	(5.8)	520	(2.9)	24	(4.9)	1.34	0.13	19.7	(6.1)	-0.3	(0.1)
New Zealand	37.3	(0.9)	516	(3.4)	493	(2.5)	23	(3.7)	1.35	0.09	17.9	(3.6)	-0.2	(0.0)
Norway	45.0	(1.2)	514	(2.9)	476	(3.1)	38	(3.0)	1.90	0.15	33.1	(3.6)	-0.4	(0.0)
Poland	47.4	(1.1)	539	(4.3)	499	(3.3)	40	(3.2)	1.80	0.14	29.5	(3.8)	-0.5	(0.0)
Portugal	50.1	(1.3)	510	(3.9)	470	(4.2)	40	(4.2)	1.72	0.14	26.3	(3.8)	-0.4	(0.0)
Slovak Republic	60.6	(1.1)	503	(3.6)	455	(3.9)	49	(3.8)	2.05	0.15	29.2	(2.7)	-0.5	(0.0)
Slovenia	60.5	(0.7)	521	(2.1)	475	(2.2)	46	(3.5)	1.86	0.14	25.4	(3.0)	-0.5	(0.0)
Spain	57.0	(0.7)	502	(2.0)	465	(2.1)	37	(1.9)	1.78	0.10	25.0	(2.3)	-0.4	(0.0)
Sweden	34.8	(0.8)	499	(3.1)	473	(2.3)	26	(3.3)	1.35	0.09	18.7	(3.8)	-0.3	(0.0)
Switzerland	37.9	(0.9)	545	(4.0)	525	(3.0)	20	(3.2)	1.21	0.08	11.6	(4.0)	-0.2	(0.0)
Turkey	59.6	(0.9)	456	(5.6)	439	(4.7)	17	(4.2)	1.22	0.10	8.2	(3.3)	-0.2	(0.0)
United Kingdom	38.6	(0.9)	521	(3.1)	484	(3.8)	37	(4.1)	1.58	0.09	26.3	(3.3)	-0.4	(0.0)
United States	39.1	(1.0)	498	(4.4)	475	(3.4)	23	(2.8)	1.38	0.11	18.7	(4.3)	-0.3	(0.0)
OECD average	47.6	(0.2)	513	(0.6)	481	(0.5)	32	(0.6)	1.59	0.02	21.8	(0.6)	-0.4	(0.0)
Albania	79.6	(0.8)	393	(2.3)	397	(3.7)	-4	(4.1)	0.98	0.06	-0.4	(1.3)	0.0	(0.0)
Argentina	53.6	(1.2)	395	(3.5)	390	(3.8)	6	(2.5)	1.09	0.08	4.0	(3.3)	-0.1	(0.0)
Brazil	51.6	(0.6)	391	(2.5)	400	(2.0)	-9	(1.9)	0.81	0.04	-9.8	(2.3)	0.1	(0.0)
Bulgaria	63.8	(1.2)	464	(4.2)	405	(4.3)	58	(5.2)	2.18	0.18	29.9	(3.4)	-0.7	(0.1)
Colombia	54.7	(1.0)	380	(3.2)	379	(2.8)	1	(2.2)	0.98	0.06	-0.9	(2.9)	0.0	(0.0)
Costa Rica	33.6	(1.1)	418	(3.8)	405	(2.9)	14	(3.1)	1.20	0.09	11.9	(4.7)	-0.2	(0.0)
Croatia	33.2	(0.9)	502	(5.9)	461	(3.0)	41	(5.3)	1.80	0.14	34.8	(3.9)	-0.5	(0.1)
Cyprus*	44.5	(0.7)	459	(1.8)	431	(1.7)	28	(2.6)	1.43	0.07	19.3	(2.7)	-0.3	(0.0)
Hong Kong-China	49.6	(1.3)	576	(4.0)	550	(3.3)	26	(4.0)	1.48	0.11	19.6	(3.5)	-0.3	(0.0)
Indonesia	37.0	(1.2)	369	(4.3)	381	(4.3)	-12	(3.0)	0.79	0.06	-15.0	(4.4)	0.2	(0.0)
Jordan	42.0	(0.8)	400	(4.5)	381	(2.6)	19	(3.9)	1.32	0.10	15.5	(4.0)	-0.2	(0.0)
Kazakhstan	74.0	(1.0)	436	(3.2)	423	(3.5)	13	(2.9)	1.26	0.08	6.4	(1.8)	-0.2	(0.0)
Latvia	66.8	(1.0)	506	(3.1)	464	(3.2)	42	(3.5)	1.91	0.17	23.1	(3.3)	-0.5	(0.0)
Liechtenstein	53.9	(2.9)	540	(7.2)	531	(7.8)	9	(12.4)	1.09	0.25	4.1	(10.6)	-0.1	(0.1)
Lithuania	53.8	(0.9)	503	(2.8)	457	(2.9)	46	(3.2)	2.11	0.15	34.0	(2.9)	-0.5	(0.0)
Macao-China	41.2	(0.6)	554	(2.0)	530	(1.4)	25	(2.7)	1.44	0.08	20.6	(3.1)	-0.3	(0.0)
Malaysia	40.9	(0.9)	414	(4.2)	428	(3.0)	-14	(3.2)	0.71	0.05	-20.9	(4.5)	0.2	(0.0)
Montenegro	72.8	(0.7)	425	(1.5)	385	(2.3)	39	(3.1)	1.77	0.11	17.2	(2.1)	-0.5	(0.0)
Peru	72.6	(0.7)	366	(3.8)	384	(4.2)	-18	(2.9)	0.75	0.05	-7.2	(1.5)	0.2	(0.0)
Qatar	55.5	(0.5)	378	(1.2)	386	(1.3)	-7	(2.0)	0.89	0.04	-5.4	(1.8)	0.1	(0.0)
Romania	83.2	(0.9)	455	(3.8)	408	(4.4)	47	(4.3)	1.95	0.13	13.8	(1.7)	-0.6	(0.1)
Russian Federation	77.5	(0.8)	495	(3.0)	450	(4.0)	46	(4.2)	1.89	0.18	16.6	(2.6)	-0.6	(0.1)
Serbia	69.8	(0.9)	465	(3.5)	423	(3.9)	42	(4.0)	1.74	0.11	18.3	(2.3)	-0.5	(0.0)
Shanghai-China	77.0	(0.8)	623	(3.2)	582	(4.7)	41	(4.1)	1.64	0.10	12.8	(1.7)	-0.4	(0.0)
Singapore	33.3	(0.7)	591	(2.5)	567	(1.6)	24	(3.1)	1.36	0.08	19.3	(3.4)	-0.2	(0.0)
Chinese Taipei	54.4	(1.0)	595	(3.4)	523	(3.9)	72	(4.5)	2.52	0.16	40.9	(2.6)	-0.7	(0.0)
Thailand	44.0	(0.8)	426	(3.8)	428	(3.6)	-2	(2.6)	0.96	0.05	-2.3	(2.9)	0.0	(0.0)
Tunisia	32.7	(1.1)	408	(5.1)	381	(3.8)	27	(3.8)	1.47	0.10	24.1	(4.2)	-0.3	(0.0)
United Arab Emirates	45.7	(0.6)	441	(3.1)	431	(2.3)	9	(2.3)	1.17	0.06	8.6	(2.9)	-0.1	(0.0)
Uruguay	47.0	(0.9)	427	(2.7)	409	(3.2)	18	(2.9)	1.28	0.08	13.1	(3.3)	-0.2	(0.0)
Viet Nam	40.8	(1.2)	520	(5.0)	508	(5.3)	12	(4.3)	1.20	0.10	10.4	(4.7)	-0.1	(0.0)

Note: Values that are statistically significant are indicated in bold (see Annex A3).
* See notes at the beginning of this Annex.
StatLink ⋙ http://dx.doi.org/10.1787/888932964908

[Part 4/4]
Performance and selected elements of socio-economic status across countries

Table II.2.5   *Results based on students' self-reports*

		Books at home: More than 200												
		Percentage of students who reported that they have more than 200 books at home		Mean performance of students who reported that they have more than 200 books at home and of those who do not				Difference in performance between those who reported that they have more than 200 books at home and those who do not		Increased likelihood of students who reported that they did not have more than 200 books at home scoring in the bottom quarter of the mathematics performance distribution		Population relevance of students who reported that they did not have more than 200 books at home scoring in the bottom quarter of the mathematics performance distribution		Effect size on mathematics performance for students who reported that they did not have more than 200 books at home
				Yes		No								
		%	S.E.	Mean score	S.E.	Mean score	S.E.	Score dif.	S.E.	Ratio	S.E.	%	S.E.	Effect size / S.E.
OECD	Australia	26.2	(0.6)	525	(2.4)	498	(1.6)	57	(1.9)	2.29	(0.12)	48.8	(2.4)	-0. (0.0)
	Austria	22.9	(1.0)	520	(2.8)	492	(3.4)	72	(3.9)	3.23	(0.40)	63.2	(4.3)	-0. (0.0)
	Belgium	20.7	(0.7)	546	(3.1)	506	(2.2)	66	(3.9)	2.85	(0.28)	59.4	(3.4)	-0. (0.0)
	Canada	23.3	(0.6)	534	(2.5)	514	(1.8)	48	(2.4)	2.27	(0.17)	49.4	(3.3)	-0. (0.0)
	Chile	6.3	(0.4)	426	(3.1)	420	(3.5)	74	(5.6)	3.08	(0.66)	65.9	(6.7)	-0. (0.1)
	Czech Republic	22.2	(0.9)	526	(3.2)	482	(3.2)	73	(4.3)	2.90	(0.38)	59.6	(5.0)	-0. (0.0)
	Denmark	20.8	(0.8)	527	(2.9)	491	(2.4)	54	(3.8)	2.51	(0.31)	54.5	(4.9)	-0. (0.0)
	Estonia	25.2	(0.7)	529	(2.2)	502	(2.7)	55	(3.6)	2.49	(0.25)	52.7	(4.0)	-0. (0.0)
	Finland	21.2	(0.6)	537	(2.1)	505	(2.1)	56	(3.0)	2.52	(0.24)	54.4	(3.9)	-0 (0.0)
	France	19.5	(0.7)	532	(3.2)	472	(2.8)	86	(4.0)	4.58	(0.80)	74.1	(3.7)	-1 (0.0)
	Germany	28.7	(1.1)	532	(3.4)	506	(3.7)	70	(3.8)	2.77	(0.34)	55.8	(4.8)	-0 (0.0)
	Greece	18.7	(0.7)	469	(2.9)	444	(2.7)	54	(4.2)	2.09	(0.32)	47.0	(6.1)	-0 (0.1)
	Hungary	31.7	(1.0)	501	(3.9)	437	(3.5)	78	(5.4)	3.78	(0.48)	65.4	(4.1)	-0 (0.1)
	Iceland	30.8	(0.6)	506	(2.1)	466	(2.8)	50	(3.8)	2.05	(0.22)	42.0	(5.4)	-0 (0.0)
	Ireland	21.8	(0.8)	519	(2.5)	497	(2.5)	62	(3.1)	3.19	(0.37)	63.0	(4.0)	-0 (0.1)
	Israel	25.6	(1.4)	478	(5.4)	463	(4.5)	54	(6.9)	1.78	(0.21)	36.8	(5.9)	-0 (0.1)
	Italy	20.2	(0.5)	499	(2.2)	469	(2.1)	59	(2.4)	2.45	(0.16)	53.7	(2.6)	-0 (0.0)
	Japan	23.6	(0.7)	563	(4.7)	529	(3.6)	37	(3.8)	1.57	(0.13)	30.3	(4.4)	-0 (0.0)
	Korea	36.9	(1.4)	572	(4.8)	529	(4.3)	61	(4.2)	2.21	(0.16)	43.2	(3.1)	-0 (0.0)
	Luxembourg	34.6	(0.6)	509	(1.6)	472	(1.6)	78	(2.6)	3.48	(0.29)	61.8	(2.7)	-0 (0.0)
	Mexico	3.8	(0.2)	418	(1.7)	413	(1.3)	39	(4.4)	1.63	(0.17)	37.7	(6.4)	-0 (0.1)
	Netherlands	20.0	(1.0)	544	(5.8)	520	(2.9)	63	(4.5)	3.00	(0.41)	61.4	(4.8)	-0 (0.1)
	New Zealand	25.3	(0.8)	516	(3.4)	493	(2.5)	67	(4.2)	2.65	(0.32)	55.2	(4.2)	-0 (0.0)
	Norway	28.6	(1.0)	514	(2.9)	476	(3.1)	55	(3.1)	2.36	(0.20)	49.2	(3.5)	-0 (0.0)
	Poland	17.9	(1.2)	539	(4.3)	499	(3.3)	70	(6.0)	3.02	(0.41)	62.4	(4.7)	-0 (0.1)
	Portugal	13.9	(0.9)	510	(3.9)	470	(4.2)	72	(4.5)	3.26	(0.50)	65.9	(5.2)	-0 (0.1)
	Slovak Republic	13.7	(0.6)	503	(3.6)	455	(3.9)	89	(6.2)	4.22	(0.92)	73.4	(5.1)	-0 (0.1)
	Slovenia	14.8	(0.6)	521	(2.1)	475	(2.2)	71	(4.9)	3.13	(0.47)	64.5	(4.6)	-0 (0.1)
	Spain	23.0	(0.7)	502	(2.0)	465	(2.1)	62	(1.9)	2.86	(0.22)	58.8	(2.7)	-0 (0.0)
	Sweden	26.2	(0.8)	499	(3.1)	473	(2.3)	61	(3.2)	2.57	(0.26)	53.7	(4.1)	-0 (0.0)
	Switzerland	21.2	(0.8)	545	(4.0)	525	(3.0)	64	(4.4)	2.74	(0.31)	57.9	(4.7)	-0 (0.0)
	Turkey	8.9	(0.8)	456	(5.6)	439	(4.7)	70	(8.6)	2.71	(0.51)	60.7	(6.6)	-0 (0.1)
	United Kingdom	22.1	(0.8)	521	(3.1)	484	(3.8)	78	(3.9)	3.40	(0.48)	65.0	(4.6)	-0 (0.0)
	United States	15.4	(0.9)	498	(4.4)	475	(3.4)	65	(5.8)	3.13	(0.45)	64.2	(4.6)	-0 (0.1)
	OECD average	**21.6**	**(0.1)**	**513**	**(0.6)**	**481**	**(0.5)**	**64**	**(0.8)**	**2.79**	**(0.07)**	**56.2**	**(0.8)**	**-0 (0.0)**
Partners	Albania	4.4	(0.4)	393	(2.3)	397	(3.7)	1	(10.1)	1.14	(0.28)	11.6	(16.6)	0 (0.1)
	Argentina	6.2	(0.5)	395	(3.5)	390	(3.8)	49	(6.0)	2.23	(0.63)	52.5	(13.0)	-0 6 (0.1)
	Brazil	3.1	(0.2)	391	(2.5)	400	(2.0)	41	(8.1)	1.37	(0.19)	26.1	(10.1)	-0 5 (0.1)
	Bulgaria	14.5	(0.8)	464	(4.2)	405	(4.3)	67	(5.2)	3.06	(0.50)	63.6	(5.2)	-0 7 (0.1)
	Colombia	2.2	(0.3)	380	(3.2)	379	(2.8)	63	(11.9)	2.01	(0.67)	49.5	(12.3)	-0 7 (0.1)
	Costa Rica	3.4	(0.4)	418	(3.8)	405	(2.9)	67	(11.2)	3.42	(1.19)	69.6	(10.3)	-0 9 (0.1)
	Croatia	8.9	(0.5)	502	(5.9)	461	(3.0)	60	(6.6)	2.83	(0.49)	62.3	(6.8)	-0 7 (0.1)
	Cyprus*	18.3	(0.5)	459	(1.8)	431	(1.7)	51	(3.7)	1.88	(0.19)	41.6	(5.5)	-0 6 (0.0)
	Hong Kong-China	12.7	(1.0)	576	(4.0)	550	(3.3)	54	(5.3)	2.68	(0.43)	59.2	(6.7)	-0 6 (0.1)
	Indonesia	5.5	(0.5)	369	(4.3)	381	(4.3)	21	(10.3)	1.13	(0.18)	11.0	(13.3)	-0 3 (0.1)
	Jordan	8.4	(0.4)	400	(4.5)	381	(2.6)	19	(5.2)	1.25	(0.16)	18.1	(9.4)	-0 2 (0.1)
	Kazakhstan	9.8	(0.8)	436	(3.2)	423	(3.5)	26	(4.9)	1.66	(0.24)	37.0	(7.1)	-0 4 (0.1)
	Latvia	20.3	(0.8)	506	(3.1)	464	(3.2)	47	(3.7)	2.21	(0.29)	49.0	(6.5)	-0 6 (0.0)
	Liechtenstein	23.1	(2.3)	540	(7.2)	531	(7.8)	64	(13.4)	2.77	(1.64)	57.0	(14.9)	-0 7 (0.2)
	Lithuania	15.1	(0.7)	503	(2.8)	457	(2.9)	50	(4.0)	2.12	(0.34)	48.6	(6.9)	-0 6 (0.1)
	Macao-China	6.6	(0.3)	554	(2.0)	530	(1.4)	39	(5.0)	1.68	(0.22)	38.9	(8.0)	-0 4 (0.1)
	Malaysia	10.8	(0.7)	414	(4.2)	428	(3.0)	37	(5.6)	1.65	(0.22)	36.8	(7.9)	-0 4 (0.1)
	Montenegro	17.2	(0.5)	425	(1.5)	385	(2.3)	53	(4.4)	2.30	(0.30)	51.7	(5.6)	-0 6 (0.1)
	Peru	3.2	(0.3)	366	(3.8)	384	(4.2)	50	(13.1)	1.38	(0.26)	26.5	(15.5)	-0 5 (0.1)
	Qatar	16.0	(0.4)	378	(1.2)	386	(1.3)	14	(3.1)	1.15	(0.07)	10.9	(4.6)	-0 1 (0.0)
	Romania	13.0	(0.9)	455	(3.8)	408	(4.4)	63	(6.2)	2.88	(0.54)	61.9	(6.0)	-0 8 (0.1)
	Russian Federation	19.7	(0.9)	495	(3.0)	450	(4.7)	43	(4.1)	1.63	(0.17)	33.6	(5.8)	-0 5 (0.0)
	Serbia	11.4	(0.7)	465	(3.5)	423	(3.9)	63	(5.8)	2.30	(0.35)	53.5	(6.2)	-0 7 (0.1)
	Shanghai-China	12.2	(0.8)	623	(3.2)	582	(4.7)	68	(6.7)	2.78	(0.38)	61.0	(5.0)	-0 7 (0.1)
	Singapore	16.6	(0.5)	591	(2.5)	567	(1.6)	60	(4.2)	2.32	(0.26)	52.4	(5.0)	-0 6 (0.0)
	Chinese Taipei	21.0	(0.7)	595	(3.4)	523	(3.9)	77	(4.5)	2.86	(0.29)	59.4	(4.2)	-0 7 (0.1)
	Thailand	5.3	(0.5)	426	(3.8)	428	(3.6)	64	(6.5)	2.02	(0.33)	48.9	(9.2)	-0 7 (0.1)
	Tunisia	3.2	(0.3)	408	(5.1)	381	(3.8)	39	(13.6)	1.29	(0.29)	21.4	(16.8)	-0 4 (0.1)
	United Arab Emirates	13.3	(0.4)	441	(3.1)	431	(2.3)	34	(4.4)	1.35	(0.11)	23.0	(5.9)	-0 4 (0.0)
	Uruguay	6.4	(0.5)	427	(2.7)	409	(3.2)	72	(8.7)	2.41	(0.60)	56.0	(11.5)	-0 8 (0.1)
	Viet Nam	3.6	(0.3)	520	(5.0)	508	(5.3)	30	(10.3)	1.36	(0.36)	25.7	(16.1)	-0 3 (0.1)

Note: Values that are statistically significant are indicated in bold (see Annex A3).
* See notes at the beginning of this Annex.
StatLink ▪▪▪ http://dx.doi.org/10.1787/888932964908

[Part 1/1]

Relationship between mathematics performance and elements of socio-economic status

Table II.2.6 *Results based on students' self-reports*

	Score-point difference in mathematics performance associated with each of the following factors, after accounting for the other factors														Explained variation in student performance (unique,[1] common and total)							
	Intercept		Parents' highest occupational status		Parents' highest level of education		Index of cultural possessions		Index of home educational resources		Number of books at home		Wealth		Unique to:						Common explained variation (explained by more than one factor)	Total explained variation
															Parents' highest occupational status	Parents' highest level of education	Index of cultural possessions	Index home educational resources	Number of books at home	Wealth		
	Mean score	S.E.	Score dif.	S.E.	Score dif.	S.E.	Score dif.	S.E.	Score dif.	S.E.	Score dif.	S.E.	Score dif.	S.E.	%	%	%	%	%	%	%	%
OECD																						
Australia	340	(7.2)	1	(0.0)	6	(0.5)	0	(1.1)	10	(1.0)	16	(0.7)	-7	(1.2)	1.7	1.0	0.0	0.9	4.6	0.5	9.3	18.1
Austria	376	(9.1)	1	(0.1)	2	(0.7)	-2	(2.0)	6	(1.9)	21	(1.4)	3	(1.8)	1.0	0.1	0.0	0.1	6.8	0.0	14.8	22.8
Belgium	399	(8.4)	1	(0.1)	1	(0.5)	1	(1.6)	16	(1.7)	13	(1.1)	2	(1.8)	3.3	0.0	0.0	1.9	2.9	0.1	15.8	23.8
Canada	401	(6.9)	1	(0.0)	2	(0.5)	1	(1.0)	4	(1.0)	16	(0.8)	-5	(1.2)	2.3	0.0	0.0	0.0	4.7	0.0	7.8	15.0
Chile	339	(6.6)	1	(0.1)	3	(0.4)	1	(1.4)	-1	(1.2)	13	(1.2)	12	(1.3)	1.9	1.1	0.1	0.1	2.6	1.4	18.2	25.6
Czech Republic	345	(13.0)	1	(0.1)	2	(1.1)	0	(1.9)	10	(2.0)	21	(1.4)	-2	(1.8)	3.5	0.0	0.0	0.2	6.7	0.0	14.2	24.7
Denmark	396	(9.1)	1	(0.1)	1	(0.6)	1	(1.4)	14	(1.5)	14	(0.9)	1	(1.8)	2.0	0.0	0.1	1.8	3.8	0.0	14.1	21.7
Estonia	427	(9.0)	1	(0.1)	-1	(0.7)	-2	(1.5)	6	(1.6)	19	(1.3)	-5	(1.5)	3.2	0.0	0.0	0.0	7.2	0.0	7.7	18.2
Finland	396	(9.7)	1	(0.1)	2	(0.7)	5	(1.4)	-2	(1.4)	19	(1.0)	-6	(1.6)	1.4	0.1	0.0	0.0	5.9	0.2	8.8	16.4
France	344	(10.5)	1	(0.1)	4	(0.8)	7	(1.6)	3	(1.8)	21	(1.2)	6	(1.9)	1.4	0.0	0.0	0.0	6.5	0.0	22.0	29.9
Germany	371	(8.4)	1	(0.1)	2	(0.6)	-4	(1.6)	7	(2.4)	20	(1.5)	1	(2.0)	3.2	0.0	0.0	0.3	6.4	0.0	13.4	23.3
Greece	353	(9.1)	1	(0.1)	2	(0.6)	1	(1.8)	13	(1.7)	12	(1.2)	-2	(2.1)	1.9	0.0	0.0	1.3	2.4	0.0	14.4	20.0
Hungary	348	(10.5)	1	(0.1)	1	(0.7)	8	(1.8)	6	(1.7)	20	(1.3)	-6	(2.3)	0.9	0.3	0.4	0.5	6.6	0.4	22.0	31.2
Iceland	373	(11.0)	1	(0.1)	1	(0.8)	7	(2.4)	0	(2.6)	17	(1.5)	-10	(2.0)	1.7	0.0	0.4	0.1	4.8	0.7	7.1	14.9
Ireland	376	(8.0)	1	(0.1)	2	(0.7)	-4	(1.5)	4	(1.5)	21	(1.0)	1	(1.6)	1.2	0.1	0.0	0.1	9.1	0.0	11.4	21.1
Israel	264	(16.2)	1	(0.1)	7	(1.0)	-1	(2.0)	-2	(2.0)	12	(1.6)	5	(2.2)	4.0	1.3	0.2	0.2	2.3	0.4	11.7	20.3
Italy	402	(4.6)	1	(0.0)	-1	(0.3)	3	(1.1)	5	(1.0)	17	(0.8)	0	(1.0)	1.9	0.1	0.1	0.2	4.9	0.0	9.6	16.8
Japan	395	(15.2)	0	(0.1)	7	(0.9)	8	(1.8)	12	(2.3)	9	(1.1)	-5	(2.6)	0.0	1.3	0.0	0.5	0.8	0.0	11.0	13.7
Korea	403	(13.9)	0	(0.1)	4	(0.9)	-1	(1.7)	17	(2.0)	18	(1.4)	-6	(3.1)	0.3	0.1	0.0	1.9	3.9	0.0	10.5	16.8
Luxembourg	360	(5.5)	1	(0.1)	1	(0.4)	2	(1.7)	5	(1.6)	19	(1.1)	-7	(1.4)	4.1	0.5	0.0	0.1	6.2	0.3	17.4	28.6
Mexico	386	(3.7)	0	(0.1)	2	(0.2)	-1	(0.7)	4	(0.9)	6	(0.7)	6	(0.8)	0.5	0.4	0.0	0.1	0.6	0.7	8.5	10.9
Netherlands	410	(12.2)	1	(0.1)	0	(0.9)	-5	(2.4)	12	(2.6)	18	(1.5)	-5	(2.8)	3.0	0.0	0.0	1.1	6.4	0.2	7.9	18.8
New Zealand	350	(10.9)	1	(0.1)	3	(0.9)	-3	(2.0)	12	(1.7)	19	(1.5)	-1	(1.9)	2.6	0.0	0.6	1.9	6.0	0.0	11.2	22.9
Norway	387	(13.5)	1	(0.1)	1	(0.9)	6	(2.0)	2	(2.1)	18	(1.3)	-12	(1.9)	1.7	0.3	0.0	0.1	5.9	1.4	7.4	16.8
Poland	358	(9.6)	1	(0.1)	6	(0.9)	3	(1.6)	4	(1.7)	17	(1.3)	-3	(1.9)	0.7	0.9	0.0	0.0	4.0	0.0	16.1	21.6
Portugal	400	(6.9)	1	(0.1)	1	(0.5)	1	(1.6)	8	(1.6)	16	(1.4)	4	(1.8)	1.8	0.0	0.0	0.0	2.6	0.0	19.2	23.6
Slovak Republic	358	(14.6)	1	(0.1)	1	(1.0)	2	(1.8)	17	(1.9)	22	(1.6)	-4	(2.2)	0.0	0.0	0.0	1.6	5.8	0.0	24.2	31.5
Slovenia	372	(9.2)	1	(0.1)	2	(0.9)	5	(1.8)	0	(2.0)	18	(1.2)	-4	(1.6)	3.6	0.3	0.4	0.3	5.2	0.4	11.9	22.2
Spain	371	(4.9)	1	(0.1)	2	(0.4)	7	(1.1)	3	(1.0)	18	(0.8)	-2	(1.5)	1.3	0.0	0.1	0.0	5.6	0.0	15.9	23.0
Sweden	382	(9.7)	1	(0.1)	-1	(0.7)	2	(2.2)	0	(1.7)	19	(1.2)	-3	(2.5)	2.3	0.0	0.0	0.0	6.6	0.1	9.0	18.0
Switzerland	395	(7.0)	1	(0.1)	3	(0.4)	-6	(1.5)	5	(1.6)	21	(1.4)	2	(1.9)	1.5	0.2	0.4	0.3	7.5	0.1	9.9	19.7
Turkey	396	(8.2)	0	(0.1)	2	(0.6)	-3	(2.0)	10	(2.2)	15	(1.7)	7	(2.5)	0.0	0.1	0.0	0.4	2.8	0.0	14.9	18.3
United Kingdom	394	(12.7)	1	(0.1)	-1	(0.8)	0	(1.5)	6	(1.4)	22	(1.1)	-3	(1.6)	2.4	0.0	0.0	0.3	8.8	0.1	11.0	22.7
United States	373	(8.5)	1	(0.1)	1	(0.7)	2	(1.5)	5	(1.6)	17	(1.6)	2	(1.9)	2.0	0.2	0.0	0.1	5.0	0.1	12.2	19.8
OECD average	375	(1.7)	1	(0.0)	2	(0.1)	1	(0.3)	6	(0.3)	17	(0.2)	-1	(0.3)	1.9	0.3	0.1	0.5	5.1	0.2	13.0	21.0
Partners																						
Albania	m	m	m	m	m	m	m	m	m	m	m	m	m	m	m	m	m	m	m	m	m	m
Argentina	329	(7.6)	1	(0.1)	2	(0.5)	0	(1.6)	2	(1.4)	11	(1.3)	8	(2.0)	2.8	0.4	0.0	0.0	2.2	0.5	12.6	18.4
Brazil	365	(3.7)	1	(0.1)	2	(0.2)	-5	(0.9)	8	(1.1)	5	(1.0)	14	(1.7)	2.0	0.6	0.8	1.0	0.6	2.3	11.3	18.7
Bulgaria	330	(9.2)	1	(0.1)	2	(0.6)	12	(1.8)	4	(1.4)	15	(1.1)	3	(2.1)	3.4	0.4	0.9	0.3	3.9	0.2	20.3	29.4
Colombia	364	(5.9)	0	(0.1)	1	(0.3)	-4	(1.3)	0	(1.4)	10	(1.4)	20	(1.7)	1.2	0.0	0.2	0.0	1.1	4.4	13.5	20.4
Costa Rica	373	(7.0)	0	(0.1)	1	(0.4)	-1	(1.5)	0	(1.5)	11	(1.4)	14	(2.0)	2.0	0.6	0.2	0.2	2.1	3.3	14.9	23.3
Croatia	402	(8.2)	1	(0.1)	-1	(0.6)	4	(1.8)	4	(1.8)	14	(1.6)	-1	(2.2)	4.0	0.0	0.0	0.0	2.2	0.0	11.3	17.6
Cyprus*	335	(8.8)	1	(0.1)	1	(0.7)	3	(1.6)	14	(1.6)	12	(1.3)	-5	(1.6)	4.2	0.0	0.0	1.4	2.5	0.0	13.0	21.1
Hong Kong-China	470	(10.4)	0	(0.1)	2	(0.7)	0	(1.5)	9	(1.7)	16	(1.2)	-7	(2.8)	0.8	1.0	0.6	1.2	3.8	0.8	3.8	11.9
Indonesia	381	(10.6)	0	(0.1)	1	(0.6)	-5	(1.7)	14	(2.2)	2	(1.3)	7	(3.0)	1.1	0.0	0.2	1.4	0.0	0.0	10.7	13.4
Jordan	333	(8.7)	0	(0.1)	3	(0.7)	6	(2.1)	9	(1.4)	2	(1.0)	1	(1.5)	1.9	1.1	0.5	1.3	0.3	0.2	7.2	12.6
Kazakhstan	392	(22.2)	0	(0.1)	2	(1.5)	2	(1.7)	11	(1.5)	5	(1.4)	6	(2.1)	0.0	0.0	0.0	1.5	0.2	0.0	9.1	10.7
Latvia	407	(11.1)	1	(0.1)	0	(0.9)	4	(2.3)	10	(1.8)	10	(1.4)	0	(1.9)	3.7	0.0	0.0	0.7	2.0	0.0	12.8	19.2
Liechtenstein	415	(30.3)	2	(0.3)	-2	(2.2)	-4	(8.0)	4	(8.3)	18	(5.1)	-2	(7.0)	9.7	0.0	0.0	0.0	3.1	0.0	7.6	20.5
Lithuania	381	(9.7)	1	(0.1)	2	(0.7)	8	(1.6)	6	(1.7)	14	(1.3)	-1	(2.3)	1.7	0.3	0.0	0.2	2.9	0.0	13.2	18.3
Macao-China	508	(5.9)	0	(0.1)	0	(0.5)	9	(1.5)	15	(1.4)	8	(1.2)	-9	(1.9)	0.5	0.2	0.8	2.2	1.2	0.8	2.5	8.4
Malaysia	395	(8.1)	1	(0.1)	0	(0.5)	-9	(1.4)	14	(1.7)	7	(1.2)	12	(2.1)	2.1	0.1	1.3	2.7	1.0	1.7	10.8	19.7
Montenegro	339	(8.8)	1	(0.1)	0	(0.7)	10	(1.8)	8	(1.6)	12	(1.2)	-6	(1.8)	1.5	0.3	0.8	1.1	4.0	0.6	11.6	20.0
Peru	340	(5.5)	1	(0.1)	2	(0.4)	-16	(1.2)	6	(1.7)	12	(1.6)	16	(1.9)	2.0	0.6	2.5	0.4	1.6	3.4	19.8	30.4
Qatar	288	(4.9)	1	(0.1)	2	(0.3)	0	(1.1)	22	(1.0)	3	(0.8)	-16	(0.8)	4.1	0.2	0.0	4.8	0.3	4.6	6.5	20.2
Romania	362	(11.8)	1	(0.1)	0	(0.8)	11	(1.6)	7	(1.5)	12	(1.2)	-1	(1.9)	5.3	0.3	1.1	0.9	3.4	0.4	14.9	26.2
Russian Federation	347	(17.8)	1	(0.1)	4	(1.2)	8	(2.0)	10	(1.5)	9	(1.3)	-7	(3.0)	2.5	0.0	0.0	0.4	1.3	0.0	10.9	15.1
Serbia	367	(8.9)	1	(0.1)	0	(0.6)	8	(1.6)	4	(1.9)	14	(1.4)	-5	(1.9)	3.8	0.0	0.1	0.0	2.7	0.0	11.9	18.6
Shanghai-China	476	(9.5)	1	(0.1)	5	(0.6)	5	(2.1)	12	(1.9)	16	(1.5)	0	(2.8)	0.6	1.5	0.3	0.9	2.6	0.1	12.4	18.4
Singapore	440	(8.3)	1	(0.1)	3	(0.6)	3	(1.7)	16	(1.7)	14	(1.2)	-1	(2.0)	1.2	0.0	0.0	1.4	2.0	0.0	13.4	18.1
Chinese Taipei	383	(11.0)	1	(0.1)	7	(0.9)	12	(2.0)	15	(1.7)	15	(1.3)	-14	(2.0)	0.8	1.3	0.7	1.6	2.4	0.9	17.2	24.9
Thailand	378	(6.3)	1	(0.1)	2	(0.6)	-6	(1.6)	13	(1.7)	10	(1.4)	-1	(1.8)	2.4	0.5	0.5	2.2	2.0	0.2	7.1	14.9
Tunisia	367	(7.1)	1	(0.1)	0	(0.4)	4	(1.6)	10	(1.7)	4	(2.1)	4	(2.0)	4.7	0.0	0.3	1.4	0.2	0.2	11.2	18.0
United Arab Emirates	306	(7.8)	1	(0.1)	4	(0.5)	3	(1.3)	16	(1.4)	8	(1.0)	-9	(1.2)	0.7	1.3	0.1	3.0	1.5	1.7	9.1	17.4
Uruguay	348	(6.8)	1	(0.1)	1	(0.6)	3	(1.6)	9	(1.6)	12	(2.3)	12	(2.3)	3.5	0.0	0.0	0.0	1.0	0.7	19.8	24.8
Viet Nam	487	(8.5)	1	(0.1)	3	(0.6)	0	(1.8)	17	(2.2)	1	(1.4)	3	(1.9)	1.6	1.4	0.6	2.6	0.3	0.3	9.0	15.9

Note: Values that are statistically significant are indicated in bold (see Annex A3).
1. Unique variation is the variation explained by each factor after taking into account the variation explained by the other factors in the model.
* See notes at the beginning of this Annex.

StatLink ⟐ http://dx.doi.org/10.1787/888932964908

[Part 1/1]
Percentage of resilient students and low-achievers among disadvantaged students, by gender
Table II.2.7a · *Results based on students' self-reports*

		Resilient students[1]							Disadvantaged low-achievers[2]							
		All students		Boys		Girls		Difference (boys - girls)		All students		Boys		Girls		Difference (boys - girls)	
		%	S.E.	%	S.E.	%	S.E.	% dif.	S.E.	%	S.E.	%	S.E.	%	S.E.	% dif.	S.E.
OECD	Australia	6.3	(0.3)	7.1	(0.5)	5.4	(0.4)	**1.6**	(0.5)	4.9	(0.2)	4.4	(0.4)	5.3	(0.3)	-0.9	(0.5)
	Austria	6.1	(0.5)	6.9	(0.8)	5.3	(0.6)	1.6	(0.9)	4.8	(0.5)	3.9	(0.8)	5.8	(0.8)	-1.8	(1.2)
	Belgium	7.1	(0.4)	7.3	(0.5)	6.9	(0.5)	0.4	(0.6)	5.0	(0.4)	4.6	(0.5)	5.3	(0.6)	-0.7	(0.7)
	Canada	8.3	(0.4)	9.2	(0.5)	7.5	(0.5)	**1.7**	(0.6)	3.3	(0.2)	3.0	(0.3)	3.5	(0.4)	-0.5	(0.5)
	Chile	1.7	(0.3)	2.2	(0.4)	1.1	(0.3)	**1.1**	(0.5)	8.1	(0.8)	6.3	(1.0)	9.8	(1.0)	-3.5	(1.1)
	Czech Republic	5.9	(0.5)	6.6	(0.7)	5.1	(0.5)	1.5	(0.8)	5.2	(0.5)	4.7	(0.7)	5.9	(0.8)	-1.2	(0.9)
	Denmark	4.9	(0.4)	5.6	(0.5)	4.2	(0.5)	**1.4**	(0.7)	4.7	(0.5)	4.1	(0.6)	5.2	(0.8)	-1.1	(0.9)
	Estonia	9.5	(0.6)	9.3	(0.9)	9.7	(0.8)	-0.4	(1.3)	1.8	(0.3)	1.5	(0.3)	2.1	(0.3)	-0.6	(0.5)
	Finland	8.1	(0.5)	8.6	(0.6)	7.6	(0.7)	1.0	(0.9)	3.2	(0.3)	3.8	(0.5)	2.6	(0.4)	1.2	(0.6)
	France	5.4	(0.4)	6.1	(0.6)	4.8	(0.6)	1.3	(0.8)	5.8	(0.5)	5.3	(0.6)	6.3	(0.7)	-1.1	(0.9)
	Germany	7.5	(0.5)	8.7	(0.8)	6.2	(0.7)	**2.5**	(1.1)	4.3	(0.5)	4.1	(0.6)	4.5	(0.6)	-0.4	(0.7)
	Greece	3.2	(0.4)	3.5	(0.5)	2.9	(0.6)	0.6	(0.7)	7.3	(0.6)	7.3	(0.8)	7.4	(0.8)	-0.1	(1.1)
	Hungary	4.1	(0.4)	4.4	(0.6)	3.8	(0.5)	0.7	(0.7)	5.9	(0.5)	5.2	(0.8)	6.5	(0.8)	-1.3	(1.1)
	Iceland	5.2	(0.4)	5.3	(0.6)	5.2	(0.6)	0.1	(0.8)	6.5	(0.5)	6.6	(0.7)	6.4	(0.6)	0.1	(1.0)
	Ireland	6.3	(0.4)	7.3	(0.6)	5.3	(0.5)	**2.0**	(0.8)	4.1	(0.5)	3.8	(0.7)	4.5	(0.5)	-0.7	(0.7)
	Israel	3.1	(0.3)	3.8	(0.5)	2.5	(0.4)	**1.4**	(0.6)	9.9	(0.8)	8.8	(1.0)	11.0	(0.9)	-2.2	(1.2)
	Italy	6.4	(0.3)	6.9	(0.3)	5.9	(0.4)	**1.0**	(0.4)	4.7	(0.3)	4.3	(0.3)	5.3	(0.4)	**-1.0**	(0.5)
	Japan	11.3	(0.5)	12.6	(0.6)	9.9	(0.7)	**2.7**	(1.0)	2.4	(0.5)	2.6	(0.6)	2.3	(0.5)	0.2	(0.5)
	Korea	12.7	(0.9)	12.4	(1.2)	13.1	(1.0)	-0.7	(1.3)	1.9	(0.3)	2.2	(0.5)	1.6	(0.3)	0.6	(0.6)
	Luxembourg	6.1	(0.4)	7.4	(0.6)	4.8	(0.5)	**2.7**	(0.7)	5.1	(0.4)	3.7	(0.5)	6.5	(0.6)	**-2.8**	(0.8)
	Mexico	3.9	(0.2)	4.3	(0.3)	3.5	(0.3)	**0.8**	(0.3)	4.3	(0.2)	3.7	(0.3)	5.0	(0.3)	**-1.3**	(0.3)
	Netherlands	8.6	(0.8)	8.6	(0.9)	8.7	(1.1)	-0.1	(1.2)	3.7	(0.5)	3.4	(0.6)	4.0	(0.6)	-0.6	(0.7)
	New Zealand	5.3	(0.4)	5.9	(0.6)	4.6	(0.6)	1.3	(0.8)	5.8	(0.5)	5.7	(0.7)	5.9	(0.7)	-0.2	(1.0)
	Norway	5.3	(0.5)	5.6	(0.5)	5.0	(0.6)	0.6	(0.6)	6.1	(0.6)	6.1	(0.7)	6.1	(0.7)	-0.1	(0.8)
	Poland	8.4	(0.6)	7.5	(0.8)	9.2	(0.7)	**-1.7**	(0.9)	2.7	(0.3)	2.8	(0.5)	2.7	(0.4)	0.2	(0.7)
	Portugal	7.7	(0.6)	8.3	(0.9)	7.0	(0.6)	1.3	(0.9)	3.5	(0.4)	3.8	(0.6)	3.3	(0.5)	0.5	(0.7)
	Slovak Republic	3.9	(0.4)	4.1	(0.5)	3.8	(0.6)	0.3	(0.8)	8.1	(0.8)	7.0	(0.8)	9.3	(1.1)	**-2.3**	(0.9)
	Slovenia	5.9	(0.4)	5.9	(0.7)	5.8	(0.6)	0.1	(1.1)	4.1	(0.5)	3.7	(0.7)	4.5	(0.5)	-0.8	(0.7)
	Spain	6.4	(0.4)	7.1	(0.6)	5.7	(0.4)	**1.4**	(0.6)	4.1	(0.3)	3.8	(0.4)	4.5	(0.4)	-0.7	(0.5)
	Sweden	4.3	(0.3)	4.5	(0.4)	4.1	(0.4)	0.4	(0.7)	6.4	(0.5)	6.8	(0.8)	6.0	(0.6)	0.9	(0.9)
	Switzerland	9.9	(0.6)	11.7	(0.8)	8.2	(0.6)	**3.5**	(0.9)	2.9	(0.3)	2.5	(0.4)	3.3	(0.4)	-0.8	(0.5)
	Turkey	7.2	(0.5)	7.1	(0.6)	7.3	(0.7)	-0.3	(0.8)	2.4	(0.3)	2.4	(0.5)	2.4	(0.4)	0.0	(0.6)
	United Kingdom	5.8	(0.4)	6.0	(0.5)	5.5	(0.6)	0.5	(0.8)	5.2	(0.6)	4.4	(0.7)	5.9	(0.8)	-1.5	(0.9)
	United States	5.2	(0.5)	5.8	(0.6)	4.5	(0.6)	1.3	(0.7)	5.6	(0.6)	5.8	(0.8)	5.4	(0.7)	0.3	(0.8)
	OECD average	6.4	(0.1)	6.9	(0.1)	5.9	(0.1)	**1.0**	(0.1)	4.8	(0.1)	4.5	(0.1)	5.2	(0.1)	**-0.7**	(0.1)
Partners	Albania	m	m	m	m	m	m	m	m	m	m	m	m	m	m	m	m
	Argentina	1.1	(0.3)	1.2	(0.3)	0.9	(0.3)	0.3	(0.4)	10.8	(0.8)	8.7	(0.9)	12.8	(1.0)	-4.1	(1.1)
	Brazil	1.7	(0.2)	2.0	(0.3)	1.5	(0.2)	0.6	(0.4)	7.5	(0.4)	5.8	(0.5)	9.0	(0.5)	-3.2	(0.6)
	Bulgaria	2.1	(0.3)	2.2	(0.4)	2.0	(0.4)	0.1	(0.5)	10.0	(0.8)	10.4	(1.1)	9.6	(0.9)	0.8	(1.0)
	Colombia	1.5	(0.3)	2.2	(0.5)	0.8	(0.2)	**1.4**	(0.6)	8.6	(0.8)	6.7	(0.9)	10.2	(1.0)	-3.5	(1.0)
	Costa Rica	1.9	(0.3)	2.4	(0.4)	1.4	(0.3)	0.9	(0.5)	4.8	(0.7)	3.2	(0.6)	6.3	(1.0)	-3.1	(1.0)
	Croatia	5.1	(0.4)	5.4	(0.6)	4.7	(0.6)	0.7	(0.9)	4.7	(0.4)	4.3	(0.6)	5.1	(0.6)	-0.8	(0.8)
	Cyprus*	1.9	(0.2)	2.3	(0.3)	1.4	(0.3)	0.8	(0.5)	10.3	(0.5)	11.0	(0.5)	9.5	(0.8)	1.5	(0.9)
	Hong Kong-China	18.1	(1.1)	17.6	(1.2)	18.7	(1.2)	-1.1	(1.2)	0.8	(0.2)	0.8	(0.3)	0.8	(0.2)	0.0	(0.3)
	Indonesia	2.5	(0.5)	3.2	(0.8)	1.9	(0.4)	1.4	(0.9)	5.5	(0.6)	5.0	(0.7)	6.0	(0.8)	-1.0	(0.8)
	Jordan	0.9	(0.2)	0.8	(0.4)	0.9	(0.3)	-0.1	(0.5)	11.5	(0.6)	11.6	(1.0)	11.4	(0.9)	0.2	(1.4)
	Kazakhstan	2.1	(0.4)	2.4	(0.6)	1.7	(0.4)	0.7	(0.6)	7.7	(0.6)	7.8	(0.7)	7.5	(0.8)	0.3	(0.9)
	Latvia	6.4	(0.5)	6.2	(0.7)	6.5	(0.7)	-0.2	(1.0)	2.8	(0.6)	2.9	(0.8)	2.7	(0.6)	0.2	(0.8)
	Liechtenstein	10.1	(1.7)	11.8	(2.6)	8.2	(1.8)	3.6	(3.1)	3.2	(1.3)	2.2	(1.7)	4.4	(1.9)	-2.2	(2.6)
	Lithuania	5.6	(0.4)	5.8	(0.6)	5.5	(0.7)	0.3	(1.0)	5.0	(0.4)	4.8	(0.6)	5.1	(0.6)	-0.3	(0.8)
	Macao-China	16.9	(0.5)	18.2	(0.7)	15.6	(0.7)	**2.6**	(1.0)	0.7	(0.1)	0.7	(0.2)	0.7	(0.2)	0.0	(0.2)
	Malaysia	2.7	(0.3)	2.7	(0.4)	2.6	(0.5)	0.0	(0.6)	7.1	(0.5)	7.6	(0.8)	6.6	(0.6)	1.1	(1.0)
	Montenegro	1.3	(0.2)	1.5	(0.3)	1.2	(0.3)	0.3	(0.4)	12.1	(0.4)	11.5	(0.6)	12.7	(0.7)	-1.2	(1.0)
	Peru	0.5	(0.1)	0.7	(0.2)	0.4	(0.2)	0.3	(0.3)	12.6	(0.9)	10.7	(0.9)	14.5	(1.3)	-3.8	(1.3)
	Qatar	0.4	(0.1)	0.5	(0.1)	0.4	(0.1)	0.2	(0.1)	19.2	(0.4)	18.7	(0.5)	19.7	(0.6)	-1.0	(0.8)
	Romania	2.8	(0.5)	3.1	(0.6)	2.5	(0.5)	0.6	(0.5)	6.5	(0.6)	6.4	(0.7)	6.5	(0.8)	-0.1	(0.8)
	Russian Federation	5.2	(0.6)	5.6	(0.8)	4.8	(0.7)	0.8	(0.8)	5.2	(0.5)	4.7	(0.6)	5.7	(0.7)	-1.0	(0.7)
	Serbia	3.6	(0.4)	4.0	(0.5)	3.2	(0.6)	0.8	(0.7)	7.1	(0.7)	6.1	(0.8)	8.0	(0.9)	-1.9	(0.9)
	Shanghai-China	19.2	(1.0)	20.3	(1.0)	18.1	(1.2)	**2.2**	(1.1)	0.4	(0.1)	0.4	(0.2)	0.3	(0.1)	0.1	(0.2)
	Singapore	15.1	(0.5)	14.5	(0.7)	15.6	(0.7)	-1.1	(1.0)	1.3	(0.2)	1.6	(0.3)	1.0	(0.2)	0.6	(0.4)
	Chinese Taipei	12.3	(0.6)	12.6	(0.7)	12.1	(0.8)	0.5	(0.9)	2.9	(0.3)	3.2	(0.5)	2.5	(0.4)	0.7	(0.5)
	Thailand	6.3	(0.6)	5.4	(0.6)	7.0	(0.7)	**-1.6**	(0.8)	2.9	(0.4)	2.9	(0.5)	2.9	(0.5)	0.0	(0.7)
	Tunisia	2.9	(0.4)	4.1	(0.6)	1.9	(0.4)	**2.2**	(0.6)	6.2	(0.7)	4.6	(0.7)	7.6	(0.9)	-2.9	(0.8)
	United Arab Emirates	1.2	(0.2)	1.2	(0.2)	1.2	(0.2)	0.0	(0.3)	12.8	(0.6)	13.1	(0.9)	12.5	(1.0)	0.6	(1.3)
	Uruguay	2.1	(0.3)	2.3	(0.4)	1.9	(0.3)	0.4	(0.5)	9.1	(0.6)	8.0	(0.8)	10.1	(0.8)	-2.1	(1.0)
	Viet Nam	16.9	(1.0)	15.9	(1.2)	17.8	(1.2)	-1.9	(1.2)	0.4	(0.1)	0.4	(0.2)	0.4	(0.2)	0.0	(0.3)

Note: Values that are statistically significant are indicated in bold (see Annex A3).
1. A student is classified as resilient if he or she is in the bottom quarter of the *PISA index of economic, social and cultural status* (ESCS) in the country/economy of assessment and performs in the top quarter of students from all countries/economies, after accounting for socio-economic status.
2. A student is classified as a disadvantaged low-achiever if he or she is in the bottom quarter of the *PISA index of economic, social and cultural status* (ESCS) in the country/economy of assessment and performs in the bottom quarter of students from all countries/economies, after accounting for socio-economic status.
* See notes at the beginning of this Annex.
StatLink ⟐🔗 http://dx.doi.org/10.1787/888932964908

[Part 1/1]

Change between 2003 and 2012 in the percentage of resilient students among disadvantaged students, by gender

Table II.2.7b   *Results based on students' self-reports*

	PISA 2003 Resilient students[1]				PISA 2012 Resilient students				Change between 2003 and 2012 (PISA 2012 - PISA 2003) Resilient students			
	All students	Boys	Girls	Difference (boys - girls)	All students	Boys	Girls	Difference (boys - girls)	All students	Boys	Girls	Difference (boys - girls)
	% (S.E.)	% (S.E.)	% (S.E.)	% dif. (S.E.)	% (S.E.)	% (S.E.)	% (S.E.)	% dif. (S.E.)	% dif. (S.E.)	% dif. (S.E.)	% dif. (S.E.)	% dif. (S.E.)
Australia	7.6 (0.4)	8.1 (0.6)	7.1 (0.5)	1.1 (0.8)	5.7 (0.3)	6.4 (0.4)	4.9 (0.4)	**1.5** (0.5)	**-1.9** (0.5)	0.8 (0.8)	0.6 (0.6)	0.4 (0.9)
Austria	6.2 (0.4)	6.9 (0.6)	5.6 (0.6)	1.3 (0.9)	5.6 (0.5)	6.3 (0.8)	4.9 (0.6)	1.4 (0.9)	-0.6 (0.7)	1.0 (1.0)	0.9 (0.9)	0.1 (1.3)
Belgium	7.8 (0.4)	7.4 (0.4)	8.2 (0.6)	-0.7 (0.7)	6.5 (0.4)	6.8 (0.5)	6.3 (0.5)	0.6 (0.7)	**-1.2** (0.5)	0.7 (0.7)	0.8 (0.8)	1.3 (1.0)
Canada	9.1 (0.4)	9.9 (0.4)	8.3 (0.6)	**1.6** (0.6)	7.5 (0.4)	8.4 (0.5)	6.7 (0.5)	**1.7** (0.6)	**-1.6** (0.6)	0.6 (0.6)	0.8 (0.8)	0.1 (0.8)
Czech Republic	6.1 (0.4)	6.5 (0.6)	5.6 (0.6)	1.0 (0.8)	5.3 (0.4)	6.1 (0.7)	4.5 (0.6)	1.6 (0.9)	-0.7 (0.6)	0.9 (0.9)	0.8 (0.8)	0.6 (1.3)
Denmark	6.2 (0.5)	6.7 (0.7)	5.7 (0.7)	1.0 (1.0)	4.5 (0.4)	5.1 (0.5)	3.8 (0.5)	**1.3** (0.6)	**-1.7** (0.7)	0.9 (0.9)	0.9 (0.9)	0.3 (1.2)
Finland	10.7 (0.6)	11.4 (0.8)	9.9 (0.7)	1.5 (0.9)	7.4 (0.4)	7.8 (0.6)	6.9 (0.8)	0.9 (0.9)	**-3.3** (0.8)	1.0 (1.0)	1.0 (1.0)	-0.6 (1.1)
France	7.4 (0.4)	7.9 (0.8)	6.9 (0.6)	1.1 (1.1)	4.9 (0.4)	5.6 (0.5)	4.3 (0.5)	1.2 (0.7)	**-2.5** (0.6)	0.9 (0.9)	0.8 (0.8)	0.2 (1.1)
Germany	5.6 (0.5)	7.2 (0.7)	4.1 (0.5)	**3.1** (0.8)	7.0 (0.5)	8.2 (0.8)	5.7 (0.6)	**2.5** (1.0)	**1.3** (0.7)	1.0 (1.0)	0.8 (0.8)	-0.6 (1.3)
Greece	2.5 (0.3)	3.1 (0.5)	2.0 (0.3)	**1.1** (0.5)	2.9 (0.4)	3.2 (0.5)	2.7 (0.5)	0.5 (0.6)	0.4 (0.5)	0.7 (0.7)	0.6 (0.6)	-0.6 (0.8)
Hungary	3.6 (0.3)	3.4 (0.4)	3.7 (0.5)	-0.3 (0.5)	3.7 (0.4)	4.1 (0.6)	3.4 (0.4)	0.7 (0.7)	0.1 (0.5)	0.7 (0.7)	0.6 (0.6)	1.0 (1.0)
Iceland	6.2 (0.4)	4.8 (0.6)	7.6 (0.7)	**-2.8** (1.0)	4.5 (0.4)	4.5 (0.6)	4.4 (0.5)	0.1 (0.7)	**-1.7** (0.6)	0.8 (0.8)	0.9 (0.9)	**2.9** (1.2)
Ireland	5.9 (0.5)	6.4 (0.7)	5.3 (0.5)	1.2 (0.9)	5.7 (0.4)	6.6 (0.6)	4.8 (0.5)	**1.8** (0.7)	-0.2 (0.6)	0.9 (0.9)	0.7 (0.7)	0.7 (1.1)
Italy	4.1 (0.3)	4.6 (0.4)	3.7 (0.4)	0.9 (0.5)	5.9 (0.2)	6.4 (0.3)	5.4 (0.3)	**1.0** (0.4)	**1.8** (0.4)	0.5 (0.5)	0.5 (0.5)	0.1 (0.6)
Japan	10.1 (0.7)	10.5 (0.8)	9.8 (0.9)	0.7 (0.9)	10.6 (0.5)	11.9 (0.8)	9.2 (0.7)	**2.7** (1.0)	0.5 (0.9)	1.1 (1.1)	1.1 (1.1)	2.0 (1.3)
Korea	11.4 (0.7)	12.1 (0.9)	10.3 (0.9)	1.8 (1.2)	12.0 (0.8)	11.6 (1.1)	12.4 (0.9)	-0.8 (1.2)	0.6 (1.0)	1.4 (1.4)	1.3 (1.3)	-2.7 (1.7)
Luxembourg	5.8 (0.4)	7.3 (0.7)	4.3 (0.5)	**3.0** (0.8)	5.7 (0.4)	7.0 (0.6)	4.3 (0.5)	**2.6** (0.7)	-0.1 (0.6)	0.9 (0.9)	0.7 (0.7)	-0.4 (1.0)
Mexico	1.7 (0.2)	1.9 (0.3)	1.5 (0.2)	0.4 (0.3)	4.2 (0.2)	4.6 (0.3)	3.9 (0.3)	**0.8** (0.3)	**2.5** (0.3)	0.4 (0.4)	0.4 (0.4)	0.4 (0.4)
Netherlands	9.7 (0.6)	9.5 (0.9)	10.0 (0.9)	-0.5 (1.4)	8.0 (0.8)	7.9 (0.8)	8.0 (1.1)	-0.1 (1.1)	-1.7 (1.0)	1.2 (1.2)	1.4 (1.4)	0.4 (1.5)
New Zealand	7.7 (0.5)	8.0 (0.8)	7.5 (0.7)	0.5 (1.1)	4.8 (0.4)	5.4 (0.6)	4.1 (0.6)	1.3 (0.8)	**-2.9** (0.7)	1.0 (1.0)	0.9 (0.9)	0.8 (1.4)
Norway	3.7 (0.4)	3.9 (0.5)	3.4 (0.5)	0.4 (0.7)	4.8 (0.4)	5.0 (0.5)	4.5 (0.5)	0.5 (0.6)	1.1 (0.6)	0.7 (0.7)	0.7 (0.7)	0.1 (0.9)
Poland	5.3 (0.4)	5.6 (0.5)	5.0 (0.6)	0.6 (0.8)	7.8 (0.6)	7.0 (0.8)	8.6 (0.7)	-1.6 (0.9)	**2.5** (0.8)	1.0 (1.0)	0.9 (0.9)	**-2.2** (1.0)
Portugal	7.5 (0.5)	7.5 (0.8)	7.5 (0.7)	0.0 (1.1)	7.4 (0.6)	8.1 (0.9)	6.8 (0.6)	1.3 (0.9)	-0.1 (0.8)	1.2 (1.2)	0.9 (0.9)	1.3 (1.4)
Slovak Republic	4.2 (0.4)	5.2 (0.6)	3.1 (0.4)	**2.0** (0.8)	3.6 (0.3)	3.7 (0.4)	3.4 (0.6)	0.4 (0.8)	-0.6 (0.5)	0.8 (0.8)	0.7 (0.7)	-1.7 (1.0)
Spain	8.1 (0.6)	8.6 (0.8)	7.5 (0.7)	1.1 (0.8)	6.0 (0.4)	6.7 (0.5)	5.2 (0.4)	**1.5** (0.6)	**-2.1** (0.7)	1.0 (1.0)	0.8 (0.8)	0.4 (1.0)
Sweden	6.7 (0.4)	6.6 (0.6)	6.7 (0.7)	-0.1 (1.0)	3.8 (0.3)	4.0 (0.4)	3.6 (0.5)	0.4 (0.7)	**-2.9** (0.5)	0.7 (0.7)	0.9 (0.9)	0.5 (1.2)
Switzerland	8.5 (0.6)	9.8 (0.7)	7.1 (0.7)	**2.7** (0.8)	9.3 (0.5)	10.9 (0.8)	7.6 (0.6)	**3.4** (0.8)	0.8 (0.8)	1.1 (1.1)	0.9 (0.9)	0.6 (1.1)
Turkey	3.1 (0.4)	4.0 (0.5)	2.0 (0.4)	**2.0** (0.6)	7.5 (0.5)	7.4 (0.6)	7.6 (0.7)	-0.2 (0.9)	**4.4** (0.6)	0.8 (0.8)	0.9 (0.9)	-2.2 (1.1)
United States	3.8 (0.3)	4.7 (0.5)	2.9 (0.4)	**1.8** (0.7)	4.7 (0.4)	5.3 (0.6)	4.0 (0.5)	1.3 (0.7)	0.9 (0.5)	0.8 (0.8)	0.7 (0.7)	-0.5 (1.0)
OECD average 2003	6.4 (0.1)	6.9 (0.1)	5.9 (0.1)	**0.9** (0.2)	6.1 (0.1)	6.6 (0.1)	5.6 (0.1)	**1.0** (0.1)	**-0.3** (0.1)	**0.9** (0.2)	**0.8** (0.2)	0.1 (0.2)
Brazil	2.1 (0.3)	2.0 (0.4)	2.2 (0.4)	-0.1 (0.5)	1.9 (0.2)	2.2 (0.3)	1.7 (0.3)	0.5 (0.4)	-0.2 (0.3)	0.5 (0.5)	0.5 (0.5)	0.7 (0.7)
Hong Kong-China	16.9 (0.9)	18.6 (1.2)	15.2 (1.2)	**3.4** (1.5)	18.1 (1.1)	17.6 (1.2)	18.5 (1.2)	-0.9 (1.2)	1.1 (1.4)	1.8 (1.8)	1.7 (1.7)	**-4.3** (2.0)
Indonesia	2.4 (0.3)	2.9 (0.5)	1.8 (0.4)	1.1 (0.6)	3.1 (0.5)	3.8 (0.8)	2.3 (0.5)	1.4 (0.9)	0.7 (0.6)	0.9 (0.9)	0.6 (0.6)	0.3 (1.1)
Latvia	5.3 (0.6)	5.9 (1.0)	4.6 (0.7)	1.3 (1.1)	5.7 (0.5)	5.6 (0.7)	5.8 (0.7)	-0.2 (1.0)	0.4 (0.8)	1.2 (1.2)	1.0 (1.0)	-1.5 (1.4)
Liechtenstein	9.5 (1.7)	c c	c c	c c	c c	c c	c c	c c	c c	c c	c c	c c
Macao-China	19.2 (1.2)	18.7 (1.8)	19.7 (2.0)	-1.0 (3.0)	16.6 (0.5)	17.9 (0.7)	15.3 (0.7)	**2.5** (1.0)	**-2.5** (1.3)	2.0 (2.0)	2.1 (2.1)	3.6 (3.2)
Russian Federation	5.9 (0.7)	6.2 (0.8)	5.5 (0.8)	0.7 (0.8)	4.7 (0.6)	5.2 (0.7)	4.2 (0.7)	0.9 (0.9)	-1.2 (0.9)	1.1 (1.1)	1.0 (1.0)	0.2 (1.2)
Thailand	8.2 (0.8)	7.9 (1.1)	8.5 (1.0)	-0.6 (1.2)	6.7 (0.6)	5.8 (0.6)	7.3 (0.7)	-1.5 (0.8)	-1.5 (1.0)	1.2 (1.2)	1.2 (1.2)	-0.9 (1.5)
Tunisia	1.9 (0.3)	2.3 (0.5)	1.5 (0.3)	0.8 (0.5)	3.3 (0.4)	4.6 (0.6)	2.2 (0.5)	**2.4** (0.7)	**1.5** (0.5)	0.8 (0.8)	0.6 (0.6)	1.6 (0.8)
Uruguay	3.5 (0.5)	3.2 (0.5)	3.9 (0.8)	-0.7 (0.9)	2.1 (0.3)	2.3 (0.4)	1.9 (0.3)	0.4 (0.4)	**-1.5** (0.6)	0.7 (0.7)	0.9 (0.9)	1.1 (1.1)

OECD (rows Australia–OECD average 2003); *Partners* (rows Brazil–Uruguay)

Notes: Values that are statistically significant are indicated in bold (see Annex A3).
Resiliency values for 2012 may differ from those shown in Table II.2.7a as the pooled reference population for resilient students used in this table is restricted to those countries and economies with comparable data from PISA 2003 and PISA 2012.
Only countries and economies with comparable data from PISA 2003 and PISA 2012 are shown.
1. A student is classified as resilient if he or she is in the bottom quarter of the *PISA index of economic, social and cultural status* (ESCS) in the country/economy of assessment and performs in the top quarter of students from all countries/economies, after accounting for socio-economic status.
StatLink http://dx.doi.org/10.1787/888932964908

[Part 1/1]
Variation in mathematics performance
Table II.2.8a *Results based on students' self-reports*

	Mean performance[1]		Total variation in mathematics performance[2]		Variation in mathematics performance between schools[3]		Variation in mathematics performance within schools[4]		As a percentage of the average total variation in mathematics performance across OECD countries			Index of academic inclusion[5]	
	Mean score	S.E.	Variance	S.E.	Variance	S.E.	Variance	S.E.	Total variance	Between schools variance	Within schools variance	Index	S.E.
OECD													
Australia	504	(1.6)	9 273	(228)	2 602	(228)	6 720	(106)	109.4	30.7	79.3	72.	(1.8)
Austria	506	(2.7)	8 554	(315)	4 080	(373)	4 346	(113)	100.9	48.1	51.3	51.	(2.4)
Belgium	515	(2.1)	10 459	(283)	5 366	(423)	5 075	(130)	123.3	63.3	59.8	48.	(2.3)
Canada	518	(1.8)	7 896	(143)	1 563	(134)	6 342	(116)	93.1	18.4	74.7	80.	(1.4)
Chile	423	(3.1)	6 522	(237)	2 817	(243)	3 669	(95)	76.9	33.2	43.3	56.	(2.2)
Czech Republic	499	(2.9)	9 016	(308)	4 544	(445)	4 285	(148)	106.3	53.6	50.5	48.	(2.8)
Denmark	500	(2.3)	6 741	(213)	1 100	(153)	5 582	(171)	79.5	13.0	65.8	83.	(2.0)
Estonia	521	(2.0)	6 546	(189)	1 129	(187)	5 412	(156)	77.2	13.3	63.8	82.	(2.4)
Finland	519	(1.9)	7 276	(198)	530	(93)	6 533	(153)	85.8	6.3	77.0	92.	(1.2)
France	495	(2.5)	9 500	(326)	w	w	w	w	112.0	w	w		w
Germany	514	(2.9)	9 275	(317)	4 890	(389)	4 333	(100)	109.4	57.7	51.1	47.	(2.1)
Greece	453	(2.5)	7 709	(235)	2 441	(305)	5 173	(127)	90.9	28.8	61.0	67.	(2.9)
Hungary	477	(3.2)	8 767	(450)	5 346	(532)	3 296	(84)	103.4	63.0	38.9	38.	(2.5)
Iceland	493	(1.7)	8 456	(241)	834	(144)	7 610	(320)	99.7	9.8	89.7	90.	(1.7)
Ireland	501	(2.2)	7 155	(213)	1 297	(191)	5 815	(139)	84.4	15.3	68.6	81.	(2.3)
Israel	466	(4.7)	11 008	(382)	4 659	(499)	6 320	(176)	129.8	54.9	74.5	57.	(2.8)
Italy	485	(2.0)	8 609	(213)	4 381	(215)	4 130	(56)	101.5	51.7	48.7	48.	(1.3)
Japan	536	(3.6)	8 748	(409)	4 620	(441)	4 094	(106)	103.2	54.5	48.3	47.	(2.5)
Korea	554	(4.6)	9 818	(426)	3 840	(482)	5 864	(180)	115.8	45.3	69.2	60.	(3.2)
Luxembourg	490	(1.1)	9 102	(182)	4 525	(2193)	6 516	(348)	107.3	53.4	76.8	59.	(11.0)
Mexico	413	(1.4)	5 516	(107)	1 940	(108)	3 578	(54)	65.1	22.9	42.2	64.	(1.3)
Netherlands	523	(3.5)	8 394	(385)	5 534	(474)	2 858	(94)	99.0	65.3	33.7	34.	(2.2)
New Zealand	500	(2.2)	9 923	(243)	2 387	(338)	7 658	(198)	117.0	28.2	90.3	76.	(2.7)
Norway	489	(2.7)	8 188	(240)	1 045	(168)	7 063	(176)	96.5	12.3	83.3	87.	(1.8)
Poland	518	(3.6)	8 168	(341)	1 659	(329)	6 433	(152)	96.3	19.6	75.9	79.	(3.4)
Portugal	487	(3.8)	8 828	(257)	2 653	(282)	6 212	(159)	104.1	31.3	73.3	70.	(2.5)
Slovak Republic	482	(3.4)	10 171	(496)	5 008	(536)	5 020	(163)	119.9	59.1	59.2	50.	(2.9)
Slovenia	501	(1.2)	8 404	(187)	4 904	(462)	3 453	(98)	99.1	57.8	40.7	41.	(2.5)
Spain	484	(1.9)	7 698	(129)	1 454	(117)	6 263	(112)	90.8	17.2	73.9	81.	(1.3)
Sweden	478	(2.3)	8 420	(235)	1 042	(168)	7 266	(177)	99.3	12.3	85.7	87.	(1.8)
Switzerland	531	(3.0)	8 892	(274)	3 196	(296)	5 771	(151)	104.9	37.7	68.1	64.	(2.3)
Turkey	448	(4.8)	8 296	(555)	5 140	(657)	3 173	(95)	97.8	60.6	37.4	38.	(3.3)
United Kingdom	494	(3.3)	8 935	(330)	2 517	(289)	6 421	(160)	105.4	29.7	75.7	71.	(2.5)
United States	481	(3.6)	8 077	(233)	1 916	(215)	6 164	(162)	95.2	22.6	72.7	76.	(2.2)
OECD average	494	(0.5)	8 481	(51)	3 126	(87)	5 372	(27)	100.0	36.9	63.3	64.	(0.5)
Partners													
Albania	394	(2.0)	8 372	(256)	380	(87)	7 958	(219)	98.7	4.5	93.9	95.	(1.0)
Argentina	388	(3.5)	5 891	(266)	2 597	(241)	3 253	(87)	69.5	30.6	38.4	55.	(2.3)
Brazil	391	(2.1)	6 041	(253)	2 623	(277)	3 457	(80)	71.2	30.9	40.8	56.	(2.7)
Bulgaria	439	(4.0)	8 821	(411)	4 647	(470)	4 160	(108)	104.0	54.8	49.1	47.	(2.7)
Colombia	376	(2.9)	5 527	(254)	1 953	(246)	3 618	(111)	65.2	23.0	42.7	64.	(2.9)
Costa Rica	407	(3.0)	4 674	(247)	1 984	(302)	2 700	(82)	55.1	23.4	31.8	57.	(3.8)
Croatia	471	(3.5)	7 829	(451)	3 466	(509)	4 360	(133)	92.3	40.9	51.4	55.	(3.9)
Cyprus*	440	(1.1)	8 675	(158)	2 791	(581)	5 814	(156)	102.3	32.9	68.6	67.	(4.8)
Hong Kong-China	561	(3.2)	9 277	(370)	3 924	(348)	5 330	(159)	109.4	46.3	62.9	57.	(2.2)
Indonesia	375	(4.0)	5 093	(463)	2 665	(438)	2 457	(75)	60.1	31.4	29.0	48.	(4.1)
Jordan	386	(3.1)	6 019	(413)	2 166	(378)	3 852	(98)	71.0	25.5	45.4	64.	(4.1)
Kazakhstan	432	(3.0)	5 067	(250)	1 861	(241)	3 234	(87)	59.7	21.9	38.1	63.	(3.1)
Latvia	491	(2.8)	6 705	(248)	1 691	(298)	4 908	(163)	79.1	19.9	57.9	74.	(3.6)
Liechtenstein	535	(4.0)	9 111	(710)	5 513	(1419)	3 305	(336)	107.1	65.0	39.0	37.	(6.8)
Lithuania	479	(2.6)	7 942	(243)	2 424	(286)	5 463	(138)	93.6	28.6	64.4	69.	(2.7)
Macao-China	538	(1.0)	8 929	(205)	3 568	(749)	6 385	(240)	105.3	42.1	75.3	64.	(4.4)
Malaysia	421	(3.2)	6 581	(263)	2 129	(284)	4 449	(143)	77.6	25.1	52.5	67.	(3.2)
Montenegro	410	(1.1)	6 835	(177)	2 485	(737)	4 324	(174)	80.6	29.3	51.0	63.	(7.3)
Peru	368	(3.7)	7 118	(371)	3 244	(364)	3 865	(103)	83.9	38.3	45.6	54.	(2.8)
Qatar	376	(0.8)	9 973	(148)	4 722	(661)	5 487	(307)	117.6	55.7	64.7	53.	(3.7)
Romania	445	(3.8)	6 618	(361)	2 986	(330)	3 591	(98)	78.0	35.2	42.3	54.	(2.8)
Russian Federation	482	(3.0)	7 461	(270)	2 018	(250)	5 502	(151)	88.0	23.8	64.9	71.	(2.6)
Serbia	449	(3.4)	8 225	(402)	3 776	(479)	4 431	(138)	97.0	44.5	52.3	54.	(3.3)
Shanghai-China	613	(3.3)	10 199	(460)	4 767	(473)	5 401	(205)	120.3	56.2	63.7	53.	(2.7)
Singapore	573	(1.3)	11 102	(194)	4 070	(503)	7 033	(213)	130.9	48.0	82.9	63.	(3.2)
Chinese Taipei	560	(3.3)	13 368	(444)	5 613	(632)	7 710	(259)	157.6	66.2	90.9	57.9	(3.2)
Thailand	427	(3.4)	6 759	(353)	2 866	(354)	3 941	(107)	79.7	33.8	46.5	57.9	(3.0)
Tunisia	388	(3.9)	6 113	(480)	3 017	(486)	3 104	(82)	72.1	35.6	36.6	51.7	(4.1)
United Arab Emirates	434	(2.4)	8 014	(213)	3 559	(312)	4 453	(106)	94.5	42.0	52.5	55.6	(2.2)
Uruguay	409	(2.8)	7 869	(307)	3 297	(376)	4 546	(121)	92.8	38.9	53.6	55.0	(3.0)
Viet Nam	511	(4.8)	7 357	(455)	3 823	(476)	3 509	(110)	86.7	45.1	41.4	48.9	(3.2)

1. The statistics computed for this table were estimated for all students, whether they had data on socio-economic status or not.
2. The total variation in student performance is calculated from the square of the standard deviation for all students.
3. In some countries, sub-units within schools were sampled instead of schools; this may affect the estimation of between-school variation components (see Annex A3).
4. Due to the unbalanced clustered nature of the data, the sum of the between- and within-school variation components, as an estimate from a sample, does not necessarily add up to the total.
5. The *index of academic inclusion* is calculated as 100*(1-rho), where rho stands for the intra-class correlation of performance, i.e. the variation in student performance between schools, divided by the sum of the variation in student performance between schools and the variation in student performance within schools.
* See notes at the beginning of this Annex.
StatLink http://dx.doi.org/10.1787/888932964908

[Part 1/3]
Change between 2003 and 2012 in the variation in mathematics performance
Table II.2.8b   *Results based on students' self-reports*

		Mean performance[1]		Total variation in mathematics performance[2]		Variation in mathematics performance between schools[3]		Variation in mathematics performance within schools[4]		Index of academic inclusion[5]	
		Mean score	S.E.	Variance	S.E.	Variance	S.E.	Variance	S.E.	Index	S.E.
OECD	Australia	524	(2.1)	9 106	(286)	1 957	(233)	7 138	(117)	78.5	(2.1)
	Austria	506	(3.3)	8 668	(311)	4 237	(348)	4 290	(127)	50.3	(2.2)
	Belgium	529	(2.3)	12 076	(391)	6 251	(606)	5 718	(134)	47.8	(2.6)
	Canada	532	(1.8)	7 588	(170)	1 301	(121)	6 290	(128)	82.9	(1.4)
	Czech Republic	516	(3.5)	9 207	(358)	4 460	(452)	4 690	(139)	51.3	(2.8)
	Denmark	514	(2.7)	8 341	(264)	1 015	(175)	7 308	(211)	87.8	(1.9)
	Finland	544	(1.9)	7 004	(180)	318	(61)	6 664	(164)	95.4	(0.8)
	France	511	(2.5)	8 410	(329)	w	w	w	w	w	w
	Germany	503	(3.3)	10 528	(363)	5 991	(582)	4 484	(140)	42.8	(2.6)
	Greece	445	(3.9)	8 806	(329)	2 824	(397)	5 872	(186)	67.5	(3.3)
	Hungary	490	(2.8)	8 746	(366)	4 488	(438)	4 065	(89)	47.5	(2.5)
	Iceland	515	(1.4)	8 168	(218)	307	(108)	8 152	(363)	96.4	(1.2)
	Ireland	503	(2.4)	7 270	(214)	1 081	(168)	6 124	(145)	85.0	(2.0)
	Italy	466	(3.1)	9 158	(359)	4 522	(389)	4 528	(90)	50.0	(2.2)
	Japan	534	(4.0)	10 110	(553)	5 350	(595)	4 738	(163)	47.0	(2.9)
	Korea	542	(3.2)	8 536	(394)	3 523	(422)	4 972	(120)	58.5	(3.1)
	Luxembourg	493	(1.0)	8 440	(175)	4 196	(2622)	6 143	(493)	59.4	(16.0)
	Mexico	385	(3.6)	7 301	(316)	3 253	(303)	4 020	(115)	55.3	(2.4)
	Netherlands	538	(3.1)	8 562	(432)	5 198	(502)	3 343	(112)	39.1	(2.6)
	New Zealand	523	(2.3)	9 664	(229)	1 677	(234)	7 988	(217)	82.6	(2.1)
	Norway	495	(2.4)	8 473	(212)	557	(101)	7 925	(210)	93.4	(1.1)
	Poland	490	(2.5)	8 145	(242)	980	(148)	7 149	(171)	87.9	(1.6)
	Portugal	466	(3.4)	7 681	(292)	2 481	(308)	5 216	(151)	67.8	(2.9)
	Slovak Republic	498	(3.3)	8 708	(432)	3 634	(350)	4 866	(157)	57.2	(2.5)
	Spain	485	(2.4)	7 828	(223)	1 746	(211)	6 066	(154)	77.6	(2.2)
	Sweden	509	(2.6)	8 979	(340)	831	(211)	8 133	(250)	90.7	(2.2)
	Switzerland	527	(3.4)	9 680	(403)	3 532	(424)	6 098	(212)	63.3	(3.1)
	Turkey	423	(6.7)	10 973	(1116)	6 006	(1243)	4 890	(167)	44.9	(5.4)
	United States	483	(2.9)	9 074	(245)	2 198	(261)	6 807	(154)	75.6	(2.3)
	OECD average 2003	500	(0.6)	8 801	(70)	3 027	(118)	5 800	(35)	66.8	(0.7)
Partners	Brazil	356	(4.8)	9 946	(588)	4 754	(650)	5 261	(144)	52.5	(3.5)
	Hong Kong-China	550	(4.5)	10 040	(602)	4 806	(499)	5 184	(197)	51.9	(2.3)
	Indonesia	360	(3.9)	6 483	(332)	3 066	(397)	3 409	(94)	52.7	(3.4)
	Latvia	483	(3.7)	7 729	(292)	1 554	(210)	5 994	(180)	79.4	(2.3)
	Liechtenstein	536	(4.1)	9 846	(879)	5 235	(1442)	4 644	(609)	47.0	(6.7)
	Macao-China	527	(2.9)	7 566	(420)	1 163	(289)	6 410	(468)	84.6	(3.8)
	Russian Federation	468	(4.2)	8 513	(356)	2 534	(336)	6 017	(176)	70.4	(2.9)
	Thailand	417	(3.0)	6 718	(295)	2 325	(288)	4 480	(126)	65.8	(2.8)
	Tunisia	359	(2.5)	6 721	(320)	2 844	(345)	3 881	(110)	57.7	(3.1)
	Uruguay	422	(3.3)	9 938	(320)	3 959	(356)	5 920	(155)	59.9	(2.3)

Notes: Values that are statistically significant are indicated in bold (see Annex A3).
Only countries and economies with comparable data from PISA 2003 and PISA 2012 are shown.
1. The statistics computed for this table were estimated for all students, whether they had data on socio-economic status or not.
2. The total variation in student performance is calculated from the square of the standard deviation for all students.
3. In some countries, sub-units within schools were sampled instead of schools; this may affect the estimation of between-school variation components (see Annex A3).
4. Due to the unbalanced clustered nature of the data, the sum of the between- and within-school variation components, as an estimate from a sample, does not necessarily add up to the total.
5. The *index of academic inclusion* is calculated as 100*(1-rho), where rho stands for the intra-class correlation of performance, i.e. the variation in student performance between schools, divided by the sum of the variation in student performance between schools and the variation in student performance within schools.
StatLink http://dx.doi.org/10.1787/888932964908

[Part 2/3]
Change between 2003 and 2012 in the variation in mathematics performance

Table II.2.8b   *Results based on students' self-reports*

		Mean performance[1]		Total variation in mathematics performance[2]		Variation in mathematics performance between schools[3]		Variation in mathematics performance within schools[4]		Index of academic inclusion[5]	
		PISA 2012									
		Mean score	S.E.	Variance	S.E.	Variance	S.E.	Variance	S.E.	Index	S.E.
OECD	Australia	504	(1.6)	9 273	(228)	2 602	(228)	6 720	(106)	72.1	(1.8)
	Austria	506	(2.7)	8 554	(315)	4 080	(373)	4 346	(113)	51.6	(2.4)
	Belgium	515	(2.1)	10 459	(283)	5 366	(423)	5 075	(130)	48.6	(2.3)
	Canada	518	(1.8)	7 896	(143)	1 563	(134)	6 342	(116)	80.2	(1.4)
	Czech Republic	499	(2.9)	9 016	(308)	4 544	(445)	4 285	(148)	48.5	(2.8)
	Denmark	500	(2.3)	6 741	(213)	1 100	(153)	5 582	(171)	83.5	(2.0)
	Finland	519	(1.9)	7 276	(198)	530	(93)	6 533	(153)	92.5	(1.2)
	France	495	(2.5)	9 500	(326)	w	w	w	w	w	w
	Germany	514	(2.9)	9 275	(317)	4 890	(389)	4 333	(100)	47.0	(2.1)
	Greece	453	(2.5)	7 709	(235)	2 441	(305)	5 173	(127)	67.9	(2.9)
	Hungary	477	(3.2)	8 767	(450)	5 346	(532)	3 296	(84)	38.1	(2.5)
	Iceland	493	(1.7)	8 456	(241)	834	(144)	7 610	(320)	90.1	(1.7)
	Ireland	501	(2.2)	7 155	(213)	1 297	(191)	5 815	(139)	81.8	(2.3)
	Italy	485	(2.0)	8 609	(213)	4 381	(215)	4 130	(56)	48.5	(1.3)
	Japan	536	(3.6)	8 748	(409)	4 620	(441)	4 094	(106)	47.0	(2.5)
	Korea	554	(4.6)	9 818	(426)	3 840	(482)	5 864	(180)	60.4	(3.2)
	Luxembourg	490	(1.1)	9 102	(182)	4 525	(2193)	6 516	(348)	59.0	(11.0)
	Mexico	413	(1.4)	5 516	(107)	1 940	(108)	3 578	(54)	64.8	(1.3)
	Netherlands	523	(3.5)	8 394	(385)	5 534	(474)	2 858	(94)	34.1	(2.2)
	New Zealand	500	(2.2)	9 923	(243)	2 387	(338)	7 658	(198)	76.2	(2.7)
	Norway	489	(2.7)	8 188	(240)	1 045	(168)	7 063	(176)	87.1	(1.8)
	Poland	518	(3.6)	8 168	(341)	1 659	(329)	6 433	(152)	79.5	(3.4)
	Portugal	487	(3.8)	8 828	(257)	2 653	(282)	6 212	(159)	70.1	(2.5)
	Slovak Republic	482	(3.4)	10 171	(496)	5 008	(536)	5 020	(163)	50.1	(2.9)
	Spain	484	(1.9)	7 698	(129)	1 454	(117)	6 263	(112)	81.2	(1.3)
	Sweden	478	(2.3)	8 420	(235)	1 042	(168)	7 266	(177)	87.5	(1.8)
	Switzerland	531	(3.0)	8 892	(274)	3 196	(296)	5 771	(151)	64.4	(2.3)
	Turkey	448	(4.8)	8 296	(555)	5 140	(657)	3 173	(95)	38.2	(3.3)
	United States	481	(3.6)	8 077	(233)	1 916	(215)	6 164	(162)	76.3	(2.2)
	OECD average 2003	494	(0.5)	8 481	(51)	3 117	(86)	5 372	(27)	64.2	(0.5)
Partners	Brazil	391	(2.1)	6 041	(253)	2 623	(277)	3 457	(80)	56.9	(2.7)
	Hong Kong-China	561	(3.2)	9 277	(370)	3 924	(348)	5 330	(159)	57.6	(2.2)
	Indonesia	375	(4.0)	5 093	(463)	2 665	(438)	2 457	(75)	48.0	(4.1)
	Latvia	491	(2.8)	6 705	(248)	1 691	(298)	4 908	(163)	74.4	(3.6)
	Liechtenstein	535	(4.0)	9 111	(710)	5 513	(1419)	3 305	(336)	37.5	(6.8)
	Macao-China	538	(1.0)	8 931	(177)	4 442	(4943)	6 181	(254)	58.2	(27.3)
	Russian Federation	482	(3.0)	7 461	(270)	2 018	(250)	5 502	(151)	73.2	(2.6)
	Thailand	427	(3.4)	6 759	(353)	2 866	(354)	3 941	(107)	57.9	(3.0)
	Tunisia	388	(3.9)	6 113	(480)	3 017	(486)	3 104	(82)	50.7	(4.1)
	Uruguay	409	(2.8)	7 869	(307)	3 297	(376)	4 546	(121)	58.0	(3.0)

Notes: Values that are statistically significant are indicated in bold (see Annex A3).
Only countries and economies with comparable data from PISA 2003 and PISA 2012 are shown.
1. The statistics computed for this table were estimated for all students, whether they had data on socio-economic status or not.
2. The total variation in student performance is calculated from the square of the standard deviation for all students.
3. In some countries/economies, sub-units within schools were sampled instead of schools; this may affect the estimation of between-school variation components (see Annex A3).
4. Due to the unbalanced clustered nature of the data, the sum of the between- and within-school variation components, as an estimate from a sample, does not necessarily add up to the total.
5. The *index of academic inclusion* is calculated as 100*(1-rho), where rho stands for the intra-class correlation of performance, i.e. the variation in student performance between schools, divided by the sum of the variation in student performance between schools and the variation in student performance within schools.
StatLink ⟐⟐⟐ http://dx.doi.org/10.1787/888932964908

[Part 3/3]
Change between 2003 and 2012 in the variation in mathematics performance

Table II.2.8b   *Results based on students' self-reports*

		Change between 2003 and 2012 (PISA 2012 - PISA 2003)									Change between 2003 and 2012 as a percentage of 2003 variation (PISA 2012 - PISA 2003) / PISA 2003		
		Mean performance[1]		Total variation in mathematics performance[2]		Variation in mathematics performance between schools[3]		Variation in mathematics performance within schools[4]		Index of academic inclusion[5]		Total variation	Between-school variation	Within-school variation
		Score dif.	S.E.	Var. dif.	S.E.	Var. dif.	S.E.	Var. dif.	S.E.	Dif.	S.E.	Change as %	Change as %	Change as %
OECD	Australia	**-20**	(2.7)	167	(366)	**644**	(326)	**-418**	(158)	**-6.4**	(2.8)	1.8	32.9	-5.9
	Austria	0	(4.2)	-114	(443)	-157	(510)	55	(171)	1.3	(3.3)	-1.3	-3.7	1.3
	Belgium	**-15**	(3.1)	**-1 617**	(483)	-885	(739)	**-644**	(187)	0.8	(3.4)	-13.4	-14.2	-11.3
	Canada	**-14**	(2.6)	308	(222)	262	(181)	52	(172)	-2.6	(2.0)	4.1	20.1	0.8
	Czech Republic	**-17**	(4.6)	-191	(472)	84	(634)	**-405**	(203)	-2.7	(4.0)	-2.1	1.9	-8.6
	Denmark	**-14**	(3.6)	**-1 600**	(339)	85	(233)	**-1 725**	(272)	-4.3	(2.8)	-19.2	8.4	-23.6
	Finland	**-26**	(2.7)	272	(268)	212	(111)	-131	(225)	**-3.0**	(1.5)	3.9	66.8	-2.0
	France	**-16**	(3.5)	**1 089**	(463)	w	w	w	w	w	w	13.0	w	w
	Germany	11	(4.4)	**-1 253**	(482)	**-1 101**	(700)	-151	(172)	4.2	(3.4)	-11.9	-18.4	-3.4
	Greece	8	(4.6)	**-1 097**	(404)	-383	(501)	**-699**	(226)	0.4	(4.4)	-12.5	-13.6	-11.9
	Hungary	**-13**	(4.3)	20	(580)	858	(689)	**-769**	(122)	**-9.4**	(3.5)	0.2	19.1	-18.9
	Iceland	**-22**	(2.2)	288	(325)	**527**	(180)	-543	(483)	**-6.2**	(2.1)	3.5	171.5	-6.7
	Ireland	-1	(3.3)	-116	(302)	215	(254)	-309	(201)	-3.2	(3.0)	-1.6	19.9	-5.0
	Italy	20	(3.7)	-549	(417)	-140	(444)	-398	(106)	-1.5	(2.6)	-6.0	-3.1	-8.8
	Japan	2	(5.4)	**-1 362**	(688)	-730	(740)	**-644**	(194)	0.0	(3.8)	-13.5	-13.6	-13.6
	Korea	12	(5.6)	**1 282**	(581)	317	(640)	**892**	(216)	1.9	(4.5)	15.0	9.0	17.9
	Luxembourg	-3	(1.5)	**662**	(252)	329	(3 418)	373	(603)	-0.4	(19.4)	7.8	7.9	6.1
	Mexico	28	(3.9)	**-1 785**	(334)	**-1 314**	(322)	-442	(128)	**9.6**	(2.8)	-24.4	-40.4	-11.0
	Netherlands	**-15**	(4.7)	-167	(579)	336	(690)	-484	(147)	-5.1	(3.4)	-2.0	6.5	-14.5
	New Zealand	**-24**	(3.2)	260	(334)	710	(411)	-330	(294)	-6.4	(3.4)	2.7	42.4	-4.1
	Norway	-6	(3.6)	-285	(321)	**488**	(196)	**-863**	(275)	**-6.3**	(2.2)	-3.4	87.7	-10.9
	Poland	27	(4.4)	23	(418)	679	(361)	**-716**	(229)	**-8.5**	(3.8)	0.3	69.4	-10.0
	Portugal	21	(5.1)	**1 147**	(389)	172	(417)	**996**	(219)	2.3	(3.8)	14.9	6.9	19.1
	Slovak Republic	**-17**	(4.8)	**1 463**	(658)	**1 373**	(640)	154	(227)	-7.2	(3.8)	16.8	37.8	3.2
	Spain	-1	(3.1)	-130	(258)	-292	(241)	197	(190)	3.5	(2.5)	-1.7	-16.7	3.2
	Sweden	**-31**	(3.4)	-559	(413)	211	(270)	**-866**	(307)	-3.3	(2.8)	-6.2	25.4	-10.7
	Switzerland	4	(4.5)	-789	(487)	-337	(517)	-327	(260)	1.0	(3.9)	-8.1	-9.5	-5.4
	Turkey	25	(8.3)	**-2 677**	(1 246)	-865	(1 406)	**-1 717**	(192)	-6.7	(6.3)	-24.4	-14.4	-35.1
	United States	-2	(4.7)	**-997**	(338)	-282	(338)	**-642**	(223)	0.7	(3.2)	-11.0	-12.8	-9.4
	OECD average 2003	**-4**	(0.8)	**-263**	(88)	84	(148)	**-359**	(45)	**-2.3**	(0.9)	-2.5	17.3	-6.2
Partners	Brazil	35	(5.3)	**-3 905**	(640)	**-2 131**	(706)	**-1 805**	(165)	4.3	(4.4)	-39.3	-44.8	-34.3
	Hong Kong-China	11	(5.6)	-762	(707)	-882	(608)	146	(253)	5.7	(3.2)	-7.6	-18.3	2.8
	Indonesia	15	(5.6)	**-1 390**	(570)	-401	(591)	**-952**	(120)	-4.7	(5.3)	-21.4	-13.1	-27.9
	Latvia	7	(4.6)	**-1 024**	(383)	137	(364)	**-1 086**	(243)	-5.0	(4.3)	-13.2	8.8	-18.1
	Liechtenstein	-1	(5.7)	-735	(1130)	278	(2023)	**-1 339**	(695)	-9.5	(9.5)	-7.5	5.3	-28.8
	Macao-China	11	(3.0)	**1 365**	(455)	3279	(4952)	-230	(532)	-26.5	(27.5)	18.0	282.0	-3.6
	Russian Federation	14	(5.2)	**-1 051**	(447)	-516	(418)	**-515**	(232)	2.8	(3.9)	-12.4	-20.4	-8.6
	Thailand	10	(4.6)	41	(460)	541	(456)	**-539**	(166)	-7.9	(4.1)	0.6	23.3	-12.0
	Tunisia	29	(4.7)	-608	(577)	173	(596)	**-777**	(137)	-7.0	(5.1)	-9.1	6.1	-20.0
	Uruguay	**-13**	(4.3)	**-2 069**	(443)	-662	(518)	**-1 374**	(197)	-2.0	(3.7)	-20.8	-16.7	-23.2

Notes: Values that are statistically significant are indicated in bold (see Annex A3).
Only countries and economies with comparable data from PISA 2003 and PISA 2012 are shown.
1. The statistics computed for this table were estimated for all students, whether they had data on socio-economic status or not.
2. The total variation in student performance is calculated from the square of the standard deviation for all students.
3. In some countries/economies, sub-units within schools were sampled instead of schools; this may affect the estimation of between-school variation components (see Annex A3).
4. Due to the unbalanced clustered nature of the data, the sum of the between- and within-school variation components, as an estimate from a sample, does not necessarily add up to the total.
5. The *index of academic inclusion* is calculated as 100*(1-rho), where rho stands for the intra-class correlation of performance, i.e. the variation in student performance between schools, divided by the sum of the variation in student performance between schools and the variation in student performance within schools.
StatLink ⟨⟨⟨ http://dx.doi.org/10.1787/888932964908

[Part 1/2]
Relationship between mathematics performance and socio-economic status, between and within schools[1]

Table II.2.9a *Results based on students' self-reports*

	Overall association of ESCS[2] and mathematics performance		Within-school association of ESCS and mathematics performance[3]		Between-school association of ESCS and mathematics performance[4]		Percentage of the overall variation in mathematics performance explained by students' ESCS			Percentage of the overall variation in mathematics performance explained by students' and schools' ESCS		
	Student-level score-point difference associated with one-unit increase in the student-level ESCS	S.E.	Student-level score-point difference associated with one-unit increase in the student-level ESCS	S.E.	School-level score-point difference associated with one-unit increase in the school mean ESCS	S.E.	Overall	Between school	Within school	Overall	Between school	Within school
OECD												
Australia	42	(1.3)	25	(1.6)	64	(4.1)	12.3	31.2	6.0	18.1	55.	6.1
Austria	43	(2.2)	15	(1.6)	85	(5.9)	15.8	17.4	3.4	29.7	56.	3.5
Belgium	49	(1.7)	19	(1.5)	102	(6.0)	19.6	22.5	4.8	37.3	70.	4.8
Canada	31	(1.2)	23	(1.2)	41	(5.0)	9.4	27.0	7.5	12.1	41.	7.5
Chile	34	(1.6)	9	(1.3)	46	(2.3)	23.1	29.1	1.3	33.4	75.	1.4
Czech Republic	51	(2.7)	14	(1.7)	127	(6.5)	16.2	15.3	2.1	36.7	70.	2.1
Denmark	39	(1.7)	31	(1.7)	38	(4.2)	16.5	53.9	10.5	19.3	70.	10.6
Estonia	29	(1.7)	19	(1.7)	45	(6.9)	8.6	31.5	4.2	11.5	58.	4.0
Finland	33	(1.8)	29	(1.5)	22	(6.9)	9.4	33.5	9.7	10.1	38.	9.8
France	57	(2.2)	w	w	w	w	22.5	w	w	41.8		w
Germany	43	(2.0)	11	(1.4)	103	(5.6)	16.9	13.8	0.5	38.2	71.	0.4
Greece	34	(1.8)	18	(1.5)	55	(5.1)	15.5	30.6	4.7	23.7	65.	4.7
Hungary	47	(2.8)	6	(1.4)	98	(4.9)	23.1	12.1	1.2	46.9	78.	1.1
Iceland	31	(2.1)	25	(2.9)	45	(8.3)	7.7	41.5	6.0	9.3	68.	5.9
Ireland	38	(1.8)	26	(1.7)	52	(4.7)	14.6	47.8	6.8	19.7	79.	6.9
Israel	51	(2.6)	24	(2.1)	98	(7.9)	17.2	25.8	5.2	30.1	66.	5.2
Italy	30	(1.2)	7	(0.7)	83	(4.1)	10.1	8.1	1.7	25.7	48.	1.7
Japan	41	(3.9)	4	(1.7)	150	(8.2)	9.8	5.9	1.8	34.2	65.	1.8
Korea	42	(3.3)	14	(2.0)	114	(10.2)	10.1	13.2	1.5	23.2	57.	1.5
Luxembourg	37	(1.2)	20	(2.7)	68	(4.9)	18.3	57.0	6.8	31.2	93.	6.7
Mexico	19	(0.8)	5	(0.5)	29	(1.4)	10.4	16.6	0.8	16.6	46.	0.9
Netherlands	40	(3.1)	9	(1.6)	147	(10.9)	11.5	7.1	1.5	37.7	57.	1.5
New Zealand	52	(1.9)	36	(2.3)	66	(6.8)	18.4	50.7	9.8	24.1	78.	9.9
Norway	32	(2.4)	27	(2.2)	49	(7.8)	7.4	29.5	5.6	9.0	46.	5.6
Poland	41	(2.4)	32	(1.8)	36	(7.4)	16.6	41.7	9.5	19.4	56.	9.5
Portugal	35	(1.6)	23	(1.4)	33	(4.0)	19.6	43.8	9.6	23.7	62	9.6
Slovak Republic	54	(2.9)	21	(2.1)	86	(6.4)	24.6	28.0	4.7	37.5	73.	4.6
Slovenia	42	(1.5)	3	(1.5)	126	(5.6)	15.6	5.3	0.2	44.1	77.	0.1
Spain	34	(1.1)	27	(1.0)	26	(3.2)	15.8	42.8	10.3	17.8	54.	10.4
Sweden	36	(1.9)	28	(2.0)	41	(7.3)	10.6	40.5	9.7	12.8	55.	9.8
Switzerland	38	(1.8)	25	(1.5)	66	(8.9)	12.8	21.3	7.2	19.4	44.	7.2
Turkey	32	(2.4)	6	(1.0)	83	(7.4)	14.5	8.6	1.3	35.8	57.	1.4
United Kingdom	41	(2.4)	24	(1.7)	73	(6.5)	12.5	33.2	6.4	19.7	63.	6.4
United States	35	(1.7)	24	(1.9)	41	(5.4)	14.8	36.7	6.7	18.8	57.	6.8
OECD average	39	(0.4)	19	(0.3)	72	(1.1)	14.8	27.8	5.1	25.5	62.	5.2
Partners												
Albania	m	m	m	m	m	m	m	m	m	m		m
Argentina	26	(1.7)	9	(1.2)	49	(5.7)	15.1	22.4	2.4	26.9	62	2.4
Brazil	26	(1.7)	8	(0.8)	46	(3.0)	15.7	20.2	2.0	27.1	61	2.0
Bulgaria	42	(2.7)	12	(1.4)	73	(5.7)	22.3	21.2	2.5	37.7	72	2.5
Colombia	25	(1.7)	11	(1.2)	35	(3.6)	15.4	28.6	3.0	22.8	60	3.0
Costa Rica	24	(1.6)	10	(1.0)	34	(3.6)	18.9	28.6	3.5	27.9	61	3.5
Croatia	36	(2.6)	12	(1.6)	90	(9.2)	12.0	14.4	2.3	26.6	58	2.3
Cyprus*	38	(1.6)	20	(1.9)	72	(11.2)	14.1	0.0	6.0	23.5	62	6.0
Hong Kong-China	27	(2.6)	4	(1.5)	65	(7.9)	7.5	8.0	0.6	17.3	41	0.7
Indonesia	20	(3.4)	6	(1.0)	37	(6.0)	9.6	8.8	1.3	17.5	32	1.3
Jordan	22	(2.2)	11	(1.3)	47	(8.5)	8.4	18.6	4.8	15.3	42	4.8
Kazakhstan	27	(2.8)	15	(1.6)	45	(8.0)	8.0	13.3	3.2	12.2	29	3.1
Latvia	35	(2.1)	22	(1.6)	46	(5.7)	14.7	35.2	5.5	19.3	62	5.5
Liechtenstein	28	(5.8)	8	(5.3)	132	(53.5)	7.6	8.3	2.2	28.3	51	2.2
Lithuania	36	(1.8)	19	(1.5)	66	(5.8)	13.8	27.5	4.5	22.5	63	4.5
Macao-China	17	(1.5)	7	(1.5)	31	(12.2)	2.6	4.9	4.7	5.1	14	5.8
Malaysia	30	(2.1)	15	(1.5)	49	(5.8)	13.4	26.3	3.7	21.0	57	3.8
Montenegro	33	(1.3)	12	(1.8)	102	(6.0)	12.7	18.7	2.4	31.8	85	2.4
Peru	33	(2.0)	10	(1.1)	49	(2.6)	23.4	28.9	1.9	35.9	78	1.9
Qatar	27	(1.2)	10	(2.3)	73	(13.1)	5.6	0.0	1.6	14.0	29	1.7
Romania	38	(2.9)	17	(1.6)	57	(6.3)	19.3	27.2	4.4	29.6	61	4.5
Russian Federation	38	(3.2)	26	(2.2)	47	(7.0)	11.4	26.4	5.1	14.3	44	5.0
Serbia	34	(2.4)	9	(1.5)	101	(7.0)	11.7	11.9	1.0	30.8	65	1.0
Shanghai-China	41	(2.7)	10	(1.8)	88	(6.2)	15.1	14.4	1.5	31.2	65	1.6
Singapore	44	(1.4)	22	(1.8)	85	(11.5)	14.4	23.9	4.4	25.0	62	4.4
Chinese Taipei	58	(2.5)	27	(1.9)	123	(9.0)	17.9	0.0	5.2	33.3	72	5.3
Thailand	22	(2.4)	9	(1.2)	35	(5.2)	9.9	15.5	1.6	15.4	40	1.5
Tunisia	22	(2.6)	6	(1.0)	45	(5.5)	12.4	11.6	2.1	24.3	44	2.1
United Arab Emirates	33	(1.9)	12	(1.4)	71	(7.3)	9.8	12.5	1.9	19.2	46	1.9
Uruguay	37	(1.8)	15	(1.2)	52	(3.3)	22.8	33.8	4.2	33.8	71	4.3
Viet Nam	29	(2.6)	8	(1.3)	49	(6.5)	14.6	13.8	1.3	24.9	49	1.4

Note: Values that are statistically significant are indicated in bold (see Annex A3).
1. In some countries, sub-units within schools were sampled instead of schools as administrative units; this may affect the estimation of school-level effects (see Annex A3).
2. ESCS refers to the *PISA index of economic, social and cultural status*.
3. Two-level regression of mathematics performance on student ESCS and school mean ESCS: within-school slope for ESCS and student-level variation explained by the model.
4. Two-level regression of mathematics performance on student ESCS and school mean ESCS: between-school slope for ESCS and school-level variation explained by the model.
5. Two-level regression of mathematics performance on student-level ESCS, student-level ESCS squared, school mean ESCS, and school mean ESCS squared. The within-school index of curvilinearity corresponds to the coefficient of student-level ESCS squared.
6. Two-level regression of mathematics performance on student ESCS, student ESCS squared, school mean ESCS and school mean ESCS squared: between-school index of curvilinearity corresponds to the coefficient of school mean ESCS squared.

StatLink ⟪⟫ http://dx.doi.org/10.1787/888932964908

[Part 2/2]
Relationship between mathematics performance and socio-economic status, between and within schools[1]

Table II.2.9a   *Results based on students' self-reports*

	Within-school index of curvilinearity of ESCS[5]		Between-school index of curvilinearity of ESCS[6]		Percentage of the overall variation in mathematics performance explained by students' study programmes		Percentage of the overall variation in mathematics performance explained by students' study programmes and students' and schools' ESCS	
	Student-level score-point difference associated with one-unit increase in the student-level ESCS	S.E.	School-level score-point difference associated with one-unit increase in the school mean ESCS	S.E.	Between school	Within school	Between school	Within school
Australia	0	(1.1)	11	(6.5)	7.6	4.6	58.6	8.9
Austria	-3	(1.3)	**-24**	(7.7)	65.0	1.7	72.1	4.2
Belgium	1	(1.0)	3	(8.3)	79.0	19.9	88.9	21.3
Canada	1	(1.0)	9	(9.5)	0.4	6.2	33.4	10.7
Chile	-1	(0.7)	4	(2.0)	8.4	3.2	78.0	4.6
Czech Republic	-4	(1.8)	-1	(10.1)	47.1	1.6	75.7	3.5
Denmark	1	(1.3)	-2	(7.7)	7.3	0.7	70.8	10.6
Estonia	2	(1.9)	**48**	(8.6)	0.0	0.0	58.0	4.0
Finland	1	(1.4)	-3	(10.9)	0.0	0.0	38.3	9.8
France	w	w	w	w	w	w	w	w
Germany	-2	(1.3)	-14	(8.3)	82.1	0.8	85.3	2.5
Greece	1	(1.1)	-2	(5.4)	59.8	0.4	80.8	4.7
Hungary	-1	(1.1)	**13**	(4.9)	62.1	0.8	82.7	1.4
Iceland	1	(2.1)	25	(16.2)	0.0	0.0	68.8	5.9
Ireland	2	(1.5)	**-25**	(6.4)	-1.7	3.3	76.4	9.5
Israel	3	(1.4)	9	(14.2)	4.7	3.0	68.1	7.2
Italy	0	(0.6)	**-25**	(5.4)	39.9	0.8	54.6	1.7
Japan	-1	(1.7)	-7	(17.7)	13.1	1.7	66.9	1.8
Korea	4	(1.8)	-4	(20.7)	35.2	0.2	61.3	1.8
Luxembourg	0	(0.9)	3	(9.7)	82.4	37.1	91.8	37.8
Mexico	0	(0.3)	2	(1.0)	26.4	0.2	58.5	0.9
Netherlands	1	(1.0)	-38	(23.5)	87.7	22.4	88.1	22.8
New Zealand	-1	(2.3)	-5	(9.1)	4.0	3.4	76.9	11.8
Norway	-3	(1.6)	8	(19.9)	0.0	0.0	46.5	5.6
Poland	-5	(1.7)	**31**	(9.9)	0.0	0.0	56.8	9.5
Portugal	-1	(1.0)	**-11**	(3.7)	76.3	26.3	85.7	29.9
Slovak Republic	-2	(1.3)	**16**	(5.9)	54.2	3.0	79.7	7.0
Slovenia	-1	(1.3)	14	(9.9)	78.6	0.4	84.1	0.4
Spain	-1	(0.7)	-4	(4.0)	0.0	0.0	54.7	10.4
Sweden	-1	(1.3)	-7	(11.1)	16.2	3.5	59.5	9.8
Switzerland	-4	(1.2)	15	(16.1)	24.5	0.8	53.1	7.7
Turkey	-1	(0.7)	14	(7.3)	46.6	6.8	73.4	7.6
United Kingdom	2	(1.5)	8	(13.2)	6.4	2.0	63.6	6.4
United States	6	(1.1)	0	(7.1)	14.5	7.8	62.8	12.6
OECD average	0	(0.2)	2	(1.9)	40.0	10.4	71.2	13.9
Albania	m	m	m	m	m	m	m	m
Argentina	1	(0.7)	8	(8.2)	34.2	9.7	72.7	11.3
Brazil	0	(0.5)	**14**	(2.3)	21.8	6.5	70.1	8.0
Bulgaria	-1	(0.8)	**19**	(3.8)	25.1	2.2	70.1	3.8
Colombia	1	(0.7)	**9**	(3.0)	19.7	14.3	63.1	15.9
Costa Rica	1	(0.6)	**8**	(2.7)	15.3	8.0	66.1	10.8
Croatia	-2	(1.1)	30	(16.8)	70.0	15.2	73.5	15.7
Cyprus*	0	(1.3)	11	(14.1)	0.0	0.0	62.9	6.0
Hong Kong-China	0	(1.2)	**-44**	(11.5)	7.6	6.1	44.3	6.2
Indonesia	0	(0.7)	**16**	(3.3)	19.2	0.3	38.2	1.3
Jordan	0	(0.7)	**29**	(4.7)	0.0	0.0	42.6	4.8
Kazakhstan	0	(1.4)	22	(12.5)	-2.7	2.3	28.9	4.8
Latvia	-3	(1.4)	22	(7.1)	5.0	2.5	63.0	7.6
Liechtenstein	-5	(2.5)	-131	(148.9)	10.9	2.7	54.0	4.3
Lithuania	-2	(1.5)	19	(9.5)	34.7	1.2	67.6	5.2
Macao-China	2	(1.3)	-18	(16.5)	33.4	21.1	37.3	21.2
Malaysia	2	(0.9)	24	(6.7)	32.6	26.9	63.5	28.1
Montenegro	0	(1.2)	12	(9.6)	55.0	7.2	83.7	8.3
Peru	0	(0.5)	**9**	(1.9)	20.8	9.4	78.9	10.6
Qatar	-1	(1.0)	**50**	(19.4)	68.3	4.2	75.5	4.9
Romania	2	(0.9)	**17**	(4.1)	1.2	0.2	61.9	4.5
Russian Federation	-4	(1.8)	**46**	(8.2)	0.8	4.2	42.7	8.2
Serbia	-1	(1.3)	13	(11.9)	58.2	5.2	72.4	5.9
Shanghai-China	-5	(1.3)	14	(8.7)	58.8	1.9	85.0	3.0
Singapore	-1	(1.3)	**-43**	(17.2)	0.0	0.0	61.2	4.4
Chinese Taipei	-4	(1.4)	-22	(13.8)	35.3	2.6	79.0	7.1
Thailand	3	(0.7)	**20**	(5.5)	20.1	2.0	47.9	3.4
Tunisia	2	(0.6)	12	(4.8)	59.0	2.3	74.9	3.5
United Arab Emirates	0	(0.8)	**23**	(10.4)	0.0	0.0	41.6	1.9
Uruguay	1	(0.8)	**-9**	(3.7)	53.5	12.2	83.8	14.6
Viet Nam	1	(0.7)	-5	(6.6)	32.8	0.0	60.2	1.4

Note: Values that are statistically significant are indicated in bold (see Annex A3).
1. In some countries, sub-units within schools were sampled instead of schools as administrative units; this may affect the estimation of school-level effects (see Annex A3).
2. ESCS refers to the *PISA index of economic, social and cultural status*.
3. Two-level regression of mathematics performance on student ESCS and school mean ESCS: within-school slope for ESCS and student-level variation explained by the model.
4. Two-level regression of mathematics performance on student ESCS and school mean ESCS: between-school slope for ESCS and school-level variation explained by the model.
5. Two-level regression of mathematics performance on student-level ESCS, student-level ESCS squared, school mean ESCS, and school mean ESCS squared. The within-school index of curvilinearity corresponds to the coefficient of student-level ESCS squared.
6. Two-level regression of mathematics performance on student ESCS, student ESCS squared, school mean ESCS and school mean ESCS squared: between-school index of curvilinearity corresponds to the coefficient of school mean ESCS squared.

StatLink ⟨⟩ http://dx.doi.org/10.1787/888932964908

[Part 1/3]
Change between 2003 and 2012 in the relationship between mathematics performance and socio-economic status, between and within schools

Table II.2.9b *Results based on students' self-reports*

	PISA 2003											
	Overall association of ESCS[1] and mathematics performance		Within-school association of ESCS and mathematics performance[2]		Between-school association of ESCS and mathematics performance[3]		Strength of the relationship between ESCS and mathematics performance		Within-school strength of the relationship between ESCS and mathematics performance[2]		Between-school strength of the relationship between ESCS and mathematics performance[3]	
	Student-level score-point difference associated with one-unit increase in ESCS	S.E.	Student-level score-point difference associated with one-unit increase in student-level ESCS	S.E.	School-level score-point difference associated with one-unit increase in school mean ESCS	S.E.	Percentage of the overall variation in student performance explained by students' socio-economic status	S.E.	Percentage of the within-school variation in student performance explained by students' socio-economic status	S.E.	Percentage of the between-school variation in student performance explained by schools' socio-economic status	S.E.
OECD Australia	40	(1.8)	26	(1.1)	54	(4.1)	**14.0**	(1.1)	6.2	(0.5)	69.2	(7.2)
Austria	42	(2.2)	9	(1.4)	100	(5.8)	**15.1**	(1.5)	1.5	(0.9)	70.7	(1.9)
Belgium	51	(1.9)	22	(1.3)	88	(5.8)	**23.0**	(1.4)	5.8	(0.7)	73.9	(1.2)
Canada	30	(1.3)	23	(1.0)	31	(3.7)	**10.2**	(0.8)	4.6	(0.6)	44.	(4.0)
Czech Republic	46	(2.0)	17	(1.6)	94	(5.3)	**18.5**	(1.3)	3.0	(0.9)	75.	(2.9)
Denmark	39	(1.8)	32	(1.7)	28	(5.0)	**17.3**	(1.5)	11.9	(0.8)	71.	(5.5)
Finland	28	(1.4)	28	(1.3)	0	(5.6)	**10.5**	(1.0)	10.2	(0.7)	26.	(21.3)
France	43	(2.2)	w	w	w	w	**20.2**	(1.8)	w	w		w
Germany	44	(1.6)	15	(1.5)	82	(4.6)	**23.8**	(1.4)	3.2	(1.0)	83.	(2.4)
Greece	36	(2.0)	17	(1.7)	58	(6.0)	**16.0**	(1.9)	3.9	(1.0)	70.	(4.3)
Hungary	50	(2.1)	12	(1.6)	86	(3.6)	**25.7**	(1.8)	1.8	(0.7)	85.	(1.2)
Iceland	26	(1.6)	26	(1.7)	8	(5.7)	**7.1**	(0.9)	5.9	(1.4)	54.	(16.3)
Ireland	36	(1.7)	27	(1.5)	40	(5.1)	**15.7**	(1.4)	8.3	(0.7)	77.	(6.6)
Italy	31	(1.8)	8	(1.0)	69	(5.5)	**12.3**	(1.3)	1.1	(0.6)	51.	(2.7)
Japan	43	(4.5)	5	(1.8)	121	(11.4)	**11.8**	(2.1)	0.6	(1.1)	60.	(4.8)
Korea	38	(2.8)	12	(1.5)	78	(6.9)	**14.5**	(2.0)	2.1	(0.7)	65.	(6.6)
Luxembourg	35	(1.2)	19	(4.4)	72	(7.2)	**16.6**	(1.0)	5.5	(2.8)	95.	(1.4)
Mexico	30	(1.9)	7	(0.9)	53	(3.3)	**17.2**	(2.0)	1.6	(0.9)	68.	(4.0)
Netherlands	39	(2.2)	12	(1.4)	105	(5.5)	**18.3**	(1.8)	2.0	(1.0)	77.	(3.6)
New Zealand	44	(1.7)	35	(1.8)	53	(5.8)	**16.6**	(1.2)	10.5	(0.8)	71.	(2.8)
Norway	41	(1.8)	38	(2.0)	20	(7.0)	**12.1**	(1.1)	9.9	(0.8)	48.	(6.0)
Poland	40	(1.6)	33	(1.7)	26	(4.7)	**16.5**	(1.2)	10.7	(0.7)	68.	(7.7)
Portugal	28	(1.2)	18	(1.1)	37	(3.9)	**18.5**	(1.6)	9.2	(0.9)	60.	(3.6)
Slovak Republic	48	(2.5)	20	(1.7)	79	(4.5)	**23.6**	(2.0)	5.1	(1.0)	81.	(2.9)
Spain	27	(1.4)	18	(1.3)	31	(3.5)	**12.6**	(1.2)	5.4	(0.8)	55.	(2.1)
Sweden	36	(1.9)	32	(1.8)	28	(6.9)	**14.3**	(1.3)	11.2	(0.9)	58.	(5.5)
Switzerland	41	(1.8)	23	(1.8)	62	(7.2)	**18.0**	(1.3)	7.2	(1.2)	59.	(4.1)
Turkey	50	(5.0)	11	(1.5)	87	(7.0)	**24.9**	(3.9)	1.7	(1.1)	78.	(2.4)
United States	42	(1.4)	29	(1.5)	46	(4.3)	**19.0**	(1.1)	9.6	(0.9)	66.	(1.9)
OECD average 2003	39	(0.4)	20	(0.3)	59	(1.1)	**16.7**	(0.3)	5.7	(0.2)	66.	(1.2)
Partners Brazil	31	(2.8)	4	(1.4)	63	(4.8)	**15.1**	(2.3)	1.0	(0.9)	61.	(4.4)
Hong Kong-China	30	(2.7)	6	(1.9)	90	(10.8)	**7.9**	(1.4)	0.4	(1.2)	46.	(5.5)
Indonesia	22	(2.6)	1	(1.2)	62	(5.9)	**7.2**	(1.7)	0.0	(0.9)	44.	(2.8)
Latvia	35	(2.0)	26	(1.9)	39	(7.4)	**11.9**	(1.3)	7.0	(0.9)	47.	(3.2)
Liechtenstein	47	(4.7)	12	(3.7)	109	(10.3)	**22.5**	(4.1)	2.2	(4.0)	90.	(5.7)
Macao-China	13	(3.2)	7	(2.9)	24	(12.5)	1.8	(0.9)	0.6	(1.6)	19.	(4.6)
Russian Federation	31	(1.9)	18	(1.5)	55	(6.9)	**10.6**	(1.2)	4.0	(0.9)	48.	(4.2)
Thailand	23	(2.1)	7	(1.4)	36	(4.0)	**11.4**	(1.9)	0.8	(0.9)	54.	(8.4)
Tunisia	25	(2.3)	8	(1.2)	47	(4.6)	**13.8**	(2.5)	2.3	(0.9)	56.	(7.3)
Uruguay	35	(1.9)	13	(1.4)	62	(3.7)	**15.9**	(1.7)	2.6	(0.8)	67.	(4.3)

Notes: Values that are statistically significant are indicated in bold (see Annex A3).
Only countries and economies with comparable data from PISA 2003 and PISA 2012 are shown.
For comparability over time, PISA 2003 values on the *PISA index of economic, social and cultural status* have been rescaled to the PISA 2012 scale of the index. PISA 2003 results reported in this table may thus differ from those presented in *Learning for Tomorrow's World: First Results from PISA 2003* (OECD, 2004) (see Annex A5 for more details).
1. ESCS refers to the *PISA index of economic, social and cultural status*.
2. Two-level regression of mathematics performance on student ESCS and school mean ESCS: within-school slope for ESCS and student-level variation explained by the model.
3. Two-level regression of mathematics performance on student ESCS and school mean ESCS: between-school slope for ESCS and school-level variation explained by the model.
StatLink ᴍᴸ﹗ http://dx.doi.org/10.1787/888932964908

EXCELLENCE THROUGH EQUITY: GIVING EVERY STUDENT THE CHANCE TO SUCCEED – VOLUME II

[Part 2/3]
Change between 2003 and 2012 in the relationship between mathematics performance and socio-economic status, between and within schools

Table II.2.9b *Results based on students' self-reports*

	PISA 2012											
	Overall association of ESCS[1] and mathematics performance		Within-school association of ESCS and mathematics performance[2]		Between-school association of ESCS and mathematics performance[3]		Strength of the relationship between ESCS and mathematics performance		Within-school strength of the relationship between ESCS and mathematics performance[2]		Between-school strength of the relationship between ESCS and mathematics performance[3]	
	Student-level score-point difference associated with one-unit increase in ESCS	S.E.	Student-level score-point difference associated with one-unit increase in student-level ESCS	S.E.	School-level score-point difference associated with one-unit increase in school mean ESCS	S.E.	Percentage of the overall variation in student performance explained by students' socio-economic status	S.E.	Percentage of the within-school variation in student performance explained by students' socio-economic status	S.E.	Percentage of the between-school variation in student performance explained by schools' socio-economic status	S.E.
OECD												
Australia	42	(1.3)	25	(1.3)	64	(4.1)	12.3	(0.8)	6.1	(0.5)	55.5	(4.3)
Austria	43	(2.2)	15	(1.6)	85	(5.9)	15.8	(1.5)	3.5	(0.8)	56.3	(2.2)
Belgium	49	(1.7)	19	(1.5)	102	(6.0)	19.6	(1.4)	4.8	(0.8)	70.1	(2.3)
Canada	31	(1.2)	23	(1.2)	41	(5.0)	9.4	(0.7)	7.5	(0.5)	41.8	(3.9)
Czech Republic	51	(2.7)	14	(1.7)	127	(6.5)	16.2	(1.5)	2.1	(1.1)	70.5	(3.2)
Denmark	39	(1.7)	31	(1.7)	38	(4.2)	16.5	(1.4)	10.6	(0.9)	70.9	(2.2)
Finland	33	(1.8)	29	(1.5)	22	(6.9)	9.4	(0.9)	9.8	(0.7)	38.3	(10.1)
France	57	(2.2)	w	w	w	w	22.5	(1.3)	w	w	w	w
Germany	43	(2.0)	11	(1.4)	103	(5.6)	16.9	(1.4)	0.4	(1.5)	71.3	(3.4)
Greece	34	(1.8)	18	(1.5)	55	(5.1)	15.5	(1.5)	4.7	(0.7)	65.1	(4.4)
Hungary	47	(2.8)	6	(1.4)	98	(4.9)	23.1	(2.3)	1.1	(0.8)	78.4	(3.3)
Iceland	31	(2.1)	25	(2.9)	45	(8.3)	7.7	(1.0)	5.9	(1.7)	68.8	(9.7)
Ireland	38	(1.8)	26	(1.7)	52	(4.7)	14.6	(1.2)	6.9	(1.1)	79.3	(1.5)
Italy	30	(1.2)	7	(0.7)	83	(4.1)	10.1	(0.6)	1.7	(0.4)	48.4	(1.9)
Japan	41	(3.9)	4	(1.7)	150	(8.2)	9.8	(1.6)	1.8	(0.8)	65.9	(5.2)
Korea	42	(3.3)	14	(2.0)	114	(10.2)	10.1	(1.4)	1.5	(1.0)	57.3	(5.3)
Luxembourg	37	(1.2)	20	(2.7)	68	(4.9)	18.3	(1.1)	6.7	(2.8)	93.8	(3.2)
Mexico	19	(0.8)	5	(0.5)	29	(1.4)	10.4	(0.8)	0.9	(0.5)	46.1	(0.4)
Netherlands	40	(3.1)	9	(1.6)	147	(10.9)	11.5	(1.7)	1.5	(1.0)	57.8	(5.7)
New Zealand	52	(1.9)	36	(2.3)	66	(6.8)	18.4	(1.3)	9.9	(0.8)	78.4	(3.1)
Norway	32	(2.4)	27	(2.2)	49	(7.8)	7.4	(1.0)	5.6	(1.4)	46.5	(2.5)
Poland	41	(2.4)	32	(1.8)	36	(7.4)	16.6	(1.7)	9.5	(1.1)	56.8	(9.1)
Portugal	35	(1.6)	23	(1.4)	33	(4.0)	19.6	(1.8)	9.6	(0.9)	62.1	(5.3)
Slovak Republic	54	(2.9)	21	(2.1)	86	(6.4)	24.6	(2.1)	4.6	(1.1)	73.8	(3.4)
Spain	34	(1.1)	27	(1.0)	26	(3.2)	15.8	(1.0)	10.4	(0.5)	54.7	(3.8)
Sweden	36	(1.9)	28	(2.0)	41	(7.3)	10.6	(1.1)	9.8	(0.7)	55.5	(4.9)
Switzerland	38	(1.8)	25	(1.5)	66	(8.9)	12.8	(1.2)	7.2	(2.0)	44.0	(7.0)
Turkey	32	(2.4)	6	(1.0)	83	(7.4)	14.5	(1.8)	1.4	(0.9)	57.6	(7.2)
United States	35	(1.7)	24	(1.9)	41	(5.4)	14.8	(1.3)	6.8	(0.8)	57.8	(3.4)
OECD average 2003	39	(0.4)	20	(0.3)	71	(1.2)	14.7	(0.3)	5.4	(0.2)	61.9	(0.9)
Partners												
Brazil	26	(1.7)	8	(0.8)	46	(3.0)	15.7	(1.6)	2.0	(0.7)	61.5	(3.5)
Hong Kong-China	27	(2.6)	4	(1.5)	65	(7.9)	7.5	(1.5)	0.7	(0.9)	41.9	(8.1)
Indonesia	20	(3.4)	6	(1.0)	37	(6.0)	9.6	(3.0)	1.3	(1.0)	32.7	(12.4)
Latvia	35	(2.1)	22	(1.6)	46	(5.7)	14.7	(1.7)	5.5	(1.0)	62.2	(6.7)
Liechtenstein	28	(5.8)	8	(5.3)	132	(53.5)	7.6	(3.1)	2.2	(3.2)	51.0	(18.5)
Macao-China	17	(1.5)	7	(1.5)	31	(12.2)	2.6	(0.4)	5.8	(1.2)	14.2	(6.8)
Russian Federation	38	(3.2)	26	(2.2)	47	(7.0)	11.4	(1.7)	5.0	(0.8)	44.5	(7.5)
Thailand	22	(2.4)	9	(1.2)	35	(5.2)	9.9	(2.2)	1.5	(0.8)	40.0	(12.8)
Tunisia	22	(2.6)	6	(1.0)	45	(5.5)	12.4	(2.4)	2.1	(0.8)	48.3	(4.3)
Uruguay	37	(1.8)	15	(1.2)	52	(3.3)	22.8	(1.9)	4.3	(0.8)	74.1	(1.2)

Notes: Values that are statistically significant are indicated in bold (see Annex A3).
Only countries and economies with comparable data from PISA 2003 and PISA 2012 are shown.
For comparability over time, PISA 2003 values on the *PISA index of economic, social and cultural status* have been rescaled to the PISA 2012 scale of the index. PISA 2003 results reported in this table may thus differ from those presented in *Learning for Tomorrow's World: First Results from PISA 2003* (OECD, 2004) (see Annex A5 for more details).
1. ESCS refers to the *PISA index of economic, social and cultural status*.
2. Two-level regression of mathematics performance on student ESCS and school mean ESCS: within-school slope for ESCS and student-level variation explained by the model.
3. Two-level regression of mathematics performance on student ESCS and school mean ESCS: between-school slope for ESCS and school-level variation explained by the model.
StatLink ⏱ http://dx.doi.org/10.1787/888932964908

[Part 3/3]
Change between 2003 and 2012 in the relationship between mathematics performance and socio-economic status, between and within schools

Table II.2.9b   *Results based on students' self-reports*

	Change between 2003 and 2012 (PISA 2012 - PISA 2003)											
	Overall association of ESCS[1] and mathematics performance		Within-school association of ESCS and mathematics performance[2]		Between-school association of ESCS and mathematics performance[3]		Strength of the relationship between ESCS and mathematics performance		Within-school strength of the relationship between ESCS and mathematics performance[2]		Between-school strength of the relationship between ESCS and mathematics performance[3]	
	Change in the student-level score-point difference associated with one-unit increase in ESCS	S.E.	Change in the student-level score-point difference associated with one-unit increase in the student-level ESCS	S.E.	Change in the school-level score point-difference associated with one-unit increase in school mean ESCS	S.E.	Change in the percentage of the overall variation in student performance explained by students' socio-economic status	S.E.	Change in the percentage of the within-school variation in student performance explained by students' socio-economic status	S.E.	Change in the percentage of the between-school variation in student performance explained by schools' socio-economic status	S.E.
OECD												
Australia	2	(2.2)	-1	(1.7)	10	(5.9)	-1.6	(1.3)	-0.1	(0.7)	**-13.7**	(8.4)
Austria	2	(3.1)	**7**	(2.1)	-15	(8.3)	0.8	(2.1)	2.0	(1.2)	**-14.4**	(2.9)
Belgium	-2	(2.6)	-4	(2.0)	12	(8.4)	-3.4	(1.9)	-1.4	(1.0)	-1.5	(2.6)
Canada	1	(1.8)	0	(1.6)	9	(6.2)	-0.8	(1.1)	**2.9**	(0.8)	-2.5	(5.6)
Czech Republic	5	(3.4)	-3	(2.4)	**33**	(8.4)	-2.3	(2.0)	-0.9	(1.4)	-5.2	(4.4)
Denmark	1	(2.5)	-1	(2.4)	10	(6.5)	-0.8	(2.0)	-1.3	(1.2)	-0.8	(5.9)
Finland	**5**	(2.3)	2	(2.0)	**22**	(8.9)	-1.1	(1.4)	-0.4	(1.0)	11.7	(23.5)
France	**14**	(3.1)	w	w	w	w	2.2	(2.3)	w	w	w	w
Germany	-1	(2.5)	**-4**	(2.1)	**21**	(7.2)	**-6.9**	(2.0)	-2.8	(1.8)	**-11.8**	(4.2)
Greece	-2	(2.8)	0	(2.3)	-3	(7.9)	-0.5	(2.4)	0.8	(1.2)	-5.2	(6.2)
Hungary	-3	(3.5)	**-5**	(2.1)	**12**	(6.1)	-2.6	(2.9)	-0.6	(1.0)	-6.0	(3.5)
Iceland	5	(2.6)	-1	(3.4)	**36**	(10.1)	0.6	(1.3)	0.0	(2.2)	14.4	(19.0)
Ireland	2	(2.5)	-1	(2.3)	13	(6.9)	-1.1	(1.9)	-1.4	(1.3)	1.8	(6.8)
Italy	-1	(2.2)	-1	(1.2)	**14**	(6.9)	-2.2	(1.4)	0.6	(0.8)	-3.0	(3.3)
Japan	-2	(6.0)	-1	(2.5)	**29**	(14.0)	-2.0	(2.6)	1.3	(1.3)	5.4	(7.1)
Korea	5	(4.3)	2	(2.5)	**36**	(12.3)	-4.4	(2.4)	-0.6	(1.2)	-8.0	(8.5)
Luxembourg	2	(1.7)	1	(5.2)	-4	(8.7)	1.7	(1.5)	1.2	(3.9)	-1.4	(3.5)
Mexico	**-11**	(2.0)	-2	(1.1)	**-24**	(3.6)	**-6.8**	(2.2)	-0.7	(1.0)	**-22.0**	(4.0)
Netherlands	0	(3.8)	-3	(2.2)	**41**	(12.2)	**-6.8**	(2.4)	-0.6	(1.4)	**-20.0**	(6.8)
New Zealand	**8**	(2.5)	1	(2.9)	13	(8.9)	1.8	(1.8)	-0.6	(1.1)	6..	(4.1)
Norway	**-8**	(3.1)	**-11**	(3.0)	**29**	(10.5)	**-4.7**	(1.5)	**-4.3**	(1.6)	-1..	(6.5)
Poland	1	(2.9)	-2	(2.5)	10	(8.8)	0.2	(2.0)	-1.2	(1.3)	-12..	(11.9)
Portugal	**7**	(2.0)	**5**	(1.8)	-4	(5.5)	1.1	(2.4)	0.4	(1.3)	1..	(6.4)
Slovak Republic	6	(3.8)	0	(2.7)	7	(7.8)	1.0	(2.9)	-0.5	(1.4)	-7..	(4.5)
Spain	**6**	(1.8)	**9**	(1.6)	-5	(4.7)	**3.2**	(1.6)	**4.9**	(0.9)	-0..	(4.3)
Sweden	-1	(2.7)	-4	(2.6)	12	(10.0)	**-3.7**	(1.7)	-1.4	(1.1)	-2..	(7.4)
Switzerland	-3	(2.6)	2	(2.4)	4	(11.4)	**-5.2**	(1.8)	0.0	(2.3)	-15..	(8.1)
Turkey	**-18**	(5.6)	**-5**	(1.8)	-4	(10.2)	**-10.4**	(4.3)	-0.4	(1.4)	-21..	(7.6)
United States	**-7**	(2.2)	**-6**	(2.4)	-5	(6.9)	**-4.2**	(1.8)	**-2.8**	(1.2)	**-8.**	(3.9)
OECD average 2003	0	(0.6)	-0.8	(0.5)	**12.0**	(1.6)	**-2.0**	(0.4)	-0.3	(0.3)	**-4.**	(1.5)
Partners												
Brazil	-5	(3.2)	**4**	(1.6)	-17	(5.7)	0.7	(2.8)	1.1	(1.1)	0..	(5.7)
Hong Kong-China	-3	(3.8)	-1	(2.4)	-25	(13.4)	-0.4	(2.0)	0.2	(1.5)	-4..	(9.8)
Indonesia	-1	(4.3)	**5**	(1.5)	**-25**	(8.4)	2.4	(3.4)	1.3	(1.3)	-11..	(12.7)
Latvia	1	(2.9)	-4	(2.5)	7	(9.3)	2.8	(2.2)	-1.5	(1.3)	15..	(7.4)
Liechtenstein	**-19**	(7.5)	-3	(6.5)	23	(54.5)	**-14.9**	(5.1)	0.0	(5.2)	**-39.**	(19.3)
Macao-China	5	(3.5)	0	(3.3)	7	(17.5)	0.8	(1.0)	**5.2**	(2.0)	-5..	(8.2)
Russian Federation	7	(3.7)	**8**	(2.6)	-8	(9.9)	0.8	(2.1)	1.1	(1.2)	-3..	(8.6)
Thailand	-1	(3.2)	2	(1.8)	-2	(6.5)	-1.5	(2.9)	0.7	(1.2)	-14..	(15.3)
Tunisia	-3	(3.5)	-2	(1.5)	-2	(7.2)	-1.4	(3.4)	-0.2	(1.2)	-8..	(8.5)
Uruguay	3	(2.6)	2	(1.8)	-10	(4.9)	**6.9**	(2.5)	1.7	(1.1)	6..	(4.5)

Notes: Values that are statistically significant are indicated in bold (see Annex A3).

Only countries and economies with comparable data from PISA 2003 and PISA 2012 are shown.

For comparability over time, PISA 2003 values on the *PISA index of economic, social and cultural status* have been rescaled to the PISA 2012 scale of the index. PISA 2003 results reported in this table may thus differ from those presented in *Learning for Tomorrow's World: First Results from PISA 2003* (OECD, 2004) (see Annex A5 for more details).

1. ESCS refers to the *PISA index of economic, social and cultural status*.

2. Two-level regression of mathematics performance on student ESCS and school mean ESCS: within-school slope for ESCS and student-level variation explained by the model.

3. Two-level regression of mathematics performance on student ESCS and school mean ESCS: between-school slope for ESCS and school-level variation explained by the model.

StatLink http://dx.doi.org/10.1787/888932964908

[Part 1/3]

Parents' education and occupation, and students' home possessions, by schools' socio-economic profile

Table II.2.10 *Results based on students' self-reports*

	Parents' highest education: Percentage of students with at least one parent whose highest educational attainment is lower secondary (ISCED 2 or less)						Parents' highest education: Percentage of students with at least one parent whose educational attainment is upper secondary or post-secondary non-tertiary (ISCED 3 or 4)						Parents' highest education: Percentage of students with at least one parent whose educational attainment is tertiary or advanced research (ISCED 5 or 6)					
	Socio-economically disadvantaged schools[1]		Socio-economically average schools[1]		Socio-economically advantaged schools[1]		Socio-economically disadvantaged schools[1]		Socio-economically average schools[1]		Socio-economically advantaged schools[1]		Socio-economically disadvantaged schools[1]		Socio-economically average schools[1]		Socio-economically advantaged schools[1]	
	%	S.E.	%	S.E.	%	S.E.	%	S.E.	%	S.E.	%	S.E.	%	S.E.	%	S.E.	%	S.E.
Australia	20.6	(0.8)	9.8	(0.4)	2.4	(0.3)	44.5	(0.8)	36.2	(0.6)	20.7	(0.8)	34.9	(0.8)	54.0	(0.7)	76.9	(0.9)
Austria	9.2	(1.1)	3.8	(0.5)	0.6	(0.2)	56.7	(1.8)	49.6	(1.5)	32.0	(2.5)	34.1	(1.6)	46.6	(1.4)	67.4	(2.5)
Belgium	10.7	(1.1)	3.8	(0.4)	1.5	(0.2)	48.1	(1.9)	34.5	(1.0)	17.0	(2.0)	41.2	(1.7)	61.7	(1.0)	81.5	(0.8)
Canada	8.4	(0.8)	2.4	(0.2)	0.8	(0.2)	37.0	(1.2)	25.8	(0.6)	11.4	(0.6)	54.7	(1.5)	71.8	(0.7)	87.8	(0.7)
Chile	41.2	(2.3)	17.8	(1.2)	2.4	(0.4)	45.8	(2.0)	53.1	(1.5)	32.0	(2.3)	13.0	(0.8)	29.1	(1.0)	65.6	(2.5)
Czech Republic	2.8	(1.0)	1.0	(0.3)	0.2	(0.1)	82.3	(1.9)	69.7	(1.1)	39.8	(1.6)	14.9	(1.4)	29.3	(1.1)	60.0	(1.6)
Denmark	11.5	(1.3)	5.5	(0.5)	1.2	(0.2)	41.0	(2.3)	27.2	(0.9)	13.6	(1.2)	47.4	(2.0)	67.3	(1.0)	85.2	(1.1)
Estonia	4.3	(0.8)	2.5	(0.4)	0.2	(0.1)	60.4	(2.2)	41.2	(1.2)	20.3	(1.1)	35.2	(2.0)	56.3	(1.1)	79.5	(1.1)
Finland	5.7	(0.9)	2.7	(0.2)	1.3	(0.2)	24.3	(1.7)	18.3	(0.6)	10.1	(1.0)	70.0	(1.8)	79.1	(0.6)	88.6	(1.0)
France	w	w	w	w	w	w	w	w	w	w	w	w	w	w	w	w	w	w
Germany	43.1	(1.7)	21.6	(1.0)	6.8	(0.6)	25.5	(1.5)	29.7	(0.9)	22.8	(1.7)	31.5	(1.5)	48.7	(1.0)	70.4	(1.9)
Greece	25.0	(1.6)	8.1	(0.6)	1.8	(0.4)	44.7	(2.0)	39.5	(1.0)	24.1	(1.3)	30.2	(1.9)	52.4	(1.0)	74.1	(1.2)
Hungary	22.8	(1.9)	5.9	(0.7)	1.0	(0.3)	57.7	(1.9)	53.0	(1.1)	30.7	(2.1)	19.5	(1.1)	41.1	(1.2)	68.3	(2.1)
Iceland	16.4	(1.5)	7.1	(0.6)	2.2	(0.5)	38.2	(1.9)	27.5	(0.9)	18.1	(1.3)	45.4	(2.1)	65.4	(1.1)	79.6	(1.3)
Ireland	18.8	(1.7)	7.5	(0.5)	2.1	(0.4)	47.1	(2.2)	39.3	(1.0)	21.9	(1.6)	34.1	(1.6)	53.2	(0.9)	76.0	(1.6)
Israel	10.7	(1.3)	3.0	(0.5)	0.5	(0.1)	51.7	(1.8)	34.9	(1.6)	16.9	(1.0)	37.6	(1.6)	62.0	(1.7)	82.7	(1.0)
Italy	37.6	(0.8)	18.8	(0.5)	6.3	(0.4)	41.4	(0.7)	45.6	(0.6)	39.2	(0.8)	21.0	(0.6)	35.6	(0.6)	54.5	(0.9)
Japan	4.1	(0.6)	1.0	(0.2)	0.3	(0.1)	57.5	(1.6)	35.7	(1.5)	14.0	(1.0)	38.5	(1.7)	63.3	(1.5)	85.7	(1.0)
Korea	6.7	(0.8)	2.5	(0.4)	1.0	(0.3)	60.4	(1.6)	41.1	(1.2)	16.4	(1.4)	32.9	(1.7)	56.4	(1.2)	82.7	(1.5)
Luxembourg	32.6	(1.0)	14.1	(1.3)	6.6	(0.6)	33.1	(1.0)	32.7	(1.7)	22.9	(1.0)	34.3	(1.0)	53.1	(1.8)	70.6	(1.0)
Mexico	76.2	(0.9)	50.6	(0.8)	18.8	(0.9)	9.1	(0.5)	16.7	(0.5)	18.4	(0.6)	14.7	(0.6)	32.8	(0.5)	62.8	(1.1)
Netherlands	11.1	(1.3)	6.3	(0.6)	1.5	(0.4)	43.9	(2.2)	32.5	(1.4)	16.0	(1.0)	45.0	(2.0)	61.2	(1.3)	82.6	(1.1)
New Zealand	16.6	(1.8)	6.0	(0.6)	2.4	(0.4)	50.7	(2.0)	43.0	(1.2)	25.3	(1.9)	32.6	(2.0)	51.0	(1.3)	72.3	(1.9)
Norway	5.9	(1.2)	3.1	(0.3)	0.3	(0.2)	46.0	(2.3)	30.3	(0.8)	15.7	(1.5)	48.2	(2.1)	66.7	(0.9)	84.1	(1.5)
Poland	6.1	(0.8)	2.5	(0.4)	0.7	(0.4)	86.6	(1.0)	73.7	(1.0)	43.9	(2.4)	7.3	(0.7)	23.7	(1.0)	55.4	(2.5)
Portugal	71.2	(1.5)	47.5	(1.4)	15.9	(2.1)	18.5	(1.1)	28.0	(1.1)	23.9	(2.3)	10.4	(1.0)	24.6	(0.8)	60.2	(3.4)
Slovak Republic	11.1	(2.0)	0.9	(0.2)	0.1	(0.1)	76.1	(1.9)	72.3	(1.2)	45.7	(2.6)	12.8	(1.1)	26.8	(1.1)	54.2	(2.7)
Slovenia	7.9	(0.8)	3.7	(0.4)	0.4	(0.2)	71.8	(1.4)	55.1	(1.1)	31.1	(1.4)	20.3	(1.1)	41.3	(1.0)	68.5	(1.4)
Spain	43.1	(1.4)	22.6	(0.8)	7.5	(0.5)	30.0	(1.2)	29.9	(0.6)	19.5	(1.1)	26.8	(0.9)	47.4	(1.0)	73.0	(1.3)
Sweden	9.8	(1.5)	5.5	(0.5)	2.1	(0.4)	34.7	(1.9)	27.0	(0.8)	14.7	(1.2)	55.6	(2.0)	67.5	(0.9)	83.2	(1.2)
Switzerland	21.8	(1.1)	12.7	(0.6)	4.4	(0.7)	36.3	(1.4)	33.6	(0.8)	21.1	(1.1)	41.8	(1.3)	53.7	(0.8)	74.5	(1.3)
Turkey	78.9	(1.0)	61.7	(1.2)	32.7	(2.2)	10.7	(0.8)	17.9	(1.0)	19.9	(1.1)	10.4	(0.7)	20.4	(0.7)	47.4	(2.5)
United Kingdom	8.4	(0.9)	2.8	(0.3)	1.1	(0.4)	46.3	(1.8)	38.8	(1.1)	24.5	(1.2)	45.3	(1.5)	58.3	(1.0)	74.4	(1.3)
United States	22.8	(2.0)	6.0	(0.7)	1.4	(0.4)	43.3	(1.4)	36.1	(1.4)	17.4	(1.2)	33.9	(1.7)	58.0	(1.4)	81.2	(1.2)
OECD average	21.9	(0.2)	11.1	(0.1)	3.9	(0.1)	45.5	(0.3)	38.5	(0.2)	23.1	(0.3)	32.6	(0.3)	50.4	(0.2)	73.0	(0.3)
Albania	m	m	m	m	m	m	m	m	m	m	m	m	m	m	m	m	m	m
Argentina	54.4	(1.5)	29.3	(1.6)	10.2	(0.9)	21.1	(1.3)	25.6	(1.0)	17.6	(1.2)	24.5	(1.1)	45.0	(1.4)	72.1	(1.6)
Brazil	60.8	(0.9)	35.4	(0.9)	8.7	(0.8)	28.1	(0.9)	43.2	(0.9)	36.9	(2.0)	11.0	(0.5)	21.4	(0.7)	54.4	(2.3)
Bulgaria	16.7	(1.8)	3.8	(0.7)	0.4	(0.1)	60.3	(1.4)	53.2	(1.2)	29.4	(1.3)	23.0	(1.2)	43.1	(1.1)	70.2	(1.4)
Colombia	64.7	(1.9)	36.4	(1.3)	12.5	(1.1)	18.2	(1.3)	18.2	(1.4)	14.7	(1.3)	23.0	(1.3)	45.4	(1.2)	72.8	(1.6)
Costa Rica	50.2	(2.3)	26.2	(1.0)	4.6	(1.0)	18.4	(1.4)	28.3	(1.5)	19.6	(1.4)	31.4	(2.3)	45.5	(1.2)	75.8	(1.8)
Croatia	10.7	(0.9)	2.7	(0.4)	0.3	(0.2)	55.0	(1.7)	51.3	(1.1)	32.7	(1.7)	34.3	(1.4)	46.0	(1.0)	66.9	(1.8)
Cyprus*	10.2	(0.8)	3.8	(0.5)	0.6	(0.2)	57.0	(1.2)	43.4	(1.2)	23.0	(1.2)	32.8	(1.2)	52.9	(1.3)	76.4	(1.2)
Hong Kong-China	47.6	(1.6)	28.3	(1.1)	6.6	(0.9)	45.5	(1.4)	54.8	(1.3)	42.2	(3.0)	6.9	(0.8)	16.9	(1.0)	51.2	(3.6)
Indonesia	69.4	(1.3)	48.2	(1.6)	16.9	(1.5)	23.3	(1.5)	36.9	(1.7)	39.0	(2.4)	7.3	(0.8)	14.9	(0.9)	44.1	(3.3)
Jordan	25.9	(1.5)	10.5	(0.7)	2.0	(0.4)	38.4	(1.8)	32.4	(1.1)	17.7	(1.6)	35.7	(1.7)	57.1	(1.2)	80.3	(1.7)
Kazakhstan	3.0	(0.7)	1.2	(0.3)	0.5	(0.2)	22.4	(2.1)	12.2	(1.0)	4.3	(0.5)	74.6	(2.1)	86.6	(0.9)	95.2	(0.6)
Latvia	7.0	(1.5)	2.3	(0.4)	0.3	(0.1)	66.4	(2.4)	45.1	(1.3)	22.2	(1.3)	26.6	(2.2)	52.6	(1.4)	77.5	(1.3)
Liechtenstein	c	c	10.5	(2.6)	c	c	c	c	35.8	(3.5)	c	c	c	c	53.7	(4.0)	c	c
Lithuania	3.2	(0.6)	1.2	(0.2)	0.5	(0.2)	58.1	(1.6)	33.4	(1.0)	13.4	(1.0)	38.7	(1.6)	65.4	(1.1)	86.1	(1.1)
Macao-China	61.0	(1.0)	51.3	(1.6)	28.3	(1.1)	29.5	(0.8)	33.4	(1.4)	36.3	(1.2)	9.4	(0.6)	15.3	(1.1)	35.4	(1.1)
Malaysia	32.7	(1.8)	16.2	(1.0)	5.8	(0.7)	56.5	(1.6)	57.6	(1.5)	43.8	(2.0)	10.8	(1.0)	26.2	(1.1)	50.3	(2.4)
Montenegro	7.1	(0.6)	3.6	(0.7)	1.2	(0.3)	44.8	(1.1)	41.9	(1.3)	26.6	(1.0)	48.1	(1.1)	54.5	(1.4)	72.2	(1.0)
Peru	52.6	(1.6)	21.9	(1.4)	4.3	(0.5)	33.4	(1.3)	47.1	(1.5)	37.6	(2.1)	14.0	(0.8)	31.0	(1.2)	58.1	(2.3)
Qatar	20.4	(0.6)	8.3	(0.6)	2.3	(0.2)	23.9	(0.7)	19.7	(0.9)	13.9	(0.5)	55.7	(0.7)	71.9	(1.0)	83.9	(0.5)
Romania	13.2	(1.8)	4.0	(0.5)	0.6	(0.2)	52.8	(1.9)	44.6	(1.5)	28.6	(2.0)	34.0	(2.3)	51.4	(1.5)	70.8	(2.1)
Russian Federation	2.7	(0.8)	1.2	(0.3)	0.2	(0.1)	16.8	(1.6)	7.5	(0.5)	2.3	(0.4)	80.5	(1.7)	91.3	(0.7)	97.5	(0.4)
Serbia	9.3	(1.2)	3.9	(0.5)	0.6	(0.3)	50.0	(1.6)	42.8	(1.3)	23.3	(1.7)	40.7	(1.3)	53.3	(1.2)	76.1	(1.8)
Shanghai-China	49.6	(2.0)	22.4	(1.5)	5.9	(0.7)	30.3	(1.5)	35.5	(1.2)	25.3	(1.3)	20.1	(1.0)	42.1	(1.2)	68.8	(1.5)
Singapore	17.8	(0.9)	9.3	(0.7)	1.4	(0.3)	51.1	(1.1)	45.7	(1.0)	24.8	(1.3)	31.1	(1.1)	45.0	(1.3)	73.8	(1.3)
Chinese Taipei	21.3	(1.5)	10.9	(0.7)	3.0	(0.6)	45.3	(1.1)	39.4	(1.0)	23.8	(1.4)	33.3	(1.4)	49.8	(1.2)	73.2	(1.6)
Thailand	72.4	(1.2)	47.8	(1.3)	23.1	(1.3)	22.5	(1.1)	37.8	(1.2)	34.4	(1.5)	5.2	(0.5)	14.4	(1.0)	42.4	(2.2)
Tunisia	52.7	(1.8)	27.8	(1.0)	8.2	(0.9)	34.7	(1.9)	48.2	(1.3)	39.9	(2.0)	12.6	(1.0)	24.0	(1.1)	51.8	(2.3)
United Arab Emirates	21.5	(1.0)	7.6	(0.7)	1.1	(0.2)	38.7	(0.9)	24.8	(1.1)	10.6	(0.6)	39.8	(1.2)	67.6	(1.5)	88.4	(0.6)
Uruguay	65.9	(1.5)	43.3	(1.1)	11.0	(1.8)	15.3	(1.0)	23.0	(1.0)	20.3	(1.2)	18.8	(0.9)	33.8	(0.9)	68.7	(2.4)
Viet Nam	77.8	(1.4)	50.6	(1.6)	26.2	(2.8)	19.1	(1.3)	32.1	(1.2)	45.6	(2.2)	3.0	(0.5)	7.5	(0.7)	28.2	(2.9)

1. A socio-economically disadvantaged school is one whose students' mean socio-economic status is statistically significantly below the mean socio-economic status of the country/economy; an average school is one where there is no difference between the students' and the country's/economy's mean socio-economic status; and an advantaged school is one whose students' mean socio-economic status is statistically significantly above the country's/ economy's mean socio-economic status.
* See notes at the beginning of this Annex.
StatLink ⫘⫘⫘ http://dx.doi.org/10.1787/888932964908

[Part 2/3]
Parents' education and occupation, and students' home possessions, by schools' socio-economic profile
Table II.2.10 *Results based on students' self-reports*

| | Parents' highest occupation: Percentage of students with at least one parent working in an occupation considered as elementary (ISCO 9) | | | | | | Parents' highest occupation: Percentage of students with at least one parent working in an occupation considered as semi-skilled blue-collar (ISCO 6, 7 and 8) | | | | | | Parents' highest occupation: Percentage of students with at least one parent working in an occupation considered as semi-skilled white-collar (ISCO 4 and 5) | | | | | |
| | Socio-economically disadvantaged schools[1] | | Socio-economically average schools[1] | | Socio-economically advantaged schools[1] | | Socio-economically disadvantaged schools[1] | | Socio-economically average schools[1] | | Socio-economically advantaged schools[1] | | Socio-economically disadvantaged schools[1] | | Socio-economically average schools[1] | | Socio-economically advantaged schools[1] | |
	%	S.E.	%	S.E.	%	S.E.	%	S.E.	%	S.E.	%	S.E.	%	S.E.	%	S.E.	%	S.E.
OECD																		
Australia	8.7	(0.6)	3.7	(0.3)	1.1	(0.2)	20.0	(0.9)	10.0	(0.4)	2.6	(0.4)	25.3	(0.9)	19.2	(0.5)	7.8	(0.6)
Austria	4.8	(0.7)	1.8	(0.3)	0.7	(0.2)	28.8	(1.8)	15.5	(1.2)	3.9	(0.5)	38.6	(1.5)	32.2	(1.2)	5.8	(1.4)
Belgium	10.5	(0.8)	3.8	(0.4)	0.9	(0.2)	29.2	(1.5)	14.2	(0.8)	4.8	(0.5)	31.8	(0.9)	27.1	(0.8)	4.7	(0.8)
Canada	5.7	(0.7)	2.6	(0.2)	0.6	(0.2)	18.6	(1.0)	9.9	(0.5)	3.9	(0.5)	30.6	(1.4)	23.1	(0.6)	2.9	(0.8)
Chile	21.7	(1.6)	10.4	(1.1)	2.3	(0.4)	36.6	(1.3)	25.3	(1.2)	10.5	(0.9)	28.9	(1.2)	35.3	(1.7)	1.0	(1.3)
Czech Republic	3.6	(0.9)	1.0	(0.2)	0.2	(0.2)	32.0	(2.0)	19.7	(0.8)	3.9	(0.6)	44.0	(2.1)	35.2	(1.0)	1.6	(1.5)
Denmark	5.7	(0.8)	2.5	(0.3)	1.0	(0.3)	15.4	(1.2)	8.7	(0.6)	1.6	(0.4)	38.8	(1.6)	29.8	(0.9)	3.7	(1.3)
Estonia	3.5	(0.7)	1.9	(0.2)	0.4	(0.2)	36.3	(1.5)	19.0	(1.0)	4.6	(0.7)	31.0	(1.7)	25.8	(1.0)	1.5	(0.8)
Finland	1.7	(0.4)	0.9	(0.1)	0.2	(0.1)	19.4	(1.7)	9.4	(0.5)	2.6	(0.6)	31.5	(1.2)	24.1	(0.7)	4.1	(1.1)
France	w	w	w	w	w	w	w	w	w	w	w	w	w	w	w	w	w	w
Germany	4.3	(0.7)	1.8	(0.3)	0.4	(0.2)	25.4	(1.5)	13.9	(0.9)	3.2	(0.5)	42.6	(1.6)	31.7	(1.0)	7.0	(1.4)
Greece	11.0	(1.2)	4.2	(0.4)	1.2	(0.3)	35.8	(1.7)	17.4	(1.1)	6.1	(0.7)	32.4	(2.0)	30.5	(1.1)	8.0	(1.0)
Hungary	8.0	(1.1)	2.6	(0.5)	1.0	(0.2)	44.4	(2.1)	21.3	(1.2)	7.5	(0.9)	29.0	(1.8)	36.4	(1.2)	0.5	(1.4)
Iceland	6.1	(1.1)	2.4	(0.3)	0.6	(0.3)	19.0	(1.6)	9.0	(0.7)	3.4	(0.6)	29.0	(2.0)	22.0	(0.9)	4.6	(1.1)
Ireland	9.2	(1.4)	2.4	(0.3)	0.7	(0.2)	18.7	(2.1)	12.4	(0.7)	5.0	(0.8)	37.5	(2.1)	30.4	(0.9)	6.0	(1.4)
Israel	4.3	(0.7)	1.3	(0.3)	0.4	(0.2)	25.9	(2.1)	9.5	(1.2)	2.1	(0.4)	24.2	(1.9)	19.1	(1.0)	7.0	(0.7)
Italy	6.9	(0.4)	3.0	(0.2)	0.8	(0.1)	40.7	(1.0)	22.1	(0.6)	9.0	(0.5)	33.8	(0.8)	33.3	(0.6)	4.6	(0.9)
Japan	5.9	(0.6)	3.3	(0.4)	1.6	(0.3)	19.7	(1.2)	10.5	(0.6)	3.4	(0.4)	41.6	(1.3)	35.9	(1.0)	6.3	(1.3)
Korea	6.9	(0.8)	1.8	(0.3)	0.8	(0.3)	15.8	(1.3)	7.8	(0.5)	3.5	(0.5)	38.8	(1.5)	33.1	(1.0)	1.1	(1.3)
Luxembourg	6.9	(0.6)	3.0	(0.7)	1.5	(0.3)	31.2	(0.9)	17.5	(1.2)	6.3	(0.5)	34.2	(1.1)	29.0	(1.7)	9.6	(0.9)
Mexico	36.7	(1.4)	12.0	(0.8)	3.4	(0.2)	29.2	(0.8)	27.0	(0.6)	12.4	(0.6)	22.5	(0.9)	35.6	(0.8)	8.5	(0.9)
Netherlands	4.0	(0.8)	1.3	(0.3)	0.8	(0.5)	17.9	(1.2)	7.3	(0.7)	2.6	(0.6)	32.3	(1.6)	21.4	(0.9)	8.7	(0.9)
New Zealand	6.8	(1.0)	2.8	(0.4)	0.6	(0.3)	26.2	(2.2)	12.5	(0.6)	3.5	(0.6)	24.5	(1.5)	19.0	(0.8)	7.8	(0.9)
Norway	2.6	(0.6)	1.5	(0.2)	0.0	(0.0)	10.0	(1.6)	6.5	(0.4)	2.3	(0.5)	32.2	(2.2)	22.2	(0.7)	9.4	(1.0)
Poland	2.5	(0.4)	1.5	(0.3)	0.6	(0.2)	53.8	(2.3)	27.8	(1.1)	9.4	(1.3)	25.3	(1.6)	26.5	(0.9)	4.7	(1.2)
Portugal	12.1	(1.2)	6.1	(0.6)	1.3	(0.3)	40.4	(1.8)	24.7	(1.3)	6.6	(1.4)	31.0	(1.5)	35.0	(1.3)	21.3	(2.9)
Slovak Republic	12.0	(1.7)	4.1	(0.7)	1.3	(0.3)	37.0	(2.3)	25.8	(1.3)	7.4	(1.2)	40.8	(2.0)	38.1	(1.5)	26.9	(1.2)
Slovenia	5.0	(0.5)	2.9	(0.5)	0.8	(0.3)	32.9	(1.3)	13.9	(0.8)	4.4	(0.7)	29.0	(1.2)	28.5	(1.1)	4.3	(1.0)
Spain	10.2	(0.7)	6.0	(0.5)	1.7	(0.3)	34.9	(1.2)	21.4	(0.6)	7.3	(0.7)	32.5	(1.4)	32.7	(0.9)	21.2	(1.3)
Sweden	3.2	(0.7)	1.5	(0.3)	0.5	(0.2)	15.5	(1.4)	9.1	(0.6)	1.7	(0.4)	39.0	(2.0)	27.7	(0.8)	11.8	(0.9)
Switzerland	2.2	(0.4)	1.4	(0.2)	0.4	(0.2)	21.2	(1.3)	11.4	(0.7)	3.1	(0.3)	32.8	(1.3)	25.5	(0.9)	9.8	(0.8)
Turkey	12.4	(1.3)	9.8	(0.8)	4.0	(0.7)	43.4	(2.5)	33.0	(1.5)	19.2	(1.4)	34.3	(2.1)	38.4	(1.7)	37.4	(2.1)
United Kingdom	5.1	(0.6)	1.9	(0.3)	0.5	(0.1)	14.2	(1.5)	6.0	(0.4)	2.3	(0.4)	36.6	(1.8)	27.2	(0.8)	12.6	(1.0)
United States	12.2	(1.2)	4.9	(0.7)	1.4	(0.3)	14.9	(1.4)	7.2	(0.6)	3.5	(0.5)	28.7	(1.5)	23.5	(0.8)	12.9	(1.2)
OECD average	7.9	(0.2)	3.4	(0.1)	1.0	(0.0)	27.4	(0.3)	15.3	(0.1)	5.2	(0.1)	33.0	(0.3)	28.9	(0.2)	16.7	(0.2)
Partners																		
Albania	m	m	m	m	m	m	m	m	m	m	m	m	m	m	m	m	m	m
Argentina	14.1	(1.0)	9.8	(1.4)	2.2	(0.4)	43.3	(1.3)	28.4	(1.3)	11.8	(1.6)	26.8	(1.3)	32.5	(1.7)	28.5	(2.2)
Brazil	19.0	(0.9)	10.0	(0.7)	1.8	(0.3)	26.7	(1.0)	20.4	(0.8)	6.4	(0.6)	35.1	(0.9)	41.4	(0.8)	26.4	(1.5)
Bulgaria	8.2	(1.0)	3.0	(0.6)	0.7	(0.2)	42.6	(1.9)	23.1	(1.2)	6.7	(0.8)	29.9	(1.6)	32.1	(1.5)	19.3	(1.2)
Colombia	10.1	(0.8)	9.0	(0.7)	3.4	(0.6)	51.8	(1.6)	34.1	(1.6)	16.5	(1.6)	28.9	(1.4)	36.1	(1.6)	36.3	(1.3)
Costa Rica	23.4	(2.7)	10.1	(1.0)	1.8	(0.5)	30.9	(3.3)	20.6	(1.2)	8.8	(1.3)	30.2	(1.8)	38.6	(1.6)	20.5	(1.9)
Croatia	3.0	(0.5)	1.3	(0.3)	0.4	(0.2)	36.6	(1.4)	18.1	(1.1)	5.8	(0.8)	39.6	(1.5)	41.2	(1.1)	21.6	(2.1)
Cyprus*	4.3	(0.5)	2.1	(0.4)	0.8	(0.3)	29.6	(1.3)	13.7	(0.8)	5.3	(0.6)	42.6	(1.2)	43.1	(1.3)	26.6	(1.3)
Hong Kong-China	11.9	(0.8)	6.4	(0.7)	1.1	(0.4)	23.2	(1.0)	16.4	(0.9)	5.3	(0.9)	41.7	(1.5)	36.8	(1.1)	18.6	(1.9)
Indonesia	28.0	(3.4)	25.2	(3.3)	8.2	(1.5)	43.9	(3.1)	29.7	(3.9)	17.6	(2.3)	20.1	(1.8)	28.0	(2.8)	28.9	(2.7)
Jordan	3.8	(0.7)	1.9	(0.4)	0.4	(0.2)	31.6	(1.3)	20.8	(0.9)	6.9	(1.2)	21.5	(1.3)	17.8	(0.9)	9.1	(1.0)
Kazakhstan	6.1	(0.8)	3.3	(0.5)	1.1	(0.2)	30.9	(2.2)	19.4	(1.1)	7.3	(0.8)	18.3	(1.9)	21.3	(1.2)	14.6	(1.1)
Latvia	12.5	(1.7)	4.9	(0.6)	0.9	(0.3)	30.9	(2.5)	15.9	(1.0)	6.0	(0.7)	35.4	(2.5)	32.6	(1.1)	16.5	(1.3)
Liechtenstein	c	c	2.8	(1.4)	c	c	c	c	9.9	(2.4)	c	c	c	c	15.6	(2.7)	c	c
Lithuania	9.9	(0.9)	3.5	(0.4)	1.4	(0.4)	39.6	(1.4)	22.8	(1.0)	7.5	(0.9)	23.6	(1.5)	23.2	(0.7)	14.1	(1.2)
Macao-China	7.5	(0.5)	3.4	(0.7)	1.9	(0.4)	12.6	(0.6)	7.7	(0.8)	4.2	(0.6)	63.6	(1.0)	61.9	(1.5)	46.3	(1.2)
Malaysia	21.6	(2.0)	8.6	(0.8)	3.1	(0.6)	38.4	(1.7)	26.4	(1.1)	11.4	(1.3)	20.2	(1.3)	29.0	(1.2)	20.4	(1.3)
Montenegro	6.4	(0.7)	4.0	(0.6)	1.6	(0.3)	30.1	(1.3)	18.1	(1.4)	8.1	(0.7)	35.8	(1.2)	35.6	(1.8)	27.7	(1.2)
Peru	44.2	(1.9)	15.2	(1.3)	4.2	(0.6)	29.3	(1.2)	31.1	(1.3)	16.1	(1.5)	21.2	(1.3)	37.4	(1.4)	35.8	(1.3)
Qatar	1.1	(0.2)	0.9	(0.2)	0.1	(0.1)	12.1	(0.6)	8.6	(0.6)	3.2	(0.3)	20.5	(0.8)	17.2	(0.9)	10.2	(0.4)
Romania	8.8	(1.2)	3.7	(0.5)	0.6	(0.2)	49.3	(2.0)	31.7	(1.5)	13.3	(1.3)	27.5	(1.8)	33.3	(1.4)	20.7	(1.7)
Russian Federation	3.8	(0.7)	1.3	(0.2)	0.4	(0.1)	29.3	(1.5)	15.1	(1.0)	4.9	(0.7)	34.6	(1.8)	29.4	(1.1)	17.6	(1.1)
Serbia	5.7	(0.8)	3.5	(0.4)	1.2	(0.4)	18.5	(1.4)	12.1	(0.8)	5.5	(0.8)	53.9	(1.6)	43.6	(1.2)	23.0	(1.9)
Shanghai-China	3.1	(0.4)	1.3	(0.2)	0.3	(0.1)	29.1	(1.9)	13.3	(0.7)	4.2	(0.5)	33.0	(1.4)	29.1	(1.3)	17.1	(1.4)
Singapore	4.9	(0.5)	2.2	(0.3)	0.5	(0.2)	11.3	(0.8)	8.9	(0.7)	1.5	(0.4)	28.9	(1.0)	22.0	(1.0)	6.3	(0.7)
Chinese Taipei	5.5	(0.5)	3.4	(0.4)	0.7	(0.2)	34.4	(1.5)	20.9	(1.0)	9.1	(1.0)	37.6	(1.3)	34.0	(0.9)	21.6	(1.5)
Thailand	16.9	(1.3)	11.8	(1.0)	4.7	(0.4)	54.7	(2.0)	40.7	(1.7)	16.5	(1.3)	17.3	(1.3)	27.3	(1.5)	33.9	(1.4)
Tunisia	57.4	(2.1)	23.9	(1.5)	4.6	(0.8)	16.3	(1.3)	25.5	(1.6)	12.8	(1.2)	16.1	(1.3)	24.5	(1.4)	25.0	(1.7)
United Arab Emirates	1.7	(0.3)	0.7	(0.2)	0.1	(0.0)	10.2	(0.9)	4.1	(0.5)	1.0	(0.3)	23.9	(1.7)	14.0	(0.9)	4.8	(0.5)
Uruguay	26.2	(1.2)	15.4	(1.1)	2.0	(0.6)	27.9	(1.2)	20.9	(1.0)	7.2	(1.1)	36.7	(1.0)	39.6	(1.4)	26.5	(2.0)
Viet Nam	3.4	(1.1)	2.0	(0.5)	3.4	(0.7)	86.2	(1.6)	69.4	(2.0)	30.9	(3.8)	7.0	(0.9)	17.7	(1.6)	34.5	(2.1)

1. A socio-economically disadvantaged school is one whose students' mean socio-economic status is statistically significantly below the mean socio-economic status of the country/economy; an average school is one where there is no difference between the students' and the country's/economy's mean socio-economic status; and an advantaged school is one whose students' mean socio-economic status is statistically significantly above the country's/ economy's mean socio-economic status.
* See notes at the beginning of this Annex.
StatLink http://dx.doi.org/10.1787/888932964908

[Part 3/3]

Parents' education and occupation, and students' home possessions, by schools' socio-economic profile

Table II.2.10 *Results based on students' self-reports*

	Parents' highest occupation: Percentage of students with at least one parent working in an occupation considered as skilled (ISCO 1, 2 and 3)						Cultural possessions: Percentage of students who reported that they have poetry books at home						Number of books at home: Percentage of students who reported that they have at least 200 books at home					
	Socio-economically disadvantaged schools[1]		Socio-economically average schools[1]		Socio-economically advantaged schools[1]		Socio-economically disadvantaged schools[1]		Socio-economically average schools[1]		Socio-economically advantaged schools[1]		Socio-economically disadvantaged schools[1]		Socio-economically average schools[1]		Socio-economically advantaged schools[1]	
	%	S.E.	%	S.E.	%	S.E.	%	S.E.	%	S.E.	%	S.E.	%	S.E.	%	S.E.	%	S.E.
Australia	45.9	(1.0)	67.1	(0.6)	88.5	(0.7)	25.3	(0.7)	33.9	(0.8)	49.1	(1.0)	15.9	(0.7)	24.3	(0.8)	39.9	(1.2)
Austria	27.8	(1.4)	50.6	(1.5)	79.6	(1.7)	44.1	(1.5)	56.1	(1.2)	72.3	(2.1)	7.3	(0.8)	19.6	(1.3)	47.5	(2.8)
Belgium	28.6	(1.1)	54.9	(1.1)	79.7	(0.9)	21.0	(1.1)	28.5	(1.1)	44.0	(1.2)	8.4	(0.5)	18.3	(0.9)	33.6	(1.3)
Canada	45.1	(1.1)	64.3	(0.7)	82.6	(1.0)	26.2	(1.5)	32.5	(0.8)	43.0	(1.2)	12.7	(1.0)	22.6	(0.7)	33.4	(1.1)
Chile	12.8	(1.0)	28.9	(1.4)	66.1	(1.9)	52.1	(1.1)	56.4	(1.9)	54.4	(1.4)	2.0	(0.3)	4.3	(0.6)	13.0	(0.9)
Czech Republic	20.4	(1.8)	44.1	(1.1)	74.3	(1.5)	28.1	(2.3)	43.2	(1.4)	60.0	(1.7)	10.6	(1.4)	18.7	(1.0)	43.9	(2.1)
Denmark	40.1	(2.1)	59.0	(1.0)	83.8	(1.3)	18.4	(1.5)	27.1	(0.8)	46.6	(2.1)	10.8	(1.1)	19.0	(0.8)	34.0	(2.1)
Estonia	29.3	(1.5)	53.3	(1.2)	83.5	(1.1)	64.4	(2.0)	70.8	(1.1)	81.7	(1.2)	15.5	(1.2)	23.0	(0.9)	39.2	(1.7)
Finland	47.4	(1.9)	65.5	(0.9)	83.1	(1.1)	40.8	(1.9)	52.3	(1.0)	59.0	(1.5)	12.9	(1.3)	20.3	(0.8)	32.5	(2.0)
France	w	w	w	w	w	w	w	w	w	w	w	w	w	w	w	w	w	w
Germany	27.7	(1.5)	52.6	(1.2)	79.4	(1.6)	47.3	(1.7)	56.3	(1.1)	70.2	(1.3)	12.2	(1.0)	25.9	(1.7)	49.5	(2.3)
Greece	20.8	(1.5)	47.8	(1.2)	74.6	(1.2)	33.0	(1.7)	42.8	(1.2)	58.6	(1.7)	8.8	(0.9)	16.8	(0.9)	31.8	(1.5)
Hungary	18.7	(1.3)	39.7	(1.4)	70.9	(1.2)	44.9	(2.4)	66.6	(1.7)	85.8	(1.1)	10.9	(1.2)	27.0	(1.2)	56.0	(2.0)
Iceland	46.0	(1.7)	66.6	(0.9)	81.5	(1.2)	62.5	(1.8)	71.0	(0.9)	79.4	(1.2)	21.0	(1.7)	28.9	(0.8)	40.2	(1.5)
Ireland	34.6	(2.3)	54.8	(0.9)	78.4	(1.4)	24.1	(2.3)	34.7	(1.2)	45.0	(1.5)	7.4	(1.2)	19.2	(0.8)	37.0	(1.8)
Israel	45.6	(2.3)	70.0	(1.5)	90.5	(0.9)	47.6	(2.1)	49.1	(1.8)	59.9	(1.6)	17.2	(2.1)	23.4	(2.3)	35.7	(3.2)
Italy	18.7	(0.7)	41.6	(0.6)	65.6	(0.9)	42.2	(1.1)	54.4	(0.8)	74.3	(0.8)	7.9	(0.5)	16.6	(0.6)	37.0	(1.0)
Japan	32.8	(1.0)	50.3	(1.0)	68.7	(1.4)	13.8	(1.0)	25.2	(1.0)	39.4	(1.7)	18.2	(1.0)	21.0	(0.9)	33.4	(1.7)
Korea	38.4	(1.5)	57.4	(1.1)	74.6	(1.4)	46.5	(1.5)	65.1	(1.1)	76.5	(1.5)	17.7	(1.4)	37.1	(1.5)	56.9	(2.4)
Luxembourg	27.7	(1.0)	50.4	(1.6)	72.6	(1.0)	41.0	(1.0)	54.7	(1.9)	65.3	(1.0)	16.6	(0.7)	37.3	(1.7)	56.8	(1.1)
Mexico	11.5	(0.4)	25.5	(0.5)	55.6	(1.1)	39.5	(1.0)	44.7	(0.8)	50.1	(0.9)	1.8	(0.2)	2.5	(0.2)	7.4	(0.6)
Netherlands	45.8	(1.6)	70.0	(1.1)	87.9	(0.9)	20.2	(1.6)	24.3	(1.3)	42.9	(1.9)	8.5	(1.1)	16.6	(1.5)	36.8	(2.0)
New Zealand	42.6	(2.4)	65.7	(0.9)	88.0	(1.3)	29.1	(1.4)	36.3	(1.2)	47.4	(2.0)	12.9	(1.2)	23.7	(1.2)	40.3	(1.9)
Norway	55.2	(2.2)	69.9	(0.8)	88.3	(1.2)	31.8	(2.5)	42.9	(1.2)	62.3	(2.5)	17.8	(2.2)	26.1	(0.9)	46.1	(3.0)
Poland	18.4	(1.0)	44.3	(1.0)	75.3	(1.8)	33.7	(1.3)	47.1	(1.1)	64.5	(2.0)	6.3	(0.8)	14.2	(1.0)	40.2	(2.7)
Portugal	16.5	(1.0)	34.2	(0.8)	70.9	(4.1)	35.6	(1.3)	50.1	(1.3)	72.8	(2.1)	4.7	(0.6)	11.9	(0.7)	32.9	(1.9)
Slovak Republic	10.2	(1.2)	32.0	(1.3)	64.5	(2.0)	45.2	(2.1)	61.5	(1.1)	74.4	(1.5)	4.3	(0.8)	10.8	(0.9)	28.8	(1.9)
Slovenia	33.2	(1.2)	54.7	(1.2)	80.5	(1.3)	44.6	(1.2)	57.7	(1.2)	78.8	(1.3)	4.8	(0.6)	10.7	(0.7)	30.3	(1.6)
Spain	22.3	(0.8)	39.9	(0.8)	69.7	(1.5)	47.8	(1.1)	55.6	(0.9)	68.7	(1.3)	10.4	(0.6)	21.7	(0.6)	38.3	(1.2)
Sweden	42.3	(1.8)	61.6	(0.9)	85.9	(1.0)	25.1	(1.5)	32.4	(1.0)	48.5	(2.1)	14.2	(1.5)	25.2	(1.0)	37.9	(1.8)
Switzerland	43.7	(1.7)	61.8	(0.9)	86.7	(1.0)	29.7	(1.5)	35.2	(1.0)	50.8	(2.0)	11.5	(0.9)	16.6	(1.1)	39.2	(1.9)
Turkey	9.9	(0.9)	18.8	(0.8)	39.4	(2.3)	51.9	(1.7)	59.6	(1.2)	69.4	(2.1)	2.9	(0.5)	6.6	(0.7)	20.3	(2.2)
United Kingdom	44.1	(2.5)	64.9	(0.9)	84.6	(1.2)	27.3	(1.9)	36.6	(1.1)	53.8	(1.4)	9.6	(0.7)	20.0	(1.1)	39.1	(2.0)
United States	44.2	(1.9)	64.5	(1.2)	82.2	(1.5)	33.2	(1.7)	38.0	(1.4)	46.0	(1.5)	5.7	(0.5)	16.3	(1.2)	22.7	(1.5)
OECD average	31.7	(0.3)	52.5	(0.2)	77.0	(0.3)	36.4	(0.3)	46.5	(0.2)	60.5	(0.3)	10.5	(0.2)	19.5	(0.2)	36.7	(0.3)
Albania	m	m	m	m	m	m	m	m	m	m	m	m	m	m	m	m	m	m
Argentina	15.8	(1.2)	29.2	(1.4)	57.5	(3.4)	50.5	(1.7)	54.4	(2.3)	55.8	(1.8)	2.1	(0.4)	5.9	(0.7)	10.8	(1.1)
Brazil	19.1	(0.7)	28.1	(0.8)	65.4	(2.0)	50.8	(1.1)	52.8	(1.1)	50.7	(1.3)	1.5	(0.2)	2.4	(0.3)	6.5	(0.8)
Bulgaria	19.2	(1.0)	41.7	(1.6)	73.3	(1.7)	44.6	(1.9)	63.0	(1.7)	83.4	(0.9)	5.5	(0.7)	11.5	(0.9)	26.3	(1.5)
Colombia	9.3	(0.8)	20.7	(1.2)	43.8	(2.2)	48.6	(2.1)	55.7	(1.3)	59.1	(1.7)	0.7	(0.3)	1.7	(0.2)	4.4	(0.8)
Costa Rica	15.5	(1.7)	30.7	(1.1)	68.9	(2.5)	23.7	(1.1)	33.3	(1.4)	46.2	(2.2)	0.4	(0.1)	1.8	(0.3)	10.2	(1.5)
Croatia	20.8	(1.1)	39.5	(1.3)	72.3	(2.2)	18.9	(1.1)	31.8	(1.1)	55.1	(2.3)	3.1	(0.4)	7.2	(0.7)	20.1	(1.6)
Cyprus*	23.4	(1.2)	41.1	(1.3)	67.3	(1.3)	35.6	(1.2)	43.3	(1.3)	56.6	(1.2)	11.0	(0.6)	17.0	(0.9)	28.5	(1.1)
Hong Kong-China	23.2	(1.0)	40.4	(1.3)	75.0	(2.6)	37.5	(1.8)	50.4	(1.5)	66.0	(2.3)	3.8	(0.5)	11.0	(0.8)	28.2	(2.1)
Indonesia	7.9	(0.9)	17.2	(1.3)	45.3	(3.8)	33.2	(2.1)	39.2	(2.0)	39.9	(2.3)	3.0	(0.5)	5.3	(0.7)	9.5	(1.3)
Jordan	43.0	(1.4)	59.4	(1.2)	83.7	(1.3)	38.5	(1.3)	40.6	(1.0)	49.6	(2.2)	5.4	(0.6)	7.9	(0.4)	12.7	(1.3)
Kazakhstan	44.6	(2.0)	56.1	(1.1)	77.0	(1.4)	69.8	(2.4)	74.6	(1.6)	76.1	(1.8)	3.5	(0.7)	7.9	(0.9)	17.0	(1.9)
Latvia	21.3	(2.2)	46.6	(1.2)	76.6	(1.4)	49.9	(2.7)	61.3	(1.4)	80.2	(1.3)	10.0	(1.7)	17.8	(1.0)	31.4	(1.8)
Liechtenstein	c	c	71.6	(3.5)	c	c	c	c	54.7	(4.1)	c	c	c	c	19.3	(3.6)	c	c
Lithuania	26.9	(1.4)	50.5	(1.0)	77.0	(1.5)	34.7	(1.4)	53.2	(1.4)	72.5	(1.5)	5.6	(0.8)	14.1	(0.8)	26.4	(1.8)
Macao-China	16.3	(0.8)	26.9	(1.3)	47.6	(1.2)	39.4	(0.9)	36.3	(1.5)	47.0	(1.2)	4.1	(0.3)	4.9	(0.8)	11.5	(0.8)
Malaysia	19.9	(1.3)	36.0	(1.2)	65.1	(2.2)	43.2	(1.7)	40.1	(1.3)	39.6	(1.6)	6.9	(0.9)	10.2	(1.0)	15.6	(1.5)
Montenegro	27.7	(1.1)	42.2	(1.7)	62.6	(1.4)	62.4	(1.1)	74.0	(1.4)	82.1	(1.0)	10.1	(0.8)	14.2	(1.2)	26.3	(1.0)
Peru	5.2	(0.6)	16.3	(1.1)	43.9	(2.4)	77.1	(1.3)	73.9	(1.4)	66.9	(1.3)	1.9	(0.3)	2.4	(0.3)	5.3	(0.8)
Qatar	66.3	(0.9)	73.3	(1.0)	86.4	(0.5)	53.8	(1.0)	54.2	(1.0)	57.3	(0.7)	10.9	(0.5)	14.6	(0.8)	20.5	(0.6)
Romania	14.3	(1.1)	31.4	(1.4)	65.4	(2.6)	73.7	(1.6)	82.4	(1.3)	94.0	(0.7)	4.1	(0.7)	8.5	(0.7)	28.9	(2.0)
Russian Federation	32.3	(1.3)	54.2	(1.0)	77.2	(1.5)	62.5	(1.8)	76.6	(1.0)	90.4	(0.8)	8.3	(0.9)	17.4	(1.0)	32.7	(1.5)
Serbia	21.9	(1.2)	40.8	(1.1)	70.3	(2.1)	56.9	(1.8)	69.8	(1.2)	85.5	(1.3)	3.5	(0.5)	9.2	(0.7)	25.6	(1.8)
Shanghai-China	34.8	(1.6)	56.3	(1.2)	78.3	(1.6)	66.9	(1.7)	76.4	(1.2)	86.5	(1.0)	3.9	(0.4)	8.1	(0.7)	24.3	(1.7)
Singapore	54.9	(1.0)	66.8	(1.0)	91.6	(0.8)	24.5	(1.0)	29.7	(1.0)	50.6	(1.7)	7.4	(0.6)	14.6	(0.8)	31.7	(1.5)
Chinese Taipei	22.5	(1.0)	41.7	(1.1)	68.5	(1.9)	38.5	(1.2)	53.4	(1.2)	72.7	(1.9)	10.3	(0.8)	19.0	(0.8)	35.8	(1.4)
Thailand	11.1	(0.9)	20.1	(1.3)	44.9	(2.1)	44.7	(1.4)	43.0	(1.6)	44.3	(1.6)	2.1	(0.4)	3.1	(0.6)	11.7	(1.0)
Tunisia	10.2	(1.0)	26.1	(1.3)	57.6	(2.2)	24.5	(1.6)	32.8	(1.3)	41.7	(2.0)	1.1	(0.3)	2.5	(0.4)	6.6	(0.9)
United Arab Emirates	64.2	(1.7)	81.2	(1.1)	94.1	(0.6)	41.2	(1.3)	44.7	(1.1)	50.4	(0.9)	6.4	(0.4)	11.5	(0.6)	20.3	(1.1)
Uruguay	9.2	(0.6)	24.1	(0.9)	64.4	(2.8)	40.0	(1.3)	49.2	(1.5)	54.8	(2.3)	2.6	(0.4)	4.5	(0.6)	15.8	(1.8)
Viet Nam	3.4	(0.5)	10.8	(1.0)	31.2	(3.0)	38.1	(2.3)	41.1	(2.3)	44.6	(1.4)	1.9	(0.4)	4.2	(0.5)	5.3	(0.9)

1. A socio-economically disadvantaged school is one whose students' mean socio-economic status is statistically significantly below the mean socio-economic status of the country/economy; an average school is one where there is no difference between the students' and the country's/economy's mean socio-economic status; and an advantaged school is one whose students' mean socio-economic status is statistically significantly above the country's/ economy's mean socio-economic status.
* See notes at the beginning of this Annex.
StatLink http://dx.doi.org/10.1787/888932964908

[Part 1/2]
School performance and schools' socio-economic profile
Table II.2.11   *Results based on students' self-reports*

| | Percentage of students (across schools of all socio-economic profiles) | | | | | | Percentage of students in schools that are socio-economically disadvantaged and ... | | | | | |
| | Schools with low achievement in mathematics[1] | | Schools with average achievement in mathematics[1] | | Schools with high achievement in mathematics[1] | | have low achievement in mathematics[1] | | have average achievement in mathematics[1] | | have high achievement in mathematics[1] | |
	%	S.E.	%	S.E.	%	S.E.	%	S.E.	%	S.E.	%	S.E.
Australia	24.4	(1.6)	51.2	(2.1)	24.4	(1.5)	13.6	(1.1)	9.8	(1.3)	0.4	(0.3)
Austria	37.1	(2.4)	20.6	(3.0)	42.3	(2.9)	25.1	(2.7)	7.1	(2.3)	0.3	(0.6)
Belgium	33.7	(1.9)	27.6	(2.4)	38.7	(2.0)	23.5	(2.0)	4.4	(1.3)	1.1	(0.7)
Canada	22.9	(2.3)	54.6	(2.8)	22.5	(2.1)	9.5	(1.6)	10.2	(1.7)	1.7	(0.8)
Chile	42.7	(3.5)	23.3	(3.9)	34.0	(3.3)	31.6	(3.3)	8.2	(2.0)	3.0	(1.5)
Czech Republic	31.3	(3.1)	37.3	(3.8)	31.4	(2.5)	13.0	(2.2)	8.5	(2.4)	0.2	(0.1)
Denmark	18.4	(2.9)	58.9	(3.8)	22.7	(2.9)	10.1	(2.3)	11.2	(2.5)	0.0	(0.1)
Estonia	19.9	(2.7)	59.4	(3.5)	20.7	(2.3)	7.8	(1.7)	10.9	(1.8)	0.3	(0.6)
Finland	12.9	(2.5)	73.0	(3.5)	14.0	(2.4)	4.0	(1.4)	11.8	(2.6)	0.1	(0.3)
France	w	w	w	w	w	w	w	w	w	w	w	w
Germany	36.1	(2.4)	25.2	(2.8)	38.7	(2.2)	21.4	(2.3)	5.6	(1.5)	1.0	(0.7)
Greece	23.2	(2.8)	43.2	(4.0)	33.6	(3.3)	17.8	(2.6)	6.7	(1.9)	0.7	(0.7)
Hungary	36.2	(2.4)	23.4	(2.7)	40.4	(2.6)	25.2	(2.2)	6.4	(2.3)	0.0	(0.1)
Iceland	19.0	(2.6)	56.2	(3.1)	24.7	(1.1)	7.1	(0.3)	8.8	(0.3)	0.4	(0.3)
Ireland	18.9	(2.8)	60.5	(3.5)	20.6	(2.5)	14.5	(2.3)	2.7	(1.3)	0.0	(0.0)
Israel	32.4	(2.7)	28.0	(3.3)	39.6	(3.7)	22.4	(2.6)	7.3	(2.1)	0.0	(0.0)
Italy	38.6	(1.7)	21.3	(2.0)	40.0	(1.9)	22.1	(1.4)	3.8	(0.9)	2.9	(0.7)
Japan	40.5	(2.9)	22.2	(3.1)	37.3	(3.0)	23.7	(2.4)	4.4	(1.6)	1.4	(1.0)
Korea	30.6	(2.6)	33.2	(3.8)	36.2	(3.5)	20.8	(2.4)	5.2	(1.8)	0.7	(0.7)
Luxembourg	42.6	(0.4)	15.4	(0.4)	42.0	(0.5)	39.7	(0.1)	8.2	(0.1)	0.0	(0.0)
Mexico	29.5	(1.5)	40.7	(2.0)	29.8	(1.7)	17.5	(1.4)	13.9	(1.3)	2.8	(0.6)
Netherlands	40.7	(2.9)	13.9	(2.9)	45.4	(2.5)	20.5	(2.6)	2.9	(0.9)	0.0	(0.0)
New Zealand	25.6	(2.6)	48.9	(3.4)	25.5	(2.3)	14.6	(2.3)	6.8	(2.2)	0.1	(0.1)
Norway	18.2	(3.1)	62.1	(3.7)	19.7	(3.1)	4.1	(1.6)	5.8	(1.8)	0.2	(0.3)
Poland	26.2	(3.8)	53.9	(4.2)	19.9	(3.1)	15.3	(3.0)	12.1	(2.5)	0.1	(0.4)
Portugal	28.8	(3.3)	37.7	(4.1)	33.5	(3.7)	21.4	(3.0)	10.8	(3.0)	1.4	(1.5)
Slovak Republic	30.2	(3.3)	38.9	(4.0)	30.9	(2.5)	19.5	(2.6)	7.0	(1.5)	0.4	(0.4)
Slovenia	42.0	(0.8)	16.9	(1.4)	41.0	(1.1)	24.3	(0.6)	4.0	(0.7)	1.1	(0.5)
Spain	25.3	(2.3)	49.9	(3.1)	24.8	(2.2)	17.3	(2.4)	12.0	(2.2)	0.1	(0.1)
Sweden	18.5	(3.0)	64.2	(4.2)	17.3	(2.9)	8.1	(2.2)	9.3	(2.4)	0.6	(0.6)
Switzerland	35.5	(3.1)	37.1	(3.1)	27.4	(2.8)	16.1	(2.7)	8.0	(1.6)	2.4	(1.3)
Turkey	52.5	(3.6)	19.3	(2.7)	28.2	(2.8)	25.4	(3.1)	5.3	(1.9)	1.4	(1.0)
United Kingdom	26.9	(3.2)	47.7	(3.8)	25.4	(2.8)	14.9	(2.9)	9.2	(2.2)	0.1	(0.2)
United States	32.9	(3.9)	37.9	(4.3)	29.2	(3.8)	21.1	(3.1)	5.6	(2.0)	0.0	(0.0)
OECD average	30.3	(0.5)	38.8	(0.6)	30.8	(0.5)	18.1	(0.4)	7.5	(0.3)	0.8	(0.1)
Albania	9.4	(2.6)	77.8	(3.8)	12.8	(2.6)	m	m	m	m	m	m
Argentina	33.4	(3.5)	29.4	(3.5)	37.2	(3.9)	24.2	(3.1)	9.0	(2.2)	0.2	(0.3)
Brazil	33.3	(2.3)	39.8	(3.0)	26.9	(2.1)	17.8	(1.9)	12.1	(2.1)	2.3	(1.0)
Bulgaria	40.5	(3.4)	25.7	(3.5)	33.9	(2.8)	27.7	(3.0)	4.8	(1.8)	1.2	(1.1)
Colombia	28.7	(3.1)	44.1	(3.8)	27.3	(3.4)	19.0	(2.8)	9.3	(2.3)	0.4	(0.4)
Costa Rica	32.3	(3.4)	41.0	(3.4)	26.7	(3.4)	18.9	(3.0)	9.5	(2.5)	0.1	(0.3)
Croatia	37.2	(3.3)	32.6	(3.4)	30.2	(2.5)	19.8	(2.8)	12.4	(2.3)	0.8	(0.7)
Cyprus*	29.6	(0.8)	34.7	(1.8)	35.7	(1.4)	20.1	(1.1)	13.4	(0.7)	1.1	(1.1)
Hong Kong-China	35.9	(3.4)	23.0	(3.7)	41.1	(2.8)	25.5	(3.0)	6.6	(2.4)	3.3	(1.5)
Indonesia	36.5	(3.5)	34.1	(4.4)	29.4	(3.7)	18.8	(3.3)	14.6	(3.6)	6.5	(2.1)
Jordan	31.4	(3.8)	43.5	(4.2)	25.1	(3.1)	10.9	(2.1)	7.8	(2.2)	2.0	(1.1)
Kazakhstan	39.4	(3.3)	35.3	(3.8)	25.3	(3.4)	15.7	(3.2)	4.4	(1.8)	2.7	(1.2)
Latvia	20.5	(3.2)	54.7	(3.8)	24.9	(2.8)	9.0	(1.9)	11.2	(2.4)	0.0	(0.0)
Liechtenstein	c	c	c	c	c	c	c	c	c	c	c	c
Lithuania	27.1	(3.2)	44.2	(4.1)	28.6	(2.9)	15.7	(2.2)	6.9	(1.4)	0.3	(0.3)
Macao-China	33.8	(0.1)	22.5	(1.4)	43.7	(1.4)	26.4	(0.0)	9.0	(0.6)	16.2	(0.6)
Malaysia	35.5	(3.7)	39.3	(3.9)	25.2	(3.2)	21.0	(2.6)	7.5	(2.2)	0.1	(0.3)
Montenegro	46.4	(2.1)	22.3	(2.4)	31.4	(3.4)	37.2	(0.7)	1.5	(0.7)	0.0	(0.0)
Peru	36.9	(2.7)	29.1	(3.5)	34.0	(3.4)	26.9	(2.5)	7.7	(1.9)	0.4	(0.4)
Qatar	56.1	(0.4)	7.2	(0.5)	36.7	(0.4)	23.2	(0.3)	1.9	(0.3)	8.6	(0.1)
Romania	40.3	(3.5)	29.5	(3.5)	30.1	(2.9)	22.8	(3.2)	6.4	(1.9)	1.6	(1.1)
Russian Federation	27.3	(2.9)	47.5	(3.5)	25.3	(3.1)	12.5	(2.1)	7.3	(2.0)	2.1	(1.0)
Serbia	42.0	(3.4)	22.8	(3.2)	35.3	(2.9)	25.2	(3.1)	6.9	(2.2)	0.1	(0.5)
Shanghai-China	37.2	(2.6)	25.1	(3.2)	37.7	(2.4)	25.6	(2.8)	3.6	(1.5)	0.3	(0.6)
Singapore	35.6	(2.3)	36.6	(2.6)	27.8	(0.7)	19.9	(1.8)	10.6	(1.8)	0.0	(0.0)
Chinese Taipei	36.8	(3.2)	30.8	(4.1)	32.4	(3.3)	25.8	(2.9)	3.7	(1.5)	0.6	(0.7)
Thailand	39.6	(3.2)	32.5	(3.7)	27.9	(3.4)	23.9	(3.0)	10.3	(2.3)	4.9	(1.5)
Tunisia	39.2	(3.6)	23.2	(4.0)	37.5	(3.5)	20.0	(3.0)	6.8	(2.0)	2.7	(1.4)
United Arab Emirates	37.8	(2.9)	32.5	(2.9)	29.7	(2.0)	17.4	(1.5)	7.5	(1.4)	0.4	(0.5)
Uruguay	38.4	(2.6)	27.2	(3.2)	34.4	(2.3)	29.3	(2.5)	9.7	(2.1)	1.3	(1.1)
Viet Nam	30.0	(3.7)	34.4	(4.8)	35.6	(4.2)	21.7	(3.3)	14.2	(2.7)	3.5	(1.3)

1. A socio-economically disadvantaged school is one whose students' mean socio-economic status is statistically significantly below the mean socio-economic status of the country/economy; an average school is one where there is no difference between the students' and the country's/economy's mean socio-economic status; and an advantaged school is one whose students' mean socio-economic status is statistically significantly above the country's/economy's mean socio-economic status. The classification by performance is done in an analogue way.
* See notes at the beginning of this Annex.
StatLink ᴍ⬚ᴩ http://dx.doi.org/10.1787/888932964908

[Part 2/2]
School performance and schools' socio-economic profile
Table II.2.11   *Results based on students' self-reports*

| | Percentage of students in schools that are socio-economically average and... | | | | | | Percentage of students in schools that are socio-economically advantaged and... | | | | | |
| | have low achievement in mathematics[1] | | have average achievement in mathematics[1] | | have high achievement in mathematics[1] | | have low achievement in mathematics[1] | | have average achievement in mathematics[1] | | have high achievement in mathematics[1] | |
	%	S.E.	%	S.E.	%	S.E.	%	S.E.	%	S.E.	%	S.E.
Australia	10.1	(1.3)	34.1	(2.1)	7.1	(1.0)	0.6	(0.4)	7.4	(1.1)	17.0	(1.3)
Austria	10.8	(2.1)	10.1	(2.6)	20.5	(2.8)	1.2	(0.8)	3.5	(1.9)	21.5	(2.5)
Belgium	9.4	(1.7)	17.8	(2.4)	10.0	(1.9)	0.7	(0.6)	5.4	(1.6)	27.6	(1.9)
Canada	12.5	(1.8)	33.7	(2.7)	6.4	(1.2)	1.0	(0.7)	10.6	(1.4)	14.4	(1.8)
Chile	9.5	(2.5)	8.9	(2.7)	4.4	(1.9)	1.6	(1.0)	6.2	(2.1)	26.7	(2.6)
Czech Republic	18.3	(2.5)	27.4	(3.0)	12.0	(2.3)	0.0	(0.0)	1.5	(0.7)	19.2	(1.9)
Denmark	8.3	(1.8)	39.8	(3.5)	8.0	(2.3)	0.0	(0.0)	8.0	(2.0)	14.6	(2.2)
Estonia	11.6	(2.5)	39.3	(3.4)	7.2	(2.0)	0.5	(0.6)	9.2	(1.3)	13.3	(1.5)
Finland	8.5	(2.0)	50.5	(3.8)	8.0	(2.3)	0.4	(0.2)	10.7	(1.7)	5.9	(1.5)
France	w	w	w	w	w	w	w	w	w	w	w	w
Germany	13.6	(2.2)	18.4	(2.5)	13.2	(2.3)	0.7	(0.6)	1.1	(0.8)	24.9	(2.1)
Greece	5.4	(1.6)	29.5	(3.9)	13.5	(2.7)	0.0	(0.0)	7.0	(2.2)	19.4	(2.9)
Hungary	10.6	(2.3)	14.7	(2.9)	9.7	(2.1)	0.4	(0.3)	2.3	(1.2)	30.7	(2.4)
Iceland	11.9	(2.8)	39.6	(2.6)	4.4	(1.9)	0.0	(0.0)	7.8	(0.8)	20.0	(0.8)
Ireland	4.3	(1.7)	45.8	(3.8)	6.9	(2.0)	0.1	(0.4)	12.0	(2.5)	13.7	(2.1)
Israel	9.3	(2.3)	16.0	(2.8)	13.1	(3.0)	1.0	(1.0)	4.5	(1.8)	26.4	(3.1)
Italy	14.8	(1.3)	12.1	(1.5)	14.3	(1.2)	1.8	(0.5)	5.4	(1.1)	22.8	(1.7)
Japan	14.3	(2.8)	14.2	(2.9)	14.6	(2.3)	2.3	(1.2)	3.6	(1.2)	21.4	(2.1)
Korea	9.1	(2.1)	22.5	(3.3)	17.0	(2.9)	0.7	(0.7)	5.5	(1.9)	18.5	(3.1)
Luxembourg	2.9	(0.4)	2.6	(0.5)	9.5	(0.4)	0.0	(0.0)	4.5	(0.2)	32.6	(0.2)
Mexico	10.3	(1.3)	17.1	(1.6)	7.8	(1.1)	1.4	(0.3)	9.7	(1.2)	19.3	(1.4)
Netherlands	19.2	(3.3)	9.2	(2.4)	22.5	(3.1)	1.0	(0.8)	1.7	(1.1)	22.9	(3.2)
New Zealand	11.0	(2.9)	36.7	(3.5)	7.7	(2.3)	0.0	(0.0)	5.4	(1.5)	17.7	(2.3)
Norway	14.1	(2.9)	49.9	(3.7)	9.3	(2.5)	0.0	(0.0)	6.4	(1.8)	10.2	(2.3)
Poland	9.2	(3.0)	36.5	(3.8)	4.5	(1.9)	1.6	(1.0)	5.4	(2.0)	15.2	(2.6)
Portugal	7.4	(1.7)	21.9	(3.9)	16.6	(3.2)	0.0	(0.0)	5.1	(2.4)	15.4	(2.9)
Slovak Republic	10.3	(2.2)	29.2	(3.8)	7.8	(2.1)	0.4	(0.6)	2.7	(1.5)	22.7	(2.0)
Slovenia	17.4	(0.8)	10.8	(1.0)	12.0	(0.6)	0.3	(0.1)	2.1	(0.3)	27.9	(0.6)
Spain	7.9	(1.2)	27.7	(3.0)	7.2	(1.2)	0.1	(0.1)	10.2	(2.0)	17.4	(2.1)
Sweden	9.7	(2.1)	43.1	(3.8)	6.1	(1.7)	0.7	(0.7)	11.8	(2.5)	10.6	(2.3)
Switzerland	16.9	(2.4)	24.6	(2.9)	5.8	(1.8)	2.6	(1.1)	4.4	(1.5)	19.3	(2.1)
Turkey	24.8	(3.6)	10.0	(2.6)	8.4	(1.5)	2.3	(1.5)	4.1	(1.4)	18.4	(2.3)
United Kingdom	12.0	(2.4)	31.9	(2.9)	8.2	(1.9)	0.0	(0.0)	6.6	(1.7)	17.1	(2.1)
United States	10.5	(3.5)	23.8	(4.1)	10.0	(2.5)	1.3	(0.9)	8.6	(2.4)	19.1	(3.3)
OECD average	11.4	(0.4)	25.4	(0.5)	10.4	(0.4)	0.8	(0.1)	6.0	(0.3)	19.7	(0.4)
Albania	m	m	m	m	m	m	m	m	m	m	m	m
Argentina	9.2	(2.5)	13.4	(2.4)	12.1	(2.8)	0.0	(0.0)	7.0	(2.6)	24.9	(3.4)
Brazil	14.9	(2.0)	23.1	(2.2)	5.9	(1.4)	0.6	(0.4)	4.6	(1.2)	18.7	(1.5)
Bulgaria	12.2	(2.7)	15.6	(2.9)	4.7	(1.5)	0.6	(0.4)	5.2	(1.8)	28.0	(2.6)
Colombia	9.6	(1.9)	24.5	(3.5)	7.5	(2.5)	0.0	(0.0)	10.3	(2.8)	19.3	(2.6)
Costa Rica	12.6	(2.4)	26.2	(3.0)	9.9	(3.1)	0.8	(0.4)	5.2	(2.0)	16.7	(2.5)
Croatia	17.1	(3.0)	18.2	(2.8)	8.3	(2.2)	0.3	(0.3)	2.0	(1.1)	21.1	(1.8)
Cyprus*	7.7	(0.5)	15.9	(0.9)	13.4	(1.0)	1.8	(0.0)	5.5	(1.5)	21.2	(1.5)
Hong Kong-China	9.7	(2.6)	12.4	(2.7)	18.0	(2.5)	0.7	(0.8)	3.9	(1.6)	19.8	(3.7)
Indonesia	14.8	(2.7)	12.1	(3.1)	6.0	(2.0)	2.9	(1.2)	7.4	(2.6)	16.9	(3.0)
Jordan	19.8	(3.2)	29.6	(3.7)	10.0	(2.5)	0.7	(0.7)	6.1	(2.0)	13.1	(1.7)
Kazakhstan	21.4	(3.4)	15.9	(2.8)	8.1	(2.0)	2.3	(1.5)	15.1	(3.1)	14.5	(2.8)
Latvia	11.5	(2.3)	34.9	(3.7)	3.8	(1.6)	0.1	(0.4)	8.2	(2.3)	21.3	(2.5)
Liechtenstein	c	c	c	c	c	c	c	c	c	c	c	c
Lithuania	11.3	(2.4)	30.9	(3.7)	10.9	(2.5)	0.1	(0.4)	6.5	(1.9)	17.5	(2.3)
Macao-China	3.4	(0.1)	6.0	(1.3)	8.1	(1.3)	4.0	(0.0)	7.5	(0.2)	19.3	(0.2)
Malaysia	13.1	(2.8)	25.2	(3.7)	4.6	(1.8)	1.4	(1.0)	6.6	(2.3)	20.6	(3.0)
Montenegro	8.9	(1.8)	8.2	(2.1)	6.5	(2.2)	0.3	(0.2)	12.5	(2.0)	24.8	(2.0)
Peru	9.9	(2.0)	16.4	(2.8)	5.5	(1.7)	0.1	(0.3)	5.0	(1.8)	28.1	(3.0)
Qatar	16.1	(0.2)	2.9	(0.5)	3.5	(0.4)	16.8	(0.1)	2.3	(0.1)	24.6	(0.2)
Romania	17.0	(3.2)	15.4	(2.9)	8.1	(2.3)	0.5	(0.6)	7.7	(2.2)	20.4	(2.9)
Russian Federation	14.6	(3.0)	29.4	(3.2)	6.2	(2.2)	0.2	(0.4)	10.7	(2.5)	17.0	(2.3)
Serbia	16.7	(3.0)	13.8	(3.1)	12.7	(2.6)	0.0	(0.0)	2.0	(1.1)	22.4	(2.3)
Shanghai-China	10.6	(2.0)	16.6	(3.4)	10.2	(2.2)	1.0	(0.9)	5.0	(1.9)	27.2	(2.6)
Singapore	15.7	(1.0)	20.8	(0.8)	8.8	(0.6)	0.0	(0.0)	5.2	(0.9)	19.0	(0.8)
Chinese Taipei	10.9	(2.1)	21.5	(4.0)	9.8	(2.5)	0.1	(0.0)	5.6	(2.2)	22.0	(2.6)
Thailand	12.8	(2.2)	13.0	(2.8)	5.9	(1.9)	2.9	(1.2)	9.3	(2.2)	17.0	(2.7)
Tunisia	17.6	(3.1)	11.8	(3.1)	14.8	(2.8)	1.6	(0.9)	4.7	(1.4)	20.0	(2.9)
United Arab Emirates	15.5	(2.0)	14.0	(2.0)	10.5	(1.3)	4.9	(1.6)	10.9	(2.1)	18.8	(1.9)
Uruguay	9.1	(1.8)	16.1	(2.6)	12.2	(2.0)	0.0	(0.0)	1.3	(0.7)	20.9	(2.2)
Viet Nam	6.9	(1.6)	14.2	(3.2)	13.3	(2.9)	1.5	(1.1)	6.0	(2.6)	18.7	(3.4)

1. A socio-economically disadvantaged school is one whose students' mean socio-economic status is statistically significantly below the mean socio-economic status of the country/economy; an average school is one where there is no difference between the students' and the country's/economy's mean socio-economic status; and an advantaged school is one whose students' mean socio-economic status is statistically significantly above the country's/economy's mean socio-economic status. The classification by performance is done in an analogue way.
* See notes at the beginning of this Annex.

StatLink http://dx.doi.org/10.1787/888932964908

[Part 1/2]

Table II.2.12 **Change between 2003 and 2012 in enrolment of 15-year-olds**

		PISA 2003			PISA 2012			Change between 2003 and 2012 (PISA 2012 - PISA 2003)	
		Total population of 15-year-olds	Total population of 15-year-olds enrolled at Grade 7 or above	Coverage index 3: Percentage of enrolled population	Total population of 15-year-olds	Total population of 15-year-olds enrolled at Grade 7 or above	Coverage index 3: Percentage of enrolled population	Total population of 15-year-olds	Total population of 15-year-olds enrolled at Grade 7 or above	Coverage index 3: Percentage of enrolled population
OECD	Australia	268 164	250 635	93	291 967	288 159	99	23 803	37 524	5.2
	Austria	94 515	89 049	94	93 537	89 073	95	- 978	24	1.0
	Belgium	120 802	118 185	98	123 469	121 493	98	2 667	3 308	0.6
	Canada	399 265	399 265	100	417 873	409 453	98	18 608	10 188	-2.0
	Chile	m	m	m	274 803	252 733	92	m	m	m
	Czech Republic	130 679	126 348	97	96 946	93 214	96	-33 733	-33 134	-0.5
	Denmark	59 156	58 188	98	72 310	70 854	98	13 154	12 666	-0.4
	Estonia	m	m	m	12 649	12 438	98	m	m	m
	Finland	61 107	61 107	100	62 523	62 195	99	1 416	1 088	-0.5
	France	809 053	808 276	100	792 983	755 447	95	-16 070	-52 829	-4.6
	Germany	951 800	916 869	96	798 136	798 136	100	-153 664	-118 733	3.7
	Greece	111 286	108 314	97	110 521	105 096	95	- 765	-3 218	-2.2
	Hungary	129 138	123 762	96	111 761	108 816	97	-17 377	-14 946	1.5
	Iceland	4 168	4 112	99	4 505	4 491	100	337	379	1.0
	Ireland	61 535	58 997	96	59 296	57 979	98	-2 239	-1 018	1.9
	Israel	m	m	m	118 953	113 278	95	m	m	m
	Italy	574 611	574 611	100	605 490	566 973	94	30 879	-7 638	-6.4
	Japan	1 365 471	1 328 498	97	1 241 786	1 214 756	98	-123 685	-113 742	0.5
	Korea	606 722	606 370	100	687 104	672 101	98	80 382	65 731	-2.1
	Luxembourg	4 204	4 204	100	6 187	6 082	98	1 983	1 878	-1.7
	Mexico	2 192 452	1 273 163	58	2 114 745	1 472 875	70	-77 707	199 712	11.6
	Netherlands	194 216	194 216	100	194 000	193 190	100	- 216	-1 026	-0.4
	New Zealand	55 440	53 293	96	60 940	59 118	97	5 500	5 825	0.9
	Norway	56 060	55 648	99	64 917	64 777	100	8 857	9 129	0.5
	Poland	589 506	569 294	97	425 597	410 700	96	-163 909	-158 594	-0.1
	Portugal	109 149	99 216	91	127 537	127 537	100	18 388	28 321	9.1
	Slovak Republic	84 242	81 945	97	59 723	59 367	99	-24 519	-22 578	2.1
	Slovenia	m	m	m	19 471	18 935	97	m	m	m
	Spain	454 064	418 005	92	423 444	404 374	95	-30 620	-13 631	3.4
	Sweden	112 258	112 258	100	102 087	102 027	100	-10 171	-10 231	-0.1
	Switzerland	83 247	81 020	97	87 200	85 239	98	3 953	4 219	0.4
	Turkey	1 351 492	725 030	54	1 266 638	965 736	76	-84 854	240 706	22.6
	United Kingdom	768 180	736 785	96	745 581	745 581	100	-22 599	8 796	4.1
	United States	3 979 116	3 979 116	100	4 074 457	4 074 457	100	95 341	95 341	0.0
Partners	Albania	m	m	m	76 910	50 157	65	m	m	m
	Argentina	m	m	m	684 879	637 603	93	m	m	m
	Brazil	3 618 332	2 359 854	65	3 574 928	2 786 064	78	-43 404	426 210	12.7
	Bulgaria	m	m	m	70 188	59 684	85	m	m	m
	Colombia	m	m	m	889 729	620 422	70	m	m	m
	Costa Rica	m	m	m	81 489	64 326	79	m	m	m
	Croatia	m	m	m	48 155	46 550	97	m	m	m
	Cyprus*	m	m	m	m	m	m	m	m	m
	Hong Kong-China	75 000	72 631	97	84 200	77 864	92	9 200	5 233	-4.4
	Indonesia	4 281 895	3 113 548	73	4 174 217	3 599 844	86	-107 678	486 296	13.5
	Jordan	m	m	m	129 492	125 333	97	m	m	m
	Kazakhstan	m	m	m	258 716	247 048	95	m	m	m
	Latvia	37 544	37 138	99	18 789	18 389	98	-18 755	-18 749	-1.0
	Liechtenstein	402	348	87	417	383	92	15	35	5.3
	Lithuania	m	m	m	38 524	35 567	92	m	m	m
	Macao-China	8 318	6 939	83	6 600	5 416	82	-1 718	-1 523	-1.4
	Malaysia	m	m	m	544 302	457 999	84	m	m	m
	Montenegro	m	m	m	8 600	8 600	100	m	m	m
	Peru	m	m	m	584 294	508 969	87	m	m	m
	Qatar	m	m	m	11 667	11 532	99	m	m	m
	Romania	m	m	m	146 243	146 243	100	m	m	m
	Russian Federation	2 496 216	2 366 285	95	1 272 632	1 268 814	100	-1223 584	-1097 471	4.9
	Serbia	98 729	92 617	94	80 089	75 870	95	-18 640	-16 747	0.9
	Shanghai-China	m	m	m	108 056	90 796	84	m	m	m
	Singapore	m	m	m	53 637	52 163	97	m	m	m
	Chinese Taipei	m	m	m	328 356	328 336	100	m	m	m
	Thailand	927 070	778 267	84	982 080	784 897	80	55 010	6 630	-4.0
	Tunisia	164 758	164 758	100	132 313	132 313	100	-32 445	-32 445	0.0
	United Arab Emirates	m	m	m	48 824	48 446	99	m	m	m
	Uruguay	53 948	40 023	74	54 638	46 442	85	690	6 419	10.8
	Viet Nam	m	m	m	1 717 996	1 091 462	64	m	m	m

Note: These data come from Annex 2 in PISA 2003 and Annex A2 in this publication. If the proportion of students enrolled in Grade 7 or above were higher than 100, then the figure for the total population of 15-year-olds was set to the proportion of 15-year-olds enrolled. These data are collected from different national data sources: for example, total population is collected from national censuses, which are conducted only in certain years. It is therefore possible that the population data are based on an older source than the enrolment data. These differences may result in an estimated enrolled population that is larger than the total population, which is clearly not possible.

* See notes at the beginning of this Annex.

StatLink ⟨⟩ http://dx.doi.org/10.1787/888932964908

[Part 2/2]
Table II.2.12 **Change between 2003 and 2012 in enrolment of 15-year-olds**

	Percentage change between 2003 and 2012 (PISA 2012 - PISA 2003)/(PISA 203) Total population of 15-year-olds enrolled at Grade 7 or above	Mean mathematics performance in PISA 2012	Mean mathematics performance in PISA 2012 if those not enrolled performed at the bottom of proficiency Level 1 (i.e. 357.77 score points)	Difference in mathematics performance after accounting for those who are not attending school at age 15	Performance rank among all countries before accounting	Performance rank among all countries after accounting	Difference in performance rank after accounting (before-after)
Australia	15.0	504	502	2	19	17	2
Austria	0.0	506	498	7	18	18	0
Belgium	2.8	515	512	3	15	14	1
Canada	2.6	518	515	3	13	12	1
Chile	m	423	417	5	52	49	3
Czech Republic	-26.2	499	494	5	24	24	0
Denmark	21.8	500	497	3	22	21	1
Estonia	m	521	518	3	11	11	0
Finland	1.8	519	518	1	12	10	2
France	-6.5	495	488	6	25	27	-2
Germany	-12.9	514	514	0	16	13	3
Greece	-3.0	453	448	5	43	42	1
Hungary	-12.1	477	474	3	40	37	3
Iceland	9.2	493	492	0	28	25	3
Ireland	-1.7	501	498	3	20	19	1
Israel	m	466	461	5	42	40	2
Italy	-1.3	485	477	8	33	36	-3
Japan	-8.6	536	533	4	7	6	1
Korea	10.8	554	549	4	5	4	1
Luxembourg	44.7	490	488	2	30	29	1
Mexico	15.7	413	396	17	54	55	-1
Netherlands	-0.5	523	522	1	10	8	2
New Zealand	10.9	500	496	4	23	22	1
Norway	16.4	489	489	0	31	26	5
Poland	-27.9	518	512	6	14	15	-1
Portugal	28.5	487	487	0	32	30	2
Slovak Republic	-27.6	482	481	1	36	33	3
Slovenia	m	501	497	4	21	20	1
Spain	-3.3	484	479	6	34	34	0
Sweden	-9.1	478	478	0	39	35	4
Switzerland	5.2	531	527	4	9	7	2
Turkey	33.2	448	427	21	45	48	-3
United Kingdom	1.2	494	494	0	27	23	4
United States	2.4	481	481	0	37	32	5
Albania	m	394	382	13	58	60	-2
Argentina	m	388	386	2	60	57	3
Brazil	18.1	391	384	7	59	59	0
Bulgaria	m	439	427	12	48	47	1
Colombia	m	376	371	6	63	63	0
Costa Rica	m	407	397	10	57	54	3
Croatia	m	471	467	4	41	39	2
Cyprus*	m	440	m	m	m	m	m
Hong Kong-China	7.2	561	546	15	3	5	-2
Indonesia	15.6	375	373	2	65	62	3
Jordan	m	386	385	1	62	58	4
Kazakhstan	m	432	428	3	50	46	4
Latvia	-50.5	491	488	3	29	28	1
Liechtenstein	10.1	535	521	14	8	9	-1
Lithuania	m	479	470	9	38	38	0
Macao-China	-21.9	538	506	32	6	16	-10
Malaysia	m	421	411	10	53	51	2
Montenegro	m	410	410	0	55	52	3
Peru	m	368	367	1	66	64	2
Qatar	m	376	376	0	64	61	3
Romania	m	445	445	0	46	43	3
Russian Federation	-46.4	482	482	0	35	31	4
Serbia	-18.1	449	444	5	44	44	0
Shanghai-China	m	613	572	41	1	1	0
Singapore	m	573	568	6	2	2	0
Chinese Taipei	m	560	560	0	4	3	1
Thailand	0.9	427	413	14	51	50	1
Tunisia	-19.7	388	388	0	61	56	5
United Arab Emirates	m	434	433	1	49	45	4
Uruguay	16.0	409	402	8	56	53	3
Viet Nam	m	511	455	56	17	41	-24

Note: These data come from Annex 2 in PISA 2003 and Annex A2 in this publication. If the proportion of students enrolled in Grade 7 or above were higher than 100, then the figure for the total population of 15-year-olds was set to the proportion of 15-year-olds enrolled. These data are collected from different national data sources: for example, total population is collected from national censuses, which are conducted only in certain years. It is therefore possible that the population data are based on an older source than the enrolment data. These differences may result in an estimated enrolled population that is larger than the total population, which is clearly not possible.
* See notes at the beginning of this Annex.
StatLink http://dx.doi.org/10.1787/888932964908

[Part 1/2]
Students' socio-economic status
Table II.2.13a   *Results based on students' self-reports*

	PISA index of economic, social and cultural status (ESCS)		Variation in ESCS		Skewness of the distribution of ESCS		Percentage of students with low ESCS[1] — Approximated by the percentage of students with a value of ESCS lower than -1		Variation in distribution of students across ESCS — 25th percentile of ESCS		75th percentile of ESCS		Interquartile range of distribution of students across ESCS	
	Mean index	S.E.	S.D.	S.E.	Skewness	S.E.	%	S.E.	Index	S.E.	Index	S.E.	Range	S.E.
OECD														
Australia	0.25	(0.01)	0.79	(0.01)	-0.46	(0.03)	6.8	(0.3)	-0.31	(0.02)	0.86	(0.01)	1.1	(0.02)
Austria	0.08	(0.02)	0.85	(0.01)	0.02	(0.05)	8.3	(0.6)	-0.53	(0.02)	0.66	(0.03)	1.1	(0.03)
Belgium	0.15	(0.02)	0.91	(0.02)	-0.33	(0.18)	10.5	(0.6)	-0.57	(0.03)	0.89	(0.03)	1.4	(0.02)
Canada	0.41	(0.02)	0.86	(0.01)	-0.39	(0.05)	5.6	(0.4)	-0.20	(0.02)	1.08	(0.01)	1.2	(0.02)
Chile	-0.58	(0.04)	1.13	(0.02)	0.13	(0.04)	37.7	(1.5)	-1.38	(0.05)	0.26	(0.06)	1.6	(0.06)
Czech Republic	-0.07	(0.02)	0.75	(0.01)	0.14	(0.06)	9.1	(0.6)	-0.62	(0.01)	0.47	(0.04)	1.0	(0.03)
Denmark	0.43	(0.02)	0.84	(0.01)	-0.35	(0.04)	4.3	(0.4)	-0.23	(0.03)	1.09	(0.03)	1.3	(0.03)
Estonia	0.11	(0.01)	0.81	(0.01)	0.01	(0.04)	7.8	(0.5)	-0.55	(0.02)	0.78	(0.02)	1.3	(0.02)
Finland	0.36	(0.02)	0.77	(0.01)	-0.44	(0.04)	4.0	(0.3)	-0.21	(0.02)	0.99	(0.02)	1.2	(0.02)
France	-0.04	(0.02)	0.80	(0.01)	-0.33	(0.03)	11.8	(0.6)	-0.62	(0.02)	0.58	(0.02)	1.2	(0.02)
Germany	0.19	(0.02)	0.93	(0.01)	-0.08	(0.04)	9.8	(0.6)	-0.49	(0.03)	0.95	(0.04)	1.4	(0.03)
Greece	-0.06	(0.03)	1.00	(0.01)	-0.09	(0.04)	18.6	(1.0)	-0.81	(0.03)	0.78	(0.04)	1.5	(0.03)
Hungary	-0.25	(0.03)	0.96	(0.02)	-0.06	(0.07)	23.7	(1.0)	-0.97	(0.03)	0.52	(0.05)	1.4	(0.03)
Iceland	0.78	(0.01)	0.81	(0.01)	-0.48	(0.04)	1.9	(0.2)	0.20	(0.02)	1.42	(0.01)	1.2	(0.02)
Ireland	0.13	(0.02)	0.85	(0.01)	-0.15	(0.03)	9.2	(0.6)	-0.53	(0.02)	0.81	(0.03)	1.3	(0.03)
Israel	0.17	(0.03)	0.85	(0.02)	-0.77	(0.08)	8.8	(0.6)	-0.40	(0.03)	0.82	(0.02)	1.2	(0.02)
Italy	-0.05	(0.01)	0.97	(0.01)	0.08	(0.02)	18.4	(0.4)	-0.76	(0.02)	0.66	(0.02)	1.4	(0.02)
Japan	-0.07	(0.02)	0.71	(0.01)	-0.02	(0.03)	10.0	(0.6)	-0.62	(0.02)	0.49	(0.02)	1.1	(0.02)
Korea	0.01	(0.03)	0.74	(0.01)	-0.28	(0.04)	9.5	(0.6)	-0.54	(0.02)	0.59	(0.03)	1.1	(0.02)
Luxembourg	0.07	(0.01)	1.10	(0.01)	-0.29	(0.02)	18.7	(0.6)	-0.71	(0.03)	0.99	(0.02)	1.7	(0.02)
Mexico	-1.11	(0.02)	1.27	(0.01)	0.21	(0.02)	55.9	(0.8)	-2.07	(0.02)	-0.19	(0.04)	1.8	(0.03)
Netherlands	0.23	(0.02)	0.78	(0.01)	-0.50	(0.05)	5.9	(0.5)	-0.31	(0.02)	0.83	(0.03)	1.1	(0.02)
New Zealand	0.04	(0.02)	0.82	(0.01)	-0.26	(0.04)	11.5	(0.6)	-0.56	(0.03)	0.68	(0.02)	1.2	(0.02)
Norway	0.46	(0.02)	0.76	(0.01)	-0.55	(0.09)	2.6	(0.3)	-0.06	(0.03)	1.01	(0.02)	1.0	(0.03)
Poland	-0.21	(0.03)	0.90	(0.01)	0.41	(0.04)	19.1	(1.0)	-0.92	(0.02)	0.54	(0.07)	1.4	(0.06)
Portugal	-0.48	(0.05)	1.19	(0.02)	0.43	(0.05)	39.8	(1.6)	-1.42	(0.04)	0.34	(0.11)	1.7	(0.09)
Slovak Republic	-0.18	(0.03)	0.92	(0.02)	0.06	(0.07)	15.0	(0.9)	-0.79	(0.02)	0.42	(0.04)	1.2	(0.04)
Slovenia	0.07	(0.01)	0.87	(0.01)	0.08	(0.04)	11.2	(0.4)	-0.63	(0.02)	0.77	(0.02)	1.4	(0.02)
Spain	-0.19	(0.03)	1.03	(0.01)	0.01	(0.03)	23.5	(0.8)	-0.96	(0.03)	0.65	(0.04)	1.6	(0.03)
Sweden	0.28	(0.02)	0.82	(0.01)	-0.41	(0.05)	5.7	(0.3)	-0.33	(0.02)	0.93	(0.02)	1.2	(0.02)
Switzerland	0.17	(0.02)	0.89	(0.02)	-0.21	(0.03)	10.4	(0.6)	-0.47	(0.03)	0.90	(0.03)	1.3	(0.02)
Turkey	-1.46	(0.04)	1.10	(0.02)	0.43	(0.04)	68.7	(1.3)	-2.28	(0.03)	-0.71	(0.07)	1.5	(0.05)
United Kingdom	0.27	(0.02)	0.80	(0.01)	-0.19	(0.03)	5.6	(0.3)	-0.33	(0.02)	0.90	(0.02)	1.2	(0.02)
United States	0.17	(0.04)	0.97	(0.02)	-0.33	(0.04)	13.4	(1.0)	-0.52	(0.05)	0.91	(0.05)	1.4	(0.04)
OECD average	0.00	(0.00)	0.90	(0.00)	-0.16	(0.07)	15.4	(0.1)	-0.66	(0.00)	0.70	(0.01)	1.3	(0.01)
Partners														
Albania	m	m	m	m	m	m	m	m	m	m	m	m	m	m
Argentina	-0.72	(0.04)	1.11	(0.02)	-0.06	(0.05)	41.2	(1.5)	-1.51	(0.04)	0.15	(0.06)	1.6	(0.06)
Brazil	-1.17	(0.02)	1.17	(0.01)	0.15	(0.02)	57.5	(0.9)	-2.04	(0.03)	-0.33	(0.03)	1.7	(0.03)
Bulgaria	-0.28	(0.04)	1.05	(0.03)	-0.38	(0.12)	24.3	(1.2)	-0.99	(0.03)	0.54	(0.05)	1.5	(0.04)
Colombia	-1.26	(0.04)	1.18	(0.03)	-0.07	(0.04)	56.4	(1.4)	-2.15	(0.06)	-0.40	(0.06)	1.4	(0.05)
Costa Rica	-0.98	(0.04)	1.24	(0.02)	-0.14	(0.04)	49.2	(1.5)	-1.90	(0.05)	0.02	(0.07)	1.2	(0.06)
Croatia	-0.34	(0.02)	0.85	(0.01)	0.23	(0.03)	21.7	(0.7)	-0.94	(0.02)	0.26	(0.04)	1.0	(0.03)
Cyprus*	0.09	(0.01)	0.91	(0.01)	-0.06	(0.03)	10.7	(0.5)	-0.60	(0.02)	0.82	(0.01)	1.2	(0.02)
Hong Kong-China	-0.79	(0.05)	0.97	(0.02)	0.09	(0.05)	45.2	(2.0)	-1.53	(0.04)	-0.03	(0.08)	1.9	(0.06)
Indonesia	-1.80	(0.05)	1.10	(0.03)	0.41	(0.06)	76.7	(1.9)	-2.64	(0.04)	-1.09	(0.09)	1.5	(0.07)
Jordan	-0.42	(0.02)	1.02	(0.01)	-0.54	(0.05)	27.8	(0.9)	-1.10	(0.03)	0.36	(0.03)	1.5	(0.03)
Kazakhstan	-0.32	(0.02)	0.75	(0.01)	-0.35	(0.05)	20.1	(0.9)	-0.89	(0.03)	0.28	(0.03)	1.7	(0.03)
Latvia	-0.26	(0.03)	0.89	(0.01)	0.01	(0.04)	24.3	(1.3)	-0.98	(0.03)	0.49	(0.03)	1.7	(0.03)
Liechtenstein	0.30	(0.05)	0.91	(0.03)	-0.25	(0.11)	9.4	(1.6)	-0.28	(0.05)	0.97	(0.06)	1.5	(0.06)
Lithuania	-0.13	(0.02)	0.92	(0.01)	-0.18	(0.04)	21.5	(0.8)	-0.89	(0.03)	0.65	(0.02)	1.4	(0.03)
Macao-China	-0.89	(0.01)	0.87	(0.01)	0.36	(0.03)	48.6	(0.6)	-1.49	(0.01)	-0.35	(0.01)	1.4	(0.02)
Malaysia	-0.72	(0.02)	0.99	(0.02)	-0.17	(0.04)	40.5	(1.4)	-1.37	(0.03)	0.04	(0.04)	1.1	(0.03)
Montenegro	-0.25	(0.01)	0.89	(0.01)	-0.13	(0.03)	21.4	(0.5)	-0.89	(0.02)	0.44	(0.02)	1.3	(0.02)
Peru	-1.23	(0.05)	1.23	(0.02)	0.13	(0.04)	59.9	(1.7)	-2.11	(0.06)	-0.38	(0.09)	1.3	(0.07)
Qatar	0.44	(0.01)	0.89	(0.01)	-0.75	(0.01)	7.0	(0.2)	-0.03	(0.01)	1.02	(0.01)	1.5	(0.01)
Romania	-0.47	(0.04)	0.94	(0.03)	-0.27	(0.15)	25.9	(1.3)	-1.02	(0.02)	0.15	(0.07)	1.7	(0.06)
Russian Federation	-0.11	(0.02)	0.76	(0.01)	-0.28	(0.04)	12.3	(0.7)	-0.65	(0.03)	0.51	(0.02)	1.6	(0.02)
Serbia	-0.30	(0.02)	0.90	(0.01)	0.23	(0.03)	24.0	(1.0)	-0.98	(0.03)	0.39	(0.04)	1.7	(0.03)
Shanghai-China	-0.36	(0.04)	0.96	(0.01)	-0.26	(0.04)	27.2	(1.4)	-1.08	(0.04)	0.43	(0.04)	1.5	(0.04)
Singapore	-0.26	(0.01)	0.92	(0.01)	-0.27	(0.04)	21.3	(0.5)	-0.88	(0.02)	0.45	(0.02)	1.3	(0.03)
Chinese Taipei	-0.40	(0.02)	0.84	(0.01)	-0.08	(0.04)	24.7	(1.0)	-1.00	(0.03)	0.22	(0.04)	1.2	(0.03)
Thailand	-1.35	(0.02)	1.17	(0.02)	0.40	(0.04)	64.4	(1.5)	-2.26	(0.03)	-0.56	(0.07)	1.70	(0.05)
Tunisia	-1.19	(0.05)	1.26	(0.02)	-0.10	(0.04)	54.4	(1.6)	-2.15	(0.06)	-0.26	(0.08)	1.89	(0.07)
United Arab Emirates	0.32	(0.02)	0.85	(0.01)	-0.81	(0.04)	7.2	(0.4)	-0.14	(0.02)	0.90	(0.01)	1.03	(0.02)
Uruguay	-0.88	(0.04)	1.13	(0.02)	0.32	(0.03)	50.4	(1.1)	-1.77	(0.02)	-0.06	(0.05)	1.71	(0.04)
Viet Nam	-1.81	(0.05)	1.12	(0.03)	0.62	(0.04)	78.9	(1.6)	-2.57	(0.03)	-1.20	(0.08)	1.86	(0.07)

1. Students with low ESCS are those with a value on the *PISA index of economic, social and cultural status* lower than -1.
2. Distribution of the school mean ESCS, percentiles calculated at the student level.
3. The *index of social inclusion* is calculated as 100*(1-rho), where rho stands for the intra-class correlation of socio-economic status, i.e. the between-school variation in the *PISA index of social, economic and cultural status* of students, divided by the sum of the between-school variation in students' socio-economic status and the within-school variation in students' socio-economic status.
* See notes at the beginning of this Annex.
StatLink ﹏ http://dx.doi.org/10.1787/888932964908

[Part 2/2]
Students' socio-economic status
Table II.2.13a   *Results based on students' self-reports*

		Variation in distribution of schools across ESCS[2]						
		25th percentile of school mean ESCS		75th percentile of school mean ESCS		Interquartile range of distribution of schools across ESCS		Index of social inclusion[3]	
		Index	S.E.	Index	S.E.	Range	S.E.	Index	S.E.
OECD	Australia	-0.05	(0.02)	0.54	(0.01)	0.60	(0.02)	76.5	(1.1)
	Austria	-0.23	(0.04)	0.36	(0.02)	0.60	(0.04)	71.2	(2.8)
	Belgium	-0.24	(0.07)	0.51	(0.05)	0.75	(0.09)	72.4	(2.1)
	Canada	0.15	(0.02)	0.70	(0.02)	0.54	(0.03)	82.8	(1.2)
	Chile	-1.13	(0.07)	-0.08	(0.08)	1.06	(0.11)	47.2	(2.2)
	Czech Republic	-0.34	(0.02)	0.17	(0.02)	0.50	(0.03)	76.4	(2.2)
	Denmark	0.16	(0.04)	0.68	(0.04)	0.52	(0.05)	82.3	(1.6)
	Estonia	-0.14	(0.02)	0.34	(0.04)	0.48	(0.04)	81.5	(2.0)
	Finland	0.20	(0.03)	0.55	(0.01)	0.35	(0.03)	91.1	(1.0)
	France	w	w	w	w	w	w	w	w
	Germany	-0.18	(0.03)	0.60	(0.03)	0.78	(0.05)	73.6	(1.9)
	Greece	-0.41	(0.11)	0.27	(0.06)	0.69	(0.11)	73.5	(2.6)
	Hungary	-0.70	(0.07)	0.25	(0.08)	0.95	(0.10)	62.6	(2.6)
	Iceland	0.54	(0.00)	1.04	(0.00)	0.49	(0.00)	86.4	(1.9)
	Ireland	-0.09	(0.03)	0.39	(0.03)	0.48	(0.04)	79.7	(2.1)
	Israel	-0.18	(0.04)	0.54	(0.04)	0.72	(0.05)	74.6	(2.0)
	Italy	-0.43	(0.02)	0.32	(0.02)	0.75	(0.03)	75.9	(1.1)
	Japan	-0.32	(0.02)	0.18	(0.03)	0.50	(0.03)	77.8	(1.7)
	Korea	-0.24	(0.06)	0.23	(0.04)	0.46	(0.07)	78.3	(1.9)
	Luxembourg	-0.46	(0.00)	0.57	(0.00)	1.03	(0.00)	73.6	(3.4)
	Mexico	-1.64	(0.01)	-0.62	(0.04)	1.02	(0.03)	56.5	(1.5)
	Netherlands	0.00	(0.03)	0.51	(0.04)	0.51	(0.05)	81.8	(1.8)
	New Zealand	-0.21	(0.01)	0.27	(0.02)	0.48	(0.02)	77.5	(2.4)
	Norway	0.30	(0.02)	0.60	(0.03)	0.30	(0.03)	91.0	(1.4)
	Poland	-0.54	(0.05)	0.05	(0.06)	0.59	(0.07)	76.4	(2.2)
	Portugal	-0.98	(0.05)	-0.19	(0.07)	0.79	(0.07)	68.6	(3.3)
	Slovak Republic	-0.48	(0.05)	0.14	(0.04)	0.62	(0.06)	64.4	(3.0)
	Slovenia	-0.29	(0.01)	0.52	(0.00)	0.81	(0.01)	74.6	(1.9)
	Spain	-0.57	(0.04)	0.21	(0.05)	0.78	(0.06)	75.2	(1.4)
	Sweden	0.04	(0.02)	0.53	(0.06)	0.49	(0.06)	86.9	(1.4)
	Switzerland	-0.14	(0.03)	0.48	(0.04)	0.62	(0.04)	82.7	(1.5)
	Turkey	-1.83	(0.03)	-1.13	(0.05)	0.70	(0.06)	72.3	(2.9)
	United Kingdom	-0.02	(0.04)	0.53	(0.02)	0.54	(0.04)	79.4	(2.0)
	United States	-0.15	(0.05)	0.54	(0.06)	0.69	(0.08)	73.8	(2.4)
	OECD average	-0.33	(0.01)	0.32	(0.01)	0.64	(0.01)	75.6	(0.4)
Partners	Albania	m	m	m	m	m	m	m	m
	Argentina	-1.24	(0.04)	-0.23	(0.09)	1.02	(0.10)	66.5	(2.6)
	Brazil	-1.66	(0.02)	-0.85	(0.04)	0.81	(0.04)	62.8	(2.3)
	Bulgaria	-0.68	(0.05)	0.18	(0.11)	0.87	(0.12)	59.6	(3.0)
	Colombia	-1.75	(0.08)	-0.83	(0.06)	0.92	(0.09)	63.2	(2.7)
	Costa Rica	-1.47	(0.08)	-0.65	(0.07)	0.81	(0.10)	61.8	(3.1)
	Croatia	-0.66	(0.03)	-0.12	(0.03)	0.54	(0.04)	75.9	(2.2)
	Cyprus*	-0.25	(0.00)	0.42	(0.00)	0.67	(0.00)	76.6	(3.2)
	Hong Kong-China	-1.20	(0.03)	-0.49	(0.15)	0.71	(0.14)	67.7	(3.2)
	Indonesia	-2.27	(0.03)	-1.38	(0.12)	0.89	(0.11)	63.1	(4.3)
	Jordan	-0.71	(0.03)	-0.17	(0.03)	0.54	(0.04)	79.6	(2.8)
	Kazakhstan	-0.57	(0.02)	-0.04	(0.02)	0.53	(0.03)	76.8	(2.1)
	Latvia	-0.58	(0.04)	0.05	(0.08)	0.64	(0.09)	74.7	(2.5)
	Liechtenstein	0.07	(0.00)	0.64	(0.00)	0.56	(0.00)	85.5	(4.1)
	Lithuania	-0.45	(0.02)	0.16	(0.03)	0.61	(0.03)	78.7	(1.9)
	Macao-China	-1.21	(0.00)	-0.71	(0.00)	0.50	(0.00)	73.7	(4.7)
	Malaysia	-1.08	(0.03)	-0.37	(0.07)	0.72	(0.08)	71.5	(2.4)
	Montenegro	-0.53	(0.00)	-0.01	(0.00)	0.52	(0.00)	80.6	(5.2)
	Peru	-1.84	(0.05)	-0.62	(0.11)	1.23	(0.10)	54.2	(2.6)
	Qatar	0.21	(0.00)	0.71	(0.00)	0.50	(0.00)	75.5	(3.2)
	Romania	-0.80	(0.05)	-0.12	(0.06)	0.68	(0.07)	64.4	(3.6)
	Russian Federation	-0.39	(0.05)	0.15	(0.03)	0.53	(0.05)	75.0	(2.4)
	Serbia	-0.62	(0.02)	-0.03	(0.06)	0.59	(0.06)	78.0	(2.3)
	Shanghai-China	-0.73	(0.08)	0.07	(0.06)	0.81	(0.09)	66.8	(2.5)
	Singapore	-0.59	(0.00)	-0.02	(0.03)	0.57	(0.03)	76.4	(2.5)
	Chinese Taipei	-0.70	(0.02)	-0.10	(0.05)	0.60	(0.06)	76.7	(2.0)
	Thailand	-1.87	(0.03)	-0.85	(0.04)	1.01	(0.04)	61.6	(2.9)
	Tunisia	-1.71	(0.08)	-0.70	(0.13)	1.01	(0.14)	67.2	(3.0)
	United Arab Emirates	0.00	(0.02)	0.68	(0.01)	0.68	(0.02)	73.9	(1.8)
	Uruguay	-1.44	(0.04)	-0.61	(0.03)	0.82	(0.04)	60.2	(3.5)
	Viet Nam	-2.25	(0.02)	-1.45	(0.12)	0.79	(0.12)	58.3	(3.4)

1. Students with low ESCS are those with a value on the *PISA index of economic, social and cultural status* lower than -1.
2. Distribution of the school mean ESCS, percentiles calculated at the student level.
3. The *index of social inclusion* is calculated as 100*(1-rho), where rho stands for the intra-class correlation of socio-economic status, i.e. the between-school variation in the *PISA index of social, economic and cultural status* of students, divided by the sum of the between-school variation in students' socio-economic status and the within-school variation in students' socio-economic status.
* See notes at the beginning of this Annex.
StatLink ⫘⬛ http://dx.doi.org/10.1787/888932964908

Change between 2003 and 2012 in the socio-economic status of students
Table II.2.13b   *Results based on students' self-reports*

		PISA 2003								
	ESCS[1]		Variability in the ESCS		Skewness of the distribution of the ESCS		Percentage of students with low ESCS[2]		Index of social inclusion[3]	
	Mean index	S.E.	S.D.	S.E.	Skewness	S.E.	%	S.E.	Index	S.E.
Australia	0.04	(0.02)	0.88	(0.01)	-0.08	(0.02)	12.4	(0.5)	75.5	(1.7)
Austria	-0.26	(0.03)	0.86	(0.01)	0.20	(0.05)	20.2	(1.1)	71.6	(1.9)
Belgium	-0.03	(0.02)	1.01	(0.01)	-0.14	(0.03)	18.0	(0.7)	70.9	(1.9)
Canada	0.21	(0.02)	0.93	(0.01)	-0.07	(0.02)	10.0	(0.4)	81.6	(1.2)
Czech Republic	-0.05	(0.02)	0.87	(0.01)	0.14	(0.03)	15.1	(0.7)	74.3	(2.0)
Denmark	0.08	(0.03)	0.98	(0.01)	-0.08	(0.03)	14.2	(0.8)	83.1	(2.3)
Finland	0.06	(0.02)	0.97	(0.01)	-0.12	(0.03)	14.7	(0.6)	89.4	(1.5)
France	-0.32	(0.03)	0.96	(0.01)	-0.02	(0.03)	24.8	(1.1)	w	w
Germany	0.01	(0.03)	1.08	(0.01)	-0.03	(0.04)	15.9	(0.8)	69.2	(1.9)
Greece	-0.30	(0.05)	1.04	(0.02)	0.21	(0.04)	26.0	(1.3)	71.5	(4.0)
Hungary	-0.31	(0.02)	0.95	(0.01)	0.28	(0.04)	25.4	(1.0)	60.3	(2.5)
Iceland	0.55	(0.02)	0.93	(0.01)	-0.33	(0.04)	5.5	(0.4)	85.4	(2.8)
Ireland	-0.26	(0.03)	0.93	(0.01)	0.06	(0.04)	21.9	(1.0)	81.4	(2.4)
Italy	-0.29	(0.03)	1.08	(0.01)	0.19	(0.03)	28.8	(0.9)	70.8	(1.9)
Japan	-0.42	(0.02)	0.80	(0.01)	0.05	(0.05)	25.4	(1.1)	71.5	(2.2)
Korea	-0.36	(0.03)	0.94	(0.02)	0.03	(0.04)	24.5	(0.9)	70.7	(2.4)
Luxembourg	-0.09	(0.01)	1.07	(0.01)	-0.26	(0.02)	20.7	(0.6)	76.7	(4.3)
Mexico	-1.32	(0.05)	1.19	(0.02)	0.38	(0.05)	62.7	(1.9)	61.7	(2.6)
Netherlands	-0.08	(0.03)	0.97	(0.01)	-0.07	(0.04)	18.7	(0.9)	77.4	(2.1)
New Zealand	-0.13	(0.02)	0.90	(0.01)	-0.35	(0.04)	16.3	(0.7)	84.5	(1.9)
Norway	0.19	(0.02)	0.79	(0.01)	-0.25	(0.04)	6.9	(0.4)	90.0	(1.7)
Poland	-0.41	(0.02)	0.92	(0.01)	0.46	(0.03)	28.8	(1.1)	79.7	(1.9)
Portugal	-0.91	(0.05)	1.34	(0.02)	0.46	(0.03)	53.0	(1.5)	76.6	(2.8)
Slovak Republic	-0.25	(0.03)	0.94	(0.02)	0.21	(0.04)	21.8	(1.2)	69.8	(2.3)
Spain	-0.51	(0.04)	1.15	(0.01)	0.18	(0.04)	36.0	(1.5)	73.2	(1.9)
Sweden	0.08	(0.03)	0.98	(0.01)	-0.25	(0.04)	14.5	(0.8)	89.4	(1.4)
Switzerland	-0.23	(0.03)	1.02	(0.01)	0.06	(0.03)	22.9	(1.0)	76.1	(2.4)
Turkey	-1.15	(0.06)	1.05	(0.03)	0.63	(0.05)	61.3	(2.4)	59.4	(4.6)
United States	0.05	(0.03)	0.98	(0.02)	-0.20	(0.04)	14.4	(0.8)	77.0	(2.4)
OECD average 2003	-0.22	(0.01)	0.98	(0.00)	0.04	(0.01)	23.5	(0.2)	75.5	(0.5)
Brazil	-1.56	(0.05)	1.23	(0.02)	0.22	(0.04)	67.3	(1.5)	61.1	(3.3)
Hong Kong-China	-1.27	(0.04)	0.95	(0.02)	0.49	(0.04)	65.6	(1.6)	76.6	(2.7)
Indonesia	-1.86	(0.04)	1.00	(0.01)	0.30	(0.04)	79.4	(1.3)	69.4	(2.3)
Latvia	-0.34	(0.03)	0.87	(0.01)	0.12	(0.04)	24.5	(1.2)	82.2	(2.0)
Liechtenstein	-0.31	(0.04)	1.00	(0.04)	0.02	(0.11)	27.6	(2.2)	71.9	(6.6)
Macao-China	-1.60	(0.03)	0.93	(0.02)	0.41	(0.09)	75.1	(1.4)	76.9	(5.0)
Russian Federation	-0.61	(0.03)	0.96	(0.01)	0.17	(0.04)	38.4	(1.3)	79.3	(2.0)
Thailand	-1.86	(0.04)	1.21	(0.02)	0.72	(0.04)	78.0	(1.0)	58.0	(2.8)
Tunisia	-1.69	(0.04)	1.22	(0.03)	0.46	(0.04)	72.2	(1.4)	66.9	(3.1)
Uruguay	-0.76	(0.04)	1.15	(0.01)	0.06	(0.03)	43.0	(1.2)	68.2	(2.5)

Notes: Values that are statistically significant are indicated in bold (see Annex A3).
Only countries and economies with comparable data from PISA 2003 and PISA 2012 are shown.
For comparability over time, PISA 2003 values on the *PISA index of economic, social and cultural status* have been rescaled to the PISA 2012 scale of the index. PISA 2003 results reported in this table may thus differ from those presented in *Learning for Tomorrow's World: First Results from PISA 2003* (OECD, 2004) (see Annex A5 for more details).
1. ESCS refers to the *PISA index of economic, social and cultural status*.
2. Students with low ESCS are those with a value on the *PISA index of economic, social and cultural status* lower than -1.
3. The *index of social inclusion* is calculated as 100*(1-rho), where rho stands for the intra-class correlation of socio-economic status, i.e. the between-school variance in the *PISA index of social, economic and cultural status* of students, divided by the sum of the between-school variance in students' socio-economic status and the within-school variance in students' socio-economic status.
StatLink ⟨⟩ http://dx.doi.org/10.1787/888932964908

[Part 2/3]
Change between 2003 and 2012 in the socio-economic status of students
Table II.2.13b *Results based on students' self-reports*

	PISA 2012									
	ESCS[1]		Variability in the ESCS		Skewness of the distribution of the ESCS		Percentage of students with low ESCS[2]		Index of social inclusion[3]	
	Mean index	S.E.	S.D.	S.E.	Skewness	S.E.	%	S.E.	Index	S.E.
Australia	0.25	(0.01)	0.79	(0.01)	-0.46	(0.03)	6.8	(0.3)	76.5	(1.1)
Austria	0.08	(0.02)	0.85	(0.01)	0.02	(0.05)	8.3	(0.6)	71.2	(2.8)
Belgium	0.15	(0.02)	0.91	(0.02)	-0.33	(0.09)	10.5	(0.6)	72.4	(2.1)
Canada	0.41	(0.02)	0.86	(0.01)	-0.39	(0.05)	5.6	(0.4)	82.8	(1.2)
Czech Republic	-0.07	(0.02)	0.75	(0.01)	0.14	(0.06)	9.1	(0.6)	76.4	(2.2)
Denmark	0.43	(0.02)	0.84	(0.01)	-0.35	(0.04)	4.3	(0.4)	82.3	(1.6)
Finland	0.36	(0.02)	0.77	(0.01)	-0.44	(0.04)	4.0	(0.3)	91.1	(1.0)
France	-0.04	(0.02)	0.80	(0.01)	-0.33	(0.03)	11.8	(0.6)	w	w
Germany	0.19	(0.02)	0.93	(0.01)	-0.08	(0.04)	9.8	(0.6)	73.6	(1.9)
Greece	-0.06	(0.03)	1.00	(0.01)	-0.09	(0.04)	18.6	(1.0)	73.5	(2.6)
Hungary	-0.25	(0.03)	0.96	(0.02)	-0.06	(0.07)	23.7	(1.0)	62.6	(2.6)
Iceland	0.78	(0.01)	0.81	(0.01)	-0.48	(0.04)	1.9	(0.2)	86.4	(1.9)
Ireland	0.13	(0.02)	0.85	(0.01)	-0.15	(0.03)	9.2	(0.6)	79.7	(2.1)
Italy	-0.05	(0.01)	0.97	(0.01)	0.08	(0.02)	18.4	(0.4)	75.9	(1.1)
Japan	-0.07	(0.02)	0.71	(0.01)	-0.02	(0.03)	10.0	(0.6)	77.8	(1.7)
Korea	0.01	(0.03)	0.74	(0.01)	-0.28	(0.04)	9.5	(0.6)	78.3	(1.9)
Luxembourg	0.07	(0.01)	1.10	(0.01)	-0.29	(0.02)	18.7	(0.6)	73.6	(3.4)
Mexico	-1.11	(0.02)	1.27	(0.01)	0.21	(0.02)	55.9	(0.8)	56.5	(1.5)
Netherlands	0.23	(0.02)	0.78	(0.01)	-0.50	(0.05)	5.9	(0.5)	81.8	(1.8)
New Zealand	0.04	(0.02)	0.82	(0.01)	-0.26	(0.04)	11.5	(0.6)	77.5	(2.4)
Norway	0.46	(0.02)	0.76	(0.01)	-0.55	(0.09)	2.6	(0.3)	91.0	(1.4)
Poland	-0.21	(0.03)	0.90	(0.01)	0.41	(0.04)	19.1	(1.0)	76.4	(2.2)
Portugal	-0.48	(0.05)	1.19	(0.02)	0.43	(0.05)	39.8	(1.6)	68.6	(3.3)
Slovak Republic	-0.18	(0.03)	0.92	(0.02)	0.06	(0.07)	15.0	(0.9)	64.4	(3.0)
Spain	-0.19	(0.03)	1.03	(0.01)	0.01	(0.03)	23.5	(0.8)	75.2	(1.4)
Sweden	0.28	(0.02)	0.82	(0.01)	-0.41	(0.05)	5.7	(0.3)	86.9	(1.4)
Switzerland	0.17	(0.02)	0.89	(0.01)	-0.21	(0.03)	10.4	(0.6)	82.7	(1.5)
Turkey	-1.46	(0.04)	1.10	(0.02)	0.43	(0.04)	68.7	(1.3)	72.3	(2.9)
United States	0.17	(0.04)	0.97	(0.02)	-0.33	(0.04)	13.4	(1.0)	73.8	(2.4)
OECD average 2003	0.00	(0.00)	0.90	(0.00)	-0.15	(0.01)	15.6	(0.1)	76.3	(0.4)
Brazil	-1.17	(0.02)	1.17	(0.01)	0.15	(0.02)	57.5	(0.9)	62.8	(2.3)
Hong Kong-China	-0.79	(0.05)	0.97	(0.02)	0.09	(0.05)	45.2	(2.0)	67.7	(3.2)
Indonesia	-1.80	(0.05)	1.10	(0.03)	0.41	(0.06)	76.7	(1.9)	63.1	(4.3)
Latvia	-0.26	(0.03)	0.89	(0.01)	0.01	(0.04)	24.3	(1.3)	74.7	(2.5)
Liechtenstein	0.30	(0.05)	0.91	(0.03)	-0.25	(0.11)	9.4	(1.6)	85.5	(4.1)
Macao-China	-0.89	(0.01)	0.87	(0.01)	0.36	(0.03)	48.6	(0.6)	73.7	(4.7)
Russian Federation	-0.11	(0.02)	0.76	(0.01)	-0.28	(0.04)	12.3	(0.7)	75.0	(2.4)
Thailand	-1.35	(0.04)	1.17	(0.02)	0.40	(0.04)	64.4	(1.5)	61.6	(2.9)
Tunisia	-1.19	(0.05)	1.26	(0.02)	-0.10	(0.04)	54.4	(1.6)	67.2	(3.0)
Uruguay	-0.88	(0.03)	1.13	(0.02)	0.32	(0.03)	50.4	(1.1)	60.2	(3.5)

Notes: Values that are statistically significant are indicated in bold (see Annex A3).
Only countries and economies with comparable data from PISA 2003 and PISA 2012 are shown.
For comparability over time, PISA 2003 values on the *PISA index of economic, social and cultural status* have been rescaled to the PISA 2012 scale of the index. PISA 2003 results reported in this table may thus differ from those presented in *Learning for Tomorrow's World: First Results from PISA 2003* (OECD, 2004) (see Annex A5 for more details).
1. ESCS refers to the *PISA index of economic, social and cultural status*.
2. Students with low ESCS are those with a value on the *PISA index of economic, social and cultural status* lower than -1.
3. The *index of social inclusion* is calculated as 100*(1-rho), where rho stands for the intra-class correlation of socio-economic status, i.e. the between-school variance in the *PISA index of social, economic and cultural status* of students, divided by the sum of the between-school variance in students' socio-economic status and the within-school variance in students' socio-economic status.
StatLink http://dx.doi.org/10.1787/888932964908

[Part 3/3]
Change between 2003 and 2012 in the socio-economic status of students
Table II.2.13b   *Results based on students' self-reports*

		Change between 2003 and 2012 (PISA 2012 - PISA 2003)								
		ESCS[1]		Variability in the ESCS		Skewness of the distribution of the ESCS		Percentage of students with low ESCS[2]		Index of social inclusion[3]	
		Dif.	S.E.	S.D. dif.	S.E.	Dif.	S.E.	% dif.	S.E.	Dif.	S.E.
OECD	Australia	**0.21**	(0.02)	**-0.09**	(0.01)	**-0.38**	(0.04)	**-5.6**	(0.6)	1.0	(2.0)
	Austria	**0.34**	(0.04)	-0.01	(0.02)	**-0.17**	(0.07)	**-12.0**	(1.2)	-0.3	(3.4)
	Belgium	**0.17**	(0.03)	**-0.10**	(0.02)	**-0.22**	(0.10)	**-7.5**	(0.9)	1.4	(2.9)
	Canada	**0.20**	(0.02)	**-0.07**	(0.01)	**-0.33**	(0.06)	**-4.3**	(0.5)	1.2	(1.8)
	Czech Republic	-0.01	(0.03)	**-0.12**	(0.01)	0.00	(0.07)	**-6.0**	(0.9)	2.0	(3.0)
	Denmark	**0.35**	(0.04)	**-0.14**	(0.02)	**-0.27**	(0.05)	**-9.9**	(0.9)	-0.8	(2.8)
	Finland	**0.31**	(0.03)	**-0.20**	(0.01)	**-0.33**	(0.05)	**-10.7**	(0.6)	1.7	(1.8)
	France	**0.28**	(0.03)	**-0.15**	(0.02)	**-0.30**	(0.04)	**-13.0**	(1.2)	w	w
	Germany	**0.19**	(0.04)	**-0.15**	(0.02)	-0.05	(0.05)	**-6.1**	(1.0)	4.4	(2.7)
	Greece	**0.24**	(0.06)	-0.04	(0.03)	**-0.31**	(0.06)	**-7.5**	(1.7)	2.0	(4.7)
	Hungary	0.06	(0.04)	0.01	(0.02)	**-0.34**	(0.08)	-1.7	(1.4)	2.2	(3.6)
	Iceland	**0.23**	(0.02)	**-0.12**	(0.01)	**-0.15**	(0.05)	**-3.6**	(0.5)	1.0	(3.4)
	Ireland	**0.39**	(0.04)	**-0.08**	(0.01)	**-0.21**	(0.05)	**-12.7**	(1.2)	-1.7	(3.2)
	Italy	**0.23**	(0.03)	**-0.11**	(0.01)	**-0.11**	(0.03)	**-10.4**	(1.0)	**5.1**	(2.3)
	Japan	**0.35**	(0.03)	**-0.09**	(0.01)	-0.08	(0.05)	**-15.5**	(1.2)	**6.3**	(2.8)
	Korea	**0.38**	(0.04)	**-0.20**	(0.02)	**-0.31**	(0.05)	**-14.9**	(1.1)	**7.6**	(3.1)
	Luxembourg	**0.16**	(0.02)	0.03	(0.01)	-0.03	(0.03)	**-2.0**	(0.8)	-3.1	(5.5)
	Mexico	**0.21**	(0.06)	**0.08**	(0.02)	**-0.17**	(0.05)	**-6.8**	(2.1)	-5.2	(3.0)
	Netherlands	**0.32**	(0.03)	**-0.18**	(0.02)	**-0.44**	(0.06)	**-12.8**	(1.0)	4.5	(2.8)
	New Zealand	**0.17**	(0.03)	**-0.09**	(0.01)	0.09	(0.05)	**-4.8**	(0.9)	**-6.9**	(3.1)
	Norway	**0.28**	(0.03)	-0.03	(0.01)	**-0.30**	(0.10)	**-4.3**	(0.5)	1.0	(2.2)
	Poland	**0.20**	(0.04)	-0.01	(0.02)	-0.05	(0.05)	**-9.7**	(1.4)	-3.2	(2.9)
	Portugal	**0.42**	(0.07)	**-0.16**	(0.03)	-0.03	(0.06)	**-13.2**	(2.2)	-8.0	(4.3)
	Slovak Republic	0.06	(0.04)	-0.02	(0.02)	-0.15	(0.08)	**-6.8**	(1.5)	-5.4	(3.8)
	Spain	**0.32**	(0.05)	**-0.12**	(0.02)	**-0.17**	(0.05)	**-12.5**	(1.7)	2.0	(2.4)
	Sweden	**0.19**	(0.03)	**-0.16**	(0.02)	**-0.17**	(0.06)	**-8.8**	(0.9)	-2.5	(2.0)
	Switzerland	**0.40**	(0.04)	**-0.13**	(0.02)	**-0.27**	(0.05)	**-12.6**	(1.2)	**6.6**	(2.8)
	Turkey	**-0.31**	(0.07)	0.05	(0.04)	**-0.20**	(0.07)	7.4	(2.8)	**13.0**	(5.4)
	United States	**0.12**	(0.05)	-0.01	(0.05)	-0.13	(0.06)	-1.0	(1.3)	-3.2	(3.4)
	OECD average 2003	**0.22**	(0.01)	**-0.08**	(0.00)	**-0.19**	(0.01)	**-7.9**	(0.2)	0.8	(0.6)
Partners	Brazil	**0.39**	(0.05)	-0.07	(0.03)	-0.07	(0.05)	**-9.8**	(1.7)	1.7	(4.0)
	Hong Kong-China	**0.48**	(0.06)	0.02	(0.03)	**-0.40**	(0.06)	**-20.4**	(2.6)	**-8.9**	(4.2)
	Indonesia	0.06	(0.06)	**0.09**	(0.04)	0.11	(0.07)	-2.7	(2.3)	-6.2	(4.9)
	Latvia	0.09	(0.04)	0.02	(0.02)	**-0.11**	(0.06)	-0.3	(1.7)	-7.5	(3.2)
	Liechtenstein	**0.61**	(0.07)	-0.09	(0.05)	-0.26	(0.15)	**-18.2**	(2.8)	13.6	(7.8)
	Macao-China	**0.71**	(0.03)	**-0.06**	(0.02)	-0.05	(0.09)	**-26.5**	(1.5)	-3.2	(6.9)
	Russian Federation	**0.50**	(0.04)	**-0.20**	(0.02)	**-0.45**	(0.05)	**-26.1**	(1.5)	-4.3	(3.1)
	Thailand	**0.52**	(0.06)	-0.04	(0.03)	**-0.32**	(0.05)	**-13.6**	(1.8)	3.6	(4.0)
	Tunisia	**0.50**	(0.06)	0.05	(0.03)	**-0.56**	(0.05)	**-17.9**	(2.1)	0.4	(4.3)
	Uruguay	**-0.12**	(0.05)	-0.02	(0.02)	**0.27**	(0.04)	7.4	(1.6)	-8.0	(4.3)

Notes: Values that are statistically significant are indicated in bold (see Annex A3).
Only countries and economies with comparable data from PISA 2003 and PISA 2012 are shown.
For comparability over time, PISA 2003 values on the *PISA index of economic, social and cultural status* have been rescaled to the PISA 2012 scale of the index. PISA 2003 results reported in this table may thus differ from those presented in *Learning for Tomorrow's World: First Results from PISA 2003* (OECD, 2004) (see Annex A5 for more details).
1. ESCS refers to the *PISA index of economic, social and cultural status*.
2. Students with low ESCS are those with a value on the *PISA index of economic, social and cultural status* lower than -1.
3. The *index of social inclusion* is calculated as 100*(1-rho), where rho stands for the intra-class correlation of socio-economic status, i.e. the between-school variance in the *PISA index of social, economic and cultural status* of students, divided by the sum of the between-school variance in students' socio-economic status and the within-school variance in students' socio-economic status. .
StatLink http://dx.doi.org/10.1787/888932964908

[Part 1/2]
Mathematics performance and type of family

Table II.3.1 *Results based on students' self-reports*

		Percentage of students				PISA index of economic, social and cultural status (ESCS)				Mathematics performance			
		Students from single-parent families		Students from other types of families		Students from single-parent families		Students from other types of families		Students from single-parent families		Students from other types of families	
		%	S.E.	%	S.E.	Mean index	S.E.	Mean index	S.E.	Mean score	S.E.	Mean score	S.E.
OECD	Australia	13.5	(0.4)	86.5	(0.4)	-0.07	(0.02)	0.33	(0.01)	495	(2.6)	513	(1.8)
	Austria	13.5	(0.7)	86.5	(0.7)	-0.05	(0.04)	0.11	(0.02)	503	(4.9)	510	(2.7)
	Belgium	13.6	(0.5)	86.4	(0.5)	-0.12	(0.05)	0.21	(0.02)	493	(4.9)	525	(2.2)
	Canada	12.7	(0.3)	87.3	(0.3)	0.11	(0.03)	0.48	(0.02)	511	(3.2)	525	(1.9)
	Chile	22.6	(0.7)	77.4	(0.7)	-0.60	(0.04)	-0.52	(0.04)	426	(3.6)	430	(3.1)
	Czech Republic	17.6	(0.5)	82.4	(0.5)	-0.30	(0.02)	0.00	(0.02)	486	(4.3)	506	(2.9)
	Denmark	15.1	(0.6)	84.9	(0.6)	0.12	(0.04)	0.50	(0.02)	485	(4.0)	508	(2.1)
	Estonia	19.2	(0.7)	80.8	(0.7)	-0.15	(0.03)	0.19	(0.01)	525	(3.4)	524	(2.3)
	Finland	15.9	(0.6)	84.1	(0.6)	0.02	(0.03)	0.45	(0.01)	507	(3.3)	528	(1.8)
	France	15.1	(0.6)	84.9	(0.6)	-0.26	(0.03)	0.03	(0.02)	484	(4.4)	505	(2.7)
	Germany	13.3	(0.6)	86.7	(0.6)	0.03	(0.05)	0.24	(0.02)	520	(4.9)	524	(3.1)
	Greece	8.7	(0.5)	91.3	(0.5)	-0.09	(0.06)	-0.04	(0.03)	444	(6.8)	458	(2.5)
	Hungary	20.6	(0.8)	79.4	(0.8)	-0.40	(0.04)	-0.18	(0.03)	474	(4.8)	485	(3.1)
	Iceland	10.7	(0.5)	89.3	(0.5)	0.52	(0.04)	0.83	(0.01)	481	(5.9)	500	(1.9)
	Ireland	10.9	(0.6)	89.1	(0.6)	-0.20	(0.04)	0.21	(0.02)	486	(3.9)	510	(2.1)
	Israel	m	m	m	m	m	m	m	m	m	m	m	m
	Italy	9.5	(0.3)	90.5	(0.3)	-0.14	(0.03)	-0.03	(0.02)	482	(3.0)	488	(2.1)
	Japan	12.1	(0.6)	87.9	(0.6)	-0.47	(0.03)	-0.01	(0.01)	516	(5.8)	544	(3.5)
	Korea	8.8	(0.5)	91.2	(0.5)	-0.39	(0.05)	0.08	(0.03)	549	(6.8)	560	(4.7)
	Luxembourg	12.2	(0.5)	87.8	(0.5)	-0.08	(0.04)	0.11	(0.02)	485	(3.8)	494	(1.4)
	Mexico	15.2	(0.4)	84.8	(0.4)	-1.02	(0.03)	-1.06	(0.03)	423	(2.2)	422	(1.3)
	Netherlands	11.2	(0.5)	88.8	(0.5)	0.02	(0.05)	0.27	(0.02)	501	(6.3)	530	(3.4)
	New Zealand	19.6	(0.8)	80.4	(0.8)	-0.23	(0.03)	0.11	(0.02)	489	(3.8)	507	(2.5)
	Norway	10.7	(0.6)	89.3	(0.6)	0.13	(0.04)	0.52	(0.02)	481	(5.5)	495	(2.7)
	Poland	16.4	(0.7)	83.6	(0.7)	-0.39	(0.04)	-0.16	(0.03)	500	(5.5)	524	(3.4)
	Portugal	12.3	(0.5)	87.7	(0.5)	-0.62	(0.08)	-0.44	(0.05)	489	(5.7)	494	(3.6)
	Slovak Republic	14.9	(0.7)	85.1	(0.7)	-0.28	(0.04)	-0.13	(0.03)	481	(5.3)	492	(3.5)
	Slovenia	10.8	(0.5)	89.2	(0.5)	-0.05	(0.05)	0.10	(0.01)	495	(4.9)	507	(1.3)
	Spain	10.2	(0.3)	89.8	(0.3)	-0.43	(0.04)	-0.15	(0.02)	479	(3.0)	489	(1.8)
	Sweden	9.4	(0.5)	90.6	(0.5)	-0.09	(0.04)	0.33	(0.02)	468	(5.4)	487	(2.1)
	Switzerland	13.6	(0.4)	86.4	(0.4)	0.11	(0.04)	0.19	(0.02)	527	(3.9)	536	(3.3)
	Turkey	4.2	(0.3)	95.8	(0.3)	-1.33	(0.10)	-1.42	(0.04)	456	(8.3)	457	(4.9)
	United Kingdom	16.6	(0.6)	83.4	(0.6)	-0.01	(0.03)	0.37	(0.02)	481	(4.4)	507	(3.0)
	United States	20.3	(0.9)	79.7	(0.9)	-0.19	(0.04)	0.30	(0.04)	468	(5.0)	492	(3.7)
	OECD average	13.7	(0.1)	86.3	(0.1)	-0.21	(0.01)	0.06	(0.00)	488	(0.8)	502	(0.5)
Partners	Albania	m	m	m	m	m	m	m	m	m	m	m	m
	Argentina	19.5	(0.7)	80.5	(0.7)	-0.80	(0.07)	-0.64	(0.04)	395	(4.1)	399	(3.7)
	Brazil	20.6	(0.5)	79.4	(0.5)	-1.20	(0.03)	-1.10	(0.03)	396	(2.7)	401	(2.3)
	Bulgaria	12.7	(0.6)	87.3	(0.6)	-0.39	(0.05)	-0.20	(0.04)	442	(5.4)	450	(3.8)
	Colombia	23.9	(0.8)	76.1	(0.8)	-1.19	(0.05)	-1.17	(0.05)	387	(3.4)	389	(3.3)
	Costa Rica	22.6	(0.7)	77.4	(0.7)	-1.08	(0.05)	-0.89	(0.05)	408	(3.5)	414	(3.1)
	Croatia	8.1	(0.5)	91.9	(0.5)	-0.40	(0.04)	-0.33	(0.02)	478	(5.3)	473	(3.7)
	Cyprus*	8.9	(0.4)	91.1	(0.4)	-0.26	(0.04)	0.14	(0.01)	425	(4.7)	448	(1.3)
	Hong Kong-China	13.3	(0.5)	86.7	(0.5)	-1.01	(0.06)	-0.75	(0.05)	555	(4.3)	566	(3.4)
	Indonesia	7.4	(0.5)	92.6	(0.5)	-1.91	(0.09)	-1.75	(0.06)	383	(5.8)	385	(4.3)
	Jordan	9.7	(0.6)	90.3	(0.6)	-0.58	(0.07)	-0.37	(0.02)	367	(5.6)	400	(3.1)
	Kazakhstan	14.1	(0.6)	85.9	(0.6)	-0.47	(0.04)	-0.29	(0.02)	435	(4.3)	433	(3.1)
	Latvia	20.1	(0.8)	79.9	(0.8)	-0.41	(0.06)	-0.17	(0.03)	498	(4.0)	496	(2.9)
	Liechtenstein	15.0	(2.2)	85.0	(2.2)	0.18	(0.14)	0.31	(0.06)	518	(13.8)	541	(5.0)
	Lithuania	15.7	(0.6)	84.3	(0.6)	-0.35	(0.04)	-0.05	(0.02)	474	(4.1)	485	(2.7)
	Macao-China	13.6	(0.5)	86.4	(0.5)	-1.03	(0.03)	-0.86	(0.01)	533	(3.6)	543	(1.1)
	Malaysia	12.3	(0.6)	87.7	(0.6)	-0.85	(0.06)	-0.67	(0.04)	411	(3.9)	429	(3.3)
	Montenegro	6.4	(0.4)	93.6	(0.4)	-0.26	(0.05)	-0.23	(0.01)	423	(6.1)	415	(1.3)
	Peru	17.0	(0.5)	83.0	(0.5)	-1.15	(0.07)	-1.21	(0.05)	382	(4.4)	372	(3.9)
	Qatar	10.9	(0.3)	89.1	(0.3)	0.23	(0.03)	0.51	(0.01)	340	(3.0)	400	(1.1)
	Romania	13.8	(0.7)	86.2	(0.7)	-0.54	(0.05)	-0.42	(0.04)	443	(4.5)	451	(4.0)
	Russian Federation	22.3	(0.7)	77.7	(0.7)	-0.26	(0.04)	-0.04	(0.03)	488	(3.8)	488	(3.2)
	Serbia	8.8	(0.4)	91.2	(0.4)	-0.41	(0.05)	-0.25	(0.02)	448	(5.3)	456	(3.3)
	Shanghai-China	9.4	(0.4)	90.6	(0.4)	-0.42	(0.05)	-0.35	(0.04)	615	(4.8)	615	(3.1)
	Singapore	9.2	(0.4)	90.8	(0.4)	-0.45	(0.04)	-0.22	(0.02)	564	(5.5)	579	(1.5)
	Chinese Taipei	12.9	(0.4)	87.1	(0.4)	-0.72	(0.04)	-0.34	(0.03)	531	(5.4)	568	(3.4)
	Thailand	14.7	(0.6)	85.3	(0.6)	-1.35	(0.06)	-1.28	(0.05)	429	(4.7)	435	(3.6)
	Tunisia	6.2	(0.5)	93.8	(0.5)	-1.27	(0.09)	-1.13	(0.05)	379	(6.9)	396	(4.3)
	United Arab Emirates	9.8	(0.4)	90.2	(0.4)	0.07	(0.04)	0.40	(0.02)	411	(4.4)	446	(2.5)
	Uruguay	18.4	(0.6)	81.6	(0.6)	-1.01	(0.05)	-0.79	(0.03)	417	(4.1)	421	(2.6)
	Viet Nam	7.8	(0.4)	92.2	(0.4)	-1.92	(0.06)	-1.78	(0.05)	525	(6.2)	514	(4.8)

Note: This table was calculated considering only students with data on the *PISA index of economic, social and cultural status*. Values that are statistically significant are indicated in bold (see Annex A3).
* See notes at the beginning of this Annex.
StatLink ᵐˢ🔗 http://dx.doi.org/10.1787/888932964927

[Part 2/2]
Mathematics performance and type of family
Table II.3.1   *Results based on students' self-reports*

	Difference in mathematics performance between students from single-parent families and those from other types of families, before accounting for ESCS		Difference in mathematics performance between students from single-parent families and those from other types of families, after accounting for ESCS		Increased likelihood of students from single-parent families scoring in the bottom quarter of the mathematics performance distribution		Population relevance of students from single-parent families scoring in the bottom quarter of the mathematics performance distribution		Effect size for students from single-parent families and other types of families in mathematics performance	
	Score dif.	S.E.	Score dif.	S.E.	Ratio	S.E.	%	S.E.	Effect size	S.E.
Australia	-18	(2.5)	-1	(2.5)	1.27	(0.06)	3.5	(0.7)	-0.2	(0.0)
Austria	-7	(4.9)	-1	(4.8)	1.09	(0.10)	1.2	(1.3)	-0.1	(0.1)
Belgium	-33	(4.8)	-17	(4.2)	1.43	(0.10)	5.5	(1.2)	-0.3	(0.0)
Canada	-14	(3.1)	-3	(3.0)	1.24	(0.07)	3.0	(0.9)	-0.2	(0.0)
Chile	-4	(3.5)	-1	(3.3)	1.06	(0.09)	1.3	(2.0)	0.0	(0.0)
Czech Republic	-20	(4.2)	-5	(4.5)	1.24	(0.09)	4.0	(1.5)	-0.2	(0.0)
Denmark	-22	(3.8)	-8	(3.5)	1.49	(0.12)	6.9	(1.6)	-0.3	(0.0)
Estonia	0	(3.8)	10	(3.7)	0.95	(0.08)	-1.0	(1.5)	0.0	(0.0)
Finland	-21	(3.2)	-7	(3.0)	1.41	(0.09)	6.1	(1.3)	-0.2	(0.0)
France	-21	(4.7)	-4	(4.2)	1.25	(0.12)	3.6	(1.7)	-0.2	(0.0)
Germany	-4	(4.7)	5	(3.9)	1.07	(0.09)	1.0	(1.2)	0.0	(0.0)
Greece	-14	(6.5)	-12	(6.0)	1.33	(0.13)	2.8	(1.1)	-0.2	(0.1)
Hungary	-10	(4.0)	-1	(3.8)	1.16	(0.09)	3.1	(1.7)	-0.1	(0.0)
Iceland	-19	(6.3)	-10	(6.1)	1.41	(0.14)	4.2	(1.4)	-0.2	(0.1)
Ireland	-24	(3.7)	-10	(3.4)	1.42	(0.12)	4.4	(1.2)	-0.3	(0.0)
Israel	m	m	m	m	m	m	m	m	m	m
Italy	-6	(2.7)	-3	(2.7)	1.10	(0.06)	0.9	(0.6)	-0.1	(0.0)
Japan	-28	(5.1)	-10	(4.0)	1.47	(0.12)	5.3	(1.3)	-0.3	(0.1)
Korea	-11	(5.3)	9	(5.5)	1.11	(0.09)	1.0	(0.8)	-0.1	(0.1)
Luxembourg	-9	(4.4)	-2	(3.8)	1.06	(0.09)	0.7	(1.1)	-0.1	(0.0)
Mexico	1	(2.1)	0	(2.0)	0.99	(0.06)	-0.2	(0.9)	0.0	(0.0)
Netherlands	-29	(5.4)	-19	(5.3)	1.45	(0.13)	4.8	(1.3)	-0.3	(0.1)
New Zealand	-19	(4.0)	-1	(4.0)	1.32	(0.10)	5.9	(1.7)	-0.2	(0.0)
Norway	-14	(5.4)	-2	(5.1)	1.21	(0.11)	2.2	(1.2)	-0.2	(0.1)
Poland	-24	(4.0)	-15	(4.0)	1.49	(0.10)	7.4	(1.4)	-0.3	(0.0)
Portugal	-5	(4.8)	1	(4.4)	1.04	(0.09)	0.4	(1.1)	-0.1	(0.1)
Slovak Republic	-10	(5.3)	-2	(5.0)	1.12	(0.09)	1.7	(1.3)	-0.1	(0.1)
Slovenia	-12	(5.1)	-6	(4.7)	1.18	(0.12)	1.9	(1.2)	-0.1	(0.1)
Spain	-10	(2.6)	-1	(2.3)	1.15	(0.07)	1.5	(0.7)	-0.1	(0.0)
Sweden	-19	(5.3)	-4	(5.5)	1.34	(0.13)	3.1	(1.1)	-0.2	(0.1)
Switzerland	-9	(3.7)	-6	(3.6)	1.10	(0.09)	1.3	(1.2)	-0.1	(0.0)
Turkey	-1	(6.9)	-4	(6.5)	1.05	(0.16)	0.2	(0.7)	0.0	(0.1)
United Kingdom	-26	(4.3)	-11	(3.8)	1.33	(0.09)	5.1	(1.4)	-0.3	(0.0)
United States	-24	(4.3)	-7	(3.5)	1.38	(0.10)	7.2	(1.7)	-0.3	(0.0)
OECD average	-15	(0.8)	-4	(0.7)	1.23	(0.02)	3.0	(0.2)	-0.2	(0.0)
Albania	m	m	m	m	m	m	m	m	m	m
Argentina	-4	(3.6)	0	(3.5)	1.06	(0.10)	1.1	(1.8)	-0.1	(0.0)
Brazil	-5	(2.6)	-3	(2.6)	1.08	(0.07)	1.6	(1.3)	-0.1	(0.0)
Bulgaria	-8	(4.3)	0	(4.0)	1.09	(0.09)	1.2	(1.1)	-0.1	(0.0)
Colombia	-2	(3.3)	-1	(3.2)	0.98	(0.09)	-0.5	(2.1)	0.0	(0.0)
Costa Rica	-5	(3.1)	-1	(2.8)	1.09	(0.09)	2.0	(1.8)	-0.1	(0.0)
Croatia	5	(5.5)	8	(5.1)	0.94	(0.11)	-0.5	(0.9)	0.1	(0.1)
Cyprus*	-23	(5.2)	-8	(5.0)	1.33	(0.11)	2.9	(1.0)	-0.2	(0.1)
Hong Kong-China	-11	(4.4)	-4	(4.3)	1.20	(0.09)	2.6	(1.2)	-0.1	(0.0)
Indonesia	-2	(4.0)	2	(4.1)	1.06	(0.11)	0.4	(0.8)	0.0	(0.1)
Jordan	-33	(4.6)	-28	(4.9)	1.79	(0.13)	7.1	(1.1)	-0.4	(0.1)
Kazakhstan	2	(3.6)	7	(3.5)	0.92	(0.08)	-1.1	(1.1)	0.0	(0.1)
Latvia	2	(3.9)	10	(3.7)	0.98	(0.10)	-0.5	(2.0)	0.0	(0.0)
Liechtenstein	-24	(15.5)	-20	(15.8)	1.21	(0.34)	3.0	(5.1)	-0.3	(0.2)
Lithuania	-11	(4.2)	-1	(3.9)	1.27	(0.10)	4.0	(1.5)	-0.1	(0.0)
Macao-China	-10	(4.0)	-7	(4.0)	1.19	(0.09)	2.5	(1.2)	-0.1	(0.0)
Malaysia	-17	(3.5)	-12	(3.4)	1.32	(0.10)	3.8	(1.1)	-0.2	(0.0)
Montenegro	8	(6.2)	9	(6.0)	0.90	(0.13)	-0.7	(0.8)	0.1	(0.1)
Peru	10	(3.0)	8	(2.7)	0.83	(0.08)	-3.0	(1.4)	0.1	(0.0)
Qatar	-59	(3.2)	-52	(3.1)	2.09	(0.09)	10.6	(0.8)	-0.6	(0.0)
Romania	-8	(3.7)	-4	(3.4)	1.10	(0.08)	1.3	(1.1)	-0.1	(0.0)
Russian Federation	0	(3.6)	8	(2.8)	1.00	(0.06)	-0.1	(1.4)	0.0	(0.0)
Serbia	-8	(4.5)	-3	(4.3)	1.09	(0.10)	0.8	(0.8)	-0.1	(0.1)
Shanghai-China	1	(4.2)	3	(3.7)	0.89	(0.09)	-1.1	(0.9)	0.0	(0.0)
Singapore	-15	(5.9)	-5	(5.5)	1.24	(0.11)	2.2	(0.9)	-0.1	(0.1)
Chinese Taipei	-37	(5.4)	-15	(4.5)	1.47	(0.10)	5.7	(1.2)	-0.3	(0.0)
Thailand	-5	(3.7)	-4	(3.7)	1.03	(0.10)	0.4	(1.4)	-0.1	(0.0)
Tunisia	-17	(6.2)	-14	(6.1)	1.38	(0.16)	2.3	(1.0)	-0.2	(0.1)
United Arab Emirates	-35	(3.9)	-25	(3.8)	1.69	(0.11)	6.4	(1.0)	-0.4	(0.1)
Uruguay	-4	(3.8)	3	(3.2)	1.03	(0.07)	0.5	(1.2)	-0.1	(0.0)
Viet Nam	11	(4.6)	15	(4.4)	0.85	(0.09)	-1.2	(0.7)	0.1	(0.1)

Note: This table was calculated considering only students with data on the *PISA index of economic, social and cultural status*. Values that are statistically significant are indicated in bold (see Annex A3).
* See notes at the beginning of this Annex.
StatLink http://dx.doi.org/10.1787/888932964927

[Part 1/3]
Mathematics performance, parents' work status and socio-economic status
Table II.3.2 *Results based on students' self-reports*

	Percentage of students								PISA index of economic, social and cultural status (ESCS)							
	Father's current job status				Mother's current job status				Father's current job status				Mother's current job status			
	Working full- or part-time <for pay>		Not working, but looking for a job or having another status (e.g. home duties, retired)		Working full- or part-time <for pay>		Not working, but looking for a job or having another status (e.g. home duties, retired)		Working full- or part-time <for pay>		Not working, but looking for a job or having another status (e.g. home duties, retired)		Working full- or part-time <for pay>		Not working, but looking for a job or having another status (e.g. home duties, retired)	
	%	S.E.	%	S.E.	%	S.E.	%	S.E.	Mean index	S.E.	Mean index	S.E.	Mean index	S.E.	Mean index	S.E.
Australia	90.9	(0.3)	9.1	(0.3)	74.8	(0.6)	25.2	(0.6)	0.31	(0.01)	-0.05	(0.03)	0.34	(0.01)	0.01	(0.02)
Austria	92.6	(0.5)	7.4	(0.5)	80.0	(0.6)	20.0	(0.6)	0.13	(0.02)	-0.32	(0.07)	0.14	(0.02)	-0.15	(0.04)
Belgium	88.8	(0.5)	11.2	(0.5)	76.6	(0.7)	23.4	(0.7)	0.25	(0.02)	-0.36	(0.06)	0.29	(0.02)	-0.27	(0.04)
Canada	91.7	(0.3)	8.3	(0.3)	78.4	(0.5)	21.6	(0.5)	0.47	(0.02)	0.15	(0.03)	0.48	(0.01)	0.22	(0.03)
Chile	90.0	(0.5)	10.0	(0.5)	53.5	(0.9)	46.5	(0.9)	-0.48	(0.03)	-1.03	(0.08)	-0.35	(0.03)	-0.82	(0.04)
Czech Republic	93.4	(0.5)	6.6	(0.5)	82.8	(0.8)	17.2	(0.8)	-0.02	(0.02)	-0.41	(0.07)	0.00	(0.02)	-0.35	(0.04)
Denmark	89.2	(0.5)	10.8	(0.5)	82.5	(0.8)	17.5	(0.8)	0.51	(0.02)	-0.05	(0.04)	0.54	(0.02)	-0.05	(0.04)
Estonia	91.0	(0.5)	9.0	(0.5)	82.0	(0.6)	18.0	(0.6)	0.18	(0.01)	-0.19	(0.05)	0.17	(0.02)	-0.12	(0.03)
Finland	87.5	(0.5)	12.5	(0.5)	85.2	(0.6)	14.8	(0.6)	0.44	(0.02)	-0.01	(0.04)	0.44	(0.01)	0.01	(0.04)
France	90.2	(0.5)	9.8	(0.5)	78.4	(0.8)	21.6	(0.8)	0.04	(0.02)	-0.41	(0.05)	0.08	(0.02)	-0.39	(0.03)
Germany	93.3	(0.4)	6.7	(0.4)	77.2	(0.8)	22.8	(0.8)	0.26	(0.02)	-0.19	(0.08)	0.26	(0.02)	-0.02	(0.04)
Greece	81.4	(0.6)	18.6	(0.6)	56.8	(1.1)	43.2	(1.1)	0.02	(0.03)	-0.38	(0.05)	0.19	(0.03)	-0.39	(0.03)
Hungary	85.5	(0.7)	14.5	(0.7)	74.3	(0.8)	25.7	(0.8)	-0.14	(0.03)	-0.72	(0.07)	-0.07	(0.03)	-0.75	(0.05)
Iceland	93.9	(0.4)	6.1	(0.4)	84.2	(0.6)	15.8	(0.6)	0.82	(0.01)	0.44	(0.06)	0.86	(0.02)	0.42	(0.04)
Ireland	81.7	(0.6)	18.3	(0.6)	62.8	(0.8)	37.2	(0.8)	0.24	(0.02)	-0.25	(0.03)	0.28	(0.02)	-0.12	(0.04)
Israel	88.4	(0.7)	11.6	(0.7)	71.9	(1.1)	28.1	(1.1)	0.28	(0.03)	-0.35	(0.05)	0.36	(0.03)	-0.25	(0.04)
Italy	91.7	(0.3)	8.3	(0.3)	62.8	(0.5)	37.2	(0.5)	0.00	(0.01)	-0.45	(0.04)	0.18	(0.02)	-0.43	(0.02)
Japan	96.9	(0.2)	3.1	(0.2)	77.9	(0.8)	22.1	(0.8)	-0.02	(0.02)	-0.27	(0.06)	-0.09	(0.01)	0.01	(0.03)
Korea	90.4	(0.6)	9.6	(0.6)	59.4	(0.9)	40.6	(0.9)	0.07	(0.03)	-0.26	(0.05)	0.03	(0.03)	0.02	(0.04)
Luxembourg	90.3	(0.5)	9.7	(0.5)	72.1	(0.7)	27.9	(0.7)	0.16	(0.02)	-0.35	(0.05)	0.11	(0.02)	0.00	(0.03)
Mexico	84.8	(0.4)	15.2	(0.4)	40.7	(0.5)	59.3	(0.5)	-0.95	(0.03)	-1.73	(0.04)	-0.69	(0.03)	-1.36	(0.02)
Netherlands	91.8	(0.4)	8.2	(0.4)	77.6	(0.7)	22.4	(0.7)	0.29	(0.04)	-0.16	(0.07)	0.32	(0.04)	-0.02	(0.03)
New Zealand	91.3	(0.5)	8.7	(0.5)	76.2	(0.7)	23.8	(0.7)	0.11	(0.02)	-0.31	(0.05)	0.12	(0.02)	-0.18	(0.03)
Norway	92.3	(0.5)	7.7	(0.5)	86.0	(0.7)	14.0	(0.7)	0.52	(0.02)	0.08	(0.05)	0.53	(0.02)	0.12	(0.04)
Poland	87.4	(0.7)	12.6	(0.7)	70.0	(0.8)	30.0	(0.8)	-0.13	(0.02)	-0.58	(0.04)	-0.03	(0.02)	-0.62	(0.03)
Portugal	85.8	(0.6)	14.2	(0.6)	74.2	(0.9)	25.8	(0.9)	-0.36	(0.05)	-0.91	(0.06)	-0.30	(0.05)	-0.96	(0.05)
Slovak Republic	85.8	(0.8)	14.2	(0.8)	75.8	(0.8)	24.2	(0.8)	-0.06	(0.02)	-0.82	(0.05)	-0.01	(0.02)	-0.70	(0.03)
Slovenia	88.6	(0.6)	11.4	(0.6)	84.3	(0.6)	15.7	(0.6)	0.13	(0.02)	-0.28	(0.05)	0.16	(0.01)	-0.42	(0.04)
Spain	84.5	(0.5)	15.5	(0.5)	66.7	(0.6)	33.3	(0.6)	-0.06	(0.02)	-0.71	(0.03)	-0.04	(0.03)	-0.48	(0.03)
Sweden	93.1	(0.5)	6.9	(0.5)	88.6	(0.6)	11.4	(0.6)	0.33	(0.02)	-0.23	(0.06)	0.34	(0.02)	-0.17	(0.04)
Switzerland	94.2	(0.3)	5.8	(0.3)	75.9	(0.6)	24.1	(0.6)	0.21	(0.02)	-0.19	(0.05)	0.23	(0.02)	0.01	(0.03)
Turkey	71.1	(0.9)	28.9	(0.9)	14.5	(0.8)	85.5	(0.8)	-1.27	(0.04)	-1.83	(0.04)	-0.83	(0.08)	-1.52	(0.03)
United Kingdom	89.6	(0.4)	10.4	(0.4)	76.3	(1.0)	23.7	(1.0)	0.35	(0.02)	-0.09	(0.03)	0.35	(0.02)	0.06	(0.04)
United States	86.0	(0.8)	14.0	(0.8)	73.8	(0.9)	26.2	(0.9)	0.27	(0.04)	-0.14	(0.04)	0.25	(0.03)	-0.03	(0.07)
OECD average	89.0	(0.1)	11.0	(0.1)	72.2	(0.1)	27.8	(0.1)	0.09	(0.00)	-0.39	(0.01)	0.14	(0.00)	-0.28	(0.01)
Albania	m	m	m	m	m	m	m	m	m	m	m	m	m	m	m	m
Argentina	88.8	(0.6)	11.2	(0.6)	53.8	(1.2)	46.2	(1.2)	-0.59	(0.04)	-1.19	(0.08)	-0.38	(0.05)	-1.04	(0.04)
Brazil	80.8	(0.4)	19.2	(0.4)	56.5	(0.5)	43.5	(0.5)	-1.01	(0.02)	-1.60	(0.03)	-0.88	(0.03)	-1.51	(0.03)
Bulgaria	86.4	(0.7)	13.6	(0.7)	79.3	(0.9)	20.7	(0.9)	-0.17	(0.03)	-0.86	(0.08)	-0.11	(0.03)	-0.87	(0.06)
Colombia	84.3	(0.9)	15.7	(0.9)	53.4	(1.0)	46.6	(1.0)	-1.12	(0.04)	-1.70	(0.07)	-1.05	(0.04)	-1.47	(0.05)
Costa Rica	87.9	(0.8)	12.1	(0.8)	44.7	(1.1)	55.3	(1.1)	-0.85	(0.04)	-1.32	(0.08)	-0.61	(0.04)	-1.25	(0.04)
Croatia	71.6	(0.8)	28.4	(0.8)	62.2	(1.0)	37.8	(1.0)	-0.21	(0.02)	-0.63	(0.04)	-0.12	(0.02)	-0.70	(0.02)
Cyprus*	90.3	(0.5)	9.7	(0.5)	72.7	(0.6)	27.3	(0.6)	0.18	(0.01)	-0.52	(0.04)	0.25	(0.01)	-0.27	(0.03)
Hong Kong-China	88.1	(0.5)	11.9	(0.5)	62.5	(1.0)	37.5	(1.0)	-0.73	(0.05)	-1.14	(0.05)	-0.75	(0.06)	-0.86	(0.05)
Indonesia	80.1	(1.0)	19.9	(1.0)	38.9	(1.1)	61.1	(1.1)	-1.71	(0.06)	-2.05	(0.05)	-1.65	(0.07)	-1.86	(0.05)
Jordan	75.1	(0.7)	24.9	(0.7)	17.4	(0.7)	82.6	(0.7)	-0.29	(0.02)	-0.75	(0.05)	0.09	(0.03)	-0.53	(0.02)
Kazakhstan	76.5	(1.1)	23.5	(1.1)	61.6	(1.3)	38.4	(1.3)	-0.19	(0.02)	-0.65	(0.04)	-0.13	(0.02)	-0.60	(0.03)
Latvia	86.3	(0.7)	13.7	(0.7)	78.7	(0.8)	21.3	(0.8)	-0.16	(0.03)	-0.58	(0.06)	-0.17	(0.03)	-0.52	(0.05)
Liechtenstein	91.4	(1.9)	8.6	(1.9)	66.3	(2.8)	33.7	(2.8)	0.30	(0.06)	c	c	0.32	(0.06)	0.21	(0.09)
Lithuania	82.5	(0.6)	17.5	(0.6)	74.8	(0.8)	25.2	(0.8)	-0.01	(0.02)	-0.51	(0.04)	0.02	(0.02)	-0.56	(0.04)
Macao-China	88.8	(0.4)	11.2	(0.4)	76.3	(0.6)	23.7	(0.6)	-0.84	(0.01)	-1.13	(0.04)	-0.86	(0.01)	-0.97	(0.02)
Malaysia	86.0	(0.6)	14.0	(0.6)	39.6	(1.0)	60.4	(1.0)	-0.67	(0.04)	-0.95	(0.05)	-0.37	(0.04)	-0.95	(0.02)
Montenegro	73.8	(0.7)	26.2	(0.7)	50.5	(0.8)	49.5	(0.8)	-0.10	(0.02)	-0.61	(0.02)	0.03	(0.02)	-0.52	(0.02)
Peru	84.0	(0.8)	16.0	(0.8)	51.4	(0.8)	48.6	(0.8)	-1.08	(0.05)	-1.80	(0.07)	-1.08	(0.06)	-1.36	(0.05)
Qatar	86.4	(0.3)	13.6	(0.3)	38.0	(0.4)	62.0	(0.4)	0.51	(0.01)	0.06	(0.03)	0.65	(0.01)	0.32	(0.01)
Romania	74.1	(1.0)	25.9	(1.0)	60.5	(1.2)	39.5	(1.2)	-0.28	(0.04)	-0.95	(0.05)	-0.19	(0.04)	-0.88	(0.04)
Russian Federation	86.3	(0.6)	13.7	(0.6)	76.2	(0.9)	23.8	(0.9)	-0.02	(0.03)	-0.37	(0.03)	-0.03	(0.02)	-0.33	(0.04)
Serbia	77.2	(0.8)	22.8	(0.8)	59.4	(1.1)	40.6	(1.1)	-0.18	(0.02)	-0.61	(0.02)	-0.08	(0.03)	-0.60	(0.03)
Shanghai-China	87.3	(0.5)	12.7	(0.5)	75.0	(0.9)	25.0	(0.9)	-0.28	(0.03)	-0.89	(0.06)	-0.25	(0.03)	-0.69	(0.05)
Singapore	92.6	(0.4)	7.4	(0.4)	63.3	(0.6)	36.7	(0.6)	-0.23	(0.02)	-0.44	(0.05)	-0.21	(0.02)	-0.34	(0.03)
Chinese Taipei	87.9	(0.5)	12.1	(0.5)	69.6	(0.6)	30.4	(0.6)	-0.34	(0.02)	-0.70	(0.04)	-0.35	(0.03)	-0.46	(0.03)
Thailand	81.8	(0.6)	18.2	(0.6)	70.9	(0.6)	29.1	(0.6)	-1.27	(0.05)	-1.55	(0.05)	-1.31	(0.05)	-1.40	(0.04)
Tunisia	84.0	(0.7)	16.0	(0.7)	23.9	(1.1)	76.1	(1.1)	-1.07	(0.05)	-1.68	(0.07)	-0.51	(0.09)	-1.39	(0.04)
United Arab Emirates	80.9	(0.6)	19.1	(0.6)	27.0	(0.6)	73.0	(0.6)	0.44	(0.01)	-0.08	(0.04)	0.65	(0.02)	0.21	(0.02)
Uruguay	89.5	(0.5)	10.5	(0.5)	65.5	(0.8)	34.5	(0.8)	-0.76	(0.03)	-1.25	(0.05)	-0.65	(0.03)	-1.29	(0.03)
Viet Nam	53.2	(1.6)	46.8	(1.6)	36.3	(1.7)	63.7	(1.7)	-1.46	(0.06)	-2.16	(0.04)	-1.35	(0.08)	-2.06	(0.03)

Note: This table was calculated considering only students with data on the *PISA index of economic, social and cultural status*. Values that are statistically significant are indicated in bold (see Annex A3).
* See notes at the beginning of this Annex.
StatLink ⟨⟩ http://dx.doi.org/10.1787/888932964927

[Part 2/3]
Mathematics performance, parents' work status and socio-economic status
Table II.3.2 *Results based on students' self-reports*

	Mean mathematics performance								Difference in mathematics performance between students whose fathers are working and those whose fathers are not working		Difference in mathematics performance between students whose mothers are working and those whose mothers are not working		Difference in mathematics performance between students whose fathers are working and those whose fathers are not working, accounting for ESCS	
	Father's current job status				Mother's current job status									
	Working full- or part-time <for pay>		Not working, but looking for a job or having another status (e.g. home duties, retired)		Working full- or part-time <for pay>		Not working, but looking for a job or having another status (e.g. home duties, retired)							
	Mean score	S.E.	Mean score	S.E.	Mean score	S.E.	Mean score	S.E.	Score dif.	S.E.	Score dif.	S.E.	Score dif.	S.E.
Australia	511	(1.7)	487	(3.5)	511	(1.8)	497	(2.5)	**24**	(3.3)	**15**	(2.3)		(3.2)
Austria	509	(2.6)	488	(7.8)	511	(2.6)	492	(4.4)	**21**	(7.5)	**19**	(4.1)		(5.9)
Belgium	526	(2.1)	482	(4.8)	530	(2.0)	481	(3.7)	**45**	(4.6)	**49**	(3.4)	1	(4.0)
Canada	524	(1.8)	515	(4.2)	523	(1.9)	516	(2.6)	**9**	(4.0)	7	(2.4)		(3.8)
Chile	426	(3.1)	415	(5.1)	430	(3.3)	418	(3.2)	12	(4.6)	**12**	(2.5)		(3.9)
Czech Republic	504	(2.8)	469	(9.1)	506	(2.6)	472	(5.9)	**35**	(8.8)	**34**	(5.6)	1	(7.2)
Denmark	508	(2.2)	474	(3.1)	509	(2.1)	472	(3.2)	**34**	(3.6)	**38**	(3.2)	1	(3.5)
Estonia	524	(2.1)	508	(5.3)	525	(2.1)	509	(3.8)	**15**	(4.9)	**15**	(3.8)		(4.8)
Finland	525	(1.8)	504	(4.1)	524	(1.8)	509	(4.3)	**21**	(4.0)	**15**	(4.1)		(3.7)
France	503	(2.5)	479	(5.2)	509	(2.7)	465	(4.1)	**24**	(5.1)	**44**	(4.5)		(5.1)
Germany	523	(3.0)	502	(7.4)	526	(3.3)	500	(4.7)	**22**	(7.0)	**26**	(4.9)		(5.9)
Greece	459	(2.5)	440	(4.2)	466	(2.6)	440	(2.8)	**18**	(4.1)	**27**	(2.5)		(3.5)
Hungary	485	(3.4)	446	(6.2)	490	(3.4)	448	(4.5)	**40**	(6.8)	**42**	(4.6)	1	(4.2)
Iceland	498	(1.8)	473	(6.7)	500	(1.9)	472	(3.4)	**25**	(6.7)	**28**	(3.8)	1	(6.2)
Ireland	510	(2.1)	480	(4.1)	509	(2.1)	492	(3.1)	**30**	(3.6)	**17**	(2.7)	1	(3.0)
Israel	477	(4.6)	442	(6.7)	490	(4.7)	423	(5.0)	**34**	(6.3)	**67**	(5.4)		(5.9)
Italy	489	(2.0)	471	(3.5)	497	(2.2)	468	(2.3)	**17**	(3.2)	**29**	(2.2)		(2.9)
Japan	542	(3.6)	526	(9.3)	538	(3.5)	546	(5.0)	16	(9.4)	-8	(3.6)		(7.9)
Korea	558	(4.7)	541	(6.5)	557	(4.3)	554	(5.7)	**17**	(6.2)	2	(3.4)		(5.6)
Luxembourg	496	(1.2)	473	(4.6)	494	(1.3)	491	(2.9)	**23**	(4.9)	3	(3.2)		(4.6)
Mexico	417	(1.3)	405	(2.4)	418	(1.6)	412	(1.4)	**11**	(2.2)	**6**	(1.3)		(1.9)
Netherlands	528	(3.5)	515	(5.7)	529	(3.4)	518	(4.7)	13	(5.2)	11	(3.4)		(5.2)
New Zealand	509	(2.2)	469	(6.2)	508	(2.2)	492	(4.7)	**40**	(5.8)	**16**	(4.6)	1	(5.1)
Norway	495	(2.6)	472	(6.7)	496	(2.6)	466	(4.2)	**23**	(6.5)	**30**	(3.9)		(6.3)
Poland	522	(3.7)	503	(4.8)	528	(3.8)	496	(3.7)	**19**	(4.3)	**32**	(3.3)		(4.2)
Portugal	496	(3.5)	468	(5.2)	498	(3.8)	471	(4.2)	**28**	(4.1)	**27**	(3.7)	1	(3.7)
Slovak Republic	493	(3.1)	431	(6.5)	497	(3.2)	440	(5.8)	**62**	(6.4)	**57**	(5.1)	2	(4.8)
Slovenia	504	(1.4)	497	(4.5)	507	(1.4)	481	(4.0)	8	(4.9)	**26**	(4.3)	-1	(4.5)
Spain	492	(2.0)	461	(2.9)	492	(2.0)	474	(2.2)	**31**	(3.1)	**18**	(2.2)		(3.1)
Sweden	486	(2.2)	448	(6.2)	486	(2.2)	452	(5.2)	**38**	(6.4)	**34**	(5.4)		(6.2)
Switzerland	535	(3.2)	509	(6.1)	535	(3.0)	524	(4.1)	**26**	(6.1)	11	(3.0)		(5.8)
Turkey	455	(5.0)	441	(5.7)	469	(7.6)	450	(4.6)	13	(4.1)	**19**	(5.5)		(3.7)
United Kingdom	503	(3.0)	481	(4.7)	502	(2.9)	485	(5.1)	**22**	(3.9)	**17**	(4.5)		(3.8)
United States	488	(3.7)	467	(5.3)	485	(3.6)	477	(4.5)	**21**	(4.7)	**8**	(3.6)		(4.3)
OECD average	501	(0.5)	476	(1.0)	503	(0.5)	480	(0.7)	**25**	(0.9)	**23**	(0.7)		(0.8)
Albania	m	m	m	m	m	m	m	m	m	m	m	m		m
Argentina	395	(3.5)	372	(5.2)	401	(3.4)	382	(3.8)	**23**	(4.2)	**19**	(2.2)		(4.5)
Brazil	397	(2.3)	384	(2.4)	402	(2.4)	382	(2.1)	**14**	(2.5)	**19**	(1.9)		(2.0)
Bulgaria	445	(3.7)	418	(6.1)	450	(3.9)	410	(5.5)	**28**	(5.0)	**40**	(5.3)		(4.4)
Colombia	378	(3.1)	378	(4.4)	379	(3.0)	376	(3.3)	0	(3.4)	3	(2.5)		(3.1)
Costa Rica	410	(3.1)	404	(5.2)	415	(3.8)	403	(3.1)	7	(4.6)	**12**	(3.2)		(3.9)
Croatia	478	(3.9)	459	(3.8)	484	(4.1)	453	(3.4)	**19**	(3.2)	**31**	(3.7)		(3.0)
Cyprus*	448	(1.3)	410	(4.1)	451	(1.6)	426	(2.4)	**38**	(4.3)	**25**	(3.2)		(4.3)
Hong Kong-China	565	(3.3)	557	(4.7)	564	(3.6)	563	(3.6)	8	(4.6)	1	(3.5)		(4.1)
Indonesia	381	(4.2)	365	(4.5)	377	(4.9)	378	(3.8)	**16**	(3.5)	-1	(3.0)		(3.3)
Jordan	396	(2.9)	378	(4.0)	401	(5.8)	389	(2.6)	**17**	(3.2)	**12**	(4.5)		(3.3)
Kazakhstan	437	(3.5)	417	(4.2)	437	(3.4)	424	(3.3)	**20**	(4.5)	**13**	(3.1)		(3.9)
Latvia	493	(3.0)	489	(5.8)	494	(3.1)	483	(3.5)	4	(6.0)	**11**	(3.9)	-1	(5.2)
Liechtenstein	538	(4.3)	c	c	532	(5.9)	548	(8.0)	c	c	-16	(11.2)	c	c
Lithuania	486	(3.4)	466	(4.3)	488	(2.6)	458	(3.5)	**20**	(3.7)	**29**	(3.0)		(3.4)
Macao-China	540	(1.1)	540	(4.2)	539	(1.2)	540	(2.6)	0	(4.6)	0	(3.1)		(4.4)
Malaysia	425	(3.3)	402	(4.2)	431	(4.1)	415	(2.9)	**23**	(3.9)	**16**	(2.9)		(4.0)
Montenegro	416	(1.5)	398	(2.4)	428	(1.7)	396	(1.6)	**18**	(3.1)	**32**	(2.5)	1	(3.0)
Peru	373	(3.9)	352	(4.6)	368	(4.1)	370	(3.7)	**21**	(3.7)	-2	(2.6)		(2.7)
Qatar	389	(1.0)	332	(2.1)	386	(1.7)	379	(1.1)	**57**	(2.4)	7	(2.2)		(2.4)
Romania	454	(4.1)	424	(4.0)	459	(4.2)	425	(3.8)	**30**	(3.8)	**33**	(3.7)		(2.9)
Russian Federation	487	(3.0)	468	(6.1)	488	(2.9)	470	(4.5)	**19**	(5.6)	**18**	(3.5)		(5.4)
Serbia	455	(3.6)	439	(4.1)	462	(3.8)	433	(3.8)	**15**	(3.6)	**29**	(3.8)		(3.1)
Shanghai-China	617	(3.1)	586	(6.7)	622	(3.0)	588	(5.3)	**31**	(5.6)	**33**	(4.3)		(4.8)
Singapore	576	(1.5)	568	(5.7)	578	(1.7)	569	(2.8)	8	(6.2)	9	(3.6)		(5.7)
Chinese Taipei	565	(3.2)	538	(6.1)	563	(3.5)	558	(4.5)	**27**	(5.7)	5	(4.2)		(5.2)
Thailand	428	(3.6)	429	(4.5)	426	(3.6)	433	(4.0)	-1	(3.7)	-8	(2.9)		(3.5)
Tunisia	391	(4.3)	385	(4.9)	412	(7.9)	384	(3.4)	6	(4.5)	**28**	(6.7)		(3.7)
United Arab Emirates	446	(2.5)	399	(2.7)	455	(3.0)	429	(2.6)	**47**	(3.0)	**26**	(2.9)		(2.7)
Uruguay	416	(2.8)	397	(4.3)	423	(2.8)	393	(3.2)	**19**	(4.5)	**30**	(2.9)		(4.2)
Viet Nam	519	(5.9)	505	(4.7)	526	(6.4)	504	(4.5)	14	(5.1)	**22**	(4.9)		(3.8)

Note: This table was calculated considering only students with data on the *PISA index of economic, social and cultural status*. Values that are statistically significant are indicated in bold (see Annex A3).
* See notes at the beginning of this Annex.
StatLink ⬛⬛⬛ http://dx.doi.org/10.1787/888932964927

EXCELLENCE THROUGH EQUITY: GIVING EVERY STUDENT THE CHANCE TO SUCCEED – VOLUME II

[Part 3/3]
Mathematics performance, parents' work status and socio-economic status
Table II.3.2   *Results based on students' self-reports*

	Difference in mathematics performance between students whose mothers are working and those whose mothers are not working, accounting for ESCS		Increased likelihood of students whose fathers are not working scoring in the bottom quarter of the mathematics performance distribution		Population relevance of students whose fathers are not working scoring in the bottom quarter of the mathematics performance distribution		Increased likelihood of students whose mothers are not working scoring in the bottom quarter of the mathematics performance distribution		Population relevance of students whose mothers are not working scoring in the bottom quarter of the mathematics performance distribution		Effect size in mathematics performance for students whose fathers are not working		Effect size in mathematics performance for students whose mothers are not working	
	Score dif.	S.E.	Ratio	S.E.	%	S.E.	Ratio	S.E.	%	S.E.	Effect size	S.E.	Effect size	S.E.
Australia	1	(2.2)	**1.40**	(0.08)	3.5	(0.7)	**1.29**	(0.06)	6.7	(1.2)	**-0.25**	(0.04)	**-0.15**	(0.02)
Austria	6	(3.6)	**1.47**	(0.15)	3.4	(1.1)	**1.41**	(0.09)	7.6	(1.7)	**-0.22**	(0.08)	**-0.20**	(0.04)
Belgium	24	(2.6)	**1.78**	(0.10)	8.0	(1.0)	**1.86**	(0.09)	16.8	(1.6)	**-0.45**	(0.04)	**-0.50**	(0.03)
Canada	-1	(2.1)	**1.20**	(0.08)	1.7	(0.6)	**1.15**	(0.05)	3.1	(1.1)	**-0.10**	(0.05)	**-0.08**	(0.03)
Chile	-4	(2.1)	1.23	(0.14)	2.3	(1.3)	**1.21**	(0.08)	9.0	(3.0)	-0.15	(0.06)	**-0.15**	(0.03)
Czech Republic	17	(4.9)	**1.64**	(0.21)	4.0	(1.4)	**1.53**	(0.12)	8.4	(1.9)	**-0.35**	(0.09)	**-0.35**	(0.05)
Denmark	16	(3.0)	**1.64**	(0.10)	6.4	(0.9)	**1.81**	(0.10)	12.4	(1.4)	**-0.42**	(0.05)	**-0.47**	(0.04)
Estonia	7	(3.7)	**1.27**	(0.14)	2.4	(1.2)	**1.29**	(0.12)	5.0	(1.9)	**-0.19**	(0.06)	**-0.19**	(0.05)
Finland	1	(3.5)	**1.43**	(0.09)	5.1	(1.1)	**1.35**	(0.09)	5.0	(1.3)	**-0.24**	(0.05)	**-0.18**	(0.05)
France	18	(4.2)	**1.40**	(0.13)	3.8	(1.2)	**1.88**	(0.15)	16.0	(2.5)	**-0.25**	(0.05)	**-0.45**	(0.05)
Germany	14	(4.1)	**1.46**	(0.16)	3.0	(1.0)	**1.47**	(0.12)	9.6	(2.2)	**-0.22**	(0.07)	**-0.26**	(0.05)
Greece	7	(2.3)	**1.36**	(0.09)	6.2	(1.5)	**1.45**	(0.07)	16.3	(2.3)	**-0.21**	(0.05)	**-0.31**	(0.03)
Hungary	12	(3.7)	**1.79**	(0.15)	10.3	(1.9)	**1.91**	(0.14)	19.0	(2.5)	**-0.42**	(0.07)	**-0.46**	(0.05)
Iceland	16	(3.8)	**1.33**	(0.13)	2.0	(0.8)	**1.46**	(0.12)	6.8	(1.6)	**-0.28**	(0.07)	**-0.32**	(0.04)
Ireland	2	(2.5)	**1.57**	(0.10)	9.4	(1.5)	**1.35**	(0.07)	11.6	(2.1)	**-0.36**	(0.04)	**-0.20**	(0.03)
Israel	41	(4.8)	**1.52**	(0.13)	5.7	(1.4)	**2.37**	(0.19)	27.8	(2.9)	**-0.32**	(0.06)	**-0.68**	(0.05)
Italy	12	(2.0)	**1.29**	(0.08)	2.4	(0.6)	**1.49**	(0.06)	15.4	(1.6)	**-0.19**	(0.03)	**-0.32**	(0.02)
Japan	-4	(3.2)	1.17	(0.18)	0.5	(0.6)	0.94	(0.05)	-1.2	(1.2)	-0.17	(0.10)	0.09	(0.04)
Korea	2	(3.0)	1.25	(0.11)	2.3	(1.0)	**1.13**	(0.06)	4.9	(2.2)	-0.17	(0.06)	-0.02	(0.03)
Luxembourg	-2	(2.7)	**1.36**	(0.14)	3.4	(1.3)	1.05	(0.06)	1.5	(1.7)	**-0.25**	(0.05)	-0.03	(0.03)
Mexico	**-7**	(1.2)	**1.23**	(0.05)	3.4	(0.7)	**1.09**	(0.04)	5.0	(1.9)	**-0.16**	(0.03)	**-0.08**	(0.02)
Netherlands	-2	(3.3)	**1.20**	(0.10)	1.6	(0.8)	**1.22**	(0.10)	4.6	(2.0)	**-0.15**	(0.06)	**-0.13**	(0.04)
New Zealand	1	(4.2)	**1.74**	(0.15)	6.0	(1.2)	**1.35**	(0.11)	7.7	(2.2)	**-0.40**	(0.06)	**-0.16**	(0.05)
Norway	18	(3.8)	**1.41**	(0.14)	3.1	(1.0)	**1.52**	(0.09)	6.8	(1.2)	**-0.25**	(0.08)	**-0.34**	(0.04)
Poland	8	(3.0)	**1.26**	(0.10)	3.2	(1.2)	**1.56**	(0.11)	14.4	(2.3)	**-0.21**	(0.05)	**-0.36**	(0.04)
Portugal	5	(3.1)	**1.45**	(0.14)	6.0	(1.6)	**1.47**	(0.10)	10.7	(2.0)	**-0.31**	(0.04)	**-0.29**	(0.04)
Slovak Republic	22	(4.1)	**2.23**	(0.16)	14.9	(1.9)	**2.18**	(0.13)	22.2	(2.0)	**-0.60**	(0.06)	**-0.57**	(0.05)
Slovenia	2	(4.1)	1.15	(0.14)	1.7	(1.5)	**1.35**	(0.11)	5.2	(1.5)	-0.08	(0.05)	**-0.29**	(0.05)
Spain	3	(1.9)	**1.52**	(0.08)	7.5	(1.1)	**1.30**	(0.06)	9.0	(1.6)	**-0.36**	(0.04)	**-0.21**	(0.03)
Sweden	17	(5.1)	**1.74**	(0.15)	4.9	(0.9)	**1.58**	(0.13)	6.2	(1.4)	**-0.41**	(0.07)	**-0.38**	(0.06)
Switzerland	3	(2.9)	**1.46**	(0.13)	2.6	(0.7)	**1.17**	(0.07)	4.0	(1.5)	**-0.27**	(0.07)	**-0.12**	(0.03)
Turkey	-2	(3.5)	**1.22**	(0.08)	5.9	(2.0)	1.03	(0.10)	2.8	(7.6)	**-0.15**	(0.05)	**-0.20**	(0.05)
United Kingdom	6	(3.6)	**1.35**	(0.09)	3.5	(0.8)	**1.33**	(0.12)	7.2	(2.6)	**-0.24**	(0.04)	**-0.18**	(0.05)
United States	-2	(3.0)	**1.39**	(0.10)	5.2	(1.4)	**1.16**	(0.08)	4.1	(1.9)	**-0.24**	(0.05)	**-0.09**	(0.04)
OECD average	8	(0.6)	**1.44**	(0.02)	4.6	(0.2)	**1.43**	(0.02)	9.2	(0.4)	**-0.27**	(0.01)	**-0.25**	(0.01)
Albania	m	m	m	m	m	m	m	m	m	m	m	m	m	m
Argentina	2	(2.3)	**1.46**	(0.12)	4.9	(1.3)	**1.35**	(0.08)	13.9	(2.8)	**-0.30**	(0.05)	**-0.25**	(0.03)
Brazil	3	(1.7)	**1.19**	(0.05)	3.5	(0.9)	**1.31**	(0.05)	11.8	(1.8)	**-0.18**	(0.03)	**-0.25**	(0.02)
Bulgaria	9	(3.7)	**1.49**	(0.11)	6.2	(1.4)	**1.75**	(0.14)	13.4	(2.2)	**-0.30**	(0.05)	**-0.44**	(0.05)
Colombia	**-7**	(2.6)	1.00	(0.09)	0.0	(1.4)	1.07	(0.07)	3.2	(3.3)	0.00	(0.05)	-0.04	(0.03)
Costa Rica	-3	(2.8)	1.12	(0.11)	1.5	(1.3)	1.14	(0.08)	7.0	(4.0)	-0.10	(0.07)	**-0.18**	(0.05)
Croatia	11	(3.2)	**1.28**	(0.07)	7.4	(1.8)	**1.54**	(0.12)	17.0	(3.0)	**-0.21**	(0.04)	**-0.36**	(0.04)
Cyprus*	5	(3.0)	**1.67**	(0.13)	6.1	(1.2)	**1.37**	(0.08)	9.1	(1.8)	**-0.42**	(0.05)	**-0.28**	(0.04)
Hong Kong-China	-2	(3.2)	1.11	(0.08)	1.3	(0.9)	0.99	(0.06)	-0.3	(2.2)	-0.08	(0.05)	-0.01	(0.04)
Indonesia	-5	(2.7)	**1.32**	(0.11)	6.1	(1.9)	0.92	(0.07)	-5.5	(5.0)	**-0.23**	(0.05)	0.01	(0.04)
Jordan	-2	(3.9)	**1.37**	(0.11)	8.3	(2.2)	1.08	(0.10)	6.4	(6.8)	**-0.23**	(0.05)	**-0.16**	(0.05)
Kazakhstan	1	(2.8)	**1.47**	(0.14)	9.9	(2.6)	**1.28**	(0.09)	9.6	(2.8)	**-0.28**	(0.06)	**-0.18**	(0.04)
Latvia	-1	(3.4)	1.14	(0.13)	1.9	(1.7)	1.16	(0.09)	3.3	(1.8)	-0.05	(0.07)	**-0.14**	(0.05)
Liechtenstein	-20	(10.9)	c	c	c	c	0.77	(0.26)	-8.7	(10.6)	c	c	0.17	(0.12)
Lithuania	9	(2.9)	**1.37**	(0.09)	6.2	(1.5)	**1.52**	(0.11)	11.7	(1.8)	**-0.23**	(0.04)	**-0.34**	(0.03)
Macao-China	-2	(3.1)	0.97	(0.09)	-0.3	(1.0)	1.05	(0.06)	1.1	(1.4)	0.00	(0.05)	0.00	(0.03)
Malaysia	-1	(2.5)	**1.41**	(0.11)	5.4	(1.4)	**1.18**	(0.08)	10.0	(4.1)	**-0.29**	(0.05)	**-0.19**	(0.03)
Montenegro	16	(2.6)	**1.39**	(0.10)	9.3	(2.1)	**1.70**	(0.11)	25.9	(2.9)	**-0.22**	(0.04)	**-0.40**	(0.03)
Peru	**-11**	(2.3)	**1.35**	(0.10)	5.3	(1.4)	0.91	(0.05)	-4.8	(2.6)	**-0.25**	(0.04)	0.02	(0.03)
Qatar	-2	(2.1)	**1.79**	(0.08)	9.7	(0.9)	0.97	(0.05)	-2.0	(3.2)	**-0.64**	(0.03)	-0.07	(0.02)
Romania	8	(2.7)	**1.55**	(0.09)	12.5	(1.8)	**1.61**	(0.11)	19.4	(2.9)	**-0.38**	(0.05)	**-0.42**	(0.04)
Russian Federation	7	(3.3)	**1.30**	(0.14)	3.9	(1.8)	**1.25**	(0.08)	5.6	(1.7)	**-0.21**	(0.06)	**-0.21**	(0.04)
Serbia	12	(3.2)	**1.18**	(0.08)	4.0	(1.7)	**1.44**	(0.10)	15.2	(2.9)	**-0.17**	(0.04)	**-0.32**	(0.04)
Shanghai-China	16	(3.7)	**1.45**	(0.13)	5.4	(1.6)	**1.60**	(0.09)	13.1	(1.9)	**-0.31**	(0.05)	**-0.33**	(0.04)
Singapore	4	(3.2)	1.09	(0.09)	0.7	(0.7)	**1.12**	(0.06)	4.2	(2.1)	-0.08	(0.06)	**-0.09**	(0.03)
Chinese Taipei	-1	(3.6)	**1.37**	(0.10)	4.3	(1.1)	1.09	(0.07)	2.7	(2.0)	**-0.23**	(0.05)	-0.04	(0.04)
Thailand	**-10**	(2.7)	0.96	(0.07)	-0.7	(1.3)	0.85	(0.06)	-4.7	(1.8)	0.01	(0.04)	0.10	(0.04)
Tunisia	9	(4.5)	1.11	(0.11)	1.7	(1.8)	**1.26**	(0.14)	16.5	(6.9)	-0.08	(0.06)	**-0.34**	(0.07)
United Arab Emirates	12	(2.9)	**1.74**	(0.08)	12.4	(1.1)	**1.38**	(0.09)	21.8	(4.1)	**-0.56**	(0.03)	**-0.29**	(0.03)
Uruguay	6	(2.6)	**1.27**	(0.12)	2.7	(1.2)	**1.47**	(0.10)	13.9	(2.4)	**-0.22**	(0.05)	**-0.34**	(0.04)
Viet Nam	1	(3.7)	**1.19**	(0.10)	8.0	(4.0)	**1.29**	(0.12)	15.4	(5.6)	**-0.16**	(0.06)	**-0.25**	(0.06)

Note: This table was calculated considering only students with data on the *PISA index of economic, social and cultural status*. Values that are statistically significant are indicated in bold (see Annex A3).
* See notes at the beginning of this Annex.
StatLink ⟐⟐⟐ http://dx.doi.org/10.1787/888932964927

[Part 1/2]

Relationship between mathematics performance and school location

Table II.3.3a   *Results based on students' self-reports and school principals' reports*

	Percentage of students						PISA index of economic, social and cultural status (ESCS)						Average performance in mathematics					
	Students attending schools located in a village, hamlet or rural area (fewer than 3 000 people)		Students attending schools located in a town (3 000 to 100 000 people)		Students attending schools located in a city or large city (over 100 000 people)		Students attending schools located in a village, hamlet or rural area (fewer than 3 000 people)		Students attending schools located in a town (3 000 to 100 000 people)		Students attending schools located in a city or large city (over 100 000 people)		Students attending schools located in a village, hamlet or rural area (fewer than 3 000 people)		Students attending schools located in a town (3 000 to 100 000 people)		Students attending schools located in a city or large city (over 100 000 people)	
	%	S.E.	%	S.E.	%	S.E.	Mean index	S.E.	Mean index	S.E.	Mean index	S.E.	Mean score	S.E.	Mean score	S.E.	Mean score	S.E.
OECD Australia	5.9	(0.9)	28.7	(1.2)	65.4	(1.3)	-0.09	(0.0)	0.13	(0.0)	0.33	(0.0)	470	(5.4)	489	(2.7)	517	(2.0)
Austria	9.8	(2.3)	54.7	(3.5)	35.5	(3.0)	0.02	(0.1)	0.02	(0.0)	0.18	(0.0)	512	(17.9)	503	(4.6)	510	(7.3)
Belgium	2.6	(1.0)	74.9	(2.8)	22.6	(2.5)	0.09	(0.0)	0.15	(0.0)	0.11	(0.1)	482	(34.7)	523	(3.1)	502	(9.3)
Canada	8.1	(0.8)	37.7	(2.1)	54.2	(2.0)	0.25	(0.0)	0.37	(0.0)	0.47	(0.0)	510	(4.8)	518	(2.3)	524	(3.3)
Chile	3.5	(1.2)	38.6	(3.7)	57.9	(3.8)	-1.72	(0.2)	-0.83	(0.1)	-0.34	(0.0)	358	(10.4)	417	(4.3)	431	(4.3)
Czech Republic	7.8	(1.6)	65.5	(3.1)	26.7	(2.9)	-0.22	(0.0)	-0.11	(0.0)	0.08	(0.0)	491	(8.3)	494	(5.2)	512	(6.9)
Denmark	23.9	(2.7)	60.7	(3.2)	15.3	(2.5)*	0.33	(0.1)	0.47	(0.0)	0.42	(0.1)	493	(5.7)	505	(2.9)	501	(7.6)
Estonia	24.3	(1.9)	45.5	(1.9)	30.2	(0.7)	-0.25	(0.0)	0.13	(0.0)	0.38	(0.0)	510	(4.0)	519	(2.7)	535	(3.8)
Finland	7.4	(1.6)	65.7	(2.9)	26.9	(2.5)	0.02	(0.1)	0.33	(0.0)	0.53	(0.0)	517	(6.9)	518	(2.6)	525	(3.1)
France	w	w	w	w	w	w	w	w	w	w	w	w	w	w	w	w	w	w
Germany	1.3	(0.7)	74.3	(3.3)	24.4	(3.2)	c	c	0.16	(0.0)	0.29	(0.1)	c	c	518	(4.5)	526	(10.6)
Greece	8.3	(1.9)	62.3	(3.3)	29.4	(2.9)	-0.62	(0.1)	-0.12	(0.0)	0.20	(0.1)	432	(7.5)	448	(3.7)	471	(6.7)
Hungary	2.9	(0.9)	58.4	(4.1)	38.7	(4.1)	-1.09	(0.2)	-0.34	(0.1)	-0.04	(0.1)	395	(21.9)	470	(6.0)	496	(8.6)
Iceland	21.7	(0.2)	47.5	(0.2)	30.9	(0.2)	0.45	(0.0)	0.84	(0.0)	0.94	(0.0)	477	(3.4)	495	(2.6)	508	(2.9)
Ireland	22.6	(3.0)	50.8	(3.7)	26.6	(3.1)	0.06	(0.0)	0.12	(0.0)	0.19	(0.1)	506	(3.2)	502	(3.3)	499	(6.3)
Israel	15.5	(2.7)	45.8	(3.3)	38.7	(3.8)	0.36	(0.1)	0.09	(0.0)	0.19	(0.0)	480	(14.3)	457	(6.5)	479	(9.3)
Italy	2.4	(0.7)	67.1	(2.0)	30.5	(1.9)	-0.41	(0.1)	-0.11	(0.0)	0.12	(0.0)	451	(9.1)	484	(2.7)	497	(4.6)
Japan	0.0	c	27.5	(2.8)	72.5	(2.8)	c	c	-0.24	(0.0)	-0.01	(0.0)	c	c	514	(7.3)	548	(5.0)
Korea	2.4	(0.8)	11.4	(1.7)	86.1	(1.8)	c	c	-0.08	(0.1)	0.03	(0.0)	c	c	546	(12.7)	556	(4.6)
Luxembourg	0.5	(0.2)	99.5	(0.0)	0.0	c	c	c	0.07	(0.0)	c	c	c	c	491	(1.2)	c	c
Mexico	15.1	(1.0)	42.0	(1.8)	43.0	(1.7)	-2.18	(0.0)	-1.32	(0.0)	-0.53	(0.0)	375	(2.9)	408	(2.4)	433	(1.9)
Netherlands	0.0	c	72.4	(4.2)	27.6	(4.2)	c	c	0.19	(0.0)	0.27	(0.1)	c	c	521	(5.9)	521	(11.1)
New Zealand	6.3	(1.0)	37.9	(3.5)	55.8	(3.4)	-0.38	(0.1)	-0.07	(0.0)	0.18	(0.0)	460	(6.4)	494	(5.1)	516	(3.3)
Norway	18.4	(2.0)	60.9	(3.2)	20.7	(2.9)	0.28	(0.0)	0.48	(0.0)	0.60	(0.1)	478	(8.4)	493	(2.9)	501	(6.0)
Poland	32.5	(2.4)	46.8	(2.5)	20.8	(0.8)	-0.54	(0.0)	-0.19	(0.0)	0.26	(0.1)	498	(3.4)	517	(4.7)	548	(11.4)
Portugal	6.0	(2.1)	72.2	(4.1)	21.9	(3.6)	-1.14	(0.1)	-0.55	(0.1)	-0.08	(0.1)	457	(20.4)	491	(4.3)	492	(10.8)
Slovak Republic	13.6	(1.9)	72.9	(2.8)	13.6	(2.8)	-0.67	(0.1)	-0.18	(0.0)	0.28	(0.1)	431	(10.6)	486	(4.9)	517	(10.9)
Slovenia	1.2	(0.4)	59.7	(0.7)	39.1	(0.6)	0.01	(0.3)	0.01	(0.0)	0.20	(0.0)	433	(12.1)	498	(1.5)	516	(2.7)
Spain	3.3	(0.6)	58.8	(2.4)	37.9	(2.4)	-0.61	(0.1)	-0.28	(0.0)	-0.02	(0.0)	467	(8.2)	484	(2.7)	495	(3.3)
Sweden	17.8	(2.4)	56.6	(3.0)	25.6	(2.4)	0.09	(0.0)	0.27	(0.0)	0.42	(0.0)	469	(4.7)	481	(3.0)	490	(5.9)
Switzerland	7.9	(1.7)	74.5	(2.9)	17.6	(2.6)	-0.09	(0.1)	0.15	(0.0)	0.38	(0.1)	522	(5.5)	531	(4.0)	538	(10.1)
Turkey	2.3	(1.0)	41.3	(4.6)	56.4	(4.4)	-1.63	(0.3)	-1.51	(0.1)	-1.41	(0.1)	480	(31.4)	457	(11.0)	441	(6.3)
United Kingdom	8.1	(1.6)	63.8	(3.1)	28.1	(2.9)	0.43	(0.1)	0.28	(0.0)	0.26	(0.0)	499	(10.4)	497	(4.1)	501	(6.7)
United States	10.9	(2.9)	52.4	(4.1)	36.7	(3.6)	0.02	(0.0)	0.27	(0.1)	0.12	(0.1)	473	(9.1)	491	(5.5)	476	(7.0)
OECD average	9.4	(0.3)	55.9	(0.5)	34.7	(0.5)	-0.33	(0.0)	-0.04	(0.0)	0.15	(0.0)	468	(2.4)	493	(0.9)	504	(1.2)
Partners Albania	m	m	m	m	m	m	m	m	m	m	m	m	m	m	m	m	m	m
Argentina	8.5	(1.9)	53.9	(3.7)	37.5	(3.5)	-1.38	(0.2)	-0.71	(0.1)	-0.59	(0.1)	369	(12.4)	386	(4.8)	400	(5.2)
Brazil	1.1	(0.4)	49.5	(2.3)	49.3	(2.3)	-1.99	(0.0)	-1.51	(0.0)	-0.80	(0.0)	365	(9.8)	378	(2.9)	406	(3.7)
Bulgaria	3.8	(1.1)	60.2	(2.2)	36.0	(2.2)	-1.52	(0.3)	-0.42	(0.0)	0.09	(0.0)	364	(13.2)	426	(4.8)	471	(7.6)
Colombia	13.0	(1.2)	31.4	(3.9)	55.5	(3.7)	-2.31	(0.1)	-1.41	(0.1)	-0.93	(0.0)	339	(6.7)	371	(5.8)	389	(4.0)
Costa Rica	23.5	(2.9)	61.7	(3.6)	14.8	(2.6)	-1.55	(0.1)	-0.87	(0.1)	-0.52	(0.1)	388	(5.2)	411	(5.0)	424	(11.2)
Croatia	0.8	(0.5)	62.2	(1.7)	37.0	(1.6)	c	c	-0.49	(0.0)	-0.07	(0.0)	c	c	461	(3.5)	490	(7.7)
Cyprus*	4.0	(0.1)	61.4	(0.1)	34.6	(0.1)	-0.24	(0.0)	-0.05	(0.0)	0.36	(0.0)	420	(4.7)	431	(1.5)	463	(1.7)
Hong Kong-China	0.0	c	0.0	c	100.0	c	c	c	c	c	-0.79	(0.0)	c	c	c	c	563	(3.2)
Indonesia	29.1	(3.5)	50.4	(4.1)	20.5	(3.6)	-2.11	(0.1)	-1.87	(0.1)	-1.18	(0.1)	359	(9.0)	371	(5.3)	407	(9.4)
Jordan	10.4	(1.7)	46.7	(3.4)	42.9	(3.0)	-0.84	(0.1)	-0.52	(0.1)	-0.22	(0.0)	370	(6.3)	373	(4.5)	408	(4.9)
Kazakhstan	32.9	(2.9)	23.9	(3.0)	43.2	(3.2)	-0.59	(0.0)	-0.33	(0.1)	-0.10	(0.0)	420	(4.5)	428	(6.2)	443	(6.1)
Latvia	24.8	(1.6)	44.2	(1.8)	31.0	(1.9)	-0.79	(0.0)	-0.22	(0.0)	0.12	(0.0)	461	(5.1)	493	(3.3)	513	(5.9)
Liechtenstein	0.0	c	100.0	c	0.0	c	c	c	0.30	(0.1)	c	c	c	c	537	(4.1)	c	c
Lithuania	20.0	(1.3)	42.7	(1.5)	37.4	(1.0)	-0.67	(0.0)	-0.15	(0.0)	0.18	(0.0)	442	(4.4)	479	(4.6)	499	(3.8)
Macao-China	0.2	(0.0)	0.0	c	99.8	(0.0)	c	c	c	c	-0.89	(0.0)	c	c	c	c	540	(1.0)
Malaysia	13.4	(2.3)	59.7	(3.8)	26.9	(3.3)	-1.20	(0.1)	-0.77	(0.0)	-0.38	(0.1)	382	(4.6)	419	(4.2)	445	(8.1)
Montenegro	0.0	c	69.7	(0.1)	30.3	(0.1)	c	c	-0.29	(0.0)	-0.14	(0.0)	c	c	406	(1.2)	420	(2.1)
Peru	18.8	(2.4)	40.4	(3.5)	40.9	(3.2)	-2.13	(0.1)	-1.42	(0.1)	-0.64	(0.1)	313	(6.2)	359	(4.7)	402	(6.1)
Qatar	10.1	(0.1)	41.7	(0.1)	48.2	(0.1)	0.18	(0.0)	0.28	(0.0)	0.62	(0.0)	349	(2.0)	354	(1.3)	407	(1.2)
Romania	8.2	(1.4)	57.1	(3.7)	34.7	(3.5)	-1.09	(0.1)	-0.57	(0.0)	-0.15	(0.0)	406	(10.4)	438	(4.8)	466	(8.3)
Russian Federation	20.4	(2.2)	33.2	(2.4)	46.4	(2.6)	-0.53	(0.0)	-0.17	(0.0)	0.13	(0.0)	460	(6.6)	470	(5.7)	501	(4.7)
Serbia	0.4	(0.4)	58.2	(3.6)	41.4	(3.6)	c	c	-0.45	(0.0)	-0.09	(0.1)	c	c	434	(4.6)	470	(7.2)
Shanghai-China	0.0	c	0.0	c	100.0	c	c	c	c	c	-0.36	(0.0)	c	c	c	c	613	(3.3)
Singapore	0.0	c	0.0	c	100.0	c	c	c	c	c	-0.26	(0.0)	c	c	c	c	575	(1.3)
Chinese Taipei	1.7	(0.9)	36.5	(2.9)	61.8	(2.8)	c	c	-0.57	(0.0)	-0.28	(0.0)	c	c	536	(4.9)	578	(4.3)
Thailand	15.7	(2.1)	52.3	(3.5)	32.0	(3.3)	-2.06	(0.1)	-1.47	(0.1)	-0.79	(0.1)	414	(9.8)	450	(4.2)	450	(6.9)
Tunisia	4.4	(1.8)	72.1	(3.3)	23.5	(3.2)	-1.74	(0.2)	-1.32	(0.2)	-0.70	(0.1)	370	(11.7)	383	(4.1)	410	(11.5)
United Arab Emirates	8.0	(1.1)	31.6	(2.3)	60.5	(2.2)	0.04	(0.1)	0.08	(0.0)	0.49	(0.0)	414	(6.4)	409	(5.4)	450	(3.3)
Uruguay	7.1	(1.4)	56.5	(2.8)	36.4	(2.7)	-1.43	(0.1)	-1.08	(0.0)	-0.47	(0.1)	365	(12.0)	397	(3.6)	439	(5.9)
Viet Nam	45.0	(3.1)	30.3	(3.0)	24.7	(3.0)	-2.26	(0.1)	-1.87	(0.1)	-0.92	(0.0)	488	(5.8)	514	(8.1)	550	(11.4)

Note: This table was calculated considering only students with data on the *PISA index of economic, social and cultural status*. Values that are statistically significant are indicated in bold (see Annex.A3).

* See notes at the beginning of this Annex.

StatLink http://dx.doi.org/10.1787/888932964927

[Part 2/2]
Relationship between mathematics performance and school location
Table II.3.3a *Results based on students' self-reports and school principals' reports*

	Average performance in mathematics after accounting for ESCS						Difference in mathematics score											
							BEFORE accounting for the PISA index of economic, social and cultural status of students (ESCS)						AFTER accounting for the PISA index of economic, social and cultural status of students (ESCS)					
	Students attending schools located in a village, hamlet or rural area (fewer than 3 000 people)		Students attending schools located in a town (3 000 to 100 000 people)		Students attending schools located in a city or large city (over 100 000 people)		Students in town schools compared with rural schools		Students in city schools compared with town schools		Students in city schools compared with rural schools		Students in town schools compared with rural schools		Students in city schools compared with town schools		Students in city schools compared with rural schools	
	Mean score	S.E.	Mean score	S.E.	Mean score	S.E.	Score dif.	S.E.	Score dif.	S.E.	Score dif.	S.E.	Score dif.	S.E.	Score dif.	S.E.	Score dif.	S.E.
OECD																		
Australia	474	(5.2)	484	(2.5)	504	(1.8)	19	(6.0)	28	(3.4)	47	(5.7)	11	(5.6)	20	(2.8)	30	(5.3)
Austria	511	(14.5)	502	(4.1)	502	(6.3)	-9	(20.1)	7	(9.9)	-2	(19.8)	-9	(16.7)	0	(8.5)	-10	(16.1)
Belgium	477	(27.3)	515	(2.4)	496	(6.5)	41	(35.8)	-21	(10.9)	20	(36.2)	38	(28.2)	-19	(7.6)	19	(28.5)
Canada	502	(4.2)	506	(2.1)	509	(2.8)	8	(5.4)	6	(4.0)	14	(6.6)	5	(4.8)	3	(3.5)	7	(5.8)
Chile	416	(7.9)	446	(3.9)	443	(3.5)	59	(12.3)	14	(7.2)	73	(11.5)	31	(8.3)	-2	(4.9)	24	(8.6)
Czech Republic	502	(7.1)	500	(4.4)	508	(5.3)	3	(10.3)	17	(9.6)	20	(10.6)	-2	(8.4)	8	(7.4)	9	(9.6)
Denmark	480	(4.2)	487	(2.4)	484	(4.7)	12	(6.3)	-5	(8.5)	8	(10.3)	7	(4.9)	-2	(5.3)	4	(7.0)
Estonia	517	(4.0)	515	(2.5)	524	(3.7)	9	(4.8)	16	(4.4)	25	(5.7)	-1	(4.8)	8	(4.1)	8	(5.9)
Finland	516	(5.4)	508	(2.6)	507	(2.8)	1	(7.1)	7	(4.3)	8	(7.6)	-8	(5.7)	0	(3.8)	-11	(6.0)
France	w	w	w	w	w	w	w	w	w	w	w	w	w	w	w	w	w	w
Germany	c	c	511	(3.6)	513	(7.8)	c	c	8	(12.6)	c	c	c	c	2	(9.3)	c	c
Greece	453	(5.9)	452	(2.7)	464	(5.2)	16	(8.5)	23	(8.7)	39	(10.2)	0	(6.6)	12	(6.7)	10	(8.6)
Hungary	444	(17.2)	486	(4.4)	498	(6.1)	76	(23.0)	26	(13.0)	102	(24.2)	41	(17.7)	12	(8.9)	58	(19.4)
Iceland	463	(3.3)	469	(2.9)	479	(3.3)	18	(4.6)	13	(3.4)	31	(4.7)	8	(4.6)	10	(3.4)	17	(4.9)
Ireland	504	(2.6)	497	(2.6)	492	(4.4)	-4	(4.6)	-3	(7.7)	-7	(7.2)	-6	(3.7)	-6	(5.1)	-12	(4.7)
Israel	462	(11.8)	452	(4.8)	469	(7.6)	-23	(17.3)	22	(11.5)	-1	(17.0)	-9	(13.7)	17	(9.1)	8	(13.9)
Italy	464	(8.1)	488	(2.4)	493	(3.9)	33	(9.2)	12	(5.6)	46	(10.3)	24	(8.3)	5	(4.7)	29	(9.3)
Japan	c	c	523	(6.3)	548	(4.5)	c	c	34	(10.1)	c	c	c	c	25	(8.8)	c	c
Korea	c	c	550	(10.6)	555	(4.1)	c	c	10	(13.5)	c	c	c	c	5	(11.5)	c	c
Luxembourg	c	c	c	c	488	(1.3)	c	c	c	c	c	c	c	c	c	c	c	c
Mexico	411	(3.5)	433	(2.2)	442	(1.7)	33	(3.7)	25	(3.4)	58	(3.4)	23	(3.9)	13	(2.9)	32	(3.3)
Netherlands	c	c	514	(5.5)	510	(10.0)	c	c	-1	(14.3)	c	c	c	c	-4	(12.9)	c	c
New Zealand	479	(5.9)	498	(4.4)	507	(2.5)	34	(8.4)	22	(6.2)	55	(7.0)	21	(7.5)	9	(4.8)	26	(6.5)
Norway	469	(8.3)	477	(2.8)	482	(5.3)	14	(8.7)	8	(6.7)	22	(10.8)	8	(8.3)	4	(5.6)	12	(10.1)
Poland	520	(3.7)	525	(4.0)	538	(8.6)	19	(5.7)	31	(11.7)	50	(12.0)	6	(4.9)	12	(8.8)	21	(10.0)
Portugal	496	(16.7)	511	(3.0)	495	(7.1)	35	(21.2)	1	(12.1)	36	(23.1)	-16	(17.7)	-12	(17.1)		
Slovak Republic	466	(8.4)	495	(3.4)	502	(8.2)	54	(11.9)	32	(12.7)	86	(15.3)	29	(9.2)	8	(9.1)	35	(11.3)
Slovenia	432	(12.1)	497	(1.5)	508	(2.8)	65	(12.2)	18	(3.4)	83	(12.4)	65	(11.6)	10	(3.3)	74	(12.7)
Spain	488	(6.1)	490	(2.3)	495	(2.5)	13	(8.5)	14	(4.2)	28	(8.9)	3	(6.7)	6	(3.4)	6	(6.5)
Sweden	466	(4.6)	471	(2.7)	475	(4.7)	12	(5.5)	9	(7.2)	21	(7.7)	6	(5.3)	4	(5.9)	8	(6.8)
Switzerland	526	(6.3)	526	(3.4)	524	(8.3)	9	(6.7)	7	(11.4)	15	(12.2)	0	(7.1)	-2	(9.2)	-1	(11.2)
Turkey	532	(23.4)	505	(11.2)	486	(6.6)	-24	(33.7)	-16	(14.4)	-40	(32.4)	-28	(24.7)	-19	(11.6)	-46	(24.1)
United Kingdom	481	(8.3)	485	(3.4)	490	(5.3)	-2	(11.5)	4	(8.0)	2	(10.6)	4	(8.9)	5	(6.4)	9	(8.4)
United States	472	(9.0)	481	(4.2)	471	(5.4)	18	(11.1)	-15	(9.6)	3	(11.5)	10	(10.4)	-10	(7.5)	-1	(10.5)
OECD average	479	(2.0)	494	(0.7)	498	(1.0)	20	(2.6)	11	(1.6)	31	(2.8)	11	(2.1)	4	(1.3)	13	(2.2)
Partners																		
Albania	m	m	m	m	m	m	m	m	m	m	m	m	m	m	m	m	m	m
Argentina	406	(11.5)	404	(4.1)	415	(4.0)	16	(13.1)	14	(7.0)	31	(12.8)	1	(11.6)	11	(5.5)	9	(11.6)
Brazil	417	(10.4)	416	(3.6)	426	(3.7)	13	(9.6)	28	(5.2)	42	(10.9)	4	(9.7)	10	(3.9)	5	(10.6)
Bulgaria	426	(12.4)	443	(4.1)	467	(5.9)	62	(14.1)	45	(9.0)	107	(15.1)	24	(12.7)	25	(7.1)	43	(13.6)
Colombia	392	(7.1)	406	(5.5)	411	(3.8)	33	(8.9)	18	(7.2)	50	(7.8)	17	(7.9)	6	(5.6)	17	(6.9)
Costa Rica	425	(4.2)	431	(4.2)	436	(8.7)	22	(8.1)	13	(13.3)	35	(12.1)	7	(5.8)	5	(10.4)	12	(9.6)
Croatia	c	c	478	(3.5)	492	(7.1)	c	c	29	(8.7)	c	c	c	c	14	(7.7)	c	c
Cyprus*	429	(4.8)	433	(1.5)	450	(1.9)	11	(4.9)	32	(2.3)	43	(4.8)	5	(4.9)	17	(2.4)	17	(5.3)
Hong Kong-China	c	c	c	c	584	(3.1)	c	c	c	c	c	c	c	c	c	c	c	c
Indonesia	400	(14.2)	409	(7.5)	428	(9.5)	12	(10.3)	36	(11.5)	48	(13.7)	8	(9.6)	25	(10.1)	28	(15.2)
Jordan	387	(7.1)	384	(4.7)	412	(4.8)	4	(7.7)	34	(7.0)	38	(7.6)	0	(7.6)	28	(6.6)	23	(7.3)
Kazakhstan	435	(4.6)	437	(6.0)	446	(5.4)	8	(7.8)	15	(9.3)	23	(7.7)	3	(7.6)	9	(8.3)	11	(6.9)
Latvia	486	(5.2)	501	(2.8)	508	(4.9)	32	(6.4)	19	(6.6)	52	(7.6)	16	(5.8)	8	(5.4)	21	(7.0)
Liechtenstein	c	c	528	(4.5)	c	c	c	c	c	c	c	c	c	c	c	c	c	c
Lithuania	464	(4.1)	484	(3.8)	493	(3.2)	37	(6.4)	20	(5.9)	57	(5.2)	20	(5.7)	10	(5.1)	31	(5.1)
Macao-China	c	c	c	c	555	(1.6)	c	c	c	c	c	c	c	c	c	c	c	c
Malaysia	416	(5.0)	442	(4.1)	455	(6.8)	36	(6.3)	26	(9.6)	62	(9.6)	26	(5.5)	15	(7.9)	38	(8.0)
Montenegro	c	c	416	(1.3)	425	(2.2)	c	c	14	(2.4)	c	c	c	c	9	(2.4)	c	c
Peru	375	(7.5)	406	(4.9)	420	(4.4)	46	(7.2)	43	(7.9)	89	(8.5)	30	(6.3)	20	(5.9)	50	(7.2)
Qatar	344	(2.0)	348	(1.4)	394	(1.2)	6	(2.2)	52	(1.8)	58	(2.4)	4	(2.3)	45	(1.8)	46	(2.5)
Romania	446	(11.5)	459	(4.0)	471	(6.4)	32	(11.1)	28	(10.2)	59	(13.1)	17	(11.3)	12	(7.4)	21	(12.3)
Russian Federation	480	(6.6)	476	(5.1)	497	(4.3)	9	(8.7)	32	(7.9)	41	(7.0)	-3	(8.2)	21	(6.8)	18	(6.2)
Serbia	c	c	448	(4.5)	473	(6.3)	c	c	36	(9.5)	c	c	c	c	25	(8.3)	c	c
Shanghai-China	c	c	c	c	627	(2.7)	c	c	c	c	c	c	c	c	c	c	c	c
Singapore	c	c	c	c	587	(1.4)	c	c	c	c	c	c	c	c	c	c	c	c
Chinese Taipei	c	c	568	(3.8)	593	(3.5)	c	c	42	(6.9)	c	c	c	c	26	(5.4)	c	c
Thailand	460	(11.7)	448	(5.0)	466	(6.5)	3	(10.6)	34	(8.5)	36	(11.3)	-4	(10.4)	18	(7.0)	9	(11.2)
Tunisia	408	(13.2)	411	(5.1)	424	(10.6)	12	(12.5)	27	(12.5)	39	(17.4)	5	(12.7)	14	(10.4)	9	(15.7)
United Arab Emirates	413	(5.3)	407	(4.6)	436	(3.0)	-5	(8.6)	41	(6.4)	36	(7.3)	-6	(7.3)	29	(6.0)	22	(6.1)
Uruguay	417	(8.8)	436	(3.4)	436	(9.3)	32	(12.6)	42	(7.3)	74	(13.4)	22	(9.8)	21	(5.4)	35	(9.3)
Viet Nam	547	(7.8)	569	(8.6)	574	(9.0)	25	(10.3)	36	(13.5)	62	(13.0)	16	(9.7)	11	(12.1)	29	(13.0)

Note: This table was calculated considering only students with data on the *PISA index of economic, social and cultural status*. Values that are statistically significant are indicated in bold (see Annex A3).
* See notes at the beginning of this Annex.
StatLink ⟨≡⟩ http://dx.doi.org/10.1787/888932964927

[Part 1/3]
Change between 2003 and 2012 in the relationship between mathematics performance and school location

Table II.3.3b   *Results based on students' self-reports and school principals' reports*

		PISA 2003										
		Percentage of students						Average performance in mathematics				
		Students attending schools located in a village, hamlet or rural area (fewer than 3 000 people)		Students attending schools located in a town (3 000 to 100 000 people)		Students attending schools located in a city or large city (over 100 000 people)		Students attending schools located in a village, hamlet or rural area (fewer than 3 000 people)		Students attending schools located in a town (3 000 to 100 000 people)		Students attending schools located in a city or large city (over 100 000 people)	
		%	S.E.	%	S.E.	%	S.E.	Mean score	S.E.	Mean score	S.E.	Mean score	S.E.
OECD	Australia	6.1	(1.3)	31.1	(2.5)	62.7	(2.5)	490	(10.8)	517	(3.4)	532	(2.7)
	Austria	13.2	(2.6)	58.0	(4.3)	28.8	(3.3)	465	(8.4)	509	(4.5)	518	(9.5)
	Belgium	2.8	(1.1)	76.5	(2.7)	20.7	(2.5)	483	(30.6)	535	(3.3)	535	(10.7)
	Canada	8.8	(0.8)	46.5	(1.7)	44.7	(1.7)	515	(3.5)	534	(2.4)	542	(2.8)
	Czech Republic	8.4	(1.5)	68.4	(2.6)	23.2	(2.6)	481	(8.3)	519	(3.8)	546	(8.4)
	Denmark	21.9	(2.7)	65.0	(3.2)	13.0	(2.0)	505	(6.4)	518	(3.0)	522	(9.2)
	Finland	11.7	(2.1)	67.2	(3.4)	21.2	(2.7)	543	(4.3)	543	(2.0)	550	(5.5)
	France	w	w	w	w	w	w	w	w	w	w	w	w
	Germany	5.2	(1.4)	63.2	(3.5)	31.6	(3.3)	490	(15.0)	510	(6.1)	517	(9.1)
	Greece	4.1	(1.1)	71.1	(4.1)	24.8	(3.9)	403	(10.2)	441	(3.8)	465	(9.3)
	Hungary	2.2	(0.7)	52.9	(3.6)	44.9	(3.5)	363	(14.6)	477	(6.1)	512	(5.9)
	Iceland	25.7	(0.2)	53.6	(0.2)	20.8	(0.1)	508	(3.2)	516	(2.2)	524	(3.5)
	Ireland	23.2	(3.6)	46.2	(4.9)	30.6	(4.1)	491	(4.9)	505	(4.1)	508	(7.0)
	Italy	0.9	(1.0)	68.0	(3.1)	31.1	(3.0)	468	(12.1)	462	(4.5)	474	(7.3)
	Japan	0.0	c	34.9	(3.7)	65.1	(3.7)	c	c	518	(8.7)	543	(6.6)
	Korea	1.3	(0.9)	15.1	(1.9)	83.6	(1.7)	c	c	505	(12.0)	551	(3.4)
	Luxembourg	0.0	c	100.0	c	0.0	c	c	c	493	(1.0)	c	c
	Mexico	23.3	(2.7)	36.4	(3.1)	40.4	(3.1)	335	(8.4)	379	(4.5)	419	(6.3)
	Netherlands	0.9	(0.7)	64.8	(4.1)	34.4	(4.2)	c	c	539	(5.2)	548	(8.1)
	New Zealand	6.2	(1.7)	47.3	(3.2)	46.5	(2.7)	503	(14.5)	521	(3.5)	530	(3.7)
	Norway	38.5	(3.3)	45.2	(3.9)	16.3	(2.7)	488	(3.8)	495	(3.0)	507	(6.9)
	Poland	37.5	(1.4)	38.9	(2.4)	23.6	(2.0)	471	(4.8)	493	(3.1)	516	(5.0)
	Portugal	6.8	(2.1)	73.8	(3.8)	19.5	(3.4)	433	(13.7)	461	(4.5)	498	(7.2)
	Slovak Republic	10.6	(1.7)	71.9	(2.7)	17.4	(2.4)	447	(9.8)	497	(3.9)	533	(7.3)
	Spain	4.2	(1.4)	53.2	(3.8)	42.6	(3.6)	474	(7.4)	480	(3.6)	493	(5.1)
	Sweden	21.0	(2.7)	57.9	(2.8)	21.1	(1.7)	508	(3.9)	510	(3.0)	508	(8.6)
	Switzerland	15.0	(2.5)	72.4	(3.6)	12.6	(2.4)	516	(6.3)	525	(4.3)	552	(19.2)
	Turkey	0.5	(0.4)	46.3	(4.7)	53.2	(4.7)	c	c	403	(9.0)	443	(9.3)
	United States	10.5	(1.8)	58.7	(2.9)	30.8	(2.6)	485	(5.0)	498	(3.3)	462	(8.2)
	OECD average 2003	11.1	(0.4)	56.6	(0.6)	32.3	(0.6)	472	(2.3)	497	(0.9)	513	(1.5)
Partners	Brazil	8.7	(1.8)	41.8	(4.2)	49.5	(4.3)	319	(15.3)	342	(8.2)	377	(7.4)
	Hong Kong-China	0.0	c	0.0	c	100.0	c	c	c	c	c	550	(4.5)
	Indonesia	31.6	(3.5)	39.4	(3.9)	29.0	(3.1)	335	(6.0)	359	(5.8)	389	(9.5)
	Latvia	29.1	(3.0)	37.8	(3.3)	33.2	(2.4)	460	(5.6)	492	(5.8)	494	(7.0)
	Liechtenstein	0.0	c	100.0	c	0.0	c	c	c	536	(4.1)	c	c
	Macao-China	0.0	c	0.0	c	100.0	c	c	c	c	c	527	(2.9)
	Russian Federation	13.8	(2.5)	41.1	(3.9)	45.1	(3.5)	439	(9.3)	460	(4.9)	485	(6.4)
	Thailand	27.0	(2.8)	47.3	(3.9)	25.7	(3.1)	389	(4.8)	412	(4.8)	453	(8.3)
	Tunisia	4.2	(1.7)	80.0	(3.3)	15.8	(3.1)	315	(7.6)	358	(3.1)	378	(13.6)
	Uruguay	7.0	(1.4)	50.8	(3.2)	42.2	(3.1)	370	(11.9)	406	(5.3)	450	(6.2)

Notes: This table was calculated considering only students with data on the *PISA index of economic, social and cultural status*. Values that are statistically significant are indicated in bold (see Annex A3).
For comparability over time, PISA 2003 values on the *PISA index of economic, social and cultural status* have been rescaled to the PISA 2012 scale of the index. PISA 2003 results reported in this table may thus differ from those presented in *Learning for Tomorrow's World: First Results from PISA 2003* (OECD, 2004) (see Annex A5 for more details).
Only countries and economies with comparable data from PISA 2003 and PISA 2012 are shown.
1. ESCS refers to the *PISA index of economic, social and cultural status*.
StatLink ⟐⟐⟐ http://dx.doi.org/10.1787/888932964927

[Part 2/3]
Change between 2003 and 2012 in the relationship between mathematics performance and school location

Table II.3.3b   *Results based on students' self-reports and school principals' reports*

	PISA 2012											
	Percentage of students						Average performance in mathematics					
	Students attending schools located in a village, hamlet or rural area (fewer than 3 000 people)		Students attending schools located in a town (3 000 to 100 000 people)		Students attending schools located in a city or large city (over 100 000 people)		Students attending schools located in a village, hamlet or rural area (fewer than 3 000 people)		Students attending schools located in a town (3 000 to 100 000 people)		Students attending schools located in a city or large city (over 100 000 people)	
	%	S.E.	%	S.E.	%	S.E.	Mean score	S.E.	Mean score	S.E.	Mean score	S.E.
OECD												
Australia	5.9	(0.9)	28.7	(1.2)	65.4	(1.3)	470	(5.4)	489	(2.7)	517	(2.0)
Austria	9.8	(2.3)	54.7	(3.5)	35.5	(3.0)	512	(17.9)	503	(4.6)	510	(7.3)
Belgium	2.6	(1.0)	74.9	(2.8)	22.6	(2.5)	482	(34.7)	523	(3.1)	502	(9.3)
Canada	8.1	(0.8)	37.7	(2.1)	54.2	(2.0)	510	(4.8)	518	(2.3)	524	(3.3)
Czech Republic	7.8	(1.6)	65.5	(3.1)	26.7	(2.9)	491	(8.3)	494	(5.2)	512	(6.9)
Denmark	23.9	(2.7)	60.7	(3.2)	15.3	(2.5)	493	(5.7)	505	(2.9)	501	(7.6)
Finland	7.4	(1.6)	65.7	(2.9)	26.9	(2.5)	517	(6.9)	518	(2.6)	525	(3.1)
France	w	w	w	w	w	w	w	w	w	w	w	w
Germany	1.3	(0.7)	74.3	(3.3)	24.4	(3.2)	c	c	518	(4.5)	526	(10.6)
Greece	8.3	(1.9)	62.3	(3.3)	29.4	(2.9)	432	(7.5)	448	(3.7)	471	(6.7)
Hungary	2.9	(0.7)	58.4	(4.1)	38.7	(4.1)	395	(21.9)	470	(6.0)	496	(8.6)
Iceland	21.7	(0.2)	47.5	(0.2)	30.9	(0.2)	477	(3.4)	495	(2.6)	508	(2.9)
Ireland	22.6	(3.0)	50.8	(3.7)	26.6	(3.1)	506	(3.2)	502	(3.3)	499	(6.3)
Italy	2.4	(0.7)	67.1	(2.0)	30.5	(1.9)	451	(9.1)	484	(2.7)	497	(4.6)
Japan	0.0	c	27.5	(2.8)	72.5	(2.8)	c	c	514	(7.3)	548	(5.0)
Korea	2.4	(0.8)	11.4	(1.8)	86.1	(1.8)	c	c	546	(12.7)	556	(4.6)
Luxembourg	0.5	(0.0)	99.5	(0.0)	0.0	c	c	c	491	(1.2)	c	c
Mexico	15.1	(1.0)	42.0	(1.8)	43.0	(1.7)	375	(2.9)	408	(2.4)	433	(1.9)
Netherlands	0.0	c	72.4	(4.2)	27.6	(4.2)	c	c	521	(5.9)	521	(11.1)
New Zealand	6.3	(1.0)	37.9	(3.5)	55.8	(3.4)	460	(6.4)	494	(5.1)	516	(3.3)
Norway	18.4	(2.0)	60.9	(3.2)	20.7	(2.9)	478	(8.4)	493	(2.9)	501	(6.0)
Poland	32.5	(2.4)	46.8	(2.5)	20.8	(0.8)	498	(3.4)	517	(4.7)	548	(11.4)
Portugal	6.0	(2.1)	72.2	(4.1)	21.9	(3.6)	457	(20.4)	491	(4.3)	492	(10.8)
Slovak Republic	13.6	(1.9)	72.9	(2.8)	13.6	(1.8)	431	(10.6)	486	(4.9)	517	(10.9)
Spain	3.3	(0.6)	58.8	(2.4)	37.9	(2.4)	467	(8.2)	480	(2.4)	495	(3.3)
Sweden	17.8	(2.4)	56.6	(3.0)	25.6	(2.4)	469	(4.7)	481	(3.0)	490	(5.9)
Switzerland	7.9	(1.7)	74.5	(2.9)	17.6	(2.6)	522	(5.5)	531	(4.0)	538	(10.1)
Turkey	2.3	(1.0)	41.3	(4.6)	56.4	(4.4)	480	(31.4)	457	(11.0)	441	(6.3)
United States	10.9	(2.9)	52.4	(4.1)	36.7	(3.6)	473	(9.1)	491	(5.5)	476	(7.0)
OECD average 2003	9.3	(0.3)	56.3	(0.6)	34.4	(0.5)	472	(2.8)	495	(1.0)	507	(1.4)
Partners												
Brazil	1.1	(0.4)	49.5	(2.3)	49.3	(2.3)	365	(9.8)	378	(2.9)	406	(3.7)
Hong Kong-China	0.0	c	0.0	c	100.0	c	c	c	c	c	563	(3.2)
Indonesia	29.1	(3.5)	50.4	(4.1)	20.5	(3.6)	359	(9.0)	371	(5.3)	407	(9.4)
Latvia	24.8	(1.6)	44.2	(1.8)	31.0	(1.9)	461	(5.1)	493	(3.3)	513	(5.9)
Liechtenstein	0.0	c	100.0	c	0.0	c	c	c	537	(4.1)	c	c
Macao-China	0.2	(0.0)	0.0	c	99.8	(0.0)	c	c	c	c	540	(1.0)
Russian Federation	20.4	(2.2)	33.2	(2.4)	46.4	(2.6)	460	(6.6)	470	(5.7)	501	(4.7)
Thailand	15.7	(2.1)	52.3	(3.5)	32.0	(3.3)	414	(9.8)	417	(4.0)	450	(6.9)
Tunisia	4.4	(1.8)	72.1	(3.3)	23.5	(3.2)	370	(11.7)	383	(4.1)	410	(11.5)
Uruguay	7.1	(1.4)	56.5	(2.8)	36.4	(2.7)	365	(12.0)	397	(3.6)	439	(5.9)

Notes: This table was calculated considering only students with data on the *PISA index of economic, social and cultural status*. Values that are statistically significant are indicated in bold (see Annex A3).
For comparability over time, PISA 2003 values on the *PISA index of economic, social and cultural status* have been rescaled to the PISA 2012 scale of the index. PISA 2003 results reported in this table may thus differ from those presented in *Learning for Tomorrow's World: First Results from PISA 2003* (OECD, 2004) (see Annex A5 for more details). Only countries and economies with comparable data from PISA 2003 and PISA 2012 are shown.
1. ESCS refers to the *PISA index of economic, social and cultural status*.
StatLink ⎘ http://dx.doi.org/10.1787/888932964927

[Part 3/3]
Change between 2003 and 2012 in the relationship between mathematics performance and school location

Table II.3.3b   *Results based on students' self-reports and school principals' reports*

	Change between 2003 and 2012 (PISA 2012 - PISA 2003)					
	Change in average performance in mathematics			Change in average performance in mathematics AFTER accounting for ESCS[1]		
	Students attending schools located in a village, hamlet or rural area (fewer than 3 000 people)	Students attending schools located in a town (3 000 to 100 000 people)	Students attending schools located in a city or large city (over 100 000 people)	Students attending schools located in a village, hamlet or rural area (fewer than 3 000 people)	Students attending schools located in a town (3 000 to 100 000 people)	Students attending schools located in a city or large city (over 100 000 people)
	Score dif. / S.E.	Score dif. / S.E.	Score dif. / S.E.	Score dif. / S.E.	Score dif. / S.E.	Score dif. / S.E.
Australia	-20 (12.3)	**-27** (4.8)	**-15** (3.9)	**-29** (10.4)	**-35** (4.2)	**-23** (3.6)
Austria	47 (19.8)	-6 (6.7)	-8 (12.2)	27 (17.5)	**-16** (5.7)	**-24** (9.8)
Belgium	-1 (46.3)	**-13** (4.9)	**-33** (14.3)	-23 (29.5)	**-24** (3.8)	**-32** (9.9)
Canada	-6 (6.3)	**-16** (3.8)	**-18** (4.7)	**-13** (6.0)	**-23** (3.7)	**-21** (4.0)
Czech Republic	10 (11.9)	**-24** (6.7)	**-34** (11.0)	5 (10.9)	**-25** (5.6)	**-26** (8.5)
Denmark	-11 (8.8)	**-13** (4.6)	-21 (12.1)	**-28** (6.8)	**-26** (3.8)	**-28** (6.9)
Finland	**-26** (8.3)	**-25** (3.8)	**-24** (6.6)	**-36** (7.5)	**-33** (3.7)	**-31** (5.6)
France	w w	w w	w w	w w	w w	w w
Germany	c c	8 (7.8)	9 (14.2)	c c	1 (6.3)	1 (8.5)
Greece	29 (12.7)	7 (5.7)	6 (11.6)	20 (12.1)	-1 (4.6)	-2 (8.7)
Hungary	31 (26.4)	-7 (8.8)	-16 (10.6)	27 (24.6)	**-15** (6.3)	**-16** (7.3)
Iceland	**-31** (5.1)	**-21** (3.9)	**-17** (5.0)	**-39** (5.2)	**-27** (3.9)	**-20** (5.2)
Ireland	**15** (6.1)	-3 (5.6)	-8 (9.6)	2 (5.4)	**-16** (4.4)	**-25** (5.9)
Italy	-17 (15.3)	22 (5.6)	23 (8.8)	-16 (12.8)	14 (4.9)	17 (8.1)
Japan	c c	-4 (11.5)	5 (8.5)	c c	-16 (9.8)	-10 (7.5)
Korea	c c	41 (17.6)	5 (6.1)	c c	19 (17.2)	-6 (5.5)
Luxembourg	c c	-3 (2.5)	c c	c c	**-8** (2.5)	c c
Mexico	39 (9.1)	29 (5.5)	15 (6.9)	41 (8.0)	28 (5.2)	7 (5.3)
Netherlands	c c	**-18** (8.1)	-27 (13.9)	c c	**-32** (8.1)	**-36** (11.7)
New Zealand	**-42** (16.0)	**-27** (6.5)	**-14** (5.3)	**-42** (14.0)	**-33** (5.6)	**-25** (4.1)
Norway	-10 (9.4)	-3 (4.6)	-7 (9.4)	-19 (9.6)	**-11** (4.4)	**-18** (6.6)
Poland	28 (6.2)	24 (6.0)	32 (12.6)	20 (5.4)	17 (5.2)	25 (8.7)
Portugal	23 (24.7)	30 (6.5)	-6 (13.2)	13 (22.6)	17 (5.6)	-15 (8.8)
Slovak Republic	-15 (14.6)	-12 (6.6)	-16 (13.2)	-21 (11.3)	**-16** (4.6)	-21 (10.6)
Spain	-7 (11.2)	0 (4.7)	2 (6.3)	-9 (9.7)	**-9** (4.2)	**-10** (4.8)
Sweden	**-39** (6.4)	**-29** (4.6)	-18 (10.6)	**-43** (6.1)	**-35** (4.1)	**-28** (6.9)
Switzerland	6 (8.6)	7 (6.2)	-15 (21.7)	-4 (8.4)	-9 (5.5)	-26 (15.3)
Turkey	c c	54 (14.4)	-2 (11.4)	c c	59 (10.6)	15 (8.8)
United States	-13 (10.6)	-7 (6.7)	14 (11.0)	-18 (10.1)	**-11** (5.5)	9 (9.1)
OECD average 2003	0 (3.5)	-1 (1.4)	**-8** (2.1)	**-8** (2.8)	**-10** (1.2)	**-14** (1.5)
Brazil	46 (18.2)	36 (8.9)	29 (8.5)	48 (14.3)	30 (7.5)	14 (7.5)
Hong Kong-China	c c	c c	13 (5.8)	c c	c c	-1 (5.2)
Indonesia	24 (11.0)	12 (8.1)	18 (13.5)	24 (9.8)	11 (7.5)	12 (10.7)
Latvia	0 (7.8)	1 (7.0)	19 (9.3)	4 (7.5)	-3 (6.1)	13 (9.0)
Liechtenstein	c c	1 (6.1)	c c	c c	**-23** (6.8)	c c
Macao-China	c c	c c	12 (3.6)	c c	c c	2 (3.6)
Russian Federation	21 (11.6)	9 (7.8)	17 (8.2)	7 (13.0)	-7 (7.0)	1 (7.3)
Thailand	25 (11.0)	4 (6.5)	-3 (11.0)	27 (11.6)	-4 (6.3)	-13 (9.0)
Tunisia	55 (14.1)	25 (5.5)	31 (17.9)	53 (15.1)	15 (5.5)	23 (14.2)
Uruguay	-6 (17.0)	-9 (6.7)	-11 (8.7)	-8 (14.3)	-5 (5.5)	-10 (6.1)

OECD (left margin label for the first section); *Partners* (left margin label for the second section)

Notes: This table was calculated considering only students with data on the *PISA index of economic, social and cultural status*. Values that are statistically significant are indicated in bold (see Annex A3).
For comparability over time, PISA 2003 values on the *PISA index of economic, social and cultural status* have been rescaled to the PISA 2012 scale of the index. PISA 2003 results reported in this table may thus differ from those presented in *Learning for Tomorrow's World: First Results from PISA 2003* (OECD, 2004) (see Annex A5 for more details).
Only countries and economies with comparable data from PISA 2003 and PISA 2012 are shown.
1. ESCS refers to the *PISA index of economic, social and cultural status*.

StatLink http://dx.doi.org/10.1787/888932964927

[Part 1/2]
Mathematics performance and immigrant background

Table II.3.4a *Results based on students' self-reports*

	Percentage of students				PISA index of economic, social and cultural status (ESCS)				Mathematics performance				Difference in mathematics performance between non-immigrant and immigrant students	
	Non-immigrant		Immigrant		Non-immigrant		Immigrant		Non-immigrant		Immigrant			
	%	S.E.	%	S.E.	Mean index	S.E.	Mean index	S.E.	Mean score	S.E.	Mean score	S.E.	Score dif.	S.E.
Australia	77.3	(0.7)	22.7	(0.7)	0.28	(0.01)	0.21	(0.02)	503	(1.5)	528	(3.8)	-26	(3.6)
Austria	83.6	(1.1)	16.4	(1.1)	0.19	(0.02)	-0.49	(0.05)	517	(2.7)	457	(4.9)	59	(5.2)
Belgium	84.9	(0.9)	15.1	(0.9)	0.23	(0.02)	-0.29	(0.06)	530	(2.1)	455	(5.2)	75	(5.0)
Canada	70.5	(1.3)	29.5	(1.3)	0.45	(0.02)	0.32	(0.04)	522	(1.8)	520	(4.2)	2	(4.4)
Chile	99.1	(0.2)	0.9	(0.2)	-0.58	(0.04)	-0.27	(0.17)	424	(3.0)	422	(14.1)	1	(13.3)
Czech Republic	96.8	(0.4)	3.2	(0.4)	-0.06	(0.02)	-0.16	(0.07)	501	(2.8)	475	(12.2)	26	(11.8)
Denmark	91.1	(0.6)	8.9	(0.6)	0.49	(0.02)	-0.23	(0.04)	508	(2.2)	442	(3.2)	66	(3.6)
Estonia	91.8	(0.5)	8.2	(0.5)	0.11	(0.01)	0.09	(0.05)	524	(2.0)	494	(5.9)	30	(5.8)
Finland	96.7	(0.2)	3.3	(0.2)	0.39	(0.02)	-0.26	(0.04)	523	(1.9)	439	(5.0)	85	(5.0)
France	85.2	(1.1)	14.8	(1.1)	0.05	(0.02)	-0.53	(0.04)	508	(2.7)	441	(6.0)	67	(6.9)
Germany	86.9	(0.8)	13.1	(0.8)	0.30	(0.03)	-0.41	(0.04)	528	(3.2)	475	(5.5)	54	(6.0)
Greece	89.5	(0.8)	10.5	(0.8)	0.00	(0.03)	-0.68	(0.04)	459	(2.6)	408	(5.9)	51	(6.4)
Hungary	98.3	(0.2)	1.7	(0.2)	-0.26	(0.03)	0.12	(0.10)	478	(3.1)	508	(14.1)	-31	(13.3)
Iceland	96.5	(0.3)	3.5	(0.3)	0.81	(0.01)	0.09	(0.08)	498	(1.8)	445	(8.5)	52	(8.6)
Ireland	89.9	(0.7)	10.1	(0.7)	0.12	(0.02)	0.18	(0.06)	503	(2.3)	501	(4.6)	2	(4.8)
Israel	81.7	(1.2)	18.3	(1.2)	0.21	(0.03)	0.04	(0.06)	470	(4.6)	477	(6.9)	-7	(5.7)
Italy	92.5	(0.3)	7.5	(0.3)	-0.01	(0.01)	-0.55	(0.03)	490	(2.0)	442	(3.3)	48	(3.5)
Japan	99.7	(0.1)	0.3	(0.1)	-0.07	(0.02)	c	c	539	(3.5)	c	c	c	c
Korea	100.0	(0.0)	0.0	(0.0)	0.01	(0.03)	c	c	555	(4.6)	c	c	c	c
Luxembourg	53.6	(0.7)	46.4	(0.7)	0.47	(0.01)	-0.39	(0.02)	511	(1.7)	470	(2.3)	40	(3.3)
Mexico	98.7	(0.1)	1.3	(0.1)	-1.10	(0.02)	-1.46	(0.14)	416	(1.3)	343	(5.7)	73	(5.5)
Netherlands	89.4	(1.0)	10.6	(1.0)	0.31	(0.02)	-0.31	(0.05)	531	(3.4)	474	(7.5)	57	(7.1)
New Zealand	73.7	(1.5)	26.3	(1.5)	0.05	(0.02)	0.02	(0.04)	503	(2.7)	503	(4.7)	0	(5.4)
Norway	90.6	(0.9)	9.4	(0.9)	0.52	(0.02)	-0.08	(0.05)	496	(2.8)	450	(6.1)	46	(6.6)
Poland	99.8	(0.1)	0.2	(0.1)	-0.21	(0.03)	c	c	518	(3.6)	c	c	c	c
Portugal	93.1	(0.6)	6.9	(0.6)	-0.47	(0.05)	-0.62	(0.10)	493	(3.7)	449	(7.2)	44	(7.2)
Slovak Republic	99.3	(0.2)	0.7	(0.2)	-0.18	(0.02)	-0.18	(0.17)	484	(3.4)	489	(21.2)	-5	(21.1)
Slovenia	91.4	(0.4)	8.6	(0.4)	0.12	(0.01)	-0.50	(0.05)	506	(1.2)	456	(4.8)	51	(5.0)
Spain	90.1	(0.6)	9.9	(0.6)	-0.14	(0.03)	-0.64	(0.04)	491	(1.7)	439	(4.6)	52	(4.3)
Sweden	85.5	(0.9)	14.5	(0.9)	0.36	(0.02)	-0.21	(0.05)	490	(2.3)	432	(4.9)	58	(5.1)
Switzerland	75.9	(0.9)	24.1	(0.9)	0.34	(0.02)	-0.34	(0.04)	548	(3.0)	484	(3.9)	63	(3.2)
Turkey	99.1	(0.2)	0.9	(0.2)	-1.46	(0.04)	-1.21	(0.20)	449	(4.8)	452	(30.9)	-3	(31.1)
United Kingdom	87.3	(1.1)	12.7	(1.1)	0.28	(0.02)	0.19	(0.06)	499	(2.8)	489	(8.2)	9	(7.9)
United States	78.5	(2.0)	21.5	(2.0)	0.34	(0.03)	-0.40	(0.08)	487	(3.6)	474	(6.2)	13	(5.5)
OECD average	88.8	(0.1)	11.2	(0.1)	0.06	(0.00)	-0.29	(0.01)	500	(0.5)	462	(1.7)	34	(1.7)
Albania	0.0	c	0.0	c	m	m	m	m	m	m	m	m	c	c
Argentina	96.1	(0.4)	3.9	(0.4)	-0.68	(0.04)	-1.45	(0.09)	392	(3.4)	355	(7.1)	37	(6.7)
Brazil	99.3	(0.1)	0.7	(0.1)	-1.16	(0.02)	-0.88	(0.21)	394	(2.1)	338	(11.4)	56	(11.0)
Bulgaria	99.5	(0.2)	0.5	(0.2)	-0.27	(0.04)	c	c	442	(3.9)	c	c	c	c
Colombia	99.7	(0.1)	0.3	(0.1)	-1.26	(0.04)	-1.36	(0.30)	378	(2.9)	309	(13.1)	69	(13.0)
Costa Rica	94.5	(0.7)	5.5	(0.7)	-0.94	(0.04)	-1.60	(0.15)	409	(2.9)	380	(9.9)	29	(9.6)
Croatia	87.9	(0.8)	12.1	(0.8)	-0.30	(0.02)	-0.59	(0.04)	474	(3.6)	455	(5.4)	19	(5.2)
Cyprus*	91.5	(0.4)	8.5	(0.4)	0.10	(0.01)	-0.07	(0.04)	444	(1.2)	424	(4.7)	21	(5.0)
Hong Kong-China	65.3	(1.5)	34.7	(1.5)	-0.56	(0.06)	-1.22	(0.03)	566	(3.7)	559	(3.8)	8	(4.4)
Indonesia	99.8	(0.1)	0.2	(0.1)	-1.80	(0.05)	c	c	376	(4.0)	c	c	c	c
Jordan	86.6	(0.7)	13.4	(0.7)	-0.47	(0.02)	-0.19	(0.05)	388	(2.8)	410	(5.1)	-22	(4.4)
Kazakhstan	83.9	(1.7)	16.1	(1.7)	-0.29	(0.02)	-0.46	(0.05)	433	(3.1)	427	(5.8)	7	(5.8)
Latvia	95.5	(0.5)	4.5	(0.5)	-0.26	(0.03)	-0.13	(0.09)	492	(2.8)	486	(8.1)	6	(7.8)
Liechtenstein	66.7	(2.9)	33.3	(2.9)	0.44	(0.05)	0.02	(0.11)	554	(5.6)	504	(8.6)	50	(11.5)
Lithuania	98.3	(0.3)	1.7	(0.3)	-0.13	(0.02)	-0.11	(0.10)	480	(2.7)	479	(9.3)	1	(9.8)
Macao-China	34.9	(0.6)	65.1	(0.6)	-0.69	(0.03)	-0.99	(0.01)	530	(2.1)	545	(1.3)	-16	(2.8)
Malaysia	98.3	(0.3)	1.7	(0.3)	-0.71	(0.03)	-1.33	(0.13)	423	(3.2)	402	(8.5)	21	(8.9)
Montenegro	94.2	(0.4)	5.8	(0.4)	-0.26	(0.01)	-0.12	(0.05)	410	(1.2)	431	(6.2)	-21	(6.5)
Peru	99.5	(0.1)	0.5	(0.1)	-1.22	(0.05)	-1.35	(0.21)	370	(3.6)	280	(23.0)	90	(22.5)
Qatar	48.0	(0.4)	52.0	(0.4)	0.42	(0.01)	0.45	(0.01)	335	(1.1)	424	(1.3)	-89	(1.7)
Romania	99.8	(0.1)	0.2	(0.1)	-0.47	(0.04)	c	c	445	(3.8)	c	c	c	c
Russian Federation	89.1	(0.8)	10.9	(0.8)	-0.10	(0.02)	-0.17	(0.05)	486	(3.2)	464	(4.3)	22	(4.5)
Serbia	91.5	(0.8)	8.5	(0.8)	-0.30	(0.02)	-0.29	(0.06)	449	(3.4)	464	(7.0)	-15	(6.2)
Shanghai-China	99.1	(0.2)	0.9	(0.2)	-0.35	(0.04)	-1.05	(0.19)	615	(3.3)	489	(15.2)	126	(14.6)
Singapore	81.7	(0.8)	18.3	(0.8)	-0.34	(0.01)	0.12	(0.04)	570	(1.6)	596	(3.6)	-26	(4.3)
Chinese Taipei	99.5	(0.1)	0.5	(0.1)	-0.39	(0.02)	-0.92	(0.17)	562	(3.3)	530	(23.6)	32	(23.1)
Thailand	99.3	(0.4)	0.7	(0.4)	-1.34	(0.04)	-3.24	(0.13)	428	(3.3)	411	(57.1)	17	(56.4)
Tunisia	99.6	(0.1)	0.4	(0.1)	-1.19	(0.05)	c	c	389	(4.0)	c	c	c	c
United Arab Emirates	45.1	(1.4)	54.9	(1.4)	0.27	(0.03)	0.37	(0.02)	400	(2.4)	466	(2.6)	-66	(3.1)
Uruguay	99.5	(0.1)	0.5	(0.1)	-0.88	(0.03)	c	c	412	(2.6)	c	c	c	c
Viet Nam	99.9	(0.1)	0.1	(0.1)	-1.81	(0.05)	c	c	512	(4.8)	c	c	c	c

Notes: This table was calculated considering only students with data on the *PISA index of economic, social and cultural status*. Values that are statistically significant are indicated in bold (see Annex A3).
Students with an immigrant background are students whose parents were born in a country/economy other than the country/economy of assessment.
* See notes at the beginning of this Annex.
StatLink ᴀᴦᴤ http://dx.doi.org/10.1787/888932964927

[Part 2/2]
Mathematics performance and immigrant background
Table II.3.4a *Results based on students' self-reports*

	Difference in mathematics performance between non-immigrant and immigrant students AFTER accounting for socio-economic status		Increased likelihood of immigrant students scoring in the bottom quarter of the mathematics performance distribution		Population relevance of immigrant students scoring in the bottom quarter of the mathematics performance distribution		Effect size in mathematics performance for immigrant background (positive number implies an advantage for non-immigrant students)		Increased likelihood of non-immigrant students scoring in the bottom quarter of the mathematics performance distribution		Population relevance of non-immigrant students scoring in the bottom quarter of the mathematics performance distribution	
	Score dif.	S.E.	Ratio	S.E.	%	S.E.	Effect size	S.E.	Ratio	S.E.	%	S.E.
Australia	-29	(3.4)	0.80	(0.04)	-4.8	(1.0)	0.27	(0.03)	1.25	(0.06)	16.3	(3.4)
Austria	33	(4.9)	2.16	(0.16)	16.0	(1.8)	-0.66	(0.06)	0.46	(0.03)	-81.6	(9.8)
Belgium	52	(3.9)	2.37	(0.15)	17.2	(1.8)	-0.78	(0.05)	0.42	(0.03)	-96.6	(8.5)
Canada	-2	(3.9)	1.07	(0.07)	2.1	(2.0)	-0.02	(0.05)	0.93	(0.06)	-5.1	(4.8)
Chile	12	(11.1)	1.04	(0.33)	0.0	(0.3)	-0.02	(0.16)	0.98	(0.30)	-3.8	(32.2)
Czech Republic	20	(11.4)	1.34	(0.23)	1.1	(0.8)	-0.25	(0.11)	0.75	(0.13)	-32.5	(21.9)
Denmark	40	(3.2)	2.43	(0.15)	11.2	(1.3)	-0.84	(0.05)	0.41	(0.03)	-115.5	(10.6)
Estonia	30	(5.2)	1.53	(0.14)	4.1	(1.1)	-0.38	(0.07)	0.65	(0.06)	-46.5	(12.0)
Finland	65	(4.6)	2.65	(0.11)	5.2	(0.4)	-0.99	(0.05)	0.38	(0.02)	-151.5	(9.7)
France	37	(6.4)	2.31	(0.20)	16.2	(2.5)	-0.71	(0.08)	0.43	(0.04)	-93.6	(11.4)
Germany	25	(5.6)	1.86	(0.16)	10.1	(1.8)	-0.57	(0.06)	0.54	(0.05)	-66.9	(11.3)
Greece	28	(6.4)	1.93	(0.19)	8.9	(1.8)	-0.61	(0.08)	0.52	(0.05)	-76.1	(13.9)
Hungary	-13	(13.2)	0.66	(0.25)	-0.6	(0.4)	0.33	(0.14)	1.59	(0.65)	34.1	(24.4)
Iceland	31	(8.4)	1.83	(0.22)	2.8	(0.8)	-0.58	(0.10)	0.55	(0.07)	-78.1	(19.6)
Ireland	4	(4.5)	1.04	(0.11)	0.4	(1.1)	-0.02	(0.06)	0.97	(0.10)	-3.1	(9.6)
Israel	-16	(4.8)	0.81	(0.09)	-3.5	(1.9)	0.07	(0.06)	1.23	(0.16)	15.8	(8.2)
Italy	32	(3.3)	1.84	(0.09)	5.9	(0.6)	-0.52	(0.04)	0.54	(0.03)	-73.0	(7.5)
Japan	c	c	c	c	c	c	c	c	c	c	c	c
Korea	c	c	c	c	c	c	c	c	c	c	c	c
Luxembourg	10	(3.3)	1.98	(0.13)	31.2	(2.9)	-0.44	(0.04)	0.51	(0.03)	-36.1	(3.3)
Mexico	66	(4.3)	2.70	(0.16)	2.2	(0.3)	-1.02	(0.09)	0.37	(0.02)	-163.7	(15.6)
Netherlands	35	(7.2)	1.96	(0.19)	9.2	(1.7)	-0.65	(0.07)	0.51	(0.04)	-77.6	(13.8)
New Zealand	-2	(4.4)	1.17	(0.13)	4.4	(3.1)	0.00	(0.05)	0.85	(0.09)	-12.2	(8.4)
Norway	29	(6.6)	1.99	(0.15)	8.5	(1.5)	-0.52	(0.08)	0.50	(0.04)	-82.0	(11.0)
Poland	c	c	c	c	c	c	c	c	c	c	c	c
Portugal	39	(7.8)	1.88	(0.19)	5.7	(1.2)	-0.47	(0.08)	0.53	(0.05)	-76.9	(15.4)
Slovak Republic	-6	(18.8)	1.24	(0.35)	0.2	(0.3)	0.05	(0.20)	0.81	(0.21)	-24.2	(34.5)
Slovenia	26	(4.6)	1.93	(0.16)	7.4	(1.2)	-0.58	(0.06)	0.52	(0.04)	-78.5	(12.2)
Spain	36	(4.3)	2.00	(0.12)	9.0	(1.2)	-0.62	(0.05)	0.50	(0.03)	-82.4	(9.3)
Sweden	40	(4.9)	2.11	(0.16)	13.9	(2.1)	-0.66	(0.06)	0.47	(0.04)	-81.9	(9.6)
Switzerland	42	(3.0)	2.30	(0.10)	23.9	(1.5)	-0.70	(0.03)	0.43	(0.02)	-75.1	(4.6)
Turkey	5	(27.3)	1.48	(0.46)	0.4	(0.5)	0.03	(0.29)	0.69	(0.20)	-46.9	(45.5)
United Kingdom	6	(6.2)	1.30	(0.13)	3.7	(1.6)	-0.10	(0.08)	0.77	(0.08)	-25.0	(10.7)
United States	-15	(4.9)	1.26	(0.12)	5.3	(2.3)	-0.14	(0.07)	0.79	(0.08)	-19.0	(8.5)
OECD average	21	(1.5)	1.71	(0.03)	7.0	(0.3)	-0.39	(0.02)	0.67	(0.03)	-56.	(3.0)
Albania	m	m	c	c	c	c	c	c	c	c	c	c
Argentina	17	(6.3)	1.54	(0.23)	2.1	(0.8)	-0.50	(0.08)	0.65	(0.10)	-51.0	(21.2)
Brazil	63	(11.7)	2.27	(0.29)	0.9	(0.3)	-0.71	(0.16)	0.44	(0.06)	-124.	(28.2)
Bulgaria	c	c	c	c	c	c	c	c	c	c	c	c
Colombia	67	(13.0)	2.44	(0.57)	0.5	(0.3)	-1.05	(0.20)	0.41	(0.09)	-143.	(56.5)
Costa Rica	14	(6.7)	1.79	(0.26)	4.2	(1.6)	-0.42	(0.13)	0.56	(0.10)	-71.	(22.5)
Croatia	9	(4.8)	1.23	(0.11)	2.7	(1.4)	-0.22	(0.06)	0.81	(0.08)	-20.	(9.3)
Cyprus*	14	(4.6)	1.46	(0.12)	3.8	(1.0)	-0.22	(0.05)	0.68	(0.05)	-40.	(10.1)
Hong Kong-China	-11	(3.8)	1.16	(0.09)	5.2	(3.0)	-0.08	(0.05)	0.86	(0.08)	-9.	(5.8)
Indonesia	c	c	c	c	c	c	c	c	c	c	c	c
Jordan	-15	(3.9)	0.69	(0.10)	-4.4	(1.6)	0.29	(0.06)	1.47	(0.25)	28.	(9.8)
Kazakhstan	2	(5.3)	1.13	(0.11)	2.0	(1.7)	-0.09	(0.08)	0.89	(0.08)	-10.	(8.5)
Latvia	10	(7.7)	1.16	(0.21)	0.7	(1.0)	-0.07	(0.09)	0.87	(0.14)	-14.	(19.7)
Liechtenstein	40	(11.9)	2.20	(0.54)	28.3	(9.6)	-0.55	(0.14)	0.46	(0.12)	-56.	(18.7)
Lithuania	2	(9.3)	0.99	(0.30)	0.0	(0.5)	-0.01	(0.11)	1.06	(0.38)	1.	(29.6)
Macao-China	-22	(2.8)	0.79	(0.05)	-16.0	(4.0)	0.17	(0.03)	1.27	(0.07)	8.	(2.1)
Malaysia	2	(9.9)	1.27	(0.27)	0.5	(0.5)	-0.28	(0.12)	0.79	(0.16)	-26.	(26.2)
Montenegro	-16	(6.0)	0.67	(0.14)	-2.0	(0.8)	0.26	(0.08)	1.51	(0.33)	31.	(13.7)
Peru	86	(20.8)	2.89	(0.41)	1.0	(0.3)	-0.97	(0.29)	0.35	(0.05)	-185.	(40.2)
Qatar	-88	(1.6)	0.30	(0.01)	-56.8	(1.7)	1.02	(0.02)	3.30	(0.14)	52.	(1.6)
Romania	c	c	c	c	c	c	c	c	c	c	c	c
Russian Federation	19	(4.4)	1.32	(0.11)	3.3	(1.0)	-0.26	(0.05)	0.76	(0.06)	-27.	(9.0)
Serbia	-14	(5.6)	0.85	(0.12)	-1.3	(1.0)	0.16	(0.07)	1.18	(0.15)	13.	(10.9)
Shanghai-China	98	(14.7)	3.06	(0.28)	1.9	(0.4)	-1.33	(0.17)	0.33	(0.03)	-200.	(26.8)
Singapore	-7	(4.6)	0.67	(0.05)	-6.4	(1.1)	0.26	(0.04)	1.50	(0.11)	28.	(4.6)
Chinese Taipei	1	(20.1)	1.49	(0.39)	0.2	(0.2)	-0.28	(0.21)	0.68	(0.26)	-48.	(39.0)
Thailand	-26	(53.6)	1.78	(0.68)	0.5	(0.7)	-0.17	(0.57)	0.58	(0.24)	-77.	(67.0)
Tunisia	c	c	c	c	c	c	c	c	c	c	c	c
United Arab Emirates	-63	(3.1)	0.41	(0.03)	-48.1	(3.8)	0.81	(0.04)	2.45	(0.16)	39.	(2.7)
Uruguay	c	c	c	c	c	c	c	c	c	c	c	c
Viet Nam	c	c	c	c	c	c	c	c	c	c	c	c

Notes: This table was calculated considering only students with data on the *PISA index of economic, social and cultural status*. Values that are statistically significant are indicated in bold (see Annex A3).
Students with an immigrant background are students whose parents were born in a country/economy other than the country/economy of assessment.
* See notes at the beginning of this Annex.
StatLink ⧉ http://dx.doi.org/10.1787/888932964927

[Part 1/3]
Change between 2003 and 2012 in the relationship between mathematics performance and immigrant background

Table II.3.4b *Results based on students' self-reports*

	PISA 2003													
	Percentage of students				Average performance in mathematics				PISA index of economic, social and cultural status (ESCS)				Difference in mathematics performance between non-immigrant and immigrant students		Difference in mathematics performance between non-immigrant and immigrant students AFTER accounting for socio-economic status	
	Non-immigrant		Immigrant		Non-immigrant		Immigrant		Non-immigrant		Immigrant					
	%	S.E.	%	S.E.	Mean score	S.E.	Mean score	S.E.	Mean index	S.E.	Mean index	S.E.	Score dif.	S.E.	Score dif.	S.E.
OECD																
Australia	77.3	(1.1)	22.7	(1.1)	527	(2.1)	523	(4.2)	0.08	(0.02)	-0.05	(0.04)	3	(4.1)	-1	(3.5)
Austria	86.9	(1.0)	13.1	(1.0)	516	(3.2)	456	(5.1)	-0.18	(0.03)	-0.77	(0.05)	**60**	(5.5)	**37**	(5.3)
Belgium	88.2	(0.9)	11.8	(0.9)	546	(2.5)	446	(6.9)	0.06	(0.03)	-0.66	(0.06)	**100**	(7.0)	**67**	(6.0)
Canada	79.9	(1.1)	20.1	(1.1)	537	(1.6)	536	(3.8)	0.21	(0.02)	0.26	(0.04)	1	(3.9)	2	(3.6)
Czech Republic	98.7	(0.2)	1.3	(0.2)	523	(3.2)	487	(13.7)	-0.05	(0.02)	-0.31	(0.11)	**36**	(13.8)	24	(14.1)
Denmark	93.5	(0.8)	6.5	(0.8)	520	(2.5)	452	(8.3)	0.13	(0.03)	-0.51	(0.09)	**68**	(8.0)	**44**	(7.6)
Finland	98.1	(0.2)	1.9	(0.2)	546	(1.9)	473	(10.5)	0.06	(0.02)	-0.14	(0.11)	**73**	(10.6)	**68**	(9.4)
France	85.7	(1.3)	14.3	(1.3)	520	(2.4)	466	(6.6)	-0.20	(0.03)	-0.99	(0.06)	**54**	(7.0)	**22**	(5.7)
Germany	84.6	(1.1)	15.4	(1.1)	525	(3.5)	444	(6.4)	0.20	(0.03)	-0.91	(0.06)	**81**	(6.9)	**38**	(6.4)
Greece	92.6	(0.6)	7.4	(0.6)	449	(3.9)	406	(6.2)	-0.27	(0.05)	-0.72	(0.06)	**43**	(6.2)	**28**	(5.9)
Hungary	97.7	(0.2)	2.3	(0.2)	491	(3.0)	486	(10.5)	-0.31	(0.02)	-0.33	(0.10)	5	(10.2)	4	(8.7)
Iceland	99.0	(0.2)	1.0	(0.2)	517	(1.4)	482	(13.3)	0.55	(0.01)	0.31	(0.22)	**35**	(13.4)	29	(14.6)
Ireland	96.5	(0.3)	3.5	(0.3)	503	(2.4)	499	(10.2)	-0.27	(0.03)	0.10	(0.10)	4	(10.3)	18	(9.3)
Italy	97.9	(0.3)	2.1	(0.3)	468	(3.0)	445	(12.6)	-0.27	(0.03)	-0.44	(0.11)	22	(11.9)	17	(11.3)
Japan	99.9	(0.0)	0.1	(0.0)	535	(4.0)	c	c	-0.41	(0.02)	c	c	c	c	c	c
Korea	100.0	(0.0)	0.0	(0.0)	543	(3.2)	c	c	-0.36	(0.03)	c	c	c	c	c	c
Luxembourg	66.7	(0.6)	33.3	(0.6)	507	(1.3)	469	(2.2)	0.15	(0.01)	-0.56	(0.03)	**38**	(2.8)	**15**	(2.9)
Mexico	97.7	(0.3)	2.3	(0.3)	392	(3.6)	301	(12.6)	-1.27	(0.03)	-1.87	(0.11)	**92**	(12.1)	**75**	(11.5)
Netherlands	89.0	(1.4)	11.0	(1.4)	551	(3.0)	485	(8.2)	0.00	(0.03)	-0.70	(0.07)	**66**	(9.0)	**41**	(7.4)
New Zealand	80.2	(1.1)	19.8	(1.1)	528	(2.6)	514	(5.3)	-0.11	(0.02)	-0.23	(0.04)	**14**	(6.0)	9	(4.8)
Norway	94.4	(0.7)	5.6	(0.7)	499	(2.3)	447	(7.7)	0.21	(0.02)	-0.15	(0.07)	**52**	(7.6)	**38**	(6.9)
Poland	100.0	(0.0)	0.0	(0.0)	491	(2.5)	c	c	-0.41	(0.02)	c	c	c	c	c	c
Portugal	95.0	(1.4)	5.0	(1.4)	470	(2.9)	409	(19.3)	-0.91	(0.05)	-0.87	(0.11)	**61**	(19.1)	**62**	(17.1)
Slovak Republic	99.1	(0.2)	0.9	(0.2)	499	(3.2)	435	(21.3)	-0.24	(0.03)	-0.36	(0.14)	**64**	(20.0)	**58**	(19.5)
Spain	96.6	(0.4)	3.4	(0.4)	487	(2.4)	442	(10.9)	-0.50	(0.04)	-0.79	(0.10)	**45**	(10.5)	**38**	(9.4)
Sweden	88.5	(0.9)	11.5	(0.9)	517	(2.2)	454	(8.5)	0.16	(0.02)	-0.42	(0.07)	**64**	(8.3)	**44**	(7.4)
Switzerland	80.0	(0.9)	20.0	(0.9)	543	(3.3)	467	(4.7)	-0.08	(0.03)	-0.79	(0.04)	**76**	(4.5)	**51**	(4.2)
Turkey	99.0	(0.2)	1.0	(0.2)	425	(6.7)	392	(25.3)	-1.15	(0.06)	-1.04	(0.26)	33	(24.7)	**38**	(19.0)
United States	85.6	(1.0)	14.4	(1.0)	490	(2.8)	462	(6.5)	0.15	(0.03)	-0.39	(0.08)	**28**	(6.3)	6	(4.9)
OECD average 2003	91.3	(0.1)	8.7	(0.1)	506	(0.6)	457	(2.2)	-0.17	(0.01)	-0.51	(0.02)	**47**	(2.1)	**33**	(1.9)
Partners																
Brazil	99.2	(0.2)	0.8	(0.2)	359	(4.7)	c	c	-1.55	(0.05)	c	c	c	c	c	c
Hong Kong-China	56.7	(1.4)	43.3	(1.4)	557	(4.5)	545	(4.8)	-1.06	(0.04)	-1.55	(0.03)	**12**	(3.6)	-2	(3.6)
Indonesia	99.7	(0.1)	0.3	(0.1)	363	(4.0)	c	c	-1.86	(0.04)	c	c	c	c	c	c
Latvia	90.6	(0.9)	9.4	(0.9)	484	(3.8)	482	(6.1)	-0.37	(0.03)	-0.14	(0.05)	3	(5.7)	10	(5.2)
Liechtenstein	82.9	(2.0)	17.1	(2.0)	545	(5.0)	494	(13.9)	-0.20	(0.04)	-0.87	(0.16)	**51**	(15.9)	20	(15.7)
Macao-China	23.9	(1.4)	76.1	(1.4)	528	(5.9)	528	(3.6)	-1.29	(0.08)	-1.69	(0.03)	-1	(7.3)	-6	(7.3)
Russian Federation	86.5	(0.7)	13.5	(0.7)	472	(4.4)	454	(5.1)	-0.59	(0.03)	-0.66	(0.05)	**17**	(4.8)	**15**	(4.5)
Thailand	99.9	(0.1)	0.1	(0.1)	419	(3.0)	c	c	-1.86	(0.04)	c	c	c	c	c	c
Tunisia	99.7	(0.1)	0.3	(0.1)	360	(2.5)	c	c	-1.69	(0.04)	c	c	c	c	c	c
Uruguay	99.2	(0.2)	0.8	(0.2)	423	(3.2)	424	(20.1)	-0.76	(0.04)	-0.39	(0.23)	-1	(19.3)	12	(19.5)

Notes: This table was calculated considering only students with data on the *PISA index of economic, social and cultural status*. Values that are statistically significant are indicated in bold (see Annex A3).

Students with an immigrant background are students whose parents were born in a country/economy other than the country/economy of assessment.

For comparability over time, PISA 2003 values on the *PISA index of economic, social and cultural status* have been rescaled to the PISA 2012 scale of the index. PISA 2003 results reported in this table may thus differ from those presented in *Learning for Tomorrow's World: First Results from PISA 2003* (OECD, 2004) (see Annex A5 for more details). Only countries and economies with comparable data from PISA 2003 and PISA 2012 are shown.

StatLink ᵐˢᵖ http://dx.doi.org/10.1787/888932964927

[Part 2/3]
Change between 2003 and 2012 in the relationship between mathematics performance and immigrant background

Table II.3.4b   *Results based on students' self-reports*

		PISA 2012												
		Percentage of students				Average performance in mathematics				PISA index of economic, social and cultural status (ESCS)				Difference in mathematics performance between non-immigrant and immigrant students		Difference in mathematics performance between non-immigrant and immigrant students AFTER accounting for socio-economic status	
		Non-immigrant		Immigrant		Non-immigrant		Immigrant		Non-immigrant		Immigrant					
		%	S.E.	%	S.E.	Mean score	S.E.	Mean score	S.E.	Mean index	S.E.	Mean index	S.E.	Score dif.	S.E.	Score dif.	S.E.
OECD	Australia	77.3	(0.7)	22.7	(0.7)	503	(1.5)	528	(3.8)	0.28	(0.01)	0.21	(0.02)	**-26**	(3.6)	**-29**	(3.4)
	Austria	83.6	(1.1)	16.4	(1.1)	517	(2.7)	457	(4.9)	0.19	(0.02)	-0.49	(0.05)	**59**	(5.2)	**33**	(4.9)
	Belgium	84.9	(0.9)	15.1	(0.9)	530	(2.1)	455	(5.2)	0.23	(0.02)	-0.29	(0.06)	**75**	(5.0)	**52**	(3.9)
	Canada	70.5	(1.3)	29.5	(1.3)	522	(1.8)	520	(4.2)	0.45	(0.02)	0.32	(0.04)	2	(4.4)	-2	(3.9)
	Czech Republic	96.8	(0.4)	3.2	(0.4)	501	(2.8)	475	(12.2)	-0.06	(0.02)	-0.16	(0.07)	**26**	(11.8)	20	(11.4)
	Denmark	91.1	(0.6)	8.9	(0.6)	508	(2.2)	442	(3.2)	0.49	(0.02)	-0.23	(0.04)	**66**	(3.6)	**40**	(3.2)
	Finland	96.7	(0.2)	3.3	(0.2)	523	(1.9)	439	(5.0)	0.39	(0.02)	-0.26	(0.04)	**85**	(5.0)	**65**	(4.6)
	France	85.2	(1.1)	14.8	(1.1)	508	(2.7)	441	(6.0)	0.05	(0.02)	-0.53	(0.04)	**67**	(6.9)	**37**	(6.4)
	Germany	86.9	(0.8)	13.1	(0.8)	528	(3.2)	475	(5.5)	0.30	(0.03)	-0.41	(0.04)	**54**	(6.0)	**25**	(5.6)
	Greece	89.5	(0.8)	10.5	(0.8)	459	(2.6)	408	(5.9)	0.00	(0.03)	-0.68	(0.04)	**51**	(6.4)	**28**	(6.4)
	Hungary	98.3	(0.2)	1.7	(0.2)	478	(3.1)	508	(14.1)	-0.26	(0.03)	0.12	(0.10)	**-31**	(13.3)	-13	(13.2)
	Iceland	96.5	(0.3)	3.5	(0.3)	498	(1.8)	445	(8.5)	0.81	(0.01)	0.09	(0.08)	**52**	(8.6)	**31**	(8.4)
	Ireland	89.9	(0.7)	10.1	(0.7)	503	(2.3)	501	(4.6)	0.12	(0.02)	0.18	(0.06)	2	(4.8)	4	(4.5)
	Italy	92.5	(0.3)	7.5	(0.3)	490	(2.0)	442	(3.3)	-0.01	(0.01)	-0.55	(0.03)	**48**	(3.5)	**32**	(3.3)
	Japan	99.7	(0.1)	0.3	(0.1)	539	(3.5)	c	c	-0.07	(0.02)	c	c	c	c	c	c
	Korea	100.0	(0.0)	0.0	(0.0)	555	(4.6)	c	c	0.01	(0.03)	c	c	c	c	c	c
	Luxembourg	53.6	(0.7)	46.4	(0.7)	511	(1.7)	470	(2.3)	0.47	(0.01)	-0.39	(0.02)	**40**	(3.3)	**10**	(3.3)
	Mexico	98.7	(0.1)	1.3	(0.1)	416	(1.3)	343	(5.7)	-1.10	(0.02)	-1.46	(0.14)	**73**	(5.5)	**66**	(4.3)
	Netherlands	89.4	(1.0)	10.6	(1.0)	531	(3.4)	474	(7.5)	0.31	(0.02)	-0.31	(0.05)	**57**	(7.1)	**35**	(7.2)
	New Zealand	73.7	(1.5)	26.3	(1.5)	503	(2.7)	503	(4.7)	0.05	(0.02)	0.02	(0.04)	0	(5.4)	-2	(4.4)
	Norway	90.6	(0.9)	9.4	(0.9)	496	(2.8)	450	(6.1)	0.52	(0.02)	-0.08	(0.05)	**46**	(6.6)	**29**	(6.6)
	Poland	99.8	(0.1)	0.2	(0.1)	518	(3.6)	c	c	-0.21	(0.03)	c	c	c	c	c	c
	Portugal	93.1	(0.6)	6.9	(0.6)	493	(3.7)	449	(7.2)	-0.47	(0.05)	-0.62	(0.10)	**44**	(7.2)	**39**	(7.8)
	Slovak Republic	99.3	(0.2)	0.7	(0.2)	484	(3.4)	489	(21.2)	-0.18	(0.03)	-0.18	(0.17)	-5	(21.1)	-6	(18.8)
	Spain	90.1	(0.6)	9.9	(0.6)	491	(1.7)	439	(4.6)	-0.14	(0.03)	-0.64	(0.04)	**52**	(4.3)	**36**	(4.3)
	Sweden	85.5	(0.9)	14.5	(0.9)	490	(2.3)	432	(4.9)	0.36	(0.02)	-0.21	(0.05)	**58**	(5.1)	**40**	(4.9)
	Switzerland	75.9	(0.9)	24.1	(0.9)	548	(3.0)	484	(3.9)	0.34	(0.02)	-0.34	(0.04)	**63**	(3.2)	**42**	(3.0)
	Turkey	99.1	(0.2)	0.9	(0.2)	449	(4.8)	452	(30.9)	-1.46	(0.04)	-1.21	(0.20)	-3	(31.1)		(27.3)
	United States	78.5	(2.0)	21.5	(2.0)	487	(3.6)	474	(6.2)	0.34	(0.03)	-0.40	(0.08)	**13**	(5.9)	-11	(4.9)
	OECD average 2003	**88.5**	**(0.1)**	**11.5**	**(0.1)**	**503**	**(0.5)**	**461**	**(1.9)**	**0.06**	**(0.00)**	**-0.33**	**(0.02)**	**37**	**(1.9)**	**2**	**(1.7)**
Partners	Brazil	99.3	(0.1)	0.7	(0.1)	394	(2.1)	338	(11.4)	-1.16	(0.02)	-0.88	(0.21)	**56**	(11.0)	6	(11.7)
	Hong Kong-China	65.3	(1.5)	34.7	(1.5)	566	(3.7)	559	(3.8)	-0.56	(0.06)	-1.22	(0.03)	8	(4.4)	-1	(3.8)
	Indonesia	99.8	(0.1)	0.2	(0.1)	376	(4.0)	c	c	-1.80	(0.05)	c	c	c	c	c	c
	Latvia	95.5	(0.5)	4.5	(0.5)	492	(2.8)	486	(8.1)	-0.26	(0.03)	-0.13	(0.09)	6	(7.8)	1	(7.7)
	Liechtenstein	66.7	(2.9)	33.3	(2.9)	554	(5.6)	504	(8.6)	0.44	(0.05)	0.02	(0.11)	**50**	(11.5)	4	(11.9)
	Macao-China	34.9	(0.6)	65.1	(0.6)	530	(2.1)	545	(1.3)	-0.69	(0.02)	-0.99	(0.01)	**-16**	(2.8)	-2	(2.8)
	Russian Federation	89.1	(0.8)	10.9	(0.8)	486	(3.2)	464	(4.3)	-0.10	(0.02)	-0.17	(0.05)	**22**	(4.5)	1	(4.4)
	Thailand	99.3	(0.4)	0.7	(0.4)	428	(3.3)	411	(57.1)	-1.34	(0.04)	-3.24	(0.13)	17	(56.4)	-2	(53.6)
	Tunisia	99.6	(0.1)	0.4	(0.1)	389	(4.0)	c	c	-1.19	(0.05)	c	c	c	c	c	c
	Uruguay	99.5	(0.1)	0.5	(0.1)	412	(2.6)	c	c	-0.88	(0.03)	c	c	c	c	c	c

Notes: This table was calculated considering only students with data on the *PISA index of economic, social and cultural status*. Values that are statistically significant are indicated in bold (see Annex A3).

Students with an immigrant background are students whose parents were born in a country/economy other than the country/economy of assessment.

For comparability over time, PISA 2003 values on the *PISA index of economic, social and cultural status* have been rescaled to the PISA 2012 scale of the index. PISA 2003 results reported in this table may thus differ from those presented in *Learning for Tomorrow's World: First Results from PISA 2003* (OECD, 2004) (see Annex A5 for more details). Only countries and economies with comparable data from PISA 2003 and PISA 2012 are shown.

StatLink ⟋ᴤ⟍ http://dx.doi.org/10.1787/888932964927

[Part 3/3]
Change between 2003 and 2012 in the relationship between mathematics performance and immigrant background

Table II.3.4b   *Results based on students' self-reports*

		Change between PISA 2003 and PISA 2012 (PISA 2012-PISA 2003)														
		Percentage of students				Average performance in mathematics				PISA index of economic, social and cultural status (ESCS)				Difference in mathematics performance between non-immigrant and immigrant students		Difference in mathematics performance between non-immigrant and immigrant students AFTER accounting for socio-economic status	
		Non-immigrant		Immigrant		Non-immigrant		Immigrant		Non-immigrant		Immigrant					
		% dif.	S.E.	% dif.	S.E.	Score dif.	S.E.	Score dif.	S.E.	Dif.	S.E.	Dif.	S.E.	Score dif.	S.E.	Score dif.	S.E.
OECD	Australia	0.1	(1.4)	-0.1	(1.4)	-24	(3.2)	5	(5.9)	**0.20**	(0.02)	**0.25**	(0.04)	**-29**	(5.5)	**-27**	(4.9)
	Austria	-3.3	(1.4)	**3.3**	(1.4)	0	(4.6)	1	(7.3)	**0.37**	(0.03)	**0.28**	(0.07)	0	(7.4)	-4	(6.7)
	Belgium	**-3.3**	(1.3)	**3.3**	(1.3)	**-16**	(3.8)	9	(8.8)	**0.17**	(0.03)	**0.37**	(0.08)	**-25**	(8.6)	**-16**	(7.1)
	Canada	**-9.3**	(1.7)	**9.3**	(1.7)	**-15**	(3.1)	**-16**	(6.0)	**0.24**	(0.02)	0.06	(0.05)	1	(5.9)	-4	(5.2)
	Czech Republic	**-1.9**	(0.4)	**1.9**	(0.4)	**-22**	(4.6)	-12	(18.5)	-0.01	(0.03)	0.14	(0.13)	-10	(17.2)	-3	(17.4)
	Denmark	**-2.4**	(1.0)	**2.4**	(1.0)	**-11**	(3.9)	-10	(9.1)	**0.37**	(0.04)	**0.28**	(0.10)	-2	(8.9)	-5	(8.0)
	Finland	**-1.5**	(0.3)	**1.5**	(0.3)	**-23**	(3.3)	**-34**	(11.8)	**0.32**	(0.03)	-0.13	(0.12)	12	(11.6)	-1	(10.2)
	France	-0.5	(1.7)	0.5	(1.7)	**-12**	(4.1)	**-26**	(9.1)	**0.25**	(0.03)	**0.47**	(0.07)	14	(9.0)	**24**	(7.5)
	Germany	2.3	(1.4)	-2.3	(1.4)	3	(5.1)	**30**	(8.6)	**0.10**	(0.04)	**0.50**	(0.07)	**-27**	(8.7)	-12	(7.6)
	Greece	**-3.1**	(1.1)	**3.1**	(1.1)	10	(5.1)	3	(8.8)	**0.28**	(0.06)	0.04	(0.08)	8	(8.6)	-1	(8.8)
	Hungary	0.5	(0.3)	-0.5	(0.3)	-13	(4.7)	22	(17.7)	0.05	(0.04)	**0.45**	(0.15)	**-35**	(17.6)	-16	(16.7)
	Iceland	**-2.5**	(0.4)	**2.5**	(0.4)	**-19**	(3.0)	**-36**	(15.9)	**0.25**	(0.02)	-0.22	(0.24)	17	(14.3)	4	(15.4)
	Ireland	**-6.7**	(0.8)	**6.7**	(0.8)	0	(3.9)	2	(11.4)	**0.39**	(0.04)	0.08	(0.11)	-2	(11.0)	-14	(10.5)
	Italy	**-5.3**	(0.4)	**5.3**	(0.4)	**23**	(4.1)	-3	(13.1)	**0.26**	(0.03)	-0.11	(0.11)	**26**	(11.8)	15	(11.2)
	Japan	**-0.2**	(0.1)	**0.2**	(0.1)	4	(5.7)	c	c	**0.34**	(0.03)	c	c	c	c	c	c
	Korea	0.0	(0.0)	0.0	(0.0)	12	(5.9)	c	c	**0.37**	(0.04)	c	c	c	c	c	c
	Luxembourg	**-13.1**	(0.9)	**13.1**	(0.9)	1	(3.7)	1	(3.7)	**0.33**	(0.02)	**0.17**	(0.04)	2	(4.3)	-3	(4.2)
	Mexico	**1.0**	(0.3)	**-1.0**	(0.3)	**24**	(4.3)	**42**	(14.0)	**0.18**	(0.06)	**0.41**	(0.18)	-18	(13.6)	-13	(12.4)
	Netherlands	0.4	(1.7)	-0.4	(1.7)	**-20**	(4.9)	-11	(11.3)	**0.31**	(0.04)	**0.39**	(0.09)	-9	(12.2)	-6	(10.6)
	New Zealand	**-6.5**	(1.9)	**6.5**	(1.9)	**-25**	(4.2)	-11	(7.3)	**0.16**	(0.03)	**0.24**	(0.06)	**-14**	(6.9)	-10	(5.9)
	Norway	**-3.8**	(1.1)	**3.8**	(1.1)	-3	(4.1)	3	(10.0)	**0.32**	(0.03)	0.06	(0.09)	-6	(9.5)	-14	(8.6)
	Poland	-0.1	(0.1)	0.1	(0.1)	**28**	(4.8)	c	c	**0.20**	(0.04)	c	c	c	c	c	c
	Portugal	-1.8	(1.6)	1.8	(1.6)	**23**	(5.1)	**40**	(20.7)	**0.43**	(0.07)	0.24	(0.14)	-17	(20.6)	-23	(18.6)
	Slovak Republic	0.1	(0.2)	-0.1	(0.2)	**-15**	(5.0)	54	(30.1)	0.07	(0.04)	0.18	(0.22)	**-70**	(28.3)	**-64**	(26.5)
	Spain	**-6.5**	(0.7)	**6.5**	(0.7)	4	(3.5)	-3	(12.0)	**0.36**	(0.05)	0.15	(0.11)	7	(11.2)	1	(10.1)
	Sweden	**-3.0**	(1.2)	**3.0**	(1.2)	**-27**	(3.7)	**-21**	(10.0)	**0.20**	(0.03)	**0.21**	(0.09)	-6	(9.8)	-6	(9.1)
	Switzerland	**-4.1**	(1.3)	**4.1**	(1.3)	5	(4.9)	**18**	(6.4)	**0.42**	(0.04)	**0.45**	(0.05)	**-12**	(5.1)	**-11**	(4.6)
	Turkey	0.1	(0.3)	-0.1	(0.3)	**24**	(8.5)	60	(40.0)	**-0.31**	(0.07)	-0.18	(0.33)	-36	(33.6)	-31	(29.3)
	United States	**-7.0**	(2.2)	**7.0**	(2.2)	-3	(5.0)	12	(9.2)	**0.19**	(0.04)	-0.01	(0.11)	-15	(8.6)	**-23**	(6.5)
	OECD average 2003	**-2.8**	(0.2)	**2.8**	(0.2)	**-3**	(0.9)	5	(2.9)	**0.23**	(0.01)	**0.18**	(0.03)	**-10**	(2.7)	**-10**	(2.5)
Partners	Brazil	0.0	(0.2)	0.0	(0.2)	**35**	(5.5)	c	c	**0.39**	(0.05)	c	c	c	c	c	c
	Hong Kong-China	**8.6**	(2.1)	**-8.6**	(2.1)	10	(6.2)	14	(6.4)	**0.50**	(0.07)	**0.32**	(0.04)	-5	(5.4)	-10	(5.1)
	Indonesia	0.1	(0.1)	-0.1	(0.1)	13	(6.0)	c	c	0.06	(0.06)	c	c	c	c	c	c
	Latvia	**4.9**	(1.1)	**-4.9**	(1.1)	8	(5.1)	4	(10.4)	**0.10**	(0.04)	0.01	(0.10)	3	(8.9)	0	(8.3)
	Liechtenstein	**-16.2**	(3.5)	**16.2**	(3.5)	9	(7.7)	10	(16.4)	**0.63**	(0.07)	**0.90**	(0.19)	-1	(18.7)	9	(16.6)
	Macao-China	**11.0**	(1.5)	**-11.0**	(1.5)	2	(6.5)	**17**	(4.3)	**0.60**	(0.08)	**0.69**	(0.03)	-15	(7.6)	-13	(7.6)
	Russian Federation	**2.6**	(1.1)	**-2.6**	(1.1)	14	(5.8)	10	(6.9)	**0.50**	(0.04)	**0.49**	(0.07)	4	(5.2)	4	(4.9)
	Thailand	-0.5	(0.4)	0.5	(0.4)	9	(4.9)	c	c	**0.52**	(0.06)	c	c	c	c	c	c
	Tunisia	-0.2	(0.1)	0.2	(0.1)	**29**	(5.1)	c	c	**0.50**	(0.06)	c	c	c	c	c	c
	Uruguay	0.3	(0.2)	-0.3	(0.2)	-11	(4.6)	c	c	**-0.12**	(0.05)	c	c	c	c	c	c

Notes: This table was calculated considering only students with data on the *PISA index of economic, social and cultural status*. Values that are statistically significant are indicated in bold (see Annex A3).

Students with an immigrant background are students whose parents were born in a country/economy other than the country/economy of assessment.

For comparability over time, PISA 2003 values on the *PISA index of economic, social and cultural status* have been rescaled to the PISA 2012 scale of the index. PISA 2003 results reported in this table may thus differ from those presented in *Learning for Tomorrow's World: First Results from PISA 2003* (OECD, 2004) (see Annex A5 for more details). Only countries and economies with comparable data from PISA 2003 and PISA 2012 are shown.

StatLink ⟨ᵐˢᴵ⟩ http://dx.doi.org/10.1787/888932964927

[Part 1/4]
Mathematics performance, immigrant background and language spoken at home
Table II.3.5   *Results based on students' self-reports*

	Percentage of students								Average socio-economic status							
	Non-immigrant students who speak the language of assessment at home		Non-immigrant students who speak another language at home		Immigrant students who speak the language of assessment at home		Immigrant students who speak another language at home		Non-immigrant students who speak the language of assessment at home		Non-immigrant students who speak another language at home		Immigrant students who speak the language of assessment at home		Immigrant students who speak another language at home	
	%	S.E.	%	S.E.	%	S.E.	%	S.E.	Mean index	S.E.	Mean index	S.E.	Mean index	S.E.	Mean index	S.E.
Australia	76.0	(0.8)	2.0	(0.2)	14.8	(0.5)	7.2	(0.5)	0.28	(0.01)	0.08	(0.06)	0.33	(0.02)	0.00	(0.05)
Austria	85.1	(0.9)	1.4	(0.2)	3.7	(0.4)	9.7	(0.8)	0.19	(0.02)	0.16	(0.18)	0.02	(0.09)	-0.54	(0.06)
Belgium	72.1	(1.1)	14.3	(0.7)	6.6	(0.6)	6.9	(0.5)	0.28	(0.02)	0.01	(0.04)	-0.08	(0.08)	-0.46	(0.08)
Canada	68.1	(1.4)	3.1	(0.4)	14.8	(0.8)	14.0	(0.8)	0.46	(0.02)	0.49	(0.05)	0.41	(0.04)	0.24	(0.04)
Chile	98.5	(0.2)	0.6	(0.1)	0.9	(0.2)	0.0	(0.0)	-0.58	(0.04)	-0.47	(0.26)	-0.31	(0.17)	c	c
Czech Republic	96.3	(0.4)	0.8	(0.1)	0.9	(0.2)	2.0	(0.3)	-0.06	(0.02)	0.08	(0.24)	-0.14	(0.15)	-0.15	(0.08)
Denmark	92.2	(0.5)	0.5	(0.1)	3.5	(0.3)	3.8	(0.3)	0.50	(0.02)	-0.10	(0.22)	-0.13	(0.06)	-0.27	(0.05)
Estonia	88.1	(0.7)	3.8	(0.4)	6.4	(0.5)	1.7	(0.2)	0.12	(0.02)	0.04	(0.05)	0.10	(0.07)	0.08	(0.09)
Finland	94.9	(0.3)	1.8	(0.1)	0.6	(0.1)	2.7	(0.2)	0.38	(0.02)	0.62	(0.03)	-0.12	(0.09)	-0.29	(0.05)
France	84.3	(1.2)	2.3	(0.4)	8.0	(0.8)	5.5	(0.5)	0.06	(0.02)	-0.12	(0.07)	-0.42	(0.05)	-0.64	(0.06)
Germany	86.9	(0.8)	1.6	(0.4)	6.8	(0.5)	4.8	(0.5)	0.32	(0.02)	-0.18	(0.17)	-0.37	(0.05)	-0.41	(0.07)
Greece	88.9	(0.8)	1.1	(0.2)	6.0	(0.5)	4.0	(0.5)	0.01	(0.03)	-0.30	(0.31)	-0.61	(0.06)	-0.79	(0.08)
Hungary	97.7	(0.2)	0.7	(0.1)	1.3	(0.2)	0.3	(0.1)	-0.26	(0.03)	0.08	(0.21)	0.18	(0.12)	c	c
Iceland	95.5	(0.4)	1.2	(0.2)	0.7	(0.1)	2.7	(0.3)	0.81	(0.01)	0.63	(0.15)	c	c	-0.09	(0.10)
Ireland	90.1	(0.7)	0.3	(0.1)	5.1	(0.4)	4.5	(0.5)	0.12	(0.02)	c	c	0.32	(0.07)	0.05	(0.08)
Israel	79.4	(1.2)	3.0	(0.3)	9.6	(0.7)	8.0	(0.8)	0.21	(0.03)	0.16	(0.08)	-0.03	(0.06)	0.15	(0.06)
Italy	83.2	(0.4)	9.8	(0.3)	2.6	(0.2)	4.4	(0.2)	0.07	(0.01)	-0.48	(0.03)	-0.35	(0.05)	-0.67	(0.04)
Japan	99.5	(0.1)	0.2	(0.1)	0.2	(0.0)	0.2	(0.1)	-0.07	(0.02)	c	c	c	c	c	c
Korea	99.9	(0.0)	0.0	(0.0)	0.0	(0.0)	0.0	(0.0)	0.01	(0.03)	c	c	c	c	c	c
Luxembourg	3.1	(0.2)	53.1	(0.6)	11.6	(0.4)	32.2	(0.7)	0.69	(0.07)	0.47	(0.02)	0.62	(0.04)	0.69	(0.03)
Mexico	95.9	(0.3)	2.8	(0.3)	1.0	(0.1)	0.2	(0.1)	-1.07	(0.02)	-2.22	(0.09)	-1.49	(0.10)	-1.68	(0.33)
Netherlands	89.2	(1.0)	1.4	(0.2)	4.6	(0.6)	4.7	(0.5)	0.31	(0.02)	0.07	(0.10)	-0.18	(0.07)	-0.48	(0.07)
New Zealand	70.8	(1.4)	2.8	(0.3)	13.3	(0.7)	13.1	(1.1)	0.07	(0.02)	-0.12	(0.11)	0.18	(0.05)	0.13	(0.06)
Norway	89.6	(0.8)	1.6	(0.2)	3.0	(0.3)	5.8	(0.6)	0.52	(0.02)	0.58	(0.08)	0.16	(0.09)	0.17	(0.06)
Poland	99.0	(0.3)	0.8	(0.3)	0.1	(0.0)	0.1	(0.0)	-0.21	(0.03)	-0.04	(0.25)	c	c	c	c
Portugal	92.7	(0.6)	0.8	(0.1)	4.7	(0.5)	1.8	(0.3)	-0.47	(0.05)	-0.29	(0.22)	-0.59	(0.10)	-0.67	(0.16)
Slovak Republic	92.3	(0.9)	7.1	(0.8)	0.5	(0.1)	0.2	(0.1)	-0.10	(0.02)	-1.08	(0.10)	c	c	c	c
Slovenia	90.8	(0.5)	1.3	(0.2)	3.3	(0.3)	4.6	(0.4)	0.13	(0.01)	0.00	(0.09)	-0.38	(0.08)	-0.62	(0.06)
Spain	76.7	(1.2)	13.7	(0.9)	4.9	(0.3)	4.7	(0.5)	-0.10	(0.03)	-0.32	(0.04)	-0.56	(0.05)	-0.73	(0.06)
Sweden	85.9	(0.8)	1.6	(0.3)	4.2	(0.3)	8.4	(0.6)	0.37	(0.02)	0.38	(0.14)	-0.16	(0.06)	-0.25	(0.07)
Switzerland	73.2	(1.0)	4.1	(0.4)	10.5	(0.5)	12.1	(0.6)	0.34	(0.02)	0.32	(0.06)	-0.07	(0.06)	-0.55	(0.04)
Turkey	93.0	(0.8)	6.0	(0.8)	0.8	(0.2)	0.2	(0.1)	-1.40	(0.04)	-2.32	(0.08)	-1.05	(0.19)	c	c
United Kingdom	86.5	(1.1)	1.3	(0.1)	6.6	(0.6)	5.7	(0.7)	0.28	(0.02)	0.32	(0.09)	0.32	(0.06)	0.06	(0.10)
United States	77.0	(2.0)	1.9	(0.3)	9.0	(1.0)	12.2	(1.2)	0.36	(0.03)	-0.26	(0.10)	-0.04	(0.10)	-0.65	(0.08)
OECD average	85.1	(0.1)	4.4	(0.1)	5.0	(0.1)	5.5	(0.1)	0.08	(0.00)	-0.12	(0.03)	-0.15	(0.02)	-0.39	(0.02)
Albania	0.0	c	0.0	c	0.0	c	0.0	c	c	c	c	c	c	c	c	c
Argentina	95.3	(0.5)	1.0	(0.2)	3.2	(0.3)	0.6	(0.1)	-0.68	(0.04)	-1.19	(0.18)	-1.39	(0.11)	-1.65	(0.28)
Brazil	98.3	(0.2)	0.9	(0.1)	0.6	(0.1)	0.2	(0.1)	-1.16	(0.02)	-1.11	(0.15)	-1.17	(0.22)	c	c
Bulgaria	89.1	(1.2)	10.4	(1.2)	0.3	(0.1)	0.2	(0.1)	-0.14	(0.03)	-1.33	(0.09)	c	c	c	c
Colombia	99.0	(0.2)	0.6	(0.2)	0.3	(0.1)	0.0	(0.0)	-1.26	(0.04)	-1.30	(0.45)	c	c	c	c
Costa Rica	93.5	(0.8)	1.0	(0.2)	5.3	(0.7)	0.2	(0.1)	-0.94	(0.04)	-0.30	(0.20)	-1.64	(0.16)	c	c
Croatia	87.3	(0.8)	0.9	(0.2)	11.5	(0.8)	0.3	(0.1)	-0.30	(0.02)	-0.42	(0.11)	-0.59	(0.04)	c	c
Cyprus*	78.0	(0.7)	14.3	(0.3)	3.7	(0.3)	4.0	(0.2)	-0.02	(0.01)	0.73	(0.03)	-0.01	(0.07)	0.08	(0.06)
Hong Kong-China	62.5	(1.6)	3.0	(0.7)	30.8	(1.3)	3.8	(0.5)	-0.58	(0.06)	-0.27	(0.21)	-1.21	(0.03)	-1.36	(0.08)
Indonesia	40.8	(2.4)	59.0	(2.4)	0.1	(0.0)	0.1	(0.0)	-1.39	(0.09)	-2.09	(0.04)	c	c	c	c
Jordan	83.0	(0.8)	3.6	(0.3)	12.5	(0.9)	0.8	(0.1)	-0.49	(0.03)	-0.24	(0.08)	-0.21	(0.06)	-0.03	(0.19)
Kazakhstan	74.2	(1.7)	9.7	(0.8)	14.7	(1.7)	1.4	(0.3)	-0.31	(0.02)	-0.15	(0.06)	-0.48	(0.05)	-0.18	(0.10)
Latvia	86.2	(1.4)	9.3	(1.2)	3.4	(0.5)	1.1	(0.3)	-0.24	(0.03)	-0.51	(0.08)	-0.10	(0.10)	-0.26	(0.20)
Liechtenstein	66.4	(3.0)	0.7	(0.5)	21.5	(2.8)	11.4	(1.8)	0.44	(0.06)	c	c	0.52	(0.12)	c	c
Lithuania	95.3	(0.6)	3.1	(0.5)	1.2	(0.2)	0.4	(0.1)	-0.12	(0.02)	-0.30	(0.09)	-0.04	(0.12)	c	c
Macao-China	28.2	(0.6)	6.6	(0.3)	58.2	(0.6)	7.0	(0.3)	-0.80	(0.02)	-0.24	(0.04)	-1.06	(0.01)	-0.48	(0.04)
Malaysia	56.5	(2.4)	41.7	(2.5)	1.3	(0.3)	0.4	(0.1)	-0.81	(0.04)	-0.58	(0.05)	-1.39	(0.14)	c	c
Montenegro	93.3	(0.5)	0.8	(0.1)	5.6	(0.4)	0.2	(0.1)	-0.26	(0.01)	-0.29	(0.20)	-0.10	(0.05)	c	c
Peru	93.4	(0.9)	6.0	(0.9)	0.4	(0.1)	0.1	(0.0)	-1.16	(0.05)	-2.20	(0.10)	c	c	c	c
Qatar	34.7	(0.4)	13.1	(0.2)	26.1	(0.4)	26.0	(0.3)	0.26	(0.02)	0.80	(0.02)	0.43	(0.02)	0.47	(0.01)
Romania	98.2	(0.4)	1.6	(0.4)	0.1	(0.0)	0.1	(0.0)	-0.47	(0.04)	-0.56	(0.19)	c	c	c	c
Russian Federation	82.0	(1.7)	7.1	(1.6)	9.4	(0.8)	1.5	(0.3)	-0.07	(0.02)	-0.31	(0.06)	-0.12	(0.05)	-0.45	(0.12)
Serbia	88.0	(0.8)	3.5	(0.5)	7.8	(0.7)	0.7	(0.1)	-0.29	(0.02)	-0.49	(0.10)	-0.26	(0.05)	-0.63	(0.23)
Shanghai-China	98.0	(0.2)	1.1	(0.2)	0.6	(0.1)	0.3	(0.1)	-0.35	(0.03)	-1.13	(0.14)	-1.15	(0.18)	c	c
Singapore	40.8	(0.8)	40.7	(1.1)	4.8	(0.4)	13.7	(0.7)	0.13	(0.02)	-0.77	(0.02)	0.59	(0.04)	-0.04	(0.04)
Chinese Taipei	83.1	(1.1)	16.4	(1.1)	0.5	(0.1)	0.0	(0.0)	-0.28	(0.02)	-0.89	(0.04)	c	c	c	c
Thailand	55.3	(1.7)	44.1	(1.7)	0.1	(0.1)	0.5	(0.3)	-0.99	(0.06)	-1.76	(0.04)	c	c	c	c
Tunisia	98.6	(0.2)	1.0	(0.2)	0.4	(0.1)	0.1	(0.0)	-1.19	(0.05)	-0.76	(0.20)	c	c	c	c
United Arab Emirates	35.9	(1.2)	8.9	(1.0)	30.6	(1.2)	24.6	(0.9)	0.15	(0.03)	0.74	(0.03)	0.35	(0.03)	0.39	(0.03)
Uruguay	97.7	(0.4)	1.8	(0.3)	0.3	(0.1)	0.1	(0.0)	-0.88	(0.03)	-1.32	(0.15)	c	c	c	c
Viet Nam	97.8	(0.4)	2.1	(0.4)	0.0	(0.0)	0.1	(0.0)	-1.78	(0.05)	-2.97	(0.17)	c	c	c	c

Notes: This table was calculated considering only students with data on the *PISA index of economic, social and cultural status*. Values that are statistically significant are indicated in bold (see Annex A3).
The percentages of immigrant and non-immigrant students who speak the language of assessment at home and those who do not speak the language of assessment at home are calculated over the total student population. The percentages of first- and second-generation students who speak the language of assessment at home and those who do not speak the language of assessment at home are calculated over the total immigrant student population.
* See notes at the beginning of this Annex.
StatLink ⫶⫶⫶ http://dx.doi.org/10.1787/888932964927

EXCELLENCE THROUGH EQUITY: GIVING EVERY STUDENT THE CHANCE TO SUCCEED – VOLUME II

[Part 2/4]
Mathematics performance, immigrant background and language spoken at home
Table II.3.5 — *Results based on students' self-reports*

	Average performance in mathematics								Performance differences before accounting for ESCS					
	Non-immigrant students who speak the language of assessment at home		Non-immigrant students who speak another language at home		Immigrant students who speak the language of assessment at home		Immigrant students who speak another language at home		Performance difference across non-immigrant students, by home language		Performance difference across immigrant students, by home language		Performance difference between immigrant students who do not speak the language of assessment at home and non-immigrant students who do	
	Mean score	S.E.	Mean score	S.E.	Mean score	S.E.	Mean score	S.E.	Score dif.	S.E.	Score dif.	S.E.	Score dif.	S.E.
OECD														
Australia	505	(1.4)	466	(8.8)	528	(3.8)	541	(6.0)	39	(8.8)	-13	(5.5)	-36	(5.9)
Austria	520	(2.7)	487	(14.5)	498	(9.4)	457	(6.0)	33	(14.5)	41	(10.6)	63	(6.3)
Belgium	535	(2.1)	513	(5.3)	469	(7.4)	448	(7.2)	23	(5.3)	21	(10.6)	88	(7.4)
Canada	523	(1.8)	521	(7.6)	518	(5.0)	530	(4.4)	3	(7.8)	-12	(4.3)	-7	(4.7)
Chile	424	(3.0)	404	(19.0)	417	(13.8)	c	c	20	(18.6)	c	c	c	c
Czech Republic	503	(2.7)	461	(30.1)	469	(22.2)	490	(16.3)	42	(30.1)	-21	(27.6)	13	(15.9)
Denmark	509	(2.3)	456	(12.8)	450	(5.4)	453	(3.6)	53	(12.8)	-3	(6.6)	56	(4.2)
Estonia	526	(2.1)	509	(5.5)	497	(6.8)	488	(11.5)	17	(5.7)	9	(12.7)	38	(11.6)
Finland	524	(1.9)	518	(7.6)	460	(9.5)	434	(5.9)	5	(7.9)	25	(11.5)	90	(5.7)
France	511	(2.8)	465	(17.1)	450	(7.5)	440	(8.6)	46	(17.0)	11	(9.9)	71	(9.3)
Germany	530	(3.2)	504	(24.4)	493	(6.7)	470	(8.2)	26	(24.2)	23	(10.3)	60	(8.6)
Greece	461	(2.6)	408	(19.7)	416	(6.8)	401	(8.7)	53	(19.8)	15	(10.3)	60	(9.3)
Hungary	478	(3.1)	454	(20.8)	503	(16.4)	c	c	24	(21.0)	c	c	c	c
Iceland	499	(1.7)	456	(18.1)	c	c	443	(9.9)	43	(18.0)	c	c	56	(10.0)
Ireland	504	(2.3)	c	c	508	(6.1)	499	(6.9)	c	c	9	(8.9)	5	(6.6)
Israel	473	(4.4)	453	(12.1)	476	(7.4)	490	(7.4)	20	(10.3)	-14	(7.6)	-16	(7.3)
Italy	499	(2.1)	463	(3.1)	461	(6.2)	442	(4.1)	36	(3.0)	19	(7.5)	57	(4.7)
Japan	540	(3.6)	c	c	c	c	c	c	c	c	c	c	c	c
Korea	555	(4.5)	c	c	c	c	c	c	c	c	c	c	c	c
Luxembourg	527	(7.8)	514	(1.8)	536	(3.9)	461	(3.0)	12	(8.4)	75	(4.7)	65	(8.1)
Mexico	418	(1.3)	371	(4.4)	342	(5.3)	335	(13.7)	47	(4.4)	7	(13.4)	83	(13.6)
Netherlands	533	(3.4)	502	(13.7)	490	(8.7)	473	(9.2)	32	(13.6)	16	(10.3)	60	(8.4)
New Zealand	508	(2.5)	421	(8.7)	516	(4.9)	492	(8.0)	87	(8.8)	24	(9.3)	16	(8.5)
Norway	497	(2.8)	482	(12.1)	464	(7.7)	451	(6.8)	15	(12.3)	13	(7.9)	46	(7.3)
Poland	519	(3.6)	514	(20.0)	c	c	c	c	5	(18.8)	c	c	c	c
Portugal	494	(3.7)	485	(19.4)	445	(7.4)	471	(11.6)	9	(19.4)	-26	(12.1)	23	(11.2)
Slovak Republic	493	(3.3)	394	(11.5)	c	c	c	c	99	(12.3)	c	c	c	c
Slovenia	508	(1.1)	448	(10.5)	479	(7.1)	449	(6.6)	61	(10.5)	30	(10.5)	59	(6.7)
Spain	493	(1.8)	484	(2.9)	442	(5.5)	439	(6.2)	9	(3.0)	3	(7.0)	54	(6.0)
Sweden	494	(2.3)	469	(23.3)	448	(6.9)	438	(6.7)	25	(23.4)	10	(9.2)	56	(7.1)
Switzerland	551	(3.2)	527	(6.3)	501	(4.7)	478	(5.0)	24	(6.6)	23	(5.9)	73	(4.4)
Turkey	452	(4.9)	400	(14.2)	471	(33.9)	c	c	52	(14.7)	c	c	c	c
United Kingdom	500	(2.8)	480	(10.3)	485	(8.2)	501	(11.3)	20	(10.7)	-16	(10.3)	-1	(11.3)
United States	489	(3.7)	443	(8.8)	494	(8.5)	461	(5.8)	45	(8.7)	33	(7.6)	28	(5.7)
OECD average	503	(0.5)	467	(2.6)	473	(2.0)	462	(1.6)	33	(2.6)	12	(2.1)	43	(1.6)
Partners														
Albania	c	c	c	c	c	c	c	c	c	c	c	c	c	c
Argentina	393	(3.4)	348	(16.3)	358	(6.4)	336	(26.1)	45	(16.3)	23	(25.9)	57	(25.2)
Brazil	395	(2.1)	397	(11.0)	322	(11.8)	c	c	-2	(10.8)	c	c	c	c
Bulgaria	451	(3.9)	374	(7.1)	c	c	c	c	77	(7.5)	c	c	c	c
Colombia	379	(2.9)	343	(16.3)	c	c	c	c	36	(15.8)	c	c	c	c
Costa Rica	410	(3.0)	429	(15.9)	377	(9.8)	c	c	-19	(16.0)	c	c	c	c
Croatia	475	(3.6)	470	(19.3)	458	(5.4)	c	c	4	(19.1)	c	c	c	c
Cyprus*	436	(1.3)	497	(3.4)	437	(6.5)	423	(6.6)	-61	(3.6)	14	(8.7)	13	(6.8)
Hong Kong-China	569	(3.8)	529	(12.7)	566	(3.5)	514	(10.7)	41	(12.9)	52	(10.4)	55	(11.7)
Indonesia	378	(6.5)	374	(4.1)	c	c	c	c	4	(6.8)	c	c	c	c
Jordan	388	(2.8)	387	(6.8)	411	(5.5)	404	(15.6)	1	(7.0)	7	(16.8)	-16	(15.8)
Kazakhstan	432	(3.0)	444	(7.5)	426	(6.2)	433	(10.0)	-12	(6.9)	-7	(11.7)	-1	(9.8)
Latvia	494	(3.0)	476	(6.0)	488	(8.6)	480	(20.4)	18	(6.5)	8	(21.9)	14	(20.4)
Liechtenstein	559	(5.7)	c	c	524	(12.0)	c	c	c	c	c	c	c	c
Lithuania	484	(2.8)	440	(11.1)	490	(10.1)	c	c	44	(11.4)	c	c	c	c
Macao-China	528	(2.4)	548	(4.8)	548	(1.6)	548	(4.8)	-20	(5.3)	1	(5.3)	-20	(5.2)
Malaysia	410	(3.2)	441	(4.6)	408	(8.5)	c	c	-31	(4.8)	c	c	c	c
Montenegro	410	(1.2)	389	(15.6)	433	(6.0)	c	c	21	(15.8)	c	c	c	c
Peru	376	(3.5)	300	(8.1)	c	c	c	c	76	(7.9)	c	c	c	c
Qatar	323	(1.5)	370	(2.6)	408	(2.4)	444	(1.8)	-46	(3.2)	-35	(3.3)	-120	(2.4)
Romania	446	(3.8)	415	(13.3)	c	c	c	c	30	(12.9)	c	c	c	c
Russian Federation	487	(3.4)	472	(6.4)	471	(4.1)	426	(12.6)	15	(6.4)	45	(12.0)	61	(12.7)
Serbia	450	(3.4)	442	(6.8)	463	(6.8)	478	(25.4)	7	(7.0)	-15	(24.9)	-28	(25.1)
Shanghai-China	616	(3.1)	502	(14.9)	493	(21.2)	c	c	115	(14.2)	c	c	c	c
Singapore	602	(2.2)	549	(2.1)	609	(6.3)	597	(4.4)	53	(3.2)	12	(7.4)	5	(5.1)
Chinese Taipei	577	(3.3)	517	(5.6)	c	c	c	c	60	(5.8)	c	c	c	c
Thailand	434	(4.7)	422	(3.8)	c	c	c	c	12	(5.6)	c	c	c	c
Tunisia	389	(4.0)	378	(15.8)	c	c	c	c	12	(15.5)	c	c	c	c
United Arab Emirates	395	(2.6)	424	(5.6)	458	(3.1)	479	(3.8)	-28	(5.3)	-20	(4.4)	-83	(4.4)
Uruguay	413	(2.6)	396	(12.4)	c	c	c	c	17	(12.0)	c	c	c	c
Viet Nam	513	(4.8)	461	(12.0)	c	c	c	c	52	(11.4)	c	c	c	c

Notes: This table was calculated considering only students with data on the *PISA index of economic, social and cultural status*. Values that are statistically significant are indicated in bold (see Annex A3).

The percentages of immigrant and non-immigrant students who speak the language of assessment at home and those who do not speak the language of assessment at home are calculated over the total student population. The percentages of first- and second-generation students who speak the language of assessment at home and those who do not speak the language of assessment at home are calculated over the total immigrant student population.

* See notes at the beginning of this Annex.

StatLink http://dx.doi.org/10.1787/888932964927

[Part 3/4]
Mathematics performance, immigrant background and language spoken at home
Table II.3.5 *Results based on students' self-reports*

| | Performance differences after accounting for ESCS | | | | | | Increased likelihood of non-immigrant students who speak the language of assessment at home scoring in the bottom quarter of the mathematics performance distribution | | Population relevance of non-immigrant students who speak the language of assessment at home scoring in the bottom quarter of the mathematics performance distribution | | Increased likelihood of non-immigrant students who do not speak the language of assessment at home scoring in the bottom quarter of the mathematics performance distribution | | Population relevance of non-immigrant students language of assessment at home scoring in the bottom quarter of the mathematics performance distribution | |
| | Performance difference across non-immigrant students, by home language | | Performance difference across immigrant students, by home language | | Performance difference between immigrant students who do not speak the language of assessment at home and non-immigrant students who do | | | | | | | | | |
	Score dif.	S.E.	Score dif.	S.E.	Score dif.	S.E.	Ratio	S.E.	%	S.E.	Ratio	S.E.	%	S.E.
OECD														
Australia	**30**	(7.7)	**-26**	(5.1)	**-48**	(5.3)	**1.17**	(0.06)	**11.4**	(3.6)	**1.75**	(0.18)	1.5	(0.4)
Austria	**32**	(13.4)	13	(8.7)	**31**	(6.1)	**0.52**	(0.04)	**-69.6**	(9.5)	1.33	(0.35)	0.5	(0.5)
Belgium	**10**	(4.5)	10	(9.1)	**53**	(5.6)	**0.53**	(0.04)	**-51.8**	(5.7)	**1.10**	(0.09)	1.3	(1.3)
Canada	3	(6.6)	**-18**	(4.4)	**-13**	(4.5)	0.96	(0.06)	-2.8	(4.4)	1.06	(0.12)	0.2	(0.4)
Chile	24	(14.2)	c	c	c	c	0.83	(0.17)	-21.2	(25.3)	1.47	(0.45)	0.3	(0.3)
Czech Republic	50	(23.2)	-21	(26.6)	9	(16.0)	0.74	(0.14)	-33.7	(22.0)	1.63	(0.53)	0.5	(0.4)
Denmark	**31**	(12.3)	-6	(6.7)	**28**	(4.4)	**0.45**	(0.03)	**-103.5**	(11.8)	**2.08**	(0.50)	0.6	(0.3)
Estonia	**14**	(5.7)	9	(11.7)	**37**	(10.7)	**0.71**	(0.06)	**-34.0**	(8.4)	1.10	(0.15)	0.4	(0.6)
Finland	**13**	(6.7)	**21**	(9.9)	**69**	(5.3)	**0.47**	(0.02)	**-102.6**	(8.4)	1.11	(0.13)	0.2	(0.2)
France	**36**	(15.3)	3	(9.9)	**33**	(9.4)	**0.46**	(0.04)	**-84.0**	(11.1)	**1.52**	(0.32)	1.2	(0.6)
Germany	6	(20.5)	**21**	(9.4)	**31**	(7.9)	**0.60**	(0.05)	**-52.7**	(11.5)	1.31	(0.46)	0.5	(0.6)
Greece	**42**	(12.8)	12	(10.1)	**33**	(9.4)	**0.52**	(0.04)	**-73.5**	(12.6)	**1.83**	(0.44)	0.9	(0.6)
Hungary	**40**	(18.0)	c	c	c	c	1.18	(0.33)	13.5	(24.0)	1.53	(0.45)	0.4	(0.3)
Iceland	**37**	(16.5)	c	c	**30**	(9.3)	**0.55**	(0.05)	**-74.1**	(16.6)	1.69	(0.42)	0.4	(0.5)
Ireland	c	c	1	(8.3)	2	(6.3)	0.98	(0.10)	-1.6	(9.4)	c	c		c
Israel	17	(9.7)	-8	(6.6)	**-19**	(5.6)	1.15	(0.12)	10.8	(7.1)	**1.41**	(0.20)	1.1	(0.6)
Italy	**21**	(2.6)	10	(7.1)	**36**	(4.6)	**0.56**	(0.02)	**-57.8**	(4.5)	**1.56**	(0.06)	5.1	(0.6)
Japan	c	c	c	c	c	c	0.48	(0.10)	-108.5	(40.5)	c	c		c
Korea	c	c	c	c	c	c	c	c	c	c	c	c		c
Luxembourg	4	(7.7)	**38**	(5.2)	**32**	(8.2)	0.49	(0.14)	-1.6	(0.5)	**0.58**	(0.04)	-28.	(3.3)
Mexico	**26**	(4.1)	3	(11.4)	**71**	(10.9)	**0.44**	(0.02)	**-115.6**	(9.2)	**1.97**	(0.12)	2.	(0.5)
Netherlands	22	(13.0)	13	(10.3)	**29**	(8.7)	**0.55**	(0.05)	**-66.1**	(11.8)	1.27	(0.30)	0.	(0.4)
New Zealand	**78**	(9.2)	7	(7.0)	6	(6.5)	**0.72**	(0.06)	**-25.0**	(6.6)	**2.52**	(0.33)	4.	(1.1)
Norway	17	(12.1)	5	(7.9)	**25**	(7.4)	**0.56**	(0.04)	**-64.6**	(9.2)	1.07	(0.28)	0.	(0.4)
Poland	12	(13.2)	c	c	c	c	0.87	(0.24)	-15.4	(31.4)	1.13	(0.38)	0.	(0.3)
Portugal	15	(14.7)	**-29**	(11.6)	16	(11.2)	0.59	(0.05)	-62.2	(13.6)	0.82	(0.35)	-0.	(0.3)
Slovak Republic	**50**	(10.2)	c	c	c	c	**0.38**	(0.04)	**-133.7**	(20.8)	**2.75**	(0.30)	11.	(2.1)
Slovenia	**56**	(9.8)	23	(11.0)	**30**	(6.5)	**0.53**	(0.05)	**-75.2**	(12.6)	**2.05**	(0.35)	1.	(0.6)
Spain	2	(2.7)	-1	(6.7)	**34**	(5.5)	**0.69**	(0.03)	**-30.7**	(4.5)	0.95	(0.06)	-0.	(0.8)
Sweden	25	(21.4)	8	(9.0)	**36**	(6.9)	**0.50**	(0.04)	**-75.2**	(10.4)	1.66	(0.34)	1.	(0.5)
Switzerland	**24**	(6.3)	10	(5.5)	**45**	(4.4)	**0.47**	(0.02)	**-63.9**	(4.7)	1.08	(0.13)	0.	(0.5)
Turkey	24	(13.6)	c	c	c	c	0.56	(0.09)	-69.1	(25.0)	1.81	(0.32)	4.	(1.9)
United Kingdom	**21**	(9.3)	**-27**	(9.3)	-10	(8.5)	0.79	(0.07)	-22.8	(9.8)	1.15	(0.19)	0.	(0.2)
United States	**21**	(8.5)	**14**	(6.2)	-9	(5.2)	0.75	(0.08)	-23.8	(8.3)	**1.71**	(0.23)	1.	(0.4)
OECD average	**26**	(2.2)	3	(1.9)	**23**	(1.5)	**0.66**	(0.02)	**-50.9**	(2.7)	**1.48**	(0.06)	0.	(0.2)
Partners														
Albania	c	c	c	c	c	c	c	c	c	c	c	c		c
Argentina	31	(13.8)	19	(30.3)	31	(29.2)	0.62	(0.08)	-55.9	(17.8)	**1.80**	(0.48)	0	(0.5)
Brazil	0	(11.1)	c	c	c	c	0.61	(0.07)	-63.2	(17.9)	1.13	(0.19)	0	(0.2)
Bulgaria	**31**	(5.6)	c	c	c	c	**0.40**	(0.04)	**-114.0**	(16.6)	**2.47**	(0.24)	13	(2.1)
Colombia	35	(18.2)	c	c	c	c	0.54	(0.12)	-85.4	(39.4)	1.53	(0.63)	0	(0.4)
Costa Rica	-4	(14.3)	c	c	c	c	0.62	(0.11)	-55.2	(21.2)	0.81	(0.32)	-0	(0.3)
Croatia	0	(17.8)	c	c	c	c	0.83	(0.08)	-17.4	(8.6)	1.01	(0.32)	0	(0.3)
Cyprus*	**-37**	(3.5)	11	(8.0)	11	(6.4)	**1.36**	(0.11)	21.9	(4.9)	0.43	(0.05)	-8	(0.9)
Hong Kong-China	**50**	(12.0)	**49**	(9.9)	**31**	(10.5)	0.82	(0.07)	-12.4	(5.4)	**1.54**	(0.22)	1	(0.8)
Indonesia	**-11**	(4.5)	c	c	c	c	1.00	(0.09)	-0.1	(3.7)	1.00	(0.09)	0	(5.4)
Jordan	7	(6.7)	13	(14.7)	-4	(14.1)	**1.35**	(0.17)	22.2	(8.1)	1.03	(0.15)	0	(0.6)
Kazakhstan	-8	(6.4)	0	(11.2)	2	(9.9)	1.00	(0.10)	0.0	(6.7)	0.81	(0.12)	-1	(1.2)
Latvia	8	(6.1)	4	(22.1)	14	(20.8)	0.79	(0.08)	-21.9	(10.8)	1.28	(0.17)	2	(1.6)
Liechtenstein	c	c	c	c	c	c	0.48	(0.12)	-52.7	(18.0)	c	c		c
Lithuania	**37**	(10.7)	c	c	c	c	0.69	(0.09)	-41.4	(15.1)	**1.70**	(0.21)	2	(0.7)
Macao-China	-8	(5.2)	**12**	(5.3)	**-12**	(5.2)	**1.38**	(0.09)	9.6	(2.0)	0.83	(0.09)	-1	(0.6)
Malaysia	**-25**	(4.2)	c	c	c	c	**1.27**	(0.11)	13.2	(4.5)	0.77	(0.07)	-10	(3.6)
Montenegro	20	(14.5)	c	c	c	c	1.34	(0.24)	23.6	(12.7)	1.34	(0.43)	0	(0.3)
Peru	**43**	(7.2)	c	c	c	c	0.37	(0.03)	-144.3	(16.8)	**2.65**	(0.24)	9	(1.9)
Qatar	**-40**	(3.0)	**-34**	(3.2)	**-117**	(2.3)	**3.06**	(0.12)	41.6	(1.5)	1.03	(0.05)	0	(0.7)
Romania	**27**	(10.5)	c	c	c	c	0.69	(0.18)	-45.6	(30.8)	1.61	(0.33)	1	(0.6)
Russian Federation	6	(7.0)	**34**	(14.2)	**46**	(14.9)	0.79	(0.06)	-21.4	(6.9)	1.15	(0.15)	1	(1.0)
Serbia	1	(7.4)	-30	(20.6)	-40	(21.2)	1.14	(0.09)	10.7	(6.8)	1.00	(0.18)	0	(0.6)
Shanghai-China	**84**	(13.7)	c	c	c	c	**0.34**	(0.02)	**-184.4**	(18.6)	**2.74**	(0.30)	1	(0.4)
Singapore	**19**	(3.8)	-12	(7.9)	-2	(5.5)	0.61	(0.03)	-19.0	(2.0)	**1.91**	(0.10)	27	(2.2)
Chinese Taipei	**27**	(4.8)	c	c	c	c	0.52	(0.03)	-67.4	(7.9)	**1.94**	(0.13)	13	(1.7)
Thailand	-7	(4.3)	c	c	c	c	0.98	(0.09)	-1.0	(5.0)	1.00	(0.08)	0	(3.7)
Tunisia	21	(15.7)	c	c	c	c	0.89	(0.26)	-12.0	(28.0)	1.11	(0.37)	0	(0.4)
United Arab Emirates	**-17**	(5.2)	**-19**	(4.2)	**-77**	(4.1)	**2.42**	(0.14)	33.8	(2.3)	1.05	(0.08)	0	(0.7)
Uruguay	0	(9.2)	c	c	c	c	0.82	(0.13)	-22.8	(23.4)	1.34	(0.25)	0	(0.5)
Viet Nam	17	(11.9)	c	c	c	c	0.54	(0.10)	-83.6	(36.6)	1.82	(0.39)	7	(0.7)

Notes: This table was calculated considering only students with data on the *PISA index of economic, social and cultural status*. Values that are statistically significant are indicated in bold (see Annex A3).

The percentages of immigrant and non-immigrant students who speak the language of assessment at home and those who do not speak the language of assessment at home are calculated over the total student population. The percentages of first- and second-generation students who speak the language of assessment at home and those who do not speak the language of assessment at home are calculated over the total immigrant student population.

* See notes at the beginning of this Annex.

StatLink ᴍᴸᴾ http://dx.doi.org/10.1787/888932964927

[Part 4/4]

Table II.3.5 Mathematics performance, immigrant background and language spoken at home

Results based on students' self-reports

		Increased likelihood of immigrant students who speak the language of assessment at home scoring in the bottom quarter of the mathematics performance distribution		Population relevance of immigrant students who speak the language of assessment at home scoring in the bottom quarter of the mathematics performance distribution		Increased likelihood of immigrant students who do not speak the language of assessment at home scoring in the bottom quarter of the mathematics performance distribution		Population relevance of immigrant students who do not speak the language of assessment at home scoring in the bottom quarter of the mathematics performance distribution		Effect size in mathematics performance for non-immigrant students who speak the language of assessment at home (positive number implies an advantage for non-immigrant students)		Effect size in mathematics performance for non-immigrant students who speak the language of assessment at home (positive number implies an advantage for non-immigrant students)		Effect size in mathematics performance for immigrant students who speak the language of assessment at home (positive number implies an advantage for non-immigrant students)		Effect size in mathematics performance for immigrant students who do not speak the language of assessment at home (positive number implies an advantage for non-immigrant students)	
		Ratio	S.E.	%	S.E.	Ratio	S.E.	%	S.E.	Effect size	S.E.	Effect size	S.E.	Effect size	S.E.	Effect size	S.E.
OECD	**Australia**	0.83	(0.05)	-2.6	(0.8)	0.71	(0.06)	-2.1	(0.5)	**-0.23**	(0.04)	**-0.47**	(0.09)	**0.22**	(0.03)	**0.34**	(0.05)
	Austria	1.28	(0.17)	1.0	(0.6)	**2.12**	(0.17)	9.8	(1.6)	**0.55**	(0.06)	-0.28	(0.15)	-0.16	(0.10)	**-0.69**	(0.07)
	Belgium	**1.93**	(0.17)	5.8	(1.3)	**2.33**	(0.17)	8.5	(1.1)	**0.50**	(0.04)	-0.10	(0.05)	**-0.59**	(0.08)	**-0.82**	(0.07)
	Canada	1.08	(0.09)	1.2	(1.4)	0.98	(0.07)	-0.3	(1.0)	0.00	(0.05)	-0.03	(0.09)	-0.08	(0.05)	0.09	(0.05)
	Chile	1.11	(0.34)	0.1	(0.3)	c	c	c	c	0.11	(0.12)	-0.23	(0.21)	-0.08	(0.16)	c	c
	Czech Republic	1.47	(0.37)	0.4	(0.3)	1.18	(0.31)	0.4	(0.6)	**0.23**	(0.10)	-0.37	(0.25)	-0.32	(0.21)	-0.12	(0.15)
	Denmark	**2.17**	(0.20)	3.9	(0.8)	**2.06**	(0.16)	3.9	(0.6)	**0.74**	(0.05)	**-0.62**	(0.16)	**-0.72**	(0.07)	**-0.69**	(0.06)
	Estonia	**1.49**	(0.15)	3.0	(0.9)	**1.51**	(0.30)	0.9	(0.5)	**0.33**	(0.06)	**-0.18**	(0.08)	**-0.34**	(0.08)	**-0.43**	(0.13)
	Finland	**1.98**	(0.24)	0.6	(0.2)	**2.77**	(0.11)	4.6	(0.4)	**0.63**	(0.05)	-0.03	(0.09)	**-0.75**	(0.12)	**-1.03**	(0.06)
	France	**1.94**	(0.17)	7.0	(1.4)	**2.16**	(0.21)	6.0	(1.2)	**0.65**	(0.08)	**-0.37**	(0.17)	**-0.57**	(0.09)	**-0.69**	(0.11)
	Germany	**1.42**	(0.16)	2.8	(1.0)	**1.88**	(0.19)	4.1	(0.9)	**0.47**	(0.07)	-0.20	(0.24)	**-0.36**	(0.08)	**-0.61**	(0.09)
	Greece	**1.61**	(0.19)	3.5	(1.1)	**2.08**	(0.25)	4.1	(1.2)	**0.60**	(0.07)	**-0.51**	(0.21)	**-0.50**	(0.09)	**-0.66**	(0.11)
	Hungary	0.66	(0.26)	-0.5	(0.4)	c	c	c	c	-0.16	(0.11)	-0.26	(0.22)	0.26	(0.16)	c	c
	Iceland	c	c	c	c	**1.81**	(0.25)	2.1	(0.7)	**0.53**	(0.09)	**-0.40**	(0.18)	c	c	**-0.64**	(0.13)
	Ireland	0.89	(0.13)	-0.6	(0.6)	1.15	(0.16)	0.7	(0.7)	0.00	(0.06)	c	c	0.06	(0.08)	-0.06	(0.08)
	Israel	0.87	(0.10)	-1.3	(1.0)	0.70	(0.11)	-2.5	(1.1)	-0.04	(0.05)	**-0.21**	(0.10)	0.01	(0.06)	**0.17**	(0.07)
	Italy	**1.55**	(0.13)	1.4	(0.4)	**1.90**	(0.13)	3.8	(0.5)	**0.46**	(0.03)	**-0.35**	(0.03)	**-0.34**	(0.06)	**-0.58**	(0.05)
	Japan	c	c	c	c	c	c	c	c	**0.50**	(0.23)	c	c	c	c	c	c
	Korea	c	c	c	c	c	c	c	c	c	c	c	c	c	c	c	c
	Luxembourg	0.59	(0.06)	-5.0	(0.8)	**2.24**	(0.15)	28.6	(2.6)	**0.32**	(0.10)	**0.33**	(0.04)	**0.44**	(0.05)	**-0.65**	(0.04)
	Mexico	**2.72**	(0.18)	1.7	(0.2)	**2.80**	(0.37)	0.4	(0.1)	**0.78**	(0.05)	**-0.65**	(0.06)	**-1.04**	(0.09)	**-1.15**	(0.20)
	Netherlands	**1.55**	(0.24)	2.5	(1.1)	**2.01**	(0.25)	4.6	(1.1)	**0.56**	(0.07)	**-0.31**	(0.16)	**-0.46**	(0.09)	**-0.65**	(0.09)
	New Zealand	0.83	(0.11)	-2.4	(1.5)	**1.51**	(0.17)	6.2	(2.0)	**0.12**	(0.05)	**-0.96**	(0.11)	**0.14**	(0.06)	-0.14	(0.08)
	Norway	**1.61**	(0.17)	1.8	(0.5)	**1.93**	(0.18)	5.2	(1.1)	**0.43**	(0.07)	-0.13	(0.14)	**-0.35**	(0.09)	**-0.50**	(0.09)
	Poland	c	c	c	c	c	c	c	c	0.02	(0.19)	-0.06	(0.20)	c	c	c	c
	Portugal	**1.90**	(0.20)	4.0	(1.0)	**1.47**	(0.23)	0.9	(0.4)	**0.41**	(0.07)	-0.07	(0.22)	**-0.52**	(0.08)	-0.22	(0.12)
	Slovak Republic	c	c	c	c	c	c	c	c	**0.90**	(0.12)	**-1.02**	(0.13)	c	c	c	c
	Slovenia	**1.34**	(0.18)	1.1	(0.6)	**2.08**	(0.21)	4.8	(1.0)	**0.56**	(0.06)	**-0.66**	(0.13)	**-0.28**	(0.08)	**-0.68**	(0.10)
	Spain	**1.86**	(0.14)	4.1	(0.7)	**1.90**	(0.14)	4.0	(0.7)	**0.32**	(0.03)	-0.04	(0.04)	**-0.56**	(0.06)	**-0.59**	(0.07)
	Sweden	**1.64**	(0.20)	2.6	(0.8)	**2.00**	(0.16)	7.8	(1.4)	**0.55**	(0.08)	-0.18	(0.24)	**-0.46**	(0.08)	**-0.61**	(0.09)
	Switzerland	**1.66**	(0.10)	6.5	(0.9)	**2.18**	(0.11)	12.5	(1.2)	**0.62**	(0.03)	-0.11	(0.07)	**-0.43**	(0.05)	**-0.71**	(0.05)
	Turkey	1.17	(0.52)	0.1	(0.4)	c	c	c	c	**0.50**	(0.16)	**-0.60**	(0.17)	0.20	(0.32)	c	c
	United Kingdom	**1.42**	(0.16)	2.7	(1.1)	1.07	(0.18)	0.4	(1.0)	0.09	(0.08)	-0.21	(0.13)	-0.15	(0.08)	0.02	(0.12)
	United States	0.92	(0.12)	-0.7	(1.1)	**1.48**	(0.14)	5.5	(1.6)	**0.18**	(0.06)	**-0.49**	(0.10)	0.11	(0.09)	**-0.31**	(0.06)
	OECD average	**1.43**	(0.04)	1.5	(0.2)	**1.78**	(0.04)	4.6	(0.2)	**0.37**	(0.02)	**-0.32**	(0.03)	**-0.26**	(0.02)	**-0.47**	(0.02)
Partners	**Albania**	c	c	c	c	c	c	c	c	c	c	c	c	c	c	c	c
	Argentina	**1.51**	(0.26)	1.6	(0.8)	1.58	(0.55)	0.3	(0.3)	**0.52**	(0.08)	**-0.59**	(0.21)	**-0.46**	(0.09)	**-0.63**	(0.27)
	Brazil	**2.58**	(0.31)	0.9	(0.2)	c	c	c	c	**0.29**	(0.11)	0.03	(0.13)	**-1.04**	(0.18)	c	c
	Bulgaria	c	c	c	c	c	c	c	c	**0.91**	(0.08)	**-0.91**	(0.08)	c	c	c	c
	Colombia	c	c	c	c	c	c	c	c	**0.65**	(0.14)	**-0.47**	(0.20)	c	c	c	c
	Costa Rica	**1.82**	(0.28)	4.2	(1.7)	c	c	c	c	**0.30**	(0.13)	0.28	(0.22)	**-0.50**	(0.14)	c	c
	Croatia	1.20	(0.11)	2.2	(1.3)	c	c	c	c	**0.19**	(0.06)	-0.03	(0.22)	**-0.20**	(0.06)	c	c
	Cyprus*	1.20	(0.17)	0.7	(0.6)	**1.54**	(0.18)	2.1	(0.7)	**-0.40**	(0.04)	**0.68**	(0.04)	-0.08	(0.07)	**-0.23**	(0.07)
	Hong Kong-China	1.01	(0.08)	0.3	(2.5)	**1.82**	(0.23)	3.0	(0.8)	**0.12**	(0.05)	**-0.37**	(0.12)	0.02	(0.04)	**-0.54**	(0.11)
	Indonesia	c	c	c	c	c	c	c	c	0.06	(0.09)	-0.06	(0.09)	c	c	c	c
	Jordan	0.67	(0.10)	-4.3	(1.4)	0.83	(0.36)	-0.1	(0.3)	**-0.23**	(0.05)	-0.06	(0.10)	**0.30**	(0.06)	0.17	(0.19)
	Kazakhstan	1.16	(0.12)	2.2	(1.7)	0.85	(0.23)	-0.2	(0.3)	-0.02	(0.07)	0.18	(0.10)	-0.10	(0.09)	0.01	(0.14)
	Latvia	1.09	(0.20)	0.3	(0.7)	1.42	(0.57)	0.5	(0.7)	**0.18**	(0.07)	**-0.21**	(0.08)	-0.05	(0.10)	-0.15	(0.26)
	Liechtenstein	1.40	(0.36)	7.7	(7.1)	c	c	c	c	**0.57**	(0.13)	c	c	-0.23	(0.15)	c	c
	Lithuania	0.81	(0.29)	-0.2	(0.4)	c	c	c	c	**0.32**	(0.10)	**-0.49**	(0.12)	0.09	(0.12)	c	c
	Macao-China	0.81	(0.06)	-12.2	(4.2)	0.89	(0.11)	-0.8	(0.8)	**-0.22**	(0.03)	0.07	(0.05)	**0.15**	(0.03)	0.06	(0.06)
	Malaysia	1.13	(0.32)	0.2	(0.4)	c	c	c	c	**-0.37**	(0.06)	**0.39**	(0.06)	-0.20	(0.13)	c	c
	Montenegro	0.62	(0.13)	-2.2	(0.8)	c	c	c	c	**-0.19**	(0.08)	-0.28	(0.21)	**0.29**	(0.07)	c	c
	Peru	c	c	c	c	c	c	c	c	**0.98**	(0.11)	**-0.97**	(0.11)	c	c	c	c
	Qatar	0.55	(0.04)	-13.2	(1.2)	0.26	(0.02)	-24.0	(1.0)	**-1.07**	(0.02)	**-0.16**	(0.03)	**0.35**	(0.03)	**0.88**	(0.03)
	Romania	c	c	c	c	c	c	c	c	0.29	(0.16)	**-0.37**	(0.16)	c	c	c	c
	Russian Federation	1.16	(0.10)	1.4	(0.9)	**2.06**	(0.30)	1.6	(0.5)	**0.23**	(0.04)	-0.15	(0.08)	**-0.17**	(0.05)	**-0.70**	(0.14)
	Serbia	0.88	(0.11)	-1.0	(0.9)	0.47	(0.41)	-0.4	(0.3)	-0.09	(0.05)	-0.10	(0.08)	**0.15**	(0.06)	0.31	(0.29)
	Shanghai-China	**2.93**	(0.40)	1.1	(0.4)	c	c	c	c	**1.23**	(0.13)	**-1.12**	(0.16)	**-1.23**	(0.22)	c	c
	Singapore	0.55	(0.11)	-2.2	(0.6)	0.78	(0.07)	-3.1	(1.0)	**0.37**	(0.03)	**-0.53**	(0.03)	**0.30**	(0.07)	**0.19**	(0.05)
	Chinese Taipei	c	c	c	c	c	c	c	c	**0.53**	(0.05)	**-0.53**	(0.05)	c	c	c	c
	Thailand	c	c	c	c	c	c	c	c	**0.14**	(0.07)	**-0.14**	(0.07)	c	c	c	c
	Tunisia	c	c	c	c	c	c	c	c	0.10	(0.15)	-0.15	(0.20)	c	c	c	c
	United Arab Emirates	0.65	(0.04)	-12.2	(1.6)	0.38	(0.05)	-18.0	(1.7)	**-0.81**	(0.04)	**-0.18**	(0.06)	**0.34**	(0.04)	**0.63**	(0.05)
	Uruguay	c	c	c	c	c	c	c	c	0.11	(0.13)	-0.19	(0.14)	c	c	c	c
	Viet Nam	c	c	c	c	c	c	c	c	**0.67**	(0.13)	**-0.65**	(0.13)	c	c	c	c

Notes: This table was calculated considering only students with data on the *PISA index of economic, social and cultural status*. Values that are statistically significant are indicated in bold (see Annex A3).

The percentages of immigrant and non-immigrant students who speak the language of assessment at home and those who do not speak the language of assessment at home are calculated over the total student population. The percentages of first- and second-generation students who speak the language of assessment at home and those who do not speak the language of assessment at home are calculated over the total immigrant student population.

* See notes at the beginning of this Annex.

StatLink http://dx.doi.org/10.1787/888932964927

[Part 1/3]

Mathematics performance and immigrant background for first- and second-generation students

Table II.3.6a — *Results based on students' self-reports*

		Percentage of students						PISA index of economic, social and cultural status (ESCS)						Mathematics performance					
		Non-immigrant		First-generation		Second-generation		Non-immigrant		First-generation		Second-generation		Non-immigrant		First-generation		Second-generation	
		%	S.E.	%	S.E.	%	S.E.	Mean index	S.E.	Mean index	S.E.	Mean index	S.E.	Mean score	S.E.	Mean score	S.E.	Mean score	S.E.
OECD	Australia	77.3	(0.7)	10.2	(0.4)	12.4	(0.6)	0.28	(0.01)	0.26	(0.03)	0.16	(0.03)	503	(1.5)	516	(3.7)	539	(5.3)
	Austria	83.6	(1.1)	5.5	(0.5)	10.8	(0.7)	0.19	(0.02)	-0.50	(0.10)	-0.49	(0.04)	517	(2.7)	454	(8.6)	458	(5.3)
	Belgium	84.9	(0.9)	7.2	(0.6)	7.9	(0.6)	0.23	(0.02)	-0.26	(0.07)	-0.32	(0.07)	530	(2.1)	448	(6.5)	461	(6.6)
	Canada	70.5	(1.3)	13.0	(0.7)	16.5	(0.8)	0.45	(0.02)	0.49	(0.04)	0.19	(0.04)	522	(1.8)	528	(5.2)	514	(4.5)
	Chile	99.1	(0.2)	0.7	(0.1)	0.2	(0.1)	-0.58	(0.04)	-0.16	(0.19)	c	c	424	(3.0)	423	(13.3)	c	c
	Czech Republic	96.8	(0.4)	1.8	(0.2)	1.4	(0.3)	-0.06	(0.02)	-0.17	(0.09)	-0.15	(0.09)	501	(2.8)	486	(12.0)	461	(21.0)
	Denmark	91.1	(0.6)	2.9	(0.3)	6.0	(0.4)	0.49	(0.02)	-0.20	(0.06)	-0.25	(0.05)	508	(2.2)	430	(5.4)	448	(4.0)
	Estonia	91.8	(0.5)	0.7	(0.2)	7.5	(0.5)	0.11	(0.01)	c	c	0.06	(0.06)	524	(2.0)	c	c	496	(6.2)
	Finland	96.7	(0.2)	1.9	(0.1)	1.5	(0.1)	0.39	(0.02)	-0.38	(0.06)	-0.12	(0.05)	523	(1.9)	427	(8.0)	454	(5.0)
	France	85.2	(1.1)	4.9	(0.5)	9.9	(0.8)	0.05	(0.02)	-0.52	(0.10)	-0.53	(0.06)	508	(2.7)	425	(10.5)	448	(6.9)
	Germany	86.9	(0.8)	2.7	(0.3)	10.5	(0.7)	0.30	(0.03)	-0.24	(0.10)	-0.46	(0.05)	528	(3.2)	462	(11.2)	478	(5.8)
	Greece	89.5	(0.8)	6.3	(0.6)	4.3	(0.4)	0.00	(0.03)	-0.83	(0.06)	-0.47	(0.07)	459	(2.6)	404	(7.3)	414	(7.7)
	Hungary	98.3	(0.2)	0.7	(0.2)	1.0	(0.2)	-0.26	(0.03)	c	c	0.18	(0.12)	478	(3.1)	c	c	522	(15.2)
	Iceland	96.5	(0.3)	2.8	(0.3)	0.7	(0.1)	0.81	(0.01)	-0.02	(0.09)	c	c	498	(1.8)	437	(9.7)	c	c
	Ireland	89.9	(0.7)	8.4	(0.7)	1.7	(0.1)	0.12	(0.02)	0.17	(0.07)	0.24	(0.11)	503	(2.3)	501	(4.8)	503	(12.1)
	Israel	81.7	(1.2)	5.5	(0.6)	12.7	(0.8)	0.21	(0.03)	-0.07	(0.08)	0.08	(0.06)	470	(4.6)	469	(7.7)	480	(8.3)
	Italy	92.5	(0.3)	5.5	(0.3)	2.0	(0.2)	-0.01	(0.01)	-0.59	(0.03)	-0.45	(0.06)	490	(2.0)	435	(3.3)	461	(7.4)
	Japan	99.7	(0.1)	0.1	(0.0)	0.2	(0.1)	-0.07	(0.07)	c	c	c	c	539	(3.5)	c	c	c	c
	Korea	100.0	(0.0)	0.0	(0.0)	0.0	(0.0)	0.01	(0.03)	c	c	c	c	555	(4.6)	c	c	c	c
	Luxembourg	53.6	(0.7)	17.4	(0.5)	28.9	(0.6)	0.47	(0.01)	-0.27	(0.04)	-0.46	(0.03)	511	(1.7)	470	(4.1)	470	(2.5)
	Mexico	98.7	(0.1)	0.8	(0.1)	0.5	(0.1)	-1.10	(0.02)	-1.60	(0.16)	-1.22	(0.17)	416	(1.3)	333	(6.3)	359	(9.9)
	Netherlands	89.4	(1.0)	2.7	(0.4)	7.9	(0.9)	0.31	(0.02)	-0.19	(0.10)	-0.35	(0.06)	531	(3.4)	471	(10.1)	475	(9.0)
	New Zealand	73.7	(1.5)	16.8	(1.0)	9.5	(0.8)	0.05	(0.02)	0.14	(0.04)	-0.20	(0.06)	503	(2.7)	509	(5.2)	492	(7.1)
	Norway	90.6	(0.9)	4.7	(0.5)	4.7	(0.6)	0.52	(0.02)	-0.17	(0.07)	0.00	(0.07)	496	(2.8)	442	(6.2)	457	(9.2)
	Poland	99.8	(0.1)	0.0	(0.0)	0.2	(0.1)	-0.21	(0.03)	c	c	c	c	518	(3.6)	c	c	c	c
	Portugal	93.1	(0.6)	3.6	(0.5)	3.3	(0.4)	-0.47	(0.05)	-0.67	(0.08)	-0.57	(0.16)	493	(3.7)	451	(8.2)	445	(10.1)
	Slovak Republic	99.3	(0.2)	0.3	(0.1)	0.4	(0.1)	-0.18	(0.03)	c	c	c	c	484	(3.4)	c	c	c	c
	Slovenia	91.4	(0.4)	2.1	(0.2)	6.5	(0.4)	0.12	(0.01)	-0.58	(0.09)	-0.48	(0.06)	506	(1.2)	433	(10.3)	463	(5.3)
	Spain	90.1	(0.6)	8.4	(0.5)	1.5	(0.2)	-0.14	(0.01)	-0.68	(0.04)	-0.40	(0.12)	491	(1.9)	436	(4.8)	457	(8.5)
	Sweden	85.5	(0.9)	5.9	(0.5)	8.6	(0.7)	0.36	(0.02)	-0.38	(0.08)	-0.10	(0.06)	490	(2.3)	414	(7.3)	445	(5.3)
	Switzerland	75.9	(0.9)	6.7	(0.4)	17.4	(0.7)	0.34	(0.02)	-0.27	(0.07)	-0.37	(0.04)	548	(3.0)	472	(5.8)	489	(3.8)
	Turkey	99.1	(0.2)	0.2	(0.1)	0.7	(0.2)	-1.46	(0.04)	c	c	-1.03	(0.19)	449	(4.8)	c	c	476	(35.4)
	United Kingdom	87.3	(1.1)	7.1	(0.8)	5.6	(0.5)	0.28	(0.02)	0.19	(0.09)	0.20	(0.06)	499	(2.8)	495	(11.7)	483	(7.3)
	United States	78.5	(2.0)	6.7	(0.8)	14.8	(1.4)	0.34	(0.03)	-0.43	(0.10)	-0.39	(0.08)	487	(3.6)	463	(9.3)	478	(6.6)
	OECD average	88.8	(0.1)	4.8	(0.1)	6.4	(0.1)	0.06	(0.00)	-0.29	(0.02)	-0.27	(0.02)	500	(0.5)	453	(1.6)	469	(2.0)
Partners	Albania	0.0	c	0.0	c	0.0	c	m	m	m	m	m	m	c	c	c	c	c	c
	Argentina	96.1	(0.4)	1.5	(0.2)	2.4	(0.3)	-0.68	(0.04)	-1.54	(0.14)	-1.39	(0.13)	392	(3.4)	351	(9.5)	358	(9.4)
	Brazil	99.3	(0.1)	0.4	(0.1)	0.4	(0.1)	-1.16	(0.02)	-1.16	(0.21)	-0.62	(0.29)	394	(2.1)	339	(18.6)	337	(17.4)
	Bulgaria	99.5	(0.2)	0.2	(0.1)	0.4	(0.1)	-0.27	(0.03)	c	c	c	c	442	(3.9)	c	c	c	c
	Colombia	99.7	(0.1)	0.1	(0.1)	0.2	(0.0)	-1.26	(0.04)	c	c	c	c	378	(2.9)	c	c	c	c
	Costa Rica	94.5	(0.7)	2.1	(0.3)	3.5	(0.7)	-0.94	(0.04)	-1.34	(0.17)	-1.76	(0.20)	409	(2.9)	390	(9.9)	374	(14.1)
	Croatia	87.9	(0.8)	3.7	(0.4)	8.4	(0.5)	-0.30	(0.02)	-0.71	(0.07)	-0.54	(0.05)	474	(3.6)	453	(10.2)	456	(5.0)
	Cyprus*	91.5	(0.4)	6.7	(0.3)	1.8	(0.3)	0.10	(0.01)	-0.18	(0.05)	0.32	(0.10)	444	(1.2)	420	(5.2)	439	(11.0)
	Hong Kong-China	65.3	(1.5)	14.2	(1.0)	20.5	(0.8)	-0.56	(0.06)	-1.35	(0.04)	-1.14	(0.03)	566	(3.7)	543	(5.2)	570	(4.2)
	Indonesia	99.8	(0.1)	0.1	(0.0)	0.1	(0.0)	-1.80	(0.05)	c	c	c	c	376	(4.0)	c	c	c	c
	Jordan	86.6	(0.7)	2.8	(0.3)	10.6	(0.6)	-0.47	(0.02)	-0.07	(0.10)	-0.22	(0.06)	388	(2.8)	416	(8.9)	408	(5.1)
	Kazakhstan	83.9	(1.7)	6.5	(1.2)	9.6	(1.0)	-0.29	(0.02)	-0.67	(0.05)	-0.31	(0.06)	433	(3.1)	407	(5.8)	440	(8.2)
	Latvia	95.5	(0.5)	0.4	(0.1)	4.1	(0.5)	-0.26	(0.03)	c	c	-0.15	(0.09)	492	(2.8)	c	c	487	(8.4)
	Liechtenstein	66.7	(2.9)	13.4	(2.2)	19.9	(2.3)	0.44	(0.05)	0.06	(0.19)	0.00	(0.13)	554	(5.6)	499	(14.6)	507	(11.9)
	Lithuania	98.3	(0.3)	0.2	(0.1)	1.4	(0.1)	-0.13	(0.02)	c	c	-0.12	(0.10)	480	(2.7)	c	c	473	(8.5)
	Macao-China	34.9	(0.6)	15.5	(0.4)	49.7	(0.7)	-0.69	(0.02)	-0.90	(0.03)	-1.02	(0.01)	530	(2.1)	541	(3.0)	546	(1.8)
	Malaysia	98.3	(0.3)	0.1	(0.0)	1.7	(0.3)	-0.71	(0.03)	c	c	-1.36	(0.14)	423	(3.2)	c	c	404	(9.1)
	Montenegro	94.2	(0.4)	3.1	(0.3)	2.7	(0.2)	-0.26	(0.01)	-0.21	(0.07)	-0.01	(0.08)	410	(1.2)	427	(8.4)	436	(8.1)
	Peru	99.5	(0.1)	0.2	(0.1)	0.3	(0.1)	-1.22	(0.05)	c	c	c	c	370	(3.6)	c	c	c	c
	Qatar	48.0	(0.4)	34.7	(0.4)	17.3	(0.4)	0.42	(0.01)	0.55	(0.01)	0.25	(0.02)	335	(1.1)	443	(1.5)	388	(2.2)
	Romania	99.8	(0.1)	0.1	(0.0)	0.0	(0.0)	-0.47	(0.04)	c	c	c	c	445	(3.8)	c	c	c	c
	Russian Federation	89.1	(0.8)	3.2	(0.4)	7.7	(0.6)	-0.10	(0.02)	-0.18	(0.06)	-0.17	(0.06)	486	(3.2)	457	(7.9)	467	(4.9)
	Serbia	91.5	(0.8)	1.9	(0.3)	6.6	(0.6)	-0.30	(0.02)	-0.36	(0.12)	-0.27	(0.06)	449	(3.4)	439	(13.1)	471	(7.0)
	Shanghai-China	99.1	(0.2)	0.6	(0.1)	0.3	(0.1)	-0.35	(0.04)	-1.03	(0.24)	c	c	615	(3.2)	510	(14.6)	c	c
	Singapore	81.7	(0.8)	12.4	(0.7)	5.9	(0.3)	-0.34	(0.01)	0.22	(0.04)	-0.10	(0.05)	570	(1.6)	591	(4.3)	609	(6.4)
	Chinese Taipei	99.5	(0.1)	0.1	(0.0)	0.4	(0.1)	-0.39	(0.02)	c	c	c	c	562	(3.3)	c	c	c	c
	Thailand	99.3	(0.4)	0.0	(0.0)	0.6	(0.4)	-1.34	(0.04)	c	c	-3.29	(0.16)	428	(3.3)	c	c	412	(58.0)
	Tunisia	99.6	(0.1)	0.1	(0.0)	0.4	(0.1)	-1.19	(0.05)	c	c	c	c	389	(4.0)	c	c	c	c
	United Arab Emirates	45.1	(1.4)	31.6	(1.0)	23.3	(0.7)	0.27	(0.03)	0.47	(0.02)	0.23	(0.03)	400	(2.4)	483	(2.9)	443	(2.9)
	Uruguay	99.5	(0.1)	0.3	(0.1)	0.2	(0.1)	-0.88	(0.04)	c	c	c	c	412	(2.0)	c	c	c	c
	Viet Nam	99.9	(0.1)	0.0	(0.0)	0.1	(0.1)	-1.81	(0.05)	c	c	c	c	512	(4.8)	c	c	c	c

Notes: This table was calculated considering only students with data on the *PISA index of economic, social and cultural status*. Values that are statistically significant are indicated in bold (see Annex A3).

Students with an immigrant background are those whose parents were born in a country/economy other than the country/economy of assessment. Second-generation immigrant students were born in the country/economy of assessment but their parents were not. First-generation immigrant students were not born in the country/economy of assessment and their parents were also not born in the country/economy of assessment.

* See notes at the beginning of this Annex.

StatLink ᐧᐧᐧ http://dx.doi.org/10.1787/888932964927

[Part 2/3]

Mathematics performance and immigrant background for first- and second-generation students

Table II.3.6a   *Results based on students' self-reports*

	Difference in mathematics performance between non-immigrant and first-generation students		Difference in mathematics performance between non-immigrant and second-generation students		Difference in mathematics performance between second- and first-generation students		Difference in mathematics performance between non-immigrant and first-generation students, AFTER accounting for socio-economic status		Difference in mathematics performance between non-immigrant and second-generation students, AFTER accounting for socio-economic status		Difference in mathematics performance between second- and first-generation students AFTER accounting for socio-economic status		Increased likelihood of first-generation students scoring in the bottom quarter of the mathematics performance distribution	
	Score dif.	S.E.	Score dif.	S.E.	Score dif.	S.E.	Score dif.	S.E.	Score dif.	S.E.	Score dif.	S.E.	Ratio	S.E.
Australia	-13	(3.6)	-36	(5.1)	23	(5.7)	-14	(3.1)	-41	(4.9)	-27	(5.3)	0.98	(0.06)
Austria	62	(9.1)	58	(5.3)	4	(9.3)	35	(7.7)	32	(5.6)	-4	(8.3)	2.02	(0.20)
Belgium	82	(6.4)	69	(6.4)	13	(8.1)	59	(5.0)	44	(5.1)	-15	(6.9)	2.27	(0.17)
Canada	-6	(5.4)	8	(4.7)	-14	(5.0)	-5	(4.7)	0	(4.3)	5	(4.5)	0.98	(0.08)
Chile	1	(12.9)	c	c	c	c	15	(11.1)	c	c	c	c	1.11	(0.40)
Czech Republic	15	(12.0)	40	(20.5)	-25	(23.1)	9	(11.4)	35	(20.3)	26	(22.9)	1.05	(0.31)
Denmark	79	(5.3)	60	(4.6)	18	(6.7)	53	(5.0)	33	(3.8)	-20	(5.9)	2.50	(0.16)
Estonia	c	c	28	(6.2)	c	c	c	c	27	(5.4)	c	c	c	c
Finland	97	(7.8)	70	(5.3)	27	(9.8)	73	(7.3)	54	(5.0)	-20	(9.0)	2.80	(0.13)
France	83	(11.5)	60	(7.2)	23	(12.2)	51	(10.5)	29	(6.8)	-24	(11.4)	2.41	(0.25)
Germany	66	(11.1)	51	(6.5)	15	(11.8)	44	(10.9)	20	(6.0)	-23	(11.6)	2.00	(0.22)
Greece	55	(7.9)	45	(8.0)	10	(9.3)	28	(8.3)	29	(7.3)	-3	(9.6)	1.94	(0.21)
Hungary	c	c	-44	(14.1)	c	c	c	c	-24	(13.0)	c	c	c	c
Iceland	60	(9.8)	c	c	c	c	36	(9.5)	c	c	c	c	1.94	(0.23)
Ireland	2	(4.7)	0	(12.5)	2	(12.6)	4	(4.7)	5	(12.2)	0	(12.9)	1.04	(0.12)
Israel	1	(7.9)	-11	(6.8)	11	(9.1)	-14	(6.8)	-17	(5.9)	-6	(8.6)	0.95	(0.15)
Italy	55	(3.7)	30	(7.3)	25	(7.9)	38	(3.5)	17	(6.5)	-21	(7.4)	1.96	(0.10)
Japan	c	c	c	c	c	c	c	c	c	c	c	c	c	c
Korea	c	c	c	c	c	c	c	c	c	c	c	c	c	c
Luxembourg	41	(4.7)	40	(3.4)	0	(4.6)	11	(4.6)	11	(3.5)	-7	(4.5)	1.64	(0.10)
Mexico	82	(6.2)	57	(9.8)	25	(11.9)	73	(5.3)	55	(8.3)	-19	(10.3)	2.78	(0.19)
Netherlands	60	(10.2)	56	(8.5)	4	(12.6)	41	(10.8)	32	(8.9)	-6	(12.9)	1.83	(0.31)
New Zealand	-6	(5.7)	11	(7.9)	-17	(8.1)	-2	(4.6)	-1	(7.2)	-2	(7.4)	1.07	(0.09)
Norway	54	(6.6)	39	(9.7)	15	(9.5)	33	(6.9)	23	(9.0)	-11	(9.0)	2.06	(0.17)
Poland	c	c	c	c	c	c	c	c	c	c	c	c	c	c
Portugal	42	(7.9)	47	(10.3)	-6	(11.5)	35	(7.0)	44	(11.8)	9	(11.9)	1.85	(0.18)
Slovak Republic	c	c	c	c	c	c	c	c	c	c	c	c	c	c
Slovenia	74	(10.4)	43	(5.4)	30	(11.3)	45	(9.0)	20	(4.9)	-27	(10.3)	2.30	(0.26)
Spain	55	(4.5)	35	(8.2)	21	(8.6)	38	(4.6)	26	(7.9)	-14	(8.5)	2.05	(0.14)
Sweden	77	(7.4)	45	(5.6)	31	(7.8)	52	(7.5)	31	(5.1)	-25	(7.9)	2.42	(0.18)
Switzerland	76	(5.1)	59	(3.2)	17	(4.9)	55	(4.3)	37	(3.3)	-20	(4.5)	2.04	(0.11)
Turkey	c	c	-27	(35.5)	c	c	c	c	-14	(31.8)	c	c	c	c
United Kingdom	4	(11.3)	16	(7.1)	-12	(11.4)	0	(9.1)	13	(6.1)	12	(10.0)	1.21	(0.18)
United States	23	(9.3)	8	(6.3)	15	(9.7)	-6	(7.4)	-19	(5.5)	-14	(8.0)	1.45	(0.18)
OECD average	45	(1.6)	31	(2.0)	10	(2.1)	29	(1.4)	18	(1.9)	-10	(2.0)	1.80	(0.04)
Albania	c	c	c	c	c	c	m	m	m	m	m	m	c	c
Argentina	41	(10.2)	34	(8.3)	7	(12.5)	19	(10.3)	16	(8.9)	-5	(12.6)	1.63	(0.41)
Brazil	55	(17.9)	57	(17.6)	-2	(27.9)	55	(17.6)	71	(17.7)	12	(28.3)	2.29	(0.44)
Bulgaria	c	c	c	c	c	c	c	c	c	c	c	c	c	c
Colombia	c	c	c	c	c	c	c	c	c	c	c	c	c	c
Costa Rica	19	(10.3)	35	(13.7)	-16	(17.8)	10	(8.6)	16	(9.8)	5	(13.9)	1.57	(0.31)
Croatia	21	(9.9)	18	(4.9)	3	(9.7)	6	(10.2)	10	(4.4)	2	(9.8)	1.33	(0.21)
Cyprus*	25	(5.4)	6	(11.2)	19	(12.1)	14	(5.1)	14	(10.0)	5	(11.1)	1.53	(0.12)
Hong Kong-China	23	(6.2)	-3	(4.3)	26	(5.5)	0	(5.1)	-19	(4.0)	-22	(5.0)	1.41	(0.13)
Indonesia	c	c	c	c	c	c	c	c	c	c	c	c	c	c
Jordan	-28	(8.8)	-20	(4.2)	-8	(8.3)	-18	(7.6)	-14	(4.0)	4	(7.6)	0.77	(0.15)
Kazakhstan	27	(6.4)	-7	(7.9)	34	(9.9)	17	(6.3)	-7	(7.4)	-26	(10.0)	1.52	(0.18)
Latvia	c	c	5	(8.1)	c	c	c	c	9	(8.0)	c	c	c	c
Liechtenstein	55	(16.6)	47	(14.1)	9	(20.1)	46	(16.6)	36	(14.5)	-10	(19.9)	1.64	(0.46)
Lithuania	c	c	7	(9.0)	c	c	c	c	7	(8.8)	c	c	c	c
Macao-China	-12	(3.6)	-17	(3.2)	5	(3.9)	-17	(3.6)	-23	(3.2)	-7	(4.0)	0.98	(0.07)
Malaysia	c	c	19	(9.4)	c	c	c	c	0	(10.3)	c	c	c	c
Montenegro	-17	(8.7)	-26	(8.3)	10	(11.0)	-15	(8.3)	-18	(8.0)	-4	(10.5)	0.78	(0.18)
Peru	c	c	c	c	c	c	c	c	c	c	c	c	c	c
Qatar	-107	(1.9)	-53	(2.4)	-54	(2.6)	-104	(1.9)	-56	(2.3)	44	(2.7)	0.25	(0.01)
Romania	c	c	c	c	c	c	c	c	c	c	c	c	c	c
Russian Federation	28	(8.0)	19	(5.2)	10	(9.1)	25	(7.2)	16	(5.1)	-9	(8.4)	1.57	(0.23)
Serbia	10	(12.4)	-21	(6.4)	31	(13.1)	8	(10.7)	-21	(5.9)	-28	(11.6)	1.09	(0.26)
Shanghai-China	104	(13.9)	c	c	c	c	77	(14.7)	c	c	c	c	2.84	(0.31)
Singapore	-21	(4.8)	-39	(6.9)	18	(7.6)	4	(5.2)	-28	(6.5)	-30	(7.3)	0.74	(0.07)
Chinese Taipei	c	c	c	c	c	c	c	c	c	c	c	c	c	c
Thailand	c	c	16	(57.3)	c	c	c	c	c	c	-29	(54.1)	c	c
Tunisia	c	c	c	c	c	c	c	c	c	c	c	c	c	c
United Arab Emirates	-83	(3.5)	-43	(3.3)	-40	(3.0)	-77	(3.5)	-44	(3.2)	30	(2.7)	0.34	(0.03)
Uruguay	c	c	c	c	c	c	c	c	c	c	c	c	c	c
Viet Nam	c	c	c	c	c	c	c	c	c	c	c	c	c	c

Notes: This table was calculated considering only students with data on the *PISA index of economic, social and cultural status*. Values that are statistically significant are indicated in bold (see Annex A3).

Students with an immigrant background are those whose parents were born in a country/economy other than the country/economy of assessment. Second-generation immigrant students were born in the country/economy of assessment but their parents were not. First-generation immigrant students were not born in the country/economy of assessment and their parents were also not born in the country/economy of assessment.

* See notes at the beginning of this Annex.

StatLink ᓚᕐᗧ http://dx.doi.org/10.1787/888932964927

[Part 3/3]
Mathematics performance and immigrant background for first- and second-generation students
Table II.3.6a *Results based on students' self-reports*

	Increased likelihood of second-generation students scoring in the bottom quarter of the mathematics performance distribution — Ratio	S.E.	Population relevance of first-generation students scoring in the bottom quarter of the mathematics performance distribution — %	S.E.	Population relevance of second-generation students scoring in the bottom quarter of the mathematics performance distribution — %	S.E.	Effect size in mathematics performance for first-generation students (positive number implies an advantage for non-immigrant students) — Effect size	S.E.	Effect size in mathematics performance for second-generation students (positive number implies an advantage for non-immigrant students) — Effect size	S.E.	Increased likelihood of immigrant students scoring in the bottom quarter of the mathematics performance distribution — Ratio	S.E.	Population relevance of non-immigrant students scoring in the bottom quarter of the mathematics performance distribution — %	S.E.	Effect size in mathematics performance for non-immigrant students (positive number implies an advantage for non-immigrant students) — Effect size	S.E.
Australia	**0.69**	(0.05)	-0.2	(0.6)	-4.0	(0.7)	0.08	(0.04)	**0.36**	(0.05)	0.27	(0.03)	1.3	(0.1)	16.34	(3.43)
Austria	**1.95**	(0.15)	5.3	(1.1)	9.3	(1.3)	**-0.59**	(0.10)	**-0.60**	(0.06)	**-0.66**	(0.06)	0.5	(0.0)	-87.60	(9.78)
Belgium	**2.01**	(0.13)	8.3	(1.3)	7.4	(1.2)	**-0.79**	(0.07)	**-0.64**	(0.06)	**-0.78**	(0.05)	0.4	(0.0)	-96.64	(8.55)
Canada	1.13	(0.07)	-0.2	(1.1)	2.0	(1.2)	0.08	(0.06)	**-0.11**	(0.05)	-0.02	(0.05)	0.9	(0.1)	-5.07	(4.83)
Chile	c	c	0.1	(0.3)	c	c	-0.01	(0.16)	c	c	-0.02	(0.16)	1.0	(0.3)	-2.80	(32.18)
Czech Republic	**1.70**	(0.26)	0.1	(0.5)	1.0	(0.4)	-0.15	(0.12)	-0.35	(0.17)	-0.25	(0.11)	0.7	(0.1)	-32.54	(21.92)
Denmark	**2.18**	(0.17)	4.2	(0.4)	6.6	(1.1)	**-0.95**	(0.07)	**-0.73**	(0.06)	**-0.84**	(0.05)	0.4	(0.0)	-111.47	(10.60)
Estonia	**1.45**	(0.15)	c	c	3.3	(1.0)	c	c	**-0.35**	(0.08)	-0.38	(0.07)	0.7	(0.1)	-46.53	(12.03)
Finland	**2.31**	(0.15)	3.2	(0.4)	1.9	(0.2)	**-1.10**	(0.08)	**-0.82**	(0.07)	**-0.99**	(0.05)	0.4	(0.1)	-15.53	(9.69)
France	**1.94**	(0.18)	6.4	(1.4)	8.5	(1.7)	**-0.78**	(0.13)	**-0.59**	(0.08)	**-0.71**	(0.08)	0.4	(0.0)	-9.60	(11.43)
Germany	**1.72**	(0.17)	2.6	(0.6)	7.0	(1.6)	**-0.61**	(0.11)	**-0.53**	(0.07)	**-0.57**	(0.06)	0.5	(0.0)	-6.92	(11.31)
Greece	**1.71**	(0.20)	5.5	(1.3)	2.9	(0.9)	**-0.64**	(0.09)	**-0.49**	(0.09)	**-0.61**	(0.08)	0.5	(0.0)	-7.10	(13.93)
Hungary	**0.39**	(0.19)	c	c	-0.6	(0.2)	c	c	**0.51**	(0.15)	0.33	(0.14)	1.6	(0.7)	3.05	(24.38)
Iceland	c	c	2.6	(0.7)	c	c	**-0.67**	(0.12)	c	c	-0.58	(0.10)	0.5	(0.1)	-7.05	(19.56)
Ireland	1.01	(0.23)	0.3	(1.0)	0.0	(0.4)	-0.03	(0.06)	0.00	(0.15)	-0.02	(0.06)	1.0	(0.1)	-0.14	(9.55)
Israel	**0.77**	(0.09)	-0.3	(0.8)	-3.0	(1.2)	-0.02	(0.08)	0.11	(0.07)	0.07	(0.06)	1.2	(0.2)	1.77	(8.16)
Italy	**1.39**	(0.13)	5.0	(0.5)	0.8	(0.3)	**-0.59**	(0.04)	**-0.28**	(0.07)	-0.52	(0.04)	0.5	(0.0)	-7.01	(7.54)
Japan	c	c	c	c	c	c	c	c	c	c	c	c	c	c	c	c
Korea	c	c	c	c	c	c	c	c	c	c	c	c	c	c	c	c
Luxembourg	**1.47**	(0.08)	10.0	(1.5)	11.9	(1.8)	**-0.27**	(0.05)	**-0.33**	(0.03)	-0.44	(0.04)	0.5	(0.0)	-3.07	(3.28)
Mexico	**2.47**	(0.24)	1.5	(0.2)	0.7	(0.1)	**-1.18**	(0.10)	**-0.77**	(0.17)	-1.02	(0.09)	0.4	(0.0)	-16.65	(15.59)
Netherlands	**1.90**	(0.22)	2.2	(0.9)	6.7	(1.6)	**-0.64**	(0.12)	**-0.61**	(0.09)	-0.65	(0.07)	0.5	(0.0)	-7.57	(13.79)
New Zealand	**1.27**	(0.18)	1.2	(1.4)	2.5	(1.7)	0.07	(0.04)	-0.12	(0.07)	0.00	(0.07)	0.9	(0.1)	-1.25	(8.43)
Norway	**1.74**	(0.20)	4.7	(1.4)	3.3	(1.0)	**-0.59**	(0.08)	**-0.40**	(0.11)	-0.52	(0.08)	0.5	(0.0)	-8.95	(11.01)
Poland	c	c	c	c	c	c	c	c	c	c	c	c	c	c	c	c
Portugal	**1.79**	(0.22)	2.9	(0.7)	2.5	(0.8)	**-0.42**	(0.09)	**-0.49**	(0.10)	-0.47	(0.08)	0.5	(0.1)	-7.95	(15.42)
Slovak Republic	c	c	c	c	c	c	c	c	c	c	0.05	(0.20)	0.8	(0.2)	-2.19	(34.50)
Slovenia	**1.71**	(0.15)	2.7	(0.5)	4.4	(1.0)	**-0.79**	(0.15)	**-0.48**	(0.07)	-0.58	(0.06)	0.5	(0.0)	-7.49	(12.20)
Spain	**1.51**	(0.20)	8.1	(1.1)	0.8	(0.3)	**-0.66**	(0.06)	**-0.35**	(0.10)	-0.62	(0.05)	0.5	(0.0)	-8.39	(9.28)
Sweden	**1.62**	(0.13)	7.7	(1.2)	5.1	(1.1)	**-0.81**	(0.09)	**-0.47**	(0.06)	-0.66	(0.05)	0.5	(0.0)	-8.91	(9.62)
Switzerland	**1.98**	(0.09)	6.6	(0.7)	14.5	(1.1)	**-0.69**	(0.05)	**-0.57**	(0.03)	-0.70	(0.03)	0.4	(0.0)	-7.09	(4.57)
Turkey	1.05	(0.55)	c	c	0.0	(0.4)	c	c	0.26	(0.32)	0.03	(0.29)	0.7	(0.2)	-4.93	(45.54)
United Kingdom	**1.36**	(0.14)	1.5	(1.3)	2.0	(0.8)	-0.03	(0.12)	**-0.16**	(0.07)	-0.10	(0.07)	0.8	(0.1)	-2.56	(10.72)
United States	1.12	(0.09)	2.9	(1.2)	1.8	(1.2)	**-0.24**	(0.10)	-0.07	(0.07)	-0.14	(0.07)	0.8	(0.1)	-1.57	(8.49)
OECD average	**1.55**	(0.04)	3.5	(0.2)	3.5	(0.2)	**-0.48**	(0.02)	**-0.32**	(0.02)	-0.39	(0.02)	0.7	(0.0)	-5.14	(2.95)
Albania	c	c	c	c	c	c	c	c	c	c	c	c	c	c	c	c
Argentina	**1.46**	(0.20)	1.0	(0.6)	1.1	(0.4)	**-0.55**	(0.13)	**-0.44**	(0.10)	-0.50	(0.08)	0.7	(0.1)	-5.00	(21.25)
Brazil	**2.22**	(0.50)	0.5	(0.2)	0.5	(0.2)	**-0.69**	(0.26)	**-0.73**	(0.24)	-0.71	(0.16)	0.4	(0.1)	-12.46	(28.19)
Bulgaria	c	c	c	c	c	c	c	c	c	c	c	c	c	c	c	c
Colombia	c	c	c	c	c	c	c	c	c	c	-1.05	(0.20)	0.4	(0.1)	-14.29	(56.51)
Costa Rica	**1.87**	(0.36)	1.2	(0.7)	2.9	(1.5)	-0.26	(0.15)	**-0.51**	(0.20)	-0.42	(0.13)	0.6	(0.1)	-1.37	(22.47)
Croatia	1.16	(0.10)	1.2	(0.8)	1.3	(0.8)	**-0.22**	(0.11)	**-0.21**	(0.06)	-0.22	(0.06)	0.8	(0.1)	-9.98	(9.35)
Cyprus*	1.14	(0.33)	3.4	(0.7)	0.3	(0.6)	**-0.26**	(0.06)	-0.04	(0.12)	-0.22	(0.05)	0.7	(0.1)	-0.71	(10.14)
Hong Kong-China	0.92	(0.07)	5.5	(1.6)	-1.7	(1.6)	**-0.25**	(0.06)	0.08	(0.04)	-0.08	(0.05)	0.9	(0.1)	9.77	(5.75)
Indonesia	c	c	c	c	c	c	c	c	c	c	c	c	c	c	c	c
Jordan	**0.68**	(0.11)	-0.7	(0.5)	-3.5	(1.3)	**0.33**	(0.11)	**0.25**	(0.05)	0.29	(0.06)	1.5	(0.2)	3.19	(9.77)
Kazakhstan	0.84	(0.14)	3.3	(1.2)	-1.5	(1.4)	**-0.41**	(0.09)	0.12	(0.11)	-0.09	(0.08)	0.9	(0.1)	-0.57	(8.51)
Latvia	1.14	(0.21)	c	c	0.6	(0.9)	c	c	-0.06	(0.10)	-0.07	(0.09)	0.9	(0.1)	-4.83	(19.67)
Liechtenstein	**1.89**	(0.45)	7.9	(5.6)	15.1	(6.4)	**-0.49**	(0.19)	**-0.40**	(0.16)	-0.55	(0.14)	0.5	(0.1)	-6.70	(18.69)
Lithuania	1.03	(0.33)	c	c	0.0	(0.5)	c	c	-0.08	(0.11)	-0.01	(0.11)	1.1	(0.4)	-1.04	(29.56)
Macao-China	0.81	(0.05)	-0.4	(1.1)	-10.5	(2.9)	0.02	(0.04)	**0.14**	(0.03)	0.17	(0.03)	1.3	(0.1)	8.57	(2.13)
Malaysia	1.28	(0.28)	c	c	0.5	(0.5)	c	c	**-0.26**	(0.13)	-0.28	(0.12)	0.8	(0.2)	-6.64	(26.23)
Montenegro	**0.56**	(0.18)	-0.7	(0.6)	-1.2	(0.5)	0.19	(0.10)	**0.32**	(0.10)	0.26	(0.08)	1.5	(0.3)	11.60	(13.69)
Peru	c	c	c	c	c	c	c	c	c	c	-0.97	(0.29)	0.3	(0.0)	-15.77	(40.24)
Qatar	**0.72**	(0.04)	-35.2	(1.0)	-5.2	(0.8)	**1.03**	(0.02)	**0.08**	(0.03)	1.02	(0.02)	3.3	(0.1)	2.46	(1.63)
Romania	c	c	c	c	c	c	c	c	c	c	c	c	c	c	c	c
Russian Federation	1.18	(0.14)	1.8	(0.7)	1.3	(1.1)	**-0.32**	(0.09)	**-0.21**	(0.06)	-0.26	(0.05)	0.8	(0.1)	-7.26	(9.01)
Serbia	0.79	(0.14)	0.2	(0.5)	-1.4	(1.0)	-0.12	(0.13)	**0.24**	(0.07)	0.16	(0.07)	1.2	(0.1)	3.79	(10.86)
Shanghai-China	c	c	1.1	(0.3)	c	c	**-1.15**	(0.18)	c	c	-1.33	(0.17)	0.3	(0.0)	-20.46	(26.79)
Singapore	**0.58**	(0.08)	-3.3	(0.9)	-2.5	(0.5)	**0.18**	(0.05)	**0.35**	(0.07)	0.26	(0.04)	1.5	(0.1)	8.81	(4.63)
Chinese Taipei	c	c	c	c	c	c	c	c	c	c	-0.28	(0.21)	0.7	(0.3)	8.43	(39.00)
Thailand	1.74	(0.65)	c	c	0.5	(0.6)	c	c	-0.15	(0.57)	-0.17	(0.57)	0.6	(0.2)	-7.45	(67.00)
Tunisia	c	c	c	c	c	c	c	c	c	c	c	c	c	c	c	c
United Arab Emirates	0.81	(0.05)	-26.4	(1.7)	-4.8	(1.4)	**0.81**	(0.03)	**0.10**	(0.04)	0.81	(0.04)	2.5	(0.2)	9.53	(2.75)
Uruguay	c	c	c	c	c	c	c	c	c	c	c	c	c	c	c	c
Viet Nam	c	c	c	c	c	c	c	c	c	c	c	c	c	c	c	c

Notes: This table was calculated considering only students with data on the *PISA index of economic, social and cultural status*. Values that are statistically significant are indicated in bold (see Annex A3).
Students with an immigrant background are those whose parents were born in a country/economy other than the country/economy of assessment. Second-generation immigrant students were born in the country/economy of assessment but their parents were not. First-generation immigrant students were not born in the country/economy of assessment and their parents were also not born in the country/economy of assessment.
* See notes at the beginning of this Annex.
StatLink ⟋⟋⟋ http://dx.doi.org/10.1787/888932964927

[Part 1/6]

Change between 2003 and 2012 in the relationship between mathematics performance and immigrant background for first- and second-generation students

Table II.3.6b   *Results based on students' self-reports*

	PISA 2003																	
	Percentage of students						Average performance in mathematics						PISA index of economic, social and cultural status (ESCS)					
	Non-immigrant		Second-generation		First-generation		Non-immigrant		Second-generation		First-generation		Non-immigrant		Second-generation		First-generation	
	%	S.E.	%	S.E.	%	S.E.	Mean score	S.E.	Mean score	S.E.	Mean score	S.E.	Mean index	S.E.	Mean index	S.E.	Mean index	S.E.
Australia	77.3	(1.1)	11.7	(0.6)	11.0	(0.7)	527	(2.1)	522	(4.7)	525	(4.9)	0.08	(0.0)	-0.15	(0.0)	0.06	(0.0)
Austria	86.9	(1.0)	4.0	(0.5)	9.1	(0.7)	516	(3.2)	464	(8.3)	453	(5.9)	-0.18	(0.0)	-0.81	(0.1)	-0.76	(0.1)
Belgium	88.2	(0.9)	6.3	(0.6)	5.5	(0.6)	546	(2.5)	454	(7.5)	437	(10.8)	0.06	(0.0)	-0.71	(0.1)	-0.60	(0.1)
Canada	79.9	(1.1)	9.2	(0.5)	10.9	(0.8)	537	(1.6)	543	(4.3)	530	(4.7)	0.21	(0.0)	0.15	(0.0)	0.34	(0.0)
Czech Republic	98.7	(0.2)	0.5	(0.1)	0.8	(0.1)	523	(3.2)	c	c	500	(14.5)	-0.05	(0.0)	c	c	-0.30	(0.2)
Denmark	93.5	(0.8)	3.5	(0.6)	3.0	(0.4)	520	(2.5)	449	(11.2)	455	(10.1)	0.13	(0.0)	-0.61	(0.1)	-0.39	(0.1)
Finland	98.1	(0.2)	0.0	(0.0)	1.8	(0.2)	546	(1.9)	c	c	474	(10.6)	0.06	(0.0)	c	c	-0.14	(0.1)
France	85.7	(1.3)	10.8	(1.1)	3.5	(0.5)	520	(2.4)	472	(6.1)	448	(15.0)	-0.20	(0.0)	-1.00	(0.1)	-0.99	(0.1)
Germany	84.6	(1.1)	6.9	(0.8)	8.5	(0.7)	525	(3.5)	432	(9.1)	454	(7.5)	0.20	(0.0)	-0.93	(0.1)	-0.89	(0.1)
Greece	92.6	(0.6)	0.5	(0.1)	6.9	(0.7)	449	(3.9)	c	c	402	(6.3)	-0.27	(0.1)	c	c	-0.77	(0.1)
Hungary	97.7	(0.2)	0.1	(0.0)	2.2	(0.2)	491	(3.0)	c	c	488	(10.8)	-0.31	(0.0)	c	c	-0.35	(0.1)
Iceland	99.0	(0.2)	0.2	(0.1)	0.8	(0.2)	517	(1.4)	c	c	c	c	0.55	(0.0)	c	c	c	c
Ireland	96.5	(0.3)	1.0	(0.2)	2.5	(0.3)	503	(2.4)	474	(19.2)	509	(11.8)	-0.27	(0.0)	-0.07	(0.2)	0.17	(0.1)
Italy	97.9	(0.3)	0.4	(0.1)	1.7	(0.4)	468	(3.0)	461	(21.2)	441	(14.3)	-0.27	(0.0)	-0.06	(0.1)	-0.54	(0.1)
Japan	99.9	(0.0)	0.0	(0.0)	0.1	(0.0)	535	(4.0)	c	c	c	c	-0.41	(0.0)	c	c	c	c
Korea	100.0	(0.0)	0.0	(0.0)	0.0	c	543	(3.2)	c	c	c	c	-0.36	(0.0)	c	c	c	c
Luxembourg	66.7	(0.6)	15.8	(0.6)	17.4	(0.5)	507	(1.3)	476	(3.3)	462	(3.7)	0.15	(0.0)	-0.47	(0.1)	-0.65	(0.0)
Mexico	97.7	(0.3)	0.5	(0.1)	1.8	(0.2)	392	(3.6)	333	(29.3)	292	(12.7)	-1.27	(0.1)	-1.53	(0.3)	-1.96	(0.1)
Netherlands	89.0	(1.4)	7.1	(1.1)	3.9	(0.4)	551	(3.0)	492	(10.3)	472	(8.4)	0.00	(0.0)	-0.78	(0.1)	-0.55	(0.1)
New Zealand	80.2	(1.1)	6.6	(0.7)	13.3	(0.7)	528	(2.6)	496	(8.4)	523	(4.9)	-0.11	(0.0)	-0.47	(0.1)	-0.10	(0.0)
Norway	94.4	(0.7)	2.3	(0.4)	3.4	(0.4)	499	(2.3)	460	(11.7)	438	(9.3)	0.21	(0.0)	-0.06	(0.1)	-0.21	(0.1)
Poland	100.0	(0.0)	0.0	(0.0)	0.0	(0.0)	491	(2.5)	c	c	c	c	-0.41	(0.0)	c	c	c	c
Portugal	95.0	(1.4)	2.3	(0.4)	2.7	(1.1)	470	(2.9)	440	(14.7)	383	(22.0)	-0.91	(0.0)	-0.60	(0.2)	-1.09	(0.1)
Slovak Republic	99.1	(0.2)	0.6	(0.2)	0.3	(0.1)	499	(3.2)	432	(27.2)	c	c	-0.24	(0.0)	-0.38	(0.1)	c	c
Spain	96.6	(0.4)	0.6	(0.1)	2.8	(0.4)	487	(2.4)	450	(18.4)	440	(12.4)	-0.50	(0.0)	-0.81	(0.2)	-0.78	(0.1)
Sweden	88.5	(0.9)	5.7	(0.5)	5.9	(0.7)	517	(2.2)	483	(9.8)	425	(9.6)	0.16	(0.0)	-0.35	(0.1)	-0.48	(0.1)
Switzerland	80.0	(0.9)	8.9	(0.5)	11.1	(0.6)	543	(3.3)	484	(5.0)	453	(6.1)	-0.08	(0.0)	-0.73	(0.0)	-0.84	(0.1)
Turkey	99.0	(0.2)	0.5	(0.2)	0.5	(0.1)	425	(6.7)	c	c	385	(28.7)	-1.15	(0.1)	c	c	-0.95	(0.2)
United States	85.6	(1.0)	8.3	(0.7)	6.1	(0.4)	490	(2.8)	468	(7.6)	453	(7.5)	0.15	(0.0)	-0.36	(0.1)	-0.43	(0.1)
OECD average 2003	91.3	(0.1)	3.9	(0.1)	4.7	(0.1)	506	(0.6)	464	(3.1)	452	(2.4)	-0.17	(0.0)	-0.54	(0.0)	-0.55	(0.0)
Brazil	99.2	(0.2)	0.6	(0.2)	0.2	(0.1)	359	(4.7)	c	c	c	c	-1.55	(0.0)	c	c	c	c
Hong Kong-China	56.7	(1.4)	22.9	(0.9)	20.4	(1.3)	557	(4.5)	570	(4.6)	516	(5.3)	-1.06	(0.0)	-1.42	(0.0)	-1.69	(0.0)
Indonesia	99.7	(0.1)	0.2	(0.1)	0.1	(0.0)	363	(4.0)	c	c	c	c	-1.86	(0.0)	c	c	c	c
Latvia	90.6	(0.9)	8.3	(0.8)	1.1	(0.2)	484	(3.8)	479	(6.6)	498	(11.8)	-0.37	(0.0)	-0.18	(0.1)	0.15	(0.1)
Liechtenstein	82.9	(2.0)	7.6	(1.3)	9.4	(1.4)	545	(5.0)	c	c	482	(20.9)	-0.20	(0.0)	c	c	-0.91	(0.2)
Macao-China	23.9	(1.4)	57.9	(1.5)	18.2	(1.4)	528	(5.9)	532	(4.1)	517	(9.2)	-1.29	(0.1)	-1.67	(0.0)	-1.75	(0.1)
Russian Federation	86.5	(0.7)	6.4	(0.5)	7.0	(0.5)	472	(4.4)	457	(7.2)	452	(5.9)	-0.59	(0.0)	-0.63	(0.1)	-0.68	(0.1)
Thailand	99.9	(0.1)	0.1	(0.1)	0.0	(0.0)	419	(3.0)	c	c	c	c	-1.86	(0.0)	c	c	c	c
Tunisia	99.7	(0.1)	0.2	(0.1)	0.1	(0.0)	360	(2.5)	c	c	c	c	-1.69	(0.0)	c	c	c	c
Uruguay	99.2	(0.2)	0.4	(0.1)	0.4	(0.1)	423	(3.2)	c	c	c	c	-0.76	(0.0)	c	c	c	c

Notes: This table was calculated considering only students with data on the *PISA index of economic, social and cultural status*. Values that are statistically significant are indicated in bold (see Annex A3).

Students with an immigrant background are those whose parents were born in a country/economy other than the country/economy of assessment. Second-generation immigrant students were born in in the country/economy of assessment but their parents were not. First-generation immigrant students were not born in the country/economy of assessment and their parents were also not born in the country/economy of assessment.

For comparability over time, PISA 2003 values on the *PISA index of economic, social and cultural status* have been rescaled to the PISA 2012 scale of the index. PISA 2003 results reported in this table may thus differ from those presented in *Learning for Tomorrow's World: First Results from PISA 2003* (OECD, 2004) (see Annex A5 for more details). Only countries and economies with comparable data from PISA 2003 and PISA 2012 are shown.

StatLink ⟐ http://dx.doi.org/10.1787/888932964927

[Part 2/6]

Change between 2003 and 2012 in the relationship between mathematics performance and immigrant background for first- and second-generation students

Table II.3.6b *Results based on students' self-reports*

	PISA 2003											
	Difference in mathematics performance between non-immigrant and second-generation students		Difference in mathematics performance between non-immigrant and first-generation students		Difference in mathematics performance between second- and first-generation students		Difference in mathematics performance between non-immigrant and second-generation students, AFTER accounting for socio-economic status		Difference in mathematics performance between non-immigrant and first-generation students AFTER accounting for socio-economic status		Difference in mathematics performance between second- and first-generation students AFTER accounting for socio-economic status	
	Score dif.	S.E.	Score dif.	S.E.	Score dif.	S.E.	Score dif.	S.E.	Score dif.	S.E.	Score dif.	S.E.
Australia	5	(4.7)	2	(4.9)	-3	(4.8)	-4	(4.1)	1	(4.4)	5	(4.8)
Austria	**52**	(9.0)	**63**	(6.0)	11	(9.5)	**27**	(8.3)	**41**	(5.7)	13	(8.6)
Belgium	**92**	(7.5)	**109**	(10.9)	17	(12.4)	**56**	(6.5)	**78**	(9.2)	**22**	(10.8)
Canada	-6	(4.4)	7	(4.8)	13	(5.1)	-8	(4.1)	**11**	(4.6)	**18**	(5.4)
Czech Republic	c	c	24	(14.8)	c	c	c	c	12	(16.2)	c	c
Denmark	**70**	(11.1)	**65**	(9.8)	-5	(13.5)	**43**	(10.8)	**45**	(9.3)	-2	(12.9)
Finland	c	c	**73**	(10.7)	c	c	c	c	**67**	(9.4)	c	c
France	**48**	(6.6)	**72**	(15.0)	25	(15.5)	**16**	(5.8)	**39**	(11.3)	**25**	(12.2)
Germany	**93**	(9.6)	**71**	(7.9)	-22	(11.2)	**47**	(8.7)	**27**	(7.8)	**-21**	(10.6)
Greece	c	c	**47**	(6.7)	c	c	c	c	**30**	(6.5)	c	c
Hungary	c	c	3	(10.3)	c	c	c	c	1	(8.2)	c	c
Iceland	c	c	c	c	c	c	c	c	c	c	c	c
Ireland	29	(19.2)	-5	(11.9)	-34	(22.9)	**36**	(16.2)	10	(10.9)	-25	(18.8)
Italy	6	(20.6)	26	(13.7)	20	(24.3)	13	(24.8)	18	(12.6)	8	(26.4)
Japan	c	c	c	c	c	c	c	c	c	c	c	c
Korea	c	c	c	c	c	c	c	c	c	c	c	c
Luxembourg	**31**	(3.7)	**45**	(4.1)	**14**	(5.6)	**11**	(3.9)	**18**	(4.0)	9	(5.1)
Mexico	**60**	(27.8)	**100**	(13.2)	40	(31.1)	**53**	(26.9)	**81**	(12.1)	32	(26.1)
Netherlands	**59**	(11.1)	**79**	(8.8)	19	(10.8)	**31**	(9.0)	**58**	(8.6)	**25**	(10.2)
New Zealand	**32**	(9.1)	5	(5.6)	-27	(8.0)	**17**	(7.7)	5	(4.8)	-11	(7.4)
Norway	**39**	(11.3)	**61**	(9.4)	22	(13.8)	**28**	(9.9)	**44**	(8.5)	17	(12.0)
Poland	c	c	c	c	c	c	c	c	c	c	c	c
Portugal	**30**	(14.2)	**87**	(21.9)	**57**	(19.4)	**39**	(11.4)	**82**	(21.5)	**42**	(21.2)
Slovak Republic	**67**	(25.9)	c	c	c	c	**61**	(26.3)	c	c	c	c
Spain	**38**	(18.4)	**47**	(12.0)	9	(22.3)	**29**	(15.2)	**39**	(10.9)	10	(19.1)
Sweden	**34**	(9.1)	**92**	(9.7)	**58**	(10.9)	**17**	(8.4)	**71**	(8.5)	**54**	(9.7)
Switzerland	**59**	(4.9)	**89**	(6.0)	**31**	(6.4)	**36**	(4.8)	**62**	(5.2)	**27**	(5.5)
Turkey	c	c	40	(28.3)	c	c	c	c	49	(28.7)	c	c
United States	**22**	(7.2)	**36**	(7.5)	14	(7.4)	1	(5.4)	12	(6.5)	12	(6.3)
OECD average 2003	**43**	(3.1)	**52**	(2.4)	**14**	(3.5)	**28**	(2.9)	**38**	(2.3)	**14**	(3.2)
Brazil	c	c	c	c	c	c	c	c	c	c	c	c
Hong Kong-China	-13	(4.3)	**41**	(4.5)	**54**	(5.2)	**-23**	(4.1)	**22**	(4.8)	**48**	(5.3)
Indonesia	c	c	c	c	c	c	c	c	c	c	c	c
Latvia	5	(6.2)	-13	(11.8)	-18	(12.9)	**11**	(5.6)	5	(11.6)	-6	(12.5)
Liechtenstein	c	c	**62**	(22.7)	c	c	c	c	28	(20.0)	c	c
Macao-China	-4	(7.9)	11	(10.4)	15	(10.4)	-9	(8.0)	5	(10.3)	14	(10.5)
Russian Federation	**14**	(7.2)	**20**	(5.4)	6	(8.3)	13	(7.0)	**17**	(5.3)	4	(8.4)
Thailand	c	c	c	c	c	c	c	c	c	c	c	c
Tunisia	c	c	c	c	c	c	c	c	c	c	c	c
Uruguay	c	c	c	c	c	c	c	c	c	c	c	c

Notes: This table was calculated considering only students with data on the *PISA index of economic, social and cultural status*. Values that are statistically significant are indicated in bold (see Annex A3).

Students with an immigrant background are those whose parents were born in a country/economy other than the country/economy of assessment. Second-generation immigrant students were born in in the country/economy of assessment but their parents were not. First-generation immigrant students were not born in the country/economy of assessment and their parents were also not born in the country/economy of assessment.

For comparability over time, PISA 2003 values on the *PISA index of economic, social and cultural status* have been rescaled to the PISA 2012 scale of the index. PISA 2003 results reported in this table may thus differ from those presented in *Learning for Tomorrow's World: First Results from PISA 2003* (OECD, 2004) (see Annex A5 for more details). Only countries and economies with comparable data from PISA 2003 and PISA 2012 are shown.

StatLink ⌗⌗⌗ http://dx.doi.org/10.1787/888932964927

[Part 3/6]
Change between 2003 and 2012 in the relationship between mathematics performance and immigrant background for first- and second-generation students

Table II.3.6b — *Results based on students' self-reports*

	PISA 2012																	
	Percentage of students						Average performance in mathematics						PISA index of economic, social and cultural status (ESCS)					
	Non-immigrant		Second-generation		First-generation		Non-immigrant		Second-generation		First-generation		Non-immigrant		Second-generation		First-generation	
	%	S.E.	%	S.E.	%	S.E.	Mean score	S.E.	Mean score	S.E.	Mean score	S.E.	Mean index	S.E.	Mean index	S.E.	Mean index	S.E.
OECD																		
Australia	77.3	(0.7)	12.4	(0.6)	10.2	(0.4)	503	(1.5)	539	(5.3)	516	(3.7)	0.28	(0.01)	0.16	(0.03)	0.26	(0.03)
Austria	83.6	(1.1)	10.8	(0.7)	5.5	(0.5)	517	(2.7)	458	(5.3)	454	(8.6)	0.19	(0.02)	-0.49	(0.04)	-0.50	(0.10)
Belgium	84.9	(0.9)	7.9	(0.6)	7.2	(0.6)	530	(2.1)	461	(6.6)	448	(6.5)	0.23	(0.02)	-0.32	(0.07)	-0.26	(0.07)
Canada	70.5	(1.3)	16.5	(0.8)	13.0	(0.7)	522	(1.8)	514	(4.5)	528	(5.2)	0.45	(0.02)	0.19	(0.04)	0.49	(0.04)
Czech Republic	96.8	(0.4)	1.4	(0.3)	1.8	(0.2)	501	(2.8)	461	(21.0)	486	(12.0)	-0.06	(0.02)	-0.15	(0.09)	-0.17	(0.09)
Denmark	91.1	(0.6)	6.0	(0.4)	2.9	(0.2)	508	(2.2)	448	(4.0)	430	(5.4)	0.49	(0.02)	-0.25	(0.05)	-0.20	(0.06)
Finland	96.7	(0.2)	1.5	(0.1)	1.9	(0.1)	523	(1.9)	454	(5.0)	427	(8.0)	0.39	(0.02)	-0.12	(0.05)	-0.38	(0.06)
France	85.2	(1.1)	9.9	(0.8)	4.9	(0.5)	508	(2.7)	448	(6.9)	425	(10.5)	0.05	(0.02)	-0.53	(0.05)	-0.52	(0.08)
Germany	86.9	(0.9)	10.5	(0.7)	2.7	(0.3)	528	(3.2)	478	(5.8)	462	(11.2)	0.30	(0.02)	-0.46	(0.05)	-0.24	(0.10)
Greece	89.5	(0.8)	4.3	(0.4)	6.3	(0.6)	459	(2.6)	414	(7.7)	404	(7.3)	0.00	(0.03)	-0.47	(0.07)	-0.83	(0.06)
Hungary	98.3	(0.2)	1.0	(0.2)	0.7	(0.2)	478	(3.1)	522	(15.2)	c	c	-0.26	(0.03)	0.18	(0.12)	c	c
Iceland	96.5	(0.3)	0.7	(0.1)	2.8	(0.3)	498	(1.8)	c	c	437	(9.7)	0.81	(0.01)	c	c	-0.02	(0.09)
Ireland	89.9	(0.7)	1.7	(0.2)	8.4	(0.7)	503	(2.3)	503	(12.1)	501	(4.8)	0.12	(0.02)	0.24	(0.11)	0.17	(0.07)
Italy	92.5	(0.3)	2.0	(0.2)	5.5	(0.3)	490	(2.0)	461	(7.4)	435	(3.3)	-0.01	(0.01)	-0.45	(0.06)	-0.59	(0.03)
Japan	99.7	(0.1)	0.2	(0.1)	0.1	(0.0)	539	(3.5)	c	c	c	c	-0.07	(0.02)	c	c	c	c
Korea	100.0	(0.0)	0.0	(0.0)	0.0	(0.0)	555	(4.6)	c	c	c	c	0.01	(0.03)	c	c	c	c
Luxembourg	53.6	(0.7)	28.9	(0.6)	17.4	(0.5)	511	(1.7)	470	(2.5)	470	(4.1)	0.47	(0.01)	-0.46	(0.03)	-0.27	(0.04)
Mexico	98.7	(0.1)	0.5	(0.1)	0.8	(0.1)	416	(1.3)	359	(9.9)	333	(6.3)	-1.10	(0.02)	-1.22	(0.17)	-1.60	(0.16)
Netherlands	89.4	(1.0)	7.9	(0.9)	2.7	(0.4)	531	(3.4)	475	(9.0)	471	(10.1)	0.31	(0.02)	-0.35	(0.06)	-0.19	(0.10)
New Zealand	73.7	(1.5)	9.5	(0.8)	16.8	(1.0)	503	(2.7)	492	(7.1)	509	(5.2)	0.05	(0.02)	-0.20	(0.06)	0.14	(0.04)
Norway	90.6	(0.9)	4.7	(0.6)	4.7	(0.5)	496	(2.8)	457	(9.2)	442	(6.2)	0.52	(0.02)	0.00	(0.07)	-0.17	(0.07)
Poland	99.8	(0.1)	0.2	(0.1)	0.0	(0.0)	518	(3.6)	c	c	c	c	-0.21	(0.03)	c	c	c	c
Portugal	93.1	(0.6)	3.3	(0.4)	3.6	(0.5)	493	(3.7)	445	(10.1)	451	(8.2)	-0.47	(0.05)	-0.57	(0.16)	-0.67	(0.08)
Slovak Republic	99.3	(0.2)	0.4	(0.1)	0.3	(0.1)	484	(3.4)	c	c	c	c	-0.18	(0.03)	c	c	c	c
Spain	90.1	(0.6)	1.5	(0.2)	8.4	(0.5)	491	(1.7)	457	(8.5)	436	(4.8)	-0.14	(0.03)	-0.40	(0.12)	-0.68	(0.04)
Sweden	85.5	(0.9)	8.6	(0.7)	5.9	(0.5)	490	(2.3)	445	(5.3)	414	(7.3)	0.36	(0.02)	-0.10	(0.06)	-0.38	(0.08)
Switzerland	75.9	(0.9)	17.4	(0.7)	6.7	(0.4)	548	(3.0)	489	(3.8)	472	(5.8)	0.34	(0.02)	-0.37	(0.04)	-0.27	(0.07)
Turkey	99.1	(0.2)	0.7	(0.2)	0.2	(0.1)	449	(4.8)	476	(35.4)	c	c	-1.46	(0.04)	-1.03	(0.19)	c	c
United States	78.5	(2.0)	14.8	(1.4)	6.7	(0.8)	487	(3.6)	478	(6.6)	463	(9.3)	0.34	(0.04)	-0.39	(0.08)	-0.43	(0.10)
OECD average 2003	88.5	(0.1)	6.4	(0.1)	5.1	(0.1)	503	(0.5)	467	(2.3)	453	(1.6)	0.06	(0.00)	-0.31	(0.02)	-0.32	(0.02)
Partners																		
Brazil	99.3	(0.1)	0.4	(0.1)	0.4	(0.1)	394	(2.1)	337	(17.4)	339	(18.6)	-1.16	(0.02)	-0.62	(0.29)	-1.16	(0.21)
Hong Kong-China	65.3	(1.5)	20.5	(0.8)	14.2	(1.0)	566	(3.7)	570	(4.2)	543	(5.2)	-0.56	(0.06)	-1.14	(0.03)	-1.35	(0.04)
Indonesia	99.8	(0.1)	0.1	(0.0)	0.1	(0.0)	376	(4.0)	c	c	c	c	-1.80	(0.05)	c	c	c	c
Latvia	95.5	(0.5)	4.1	(0.5)	0.4	(0.1)	492	(2.8)	487	(8.4)	c	c	-0.26	(0.03)	-0.15	(0.09)	c	c
Liechtenstein	66.7	(2.9)	19.9	(2.3)	13.4	(2.2)	554	(5.6)	507	(11.9)	499	(14.6)	0.44	(0.05)	0.00	(0.13)	0.06	(0.19)
Macao-China	34.9	(0.6)	49.7	(0.7)	15.5	(0.4)	530	(2.1)	546	(1.8)	541	(3.0)	-0.69	(0.02)	-1.02	(0.01)	-0.90	(0.03)
Russian Federation	89.1	(0.8)	7.7	(0.6)	3.2	(0.4)	486	(3.2)	467	(4.9)	457	(7.9)	-0.10	(0.02)	-0.17	(0.06)	-0.18	(0.06)
Thailand	99.3	(0.4)	0.6	(0.4)	0.0	(0.0)	428	(3.3)	412	(58.0)	c	c	-1.34	(0.04)	-3.29	(0.16)	c	c
Tunisia	99.6	(0.1)	0.4	(0.1)	0.1	(0.0)	389	(4.0)	c	c	c	c	-1.19	(0.05)	c	c	c	c
Uruguay	99.5	(0.1)	0.2	(0.1)	0.3	(0.1)	412	(2.6)	c	c	c	c	-0.88	(0.03)	c	c	c	c

Notes: This table was calculated considering only students with data on the *PISA index of economic, social and cultural status*. Values that are statistically significant are indicated in bold (see Annex A3).

Students with an immigrant background are those whose parents were born in a country/economy other than the country/economy of assessment. Second-generation immigrant students were born in in the country/economy of assessment but their parents were not. First-generation immigrant students were not born in the country/economy of assessment and their parents were also not born in the country/economy of assessment.

For comparability over time, PISA 2003 values on the *PISA index of economic, social and cultural status* have been rescaled to the PISA 2012 scale of the index. PISA 2003 results reported in this table may thus differ from those presented in *Learning for Tomorrow's World: First Results from PISA 2003* (OECD, 2004) (see Annex A5 for more details). Only countries and economies with comparable data from PISA 2003 and PISA 2012 are shown.

StatLink ⟨⟩ http://dx.doi.org/10.1787/888932964927

[Part4/6]
Change between 2003 and 2012 in the relationship between mathematics performance and immigrant background for first- and second-generation students

Table II.3.6b   *Results based on students' self-reports*

	PISA 2012											
	Difference in mathematics performance between non-immigrant and second-generation students		Difference in mathematics performance between non-immigrant and first-generation students		Difference in mathematics performance between second- and first-generation students		Difference in mathematics performance between non-immigrant and second-generation students, AFTER accounting for socio-economic status		Difference in mathematics performance between non-immigrant and first-generation students AFTER accounting for socio-economic status		Difference in mathematics performance between second- and first-generation students AFTER accounting for socio-economic status	
	Score dif.	S.E.	Score dif.	S.E.	Score dif.	S.E.	Score dif.	S.E.	Score dif.	S.E.	Score dif.	S.E.
OECD												
Australia	-36	(5.1)	-13	(3.6)	23	(5.7)	-41	(4.9)	-14	(3.1)	27	(5.3)
Austria	58	(5.3)	62	(9.1)	4	(9.3)	32	(5.6)	35	(7.7)	4	(8.3)
Belgium	69	(6.4)	82	(6.4)	13	(8.1)	44	(5.1)	59	(5.0)	15	(6.9)
Canada	8	(4.7)	-6	(5.4)	-14	(5.0)	0	(4.3)	-5	(4.7)	-5	(4.5)
Czech Republic	40	(20.5)	15	(12.0)	-25	(23.1)	35	(20.3)	9	(11.4)	-26	(22.9)
Denmark	60	(4.6)	79	(5.3)	18	(6.7)	33	(3.8)	53	(5.0)	20	(5.9)
Finland	70	(5.3)	97	(7.8)	27	(9.8)	54	(5.0)	73	(7.3)	20	(9.0)
France	60	(7.2)	83	(11.5)	23	(12.2)	29	(6.8)	51	(10.5)	24	(11.4)
Germany	51	(6.5)	66	(11.1)	15	(11.8)	20	(6.0)	44	(10.9)	23	(11.6)
Greece	45	(8.0)	55	(7.9)	10	(9.3)	29	(7.3)	28	(8.3)	3	(9.6)
Hungary	-44	(14.1)	c	c	c	c	-24	(13.0)	c	c	c	c
Iceland	c	c	60	(9.8)	c	c	c	c	36	(9.5)	c	c
Ireland	0	(12.5)	2	(4.7)	2	(12.6)	5	(12.2)	4	(4.7)	0	(12.9)
Italy	30	(7.3)	55	(3.7)	25	(7.9)	17	(6.5)	38	(3.5)	21	(7.4)
Japan	c	c	c	c	c	c	c	c	c	c	c	c
Korea	c	c	c	c	c	c	c	c	c	c	c	c
Luxembourg	40	(3.4)	41	(4.7)	0	(4.6)	11	(3.5)	11	(4.6)	7	(4.5)
Mexico	57	(9.8)	82	(6.2)	25	(11.9)	55	(8.3)	73	(5.3)	19	(10.3)
Netherlands	56	(8.5)	60	(10.2)	4	(12.6)	32	(8.9)	41	(10.8)	6	(12.9)
New Zealand	11	(7.9)	-6	(5.7)	-17	(8.1)	-1	(7.2)	-2	(4.6)	2	(7.4)
Norway	39	(9.7)	54	(6.6)	15	(9.5)	23	(9.0)	33	(6.9)	11	(9.0)
Poland	c	c	c	c	c	c	c	c	c	c	c	c
Portugal	47	(10.3)	42	(7.9)	-6	(11.5)	44	(11.8)	35	(7.0)	-9	(11.9)
Slovak Republic	c	c	c	c	c	c	c	c	c	c	c	c
Spain	35	(8.2)	55	(4.5)	21	(8.6)	26	(7.9)	38	(4.6)	14	(8.5)
Sweden	45	(5.6)	77	(7.4)	31	(7.8)	31	(5.1)	52	(7.5)	25	(7.9)
Switzerland	59	(3.2)	76	(5.1)	17	(4.9)	37	(3.3)	55	(4.3)	20	(4.5)
Turkey	-27	(35.5)	c	c	c	c	-14	(31.8)	c	c	c	c
United States	8	(6.3)	23	(9.3)	15	(9.7)	-19	(5.5)	-6	(7.4)	14	(8.0)
OECD average 2003	32	(2.3)	49	(1.6)	10	(2.2)	19	(2.1)	32	(1.5)	11	(2.1)
Partners												
Brazil	57	(17.6)	55	(17.9)	-2	(27.9)	71	(17.7)	55	(17.6)	-12	(28.3)
Hong Kong-China	-3	(4.3)	23	(6.2)	26	(5.5)	-19	(4.0)	0	(5.1)	22	(5.0)
Indonesia	c	c	c	c	c	c	c	c	c	c	c	c
Latvia	5	(8.1)	c	c	c	c	9	(8.0)	c	c	c	c
Liechtenstein	47	(14.1)	55	(16.6)	9	(20.1)	36	(14.5)	46	(16.6)	10	(19.9)
Macao-China	-17	(3.2)	-12	(3.6)	5	(3.9)	-23	(3.2)	-17	(3.6)	7	(4.0)
Russian Federation	19	(5.2)	28	(8.0)	10	(9.1)	16	(5.1)	25	(7.2)	9	(8.4)
Thailand	16	(57.3)	c	c	c	c	-29	(54.1)	c	c	c	c
Tunisia	c	c	c	c	c	c	c	c	c	c	c	c
Uruguay	c	c	c	c	c	c	c	c	c	c	c	c

Notes: This table was calculated considering only students with data on the *PISA index of economic, social and cultural status*. Values that are statistically significant are indicated in bold (see Annex A3).

Students with an immigrant background are those whose parents were born in a country/economy other than the country/economy of assessment. Second-generation immigrant students were born in in the country/economy of assessment but their parents were not. First-generation immigrant students were not born in the country/economy of assessment and their parents were also not born in the country/economy of assessment.

For comparability over time, PISA 2003 values on the *PISA index of economic, social and cultural status* have been rescaled to the PISA 2012 scale of the index. PISA 2003 results reported in this table may thus differ from those presented in *Learning for Tomorrow's World: First Results from PISA 2003* (OECD, 2004) (see Annex A5 for more details). Only countries and economies with comparable data from PISA 2003 and PISA 2012 are shown.

StatLink ⫯⫯⫯⫯ http://dx.doi.org/10.1787/888932964927

[Part 5/6]
Change between 2003 and 2012 in the relationship between mathematics performance and immigrant background for first- and second-generation students

Table II.3.6b *Results based on students' self-reports*

	Change between PISA 2003 and PISA 2012 (PISA 2012 - PISA 2003)																	
	Percentage of students						Average performance in mathematics						PISA index of economic, social and cultural status (ESCS)					
	Non-immigrant		Second-generation		First-generation		Non-immigrant		Second-generation		First-generation		Non-immigrant		Second-generation		First-generation	
	% dif.	S.E.	% dif.	S.E.	% dif.	S.E.	Score dif.	S.E.	Score dif.	S.E.	Score dif.	S.E.	Dif.	S.E.	Dif.	S.E.	Dif.	S.E.
Australia	0.1	(1.4)	0.7	(0.8)	-0.7	(0.8)	-24	(3.2)	17	(7.3)	-9	(6.5)	0.20	(0.02)	0.31	(0.05)	0.20	(0.06)
Austria	-3.3	(1.4)	6.9	(0.8)	-3.6	(0.9)	0	(4.6)	-6	(10.0)	1	(10.6)	0.37	(0.03)	0.32	(0.10)	0.26	(0.11)
Belgium	-3.3	(1.3)	1.6	(0.8)	1.7	(0.9)	-16	(3.8)	7	(10.2)	11	(12.7)	0.17	(0.03)	0.38	(0.10)	0.34	(0.10)
Canada	-9.3	(1.7)	7.2	(1.0)	2.1	(1.1)	-15	(3.1)	-29	(6.5)	-2	(7.3)	0.24	(0.02)	0.03	(0.06)	0.14	(0.06)
Czech Republic	-1.9	(0.4)	0.9	(0.3)	1.0	(0.3)	-22	(4.6)	c	c	-14	(18.9)	-0.01	(0.03)	c	c	0.12	(0.18)
Denmark	-2.4	(1.0)	2.5	(0.7)	-0.1	(0.4)	-11	(3.9)	-1	(12.1)	-25	(11.6)	0.37	(0.04)	0.36	(0.13)	0.20	(0.12)
Finland	-1.5	(0.3)	1.5	(0.1)	0.0	(0.3)	-23	(3.3)	c	c	-47	(13.4)	0.32	(0.03)	c	c	-0.24	(0.13)
France	-0.5	(1.7)	-0.9	(1.4)	1.4	(0.7)	-12	(4.1)	-24	(9.4)	-23	(18.4)	0.25	(0.03)	0.47	(0.07)	0.47	(0.16)
Germany	2.3	(1.4)	3.5	(1.0)	-5.8	(0.8)	3	(5.1)	46	(11.0)	8	(13.6)	0.10	(0.04)	0.47	(0.10)	0.65	(0.12)
Greece	-3.1	(1.1)	3.7	(0.4)	-0.6	(0.9)	10	(5.1)	c	c	2	(9.8)	0.28	(0.06)	c	c	-0.05	(0.08)
Hungary	0.5	(0.3)	0.9	(0.2)	-1.5	(0.3)	-13	(4.7)	c	c	c	c	0.05	(0.04)	c	c	c	c
Iceland	-2.5*	(0.4)	0.5	(0.2)	2.0	(0.4)	-19	(3.0)	c	c	c	c	0.25	(0.02)	c	c	c	c
Ireland	-6.7	(0.8)	0.7	(0.3)	5.9	(0.7)	0	(3.9)	29	(22.7)	-8	(12.9)	0.39	(0.04)	0.31	(0.23)	0.00	(0.13)
Italy	-5.3	(0.4)	1.6	(0.2)	3.8	(0.3)	23	(4.1)	-1	(22.6)	-6	(14.8)	0.26	(0.03)	-0.39	(0.21)	-0.05	(0.13)
Japan	-0.2	(0.1)	0.2	(0.1)	0.1	(0.1)	4	(5.7)	c	c	c	c	0.34	(0.03)	c	c	c	c
Korea	0.0	(0.0)	0.0	(0.0)	0.0	c	12	(5.9)	c	c	c	c	0.37	(0.04)	c	c	c	c
Luxembourg	-13.1	(0.9)	13.1	(0.9)	0.0	(0.7)	3	(2.9)	-6	(4.6)	8	(5.9)	0.33	(0.02)	0.01	(0.06)	0.38	(0.06)
Mexico	1.0	(0.3)	0.0	(0.1)	-1.0	(0.2)	24	(4.3)	26	(31.0)	41	(14.3)	0.18	(0.06)	0.31	(0.33)	0.36	(0.19)
Netherlands	0.4	(1.7)	0.9	(1.4)	-1.2	(0.6)	-20	(4.9)	-17	(13.8)	-1	(13.3)	0.31	(0.04)	0.43	(0.10)	0.36	(0.15)
New Zealand	-6.5	(1.9)	2.9	(1.0)	3.6	(1.2)	-25	(4.2)	-4	(11.2)	-14	(7.4)	0.16	(0.03)	0.27	(0.09)	0.24	(0.06)
Norway	-3.8	(1.1)	2.4	(0.7)	1.3	(0.6)	-3	(4.1)	-3	(15.0)	4	(11.3)	0.32	(0.03)	0.07	(0.14)	0.04	(0.12)
Poland	-0.1	(0.3)	0.1	(0.1)	0.0	(0.0)	28	(4.8)	c	c	c	c	0.20	(0.04)	c	c	c	c
Portugal	-1.8	(1.6)	1.0	(0.6)	0.8	(1.2)	23	(5.1)	6	(17.9)	68	(23.6)	0.43	(0.07)	0.03	(0.23)	0.42	(0.13)
Slovak Republic	0.1	(0.2)	-0.2	(0.2)	0.0	(0.1)	-15	(5.0)	c	c	c	c	0.07	(0.04)	c	c	c	c
Spain	-6.5	(0.7)	0.9	(0.2)	5.5	(0.6)	4	(3.5)	7	(20.4)	-4	(13.5)	0.36	(0.05)	0.42	(0.27)	0.11	(0.13)
Sweden	-3.0	(1.2)	3.0	(0.8)	0.0	(0.8)	-27	(3.7)	-38	(11.3)	-11	(12.2)	0.20	(0.03)	0.25	(0.10)	0.10	(0.12)
Switzerland	-4.1	(1.3)	8.5	(0.9)	-4.3	(0.7)	5	(4.9)	6	(6.6)	19	(8.6)	0.42	(0.04)	0.37	(0.06)	0.57	(0.09)
Turkey	0.1	(0.3)	0.2	(0.3)	-0.3	(0.2)	24	(8.5)	c	c	c	c	-0.31	(0.07)	c	c	c	c
United States	-7.0	(2.2)	6.4	(1.6)	0.6	(0.9)	-3	(5.0)	11	(10.2)	10	(12.1)	0.19	(0.04)	-0.03	(0.13)	-0.01	(0.13)
OECD average 2003	-2.8	(0.2)	2.4	(0.1)	0.4	(0.1)	-3	(0.9)	1	(3.4)	0	(2.8)	0.23	(0.01)	0.23	(0.04)	0.21	(0.03)
Brazil	0.0	(0.2)	-0.2	(0.2)	0.2	(0.1)	35	(5.5)	c	c	c	c	0.39	(0.05)	c	c	c	c
Hong Kong-China	8.6	(2.1)	-2.5	(1.2)	-6.1	(1.6)	10	(6.2)	0	(6.5)	27	(7.7)	0.50	(0.07)	0.28	(0.05)	0.35	(0.05)
Indonesia	0.1	(0.1)	-0.1	(0.1)	0.0	(0.0)	13	(6.0)	c	c	c	c	0.06	(0.06)	c	c	c	c
Latvia	4.9	(1.1)	-4.1	(1.0)	-0.8	(0.2)	8	(5.1)	7	(10.9)	c	c	0.10	(0.04)	0.03	(0.11)	c	c
Liechtenstein	-16.2	(3.5)	12.3	(2.6)	4.0	(2.7)	9	(7.7)	c	c	16	(25.6)	0.63	(0.07)	c	c	0.97	(0.29)
Macao-China	11.0	(1.5)	-8.2	(1.7)	-2.7	(1.4)	2	(6.5)	15	(4.9)	24	(9.9)	0.60	(0.08)	0.65	(0.03)	0.85	(0.07)
Russian Federation	2.6	(1.1)	1.3	(0.8)	-3.8	(0.7)	14	(5.8)	10	(8.9)	5	(10.1)	0.50	(0.04)	0.46	(0.09)	0.50	(0.09)
Thailand	-0.5	(0.4)	0.5	(0.4)	0.0	(0.0)	9	(4.9)	c	c	c	c	0.52	(0.06)	c	c	c	c
Tunisia	-0.2	(0.1)	0.2	(0.1)	0.0	(0.1)	29	(5.1)	c	c	c	c	0.50	(0.06)	c	c	c	c
Uruguay	0.3	(0.2)	-0.2	(0.1)	-0.1	(0.2)	-11	(4.6)	c	c	c	c	-0.12	(0.05)	c	c	c	c

Notes: This table was calculated considering only students with data on the *PISA index of economic, social and cultural status*. Values that are statistically significant are indicated in bold (see Annex A3).

Students with an immigrant background are those whose parents were born in a country/economy other than the country/economy of assessment. Second-generation immigrant students were born in the country/economy of assessment but their parents were not. First-generation immigrant students were not born in the country/economy of assessment and their parents were also not born in the country/economy of assessment.

For comparability over time, PISA 2003 values on the *PISA index of economic, social and cultural status* have been rescaled to the PISA 2012 scale of the index. PISA 2003 results reported in this table may thus differ from those presented in *Learning for Tomorrow's World: First Results from PISA 2003* (OECD, 2004) (see Annex A5 for more details). Only countries and economies with comparable data from PISA 2003 and PISA 2012 are shown.

StatLink ⟨⟩ http://dx.doi.org/10.1787/888932964927

[Part 6/6]

Change between 2003 and 2012 in the relationship between mathematics performance and immigrant background for first- and second-generation students

Table II.3.6b   *Results based on students' self-reports*

		Change between PISA 2003 and PISA 2012 (PISA 2012 - PISA 2003)										
		Difference in mathematics performance between non-immigrant and second-generation students		Difference in mathematics performance between non-immigrant and first-generation students		Difference in mathematics performance between second- and first-generation students		Difference in mathematics performance between non-immigrant and second-generation students, AFTER accounting for socio-economic status		Difference in mathematics performance between non-immigrant and first-generation students AFTER accounting for socio-economic status		Difference in mathematics performance between second- and first-generation students AFTER accounting for socio-economic status	
		Score dif.	S.E.	Score dif.	S.E.	Score dif.	S.E.	Score dif.	S.E.	Score dif.	S.E.	Score dif.	S.E.
OECD	Australia	**-41**	(7.4)	**-15**	(5.8)	**26**	(7.7)	**-37**	(6.7)	**-15**	(5.3)	**22**	(7.2)
	Austria	6	(10.8)	-1	(10.4)	-7	(13.4)	4	(9.8)	-5	(8.9)	-9	(11.7)
	Belgium	**-23**	(9.5)	**-27**	(13.4)	-4	(15.6)	-13	(8.4)	**-19**	(11.0)	-6	(14.0)
	Canada	**14**	(6.4)	-13	(7.4)	**-27**	(7.3)	8	(6.0)	**-16**	(6.6)	**-24**	(7.1)
	Czech Republic	c	c	-9	(19.0)	c	c	c	c	-2	(20.3)	c	c
	Denmark	-10	(11.9)	14	(11.3)	24	(15.0)	-10	(11.3)	7	(10.6)	20	(14.5)
	Finland	c	c	24	(13.6)	c	c	c	c	8	(12.1)	c	c
	France	12	(9.2)	11	(19.0)	-1	(20.4)	**22**	(7.8)	21	(15.3)	-1	(17.4)
	Germany	**-43**	(11.3)	-5	(13.7)	**38**	(15.8)	**-28**	(9.6)	17	(13.8)	**43**	(15.6)
	Greece	c	c	8	(10.2)	c	c	c	c	-3	(10.7)	c	c
	Hungary	c	c	c	c	c	c	c	c	c	c	c	c
	Iceland	c	c	c	c	c	c	c	c	c	c	c	c
	Ireland	-29	(21.1)	8	(12.7)	37	(24.1)	-32	(19.2)	-7	(11.9)	27	(21.8)
	Italy	23	(21.7)	**28**	(13.4)	5	(25.2)	4	(25.3)	19	(12.6)	14	(27.7)
	Japan	c	c	c	c	c	c	c	c	c	c	c	c
	Korea	c	c	c	c	c	c	c	c	c	c	c	c
	Luxembourg	10	(5.3)	-4	(5.9)	**-14**	(6.9)	0	(5.2)	-2	(5.4)	-2	(6.3)
	Mexico	-3	(30.5)	-18	(14.5)	-15	(33.9)	1	(28.7)	-13	(13.1)	-14	(31.4)
	Netherlands	-3	(15.6)	-19	(12.7)	-16	(18.2)	1	(13.8)	-17	(13.5)	-17	(18.3)
	New Zealand	-21	(11.2)	-11	(6.9)	10	(11.4)	-16	(9.4)	-7	(6.5)	8	(10.2)
	Norway	0	(14.5)	-7	(11.3)	-7	(17.0)	-9	(12.8)	-17	(10.4)	-8	(15.4)
	Poland	c	c	c	c	c	c	c	c	c	c	c	c
	Portugal	17	(17.5)	**-45**	(23.6)	**-63**	(22.3)	5	(15.8)	**-46**	(22.5)	**-49**	(22.5)
	Slovak Republic	c	c	c	c	c	c	c	c	c	c	c	c
	Spain	-3	(20.5)	8	(12.7)	11	(24.2)	-1	(16.5)	1	(11.6)	3	(20.7)
	Sweden	11	(10.9)	-16	(11.1)	**-27**	(11.8)	13	(9.8)	-19	(10.2)	-30	(10.7)
	Switzerland	0	(5.6)	-13	(7.5)	-13	(8.1)	-2	(5.1)	-8	(6.5)	-7	(7.3)
	Turkey	c	c	c	c	c	c	c	c	c	c	c	c
	United States	-14	(9.1)	-13	(11.9)	1	(11.2)	**-22**	(7.3)	**-21**	(9.1)	2	(9.8)
	OECD average 2003	-5	(3.4)	-5	(2.8)	-2	(4.1)	-6	(3.1)	-7	(2.6)	-	(3.8)
Partners	Brazil	c	c	c	c	c	c	c	c	c	c	c	c
	Hong Kong-China	10	(5.6)	**-18**	(7.4)	**-28**	(7.1)	4	(5.4)	**-22**	(6.8)	-26	(6.8)
	Indonesia	c	c	c	c	c	c	c	c	c	c	c	c
	Latvia	1	(9.5)	c	c	c	c	-2	(8.9)	c	c	c	c
	Liechtenstein	c	c	-7	(30.4)	c	c	c	c	6	(27.6)	c	c
	Macao-China	-12	(8.2)	**-22**	(11.1)	-10	(11.2)	-12	(8.3)	-18	(11.0)	-	(11.4)
	Russian Federation	5	(7.8)	9	(9.3)	4	(12.9)	3	(7.5)	9	(8.7)		(12.3)
	Thailand	c	c	c	c	c	c	c	c	c	c	c	c
	Tunisia	c	c	c	c	c	c	c	c	c	c	c	c
	Uruguay	c	c	c	c	c	c	c	c	c	c	c	c

Notes: This table was calculated considering only students with data on the *PISA index of economic, social and cultural status*. Values that are statistically significant are indicated in bold (see Annex A3).

Students with an immigrant background are those whose parents were born in a country/economy other than the country/economy of assessment. Second-generation immigrant students were born in in the country/economy of assessment but their parents were not. First-generation immigrant students were not born in the country/economy of assessment and their parents were also not born in the country/economy of assessment.

For comparability over time, PISA 2003 values on the *PISA index of economic, social and cultural status* have been rescaled to the PISA 2012 scale of the index. PISA 2003 results reported in this table may thus differ from those presented in *Learning for Tomorrow's World: First Results from PISA 2003* (OECD, 2004) (see Annex A5 for more details). Only countries and economies with comparable data from PISA 2003 and PISA 2012 are shown.

StatLink ⏱ http://dx.doi.org/10.1787/888932964927

[Part 1/1]
Proficiency levels in mathematics, by immigrant background for first- and second-generation students

Table II.3.7 *Results based on students' self-reports*

	All students Below Level 2 (under 420.07 score points)		All students Level 3 or above (above 482.38 score points)		Non-immigrant students Below Level 2 (under 420.07 score points)		Non-immigrant students Level 3 or above (above 482.38 score points)		Immigrant students Below Level 2 (under 420.07 score points)		Immigrant students Level 3 or above (above 482.38 score points)		First-generation students Below Level 2 (under 420.07 score points)		First-generation students Level 3 or above (above 482.38 score points)		Second-generation students Below Level 2 (under 420.07 score points)		Second-generation students Level 3 or above (above 482.38 score points)	
	%	S.E.	%	S.E.	%	S.E.	%	S.E.	%	S.E.	%	S.E.	%	S.E.	%	S.E.	%	S.E.	%	S.E.
Australia	19.8	(0.6)	58.4	(0.8)	19.2	(0.7)	58.0	(0.8)	15.5	(0.9)	66.5	(1.4)	17.9	(1.4)	62.4	(1.6)	13.6	(1.1)	69.9	(2.1)
Austria	18.8	(1.0)	59.4	(1.2)	14.8	(0.9)	64.2	(1.3)	37.0	(2.6)	37.6	(2.6)	38.0	(4.3)	34.8	(4.0)	36.5	(3.0)	39.0	(3.1)
Belgium	19.1	(0.8)	62.6	(1.0)	14.4	(0.8)	68.3	(1.0)	38.8	(2.6)	37.3	(2.3)	42.0	(3.8)	34.7	(3.0)	35.9	(2.9)	39.7	(3.0)
Canada	13.9	(0.6)	65.1	(0.9)	12.3	(0.5)	67.0	(0.9)	14.1	(1.1)	65.3	(1.8)	13.5	(1.4)	68.0	(2.4)	14.6	(1.4)	63.2	(2.1)
Chile	51.7	(1.7)	23.1	(1.3)	51.3	(1.7)	23.5	(1.3)	c	c	22.1	(6.3)	c	c	c	c	c	c	c	c
Czech Republic	21.2	(1.2)	57.3	(1.3)	20.7	(1.2)	57.8	(1.3)	30.3	(5.4)	48.6	(5.1)	c	c	48.8	(6.8)	c	c	48.3	(6.4)
Denmark	17.0	(1.0)	58.8	(1.2)	13.5	(0.9)	62.6	(1.3)	42.0	(2.2)	29.3	(1.9)	48.7	(3.1)	24.4	(2.9)	38.6	(2.9)	31.8	(2.4)
Estonia	10.6	(0.6)	67.5	(1.0)	9.4	(0.6)	69.2	(1.1)	19.1	(3.1)	55.9	(3.3)	c	c	c	c	17.9	(3.3)	57.4	(3.7)
Finland	12.3	(0.7)	67.2	(0.9)	10.6	(0.6)	69.2	(0.8)	45.1	(2.4)	30.7	(1.9)	51.7	(3.5)	26.2	(2.6)	36.7	(3.1)	36.4	(2.9)
France	22.5	(0.9)	55.5	(1.1)	17.8	(1.0)	60.8	(1.4)	43.5	(2.9)	31.9	(2.6)	53.2	(5.0)	27.5	(4.1)	38.7	(3.4)	34.1	(2.9)
Germany	17.8	(1.0)	62.9	(1.3)	13.8	(1.1)	68.6	(1.4)	31.3	(2.8)	46.6	(3.0)	39.0	(5.9)	38.6	(5.6)	29.2	(3.2)	48.8	(3.3)
Greece	35.8	(1.3)	37.2	(1.2)	32.8	(1.4)	39.7	(1.3)	57.9	(3.5)	18.5	(2.3)	59.4	(4.4)	17.0	(2.7)	55.6	(4.7)	20.7	(3.2)
Hungary	28.2	(1.3)	46.7	(1.5)	27.9	(1.3)	46.9	(1.5)	c	c	60.1	(7.0)	c	c	c	c	c	c	69.9	(9.6)
Iceland	21.6	(0.8)	54.9	(0.9)	19.9	(0.8)	56.8	(0.9)	39.5	(5.1)	30.5	(6.7)	41.6	(5.8)	c	c	c	c	c	c
Ireland	17.0	(1.0)	59.2	(1.2)	16.6	(1.0)	59.6	(1.3)	17.8	(2.5)	59.4	(2.9)	18.3	(2.6)	59.1	(3.1)	c	c	60.9	(6.9)
Israel	33.7	(1.7)	44.9	(1.9)	33.2	(1.7)	45.5	(1.9)	27.8	(2.8)	48.3	(2.9)	30.4	(3.6)	43.5	(3.2)	26.7	(3.3)	50.3	(3.6)
Italy	24.8	(0.8)	51.3	(1.0)	22.7	(0.8)	53.3	(1.0)	42.4	(1.8)	32.8	(1.8)	45.8	(2.2)	29.5	(1.8)	33.5	(3.4)	41.8	(3.5)
Japan	11.2	(1.0)	72.0	(1.4)	10.6	(0.9)	72.8	(1.4)	c	c	c	c	c	c	c	c	c	c	c	c
Korea	9.2	(1.0)	76.2	(1.4)	9.0	(0.9)	76.4	(1.4)	c	c	c	c	c	c	c	c	c	c	c	c
Luxembourg	24.5	(0.5)	53.3	(0.6)	16.2	(0.8)	63.0	(0.9)	32.9	(1.0)	43.2	(1.1)	36.0	(1.9)	42.9	(1.8)	31.1	(1.2)	43.5	(1.5)
Mexico	54.9	(0.8)	17.5	(0.6)	53.8	(0.8)	18.0	(0.6)	87.8	(2.7)	c	c	90.9	(2.7)	c	c	82.4	(5.3)	c	c
Netherlands	14.9	(1.3)	67.3	(1.6)	12.4	(1.2)	70.7	(1.5)	29.1	(4.5)	46.6	(4.4)	27.2	(5.4)	45.7	(8.9)	29.8	(5.2)	46.9	(5.5)
New Zealand	22.8	(0.8)	55.8	(1.0)	21.0	(1.1)	57.3	(1.3)	25.0	(2.0)	54.3	(1.7)	23.2	(1.9)	57.6	(2.1)	28.2	(3.6)	48.3	(3.0)
Norway	22.5	(1.1)	53.4	(1.2)	19.8	(1.1)	56.3	(1.1)	41.1	(2.9)	33.5	(3.0)	43.9	(3.6)	28.2	(3.4)	38.2	(4.2)	38.9	(4.2)
Poland	14.5	(0.9)	63.5	(1.4)	14.3	(0.9)	63.9	(1.4)	c	c	c	c	c	c	c	c	c	c	c	c
Portugal	25.0	(1.5)	52.3	(1.8)	22.6	(1.5)	54.5	(1.8)	42.7	(3.7)	35.7	(3.2)	43.2	(4.4)	36.5	(4.1)	42.1	(4.9)	34.7	(4.4)
Slovak Republic	27.6	(1.3)	49.4	(1.6)	26.8	(1.2)	50.2	(1.6)	c	c	c	c	c	c	c	c	c	c	c	c
Slovenia	20.3	(0.6)	56.3	(0.8)	18.3	(0.6)	58.8	(0.8)	37.3	(3.2)	34.5	(3.3)	50.0	(5.8)	23.1	(4.5)	33.0	(3.5)	38.3	(4.0)
Spain	23.7	(0.8)	51.5	(1.0)	20.8	(0.8)	54.7	(0.9)	42.9	(2.8)	30.1	(2.2)	44.2	(3.1)	28.8	(2.3)	35.7	(5.2)	37.4	(5.0)
Sweden	27.2	(1.1)	48.2	(1.1)	22.3	(1.1)	52.8	(1.2)	47.5	(2.6)	28.6	(2.6)	59.2	(3.8)	21.5	(3.0)	39.2	(2.7)	33.7	(3.3)
Switzerland	12.5	(0.7)	69.8	(1.3)	8.1	(0.5)	76.7	(1.1)	24.7	(1.5)	50.8	(2.1)	29.9	(2.6)	46.3	(2.9)	22.7	(1.5)	52.5	(2.3)
Turkey	42.2	(1.9)	32.5	(2.2)	41.7	(2.0)	32.8	(2.2)	c	c	c	c	c	c	c	c	c	c	c	c
United Kingdom	21.9	(1.3)	55.0	(1.5)	20.1	(1.1)	56.7	(1.4)	27.5	(3.0)	49.9	(3.4)	26.7	(4.1)	53.3	(4.9)	28.6	(3.5)	45.6	(3.7)
United States	26.0	(1.4)	47.9	(1.7)	23.6	(1.5)	50.6	(1.9)	30.0	(2.4)	42.3	(2.9)	35.2	(4.2)	39.6	(4.2)	27.6	(2.2)	43.6	(3.2)
OECD average	23.1	(0.2)	54.5	(0.2)	20.9	(0.2)	57.0	(0.2)	36.0	(0.6)	41.8	(0.6)	40.4	(0.8)	39.1	(0.8)	34.0	(0.7)	45.2	(0.8)
Albania	60.8	(0.9)	16.4	(1.0)	61.3	(1.0)	16.1	(1.1)	c	c	c	c	c	c	c	c	c	c	c	c
Argentina	66.7	(2.0)	11.3	(1.1)	65.5	(2.1)	11.8	(1.1)	83.3	(3.2)	c	c	86.0	(5.1)	c	c	81.5	(4.5)	c	c
Brazil	67.3	(1.0)	12.5	(0.8)	66.4	(1.1)	12.9	(0.8)	82.3	(5.9)	c	c	83.1	(8.6)	c	c	81.6	(9.0)	c	c
Bulgaria	43.9	(1.8)	31.9	(1.7)	42.4	(1.7)	32.9	(1.7)	c	c	c	c	c	c	c	c	c	c	c	c
Colombia	74.0	(1.4)	8.4	(0.8)	73.5	(1.4)	8.6	(0.9)	c	c	c	c	c	c	c	c	c	c	c	c
Costa Rica	60.1	(1.9)	13.3	(1.3)	58.8	(1.9)	13.7	(1.3)	76.9	(4.0)	c	c	70.7	(5.9)	c	c	80.7	(5.3)	c	c
Croatia	30.0	(1.3)	43.4	(1.6)	29.0	(1.4)	44.8	(1.6)	35.6	(2.6)	35.4	(3.0)	37.7	(5.1)	36.1	(5.0)	34.7	(2.7)	35.1	(3.1)
Cyprus*	42.2	(0.6)	32.5	(0.6)	40.0	(0.7)	33.9	(0.7)	52.2	(2.5)	27.1	(2.5)	54.5	(2.8)	25.3	(3.0)	43.6	(7.4)	33.7	(5.6)
Hong Kong-China	8.6	(0.8)	79.5	(1.3)	8.2	(0.9)	81.2	(1.4)	8.1	(1.1)	78.8	(1.6)	10.0	(1.6)	73.8	(2.3)	6.8	(1.3)	82.2	(1.7)
Indonesia	75.9	(2.0)	7.5	(1.4)	75.7	(2.1)	7.5	(1.5)	c	c	c	c	c	c	c	c	c	c	c	c
Jordan	68.7	(1.5)	10.5	(0.9)	68.6	(1.5)	10.2	(0.9)	59.0	(3.1)	16.5	(2.2)	55.0	(5.5)	22.6	(4.8)	60.1	(3.3)	14.9	(2.2)
Kazakhstan	45.5	(1.7)	23.2	(1.7)	44.7	(1.9)	24.0	(1.8)	48.6	(3.2)	19.9	(3.0)	59.0	(4.5)	11.4	(2.2)	41.6	(4.4)	25.7	(4.3)
Latvia	20.1	(1.1)	53.4	(1.5)	19.7	(1.1)	54.0	(1.6)	22.6	(4.7)	50.3	(4.6)	c	c	c	c	22.1	(4.8)	50.1	(4.7)
Liechtenstein	14.1	(2.0)	70.7	(2.2)	c	c	77.6	(3.0)	c	c	57.5	(5.3)	c	c	c	c	c	c	56.4	(6.7)
Lithuania	26.2	(1.2)	48.0	(1.3)	25.7	(1.2)	48.6	(1.4)	c	c	44.1	(5.0)	c	c	c	c	c	c	c	c
Macao-China	10.9	(0.5)	72.8	(0.6)	13.0	(1.1)	69.2	(1.1)	9.2	(0.5)	75.2	(0.7)	11.0	(1.3)	73.4	(1.7)	8.7	(0.7)	75.8	(0.9)
Malaysia	52.0	(1.7)	22.2	(1.5)	51.0	(1.7)	22.8	(1.5)	64.6	(5.5)	c	c	c	c	c	c	63.3	(5.8)	c	c
Montenegro	56.9	(1.0)	19.1	(0.6)	56.9	(1.0)	19.0	(0.7)	45.6	(4.0)	26.6	(3.6)	47.9	(4.9)	24.9	(5.5)	43.1	(5.2)	28.5	(5.3)
Peru	74.7	(1.7)	9.3	(1.1)	74.1	(1.8)	9.5	(1.1)	c	c	c	c	c	c	c	c	c	c	c	c
Qatar	69.7	(0.5)	15.3	(0.3)	87.1	(0.5)	4.1	(0.3)	51.0	(0.9)	27.0	(0.6)	43.0	(1.1)	33.4	(0.9)	67.2	(1.3)	14.1	(0.9)
Romania	41.0	(1.9)	30.9	(1.8)	40.9	(1.9)	30.9	(1.8)	c	c	c	c	c	c	c	c	c	c	c	c
Russian Federation	24.1	(1.1)	49.5	(1.5)	22.9	(1.2)	51.0	(1.5)	29.7	(2.7)	40.9	(2.4)	36.4	(5.3)	37.9	(5.2)	27.0	(3.2)	42.2	(2.7)
Serbia	39.1	(1.5)	34.6	(1.6)	38.9	(1.6)	34.7	(1.5)	33.5	(3.7)	39.6	(3.4)	40.0	(8.2)	c	c	31.6	(3.5)	41.8	(3.7)
Shanghai-China	3.8	(0.6)	88.7	(1.0)	3.5	(0.5)	89.3	(0.9)	c	c	c	c	c	c	c	c	c	c	c	c
Singapore	8.3	(0.5)	79.5	(0.6)	8.8	(0.6)	78.7	(0.7)	4.7	(0.7)	86.2	(1.1)	5.1	(0.9)	85.1	(1.5)	c	c	88.6	(1.9)
Chinese Taipei	12.9	(0.8)	74.0	(1.1)	12.4	(0.8)	74.6	(1.1)	c	c	c	c	c	c	c	c	c	c	c	c
Thailand	50.0	(1.7)	22.9	(1.6)	49.3	(1.7)	23.2	(1.6)	c	c	c	c	c	c	c	c	c	c	c	c
Tunisia	67.9	(1.8)	11.1	(1.4)	67.5	(1.8)	11.3	(1.4)	c	c	c	c	c	c	c	c	c	c	c	c
United Arab Emirates	46.5	(1.2)	28.9	(1.1)	62.9	(1.5)	13.8	(1.0)	31.5	(1.1)	42.3	(1.4)	24.5	(1.1)	50.0	(1.6)	41.0	(1.6)	31.7	(1.6)
Uruguay	56.0	(1.3)	21.2	(1.1)	55.2	(1.3)	21.6	(1.1)	c	c	c	c	c	c	c	c	c	c	c	c
Viet Nam	14.3	(1.8)	63.0	(2.2)	14.2	(1.7)	63.1	(2.2)	c	c	c	c	c	c	c	c	c	c	c	c

* See notes at the beginning of this Annex.
StatLink ⟲ http://dx.doi.org/10.1787/888932964927

[Part 1/2]

Mathematics performance, first-generation immigrant students, and age at arrival

Table II.3.8 *Results based on students' self-reports*

	Percentage of students (out of total number of students)						Performance in mathematics						PISA index of economic, social and cultural status (ESCS)					
	First-generation students who arrived in the country when they were 5 years old or younger		First-generation students who arrived in the country when they were between 6 and 12 years old		First-generation students who arrived in the country when they were older than 12 years		First-generation students who arrived in the country when they were 5 years old or younger		First-generation students who arrived in the country when they were between 6 and 12 years old		First-generation students who arrived in the country when they were older than 12 years		First-generation students who arrived in the country when they were 5 years old or younger		First-generation students who arrived in the country when they were between 6 and 12 years old		First-generation students who arrived in the country when they were older than 12 years	
	%	S.E.	%	S.E.	%	S.E.	Mean score	S.E.	Mean score	S.E.	Mean score	S.E.	Mean index	S.E.	Mean index	S.E.	Mean index	S.E.
OECD																		
Australia	2.9	(0.2)	4.7	(0.2)	1.6	(0.2)	536	(6.7)	515	(4.2)	490	(9.1)	0.33	(0.04)	0.30	(0.04)	0.10	(0.09)
Austria	2.4	(0.3)	2.4	(0.3)	0.0	c	455	(11.0)	453	(12.1)	c	c	-0.49	(0.11)	-0.51	(0.13)	c	c
Belgium	2.6	(0.2)	2.3	(0.2)	1.4	(0.3)	478	(8.6)	456	(8.7)	433	(18.6)	-0.18	(0.09)	-0.34	(0.09)	0.33	(0.20)
Canada	4.3	(0.3)	5.6	(0.4)	1.8	(0.2)	531	(6.3)	529	(5.5)	522	(9.0)	0.56	(0.05)	0.46	(0.04)	0.40	(0.08)
Chile	0.0	c	0.0	c	0.0	c	c	c	c	c	c	c	c	c	c	c	c	c
Czech Republic	0.6	(0.1)	0.7	(0.2)	0.0	c	499	(24.4)	480	(16.0)	c	c	-0.08	(0.13)	-0.23	(0.15)	c	c
Denmark	1.6	(0.2)	1.0	(0.1)	0.0	c	428	(5.7)	429	(8.7)	c	c	-0.15	(0.08)	-0.25	(0.10)	c	c
Estonia	0.0	c	0.0	c	0.0	c	c	c	c	c	c	c	c	c	c	c	c	c
Finland	0.7	(0.1)	0.9	(0.1)	0.2	(0.0)	443	(6.8)	417	(13.5)	420	(20.2)	-0.32	(0.08)	-0.34	(0.07)	-0.73	(0.35)
France	2.2	(0.3)	1.5	(0.2)	0.9	(0.2)	455	(16.5)	411	(11.7)	374	(11.9)	-0.19	(0.09)	-0.87	(0.14)	-0.73	(0.14)
Germany	1.2	(0.2)	0.0	c	0.0	c	466	(13.1)	c	c	c	c	-0.25	(0.13)	c	c	c	c
Greece	3.7	(0.4)	1.5	(0.3)	0.0	c	419	(7.5)	398	(13.5)	c	c	-0.88	(0.06)	-0.74	(0.13)	c	c
Hungary	0.0	c	0.0	c	0.0	c	c	c	c	c	c	c	c	c	c	c	c	c
Iceland	0.9	(0.1)	1.5	(0.2)	0.0	c	482	(15.8)	408	(12.1)	c	c	0.04	(0.18)	-0.15	(0.11)	c	c
Ireland	2.1	(0.2)	4.5	(0.4)	1.1	(0.2)	504	(10.3)	500	(5.7)	520	(16.6)	0.29	(0.10)	0.10	(0.06)	0.41	(0.18)
Israel	3.0	(0.5)	1.6	(0.2)	0.0	c	486	(9.9)	461	(14.8)	c	c	0.02	(0.07)	-0.34	(0.25)	c	c
Italy	2.5	(0.1)	3.1	(0.2)	0.7	(0.1)	454	(5.5)	442	(4.3)	392	(8.6)	-0.3	(0.0)	-0.5	(0.0)	-0.6	(0.1)
Japan	0.0	c	0.0	c	0.0	c	c	c	c	c	c	c	c	c	c	c	c	c
Korea	0.0	c	0.0	c	0.0	c	c	c	c	c	c	c	c	c	c	c	c	c
Luxembourg	7.3	(0.4)	6.4	(0.3)	1.9	(0.2)	480	(6.4)	460	(6.1)	470	(11.5)	-0.18	(0.06)	-0.41	(0.06)	-0.28	(0.14)
Mexico	0.3	(0.0)	0.0	c	0.0	c	322	(8.3)	c	c	c	c	-1.77	(0.14)	c	c	c	c
Netherlands	1.6	(0.3)	0.6	(0.1)	0.0	c	474	(13.8)	494	(14.5)	c	c	-0.16	(0.11)	-0.49	(0.19)	c	c
New Zealand	4.9	(0.5)	8.1	(0.5)	2.7	(0.3)	529	(8.3)	503	(6.6)	497	(10.8)	0.28	(0.07)	0.07	(0.06)	0.16	(0.08)
Norway	1.8	(0.2)	2.1	(0.3)	0.0	c	445	(10.6)	452	(8.7)	c	c	0.03	(0.10)	-0.16	(0.09)	c	c
Poland	0.0	c	0.0	c	0.0	c	c	c	c	c	c	c	c	c	c	c	c	c
Portugal	1.0	(0.2)	1.8	(0.3)	0.0	c	455	(18.9)	454	(10.6)	c	c	-0.43	(0.14)	-0.77	(0.14)	c	c
Slovak Republic	0.0	c	0.0	c	0.0	c	c	c	c	c	c	c	c	c	c	c	c	c
Slovenia	0.5	(0.1)	0.9	(0.1)	0.5	(0.1)	470	(27.1)	422	(13.6)	415	(18.3)	-0.17	(0.17)	-0.55	(0.15)	-0.89	(0.15)
Spain	2.5	(0.2)	4.5	(0.3)	0.7	(0.1)	455	(7.0)	431	(4.7)	418	(13.1)	-0.52	(0.08)	-0.76	(0.04)	-0.63	(0.15)
Sweden	1.8	(0.2)	3.1	(0.3)	0.8	(0.1)	417	(11.1)	410	(8.6)	402	(24.9)	-0.42	(0.11)	-0.35	(0.10)	-0.47	(0.25)
Switzerland	2.9	(0.2)	2.5	(0.3)	0.8	(0.1)	477	(9.2)	471	(9.6)	471	(14.9)	-0.32	(0.11)	-0.25	(0.11)	-0.08	(0.16)
Turkey	0.0	c	0.0	c	0.0	c	c	c	c	c	c	c	c	c	c	c	c	c
United Kingdom	2.1	(0.2)	3.0	(0.4)	1.4	(0.4)	482	(11.9)	487	(9.9)	525	(23.8)	0.00	(0.10)	0.21	(0.09)	0.60	(0.18)
United States	3.2	(0.4)	2.5	(0.4)	0.0	c	469	(9.8)	451	(14.5)	c	c	-0.37	(0.12)	-0.54	(0.14)	c	c
OECD average	1.8	(0.1)	2.0	(0.1)	0.5	(0.1)	466	(2.4)	456	(2.2)	453	(4.3)	-0.22	(0.02)	-0.31	(0.02)	-0.22	(0.05)
Partners																		
Albania	0.0	c	0.0	c	0.0	c	c	c	c	c	c	c	c	c	c	c	c	c
Argentina	0.4	(0.1)	0.5	(0.1)	0.0	c	362	(13.7)	343	(17.7)	c	c	-1.29	(0.14)	-1.54	(0.16)	c	c
Brazil	0.0	c	0.0	c	0.0	c	c	c	c	c	c	c	c	c	c	c	c	c
Bulgaria	0.0	c	0.0	c	0.0	c	c	c	c	c	c	c	c	c	c	c	c	c
Colombia	0.0	c	0.0	c	0.0	c	c	c	c	c	c	c	c	c	c	c	c	c
Costa Rica	1.1	(0.2)	0.0	c	0.0	c	396	(14.9)	c	c	c	c	-1.35	(0.21)	c	c	c	c
Croatia	2.6	(0.4)	0.0	c	0.0	c	458	(11.5)	c	c	c	c	-0.80	(0.08)	c	c	c	c
Cyprus*	2.1	(0.2)	2.9	(0.2)	0.9	(0.1)	413	(8.9)	427	(8.2)	434	(14.8)	-0.09	(0.08)	-0.25	(0.08)	-0.07	(0.10)
Hong Kong-China	5.3	(0.5)	6.5	(0.5)	1.3	(0.3)	548	(8.1)	541	(5.8)	540	(19.4)	-1.32	(0.07)	-1.37	(0.04)	-1.25	(0.15)
Indonesia	0.0	c	0.0	c	0.0	c	c	c	c	c	c	c	c	c	c	c	c	c
Jordan	1.0	(0.2)	0.9	(0.2)	0.0	c	405	(8.4)	449	(15.1)	c	c	-0.27	(0.15)	0.37	(0.09)	c	c
Kazakhstan	1.5	(0.2)	3.2	(0.8)	0.8	(0.2)	416	(8.8)	407	(6.3)	382	(15.1)	-0.64	(0.09)	-0.69	(0.05)	-0.82	(0.13)
Latvia	0.0	c	0.0	c	0.0	c	c	c	c	c	c	c	c	c	c	c	c	c
Liechtenstein	0.0	c	0.0	c	0.0	c	c	c	c	c	c	c	c	c	c	c	c	c
Lithuania	0.0	c	0.0	c	0.0	c	c	c	c	c	c	c	c	c	c	c	c	c
Macao-China	4.8	(0.3)	7.7	(0.3)	2.2	(0.2)	536	(6.1)	544	(4.3)	553	(7.9)	-0.81	(0.05)	-0.99	(0.05)	-0.81	(0.09)
Malaysia	0.0	c	0.0	c	0.0	c	c	c	c	c	c	c	c	c	c	c	c	c
Montenegro	1.7	(0.2)	0.0	c	0.0	c	433	(11.0)	c	c	c	c	-0.07	(0.10)	c	c	c	c
Peru	0.0	c	0.0	c	0.0	c	c	c	c	c	c	c	c	c	c	c	c	c
Qatar	13.0	(0.3)	12.6	(0.3)	4.6	(0.2)	431	(2.3)	459	(2.4)	457	(4.1)	0.51	(0.02)	0.63	(0.02)	0.58	(0.03)
Romania	0.0	c	0.0	c	0.0	c	c	c	c	c	c	c	c	c	c	c	c	c
Russian Federation	1.6	(0.2)	0.9	(0.2)	0.0	c	462	(10.4)	453	(13.2)	c	c	-0.11	(0.10)	-0.30	(0.11)	c	c
Serbia	0.9	(0.2)	0.0	c	0.0	c	441	(17.3)	c	c	c	c	-0.49	(0.19)	c	c	c	c
Shanghai-China	0.6	(0.1)	0.0	c	0.0	c	538	(18.3)	c	c	c	c	-0.5	(0.2)	c	c	c	c
Singapore	3.8	(0.3)	4.8	(0.4)	3.2	(0.3)	595	(8.4)	580	(7.4)	601	(7.7)	0.21	(0.05)	0.15	(0.07)	0.38	(0.06)
Chinese Taipei	0.0	c	0.0	c	0.0	c	c	c	c	c	c	c	c	c	c	c	c	c
Thailand	0.0	c	0.0	c	0.0	c	c	c	c	c	c	c	c	c	c	c	c	c
Tunisia	0.0	c	0.0	c	0.0	c	c	c	c	c	c	c	c	c	c	c	c	c
United Arab Emirates	14.0	(0.5)	11.5	(0.6)	3.6	(0.3)	481	(3.4)	491	(4.1)	496	(5.6)	0.44	(0.03)	0.54	(0.03)	0.51	(0.04)
Uruguay	0.0	c	0.0	c	0.0	c	c	c	c	c	c	c	c	c	c	c	c	c
Viet Nam	0.0	c	0.0	c	0.0	c	c	c	c	c	c	c	c	c	c	c	c	c

Note: Values that are statistically significant are indicated in bold (see Annex A3).
* See notes at the beginning of this Annex.
StatLink http://dx.doi.org/10.1787/888932964927

[Part 2/2]
Mathematics performance, first-generation immigrant students, and age at arrival

Table II.3.8   *Results based on students' self-reports*

	Difference in mathematics performance between non-immigrant students and first-generation students (dummy for second-generation included in the model but not reported)													
	Observed		After accounting for age at arrival		Late-arrival penalty (coefficient on age)		After accounting for age at arrival and student ESCS		Late-arrival penalty (coefficient on age) after accounting for student ESCS		After accounting for age at arrival and student and school ESCS		Late-arrival penalty (coefficient on age) after accounting for student and school ESCS	
	Score dif.	S.E.	Score dif.	S.E.	Score dif.	S.E.	Score dif.	S.E.	Score dif.	S.E.	Score dif.	S.E.	Score dif.	S.E.
Australia	15	(3.6)	41	(7.4)	-3	(0.8)	35	(7.0)	-2	(0.7)	30	(6.9)	-2	(0.7)
Austria	-63	(9.3)	-73	(14.4)	2	(1.8)	-42	(12.4)	1	(1.6)	-41	(10.1)	2	(1.3)
Belgium	-82	(6.4)	-61	(9.4)	-3	(1.4)	-44	(8.1)	-2	(1.1)	-40	(7.5)	-1	(0.8)
Canada	7	(5.4)	15	(8.0)	-1	(0.7)	10	(7.1)	0	(0.7)	8	(7.0)	-1	(0.7)
Chile	c	c	c	c	c	c	c	c	c	c	c	c	c	c
Czech Republic	-15	(12.1)	10	(25.0)	-3	(2.4)	3	(26.1)	-1	(2.6)	-22	(19.7)	0	(2.1)
Denmark	-79	(5.4)	-81	(9.6)	0	(1.8)	-59	(9.6)	1	(1.6)	-54	(9.6)	1	(1.6)
Estonia	c	c	c	c	c	c	c	c	c	c	c	c	c	c
Finland	-96	(7.9)	-75	(8.7)	-3	(1.6)	-57	(7.3)	-2	(1.3)	-59	(7.1)	-2	(1.2)
France	-83	(11.8)	-43	(19.4)	-6	(1.8)	-32	(17.1)	-3	(1.6)	w	w	w	w
Germany	-64	(11.3)	-62	(19.6)	0	(3.2)	-41	(18.2)	0	(3.0)	-25	(15.8)	-1	(2.6)
Greece	-55	(7.9)	-37	(9.8)	-2	(1.5)	-8	(9.8)	-2	(1.5)	-7	(8.0)	0	(1.4)
Hungary	c	c	c	c	c	c	c	c	c	c	c	c	c	c
Iceland	-61	(10.2)	5	(20.0)	-9	(2.2)	25	(18.9)	-8	(2.1)	27	(18.6)	-8	(2.0)
Ireland	0	(4.9)	2	(12.4)	0	(1.4)	-5	(11.6)	1	(1.2)	-2	(11.6)	1	(1.2)
Israel	0	(8.0)	29	(14.8)	-5	(2.3)	39	(12.5)	-4	(2.0)	33	(11.6)	-5	(2.1)
Italy	-55	(3.7)	-30	(8.0)	-3	(0.9)	-15	(8.3)	-3	(0.9)	-12	(7.8)	-2	(0.8)
Japan	c	c	c	c	c	c	c	c	c	c	c	c	c	c
Korea	c	c	c	c	c	c	c	c	c	c	c	c	c	c
Luxembourg	-40	(4.7)	-34	(7.9)	-1	(0.8)	-11	(7.4)	0	(0.7)	-19	(6.9)	0	(0.6)
Mexico	-83	(6.4)	-98	(8.5)	5	(1.7)	-83	(8.0)	2	(1.6)	-77	(7.5)	0	(1.7)
Netherlands	-60	(10.6)	-56	(16.6)	1	(2.2)	-37	(16.0)	1	(2.3)	-42	(13.9)	1	(1.9)
New Zealand	7	(5.8)	37	(11.3)	-3	(1.1)	25	(10.0)	-3	(1.0)	22	(9.3)	-2	(1.0)
Norway	-54	(6.7)	-45	(13.5)	-1	(1.5)	-34	(14.4)	0	(1.6)	-32	(13.8)	0	(1.5)
Poland	c	c	c	c	c	c	c	c	c	c	c	c	c	c
Portugal	-43	(8.0)	-14	(24.7)	-4	(2.5)	-17	(22.3)	-2	(2.3)	-14	(22.5)	-3	(2.3)
Slovak Republic	c	c	c	c	c	c	c	c	c	c	c	c	c	c
Slovenia	-74	(10.6)	-31	(24.8)	-4	(2.1)	-24	(21.9)	-2	(2.1)	-45	(21.4)	0	(2.5)
Spain	-56	(4.5)	-24	(7.3)	-4	(0.9)	-12	(7.5)	-3	(0.8)	-9	(7.2)	-4	(0.8)
Sweden	-76	(7.9)	-60	(14.6)	-2	(1.7)	-37	(14.4)	-2	(1.5)	-34	(14.3)	-2	(1.5)
Switzerland	-77	(5.1)	-70	(10.6)	-1	(1.3)	-48	(8.9)	-1	(1.1)	-51	(7.4)	-1	(1.0)
Turkey	c	c	c	c	c	c	c	c	c	c	c	c	c	c
United Kingdom	-3	(11.7)	-30	(11.9)	4	(2.0)	-12	(12.3)	2	(1.7)	2	(9.8)	0	(1.2)
United States	-23	(9.6)	-27	(12.3)	1	(1.5)	5	(10.0)	0	(1.3)	10	(9.7)	0	(1.3)
OECD average	-47	(1.6)	-31	(2.9)	-2	(0.3)	-18	(2.7)	-1	(0.3)	-18	(2.5)	-1	(0.3)
Albania	c	c	c	c	c	c	c	c	c	c	c	c	c	c
Argentina	-39	(10.0)	-33	(15.6)	-1	(1.9)	-18	(15.5)	0	(2.0)	-17	(14.5)	1	(1.9)
Brazil	c	c	c	c	c	c	c	c	c	c	c	c	c	c
Bulgaria	c	c	c	c	c	c	c	c	c	c	c	c	c	c
Colombia	c	c	c	c	c	c	c	c	c	c	c	c	c	c
Costa Rica	-20	(10.5)	-10	(17.0)	-2	(2.0)	-1	(15.2)	-2	(1.9)	-7	(14.5)	-2	(1.9)
Croatia	-21	(10.1)	-11	(13.7)	-2	(1.7)	9	(13.2)	-3	(1.8)	7	(12.0)	-3	(2.0)
Cyprus*	-23	(5.5)	-29	(10.6)	1	(1.1)	-22	(9.6)	2	(1.0)	-29	(8.9)	2	(1.0)
Hong Kong-China	-24	(6.6)	-16	(9.9)	-1	(1.2)	5	(9.2)	-1	(1.1)	6	(8.8)	-1	(1.0)
Indonesia	c	c	c	c	c	c	c	c	c	c	c	c	c	c
Jordan	29	(8.7)	21	(11.6)	3	(1.8)	17	(10.9)	1	(1.6)	10	(10.7)	0	(1.5)
Kazakhstan	-26	(6.3)	-7	(10.4)	-3	(1.2)	-2	(10.4)	-2	(1.2)	1	(10.4)	-1	(1.2)
Latvia	c	c	c	c	c	c	c	c	c	c	c	c	c	c
Liechtenstein	c	c	c	c	c	c	c	c	c	c	c	c	c	c
Lithuania	c	c	c	c	c	c	c	c	c	c	c	c	c	c
Macao-China	11	(3.7)	-2	(7.7)	2	(0.8)	3	(7.6)	2	(0.8)	8	(7.7)	2	(0.9)
Malaysia	c	c	c	c	c	c	c	c	c	c	c	c	c	c
Montenegro	19	(8.9)	27	(13.3)	-1	(1.8)	17	(12.1)	0	(1.8)	12	(10.6)	1	(1.7)
Peru	c	c	c	c	c	c	c	c	c	c	c	c	c	c
Qatar	109	(1.9)	94	(2.8)	3	(0.3)	92	(2.7)	3	(0.3)	90	(2.5)	2	(0.3)
Romania	c	c	c	c	c	c	c	c	c	c	c	c	c	c
Russian Federation	-29	(8.2)	-26	(12.6)	-1	(1.9)	-27	(14.2)	0	(1.9)	-28	(15.2)	0	(2.0)
Serbia	-10	(12.4)	1	(22.1)	-1	(3.3)	9	(18.6)	-2	(2.9)	13	(15.0)	-4	(2.4)
Shanghai-China	-104	(13.9)	-141	(25.8)	5	(3.0)	-114	(28.6)	5	(3.3)	-88	(22.3)	5	(3.0)
Singapore	20	(4.8)	20	(8.7)	0	(0.9)	-1	(7.9)	0	(0.9)	-12	(8.0)	0	(0.9)
Chinese Taipei	c	c	c	c	c	c	c	c	c	c	c	c	c	c
Thailand	c	c	c	c	c	c	c	c	c	c	c	c	c	c
Tunisia	c	c	c	c	c	c	c	c	c	c	c	c	c	c
United Arab Emirates	84	(3.5)	78	(4.2)	1	(0.4)	74	(4.3)	1	(0.4)	67	(4.9)	1	(0.3)
Uruguay	c	c	c	c	c	c	c	c	c	c	c	c	c	c
Viet Nam	c	c	c	c	c	c	c	c	c	c	c	c	c	c

Note: Values that are statistically significant are indicated in bold (see Annex A3).
* See notes at the beginning of this Annex.
StatLink http://dx.doi.org/10.1787/888932964927

[Part 1/2]
Concentration of immigrant students in school
Table II.3.9   *Results based on students' self-reports*

		Percentage of students									
		Immigrant students		In schools where the percentage of immigrant students is zero		In schools where the percentage of immigrant students is more than 0% but less than 10% (low concentration)		In schools where the percentage of immigrant students is at or above 10% but less than 25% (medium concentration)		In schools where the percentage of immigrant students is at or above 25% (high concentration)	
		%	S.E.	%	S.E.	%	S.E.	%	S.E.	%	S.E.
OECD	Australia	22.7	(0.7)	15.0	(1.3)	18.2	(1.6)	29.1	(1.9)	37.7	(1.8)
	Austria	16.4	(1.1)	15.1	(2.9)	33.6	(3.9)	29.1	(4.0)	22.2	(2.9)
	Belgium	15.1	(0.9)	17.8	(2.2)	36.6	(2.9)	24.2	(2.4)	21.4	(2.2)
	Canada	29.5	(1.3)	17.9	(1.3)	22.4	(1.6)	16.3	(1.6)	43.3	(1.9)
	Chile	0.9	(0.2)	78.4	(3.1)	21.1	(3.1)	0.5	(0.3)	c	c
	Czech Republic	3.2	(0.4)	60.8	(3.7)	26.9	(3.6)	11.5	(2.1)	0.7	(0.5)
	Denmark	8.9	(0.6)	29.8	(2.8)	41.6	(2.9)	20.9	(2.4)	7.7	(1.3)
	Estonia	8.2	(0.5)	39.7	(2.2)	34.8	(2.1)	12.5	(2.1)	13.1	(2.1)
	Finland	3.3	(0.2)	33.4	(3.0)	58.0	(3.0)	7.5	(0.4)	1.1	(0.2)
	France	w	w	w	w	w	w	w	w	w	w
	Germany	13.1	(0.8)	23.3	(2.7)	27.8	(2.8)	31.3	(3.1)	17.6	(2.4)
	Greece	10.5	(0.8)	19.9	(3.2)	49.8	(3.9)	23.3	(3.0)	7.0	(1.5)
	Hungary	1.7	(0.2)	70.7	(3.5)	27.1	(3.4)	1.8	(1.0)	0.4	(0.3)
	Iceland	3.5	(0.3)	43.2	(0.2)	50.7	(0.2)	5.5	(0.2)	0.6	(0.0)
	Ireland	10.1	(0.7)	14.3	(2.4)	40.5	(3.6)	38.7	(3.9)	6.5	(2.0)
	Israel	18.3	(1.2)	17.0	(1.9)	25.7	(3.5)	29.7	(3.6)	27.7	(3.1)
	Italy	7.5	(0.3)	30.3	(1.5)	46.1	(1.6)	18.0	(1.3)	5.6	(1.1)
	Japan	0.3	(0.1)	90.0	(2.1)	10.0	(2.1)	c	c	c	c
	Korea	0.0	(0.0)	99.3	(0.5)	0.7	(0.5)	c	c	c	c
	Luxembourg	46.4	(0.7)	c	c	0.8	(0.0)	16.0	(0.1)	83.2	(0.1)
	Mexico	1.3	(0.1)	77.2	(1.6)	20.4	(1.5)	2.1	(0.5)	0.3	(0.2)
	Netherlands	10.6	(1.0)	29.7	(3.5)	35.6	(4.0)	22.7	(3.7)	12.0	(2.1)
	New Zealand	26.3	(1.5)	7.4	(1.9)	13.9	(2.5)	41.3	(3.5)	37.3	(3.4)
	Norway	9.4	(0.9)	28.9	(3.5)	37.6	(3.6)	26.2	(3.0)	7.2	(1.7)
	Poland	0.2	(0.1)	95.9	(1.5)	4.0	(1.5)	0.1	(0.1)	c	c
	Portugal	6.9	(0.6)	34.4	(4.5)	42.0	(4.5)	16.5	(2.9)	7.2	(2.3)
	Slovak Republic	0.7	(0.2)	85.2	(2.7)	13.6	(2.7)	1.2	(0.7)	c	c
	Slovenia	8.6	(0.4)	36.0	(0.8)	35.8	(0.5)	19.8	(0.6)	8.4	(0.6)
	Spain	9.9	(0.6)	27.7	(2.4)	35.7	(2.8)	26.6	(2.7)	10.0	(1.7)
	Sweden	14.5	(0.9)	17.6	(2.5)	34.3	(3.1)	28.7	(2.9)	19.4	(2.2)
	Switzerland	24.1	(0.9)	3.9	(1.0)	14.5	(2.1)	41.4	(3.2)	40.2	(3.3)
	Turkey	0.9	(0.2)	83.0	(3.3)	15.0	(3.2)	2.0	(1.3)	c	c
	United Kingdom	12.7	(1.1)	33.1	(2.9)	29.8	(3.1)	20.7	(2.9)	16.4	(2.2)
	United States	21	(2.0)	20	(3.4)	29	(4.1)	17.3	(3.5)	34.2	(3.9)
	OECD average	**11.2**	**(0.1)**	**40.0**	**(0.4)**	**28.5**	**(0.5)**	**19.0**	**(0.4)**	**18.1**	**(0.4)**
Partners	Albania	0.0	c	0.0	c	0.0	c	0.0	c	0.0	c
	Argentina	3.9	(0.4)	56.4	(3.8)	33.1	(3.7)	7.3	(2.2)	3.2	(0.8)
	Brazil	0.7	(0.1)	86.2	(1.6)	12.3	(1.5)	1.4	(0.5)	0.1	(0.1)
	Bulgaria	0.5	(0.2)	90.3	(2.3)	8.6	(2.2)	1.0	(0.7)	0.1	(0.1)
	Colombia	0.3	(0.1)	91.1	(2.0)	8.9	(2.0)	0.1	(0.1)	c	c
	Costa Rica	5.5	(0.7)	43.7	(3.4)	37.1	(3.4)	16.4	(2.3)	2.8	(1.5)
	Croatia	12.1	(0.8)	11.4	(2.5)	34.7	(3.9)	43.9	(3.9)	10.1	(2.5)
	Cyprus*	8.5	(0.4)	15.9	(0.1)	62.5	(0.2)	14.2	(0.1)	7.4	(0.1)
	Hong Kong-China	34.7	(1.5)	c	c	7.6	(2.9)	18.6	(3.1)	73.7	(3.9)
	Indonesia	0.2	(0.1)	96.9	(1.2)	2.9	(1.1)	0.2	(0.1)	c	c
	Jordan	13.4	(0.7)	20.8	(2.7)	22.8	(2.8)	38.8	(4.0)	17.6	(3.1)
	Kazakhstan	16.1	(1.7)	15.6	(2.6)	32.8	(3.6)	35.4	(3.7)	16.1	(3.4)
	Latvia	4.5	(0.5)	58.9	(3.5)	21.7	(3.2)	16.1	(2.5)	3.2	(1.3)
	Liechtenstein	33.3	(2.9)	c	c	c	c	53.1	(1.0)	46.9	(1.0)
	Lithuania	1.7	(0.3)	79.7	(3.1)	16.3	(3.0)	2.4	(1.1)	1.5	(0.8)
	Macao-China	65.1	(0.6)	c	c	c	c	c	c	100.0	c
	Malaysia	1.7	(0.3)	72.8	(3.2)	21.6	(2.9)	5.6	(1.3)	c	c
	Montenegro	5.8	(0.4)	0.9	(0.2)	77.3	(0.2)	21.7	(0.1)	0.0	(0.0)
	Peru	0.5	(0.1)	88.0	(2.1)	11.2	(2.1)	0.6	(0.4)	0.1	(0.1)
	Qatar	52.0	(0.4)	c	c	3.6	(0.0)	20.8	(0.1)	75.6	(0.1)
	Romania	0.2	(0.1)	94.6	(1.9)	5.4	(1.9)	c	c	c	c
	Russian Federation	10.9	(0.8)	13.8	(2.0)	39.3	(3.2)	40.5	(2.7)	6.3	(2.0)
	Serbia	8.5	(0.8)	27.8	(3.6)	42.1	(4.2)	23.9	(3.0)	6.2	(1.8)
	Shanghai-China	0.9	(0.2)	80.1	(3.2)	18.9	(3.1)	0.9	(0.7)	c	c
	Singapore	18.3	(0.8)	2.1	(0.9)	21.2	(0.1)	58.6	(0.2)	18.1	(0.9)
	Chinese Taipei	0.5	(0.1)	84.8	(2.9)	15.2	(2.9)	c	c	c	c
	Thailand	0.7	(0.4)	96.8	(1.4)	1.5	(1.0)	0.7	(0.7)	1.0	(0.7)
	Tunisia	0.4	(0.1)	89.2	(2.6)	10.8	(2.6)	c	c	c	c
	United Arab Emirates	54.9	(1.4)	2.3	(1.1)	11.1	(1.7)	16.5	(1.9)	70.1	(2.2)
	Uruguay	0.5	(0.1)	88.6	(2.4)	11.0	(2.5)	0.5	(0.4)	c	c
	Viet Nam	0.1	(0.1)	97.2	(1.4)	2.8	(1.4)	c	c	c	c

Note: This table was calculated considering only students with data on the *PISA index of economic, social and cultural status*. Values that are statistically significant are indicated in bold (see Annex A3).
1. The *PISA index of economic, social and cultural status* (ESCS).
* See notes at the beginning of this Annex.
StatLink ᴍᴙᴘ▛ http://dx.doi.org/10.1787/888932964927

   EXCELLENCE THROUGH EQUITY: GIVING EVERY STUDENT THE CHANCE TO SUCCEED – VOLUME II

[Part 2/2]

Table II.3.9 **Concentration of immigrant students in school**

Results based on students' self-reports

	Estimated coefficients in a model with mathematics performance as the dependent variable																							
	Before accounting for ESCS[1]								After accounting for student ESCS								After accounting for student and school ESCS							
	Immigrant student		Low-concentration schools vs. those without immigrant students		Medium-concentration schools vs. those without immigrant students		High-concentration schools vs. those without immigrant students		Immigrant student		Low-concentration schools vs. those without immigrant students		Medium-concentration schools vs. those without immigrant students		High-concentration schools vs. those without immigrant students		Immigrant student		Low-concentration schools vs. those without immigrant students		Medium-concentration schools vs. those without immigrant students		High-concentration schools vs. those without immigrant students	
	Score dif.	S.E.	Score dif.	S.E.	Score dif.	S.E.	Score dif.	S.E.	Score dif.	S.E.	Score dif.	S.E.	Score dif.	S.E.	Score dif.	S.E.	Score dif.	S.E.	Score dif.	S.E.	Score dif.	S.E.	Score dif.	S.E.
OECD																								
Australia	**14**	(3.2)	**17**	(5.2)	**25**	(4.3)	**37**	(4.9)	**19**	(3.2)	**9**	(4.3)	**12**	(3.7)	**25**	(3.9)	**20**	(2.9)	0	(4.6)	-3	(4.2)	**14**	(4.0)
Austria	**-44**	(4.3)	26	(14.1)	25	(14.2)	-17	(14.3)	**-22**	(4.1)	17	(12.1)	12	(12.4)	-17	(11.8)	**-33**	(3.9)	5	(10.7)	0	(11.2)	4	(9.6)
Belgium	**-45**	(4.4)	-20	(10.7)	**-48**	(11.0)	**-72**	(12.6)	**-28**	(3.6)	**-22**	(8.2)	**-48**	(8.6)	**-61**	(9.1)	**-31**	(3.9)	**-23**	(6.4)	**-43**	(6.7)	**-30**	(6.5)
Canada	**-9**	(3.4)	7	(6.1)	5	(6.8)	**16**	(5.3)	0	(3.2)	2	(5.6)	-5	(6.3)	3	(4.9)	2	(3.3)	-2	(5.2)	**-14**	(6.0)	-4	(4.9)
Chile	-5	(10.3)	7	(9.2)	c	c	c	c	-4	(8.8)	-7	(6.3)	c	c	c	c	-4	(9.4)	**-15**	(5.6)	c	c	c	c
Czech Republic	**-22**	(8.5)	**28**	(9.6)	-15	(16.0)	c	c	-14	(9.2)	**17**	(8.3)	-18	(12.1)	c	c	**-19**	(7.9)	-3	(8.0)	**-21**	(9.0)	c	c
Denmark	**-60**	(3.2)	3	(5.5)	4	(6.4)	**-17**	(6.1)	**-37**	(3.1)	2	(4.3)	4	(4.9)	-10	(5.2)	**-40**	(3.2)	2	(3.8)	8	(4.4)	7	(5.7)
Estonia	**-15**	(5.5)	3	(4.1)	**-32**	(6.5)	**-21**	(7.9)	**-15**	(5.2)	-3	(3.7)	**-31**	(6.4)	**-23**	(6.7)	**-14**	(5.4)	**-10**	(3.8)	**-31**	(6.9)	**-25**	(5.9)
Finland	**-80**	(4.3)	**12**	(3.9)	0	(5.1)	**-34**	(16.2)	**-59**	(4.0)	5	(3.7)	-5	(4.4)	**-33**	(16.1)	**-61**	(4.0)	1	(3.7)	-6	(4.2)	-25	(15.8)
France	w	w	w	w	w	w	w	w	w	w	w	w	w	w	w	w	w	w	w	w	w	w	w	w
Germany	**-32**	(4.2)	18	(12.8)	-6	(13.5)	**-49**	(14.1)	**-9**	(4.6)	14	(10.6)	-4	(11.0)	**-39**	(12.0)	**-23**	(3.9)	10	(9.2)	10	(8.2)	1	(9.9)
Greece	**-20**	(5.0)	-7	(11.3)	**-33**	(11.5)	**-80**	(15.4)	-5	(5.3)	-7	(8.3)	**-28**	(9.1)	**-66**	(14.3)	-7	(5.1)	-6	(6.7)	**-20**	(8.1)	**-40**	(14.8)
Hungary	16	(10.2)	**48**	(12.9)	c	c	c	c	11	(12.4)	**29**	(9.7)	c	c	c	c	11	(9.6)	3	(7.2)	c	c	c	c
Iceland	**-47**	(9.3)	**10**	(3.1)	-13	(7.3)	c	c	**-28**	(8.9)	5	(3.1)	-7	(7.1)	c	c	**-29**	(9.0)	1	(3.2)	3	(7.2)	c	c
Ireland	4	(4.7)	-9	(8.6)	-11	(9.6)	**-33**	(14.2)	0	(4.4)	-4	(6.3)	-7	(6.8)	**-24**	(10.5)	3	(4.3)	-1	(5.1)	-4	(5.4)	-16	(9.0)
Israel	**-12**	(3.6)	**59**	(15.1)	**78**	(12.0)	**75**	(12.1)	-2	(3.4)	**41**	(11.4)	**58**	(9.6)	**62**	(9.0)	-5	(3.5)	**18**	(8.9)	**34**	(9.0)	**51**	(7.6)
Italy	**-31**	(2.7)	**20**	(6.4)	-2	(6.8)	**-50**	(8.8)	**-21**	(2.7)	**19**	(5.4)	2	(5.9)	**-38**	(7.1)	**-25**	(2.5)	**18**	(4.3)	**14**	(5.1)	-2	(5.2)
Japan	c	c	-16	(22.2)	c	c	c	c	c	c	-13	(17.4)	c	c	c	c	c	c	-4	(9.2)	c	c	c	c
Korea	c	c	c	c	c	c	c	c	c	c	c	c	c	c	c	c	c	c	c	c	c	c	c	c
Luxembourg	**-31**	(3.2)	c	c	**57**	(2.7)	-14	(11.8)	-4	(3.3)	c	c	**43**	(2.7)	**-43**	(2.7)	**-14**	(3.1)	c	c	**7**	(2.8)	-12	(12.0)
Mexico	**-52**	(4.1)	**-15**	(4.0)	**-68**	(7.0)	-14	(40.1)	**-48**	(4.0)	**-14**	(3.2)	**-49**	(7.9)	-23	(24.5)	**-50**	(3.7)	**-13**	(2.9)	**-34**	(9.0)	**-30**	(14.9)
Netherlands	**-35**	(5.5)	-11	(16.1)	-9	(16.4)	**-60**	(19.5)	**-16**	(5.8)	-13	(13.7)	-12	(15.3)	**-54**	(17.2)	**-30**	(5.2)	-13	(9.3)	-8	(14.5)	0	(12.8)
New Zealand	-10	(5.2)	23	(14.7)	**42**	(13.4)	**48**	(15.5)	-4	(4.4)	14	(14.6)	22	(14.2)	27	(14.8)	-2	(4.0)	6	(15.2)	2	(15.4)	9	(14.3)
Norway	**-46**	(5.8)	-4	(6.6)	-5	(7.7)	-1	(11.2)	**-27**	(5.8)	-4	(6.0)	-7	(7.1)	-3	(10.0)	**-30**	(5.7)	-3	(5.8)	-6	(6.9)	9	(9.9)
Poland	c	c	14	(24.2)	c	c	c	c	c	c	-7	(19.7)	c	c	c	c	c	c	-22	(18.4)	c	c	c	c
Portugal	**-31**	(7.4)	11	(9.5)	-16	(12.0)	-26	(16.6)	**-25**	(8.6)	0	(6.8)	**-26**	(8.4)	**-27**	(13.1)	**-25**	(8.1)	-7	(7.0)	**-32**	(7.1)	**-26**	(11.3)
Slovak Republic	-19	(16.1)	31	(18.2)	c	c	c	c	-10	(19.3)	16	(13.5)	c	c	c	c	-8	(17.9)	3	(10.7)	c	c	c	c
Slovenia	**-33**	(5.4)	**12**	(3.6)	**16**	(4.9)	**-53**	(5.9)	**-13**	(4.9)	**7**	(3.3)	9	(4.9)	**-42**	(5.2)	**-26**	(4.9)	1	(3.2)	1	(4.0)	8	(6.5)
Spain	**-45**	(3.7)	8	(5.5)	-7	(7.2)	-14	(7.7)	**-33**	(3.7)	7	(3.8)	-3	(5.9)	-7	(6.8)	**-34**	(3.7)	**7**	(3.4)	1	(5.6)	1	(6.7)
Sweden	**-57**	(4.6)	-4	(6.1)	6	(7.3)	-5	(8.2)	**-40**	(4.7)	-5	(5.2)	4	(6.2)	-4	(6.8)	**-43**	(4.6)	-5	(5.1)	5	(5.9)	6	(6.3)
Switzerland	**-49**	(2.5)	**35**	(15.0)	**34**	(14.8)	-11	(13.2)	**-30**	(2.6)	27	(13.8)	22	(13.0)	-17	(11.4)	**-36**	(2.7)	16	(14.9)	10	(12.9)	-14	(11.8)
Turkey	-20	(15.0)	23	(19.7)	c	c	c	c	-24	(15.2)	18	(15.9)	c	c	c	c	-19	(13.1)	8	(11.8)	c	c	c	c
United Kingdom	-9	(6.2)	8	(6.3)	14	(13.1)	1	(9.0)	-7	(5.9)	5	(5.6)	14	(9.6)	2	(7.0)	-9	(5.1)	2	(5.4)	**16**	(6.3)	6	(6.4)
United States	-5	(4.3)	**23**	(9.6)	**24**	(9.4)	-1	(10.9)	**19**	(4.5)	12	(7.7)	**19**	(7.3)	-1	(9.0)	**18**	(4.6)	4	(6.8)	**19**	(6.7)	11	(8.5)
OECD average	**-28**	(1.2)	**12**	(2.1)	2	(2.0)	**-18**	(2.9)	**-16**	(1.3)	**5**	(1.7)	-1	(1.7)	**-19**	(2.2)	**-19**	(1.2)	-1	(1.4)	**-4**	(1.5)	**-5**	(2.0)
Partners																								
Albania	c	c	c	c	c	c	c	c	c	c	c	c	c	c	c	c	c	c	c	c	c	c	c	c
Argentina	**-12**	(6.2)	-7	(8.2)	**-40**	(9.5)	**-52**	(11.6)	-1	(6.1)	-5	(6.6)	**-27**	(8.9)	**-36**	(11.0)	-8	(6.3)	-2	(5.5)	-9	(9.9)	-8	(12.1)
Brazil	**-39**	(8.4)	-7	(9.6)	-33	(19.0)	c	c	**-40**	(8.2)	-9	(7.1)	**-43**	(8.8)	c	c	**-39**	(8.4)	**-11**	(5.1)	**-53**	(10.9)	c	c
Bulgaria	c	c	**-33**	(14.6)	c	c	c	c	c	c	**-24**	(8.3)	c	c	c	c	c	c	**-19**	(7.6)	c	c	c	c
Colombia	**-37**	(12.0)	**-35**	(9.6)	c	c	c	c	**-43**	(11.5)	**-26**	(7.6)	c	c	c	c	**-40**	(11.1)	**-19**	(6.7)	c	c	c	c
Costa Rica	**-19**	(5.2)	9	(7.4)	-6	(7.2)	**-42**	(11.8)	-6	(4.8)	5	(5.9)	-5	(5.4)	**-34**	(6.1)	**-13**	(4.6)	4	(5.6)	-1	(5.4)	**-21**	(9.3)
Croatia	**-13**	(4.2)	21	(16.7)	5	(15.4)	-12	(16.5)	-3	(4.0)	15	(13.3)	1	(12.3)	-14	(13.6)	**-8**	(3.8)	5	(10.6)	-2	(9.6)	-10	(12.3)
Cyprus*	**-16**	(5.8)	**14**	(3.5)	-1	(4.1)	-6	(6.2)	-9	(5.3)	6	(3.6)	-4	(4.3)	-6	(6.2)	**-17**	(4.8)	-4	(3.6)	-7	(4.1)	-6	(5.8)
Hong Kong-China	1	(3.7)	**47**	(16.3)	**33**	(14.1)	**-47**	(16.3)	**14**	(3.6)	19	(15.6)	21	(12.1)	-21	(12.1)	**8**	(3.4)	**-62**	(17.2)	-19	(12.2)	**62**	(17.2)
Indonesia	c	c	19	(14.1)	c	c	c	c	c	c	15	(12.8)	c	c	c	c	c	c	9	(12.8)	c	c	c	c
Jordan	**13**	(3.4)	**14**	(6.8)	**19**	(9.1)	**31**	(11.7)	**10**	(3.3)	10	(6.6)	12	(8.0)	19	(10.7)	**10**	(3.0)	4	(7.6)	0	(7.4)	-2	(11.7)
Kazakhstan	-4	(4.1)	1	(10.5)	-4	(9.8)	-5	(13.3)	-1	(3.8)	-5	(10.2)	-10	(9.4)	-6	(12.8)	0	(3.6)	-14	(10.7)	-19	(10.3)	-5	(13.1)
Latvia	-5	(7.4)	**16**	(7.6)	2	(10.1)	-10	(9.0)	-8	(7.7)	9	(6.1)	-1	(8.2)	-10	(6.1)	-7	(7.6)	3	(5.8)	-3	(7.6)	-12	(8.1)
Liechtenstein	-17	(9.4)	c	c	c	c	c	c	-13	(9.4)	c	c	c	c	c	c	-14	(9.6)	c	c	c	c	c	c
Lithuania	0	(10.2)	4	(7.8)	-29	(15.1)	c	c	3	(10.5)	0	(6.9)	**-28**	(10.6)	c	c	3	(10.1)	-6	(6.7)	**-25**	(8.2)	c	c
Macao-China	**16**	(2.8)	c	c	c	c	c	c	**22**	(2.8)	c	c	c	c	c	c	**26**	(2.7)	c	c	c	c	c	c
Malaysia	-11	(8.6)	-3	(7.2)	**-20**	(8.4)	c	c	5	(10.3)	-5	(6.0)	-15	(7.9)	c	c	-2	(9.1)	-6	(5.8)	-6	(9.5)	c	c
Montenegro	**19**	(6.6)	39	(21.3)	**45**	(21.4)	c	c	**16**	(6.2)	20	(19.0)	22	(19.1)	c	c	**14**	(5.5)	-27	(16.1)	**-34**	(16.2)	c	c
Peru	**-75**	(17.1)	3	(14.1)	c	c	c	c	**-74**	(18.2)	-1	(8.8)	c	c	c	c	**-71**	(17.0)	-4	(6.2)	c	c	c	c
Qatar	**81**	(1.9)	**-10**	(4.0)	**-27**	(2.2)	**10**	(4.0)	**80**	(1.9)	**-14**	(4.1)	**-27**	(2.3)	**27**	(2.3)	**74**	(1.9)	**-24**	(3.8)	**-30**	(2.3)	**24**	(3.8)
Romania	c	c	28	(22.4)	c	c	c	c	c	c	12	(14.7)	c	c	c	c	c	c	-5	(8.5)	c	c	c	c
Russian Federation	**-19**	(4.0)	**22**	(8.7)	7	(8.6)	1	(12.5)	**-16**	(4.3)	3	(8.1)	-7	(7.4)	-7	(11.1)	**-16**	(4.2)	-14	(9.2)	**-20**	(7.8)	-13	(12.3)
Serbia	**8**	(3.9)	13	(12.0)	**38**	(12.8)	-2	(19.0)	**8**	(3.9)	12	(10.0)	**30**	(10.4)	6	(16.7)	**7**	(3.7)	9	(7.2)	12	(7.2)	24	(13.8)
Shanghai-China	**-65**	(14.1)	**-67**	(11.5)	c	c	c	c	**-55**	(15.6)	**-51**	(9.6)	c	c	c	c	**-57**	(14.3)	**-27**	(8.3)	c	c	c	c
Singapore	**9**	(4.3)	20	(11.2)	**34**	(10.9)	**99**	(12.8)	-4	(4.4)	**23**	(10.9)	**34**	(10.5)	**80**	(13.3)	-4	(4.8)	**25**	(9.8)	**33**	(9.3)	**41**	(11.7)
Chinese Taipei	-11	(17.0)	-24	(16.1)	c	c	c	c	18	(17.8)	-22	(12.5)	c	c	c	c	4	(16.6)	-17	(9.5)	c	c	c	c
Thailand	-35	(23.4)	23	(19.9)	c	c	c	c	-14	(29.5)	24	(19.2)	c	c	c	c	-28	(26.1)	26	(19.3)	c	c	c	c
Tunisia	c	c	6	(18.1)	c	c	c	c	c	c	4	(13.9)	c	c	c	c	c	c	1	(9.6)	c	c	c	c
United Arab Emirates	**64**	(3.4)	17	(11.7)	9	(11.1)	16	(10.9)	**62**	(3.2)	10	(10.1)	2	(9.0)	7	(8.6)	**53**	(3.4)	2	(10.8)	-6	(9.5)	1	(8.7)
Uruguay	c	c	32	(17.2)	c	c	c	c	c	c	13	(9.8)	c	c	c	c	c	c	-3	(6.6)	c	c	c	c
Viet Nam	c	c	c	c	c	c	c	c	c	c	c	c	c	c	c	c	c	c	c	c	c	c	c	c

Note: This table was calculated considering only students with data on the *PISA index of economic, social and cultural status*. Values that are statistically significant are indicated in bold (see Annex A3).

1. The *PISA index of economic, social and cultural status* (ESCS).

* See notes at the beginning of this Annex.

StatLink http://dx.doi.org/10.1787/888932964927

[Part 1/2]

Concentration, in school, of students who do not speak the language of assessment at home

Table II.3.10   *Results based on students' self-reports*

		Percentage of students									
		Students who do not speak the language of assessment at home		In schools where the percentage of students who do not speak the language of assessment at home is zero		In schools where the percentage of students who do not speak the language of assessment at home is more than 0% but less than 10% (low concentration)		In schools where the percentage of students who do not speak the language of assessment at home is at or above 10% but less than 25% (medium concentration)		In schools where the percentage of students who do not speak the language of assessment at home is at or above 25% (high concentration)	
		%	S.E.	%	S.E.	%	S.E.	%	S.E.	%	S.E.
OECD	Australia	9.7	(0.5)	38.2	(1.8)	25.9	(1.6)	23.7	(1.4)	12.1	(1.2)
	Austria	11.2	(0.8)	26.8	(3.0)	38.1	(3.9)	18.4	(3.2)	16.7	(2.3)
	Belgium	21.4	(0.8)	10.4	(1.8)	25.0	(2.6)	32.3	(2.6)	32.3	(2.4)
	Canada	17.3	(0.9)	22.8	(1.8)	26.6	(2.0)	23.3	(2.2)	27.2	(2.3)
	Chile	0.6	(0.1)	83.8	(2.9)	15.6	(2.9)	c	c	c	c
	Czech Republic	2.9	(0.4)	66.3	(3.5)	25.6	(3.0)	6.7	(1.5)	1.4	(0.7)
	Denmark	4.5	(0.3)	43.8	(3.3)	43.3	(3.3)	10.0	(1.4)	2.8	(0.2)
	Estonia	5.5	(0.5)	50.7	(2.4)	34.9	(2.3)	10.8	(1.7)	3.6	(1.1)
	Finland	4.5	(0.2)	31.3	(3.1)	55.9	(3.1)	9.7	(0.5)	3.1	(0.3)
	France	w	w	w	w	w	w	w	w	w	w
	Germany	7.0	(0.6)	41.0	(2.9)	36.9	(3.2)	15.4	(2.4)	6.7	(1.6)
	Greece	5.1	(0.6)	43.2	(3.6)	46.0	(3.7)	6.8	(1.7)	4.0	(1.1)
	Hungary	1.0	(0.2)	80.6	(3.2)	17.9	(3.2)	c	c	c	c
	Iceland	3.9	(0.3)	36.3	(0.3)	54.8	(0.3)	6.3	(0.1)	c	c
	Ireland	4.8	(0.5)	43.5	(3.7)	38.2	(3.4)	17.9	(3.1)	c	c
	Israel	11.1	(0.9)	16.5	(3.0)	42.3	(4.0)	28.5	(3.6)	12.8	(2.6)
	Italy	14.3	(0.4)	11.6	(1.2)	39.8	(2.2)	31.3	(2.3)	17.4	(1.1)
	Japan	c	c	88.9	(2.4)	11.1	(2.4)	c	c	c	c
	Korea	c	c	98.1	(1.0)	c	c	c	c	c	c
	Luxembourg	85.3	(0.4)	c	c	c	c	c	c	95.2	(0.0)
	Mexico	3.2	(0.3)	74.0	(1.6)	19.3	(1.6)	3.0	(0.6)	3.7	(0.6)
	Netherlands	6.3	(0.5)	35.7	(3.9)	41.2	(3.7)	19.1	(3.4)	4.0	(1.5)
	New Zealand	16.0	(1.1)	9.9	(1.8)	32.9	(3.4)	36.2	(3.6)	21.0	(2.6)
	Norway	7.5	(0.6)	26.9	(3.1)	47.3	(3.6)	21.4	(2.8)	4.5	(1.5)
	Poland	0.9	(0.3)	86.7	(2.4)	11.8	(2.2)	c	c	c	c
	Portugal	2.6	(0.3)	55.0	(3.6)	40.5	(3.7)	4.0	(1.3)	c	c
	Slovak Republic	7.4	(0.9)	55.2	(3.6)	26.6	(3.2)	9.1	(1.6)	9.1	(1.9)
	Slovenia	5.9	(0.4)	51.8	(0.7)	30.7	(0.5)	11.5	(0.6)	6.0	(0.5)
	Spain	18.6	(1.1)	34.0	(2.1)	28.4	(2.3)	11.5	(1.7)	26.1	(1.9)
	Sweden	10.1	(0.7)	33.1	(3.0)	33.3	(3.2)	22.3	(2.8)	11.3	(1.6)
	Switzerland	16.4	(0.8)	8.6	(1.6)	28.0	(3.3)	40.7	(3.3)	22.7	(2.7)
	Turkey	6.2	(0.8)	64.9	(3.1)	21.3	(3.1)	4.8	(1.3)	9.0	(1.5)
	United Kingdom	6.9	(0.7)	43.7	(3.2)	39.2	(3.2)	7.6	(1.8)	9.5	(1.8)
	United States	14	(1.3)	21	(3.3)	39	(4.3)	17.7	(3.1)	21.7	(3.0)
	OECD average	10.6	(0.1)	44.6	(0.5)	32.9	(0.5)	16.8	(0.4)	15.1	(0.3)
Partners	Albania	c	c	c	c	c	c	c	c	c	c
	Argentina	1.6	(0.2)	74.9	(3.5)	21.1	(3.3)	3.4	(1.4)	c	c
	Brazil	1.1	(0.1)	77.4	(2.2)	21.1	(2.2)	1.1	(0.5)	0.4	(0.2)
	Bulgaria	10.8	(1.2)	45.3	(3.3)	29.5	(3.3)	10.4	(2.3)	14.8	(2.2)
	Colombia	0.7	(0.2)	87.6	(2.4)	11.3	(2.3)	c	c	c	c
	Costa Rica	1.2	(0.2)	76.8	(3.1)	20.4	(3.0)	2.8	(1.1)	c	c
	Croatia	1.3	(0.3)	75.5	(3.4)	22.7	(3.4)	c	c	c	c
	Cyprus*	18.4	(0.3)	11.3	(0.1)	62.9	(0.1)	6.9	(0.1)	18.9	(0.1)
	Hong Kong-China	6.8	(0.9)	25.3	(3.9)	54.2	(3.9)	18.2	(3.0)	2.3	(1.1)
	Indonesia	58.9	(2.3)	3.0	(1.1)	9.7	(2.7)	7.0	(2.0)	80.3	(2.7)
	Jordan	4.7	(0.3)	31.0	(3.2)	56.2	(3.7)	12.6	(2.3)	c	c
	Kazakhstan	11.1	(0.9)	34.3	(2.6)	26.5	(3.3)	25.8	(3.5)	13.3	(2.0)
	Latvia	10.5	(1.4)	40.3	(3.5)	29.4	(2.8)	19.1	(2.8)	11.3	(2.2)
	Liechtenstein	12.0	(1.8)	c	c	c	c	31.9	(1.1)	c	c
	Lithuania	3.5	(0.5)	65.2	(3.2)	24.3	(3.2)	8.7	(1.7)	1.8	(0.8)
	Macao-China	13.6	(0.2)	24.5	(0.1)	56.2	(0.1)	c	c	16.0	(0.1)
	Malaysia	42.3	(2.5)	13.1	(2.4)	16.1	(3.2)	18.1	(3.1)	52.7	(3.5)
	Montenegro	1.0	(0.1)	41.5	(0.2)	58.5	(0.2)	c	c	c	c
	Peru	6.4	(0.9)	65.5	(3.3)	23.0	(3.3)	2.5	(1.0)	8.9	(1.6)
	Qatar	39.2	(0.3)	3.4	(0.1)	45.3	(0.1)	8.3	(0.1)	43.0	(0.1)
	Romania	1.7	(0.4)	76.8	(3.3)	20.2	(3.0)	c	c	c	c
	Russian Federation	8.7	(1.8)	41.9	(3.7)	41.9	(4.0)	7.2	(1.8)	9.1	(2.9)
	Serbia	4.2	(0.6)	52.5	(3.9)	38.3	(4.0)	5.6	(1.7)	3.6	(1.7)
	Shanghai-China	1.4	(0.2)	66.4	(3.3)	33.2	(3.2)	c	c	c	c
	Singapore	54.4	(0.9)	c	c	c	c	10.9	(0.2)	86.9	(0.7)
	Chinese Taipei	16.5	(1.1)	7.2	(2.0)	37.7	(3.6)	31.7	(3.4)	23.3	(3.1)
	Thailand	44.6	(1.7)	10.0	(1.8)	18.1	(2.7)	14.5	(2.5)	57.5	(2.4)
	Tunisia	1.1	(0.2)	77.2	(3.3)	21.8	(3.3)	c	c	c	c
	United Arab Emirates	33.5	(0.9)	16.7	(1.9)	32.3	(2.5)	11.7	(1.6)	39.4	(0.9)
	Uruguay	2.1	(0.4)	70.0	(3.1)	25.3	(3.0)	3.3	(1.1)	c	c
	Viet Nam	2.2	(0.4)	81.6	(2.8)	12.7	(2.5)	3.3	(1.5)	c	c

Note: This table was calculated considering only students with data on the *PISA index of economic, social and cultural status*. Values that are statistically significant are indicated in bold (see Annex A3).
1. The *PISA index of economic, social and cultural status* (ESCS).
* See notes at the beginning of this Annex.
StatLink http://dx.doi.org/10.1787/888932964927

[Part 2/2]

Table II.3.10 **Concentration, in school, of students who do not speak the language of assessment at home**

Results based on students' self-reports

		Estimated coefficients in a model with mathematics performance as the dependent variable																							
		Before accounting for ESCS[1]								After accounting for student ESCS								After accounting for student and school ESCS							
		Students who do not speak the language of assessment at home		Low-concentration schools vs. schools without students who do not speak the language of assessment at home		Medium-concentration schools vs. schools without students who do not speak the language of assessment at home		High-concentration schools vs. schools without students who do not speak the language of assessment at home		Students who do not speak the language of assessment at home		Low-concentration schools vs. schools without students who do not speak the language of assessment at home		Medium-concentration schools vs. schools without students who do not speak the language of assessment at home		High-concentration schools vs. schools without students who do not speak the language of assessment at home		Students who do not speak the language of assessment at home		Low-concentration schools vs. schools without students who do not speak the language of assessment at home		Medium-concentration schools vs. schools without students who do not speak the language of assessment at home		High-concentration schools vs. schools without students who do not speak the language of assessment at home	
		Score dif.	S.E.	Score dif.	S.E.	Score dif.	S.E.	Score dif.	S.E.	Score dif.	S.E.	Score dif.	S.E.	Score dif.	S.E.	Score dif.	S.E.	Score dif.	S.E.	Score dif.	S.E.	Score dif.	S.E.	Score dif.	S.E.
OECD	Australia	**11**	(3.9)	7	(5.0)	9	(4.8)	**31**	(10.2)	**11**	(3.9)	4	(3.8)	4	(3.8)	**33**	(8.3)	**8**	(3.7)	2	(3.4)	3	(3.5)	**42**	(6.9)
	Austria	**-24**	(6.1)	**25**	(11.2)	18	(13.1)	-11	(12.6)	**-24**	(5.7)	16	(9.8)	6	(11.8)	-10	(10.7)	**-34**	(5.2)	5	(8.5)	-4	(10.8)	11	(10.6)
	Belgium	**-18**	(4.1)	13	(14.8)	**42**	(12.9)	-3	(13.0)	**-18**	(3.7)	11	(11.0)	**37**	(9.7)	6	(9.9)	**-19**	(3.9)	9	(8.6)	**32**	(8.3)	**30**	(9.0)
	Canada	**9**	(4.0)	3	(5.4)	3	(5.4)	9	(6.8)	**9**	(3.8)	-4	(4.8)	-5	(4.8)	2	(6.0)	**8**	(3.7)	**-9**	(4.6)	**-12**	(4.8)	-2	(5.6)
	Chile	-17	(11.6)	15	(9.0)	c	c	c	c	-17	(11.5)	6	(5.6)	c	c	c	c	-12	(10.9)	0	(5.3)	c	c	c	c
	Czech Republic	-19	(9.7)	**25**	(10.5)	4	(20.0)	-48	(58.4)	-19	(9.8)	13	(8.9)	-7	(15.0)	-48	(45.2)	**-24**	(9.2)	-7	(7.9)	**-28**	(9.4)	-46	(25.0)
	Denmark	**-21**	(3.7)	7	(4.9)	**-12**	(5.3)	**-40**	(7.2)	**-21**	(4.1)	5	(3.7)	-5	(4.6)	**-26**	(6.1)	**-24**	(3.9)	6	(3.4)	5	(4.8)	-6	(6.3)
	Estonia	**-18**	(5.9)	**21**	(4.1)	4	(5.7)	0	(7.6)	**-18**	(5.7)	**12**	(3.8)	-1	(5.4)	-3	(7.9)	**-18**	(5.7)	3	(3.8)	-7	(5.5)	-4	(9.0)
	Finland	**-43**	(4.3)	**12**	(3.7)	3	(4.2)	7	(13.3)	**-43**	(3.9)	5	(3.5)	-6	(4.0)	-5	(10.6)	**-45**	(3.7)	0	(3.4)	**-11**	(3.7)	-9	(9.0)
	France	w	w	w	w	w	w	w	w	w	w	w	w	w	w	w	w	w	w	w	w	w	w	w	w
	Germany	**-17**	(5.0)	12	(12.5)	-24	(13.2)	-23	(22.0)	**-17**	(5.2)	8	(9.8)	-14	(11.0)	-12	(17.0)	**-29**	(4.8)	3	(6.0)	12	(8.1)	**25**	(11.6)
	Greece	-5	(6.7)	-2	(6.7)	**-81**	(12.7)	**-85**	(8.7)	-5	(7.1)	-5	(5.1)	**-65**	(10.7)	**-57**	(8.7)	-6	(6.8)	-7	(4.6)	**-47**	(9.7)	**-21**	(10.2)
	Hungary	0	(17.0)	18	(14.8)	c	c	c	c	0	(19.8)	9	(10.7)	c	c	c	c	13	(16.9)	-3	(8.2)	c	c	c	c
	Iceland	**-30**	(9.9)	**9**	(3.3)	**-16**	(7.5)	c	c	**-30**	(8.9)	2	(3.4)	**-15**	(7.1)	c	c	**-31**	(9.2)	-5	(3.8)	-11	(7.0)	c	c
	Ireland	4	(6.3)	-4	(5.6)	**-24**	(9.8)	c	c	4	(5.9)	-2	(4.0)	**-16**	(7.0)	c	c	6	(5.8)	0	(3.7)	-9	(5.5)	c	c
	Israel	-3	(5.1)	-8	(15.0)	2	(16.3)	26	(17.7)	-3	(4.6)	-5	(11.2)	5	(12.3)	**27**	(12.7)	-6	(4.9)	-1	(9.2)	11	(9.5)	**28**	(10.0)
	Italy	-4	(2.1)	2	(8.3)	**-31**	(8.8)	**-76**	(7.9)	-4	(2.3)	4	(7.1)	**-22**	(7.6)	**-60**	(7.2)	**-7**	(2.1)	**11**	(5.5)	4	(6.2)	-12	(7.1)
	Japan	c	c	1	(19.1)	c	c	c	c	c	c	0	(15.1)	c	c	c	c	c	c	-3	(8.4)	c	c	c	c
	Korea	c	c	c	c	c	c	c	c	c	c	c	c	c	c	c	c	c	c	c	c	c	c	c	c
	Luxembourg	-8	(4.7)	c	c	c	c	c	c	-8	(4.0)	c	c	c	c	c	c	-1	(3.8)	c	c	c	c	c	c
	Mexico	**-10**	(4.5)	-5	(3.7)	**-21**	(6.7)	**-53**	(8.9)	**-10**	(4.4)	-5	(3.1)	**-12**	(5.4)	**-32**	(8.8)	**-11**	(4.3)	-4	(3.2)	-4	(5.6)	-11	(9.2)
	Netherlands	-6	(5.9)	-10	(14.3)	**-38**	(11.4)	**-105**	(22.5)	-6	(5.5)	-11	(12.5)	**-32**	(9.8)	**-92**	(21.5)	**-18**	(5.8)	-7	(10.1)	-4	(10.0)	-27	(20.3)
	New Zealand	**-18**	(6.0)	**31**	(8.4)	**27**	(10.3)	8	(11.6)	**-18**	(5.4)	13	(7.3)	12	(8.9)	2	(10.1)	**-20**	(5.1)	-5	(8.4)	-2	(9.0)	0	(10.3)
	Norway	**-25**	(6.4)	-3	(6.8)	4	(8.0)	-9	(11.4)	**-25**	(6.2)	-4	(6.4)	1	(7.6)	-8	(11.2)	**-27**	(6.0)	-4	(6.3)	0	(7.4)	4	(11.9)
	Poland	-12	(17.4)	21	(18.7)	c	c	c	c	-12	(15.7)	9	(14.8)	c	c	c	c	-13	(15.8)	1	(12.8)	c	c	c	c
	Portugal	-1	(9.9)	-11	(8.0)	**-23**	(10.3)	c	c	-1	(9.2)	-12	(6.3)	**-22**	(8.8)	c	c	-2	(9.2)	-12	(6.3)	**-22**	(8.2)	c	c
	Slovak Republic	-21	(12.5)	-7	(12.6)	-33	(18.6)	**-75**	(26.5)	**-21**	(9.2)	-9	(9.4)	**-25**	(12.8)	**-49**	(19.1)	-18	(9.4)	-10	(7.2)	-14	(8.9)	-6	(13.1)
	Slovenia	-9	(6.1)	-5	(3.3)	**-50**	(5.2)	**-70**	(5.6)	-9	(6.0)	-5	(3.2)	**-41**	(5.1)	**-53**	(5.6)	**-19**	(5.9)	-3	(2.5)	**-15**	(5.1)	3	(8.0)
	Spain	**-12**	(4.0)	2	(5.9)	-2	(9.1)	7	(6.0)	**-12**	(3.6)	0	(4.3)	-1	(6.0)	5	(4.9)	**-12**	(3.6)	-1	(3.7)	0	(4.6)	7	(4.8)
	Sweden	**-31**	(7.4)	-2	(5.9)	**-14**	(6.2)	-4	(9.2)	**-31**	(7.1)	-3	(5.1)	-10	(5.2)	-2	(7.8)	**-34**	(6.7)	-2	(5.0)	-3	(5.0)	8	(7.7)
	Switzerland	**-19**	(3.8)	-5	(10.8)	-13	(11.3)	**-55**	(10.7)	**-19**	(3.6)	-10	(9.8)	-17	(9.4)	**-53**	(9.4)	**-25**	(3.6)	-16	(10.6)	-17	(8.9)	**-40**	(9.6)
	Turkey	9	(8.5)	-5	(16.3)	**-71**	(13.4)	**-59**	(17.2)	9	(7.9)	-4	(13.5)	**-57**	(11.4)	**-44**	(15.2)	6	(7.4)	1	(10.0)	**-20**	(9.9)	6	(13.9)
	United Kingdom	7	(6.3)	6	(7.3)	5	(18.3)	-3	(15.0)	7	(5.9)	5	(5.5)	8	(13.6)	-4	(11.0)	1	(5.4)	5	(4.3)	15	(8.2)	1	(8.2)
	United States	5	(5.1)	**20**	(9.4)	17	(13.4)	-18	(12.8)	5	(4.6)	**16**	(7.4)	17	(12.1)	-6	(10.1)	2	(4.4)	**13**	(6.4)	21	(11.9)	18	(9.2)
	OECD average	**-11**	(1.4)	**6**	(1.8)	**-13**	(2.2)	**-30**	(3.6)	**-11**	(1.3)	2	(1.4)	**-11**	(1.7)	**-23**	(2.9)	**-13**	(1.3)	-1	(1.2)	**-5**	(1.5)	-1	(2.3)
Partners	Albania	c	c	c	c	c	c	c	c	c	c	c	c	c	c	c	c	c	c	c	c	c	c	c	c
	Argentina	-10	(11.3)	**-21**	(7.9)	**-64**	(14.5)	c	c	-10	(12.7)	**-16**	(5.9)	**-44**	(13.6)	c	c	-13	(11.8)	-9	(4.7)	-21	(13.6)	c	c
	Brazil	-13	(9.1)	11	(7.6)	-15	(23.8)	40	(32.9)	-13	(8.4)	7	(5.5)	**-32**	(14.4)	**60**	(27.6)	-8	(8.6)	2	(4.0)	**-50**	(17.2)	**77**	(24.4)
	Bulgaria	0	(6.3)	**-25**	(11.3)	**-67**	(14.6)	**-91**	(10.7)	0	(5.6)	**-21**	(8.3)	**-49**	(12.3)	**-57**	(9.9)	2	(5.9)	**-14**	(5.9)	-20	(10.9)	4	(11.6)
	Colombia	**-40**	(14.4)	-11	(12.9)	c	c	c	c	**-40**	(14.4)	-14	(8.6)	c	c	c	c	**-33**	(14.0)	**-17**	(6.2)	c	c	c	c
	Costa Rica	7	(11.9)	14	(8.6)	**38**	(15.2)	c	c	7	(11.7)	8	(6.5)	10	(13.2)	c	c	11	(11.1)	2	(5.7)	-15	(12.1)	c	c
	Croatia	-9	(9.3)	-6	(9.8)	c	c	c	c	-9	(9.5)	-3	(8.2)	c	c	c	c	-11	(9.3)	3	(7.8)	c	c	c	c
	Cyprus*	1	(6.0)	4	(4.2)	-1	(5.3)	**52**	(6.5)	1	(5.4)	4	(4.0)	-3	(5.2)	**34**	(6.2)	**-11**	(4.9)	6	(4.0)	-6	(5.0)	6	(5.7)
	Hong Kong-China	**-23**	(6.3)	**-34**	(11.9)	**-54**	(16.4)	**-84**	(30.2)	**-23**	(6.0)	**-30**	(10.0)	**-45**	(14.5)	**-91**	(18.1)	**-31**	(5.7)	**-22**	(9.1)	**-28**	(12.8)	**-93**	(12.7)
	Indonesia	**25**	(4.5)	-2	(27.2)	2	(28.0)	**-47**	(18.9)	**25**	(4.2)	-5	(19.4)	-1	(22.6)	**-40**	(13.5)	**26**	(4.0)	-7	(14.2)	-3	(19.4)	**-24**	(11.7)
	Jordan	-9	(5.4)	1	(10.4)	5	(15.2)	c	c	-9	(5.3)	-2	(9.2)	-3	(12.9)	c	c	-9	(5.4)	-5	(8.1)	-18	(11.2)	c	c
	Kazakhstan	-1	(5.7)	15	(8.1)	**34**	(8.8)	21	(13.3)	-1	(5.6)	10	(7.4)	**26**	(8.1)	16	(12.5)	0	(5.7)	5	(7.1)	**16**	(8.1)	9	(12.1)
	Latvia	-6	(5.9)	**34**	(6.6)	13	(9.3)	4	(8.9)	-6	(5.8)	**18**	(5.6)	6	(8.1)	1	(7.5)	-7	(5.9)	5	(5.9)	0	(7.6)	2	(7.3)
	Liechtenstein	-4	(13.8)	c	c	c	c	c	c	-4	(15.2)	c	c	c	c	c	c	-6	(14.2)	c	c	c	c	c	c
	Lithuania	**-26**	(9.0)	**23**	(7.0)	1	(9.9)	**-40**	(13.2)	**-26**	(9.5)	**13**	(5.9)	-4	(8.6)	**-33**	(12.9)	**-27**	(8.6)	1	(5.3)	-7	(8.5)	-17	(13.0)
	Macao-China	**-11**	(5.5)	**-19**	(2.5)	c	c	6	(5.5)	**-11**	(5.6)	**-15**	(2.5)	c	c	0	(5.5)	**-12**	(5.6)	**-8**	(2.6)	c	c	**-17**	(5.5)
	Malaysia	**12**	(4.9)	10	(13.7)	-3	(9.0)	**31**	(9.8)	**12**	(4.2)	4	(10.5)	-6	(6.8)	**17**	(7.5)	**9**	(3.9)	-3	(9.1)	-10	(6.8)	3	(7.0)
	Montenegro	-19	(14.4)	**-14**	(2.2)	c	c	c	c	-19	(13.2)	**-11**	(2.2)	c	c	c	c	-16	(12.9)	-2	(2.1)	c	c	c	c
	Peru	**-15**	(5.9)	3	(10.9)	**-72**	(16.4)	**-69**	(9.3)	**-15**	(5.5)	-1	(6.8)	**-54**	(15.7)	**-43**	(6.9)	**-17**	(4.9)	-4	(4.6)	**-36**	(16.6)	**-15**	(6.8)
	Qatar	**-48**	(3.8)	-5	(4.1)	**-15**	(5.5)	**131**	(5.1)	**-48**	(3.7)	-6	(3.9)	**-17**	(5.4)	**121**	(4.9)	**-46**	(3.6)	**-9**	(4.0)	**-19**	(5.4)	**106**	(5.0)
	Romania	-7	(11.0)	19	(11.4)	c	c	c	c	-7	(10.0)	6	(8.6)	c	c	c	c	-9	(9.8)	-7	(7.0)	c	c	c	c
	Russian Federation	**-21**	(5.5)	2	(8.8)	-11	(10.4)	6	(10.0)	**-21**	(4.9)	0	(6.9)	-3	(9.8)	15	(9.4)	**-20**	(5.0)	-1	(5.7)	3	(10.1)	**25**	(11.8)
	Serbia	7	(6.7)	-9	(11.0)	-32	(21.1)	-5	(15.3)	7	(6.8)	-6	(9.1)	-26	(17.9)	7	(13.1)	4	(6.5)	2	(6.6)	-11	(14.0)	**38**	(11.1)
	Shanghai-China	**-68**	(9.7)	**-62**	(10.0)	c	c	c	c	**-68**	(9.3)	**-44**	(8.9)	c	c	c	c	**-70**	(9.0)	-13	(9.6)	c	c	c	c
	Singapore	**-10**	(3.0)	c	c	c	c	c	c	**-10**	(3.2)	c	c	c	c	c	c	-6	(3.3)	c	c	c	c	c	c
	Chinese Taipei	**-15**	(4.4)	**-55**	(20.4)	**-71**	(19.6)	**-100**	(19.3)	**-15**	(4.3)	-32	(18.1)	**-41**	(17.4)	**-61**	(17.5)	**-19**	(4.1)	19	(16.3)	29	(16.8)	**43**	(17.9)
	Thailand	**20**	(5.1)	-39	(22.1)	**-46**	(21.9)	**-59**	(19.5)	**20**	(4.6)	-31	(18.1)	-35	(18.1)	**-44**	(16.0)	**20**	(4.1)	-22	(15.0)	-22	(15.4)	-19	(13.9)
	Tunisia	**-22**	(10.9)	2	(10.0)	c	c	c	c	-22	(12.2)	3	(8.5)	c	c	c	c	-14	(10.2)	2	(7.6)	c	c	c	c
	United Arab Emirates	**-26**	(4.4)	-1	(5.3)	**17**	(7.9)	**92**	(6.7)	**-26**	(4.2)	-1	(5.0)	**14**	(7.1)	**80**	(5.9)	**-25**	(4.0)	-2	(5.8)	10	(6.9)	**63**	(5.5)
	Uruguay	14	(10.1)	-3	(12.6)	-40	(30.2)	c	c	14	(9.8)	-4	(7.2)	-33	(19.1)	c	c	14	(9.5)	-4	(4.9)	-27	(15.0)	c	c
	Viet Nam	1	(11.0)	16	(18.8)	**-64**	(20.6)	c	c	1	(11.0)	10	(14.5)	**-48**	(16.3)	c	c	-2	(11.7)	4	(11.4)	-28	(16.4)	c	c

Note: This table was calculated considering only students with data on the *PISA index of economic, social and cultural status*. Values that are statistically significant are indicated in bold (see Annex A3).

1. The *PISA index of economic, social and cultural status* (ESCS).

* See notes at the beginning of this Annex.

StatLink http://dx.doi.org/10.1787/888932964927

[Part 1/2]
Host country/economy, country of origin and mathematics performance

Table II.3.11   *Results based on students' self-reports*

Host country/economy	Country of origin	Percentage of students out of all students in the sample		Performance in mathematics		Performance in mathematics after accounting for socio-economic status within each immigrant group		Performance in mathematics after accounting for socio-economic status of the host country/economy	
		%	S.E.	Mean score	S.E.	Mean score	S.E.	Mean score	S.E.
Australia	China	2.3	(0.2)	596	(13.5)	585	(11.6)	584	(11.5)
	India	1.1	(0.1)	563	(8.9)	522	(11.0)	532	(8.0)
	New Zealand	2.3	(0.2)	485	(5.7)	484	(5.3)	486	(4.1)
	Philippines	1.0	(0.1)	517	(9.1)	507	(7.6)	507	(6.5)
	United Kingdom	3.5	(0.2)	525	(4.6)	508	(5.5)	499	(3.0)
	Viet Nam	1.9	(0.2)	548	(6.9)	553	(8.1)	566	(7.0)
Austria	Bosnia and Herzegovina	3.5	(0.4)	462	(8.9)	463	(10.9)	478	(8.6)
	Former Yugoslavia	2.8	(0.3)	435	(8.3)	454	(10.2)	458	(8.2)
	Germany	0.8	(0.2)	554	(16.3)	526	(17.8)	515	(8.9)
	Romania	0.7	(0.2)	510	(23.1)	508	(20.8)	517	(14.2)
	Turkey	3.6	(0.4)	422	(8.6)	464	(11.6)	467	(8.0)
Belgium	African country	5.1	(0.5)	445	(6.6)	453	(6.2)	470	(4.7)
	East European country	1.7	(0.2)	457	(10.0)	461	(9.3)	473	(6.9)
	France	1.7	(0.5)	462	(22.1)	464	(15.0)	480	(9.9)
	Germany	0.3	(0.1)	525	(13.2)	510	(9.1)	508	(9.5)
	Netherlands Antilles	0.7	(0.2)	506	(14.5)	503	(12.3)	515	(9.3)
	Turkey	1.7	(0.3)	432	(13.8)	454	(12.7)	473	(8.9)
	Western European country	1.4	(0.2)	454	(10.6)	459	(10.3)	480	(6.3)
Czech Republic	Slovak Republic	0.8	(0.2)	458	(23.3)	488	(19.1)	489	(8.7)
	Ukraine	0.7	(0.1)	492	(16.1)	488	(18.5)	502	(12.6)
	Viet Nam	0.5	(0.1)	524	(14.9)	521	(17.0)	532	(24.7)
Denmark	Afghanistan	0.4	(0.1)	444	(11.0)	445	(10.9)	453	(12.3)
	Former Yugoslavia	0.8	(0.1)	459	(8.0)	460	(7.5)	462	(7.3)
	Iraq	1.0	(0.1)	429	(8.5)	433	(8.5)	436	(7.7)
	Lebanon	0.6	(0.1)	423	(7.5)	429	(8.7)	438	(6.5)
	Pakistan	0.7	(0.3)	433	(14.6)	444	(14.4)	446	(12.4)
	Somalia	0.5	(0.1)	406	(9.2)	404	(10.1)	424	(11.8)
	Turkey	1.1	(0.1)	423	(5.7)	428	(7.2)	446	(5.7)
Estonia	Russian Federation	6.2	(0.5)	500	(5.5)	497	(5.6)	507	(4.4)
Finland	Estonia	0.4	(0.0)	467	(8.9)	469	(7.8)	488	(6.5)
	Former Yugoslavia	0.2	(0.0)	445	(10.7)	451	(11.4)	471	(17.3)
	Iraq	0.2	(0.0)	445	(12.8)	455	(13.1)	460	(11.9)
	Russian Federation	0.6	(0.1)	471	(9.1)	469	(9.9)	477	(8.7)
	Somalia	0.4	(0.1)	385	(6.5)	394	(6.7)	402	(6.7)
	Turkey	0.1	(0.0)	428	(21.5)	427	(21.9)	473	(11.6)
Germany	Poland	1.5	(0.2)	505	(13.8)	505	(13.7)	504	(9.5)
	Russian Federation	3.9	(0.4)	489	(8.7)	497	(7.7)	501	(7.5)
	Turkey	3.6	(0.4)	453	(9.4)	472	(11.6)	480	(7.1)
Greece	Albania	5.7	(0.5)	407	(7.1)	420	(8.0)	439	(7.0)
	Russian Federation	2.3	(0.4)	405	(12.3)	421	(10.9)	436	(9.0)
Ireland	United Kingdom	2.8	(0.3)	517	(9.3)	505	(9.6)	503	(3.5)
Israel	Ethiopia	1.5	(0.3)	387	(12.8)	386	(24.0)	463	(15.6)
	France	1.2	(0.2)	471	(18.1)	447	(19.0)	463	(14.0)
	Russian Federation	8.0	(0.9)	492	(7.9)	487	(7.3)	484	(6.3)
	South and Central America	0.8	(0.1)	486	(16.7)	465	(14.7)	483	(10.7)
	United States	1.7	(0.4)	521	(9.2)	501	(10.9)	504	(9.1)
Italy	European Union	2.3	(0.2)	440	(6.1)	457	(6.2)	475	(3.7)
Luxembourg	Belgium	2.0	(0.2)	533	(8.3)	524	(10.2)	506	(6.0)
	Cape Verde	2.7	(0.2)	413	(7.6)	426	(12.7)	450	(7.4)
	European Union	3.1	(0.2)	537	(8.6)	491	(11.3)	506	(6.4)
	Former Yugoslavia	4.9	(0.3)	447	(6.8)	453	(7.6)	463	(6.6)
	France	4.0	(0.3)	521	(6.3)	503	(6.3)	501	(4.4)
	Germany	1.7	(0.2)	551	(10.2)	515	(14.3)	510	(5.4)
	Italy	2.0	(0.2)	476	(9.6)	470	(9.0)	466	(6.9)
	Portugal	19.7	(0.5)	442	(2.9)	448	(3.7)	473	(2.7)
Netherlands	Morocco	1.8	(0.3)	456	(14.2)	455	(17.4)	474	(13.4)
	Suriname	0.9	(0.2)	479	(12.0)	478	(11.8)	476	(9.5)
	Turkey	2.8	(0.4)	460	(14.1)	467	(16.5)	482	(12.5)

Note: A student's country of origin is determined using both the country of birth the student reported for both their father and mother (only students with valid answers for both these variables are included in this analysis). Only students with an immigrant background (first- and second-generation students) are considered for this analysis. Only those students who reported a specific country of origin (that is, a country "other than the test country") were included in this analysis. If both parents share the same country of birth (different from the test country), then the student's country of origin is the same as his/her parents' country of birth. If they are different, then the father's country of birth is used.
* See notes at the beginning of this Annex.

StatLink http://dx.doi.org/10.1787/888932964927

[Part 2/2]
Host country/economy, country of origin and mathematics performance
Table II.3.11 *Results based on students' self-reports*

Host country/economy	Country of origin	Percentage of students out of all students in the sample %	S.E.	Performance in mathematics Mean score	S.E.	Performance in mathematics after accounting for socio-economic status within each immigrant group Mean score	S.E.	Performance in mathematics after accounting for socio-economic status of the host country/economy Mean score	S.E.
New Zealand	China	2.3	(0.4)	588	(12.2)	582	(11.7)	581	(10.2)
	Fiji	1.7	(0.2)	465	(13.8)	472	(13.1)	480	(11.7)
	Korea	1.2	(0.2)	586	(14.6)	569	(18.2)	566	(13.8)
	Samoa	2.8	(0.4)	416	(7.6)	433	(12.5)	451	(7.0)
	South Africa	1.7	(0.2)	507	(9.2)	487	(11.4)	494	(9.0)
	United Kingdom	3.5	(0.3)	528	(7.8)	505	(7.8)	515	(4.4)
Portugal	African country (Portuguese speaking)	3.4	(0.5)	440	(7.7)	469	(8.3)	493	(4.7)
	Brazil	1.0	(0.2)	443	(11.4)	444	(13.3)	471	(9.8)
	East European country (not EU)	0.5	(0.1)	504	(16.1)	507	(14.7)	515	(15.3)
	European Union	0.7	(0.1)	485	(16.3)	488	(16.9)	511	(5.9)
Switzerland	Albania	0.5	(0.1)	417	(17.7)	435	(32.8)	448	(17.3)
	Former Yugoslavia	7.9	(0.5)	472	(5.5)	481	(6.2)	492	(5.0)
	France	0.7	(0.1)	524	(11.3)	508	(12.5)	526	(6.1)
	Germany	1.6	(0.2)	524	(10.3)	489	(19.3)	513	(6.6)
	Italy	1.9	(0.2)	476	(10.0)	483	(8.0)	498	(6.8)
	Portugal	3.1	(0.2)	487	(6.9)	506	(14.8)	521	(6.2)
	Spain	0.6	(0.1)	494	(14.2)	500	(16.5)	515	(10.4)
	Turkey	1.5	(0.2)	462	(12.0)	475	(10.1)	490	(10.5)
Argentina	Bolivia (Plurinational State of)	1.4	(0.2)	353	(12.3)	368	(33.4)	396	(10.1)
	Paraguay	1.1	(0.3)	360	(13.1)	388	(18.4)	398	(10.9)
Costa Rica	Nicaragua	4.2	(0.7)	365	(10.2)	393	(12.9)	417	(6.2)
Croatia	Bosnia and Herzegovina	9.6	(0.6)	457	(5.8)	471	(6.6)	481	(5.1)
	Other former Yugoslavia	1.1	(0.2)	459	(11.8)	475	(14.8)	498	(8.6)
Cyprus*	East European country	0.8	(0.1)	432	(15.0)	439	(15.9)	445	(8.9)
	Greece	1.4	(0.2)	427	(11.4)	429	(11.0)	431	(7.1)
	Russian Federation	1.6	(0.2)	461	(11.1)	457	(9.7)	460	(8.2)
	United Kingdom	1.0	(0.1)	447	(14.3)	419	(15.6)	438	(6.1)
Hong Kong-China	China	31.7	(1.4)	562	(3.4)	594	(5.2)	596	(3.7)
	Macao-China	0.8	(0.1)	554	(14.5)	572	(23.4)	578	(12.9)
Kazakhstan	Russian Federation	12.1	(1.5)	432	(7.0)	442	(6.3)	448	(5.4)
Latvia	Belarus	0.7	(0.1)	507	(13.7)	508	(11.8)	502	(8.7)
	Russian Federation	1.8	(0.3)	486	(11.4)	485	(10.9)	494	(5.0)
	Ukraine	1.0	(0.3)	496	(20.1)	508	(16.7)	502	(8.5)
Macao-China	China	57.4	(0.7)	548	(1.4)	570	(2.7)	568	(1.8)
	Hong Kong-China	2.5	(0.3)	526	(8.1)	540	(11.0)	543	(5.8)
	Philippines	1.0	(0.1)	467	(13.1)	478	(12.4)	467	(11.6)
Montenegro	Bosnia and Herzegovina	1.3	(0.2)	455	(9.7)	453	(9.7)	442	(5.2)
	Serbia	2.9	(0.3)	424	(8.2)	427	(7.5)	426	(3.7)
Qatar	Egypt	7.0	(0.2)	416	(3.7)	393	(4.8)	397	(3.6)
	Jordan	1.6	(0.1)	411	(9.0)	371	(13.2)	388	(8.0)
	Palestinian Authority	2.3	(0.1)	396	(6.2)	377	(8.1)	375	(5.4)
	Yemen	2.8	(0.2)	349	(4.9)	351	(4.8)	350	(4.4)
Russian Federation	Other former USSR	8.3	(0.7)	473	(4.6)	477	(4.1)	491	(3.2)
Serbia	Other former Yugoslavia	7.4	(0.7)	468	(7.2)	481	(6.1)	479	(4.8)

Note: A student's country of origin is determined using both the country of birth the student reported for both their father and mother (only students with valid answers for both these variables are included in this analysis). Only students with an immigrant background (first- and second-generation students) are considered for this analysis. Only those students who reported a specific country of origin (that is, a country "other than the test country") were included in this analysis. If both parents share the same country of birth (different from the test country), then the student's country of origin is the same as his/her parents' country of birth. If they are different, then the father's country of birth is used.
* See notes at the beginning of this Annex.
StatLink http://dx.doi.org/10.1787/888932964927

[Part 1/3]
Table II.4.1 **Equity in opportunity to learn: Formal mathematics**
Results based on students' self-reports

		Descriptive statistics												Average index of opportunity to learn, by national quarter of the ESCS[1]							
		Mean index		First quartile: 25% of students are below this value		Third quartile: 25% of students are above this value		Interquartile range: difference between top and bottom quartiles		Standard deviation across all students		Skewness		Bottom quarter		Second quarter		Third quarter		Top quarter	
		Mean index	S.E.	Mean index	S.E.	Mean index	S.E.	Dif.	S.E.	S.D.	S.E.	Coef.	S.E.	Mean index	S.E.	Mean index	S.E.	Mean index	S.E.	Mean index	S.E.
OECD	Australia	1.69	(0.01)	1.17	(0.03)	2.25	(0.02)	**1.08**	(0.03)	0.70	(0.01)	-0.01	(1.62)	0.78	(0.01)	1.44	(0.02)	1.97	(0.02)	2.59	(0.01)
	Austria	1.54	(0.02)	1.00	(0.03)	2.08	(0.04)	**1.08**	(0.05)	0.69	(0.01)	0.01	(1.56)	0.66	(0.02)	1.28	(0.02)	1.80	(0.03)	2.43	(0.02)
	Belgium	1.83	(0.01)	1.39	(0.04)	2.36	(0.04)	**0.97**	(0.05)	0.72	(0.01)	-0.55	(1.81)	0.81	(0.02)	1.70	(0.02)	2.17	(0.01)	2.64	(0.01)
	Canada	1.98	(0.01)	1.58	(0.02)	2.44	(0.01)	**0.86**	(0.02)	0.61	(0.01)	-0.36	(1.92)	1.16	(0.02)	1.83	(0.01)	2.25	(0.01)	2.70	(0.01)
	Chile	1.70	(0.02)	1.28	(0.04)	2.11	(0.03)	**0.83**	(0.03)	0.58	(0.01)	-0.18	(1.82)	0.95	(0.02)	1.50	(0.02)	1.91	(0.02)	2.44	(0.02)
	Czech Republic	1.80	(0.02)	1.44	(0.02)	2.19	(0.04)	**0.75**	(0.04)	0.53	(0.01)	-0.33	(1.87)	1.10	(0.03)	1.65	(0.02)	2.00	(0.02)	2.46	(0.02)
	Denmark	1.62	(0.02)	1.19	(0.03)	2.06	(0.03)	**0.86**	(0.03)	0.60	(0.01)	0.01	(1.60)	0.85	(0.02)	1.42	(0.02)	1.83	(0.02)	2.39	(0.02)
	Estonia	2.00	(0.01)	1.75	(0.02)	2.31	(0.00)	**0.56**	(0.02)	0.45	(0.01)	-0.58	(2.01)	1.39	(0.02)	1.91	(0.01)	2.19	(0.01)	2.52	(0.01)
	Finland	1.72	(0.01)	1.31	(0.03)	2.14	(0.03)	**0.83**	(0.05)	0.59	(0.01)	-0.07	(1.62)	0.93	(0.02)	1.54	(0.02)	1.94	(0.02)	2.45	(0.01)
	France	1.87	(0.01)	1.53	(0.04)	2.28	(0.02)	**0.75**	(0.04)	0.56	(0.01)	-0.64	(1.88)	1.10	(0.03)	1.76	(0.02)	2.12	(0.01)	2.51	(0.01)
	Germany	1.66	(0.02)	1.19	(0.04)	2.17	(0.02)	**0.97**	(0.03)	0.66	(0.01)	-0.21	(1.67)	0.78	(0.02)	1.46	(0.02)	1.93	(0.02)	2.47	(0.02)
	Greece	1.91	(0.01)	1.58	(0.01)	2.33	(0.01)	**0.75**	(0.02)	0.58	(0.01)	-0.46	(1.91)	1.15	(0.03)	1.77	(0.02)	2.11	(0.01)	2.61	(0.01)
	Hungary	1.96	(0.02)	1.64	(0.04)	2.33	(0.03)	**0.69**	(0.04)	0.54	(0.01)	-0.73	(2.00)	1.22	(0.03)	1.85	(0.02)	2.19	(0.02)	2.57	(0.01)
	Iceland	1.14	(0.01)	0.67	(0.00)	1.50	(0.03)	**0.83**	(0.03)	0.62	(0.01)	0.80	(1.14)	0.45	(0.01)	0.86	(0.01)	1.25	(0.02)	2.01	(0.03)
	Ireland	1.47	(0.01)	1.00	(0.04)	1.92	(0.02)	**0.92**	(0.05)	0.60	(0.01)	0.00	(1.46)	0.69	(0.02)	1.26	(0.02)	1.69	(0.02)	2.24	(0.02)
	Israel	1.81	(0.02)	1.42	(0.05)	2.25	(0.04)	**0.83**	(0.04)	0.64	(0.01)	-0.42	(1.82)	0.94	(0.04)	1.67	(0.03)	2.08	(0.02)	2.56	(0.02)
	Italy	1.83	(0.01)	1.39	(0.02)	2.31	(0.04)	**0.92**	(0.04)	0.63	(0.01)	-0.29	(1.84)	0.99	(0.01)	1.64	(0.02)	2.08	(0.02)	2.61	(0.01)
	Japan	2.05	(0.02)	1.81	(0.03)	2.36	(0.03)	**0.56**	(0.04)	0.47	(0.01)	-0.83	(2.05)	1.43	(0.03)	1.96	(0.01)	2.22	(0.02)	2.60	(0.02)
	Korea	2.07	(0.02)	1.78	(0.03)	2.42	(0.03)	**0.64**	(0.04)	0.52	(0.01)	-0.83	(2.07)	1.34	(0.03)	1.99	(0.02)	2.31	(0.02)	2.64	(0.02)
	Luxembourg	1.45	(0.01)	0.92	(0.03)	2.00	(0.02)	**1.08**	(0.03)	0.71	(0.01)	0.23	(1.45)	0.57	(0.01)	1.14	(0.02)	1.68	(0.02)	2.40	(0.01)
	Mexico	1.78	(0.01)	1.31	(0.02)	2.28	(0.02)	**0.97**	(0.03)	0.65	(0.00)	-0.20	(1.80)	0.90	(0.01)	1.58	(0.01)	2.04	(0.01)	2.59	(0.01)
	Netherlands	1.50	(0.02)	1.00	(0.04)	1.97	(0.03)	**0.97**	(0.03)	0.67	(0.01)	-0.10	(1.48)	0.61	(0.03)	1.31	(0.03)	1.76	(0.02)	2.33	(0.02)
	New Zealand	1.51	(0.02)	0.97	(0.04)	2.06	(0.04)	**1.08**	(0.05)	0.71	(0.01)	0.01	(1.51)	0.59	(0.02)	1.25	(0.02)	1.78	(0.02)	2.44	(0.02)
	Norway	m	m	m	m	m	m	m	m	m	m	m	m	m	m	m	m	m	m	m	m
	Poland	1.83	(0.02)	1.44	(0.02)	2.25	(0.03)	**0.81**	(0.04)	0.55	(0.01)	-0.15	(1.85)	1.12	(0.02)	1.66	(0.02)	2.03	(0.02)	2.52	(0.02)
	Portugal	1.73	(0.02)	1.33	(0.04)	2.19	(0.04)	**0.86**	(0.04)	0.60	(0.01)	-0.27	(1.71)	0.91	(0.02)	1.56	(0.02)	1.96	(0.02)	2.47	(0.02)
	Slovak Republic	1.70	(0.01)	1.33	(0.01)	2.06	(0.03)	**0.72**	(0.03)	0.56	(0.01)	-0.14	(1.72)	0.98	(0.02)	1.53	(0.02)	1.88	(0.02)	2.41	(0.03)
	Slovenia	1.93	(0.01)	1.56	(0.01)	2.33	(0.00)	**0.78**	(0.01)	0.56	(0.01)	-0.28	(1.88)	1.19	(0.02)	1.77	(0.01)	2.14	(0.01)	2.61	(0.01)
	Spain	1.87	(0.01)	1.39	(0.02)	2.39	(0.02)	**1.00**	(0.03)	0.66	(0.01)	-0.35	(1.91)	0.98	(0.01)	1.67	(0.02)	2.16	(0.01)	2.68	(0.01)
	Sweden	0.77	(0.01)	0.33	(0.09)	1.00	(0.00)	**0.67**	(0.09)	0.56	(0.02)	1.74	(0.77)	0.29	(0.01)	0.48	(0.01)	0.76	(0.02)	1.56	(0.04)
	Switzerland	1.41	(0.02)	0.86	(0.04)	1.94	(0.04)	**1.08**	(0.05)	0.71	(0.01)	0.14	(1.48)	0.53	(0.02)	1.11	(0.03)	1.64	(0.03)	2.37	(0.02)
	Turkey	1.92	(0.01)	1.61	(0.02)	2.33	(0.03)	**0.72**	(0.03)	0.55	(0.01)	-0.61	(1.92)	1.16	(0.02)	1.82	(0.02)	2.15	(0.02)	2.55	(0.01)
	United Kingdom	1.63	(0.02)	1.11	(0.03)	2.14	(0.03)	**1.03**	(0.04)	0.66	(0.01)	0.02	(1.49)	0.76	(0.02)	1.41	(0.03)	1.90	(0.02)	2.45	(0.02)
	United States	2.00	(0.02)	1.56	(0.05)	2.50	(0.03)	**0.94**	(0.06)	0.64	(0.01)	-0.47	(2.01)	1.12	(0.03)	1.83	(0.02)	2.28	(0.02)	2.76	(0.02)
	OECD average	1.70	(0.00)	1.29	(0.01)	2.13	(0.00)	**0.84**	(0.01)	0.60	(0.00)	-0.29	(0.29)	0.92	(0.00)	1.52	(0.00)	1.92	(0.00)	2.43	(0.00)
Partners	Albania	2.09	(0.01)	1.71	(0.03)	2.56	(0.00)	**0.85**	(0.03)	0.65	(0.01)	-0.67	(2.08)	1.19	(0.03)	1.97	(0.02)	2.40	(0.01)	2.80	(0.01)
	Argentina	1.35	(0.03)	0.83	(0.04)	1.83	(0.05)	**1.00**	(0.06)	0.69	(0.01)	0.22	(1.40)	0.49	(0.02)	1.06	(0.03)	1.56	(0.03)	2.28	(0.04)
	Brazil	1.43	(0.02)	0.89	(0.02)	1.94	(0.03)	**1.06**	(0.03)	0.71	(0.01)	0.25	(1.42)	0.54	(0.02)	1.14	(0.02)	1.67	(0.02)	2.38	(0.02)
	Bulgaria	1.96	(0.02)	1.56	(0.03)	2.47	(0.03)	**0.92**	(0.04)	0.67	(0.01)	-0.66	(1.98)	1.03	(0.04)	1.83	(0.03)	2.27	(0.02)	2.71	(0.01)
	Colombia	1.76	(0.02)	1.22	(0.03)	2.31	(0.04)	**1.08**	(0.04)	0.71	(0.01)	-0.20	(1.78)	0.80	(0.02)	1.53	(0.03)	2.06	(0.02)	2.64	(0.02)
	Costa Rica	1.53	(0.03)	0.97	(0.04)	2.08	(0.05)	**1.11**	(0.05)	0.72	(0.01)	0.14	(1.53)	0.63	(0.02)	1.23	(0.03)	1.78	(0.03)	2.49	(0.04)
	Croatia	2.07	(0.01)	1.72	(0.03)	2.44	(0.03)	**0.72**	(0.04)	0.57	(0.01)	-0.49	(2.06)	1.32	(0.02)	1.93	(0.02)	2.29	(0.01)	2.74	(0.01)
	Cyprus*	1.87	(0.01)	1.47	(0.03)	2.33	(0.00)	**0.86**	(0.03)	0.64	(0.01)	-0.40	(1.84)	1.02	(0.02)	1.71	(0.01)	2.12	(0.01)	2.64	(0.01)
	Hong Kong-China	1.83	(0.02)	1.33	(0.04)	2.33	(0.01)	**1.00**	(0.04)	0.64	(0.01)	-0.07	(1.83)	1.01	(0.02)	1.60	(0.02)	2.06	(0.02)	2.65	(0.02)
	Indonesia	1.60	(0.02)	1.19	(0.03)	2.00	(0.02)	**0.81**	(0.03)	0.58	(0.01)	0.02	(1.61)	0.86	(0.02)	1.40	(0.02)	1.80	(0.02)	2.33	(0.03)
	Jordan	2.15	(0.02)	1.75	(0.07)	2.67	(0.04)	**0.92**	(0.06)	0.76	(0.01)	-0.93	(2.13)	1.02	(0.04)	2.11	(0.02)	2.56	(0.01	2.90	(0.01)
	Kazakhstan	1.97	(0.02)	1.64	(0.04)	2.33	(0.02)	**0.69**	(0.03)	0.56	(0.01)	-0.64	(1.98)	1.20	(0.03)	1.86	(0.02)	2.21	(0.02)	2.61	(0.02)
	Latvia	2.03	(0.01)	1.75	(0.04)	2.33	(0.02)	**0.58**	(0.03)	0.47	(0.01)	-0.67	(2.06)	1.39	(0.02)	1.94	(0.01)	2.21	(0.01	2.57	(0.02)
	Liechtenstein	1.55	(0.05)	0.94	(0.05)	2.19	(0.07)	**1.25**	(0.08)	0.75	(0.02)	0.15	(1.57)	0.63	(0.05)	1.20	(0.05)	1.82	(0.08	2.57	(0.05)
	Lithuania	1.65	(0.01)	1.31	(0.03)	2.00	(0.02)	**0.69**	(0.04)	0.52	(0.01)	-0.23	(1.65)	0.96	(0.02)	1.50	(0.02)	1.84	(0.01	2.28	(0.01)
	Macao-China	2.20	(0.01)	1.83	(0.01)	2.67	(0.00)	**0.83**	(0.01)	0.57	(0.01)	-0.70	(2.20)	1.41	(0.02)	2.07	(0.01)	2.47	(0.01	2.84	(0.01)
	Malaysia	1.59	(0.02)	1.19	(0.03)	2.00	(0.04)	**0.81**	(0.04)	0.60	(0.01)	-0.20	(1.60)	0.79	(0.02)	1.42	(0.02)	1.81	(0.02	2.33	(0.02)
	Montenegro	1.90	(0.01)	1.50	(0.03)	2.33	(0.01)	**0.83**	(0.04)	0.63	(0.01)	-0.42	(1.91)	1.04	(0.02)	1.75	(0.02)	2.15	(0.01	2.65	(0.01)
	Peru	1.79	(0.02)	1.25	(0.04)	2.33	(0.01)	**1.08**	(0.03)	0.72	(0.01)	-0.14	(1.79)	0.84	(0.02)	1.56	(0.03)	2.09	(0.03	2.68	(0.02)
	Qatar	1.72	(0.01)	1.03	(0.03)	2.39	(0.02)	**1.36**	(0.04)	0.82	(0.01)	-0.07	(1.71)	0.65	(0.01)	1.39	(0.02)	2.07	(0.02	2.75	(0.01)
	Romania	2.02	(0.02)	1.67	(0.05)	2.50	(0.02)	**0.83**	(0.05)	0.63	(0.01)	-0.68	(2.03)	1.13	(0.04)	1.91	(0.03)	2.32	(0.02	2.72	(0.01)
	Russian Federation	2.10	(0.01)	1.92	(0.04)	2.33	(0.02)	**0.42**	(0.04)	0.41	(0.01)	-1.25	(2.10)	1.56	(0.02)	2.10	(0.01)	2.24	(0.00	2.52	(0.01)
	Serbia	2.04	(0.01)	1.75	(0.02)	2.42	(0.02)	**0.67**	(0.03)	0.54	(0.01)	-0.75	(2.04)	1.31	(0.03)	1.94	(0.01)	2.26	(0.01	2.65	(0.01)
	Shanghai-China	2.30	(0.01)	2.11	(0.00)	2.56	(0.01)	**0.44**	(0.01)	0.46	(0.02)	-1.32	(2.29)	1.70	(0.04)	2.24	(0.01)	2.49	(0.01	2.76	(0.01)
	Singapore	2.23	(0.01)	1.81	(0.04)	2.75	(0.03)	**0.94**	(0.05)	0.64	(0.01)	-0.73	(2.21)	1.31	(0.02)	2.10	(0.02)	2.57	(0.01	2.92	(0.01)
	Chinese Taipei	1.98	(0.01)	1.64	(0.03)	2.39	(0.03)	**0.75**	(0.03)	0.57	(0.01)	-0.54	(1.97)	1.22	(0.02)	1.84	(0.02)	2.21	(0.01	2.66	(0.01)
	Thailand	1.70	(0.01)	1.33	(0.01)	2.08	(0.03)	**0.75**	(0.03)	0.54	(0.01)	-0.18	(1.77)	1.00	(0.02)	1.54	(0.02)	1.90	(0.01	2.37	(0.01)
	Tunisia	1.23	(0.01)	0.81	(0.04)	1.58	(0.03)	**0.78**	(0.04)	0.60	(0.01)	0.63	(1.23)	0.54	(0.01)	0.98	(0.01)	1.36	(0.02	2.04	(0.03)
	United Arab Emirates	2.13	(0.02)	1.69	(0.04)	2.67	(0.00)	**0.97**	(0.04)	0.71	(0.01)	-0.64	(2.09)	1.12	(0.03)	2.01	(0.02)	2.48	(0.01	2.90	(0.01)
	Uruguay	1.64	(0.02)	1.14	(0.04)	2.14	(0.03)	**1.00**	(0.04)	0.68	(0.01)	-0.18	(1.64)	0.73	(0.02)	1.43	(0.02)	1.91	(0.02	2.48	(0.02)
	Viet Nam	1.96	(0.02)	1.67	(0.01)	2.31	(0.04)	**0.64**	(0.03)	0.47	(0.01)	-0.41	(1.95)	1.34	(0.03)	1.83	(0.02)	2.13	(0.02	2.52	(0.02)

Note: Values that are statistically significant are indicated in bold (see Annex A3).
1. ESCS refers to the *PISA index of economic, social and cultural status.*
* See notes at the beginning of this Annex.
StatLink http://dx.doi.org/10.1787/888932964946

[Part 2/3]
Equity in opportunity to learn: Formal mathematics
Table II.4.1 *Results based on students' self-reports*

	Mathematics score, by national quarters of this index								Strength of the opportunity gradient: explained variation in student performance (r-squared x 100)		Slope of the opportunity gradient: change in mathematics score per unit of this index		Index of curvilinearity: change in mathematics score per unit of this index squared	
	Bottom quarter		Second quarter		Third quarter		Top quarter							
	Mean score	S.E.	Mean score	S.E.	Mean score	S.E.	Mean score	S.E.	%	S.E.	Score dif.	S.E.	Score dif.	S.E.
OECD														
Australia	431	(1.9)	485	(2.6)	528	(2.8)	587	(3.2)	**39**	(1.0)	**85**	(1.6)	3	(1.9)
Austria	445	(4.0)	489	(4.5)	525	(4.8)	574	(5.2)	**28**	(2.2)	**71**	(3.0)	-5	(3.4)
Belgium	437	(3.5)	512	(3.3)	552	(3.1)	584	(3.5)	**33**	(1.4)	**80**	(1.9)	-1	(2.7)
Canada	464	(2.6)	507	(2.5)	540	(2.9)	569	(2.8)	**22**	(1.0)	**68**	(1.7)	-2	(2.4)
Chile	373	(3.9)	402	(4.5)	437	(4.1)	478	(4.4)	**25**	(1.6)	**71**	(2.8)	7	(3.4)
Czech Republic	448	(4.5)	490	(5.7)	521	(4.6)	562	(4.6)	**24**	(1.9)	**83**	(3.5)	2	(5.4)
Denmark	456	(3.8)	494	(2.8)	518	(3.4)	544	(3.6)	**19**	(1.7)	**57**	(3.0)	**-11**	(3.0)
Estonia	488	(3.4)	514	(3.9)	535	(3.8)	549	(4.1)	**9**	(1.1)	**55**	(3.3)	**-11**	(5.7)
Finland	472	(2.8)	503	(2.9)	538	(2.5)	571	(3.3)	**23**	(1.6)	**67**	(2.5)	4	(3.4)
France	417	(4.7)	488	(4.7)	526	(4.3)	557	(4.4)	**31**	(2.2)	**95**	(3.9)	-8	(5.3)
Germany	450	(3.5)	503	(5.4)	549	(4.5)	591	(4.1)	**33**	(1.7)	**82**	(2.8)	-4	(3.5)
Greece	409	(6.0)	458	(4.0)	467	(3.9)	474	(3.8)	**9**	(1.3)	**46**	(3.5)	**-18**	(3.0)
Hungary	414	(4.2)	459	(5.1)	500	(4.7)	539	(6.9)	**27**	(2.2)	**91**	(5.5)	12	(6.0)
Iceland	466	(4.6)	494	(4.1)	512	(3.7)	515	(4.2)	**3**	(0.9)	**26**	(3.8)	**-31**	(4.0)
Ireland	440	(4.2)	496	(3.9)	523	(3.3)	552	(3.3)	**26**	(1.5)	**71**	(2.5)	**-22**	(3.4)
Israel	404	(6.3)	454	(6.5)	498	(5.6)	522	(6.5)	**20**	(1.7)	**73**	(3.6)	-7	(4.3)
Italy	427	(2.8)	469	(2.4)	503	(3.0)	545	(3.5)	**23**	(1.2)	**71**	(2.3)	4	(2.1)
Japan	472	(5.4)	529	(4.4)	557	(4.5)	598	(5.5)	**30**	(1.8)	**106**	(4.0)	2	(4.6)
Korea	471	(5.5)	537	(5.4)	583	(5.9)	622	(7.5)	**36**	(1.9)	**115**	(4.6)	13	(6.3)
Luxembourg	442	(3.2)	475	(3.4)	509	(3.0)	542	(3.1)	**16**	(1.3)	**53**	(2.3)	**-11**	(3.2)
Mexico	373	(1.9)	404	(2.0)	428	(1.8)	451	(2.4)	**16**	(0.9)	**46**	(1.5)	-3	(1.5)
Netherlands	448	(5.8)	514	(5.3)	556	(4.6)	597	(5.2)	**42**	(2.5)	**87**	(3.4)	**-11**	(3.9)
New Zealand	425	(3.3)	482	(4.2)	522	(4.1)	583	(5.1)	**36**	(2.1)	**84**	(2.9)	-1	(4.5)
Norway	m	m	m	m	m	m	m	m	m	m	m	m	m	m
Poland	473	(4.4)	503	(4.5)	534	(3.9)	560	(8.5)	**15**	(1.9)	**64**	(4.8)	-4	(6.2)
Portugal	426	(5.2)	475	(6.0)	515	(4.9)	543	(4.7)	**23**	(1.7)	**74**	(3.1)	-8	(3.4)
Slovak Republic	405	(5.6)	472	(5.3)	505	(5.1)	552	(5.9)	**30**	(2.0)	**99**	(4.0)	-7	(5.4)
Slovenia	455	(3.5)	493	(3.8)	517	(4.2)	546	(4.7)	**15**	(1.6)	**62**	(3.9)	-8	(5.7)
Spain	419	(2.7)	473	(3.1)	509	(2.2)	542	(2.9)	**29**	(1.2)	**71**	(1.8)	-8	(1.9)
Sweden	458	(3.3)	483	(3.5)	494	(3.9)	486	(4.9)	**1**	(0.5)	**13**	(4.3)	**-22**	(4.9)
Switzerland	472	(3.9)	520	(4.1)	549	(4.3)	589	(4.8)	**22**	(1.6)	**62**	(2.6)	**-12**	(3.2)
Turkey	398	(4.1)	436	(5.9)	466	(5.8)	491	(8.3)	**15**	(1.5)	**64**	(4.8)	5	(4.4)
United Kingdom	421	(4.6)	480	(4.7)	519	(5.1)	564	(4.0)	**35**	(1.9)	**84**	(3.0)	-5	(3.5)
United States	416	(4.5)	466	(4.5)	498	(4.8)	545	(5.6)	**29**	(1.6)	**76**	(3.1)	9	(2.9)
OECD average	437	(0.7)	484	(0.8)	516	(0.7)	549	(0.9)	**24**	(0.3)	**71**	(0.6)	**-5**	(0.7)
Partners														
Albania	395	(4.3)	394	(4.8)	395	(5.1)	388	(6.1)	**0**	(0.1)	**-4**	(3.6)	-2	(4.0)
Argentina	350	(4.9)	382	(5.0)	413	(5.0)	426	(4.6)	**16**	(1.9)	**43**	(3.0)	-15	(3.3)
Brazil	350	(2.4)	376	(2.8)	403	(3.0)	446	(4.7)	**23**	(1.8)	**52**	(2.6)	2	(2.9)
Bulgaria	376	(5.6)	435	(5.1)	471	(5.7)	484	(5.6)	**20**	(1.9)	**62**	(3.8)	-7	(3.7)
Colombia	334	(3.6)	369	(3.8)	396	(4.2)	425	(4.5)	**22**	(1.8)	**49**	(2.6)	0	(2.5)
Costa Rica	373	(4.5)	393	(3.9)	419	(4.3)	450	(5.4)	**19**	(2.3)	**42**	(2.9)	2	(3.1)
Croatia	414	(3.9)	462	(4.2)	489	(4.9)	518	(6.1)	**20**	(1.7)	**70**	(4.3)	-1	(4.0)
Cyprus*	385	(3.4)	438	(3.7)	465	(3.2)	486	(3.4)	**18**	(1.5)	**61**	(2.8)	-8	(2.9)
Hong Kong-China	516	(5.8)	543	(4.4)	575	(4.4)	619	(4.4)	**17**	(1.5)	**61**	(3.4)	13	(4.8)
Indonesia	345	(4.8)	373	(3.6)	388	(5.2)	399	(8.3)	**9**	(2.2)	**37**	(5.6)	-7	(4.4)
Jordan	342	(3.7)	378	(3.8)	414	(4.2)	415	(7.2)	**14**	(1.7)	**38**	(3.3)	5	(3.5)
Kazakhstan	401	(3.7)	433	(4.4)	448	(4.4)	448	(4.3)	**7**	(1.2)	**33**	(3.1)	-12	(4.2)
Latvia	441	(4.6)	486	(5.2)	513	(4.8)	526	(4.6)	**17**	(1.9)	**73**	(4.7)	-7	(5.7)
Liechtenstein	458	(12.7)	511	(11.4)	571	(15.6)	602	(12.3)	**34**	(6.3)	**74**	(8.4)	-26	(11.7)
Lithuania	436	(3.7)	467	(4.0)	494	(4.2)	520	(4.4)	**14**	(1.3)	**63**	(3.5)	-11	(5.0)
Macao-China	471	(2.9)	526	(3.5)	558	(3.5)	598	(2.4)	**28**	(1.3)	**85**	(2.5)	15	(3.9)
Malaysia	368	(3.6)	407	(4.2)	442	(4.6)	472	(5.4)	**23**	(1.9)	**66**	(3.2)	-4	(4.3)
Montenegro	370	(3.7)	406	(3.8)	425	(3.7)	446	(3.6)	**13**	(1.5)	**46**	(2.9)	-5	(2.7)
Peru	318	(3.5)	355	(4.3)	390	(4.8)	429	(6.6)	**24**	(1.7)	**57**	(3.0)	-1	(2.5)
Qatar	322	(2.1)	348	(2.2)	406	(2.6)	449	(2.8)	**23**	(0.9)	**59**	(1.3)	3	(1.6)
Romania	405	(4.3)	429	(4.8)	458	(5.1)	487	(5.7)	**15**	(1.7)	**49**	(3.6)	13	(3.8)
Russian Federation	442	(4.7)	485	(4.9)	511	(4.2)	493	(5.1)	**7**	(1.1)	**57**	(5.2)	-24	(4.2)
Serbia	397	(4.7)	448	(4.1)	471	(5.0)	485	(5.0)	**14**	(1.5)	**61**	(4.0)	-6	(4.4)
Shanghai-China	546	(8.7)	627	(4.3)	634	(3.7)	646	(5.4)	**17**	(1.9)	**93**	(5.4)	-18	(5.6)
Singapore	480	(3.1)	545	(3.5)	618	(3.1)	652	(2.9)	**40**	(1.3)	**105**	(2.5)	20	(3.1)
Chinese Taipei	477	(5.7)	541	(4.8)	587	(4.9)	635	(5.1)	**29**	(1.8)	**109**	(4.0)	-8	(3.9)
Thailand	386	(4.4)	415	(4.1)	436	(4.0)	466	(6.1)	**14**	(1.9)	**58**	(4.5)	10	(4.6)
Tunisia	378	(4.2)	386	(4.7)	392	(4.7)	402	(7.2)	**2**	(1.0)	**20**	(4.7)	0	(5.1)
United Arab Emirates	374	(2.9)	424	(3.8)	458	(2.8)	489	(3.6)	**23**	(1.2)	**61**	(1.9)	3	(2.7)
Uruguay	347	(3.7)	405	(4.4)	433	(4.5)	467	(4.8)	**26**	(1.9)	**65**	(2.8)	-10	(3.5)
Viet Nam	463	(5.8)	503	(5.4)	528	(6.9)	554	(6.5)	**18**	(2.0)	**77**	(5.6)	-5	(5.8)

Note: Values that are statistically significant are indicated in bold (see Annex A3).
1. ESCS refers to the *PISA index of economic, social and cultural status*.
* See notes at the beginning of this Annex.
StatLink ⟐ http://dx.doi.org/10.1787/888932964946

[Part 3/3]
Equity in opportunity to learn: Formal mathematics
Table II.4.1 *Results based on students' self-reports*

		Slope of the opportunity gradient: change in mathematics score per unit of this index, AFTER accounting for student's ESCS[1]		Slope of the opportunity gradient: change in mathematics score per unit of this index, AFTER accounting for student's and school's ESCS		Total variation of this index		Variance-component: between-school variance of this index		Variance-component: within-school variance of this index		Percentage of the variance observed within schools: within-school variance as a proportion of the sum of the between and within variance	
		Score dif.	S.E.	Score dif.	S.E.	Overall	S.E.	Between	S.E.	Within	S.E.	%	S.E.
OECD	Australia	78	(1.7)	74	(1.6)	0.49	(0.01)	0.10	(0.01)	0.40	(0.01)	80.1	(1.33)
	Austria	61	(3.1)	47	(3.5)	0.47	(0.01)	0.20	(0.02)	0.27	(0.01)	57.3	(2.27)
	Belgium	67	(2.0)	55	(2.0)	0.52	(0.01)	0.14	(0.01)	0.37	(0.01)	72.1	(2.00)
	Canada	61	(1.6)	59	(1.5)	0.37	(0.01)	0.04	(0.00)	0.33	(0.01)	89.0	(1.01)
	Chile	52	(2.7)	43	(2.8)	0.34	(0.01)	0.08	(0.01)	0.25	(0.01)	75.2	(1.83)
	Czech Republic	72	(3.2)	54	(2.9)	0.29	(0.01)	0.08	(0.01)	0.21	(0.01)	71.2	(2.47)
	Denmark	45	(2.8)	44	(2.7)	0.36	(0.01)	0.04	(0.01)	0.32	(0.01)	87.7	(1.93)
	Estonia	47	(3.2)	46	(3.2)	0.21	(0.01)	0.02	(0.00)	0.19	(0.01)	92.0	(1.34)
	Finland	61	(2.6)	60	(2.7)	0.35	(0.01)	0.04	(0.01)	0.31	(0.01)	87.9	(1.69)
	France	75	(4.1)	w	w	0.32	(0.01)	w	w	w	w	w	w
	Germany	72	(2.8)	55	(2.9)	0.43	(0.01)	0.14	(0.01)	0.29	(0.01)	66.7	(2.09)
	Greece	33	(3.2)	29	(2.9)	0.34	(0.01)	0.02	(0.01)	0.30	(0.01)	93.1	(1.68)
	Hungary	71	(5.0)	48	(4.0)	0.29	(0.01)	0.08	(0.01)	0.20	(0.01)	72.4	(2.56)
	Iceland	20	(3.7)	19	(3.6)	0.39	(0.01)	0.02	(0.00)	0.37	(0.01)	95.8	(1.08)
	Ireland	60	(2.4)	57	(2.4)	0.37	(0.01)	0.03	(0.01)	0.33	(0.01)	90.9	(1.59)
	Israel	58	(3.5)	53	(3.6)	0.41	(0.02)	0.08	(0.02)	0.33	(0.01)	80.0	(3.76)
	Italy	63	(2.1)	51	(1.9)	0.39	(0.01)	0.12	(0.01)	0.26	(0.01)	68.0	(1.34)
	Japan	96	(3.2)	70	(3.5)	0.22	(0.01)	0.06	(0.01)	0.16	(0.01)	71.6	(2.61)
	Korea	105	(4.5)	91	(4.2)	0.27	(0.01)	0.07	(0.01)	0.20	(0.01)	73.6	(2.52)
	Luxembourg	38	(2.4)	29	(2.3)	0.51	(0.01)	0.07	(0.02)	0.44	(0.01)	85.8	(4.23)
	Mexico	39	(1.3)	36	(1.3)	0.43	(0.01)	0.08	(0.00)	0.35	(0.01)	82.3	(1.06)
	Netherlands	82	(3.3)	66	(3.9)	0.45	(0.01)	0.14	(0.01)	0.31	(0.01)	68.2	(2.17)
	New Zealand	72	(3.2)	68	(3.3)	0.51	(0.01)	0.09	(0.01)	0.42	(0.01)	82.7	(2.10)
	Norway	m	m	m	m	m	m	m	m	m	m	m	m
	Poland	51	(3.9)	50	(3.3)	0.30	(0.01)	0.02	(0.01)	0.28	(0.01)	92.5	(2.31)
	Portugal	59	(3.1)	57	(3.2)	0.37	(0.01)	0.04	(0.01)	0.33	(0.01)	89.5	(1.67)
	Slovak Republic	76	(3.4)	57	(3.7)	0.32	(0.02)	0.11	(0.01)	0.22	(0.01)	67.2	(2.77)
	Slovenia	49	(3.8)	25	(3.2)	0.32	(0.01)	0.07	(0.01)	0.25	(0.01)	78.7	(2.23)
	Spain	60	(2.0)	59	(2.0)	0.44	(0.01)	0.05	(0.01)	0.39	(0.01)	88.0	(1.19)
	Sweden	6	(4.3)	5	(4.0)	0.31	(0.02)	0.02	(0.01)	0.28	(0.01)	92.5	(2.89)
	Switzerland	53	(2.5)	46	(2.6)	0.50	(0.01)	0.20	(0.02)	0.30	(0.01)	59.6	(2.53)
	Turkey	53	(3.8)	38	(3.2)	0.30	(0.01)	0.04	(0.01)	0.26	(0.01)	85.1	(1.90)
	United Kingdom	76	(2.4)	71	(2.2)	0.43	(0.01)	0.08	(0.01)	0.36	(0.01)	82.2	(2.19)
	United States	65	(3.1)	63	(3.1)	0.41	(0.01)	0.04	(0.01)	0.37	(0.01)	89.5	(1.43)
	OECD average	60	(0.5)	51	(0.5)	0.37	(0.00)	0.08	(0.00)	0.29	(0.00)	80.4	(0.37)
Partners	Albania	m	m	m	m	0.42	(0.01)	0.03	(0.00)	0.40	(0.02)	93.1	(1.16)
	Argentina	33	(2.7)	25	(2.6)	0.48	(0.02)	0.12	(0.01)	0.37	(0.01)	74.7	(2.37)
	Brazil	42	(2.2)	34	(2.0)	0.51	(0.01)	0.14	(0.01)	0.37	(0.01)	72.4	(2.19)
	Bulgaria	46	(2.9)	34	(2.9)	0.45	(0.02)	0.08	(0.01)	0.36	(0.01)	82.0	(2.44)
	Colombia	40	(2.1)	36	(2.0)	0.51	(0.01)	0.08	(0.01)	0.43	(0.01)	83.6	(2.21)
	Costa Rica	32	(2.5)	27	(2.2)	0.52	(0.02)	0.11	(0.02)	0.42	(0.01)	79.4	(3.30)
	Croatia	61	(3.7)	52	(3.3)	0.32	(0.01)	0.04	(0.00)	0.29	(0.01)	87.7	(1.46)
	Cyprus*	49	(3.0)	44	(3.0)	0.40	(0.01)	0.04	(0.01)	0.37	(0.01)	89.5	(2.19)
	Hong Kong-China	55	(3.3)	55	(2.8)	0.40	(0.01)	0.03	(0.00)	0.38	(0.01)	92.8	(1.20)
	Indonesia	30	(3.9)	24	(3.2)	0.33	(0.01)	0.06	(0.01)	0.28	(0.01)	81.9	(2.49)
	Jordan	34	(2.8)	34	(2.3)	0.57	(0.02)	0.09	(0.01)	0.49	(0.02)	84.8	(1.59)
	Kazakhstan	27	(2.6)	24	(2.3)	0.32	(0.01)	0.03	(0.00)	0.30	(0.01)	90.1	(1.42)
	Latvia	59	(4.6)	56	(4.7)	0.22	(0.01)	0.02	(0.00)	0.19	(0.01)	88.4	(1.58)
	Liechtenstein	66	(9.6)	48	(12.7)	0.57	(0.04)	0.25	(0.07)	0.29	(0.03)	53.3	(8.68)
	Lithuania	53	(3.1)	48	(3.2)	0.27	(0.01)	0.02	(0.01)	0.25	(0.01)	91.5	(1.19)
	Macao-China	83	(2.4)	84	(2.5)	0.32	(0.01)	0.04	(0.01)	0.28	(0.02)	86.7	(2.91)
	Malaysia	57	(2.9)	52	(2.6)	0.36	(0.01)	0.04	(0.01)	0.32	(0.01)	88.4	(1.95)
	Montenegro	39	(2.8)	33	(2.7)	0.40	(0.01)	0.03	(0.01)	0.38	(0.02)	92.4	(1.69)
	Peru	42	(2.3)	35	(2.1)	0.51	(0.01)	0.10	(0.01)	0.41	(0.01)	79.5	(1.97)
	Qatar	55	(1.3)	52	(1.3)	0.67	(0.01)	0.16	(0.02)	0.51	(0.04)	76.1	(2.96)
	Romania	36	(2.9)	29	(2.7)	0.40	(0.01)	0.09	(0.01)	0.31	(0.01)	78.3	(2.47)
	Russian Federation	42	(5.3)	40	(5.3)	0.16	(0.00)	0.01	(0.00)	0.16	(0.01)	94.2	(1.12)
	Serbia	50	(3.7)	41	(3.6)	0.29	(0.01)	0.03	(0.00)	0.27	(0.01)	89.7	(1.48)
	Shanghai-China	74	(4.9)	59	(6.0)	0.21	(0.02)	0.04	(0.01)	0.17	(0.01)	82.7	(3.81)
	Singapore	95	(2.6)	87	(2.6)	0.41	(0.01)	0.07	(0.01)	0.35	(0.01)	83.4	(1.74)
	Chinese Taipei	91	(3.6)	74	(3.3)	0.33	(0.01)	0.06	(0.01)	0.27	(0.01)	81.9	(2.00)
	Thailand	47	(3.8)	42	(3.5)	0.29	(0.01)	0.04	(0.01)	0.24	(0.01)	85.5	(1.73)
	Tunisia	13	(3.7)	11	(2.8)	0.36	(0.01)	0.02	(0.01)	0.35	(0.01)	94.3	(2.83)
	United Arab Emirates	56	(1.8)	51	(1.8)	0.50	(0.01)	0.10	(0.01)	0.40	(0.01)	80.3	(1.61)
	Uruguay	50	(2.5)	42	(2.5)	0.47	(0.01)	0.11	(0.01)	0.36	(0.01)	76.3	(2.34)
	Viet Nam	65	(4.3)	56	(3.6)	0.22	(0.01)	0.04	(0.01)	0.18	(0.01)	83.3	(2.16)

Note: Values that are statistically significant are indicated in bold (see Annex A3).
1. ESCS refers to the *PISA index of economic, social and cultural status*.
* See notes at the beginning of this Annex.
StatLink ⬛᎒⬛ http://dx.doi.org/10.1787/888932964946

[Part 1/4]

Table II.4.2 **Mathematics performance and student population, by schools' socio-economic profile**

Results based on students' self-reports

		Percentage of students						Mean ESCS[1]						Mean mathematics performance					
		Socio-economically disadvantaged schools[2]		Socio-economically average schools[2]		Socio-economically advantaged schools[2]		Socio-economically disadvantaged schools[2]		Socio-economically average schools[2]		Socio-economically advantaged schools[2]		Socio-economically disadvantaged schools[2]		Socio-economically average schools[2]		Socio-economically advantaged schools[2]	
		%	S.E.	%	S.E.	%	S.E.	Mean index	S.E.	Mean index	S.E.	Mean index	S.E.	Mean score	S.E.	Mean score	S.E.	Mean score	S.E.
OECD	Australia	23.8	(1.2)	51.2	(1.7)	25.0	(1.4)	-0.30	(0.02)	0.24	(0.01)	0.77	(0.01)	459	(3.1)	499	(2.1)	558	(3.6)
	Austria	32.5	(2.8)	41.4	(3.5)	26.1	(2.8)	-0.41	(0.03)	0.07	(0.02)	0.68	(0.05)	445	(5.3)	521	(5.5)	558	(5.5)
	Belgium	29.0	(2.2)	37.3	(2.9)	33.8	(2.1)	-0.46	(0.03)	0.12	(0.02)	0.68	(0.02)	437	(4.6)	512	(3.6)	584	(4.2)
	Canada	21.4	(2.1)	52.6	(2.9)	26.0	(2.0)	-0.12	(0.02)	0.38	(0.01)	0.90	(0.02)	489	(4.1)	511	(2.0)	556	(3.4)
	Chile	42.8	(3.0)	22.8	(3.5)	34.4	(2.4)	-1.29	(0.04)	-0.66	(0.02)	0.36	(0.05)	387	(3.8)	408	(6.2)	476	(5.4)
	Czech Republic	21.7	(2.6)	57.7	(3.0)	20.6	(2.0)	-0.55	(0.03)	-0.09	(0.01)	0.51	(0.02)	434	(7.5)	492	(3.6)	588	(4.4)
	Denmark	21.4	(3.0)	56.0	(3.3)	22.6	(2.3)	-0.08	(0.03)	0.39	(0.01)	0.97	(0.02)	467	(5.0)	497	(2.1)	538	(4.1)
	Estonia	19.0	(2.0)	58.1	(2.7)	22.9	(1.7)	-0.40	(0.03)	0.06	(0.01)	0.66	(0.02)	498	(4.1)	513	(2.7)	558	(3.8)
	Finland	16.0	(2.4)	67.0	(3.0)	17.0	(1.9)	-0.04	(0.03)	0.36	(0.01)	0.77	(0.02)	499	(4.3)	519	(2.5)	538	(4.1)
	France	w	w	w	w	w	w	w	w	w	w	w	w	w	w	w	w	w	w
	Germany	28.0	(2.8)	45.2	(3.3)	26.8	(2.2)	-0.44	(0.02)	0.19	(0.02)	0.82	(0.03)	446	(5.8)	514	(5.0)	586	(4.5)
	Greece	25.3	(3.1)	48.3	(4.0)	26.5	(3.3)	-0.77	(0.04)	-0.07	(0.02)	0.61	(0.03)	397	(6.2)	457	(2.9)	498	(4.3)
	Hungary	31.6	(2.7)	35.0	(3.3)	33.4	(2.5)	-0.95	(0.05)	-0.27	(0.02)	0.42	(0.04)	409	(6.1)	465	(4.9)	554	(6.0)
	Iceland	16.3	(0.2)	55.9	(0.2)	27.8	(0.2)	0.27	(0.03)	0.74	(0.02)	1.16	(0.02)	466	(3.8)	486	(2.3)	522	(2.8)
	Ireland	17.2	(2.3)	57.0	(3.6)	25.8	(2.8)	-0.51	(0.04)	0.09	(0.01)	0.63	(0.03)	439	(5.4)	505	(2.2)	536	(3.3)
	Israel	29.7	(3.1)	38.4	(3.8)	31.9	(3.2)	-0.39	(0.03)	0.18	(0.02)	0.67	(0.02)	397	(5.6)	467	(7.9)	529	(6.8)
	Italy	28.8	(1.6)	41.2	(2.2)	29.9	(1.7)	-0.65	(0.02)	-0.08	(0.01)	0.55	(0.02)	428	(3.4)	484	(2.7)	543	(3.4)
	Japan	29.5	(2.5)	43.1	(3.3)	27.4	(2.2)	-0.49	(0.02)	-0.08	(0.01)	0.37	(0.02)	474	(6.7)	540	(5.2)	599	(6.2)
	Korea	26.7	(2.6)	48.6	(3.7)	24.8	(3.5)	-0.46	(0.02)	0.03	(0.02)	0.48	(0.03)	493	(6.8)	557	(4.7)	613	(9.1)
	Luxembourg	47.9	(0.1)	15.0	(0.1)	37.1	(0.1)	-0.45	(0.02)	0.17	(0.03)	0.71	(0.02)	444	(1.3)	497	(2.4)	546	(1.8)
	Mexico	34.3	(1.4)	35.3	(1.8)	30.5	(1.7)	-1.99	(0.02)	-1.12	(0.01)	-0.10	(0.04)	384	(2.4)	409	(1.9)	451	(2.3)
	Netherlands	23.4	(2.7)	50.9	(4.2)	25.7	(3.3)	-0.26	(0.03)	0.23	(0.02)	0.68	(0.02)	440	(5.7)	527	(5.9)	591	(7.2)
	New Zealand	21.5	(3.1)	55.3	(4.0)	23.2	(2.6)	-0.51	(0.04)	0.02	(0.02)	0.58	(0.03)	443	(4.9)	497	(4.4)	558	(4.1)
	Norway	10.0	(2.2)	73.3	(2.8)	16.6	(2.6)	0.03	(0.03)	0.42	(0.01)	0.91	(0.03)	467	(7.4)	484	(3.2)	527	(4.6)
	Poland	27.5	(3.1)	50.2	(3.9)	22.3	(3.1)	-0.74	(0.03)	-0.22	(0.02)	0.47	(0.04)	484	(3.7)	513	(3.4)	566	(8.4)
	Portugal	33.6	(3.6)	45.8	(4.7)	20.5	(3.8)	-1.15	(0.03)	-0.49	(0.02)	0.61	(0.09)	441	(7.1)	496	(3.9)	543	(5.8)
	Slovak Republic	26.9	(2.7)	47.3	(2.8)	25.8	(1.9)	-0.86	(0.04)	-0.17	(0.02)	0.50	(0.04)	412	(6.3)	477	(3.7)	563	(6.8)
	Slovenia	29.5	(0.6)	40.2	(0.7)	30.3	(0.5)	-0.47	(0.01)	0.03	(0.02)	0.66	(0.02)	437	(1.9)	492	(1.9)	579	(2.2)
	Spain	29.5	(2.4)	42.9	(3.2)	27.7	(2.5)	-0.79	(0.02)	-0.23	(0.01)	0.52	(0.03)	450	(3.3)	484	(2.3)	522	(2.6)
	Sweden	18.0	(2.7)	58.9	(3.4)	23.1	(2.6)	-0.17	(0.03)	0.22	(0.01)	0.74	(0.02)	453	(6.0)	474	(2.5)	508	(5.3)
	Switzerland	26.5	(3.1)	47.2	(3.4)	26.3	(2.6)	-0.28	(0.02)	0.11	(0.02)	0.73	(0.03)	497	(5.3)	516	(3.4)	592	(6.2)
	Turkey	32.0	(3.2)	43.1	(4.1)	24.8	(2.8)	-2.05	(0.03)	-1.49	(0.02)	-0.63	(0.07)	402	(4.5)	435	(5.3)	529	(11.5)
	United Kingdom	24.2	(2.6)	52.1	(3.0)	23.7	(2.3)	-0.23	(0.03)	0.26	(0.01)	0.79	(0.02)	449	(7.9)	489	(3.5)	552	(5.6)
	United States	26.6	(3.5)	44.4	(4.3)	29.0	(3.3)	-0.48	(0.04)	0.17	(0.02)	0.78	(0.04)	435	(5.0)	485	(4.8)	519	(4.8)
	OECD average	26.4	(0.4)	47.2	(0.6)	26.5	(0.4)	-0.56	(0.01)	-0.02	(0.00)	0.60	(0.01)	444	(0.9)	492	(0.7)	548	(0.9)
Partners	Albania	m	m	m	m	m	m	m	m	m	m	m	m	m	m	m	m	m	m
	Argentina	33.4	(3.0)	34.6	(3.6)	31.9	(3.4)	-1.43	(0.04)	-0.75	(0.03)	0.05	(0.05)	342	(4.4)	389	(6.1)	436	(5.3)
	Brazil	33.1	(2.0)	42.6	(2.2)	24.3	(1.6)	-1.87	(0.02)	-1.23	(0.02)	-0.11	(0.05)	363	(2.8)	378	(1.9)	454	(5.7)
	Bulgaria	33.7	(3.0)	32.4	(3.6)	33.8	(2.7)	-0.97	(0.05)	-0.29	(0.03)	0.46	(0.04)	381	(5.0)	425	(4.9)	510	(5.7)
	Colombia	28.8	(3.1)	41.7	(3.8)	29.6	(3.1)	-2.12	(0.04)	-1.28	(0.02)	-0.40	(0.06)	339	(4.1)	372	(3.5)	419	(5.8)
	Costa Rica	28.5	(3.2)	48.7	(3.5)	22.8	(2.1)	-1.88	(0.05)	-0.99	(0.02)	0.16	(0.05)	372	(3.7)	402	(3.7)	461	(6.5)
	Croatia	33.1	(3.0)	43.6	(3.4)	23.4	(1.8)	-0.79	(0.02)	-0.35	(0.02)	0.32	(0.03)	430	(4.1)	463	(5.2)	546	(8.6)
	Cyprus*	34.5	(0.1)	37.0	(0.1)	28.5	(0.1)	-0.38	(0.02)	0.08	(0.02)	0.65	(0.02)	399	(1.7)	442	(2.0)	487	(2.3)
	Hong Kong-China	35.3	(3.4)	40.2	(3.8)	24.5	(3.6)	-1.33	(0.02)	-0.84	(0.02)	0.05	(0.06)	510	(6.4)	573	(5.8)	615	(6.9)
	Indonesia	39.9	(3.8)	32.9	(3.5)	27.1	(3.3)	-2.38	(0.02)	-1.88	(0.03)	-0.85	(0.09)	360	(6.0)	358	(4.5)	417	(8.7)
	Jordan	20.8	(2.5)	59.3	(3.5)	19.9	(2.3)	-1.02	(0.04)	-0.46	(0.02)	0.30	(0.04)	362	(4.7)	376	(3.9)	438	(9.2)
	Kazakhstan	22.7	(3.0)	45.4	(3.6)	31.9	(3.2)	-0.81	(0.02)	-0.37	(0.02)	0.12	(0.02)	410	(7.5)	423	(4.0)	460	(6.2)
	Latvia	20.2	(2.5)	50.3	(3.4)	29.5	(2.9)	-0.95	(0.04)	-0.32	(0.02)	0.32	(0.03)	452	(5.5)	480	(2.9)	534	(4.9)
	Liechtenstein	14.8	(0.9)	51.2	(0.9)	34.1	(0.4)	c	c	0.24	(0.08)	c	c	c	c	506	(5.3)	c	c
	Lithuania	22.8	(2.1)	53.1	(3.2)	24.1	(2.6)	-0.76	(0.03)	-0.13	(0.02)	0.45	(0.03)	430	(4.5)	475	(3.5)	534	(5.3)
	Macao-China	51.6	(0.1)	17.5	(0.0)	30.8	(0.1)	-1.22	(0.01)	-0.89	(0.02)	-0.32	(0.02)	527	(1.5)	535	(2.4)	558	(1.9)
	Malaysia	28.6	(2.7)	42.9	(4.0)	28.6	(3.2)	-1.36	(0.04)	-0.76	(0.02)	-0.04	(0.05)	387	(3.5)	408	(3.9)	473	(6.6)
	Montenegro	38.7	(0.2)	23.6	(0.1)	37.7	(0.1)	-0.63	(0.02)	-0.30	(0.03)	0.17	(0.02)	363	(1.5)	413	(2.5)	455	(1.9)
	Peru	35.0	(2.7)	31.8	(3.0)	33.2	(2.8)	-2.13	(0.04)	-1.25	(0.03)	-0.28	(0.07)	318	(3.7)	359	(3.6)	429	(5.5)
	Qatar	33.8	(0.1)	22.6	(0.1)	43.7	(0.1)	-0.03	(0.01)	0.42	(0.02)	0.81	(0.01)	353	(1.3)	344	(1.6)	412	(1.1)
	Romania	30.9	(3.3)	40.5	(4.2)	28.7	(3.5)	-1.07	(0.05)	-0.51	(0.02)	0.22	(0.05)	403	(5.5)	434	(4.4)	505	(6.9)
	Russian Federation	21.9	(2.8)	50.2	(3.3)	27.9	(2.6)	-0.62	(0.03)	-0.16	(0.02)	0.39	(0.03)	450	(6.2)	474	(4.9)	523	(5.2)
	Serbia	32.3	(3.3)	43.2	(4.0)	24.4	(2.4)	-0.74	(0.02)	-0.33	(0.02)	0.36	(0.04)	398	(5.0)	444	(5.1)	525	(7.4)
	Shanghai-China	29.4	(3.1)	37.4	(3.7)	33.2	(3.1)	-1.06	(0.05)	-0.35	(0.02)	0.25	(0.04)	541	(6.2)	611	(5.2)	678	(6.4)
	Singapore	30.5	(0.2)	45.3	(0.9)	24.2	(0.9)	-0.71	(0.02)	-0.33	(0.02)	0.45	(0.02)	526	(2.4)	562	(2.1)	655	(3.4)
	Chinese Taipei	30.0	(3.1)	42.2	(3.9)	27.7	(2.8)	-0.86	(0.03)	-0.44	(0.02)	0.15	(0.04)	485	(5.5)	560	(4.5)	641	(6.7)
	Thailand	39.1	(2.9)	31.7	(3.0)	29.2	(2.6)	-2.04	(0.03)	-1.37	(0.02)	-0.40	(0.05)	404	(4.5)	415	(4.2)	471	(6.2)
	Tunisia	29.5	(2.9)	44.2	(3.9)	26.4	(3.0)	-2.04	(0.05)	-1.22	(0.03)	-0.22	(0.06)	353	(4.7)	380	(5.4)	440	(8.5)
	United Arab Emirates	25.4	(1.5)	40.0	(2.3)	34.6	(2.0)	-0.26	(0.03)	0.29	(0.02)	0.80	(0.02)	390	(2.9)	426	(3.4)	476	(5.1)
	Uruguay	40.4	(2.9)	37.4	(3.0)	22.2	(2.1)	-1.51	(0.02)	-0.89	(0.02)	0.26	(0.08)	365	(4.1)	413	(4.3)	483	(5.5)
	Viet Nam	39.4	(3.3)	34.4	(3.7)	26.2	(3.1)	-2.46	(0.03)	-1.85	(0.02)	-0.78	(0.09)	471	(6.9)	517	(4.9)	565	(8.0)

Note: Values that are statistically significant are indicated in bold (see Annex A3).

1. ESCS refers to the *PISA index of economic, social and cultural status.*

2. Advantaged (disadvantaged) schools are those where the typical student in the school, or the socio-economic profile of the school, is above (below) the ESCS of the typical student in the country/economy, the country mean ESCS. In each school, a random sample of 35 students are to take part in PISA (for more details see the *PISA 2012 Technical Report,* OECD, forthcoming). The socio-economic profile of the school is calculated using the information provided by these students. Therefore, the precision of the estimate depends on the number of students that actually take the test in the school and the diversity of their answers. This precision was taken into account when classifying schools as advantaged, disadvantaged or average. If the difference between the school socio-economic profile and the ESCS of the typical student in the country/economy (the mean ESCS at the country level) was not statistically significant, the school was classified as a school with an average socio-economic profile. If the school profile was statistically significantly above the country mean, the school is classified as a socio-economically advantaged school. If the profile was below the country mean, the school is classified as a socio-economically disadvantaged school.

* See notes at the beginning of this Annex.

StatLink http://dx.doi.org/10.1787/888932964946

[Part 2/4]
Mathematics performance and student population, by schools' socio-economic profile
Table II.4.2   *Results based on students' self-reports*

| | Percentage of immigrant students | | | | | | Percentage of immigrant students who do not speak the language of assessment at home | | | | | | Percentage of students in rural schools (schools located in a village, hamlet or rural area; fewer than 3 000 people) | | | | | |
| | Socio-economically disadvantaged schools[2] | | Socio-economically average schools[2] | | Socio-economically advantaged schools[2] | | Socio-economically disadvantaged schools[2] | | Socio-economically average schools[2] | | Socio-economically advantaged schools[2] | | Socio-economically disadvantaged schools[2] | | Socio-economically average schools[2] | | Socio-economically advantaged schools[2] | |
	%	S.E.	%	S.E.	%	S.E.	%	S.E.	%	S.E.	%	S.E.	%	S.E.	%	S.E.	%	S.E.
OECD																		
Australia	22.3	(2.0)	6.5	(0.5)	25.8	(1.5)	8.0	(1.3)	6.5	(0.5)	8.0	(1.0)	61.9	(7.2)	33.5	(7.4)	4.6	(3.0)
Austria	24.3	(2.4)	8.3	(1.1)	11.0	(1.4)	15.2	(1.9)	8.3	(1.1)	6.2	(0.6)	35.2	(12.0)	41.6	(12.2)	3.2	(11.6)
Belgium	24.9	(2.8)	13.1	(1.5)	9.7	(1.1)	12.9	(1.5)	6.1	(0.7)	3.4	(0.6)	38.1	(18.7)	25.9	(16.6)	5.9	(19.6)
Canada	38.9	(3.8)	10.8	(0.9)	35.7	(2.9)	19.0	(2.5)	10.8	(0.9)	16.8	(1.5)	29.3	(5.2)	60.0	(6.1)	0.7	(5.1)
Chile	0.5	(0.2)	0.0	(0.0)	1.0	(0.2)	0.0	(0.0)	0.0	(0.0)	0.1	(0.1)	93.2	(5.0)	0.0	c	6.8	(5.0)
Czech Republic	2.5	(0.7)	2.0	(0.4)	4.1	(0.6)	1.1	(0.5)	2.0	(0.4)	3.3	(0.5)	16.6	(9.4)	80.0	(9.6)	3.3	(3.3)
Denmark	17.4	(2.5)	3.7	(0.3)	3.8	(0.7)	7.6	(0.9)	3.7	(0.3)	1.4	(0.4)	24.7	(7.1)	67.5	(7.7)	7.8	(4.7)
Estonia	8.8	(1.7)	1.5	(0.3)	5.5	(1.5)	1.8	(0.9)	1.5	(0.3)	1.9	(0.5)	36.6	(6.6)	61.3	(6.7)	2.2	(2.2)
Finland	4.8	(0.8)	2.5	(0.1)	3.4	(0.3)	3.9	(0.8)	2.5	(0.1)	2.6	(0.3)	61.2	(13.5)	38.7	(13.5)	0.2	(0.0)
France	w	w	w	w	w	w	w	w	w	w	w	w	w	w	w	w	w	w
Germany	20.0	(2.1)	4.5	(0.6)	7.7	(1.1)	8.4	(1.2)	4.5	(0.6)	2.6	(0.6)	60.3	(27.2)	39.7	(27.2)	0.0	c
Greece	18.6	(3.2)	2.5	(0.4)	5.4	(0.7)	9.9	(2.3)	2.5	(0.4)	1.4	(0.4)	57.5	(13.3)	32.0	(12.5)	0.5	(9.4)
Hungary	0.6	(0.2)	0.5	(0.3)	2.4	(0.5)	0.0	(0.0)	0.5	(0.3)	0.4	(0.3)	76.1	(17.3)	23.9	(17.3)	0.0	c
Iceland	6.9	(0.8)	2.2	(0.4)	2.5	(0.5)	6.1	(0.7)	2.2	(0.4)	1.7	(0.5)	37.9	(0.7)	57.9	(0.6)	4.2	(0.2)
Ireland	13.3	(2.1)	4.7	(0.7)	8.4	(1.1)	7.1	(1.5)	4.7	(0.7)	2.6	(0.6)	8.3	(4.6)	83.0	(6.6)	8.8	(5.0)
Israel	16.7	(2.5)	9.1	(1.3)	16.1	(1.9)	6.3	(1.3)	9.1	(1.3)	8.3	(1.7)	21.8	(8.2)	15.2	(7.1)	63.1	(9.5)
Italy	10.8	(0.7)	4.3	(0.4)	4.0	(0.3)	7.6	(0.6)	4.3	(0.4)	1.9	(0.2)	45.3	(13.3)	54.2	(13.4)	0.4	(0.4)
Japan	0.5	(0.1)	0.0	(0.0)	0.4	(0.2)	0.3	(0.1)	0.0	(0.0)	0.3	(0.1)	0.0	c	0.0	c	0.0	c
Korea	0.0	(0.0)	0.0	(0.0)	0.0	(0.0)	0.0	(0.0)	0.0	(0.0)	0.0	(0.0)	73.6	(26.0)	0.0	c	26.4	(26.0)
Luxembourg	58.0	(1.0)	23.2	(1.8)	36.9	(0.8)	48.1	(1.1)	23.2	(1.8)	16.7	(0.8)	0.0	c	0.0	c	100.0	c
Mexico	1.7	(0.2)	0.0	(0.0)	0.9	(0.2)	0.5	(0.1)	0.0	(0.0)	0.2	(0.1)	87.0	(2.2)	12.0	(2.2)	1.0	(0.6)
Netherlands	17.5	(3.3)	5.0	(0.9)	5.4	(1.0)	7.9	(1.8)	5.0	(0.9)	1.9	(0.5)	0.0	c	0.0	c	0.0	c
New Zealand	29.9	(3.4)	11.0	(1.4)	31.7	(2.7)	17.0	(2.3)	11.0	(1.4)	15.1	(2.4)	63.6	(13.5)	36.4	(13.5)	0.0	c
Norway	21.4	(5.6)	5.5	(0.5)	6.7	(1.7)	12.8	(4.0)	5.5	(0.5)	3.8	(0.9)	17.0	(6.1)	83.0	(6.1)	0.0	c
Poland	0.1	(0.1)	0.0	(0.0)	0.5	(0.3)	0.1	(0.1)	0.0	(0.0)	0.2	(0.2)	54.1	(7.0)	43.3	(7.0)	2.5	(2.2)
Portugal	6.7	(1.3)	2.4	(0.5)	4.6	(0.9)	1.7	(0.5)	2.4	(0.5)	0.9	(0.2)	81.2	(14.5)	18.8	(14.5)	0.0	c
Slovak Republic	0.7	(0.3)	0.1	(0.1)	0.8	(0.2)	0.1	(0.1)	0.1	(0.1)	0.3	(0.2)	51.4	(8.1)	48.6	(8.1)	0.0	c
Slovenia	13.2	(1.1)	3.8	(0.6)	5.7	(0.6)	8.2	(0.8)	3.8	(0.6)	2.3	(0.5)	6.1	(3.4)	93.9	(3.4)	0.0	c
Spain	13.3	(1.4)	4.7	(0.7)	5.0	(0.7)	7.1	(1.2)	4.7	(0.7)	2.1	(0.5)	65.9	(11.5)	30.4	(11.5)	3.7	(1.7)
Sweden	22.8	(4.3)	8.5	(0.8)	10.0	(1.5)	14.9	(3.2)	8.5	(0.8)	4.6	(1.2)	34.1	(9.2)	59.7	(9.4)	6.2	(4.2)
Switzerland	29.8	(2.2)	13.1	(0.8)	16.8	(1.2)	16.6	(1.8)	13.1	(0.8)	6.6	(0.6)	48.4	(10.8)	49.4	(10.8)	2.3	(3.3)
Turkey	0.7	(0.4)	0.2	(0.1)	1.0	(0.5)	0.2	(0.2)	0.2	(0.1)	0.1	(0.1)	27.4	(17.5)	39.1	(23.7)	33.5	(20.5)
United Kingdom	20.9	(2.8)	3.2	(0.7)	14.6	(2.6)	10.2	(1.6)	3.2	(0.7)	6.9	(1.8)	11.6	(7.0)	47.6	(10.5)	40.8	(10.6)
United States	40.0	(3.4)	8.4	(1.6)	12.7	(2.6)	25.4	(2.6)	8.4	(1.6)	6.2	(1.3)	22.8	(12.7)	77.2	(12.7)	0.0	c
OECD average	15.7	(0.4)	10.1	(0.2)	9.1	(0.2)	8.7	(0.3)	4.8	(0.1)	3.9	(0.1)	41.2	(2.2)	41.2	(2.3)	11.7	(2.1)
Partners																		
Albania	m	m	m	m	m	m	m	m	m	m	m	m	m	m	m	m	m	m
Argentina	6.6	(1.0)	0.5	(0.3)	1.4	(0.4)	1.1	(0.3)	0.5	(0.3)	0.1	(0.1)	51.4	(12.8)	48.6	(12.8)	0.0	c
Brazil	0.5	(0.1)	0.1	(0.1)	1.0	(0.4)	0.0	(0.0)	0.1	(0.1)	0.4	(0.2)	88.8	(6.6)	11.2	(6.6)	0.0	c
Bulgaria	0.4	(0.2)	0.3	(0.2)	0.4	(0.2)	0.1	(0.1)	0.3	(0.2)	0.3	(0.2)	88.1	(8.5)	11.9	(8.5)	0.0	c
Colombia	0.5	(0.2)	0.0	(0.0)	0.1	(0.0)	0.0	(0.0)	0.0	(0.0)	0.0	(0.0)	87.5	(6.1)	12.4	(6.0)	0.2	(0.1)
Costa Rica	7.2	(2.0)	0.1	(0.0)	4.4	(0.8)	0.0	(0.0)	0.1	(0.0)	0.8	(0.3)	66.7	(7.3)	26.0	(6.9)	7.3	(4.1)
Croatia	13.9	(1.5)	0.2	(0.1)	10.3	(1.1)	0.4	(0.1)	0.2	(0.1)	0.1	(0.1)	62.6	(34.5)	37.4	(34.5)	0.0	c
Cyprus*	7.6	(0.6)	3.9	(0.4)	9.2	(0.7)	4.4	(0.4)	3.9	(0.4)	3.8	(0.5)	54.6	(0.6)	45.4	(0.6)	c	c
Hong Kong-China	42.5	(1.9)	3.4	(0.4)	18.0	(2.2)	5.6	(1.1)	3.4	(0.4)	1.6	(0.5)	0.0	c	0.0	c	0.0	c
Indonesia	0.1	(0.1)	0.1	(0.1)	0.2	(0.1)	0.0	(0.0)	0.1	(0.1)	0.1	(0.1)	61.7	(7.3)	31.8	(6.8)	6.4	(4.7)
Jordan	8.6	(1.6)	0.6	(0.1)	19.9	(2.4)	0.3	(0.1)	0.6	(0.1)	2.0	(0.5)	52.3	(11.1)	34.6	(10.8)	13.1	(8.4)
Kazakhstan	28.2	(5.0)	1.0	(0.0)	13.3	(1.6)	0.6	(0.3)	1.0	(0.2)	2.6	(0.6)	45.0	(5.4)	52.3	(5.8)	2.7	(2.2)
Latvia	3.8	(0.9)	1.1	(0.4)	4.2	(0.9)	1.5	(0.8)	1.1	(0.4)	0.8	(0.2)	52.9	(7.0)	44.1	(7.1)	2.9	(2.1)
Liechtenstein	c	c	12.5	(2.8)	c	c	c	c	12.5	(2.8)	c	c	c	c	c	c	0.0	c
Lithuania	0.8	(0.2)	0.5	(0.1)	1.6	(0.6)	0.4	(0.2)	0.5	(0.1)	0.3	(0.2)	65.2	(6.6)	34.8	(6.6)	0.0	c
Macao-China	74.1	(0.8)	4.0	(0.5)	50.4	(1.3)	1.1	(0.2)	4.0	(0.5)	18.4	(0.9)	0.0	c	100.0	c	0.0	c
Malaysia	1.7	(0.6)	0.4	(0.2)	1.0	(0.3)	0.3	(0.2)	0.4	(0.2)	0.6	(0.3)	69.8	(10.0)	30.2	(10.0)	0.0	c
Montenegro	4.3	(0.5)	0.0	(0.0)	7.5	(0.7)	0.0	(0.0)	0.0	(0.0)	0.5	(0.2)	0.0	c	0.0	c	0.0	c
Peru	0.7	(0.2)	0.1	(0.1)	0.3	(0.1)	0.2	(0.1)	0.1	(0.1)	0.0	(0.0)	80.9	(5.9)	16.2	(5.4)	2.9	(2.9)
Qatar	52.4	(0.7)	11.4	(0.4)	53.9	(0.5)	27.7	(0.5)	11.4	(0.4)	32.0	(0.5)	35.9	(0.3)	18.5	(0.2)	45.6	(0.3)
Romania	0.1	(0.1)	0.0	(0.0)	0.4	(0.2)	0.0	(0.0)	0.0	(0.0)	0.2	(0.1)	67.5	(12.5)	32.5	(12.5)	0.0	c
Russian Federation	12.4	(1.8)	1.2	(0.2)	10.5	(1.0)	3.3	(1.0)	1.2	(0.2)	0.7	(0.2)	47.5	(5.5)	52.5	(5.5)	0.0	c
Serbia	8.9	(1.5)	0.9	(0.6)	8.1	(0.9)	0.8	(0.3)	0.9	(0.6)	0.4	(0.2)	100.0	c	0.0	c	0.0	c
Shanghai-China	2.0	(0.5)	0.3	(0.2)	0.3	(0.2)	0.4	(0.2)	0.3	(0.2)	0.1	(0.1)	0.0	c	0.0	c	0.0	c
Singapore	15.0	(0.8)	12.0	(0.7)	28.4	(2.1)	13.6	(0.7)	12.0	(0.7)	17.0	(1.7)	0.0	c	0.0	c	0.0	c
Chinese Taipei	0.5	(0.2)	0.1	(0.1)	0.2	(0.1)	0.0	(0.0)	0.1	(0.1)	0.0	(0.0)	67.0	(27.0)	32.5	(27.1)	0.6	(0.4)
Thailand	1.7	(1.1)	0.1	(0.1)	0.0	(0.0)	1.4	(0.9)	0.1	(0.1)	0.0	(0.0)	74.2	(7.5)	21.7	(7.0)	4.1	(4.0)
Tunisia	0.4	(0.2)	0.1	(0.1)	0.5	(0.2)	0.0	(0.0)	0.1	(0.1)	0.1	(0.1)	79.4	(17.1)	20.6	(17.1)	0.0	c
United Arab Emirates	41.5	(2.1)	25.1	(2.2)	66.9	(3.3)	14.9	(1.8)	25.1	(2.2)	31.0	(2.6)	52.4	(7.4)	28.7	(5.2)	18.9	(4.7)
Uruguay	0.3	(0.1)	0.1	(0.1)	0.9	(0.3)	0.1	(0.1)	0.1	(0.1)	0.3	(0.2)	70.2	(10.4)	29.8	(10.4)	0.0	c
Viet Nam	0.1	(0.1)	0.0	(0.0)	0.2	(0.2)	0.0	(0.0)	0.0	(0.0)	0.2	(0.2)	66.0	(5.8)	28.2	(5.4)	5.8	(2.9)

Note: Values that are statistically significant are indicated in bold (see Annex A3).
1. ESCS refers to the *PISA index of economic, social and cultural status*.
2. Advantaged (disadvantaged) schools are those where the typical student in the school, or the socio-economic profile of the school, is above (below) the ESCS of the typical student in the country/economy, the country mean ESCS. In each school, a random sample of 35 students are to take part in PISA (for more details see the *PISA 2012 Technical Report*, OECD, forthcoming). The socio-economic profile of the school is calculated using the information provided by these students. Therefore, the precision of the estimate depends on the number of students that actually take the test in the school and the diversity of their answers. This precision was taken into account when classifying schools as advantaged, disadvantaged or average. If the difference between the school socio-economic profile and the ESCS of the typical student in the country/economy (the mean ESCS at the country level) was not statistically significant, the school was classified as a school with an average socio-economic profile. If the school profile was statistically significantly above the country mean, the school is classified as a socio-economically advantaged school. If the profile was below the country mean, the school is classified as a socio-economically disadvantaged school.
* See notes at the beginning of this Annex.
StatLink ⌧ http://dx.doi.org/10.1787/888932964946

[Part 3/4]

Mathematics performance and student population, by schools' socio-economic profile

Table II.4.2 *Results based on students' self-reports*

	Percentage of students in schools located in a city or large city (over 100 000 people)						Difference in performance between students in socio-economically average versus disadvantaged schools				Difference in performance between students in socio-economically advantaged versus average schools			
	Socio-economically disadvantaged schools[2]		Socio-economically average schools[2]		Socio-economically advantaged schools[2]		Before accounting for student's ESCS[1]		After accounting for student's ESCS		Before accounting for student's ESCS		After accounting for student's ESCS	
	%	S.E.	%	S.E.	%	S.E.	Score dif.	S.E.	Score dif.	S.E.	Score dif.	S.E.	Score dif.	S.E.
OECD														
Australia	18.0	(1.5)	49.2	(2.2)	32.8	(1.9)	41	(3.6)	24	(3.4)	58	(4.1)	42	(4.4)
Austria	31.0	(4.4)	35.4	(7.3)	33.6	(6.5)	75	(7.8)	63	(7.7)	37	(7.7)	23	(7.8)
Belgium	35.7	(5.8)	24.3	(5.6)	40.0	(7.0)	75	(5.9)	58	(5.9)	72	(6.0)	57	(6.1)
Canada	21.7	(3.0)	44.4	(3.7)	33.9	(3.2)	22	(4.7)	9	(4.6)	45	(4.0)	31	(4.0)
Chile	29.4	(3.9)	29.3	(5.0)	41.3	(4.3)	21	(7.6)	11	(7.5)	68	(8.1)	46	(7.9)
Czech Republic	11.4	(4.7)	56.2	(7.3)	32.4	(5.6)	57	(8.7)	45	(8.3)	96	(5.2)	84	(5.3)
Denmark	24.9	(8.0)	45.0	(8.3)	30.1	(8.3)	30	(5.4)	13	(4.2)	41	(4.6)	22	(4.1)
Estonia	6.8	(2.3)	46.1	(5.4)	47.1	(4.9)	15	(5.1)	5	(5.1)	44	(4.4)	30	(4.3)
Finland	5.3	(0.5)	61.0	(4.7)	33.7	(4.6)	20	(4.9)	7	(4.5)	19	(5.1)	6	(4.3)
France	w	w	w	w	w	w	w	w	w	w	w	w	w	w
Germany	25.2	(6.4)	38.1	(6.5)	36.6	(6.7)	69	(7.7)	59	(7.9)	72	(6.9)	62	(6.9)
Greece	15.7	(4.7)	41.0	(7.8)	43.3	(7.1)	60	(7.1)	46	(6.9)	41	(5.1)	25	(4.8)
Hungary	18.9	(5.2)	38.2	(5.4)	42.8	(6.1)	55	(8.5)	44	(8.1)	90	(7.5)	78	(6.7)
Iceland	5.9	(0.1)	48.4	(0.4)	45.7	(0.4)	20	(4.4)	9	(4.8)	36	(3.2)	24	(3.5)
Ireland	29.5	(5.3)	26.1	(6.7)	44.5	(6.5)	65	(5.8)	49	(5.6)	31	(3.9)	15	(3.4)
Israel	21.7	(5.1)	53.3	(6.7)	25.0	(5.7)	69	(9.7)	55	(9.1)	62	(9.8)	43	(9.5)
Italy	18.2	(3.1)	41.4	(4.1)	40.4	(3.4)	56	(4.4)	49	(4.6)	59	(4.6)	53	(4.7)
Japan	22.5	(2.9)	43.5	(4.2)	34.0	(3.1)	66	(8.8)	60	(8.3)	60	(7.3)	54	(7.1)
Korea	24.4	(2.5)	50.1	(3.9)	25.5	(3.6)	65	(8.3)	57	(8.4)	55	(9.8)	45	(9.9)
Luxembourg	0.0	c	0.0	c	0.0	c	53	(2.6)	41	(2.9)	48	(3.1)	35	(3.6)
Mexico	7.9	(1.5)	36.5	(3.1)	55.6	(3.0)	25	(3.4)	18	(3.5)	42	(3.4)	32	(2.7)
Netherlands	22.8	(5.5)	44.2	(7.5)	33.0	(7.1)	87	(8.2)	79	(8.1)	65	(9.9)	58	(9.9)
New Zealand	14.1	(3.8)	47.0	(5.8)	38.9	(4.6)	54	(6.6)	32	(5.6)	60	(6.2)	36	(6.2)
Norway	10.4	(5.2)	50.9	(7.3)	38.7	(7.6)	16	(8.1)	5	(7.9)	43	(5.6)	28	(5.3)
Poland	6.6	(4.6)	33.4	(9.4)	60.0	(9.5)	29	(5.1)	12	(5.2)	53	(8.1)	31	(7.5)
Portugal	29.8	(8.2)	29.5	(9.0)	40.7	(8.7)	54	(8.3)	36	(8.0)	47	(6.8)	17	(5.6)
Slovak Republic	6.9	(4.9)	33.9	(6.2)	59.3	(6.4)	65	(7.5)	43	(7.1)	86	(7.7)	66	(7.4)
Slovenia	22.1	(0.8)	38.0	(1.6)	39.9	(1.3)	54	(2.7)	47	(3.0)	87	(3.0)	80	(3.0)
Spain	18.7	(3.6)	42.8	(4.2)	38.4	(3.6)	34	(3.4)	19	(3.7)	39	(3.4)	18	(3.7)
Sweden	12.6	(4.4)	45.8	(7.7)	41.6	(6.9)	21	(6.5)	9	(5.8)	34	(6.2)	16	(6.0)
Switzerland	14.1	(5.7)	37.1	(8.4)	48.8	(8.5)	20	(6.4)	9	(6.3)	76	(6.7)	60	(6.7)
Turkey	32.2	(5.4)	42.4	(5.5)	25.4	(4.4)	33	(7.2)	26	(7.3)	94	(12.8)	81	(13.1)
United Kingdom	29.3	(6.3)	42.4	(6.7)	28.2	(4.8)	39	(9.1)	24	(7.6)	63	(6.6)	45	(6.6)
United States	35.8	(6.1)	31.9	(7.1)	32.3	(6.2)	50	(7.2)	34	(7.7)	34	(6.5)	14	(6.0)
OECD average	19.2	(0.8)	40.0	(1.1)	37.9	(1.0)	47	(1.1)	34	(1.1)	57	(1.1)	41	(1.1)
Partners														
Albania	m	m	m	m	m	m	m	m	m	m	m	m	m	m
Argentina	32.8	(5.4)	30.5	(5.7)	36.6	(5.9)	46	(7.8)	39	(7.5)	47	(8.1)	35	(7.9)
Brazil	12.1	(2.1)	47.4	(3.3)	40.6	(3.2)	15	(3.4)	8	(3.4)	76	(6.0)	58	(5.1)
Bulgaria	14.6	(3.8)	32.2	(5.8)	53.2	(4.8)	44	(7.2)	32	(6.8)	85	(7.0)	70	(6.5)
Colombia	12.5	(2.6)	44.1	(4.6)	43.4	(4.1)	32	(5.3)	23	(5.2)	48	(6.2)	33	(6.0)
Costa Rica	5.7	(4.0)	53.2	(8.4)	41.2	(8.2)	30	(5.1)	19	(5.0)	59	(7.5)	41	(7.1)
Croatia	12.4	(3.9)	47.4	(4.3)	40.3	(3.4)	33	(6.9)	26	(6.8)	83	(10.3)	73	(10.3)
Cyprus*	18.2	(0.2)	24.0	(0.1)	57.8	(0.2)	43	(2.8)	32	(2.8)	45	(3.0)	27	(3.2)
Hong Kong-China	35.3	(3.4)	40.2	(3.8)	24.5	(3.6)	63	(8.5)	59	(8.4)	42	(9.5)	35	(9.1)
Indonesia	6.1	(3.8)	28.5	(8.6)	65.4	(9.0)	-2	(7.9)	-5	(8.1)	59	(9.9)	44	(8.9)
Jordan	11.9	(3.6)	55.7	(5.6)	32.4	(4.3)	14	(6.5)	8	(6.1)	62	(9.9)	48	(9.5)
Kazakhstan	8.9	(3.7)	39.5	(5.9)	51.6	(6.0)	13	(9.3)	5	(9.2)	38	(7.1)	28	(6.9)
Latvia	4.5	(2.6)	38.2	(6.5)	57.2	(6.5)	29	(6.1)	13	(5.7)	54	(5.4)	37	(5.3)
Liechtenstein	0.0	c	0.0	c	0.0	c	c	c	c	c	c	c	c	c
Lithuania	5.0	(2.4)	48.2	(5.6)	46.8	(5.2)	45	(5.9)	30	(5.9)	59	(6.7)	47	(6.4)
Macao-China	51.8	(0.1)	17.3	(0.0)	30.9	(0.1)	8	(3.1)	5	(3.3)	24	(3.0)	19	(3.0)
Malaysia	6.9	(3.8)	40.3	(7.9)	52.8	(8.0)	21	(5.3)	12	(5.1)	65	(7.7)	50	(7.4)
Montenegro	30.9	(0.2)	26.3	(0.3)	42.8	(0.2)	50	(3.2)	45	(3.3)	41	(3.0)	32	(3.1)
Peru	5.8	(2.4)	32.2	(5.1)	62.0	(5.3)	40	(5.3)	28	(5.1)	71	(6.9)	53	(5.7)
Qatar	22.1	(0.1)	17.1	(0.1)	60.7	(0.1)	-9	(1.8)	-14	(2.1)	68	(2.0)	59	(2.2)
Romania	15.2	(4.7)	39.7	(6.1)	45.1	(6.2)	31	(6.8)	21	(6.8)	71	(7.8)	51	(6.6)
Russian Federation	8.6	(2.8)	41.6	(4.8)	49.8	(4.7)	23	(8.3)	10	(8.2)	49	(6.6)	33	(6.1)
Serbia	22.4	(4.7)	37.2	(5.4)	40.4	(5.1)	46	(7.7)	41	(7.6)	80	(9.8)	72	(9.6)
Shanghai-China	29.4	(3.1)	37.4	(3.7)	33.2	(3.1)	70	(8.0)	58	(7.8)	68	(8.2)	60	(8.1)
Singapore	30.5	(0.3)	45.5	(0.6)	24.1	(0.7)	35	(3.4)	25	(3.3)	93	(4.4)	73	(4.6)
Chinese Taipei	23.2	(3.6)	40.1	(5.3)	36.7	(4.0)	74	(7.3)	60	(6.7)	82	(8.6)	61	(8.6)
Thailand	12.2	(3.4)	29.6	(4.9)	58.2	(5.7)	11	(6.5)	9	(6.4)	56	(7.0)	37	(6.5)
Tunisia	14.4	(6.3)	36.9	(8.4)	48.7	(7.7)	27	(7.6)	22	(7.7)	60	(10.3)	46	(9.1)
United Arab Emirates	13.1	(2.0)	39.1	(2.8)	47.8	(2.9)	37	(4.7)	28	(4.5)	50	(6.5)	39	(6.5)
Uruguay	22.8	(4.4)	35.2	(3.9)	41.9	(4.6)	49	(6.1)	36	(6.1)	70	(6.6)	45	(5.5)
Viet Nam	3.5	(3.5)	15.4	(5.8)	81.1	(6.4)	46	(8.7)	38	(9.0)	49	(9.9)	33	(9.8)

Note: Values that are statistically significant are indicated in bold (see Annex A3).
1. ESCS refers to the *PISA index of economic, social and cultural status.*
2. Advantaged (disadvantaged) schools are those where the typical student in the school, or the socio-economic profile of the school, is above (below) the ESCS of the typical student in the country/economy, the country mean ESCS. In each school, a random sample of 35 students are to take part in PISA (for more details see the *PISA 2012 Technical Report,* OECD, forthcoming). The socio-economic profile of the school is calculated using the information provided by these students. Therefore, the precision of the estimate depends on the number of students that actually take the test in the school and the diversity of their answers. This precision was taken into account when classifying schools as advantaged, disadvantaged or average. If the difference between the school socio-economic profile and the ESCS of the typical student in the country/economy (the mean ESCS at the country level) was not statistically significant, the school was classified as a school with an average socio-economic profile. If the school profile was statistically significantly above the country mean, the school is classified as a socio-economically advantaged school. If the profile was below the country mean, the school is classified as a socio-economically disadvantaged school.
* See notes at the beginning of this Annex.
StatLink ᘓᕯᑩᕮ http://dx.doi.org/10.1787/888932964946

[Part4/4]

Table II.4.2 **Mathematics performance and student population, by schools' socio-economic profile**
Results based on students' self-reports

		Relative risk and population relevance of scoring in the bottom quarter of the performance distribution												Effect size					
		Students in socio-economically disadvantaged schools[2]				Students in socio-economically average schools[2]				Students in socio-economically advantaged schools[2]				Mean among students in socio-economically disadvantaged schools		Mean among students in socio-economically average schools		ean among students in socio- onomically dvantaged schools	
		Relative risk	S.E.	Population relevance	S.E.	Relative risk	S.E.	Population relevance	S.E.	Relative risk	S.E.	Population relevance	S.E.	Effect size	S.E.	Effect size	S.E.	fect ize	S.E.
OECD	Australia	**2.1**	(0.1)	20.6	(1.7)	1.0	(0.1)	0.1	(2.6)	0.3	(0.0)	-21.0	(1.8)	**-0.65**	(0.04)	**-0.10**	(0.04)	**.79**	(0.04)
	Austria	**3.4**	(0.4)	43.5	(5.1)	0.6	(0.1)	-17.9	(6.4)	0.2	(0.1)	-25.5	(3.7)	**-1.10**	(0.09)	**0.28**	(0.09)	**.84**	(0.08)
	Belgium	**4.0**	(0.3)	46.4	(3.2)	0.8	(0.1)	-8.8	(3.2)	0.1	(0.0)	-41.4	(3.5)	**-1.22**	(0.06)	-0.04	(0.06)	**.19**	(0.07)
	Canada	**1.6**	(0.1)	12.1	(2.0)	**1.1**	(0.1)	6.7	(3.1)	0.4	(0.0)	-17.2	(2.1)	**-0.42**	(0.06)	**-0.17**	(0.04)	**.61**	(0.05)
	Chile	**2.5**	(0.3)	38.3	(5.5)	1.1	(0.2)	3.3	(3.5)	0.2	(0.0)	-37.3	(3.5)	**-0.84**	(0.09)	**-0.25**	(0.09)	**.14**	(0.09)
	Czech Republic	**2.6**	(0.3)	25.6	(3.9)	1.0	(0.1)	-2.5	(7.1)	0.1	(0.0)	-23.9	(2.9)	**-0.94**	(0.10)	**-0.18**	(0.08)	**.40**	(0.08)
	Denmark	**1.9**	(0.2)	16.4	(3.5)	1.0	(0.1)	1.6	(5.9)	0.3	(0.1)	-17.5	(2.6)	**-0.53**	(0.07)	-0.08	(0.06)	**.64**	(0.06)
	Estonia	**1.5**	(0.1)	8.0	(2.1)	**1.2**	(0.1)	12.1	(4.6)	0.4	(0.0)	-15.0	(1.9)	**-0.36**	(0.06)	**-0.21**	(0.05)	**.61**	(0.05)
	Finland	**1.4**	(0.1)	6.1	(1.6)	1.0	(0.1)	-1.7	(4.5)	0.7	(0.1)	-5.5	(1.5)	**-0.28**	(0.05)	0.00	(0.05)	**.27**	(0.06)
	France	w	w	w	w	w	w	w	w	w	w	w	w	w	w	w	w	w	w
	Germany	**3.5**	(0.4)	41.3	(4.4)	0.7	(0.1)	-13.4	(5.7)	0.1	(0.0)	-30.6	(3.4)	**-1.12**	(0.09)	0.00	(0.09)	**.19**	(0.09)
	Greece	**3.1**	(0.3)	34.4	(4.1)	0.7	(0.1)	-16.4	(6.0)	0.3	(0.0)	-23.4	(4.0)	**-0.93**	(0.09)	0.10	(0.07)	**.75**	(0.07)
	Hungary	**4.0**	(0.6)	48.6	(4.7)	0.8	(0.1)	-6.0	(5.3)	0.1	(0.0)	-44.0	(4.8)	**-1.26**	(0.11)	**-0.22**	(0.08)	**.53**	(0.09)
	Iceland	**1.6**	(0.1)	9.1	(1.7)	**1.2**	(0.1)	10.9	(3.1)	0.5	(0.0)	-17.2	(1.7)	**-0.35**	(0.05)	**-0.17**	(0.03)	**.46**	(0.04)
	Ireland	**2.8**	(0.2)	23.7	(3.1)	0.8	(0.1)	-13.8	(5.1)	0.4	(0.0)	-18.5	(2.7)	**-0.93**	(0.08)	0.09	(0.06)	**.57**	(0.05)
	Israel	**3.2**	(0.4)	40.0	(5.0)	0.8	(0.1)	-7.7	(5.5)	0.2	(0.0)	-34.3	(5.4)	**-1.04**	(0.09)	0.01	(0.10)	**.98**	(0.10)
	Italy	**3.0**	(0.2)	36.7	(2.4)	0.8	(0.1)	-7.0	(2.5)	0.2	(0.0)	-31.4	(2.9)	**-0.96**	(0.06)	-0.02	(0.05)	**.98**	(0.05)
	Japan	**3.2**	(0.5)	39.5	(5.6)	0.7	(0.1)	-15.6	(5.0)	0.2	(0.1)	-26.1	(3.5)	**-1.06**	(0.10)	0.06	(0.08)	**.03**	(0.09)
	Korea	**2.8**	(0.3)	32.1	(4.1)	0.7	(0.1)	-16.3	(6.5)	0.3	(0.1)	-20.2	(4.2)	**-0.93**	(0.10)	0.07	(0.09)	**.84**	(0.11)
	Luxembourg	**3.8**	(0.2)	57.5	(1.8)	0.8	(0.1)	-3.6	(0.8)	0.2	(0.0)	-42.9	(1.2)	**-1.04**	(0.02)	**0.10**	(0.03)	**.05**	(0.03)
	Mexico	**2.2**	(0.1)	29.2	(2.5)	0.9	(0.1)	-2.4	(2.3)	0.3	(0.0)	-25.4	(2.1)	**-0.62**	(0.04)	**-0.09**	(0.04)	**.77**	(0.04)
	Netherlands	**4.2**	(0.5)	42.7	(5.3)	0.6	(0.1)	-23.5	(9.1)	0.1	(0.1)	-28.5	(6.0)	**-1.42**	(0.10)	0.08	(0.13)	**1.16**	(0.17)
	New Zealand	**2.5**	(0.2)	23.9	(4.0)	0.9	(0.1)	-8.9	(6.3)	0.3	(0.0)	-19.2	(3.0)	**-0.77**	(0.07)	-0.05	(0.08)	**0.80**	(0.06)
	Norway	**1.4**	(0.2)	3.8	(1.6)	**1.3**	(0.1)	19.3	(7.0)	0.4	(0.1)	-10.2	(2.1)	**-0.27**	(0.09)	**-0.23**	(0.07)	**0.52**	(0.06)
	Poland	**1.8**	(0.2)	18.8	(3.5)	1.0	(0.1)	-2.3	(5.1)	0.4	(0.1)	-16.1	(3.1)	**-0.52**	(0.06)	-0.09	(0.07)	**0.72**	(0.09)
	Portugal	**2.7**	(0.3)	36.3	(4.6)	0.7	(0.1)	-17.2	(6.2)	0.2	(0.1)	-18.6	(4.1)	**-0.78**	(0.10)	**0.17**	(0.08)	**0.81**	(0.08)
	Slovak Republic	**3.0**	(0.3)	35.3	(4.2)	0.9	(0.1)	-6.7	(5.2)	0.1	(0.0)	-30.0	(2.9)	**-1.05**	(0.08)	-0.09	(0.08)	**1.26**	(0.10)
	Slovenia	**3.5**	(0.2)	42.1	(2.3)	0.9	(0.1)	-3.8	(2.6)	0.1	(0.0)	-39.3	(1.2)	**-1.17**	(0.04)	**-0.20**	(0.03)	**1.47**	(0.04)
	Spain	**2.0**	(0.1)	23.1	(2.8)	0.9	(0.1)	-2.2	(3.0)	0.4	(0.0)	-20.8	(2.6)	**-0.58**	(0.04)	-0.02	(0.04)	**0.63**	(0.04)
	Sweden	**1.5**	(0.2)	8.0	(2.6)	1.1	(0.1)	6.3	(5.6)	0.5	(0.1)	-11.9	(2.7)	**-0.34**	(0.07)	-0.11	(0.06)	**0.44**	(0.07)
	Switzerland	**1.8**	(0.1)	17.3	(3.0)	**1.2**	(0.1)	10.3	(4.8)	0.2	(0.0)	-24.6	(3.2)	**-0.51**	(0.06)	**-0.30**	(0.07)	**0.96**	(0.08)
	Turkey	**2.0**	(0.2)	24.3	(4.6)	1.1	(0.1)	3.6	(4.8)	0.2	(0.1)	-24.7	(3.8)	**-0.83**	(0.09)	**-0.26**	(0.09)	**1.32**	(0.17)
	United Kingdom	**2.1**	(0.2)	21.1	(4.5)	1.0	(0.1)	1.1	(6.6)	0.3	(0.0)	-21.6	(2.7)	**-0.66**	(0.10)	-0.12	(0.09)	**0.87**	(0.08)
	United States	**2.4**	(0.3)	26.9	(4.9)	0.8	(0.1)	-9.0	(5.1)	0.4	(0.1)	-20.8	(3.9)	**-0.76**	(0.08)	0.07	(0.08)	**0.61**	(0.07)
	OECD average	**2.6**	(0.0)	28.8	(0.6)	0.9	(0.0)	-4.4	(0.9)	0.3	(0.0)	-24.8	(0.6)	**-0.81**	(0.01)	**-0.06**	(0.01)	**0.89**	(0.01)
Partners	Albania	m	m	m	m	m	m	m	m	m	m	m	m	m	m	m	m	m	m
	Argentina	**3.2**	(0.4)	42.1	(5.1)	0.8	(0.1)	-6.1	(5.1)	0.2	(0.0)	-35.4	(5.2)	**-1.01**	(0.09)	0.01	(0.11)	**1.02**	(0.10)
	Brazil	**1.8**	(0.1)	20.8	(2.9)	**1.2**	(0.1)	7.4	(3.1)	0.2	(0.0)	-24.0	(2.3)	**-0.58**	(0.05)	**-0.31**	(0.05)	**1.14**	(0.07)
	Bulgaria	**3.3**	(0.4)	43.6	(5.1)	1.0	(0.1)	-1.0	(3.9)	0.1	(0.0)	-42.6	(5.2)	**-1.07**	(0.09)	**-0.23**	(0.08)	**1.36**	(0.09)
	Colombia	**2.3**	(0.3)	27.0	(4.4)	1.0	(0.1)	-0.3	(4.0)	0.3	(0.0)	-27.0	(3.7)	**-0.76**	(0.08)	-0.11	(0.07)	**0.87**	(0.09)
	Costa Rica	**2.4**	(0.3)	27.9	(4.6)	0.9	(0.1)	-4.1	(5.8)	0.2	(0.1)	-23.1	(3.5)	**-0.78**	(0.08)	-0.14	(0.09)	**1.09**	(0.11)
	Croatia	**2.3**	(0.3)	30.2	(5.1)	1.0	(0.1)	-0.2	(5.4)	0.1	(0.0)	-26.2	(2.7)	**-0.76**	(0.08)	-0.17	(0.10)	**1.26**	(0.11)
	Cyprus*	**2.4**	(0.1)	32.3	(2.0)	0.8	(0.0)	-6.9	(1.9)	0.3	(0.0)	-23.5	(1.5)	**-0.71**	(0.03)	0.04	(0.03)	**0.74**	(0.03)
	Hong Kong-China	**3.0**	(0.4)	41.7	(5.6)	0.6	(0.1)	-17.9	(6.4)	0.3	(0.1)	-21.6	(5.1)	**-0.88**	(0.10)	**0.21**	(0.10)	**0.81**	(0.12)
	Indonesia	**1.5**	(0.2)	16.0	(6.4)	1.3	(0.2)	8.7	(5.1)	0.4	(0.1)	-21.2	(4.2)	**-0.35**	(0.12)	**-0.37**	(0.10)	**0.83**	(0.13)
	Jordan	**1.5**	(0.2)	8.8	(2.7)	**1.3**	(0.1)	14.4	(5.5)	0.3	(0.1)	-16.0	(2.3)	**-0.40**	(0.08)	**-0.30**	(0.07)	**0.87**	(0.10)
	Kazakhstan	**1.7**	(0.2)	13.8	(4.3)	1.2	(0.2)	8.5	(5.8)	0.4	(0.1)	-22.4	(4.0)	**-0.40**	(0.14)	**-0.24**	(0.10)	**0.61**	(0.10)
	Latvia	**2.0**	(0.2)	16.8	(3.0)	**1.3**	(0.1)	11.3	(4.7)	0.3	(0.0)	-26.9	(3.9)	**-0.62**	(0.08)	**-0.25**	(0.05)	**0.81**	(0.08)
	Liechtenstein	c	c	c	c	c	c	c	c	c	c	c	c	c	c	c	c	c	c
	Lithuania	**2.3**	(0.2)	22.8	(3.6)	1.0	(0.1)	-0.9	(6.0)	0.2	(0.0)	-22.7	(3.2)	**-0.76**	(0.07)	-0.10	(0.07)	**0.89**	(0.08)
	Macao-China	**1.4**	(0.1)	16.0	(2.4)	1.1	(0.1)	1.8	(1.1)	0.6	(0.0)	-13.4	(1.2)	**-0.24**	(0.03)	-0.04	(0.03)	**0.32**	(0.03)
	Malaysia	**1.8**	(0.2)	18.0	(3.6)	**1.3**	(0.1)	9.8	(4.4)	0.3	(0.1)	-25.9	(4.0)	**-0.62**	(0.07)	**-0.28**	(0.08)	**0.97**	(0.10)
	Montenegro	**3.2**	(0.3)	46.3	(3.1)	0.8	(0.1)	-6.2	(2.4)	0.3	(0.0)	-38.0	(1.9)	**-1.04**	(0.04)	0.06	(0.04)	**0.96**	(0.03)
	Peru	**3.2**	(0.3)	43.5	(3.5)	0.9	(0.1)	-2.1	(3.3)	0.1	(0.0)	-40.2	(5.0)	**-1.03**	(0.07)	**-0.17**	(0.08)	**1.25**	(0.08)
	Qatar	**1.4**	(0.0)	11.9	(1.1)	**1.5**	(0.1)	10.6	(1.0)	0.5	(0.0)	-28.6	(1.6)	**-0.37**	(0.02)	**-0.45**	(0.02)	**0.65**	(0.02)
	Romania	**2.5**	(0.3)	30.9	(5.5)	1.1	(0.2)	2.9	(5.9)	0.1	(0.0)	-32.3	(5.4)	**-0.83**	(0.10)	**-0.23**	(0.10)	**1.16**	(0.10)
	Russian Federation	**1.7**	(0.2)	13.1	(3.3)	1.2	(0.1)	9.2	(5.5)	0.4	(0.1)	-20.5	(3.3)	**-0.49**	(0.09)	**-0.20**	(0.08)	**0.68**	(0.08)
	Serbia	**2.7**	(0.3)	35.9	(5.3)	0.9	(0.1)	-6.4	(5.7)	0.1	(0.0)	-27.4	(3.2)	**-0.93**	(0.09)	-0.09	(0.10)	**1.26**	(0.11)
	Shanghai-China	**3.5**	(0.4)	42.3	(5.3)	0.8	(0.1)	-8.1	(5.0)	0.2	(0.1)	-37.2	(5.1)	**-1.13**	(0.08)	-0.03	(0.09)	**1.12**	(0.11)
	Singapore	**1.9**	(0.1)	21.9	(1.7)	**1.2**	(0.1)	6.6	(2.1)	0.2	(0.0)	-24.8	(1.2)	**-0.69**	(0.03)	**-0.20**	(0.03)	**1.16**	(0.05)
	Chinese Taipei	**3.0**	(0.3)	38.0	(3.7)	0.8	(0.1)	-9.0	(4.2)	0.2	(0.0)	-29.6	(3.6)	**-1.03**	(0.06)	0.00	(0.07)	**1.11**	(0.08)
	Thailand	**1.7**	(0.2)	20.3	(4.4)	1.1	(0.1)	4.3	(3.5)	0.4	(0.1)	-21.6	(3.8)	**-0.48**	(0.08)	**-0.22**	(0.08)	**0.77**	(0.09)
	Tunisia	**2.0**	(0.3)	22.1	(5.5)	1.1	(0.2)	3.1	(6.8)	0.3	(0.1)	-23.5	(4.3)	**-0.68**	(0.10)	-0.18	(0.11)	**0.94**	(0.11)
	United Arab Emirates	**2.1**	(0.2)	22.4	(2.8)	1.1	(0.1)	3.2	(3.4)	0.4	(0.0)	-28.6	(3.1)	**-0.73**	(0.05)	**-0.15**	(0.06)	**0.75**	(0.07)
	Uruguay	**3.0**	(0.4)	44.2	(5.2)	0.7	(0.1)	-11.2	(4.5)	0.1	(0.0)	-24.9	(3.1)	**-0.94**	(0.08)	0.08	(0.08)	**1.23**	(0.07)
	Viet Nam	**2.8**	(0.4)	41.3	(5.6)	0.7	(0.1)	-10.2	(5.5)	0.2	(0.1)	-24.8	(4.8)	**-0.84**	(0.10)	0.10	(0.11)	**0.93**	(0.12)

Note: Values that are statistically significant are indicated in bold (see Annex A3).
1. ESCS refers to the *PISA index of economic, social and cultural status*.
2. Advantaged (disadvantaged) schools are those where the typical student in the school, or the socio-economic profile of the school, is above (below) the CS of the typical student in the country/economy, the country mean ESCS. In each school, a random sample of 35 students are to take part in PISA (for more details see the *PI A 2012 Technical Report*, OECD, forthcoming). The socio-economic profile of the school is calculated using the information provided by these students. Therefore, the precis n of the estimate depends on the number of students that actually take the test in the school and the diversity of their answers. This precision was taken into account when assifying schools as advantaged, disadvantaged or average. If the difference between the school socio-economic profile and the ESCS of the typical student in the country/e nomy (the mean ESCS at the country level) was not statistically significant, the school was classified as a school with an average socio-economic profile. If the school prof e was statistically significantly above the country mean, the school is classified as a socio-economically advantaged school. If the profile was below the country mean, the hool is classified as a socio-economically disadvantaged school.
* See notes at the beginning of this Annex.

StatLink http://dx.doi.org/10.1787/888932964946

[Part 1/2]

Table II.4.3 Inequity in access to instructional content: Formal mathematics

Results based on students' self-reports

		Formal mathematics																			
		Percentage of the variation explained by student ESCS[1]		Percentage of the variation explained by student and school mean ESCS		Percentage of the variation explained by student and school mean and standard deviation of ESCS		Mean among students in socio-economically disadvantaged schools,[2] relative to the country mean ESCS		Mean among students in socio-economically average schools,[2] relative to the country mean ESCS		Mean among students in socio-economically advantaged schools,[2] relative to the country mean ESCS		Difference between students in disadvantaged and average schools		Difference between students in average and advantaged schools		Mean among non-immigrant students		Mean among immigrant students	
		%	S.E.	%	S.E.	%	S.E.	Mean index	S.E.	Mean index	S.E.	Mean index	S.E.	Dif.	S.E.	Dif.	S.E.	Mean index	S.E.	Mean index	S.E.
OECD	Australia	10.5	(0.7)	13.2	(1.0)	13.7	(1.0)	1.43	(0.02)	1.66	(0.02)	2.01	(0.02)	**0.23**	(0.03)	**0.35**	(0.03)	1.62	(0.01)	1.95	(0.02)
	Austria	15.7	(1.7)	28.0	(2.4)	28.0	(2.4)	1.13	(0.04)	1.59	(0.04)	1.97	(0.04)	**0.46**	(0.06)	**0.38**	(0.06)	1.57	(0.02)	1.41	(0.04)
	Belgium	13.4	(1.2)	19.3	(1.6)	19.6	(1.6)	1.46	(0.04)	1.78	(0.03)	2.17	(0.02)	**0.32**	(0.05)	**0.39**	(0.03)	1.86	(0.01)	1.68	(0.04)
	Canada	6.6	(0.7)	7.6	(0.8)	8.2	(0.8)	1.85	(0.02)	1.95	(0.01)	2.16	(0.02)	**0.10**	(0.03)	**0.21**	(0.02)	1.94	(0.01)	2.10	(0.02)
	Chile	14.7	(1.6)	19.4	(1.8)	19.5	(1.8)	1.49	(0.02)	1.65	(0.03)	1.99	(0.03)	**0.16**	(0.04)	**0.34**	(0.05)	1.70	(0.02)	1.82	(0.10)
	Czech Republic	8.6	(1.1)	16.3	(2.1)	17.1	(2.3)	1.59	(0.04)	1.74	(0.02)	2.16	(0.03)	**0.14**	(0.04)	**0.42**	(0.03)	1.80	(0.02)	1.84	(0.07)
	Denmark	9.8	(1.2)	11.0	(1.4)	11.1	(1.5)	1.49	(0.04)	1.57	(0.02)	1.86	(0.03)	0.07	(0.05)	**0.29**	(0.04)	1.63	(0.02)	1.58	(0.03)
	Estonia	3.0	(0.7)	3.2	(0.8)	3.1	(0.7)	1.95	(0.02)	1.99	(0.02)	2.07	(0.02)	0.05	(0.03)	**0.07**	(0.03)	1.99	(0.01)	2.15	(0.04)
	Finland	5.1	(0.6)	5.1	(0.6)	6.1	(0.6)	1.58	(0.04)	1.74	(0.01)	1.75	(0.02)	**0.16**	(0.04)	0.01	(0.03)	1.73	(0.01)	1.48	(0.03)
	France	13.8	(1.4)	w	w	w	w	w	w	w	w	w	w	w	w	w	w	1.91	(0.02)	1.69	(0.04)
	Germany	11.9	(1.4)	22.5	(2.0)	22.5	(2.0)	1.31	(0.03)	1.60	(0.03)	2.05	(0.03)	**0.30**	(0.05)	**0.45**	(0.04)	1.69	(0.02)	1.47	(0.03)
	Greece	5.4	(0.8)	6.4	(1.0)	6.4	(1.0)	1.72	(0.03)	1.94	(0.02)	2.03	(0.02)	**0.23**	(0.03)	**0.09**	(0.03)	1.93	(0.01)	1.74	(0.04)
	Hungary	12.1	(1.5)	20.1	(2.0)	21.3	(2.1)	1.70	(0.03)	1.95	(0.03)	2.22	(0.02)	**0.25**	(0.05)	**0.28**	(0.03)	1.95	(0.02)	2.08	(0.09)
	Iceland	3.1	(0.7)	3.6	(0.7)	3.6	(0.7)	1.07	(0.03)	1.11	(0.02)	1.26	(0.02)	0.04	(0.04)	**0.15**	(0.03)	1.14	(0.01)	1.18	(0.08)
	Ireland	9.2	(1.2)	10.0	(1.3)	10.2	(1.3)	1.19	(0.03)	1.51	(0.02)	1.59	(0.02)	**0.32**	(0.04)	**0.08**	(0.03)	1.46	(0.01)	1.59	(0.04)
	Israel	7.4	(1.2)	8.1	(1.3)	8.2	(1.3)	1.63	(0.03)	1.83	(0.04)	1.94	(0.03)	**0.20**	(0.05)	**0.11**	(0.05)	1.82	(0.02)	1.82	(0.04)
	Italy	6.8	(0.6)	13.6	(1.2)	13.8	(1.2)	1.56	(0.02)	1.81	(0.02)	2.11	(0.03)	**0.25**	(0.03)	**0.30**	(0.03)	1.85	(0.01)	1.62	(0.02)
	Japan	7.8	(1.3)	18.9	(2.0)	19.4	(1.9)	1.82	(0.03)	2.05	(0.02)	2.29	(0.02)	**0.23**	(0.04)	**0.24**	(0.03)	2.05	(0.02)	c	c
	Korea	11.6	(1.3)	19.5	(2.3)	19.6	(2.2)	1.78	(0.03)	2.09	(0.02)	2.35	(0.03)	**0.31**	(0.04)	**0.26**	(0.04)	2.07	(0.02)	c	c
	Luxembourg	12.5	(1.3)	15.9	(1.4)	16.9	(1.4)	1.25	(0.02)	1.45	(0.03)	1.70	(0.02)	**0.20**	(0.04)	**0.26**	(0.04)	1.49	(0.02)	1.41	(0.02)
	Mexico	5.3	(0.5)	7.0	(0.7)	7.1	(0.7)	1.62	(0.02)	1.74	(0.01)	2.00	(0.02)	**0.12**	(0.02)	**0.26**	(0.02)	1.79	(0.01)	1.43	(0.05)
	Netherlands	8.5	(1.3)	20.6	(2.8)	20.6	(2.8)	1.07	(0.03)	1.49	(0.03)	1.87	(0.04)	**0.42**	(0.05)	**0.39**	(0.05)	1.52	(0.02)	1.36	(0.07)
	New Zealand	10.8	(1.2)	13.2	(1.4)	13.2	(1.4)	1.28	(0.05)	1.46	(0.03)	1.86	(0.04)	**0.18**	(0.05)	**0.40**	(0.05)	1.43	(0.02)	1.74	(0.04)
	Norway	m	m	m	m	m	m	m	m	m	m	m	m	m	m	m	m	m	m	m	m
	Poland	4.7	(0.9)	4.8	(1.0)	5.1	(1.1)	1.76	(0.02)	1.82	(0.02)	1.95	(0.04)	0.06	(0.03)	**0.13**	(0.04)	1.84	(0.02)	c	c
	Portugal	7.7	(1.4)	8.2	(1.5)	8.9	(1.5)	1.57	(0.04)	1.75	(0.02)	1.93	(0.03)	**0.17**	(0.05)	**0.18**	(0.04)	1.74	(0.02)	1.62	(0.04)
	Slovak Republic	14.4	(1.6)	24.0	(2.4)	24.2	(2.4)	1.40	(0.03)	1.64	(0.02)	2.09	(0.03)	**0.24**	(0.03)	**0.45**	(0.04)	1.70	(0.01)	c	c
	Slovenia	6.2	(1.0)	13.6	(1.4)	13.9	(1.4)	1.69	(0.02)	1.90	(0.02)	2.18	(0.02)	**0.21**	(0.03)	**0.27**	(0.02)	1.94	(0.01)	1.77	(0.05)
	Spain	13.6	(0.9)	14.4	(0.9)	14.4	(0.9)	1.67	(0.02)	1.85	(0.02)	2.12	(0.02)	**0.18**	(0.03)	**0.27**	(0.03)	1.91	(0.01)	1.60	(0.03)
	Sweden	2.2	(0.6)	2.6	(0.8)	2.6	(0.8)	0.72	(0.03)	0.73	(0.01)	0.93	(0.04)	0.00	(0.04)	**0.20**	(0.05)	0.76	(0.01)	0.88	(0.04)
	Switzerland	8.6	(1.0)	14.8	(2.0)	15.4	(2.1)	1.19	(0.05)	1.34	(0.04)	1.78	(0.05)	**0.15**	(0.06)	**0.44**	(0.07)	1.43	(0.02)	1.36	(0.03)
	Turkey	5.6	(1.0)	9.7	(1.5)	10.1	(1.6)	1.78	(0.02)	1.88	(0.02)	2.17	(0.02)	**0.09**	(0.03)	**0.29**	(0.03)	1.92	(0.02)	c	c
	United Kingdom	9.4	(1.0)	11.8	(1.6)	12.7	(1.4)	1.44	(0.05)	1.59	(0.02)	1.90	(0.03)	**0.15**	(0.06)	**0.31**	(0.04)	1.61	(0.02)	1.80	(0.07)
	United States	10.0	(1.3)	10.4	(1.4)	10.4	(1.4)	1.83	(0.03)	1.98	(0.03)	2.18	(0.03)	**0.16**	(0.04)	**0.20**	(0.04)	2.01	(0.02)	2.01	(0.04)
	OECD average	8.7	(0.2)	12.9	(0.3)	13.3	(0.3)	1.48	(0.01)	1.68	(0.00)	1.93	(0.00)	**0.19**	(0.01)	**0.26**	(0.01)	1.70	(0.00)	1.62	(0.01)
Partners	Albania	m	m	m	m	m	m	m	m	m	m	m	m	m	m	m	m	2.10	(0.02)	m	m
	Argentina	8.8	(1.3)	13.7	(1.8)	14.0	(1.8)	1.08	(0.03)	1.31	(0.05)	1.65	(0.05)	**0.23**	(0.06)	**0.34**	(0.07)	1.35	(0.03)	1.31	(0.07)
	Brazil	11.7	(1.2)	18.0	(2.0)	18.0	(2.0)	1.22	(0.02)	1.31	(0.02)	1.92	(0.04)	**0.09**	(0.03)	**0.61**	(0.05)	1.44	(0.02)	1.21	(0.10)
	Bulgaria	10.9	(1.6)	15.7	(2.2)	16.0	(2.2)	1.69	(0.03)	1.95	(0.03)	2.23	(0.02)	**0.26**	(0.04)	**0.28**	(0.04)	1.97	(0.02)	c	c
	Colombia	10.4	(1.4)	12.6	(1.6)	12.7	(1.6)	1.57	(0.04)	1.68	(0.03)	2.04	(0.03)	**0.12**	(0.05)	**0.36**	(0.04)	1.77	(0.02)	c	c
	Costa Rica	10.0	(1.4)	13.5	(2.1)	13.7	(2.1)	1.28	(0.04)	1.49	(0.04)	1.96	(0.06)	**0.21**	(0.05)	**0.47**	(0.07)	1.54	(0.03)	1.40	(0.11)
	Croatia	4.9	(0.8)	7.7	(1.3)	7.8	(1.3)	1.92	(0.03)	2.05	(0.02)	2.31	(0.03)	**0.13**	(0.04)	**0.26**	(0.04)	2.07	(0.01)	2.04	(0.03)
	Cyprus*	8.7	(1.0)	10.3	(1.0)	11.0	(1.1)	1.69	(0.02)	1.89	(0.02)	2.07	(0.02)	**0.20**	(0.03)	**0.18**	(0.03)	1.88	(0.01)	1.84	(0.04)
	Hong Kong-China	3.5	(0.8)	3.5	(0.8)	3.5	(0.8)	1.71	(0.03)	1.89	(0.02)	1.91	(0.03)	**0.18**	(0.04)	0.02	(0.04)	1.87	(0.02)	1.77	(0.02)
	Indonesia	6.2	(1.9)	9.2	(2.7)	9.2	(2.8)	1.49	(0.03)	1.51	(0.03)	1.86	(0.05)	0.02	(0.04)	**0.36**	(0.06)	1.60	(0.02)	c	c
	Jordan	2.9	(0.8)	2.9	(0.8)	3.5	(0.9)	2.14	(0.05)	2.11	(0.03)	2.26	(0.06)	-0.03	(0.06)	**0.14**	(0.07)	2.16	(0.02)	2.22	(0.04)
	Kazakhstan	4.3	(0.9)	5.4	(1.2)	5.5	(1.3)	1.80	(0.04)	1.97	(0.02)	2.09	(0.03)	**0.17**	(0.05)	**0.11**	(0.03)	1.98	(0.02)	1.91	(0.03)
	Latvia	6.8	(1.3)	8.1	(1.5)	8.1	(1.6)	1.87	(0.02)	2.00	(0.02)	2.17	(0.02)	**0.13**	(0.03)	**0.16**	(0.03)	2.02	(0.01)	2.18	(0.07)
	Liechtenstein	11.7	(5.6)	30.8	(6.0)	33.7	(5.7)	c	c	1.32	(0.06)	c	c	c	c	c	c	1.62	(0.06)	1.44	(0.09)
	Lithuania	4.3	(0.7)	5.6	(0.9)	5.7	(0.9)	1.49	(0.03)	1.66	(0.02)	1.77	(0.02)	**0.16**	(0.03)	**0.12**	(0.03)	1.65	(0.01)	1.69	(0.07)
	Macao-China	1.9	(0.5)	1.9	(0.5)	2.0	(0.5)	2.19	(0.01)	2.23	(0.02)	2.18	(0.02)	0.04	(0.02)	**-0.05**	(0.02)	2.16	(0.02)	2.22	(0.01)
	Malaysia	7.6	(1.2)	9.1	(1.4)	9.1	(1.4)	1.43	(0.03)	1.53	(0.02)	1.82	(0.03)	**0.10**	(0.03)	**0.29**	(0.04)	1.60	(0.02)	1.53	(0.05)
	Montenegro	2.6	(0.7)	3.9	(0.8)	4.8	(0.8)	1.78	(0.02)	1.92	(0.02)	2.01	(0.02)	**0.14**	(0.03)	**0.09**	(0.03)	1.90	(0.01)	1.83	(0.06)
	Peru	14.4	(1.8)	17.6	(1.9)	17.7	(1.8)	1.48	(0.02)	1.76	(0.03)	2.12	(0.04)	**0.27**	(0.04)	**0.36**	(0.05)	1.80	(0.02)	c	c
	Qatar	4.2	(0.4)	5.7	(0.5)	14.0	(0.7)	1.62	(0.02)	1.59	(0.02)	1.85	(0.02)	-0.03	(0.03)	**0.26**	(0.03)	1.44	(0.02)	1.98	(0.01)
	Romania	8.4	(1.5)	11.8	(1.9)	11.9	(1.9)	1.81	(0.04)	1.97	(0.03)	2.32	(0.03)	**0.17**	(0.05)	**0.34**	(0.04)	2.02	(0.02)	c	c
	Russian Federation	5.1	(0.7)	5.4	(0.8)	5.5	(0.8)	2.01	(0.02)	2.10	(0.01)	2.19	(0.01)	**0.09**	(0.02)	**0.09**	(0.02)	2.11	(0.01)	2.10	(0.02)
	Serbia	5.0	(0.7)	7.0	(0.9)	7.0	(0.9)	1.87	(0.02)	2.07	(0.02)	2.21	(0.02)	**0.20**	(0.03)	**0.14**	(0.03)	2.05	(0.01)	2.01	(0.04)
	Shanghai-China	7.9	(1.6)	10.6	(2.2)	10.7	(2.1)	2.12	(0.03)	2.33	(0.01)	2.42	(0.03)	**0.20**	(0.03)	**0.10**	(0.03)	2.30	(0.01)	c	c
	Singapore	12.6	(1.2)	16.2	(1.2)	16.2	(1.2)	1.98	(0.02)	2.20	(0.01)	2.58	(0.02)	**0.22**	(0.02)	**0.38**	(0.02)	2.23	(0.01)	2.24	(0.02)
	Chinese Taipei	12.8	(1.2)	17.4	(1.5)	17.4	(1.6)	1.74	(0.03)	1.98	(0.02)	2.24	(0.03)	**0.24**	(0.04)	**0.25**	(0.03)	1.98	(0.01)	c	c
	Thailand	9.2	(1.1)	10.9	(1.2)	11.0	(1.3)	1.56	(0.02)	1.68	(0.02)	1.90	(0.02)	**0.12**	(0.03)	**0.22**	(0.03)	1.70	(0.01)	c	c
	Tunisia	2.8	(0.9)	2.9	(1.1)	3.2	(0.9)	1.18	(0.02)	1.21	(0.02)	1.32	(0.04)	0.03	(0.03)	**0.11**	(0.04)	1.23	(0.01)	c	c
	United Arab Emirates	3.8	(0.6)	5.5	(0.9)	5.8	(1.0)	1.99	(0.03)	2.10	(0.03)	2.27	(0.03)	**0.10**	(0.05)	**0.17**	(0.05)	1.99	(0.02)	2.26	(0.02)
	Uruguay	12.2	(1.3)	16.5	(1.7)	17.0	(1.7)	1.37	(0.03)	1.69	(0.03)	2.00	(0.04)	**0.32**	(0.04)	**0.31**	(0.05)	1.64	(0.02)	c	c
	Viet Nam	5.1	(1.2)	7.7	(1.7)	7.7	(1.7)	1.83	(0.03)	1.99	(0.02)	2.10	(0.03)	**0.16**	(0.04)	**0.11**	(0.03)	1.96	(0.02)	c	c

Note: Values that are statistically significant are indicated in bold (see Annex A3).

1. ESCS refers to the *PISA index of economic, social and cultural status*.

2. A socio-economically disadvantaged school is one whose students' mean ESCS is statistically significantly below the mean ESCS of the country/economy; an average school is one where there is no difference between the students' and the country's/economy's mean ESCS; and an advantaged school is one whose students' mean ESCS is statistically significantly above the country/economy mean.

* See notes at the beginning of this Annex.

StatLink http://dx.doi.org/10.1787/888932964946

[Part 2/2]
Table II.4.3 Inequity in access to instructional content: Formal mathematics
Results based on students' self-reports

	Formal mathematics: Difference between non-immigrant and immigrant students		Mean among students who speak the language of assessment at home		Mean among students who do not speak the language of assessment at home		Difference between students who speak the language of assessment at home and those who do not		Mean among students in rural schools		Mean among students in town schools (small town and town)		Mean among students in urban schools (city and large city)		Difference between students in rural and town schools		Difference between students in town and urban schools		Difference between students in rural and urban schools	
	Dif.	S.E.	Mean index	S.E.	Mean index	S.E.	Dif.	S.E.	Mean index	S.E.	Mean index	S.E.	Mean index	S.E.	Dif.	S.E.	Dif.	S.E.	Dif.	S.E.
OECD																				
Australia	**0.33**	(0.02)	1.63	(0.01)	2.07	(0.04)	**-0.45**	(0.04)	1.44	(0.03)	1.54	(0.02)	1.79	(0.01)	**-0.10**	(0.04)	**-0.25**	(0.02)	**0.35**	(0.03)
Austria	**-0.15**	(0.05)	1.58	(0.02)	1.41	(0.05)	**0.17**	(0.05)	1.51	(0.15)	1.46	(0.03)	1.68	(0.05)	0.05	(0.16)	**-0.23**	(0.06)	0.17	(0.15)
Belgium	**-0.19**	(0.04)	1.91	(0.02)	1.59	(0.06)	**0.32**	(0.06)	1.92	(0.15)	1.81	(0.02)	1.88	(0.05)	0.11	(0.16)	-0.07	(0.06)	-0.05	(0.16)
Canada	**0.16**	(0.02)	1.94	(0.01)	2.13	(0.03)	**-0.18**	(0.03)	1.86	(0.02)	1.91	(0.01)	2.05	(0.02)	-0.05	(0.03)	**-0.14**	(0.02)	**0.19**	(0.03)
Chile	0.12	(0.10)	1.70	(0.02)	c	c	c	c	1.39	(0.06)	1.66	(0.04)	1.74	(0.03)	**-0.26**	(0.08)	-0.09	(0.05)	**0.35**	(0.07)
Czech Republic	0.04	(0.07)	1.81	(0.02)	1.87	(0.09)	-0.07	(0.09)	1.66	(0.08)	1.81	(0.02)	1.79	(0.05)	-0.15	(0.08)	0.02	(0.05)	0.13	(0.09)
Denmark	-0.05	(0.03)	1.63	(0.02)	1.58	(0.05)	0.05	(0.04)	1.55	(0.04)	1.62	(0.02)	1.72	(0.04)	-0.07	(0.04)	-0.09	(0.05)	**0.16**	(0.06)
Estonia	**0.16**	(0.04)	1.99	(0.01)	2.06	(0.06)	-0.08	(0.07)	1.90	(0.03)	1.99	(0.01)	2.10	(0.02)	**-0.10**	(0.03)	**-0.11**	(0.02)	**0.21**	(0.03)
Finland	**-0.24**	(0.03)	1.73	(0.01)	1.49	(0.03)	**0.24**	(0.03)	1.59	(0.09)	1.71	(0.01)	1.76	(0.02)	-0.12	(0.09)	**-0.05**	(0.03)	0.17	(0.09)
France	**-0.23**	(0.04)	1.92	(0.02)	1.65	(0.06)	**0.27**	(0.06)	w	w	w	w	w	w	w	w	w	w	w	w
Germany	**-0.22**	(0.04)	1.70	(0.02)	1.47	(0.06)	**0.23**	(0.07)	c	c	1.65	(0.03)	1.72	(0.05)	c	c	-0.07	(0.07	c	c
Greece	**-0.19**	(0.04)	1.94	(0.01)	1.67	(0.06)	**0.26**	(0.06)	1.83	(0.05)	1.91	(0.02)	1.92	(0.03)	-0.08	(0.05)	-0.01	(0.03	0.09	(0.05)
Hungary	0.12	(0.09)	1.96	(0.02)	c	c	c	c	1.59	(0.12)	1.95	(0.03)	2.01	(0.04)	**-0.36**	(0.13)	-0.07	(0.05	**0.42**	(0.13)
Iceland	0.04	(0.08)	1.14	(0.01)	1.23	(0.09)	-0.09	(0.09)	1.07	(0.03)	1.12	(0.02)	1.24	(0.03)	-0.05	(0.04)	**-0.12**	(0.04	**0.17**	(0.03)
Ireland	**0.14**	(0.04)	1.46	(0.01)	1.60	(0.07)	**-0.14**	(0.07)	1.53	(0.03)	1.48	(0.02)	1.40	(0.04)	0.05	(0.04)	0.08	(0.04	**-0.14**	(0.05)
Israel	0.00	(0.03)	1.82	(0.02)	1.83	(0.06)	-0.01	(0.06)	1.78	(0.04)	1.84	(0.02)	1.79	(0.05)	-0.06	(0.05)	0.05	(0.05	0.01	(0.06)
Italy	**-0.23**	(0.03)	1.89	(0.01)	1.54	(0.03)	**0.35**	(0.03)	1.46	(0.07)	1.83	(0.02)	1.88	(0.03)	**-0.37**	(0.07)	-0.05	(0.03	**0.42**	(0.08)
Japan	c	c	2.06	(0.02)	c	c	c	c	c	c	1.96	(0.03)	2.09	(0.02)	c	c	**-0.13**	(0.04	c	c
Korea	c	c	2.07	(0.02)	c	c	c	c	c	c	2.04	(0.06)	2.08	(0.02)	c	c	-0.04	(0.06	c	c
Luxembourg	**-0.08**	(0.02)	1.70	(0.07)	1.29	(0.03)	**0.40**	(0.07)	c	c	1.44	(0.01)	c	c	c	c	c	c	c	c
Mexico	**-0.35**	(0.05)	1.79	(0.01)	1.36	(0.12)	**0.43**	(0.12)	1.58	(0.02)	1.75	(0.01)	1.87	(0.01)	**-0.18**	(0.02)	**-0.12**	(0.02	**0.30**	(0.03)
Netherlands	**-0.16**	(0.07)	1.53	(0.02)	1.31	(0.08)	**0.22**	(0.08)	c	c	1.48	(0.03)	1.50	(0.06)	c	c	-0.02	(0.07	c	c
New Zealand	**0.31**	(0.04)	1.45	(0.02)	1.79	(0.05)	**-0.34**	(0.06)	1.12	(0.07)	1.39	(0.04)	1.66	(0.03)	**-0.27**	(0.08)	**-0.27**	(0.05	**0.53**	(0.07)
Norway	m	m	m	m	m	m	m	m	m	m	m	m	m	m	m	m	m	m	m	m
Poland	c	c	1.84	(0.02)	c	c	c	c	1.81	(0.02)	1.82	(0.02)	1.90	(0.04)	-0.01	(0.03)	-0.07	(0.04	0.09	(0.05)
Portugal	**-0.11**	(0.03)	1.74	(0.02)	1.73	(0.07)	0.01	(0.07)	1.70	(0.18)	1.72	(0.02)	1.75	(0.05)	-0.03	(0.18)	-0.03	(0.06	0.05	(0.18)
Slovak Republic	c	c	1.73	(0.02)	c	c	c	c	1.39	(0.04)	1.72	(0.02)	1.88	(0.07)	**-0.33**	(0.04)	**-0.16**	(0.07	**0.49**	(0.08)
Slovenia	**-0.17**	(0.06)	1.94	(0.01)	1.64	(0.07)	**0.30**	(0.07)	c	c	1.91	(0.01)	1.96	(0.02)	c	c	**-0.05**	(0.02	c	c
Spain	**-0.31**	(0.03)	1.93	(0.01)	1.59	(0.04)	**0.33**	(0.05)	1.78	(0.04)	1.83	(0.01)	1.95	(0.02)	-0.05	(0.04)	**-0.12**	(0.03	**0.17**	(0.05)
Sweden	**0.12**	(0.04)	0.74	(0.01)	0.93	(0.05)	**-0.19**	(0.05)	0.74	(0.03)	0.74	(0.01)	0.88	(0.04)	0.00	(0.04)	**-0.14**	(0.04	**0.14**	(0.05)
Switzerland	**-0.08**	(0.03)	1.44	(0.03)	1.30	(0.04)	**0.14**	(0.04)	1.15	(0.07)	1.41	(0.03)	1.54	(0.08)	**-0.26**	(0.08)	-0.12	(0.09	**0.39**	(0.12)
Turkey	c	c	1.94	(0.01)	c	c	c	c	1.65	(0.20)	1.93	(0.03)	1.92	(0.02)	-0.29	(0.20)	0.02	(0.05	0.27	(0.20)
United Kingdom	**0.19**	(0.06)	1.61	(0.02)	1.86	(0.08)	**-0.25**	(0.08)	1.70	(0.06)	1.58	(0.03)	1.71	(0.04)	0.12	(0.06)	**-0.13**	(0.05	0.01	(0.06)
United States	0.00	(0.05)	2.01	(0.02)	1.93	(0.05)	0.08	(0.05)	1.81	(0.06)	2.02	(0.03)	2.03	(0.03)	**-0.21**	(0.07)	-0.01	(0.05	**0.22**	(0.07)
OECD average	**-0.04**	(0.01)	1.71	(0.00)	1.59	(0.01)	**0.07**	(0.01)	1.54	(0.02)	1.67	(0.00)	1.76	(0.01)	**-0.12**	(0.02)	**-0.08**	(0.01	**0.20**	(0.02)
Partners																				
Albania	m	m	2.10	(0.02)	m	m	m	m	2.00	(0.04)	2.12	(0.03)	2.12	(0.03)	**-0.11**	(0.04)	-0.01	(0.04	**0.12**	(0.05)
Argentina	-0.04	(0.07)	1.35	(0.03)	c	c	c	c	1.08	(0.09)	1.34	(0.04)	1.41	(0.04)	**-0.26**	(0.10)	-0.07	(0.05	**0.33**	(0.09)
Brazil	**-0.23**	(0.10)	1.44	(0.02)	c	c	c	c	1.24	(0.11)	1.34	(0.03)	1.53	(0.03)	-0.10	(0.12)	**-0.19**	(0.04	**0.29**	(0.12)
Bulgaria	c	c	2.02	(0.02)	c	c	c	c	1.40	(0.14)	1.92	(0.03)	2.08	(0.03)	**-0.52**	(0.14)	**-0.16**	(0.04	**0.69**	(0.14)
Colombia	c	c	1.77	(0.02)	c	c	c	c	1.49	(0.06)	1.73	(0.05)	1.84	(0.03)	**-0.24**	(0.08)	-0.10	(0.0	**0.34**	(0.06)
Costa Rica	-0.15	(0.11)	1.55	(0.03)	c	c	c	c	1.36	(0.04)	1.58	(0.04)	1.63	(0.08)	**-0.22**	(0.07)	-0.05	(0.1	**0.27**	(0.09)
Croatia	-0.03	(0.03)	2.08	(0.01)	c	c	c	c	c	c	2.04	(0.02)	2.12	(0.03)	c	c	**-0.07**	(0.0	c	c
Cyprus*	-0.03	(0.05)	1.85	(0.01)	1.85	(0.06)	0.00	(0.06)	1.71	(0.04)	1.84	(0.02)	1.95	(0.02)	**-0.13**	(0.05)	**-0.11**	(0.0	**0.24**	(0.05)
Hong Kong-China	**-0.10**	(0.02)	1.86	(0.02)	1.59	(0.06)	**0.27**	(0.06)	c	c	c	c	1.83	(0.02)	c	c	c	[illegible]	c	c
Indonesia	c	c	1.67	(0.04)	c	c	c	c	1.53	(0.05)	1.57	(0.03)	1.77	(0.07)	-0.04	(0.06)	**-0.20**	(0.0	**0.24**	(0.07)
Jordan	0.06	(0.05)	2.16	(0.02)	c	c	c	c	2.08	(0.08)	2.08	(0.03)	2.24	(0.02)	0.00	(0.09)	**-0.16**	(0.0	0.17	(0.09)
Kazakhstan	**-0.07**	(0.03)	1.98	(0.02)	1.86	(0.10)	0.11	(0.10)	1.92	(0.03)	1.95	(0.04)	2.02	(0.03)	-0.03	(0.05)	-0.08	(0.0	**0.11**	(0.04)
Latvia	**0.16**	(0.07)	2.02	(0.01)	c	c	c	c	1.89	(0.03)	2.01	(0.02)	2.15	(0.02)	**-0.12**	(0.03)	**-0.14**	(0.0	**0.26**	(0.04)
Liechtenstein	-0.18	(0.11)	1.64	(0.06)	c	c	c	c	c	c	1.55	(0.05)	c	c	c	c	c	[illegible]	c	c
Lithuania	0.04	(0.08)	1.65	(0.01)	c	c	c	c	1.52	(0.03)	1.64	(0.02)	1.73	(0.02)	**-0.12**	(0.04)	**-0.09**	(0.0	**0.21**	(0.03)
Macao-China	**0.05**	(0.02)	2.21	(0.01)	2.00	(0.04)	**0.20**	(0.04)	c	c	c	c	2.20	(0.01)	c	c	c	[illegible]	c	c
Malaysia	-0.07	(0.05)	1.56	(0.02)	c	c	c	c	1.42	(0.05)	1.59	(0.02)	1.67	(0.04)	**-0.17**	(0.06)	-0.08	(0.0	**0.25**	(0.07)
Montenegro	-0.07	(0.06)	1.90	(0.01)	c	c	c	c	c	c	1.92	(0.01)	1.86	(0.02)	c	c	0.06	(0.0	c	c
Peru	c	c	1.83	(0.02)	c	c	c	c	1.48	(0.04)	1.74	(0.04)	1.97	(0.04)	**-0.26**	(0.05)	**-0.23**	(0.0	**0.49**	(0.05)
Qatar	**0.54**	(0.02)	1.37	(0.02)	2.11	(0.02)	**-0.74**	(0.02)	1.46	(0.03)	1.57	(0.02)	1.89	(0.01)	**-0.11**	(0.03)	**-0.32**	(0.0	**0.44**	(0.03)
Romania	c	c	2.03	(0.02)	c	c	c	c	1.87	(0.04)	2.00	(0.03)	2.10	(0.05)	**-0.12**	(0.05)	-0.10	(0.0	**0.22**	(0.06)
Russian Federation	-0.01	(0.02)	2.11	(0.01)	2.06	(0.05)	0.05	(0.05)	2.09	(0.02)	2.06	(0.01)	2.14	(0.01)	0.02	(0.03)	**-0.08**	(0.0	**0.06**	(0.03)
Serbia	-0.03	(0.04)	2.05	(0.01)	c	c	c	c	c	c	2.03	(0.02)	2.07	(0.03)	c	c	-0.03	(0.0	c	c
Shanghai-China	c	c	2.31	(0.01)	c	c	c	c	c	c	c	c	2.30	(0.01)	c	c	c	[illegible]	c	c
Singapore	0.01	(0.03)	2.40	(0.02)	2.21	(0.03)	**0.18**	(0.03)	c	c	c	c	2.23	(0.01)	c	c	c	[illegible]	c	c
Chinese Taipei	c	c	2.03	(0.01)	c	c	c	c	c	c	1.87	(0.02)	2.06	(0.02)	c	c	**-0.19**	(0.0	c	c
Thailand	c	c	1.74	(0.02)	c	c	c	c	1.57	(0.04)	1.68	(0.02)	1.79	(0.03)	**-0.11**	(0.05)	**-0.11**	(0.0	**0.22**	(0.05)
Tunisia	c	c	1.23	(0.01)	c	c	c	c	1.24	(0.07)	1.21	(0.01)	1.29	(0.05)	0.03	(0.07)	-0.07	(0.0	0.04	(0.09)
United Arab Emirates	**0.28**	(0.02)	1.98	(0.03)	2.28	(0.03)	**-0.30**	(0.04)	2.11	(0.04)	2.05	(0.04)	2.17	(0.02)	0.06	(0.06)	**-0.12**	(0.0	0.06	(0.05)
Uruguay	c	c	1.64	(0.02)	c	c	c	c	1.44	(0.10)	1.59	(0.02)	1.75	(0.04)	-0.15	(0.10)	**-0.16**	(0.0	**0.31**	(0.11)
Viet Nam	c	c	1.96	(0.02)	c	c	c	c	1.89	(0.02)	1.95	(0.03)	2.08	(0.04)	-0.06	(0.04)	**-0.13**	(0.0	**0.18**	(0.04)

Note: Values that are statistically significant are indicated in bold (see Annex A3).
1. ESCS refers to the *PISA index of economic, social and cultural status.*
2. A socio-economically disadvantaged school is one whose students' mean ESCS is statistically significantly below the mean ESCS of the country/economy; [illegible]n average school is one where there is no difference between the students' and the country's/economy's mean ESCS; and an advantaged school is one whose students' mean E[illegible]CS is statistically significantly above the country/economy mean.
* See notes at the beginning of this Annex.

StatLink http://dx.doi.org/10.1787/888932964946

[Part 1/1]
Correlation between student performance and selected student and school characteristics

Table II.4.4   *Results based on students' self-reports*

	Study behaviour				Student and teacher profile				School climate					
	Attendance in after-school lessons		Homework or other study set by your teachers		Student-teacher ratio		Proportion of teachers with a univerity degree		Student-related factors affecting school climate		Behavioural outcomes: Dropout		Parental pressure to achieve	
	Corr.	S.E.	Corr.	S.E.	Corr.	S.E.	Corr.	S.E.	Corr.	S.E.	Corr.	S.E.	Corr.	S.E.
Australia	**0.13**	(0.02)	**0.32**	(0.01)	0.00	(0.02)	-0.01	(0.02)	**0.27**	(0.01)	**-0.17**	(0.01)	**0.20**	(0.02)
Austria	-0.03	(0.02)	**0.17**	(0.02)	-0.07	(0.04)	**0.42**	(0.03)	**0.16**	(0.04)	**-0.19**	(0.05)	**0.14**	(0.06)
Belgium	**0.07**	(0.02)	**0.29**	(0.02)	**0.43**	(0.03)	**0.43**	(0.03)	**0.39**	(0.04)	**-0.34**	(0.03)	**0.21**	(0.04)
Canada	-0.01	(0.02)	**0.17**	(0.01)	**0.10**	(0.02)	0.03	(0.02)	**0.22**	(0.02)	**-0.11**	(0.02)	**0.17**	(0.02)
Chile	0.04	(0.03)	**0.23**	(0.02)	0.06	(0.05)	**0.12**	(0.04)	**0.33**	(0.04)	**-0.22**	(0.04)	**0.34**	(0.03)
Czech Republic	**-0.06**	(0.02)	**0.14**	(0.02)	0.03	(0.04)	**0.23**	(0.05)	**0.24**	(0.04)	**-0.12**	(0.04)	**0.21**	(0.06)
Denmark	**-0.11**	(0.02)	**0.07**	(0.02)	0.07	(0.05)	0.03	(0.03)	**0.17**	(0.02)	**-0.16**	(0.05)	**0.12**	(0.03)
Estonia	**-0.12**	(0.02)	0.04	(0.02)	**0.11**	(0.02)	c	c	**0.08**	(0.02)	-0.05	(0.03)	0.04	(0.03)
Finland	**-0.11**	(0.02)	**0.05**	(0.02)	0.05	(0.03)	**0.05**	(0.02)	**0.09**	(0.02)	-0.05	(0.04)	0.03	(0.02)
France	0.03	(0.02)	**0.26**	(0.02)	w	w	w	w	w	w	w	w	w	w
Germany	-0.01	(0.02)	**0.08**	(0.03)	**0.14**	(0.04)	c	c	**0.30**	(0.04)	**-0.19**	(0.05)	0.06	(0.06)
Greece	**0.18**	(0.02)	**0.27**	(0.02)	**0.12**	(0.04)	**0.18**	(0.05)	0.07	(0.04)	**-0.32**	(0.02)	**0.18**	(0.03)
Hungary	**0.10**	(0.02)	**0.29**	(0.02)	0.02	(0.06)	**0.09**	(0.04)	**0.37**	(0.05)	**-0.30**	(0.03)	**0.40**	(0.05)
Iceland	**-0.16**	(0.03)	0.05	(0.03)	**0.04**	(0.02)	**0.05**	(0.02)	**0.05**	(0.02)	-0.02	(0.02)	**0.05**	(0.02)
Ireland	**0.08**	(0.02)	**0.25**	(0.02)	**0.15**	(0.05)	0.00	(0.03)	**0.21**	(0.03)	**-0.18**	(0.04)	**0.26**	(0.03)
Israel	**-0.13**	(0.02)	**0.14**	(0.02)	-0.04	(0.07)	0.08	(0.04)	**0.12**	(0.05)	-0.06	(0.05)	**0.25**	(0.04)
Italy	**0.06**	(0.01)	**0.30**	(0.01)	**0.34**	(0.03)	**0.14**	(0.04)	**0.31**	(0.03)	**-0.24**	(0.03)	**0.21**	(0.03)
Japan	**0.26**	(0.02)	**0.32**	(0.02)	**0.24**	(0.04)	**0.11**	(0.04)	**0.28**	(0.06)	**-0.34**	(0.04)	**0.38**	(0.04)
Korea	**0.29**	(0.03)	**0.32**	(0.03)	0.10	(0.08)	0.01	(0.03)	**0.29**	(0.05)	**-0.27**	(0.06)	**0.26**	(0.05)
Luxembourg	-0.02	(0.02)	**0.20**	(0.02)	**0.11**	(0.01)	**0.24**	(0.01)	**0.23**	(0.01)	**-0.20**	(0.01)	**-0.08**	(0.01)
Mexico	**0.14**	(0.01)	**0.33**	(0.01)	0.03	(0.02)	0.00	(0.02)	**0.11**	(0.02)	0.00	(0.02)	0.03	(0.02)
Netherlands	**0.08**	(0.03)	**0.27**	(0.02)	**0.41**	(0.08)	**0.43**	(0.08)	**0.27**	(0.05)	**-0.30**	(0.04)	**0.29**	(0.06)
New Zealand	**0.08**	(0.03)	**0.28**	(0.02)	**0.09**	(0.04)	**0.08**	(0.03)	**0.27**	(0.03)	**-0.41**	(0.02)	**0.25**	(0.03)
Norway	-0.04	(0.03)	**0.16**	(0.02)	-0.02	(0.04)	c	c	**0.15**	(0.03)	c	c	**0.11**	(0.04)
Poland	**-0.07**	(0.02)	**0.15**	(0.02)	**0.13**	(0.04)	-0.01	(0.05)	0.06	(0.06)	-0.06	(0.04)	0.05	(0.05)
Portugal	**0.10**	(0.02)	**0.25**	(0.02)	**0.23**	(0.04)	-0.03	(0.06)	**0.16**	(0.04)	0.07	(0.04)	**0.19**	(0.05)
Slovak Republic	**-0.10**	(0.03)	**0.13**	(0.03)	-0.05	(0.05)	**-0.11**	(0.04)	**0.19**	(0.04)	**-0.22**	(0.04)	**0.20**	(0.05)
Slovenia	**-0.11**	(0.03)	**0.11**	(0.04)	**0.18**	(0.01)	**0.36**	(0.01)	**0.27**	(0.01)	**-0.24**	(0.01)	**0.21**	(0.02)
Spain	0.02	(0.01)	**0.20**	(0.01)	0.07	(0.05)	-0.03	(0.03)	**0.20**	(0.02)	**-0.16**	(0.02)	**0.10**	(0.02)
Sweden	**-0.09**	(0.02)	**0.08**	(0.02)	**0.05**	(0.03)	0.03	(0.03)	**0.13**	(0.03)	**-0.19**	(0.04)	**0.12**	(0.03)
Switzerland	**-0.08**	(0.02)	**0.11**	(0.02)	**0.07**	(0.03)	**0.18**	(0.04)	**0.11**	(0.04)	c	c	**-0.17**	(0.03)
Turkey	**0.07**	(0.02)	**0.12**	(0.02)	**-0.29**	(0.04)	0.01	(0.07)	**0.34**	(0.07)	**-0.23**	(0.03)	**0.18**	(0.06)
United Kingdom	**0.09**	(0.02)	**0.32**	(0.02)	-0.06	(0.05)	-0.02	(0.03)	**0.19**	(0.05)	**-0.13**	(0.04)	**0.22**	(0.04)
United States	**0.08**	(0.02)	**0.35**	(0.02)	0.01	(0.04)	0.01	(0.07)	**0.19**	(0.05)	**-0.16**	(0.04)	**0.18**	(0.05)
OECD average	**0.02**	(0.00)	**0.20**	(0.00)	**0.08**	(0.01)	**0.10**	(0.01)	**0.23**	(0.05)	**-0.20**	(0.03)	**0.15**	(0.05)
Albania	0.03	(0.02)	0.01	(0.02)	c	c	0.01	(0.02)	-0.02	(0.02)	-0.03	(0.02)	0.03	(0.02)
Argentina	0.03	(0.02)	**0.19**	(0.03)	0.02	(0.04)	**0.15**	(0.05)	**0.31**	(0.05)	**-0.13**	(0.04)	0.08	(0.05)
Brazil	0.01	(0.02)	**0.17**	(0.02)	**-0.15**	(0.02)	-0.02	(0.05)	**0.23**	(0.03)	**-0.12**	(0.03)	**0.14**	(0.04)
Bulgaria	**0.13**	(0.02)	**0.35**	(0.03)	-0.02	(0.04)	c	c	**0.25**	(0.05)	**-0.31**	(0.04)	**0.28**	(0.05)
Colombia	**0.19**	(0.02)	**0.34**	(0.02)	**-0.08**	(0.04)	0.01	(0.07)	**0.19**	(0.05)	-0.04	(0.05)	0.03	(0.04)
Costa Rica	**0.10**	(0.05)	**0.31**	(0.03)	0.16	(0.10)	0.02	(0.10)	**0.32**	(0.05)	**-0.35**	(0.04)	**0.14**	(0.05)
Croatia	0.00	(0.02)	**0.24**	(0.03)	**0.19**	(0.05)	**0.32**	(0.04)	**0.23**	(0.05)	**-0.20**	(0.03)	**0.15**	(0.05)
Cyprus*	-0.01	(0.02)	**0.24**	(0.02)	**0.34**	(0.01)	**-0.04**	(0.01)	0.03	(0.01)	**-0.25**	(0.01)	**0.19**	(0.01)
Hong Kong-China	**0.21**	(0.02)	**0.30**	(0.02)	**0.34**	(0.05)	0.05	(0.03)	**0.22**	(0.05)	**-0.13**	(0.05)	**-0.18**	(0.06)
Indonesia	**0.14**	(0.02)	**0.25**	(0.02)	-0.04	(0.06)	0.06	(0.09)	**0.16**	(0.07)	0.04	(0.08)	-0.03	(0.06)
Jordan	-0.04	(0.02)	**0.19**	(0.02)	-0.09	(0.06)	0.02	(0.05)	**0.12**	(0.06)	**-0.12**	(0.03)	0.09	(0.05)
Kazakhstan	0.05	(0.03)	**0.20**	(0.03)	-0.04	(0.04)	0.03	(0.05)	-0.01	(0.05)	-0.03	(0.03)	0.10	(0.05)
Latvia	**-0.04**	(0.02)	**0.15**	(0.02)	**0.13**	(0.04)	0.03	(0.04)	0.07	(0.04)	**-0.08**	(0.04)	0.04	(0.04)
Liechtenstein	-0.03	(0.05)	0.06	(0.07)	**0.56**	(0.04)	**0.45**	(0.04)	**0.12**	(0.04)	c	c	**-0.43**	(0.03)
Lithuania	-0.04	(0.02)	**0.18**	(0.02)	0.01	(0.04)	0.03	(0.03)	**0.17**	(0.04)	**-0.15**	(0.03)	0.03	(0.04)
Macao-China	**0.12**	(0.02)	**0.29**	(0.01)	**0.20**	(0.01)	**-0.05**	(0.01)	**0.26**	(0.01)	**-0.26**	(0.01)	**-0.05**	(0.01)
Malaysia	**0.25**	(0.02)	**0.43**	(0.02)	0.03	(0.05)	-0.07	(0.05)	**0.26**	(0.04)	**-0.12**	(0.03)	**0.22**	(0.05)
Montenegro	0.01	(0.03)	**0.25**	(0.02)	**0.24**	(0.01)	**0.19**	(0.01)	**0.13**	(0.02)	**-0.13**	(0.01)	0.00	(0.01)
Peru	**0.11**	(0.02)	**0.24**	(0.02)	**0.15**	(0.04)	-0.08	(0.07)	**0.21**	(0.04)	**-0.12**	(0.04)	**0.13**	(0.06)
Qatar	-0.01	(0.01)	**0.32**	(0.01)	**0.04**	(0.01)	**-0.09**	(0.01)	**0.10**	(0.01)	**-0.12**	(0.01)	**0.29**	(0.01)
Romania	**0.17**	(0.03)	**0.37**	(0.02)	-0.02	(0.04)	0.05	(0.08)	**0.20**	(0.04)	**-0.25**	(0.04)	0.04	(0.06)
Russian Federation	0.04	(0.02)	**0.19**	(0.02)	0.08	(0.04)	**0.13**	(0.04)	**0.15**	(0.04)	**-0.21**	(0.04)	0.08	(0.04)
Serbia	-0.03	(0.02)	**0.13**	(0.02)	**0.18**	(0.05)	0.06	(0.05)	**0.21**	(0.05)	**-0.21**	(0.04)	**0.22**	(0.05)
Shanghai-China	**0.27**	(0.02)	**0.49**	(0.02)	**-0.25**	(0.05)	**0.20**	(0.04)	**0.21**	(0.05)	**-0.26**	(0.05)	0.09	(0.06)
Singapore	**0.22**	(0.02)	**0.38**	(0.01)	0.04	(0.02)	**0.24**	(0.01)	**0.35**	(0.01)	**-0.17**	(0.01)	**0.21**	(0.01)
Chinese Taipei	**0.30**	(0.02)	**0.42**	(0.02)	**-0.08**	(0.04)	0.02	(0.05)	**0.22**	(0.04)	**-0.09**	(0.04)	**0.17**	(0.05)
Thailand	**0.23**	(0.02)	**0.35**	(0.02)	0.00	(0.04)	**0.11**	(0.04)	**0.20**	(0.04)	**-0.29**	(0.03)	**0.21**	(0.03)
Tunisia	**-0.09**	(0.02)	**0.12**	(0.02)	-0.07	(0.02)	**0.14**	(0.07)	-0.07	(0.06)	-0.08	(0.06)	**0.17**	(0.07)
United Arab Emirates	0.03	(0.02)	**0.29**	(0.02)	0.05	(0.04)	0.01	(0.04)	**0.22**	(0.03)	**-0.14**	(0.02)	**0.22**	(0.03)
Uruguay	0.04	(0.03)	**0.16**	(0.03)	-0.03	(0.03)	**0.14**	(0.07)	**0.36**	(0.04)	**-0.18**	(0.06)	0.13	(0.07)
Viet Nam	**0.26**	(0.03)	**0.33**	(0.02)	0.12	(0.07)	**0.17**	(0.07)	**0.17**	(0.07)	**-0.21**	(0.06)	**0.25**	(0.06)

Note: Values that are statistically significant are indicated in bold (see Annex A3).
* See notes at the beginning of this Annex.
StatLink ᴍᴤᴾ http://dx.doi.org/10.1787/888932964946

[Part 1/1]
Correlation between student socio-economic status and selected student and school characteristics
Table II.4.5   *Results based on students' self-reports*

| | Study behaviour | | | | Student and teacher profile | | | | School climate | | | | | |
| | Attendance in after-school lessons | | Homework or other study set by your teachers | | Student-teacher ratio | | Proportion of teachers with a univeristy degree | | Student-related factors affecting school climate | | Behavioural outcomes: Dropout | | Parental pressure to achieve | |
	Corr.	S.E.	Corr.	S.E.	Corr.	S.E.	Corr.	S.E.	Corr.	S.E.	Corr.	S.E.	Corr.	S.E.
OECD														
Australia	0.14	(0.01)	0.19	(0.01)	-0.03	(0.02)	0.01	(0.02)	0.28	(0.01)	-0.16	(0.01)	0.1	(0.02)
Austria	0.11	(0.02)	0.13	(0.02)	-0.06	(0.03)	0.35	(0.03)	0.13	(0.04)	-0.12	(0.03)	0.1	(0.06)
Belgium	0.13	(0.02)	0.20	(0.02)	0.33	(0.03)	0.33	(0.03)	0.30	(0.02)	-0.19	(0.03)	0.1	(0.03)
Canada	0.12	(0.01)	0.15	(0.01)	0.09	(0.02)	0.01	(0.01)	0.17	(0.02)	-0.14	(0.03)	0.1	(0.02)
Chile	0.08	(0.02)	0.13	(0.02)	-0.03	(0.04)	0.14	(0.07)	0.33	(0.04)	-0.25	(0.03)	0.3	(0.04)
Czech Republic	0.09	(0.02)	0.12	(0.02)	0.03	(0.03)	0.15	(0.03)	0.17	(0.03)	-0.10	(0.03)	0.1	(0.04)
Denmark	0.03	(0.03)	0.08	(0.02)	0.09	(0.04)	0.04	(0.02)	0.17	(0.02)	-0.13	(0.03)	0.1	(0.03)
Estonia	0.06	(0.02)	0.06	(0.02)	0.22	(0.02)	c	c	0.05	(0.03)	-0.06	(0.02)	0.0	(0.03)
Finland	0.06	(0.01)	0.08	(0.02)	0.13	(0.02)	0.01	(0.03)	0.00	(0.02)	0.00	(0.02)	0.0	(0.02)
France	0.11	(0.02)	0.21	(0.02)	w	w	w	w	w	w	w	w		w
Germany	0.11	(0.02)	0.08	(0.02)	0.11	(0.03)	m	m	0.17	(0.03)	-0.10	(0.02)	0.0	(0.04)
Greece	0.23	(0.02)	0.17	(0.02)	0.10	(0.04)	0.11	(0.05)	0.08	(0.03)	-0.21	(0.03)	0.1	(0.03)
Hungary	0.17	(0.02)	0.22	(0.03)	-0.03	(0.04)	0.11	(0.03)	0.30	(0.04)	-0.28	(0.03)	0.2	(0.04)
Iceland	0.03	(0.02)	0.05	(0.02)	0.18	(0.02)	0.07	(0.02)	0.00	(0.02)	-0.03	(0.01)	0.1	(0.02)
Ireland	0.15	(0.02)	0.18	(0.02)	0.15	(0.04)	-0.04	(0.06)	0.20	(0.03)	-0.16	(0.04)	0.2	(0.03)
Israel	0.01	(0.02)	0.07	(0.01)	-0.02	(0.05)	0.11	(0.04)	0.07	(0.04)	-0.11	(0.04)	0.2	(0.04)
Italy	0.18	(0.01)	0.22	(0.01)	0.22	(0.02)	0.16	(0.02)	0.22	(0.02)	-0.19	(0.02)	0.5	(0.02)
Japan	0.22	(0.02)	0.19	(0.02)	0.15	(0.03)	0.08	(0.03)	0.16	(0.04)	-0.19	(0.03)	0.2	(0.03)
Korea	0.33	(0.02)	0.21	(0.02)	0.13	(0.05)	0.01	(0.02)	0.12	(0.04)	-0.12	(0.05)	0.1	(0.03)
Luxembourg	0.14	(0.02)	0.15	(0.02)	0.09	(0.01)	0.25	(0.01)	0.25	(0.01)	-0.21	(0.01)	-0.3	(0.01)
Mexico	0.10	(0.01)	0.11	(0.01)	0.02	(0.01)	0.00	(0.03)	0.09	(0.02)	-0.02	(0.02)	0.7	(0.02)
Netherlands	0.08	(0.02)	0.10	(0.02)	0.20	(0.05)	0.24	(0.05)	0.10	(0.03)	-0.15	(0.03)	0.8	(0.03)
New Zealand	0.17	(0.03)	0.20	(0.02)	0.07	(0.04)	0.11	(0.03)	0.28	(0.03)	-0.42	(0.02)	0.3	(0.03)
Norway	0.08	(0.02)	0.12	(0.02)	0.10	(0.03)	m	m	0.10	(0.02)	c	c	0.7	(0.03)
Poland	0.06	(0.02)	0.07	(0.02)	0.03	(0.03)	-0.03	(0.04)	0.02	(0.05)	-0.02	(0.04)	0.3	(0.05)
Portugal	0.18	(0.02)	0.19	(0.02)	0.23	(0.05)	-0.09	(0.06)	0.10	(0.05)	0.05	(0.05)	0.2	(0.05)
Slovak Republic	0.04	(0.02)	0.11	(0.03)	0.03	(0.05)	-0.09	(0.03)	0.15	(0.03)	-0.18	(0.03)	0.9	(0.05)
Slovenia	0.04	(0.02)	0.09	(0.02)	0.14	(0.01)	0.24	(0.01)	0.15	(0.01)	-0.13	(0.01)	0.5	(0.02)
Spain	0.10	(0.01)	0.12	(0.02)	0.09	(0.06)	-0.02	(0.03)	0.23	(0.03)	-0.16	(0.03)	0.4	(0.03)
Sweden	0.12	(0.02)	0.13	(0.02)	0.11	(0.03)	0.05	(0.03)	0.18	(0.03)	-0.21	(0.03)	0.7	(0.03)
Switzerland	0.07	(0.02)	0.09	(0.02)	-0.03	(0.03)	0.09	(0.04)	0.04	(0.03)	c	c	-0.4	(0.03)
Turkey	0.11	(0.02)	0.00	(0.02)	-0.21	(0.04)	0.02	(0.04)	0.17	(0.04)	-0.11	(0.03)	0.2	(0.04)
United Kingdom	0.15	(0.02)	0.24	(0.02)	-0.09	(0.04)	0.00	(0.03)	0.17	(0.03)	-0.15	(0.02)	0.4	(0.03)
United States	0.15	(0.02)	0.22	(0.02)	0.01	(0.03)	-0.01	(0.07)	0.22	(0.04)	-0.17	(0.05)	0.5	(0.04)
OECD average	0.12	(0.00)	0.14	(0.00)	0.07	(0.01)	0.08	(0.01)	0.16	(0.01)	-0.15	(0.01)	0.6	(0.01)
Partners														
Albania	m	m	m	m	m	m	m	m	m	m	m	m	m	m
Argentina	0.08	(0.02)	0.10	(0.02)	0.03	(0.03)	0.10	(0.05)	0.20	(0.05)	-0.15	(0.04)	0.09	(0.05)
Brazil	0.09	(0.02)	0.09	(0.01)	-0.13	(0.03)	-0.01	(0.04)	0.24	(0.03)	-0.14	(0.03)	0.20	(0.03)
Bulgaria	0.20	(0.02)	0.26	(0.03)	-0.02	(0.03)	c	c	0.15	(0.04)	-0.25	(0.04)	0.27	(0.03)
Colombia	0.16	(0.02)	0.17	(0.02)	-0.04	(0.04)	-0.02	(0.06)	0.16	(0.04)	-0.04	(0.04)	0.05	(0.05)
Costa Rica	0.15	(0.03)	0.14	(0.02)	0.12	(0.07)	0.10	(0.10)	0.28	(0.04)	-0.27	(0.04)	0.14	(0.05)
Croatia	0.11	(0.02)	0.15	(0.02)	0.12	(0.05)	0.21	(0.03)	0.11	(0.04)	-0.11	(0.04)	0.10	(0.04)
Cyprus*	0.09	(0.02)	0.19	(0.02)	0.26	(0.01)	0.03	(0.02)	0.08	(0.01)	-0.14	(0.01)	0.17	(0.01)
Hong Kong-China	0.19	(0.02)	0.10	(0.02)	0.02	(0.05)	0.02	(0.03)	0.12	(0.05)	0.01	(0.06)	-0.04	(0.05)
Indonesia	0.14	(0.02)	0.11	(0.03)	-0.07	(0.05)	0.12	(0.04)	0.11	(0.05)	-0.12	(0.04)	-0.04	(0.05)
Jordan	0.05	(0.02)	0.05	(0.02)	-0.04	(0.03)	0.00	(0.03)	0.03	(0.04)	-0.09	(0.04)	0.09	(0.04)
Kazakhstan	0.14	(0.02)	0.14	(0.03)	0.12	(0.04)	0.11	(0.04)	-0.02	(0.04)	-0.02	(0.01)	0.10	(0.04)
Latvia	0.12	(0.02)	0.14	(0.02)	0.21	(0.04)	0.10	(0.04)	0.00	(0.04)	-0.08	(0.04)	0.07	(0.04)
Liechtenstein	0.21	(0.07)	0.16	(0.08)	0.19	(0.06)	0.17	(0.07)	0.18	(0.06)	c	c	-0.22	(0.06)
Lithuania	0.08	(0.02)	0.12	(0.02)	0.02	(0.04)	0.03	(0.03)	0.12	(0.03)	-0.09	(0.03)	0.08	(0.03)
Macao-China	0.15	(0.01)	0.13	(0.02)	-0.03	(0.01)	-0.05	(0.01)	0.13	(0.01)	-0.12	(0.01)	0.08	(0.01)
Malaysia	0.17	(0.02)	0.18	(0.02)	0.05	(0.03)	-0.05	(0.04)	0.23	(0.04)	-0.12	(0.03)	0.17	(0.05)
Montenegro	0.07	(0.02)	0.07	(0.02)	0.18	(0.01)	0.12	(0.01)	0.09	(0.01)	-0.11	(0.01)	-0.03	(0.01)
Peru	0.15	(0.02)	0.11	(0.02)	0.13	(0.03)	-0.04	(0.07)	0.20	(0.04)	-0.10	(0.04)	0.13	(0.05)
Qatar	0.04	(0.01)	0.11	(0.01)	0.03	(0.01)	-0.04	(0.01)	-0.01	(0.01)	-0.03	(0.01)	0.09	(0.01)
Romania	0.18	(0.02)	0.21	(0.02)	-0.11	(0.04)	0.15	(0.03)	0.17	(0.04)	-0.15	(0.03)	0.04	(0.05)
Russian Federation	0.11	(0.02)	0.10	(0.02)	0.19	(0.03)	0.15	(0.03)	0.11	(0.05)	-0.04	(0.02)	0.14	(0.04)
Serbia	0.12	(0.02)	0.02	(0.02)	0.14	(0.04)	0.03	(0.03)	0.12	(0.04)	-0.10	(0.03)	0.15	(0.04)
Shanghai-China	0.21	(0.02)	0.26	(0.02)	-0.16	(0.05)	0.15	(0.05)	0.10	(0.04)	-0.21	(0.05)	0.12	(0.05)
Singapore	0.18	(0.02)	0.16	(0.02)	0.05	(0.05)	0.18	(0.02)	0.23	(0.01)	-0.09	(0.04)	0.19	(0.02)
Chinese Taipei	0.28	(0.02)	0.26	(0.02)	-0.01	(0.03)	0.01	(0.03)	0.18	(0.04)	-0.10	(0.03)	0.15	(0.04)
Thailand	0.20	(0.02)	0.16	(0.02)	0.07	(0.04)	0.02	(0.03)	0.08	(0.04)	-0.19	(0.03)	0.19	(0.04)
Tunisia	0.13	(0.02)	0.06	(0.02)	0.03	(0.02)	0.02	(0.03)	-0.05	(0.05)	-0.11	(0.05)	0.14	(0.06)
United Arab Emirates	0.03	(0.02)	0.09	(0.02)	-0.03	(0.03)	-0.03	(0.02)	0.06	(0.02)	-0.11	(0.02)	0.14	(0.03)
Uruguay	0.11	(0.02)	0.07	(0.02)	-0.05	(0.04)	0.15	(0.06)	0.35	(0.04)	-0.23	(0.04)	0.16	(0.07)
Viet Nam	0.23	(0.02)	0.16	(0.03)	0.08	(0.06)	0.07	(0.06)	0.13	(0.05)	-0.17	(0.05)	0.16	(0.05)

Note: Values that are statistically significant are indicated in bold (see Annex A3).
* See notes at the beginning of this Annex.
StatLink ⟶ http://dx.doi.org/10.1787/888932964946

[Part 1/1]
Correlation between school socio-economic profile and selected student and school characteristics
Table II.4.6   *Results based on students' self-reports*

		Study behaviour				Student and teacher profile				School climate					
		Attendance in after-school lessons		Homework or other study set by your teachers		Student-teacher ratio		Proportion of teachers with a univeristy degree		Student-related factors affecting school climate		Behavioural outcomes: Dropout		Parental pressure to achieve	
		Corr.	S.E.	Corr.	S.E.	Corr.	S.E.	Corr.	S.E.	Corr.	S.E.	Corr.	S.E.	Corr.	S.E.
OECD	Australia	0.14	(0.01)	0.25	(0.01)	-0.05	(0.04)	0.02	(0.04)	0.52	(0.02)	-0.31	(0.02)	0.36	(0.04)
	Austria	0.12	(0.03)	0.23	(0.03)	-0.11	(0.05)	0.60	(0.05)	0.23	(0.07)	-0.22	(0.06)	0.25	(0.10)
	Belgium	0.17	(0.02)	0.31	(0.02)	0.59	(0.05)	0.61	(0.04)	0.56	(0.04)	-0.36	(0.05)	0.30	(0.05)
	Canada	0.10	(0.02)	0.18	(0.02)	0.20	(0.04)	0.02	(0.03)	0.36	(0.05)	-0.31	(0.06)	0.41	(0.03)
	Chile	0.08	(0.02)	0.16	(0.02)	-0.03	(0.05)	0.19	(0.09)	0.45	(0.05)	-0.34	(0.04)	0.44	(0.05)
	Czech Republic	0.02	(0.02)	0.14	(0.02)	0.05	(0.06)	0.28	(0.06)	0.31	(0.06)	-0.18	(0.06)	0.28	(0.08)
	Denmark	0.00	(0.02)	0.05	(0.03)	0.20	(0.08)	0.09	(0.05)	0.35	(0.05)	-0.30	(0.07)	0.35	(0.07)
	Estonia	0.02	(0.02)	0.04	(0.02)	0.45	(0.04)	c	c	0.09	(0.05)	-0.12	(0.05)	0.13	(0.05)
	Finland	0.05	(0.02)	0.05	(0.02)	0.36	(0.05)	0.01	(0.07)	0.01	(0.06)	0.02	(0.06)	0.14	(0.05)
	France	0.13	(0.03)	0.29	(0.03)	w	w	w	w	w	w	w	w	w	w
	Germany	0.08	(0.03)	0.14	(0.03)	0.19	(0.05)	m	m	0.29	(0.06)	-0.18	(0.04)	0.13	(0.07)
	Greece	0.21	(0.02)	0.20	(0.02)	0.18	(0.07)	0.19	(0.09)	0.14	(0.05)	-0.37	(0.04)	0.35	(0.06)
	Hungary	0.20	(0.03)	0.32	(0.03)	-0.04	(0.07)	0.16	(0.05)	0.47	(0.06)	-0.43	(0.04)	0.49	(0.06)
	Iceland	0.05	(0.02)	0.11	(0.02)	0.42	(0.01)	0.18	(0.01)	-0.01	(0.01)	-0.07	(0.00)	0.24	(0.01)
	Ireland	0.10	(0.03)	0.15	(0.03)	0.32	(0.09)	-0.08	(0.14)	0.42	(0.06)	-0.33	(0.07)	0.56	(0.04)
	Israel	-0.06	(0.02)	0.07	(0.02)	-0.03	(0.09)	0.21	(0.07)	0.14	(0.07)	-0.20	(0.08)	0.37	(0.05)
	Italy	0.24	(0.02)	0.38	(0.02)	0.40	(0.04)	0.30	(0.03)	0.41	(0.04)	-0.35	(0.03)	0.30	(0.04)
	Japan	0.31	(0.02)	0.33	(0.02)	0.30	(0.05)	0.18	(0.07)	0.34	(0.08)	-0.39	(0.06)	0.44	(0.06)
	Korea	0.36	(0.03)	0.28	(0.03)	0.27	(0.11)	0.02	(0.05)	0.25	(0.07)	-0.24	(0.11)	0.42	(0.06)
	Luxembourg	0.06	(0.02)	0.16	(0.02)	0.17	(0.00)	0.46	(0.00)	0.47	(0.00)	-0.38	(0.00)	-0.06	(0.00)
	Mexico	0.09	(0.01)	0.16	(0.01)	0.22	(0.02)	0.01	(0.04)	0.12	(0.03)	-0.02	(0.03)	0.10	(0.04)
	Netherlands	0.12	(0.03)	0.22	(0.02)	0.43	(0.09)	0.51	(0.11)	0.21	(0.07)	-0.34	(0.06)	0.39	(0.07)
	New Zealand	0.14	(0.04)	0.24	(0.03)	0.15	(0.08)	0.21	(0.07)	0.53	(0.05)	-0.80	(0.02)	0.44	(0.06)
	Norway	0.09	(0.02)	0.12	(0.02)	0.27	(0.07)	c	c	0.28	(0.06)	c	c	0.47	(0.06)
	Poland	0.01	(0.02)	0.03	(0.02)	0.07	(0.07)	-0.07	(0.08)	0.04	(0.09)	-0.05	(0.05)	0.07	(0.09)
	Portugal	0.12	(0.03)	0.17	(0.03)	0.41	(0.07)	-0.15	(0.11)	0.17	(0.09)	0.08	(0.08)	0.38	(0.07)
	Slovak Republic	-0.01	(0.03)	0.16	(0.04)	0.04	(0.08)	-0.15	(0.05)	0.25	(0.05)	-0.28	(0.04)	0.30	(0.08)
	Slovenia	0.04	(0.03)	0.16	(0.03)	0.25	(0.01)	0.43	(0.01)	0.27	(0.01)	-0.23	(0.01)	0.27	(0.02)
	Spain	0.04	(0.01)	0.08	(0.01)	0.17	(0.11)	-0.04	(0.05)	0.45	(0.04)	-0.31	(0.05)	0.27	(0.05)
	Sweden	0.11	(0.03)	0.17	(0.03)	0.26	(0.06)	0.12	(0.06)	0.43	(0.06)	-0.49	(0.06)	0.40	(0.06)
	Switzerland	0.06	(0.02)	0.12	(0.03)	-0.07	(0.06)	0.18	(0.08)	0.08	(0.07)	c	c	-0.10	(0.07)
	Turkey	0.05	(0.03)	0.04	(0.02)	-0.37	(0.06)	0.04	(0.08)	0.31	(0.07)	-0.19	(0.05)	0.21	(0.07)
	United Kingdom	0.16	(0.03)	0.31	(0.03)	-0.18	(0.10)	0.00	(0.06)	0.35	(0.06)	-0.29	(0.05)	0.48	(0.05)
	United States	0.14	(0.02)	0.25	(0.03)	0.02	(0.05)	-0.02	(0.13)	0.42	(0.06)	-0.31	(0.09)	0.47	(0.07)
	OECD average	**0.10**	**(0.00)**	**0.18**	**(0.00)**	**0.16**	**(0.01)**	**0.14**	**(0.01)**	**0.30**	**(0.01)**	**-0.28**	**(0.01)**	**0.31**	**(0.01)**
Partners	Albania	m	m	m	m	m	m	m	m	m	m	m	m	m	m
	Argentina	0.04	(0.02)	0.10	(0.03)	0.05	(0.05)	0.17	(0.08)	0.33	(0.08)	-0.24	(0.07)	0.15	(0.08)
	Brazil	0.05	(0.02)	0.13	(0.02)	-0.21	(0.05)	-0.01	(0.06)	0.38	(0.04)	-0.21	(0.05)	0.31	(0.04)
	Bulgaria	0.17	(0.02)	0.33	(0.03)	-0.02	(0.05)	c	c	0.23	(0.06)	-0.39	(0.06)	0.40	(0.05)
	Colombia	0.12	(0.03)	0.18	(0.03)	-0.07	(0.06)	-0.04	(0.10)	0.25	(0.06)	-0.06	(0.06)	0.07	(0.08)
	Costa Rica	0.13	(0.04)	0.22	(0.04)	0.18	(0.11)	0.15	(0.15)	0.43	(0.07)	-0.41	(0.05)	0.22	(0.07)
	Croatia	0.10	(0.02)	0.24	(0.03)	0.22	(0.09)	0.42	(0.04)	0.20	(0.08)	-0.22	(0.07)	0.19	(0.08)
	Cyprus*	0.06	(0.02)	0.28	(0.02)	0.53	(0.00)	0.07	(0.00)	0.15	(0.00)	-0.29	(0.00)	0.35	(0.00)
	Hong Kong-China	0.20	(0.02)	0.14	(0.03)	0.04	(0.09)	0.04	(0.05)	0.21	(0.09)	0.02	(0.10)	-0.07	(0.09)
	Indonesia	0.14	(0.02)	0.16	(0.02)	-0.11	(0.08)	0.20	(0.06)	0.17	(0.08)	-0.19	(0.06)	-0.06	(0.08)
	Jordan	-0.03	(0.02)	0.04	(0.03)	-0.07	(0.07)	-0.01	(0.06)	0.06	(0.08)	-0.18	(0.07)	0.19	(0.08)
	Kazakhstan	0.08	(0.03)	0.13	(0.03)	0.22	(0.08)	0.21	(0.08)	-0.04	(0.07)	-0.04	(0.03)	0.20	(0.07)
	Latvia	0.11	(0.03)	0.17	(0.03)	0.37	(0.07)	0.16	(0.07)	0.01	(0.08)	-0.14	(0.07)	0.13	(0.07)
	Liechtenstein	0.01	(0.06)	0.12	(0.06)	0.50	(0.01)	0.46	(0.02)	0.45	(0.02)	c	c	-0.56	(0.01)
	Lithuania	0.04	(0.02)	0.16	(0.02)	0.05	(0.07)	0.05	(0.05)	0.24	(0.06)	-0.17	(0.06)	0.15	(0.07)
	Macao-China	0.15	(0.02)	0.16	(0.02)	-0.05	(0.00)	-0.09	(0.00)	0.26	(0.00)	-0.23	(0.00)	0.16	(0.00)
	Malaysia	0.11	(0.02)	0.18	(0.02)	0.08	(0.06)	-0.10	(0.07)	0.41	(0.06)	-0.23	(0.05)	0.30	(0.09)
	Montenegro	0.05	(0.02)	0.16	(0.03)	0.40	(0.01)	0.27	(0.01)	0.20	(0.01)	-0.25	(0.00)	-0.07	(0.00)
	Peru	0.08	(0.02)	0.13	(0.02)	0.20	(0.05)	-0.05	(0.11)	0.29	(0.06)	-0.14	(0.06)	0.18	(0.08)
	Qatar	-0.03	(0.01)	0.13	(0.01)	0.07	(0.00)	-0.09	(0.00)	-0.02	(0.00)	-0.06	(0.00)	0.19	(0.00)
	Romania	0.16	(0.03)	0.25	(0.03)	-0.19	(0.06)	0.24	(0.04)	0.27	(0.06)	-0.24	(0.05)	0.06	(0.07)
	Russian Federation	0.06	(0.03)	0.09	(0.03)	0.35	(0.07)	0.27	(0.07)	0.21	(0.09)	-0.07	(0.04)	0.26	(0.07)
	Serbia	0.03	(0.02)	0.10	(0.02)	0.29	(0.08)	0.07	(0.06)	0.24	(0.08)	-0.21	(0.05)	0.31	(0.08)
	Shanghai-China	0.24	(0.02)	0.35	(0.02)	-0.26	(0.08)	0.26	(0.08)	0.17	(0.07)	-0.35	(0.08)	0.19	(0.07)
	Singapore	0.13	(0.02)	0.18	(0.02)	0.11	(0.10)	0.36	(0.02)	0.47	(0.01)	-0.17	(0.07)	0.38	(0.02)
	Chinese Taipei	0.29	(0.02)	0.36	(0.03)	-0.01	(0.07)	0.02	(0.07)	0.36	(0.07)	-0.20	(0.06)	0.29	(0.07)
	Thailand	0.22	(0.02)	0.24	(0.02)	0.11	(0.07)	0.03	(0.04)	0.12	(0.06)	-0.28	(0.04)	0.30	(0.07)
	Tunisia	0.03	(0.03)	0.07	(0.03)	0.05	(0.04)	0.03	(0.06)	-0.08	(0.08)	-0.19	(0.08)	0.23	(0.10)
	United Arab Emirates	-0.03	(0.02)	0.11	(0.02)	-0.05	(0.05)	-0.05	(0.04)	0.11	(0.04)	-0.22	(0.04)	0.26	(0.05)
	Uruguay	0.09	(0.02)	0.10	(0.02)	-0.08	(0.05)	0.23	(0.09)	0.54	(0.05)	-0.35	(0.05)	0.25	(0.10)
	Viet Nam	0.21	(0.03)	0.20	(0.03)	0.12	(0.08)	0.10	(0.10)	0.20	(0.08)	-0.26	(0.08)	0.24	(0.08)

Note: Values that are statistically significant are indicated in bold (see Annex A3).
* See notes at the beginning of this Annex.
StatLink ᘯᓂᑊ http://dx.doi.org/10.1787/888932964946

[Part 1/1]
Correlation of the variation of students' socio-economic status within a school and selected student and school characteristics

Table II.4.7 *Results based on students' self-reports*

| | Study behaviour | | | | Student and teacher profile | | | | School climate | | | | | |
| | Attendance in after-school lessons | | Homework or other study set by your teachers | | Student-teacher ratio | | Proportion of teachers with a univeristy degree | | Student-related factors affecting school climate | | Behavioural outcomes: Dropout | | Parental pressure to achieve | |
	Corr.	S.E.	Corr.	S.E.	Corr.	S.E.	Corr.	S.E.	Corr.	S.E.	Corr.	S.E.	Corr.	S.E.
Australia	0.00	(0.02)	-0.03	(0.02)	-0.01	(0.04)	-0.02	(0.03)	**-0.12**	(0.04)	0.05	(0.03)	-0.0	(0.05)
Austria	-0.05	(0.03)	**-0.05**	(0.03)	**-0.10**	(0.05)	-0.02	(0.06)	0.03	(0.09)	0.00	(0.04)	0.0	(0.07)
Belgium	-0.03	(0.02)	**-0.10**	(0.02)	-0.06	(0.06)	-0.14	(0.09)	-0.09	(0.06)	0.10	(0.09)	-0.1	(0.05)
Canada	**0.10**	(0.02)	**0.08**	(0.02)	**-0.19**	(0.05)	0.03	(0.03)	**-0.17**	(0.04)	0.03	(0.06)	-0.0	(0.06)
Chile	-0.01	(0.02)	**-0.05**	(0.01)	0.13	(0.08)	0.04	(0.02)	**-0.13**	(0.06)	0.03	(0.06)	-0.0	(0.04)
Czech Republic	0.01	(0.03)	-0.04	(0.02)	**0.12**	(0.06)	0.02	(0.05)	-0.06	(0.05)	**-0.17**	(0.04)	-0.1	(0.07)
Denmark	-0.03	(0.02)	**-0.03**	(0.01)	0.13	(0.11)	**-0.18**	(0.08)	0.11	(0.14)	0.01	(0.05)	-0.1	(0.05)
Estonia	-0.03	(0.02)	-0.01	(0.04)	**-0.42**	(0.06)	c	c	0.13	(0.07)	**-0.09**	(0.02)	-0.1	(0.05)
Finland	0.00	(0.02)	0.02	(0.02)	**-0.30**	(0.11)	0.16	(0.06)	-0.05	(0.05)	-0.09	(0.05)	0.1	(0.11)
France	-0.04	(0.03)	**-0.11**	(0.03)	w	w	w	w	w	w	w	w		w
Germany	-0.05	(0.03)	**-0.07**	(0.03)	-0.08	(0.07)	m	m	-0.11	(0.09)	**0.43**	(0.19)	-0.0	(0.07)
Greece	-0.03	(0.03)	**-0.06**	(0.03)	0.00	(0.07)	-0.01	(0.12)	0.01	(0.08)	0.00	(0.09)	-0.1	(0.07)
Hungary	-0.01	(0.02)	**-0.07**	(0.02)	**-0.17**	(0.03)	**0.07**	(0.03)	-0.01	(0.07)	**-0.14**	(0.04)	-0.0	(0.06)
Iceland	-0.01	(0.02)	**-0.05**	(0.02)	**-0.11**	(0.01)	-0.01	(0.01)	**-0.05**	(0.01)	**0.02**	(0.01)	-0.7	(0.00)
Ireland	0.01	(0.03)	0.00	(0.03)	-0.12	(0.09)	-0.09	(0.08)	-0.15	(0.08)	0.02	(0.10)	-0.3	(0.07)
Israel	0.02	(0.02)	**-0.09**	(0.03)	-0.10	(0.09)	0.01	(0.09)	**-0.12**	(0.06)	0.10	(0.07)	-0.3	(0.06)
Italy	0.01	(0.03)	0.00	(0.04)	-0.02	(0.03)	-0.09	(0.06)	0.00	(0.07)	0.02	(0.08)	0.0	(0.04)
Japan	-0.01	(0.04)	-0.02	(0.04)	-0.01	(0.09)	-0.02	(0.06)	-0.07	(0.07)	0.12	(0.10)	-0.5	(0.08)
Korea	**-0.10**	(0.04)	-0.08	(0.04)	-0.17	(0.09)	0.03	(0.02)	**-0.17**	(0.07)	0.01	(0.08)	-0.2	(0.07)
Luxembourg	**-0.05**	(0.02)	**-0.16**	(0.02)	**-0.11**	(0.00)	**-0.16**	(0.00)	**-0.40**	(0.00)	**0.14**	(0.00)	-0.2	(0.00)
Mexico	0.01	(0.01)	0.01	(0.01)	-0.01	(0.03)	0.01	(0.04)	-0.07	(0.06)	-0.03	(0.03)	0.3	(0.04)
Netherlands	0.03	(0.03)	-0.01	(0.04)	0.06	(0.10)	-0.06	(0.08)	**-0.10**	(0.04)	0.26	(0.15)	0.3	(0.05)
New Zealand	-0.01	(0.04)	**-0.08**	(0.02)	0.08	(0.07)	-0.05	(0.06)	**-0.32**	(0.05)	**0.36**	(0.05)	-0.3	(0.07)
Norway	-0.02	(0.02)	-0.04	(0.02)	**-0.15**	(0.07)	c	c	**-0.15**	(0.07)	c	c	-0.9	(0.07)
Poland	0.01	(0.02)	0.00	(0.02)	**0.17**	(0.08)	0.06	(0.06)	-0.09	(0.07)	**-0.12**	(0.06)	-0.4	(0.08)
Portugal	0.01	(0.03)	0.04	(0.04)	-0.09	(0.09)	-0.02	(0.14)	**-0.16**	(0.08)	**0.16**	(0.06)	-0.3	(0.13)
Slovak Republic	0.02	(0.03)	-0.03	(0.03)	-0.08	(0.07)	**-0.25**	(0.04)	**0.12**	(0.05)	**-0.14**	(0.04)	-0.5	(0.06)
Slovenia	0.02	(0.02)	**0.04**	(0.02)	**0.15**	(0.05)	-0.01	(0.03)	**0.07**	(0.02)	**-0.15**	(0.02)	0.5	(0.05)
Spain	0.02	(0.02)	**0.04**	(0.02)	-0.03	(0.02)	**0.16**	(0.02)	**-0.10**	(0.04)	-0.03	(0.08)	-0.0	(0.05)
Sweden	-0.01	(0.02)	-0.04	(0.03)	**-0.24**	(0.08)	-0.04	(0.07)	**-0.35**	(0.06)	**0.30**	(0.10)	-0.5	(0.06)
Switzerland	-0.03	(0.02)	-0.02	(0.02)	-0.04	(0.10)	-0.13	(0.08)	**-0.10**	(0.04)	c	c	0.3	(0.09)
Turkey	**0.06**	(0.02)	**0.06**	(0.02)	-0.14	(0.08)	**-0.13**	(0.06)	**0.32**	(0.07)	**-0.25**	(0.06)	0.9	(0.07)
United Kingdom	0.00	(0.04)	-0.05	(0.04)	-0.07	(0.09)	0.05	(0.03)	-0.02	(0.04)	-0.06	(0.13)	0.3	(0.07)
United States	0.02	(0.03)	-0.01	(0.05)	0.14	(0.13)	0.08	(0.04)	0.05	(0.14)	0.01	(0.12)	-0.8	(0.13)
OECD average	0.00	(0.00)	**-0.03**	(0.00)	**-0.06**	(0.01)	-0.02	(0.01)	**-0.08**	(0.01)	**0.04**	(0.01)	-0.6	(0.01)
Albania	m	m	m	m	m	m	m	m	m	m	m	m	m	m
Argentina	0.07	(0.06)	0.07	(0.05)	-0.11	(0.07)	-0.05	(0.09)	0.16	(0.14)	0.05	(0.07)	0.6	(0.10)
Brazil	-0.01	(0.02)	-0.02	(0.02)	-0.02	(0.06)	-0.06	(0.06)	-0.08	(0.06)	0.08	(0.07)	-0.8	(0.06)
Bulgaria	**-0.07**	(0.02)	**-0.12**	(0.02)	0.19	(0.20)	c	c	**-0.17**	(0.06)	**0.21**	(0.07)	-0.4	(0.05)
Colombia	-0.01	(0.03)	0.00	(0.04)	-0.03	(0.05)	0.05	(0.09)	-0.06	(0.04)	**0.36**	(0.17)	0.3	(0.11)
Costa Rica	0.00	(0.05)	-0.06	(0.04)	-0.09	(0.06)	0.04	(0.08)	**-0.16**	(0.06)	0.01	(0.10)	-0.4	(0.10)
Croatia	0.03	(0.02)	0.08	(0.04)	-0.01	(0.07)	**0.17**	(0.07)	0.06	(0.09)	**-0.14**	(0.06)	0.3	(0.08)
Cyprus*	**0.05**	(0.02)	**-0.12**	(0.02)	**0.06**	(0.00)	**-0.05**	(0.00)	**-0.33**	(0.00)	**-0.10**	(0.00)	-0.20	(0.00)
Hong Kong-China	0.01	(0.03)	0.02	(0.03)	**0.22**	(0.08)	-0.03	(0.08)	0.01	(0.08)	-0.06	(0.08)	-0.7	(0.08)
Indonesia	0.02	(0.04)	-0.02	(0.03)	0.03	(0.07)	0.05	(0.12)	-0.08	(0.06)	0.05	(0.09)	-0.9	(0.08)
Jordan	0.02	(0.02)	**-0.04**	(0.02)	0.10	(0.06)	-0.03	(0.07)	-0.06	(0.09)	0.08	(0.05)	-0.0	(0.08)
Kazakhstan	**-0.05**	(0.02)	-0.06	(0.03)	**-0.24**	(0.07)	**-0.14**	(0.06)	-0.01	(0.08)	-0.03	(0.03)	-0.8	(0.06)
Latvia	**-0.09**	(0.02)	-0.07	(0.04)	**-0.29**	(0.08)	**-0.19**	(0.07)	**0.11**	(0.06)	0.07	(0.10)	-0.1	(0.06)
Liechtenstein	-0.03	(0.06)	-0.07	(0.07)	**-0.14**	(0.01)	**-0.48**	(0.03)	**-0.12**	(0.04)	c	c	0.9	(0.02)
Lithuania	0.02	(0.02)	-0.03	(0.02)	0.03	(0.07)	-0.04	(0.04)	**-0.11**	(0.05)	-0.03	(0.07)	-0.7	(0.05)
Macao-China	**-0.04**	(0.02)	**-0.07**	(0.02)	**-0.14**	(0.00)	**-0.12**	(0.00)	**-0.15**	(0.00)	**0.10**	(0.00)	-0.6	(0.00)
Malaysia	-0.03	(0.02)	**-0.07**	(0.02)	0.07	(0.08)	0.07	(0.05)	**-0.16**	(0.08)	**0.17**	(0.08)	-0.8	(0.08)
Montenegro	0.01	(0.02)	0.00	(0.02)	**0.27**	(0.00)	**-0.09**	(0.01)	**-0.24**	(0.00)	**0.07**	(0.00)	0.22	(0.00)
Peru	0.01	(0.03)	-0.03	(0.03)	0.05	(0.11)	-0.21	(0.15)	**-0.16**	(0.07)	0.08	(0.07)	-0.3	(0.04)
Qatar	**-0.06**	(0.01)	**-0.23**	(0.01)	**-0.12**	(0.00)	**0.20**	(0.00)	**-0.10**	(0.00)	**0.19**	(0.00)	-0.30	(0.00)
Romania	0.04	(0.03)	-0.03	(0.03)	-0.01	(0.04)	**-0.16**	(0.07)	0.00	(0.05)	-0.07	(0.06)	-0.1	(0.05)
Russian Federation	0.00	(0.04)	0.01	(0.04)	**-0.40**	(0.05)	**-0.14**	(0.05)	-0.04	(0.07)	0.07	(0.06)	-0.8	(0.05)
Serbia	0.06	(0.04)	**0.08**	(0.04)	0.07	(0.08)	0.02	(0.06)	0.08	(0.08)	**-0.14**	(0.05)	0.20	(0.08)
Shanghai-China	-0.03	(0.04)	-0.04	(0.06)	-0.05	(0.07)	-0.01	(0.04)	0.12	(0.08)	**-0.10**	(0.04)	-0.22	(0.11)
Singapore	**-0.05**	(0.01)	**-0.08**	(0.02)	-0.08	(0.06)	**-0.08**	(0.01)	**-0.12**	(0.01)	**0.10**	(0.04)	-0.04	(0.01)
Chinese Taipei	0.00	(0.03)	-0.03	(0.03)	**-0.41**	(0.05)	0.01	(0.06)	-0.06	(0.08)	0.01	(0.05)	0.05	(0.07)
Thailand	0.04	(0.02)	0.04	(0.03)	0.10	(0.08)	-0.07	(0.08)	-0.07	(0.07)	0.04	(0.06)	-0.6	(0.09)
Tunisia	-0.02	(0.02)	**-0.06**	(0.02)	-0.01	(0.02)	0.09	(0.09)	0.02	(0.09)	0.15	(0.10)	-0.23	(0.08)
United Arab Emirates	0.00	(0.03)	**-0.07**	(0.02)	0.04	(0.05)	**0.08**	(0.04)	-0.10	(0.08)	-0.01	(0.05)	-0.20	(0.06)
Uruguay	0.05	(0.03)	0.06	(0.03)	-0.02	(0.06)	-0.04	(0.07)	-0.05	(0.04)	-0.05	(0.06)	-0.9	(0.07)
Viet Nam	0.03	(0.03)	0.02	(0.03)	-0.14	(0.09)	-0.05	(0.10)	0.07	(0.08)	-0.06	(0.09)	0.15	(0.07)

Note: Values that are statistically significant are indicated in bold (see Annex A3).
* See notes at the beginning of this Annex.
StatLink ᵍⁱˢᵖ http://dx.doi.org/10.1787/888932964946

[Part 1/2]

Table II.4.8 **Inequity in access to educational resources: Student-teacher ratio**

Results based on students' self-reports

		Student-teacher ratio																			
		Percentage of the variation explained by student ESCS[1]		Percentage of the variation explained by student and school mean ESCS		Percentage of the variation explained by student and school mean and standard deviation of ESCS		Mean among students in socio-economically disadvantaged schools,[2] relative to the country mean ESCS		Mean among students in socio-economically average schools,[2] relative to the country mean ESCS		Mean among students in socio-economically advantaged schools,[2] relative to the country mean ESCS		Difference between students in average and disadvantaged schools		Difference between students in advantaged and average schools		Difference between students in disadvantaged and advantaged schools		Mean among non-immigrant students	
		%	S.E.	%	S.E.	%	S.E.	Mean	S.E.	Mean	S.E.	Mean	S.E.	Dif.	S.E.	Dif.	S.E.	Dif.	S.E.	Mean	S.E.
OECD	Australia	0.1	(0.1)	0.3	(0.4)	0.4	(0.5)	12.7	(0.2)	13.7	(0.1)	12.4	(0.2)	**1.1**	(0.2)	-1.3	(0.2)	0.3	(0.2)	13.2	(0.1)
	Austria	0.4	(0.4)	1.2	(1.1)	2.5	(1.8)	12.8	(1.3)	10.4	(0.5)	10.0	(0.4)	-2.4	(1.5)	-0.4	(0.6)	**2.7**	(1.4)	11.1	(0.5)
	Belgium	10.6	(1.9)	34.7	(5.5)	36.6	(5.5)	6.9	(0.2)	9.1	(0.3)	11.5	(0.2)	**2.2**	(0.4)	2.4	(0.4)	**-4.6**	(0.3)	9.4	(0.1)
	Canada	0.7	(0.3)	3.6	(1.6)	5.8	(2.3)	14.7	(0.4)	15.3	(0.3)	16.9	(0.3)	0.6	(0.5)	1.6	(0.4)	**-2.2**	(0.5)	15.6	(0.2)
	Chile	0.1	(0.3)	0.1	(0.5)	1.7	(2.1)	21.4	(0.7)	23.2	(1.5)	22.4	(0.8)	1.8	(1.6)	-0.7	(1.7)	-1.0	(1.1)	22.1	(0.5)
	Czech Republic	0.1	(0.2)	0.3	(0.7)	2.1	(1.8)	12.6	(0.7)	13.7	(0.4)	12.5	(0.5)	1.0	(0.8)	-1.2	(0.6)	0.1	(0.8)	13.2	(0.3)
	Denmark	0.8	(0.7)	3.7	(3.1)	6.7	(3.9)	11.1	(0.7)	12.0	(0.3)	13.4	(0.5)	0.9	(0.7)	1.4	(0.6)	**-2.2**	(0.8)	12.1	(0.2)
	Estonia	5.0	(1.0)	20.1	(3.6)	32.0	(4.5)	9.7	(0.4)	11.2	(0.2)	13.2	(0.2)	**1.5**	(0.5)	2.0	(0.3)	**-3.5**	(0.4)	11.4	(0.1)
	Finland	1.7	(0.6)	12.6	(3.6)	17.4	(6.0)	9.2	(0.3)	10.8	(0.2)	11.4	(0.2)	**1.6**	(0.3)	0.7	(0.3)	**-2.3**	(0.4)	10.6	(0.1)
	France	0.0	(0.1)	w	w	w	w	w	w	w	w	w	w	w	w	w	w	w	w	11.7	(0.2)
	Germany	1.2	(0.6)	3.9	(1.9)	4.1	(2.0)	13.5	(0.5)	15.7	(0.3)	16.0	(0.9)	**2.1**	(0.6)	0.3	(1.0)	**-2.5**	(1.0)	15.1	(0.4)
	Greece	1.0	(0.8)	3.2	(2.5)	3.5	(2.7)	7.7	(0.3)	9.8	(0.5)	9.3	(0.4)	**2.2**	(0.6)	-0.6	(0.6)	**-1.6**	(0.5)	9.2	(0.3)
	Hungary	0.1	(0.3)	0.2	(0.8)	3.7	(2.0)	13.4	(0.7)	11.5	(0.5)	12.6	(0.3)	**-1.9**	(0.9)	1.1	(0.6)	0.9	(0.7)	12.5	(0.3)
	Iceland	3.1	(0.6)	17.7	(0.6)	18.5	(0.6)	9.8	(0.0)	10.3	(0.0)	11.7	(0.0)	**0.4**	(0.0)	1.4	(0.0)	**-1.8**	(0.0)	10.5	(0.0)
	Ireland	2.3	(1.3)	10.2	(5.6)	10.4	(5.7)	12.6	(0.5)	14.5	(0.2)	15.0	(0.4)	**1.9**	(0.6)	0.5	(0.4)	**-2.5**	(0.7)	14.3	(0.2)
	Israel	0.0	(0.2)	0.1	(0.8)	1.6	(2.3)	11.1	(0.5)	10.6	(0.4)	10.8	(0.4)	-0.6	(0.6)	0.2	(0.6)	0.3	(0.7)	11.0	(0.2)
	Italy	4.7	(0.9)	16.5	(3.2)	16.6	(3.2)	8.7	(0.2)	9.9	(0.2)	12.3	(0.2)	**1.2**	(0.3)	2.3	(0.3)	**-3.5**	(0.3)	10.4	(0.1)
	Japan	2.2	(0.8)	8.9	(3.2)	8.9	(3.4)	10.0	(0.4)	12.0	(0.5)	13.0	(0.5)	**2.0**	(0.7)	1.1	(0.8)	**-3.1**	(0.6)	11.7	(0.2)
	Korea	1.8	(1.7)	7.3	(6.7)	7.9	(7.2)	14.0	(0.5)	17.0	(0.4)	16.6	(0.7)	**3.0**	(0.7)	-0.4	(0.9)	**-2.6**	(1.0)	16.1	(0.2)
	Luxembourg	0.7	(0.2)	2.6	(0.1)	2.6	(0.1)	9.0	(0.0)	8.6	(0.0)	9.3	(0.0)	**-0.4**	(0.0)	0.7	(0.0)	**-0.3**	(0.0)	9.0	(0.0)
	Mexico	0.0	(0.0)	0.0	(0.1)	0.1	(0.1)	27.3	(0.7)	34.0	(1.9)	30.5	(1.0)	**6.7**	(1.9)	-3.5	(2.5)	**-3.2**	(1.3)	30.7	(0.8)
	Netherlands	4.0	(1.8)	17.8	(7.7)	18.9	(8.3)	14.1	(0.4)	17.6	(0.5)	18.1	(0.8)	**3.4**	(0.5)	0.5	(0.9)	**-4.0**	(0.9)	16.8	(0.4)
	New Zealand	0.5	(0.7)	1.9	(2.5)	3.8	(3.3)	14.1	(0.6)	15.4	(0.3)	15.5	(0.5)	1.3	(0.7)	0.1	(0.5)	-1.4	(0.7)	15.0	(0.2)
	Norway	1.0	(0.5)	7.3	(3.6)	8.3	(3.8)	10.7	(0.4)	10.1	(0.2)	11.6	(0.3)	-0.5	(0.4)	1.5	(0.4)	**-0.9**	(0.5)	10.4	(0.1)
	Poland	0.1	(0.3)	0.4	(1.1)	2.8	(3.1)	8.7	(0.3)	9.8	(0.3)	9.7	(0.4)	**1.1**	(0.4)	-0.1	(0.5)	**-1.0**	(0.5)	9.4	(0.2)
	Portugal	5.5	(2.3)	16.7	(6.1)	17.5	(6.5)	7.8	(0.4)	9.0	(0.3)	10.4	(0.4)	**1.1**	(0.5)	1.5	(0.5)	**-2.6**	(0.5)	8.9	(0.2)
	Slovak Republic	0.0	(0.2)	0.0	(0.6)	1.1	(1.3)	12.8	(0.6)	13.7	(0.4)	13.1	(0.4)	1.0	(0.7)	-0.7	(0.5)	-0.3	(0.7)	13.3	(0.3)
	Slovenia	1.9	(0.4)	6.1	(0.4)	7.7	(1.3)	9.5	(0.1)	10.2	(0.1)	12.0	(0.0)	**0.8**	(0.1)	1.7	(0.1)	**-2.5**	(0.1)	10.5	(0.0)
	Spain	0.8	(1.1)	2.7	(4.2)	2.8	(4.2)	11.6	(1.3)	11.8	(0.2)	14.7	(0.4)	0.2	(1.3)	2.8	(0.5)	**-3.0**	(1.4)	12.7	(0.4)
	Sweden	1.2	(0.5)	6.8	(3.2)	8.9	(4.0)	11.4	(0.5)	12.2	(0.3)	14.0	(0.5)	0.8	(0.6)	1.8	(0.6)	**-2.6**	(0.7)	12.5	(0.2)
	Switzerland	0.1	(0.2)	0.5	(0.9)	0.7	(1.2)	12.1	(0.6)	12.3	(0.5)	11.6	(0.5)	0.2	(0.9)	-0.7	(0.9)	0.5	(0.9)	12.2	(0.3)
	Turkey	4.3	(1.5)	13.5	(4.6)	13.6	(4.6)	20.7	(1.4)	16.9	(0.8)	14.2	(1.0)	**-3.8**	(1.8)	-2.8	(1.4)	**6.5**	(1.8)	17.4	(0.5)
	United Kingdom	0.9	(0.9)	3.6	(3.6)	4.5	(2.9)	14.5	(0.4)	15.4	(0.1)	13.8	(0.4)	**0.9**	(0.5)	-1.6	(0.4)	0.7	(0.6)	14.9	(0.2)
	United States	0.0	(0.1)	0.0	(0.3)	2.3	(4.6)	16.8	(1.1)	17.1	(1.1)	18.5	(2.4)	0.3	(1.5)	1.4	(2.6)	-1.7	(1.9)	17.1	(1.0)
	OECD average	1.7	(0.2)	6.6	(0.6)	8.2	(0.6)	12.5	(0.1)	13.4	(0.1)	13.8	(0.1)	**0.9**	(0.1)	0.4	(0.2)	**-1.3**	(0.1)	13.3	(0.1)
Partners	Albania	m	m	m	m	m	m	m	m	m	m	m	m	m	m	m	m	m	m	m	m
	Argentina	0.1	(0.3)	0.3	(0.7)	1.5	(2.2)	9.6	(0.7)	10.7	(3.2)	11.3	(1.3)	1.1	(3.3)	0.6	(3.4)	-1.7	(1.5)	10.6	(1.2)
	Brazil	1.7	(0.9)	4.4	(2.2)	4.7	(2.3)	31.3	(1.2)	28.6	(1.1)	22.9	(1.5)	-2.7	(1.5)	-5.7	(1.9)	**8.3**	(2.0)	28.0	(0.7)
	Bulgaria	0.0	(0.1)	0.1	(0.3)	3.8	(9.0)	13.8	(2.8)	16.5	(3.3)	13.7	(0.7)	2.7	(4.2)	-2.8	(3.4)	0.1	(2.9)	14.6	(1.5)
	Colombia	0.2	(0.4)	0.5	(0.9)	0.8	(1.2)	26.0	(1.4)	28.8	(1.0)	25.4	(0.9)	2.7	(1.7)	-3.4	(1.2)	0.6	(1.6)	27.0	(0.6)
	Costa Rica	1.5	(2.1)	3.3	(4.7)	3.4	(4.8)	16.5	(1.0)	19.7	(1.4)	25.3	(9.1)	3.1	(1.8)	5.6	(9.2)	-8.8	(9.1)	20.4	(2.6)
	Croatia	1.3	(1.1)	5.0	(4.1)	5.1	(4.1)	12.2	(0.3)	12.2	(0.3)	14.0	(0.4)	0.0	(0.4)	1.8	(0.5)	**-1.8**	(0.6)	12.6	(0.2)
	Cyprus*	6.5	(0.5)	28.3	(0.3)	29.2	(0.3)	7.0	(0.0)	8.1	(0.0)	8.9	(0.0)	**1.2**	(0.0)	0.8	(0.0)	**-1.9**	(0.0)	7.9	(0.0)
	Hong Kong-China	0.0	(0.3)	0.1	(1.0)	5.6	(3.9)	14.5	(0.2)	16.4	(0.2)	15.1	(0.4)	**1.9**	(0.3)	-1.3	(0.5)	-0.6	(0.5)	15.4	(0.2)
	Indonesia	0.5	(0.8)	1.1	(1.9)	1.3	(2.2)	17.9	(0.9)	15.6	(1.1)	16.7	(1.0)	-2.3	(1.4)	1.1	(1.5)	1.2	(1.4)	16.9	(0.6)
	Jordan	0.1	(0.3)	0.6	(1.2)	1.3	(1.7)	16.7	(0.8)	17.9	(0.6)	15.0	(1.0)	1.2	(1.2)	-3.0	(1.1)	1.8	(1.3)	16.8	(0.4)
	Kazakhstan	1.3	(0.9)	5.0	(3.4)	7.7	(4.2)	9.2	(0.5)	10.0	(0.3)	11.0	(0.4)	0.8	(0.7)	1.0	(0.5)	**-1.8**	(0.7)	10.2	(0.2)
	Latvia	4.5	(1.9)	13.9	(5.6)	18.3	(6.1)	8.1	(0.4)	10.5	(0.3)	10.4	(0.4)	**2.3**	(0.5)	-0.1	(0.5)	**-2.2**	(0.6)	10.0	(0.2)
	Liechtenstein	3.6	(2.3)	24.7	(1.7)	26.8	(1.3)	c	c	7.7	(0.1)	c	c	c	c	c	c	c	c	8.2	(0.1)
	Lithuania	0.1	(0.2)	0.2	(0.9)	0.4	(1.1)	11.2	(1.9)	11.4	(0.8)	11.6	(0.3)	0.2	(2.0)	0.2	(0.8)	-0.4	(1.9)	11.4	(0.6)
	Macao-China	0.1	(0.1)	0.3	(0.0)	2.2	(0.1)	16.4	(0.0)	14.3	(0.0)	15.2	(0.0)	**-2.1**	(0.0)	0.9	(0.0)	**1.2**	(0.0)	15.3	(0.1)
	Malaysia	0.2	(0.3)	0.7	(1.1)	1.6	(2.0)	13.3	(0.3)	13.3	(0.4)	13.7	(0.5)	0.0	(0.6)	0.4	(0.7)	-0.4	(0.6)	13.4	(0.2)
	Montenegro	3.4	(0.5)	16.1	(0.7)	24.1	(0.9)	14.6	(0.0)	15.7	(0.0)	16.8	(0.0)	**1.1**	(0.0)	1.0	(0.0)	**-2.2**	(0.0)	15.7	(0.0)
	Peru	1.8	(0.8)	3.9	(1.8)	4.2	(2.1)	17.0	(0.7)	18.3	(0.9)	20.1	(1.1)	1.3	(1.2)	1.9	(1.4)	**-3.1**	(1.1)	18.5	(0.6)
	Qatar	0.1	(0.1)	0.4	(0.0)	1.5	(0.0)	12.5	(0.0)	11.8	(0.0)	16.0	(0.0)	**-0.7**	(0.0)	4.2	(0.0)	**-3.5**	(0.0)	13.2	(0.1)
	Romania	1.3	(0.8)	3.3	(2.2)	3.9	(2.4)	18.1	(0.9)	15.4	(0.5)	15.0	(0.7)	**-2.7**	(1.0)	-0.4	(0.9)	**3.1**	(1.1)	16.1	(0.4)
	Russian Federation	3.6	(1.3)	12.5	(4.7)	20.2	(5.0)	12.2	(0.8)	14.6	(0.4)	15.5	(0.3)	**2.4**	(1.0)	0.9	(0.6)	**-3.3**	(0.9)	14.3	(0.3)
	Serbia	2.0	(1.1)	8.4	(4.4)	8.6	(4.4)	10.5	(0.4)	11.3	(0.6)	13.3	(0.6)	0.8	(0.7)	1.9	(0.9)	**-2.7**	(0.8)	11.6	(0.3)
	Shanghai-China	2.5	(1.4)	6.8	(3.8)	8.8	(4.7)	14.7	(0.8)	11.8	(0.6)	10.5	(0.3)	**-2.9**	(1.0)	-1.3	(0.7)	**4.2**	(0.9)	12.2	(0.3)
	Singapore	0.3	(0.6)	1.2	(2.3)	1.4	(2.5)	14.0	(0.0)	14.3	(0.1)	15.9	(1.3)	**0.3**	(0.1)	1.6	(1.3)	-1.9	(1.3)	14.4	(0.1)
	Chinese Taipei	0.0	(0.1)	0.0	(0.4)	16.7	(4.4)	18.0	(0.7)	16.6	(0.5)	18.0	(0.5)	-1.4	(0.9)	1.4	(0.8)	0.0	(0.9)	17.4	(0.2)
	Thailand	0.5	(0.7)	1.2	(1.7)	2.1	(2.5)	19.8	(0.7)	20.0	(0.8)	21.1	(0.7)	0.1	(1.0)	1.2	(0.9)	-1.3	(0.9)	20.3	(0.4)
	Tunisia	0.1	(0.1)	0.3	(0.4)	0.3	(0.4)	11.4	(0.3)	11.7	(0.3)	14.1	(2.9)	0.3	(0.4)	2.4	(2.9)	-2.7	(2.9)	12.2	(0.8)
	United Arab Emirates	0.1	(0.2)	0.3	(0.6)	0.3	(0.7)	12.0	(0.4)	12.6	(0.4)	12.0	(0.5)	0.6	(0.6)	-0.6	(0.6)	0.0	(0.7)	11.0	(0.2)
	Uruguay	0.3	(0.4)	0.6	(0.9)	0.8	(1.0)	15.5	(0.6)	16.9	(0.6)	13.2	(0.7)	1.4	(0.8)	-3.7	(0.9)	**2.2**	(1.0)	15.5	(0.3)
	Viet Nam	0.7	(1.0)	1.5	(2.3)	5.2	(4.0)	18.0	(0.5)	19.4	(0.6)	19.2	(1.2)	1.3	(0.8)	-0.2	(1.3)	-1.2	(1.3)	18.8	(0.4)

Note: Values that are statistically significant are indicated in bold (see Annex A3).

1. ESCS refers to the *PISA index of economic. social and cultural status*.

2. A socio-economically disadvantaged school is one whose students' mean ESCS is statistically significantly below the mean ESCS of the country/economy; an average school is one where there is no difference between the students' and the country's/economy's mean ESCS; and an advantaged school is one whose students' mean ESCS is statistically significantly above the country/economy mean.

* See notes at the beginning of this Annex.

StatLink http://dx.doi.org/10.1787/888932964946

[Part 2/2]

Table II.4.8 Inequity in access to educational resources: Student-teacher ratio

Results based on students' self-reports

		Student-teacher ratio																				
		Mean among immigrant students		Difference between non-immigrant and immigrant students		Mean among students who speak the language of assessment at home		Mean among students who do not speak the language of assessment at home		Difference between students who speak the language of assessment at home and those who do not		Mean among students in rural schools		Mean among students in town schools (small town and town)		Mean among students in urban schools (city and large city)		Difference between students in rural and town schools		Difference between students in town and urban schools		Difference between students in rural and urban schools	
		Mean	S.E.	Dif.	S.E.	Mean	S.E.	Mean	S.E.	Dif.	S.E.	Mean	S.E.	Mean	S.E.	Mean	S.E.	Dif.	S.E.	Dif.	S.E.	Dif.	S.E.
OECD	Australia	13.2	(0.1)	0.0	(0.1)	13.2	(0.1)	13.2	(0.2)	0.0	(0.2)	11.5	(0.4)	13.5	(0.1)	13.2	(0.1)	**-2.1**	(0.5)	**0.4**	(0.2	**1.7**	(0.4)
	Austria	10.7	(0.5)	-0.5	(0.5)	11.1	(0.5)	10.5	(0.6)	0.6	(0.7)	7.6	(0.6)	11.8	(0.7)	10.9	(0.8)	**-4.2**	(0.9)	0.8	(1.1	**3.4**	(1.0)
	Belgium	9.0	(0.3)	-0.4	(0.2)	9.5	(0.1)	8.7	(0.3)	**0.8**	(0.3)	7.8	(1.4)	9.2	(0.2)	9.6	(0.5)	-1.4	(1.5)	-0.4	(0.5	1.8	(1.5)
	Canada	15.7	(0.3)	0.2	(0.3)	15.6	(0.2)	15.9	(0.3)	-0.2	(0.3)	15.5	(1.1)	15.3	(0.3)	15.8	(0.3)	0.2	(1.1)	-0.5	(0.4	0.3	(1.1)
	Chile	20.6	(1.6)	-1.6	(1.5)	22.2	(0.5)	c	c	c	c	15.2	(1.1)	21.7	(0.6)	22.8	(0.8)	**-6.6**	(1.2)	-1.1	(1.0	**7.6**	(1.3)
	Czech Republic	12.8	(0.5)	-0.4	(0.4)	13.2	(0.3)	13.0	(0.6)	0.2	(0.5)	13.5	(1.4)	13.1	(0.3)	13.3	(0.6)	0.4	(1.4)	-0.2	(0.7	-0.2	(1.5)
	Denmark	12.3	(0.4)	0.2	(0.4)	12.1	(0.2)	12.1	(0.4)	0.0	(0.3)	10.4	(0.5)	12.6	(0.3)	13.2	(0.7)	**-2.2**	(0.6)	-0.7	(0.7	**2.8**	(0.9)
	Estonia	11.2	(0.3)	-0.2	(0.3)	11.4	(0.1)	11.2	(0.4)	0.1	(0.4)	8.4	(0.3)	11.9	(0.2)	13.0	(0.2)	**-3.5**	(0.3)	**-1.1**	(0.3	**4.6**	(0.4)
	Finland	10.4	(0.2)	-0.2	(0.2)	10.6	(0.1)	10.4	(0.2)	0.2	(0.2)	9.1	(0.4)	10.5	(0.2)	11.3	(0.2)	**-1.4**	(0.4)	**-0.8**	(0.2	**2.2**	(0.4)
	France	12.3	(0.3)	**0.6**	(0.3)	11.7	(0.2)	12.3	(0.3)	-0.6	(0.3)	w	w	w	w	w	w	w	w	w	[illegible]	w	w
	Germany	14.9	(0.3)	-0.2	(0.3)	15.1	(0.4)	14.5	(0.4)	0.7	(0.5)	c	c	14.9	(0.3)	15.7	(0.9)	c	c	-0.9	(0.9	c	c
	Greece	8.8	(0.3)	-0.4	(0.3)	9.2	(0.3)	8.6	(0.3)	0.6	(0.3)	7.9	(0.9)	9.6	(0.4)	8.6	(0.4)	-1.7	(1.0)	1.0	(0.6	0.7	(1.0)
	Hungary	11.9	(0.4)	-0.6	(0.4)	12.5	(0.3)	c	c	c	c	9.0	(0.9)	12.6	(0.4)	12.4	(0.6)	**-3.6**	(1.0)	0.2	(0.7	**3.4**	(1.1)
	Iceland	10.5	(0.2)	0.0	(0.2)	10.5	(0.0)	10.5	(0.2)	0.0	(0.2)	8.4	(0.0)	11.0	(0.0)	11.2	(0.0)	**-2.6**	(0.0)	**-0.2**	(0.0	**2.8**	(0.0)
	Ireland	14.3	(0.3)	0.0	(0.2)	14.3	(0.2)	14.1	(0.3)	0.2	(0.3)	13.8	(0.4)	14.8	(0.2)	13.8	(0.5)	**-1.0**	(0.5)	**1.1**	(0.5	0.0	(0.6)
	Israel	10.2	(0.2)	**-0.8**	(0.2)	10.9	(0.2)	10.0	(0.3)	**0.9**	(0.3)	10.0	(0.4)	11.4	(0.4)	10.6	(0.4)	**-1.4**	(0.6)	0.8	(0.6	0.6	(0.6)
	Italy	9.7	(0.2)	**-0.7**	(0.2)	10.6	(0.1)	9.6	(0.2)	**1.0**	(0.2)	9.2	(0.8)	10.2	(0.1)	10.8	(0.2)	-0.9	(0.9)	**-0.6**	(0.3	1.6	(0.9)
	Japan	c	c	c	c	11.7	(0.2)	c	c	c	c	c	c	10.5	(0.5)	12.1	(0.3)	c	c	**-1.6**	(0.6	c	c
	Korea	c	c	c	c	16.1	(0.2)	c	c	c	c	c	c	14.4	(0.9)	16.5	(0.3)	c	c	**-2.1**	(1.0	c	c
	Luxembourg	9.1	(0.0)	**0.2**	(0.0)	9.6	(0.1)	9.0	(0.0)	**0.6**	(0.1)	c	c	9.1	(0.0)	c	c	c	c	c	[illegible]	c	c
	Mexico	27.5	(1.5)	**-3.1**	(1.6)	30.8	(0.8)	25.8	(3.7)	5.0	(3.8)	22.1	(1.0)	33.7	(1.7)	30.5	(0.9)	**-11.6**	(2.0)	3.2	(2.0	**8.4**	(1.4)
	Netherlands	16.5	(0.5)	-0.3	(0.4)	16.9	(0.4)	16.7	(0.6)	0.2	(0.5)	c	c	16.4	(0.4)	17.6	(0.6)	c	c	-1.2	(0.7	c	c
	New Zealand	15.6	(0.3)	**0.6**	(0.2)	15.1	(0.2)	15.5	(0.3)	-0.4	(0.3)	11.8	(0.4)	14.7	(0.4)	15.9	(0.3)	**-2.9**	(0.7)	**-1.2**	(0.5	**4.1**	(0.6)
	Norway	11.0	(0.2)	**0.6**	(0.2)	10.4	(0.1)	11.0	(0.2)	**-0.6**	(0.2)	8.9	(0.3)	10.6	(0.2)	11.5	(0.3)	**-1.7**	(0.4)	**-1.0**	(0.3	**2.7**	(0.5)
	Poland	c	c	c	c	9.4	(0.2)	c	c	c	c	9.0	(0.3)	9.8	(0.3)	9.3	(0.5)	-0.8	(0.4)	0.4	(0.6	0.4	(0.6)
	Portugal	8.6	(0.3)	-0.3	(0.3)	8.9	(0.2)	8.4	(0.4)	0.5	(0.4)	9.1	(2.1)	8.6	(0.2)	9.6	(0.4)	0.4	(2.2)	-1.0	(0.5	0.6	(2.2)
	Slovak Republic	13.5	(0.5)	0.2	(0.6)	13.2	(0.3)	c	c	c	c	12.8	(0.4)	13.2	(0.3)	14.0	(0.8)	-0.5	(0.5)	-0.8	(0.8	1.2	(0.9)
	Slovenia	10.9	(0.2)	0.4	(0.2)	10.5	(0.0)	11.0	(0.3)	-0.5	(0.3)	9.1	(0.5)	10.0	(0.0)	11.5	(0.1)	-0.9	(0.5)	**-1.5**	(0.	**2.4**	(0.5)
	Spain	11.3	(0.2)	**-1.3**	(0.3)	12.8	(0.4)	10.9	(0.3)	**1.9**	(0.5)	7.9	(0.4)	11.4	(0.2)	14.7	(1.0)	**-3.5**	(0.5)	**-3.3**	(1.	**6.8**	(1.1)
	Sweden	12.2	(0.3)	-0.3	(0.2)	12.5	(0.2)	12.1	(0.3)	0.4	(0.3)	11.7	(0.6)	12.2	(0.3)	13.6	(0.5)	-0.5	(0.7)	**-1.5**	(0.	**1.9**	(0.8)
	Switzerland	11.7	(0.3)	**-0.5**	(0.2)	12.2	(0.3)	12.0	(0.3)	0.3	(0.3)	11.5	(0.7)	12.2	(0.4)	11.5	(0.8)	-0.7	(0.8)	0.7	(1.	-0.1	(1.2)
	Turkey	19.2	(2.0)	1.8	(1.9)	17.0	(0.5)	c	c	c	c	23.4	(5.7)	15.3	(0.7)	18.7	(0.8)	8.2	(5.8)	**-3.5**	(1.	-4.7	(5.8)
	United Kingdom	14.0	(0.4)	**-0.9**	(0.4)	14.9	(0.2)	14.0	(0.6)	0.9	(0.6)	14.4	(0.7)	14.8	(0.2)	14.8	(0.3)	-0.4	(0.8)	0.0	(0.	0.4	(0.7)
	United States	18.8	(1.8)	1.7	(1.3)	17.1	(1.0)	18.9	(1.9)	-1.8	(1.4)	17.5	(4.7)	16.4	(0.5)	19.0	(2.2)	1.1	(4.7)	-2.6	(1.	1.5	(5.3)
	OECD average	13.2	(0.1)	-0.2	(0.1)	13.3	(0.1)	12.6	(0.2)	**0.4**	(0.2)	11.7	(0.3)	13.2	(0.1)	13.9	(0.1)	**-1.6**	(0.3)	**-0.6**	(0.	**2.0**	(0.3)
Partners	Albania	m	m	m	m	m	m	m	m	m	m	m	m	m	m	m	m	m	m	m	[illegible]	m	m
	Argentina	8.4	(0.5)	-2.2	(1.3)	10.6	(1.3)	c	c	c	c	5.0	(0.6)	9.4	(0.6)	13.8	(3.3)	**-4.4**	(0.8)	-4.5	(3.	**8.8**	(3.4)
	Brazil	27.2	(3.5)	-0.9	(3.2)	28.0	(0.7)	c	c	c	c	18.6	(3.2)	29.0	(0.8)	27.6	(1.1)	**-10.3**	(3.4)	1.4	(1.	**9.0**	(3.4)
	Bulgaria	c	c	c	c	14.6	(1.5)	c	c	c	c	21.0	(11.1)	15.4	(2.4)	12.7	(0.4)	5.6	(11.4)	2.8	(2.	-8.3	(11.1)
	Colombia	c	c	c	c	27.0	(0.6)	c	c	c	c	24.3	(2.5)	25.3	(1.0)	28.5	(0.8)	-1.1	(2.8)	**-3.1**	(1.	4.2	(2.6)
	Costa Rica	20.9	(2.1)	0.5	(1.7)	20.5	(2.7)	c	c	c	c	17.9	(2.5)	17.5	(0.6)	34.6	(13.8)	0.4	(2.5)	-17.1	(13.	16.7	(14.0)
	Croatia	12.6	(0.2)	0.0	(0.2)	12.6	(0.2)	c	c	c	c	c	c	12.2	(0.2)	13.3	(0.3)	c	c	**-1.0**	(0.	c	c
	Cyprus*	8.1	(0.1)	**0.1**	(0.1)	7.6	(0.0)	8.2	(0.1)	**-0.6**	(0.1)	6.7	(0.0)	8.0	(0.0)	7.9	(0.0)	**-1.3**	(0.0)	**0.1**	(0.	**1.2**	(0.0)
	Hong Kong-China	15.6	(0.1)	0.3	(0.1)	15.4	(0.2)	14.9	(0.2)	**0.6**	(0.3)	c	c	c	c	15.4	(0.1)	c	c	c	c	c	c
	Indonesia	c	c	c	c	17.1	(0.8)	c	c	c	c	15.6	(1.1)	17.0	(0.7)	18.2	(1.5)	-1.4	(1.2)	-1.2	(1.	2.6	(1.9)
	Jordan	18.9	(0.7)	**2.2**	(0.6)	16.8	(0.4)	17.4	(1.6)	-0.7	(1.5)	13.1	(0.8)	16.7	(0.7)	18.3	(0.6)	**-3.7**	(0.9)	-1.6	(0	**5.3**	(1.0)
	Kazakhstan	9.9	(0.5)	-0.3	(0.5)	10.1	(0.2)	11.4	(0.3)	**-1.3**	(0.3)	7.7	(0.3)	10.2	(0.4)	11.9	(0.4)	**-2.5**	(0.5)	**-1.7**	(0	**4.2**	(0.5)
	Latvia	10.6	(0.4)	0.7	(0.4)	9.9	(0.2)	10.0	(1.0)	0.0	(1.0)	7.5	(0.2)	10.6	(0.3)	11.1	(0.4)	**-3.1**	(0.4)	-0.6	(0	**3.7**	(0.5)
	Liechtenstein	7.6	(0.1)	**-0.6**	(0.2)	8.3	(0.1)	c	c	c	c	c	c	8.0	(0.0)	c	c	c	c	c	c	c	c
	Lithuania	10.4	(1.3)	-1.0	(1.0)	11.6	(0.7)	c	c	c	c	12.3	(2.9)	11.6	(0.2)	10.8	(0.3)	0.7	(2.9)	**0.8**	(0	-1.5	(2.9)
	Macao-China	15.9	(0.1)	**0.6**	(0.2)	15.2	(0.1)	15.7	(0.2)	**-0.4**	(0.2)	c	c	c	c	15.7	(0.0)	c	c	c	c	c	c
	Malaysia	14.1	(0.5)	0.7	(0.4)	12.9	(0.2)	c	c	c	c	13.1	(0.5)	13.4	(0.3)	13.7	(0.4)	-0.3	(0.7)	-0.3	(0	0.6	(0.7)
	Montenegro	16.0	(0.2)	0.3	(0.2)	15.7	(0.0)	c	c	c	c	c	c	15.2	(0.0)	16.7	(0.0)	c	c	**-1.6**	(0	c	c
	Peru	16.9	(1.5)	-1.6	(1.5)	18.7	(0.6)	c	c	c	c	13.8	(0.8)	19.1	(0.7)	19.8	(1.1)	**-5.3**	(1.1)	-0.7	(1	**6.0**	(1.3)
	Qatar	14.9	(0.1)	**1.7**	(0.2)	10.4	(0.0)	18.1	(0.3)	**-7.7**	(0.3)	11.8	(0.0)	12.0	(0.0)	16.2	(0.0)	**-0.3**	(0.0)	**-4.1**	(0	**4.4**	(0.0)
	Romania	c	c	c	c	16.1	(0.4)	c	c	c	c	16.6	(1.4)	16.5	(0.6)	15.3	(0.5)	0.1	(1.6)	1.2	(0	-1.3	(1.6)
	Russian Federation	14.8	(0.3)	0.6	(0.3)	14.5	(0.3)	14.6	(0.8)	-0.1	(0.9)	8.2	(0.7)	15.1	(0.6)	16.3	(0.2)	**-6.9**	(0.9)	-1.2	(0	**8.1**	(0.7)
	Serbia	11.1	(0.5)	-0.5	(0.5)	11.6	(0.3)	c	c	c	c	c	c	11.2	(0.4)	11.8	(0.4)	c	c	-0.6	(0	c	c
	Shanghai-China	14.7	(2.5)	2.5	(2.4)	12.2	(0.3)	c	c	c	c	c	c	c	c	12.2	(0.3)	c	c	c	c	c	c
	Singapore	15.8	(1.8)	1.5	(1.8)	14.5	(0.1)	15.8	(1.5)	-1.3	(1.5)	c	c	c	c	14.6	(0.3)	c	c	c	c	c	c
	Chinese Taipei	17.7	(1.3)	0.3	(1.3)	17.3	(0.2)	c	c	c	c	c	c	16.5	(0.4)	18.0	(0.4)	c	c	**-1.5**	(0	c	c
	Thailand	18.9	(3.6)	-1.4	(3.5)	20.7	(0.5)	c	c	c	c	15.2	(0.8)	21.0	(0.6)	21.5	(0.7)	**-5.8**	(1.0)	-0.4	(0	**6.2**	(1.1)
	Tunisia	c	c	c	c	12.2	(0.7)	c	c	c	c	11.7	(1.0)	12.5	(1.0)	11.5	(0.4)	-0.8	(1.4)	1.0	(1	-0.2	(1.1)
	United Arab Emirates	13.1	(0.4)	**2.1**	(0.4)	11.0	(0.3)	13.2	(0.5)	**-2.2**	(0.5)	11.6	(0.4)	12.8	(0.5)	12.0	(0.4)	**-1.3**	(0.6)	0.8	(0	0.4	(0.5)
	Uruguay	c	c	c	c	15.4	(0.3)	c	c	c	c	13.6	(1.7)	15.3	(0.4)	16.1	(0.6)	-1.7	(1.8)	-0.8	(0	2.4	(1.8)
	Viet Nam	c	c	c	c	18.9	(0.4)	c	c	c	c	18.4	(0.6)	19.2	(0.8)	19.1	(1.1)	-0.8	(1.0)	0.1	(1	0.7	(1.3)

Note: Values that are statistically significant are indicated in bold (see Annex A3).

1. ESCS refers to the *PISA index of economic, social and cultural status*.

2. A socio-economically disadvantaged school is one whose students' mean ESCS is statistically significantly below the mean ESCS of the country/economy; [illegible]n average school is one where there is no difference between the students' and the country's/economy's mean ESCS; and an advantaged school is one whose students' mean E[illegible]CS is statistically significantly above the country/economy mean.

* See notes at the beginning of this Annex.

StatLink http://dx.doi.org/10.1787/888932964946

[Part 1/2]

Table II.4.9 Inequity in access to educational resources: Percentage of teachers with university-level qualifications

Results based on students' self-reports

		Percentage of teachers with a university-level qualifications																			
		Percentage of the variation explained by student ESCS[1]		Percentage of the variation explained by student and school mean ESCS		Percentage of the variance explained by student and school mean and standard deviation of ESCS		Mean among students in socio-economically disadvantaged schools,[2] relative to the country mean ESCS		Mean among students in socio-economically average schools[2], relative to the country mean ESCS		Mean among students in socio-economically advantaged schools,[2] relative to the country mean ESCS		Difference between students in average and disadvantaged schools		Difference between students in advantaged and average schools		Difference between students in disadvantaged and advantaged schools		Mean among non-immigrant students	
		%	S.E.	%	S.E.	%	S.E.	%	S.E.	%	S.E.	%	S.E.	Dif.	S.E.	Dif.	S.E.	Dif.	S.E.	%	S.E.
OECD	Australia	0.0	(0.0)	0.0	(0.2)	0.0	(0.2)	95.9	(1.4)	97.4	(0.9)	97.2	(1.2)	1.6	(1.7)	-0.3	(1.5)	-1.3	(1.8)	97.3	(0.6)
	Austria	12.1	(1.9)	35.7	(5.6)	36.2	(5.7)	18.3	(4.0)	60.1	(4.2)	83.3	(3.4)	**41.7**	(6.6)	23.2	(5.0)	**-65.0**	(5.3)	53.4	(1.9)
	Belgium	11.2	(1.8)	36.8	(5.0)	37.1	(5.1)	25.3	(1.9)	38.7	(1.6)	51.2	(1.4)	**13.4**	(2.5)	12.5	(2.0)	**-25.9**	(2.2)	39.6	(1.0)
	Canada	0.0	(0.0)	0.0	(0.1)	0.2	(0.3)	96.5	(0.7)	94.3	(1.1)	96.3	(1.4)	-2.1	(1.3)	2.0	(1.7)	0.1	(1.5)	94.9	(0.8)
	Chile	2.0	(2.0)	3.7	(3.7)	4.4	(4.1)	88.0	(2.5)	95.9	(1.5)	95.0	(2.5)	**7.9**	(2.8)	-0.9	(2.8)	**-7.0**	(3.5)	92.2	(1.4)
	Czech Republic	2.3	(0.9)	8.0	(3.1)	8.5	(3.2)	84.8	(1.9)	93.1	(0.8)	95.3	(1.7)	**8.3**	(2.3)	2.2	(2.0)	**-10.5**	(2.6)	91.8	(0.7)
	Denmark	0.1	(0.2)	0.7	(0.8)	3.4	(3.1)	88.6	(3.7)	86.5	(2.7)	94.3	(2.5)	-2.1	(4.4)	7.8	(3.7)	-5.7	(4.5)	88.4	(1.9)
	Estonia	m	m	m	m	m	m	m	m	m	m	m	m	m	m	m	m	m	m	m	m
	Finland	0.0	(0.1)	0.0	(0.4)	2.9	(1.7)	90.9	(1.6)	92.7	(1.2)	87.4	(1.7)	1.8	(2.0)	-5.4	(2.1)	3.6	(2.4)	91.7	(0.9)
	France	w	w	w	w	w	w	w	w	w	w	w	w	w	w	w	w	w	w	w	w
	Germany	m	m	m	m	m	m	m	m	m	m	m	m	m	m	m	m	m	m	m	m
	Greece	1.2	(1.3)	3.6	(3.9)	4.0	(4.1)	85.3	(2.9)	97.6	(0.7)	93.9	(3.4)	**12.3**	(2.9)	-3.7	(3.5)	**-8.5**	(4.3)	93.7	(1.4)
	Hungary	1.1	(0.7)	2.8	(1.7)	3.8	(2.1)	98.5	(0.4)	99.2	(0.4)	99.9	(0.1)	0.7	(0.6)	0.7	(0.5)	**-1.4**	(0.4)	99.3	(0.2)
	Iceland	0.6	(0.3)	3.2	(0.2)	3.8	(0.2)	68.9	(0.5)	82.0	(0.2)	89.9	(0.3)	**13.1**	(0.5)	7.9	(0.3)	**-21.1**	(0.6)	81.7	(0.3)
	Ireland	0.1	(0.5)	0.7	(2.2)	1.8	(2.4)	99.4	(0.4)	99.9	(0.0)	99.2	(0.6)	0.5	(0.4)	-0.7	(0.6)	0.2	(0.7)	99.7	(0.2)
	Israel	1.3	(0.8)	4.2	(2.7)	7.0	(3.9)	81.8	(3.7)	85.7	(3.8)	91.3	(1.7)	4.0	(4.9)	5.6	(4.2)	**-9.6**	(4.2)	86.5	(1.8)
	Italy	2.6	(0.6)	9.0	(2.0)	9.4	(2.2)	84.3	(1.2)	88.6	(1.6)	95.7	(0.9)	**4.3**	(2.1)	7.1	(1.9)	**-11.3**	(1.6)	89.9	(0.8)
	Japan	0.7	(0.6)	2.8	(2.4)	2.9	(2.5)	99.8	(0.1)	99.9	(0.1)	100.0	(0.0)	0.1	(0.1)	0.1	(0.1)	**-0.1**	(0.1)	99.9	(0.0)
	Korea	0.0	(0.1)	0.0	(0.3)	0.2	(0.5)	99.8	(0.1)	99.5	(0.3)	100.0	(0.0)	-0.2	(0.3)	0.4	(0.3)	-0.2	(0.1)	99.7	(0.1)
	Luxembourg	6.0	(0.5)	21.0	(0.2)	24.3	(0.2)	88.6	(0.0)	87.4	(0.1)	97.3	(0.0)	**-1.2**	(0.1)	9.9	(0.1)	**-8.6**	(0.0)	91.6	(0.1)
	Mexico	0.0	(0.1)	0.0	(0.2)	0.0	(0.2)	87.5	(1.7)	88.9	(1.9)	87.9	(1.7)	1.5	(2.5)	-1.1	(2.7)	-0.4	(2.6)	88.1	(1.0)
	Netherlands	5.7	(2.3)	26.7	(11.6)	26.7	(11.7)	14.3	(3.1)	31.3	(2.4)	51.6	(2.9)	**17.0**	(4.0)	20.2	(3.9)	**-37.2**	(4.3)	32.9	(1.7)
	New Zealand	1.1	(0.8)	4.3	(2.9)	4.4	(3.1)	89.3	(2.1)	92.9	(1.6)	95.9	(0.7)	3.6	(2.4)	3.0	(1.8)	**-6.6**	(2.2)	92.9	(1.1)
	Norway	c	c	c	c	c	c	100.0	c	100.0	c	100.0	c	m	m	m	m	m	m	100.0	c
	Poland	0.1	(0.3)	0.4	(1.3)	1.1	(1.7)	95.7	(2.8)	92.7	(2.9)	91.1	(4.9)	-3.0	(4.1)	-1.6	(6.1)	4.5	(5.6)	93.2	(1.8)
	Portugal	0.7	(1.1)	2.3	(3.4)	2.3	(3.7)	70.1	(8.9)	80.4	(3.8)	53.0	(9.3)	10.3	(9.5)	-27.4	(10.4)	17.1	(13.2)	70.8	(4.1)
	Slovak Republic	0.2	(0.3)	0.6	(0.8)	0.9	(1.4)	89.2	(2.8)	89.9	(1.8)	92.4	(1.0)	0.7	(3.3)	2.5	(2.0)	-3.2	(3.0)	90.5	(1.1)
	Slovenia	5.9	(0.7)	18.9	(1.2)	19.6	(1.0)	80.4	(0.5)	87.8	(0.4)	96.8	(0.2)	**7.4**	(0.6)	9.0	(0.4)	**-16.4**	(0.5)	88.5	(0.3)
	Spain	0.0	(0.1)	0.1	(0.5)	2.6	(0.7)	95.3	(2.1)	94.1	(1.4)	94.4	(1.5)	-1.1	(2.4)	0.2	(1.9)	0.9	(1.7)	94.3	(1.3)
	Sweden	0.3	(0.3)	1.6	(1.6)	1.7	(1.8)	74.9	(7.6)	72.9	(4.2)	87.6	(4.9)	-2.0	(8.5)	14.7	(6.2)	-12.7	(8.6)	77.0	(3.3)
	Switzerland	0.7	(0.6)	3.4	(2.9)	4.6	(3.6)	58.2	(4.8)	61.3	(3.6)	77.8	(6.2)	3.1	(5.9)	16.5	(6.7)	**-19.7**	(7.5)	65.6	(2.9)
	Turkey	0.0	(0.2)	0.1	(0.7)	2.4	(1.5)	92.3	(2.7)	94.7	(1.4)	92.1	(3.6)	2.3	(3.1)	-2.6	(3.6)	0.3	(4.6)	93.2	(1.5)
	United Kingdom	0.0	(0.1)	0.0	(0.3)	0.3	(0.5)	96.6	(2.1)	95.0	(1.7)	96.5	(2.6)	-1.5	(2.6)	1.5	(3.0)	0.0	(3.2)	95.5	(1.3)
	United States	0.0	(0.3)	0.0	(1.0)	0.7	(1.2)	98.3	(1.1)	98.9	(0.4)	98.8	(0.8)	0.6	(1.1)	-0.2	(0.9)	-0.5	(1.8)	98.7	(0.3)
	OECD average	1.8	(0.16)	6.2	(0.6)	7.1	(0.6)	81.4	(0.6)	85.9	(0.4)	88.8	(0.5)	**4.5**	(0.7)	2.9	(0.7)	**-7.4**	(0.8)	85.5	(0.3)
Partners	Albania	m	m	m	m	m	m	m	m	m	m	m	m	m	m	m	m	m	m	83.6	(1.6)
	Argentina	1.0	(1.0)	3.0	(2.9)	3.2	(3.2)	15.4	(2.0)	13.5	(2.4)	23.8	(3.3)	-1.9	(3.1)	10.3	(4.0)	**-8.4**	(4.0)	17.7	(1.6)
	Brazil	0.0	(0.1)	0.0	(0.3)	0.4	(0.9)	87.9	(1.4)	86.4	(2.0)	87.1	(2.6)	-1.5	(2.6)	0.7	(3.6)	0.7	(2.8)	87.0	(1.0)
	Bulgaria	m	m	m	m	m	m	m	m	m	m	m	m	m	m	m	m	m	m	m	m
	Colombia	0.1	(0.4)	0.1	(1.0)	0.3	(1.4)	92.2	(2.3)	90.2	(2.2)	90.1	(2.4)	-2.0	(3.1)	-0.1	(3.4)	2.1	(3.3)	90.7	(1.3)
	Costa Rica	1.0	(2.1)	2.2	(4.6)	3.5	(5.0)	72.3	(5.4)	90.2	(1.4)	83.3	(5.5)	**17.9**	(5.7)	-6.9	(5.6)	-11.0	(7.6)	84.2	(2.2)
	Croatia	4.6	(1.1)	17.3	(3.6)	18.7	(4.0)	89.2	(1.3)	95.1	(0.8)	99.2	(0.4)	**5.9**	(1.5)	4.1	(0.9)	**-9.9**	(1.4)	94.3	(0.6)
	Cyprus*	0.1	(0.1)	0.5	(0.0)	0.6	(0.0)	92.9	(0.0)	95.2	(0.0)	100.0	(0.0)	**2.3**	(0.0)	4.8	(0.0)	**-7.1**	(0.0)	95.4	(0.1)
	Hong Kong-China	0.0	(0.2)	0.1	(0.6)	0.2	(0.8)	97.5	(0.4)	97.0	(1.4)	98.1	(0.5)	-0.5	(1.4)	1.2	(1.5)	-0.7	(0.7)	97.4	(0.7)
	Indonesia	1.5	(1.0)	4.2	(2.6)	4.4	(2.8)	77.7	(3.2)	81.4	(2.7)	89.3	(2.2)	3.7	(4.4)	7.9	(3.5)	**-11.6**	(4.1)	82.2	(1.6)
	Jordan	0.0	(0.1)	0.0	(0.3)	0.1	(0.6)	84.4	(3.6)	85.8	(2.0)	82.1	(5.1)	1.5	(4.0)	-3.8	(5.4)	2.3	(6.2)	84.5	(1.8)
	Kazakhstan	1.1	(0.8)	4.4	(3.3)	5.0	(3.6)	79.0	(4.1)	84.8	(3.3)	91.1	(2.5)	5.9	(4.5)	6.3	(4.1)	**-12.2**	(4.8)	86.9	(1.9)
	Latvia	0.9	(0.9)	2.9	(2.8)	5.0	(3.2)	47.5	(5.3)	47.3	(3.7)	55.8	(4.9)	-0.2	(6.5)	8.4	(6.1)	-8.3	(7.7)	49.8	(2.5)
	Liechtenstein	3.0	(2.5)	20.5	(2.1)	43.9	(3.0)	c	c	68.8	(1.1)	c	c	c	c	c	c	c	c	81.1	(1.4)
	Lithuania	0.1	(0.2)	0.3	(0.6)	0.3	(0.6)	90.1	(3.1)	88.9	(2.9)	91.7	(2.8)	-1.2	(4.1)	2.8	(4.5)	-1.6	(4.2)	90.0	(1.7)
	Macao-China	0.2	(0.1)	0.9	(0.0)	1.7	(0.0)	93.3	(0.0)	88.7	(0.0)	92.0	(0.0)	**-4.6**	(0.0)	3.3	(0.0)	**1.3**	(0.0)	91.4	(0.1)
	Malaysia	0.3	(0.4)	1.0	(1.4)	1.1	(1.6)	90.4	(1.6)	88.6	(2.8)	87.5	(4.0)	-1.8	(3.4)	-1.1	(5.1)	2.8	(4.3)	88.7	(1.6)
	Montenegro	1.5	(0.4)	7.0	(0.4)	7.7	(0.3)	86.2	(0.2)	83.8	(0.1)	94.8	(0.1)	**-2.4**	(0.2)	11.0	(0.1)	**-8.6**	(0.2)	88.9	(0.1)
	Peru	0.1	(0.7)	0.3	(1.5)	5.1	(6.0)	83.1	(4.9)	69.3	(6.7)	78.1	(5.6)	-13.9	(8.3)	8.8	(9.2)	5.1	(7.0)	77.3	(3.3)
	Qatar	0.2	(0.1)	0.8	(0.0)	4.2	(0.1)	97.8	(0.0)	95.8	(0.1)	97.0	(0.0)	**-2.1**	(0.1)	1.2	(0.1)	**0.8**	(0.0)	98.4	(0.1)
	Romania	2.3	(0.9)	6.0	(2.3)	6.7	(2.8)	92.5	(2.2)	96.8	(0.7)	98.3	(0.4)	4.3	(2.3)	1.6	(0.7)	**-5.9**	(2.3)	95.9	(0.8)
	Russian Federation	2.1	(1.1)	7.4	(3.8)	7.5	(3.9)	85.1	(1.8)	86.2	(2.0)	93.4	(0.8)	1.2	(2.6)	7.1	(2.1)	**-8.3**	(2.0)	87.9	(1.2)
	Serbia	0.1	(0.3)	0.5	(1.1)	0.5	(1.2)	4.9	(1.9)	8.7	(3.7)	6.2	(1.4)	3.8	(4.2)	-2.5	(4.0)	-1.3	(2.2)	6.8	(1.8)
	Shanghai-China	2.3	(1.5)	6.6	(4.0)	6.8	(4.2)	91.9	(1.2)	96.2	(0.7)	96.6	(0.9)	**4.3**	(1.3)	0.4	(1.1)	**-4.7**	(1.4)	95.1	(0.5)
	Singapore	3.3	(0.7)	13.1	(1.1)	13.3	(1.1)	93.5	(0.0)	95.1	(0.1)	97.0	(0.1)	**1.5**	(0.1)	2.0	(0.1)	**-3.5**	(0.1)	95.0	(0.0)
	Chinese Taipei	0.0	(0.1)	0.0	(0.4)	0.1	(0.6)	89.1	(4.4)	90.9	(3.2)	91.8	(3.1)	1.8	(5.2)	0.8	(4.5)	-2.6	(5.4)	90.5	(2.2)
	Thailand	0.0	(0.1)	0.1	(0.3)	0.7	(1.3)	99.4	(0.2)	98.7	(0.4)	99.6	(0.2)	-0.7	(0.5)	0.9	(0.5)	-0.2	(0.3)	99.2	(0.2)
	Tunisia	0.0	(0.1)	0.1	(0.4)	1.1	(1.8)	89.8	(2.5)	83.1	(3.2)	92.0	(3.0)	-6.6	(4.2)	8.9	(4.5)	-2.2	(4.0)	87.2	(1.7)
	United Arab Emirates	0.1	(0.1)	0.2	(0.4)	0.7	(0.8)	92.6	(0.8)	92.2	(1.6)	89.3	(1.4)	-0.4	(1.8)	-2.9	(2.2)	**3.3**	(1.6)	93.8	(0.8)
	Uruguay	2.3	(2.0)	5.5	(4.7)	5.5	(4.8)	7.5	(1.1)	6.9	(0.8)	12.0	(1.2)	-0.6	(1.4)	5.1	(1.3)	**-4.5**	(1.7)	8.3	(0.6)
	Viet Nam	0.4	(0.9)	1.0	(2.2)	1.7	(3.1)	83.6	(3.6)	89.3	(4.3)	90.1	(4.9)	5.7	(5.3)	0.8	(6.1)	-6.5	(6.1)	87.2	(2.6)

Note: Values that are statistically significant are indicated in bold (see Annex A3).

1. ESCS refers to the *PISA index of economic, social and cultural status*.

2. A socio-economically disadvantaged school is one whose students' mean ESCS is statistically significantly below the mean ESCS of the country/economy; an average school is one where there is no difference between the students' and the country's/economy's mean ESCS; and an advantaged school is one whose students' mean ESCS is statistically significantly above the country/economy mean.

* See notes at the beginning of this Annex.

StatLink http://dx.doi.org/10.1787/888932964946

[Part 2/2]

Table II.4.9 **Inequity in access to educational resources: Percentage of teachers with university-level qualifications**

Results based on students' self-reports

Percentage of teachers with a university-level qualifications

		Mean among immigrant students		Difference between non-immigrant and immigrant students		Mean among students who speak the language of assessment at home		Mean among students who do not speak the language of assessment at home		Difference between students who speak the language of assessment at home and those who do not		Mean among students in rural schools		Mean among students in town schools (small town and town)		Mean among students in urban schools (city and large city)		Difference between students in rural and town schools		Difference between students in town and urban schools		Difference between students in rural and urban schools	
		%	S.E.	Dif.	S.E.	%	S.E.	%	S.E.	Dif.	S.E.	%	S.E.	%	S.E.	%	S.E.	Dif.	S.E.	Dif.	S.E.	Dif.	S.E.
OECD	Australia	96.8	(0.9)	-0.4	(0.7)	97.2	(0.7)	97.4	(1.0)	-0.2	(1.0)	94.3	(3.8)	97.9	(0.7)	96.8	(0.9)	-3.5	(3.8)	1.0	(1.1)	2.5	(3.9)
	Austria	49.9	(3.3)	-3.4	(3.3)	53.9	(1.9)	52.5	(3.7)	1.4	(3.7)	38.5	(10.3)	54.5	(3.0)	53.8	(3.4)	-16.0	(11.8)	0.7	(4.8)	15.2	(10.9)
	Belgium	37.7	(1.6)	-1.9	(1.5)	40.5	(1.0)	37.2	(1.6)	**3.3**	(1.6)	37.3	(9.4)	37.7	(1.1)	44.1	(2.1)	-0.4	(9.5)	**-6.3**	(2.5)	6.8	(9.6)
	Canada	96.3	(0.9)	1.4	(0.9)	95.1	(0.9)	96.5	(1.0)	-1.4	(1.1)	94.6	(1.5)	94.7	(1.2)	95.9	(1.0)	0.0	(2.0)	-1.2	(1.6)	1.2	(1.7)
	Chile	91.0	(3.4)	-1.1	(3.1)	92.2	(1.5)	c	c	c	c	85.4	(4.6)	88.9	(3.1)	95.0	(1.2)	-3.5	(5.6)	-6.1	(3.3)	**9.6**	(4.7)
	Czech Republic	91.4	(0.8)	-0.3	(0.9)	91.9	(0.7)	91.9	(1.3)	0.0	(1.3)	90.9	(2.6)	91.3	(1.0)	93.3	(1.4)	-0.4	(2.7)	-2.0	(1.9)	2.4	(3.0)
	Denmark	92.2	(1.4)	3.7	(2.0)	88.6	(1.9)	92.7	(1.5)	-4.1	(2.2)	86.8	(4.4)	90.2	(1.6)	85.5	(6.8)	-3.4	(4.6)	4.6	(7.0)	-1.2	(8.0)
	Estonia	m	m	m	m	m	m	m	m	m	m	m	m	m	m	m	m	m	m	m	m	m	m
	Finland	88.3	(1.3)	**-3.3**	(1.5)	91.8	(0.9)	88.7	(1.4)	3.1	(1.6)	92.4	(2.7)	92.0	(1.3)	90.1	(1.1)	0.3	(3.0)	1.9	(1.7)	-2.2	(3.0)
	France	w	w	w	w	w	w	w	w	w	w	w	w	w	w	w	w	w	w	w	w	w	w
	Germany	m	m	m	m	m	m	m	m	m	m	m	m	m	m	m	m	m	m	m	m	m	m
	Greece	92.3	(1.2)	-1.4	(1.1)	93.7	(1.4)	90.5	(1.5)	**3.2**	(1.6)	98.1	(1.1)	91.4	(2.0)	96.7	(0.8)	**6.7**	(2.3)	**-5.3**	(2.2)	-1.4	(1.4)
	Hungary	99.9	(0.1)	**0.6**	(0.2)	99.2	(0.2)	c	c	c	c	99.0	(1.0)	99.0	(0.3)	99.7	(0.2)	0.0	(1.0)	**-0.7**	(0.4)	0.7	(1.0)
	Iceland	83.1	(2.4)	1.4	(2.5)	81.7	(0.3)	84.5	(2.3)	-2.9	(2.3)	72.5	(0.6)	74.7	(0.3)	97.0	(0.1)	**-2.3**	(0.7)	**-22.3**	(0.3)	**24.5**	(0.6)
	Ireland	99.7	(0.2)	0.0	(0.2)	99.7	(0.2)	99.8	(0.1)	-0.1	(0.2)	100.0	(0.0)	99.6	(0.3)	99.6	(0.3)	0.4	(0.3)	0.0	(0.4)	-0.4	(0.3)
	Israel	85.5	(3.0)	-1.0	(1.7)	86.2	(1.9)	85.9	(3.2)	0.3	(2.1)	80.9	(5.0)	89.7	(2.2)	83.9	(2.9)	-8.8	(5.6)	5.8	(3.9)	3.0	(4.9)
	Italy	85.9	(1.1)	**-4.0**	(1.0)	90.6	(0.9)	84.3	(1.5)	**6.3**	(1.5)	70.8	(5.0)	89.5	(0.9)	91.3	(1.6)	**-18.7**	(5.3)	-1.9	(1.7)	**20.6**	(5.4)
	Japan	c	c	c	c	99.9	(0.0)	c	c	c	c	c	c	99.9	(0.1)	99.9	(0.0)	c	c	0.0	(0.1)	c	c
	Korea	c	c	c	c	99.7	(0.1)	c	c	c	c	c	c	100.0	(0.0)	99.7	(0.2)	c	c	**0.3**	(0.2)	c	c
	Luxembourg	91.7	(0.1)	0.0	(0.3)	95.4	(0.6)	90.7	(0.2)	**4.7**	(0.6)	c	c	91.6	(0.0)	c	c	c	c	c	c	c	c
	Mexico	87.4	(2.2)	-0.7	(1.9)	88.3	(1.0)	90.1	(4.9)	-1.8	(4.8)	92.3	(1.6)	86.0	(1.9)	88.7	(1.2)	**6.3**	(2.3)	-2.8	(2.3)	-3.6	(1.9)
	Netherlands	27.0	(2.7)	**-5.9**	(2.5)	33.2	(1.7)	28.1	(3.2)	5.1	(2.9)	c	c	30.3	(2.4)	36.0	(3.6)	c	c	-5.7	(5.0)	c	c
	New Zealand	93.9	(1.1)	1.0	(0.9)	93.1	(1.0)	93.9	(1.2)	-0.9	(1.0)	85.9	(3.4)	90.4	(2.1)	95.5	(1.1)	-4.5	(3.9)	**-5.1**	(2.4)	**9.6**	(3.5)
	Norway	100.0	c	m	m	100.0	c	100.0	c	m	m	100.0	c	100.0	c	100.0	c	m	m	m	m	m	m
	Poland	c	c	c	c	93.3	(1.8)	c	c	c	c	94.7	(2.8)	94.2	(2.7)	88.8	(3.9)	0.5	(3.9)	5.4	(4.5)	-5.9	(4.8)
	Portugal	79.0	(6.4)	8.2	(5.9)	70.7	(4.1)	78.6	(9.0)	-7.8	(8.3)	45.8	(26.5)	78.8	(4.3)	55.7	(10.1)	-33.0	(26.6)	**23.1**	(11.4)	9.9	(27.9)
	Slovak Republic	92.6	(1.3)	2.1	(1.5)	90.4	(1.2)	c	c	c	c	90.2	(2.0)	89.6	(1.6)	94.2	(1.3)	0.6	(2.6)	**-4.6**	(1.9)	4.0	(2.3)
	Slovenia	86.0	(0.9)	**-2.5**	(1.0)	88.7	(0.3)	84.2	(1.3)	**4.5**	(1.4)	68.4	(4.1)	88.2	(0.3)	89.0	(0.3)	**-19.8**	(4.1)	-0.9	(0.5)	**20.7**	(4.1)
	Spain	96.1	(0.7)	1.7	(1.0)	94.8	(1.4)	95.3	(1.3)	-0.5	(1.4)	92.2	(3.3)	95.7	(0.7)	93.1	(2.7)	-3.4	(3.2)	2.6	(2.7)	0.9	(4.2)
	Sweden	74.4	(5.2)	-2.6	(4.6)	76.9	(3.3)	74.5	(5.6)	2.3	(5.0)	78.2	(6.7)	72.1	(4.8)	86.9	(4.8)	6.1	(8.2)	**-14.8**	(6.8)	8.7	(7.9)
	Switzerland	63.0	(3.1)	-2.6	(1.8)	65.7	(2.8)	63.0	(3.2)	2.8	(2.5)	57.4	(8.5)	64.0	(3.4)	71.9	(5.9)	-6.6	(9.2)	-7.9	(6.8)	14.5	(10.5)
	Turkey	95.5	(2.6)	2.2	(2.4)	93.1	(1.5)	c	c	c	c	63.9	(18.4)	91.5	(2.7)	95.9	(0.9)	-27.6	(18.7)	-4.5	(2.8)	32.0	(18.3)
	United Kingdom	97.6	(0.7)	**2.1**	(1.1)	95.5	(1.3)	96.8	(1.2)	-1.4	(1.1)	98.5	(0.6)	95.1	(1.6)	96.5	(2.2)	3.4	(1.8)	-1.4	[illegible]	-2.0	(2.3)
	United States	98.9	(0.6)	0.2	(0.8)	98.7	(0.3)	98.9	(0.5)	-0.2	(0.8)	98.9	(0.7)	99.1	(0.3)	98.1	(0.3)	-0.2	(0.7)	**1.1**	(0.4)	-0.8	(0.8)
	OECD average	84.2	(0.5)	-0.1	(0.4)	85.8	(0.3)	82.7	(0.6)	0.4	(0.6)	80.9	(1.5)	85.0	(0.4)	86.9	(0.6)	**-4.8**	(1.5)	**-2.1**	[illegible]	**6.9**	(1.6)
Partners	Albania	m	m	m	m	83.5	(1.6)	m	m	m	m	75.1	(3.3)	87.1	(1.8)	86.4	(3.4)	**-11.9**	(3.9)	0.7	[illegible]	**11.2**	(4.5)
	Argentina	14.0	(1.8)	-3.7	(2.1)	17.9	(1.6)	c	c	c	c	16.9	(7.7)	14.9	(1.6)	22.0	(3.5)	2.0	(7.9)	-7.1	[illegible]	5.1	(8.6)
	Brazil	85.7	(3.5)	-1.3	(3.3)	87.0	(1.0)	c	c	c	c	86.4	(3.9)	86.2	(1.4)	88.0	(1.4)	0.2	(4.1)	-1.7	[illegible]	1.5	(3.9)
	Bulgaria	m	m	m	m	m	m	m	m	m	m	m	m	m	m	m	m	m	m	m	m	m	m
	Colombia	c	c	c	c	90.8	(1.3)	c	c	c	c	83.4	(5.8)	94.7	(2.1)	90.2	(1.4)	-11.3	(6.1)	4.5	[illegible]	6.8	(6.0)
	Costa Rica	80.6	(4.4)	-3.6	(3.9)	84.2	(2.2)	c	c	c	c	75.8	(5.6)	87.9	(2.3)	80.1	(5.7)	**-12.2**	(5.9)	7.9	[illegible]	4.3	(7.8)
	Croatia	93.4	(1.1)	-0.9	(0.8)	94.3	(0.6)	c	c	c	c	c	c	93.3	(0.8)	95.5	(1.0)	c	c	-2.2	[illegible]	c	c
	Cyprus*	97.2	(0.8)	1.7	(0.9)	94.7	(0.1)	96.4	(1.4)	-1.7	(1.5)	100.0	(0.0)	96.7	(0.0)	93.4	(0.0)	**3.3**	(0.0)	**3.2**	[illegible]	**-6.6**	(0.0)
	Hong Kong-China	97.5	(0.4)	0.2	(0.4)	97.4	(0.7)	96.9	(0.7)	0.5	(0.5)	c	c	c	c	97.4	(0.6)	c	c	c	c	c	c
	Indonesia	c	c	c	c	83.2	(1.9)	c	c	c	c	77.4	(3.0)	82.1	(2.6)	88.5	(3.2)	-4.7	(4.2)	-6.4	[illegible]	**11.1**	(4.5)
	Jordan	86.4	(1.9)	1.9	(1.2)	84.5	(1.8)	86.9	(3.9)	-2.4	(3.5)	83.2	(6.6)	84.3	(2.8)	85.7	(2.2)	-1.0	(7.0)	-1.4	[illegible]	2.4	(7.0)
	Kazakhstan	77.5	(4.7)	**-9.4**	(4.1)	86.7	(2.1)	92.1	(1.9)	**-5.5**	(2.4)	81.5	(2.9)	88.2	(1.9)	86.7	(3.9)	-6.7	(3.5)	1.5	[illegible]	5.2	(4.2)
	Latvia	47.8	(4.4)	-2.0	(3.8)	49.6	(2.5)	57.4	(7.6)	-7.8	(7.6)	36.5	(4.7)	53.8	(3.6)	54.6	(4.1)	**-17.2**	(6.1)	-0.9	[illegible]	**18.1**	(5.6)
	Liechtenstein	66.1	(2.6)	**-15.0**	(3.6)	82.5	(1.7)	c	c	c	c	c	c	76.5	(0.6)	c	c	c	c	c	c	c	c
	Lithuania	90.6	(4.2)	0.6	(3.9)	90.3	(1.6)	c	c	c	c	92.2	(1.5)	93.1	(2.4)	85.0	(3.4)	-0.9	(2.8)	8.0	[illegible]	**-7.1**	(3.6)
	Macao-China	92.5	(0.1)	**1.1**	(0.2)	90.9	(0.2)	93.5	(0.2)	**-2.6**	(0.3)	c	c	c	c	92.1	(0.0)	c	c	c	c	c	c
	Malaysia	93.3	(2.5)	4.6	(2.4)	92.8	(1.0)	c	c	c	c	91.5	(3.4)	86.3	(2.5)	92.9	(1.2)	5.2	(4.2)	**-6.5**	[illegible]	1.4	(3.6)
	Montenegro	91.1	(1.1)	**2.2**	(1.1)	88.9	(0.1)	c	c	c	c	c	c	86.8	(0.1)	93.9	(0.1)	c	c	**-7.2**	[illegible]	c	c
	Peru	c	c	c	c	76.3	(3.5)	c	c	c	c	78.4	(8.1)	80.5	(4.2)	74.0	(6.0)	-2.1	(8.9)	6.5	[illegible]	-4.5	(10.0)
	Qatar	95.6	(0.1)	**-2.8**	(0.2)	98.9	(0.1)	95.6	(0.2)	**3.3**	(0.2)	99.5	(0.0)	96.8	(0.0)	96.7	(0.0)	**2.8**	(0.0)	0.1	[illegible]	**-2.8**	(0.0)
	Romania	c	c	c	c	95.9	(0.8)	c	c	c	c	84.0	(7.5)	96.7	(0.5)	97.3	(0.7)	-12.7	(7.6)	-0.6	[illegible]	13.3	(7.6)
	Russian Federation	88.6	(1.1)	0.7	(0.5)	87.7	(1.3)	90.1	(1.0)	-2.4	(1.6)	83.4	(1.6)	84.3	(2.5)	92.4	(0.7)	-0.9	(2.3)	**-8.0**	[illegible]	**9.0**	(1.5)
	Serbia	6.2	(1.4)	-0.6	(1.3)	6.8	(1.8)	c	c	c	c	c	c	4.3	(1.6)	9.5	(3.2)	c	c	-5.2	[illegible]	c	c
	Shanghai-China	92.0	(2.4)	-3.1	(2.2)	95.2	(0.5)	c	c	c	c	c	c	c	c	95.1	(0.5)	c	c	c	c	c	c
	Singapore	95.7	(0.2)	**0.7**	(0.2)	95.4	(0.1)	95.5	(0.2)	-0.2	(0.2)	c	c	c	c	95.1	(0.0)	c	c	c	c	c	c
	Chinese Taipei	87.8	(9.6)	-2.8	(9.1)	90.7	(2.2)	c	c	c	c	c	c	88.0	(4.1)	92.0	(2.4)	c	c	-4.0	[illegible]	c	c
	Thailand	100.0	(0.0)	**0.8**	(0.2)	99.2	(0.2)	c	c	c	c	99.4	(0.3)	99.1	(0.3)	99.3	(0.2)	0.3	(0.4)	-0.3	[illegible]	0.0	(0.4)
	Tunisia	c	c	c	c	87.2	(1.8)	c	c	c	c	92.3	(4.0)	89.3	(1.8)	79.4	(5.3)	3.0	(4.5)	9.9	[illegible]	**-12.9**	(6.4)
	United Arab Emirates	89.2	(1.1)	**-4.6**	(1.1)	94.3	(0.9)	87.5	(1.2)	**6.7**	(1.4)	92.2	(1.3)	92.5	(1.6)	90.4	(1.1)	-0.3	(2.0)	2.1	[illegible]	-1.8	(1.7)
	Uruguay	c	c	c	c	8.3	(0.6)	c	c	c	c	8.0	(3.3)	6.8	(0.8)	10.6	(0.7)	1.1	(3.4)	**-3.8**	[illegible]	2.7	(3.4)
	Viet Nam	c	c	c	c	87.5	(2.6)	c	c	c	c	86.0	(3.5)	87.6	(4.5)	89.2	(5.4)	-1.6	(5.7)	-1.6	[illegible]	3.2	(6.4)

Note: Values that are statistically significant are indicated in bold (see Annex A3).

1. ESCS refers to the *PISA index of economic, social and cultural status*.

2. A socio-economically disadvantaged school is one whose students' mean ESCS is statistically significantly below the mean ESCS of the country/economy; an average school is one where there is no difference between the students' and the country's/economy's mean ESCS; and an advantaged school is one whose students' mean ESCS is statistically significantly above the country/economy mean.

* See notes at the beginning of this Annex.

StatLink http://dx.doi.org/10.1787/888932964946

[Part 1/2]

Table II.4.10 Inequity in access to educational resources: Disciplinary climate

Results based on students' self-reports

		Disciplinary climate																			
		Percentage of the variation explained by student ESCS[1]		Percentage of the variation explained by student and school mean ESCS		Percentage of the variation explained by student and school mean and standard deviation of ESCS		Mean among students in socio-economically disadvantaged schools,[2] relative to the country mean ESCS		Mean among students in socio-economically average schools,[2] relative to the country mean ESCS		Mean among students in socio-economically advantaged schools,[2] relative to the country mean ESCS		Difference between students in average and disadvantaged schools		Difference between students in advantaged and average schools		Difference between students in disadvantaged and advantaged schools		Mean among non-immigrant students	
		%	S.E.	%	S.E.	%	S.E.	Mean index	S.E.	Mean index	S.E.	Mean index	S.E.	Dif.	S.E.	Dif.	S.E.	Dif.	S.E.	Mean index	S.E.
OECD	Australia	3.1	(0.7)	11.2	(2.3)	11.4	(2.3)	-0.31	(0.03)	-0.16	(0.02)	0.08	(0.03)	**0.15**	(0.03)	**0.24**	(0.04)	**-0.38**	(0.04)	-0.16	(0.02)
	Austria	3.8	(1.6)	11.6	(4.8)	11.8	(5.2)	0.00	(0.06)	0.24	(0.04)	0.40	(0.06)	**0.24**	(0.08)	**0.16**	(0.07)	**-0.40**	(0.09)	0.24	(0.03)
	Belgium	3.4	(1.1)	12.1	(3.9)	13.6	(4.1)	-0.15	(0.04)	-0.01	(0.05)	0.23	(0.05)	**0.13**	(0.06)	**0.24**	(0.06)	**-0.37**	(0.06)	0.04	(0.03)
	Canada	0.4	(0.2)	1.7	(1.1)	1.7	(1.2)	-0.01	(0.03)	-0.03	(0.02)	0.08	(0.03)	-0.02	(0.04)	**0.11**	(0.04)	**-0.09**	(0.04)	-0.03	(0.01)
	Chile	1.9	(1.3)	3.5	(2.4)	3.7	(2.4)	-0.31	(0.04)	-0.23	(0.06)	-0.19	(0.04)	0.09	(0.07)	0.04	(0.08)	**-0.12**	(0.06)	-0.25	(0.02)
	Czech Republic	1.5	(0.8)	6.1	(3.1)	6.3	(3.1)	-0.14	(0.07)	0.10	(0.06)	0.34	(0.08)	**0.24**	(0.10)	**0.24**	(0.10)	**-0.48**	(0.11)	0.11	(0.04)
	Denmark	2.0	(0.8)	9.4	(3.6)	10.7	(3.6)	-0.17	(0.05)	-0.02	(0.04)	0.14	(0.05)	**0.15**	(0.06)	**0.16**	(0.06)	**-0.31**	(0.07)	-0.01	(0.03)
	Estonia	0.0	(0.1)	0.1	(0.4)	0.2	(0.9)	0.24	(0.06)	0.18	(0.04)	0.20	(0.02)	-0.06	(0.08)	0.01	(0.05)	0.04	(0.07)	0.20	(0.03)
	Finland	0.0	(0.1)	0.4	(1.0)	1.6	(1.9)	-0.42	(0.07)	-0.31	(0.02)	-0.31	(0.03)	0.11	(0.07)	0.00	(0.04)	-0.11	(0.08)	-0.32	(0.02)
	France	4.8	(1.1)	w	w	w	w	w	w	w	w	w	w	w	w	w	w	w	w	-0.27	(0.03)
	Germany	1.4	(0.9)	4.7	(2.9)	5.1	(3.1)	-0.12	(0.06)	-0.05	(0.04)	0.07	(0.04)	0.07	(0.07)	**0.11**	(0.05)	**-0.19**	(0.08)	-0.01	(0.03)
	Greece	4.6	(1.4)	15.0	(4.6)	15.1	(4.5)	-0.46	(0.05)	-0.25	(0.03)	-0.03	(0.05)	**0.21**	(0.06)	**0.22**	(0.06)	**-0.43**	(0.07)	-0.24	(0.03)
	Hungary	10.1	(2.6)	24.7	(5.5)	26.0	(5.5)	-0.25	(0.07)	-0.02	(0.06)	0.40	(0.06)	**0.23**	(0.10)	**0.42**	(0.09)	**-0.65**	(0.09)	0.05	(0.04)
	Iceland	0.0	(0.1)	0.0	(0.1)	0.2	(0.1)	0.03	(0.01)	-0.07	(0.00)	0.04	(0.00)	**-0.10**	(0.01)	**0.11**	(0.00)	-0.01	(0.01)	-0.02	(0.00)
	Ireland	1.8	(0.9)	7.8	(3.5)	9.0	(3.7)	-0.20	(0.09)	0.17	(0.04)	0.26	(0.04)	**0.37**	(0.10)	0.09	(0.06)	**-0.47**	(0.10)	0.14	(0.03)
	Israel	1.2	(1.0)	4.4	(3.5)	5.9	(3.2)	0.10	(0.06)	0.30	(0.04)	0.34	(0.04)	**0.20**	(0.07)	0.04	(0.06)	**-0.24**	(0.07)	0.24	(0.03)
	Italy	3.3	(0.7)	11.7	(2.6)	11.9	(2.6)	-0.24	(0.03)	-0.07	(0.03)	0.18	(0.03)	**0.16**	(0.04)	**0.26**	(0.04)	**-0.42**	(0.03)	-0.03	(0.02)
	Japan	5.3	(1.7)	21.7	(6.2)	23.0	(6.4)	0.39	(0.05)	0.72	(0.03)	0.88	(0.06)	**0.33**	(0.06)	**0.16**	(0.07)	**-0.49**	(0.09)	0.67	(0.03)
	Korea	3.1	(1.4)	13.0	(5.6)	13.4	(5.7)	0.02	(0.05)	0.20	(0.04)	0.36	(0.07)	**0.18**	(0.06)	**0.16**	(0.08)	**-0.34**	(0.09)	0.19	(0.03)
	Luxembourg	0.7	(0.2)	2.3	(0.1)	11.1	(0.1)	-0.03	(0.00)	0.01	(0.00)	-0.03	(0.00)	**0.05**	(0.00)	**-0.04**	(0.00)	**0.00**	(0.00)	-0.01	(0.00)
	Mexico	0.1	(0.2)	0.2	(0.4)	0.4	(0.7)	0.05	(0.02)	0.02	(0.02)	0.11	(0.02)	-0.03	(0.03)	**0.10**	(0.03)	**-0.06**	(0.03)	0.06	(0.01)
	Netherlands	0.7	(0.6)	3.6	(2.8)	3.6	(3.0)	-0.25	(0.05)	-0.16	(0.05)	-0.10	(0.05)	0.09	(0.07)	0.06	(0.06)	**-0.15**	(0.07)	-0.15	(0.03)
	New Zealand	4.8	(1.6)	18.3	(5.8)	18.7	(5.7)	-0.43	(0.06)	-0.29	(0.04)	-0.01	(0.05)	**0.14**	(0.06)	**0.28**	(0.06)	**-0.42**	(0.08)	-0.26	(0.03)
	Norway	0.0	(0.1)	0.0	(0.4)	0.1	(0.8)	0.03	(0.08)	-0.11	(0.03)	0.00	(0.05)	-0.14	(0.09)	**0.11**	(0.06)	0.03	(0.10)	-0.08	(0.03)
	Poland	0.2	(0.4)	0.9	(1.6)	1.8	(2.1)	0.15	(0.08)	0.07	(0.05)	-0.01	(0.08)	-0.08	(0.09)	-0.08	(0.09)	0.16	(0.11)	0.07	(0.04)
	Portugal	0.0	(0.2)	0.0	(0.6)	2.3	(2.5)	0.05	(0.05)	-0.06	(0.04)	0.06	(0.08)	-0.11	(0.06)	0.12	(0.09)	-0.01	(0.09)	0.01	(0.03)
	Slovak Republic	4.9	(1.6)	13.2	(4.3)	13.2	(4.4)	-0.34	(0.05)	-0.12	(0.04)	0.03	(0.05)	**0.23**	(0.06)	**0.15**	(0.06)	**-0.38**	(0.07)	-0.13	(0.03)
	Slovenia	8.3	(1.0)	27.1	(2.6)	29.1	(2.1)	-0.23	(0.02)	-0.03	(0.01)	0.45	(0.01)	**0.20**	(0.02)	**0.48**	(0.01)	**-0.68**	(0.02)	0.07	(0.01)
	Spain	1.1	(0.4)	4.0	(1.5)	4.0	(1.5)	-0.13	(0.04)	-0.06	(0.04)	0.07	(0.04)	0.06	(0.05)	**0.14**	(0.06)	**-0.20**	(0.05)	-0.04	(0.02)
	Sweden	1.7	(0.8)	10.0	(4.3)	10.5	(4.5)	-0.32	(0.07)	-0.22	(0.03)	-0.09	(0.05)	0.11	(0.08)	**0.12**	(0.06)	**-0.23**	(0.09)	-0.20	(0.03)
	Switzerland	0.0	(0.1)	0.1	(0.6)	1.6	(2.0)	0.09	(0.05)	0.05	(0.04)	0.10	(0.04)	-0.04	(0.05)	0.05	(0.06)	-0.01	(0.07)	0.09	(0.03)
	Turkey	4.0	(1.5)	12.9	(4.5)	17.3	(4.9)	-0.23	(0.04)	-0.12	(0.03)	0.14	(0.06)	**0.11**	(0.05)	**0.26**	(0.08)	**-0.37**	(0.07)	-0.09	(0.02)
	United Kingdom	1.0	(0.8)	4.0	(3.4)	4.4	(3.0)	0.14	(0.07)	0.08	(0.03)	0.28	(0.05)	-0.05	(0.07)	**0.20**	(0.06)	-0.15	(0.08)	0.14	(0.03)
	United States	5.7	(1.4)	19.6	(4.5)	21.4	(4.7)	-0.11	(0.05)	0.02	(0.04)	0.29	(0.04)	0.13	(0.07)	**0.27**	(0.07)	**-0.40**	(0.07)	0.06	(0.03)
	OECD average	2.5	(0.2)	8.5	(0.6)	9.7	(0.6)	-0.12	(0.01)	-0.02	(0.01)	0.14	(0.01)	**0.10**	(0.01)	**0.16**	(0.01)	**-0.26**	(0.01)	0.00	(0.00)
Partners	Albania	m	m	m	m	m	m	m	m	m	m	m	m	m	m	m	m	m	m	0.38	(0.03)
	Argentina	0.0	(0.3)	0.1	(0.7)	3.5	(3.5)	-0.53	(0.04)	-0.53	(0.04)	-0.47	(0.06)	0.00	(0.07)	0.06	(0.06)	-0.06	(0.07)	-0.50	(0.03)
	Brazil	0.6	(0.5)	1.4	(1.3)	2.2	(1.9)	-0.36	(0.03)	-0.40	(0.02)	-0.25	(0.05)	-0.04	(0.04)	**0.14**	(0.05)	**-0.11**	(0.06)	-0.34	(0.02)
	Bulgaria	5.0	(2.5)	11.4	(5.9)	13.0	(6.0)	-0.38	(0.05)	-0.21	(0.04)	-0.03	(0.05)	**0.17**	(0.07)	**0.18**	(0.06)	**-0.35**	(0.07)	-0.20	(0.03)
	Colombia	0.5	(0.6)	1.3	(1.4)	1.5	(2.0)	-0.05	(0.03)	-0.11	(0.04)	0.02	(0.03)	-0.05	(0.05)	**0.13**	(0.05)	-0.07	(0.05)	-0.05	(0.02)
	Costa Rica	0.2	(0.6)	0.6	(1.4)	0.6	(1.7)	0.05	(0.05)	-0.04	(0.03)	0.18	(0.07)	-0.09	(0.06)	**0.22**	(0.08)	-0.13	(0.09)	0.03	(0.03)
	Croatia	6.4	(1.6)	24.0	(5.3)	24.2	(5.7)	-0.30	(0.05)	-0.21	(0.05)	0.30	(0.08)	0.08	(0.07)	**0.51**	(0.10)	**-0.59**	(0.09)	-0.11	(0.03)
	Cyprus*	1.1	(0.2)	4.2	(0.2)	9.2	(0.3)	-0.26	(0.00)	-0.16	(0.00)	-0.16	(0.00)	**0.09**	(0.00)	**0.01**	(0.00)	**-0.10**	(0.00)	-0.19	(0.00)
	Hong Kong-China	0.2	(0.6)	0.7	(1.6)	1.4	(2.3)	0.25	(0.04)	0.30	(0.04)	0.32	(0.06)	0.04	(0.06)	0.02	(0.08)	-0.07	(0.08)	0.29	(0.03)
	Indonesia	2.4	(1.3)	6.0	(3.3)	6.3	(3.4)	0.18	(0.04)	0.12	(0.04)	0.04	(0.04)	-0.06	(0.06)	-0.08	(0.06)	**0.14**	(0.06)	0.12	(0.02)
	Jordan	0.0	(0.2)	0.0	(0.8)	0.0	(1.5)	-0.09	(0.06)	-0.32	(0.05)	-0.16	(0.09)	**-0.24**	(0.08)	0.17	(0.11)	0.07	(0.11)	-0.23	(0.03)
	Kazakhstan	1.3	(1.0)	5.0	(3.8)	7.2	(4.4)	0.53	(0.07)	0.77	(0.05)	0.77	(0.06)	**0.25**	(0.09)	-0.01	(0.08)	**-0.24**	(0.09)	0.74	(0.04)
	Latvia	0.0	(0.2)	0.1	(0.7)	0.5	(1.3)	0.13	(0.08)	0.06	(0.06)	0.08	(0.06)	-0.07	(0.10)	0.02	(0.09)	0.05	(0.10)	0.08	(0.04)
	Liechtenstein	0.1	(0.6)	0.7	(0.6)	4.1	(1.5)	c	c	0.09	(0.01)	c	c	c	c	c	c	c	c	0.24	(0.01)
	Lithuania	1.6	(0.7)	6.0	(2.8)	6.1	(2.7)	0.03	(0.05)	0.31	(0.04)	0.43	(0.05)	**0.28**	(0.06)	0.12	(0.06)	**-0.40**	(0.07)	0.28	(0.03)
	Macao-China	0.4	(0.2)	1.7	(0.1)	4.9	(0.1)	0.08	(0.00)	0.14	(0.00)	0.11	(0.00)	**0.06**	(0.00)	**-0.03**	(0.00)	**-0.03**	(0.00)	0.08	(0.00)
	Malaysia	1.8	(1.1)	5.9	(3.7)	6.2	(3.8)	-0.25	(0.04)	-0.27	(0.03)	-0.08	(0.05)	-0.02	(0.05)	**0.18**	(0.06)	**-0.17**	(0.07)	-0.21	(0.02)
	Montenegro	1.1	(0.3)	5.4	(0.4)	6.0	(0.4)	-0.08	(0.00)	-0.11	(0.00)	0.10	(0.00)	**-0.03**	(0.00)	**0.21**	(0.00)	**-0.17**	(0.00)	-0.02	(0.00)
	Peru	0.2	(0.5)	0.4	(1.1)	2.2	(3.3)	-0.05	(0.03)	0.00	(0.04)	-0.05	(0.04)	0.05	(0.05)	-0.05	(0.06)	0.00	(0.05)	-0.03	(0.02)
	Qatar	2.0	(0.2)	8.2	(0.2)	18.1	(0.2)	-0.41	(0.00)	-0.41	(0.00)	-0.24	(0.00)	0.00	(0.00)	**0.17**	(0.00)	**-0.17**	(0.00)	-0.45	(0.00)
	Romania	5.9	(2.1)	15.3	(5.2)	15.5	(5.3)	-0.14	(0.06)	-0.08	(0.05)	0.30	(0.06)	0.06	(0.08)	**0.38**	(0.08)	**-0.44**	(0.08)	0.01	(0.04)
	Russian Federation	0.2	(0.3)	0.7	(1.2)	3.0	(2.0)	0.25	(0.06)	0.37	(0.05)	0.39	(0.06)	0.11	(0.08)	0.03	(0.08)	-0.14	(0.08)	0.36	(0.03)
	Serbia	3.5	(1.4)	14.0	(5.6)	15.7	(5.9)	-0.37	(0.05)	-0.11	(0.05)	0.05	(0.07)	**0.26**	(0.08)	0.16	(0.09)	**-0.42**	(0.09)	-0.16	(0.03)
	Shanghai-China	5.9	(1.9)	16.9	(5.1)	17.2	(5.1)	0.30	(0.05)	0.58	(0.05)	0.81	(0.05)	**0.28**	(0.07)	**0.22**	(0.07)	**-0.50**	(0.07)	0.58	(0.02)
	Singapore	5.4	(0.6)	20.6	(0.8)	21.1	(0.9)	0.03	(0.00)	0.19	(0.01)	0.47	(0.01)	**0.16**	(0.01)	**0.28**	(0.01)	**-0.45**	(0.01)	0.20	(0.01)
	Chinese Taipei	7.6	(2.0)	29.7	(7.2)	30.0	(7.3)	-0.22	(0.05)	-0.02	(0.04)	0.24	(0.05)	**0.20**	(0.06)	**0.26**	(0.06)	**-0.46**	(0.07)	-0.01	(0.03)
	Thailand	0.3	(0.4)	0.8	(1.1)	1.8	(2.1)	0.12	(0.03)	0.02	(0.04)	0.04	(0.03)	**-0.11**	(0.05)	0.02	(0.05)	0.08	(0.04)	0.07	(0.02)
	Tunisia	2.8	(1.9)	8.1	(5.3)	8.1	(5.4)	-0.31	(0.04)	-0.46	(0.03)	-0.52	(0.05)	**-0.15**	(0.05)	-0.06	(0.06)	**0.21**	(0.06)	-0.43	(0.02)
	United Arab Emirates	2.9	(0.9)	9.6	(3.0)	10.1	(3.3)	-0.10	(0.03)	-0.04	(0.03)	0.18	(0.05)	0.06	(0.05)	**0.23**	(0.06)	**-0.28**	(0.06)	-0.06	(0.03)
	Uruguay	3.0	(1.6)	7.1	(3.6)	8.8	(3.7)	-0.27	(0.04)	-0.15	(0.04)	0.00	(0.06)	**0.12**	(0.06)	**0.15**	(0.08)	**-0.27**	(0.07)	-0.17	(0.03)
	Viet Nam	1.6	(1.5)	3.6	(3.3)	3.6	(3.5)	0.40	(0.03)	0.38	(0.03)	0.28	(0.04)	-0.01	(0.04)	**-0.10**	(0.05)	**0.11**	(0.05)	0.36	(0.02)

Note: Values that are statistically significant are indicated in bold (see Annex A3).

1. ESCS refers to the *PISA index of economic, social and cultural status*.

2. A socio-economically disadvantaged school is one whose students' mean ESCS is statistically significantly below the mean ESCS of the country/economy; an average school is one where there is no difference between the students' and the country's/economy's mean ESCS; and an advantaged school is one whose students' mean ESCS is statistically significantly above the country/economy mean.

* See notes at the beginning of this Annex.

StatLink http://dx.doi.org/10.1787/888932964946

[Part 2/2]

Table II.4.10 **Inequity in access to educational resources: Disciplinary climate**
Results based on students' self-reports

	Disciplinary climate																					
	Mean among immigrant students		Difference between non-immigrant and immigrant students		Mean among students who speak the language of assessment at home		Mean among students who do not speak the language of assessment at home		Difference between students who speak the language of assessment at home and those who do not		Mean among students in rural schools		Mean among students in town schools (small town and town)		Mean among students in urban schools (city and large city)		Difference between students in rural and town schools		Difference between students in town and urban schools		Difference between students in rural and urban schools	
	Mean index	S.E.	Dif.	S.E.	Mean index	S.E.	Mean index	S.E.	Dif.	S.E.	Mean index	S.E.	Mean index	S.E.	Mean index	S.E.	Dif.	S.E.	Dif.	S.E.	Dif.	S.E.
OECD																						
Australia	-0.06	(0.03)	**0.10**	(0.02)	-0.16	(0.02)	-0.04	(0.04)	**-0.12**	(0.03)	-0.24	(0.05)	-0.22	(0.03)	-0.09	(0.02)	-0.02	(0.05)	**-0.13**	(0.04)	**0.15**	(0.06)
Austria	0.04	(0.05)	**-0.19**	(0.05)	0.24	(0.03)	0.05	(0.07)	**0.19**	(0.06)	0.35	(0.16)	0.21	(0.05)	0.16	(0.05)	0.14	(0.18)	0.05	(0.07)	-0.19	(0.17)
Belgium	0.00	(0.04)	-0.05	(0.03)	0.05	(0.03)	0.02	(0.04)	0.03	(0.04)	0.04	(0.07)	0.05	(0.03)	-0.03	(0.07)	-0.01	(0.08)	0.08	(0.07)	-0.07	(0.10)
Canada	0.08	(0.02)	**0.11**	(0.02)	-0.02	(0.02)	0.10	(0.03)	**-0.12**	(0.03)	-0.10	(0.05)	-0.03	(0.02)	0.04	(0.02)	-0.07	(0.06)	**-0.07**	(0.03)	**0.15**	(0.06)
Chile	-0.25	(0.06)	0.00	(0.06)	-0.25	(0.02)	c	c	c	c	-0.32	(0.14)	-0.23	(0.05)	-0.25	(0.03)	-0.09	(0.14)	0.02	(0.06)	0.07	(0.14)
Czech Republic	0.06	(0.08)	-0.04	(0.07)	0.11	(0.04)	0.11	(0.09)	0.00	(0.08)	0.24	(0.17)	0.12	(0.05)	0.01	(0.08)	0.12	(0.17)	0.11	(0.10)	-0.23	(0.18)
Denmark	-0.05	(0.03)	-0.04	(0.03)	-0.01	(0.03)	-0.03	(0.03)	0.02	(0.03)	-0.11	(0.07)	-0.01	(0.03)	0.04	(0.04)	-0.10	(0.07)	-0.04	(0.05)	0.14	(0.08)
Estonia	0.22	(0.06)	0.02	(0.05)	0.20	(0.03)	0.12	(0.06)	0.08	(0.06)	0.24	(0.08)	0.19	(0.04)	0.17	(0.04)	0.04	(0.08)	0.02	(0.06)	-0.06	(0.09)
Finland	-0.39	(0.01)	**-0.06**	(0.02)	-0.32	(0.02)	-0.38	(0.02)	**0.06**	(0.02)	-0.26	(0.11)	-0.31	(0.03)	-0.37	(0.02)	0.06	(0.11)	0.05	(0.04)	-0.11	(0.11)
France	-0.43	(0.05)	**-0.15**	(0.04)	-0.27	(0.03)	-0.41	(0.05)	**0.14**	(0.04)	w	w	w	w	w	w	w	w	w	[illegible]	w	w
Germany	-0.11	(0.04)	**-0.10**	(0.03)	-0.02	(0.03)	-0.06	(0.05)	0.04	(0.05)	c	c	-0.04	(0.03)	-0.06	(0.06)	c	c	0.02	[illegible]	c	c
Greece	-0.28	(0.03)	-0.04	(0.03)	-0.24	(0.03)	-0.32	(0.04)	0.08	(0.04)	-0.29	(0.09)	-0.29	(0.03)	-0.14	(0.05)	0.00	(0.10)	**-0.14**	(0.07)	0.14	(0.10)
Hungary	0.11	(0.10)	0.06	(0.10)	0.05	(0.04)	c	c	c	c	-0.13	(0.15)	0.01	(0.05)	0.12	(0.07)	-0.13	(0.17)	-0.11	(0.10)	0.25	(0.16)
Iceland	0.05	(0.03)	**0.08**	(0.03)	-0.03	(0.00)	0.08	(0.04)	**-0.10**	(0.04)	-0.06	(0.01)	-0.06	(0.00)	0.04	(0.00)	0.00	(0.01)	**-0.10**	[illegible]	**0.10**	(0.01)
Ireland	0.05	(0.04)	**-0.09**	(0.02)	0.14	(0.03)	0.02	(0.05)	**0.12**	(0.04)	0.31	(0.06)	0.11	(0.04)	0.01	(0.06)	**0.19**	(0.08)	0.11	(0.07)	**-0.30**	(0.09)
Israel	0.33	(0.04)	**0.09**	(0.03)	0.25	(0.03)	0.37	(0.04)	**-0.12**	(0.04)	0.19	(0.07)	0.20	(0.05)	0.34	(0.04)	0.00	(0.09)	**-0.15**	(0.06)	0.15	(0.08)
Italy	-0.22	(0.02)	**-0.19**	(0.02)	-0.01	(0.02)	-0.24	(0.03)	**0.24**	(0.03)	-0.36	(0.14)	-0.03	(0.02)	-0.04	(0.03)	**-0.33**	(0.14)	0.02	(0.04)	**0.31**	(0.14)
Japan	c	c	c	c	0.67	(0.03)	c	c	c	c	c	c	0.67	(0.05)	0.66	(0.04)	c	c	0.00	[illegible]	c	c
Korea	c	c	c	c	0.19	(0.03)	c	c	c	c	c	c	0.15	(0.11)	0.21	(0.03)	c	c	-0.05	[illegible]	c	c
Luxembourg	-0.04	(0.00)	**-0.03**	(0.01)	-0.01	(0.02)	-0.05	(0.01)	**0.04**	(0.02)	c	c	-0.03	(0.00)	c	c	c	c	c	[illegible]	c	c
Mexico	-0.04	(0.03)	**-0.10**	(0.03)	0.06	(0.01)	0.07	(0.09)	-0.01	(0.10)	0.11	(0.02)	0.05	(0.02)	0.05	(0.02)	**0.06**	(0.03)	0.00	[illegible]	**-0.06**	(0.03)
Netherlands	-0.26	(0.05)	**-0.11**	(0.04)	-0.15	(0.03)	-0.25	(0.06)	**0.11**	(0.04)	c	c	-0.12	(0.03)	-0.28	(0.05)	c	c	**0.16**	[illegible]	c	c
New Zealand	-0.21	(0.04)	0.05	(0.04)	-0.25	(0.03)	-0.23	(0.05)	-0.02	(0.05)	-0.30	(0.11)	-0.30	(0.04)	-0.20	(0.05)	0.00	(0.11)	-0.10	[illegible]	0.10	(0.12)
Norway	-0.07	(0.04)	0.01	(0.04)	-0.08	(0.03)	-0.07	(0.05)	-0.01	(0.04)	-0.05	(0.08)	-0.11	(0.03)	0.01	(0.06)	0.06	(0.08)	-0.12	[illegible]	0.06	(0.10)
Poland	c	c	c	c	0.07	(0.04)	c	c	c	c	0.22	(0.08)	0.04	(0.06)	-0.07	(0.07)	0.18	(0.10)	0.11	[illegible]	**-0.29**	(0.11)
Portugal	-0.10	(0.03)	**-0.11**	(0.03)	0.01	(0.03)	-0.10	(0.04)	**0.11**	(0.04)	0.17	(0.12)	0.02	(0.03)	-0.07	(0.06)	0.15	(0.12)	0.09	[illegible]	-0.24	(0.14)
Slovak Republic	-0.07	(0.10)	0.07	(0.10)	-0.11	(0.03)	c	c	c	c	-0.13	(0.08)	-0.14	(0.03)	-0.15	(0.06)	0.01	(0.08)	0.01	[illegible]	-0.02	(0.10)
Slovenia	-0.04	(0.04)	**-0.11**	(0.04)	0.08	(0.01)	-0.10	(0.04)	**0.18**	(0.04)	c	c	0.02	(0.01)	0.14	(0.01)	c	c	**-0.12**	[illegible]	c	c
Spain	-0.13	(0.03)	**-0.09**	(0.02)	-0.01	(0.02)	-0.18	(0.04)	**0.17**	(0.04)	0.14	(0.06)	-0.07	(0.03)	-0.02	(0.04)	**0.22**	(0.07)	-0.06	[illegible]	**-0.16**	(0.07)
Sweden	-0.24	(0.04)	-0.04	(0.03)	-0.19	(0.03)	-0.25	(0.05)	0.06	(0.04)	-0.31	(0.07)	-0.20	(0.03)	-0.16	(0.05)	-0.11	(0.07)	-0.04	[illegible]	0.15	(0.09)
Switzerland	0.03	(0.03)	**-0.06**	(0.02)	0.09	(0.03)	0.01	(0.04)	**0.08**	(0.02)	0.27	(0.11)	0.10	(0.03)	-0.11	(0.07)	0.17	(0.11)	**0.20**	[illegible]	**-0.38**	(0.13)
Turkey	-0.14	(0.13)	-0.05	(0.13)	-0.08	(0.02)	c	c	c	c	0.43	(0.21)	-0.02	(0.04)	-0.17	(0.03)	**0.45**	(0.21)	**0.15**	[illegible]	**-0.60**	(0.21)
United Kingdom	0.17	(0.04)	0.03	(0.04)	0.14	(0.03)	0.19	(0.05)	-0.05	(0.05)	0.05	(0.11)	0.16	(0.04)	0.17	(0.05)	-0.11	(0.12)	-0.01	[illegible]	0.12	(0.12)
United States	0.08	(0.04)	0.02	(0.04)	0.06	(0.03)	0.07	(0.04)	-0.01	(0.04)	-0.05	(0.05)	0.08	(0.04)	0.07	(0.05)	-0.13	(0.07)	0.01	[illegible]	0.12	(0.07)
OECD average	-0.06	(0.01)	**-0.03**	(0.01)	0.01	(0.00)	-0.06	(0.01)	**0.04**	(0.01)	0.00	(0.02)	-0.01	(0.01)	-0.01	(0.01)	0.03	(0.02)	0.00	[illegible]	-0.03	(0.02)
Partners																						
Albania	m	m	m	m	0.38	(0.03)	m	m	m	m	0.35	(0.05)	0.41	(0.03)	0.37	(0.06)	-0.06	(0.06)	0.04	[illegible]	0.02	(0.08)
Argentina	-0.53	(0.04)	-0.03	(0.05)	-0.50	(0.03)	-0.49	(0.09)	-0.01	(0.10)	-0.18	(0.11)	-0.55	(0.03)	-0.54	(0.05)	**0.36**	(0.12)	-0.01	[illegible]	**-0.35**	(0.10)
Brazil	-0.46	(0.05)	**-0.11**	(0.05)	-0.34	(0.02)	c	c	c	c	-0.32	(0.13)	-0.34	(0.03)	-0.36	(0.03)	0.02	(0.13)	0.01	[illegible]	-0.04	(0.13)
Bulgaria	c	c	c	c	-0.18	(0.03)	c	c	c	c	-0.19	(0.14)	-0.20	(0.04)	-0.22	(0.05)	0.01	(0.14)	0.02	[illegible]	-0.03	(0.15)
Colombia	-0.17	(0.04)	**-0.12**	(0.04)	-0.05	(0.02)	c	c	c	c	-0.02	(0.06)	-0.08	(0.04)	-0.05	(0.03)	0.06	(0.08)	-0.03	[illegible]	-0.03	(0.07)
Costa Rica	0.11	(0.06)	0.08	(0.06)	0.03	(0.03)	c	c	c	c	0.01	(0.05)	0.03	(0.04)	0.07	(0.07)	-0.02	(0.07)	-0.04	[illegible]	0.06	(0.09)
Croatia	-0.19	(0.04)	**-0.08**	(0.03)	-0.11	(0.03)	c	c	c	c	c	c	-0.13	(0.04)	-0.11	(0.07)	c	c	-0.02	[illegible]	c	c
Cyprus*	-0.16	(0.01)	**0.04**	(0.02)	-0.20	(0.00)	-0.17	(0.02)	-0.03	(0.03)	-0.17	(0.00)	-0.17	(0.00)	-0.24	(0.00)	-0.01	(0.00)	**0.07**	[illegible]	**-0.07**	(0.00)
Hong Kong-China	0.29	(0.03)	0.01	(0.02)	0.29	(0.03)	0.28	(0.04)	0.01	(0.04)	c	c	c	c	0.29	(0.02)	c	c	c	c	c	c
Indonesia	c	c	c	c	0.11	(0.03)	c	c	c	c	0.19	(0.04)	0.13	(0.03)	0.00	(0.05)	0.06	(0.05)	**0.13**	[illegible]	**-0.19**	(0.07)
Jordan	-0.23	(0.04)	-0.01	(0.03)	-0.23	(0.03)	-0.18	(0.11)	-0.05	(0.10)	-0.19	(0.07)	-0.33	(0.05)	-0.15	(0.05)	0.14	(0.09)	**-0.18**	[illegible]	0.04	(0.08)
Kazakhstan	0.62	(0.05)	**-0.12**	(0.05)	0.74	(0.03)	0.65	(0.07)	0.08	(0.06)	0.75	(0.05)	0.72	(0.06)	0.69	(0.06)	0.03	(0.08)	0.03	[illegible]	-0.06	(0.08)
Latvia	0.14	(0.06)	0.06	(0.06)	0.06	(0.04)	0.30	(0.16)	-0.25	(0.16)	0.16	(0.07)	0.11	(0.05)	-0.02	(0.07)	0.05	(0.09)	0.13	[illegible]	-0.18	(0.09)
Liechtenstein	0.25	(0.02)	0.01	(0.03)	0.25	(0.01)	c	c	c	c	c	c	0.24	(0.01)	c	c	c	c	c	c	c	c
Lithuania	0.39	(0.07)	0.11	(0.06)	0.28	(0.03)	c	c	c	c	0.29	(0.06)	0.20	(0.05)	0.36	(0.04)	0.08	(0.08)	**-0.16**	[illegible]	0.08	(0.07)
Macao-China	0.11	(0.00)	**0.03**	(0.01)	0.10	(0.01)	0.03	(0.01)	**0.07**	(0.01)	c	c	c	c	0.10	(0.00)	c	c	c	c	c	c
Malaysia	-0.23	(0.05)	-0.03	(0.05)	-0.21	(0.02)	c	c	c	c	-0.29	(0.05)	-0.23	(0.03)	-0.14	(0.06)	-0.06	(0.06)	-0.09	[illegible]	0.15	(0.08)
Montenegro	-0.05	(0.02)	-0.03	(0.02)	-0.02	(0.00)	c	c	c	c	c	c	0.02	(0.00)	-0.11	(0.00)	c	c	**0.13**	[illegible]	c	c
Peru	-0.08	(0.05)	-0.05	(0.05)	-0.02	(0.02)	c	c	c	c	-0.04	(0.05)	-0.04	(0.03)	-0.03	(0.04)	0.00	(0.05)	-0.01	[illegible]	0.01	(0.06)
Qatar	-0.20	(0.00)	**0.25**	(0.01)	-0.52	(0.00)	-0.08	(0.01)	**-0.44**	(0.01)	-0.43	(0.00)	-0.42	(0.00)	-0.24	(0.00)	**-0.01**	(0.00)	**-0.18**	[illegible]	**0.20**	(0.00)
Romania	c	c	c	c	0.01	(0.04)	c	c	c	c	-0.18	(0.11)	0.03	(0.04)	0.01	(0.07)	-0.21	(0.13)	0.02	[illegible]	0.19	(0.13)
Russian Federation	0.29	(0.05)	**-0.07**	(0.03)	0.35	(0.03)	0.31	(0.09)	0.04	(0.09)	0.56	(0.07)	0.23	(0.05)	0.34	(0.05)	**0.33**	(0.08)	-0.10	[illegible]	**-0.22**	(0.08)
Serbia	-0.16	(0.05)	0.00	(0.04)	-0.16	(0.03)	-0.08	(0.10)	-0.08	(0.09)	c	c	-0.19	(0.05)	-0.11	(0.05)	c	c	-0.08	[illegible]	c	c
Shanghai-China	0.34	(0.10)	**-0.23**	(0.10)	0.58	(0.02)	c	c	c	c	c	c	c	c	0.57	(0.03)	c	c	c	c	c	c
Singapore	0.24	(0.01)	**0.04**	(0.01)	0.26	(0.01)	0.22	(0.01)	**0.04**	(0.01)	c	c	c	c	0.20	(0.00)	c	c	c	c	c	c
Chinese Taipei	-0.17	(0.05)	**-0.17**	(0.06)	0.01	(0.03)	c	c	c	c	c	c	-0.03	(0.04)	0.01	(0.03)	c	c	-0.04	[illegible]	c	c
Thailand	0.10	(0.14)	0.03	(0.14)	0.01	(0.02)	c	c	c	c	0.13	(0.05)	0.09	(0.02)	-0.01	(0.03)	0.04	(0.05)	**0.09**	[illegible]	**-0.14**	(0.06)
Tunisia	c	c	c	c	-0.43	(0.02)	c	c	c	c	-0.23	(0.13)	-0.42	(0.02)	-0.50	(0.05)	0.19	(0.13)	0.08	[illegible]	**-0.27**	(0.14)
United Arab Emirates	0.10	(0.03)	**0.16**	(0.03)	-0.08	(0.03)	0.18	(0.04)	**-0.25**	(0.05)	0.03	(0.05)	-0.10	(0.04)	0.08	(0.03)	0.13	(0.07)	**-0.18**	[illegible]	0.05	(0.06)
Uruguay	c	c	c	c	-0.16	(0.03)	c	c	c	c	-0.20	(0.10)	-0.17	(0.03)	-0.16	(0.05)	-0.03	(0.10)	0.00	[illegible]	0.04	(0.11)
Viet Nam	c	c	c	c	0.36	(0.02)	c	c	c	c	0.38	(0.03)	0.43	(0.03)	0.25	(0.05)	-0.06	(0.04)	**0.18**	[illegible]	**-0.13**	(0.06)

Note: Values that are statistically significant are indicated in bold (see Annex A3).
1. ESCS refers to the *PISA index of economic, social and cultural status.*
2. A socio-economically disadvantaged school is one whose students' mean ESCS is statistically significantly below the mean ESCS of the country/economy; [illegible]n average school is one where there is no difference between the students' and the country's/economy's mean ESCS; and an advantaged school is one whose students' mean E[illegible]CS is statistically significantly above the country/economy mean.
* See notes at the beginning of this Annex.

StatLink http://dx.doi.org/10.1787/888932964946

[Part 1/3]

Impact of socio-economic status after accounting for student characteristics and educational resources at school

Table II.4.11 *Results based on students' self-reports*

	Observed impact of ESCS[1] on mathematics performance				...after accounting for student's gender, immigrant background, language spoken at home and school location				...and school climate: parental pressure to achieve[2]				...and school disciplinary climate[3]			
	Student's socio-economic status		School socio-economic profile		Student's socio-economic status		School socio-economic profile		Student's socio-economic status		School socio-economic profile		Student's socio-economic status		School socio-economic profile	
	Coef.	S.E.	Coef.	S.E.	Coef.	S.E.	Coef.	S.E.	Coef.	S.E.	Coef.	S.E.	Coef.	S.E.	Coef.	S.E.
OECD																
Australia	24	(1.2)	64	(3.8)	24	(1.1)	58	(3.8)	24	(1.1)	53	(3.8)	24	(1.1)	43	(4.3)
Austria	15	(1.6)	86	(5.5)	10	(2.0)	87	(5.0)	10	(2.0)	86	(5.7)	11	(1.9)	72	(5.3)
Belgium	18	(1.4)	101	(5.4)	16	(1.5)	99	(5.9)	16	(1.5)	97	(6.2)	16	(1.5)	76	(5.8)
Canada	23	(1.1)	41	(4.8)	23	(1.1)	38	(4.7)	23	(1.1)	32	(5.2)	23	(1.1)	27	(4.5)
Chile	9	(1.2)	46	(2.4)	9	(1.2)	49	(2.6)	9	(1.2)	44	(2.8)	9	(1.3)	42	(3.3)
Czech Republic	14	(2.0)	127	(6.2)	14	(2.0)	133	(6.4)	14	(2.0)	129	(6.7)	14	(2.0)	112	(6.7)
Denmark	31	(1.6)	39	(4.3)	29	(1.6)	35	(4.9)	29	(1.7)	36	(4.9)	30	(1.7)	25	(5.1)
Estonia	20	(1.6)	39	(5.2)	20	(1.6)	45	(5.8)	20	(1.6)	45	(5.8)	20	(1.8)	45	(6.0)
Finland	30	(1.6)	28	(6.7)	27	(1.7)	38	(6.7)	27	(1.7)	38	(6.7)	28	(1.7)	24	(5.9)
France	w	w	w	w	w	w	w	w	w	w	w	w	w	w	w	w
Germany	11	(1.3)	104	(5.5)	8	(1.5)	108	(6.1)	8	(1.5)	111	(6.5)	8	(1.5)	94	(6.2)
Greece	18	(1.4)	54	(4.1)	17	(1.5)	56	(4.6)	17	(1.5)	54	(5.0)	17	(1.5)	48	(5.0)
Hungary	7	(1.4)	96	(4.9)	6	(1.3)	101	(5.1)	6	(1.3)	94	(5.7)	6	(1.3)	86	(6.0)
Iceland	24	(2.5)	37	(5.1)	23	(2.6)	33	(6.0)	23	(2.6)	34	(6.5)	22	(2.6)	31	(6.3)
Ireland	26	(1.6)	53	(4.6)	26	(1.6)	54	(4.2)	25	(1.7)	50	(5.4)	25	(1.7)	53	(4.6)
Israel	23	(1.9)	98	(7.5)	25	(1.8)	92	(7.1)	25	(1.9)	91	(7.2)	25	(1.9)	85	(6.4)
Italy	7	(0.7)	83	(3.8)	5	(0.8)	86	(3.9)	5	(0.9)	82	(4.3)	5	(0.8)	67	(4.9)
Japan	4	(1.8)	149	(6.8)	4	(1.7)	147	(7.6)	4	(1.7)	129	(9.5)	4	(1.7)	117	(10.0)
Korea	15	(2.0)	113	(10.5)	15	(2.0)	111	(10.4)	15	(2.0)	102	(11.1)	14	(2.1)	81	(8.3)
Luxembourg	18	(1.4)	69	(2.0)	14	(1.6)	66	(2.2)	14	(1.6)	67	(2.3)	14	(1.6)	63	(2.4)
Mexico	5	(0.5)	29	(1.3)	5	(0.5)	28	(1.6)	5	(0.5)	28	(1.6)	5	(0.5)	26	(1.6)
Netherlands	8	(1.7)	146	(10.1)	6	(1.8)	148	(11.0)	6	(1.8)	141	(14.8)	7	(1.9)	124	(14.1)
New Zealand	35	(2.0)	66	(5.2)	33	(2.3)	65	(5.1)	33	(2.3)	58	(5.7)	33	(2.3)	53	(6.3)
Norway	26	(2.3)	46	(9.9)	24	(2.2)	40	(10.9)	24	(2.2)	41	(11.8)	24	(2.2)	38	(9.2)
Poland	31	(1.9)	38	(7.1)	31	(1.9)	41	(10.0)	31	(1.9)	41	(10.1)	31	(1.9)	37	(8.0)
Portugal	23	(1.4)	33	(4.1)	23	(1.4)	39	(3.9)	23	(1.4)	41	(4.3)	23	(1.4)	39	(4.0)
Slovak Republic	23	(1.9)	81	(6.4)	21	(2.0)	81	(6.5)	21	(2.0)	80	(6.8)	21	(2.0)	75	(7.8)
Slovenia	4	(1.6)	121	(3.6)	1	(1.5)	125	(3.7)	1	(1.5)	124	(4.0)	1	(1.6)	108	(4.6)
Spain	26	(1.0)	27	(3.0)	25	(1.1)	25	(3.2)	25	(1.1)	24	(3.5)	25	(1.1)	20	(3.4)
Sweden	28	(2.0)	43	(6.9)	24	(2.0)	32	(7.1)	24	(2.0)	32	(7.6)	24	(2.0)	27	(7.2)
Switzerland	24	(1.7)	66	(6.5)	17	(1.8)	68	(6.5)	18	(1.9)	65	(6.6)	17	(1.9)	65	(6.3)
Turkey	6	(1.0)	83	(6.8)	6	(1.1)	90	(6.1)	6	(1.1)	89	(6.7)	6	(1.1)	72	(5.3)
United Kingdom	23	(1.6)	73	(6.8)	24	(1.7)	75	(7.1)	24	(1.7)	73	(8.1)	24	(1.7)	66	(9.2)
United States	24	(1.8)	41	(5.0)	25	(1.9)	42	(5.2)	26	(2.0)	39	(6.5)	25	(2.0)	34	(6.2)
OECD average	19	(0.3)	72	(1.0)	18	(0.3)	72	(1.1)	18	(0.3)	70	(1.2)	18	(0.3)	61	(1.1)
Partners																
Albania	m	m	m	m	m	m	m	m	m	m	m	m	m	m	m	m
Argentina	9	(1.1)	49	(5.7)	9	(1.2)	49	(5.3)	9	(1.2)	47	(5.1)	9	(1.2)	41	(5.4)
Brazil	8	(0.7)	46	(3.2)	8	(0.7)	50	(3.3)	8	(0.7)	51	(3.4)	8	(0.7)	47	(3.0)
Bulgaria	11	(1.5)	70	(6.0)	12	(1.5)	71	(6.9)	12	(1.5)	67	(8.4)	11	(1.5)	57	(7.2)
Colombia	11	(1.2)	35	(3.4)	10	(1.2)	40	(3.7)	10	(1.2)	40	(3.7)	10	(1.2)	37	(4.1)
Costa Rica	10	(0.9)	34	(3.0)	9	(0.9)	36	(3.7)	9	(0.9)	36	(3.8)	9	(0.9)	31	(3.6)
Croatia	12	(1.5)	89	(8.0)	10	(1.5)	97	(8.2)	10	(1.5)	95	(8.9)	10	(1.5)	67	(8.0)
Cyprus*	20	(1.8)	72	(3.1)	20	(1.7)	80	(4.0)	20	(1.8)	78	(4.2)	20	(1.8)	73	(4.4)
Hong Kong-China	5	(1.4)	65	(7.0)	5	(1.4)	66	(6.6)	5	(1.4)	64	(6.1)	5	(1.4)	59	(7.1)
Indonesia	5	(1.0)	37	(6.1)	6	(1.0)	38	(8.3)	6	(1.0)	38	(8.3)	6	(1.1)	39	(8.0)
Jordan	11	(1.3)	46	(9.0)	13	(1.2)	40	(9.6)	13	(1.3)	40	(9.9)	13	(1.3)	39	(7.4)
Kazakhstan	15	(1.7)	44	(8.8)	15	(1.7)	50	(9.3)	15	(1.7)	49	(9.5)	15	(1.7)	41	(9.8)
Latvia	21	(1.8)	42	(4.5)	22	(1.8)	46	(6.0)	22	(1.8)	42	(6.1)	22	(1.8)	43	(5.7)
Liechtenstein	8	(6.3)	129	(12.6)	4	(7.2)	120	(12.9)	4	(7.0)	94	(15.5)	2	(6.8)	118	(13.2)
Lithuania	19	(1.5)	65	(4.6)	19	(1.5)	74	(6.6)	18	(1.5)	75	(6.5)	18	(1.5)	67	(6.0)
Macao-China	7	(1.8)	38	(3.1)	9	(1.9)	48	(3.5)	9	(1.9)	49	(3.5)	9	(1.7)	34	(3.5)
Malaysia	15	(1.4)	49	(5.2)	15	(1.4)	41	(5.8)	15	(1.4)	38	(5.6)	15	(1.5)	30	(5.6)
Montenegro	12	(1.3)	100	(3.5)	12	(1.3)	101	(3.6)	12	(1.3)	102	(3.6)	12	(1.3)	99	(3.7)
Peru	10	(1.3)	48	(2.5)	10	(1.2)	46	(4.0)	10	(1.2)	45	(4.1)	9	(1.2)	45	(4.0)
Qatar	8	(1.4)	75	(2.3)	9	(1.3)	50	(2.2)	10	(1.3)	52	(2.3)	9	(1.3)	42	(2.2)
Romania	16	(1.8)	57	(6.3)	15	(1.8)	63	(7.2)	16	(1.8)	64	(7.3)	15	(1.8)	49	(8.2)
Russian Federation	26	(2.2)	42	(7.3)	26	(2.1)	41	(7.6)	26	(2.2)	43	(7.7)	26	(2.2)	28	(7.9)
Serbia	9	(1.3)	101	(6.3)	9	(1.2)	103	(7.7)	8	(1.2)	95	(7.4)	9	(1.2)	86	(7.9)
Shanghai-China	10	(1.6)	88	(5.3)	9	(1.6)	87	(5.3)	9	(1.6)	88	(5.5)	9	(1.6)	67	(5.9)
Singapore	21	(1.7)	85	(5.8)	20	(2.0)	91	(5.7)	20	(2.0)	89	(6.6)	21	(2.0)	60	(6.5)
Chinese Taipei	27	(1.7)	124	(7.1)	26	(1.8)	118	(8.2)	26	(1.8)	116	(8.4)	25	(2.0)	91	(10.4)
Thailand	8	(1.2)	33	(4.3)	10	(1.2)	44	(5.1)	10	(1.2)	42	(5.4)	10	(1.2)	39	(5.2)
Tunisia	6	(0.9)	45	(6.1)	6	(0.9)	47	(6.0)	5	(0.9)	46	(5.7)	6	(0.9)	47	(5.5)
United Arab Emirates	12	(1.3)	71	(5.8)	14	(1.2)	56	(5.1)	14	(1.2)	55	(5.1)	14	(1.2)	50	(4.8)
Uruguay	15	(1.2)	52	(3.0)	15	(1.3)	51	(3.2)	15	(1.3)	51	(3.3)	15	(1.3)	43	(4.2)
Viet Nam	8	(1.3)	50	(5.2)	7	(1.3)	65	(7.9)	7	(1.3)	60	(7.6)	7	(1.3)	66	(6.2)

Notes: Values that are statistically significant are indicated in bold (see Annex A3).

All the models presented here include student- and school-level socio-economic status. Then individual characteristics (gender, immigrant background and language at home) and school location are included. All of these variables are kept for each model. School- and student-level variables measuring availability and quality of resources are introduced one group at a time. At the end, all variables are combined in a single model: The "combined model". Some students, schools and countries do not have data for some of these variables, therefore they are not included in the combined model. Then a baseline model, with only student- and school-level socio-economic status is presented, where all students, schools and countries without data have been omitted, which allows for a more direct comparison with the estimates in the combined model.

1. ESCS refers to the *PISA index of economic, social and cultural status.*
2. Parental pressure to achieve is based on the school-level index (PARPRES).
3. School climate includes the following variables: xdisclim (aggregated to the school level from the student questionnaire), studclim and teacclim, both school-level indices measuring student and teacher factors related to school disciplinary climate.
4. Opportunity to learn includes the following variables: index of exposure to formal mathematics, index to exposure to word problems, index of exposure to applied mathematics (the simple index and the index squared), all of these indices.
5. Opportunity to learn at the school level includes all of the same opportunity-to-learn indices at both the student and the school levels (except applied mathematics squared).
6. Teacher profile includes the following variables: student-teacher ratio, composition and qualifications of mathematics teaching staff, proportion of certified teachers and teacher shortage.
7. School educational resources and physical infrastructure include: shortage of educational physical infrastructure and shortage of educational resources in school.
8. School proportion of early school-leavers includes: behavioural outcomes – dropout.
* See notes at the beginning of this Annex.

StatLink ᴹ᠍᠌ᴹ᠍ http://dx.doi.org/10.1787/888932964946

[Part 2/3]
Impact of socio-economic status after accounting for student characteristics and educational resources at school

Table II.4.11   *Results based on students' self-reports*

	...and opportunity to learn (student level)[4]				...and opportunity to learn (school level)[5]				...and teacher profile[6]				...and school educational resources and physical infrastructure[7]			
	Student's socio-economic status		School socio-economic profile		Student's socio-economic status		School socio-economic profile		Student's socio-economic status		School socio-economic profile		Student's socio-economic status		School socio-economic profile	
	Coef.	S.E.	Coef.	S.E.	Coef.	S.E.	Coef.	S.E.	Coef.	S.E.	Coef.	S.E.	Coef.	S.E.	Coef.	S.E.
OECD																
Australia	8	(1.5)	38	(3.8)	9	(1.4)	26	(4.3)	24	(1.2)	56	(4.5)	24	(1.1)	8	(4.5)
Austria	4	(2.1)	60	(5.6)	5	(2.1)	37	(8.2)	9	(2.4)	79	(7.8)	9	(2.1)	8	(6.1)
Belgium	6	(1.5)	72	(5.0)	7	(1.5)	66	(7.6)	17	(1.8)	75	(8.6)	16	(1.5)	8	(5.8)
Canada	12	(1.3)	30	(4.4)	12	(1.3)	22	(4.8)	24	(1.4)	36	(5.4)	23	(1.1)	8	(4.7)
Chile	5	(1.7)	37	(2.9)	6	(1.6)	19	(4.2)	9	(1.4)	48	(2.9)	9	(1.2)	8	(2.8)
Czech Republic	7	(2.5)	97	(7.6)	7	(2.4)	83	(10.1)	14	(2.1)	118	(7.3)	14	(2.0)	14	(6.5)
Denmark	20	(1.9)	18	(4.8)	20	(1.9)	19	(5.3)	m	m	m	m	30	(1.7)	4	(5.3)
Estonia	13	(2.0)	46	(5.8)	13	(2.0)	41	(6.1)	20	(1.7)	48	(5.8)	20	(1.7)	4	(5.9)
Finland	17	(1.7)	27	(6.2)	17	(1.7)	30	(5.9)	27	(1.6)	30	(5.9)	28	(1.6)	9	(6.9)
France	w	w	w	w	w	w	w	w	w	w	w	w	w	w	w	w
Germany	2	(2.1)	74	(5.6)	4	(2.1)	45	(6.9)	8	(1.9)	103	(8.1)	8	(1.5)	19	(6.1)
Greece	14	(1.8)	49	(5.2)	15	(1.8)	34	(6.2)	16	(2.0)	57	(6.1)	17	(1.5)	17	(4.7)
Hungary	2	(1.6)	84	(4.9)	2	(1.6)	60	(6.2)	m	m	m	m	6	(1.3)	12	(5.1)
Iceland	20	(2.8)	19	(6.6)	20	(2.8)	16	(7.5)	24	(3.0)	39	(7.0)	22	(2.7)	34	(6.3)
Ireland	16	(1.7)	42	(4.4)	16	(1.7)	40	(5.3)	25	(1.9)	58	(5.3)	25	(1.8)	51	(4.6)
Israel	18	(2.3)	82	(6.8)	18	(2.3)	68	(8.4)	25	(2.2)	101	(8.3)	25	(2.0)	96	(6.8)
Italy	2	(1.1)	66	(3.6)	3	(1.0)	40	(4.4)	5	(0.9)	71	(5.1)	5	(0.8)	35	(4.0)
Japan	0	(2.1)	112	(8.3)	1	(2.1)	59	(11.5)	m	m	m	m	4	(1.7)	48	(7.8)
Korea	5	(2.0)	71	(8.1)	7	(2.0)	12	(9.6)	15	(2.1)	120	(11.9)	14	(2.1)	99	(10.1)
Luxembourg	8	(1.9)	56	(3.0)	9	(1.8)	41	(5.3)	14	(1.6)	66	(2.6)	14	(1.6)	58	(2.2)
Mexico	3	(0.7)	22	(1.7)	3	(0.7)	15	(2.0)	5	(0.8)	26	(2.7)	5	(0.5)	27	(1.7)
Netherlands	-3	(2.2)	91	(11.8)	0	(2.2)	29	(15.2)	7	(2.5)	113	(19.9)	6	(1.8)	65	(10.9)
New Zealand	17	(2.4)	44	(4.5)	17	(2.4)	40	(5.7)	32	(2.4)	68	(6.7)	33	(2.3)	55	(5.0)
Norway	25	(2.8)	32	(11.5)	25	(2.8)	28	(11.3)	24	(2.4)	42	(12.3)	24	(2.3)	46	(10.6)
Poland	24	(1.8)	35	(8.8)	24	(1.9)	28	(8.9)	32	(2.0)	40	(11.7)	31	(1.9)	40	(9.6)
Portugal	17	(1.5)	35	(4.2)	17	(1.5)	26	(4.5)	24	(1.6)	37	(5.6)	23	(1.4)	39	(4.3)
Slovak Republic	17	(2.3)	69	(6.8)	17	(2.2)	50	(8.9)	23	(2.5)	83	(7.7)	21	(2.0)	81	(6.5)
Slovenia	0	(2.1)	113	(4.3)	0	(2.0)	90	(5.4)	1	(1.6)	126	(4.2)	1	(1.6)	26	(4.1)
Spain	13	(1.2)	20	(2.9)	13	(1.2)	18	(3.8)	24	(1.2)	22	(4.1)	25	(1.1)	25	(3.4)
Sweden	22	(2.5)	26	(7.4)	22	(2.5)	22	(8.0)	25	(2.4)	29	(7.3)	24	(2.0)	32	(7.2)
Switzerland	12	(1.9)	46	(5.4)	12	(1.8)	45	(5.7)	16	(1.9)	61	(7.0)	17	(1.9)	68	(6.5)
Turkey	3	(1.5)	82	(6.1)	4	(1.4)	57	(6.3)	6	(1.2)	93	(7.1)	6	(1.1)	90	(6.9)
United Kingdom	9	(1.8)	51	(5.4)	10	(1.8)	45	(6.5)	25	(1.9)	70	(8.2)	24	(1.7)	75	(6.9)
United States	14	(2.1)	32	(4.7)	14	(2.1)	24	(6.1)	25	(2.2)	41	(5.6)	25	(2.0)	40	(5.4)
OECD average	11	(0.3)	55	(1.0)	11	(0.3)	39	(1.3)	18	(0.3)	67	(1.4)	18	(0.3)	73	(1.1)
Partners																
Albania	m	m	m	m	m	m	m	m	m	m	m	m	m	m	m	m
Argentina	6	(1.4)	39	(5.4)	6	(1.4)	34	(6.6)	9	(1.4)	56	(5.4)	9	(1.2)	47	(6.2)
Brazil	4	(0.9)	40	(3.0)	5	(0.9)	21	(3.6)	m	m	m	m	8	(0.7)	49	(3.6)
Bulgaria	7	(1.7)	64	(7.2)	7	(1.8)	46	(10.1)	m	m	m	m	12	(1.5)	70	(7.1)
Colombia	3	(1.5)	31	(3.2)	3	(1.5)	26	(3.9)	9	(1.8)	40	(4.6)	10	(1.2)	39	(3.7)
Costa Rica	7	(1.4)	29	(3.5)	7	(1.3)	19	(4.0)	8	(1.3)	32	(5.4)	9	(0.9)	33	(3.7)
Croatia	7	(1.8)	81	(7.9)	7	(1.8)	51	(7.3)	12	(1.8)	112	(11.5)	11	(1.5)	98	(8.1)
Cyprus*	15	(2.0)	59	(4.6)	15	(2.0)	22	(5.6)	21	(1.9)	64	(5.0)	21	(1.8)	78	(4.2)
Hong Kong-China	0	(1.8)	65	(5.9)	1	(1.8)	52	(5.9)	5	(1.4)	61	(7.0)	5	(1.4)	67	(6.7)
Indonesia	5	(1.6)	32	(7.3)	6	(1.5)	13	(6.8)	5	(1.1)	21	(8.1)	6	(1.0)	35	(7.1)
Jordan	9	(1.4)	39	(9.2)	9	(1.4)	33	(8.4)	12	(1.4)	49	(7.1)	13	(1.2)	40	(9.9)
Kazakhstan	11	(2.1)	47	(9.2)	11	(2.1)	35	(9.4)	14	(1.9)	52	(9.2)	15	(1.7)	50	(9.3)
Latvia	15	(2.3)	43	(6.1)	16	(2.3)	40	(6.6)	20	(2.3)	47	(8.4)	22	(1.8)	47	(5.8)
Liechtenstein	0	(7.9)	64	(25.6)	5	(7.0)	-8	(26.7)	4	(6.0)	32	(16.5)	3	(6.9)	87	(13.5)
Lithuania	14	(1.7)	62	(6.6)	14	(1.7)	52	(7.3)	17	(1.8)	76	(7.9)	19	(1.5)	74	(6.7)
Macao-China	2	(2.0)	41	(4.5)	4	(1.8)	19	(4.5)	9	(1.8)	43	(3.7)	9	(1.9)	47	(3.5)
Malaysia	9	(1.7)	33	(5.6)	10	(1.7)	16	(6.0)	15	(1.7)	37	(6.6)	15	(1.4)	41	(5.7)
Montenegro	8	(1.6)	94	(4.1)	8	(1.6)	67	(5.5)	11	(1.8)	90	(6.9)	12	(1.3)	101	(3.6)
Peru	6	(1.4)	35	(3.7)	6	(1.4)	23	(4.3)	9	(1.4)	44	(5.0)	10	(1.2)	46	(4.0)
Qatar	4	(1.5)	49	(3.1)	5	(1.5)	40	(3.2)	8	(1.4)	47	(2.7)	9	(1.3)	52	(2.3)
Romania	12	(1.9)	53	(7.2)	12	(1.9)	40	(8.6)	15	(1.8)	66	(6.7)	15	(1.8)	63	(7.2)
Russian Federation	23	(2.5)	35	(8.0)	23	(2.5)	31	(9.3)	25	(2.3)	39	(7.9)	26	(2.1)	41	(7.8)
Serbia	7	(1.7)	86	(7.8)	7	(1.6)	68	(8.6)	7	(2.0)	103	(16.6)	9	(1.3)	102	(7.7)
Shanghai-China	7	(1.8)	73	(5.1)	8	(1.8)	53	(6.3)	9	(1.6)	79	(5.7)	9	(1.6)	87	(5.5)
Singapore	4	(2.0)	65	(4.5)	5	(2.0)	27	(5.5)	20	(2.0)	87	(5.2)	22	(2.1)	84	(5.8)
Chinese Taipei	14	(1.9)	98	(6.7)	15	(1.9)	59	(9.8)	26	(2.1)	90	(11.5)	25	(2.0)	118	(8.6)
Thailand	6	(1.4)	37	(5.5)	6	(1.4)	23	(6.5)	10	(1.2)	43	(5.8)	10	(1.2)	44	(5.2)
Tunisia	5	(1.3)	47	(5.7)	5	(1.3)	38	(5.3)	6	(1.0)	43	(6.7)	6	(0.9)	47	(6.1)
United Arab Emirates	9	(1.4)	44	(4.6)	9	(1.4)	36	(4.8)	m	m	m	m	14	(1.2)	54	(5.1)
Uruguay	10	(1.5)	35	(3.6)	11	(1.5)	22	(4.6)	15	(1.3)	49	(4.0)	15	(1.3)	47	(3.6)
Viet Nam	5	(1.6)	52	(7.1)	5	(1.6)	22	(7.7)	8	(1.4)	65	(8.3)	7	(1.3)	65	(7.9)

Notes: Values that are statistically significant are indicated in bold (see Annex A3).
All the models presented here include student- and school-level socio-economic status. Then individual characteristics (gender, immigrant background and language at home) and school location are included. All of these variables are kept for each model. School- and student-level variables measuring availability and quality of resources are introduced one group at a time. At the end, all variables are combined in a single model: The "combined model". Some students, schools and countries do not have data for some of these variables, therefore they are not included in the combined model. Then a baseline model, with only student- and school-level socio-economic status is presented, where all students, schools and countries without data have been omitted, which allows for a more direct comparison with the estimates in the combined model.
1. ESCS refers to the *PISA index of economic, social and cultural status*.
2. Parental pressure to achieve is based on the school-level index (PARPRES).
3. School climate includes the following variables: xdisclim (aggregated to the school level from the student questionnaire), studclim and teacclim, both school-level indices measuring student and teacher factors related to school disciplinary climate.
4. Opportunity to learn includes the following variables: index of exposure to formal mathematics, index to exposure to word problems, index of exposure to applied mathematics (the simple index and the index squared), all of these indices.
5. Opportunity to learn at the school level includes all of the same opportunity-to-learn indices at both the student and the school levels (except applied mathematics squared).
6. Teacher profile includes the following variables: student-teacher ratio, composition and qualifications of mathematics teaching staff, proportion of certified teachers and teacher shortage.
7. School educational resources and physical infrastructure include: shortage of educational physical infrastructure and shortage of educational resources in school.
8. School proportion of early school-leavers includes: behavioural outcomes – dropout.
* See notes at the beginning of this Annex.
StatLink ⟲ http://dx.doi.org/10.1787/888932964946

[Part 3/3]
Impact of socio-economic status after accounting for student characteristics and educational resources at school

Table II.4.11   *Results based on students' self-reports*

	...and percentage of early school-leavers[8]				Combined model				Original model with all missing observations across variables dropped			
	Student's socio-economic status		School socio-economic profile		Student's socio-economic status		School socio-economic profile		Student's socio-economic status		School socio-economic profile	
	Coef.	S.E.	Coef.	S.E.	Coef.	S.E.	Coef.	S.E.	Coef.	S.E.	Coef.	S.E.
Australia	24	(1.2)	56	(4.0)	9	(1.6)	22	(5.6)	22	(1.8)	66	(5.2)
Austria	11	(2.0)	85	(5.5)	4	(2.7)	28	(14.9)	12	(2.6)	90	(10.5)
Belgium	16	(1.7)	93	(7.4)	7	(2.2)	48	(11.3)	19	(2.1)	102	(7.4)
Canada	24	(1.2)	36	(5.6)	13	(1.8)	20	(6.7)	22	(2.0)	41	(6.2)
Chile	9	(1.3)	48	(2.7)	6	(1.8)	18	(5.4)	10	(2.0)	45	(3.0)
Czech Republic	14	(2.1)	134	(7.4)	7	(2.8)	66	(10.3)	13	(3.0)	120	(7.4)
Denmark	29	(1.7)	33	(4.9)	c	c	c	c	c	c	c	c
Estonia	20	(1.7)	45	(6.0)	13	(2.2)	43	(7.6)	18	(2.4)	42	(6.3)
Finland	27	(1.7)	36	(6.8)	17	(1.8)	28	(5.8)	31	(2.0)	16	(7.5)
France	w	w	w	w	w	w	w	w	w	w	w	w
Germany	9	(1.5)	103	(6.1)	4	(2.5)	44	(8.8)	12	(2.6)	101	(7.3)
Greece	17	(1.5)	44	(4.7)	16	(2.4)	33	(7.8)	19	(2.6)	53	(5.8)
Hungary	6	(1.3)	100	(5.1)	c	c	c	c	c	c	c	c
Iceland	23	(2.6)	34	(6.1)	17	(3.1)	12	(9.7)	23	(3.2)	32	(6.8)
Ireland	26	(1.7)	51	(4.2)	14	(2.0)	37	(8.0)	24	(2.3)	57	(6.4)
Israel	25	(1.8)	94	(7.5)	18	(2.6)	62	(10.5)	27	(2.8)	99	(9.3)
Italy	5	(0.9)	78	(4.6)	3	(1.2)	33	(5.5)	7	(1.3)	76	(5.0)
Japan	4	(1.7)	132	(9.1)	c	c	c	c	c	c	c	c
Korea	14	(2.0)	102	(10.1)	6	(2.1)	14	(10.2)	16	(2.4)	114	(10.3)
Luxembourg	15	(1.8)	64	(2.5)	11	(1.9)	63	(12.1)	18	(2.0)	62	(3.0)
Mexico	5	(0.5)	28	(1.6)	3	(1.1)	15	(3.1)	5	(1.2)	27	(2.6)
Netherlands	6	(1.9)	143	(12.9)	2	(2.9)	20	(17.2)	10	(3.4)	137	(20.8)
New Zealand	33	(2.3)	35	(8.4)	18	(2.3)	24	(8.1)	32	(2.7)	75	(6.2)
Norway	m	m	m	m	c	c	c	c	c	c	c	c
Poland	32	(1.9)	38	(10.7)	25	(2.1)	27	(9.2)	33	(2.3)	33	(9.0)
Portugal	23	(1.4)	41	(4.0)	19	(1.8)	27	(5.6)	25	(2.0)	35	(5.5)
Slovak Republic	21	(2.3)	76	(7.8)	19	(2.9)	45	(10.9)	25	(3.1)	90	(7.8)
Slovenia	1	(1.5)	122	(4.0)	0	(2.3)	85	(5.9)	4	(2.5)	125	(4.8)
Spain	25	(1.1)	21	(3.6)	12	(1.5)	15	(5.3)	24	(1.7)	31	(4.2)
Sweden	24	(2.1)	24	(8.7)	22	(2.9)	18	(11.7)	27	(2.8)	38	(7.9)
Switzerland	m	m	m	m	c	c	c	c	c	c	c	c
Turkey	6	(1.1)	89	(6.7)	4	(1.5)	53	(7.7)	5	(1.6)	87	(7.5)
United Kingdom	24	(1.8)	75	(7.8)	10	(1.9)	44	(9.2)	23	(2.5)	71	(8.7)
United States	25	(2.0)	37	(5.9)	14	(2.3)	25	(7.5)	26	(2.4)	35	(5.8)
OECD average	18	(0.3)	69	(1.2)	11	(0.4)	35	(1.7)	19	(0.5)	69	(1.5)
Albania	m	m	m	m	m	m	m	m	m	m	m	m
Argentina	9	(1.2)	47	(6.5)	8	(2.1)	35	(8.7)	11	(2.3)	51	(4.9)
Brazil	8	(0.8)	47	(3.4)	c	c	c	c	c	c	c	c
Bulgaria	12	(1.5)	66	(7.5)	c	c	c	c	c	c	c	c
Colombia	10	(1.2)	39	(3.9)	3	(2.2)	22	(5.2)	8	(2.5)	38	(4.5)
Costa Rica	10	(1.2)	29	(4.6)	6	(2.7)	14	(7.0)	10	(2.8)	32	(5.5)
Croatia	10	(1.6)	92	(8.5)	8	(2.2)	50	(9.4)	13	(2.3)	104	(11.2)
Cyprus*	20	(1.8)	69	(4.5)	17	(2.3)	23	(7.7)	23	(2.4)	61	(4.7)
Hong Kong-China	5	(1.4)	71	(7.1)	0	(1.8)	48	(5.7)	5	(2.1)	69	(8.1)
Indonesia	7	(1.1)	42	(8.2)	3	(1.8)	8	(8.4)	3	(1.9)	32	(9.3)
Jordan	14	(1.3)	39	(10.0)	8	(1.9)	46	(6.3)	13	(1.9)	63	(10.1)
Kazakhstan	15	(1.7)	50	(9.4)	10	(2.2)	34	(9.1)	12	(2.3)	52	(10.0)
Latvia	22	(1.9)	40	(6.5)	15	(2.9)	39	(9.7)	21	(3.3)	34	(7.6)
Liechtenstein	m	m	m	m	c	c	c	c	c	c	c	c
Lithuania	18	(1.5)	72	(6.7)	14	(1.8)	48	(9.1)	17	(2.0)	64	(5.6)
Macao-China	9	(1.9)	38	(3.7)	3	(1.7)	9	(5.3)	9	(2.2)	36	(5.0)
Malaysia	15	(1.5)	44	(6.4)	10	(2.1)	11	(8.1)	15	(2.3)	51	(7.2)
Montenegro	12	(1.3)	102	(3.3)	8	(2.1)	78	(12.0)	11	(2.3)	90	(6.5)
Peru	10	(1.1)	44	(4.2)	6	(1.7)	23	(5.5)	13	(1.9)	43	(3.9)
Qatar	10	(1.3)	49	(2.6)	5	(1.7)	27	(4.5)	9	(2.1)	65	(4.7)
Romania	15	(1.8)	57	(7.0)	12	(2.0)	39	(9.1)	16	(2.2)	57	(6.5)
Russian Federation	26	(2.2)	41	(7.8)	22	(3.0)	23	(11.4)	27	(3.0)	48	(8.4)
Serbia	9	(1.4)	107	(8.4)	6	(2.6)	29	(15.0)	11	(2.8)	94	(12.9)
Shanghai-China	9	(1.7)	83	(5.8)	6	(1.6)	42	(6.6)	10	(2.0)	88	(5.6)
Singapore	20	(2.0)	88	(5.4)	6	(2.1)	18	(6.2)	20	(2.4)	87	(6.4)
Chinese Taipei	26	(1.8)	119	(8.3)	15	(2.3)	38	(11.3)	27	(2.5)	119	(8.8)
Thailand	10	(1.3)	37	(5.6)	6	(1.4)	26	(6.8)	9	(1.5)	35	(4.7)
Tunisia	5	(1.1)	50	(7.4)	7	(1.7)	39	(7.0)	8	(1.7)	30	(6.2)
United Arab Emirates	15	(1.3)	49	(5.2)	c	c	c	c	c	c	c	c
Uruguay	15	(1.4)	49	(3.8)	11	(1.6)	10	(4.8)	16	(1.7)	44	(3.7)
Viet Nam	8	(1.4)	62	(8.6)	8	(1.7)	23	(9.4)	10	(1.9)	50	(6.4)

Notes: Values that are statistically significant are indicated in bold (see Annex A3).

All the models presented here include student- and school-level socio-economic status. Then individual characteristics (gender, immigrant background and language at home) and school location are included. All of these variables are kept for each model. School- and student-level variables measuring availability and quality of resources are introduced one group at a time. At the end, all variables are combined in a single model: The "combined model". Some students, schools and countries do not have data for some of these variables, therefore they are not included in the combined model. Then a baseline model, with only student- and school-level socio-economic status is presented, where all students, schools and countries without data have been omitted, which allows for a more direct comparison with the estimates in the combined model.

1. ESCS refers to the *PISA index of economic, social and cultural status*.
2. Parental pressure to achieve is based on the school-level index (PARPRES).
3. School climate includes the following variables: xdisclim (aggregated to the school level from the student questionnaire), studclim and teacclim, both school-level indices measuring student and teacher factors related to school disciplinary climate.
4. Opportunity to learn includes the following variables: index of exposure to formal mathematics, index to exposure to word problems, index of exposure to applied mathematics (the simple index and the index squared), all of these indices.
5. Opportunity to learn at the school level includes all of the same opportunity-to-learn indices at both the student and the school levels (except applied mathematics squared).
6. Teacher profile includes the following variables: student-teacher ratio, composition and qualifications of mathematics teaching staff, proportion of certified teachers and teacher shortage.
7. School educational resources and physical infrastructure include: shortage of educational physical infrastructure and shortage of educational resources in school.
8. School proportion of early school-leavers includes: behavioural outcomes – dropout.
* See notes at the beginning of this Annex.

StatLink ⌨ http://dx.doi.org/10.1787/888932964946

[Part 1/3]
Pre-primary school attendance, mathematics performance and students' socio-economic status

Table II.4.12   *Results based on students' self-reports*

	Percentage of students with						Mean ESCS[1]						Average mathematics performance of students with					
	No pre-primary school attendance		Pre-primary school attendance for one year or less		Pre-primary school attendance for more than one year		No pre-primary school attendance		Pre-primary school attendance for one year or less		Pre-primary school attendance for more than one year		No pre-primary school attendance		Pre-primary school attendance for one year or less		Pre-primary school attendance for more than one year	
	%	S.E.	%	S.E.	%	S.E.	Mean score	S.E.	Mean score	S.E.	Mean score	S.E.	Mean index	S.E.	Mean index	S.E.	Mean index	S.E.
OECD																		
Australia	4.5	(0.2)	43.6	(0.6)	51.9	(0.6)	-0.1	(0.0)	0.2	(0.0)	0.4	(0.0)	463	(5.3)	500	(1.8)	516	(2.0)
Austria	1.8	(0.3)	10.5	(0.6)	87.7	(0.7)	-0.8	(0.2)	-0.2	(0.0)	0.1	(0.0)	447	(14.4)	482	(5.9)	510	(2.6)
Belgium	2.3	(0.2)	4.5	(0.3)	93.2	(0.4)	-0.4	(0.1)	-0.2	(0.1)	0.2	(0.0)	437	(8.1)	443	(7.1)	523	(2.2)
Canada	9.0	(0.3)	40.4	(0.7)	50.6	(0.6)	0.1	(0.0)	0.3	(0.0)	0.5	(0.0)	500	(3.2)	512	(1.8)	532	(2.6)
Chile	9.2	(0.7)	56.4	(0.9)	34.4	(0.8)	-1.4	(0.1)	-0.6	(0.0)	-0.3	(0.0)	382	(5.4)	423	(3.0)	436	(3.6)
Czech Republic	3.2	(0.5)	8.7	(0.5)	88.1	(0.8)	-0.4	(0.1)	-0.2	(0.0)	0.0	(0.0)	435	(15.3)	483	(6.8)	504	(2.7)
Denmark	1.0	(0.1)	20.0	(0.6)	79.0	(0.6)	0.0	(0.1)	0.3	(0.0)	0.5	(0.0)	445	(11.4)	469	(3.3)	511	(2.2)
Estonia	7.3	(0.6)	8.7	(0.5)	84.0	(0.8)	-0.2	(0.0)	-0.1	(0.0)	0.2	(0.0)	525	(6.4)	508	(5.4)	522	(2.0)
Finland	2.4	(0.2)	34.9	(1.0)	62.7	(1.0)	-0.1	(0.1)	0.2	(0.0)	0.5	(0.0)	474	(10.7)	512	(2.6)	527	(2.2)
France	1.7	(0.2)	6.3	(0.3)	92.0	(0.4)	-0.7	(0.1)	-0.3	(0.1)	0.0	(0.0)	404	(13.6)	440	(5.6)	504	(2.5)
Germany	3.2	(0.3)	11.0	(0.6)	85.7	(0.7)	-0.1	(0.1)	-0.1	(0.1)	0.3	(0.0)	472	(8.6)	466	(5.2)	529	(3.2)
Greece	4.6	(0.5)	27.4	(0.9)	68.0	(1.0)	-0.8	(0.1)	-0.2	(0.0)	0.0	(0.0)	395	(7.8)	439	(3.9)	463	(2.5)
Hungary	0.5	(0.1)	3.9	(0.4)	95.6	(0.4)	c	c	-0.5	(0.0)	-0.2	(0.0)	c	c	433	(10.1)	480	(3.2)
Iceland	2.0	(0.2)	3.2	(0.3)	94.7	(0.4)	0.1	(0.1)	0.5	(0.1)	0.8	(0.0)	450	(12.1)	463	(9.4)	497	(1.7)
Ireland	13.6	(0.7)	43.6	(0.9)	42.8	(0.9)	-0.2	(0.0)	0.1	(0.0)	0.3	(0.0)	491	(4.2)	506	(2.8)	503	(2.7)
Israel	2.1	(0.2)	16.4	(0.8)	81.5	(0.8)	-0.7	(0.1)	0.0	(0.0)	0.2	(0.0)	383	(10.5)	425	(6.0)	481	(4.8)
Italy	4.3	(0.2)	8.0	(0.2)	87.7	(0.3)	-0.4	(0.0)	-0.1	(0.0)	0.0	(0.0)	429	(4.4)	454	(3.3)	492	(2.1)
Japan	0.8	(0.1)	2.2	(0.2)	96.9	(0.2)	-0.1	(0.1)	-0.3	(0.1)	-0.1	(0.0)	506	(18.9)	489	(8.0)	540	(3.5)
Korea	4.5	(0.4)	12.6	(0.7)	82.8	(0.9)	-0.2	(0.1)	-0.1	(0.0)	-0.1	(0.0)	533	(8.6)	542	(6.9)	557	(4.5)
Luxembourg	4.6	(0.3)	12.8	(0.4)	82.6	(0.5)	-0.4	(0.1)	-0.1	(0.0)	0.1	(0.0)	454	(6.4)	455	(4.4)	499	(1.4)
Mexico	9.4	(0.3)	18.7	(0.3)	71.8	(0.5)	-1.8	(0.0)	-1.3	(0.0)	-1.0	(0.0)	378	(2.5)	411	(1.8)	419	(1.4)
Netherlands	2.3	(0.3)	2.7	(0.3)	95.0	(0.3)	-0.1	(0.2)	0.1	(0.1)	0.2	(0.0)	484	(12.6)	522	(10.1)	526	(3.4)
New Zealand	9.1	(0.6)	19.4	(0.7)	71.5	(0.9)	-0.4	(0.0)	-0.1	(0.0)	0.1	(0.0)	454	(6.9)	491	(4.1)	513	(2.5)
Norway	7.9	(0.4)	5.7	(0.4)	86.4	(0.6)	0.1	(0.0)	0.1	(0.0)	0.5	(0.0)	465	(5.2)	461	(5.8)	496	(2.7)
Poland	2.5	(0.3)	46.4	(1.5)	51.1	(1.5)	-0.6	(0.0)	-0.5	(0.0)	0.1	(0.0)	471	(9.3)	504	(3.0)	532	(4.8)
Portugal	14.9	(0.8)	20.7	(0.8)	64.4	(1.1)	-0.9	(0.0)	-0.7	(0.1)	-0.3	(0.1)	461	(4.9)	465	(5.0)	505	(4.0)
Slovak Republic	6.8	(0.7)	13.1	(0.8)	80.1	(1.1)	-1.0	(0.1)	-0.5	(0.0)	0.0	(0.0)	391	(8.0)	463	(6.3)	494	(3.5)
Slovenia	14.6	(0.5)	12.8	(0.6)	72.6	(0.7)	-0.3	(0.0)	-0.1	(0.0)	0.2	(0.0)	484	(4.2)	484	(4.4)	509	(1.6)
Spain	5.9	(0.2)	8.3	(0.2)	85.9	(0.4)	-0.6	(0.1)	-0.4	(0.0)	-0.1	(0.0)	436	(3.2)	455	(3.9)	492	(1.8)
Sweden	8.1	(0.5)	20.4	(0.8)	71.5	(0.8)	-0.1	(0.1)	0.2	(0.0)	0.3	(0.0)	442	(6.3)	472	(3.0)	489	(2.4)
Switzerland	1.8	(0.2)	25.0	(1.8)	73.1	(1.9)	-0.4	(0.1)	0.1	(0.0)	0.2	(0.0)	458	(13.9)	537	(5.2)	532	(3.2)
Turkey	70.3	(1.4)	21.0	(1.0)	8.7	(0.8)	-1.8	(0.0)	-0.9	(0.0)	-0.3	(0.1)	433	(4.3)	480	(6.0)	495	(10.0)
United Kingdom	4.7	(0.4)	26.0	(0.6)	69.3	(0.6)	-0.1	(0.1)	0.2	(0.0)	0.3	(0.0)	448	(7.8)	481	(3.7)	507	(2.9)
United States	1.4	(0.2)	24.0	(0.9)	74.6	(0.9)	-0.3	(0.2)	-0.2	(0.0)	0.3	(0.0)	454	(11.9)	472	(3.6)	487	(4.1)
OECD average	7.1	(0.1)	18.8	(0.1)	74.1	(0.1)	-0.5	(0.0)	-0.2	(0.0)	0.1	(0.0)	451	(1.6)	475	(0.9)	504	(0.6)
Partners																		
Albania	m	m	m	m	m	m	m	m	m	m	m	m	m	m	m	m	m	m
Argentina	6.1	(0.9)	22.6	(1.0)	71.4	(1.4)	-1.3	(0.1)	-1.1	(0.1)	-0.5	(0.0)	338	(6.3)	367	(4.2)	403	(3.4)
Brazil	18.8	(0.6)	33.4	(0.7)	47.8	(0.8)	-1.6	(0.0)	-1.2	(0.0)	-0.9	(0.0)	368	(2.4)	386	(2.0)	408	(2.8)
Bulgaria	10.2	(0.7)	12.9	(0.6)	76.9	(1.0)	-0.8	(0.1)	-0.4	(0.1)	-0.2	(0.0)	399	(6.6)	427	(6.2)	448	(3.7)
Colombia	14.2	(0.8)	52.5	(0.8)	33.3	(1.1)	-1.9	(0.1)	-1.3	(0.0)	-0.9	(0.1)	351	(3.9)	379	(3.0)	385	(4.1)
Costa Rica	15.4	(0.9)	39.6	(1.1)	45.0	(1.2)	-1.5	(0.1)	-1.1	(0.1)	-0.7	(0.1)	384	(4.4)	408	(3.2)	416	(4.0)
Croatia	26.8	(1.1)	22.4	(0.8)	50.8	(1.1)	-0.7	(0.0)	-0.5	(0.0)	0.0	(0.0)	457	(3.6)	456	(4.0)	487	(5.0)
Cyprus*	3.5	(0.3)	23.4	(0.6)	73.1	(0.7)	-0.2	(0.1)	0.0	(0.0)	0.1	(0.0)	423	(8.0)	427	(2.5)	448	(1.5)
Hong Kong-China	1.6	(0.2)	3.3	(0.3)	95.1	(0.4)	-1.3	(0.1)	-1.2	(0.1)	-0.8	(0.1)	483	(15.5)	503	(8.3)	567	(3.1)
Indonesia	46.1	(2.2)	31.4	(2.0)	22.5	(1.5)	-2.2	(0.0)	-1.6	(0.1)	-1.3	(0.1)	351	(3.7)	390	(4.5)	405	(9.2)
Jordan	24.1	(1.0)	49.4	(0.9)	26.5	(1.0)	-0.8	(0.0)	-0.4	(0.0)	-0.1	(0.0)	370	(3.1)	393	(2.8)	410	(5.6)
Kazakhstan	65.0	(1.7)	11.2	(0.6)	23.8	(1.4)	-0.5	(0.0)	-0.1	(0.0)	0.0	(0.0)	425	(3.1)	434	(5.2)	449	(4.8)
Latvia	11.5	(0.8)	13.3	(0.7)	75.2	(0.9)	-0.6	(0.1)	-0.5	(0.0)	-0.2	(0.0)	485	(6.2)	482	(5.3)	494	(2.9)
Liechtenstein	0.7	(0.5)	8.6	(1.7)	90.7	(1.8)	c	c	c	c	0.3	(0.1)	c	c	c	c	541	(5.0)
Lithuania	30.4	(1.0)	13.3	(0.6)	56.3	(1.0)	-0.5	(0.0)	-0.2	(0.0)	0.1	(0.0)	457	(3.3)	472	(4.3)	493	(3.0)
Macao-China	2.4	(0.2)	11.9	(0.4)	85.7	(0.5)	-0.8	(0.1)	-1.0	(0.0)	-0.9	(0.0)	495	(8.6)	492	(4.0)	547	(1.1)
Malaysia	23.8	(1.3)	28.7	(1.0)	47.6	(1.4)	-1.0	(0.0)	-0.9	(0.0)	-0.5	(0.0)	399	(3.7)	407	(3.0)	441	(4.2)
Montenegro	32.8	(0.6)	24.8	(0.6)	42.3	(0.7)	-0.6	(0.0)	-0.3	(0.0)	0.1	(0.0)	393	(2.0)	408	(2.8)	426	(1.9)
Peru	13.8	(0.7)	25.0	(0.7)	61.1	(1.1)	-2.0	(0.1)	-1.4	(0.0)	-1.0	(0.1)	327	(3.8)	360	(4.0)	384	(4.4)
Qatar	30.5	(0.5)	41.6	(0.5)	27.9	(0.4)	0.0	(0.0)	0.6	(0.0)	0.7	(0.0)	347	(1.6)	382	(1.4)	410	(2.1)
Romania	4.5	(0.5)	9.0	(0.5)	86.6	(0.8)	-1.2	(0.2)	-0.7	(0.1)	-0.4	(0.0)	400	(7.7)	419	(5.5)	450	(3.8)
Russian Federation	18.8	(1.1)	10.1	(0.6)	71.1	(1.4)	-0.5	(0.0)	-0.2	(0.0)	0.0	(0.0)	462	(4.7)	464	(5.0)	491	(3.0)
Serbia	20.4	(0.9)	28.8	(1.1)	50.8	(1.2)	-0.6	(0.0)	-0.5	(0.0)	-0.1	(0.0)	433	(5.1)	433	(3.3)	465	(4.3)
Shanghai-China	3.6	(0.6)	8.6	(0.6)	87.8	(1.0)	-1.6	(0.1)	-0.9	(0.1)	-0.3	(0.0)	505	(9.1)	555	(8.5)	623	(2.7)
Singapore	2.3	(0.2)	7.1	(0.4)	90.6	(0.4)	-0.7	(0.1)	-0.3	(0.0)	-0.2	(0.0)	524	(9.3)	530	(5.5)	579	(1.4)
Chinese Taipei	1.5	(0.2)	14.7	(0.6)	83.8	(0.6)	-0.7	(0.1)	-0.6	(0.0)	-0.4	(0.0)	508	(19.4)	530	(5.6)	566	(3.3)
Thailand	1.7	(0.2)	10.5	(0.6)	87.8	(0.6)	-1.8	(0.1)	-1.7	(0.1)	-1.3	(0.0)	375	(11.5)	395	(4.8)	432	(3.5)
Tunisia	37.5	(1.5)	39.3	(1.1)	23.2	(1.0)	-1.8	(0.0)	-0.9	(0.0)	-0.7	(0.1)	373	(3.8)	394	(4.8)	408	(6.0)
United Arab Emirates	23.5	(0.7)	26.7	(0.6)	49.8	(0.9)	0.0	(0.0)	0.4	(0.0)	0.5	(0.0)	399	(3.0)	438	(3.4)	454	(2.8)
Uruguay	16.2	(0.8)	14.2	(0.7)	69.7	(1.0)	-1.3	(0.0)	-1.2	(0.0)	-0.7	(0.0)	370	(3.2)	390	(4.7)	426	(3.2)
Viet Nam	9.3	(1.0)	22.5	(1.2)	68.2	(1.5)	-2.4	(0.1)	-2.1	(0.0)	-1.6	(0.1)	457	(12.0)	499	(4.4)	523	(4.8)

Note: This table was calculated considering only students with data on the *PISA index of economic, social and cultural status*. Values that are statistically significant are indicated in bold (see Annex A3).
1. ESCS refers to the *PISA index of economic, social and cultural status*.
* See notes at the beginning of this Annex.

StatLink ⟶ http://dx.doi.org/10.1787/888932964946

[Part 2/3]
Pre-primary school attendance, mathematics performance and students' socio-economic status

Table II.4.12   *Results based on students' self-reports*

| | Difference in mathematics performance between students who reported having attended pre-primary school for one year or less and those who had not attended pre-primary school | | | | Difference in mathematics performance between students who reported having attended pre-primary school for more than one year and those who had not attended pre-primary school | | | | Increased likelihood of students who had not attended pre-primary school scoring in the bottom quarter of the national mathematics performance distribution | |
| | Before accounting for student's ESCS¹ | | After accounting for student's ESCS¹ | | Before accounting for student's ESCS¹ | | After accounting for student's ESCS¹ | | | |
	Score dif.	S.E.	Score dif.	S.E.	Score dif.	S.E.	Score dif.	S.E.	Ratio	S.E.
Australia	37	(5.3)	26	(5.1)	52	(5.5)	32	(5.0)	1.83	(0.1)
Austria	35	(13.9)	11	(11.7)	63	(14.4)	26	(12.4)	1.76	(0.3)
Belgium	6	(10.5)	-5	(9.6)	85	(8.0)	56	(7.7)	2.35	(0.2)
Canada	12	(3.3)	6	(3.1)	32	(3.4)	19	(3.3)	1.31	(0.1)
Chile	41	(5.2)	19	(4.9)	54	(5.3)	14	(5.5)	1.80	(0.2)
Czech Republic	48	(16.0)	36	(12.4)	69	(15.3)	51	(12.3)	2.04	(0.3)
Denmark	24	(11.3)	14	(11.1)	66	(10.9)	46	(10.5)	2.22	(0.3)
Estonia	-17	(8.2)	-19	(8.3)	-3	(6.5)	-13	(6.6)	1.03	(0.1)
Finland	38	(10.4)	27	(9.1)	53	(10.7)	34	(9.2)	1.88	(0.2)
France	36	(14.5)	16	(15.9)	100	(13.5)	61	(15.5)	2.81	(0.3)
Germany	-6	(9.5)	-4	(8.5)	57	(8.2)	42	(7.5)	1.81	(0.2)
Greece	44	(8.0)	24	(7.4)	68	(7.7)	41	(7.3)	2.21	(0.2)
Hungary	c	c	c	c	c	c	c	c	c	c
Iceland	12	(16.2)	9	(16.3)	47	(12.4)	25	(11.9)	1.64	(0.3)
Ireland	15	(4.2)	5	(4.0)	12	(4.4)	-5	(3.9)	1.17	(0.1)
Israel	42	(11.9)	15	(11.5)	98	(11.3)	50	(10.4)	2.53	(0.3)
Italy	25	(4.6)	18	(4.1)	63	(4.6)	52	(4.3)	2.01	(0.1)
Japan	-18	(19.4)	-5	(18.7)	34	(17.9)	34	(16.6)	1.70	(0.3)
Korea	9	(8.0)	0	(7.7)	24	(8.2)	13	(7.9)	1.36	(0.2)
Luxembourg	1	(8.2)	-10	(7.1)	45	(6.7)	26	(5.9)	1.64	(0.2)
Mexico	33	(2.6)	27	(2.6)	41	(2.5)	25	(2.3)	1.84	(0.1)
Netherlands	38	(15.5)	28	(15.1)	42	(12.1)	28	(12.0)	1.60	(0.2)
New Zealand	37	(7.8)	19	(7.6)	58	(6.6)	31	(6.6)	1.95	(0.1)
Norway	-4	(7.6)	-5	(7.9)	31	(4.8)	17	(4.9)	1.45	(0.1)
Poland	33	(9.5)	33	(9.2)	61	(10.5)	32	(9.7)	1.77	(0.3)
Portugal	4	(6.2)	-2	(5.6)	43	(5.0)	23	(5.0)	1.52	(0.1)
Slovak Republic	72	(8.9)	48	(7.5)	103	(9.1)	57	(6.9)	2.85	(0.2)
Slovenia	0	(6.9)	-8	(6.4)	25	(4.5)	5	(4.2)	1.33	(0.1)
Spain	19	(3.9)	13	(4.0)	56	(3.1)	40	(3.2)	1.98	(0.1)
Sweden	31	(6.4)	24	(6.0)	47	(6.2)	32	(5.9)	1.91	(0.2)
Switzerland	79	(13.0)	58	(11.5)	74	(13.1)	52	(11.2)	2.24	(0.2)
Turkey	47	(5.3)	25	(4.7)	62	(9.3)	22	(7.5)	2.10	(0.2)
United Kingdom	33	(7.0)	25	(6.8)	59	(7.5)	42	(7.2)	1.88	(0.1)
United States	18	(11.5)	16	(11.7)	33	(12.2)	12	(12.2)	1.57	(0.2)
OECD average	**25**	**(1.7)**	**15**	**(1.6)**	**53**	**(1.6)**	**31**	**(1.5)**	**1.85**	**(0.0)**
Albania	m	m	m	m	m	m	m	m	m	m
Argentina	28	(5.2)	26	(5.0)	65	(6.2)	47	(5.9)	2.19	(0.2)
Brazil	18	(2.6)	12	(2.5)	40	(3.0)	23	(2.3)	1.55	(0.1)
Bulgaria	29	(5.8)	15	(5.3)	50	(5.8)	26	(4.6)	1.96	(0.1)
Colombia	29	(3.9)	16	(3.6)	34	(4.6)	8	(3.7)	1.68	(0.1)
Costa Rica	24	(4.2)	17	(3.8)	32	(5.3)	11	(4.0)	1.52	(0.1)
Croatia	-1	(4.6)	-6	(4.4)	30	(5.5)	6	(4.8)	1.25	(0.1)
Cyprus*	4	(8.1)	-2	(7.9)	25	(8.4)	13	(8.0)	1.49	(0.1)
Hong Kong-China	20	(17.2)	19	(17.0)	83	(15.4)	69	(14.7)	2.24	(0.3)
Indonesia	39	(5.3)	32	(5.5)	54	(9.8)	40	(6.6)	2.20	(0.2)
Jordan	23	(2.8)	15	(2.6)	41	(5.9)	25	(4.8)	1.54	(0.1)
Kazakhstan	8	(5.3)	-1	(4.7)	23	(4.8)	11	(4.2)	1.42	(0.1)
Latvia	-3	(7.3)	-4	(6.7)	9	(6.3)	-6	(5.7)	1.21	(0.1)
Liechtenstein	c	c	c	c	c	c	c	c	c	c
Lithuania	15	(4.6)	4	(4.3)	36	(3.6)	15	(3.3)	1.54	(0.1)
Macao-China	-3	(9.4)	-2	(9.6)	52	(8.7)	54	(8.8)	1.70	(0.2)
Malaysia	8	(3.9)	5	(3.8)	42	(4.2)	27	(4.0)	1.48	(0.1)
Montenegro	15	(3.5)	4	(3.4)	32	(3.0)	10	(3.1)	1.55	(0.1)
Peru	33	(4.8)	17	(4.2)	56	(5.5)	25	(4.1)	1.93	(0.1)
Qatar	35	(2.0)	22	(2.2)	63	(2.8)	52	(3.0)	1.67	(0.1)
Romania	19	(8.7)	9	(8.0)	50	(8.1)	21	(7.8)	1.93	(0.2)
Russian Federation	3	(6.3)	-5	(5.9)	29	(4.0)	12	(3.5)	1.48	(0.1)
Serbia	0	(4.4)	-5	(4.0)	32	(5.5)	14	(4.8)	1.30	(0.1)
Shanghai-China	50	(10.1)	25	(11.3)	118	(8.6)	72	(8.5)	2.94	(0.2)
Singapore	6	(10.4)	-11	(9.8)	55	(9.6)	35	(9.3)	1.80	(0.2)
Chinese Taipei	22	(19.1)	14	(14.5)	58	(19.4)	38	(14.6)	1.86	(0.3)
Thailand	21	(12.1)	20	(11.9)	57	(11.3)	47	(10.9)	2.13	(0.3)
Tunisia	21	(4.8)	4	(3.8)	35	(5.8)	15	(4.5)	1.40	(0.1)
United Arab Emirates	39	(3.7)	29	(3.3)	55	(3.6)	42	(3.4)	1.98	(0.1)
Uruguay	20	(5.2)	16	(4.9)	57	(4.3)	33	(3.9)	1.92	(0.1)
Viet Nam	43	(10.9)	36	(10.2)	66	(11.2)	43	(11.0)	2.12	(0.3)

Note: This table was calculated considering only students with data on the *PISA index of economic, social and cultural status*. Values that are statistically significant are indicated in bold (see Annex A3).
1. ESCS refers to the *PISA index of economic, social and cultural status*.
* See notes at the beginning of this Annex.
StatLink ᵃˢᵖ http://dx.doi.org/10.1787/888932964946

[Part 3/3]
Pre-primary school attendance, mathematics performance and students' socio-economic status
Table II.4.12   *Results based on students' self-reports*

		Population relevance of students who had not attended pre-primary school scoring in the bottom quarter of the national mathematics performance distribution		Effect size for students who had not attended pre-primary school		Effect size for students who had attended pre-primary school for one year or less		Effect size for students who had attended pre-primary school for more than one year		Proportion of the variation in student performance explained by having attended pre-primary school for less than one year	
		%	S.E.	Effect size	S.E.	Effect size	S.E.	Effect size	S.E.	%	S.E.
OECD	Australia	3.6	(0.6)	-0.5	(0.1)	-0.1	(0.0)	0.2	(0.0)	1.6	(0.3)
	Austria	1.3	(0.6)	-0.7	(0.1)	-0.3	(0.1)	0.4	(0.1)	1.6	(0.6)
	Belgium	3.0	(0.5)	-0.8	(0.1)	-0.8	(0.1)	0.8	(0.1)	4.1	(0.6)
	Canada	2.7	(0.6)	-0.3	(0.0)	-0.2	(0.0)	0.3	(0.0)	1.8	(0.3)
	Chile	6.8	(1.5)	-0.6	(0.1)	0.0	(0.0)	0.2	(0.0)	3.3	(0.6)
	Czech Republic	3.2	(1.2)	-0.6	(0.1)	-0.2	(0.1)	0.3	(0.1)	1.9	(0.9)
	Denmark	1.2	(0.3)	-0.7	(0.1)	-0.5	(0.0)	0.5	(0.0)	4.7	(0.6)
	Estonia	0.2	(1.0)	0.0	(0.1)	-0.2	(0.1)	0.1	(0.1)	0.3	(0.2)
	Finland	2.1	(0.6)	-0.5	(0.1)	-0.2	(0.0)	0.2	(0.0)	1.5	(0.5)
	France	3.1	(0.7)	-1.0	(0.2)	-0.6	(0.1)	0.7	(0.1)	4.3	(0.7)
	Germany	2.6	(0.6)	-0.5	(0.1)	-0.6	(0.1)	0.6	(0.1)	5.0	(0.8)
	Greece	5.2	(1.2)	-0.7	(0.1)	-0.2	(0.0)	0.3	(0.0)	3.6	(0.7)
	Hungary	c	c	c	c	-0.5	(0.1)	0.5	(0.1)	1.1	(0.5)
	Iceland	1.3	(0.6)	-0.5	(0.1)	-0.4	(0.1)	0.4	(0.1)	0.9	(0.4)
	Ireland	2.3	(1.4)	-0.2	(0.0)	0.1	(0.0)	0.0	(0.0)	0.3	(0.2)
	Israel	3.0	(0.5)	-0.9	(0.1)	-0.5	(0.1)	0.6	(0.1)	5.5	(1.0)
	Italy	4.1	(0.4)	-0.6	(0.0)	-0.4	(0.0)	0.5	(0.0)	2.9	(0.4)
	Japan	0.6	(0.3)	-0.3	(0.2)	-0.6	(0.1)	0.5	(0.1)	0.8	(0.2)
	Korea	1.6	(0.7)	-0.2	(0.1)	-0.1	(0.0)	0.2	(0.0)	0.5	(0.3)
	Luxembourg	2.9	(0.8)	-0.4	(0.1)	-0.4	(0.0)	0.5	(0.0)	3.1	(0.5)
	Mexico	7.4	(0.7)	-0.5	(0.0)	0.0	(0.0)	0.3	(0.0)	2.6	(0.3)
	Netherlands	1.3	(0.5)	-0.4	(0.1)	0.0	(0.1)	0.2	(0.1)	0.5	(0.3)
	New Zealand	7.9	(0.9)	-0.5	(0.1)	-0.2	(0.0)	0.3	(0.0)	3.2	(0.6)
	Norway	3.4	(0.9)	-0.3	(0.1)	-0.4	(0.1)	0.4	(0.0)	1.5	(0.4)
	Poland	1.9	(0.6)	-0.5	(0.1)	-0.3	(0.0)	0.3	(0.0)	2.9	(0.8)
	Portugal	7.2	(1.6)	-0.4	(0.1)	-0.3	(0.1)	0.5	(0.0)	4.6	(0.8)
	Slovak Republic	11.2	(1.8)	-1.0	(0.1)	-0.2	(0.1)	0.6	(0.1)	7.2	(1.5)
	Slovenia	4.7	(1.4)	-0.2	(0.1)	-0.2	(0.1)	0.3	(0.0)	1.5	(0.4)
	Spain	5.4	(0.7)	-0.6	(0.0)	-0.4	(0.0)	0.5	(0.0)	3.5	(0.4)
	Sweden	6.8	(1.2)	-0.5	(0.1)	-0.1	(0.0)	0.3	(0.0)	2.3	(0.5)
	Switzerland	2.2	(0.5)	-0.7	(0.1)	0.1	(0.1)	0.0	(0.1)	1.2	(0.4)
	Turkey	43.6	(5.2)	-0.6	(0.1)	0.4	(0.1)	0.5	(0.1)	6.8	(1.4)
	United Kingdom	3.9	(0.6)	-0.6	(0.1)	-0.2	(0.0)	0.3	(0.0)	2.9	(0.6)
	United States	0.8	(0.4)	-0.3	(0.1)	-0.2	(0.0)	0.2	(0.0)	0.7	(0.3)
	OECD average	4.8	(0.2)	-0.5	(0.0)	-0.3	(0.0)	0.4	(0.0)	2.6	(0.1)
Partners	Albania	m	m	m	m	m	m	m	m	m	m
	Argentina	6.7	(1.3)	-0.8	(0.1)	-0.4	(0.1)	0.6	(0.1)	7.3	(1.4)
	Brazil	9.4	(1.2)	-0.4	(0.0)	-0.1	(0.0)	0.4	(0.0)	4.0	(0.5)
	Bulgaria	8.9	(1.3)	-0.5	(0.1)	-0.2	(0.0)	0.4	(0.0)	2.9	(0.7)
	Colombia	8.8	(1.8)	-0.4	(0.1)	0.1	(0.0)	0.2	(0.0)	2.2	(0.5)
	Costa Rica	7.4	(1.7)	-0.4	(0.1)	0.0	(0.0)	0.2	(0.1)	2.6	(0.8)
	Croatia	6.3	(2.4)	-0.2	(0.1)	-0.2	(0.0)	0.4	(0.0)	3.0	(0.8)
	Cyprus*	1.7	(0.5)	-0.2	(0.1)	-0.2	(0.0)	0.2	(0.0)	1.1	(0.3)
	Hong Kong-China	1.9	(0.5)	-0.8	(0.1)	-0.7	(0.1)	0.7	(0.1)	2.5	(0.6)
	Indonesia	35.6	(3.9)	-0.7	(0.1)	0.3	(0.1)	0.5	(0.1)	10.5	(2.4)
	Jordan	11.6	(2.2)	-0.4	(0.0)	0.0	(0.0)	0.3	(0.0)	3.8	(0.9)
	Kazakhstan	21.2	(5.1)	-0.3	(0.1)	0.0	(0.1)	0.3	(0.1)	1.9	(0.8)
	Latvia	2.3	(1.6)	-0.1	(0.1)	-0.1	(0.1)	0.1	(0.1)	0.3	(0.3)
	Liechtenstein	c	c	c	c	c	c	c	c	1.3	(1.4)
	Lithuania	14.0	(2.7)	-0.4	(0.0)	-0.1	(0.0)	0.4	(0.0)	3.3	(0.6)
	Macao-China	1.7	(0.5)	-0.5	(0.1)	-0.6	(0.0)	0.6	(0.0)	4.4	(0.6)
	Malaysia	10.2	(2.2)	-0.4	(0.0)	-0.3	(0.0)	0.5	(0.0)	5.6	(0.9)
	Montenegro	15.2	(2.0)	-0.3	(0.0)	0.0	(0.0)	0.3	(0.0)	2.9	(0.5)
	Peru	11.4	(1.6)	-0.6	(0.1)	-0.2	(0.1)	0.4	(0.1)	5.5	(0.9)
	Qatar	17.0	(1.2)	-0.5	(0.0)	0.0	(0.0)	0.4	(0.0)	6.0	(0.5)
	Romania	4.0	(1.0)	-0.6	(0.1)	-0.4	(0.1)	0.5	(0.1)	2.7	(0.7)
	Russian Federation	8.3	(1.7)	-0.3	(0.0)	-0.2	(0.1)	0.3	(0.0)	2.2	(0.5)
	Serbia	5.8	(1.7)	-0.2	(0.1)	-0.3	(0.0)	0.4	(0.0)	3.2	(0.8)
	Shanghai-China	6.5	(1.4)	-1.1	(0.1)	-0.6	(0.1)	0.8	(0.1)	7.9	(1.5)
	Singapore	1.8	(0.5)	-0.5	(0.1)	-0.4	(0.1)	0.5	(0.0)	2.0	(0.4)
	Chinese Taipei	1.3	(0.5)	-0.4	(0.1)	-0.3	(0.0)	0.3	(0.0)	1.5	(0.4)
	Thailand	1.8	(0.5)	-0.7	(0.1)	-0.5	(0.1)	0.5	(0.1)	2.6	(0.5)
	Tunisia	13.0	(3.7)	-0.3	(0.1)	0.1	(0.0)	0.3	(0.1)	3.2	(0.9)
	United Arab Emirates	18.7	(1.6)	-0.6	(0.0)	0.0	(0.0)	0.4	(0.0)	6.1	(0.7)
	Uruguay	13.0	(1.9)	-0.6	(0.1)	-0.3	(0.1)	0.6	(0.0)	6.5	(0.9)
	Viet Nam	9.4	(2.9)	-0.7	(0.1)	-0.2	(0.1)	0.4	(0.1)	5.5	(1.7)

Note: This table was calculated considering only students with data on the *PISA index of economic, social and cultural status*. Values that are statistically significant are indicated in bold (see Annex A3).
1. ESCS refers to the *PISA index of economic, social and cultural status*.
* See notes at the beginning of this Annex.
StatLink ⟦⟧ http://dx.doi.org/10.1787/888932964946

[Part 1/1]

Table II.4.13 **Relationship between performance, pre-primary school attendance and socio-economic status[1]**

	Difference in mathematics performance among students who had attended pre-primary school		Difference in performance among socio-economically advantaged students[2]		Additional difference in performance among advantaged students[2] who had attended pre-primary school	
	Score dif.	S.E.	Score dif.	S.E.	Score dif.	S.E.
OECD						
Australia	28	(5.6)	20	(6.0)	4	(6.1)
Austria	13	(9.2)	-1	(9.3)	12	(9.2)
Belgium	23	(8.8)	14	(8.4)	1	(8.7)
Canada	15	(3.1)	21	(3.4)	1	(3.5)
Chile	14	(6.1)	3	(3.3)	6	(3.1)
Czech Republic	19	(9.7)	6	(8.1)	7	(7.9)
Denmark	14	(9.0)	15	(8.3)	12	(8.6)
Estonia	-14	(6.7)	10	(6.5)	10	(6.9)
Finland	20	(8.0)	38	(6.6)	-13	(7.0)
France	46	(14.6)	-7	(13.5)	26	(13.4)
Germany	11	(7.8)	-2	(8.7)	11	(9.1)
Greece	22	(8.1)	17	(7.2)	0	(7.2)
Hungary	c	c	c	c	c	c
Iceland	17	(11.4)	25	(11.4)	-4	(12.0)
Ireland	0	(3.6)	27	(4.0)	-2	(4.4)
Israel	46	(12.3)	15	(7.2)	10	(6.6)
Italy	34	(3.8)	-1	(3.8)	6	(4.0)
Japan	11	(14.6)	19	(13.7)	-15	(13.9)
Korea	5	(6.8)	22	(9.2)	-7	(9.7)
Luxembourg	12	(6.0)	20	(4.3)	-6	(4.3)
Mexico	27	(4.2)	5	(2.2)	4	(1.9)
Netherlands	11	(8.6)	3	(9.8)	2	(10.2)
New Zealand	35	(6.7)	30	(8.6)	2	(9.6)
Norway	12	(5.3)	13	(5.9)	11	(6.2)
Poland	28	(12.3)	36	(10.1)	-5	(10.5)
Portugal	24	(6.5)	11	(4.6)	12	(4.8)
Slovak Republic	41	(8.7)	12	(8.7)	10	(9.2)
Slovenia	-1	(3.6)	-2	(4.7)	3	(5.1)
Spain	33	(4.0)	20	(3.6)	4	(3.5)
Sweden	21	(5.5)	27	(5.5)	-4	(5.5)
Switzerland	40	(9.4)	27	(6.7)	-11	(6.6)
Turkey	8	(4.5)	8	(3.7)	0	(2.7)
United Kingdom	36	(6.9)	20	(5.4)	3	(6.0)
United States	9	(11.5)	22	(13.5)	4	(13.2)
OECD average	20	(1.4)	15	(1.4)	3	(1.5)
Partners						
Albania	m	m	m	m	m	m
Argentina	42	(8.3)	4	(4.3)	7	(4.1)
Brazil	21	(3.1)	9	(2.3)	4	(1.8)
Bulgaria	9	(4.8)	15	(5.3)	-2	(5.4)
Colombia	6	(5.9)	14	(4.3)	-2	(3.0)
Costa Rica	14	(4.8)	11	(2.9)	4	(2.5)
Croatia	-6	(4.0)	9	(3.3)	3	(3.6)
Cyprus*	2	(7.8)	22	(6.8)	-2	(6.5)
Hong Kong-China	49	(23.5)	2	(14.4)	1	(14.4)
Indonesia	30	(7.8)	11	(4.3)	3	(3.2)
Jordan	15	(3.2)	10	(2.8)	6	(2.7)
Kazakhstan	0	(3.2)	15	(2.6)	-1	(3.0)
Latvia	-9	(5.7)	13	(5.4)	10	(6.1)
Liechtenstein	c	c	c	c	c	c
Lithuania	1	(3.4)	14	(3.0)	6	(3.4)
Macao-China	48	(9.0)	0	(7.4)	11	(7.5)
Malaysia	18	(4.1)	17	(3.4)	6	(3.1)
Montenegro	-3	(2.7)	11	(2.7)	2	(3.0)
Peru	25	(5.9)	7	(3.5)	7	(2.7)
Qatar	-6	(2.0)	-2	(1.8)	17	(2.8)
Romania	31	(9.0)	0	(7.5)	24	(7.3)
Russian Federation	6	(3.7)	16	(4.8)	11	(5.0)
Serbia	0	(4.8)	8	(3.7)	2	(3.9)
Shanghai-China	57	(17.1)	-11	(10.1)	17	(9.5)
Singapore	22	(11.5)	29	(7.8)	-11	(7.9)
Chinese Taipei	27	(17.5)	41	(15.6)	-18	(15.1)
Thailand	37	(17.7)	25	(10.5)	-2	(9.8)
Tunisia	4	(4.7)	12	(3.6)	6	(2.7)
United Arab Emirates	26	(2.6)	8	(2.5)	5	(3.1)
Uruguay	35	(5.3)	7	(3.8)	9	(3.2)
Viet Nam	37	(13.9)	9	(5.9)	4	(6.1)

Note: Values that are statistically significant are indicated in bold (see Annex A3).
1. Mathematics performance is regressed on the following variables: student had attended pre-primary school; student's socio-economic status; (student had attended pre-primary school)*(student's socio-economic status); a square of student's socio-economic status; school's socio-economic profile; gender; student with an immigrant background; school in rural area; school in a city; school size; a square of school size; and private school.
2. Socio-economically advantaged students correspond to students with a *PISA index of economic, social and cultural status* that is one unit higher than the OECD average.
* See notes at the beginning of this Annex.
StatLink ⟐ http://dx.doi.org/10.1787/888932964946

[Part 1/1]

Table II.4.14 Relationship between performance, pre-primary school attendance and immigrant background[1]

	Overall performance difference between student not attending and those that attend primary education		Overall performance difference between immigrant and non-immigrant students		Additional performance difference for immigrant students who do not attend pre-primary education	
	Score dif.	S.E.	Score dif.	S.E.	Score dif.	S.E.
Australia	**-25**	(7.0)	**25**	(3.1)	-15	(1.3)
Austria	-6	(9.8)	**-33**	(3.5)	6	(1.7)
Belgium	-20	(10.6)	**-40**	(4.0)	-8	(1.9)
Canada	**-9**	(3.8)	-3	(3.8)	**-20**	(.0)
Chile	-6	(4.4)	-7	(8.1)	c	c
Czech Republic	-11	(9.4)	**-20**	(8.7)	c	c
Denmark	-14	(15.8)	**-52**	(3.6)	-10	(1.7)
Estonia	18	(7.4)	**-21**	(5.6)	c	c
Finland	-14	(9.1)	**-71**	(4.4)	**-51**	(2.1)
France	-29	(16.5)	**-33**	(4.9)	3	(2.9)
Germany	-16	(8.9)	**-32**	(5.0)	18	(1.6)
Greece	**-27**	(7.8)	**-26**	(5.7)	16	(1.3)
Hungary	c	c	4	(8.7)	c	c
Iceland	-9	(12.8)	**-29**	(9.3)	c	c
Ireland	1	(3.9)	7	(5.1)	-9	(10.2)
Israel	**-37**	(13.6)	7	(4.8)	-12	(24.9)
Italy	**-35**	(4.0)	**-20**	(3.4)	12	(3.5)
Japan	-15	(13.8)	c	c	c	c
Korea	-7	(6.7)	c	c	c	c
Luxembourg	-20	(14.6)	**-26**	(3.1)	3	(7.1)
Mexico	**-19**	(2.3)	**-60**	(4.8)	-2	(1.6)
Netherlands	-16	(10.0)	**-29**	(7.3)	9	(5.7)
New Zealand	**-30**	(7.6)	5	(4.8)	-8	(1.2)
Norway	**-12**	(5.6)	**-36**	(6.2)	-12	(2.1)
Poland	**-31**	(9.8)	c	c	c	c
Portugal	**-13**	(5.1)	**-33**	(8.6)	-1	(5.1)
Slovak Republic	**-32**	(8.0)	-1	(16.3)	c	c
Slovenia	3	(3.7)	**-18**	(4.7)	-18	(5.0)
Spain	**-34**	(4.2)	**-42**	(3.9)	11	(1.0)
Sweden	**-18**	(5.7)	**-49**	(5.1)	-17	(1.0)
Switzerland	**-55**	(16.0)	**-54**	(2.7)	11	(5.9)
Turkey	**-8**	(3.0)	16	(21.6)	c	c
United Kingdom	**-35**	(7.9)	-4	(4.7)	5	(1.7)
United States	-5	(13.9)	4	(4.7)	c	c
OECD average	**-18**	(1.7)	**-22**	(1.3)	**-4**	(3.2)
Albania	m	m	m	m	m	m
Argentina	**-33**	(5.3)	-10	(6.1)	5	(0.2)
Brazil	**-15**	(2.2)	**-41**	(8.5)	-9	(4.0)
Bulgaria	**-10**	(5.1)	c	c	c	c
Colombia	**-9**	(3.4)	c	c	c	c
Costa Rica	-7	(3.5)	**-16**	(5.5)	-17	(0.9)
Croatia	8	(3.6)	**-11**	(4.5)	-6	(8.3)
Cyprus*	-5	(9.4)	**-19**	(4.3)	11	(3.4)
Hong Kong-China	-38	(23.2)	**12**	(3.3)	-22	(1.2)
Indonesia	**-24**	(4.3)	c	c	c	c
Jordan	**-10**	(3.1)	**10**	(4.4)	-3	(9.3)
Kazakhstan	0	(3.4)	3	(5.2)	2	(7.5)
Latvia	**14**	(5.8)	-10	(7.1)	c	c
Liechtenstein	c	c	-12	(9.1)	c	c
Lithuania	1	(3.3)	-5	(11.1)	c	c
Macao-China	**-38**	(10.7)	**22**	(2.7)	-3	(6.4)
Malaysia	**-13**	(3.4)	-18	(12.3)	14	(9.3)
Montenegro	4	(2.4)	12	(6.4)	0	(1.3)
Peru	**-12**	(3.4)	c	c	c	c
Qatar	11	(2.7)	**58**	(2.7)	**-23**	(4.3)
Romania	-7	(7.7)	c	c	c	c
Russian Federation	-2	(4.3)	**-21**	(4.3)	-2	(0.3)
Serbia	2	(4.2)	**17**	(6.9)	-4	(14.5)
Shanghai-China	**-33**	(9.9)	**-79**	(17.7)	c	c
Singapore	**-33**	(11.7)	**13**	(4.3)	5	(18.3)
Chinese Taipei	**-40**	(12.9)	-10	(17.8)	c	c
Thailand	**-38**	(10.0)	36	(58.4)	c	c
Tunisia	5	(3.7)	c	c	c	c
United Arab Emirates	**-23**	(3.4)	**53**	(4.2)	-8	(5.4)
Uruguay	**-23**	(3.8)	c	c	c	c
Viet Nam	**-28**	(8.2)	c	c	c	c

Note: Values that are statistically significant are indicated in bold (see Annex A3).
1. Mathematics performance is regressed on the following variables: student did not attend pre-primary school; student with an immigrant background; student did not attended pre-primary school)*(student with an immigrant background); student's socio-economic status; a square of student's socio-economic status; school's socio-economic profile; gender; school in rural area; school in a city; school size; a square of school size; and private school.
StatLink ⬛ http://dx.doi.org/10.1787/888932964946

ANNEX B2

RESULTS FOR REGIONS WITHIN COUNTRIES

[Part 1/4]

Relationship between mathematics performance and socio-economic status, by region

Table B2.II.1   *Results based on students' self-reports*

| | Unadjusted mathematics mean score | | Mathematics performance adjusted by mean ESCS[1] | | Strength of the relationship between mathematics performance and ESCS[2] | | Slope of the socio-economic gradient for mathematics[2] | |
| | | | | | % of explained variance in mathematics performance | | Score-point difference in mathematics associated with one-unit increase in ESCS | |
	Mean score	S.E.	Mean score	S.E.		S.E.		S.E.
Australia								
Australian Capital Territory	518	(3.6)	489	(4.6)	**12.5**	(2.7)	**52**	(5.3)
New South Wales	509	(3.6)	501	(3.2)	**12.8**	(1.6)	**44**	(3.0)
Northern Territory	452	(10.4)	448	(8.4)	**20.7**	(5.0)	**62**	(7.8)
Queensland	503	(2.9)	496	(2.5)	**14.9**	(1.6)	**46**	(2.7)
South Australia	489	(3.3)	484	(3.1)	**11.1**	(2.0)	**38**	(3.7)
Tasmania	478	(3.4)	479	(3.2)	**16.0**	(2.4)	**46**	(3.9)
Victoria	501	(3.7)	492	(3.4)	**9.0**	(1.1)	**35**	(2.5)
Western Australia	516	(3.4)	507	(2.9)	**13.4**	(1.7)	**43**	(3.1)
Belgium								
Flemish Community*	531	(3.3)	525	(2.6)	**19.9**	(1.9)	**50**	(2.3)
French Community	493	(2.9)	490	(2.6)	**20.6**	(2.0)	**48**	(2.6)
German-speaking Community	511	(2.1)	505	(2.5)	**4.4**	(1.6)	**22**	(4.0)
Canada								
Alberta	517	(4.6)	504	(4.2)	**8.9**	(1.3)	**33**	(2.4)
British Columbia	522	(4.4)	513	(4.2)	**7.1**	(1.3)	**26**	(2.6)
Manitoba	492	(2.9)	485	(2.8)	**14.1**	(2.2)	**37**	(3.0)
New Brunswick	502	(2.6)	494	(2.5)	**6.7**	(2.0)	**26**	(4.2)
Newfoundland and Labrador	490	(3.7)	482	(3.4)	**17.6**	(4.0)	**40**	(4.6)
Nova Scotia	497	(4.1)	491	(3.4)	**8.9**	(1.7)	**29**	(2.9)
Ontario	514	(4.1)	503	(3.3)	**9.6**	(1.3)	**30**	(2.4)
Prince Edward Island	479	(2.5)	471	(2.7)	**8.3**	(1.6)	**29**	(3.0)
Quebec	536	(3.4)	526	(3.0)	**11.6**	(1.5)	**36**	(2.7)
Saskatchewan	506	(3.0)	499	(2.6)	**6.2**	(1.0)	**25**	(2.2)
Italy								
Abruzzo	476	(6.4)	475	(6.2)	**7.4**	(1.5)	**27**	(2.9)
Basilicata	466	(4.3)	472	(4.3)	**10.2**	(1.6)	**28**	(2.4)
Bolzano	506	(2.1)	509	(2.1)	**6.4**	(1.1)	**27**	(2.3)
Calabria	430	(5.7)	436	(5.2)	**8.5**	(2.1)	**25**	(3.3)
Campania	453	(7.7)	458	(7.0)	**12.1**	(1.9)	**31**	(3.0)
Emilia Romagna	500	(6.4)	501	(5.5)	**14.0**	(3.0)	**38**	(4.9)
Friuli Venezia Giulia	523	(4.4)	522	(3.8)	**7.8**	(2.3)	**28**	(4.4)
Lazio	475	(6.8)	471	(6.2)	**6.4**	(2.5)	**25**	(5.1)
Liguria	488	(6.2)	487	(5.4)	**9.6**	(1.6)	**31**	(2.9)
Lombardia	517	(7.6)	515	(6.8)	**10.6**	(2.7)	**29**	(4.3)
Marche	496	(5.5)	498	(5.4)	**5.0**	(1.4)	**20**	(3.0)
Molise	466	(2.3)	469	(2.5)	**8.7**	(1.8)	**27**	(3.1)
Piemonte	499	(5.8)	500	(5.5)	**7.9**	(1.6)	**27**	(3.0)
Puglia	478	(6.1)	487	(5.4)	**11.7**	(2.4)	**29**	(3.4)
Sardegna	458	(5.3)	462	(4.4)	**11.1**	(2.5)	**29**	(3.2)
Sicilia	447	(5.1)	450	(4.7)	**11.2**	(2.3)	**26**	(3.1)
Toscana	495	(4.9)	497	(4.4)	**12.8**	(2.2)	**35**	(3.3)
Trento	524	(4.1)	524	(4.1)	**6.8**	(1.9)	**25**	(3.8)
Umbria	493	(6.8)	491	(6.5)	**5.6**	(1.9)	**23**	(4.3)
Valle d'Aosta	492	(2.2)	498	(2.4)	**7.2**	(1.9)	**23**	(3.1)
Veneto	523	(7.6)	525	(7.0)	**9.5**	(2.4)	**30**	(4.9)
Mexico								
Aguascalientes	437	(4.5)	453	(4.8)	**10.4**	(3.5)	**20**	(3.5)
Baja California	415	(5.8)	425	(7.2)	3.5	(2.5)	**13**	(4.7)
Baja California Sur	414	(5.4)	431	(4.1)	**9.5**	(2.8)	**21**	(3.2)
Campeche	396	(3.9)	415	(5.1)	**7.3**	(2.5)	**15**	(2.7)
Chiapas	373	(7.2)	391	(10.7)	2.8	(2.1)	10	(3.7)
Chihuahua	428	(7.8)	446	(8.0)	**9.9**	(2.8)	**22**	(3.5)
Coahuila	418	(8.1)	436	(8.9)	**10.3**	(4.2)	**22**	(5.1)
Colima	429	(4.5)	445	(5.1)	**11.1**	(4.6)	**21**	(4.3)
Distrito Federal	428	(5.0)	438	(4.2)	**9.1**	(2.4)	**18**	(2.5)
Durango	424	(5.7)	442	(5.7)	**8.5**	(3.0)	**18**	(3.2)
Guanajuato	412	(5.4)	439	(3.6)	**12.0**	(2.5)	**21**	(2.1)
Guerrero	367	(3.4)	390	(4.7)	**6.2**	(2.1)	**13**	(2.3)
Hidalgo	406	(5.8)	436	(7.2)	**11.6**	(3.7)	**21**	(2.9)
Jalisco	435	(5.9)	449	(5.4)	**5.1**	(2.0)	**13**	(2.5)
Mexico	417	(5.6)	433	(7.8)	5.5	(3.3)	**14**	(4.3)
Morelos	421	(8.5)	444	(8.3)	**18.3**	(5.4)	**25**	(4.8)
Nayarit	414	(5.9)	431	(5.4)	**7.2**	(2.8)	**16**	(3.0)
Nuevo León	436	(8.2)	445	(6.3)	**10.3**	(3.5)	**21**	(3.4)
Puebla	415	(4.9)	447	(4.5)	**13.4**	(3.1)	**21**	(2.5)
Querétaro	434	(6.4)	452	(7.7)	**10.8**	(6.2)	**19**	(5.4)
Quintana Roo	411	(5.4)	430	(4.5)	**10.4**	(2.3)	**20**	(2.1)
San Luis Potosí	412	(7.4)	443	(7.5)	**18.8**	(6.4)	**24**	(3.4)
Sinaloa	411	(4.2)	425	(4.5)	**5.6**	(2.3)	**15**	(3.0)
Tabasco	378	(3.8)	398	(5.6)	**7.8**	(2.3)	**16**	(2.7)
Tamaulipas	411	(7.4)	427	(7.9)	**7.4**	(2.6)	**18**	(3.6)
Tlaxcala	411	(5.0)	427	(4.0)	**5.1**	(1.8)	**14**	(2.4)
Veracruz	402	(6.3)	427	(9.0)	**9.6**	(4.7)	**17**	(4.0)
Yucatán	410	(4.6)	433	(4.7)	**11.3**	(3.2)	**19**	(2.6)
Zacatecas	408	(4.2)	429	(4.0)	**7.8**	(2.1)	**16**	(2.3)

* PISA adjudicated region.

Notes: Values that are statistically significant are indicated in bold (see Annex A3). There are no direct comparison with the OECD average in these tables.

See Table II.2.1 for national data.

1. ESCS refers to the *PISA index of economic, social and cultural status*.
2. Single-level bivariate regression of performance on ESCS, the slope is the regression coefficient for ESCS.
3. Percentiles calculated at the student level.
4. Student-level regression of mathematics performance on the ESCS index and the squared term of the ESCS, the index of curvilinearity is the regression coefficient for the squared term.

StatLink ⛶ http://dx.doi.org/10.1787/888932964965

[Part 2/4]
Relationship between mathematics performance and socio-economic status, by region
Table B2.II.1 *Results based on students' self-reports*

	Unadjusted mathematics mean score		Mathematics performance adjusted by mean ESCS[1]		Strength of the relationship between mathematics performance and ESCS[2]		Slope of the socio-economic gradient for mathematics[2]	
					% of explained variance in mathematics performance		Score-point difference in mathematics associated with one-unit increase in ESCS	
	Mean score	S.E.	Mean score	S.E.		S.E.		S.E.
Portugal								
Alentejo	489	(10.3)	501	(6.7)	**17.9**	(3.3)	33	(3.6)
Spain								
Andalusia•	472	(3.8)	484	(3.2)	**16.0**	(2.4)	32	(2.4)
Aragon•	496	(5.4)	499	(4.3)	**15.7**	(2.6)	37	(3.4)
Asturias•	500	(4.3)	501	(3.4)	**15.6**	(2.8)	37	(3.7)
Balearic Islands•	475	(4.8)	481	(4.1)	**12.5**	(2.6)	30	(3.4)
Basque Country•	505	(2.5)	507	(2.1)	**10.5**	(1.1)	29	(1.6)
Cantabria•	491	(3.5)	494	(2.9)	**10.5**	(1.9)	30	(2.7)
Castile and Leon•	509	(4.2)	512	(3.9)	**12.0**	(2.1)	29	(3.1)
Catalonia•	493	(5.2)	498	(4.0)	**17.5**	(2.9)	35	(3.1)
Extremadura•	461	(4.4)	478	(3.6)	**15.9**	(2.1)	34	(2.3)
Galicia•	489	(4.2)	494	(3.7)	**10.0**	(1.8)	27	(2.4)
La Rioja•	503	(1.9)	509	(1.9)	**15.4**	(2.0)	39	(2.8)
Madrid•	504	(3.5)	500	(3.4)	**16.0**	(2.8)	34	(3.3)
Murcia•	462	(4.7)	479	(4.5)	**14.6**	(2.2)	34	(2.9)
Navarre•	517	(3.1)	521	(2.6)	**12.8**	(1.5)	31	(2.0)
United Kingdom								
England	495	(3.9)	487	(3.1)	**12.4**	(1.4)	41	(2.8)
Northern Ireland	487	(3.1)	476	(2.7)	**16.7**	(1.9)	45	(3.0)
Scotland•	498	(2.6)	495	(2.3)	**12.9**	(1.4)	37	(2.4)
Wales	468	(2.2)	464	(2.0)	**10.4**	(1.3)	35	(2.2)
United States								
Connecticut•	506	(6.2)	482	(4.3)	**22.1**	(2.3)	51	(3.1)
Florida•	467	(5.8)	460	(4.1)	**13.9**	(2.2)	36	(3.4)
Massachusetts•	514	(6.2)	492	(3.9)	**20.5**	(3.5)	50	(4.9)
Argentina								
Ciudad Autónoma de Buenos Aires•	418	(7.3)	428	(5.3)	**28.9**	(3.6)	43	(5.1)
Brazil								
Acre	359	(5.6)	386	(9.1)	**12.8**	(5.1)	20	(4.3)
Alagoas	342	(6.0)	373	(11.0)	9.8	(4.0)	18	(4.2)
Amapá	360	(8.6)	381	(8.6)	**11.6**	(5.6)	21	(4.9)
Amazonas	356	(5.5)	374	(10.1)	7.6	(4.3)	17	(5.9)
Bahia	373	(8.7)	416	(9.4)	**19.1**	(3.0)	27	(3.3)
Ceará	378	(8.8)	415	(15.1)	**14.0**	(7.2)	24	(6.5)
Espírito Santo	414	(9.7)	450	(13.5)	**18.7**	(6.6)	30	(5.7)
Federal District	416	(9.1)	442	(8.2)	**27.3**	(6.3)	38	(5.6)
Goiás	379	(5.9)	415	(5.3)	**17.6**	(3.9)	28	(3.5)
Maranhão	343	(13.2)	377	(19.0)	12.8	(7.2)	23	(7.7)
Mato Grosso	370	(9.0)	400	(15.5)	12.6	(7.5)	23	(7.6)
Mato Grosso do Sul	408	(7.5)	438	(6.6)	**23.3**	(3.8)	29	(3.1)
Minas Gerais	403	(6.7)	431	(9.7)	12.8	(5.8)	21	(4.9)
Pará	360	(4.2)	386	(5.0)	**12.5**	(5.4)	21	(3.7)
Paraíba	395	(6.7)	433	(5.6)	**28.2**	(5.8)	33	(4.6)
Paraná	403	(11.6)	442	(19.8)	23.9	(13.4)	34	(11.5)
Pernambuco	363	(7.5)	399	(10.8)	**12.6**	(5.0)	22	(4.7)
Piauí	385	(7.4)	425	(11.5)	**25.3**	(6.0)	32	(5.4)
Rio de Janeiro	389	(6.7)	413	(8.6)	12.1	(6.5)	25	(6.6)
Rio Grande do Norte	380	(9.1)	425	(13.9)	**25.7**	(8.2)	35	(7.0)
Rio Grande do Sul	407	(5.5)	426	(6.4)	**6.7**	(2.5)	16	(3.1)
Rondônia	382	(5.3)	402	(6.8)	**7.1**	(3.2)	14	(3.2)
Roraima	362	(5.7)	391	(7.7)	**19.7**	(5.0)	28	(4.1)
Santa Catarina	415	(8.3)	443	(9.8)	**11.4**	(5.8)	23	(6.0)
São Paulo	404	(4.4)	430	(7.1)	**14.4**	(3.5)	27	(4.0)
Sergipe	384	(8.9)	408	(14.5)	9.5	(5.3)	19	(6.2)
Tocantins	366	(7.3)	396	(9.8)	**12.6**	(3.5)	23	(3.7)
Colombia								
Bogotá	393	(3.4)	414	(5.9)	**7.9**	(2.8)	19	(3.6)
Cali	379	(6.1)	401	(6.2)	**14.4**	(3.3)	27	(3.5)
Manizales	404	(4.1)	428	(6.0)	**20.5**	(3.7)	30	(3.7)
Medellín	393	(7.5)	427	(9.2)	**24.2**	(5.8)	35	(5.3)
Russian Federation								
Perm Territory region•	484	(5.5)	489	(5.1)	**10.3**	(2.0)	38	(4.9)
United Arab Emirates								
Abu Dhabi•	421	(4.0)	414	(3.1)	**8.4**	(1.6)	29	(3.2)
Ajman	403	(7.9)	405	(6.9)	**6.6**	(2.2)	21	(3.8)
Dubai•	464	(1.2)	443	(1.7)	**11.1**	(1.0)	43	(2.0)
Fujairah	411	(9.9)	411	(9.6)	4.8	(3.4)	20	(7.2)
Ras al-Khaimah	416	(6.7)	414	(5.5)	**7.6**	(2.4)	22	(3.5)
Sharjah	439	(9.0)	427	(7.2)	**6.6**	(2.6)	28	(6.6)
Umm al-Quwain	398	(4.0)	401	(4.1)	**6.9**	(3.1)	22	(5.3)

• PISA adjudicated region.
Notes: Values that are statistically significant are indicated in bold (see Annex A3). There are no direct comparison with the OECD average in these tables.
See Table II.2.1 for national data.
1. ESCS refers to the *PISA index of economic, social and cultural status*.
2. Single-level bivariate regression of performance on ESCS, the slope is the regression coefficient for ESCS.
3. Percentiles calculated at the student level.
4. Student-level regression of mathematics performance on the ESCS index and the squared term of the ESCS, the index of curvilinearity is the regression coefficient for the squared term.
StatLink ᴍᴤᴘ http://dx.doi.org/10.1787/888932964965

[Part 3/4]
Relationship between mathematics performance and socio-economic status, by region

Table B2.II.1 *Results based on students' self-reports*

| | Length of the projection of the gradient line[3] | | | | | | Index of curvilinearity[4] | |
| | 5th percentile of ESCS | | 95th percentile of ESCS | | Difference between 95th and 5th percentile of ESCS | | Score-point difference in mathematics associated with one-unit increase in ESCS squared | |
	Index	S.E.	Index	S.E.	Dif.	S.E.		S.E.
Australia								
Australian Capital Territory	-0.6	(0.07)	1.5	(0.05)	**2.1**	(0.08)	-4.2	(4.5)
New South Wales	-1.1	(0.04)	1.4	(0.04)	**2.5**	(0.06)	1.5	(1.9)
Northern Territory	-1.2	(0.20)	1.2	(0.07)	**2.4**	(0.21)	-16.1	(8.6)
Queensland	-1.2	(0.03)	1.3	(0.03)	**2.5**	(0.04)	**6.7**	(2.4)
South Australia	-1.1	(0.08)	1.3	(0.02)	**2.4**	(0.08)	1.3	(2.9)
Tasmania	-1.3	(0.05)	1.3	(0.04)	**2.6**	(0.06)	2.1	(3.7)
Victoria	-1.0	(0.05)	1.4	(0.03)	**2.4**	(0.05)	0.1	(2.5)
Western Australia	-1.1	(0.04)	1.4	(0.04)	**2.5**	(0.05)	2.7	(3.3)
Belgium								
Flemish Community*	-1.3	(0.04)	1.5	(0.03)	**2.7**	(0.05)	0.1	(1.6)
French Community	-1.3	(0.06)	1.5	(0.03)	**2.8**	(0.06)	**3.8**	(1.8)
German-speaking Community	-1.1	(0.10)	1.5	(0.03)	**2.7**	(0.10)	2.0	(4.4)
Canada								
Alberta	-0.9	(0.05)	1.7	(0.04)	**2.6**	(0.05)	2.9	(2.6)
British Columbia	-1.0	(0.04)	1.7	(0.02)	**2.6**	(0.05)	0.7	(2.5)
Manitoba	-1.2	(0.09)	1.6	(0.03)	**2.8**	(0.09)	1.4	(2.3)
New Brunswick	-1.0	(0.04)	1.6	(0.03)	**2.6**	(0.05)	1.1	(3.6)
Newfoundland and Labrador	-1.1	(0.08)	1.6	(0.07)	**2.7**	(0.10)	0.9	(4.0)
Nova Scotia	-1.1	(0.04)	1.6	(0.04)	**2.6**	(0.05)	3.2	(3.7)
Ontario	-1.1	(0.06)	1.7	(0.03)	**2.8**	(0.06)	**3.2**	(1.6)
Prince Edward Island	-1.1	(0.07)	1.5	(0.05)	**2.6**	(0.09)	2.7	(2.8)
Quebec	-1.1	(0.04)	1.5	(0.02)	**2.6**	(0.04)	0.3	(1.9)
Saskatchewan	-0.9	(0.02)	1.7	(0.02)	**2.6**	(0.03)	-0.3	(2.7)
Italy								
Abruzzo	-1.4	(0.04)	1.6	(0.05)	**3.0**	(0.06)	-1.8	(3.1)
Basilicata	-1.6	(0.03)	1.5	(0.03)	**3.1**	(0.04)	1.1	(2.5)
Bolzano	-1.4	(0.04)	1.4	(0.04)	**2.8**	(0.06)	**-4.6**	(2.2)
Calabria	-1.7	(0.02)	1.6	(0.06)	**3.3**	(0.06)	2.6	(2.5)
Campania	-1.7	(0.07)	1.6	(0.05)	**3.2**	(0.08)	2.0	(2.6)
Emilia Romagna	-1.5	(0.03)	1.6	(0.04)	**3.1**	(0.05)	**-6.1**	(3.0)
Friuli Venezia Giulia	-1.4	(0.06)	1.5	(0.05)	**2.9**	(0.07)	**-7.4**	(2.9)
Lazio	-1.4	(0.10)	1.6	(0.06)	**3.0**	(0.10)	-1.2	(2.4)
Liguria	-1.5	(0.04)	1.5	(0.04)	**3.0**	(0.06)	-1.8	(2.4)
Lombardia	-1.5	(0.04)	1.6	(0.06)	**3.0**	(0.06)	-1.5	(2.5)
Marche	-1.5	(0.05)	1.6	(0.04)	**3.1**	(0.05)	-2.7	(2.4)
Molise	-1.6	(0.04)	1.6	(0.06)	**3.1**	(0.07)	3.1	(2.8)
Piemonte	-1.6	(0.06)	1.5	(0.05)	**3.1**	(0.05)	-1.2	(2.6)
Puglia	-1.8	(0.04)	1.6	(0.06)	**3.3**	(0.06)	-1.9	(2.2)
Sardegna	-1.6	(0.02)	1.6	(0.05)	**3.2**	(0.06)	0.5	(2.9)
Sicilia	-1.7	(0.05)	1.6	(0.04)	**3.3**	(0.05)	-1.3	(2.6)
Toscana	-1.5	(0.03)	1.6	(0.06)	**3.1**	(0.06)	-4.4	(2.8)
Trento	-1.4	(0.04)	1.4	(0.03)	**2.8**	(0.04)	-5.0	(2.9)
Umbria	-1.4	(0.06)	1.6	(0.04)	**3.0**	(0.06)	-2.7	(2.6)
Valle d'Aosta	-1.7	(0.06)	1.4	(0.06)	**3.1**	(0.09)	-3.8	(3.0)
Veneto	-1.5	(0.03)	1.5	(0.05)	**3.0**	(0.04)	**-6.4**	(2.3)
Mexico								
Aguascalientes	-2.5	(0.07)	1.2	(0.10)	**3.7**	(0.11)	-0.4	(2.0)
Baja California	-2.3	(0.16)	1.0	(0.05)	**3.3**	(0.17)	**4.7**	(1.7)
Baja California Sur	-2.5	(0.10)	1.0	(0.05)	**3.5**	(0.11)	1.4	(2.0)
Campeche	-3.2	(0.10)	0.9	(0.12)	**4.1**	(0.13)	**3.1**	(1.4)
Chiapas	-3.5	(0.12)	0.6	(0.20)	**4.1**	(0.21)	**6.1**	(2.3)
Chihuahua	-2.5	(0.11)	1.0	(0.06)	**3.5**	(0.11)	3.5	(2.1)
Coahuila	-2.4	(0.11)	1.0	(0.13)	**3.4**	(0.16)	2.1	(2.4)
Colima	-2.7	(0.05)	1.2	(0.10)	**3.9**	(0.12)	**4.3**	(1.9)
Distrito Federal	-2.4	(0.12)	1.5	(0.17)	**3.9**	(0.18)	1.3	(1.7)
Durango	-2.7	(0.05)	1.0	(0.08)	**3.7**	(0.09)	**4.9**	(2.1)
Guanajuato	-3.0	(0.10)	1.1	(0.19)	**4.2**	(0.17)	-0.3	(1.5)
Guerrero	-3.5	(0.06)	0.7	(0.07)	**4.2**	(0.09)	1.7	(1.8)
Hidalgo	-3.2	(0.09)	0.9	(0.17)	**4.1**	(0.18)	1.4	(2.2)
Jalisco	-2.9	(0.08)	1.1	(0.10)	**4.0**	(0.11)	0.8	(1.6)
Mexico	-2.7	(0.03)	0.9	(0.12)	**3.6**	(0.12)	1.8	(3.4)
Morelos	-2.9	(0.06)	1.3	(0.14)	**4.2**	(0.13)	3.5	(2.4)
Nayarit	-2.9	(0.11)	1.0	(0.08)	**3.9**	(0.12)	-1.0	(2.1)
Nuevo León	-2.2	(0.24)	1.3	(0.11)	**3.5**	(0.21)	2.1	(2.3)
Puebla	-3.3	(0.13)	1.0	(0.14)	**4.3**	(0.18)	-2.0	(1.5)
Querétaro	-2.8	(0.10)	1.3	(0.10)	**4.1**	(0.13)	-1.7	(2.4)
Quintana Roo	-2.8	(0.09)	0.9	(0.09)	**3.7**	(0.12)	-0.7	(1.9)
San Luis Potosí	-3.2	(0.10)	1.2	(0.17)	**4.4**	(0.19)	1.9	(1.2)
Sinaloa	-2.8	(0.07)	0.9	(0.09)	**3.6**	(0.10)	0.6	(1.9)
Tabasco	-3.0	(0.11)	1.0	(0.05)	**4.0**	(0.09)	3.0	(2.1)
Tamaulipas	-2.6	(0.08)	1.0	(0.12)	**3.6**	(0.12)	1.7	(2.1)
Tlaxcala	-2.8	(0.06)	1.0	(0.10)	**3.8**	(0.12)	-0.5	(1.7)
Veracruz	-3.3	(0.08)	1.0	(0.16)	**4.3**	(0.17)	2.1	(2.3)
Yucatán	-3.0	(0.08)	1.1	(0.09)	**4.1**	(0.09)	2.4	(1.7)
Zacatecas	-2.9	(0.09)	1.1	(0.07)	**4.0**	(0.11)	1.0	(1.5)

* PISA adjudicated region.

Notes: Values that are statistically significant are indicated in bold (see Annex A3). There are no direct comparison with the OECD average in these tables.

See Table II.2.1 for national data.

1. ESCS refers to the *PISA index of economic, social and cultural status.*
2. Single-level bivariate regression of performance on ESCS, the slope is the regression coefficient for ESCS.
3. Percentiles calculated at the student level.
4. Student-level regression of mathematics performance on the ESCS index and the squared term of the ESCS, the index of curvilinearity is the regression coefficient for the squared term.

StatLink 🔗 http://dx.doi.org/10.1787/888932964965

[Part 4/4]
Relationship between mathematics performance and socio-economic status, by region
Table B2.II.1   *Results based on students' self-reports*

| | Length of the projection of the gradient line[3] | | | | | | Index of curvilinearity[4] | |
| | 5th percentile of ESCS | | 95th percentile of ESCS | | Difference between 95th and 5th percentile of ESCS | | Score-point difference in mathematics associated with one-unit increase in ESCS squared | |
	Index	S.E.	Index	S.E.	Dif.	S.E.		S.E.
Portugal								
Alentejo	-2.0	(0.06)	1.5	(0.08)	**3.5**	(0.07)	-0.8	(2.4)
Spain								
Andalusia•	-1.9	(0.05)	1.4	(0.02)	**3.3**	(0.05)	2.7	(2.0)
Aragon•	-1.7	(0.10)	1.5	(0.06)	**3.2**	(0.12)	**-6.7**	(1.9)
Asturias•	-1.6	(0.05)	1.5	(0.03)	**3.1**	(0.06)	1.0	(4.1)
Balearic Islands•	-1.8	(0.05)	1.5	(0.05)	**3.2**	(0.06)	-2.6	(1.9)
Basque Country•	-1.6	(0.04)	1.4	(0.02)	**3.0**	(0.05)	**-3.8**	(1.5)
Cantabria•	-1.6	(0.05)	1.5	(0.05)	**3.1**	(0.07)	4.5	(2.7)
Castile and Leon•	-1.7	(0.05)	1.5	(0.05)	**3.1**	(0.06)	-2.5	(1.8)
Catalonia•	-1.8	(0.06)	1.3	(0.03)	**3.1**	(0.06)	0.2	(2.0)
Extremadura•	-2.0	(0.07)	1.4	(0.04)	**3.4**	(0.08)	0.5	(2.2)
Galicia•	-1.7	(0.05)	1.4	(0.02)	**3.2**	(0.05)	-0.1	(1.7)
La Rioja•	-1.8	(0.06)	1.4	(0.04)	**3.2**	(0.07)	1.8	(2.5)
Madrid•	-1.6	(0.05)	1.6	(0.07)	**3.2**	(0.08)	**-6.5**	(2.2)
Murcia•	-2.1	(0.06)	1.3	(0.05)	**3.4**	(0.09)	1.4	(2.2)
Navarre•	-1.7	(0.07)	1.4	(0.04)	**3.1**	(0.07)	-0.8	(2.4)
United Kingdom								
England	-1.0	(0.03)	1.5	(0.05)	**2.5**	(0.04)	**5.3**	(1.7)
Northern Ireland	-1.0	(0.03)	1.6	(0.05)	**2.6**	(0.05)	0.8	(2.8)
Scotland•	-1.2	(0.02)	1.4	(0.03)	**2.6**	(0.03)	**7.4**	(2.2)
Wales	-1.0	(0.03)	1.4	(0.02)	**2.5**	(0.04)	**7.3**	(2.2)
United States								
Connecticut•	-1.1	(0.09)	1.8	(0.05)	**3.0**	(0.09)	**5.3**	(1.9)
Florida•	-1.3	(0.06)	1.5	(0.05)	**2.8**	(0.08)	**7.9**	(2.3)
Massachusetts•	-1.1	(0.08)	1.6	(0.08)	**2.7**	(0.09)	**9.4**	(2.9)
Argentina								
Ciudad Autónoma de Buenos Aires•	-2.3	(0.11)	1.4	(0.07)	**3.7**	(0.11)	-2.5	(2.3)
Brazil								
Acre	-3.2	(0.07)	0.7	(0.10)	**3.9**	(0.11)	4.0	(2.4)
Alagoas	-3.3	(0.08)	0.5	(0.13)	**3.8**	(0.13)	3.4	(2.1)
Amapá	-2.7	(0.08)	0.8	(0.16)	**3.4**	(0.16)	4.4	(4.2)
Amazonas	-2.9	(0.05)	0.7	(0.13)	**3.6**	(0.12)	6.3	(5.0)
Bahia	-3.3	(0.12)	0.8	(0.04)	**4.1**	(0.14)	**10.7**	(3.7)
Ceará	-3.3	(0.05)	0.7	(0.27)	**4.1**	(0.28)	**8.1**	(3.7)
Espírito Santo	-3.0	(0.08)	0.9	(0.27)	**3.9**	(0.29)	**13.0**	(2.5)
Federal District	-2.5	(0.09)	1.2	(0.23)	**3.7**	(0.27)	**7.2**	(2.2)
Goiás	-2.9	(0.04)	0.6	(0.11)	**3.5**	(0.12)	3.0	(2.2)
Maranhão	-3.2	(0.09)	0.6	(0.30)	**3.8**	(0.28)	**6.8**	(2.8)
Mato Grosso	-3.1	(0.11)	0.7	(0.15)	**3.9**	(0.18)	6.9	(3.6)
Mato Grosso do Sul	-2.8	(0.07)	0.9	(0.06)	**3.7**	(0.06)	**4.3**	(1.1)
Minas Gerais	-3.0	(0.05)	0.7	(0.20)	**3.8**	(0.22)	4.5	(4.0)
Pará	-3.0	(0.07)	0.7	(0.15)	**3.7**	(0.12)	2.3	(1.7)
Paraíba	-3.1	(0.13)	0.7	(0.17)	**3.8**	(0.26)	3.4	(3.8)
Paraná	-2.9	(0.07)	0.9	(0.31)	**3.7**	(0.32)	10.4	(5.8)
Pernambuco	-3.3	(0.07)	0.3	(0.17)	**3.6**	(0.15)	2.9	(4.1)
Piauí	-3.2	(0.06)	0.9	(0.05)	**4.1**	(0.09)	**9.2**	(1.5)
Rio de Janeiro	-2.6	(0.07)	0.7	(0.23)	**3.3**	(0.23)	4.7	(4.2)
Rio Grande do Norte	-3.2	(0.10)	0.8	(0.22)	**4.0**	(0.23)	**10.0**	(3.3)
Rio Grande do Sul	-2.8	(0.11)	0.7	(0.07)	**3.6**	(0.13)	-2.1	(1.8)
Rondônia	-3.2	(0.05)	0.7	(0.14)	**3.8**	(0.12)	**5.3**	(1.9)
Roraima	-2.9	(0.10)	0.8	(0.09)	**3.7**	(0.12)	**9.1**	(2.4)
Santa Catarina	-2.9	(0.17)	0.7	(0.14)	**3.7**	(0.18)	**7.1**	(2.3)
São Paulo	-2.7	(0.05)	0.9	(0.06)	**3.6**	(0.08)	**5.8**	(2.4)
Sergipe	-3.1	(0.07)	0.7	(0.06)	**3.7**	(0.06)	0.2	(2.8)
Tocantins	-3.1	(0.09)	0.7	(0.09)	**3.8**	(0.11)	**6.7**	(2.4)
Colombia								
Bogotá	-2.7	(0.04)	0.5	(0.10)	**3.2**	(0.08)	3.2	(3.5)
Cali	-2.5	(0.06)	0.8	(0.09)	**3.2**	(0.10)	-0.3	(1.8)
Manizales	-2.8	(0.06)	0.9	(0.06)	**3.6**	(0.07)	2.5	(1.8)
Medellín	-2.9	(0.14)	0.9	(0.11)	**3.8**	(0.16)	**10.4**	(2.5)
Russian Federation								
Perm Territory region•	-1.4	(0.07)	0.9	(0.02)	**2.3**	(0.07)	0.3	(3.2)
United Arab Emirates								
Abu Dhabi•	-1.4	(0.07)	1.5	(0.04)	**3.0**	(0.08)	0.4	(1.9)
Ajman	-1.8	(0.14)	1.2	(0.11)	**3.1**	(0.18)	3.1	(1.9)
Dubai•	-0.8	(0.04)	1.5	(0.03)	**2.4**	(0.05)	-2.6	(1.5)
Fujairah	-1.8	(0.08)	1.3	(0.07)	**3.0**	(0.10)	1.4	(2.4)
Ras al-Khaimah	-1.8	(0.25)	1.4	(0.09)	**3.2**	(0.24)	3.1	(2.0)
Sharjah	-1.0	(0.10)	1.4	(0.03)	**2.4**	(0.11)	-2.6	(4.4)
Umm al-Quwain	-1.8	(0.09)	1.2	(0.12)	**3.0**	(0.16)	4.7	(5.7)

• PISA adjudicated region.
Notes: Values that are statistically significant are indicated in bold (see Annex A3). There are no direct comparison with the OECD average in these tables.
See Table II.2.1 for national data.
1. ESCS refers to the *PISA index of economic, social and cultural status*.
2. Single-level bivariate regression of performance on ESCS, the slope is the regression coefficient for ESCS.
3. Percentiles calculated at the student level.
4. Student-level regression of mathematics performance on the ESCS index and the squared term of the ESCS, the index of curvilinearity is the regression coefficient for the squared term.
StatLink ⫘ http://dx.doi.org/10.1787/888932964965

[Part 1/2]

Table B2.II.2 Students' socio-economic status and mathematics performance, by region

By national quarters of the PISA index of economic, social and cultural status; results based on students' self-reports

	ESCS[1]										Performance on the mathematics scale, by national quarters of this index								Increased likelihood of students in the bottom quarter of the ESCS index scoring in the bottom quarter of the mathematics performance distribution	
	All students		Bottom quarter		Second quarter		Third quarter		Top quarter		Bottom quarter		Second quarter		Third quarter		Top quarter			
	Mean index	S.E.	Mean index	S.E.	Mean index	S.E.	Mean index	S.E.	Mean index	S.E.	Mean score	S.E.	Mean score	S.E.	Mean score	S.E.	Mean score	S.E.	Ratio	S.E.
OECD **Australia**																				
Australian Capital Territory	0.62	(0.02)	-0.23	(0.05)	0.49	(0.02)	0.87	(0.02)	1.33	(0.03)	467	(7.1)	513	(7.7)	552	(7.3)	552	(7.1)	**2.45**	(0.33)
New South Wales	0.25	(0.02)	-0.86	(0.03)	0.04	(0.03)	0.62	(0.02)	1.19	(0.02)	465	(4.6)	498	(4.4)	526	(6.1)	559	(5.5)	**2.23**	(0.19)
Northern Territory	0.14	(0.06)	-0.95	(0.09)	-0.04	(0.07)	0.51	(0.06)	1.06	(0.07)	394	(22.7)	453	(13.7)	476	(12.3)	505	(14.9)	**2.64**	(0.52)
Queensland	0.20	(0.02)	-0.86	(0.03)	-0.02	(0.04)	0.54	(0.03)	1.14	(0.02)	462	(4.7)	487	(4.0)	518	(5.7)	554	(4.1)	**2.19**	(0.19)
South Australia	0.19	(0.02)	-0.90	(0.05)	0.00	(0.03)	0.54	(0.02)	1.11	(0.03)	449	(6.4)	482	(5.8)	501	(5.9)	532	(6.6)	**2.26**	(0.25)
Tasmania	0.02	(0.03)	-1.05	(0.03)	-0.25	(0.04)	0.35	(0.04)	1.05	(0.03)	433	(6.7)	466	(6.3)	494	(6.0)	529	(7.3)	**2.23**	(0.24)
Victoria	0.30	(0.02)	-0.76	(0.03)	0.11	(0.04)	0.66	(0.03)	1.20	(0.02)	467	(4.4)	486	(5.1)	522	(5.8)	533	(5.8)	**1.79**	(0.15)
Western Australia	0.26	(0.03)	-0.82	(0.04)	0.04	(0.04)	0.62	(0.03)	1.19	(0.03)	476	(5.4)	502	(5.4)	530	(7.6)	567	(5.3)	**1.99**	(0.22)
Belgium																				
Flemish Community•	0.16	(0.02)	-1.04	(0.04)	-0.18	(0.03)	0.58	(0.03)	1.28	(0.02)	474	(4.8)	513	(5.4)	554	(4.3)	590	(4.9)	**2.39**	(0.20)
French Community	0.12	(0.03)	-1.05	(0.04)	-0.21	(0.04)	0.51	(0.04)	1.25	(0.03)	442	(5.0)	475	(5.3)	512	(4.7)	553	(4.3)	**2.51**	(0.19)
German-speaking Community	0.29	(0.03)	-0.81	(0.04)	-0.05	(0.04)	0.66	(0.04)	1.35	(0.03)	485	(6.2)	502	(6.6)	522	(6.8)	538	(6.8)	**1.60**	(0.21)
Canada																				
Alberta	0.51	(0.03)	-0.58	(0.04)	0.27	(0.04)	0.87	(0.04)	1.51	(0.02)	490	(5.5)	506	(7.1)	528	(6.5)	559	(5.7)	**1.78**	(0.17)
British Columbia	0.46	(0.04)	-0.67	(0.04)	0.19	(0.05)	0.84	(0.04)	1.48	(0.03)	498	(5.0)	511	(6.9)	533	(5.4)	557	(7.2)	**1.80**	(0.16)
Manitoba	0.26	(0.03)	-0.94	(0.05)	0.00	(0.04)	0.66	(0.03)	1.34	(0.03)	455	(6.1)	484	(4.1)	502	(5.2)	540	(5.8)	**2.10**	(0.26)
New Brunswick	0.37	(0.02)	-0.72	(0.03)	0.10	(0.04)	0.73	(0.03)	1.37	(0.03)	475	(5.4)	497	(5.4)	510	(6.3)	532	(6.8)	**1.57**	(0.21)
Newfoundland and Labrador	0.28	(0.04)	-0.89	(0.06)	-0.04	(0.05)	0.65	(0.05)	1.41	(0.04)	452	(9.6)	468	(5.7)	512	(6.2)	541	(4.8)	**2.20**	(0.38)
Nova Scotia	0.31	(0.03)	-0.78	(0.03)	0.04	(0.04)	0.63	(0.05)	1.33	(0.03)	470	(5.0)	489	(8.1)	505	(5.6)	534	(6.1)	**1.81**	(0.25)
Ontario	0.44	(0.04)	-0.76	(0.05)	0.20	(0.05)	0.83	(0.04)	1.49	(0.03)	482	(4.7)	504	(5.3)	525	(6.4)	554	(5.9)	**1.84**	(0.16)
Prince Edward Island	0.33	(0.02)	-0.77	(0.04)	0.09	(0.03)	0.72	(0.03)	1.31	(0.02)	452	(5.1)	467	(4.6)	490	(4.6)	513	(4.7)	**1.67**	(0.19)
Quebec	0.34	(0.03)	-0.80	(0.03)	0.09	(0.04)	0.73	(0.03)	1.34	(0.02)	498	(4.6)	528	(5.1)	549	(4.8)	578	(4.4)	**2.04**	(0.16)
Saskatchewan	0.40	(0.02)	-0.65	(0.03)	0.09	(0.03)	0.72	(0.03)	1.45	(0.03)	487	(3.7)	500	(4.3)	512	(6.0)	538	(4.4)	**1.57**	(0.14)
Italy																				
Abruzzo	0.03	(0.04)	-1.11	(0.04)	-0.30	(0.04)	0.29	(0.05)	1.26	(0.06)	446	(8.7)	466	(7.7)	486	(8.8)	507	(7.1)	**1.78**	(0.24)
Basilicata	-0.21	(0.03)	-1.37	(0.03)	-0.60	(0.03)	0.02	(0.04)	1.11	(0.04)	430	(4.5)	461	(7.0)	474	(7.8)	500	(5.8)	**2.05**	(0.28)
Bolzano	-0.07	(0.02)	-1.10	(0.03)	-0.37	(0.02)	0.17	(0.03)	1.04	(0.02)	475	(4.2)	502	(5.1)	521	(4.5)	529	(4.0)	**1.71**	(0.20)
Calabria	-0.21	(0.05)	-1.49	(0.04)	-0.62	(0.05)	0.08	(0.06)	1.18	(0.06)	401	(7.3)	422	(10.2)	434	(6.2)	465	(9.4)	**1.77**	(0.22)
Campania	-0.19	(0.06)	-1.42	(0.04)	-0.61	(0.06)	0.09	(0.07)	1.21	(0.08)	423	(8.3)	434	(8.9)	455	(10.2)	500	(10.6)	**1.72**	(0.24)
Emilia Romagna	-0.01	(0.04)	-1.21	(0.04)	-0.34	(0.04)	0.27	(0.05)	1.24	(0.05)	451	(9.1)	488	(7.8)	525	(9.1)	540	(9.8)	**1.98**	(0.29)
Friuli Venezia Giulia	0.05	(0.04)	-1.07	(0.06)	-0.25	(0.05)	0.33	(0.05)	1.19	(0.04)	486	(9.1)	527	(6.6)	533	(5.3)	548	(6.1)	**2.16**	(0.28)
Lazio	0.16	(0.05)	-1.02	(0.07)	-0.12	(0.06)	0.49	(0.06)	1.32	(0.04)	447	(10.3)	472	(7.1)	473	(9.4)	508	(10.3)	**1.56**	(0.25)
Liguria	0.03	(0.04)	-1.14	(0.05)	-0.29	(0.05)	0.32	(0.06)	1.22	(0.04)	454	(7.3)	480	(7.5)	495	(7.5)	524	(9.5)	**1.96**	(0.24)
Lombardia	0.06	(0.05)	-1.17	(0.05)	-0.28	(0.06)	0.38	(0.06)	1.31	(0.06)	481	(8.6)	512	(11.4)	521	(8.2)	555	(10.3)	**1.96**	(0.30)
Marche	-0.03	(0.04)	-1.22	(0.04)	-0.37	(0.05)	0.24	(0.05)	1.22	(0.06)	472	(7.7)	495	(6.4)	498	(6.5)	523	(7.7)	**1.65**	(0.26)
Molise	-0.12	(0.03)	-1.28	(0.03)	-0.50	(0.03)	0.15	(0.04)	1.17	(0.04)	437	(6.6)	454	(6.4)	472	(6.3)	502	(5.9)	**1.71**	(0.23)
Piemonte	-0.06	(0.04)	-1.26	(0.03)	-0.39	(0.04)	0.25	(0.05)	1.16	(0.05)	468	(6.0)	484	(7.9)	514	(8.0)	528	(8.6)	**1.74**	(0.28)
Puglia	-0.30	(0.04)	-1.56	(0.04)	-0.75	(0.05)	-0.02	(0.05)	1.11	(0.06)	441	(6.8)	468	(8.1)	493	(10.0)	512	(7.1)	**2.00**	(0.30)
Sardegna	-0.12	(0.05)	-1.38	(0.03)	-0.55	(0.05)	0.19	(0.07)	1.25	(0.06)	425	(7.7)	446	(7.8)	462	(8.6)	501	(7.4)	**1.94**	(0.32)
Sicilia	-0.11	(0.05)	-1.43	(0.05)	-0.49	(0.05)	0.20	(0.06)	1.30	(0.05)	416	(6.8)	434	(7.9)	456	(6.9)	484	(7.6)	**1.69**	(0.22)
Toscana	0.00	(0.06)	-1.20	(0.04)	-0.35	(0.07)	0.30	(0.09)	1.25	(0.08)	453	(6.2)	483	(6.9)	518	(7.9)	534	(6.8)	**2.23**	(0.27)
Trento	0.00	(0.03)	-1.07	(0.04)	-0.30	(0.03)	0.25	(0.03)	1.13	(0.04)	491	(7.1)	524	(6.3)	536	(7.1)	546	(5.5)	**1.89**	(0.23)
Umbria	0.11	(0.04)	-1.03	(0.05)	-0.23	(0.04)	0.39	(0.04)	1.33	(0.04)	468	(12.0)	485	(8.1)	503	(7.6)	517	(6.0)	**1.63**	(0.17)
Valle d'Aosta	-0.20	(0.03)	-1.42	(0.03)	-0.56	(0.04)	0.10	(0.04)	1.09	(0.04)	465	(5.1)	485	(7.1)	505	(5.5)	518	(6.6)	**1.66**	(0.25)
Veneto	-0.07	(0.04)	-1.22	(0.04)	-0.42	(0.05)	0.18	(0.05)	1.19	(0.05)	486	(9.1)	508	(10.3)	545	(10.1)	555	(10.3)	**2.15**	(0.28)
Mexico																				
Aguascalientes	-0.76	(0.08)	-2.20	(0.07)	-1.27	(0.08)	-0.39	(0.12)	0.83	(0.10)	406	(6.9)	434	(8.1)	443	(6.1)	466	(10.2)	**1.96**	(0.25)
Baja California	-0.72	(0.08)	-1.99	(0.10)	-1.12	(0.10)	-0.41	(0.09)	0.65	(0.10)	405	(7.2)	409	(6.5)	408	(8.9)	440	(10.5)	1.12	(0.27)
Baja California Sur	-0.78	(0.09)	-2.16	(0.08)	-1.19	(0.13)	-0.38	(0.11)	0.62	(0.07)	386	(8.0)	404	(9.7)	424	(7.9)	444	(6.6)	**1.94**	(0.26)
Campeche	-1.30	(0.09)	-2.88	(0.09)	-1.87	(0.10)	-0.89	(0.13)	0.44	(0.11)	378	(7.2)	382	(5.6)	399	(6.9)	425	(7.0)	**1.52**	(0.25)
Chiapas	-1.75	(0.13)	-3.17	(0.07)	-2.32	(0.11)	-1.46	(0.18)	-0.03	(0.21)	369	(7.7)	361	(8.6)	367	(9.5)	395	(13.0)	1.03	(0.23)
Chihuahua	-0.81	(0.10)	-2.20	(0.09)	-1.23	(0.11)	-0.46	(0.12)	0.67	(0.10)	407	(7.9)	412	(11.2)	424	(8.7)	471	(12.1)	1.44	(0.27)
Coahuila	-0.82	(0.12)	-2.10	(0.08)	-1.25	(0.14)	-0.51	(0.18)	0.61	(0.13)	392	(6.7)	404	(9.8)	427	(13.8)	451	(14.5)	**1.66**	(0.36)
Colima	-0.75	(0.10)	-2.33	(0.05)	-1.24	(0.10)	-0.28	(0.14)	0.84	(0.13)	401	(6.7)	414	(7.0)	436	(8.8)	466	(12.7)	**1.79**	(0.26)
Distrito Federal	-0.55	(0.12)	-2.04	(0.08)	-1.07	(0.11)	-0.16	(0.16)	1.08	(0.16)	403	(5.5)	416	(6.9)	433	(10.8)	460	(8.4)	**1.58**	(0.22)
Durango	-1.00	(0.14)	-2.44	(0.09)	-1.54	(0.15)	-0.65	(0.21)	0.63	(0.13)	403	(6.2)	409	(6.6)	430	(8.9)	456	(9.1)	**1.54**	(0.29)
Guanajuato	-1.27	(0.12)	-2.68	(0.07)	-1.83	(0.09)	-1.03	(0.15)	0.48	(0.20)	377	(8.0)	402	(8.2)	422	(10.0)	447	(5.6)	**2.04**	(0.33)
Guerrero	-1.66	(0.09)	-3.11	(0.11)	-2.19	(0.10)	-1.38	(0.09)	0.03	(0.10)	349	(7.2)	364	(5.7)	364	(5.2)	393	(5.4)	**1.51**	(0.24)
Hidalgo	-1.45	(0.10)	-2.88	(0.10)	-1.98	(0.10)	-1.16	(0.12)	0.25	(0.17)	374	(5.9)	399	(8.7)	415	(9.1)	438	(9.1)	**1.83**	(0.31)
Jalisco	-1.07	(0.12)	-2.54	(0.08)	-1.63	(0.12)	-0.73	(0.15)	0.61	(0.16)	415	(8.5)	430	(6.9)	438	(7.7)	457	(8.0)	**1.56**	(0.19)
Mexico	-1.07	(0.08)	-2.38	(0.07)	-1.53	(0.10)	-0.78	(0.11)	0.42	(0.10)	397	(7.0)	422	(7.7)	416	(8.7)	435	(9.8)	**1.62**	(0.27)
Morelos	-0.87	(0.14)	-2.53	(0.08)	-1.49	(0.12)	-0.39	(0.22)	0.93	(0.16)	382	(7.6)	409	(9.9)	426	(8.8)	470	(19.2)	**2.30**	(0.37)
Nayarit	-1.02	(0.11)	-2.59	(0.10)	-1.55	(0.12)	-0.58	(0.14)	0.67	(0.11)	387	(11.9)	412	(7.3)	415	(8.5)	441	(6.9)	**1.71**	(0.33)
Nuevo León	-0.43	(0.16)	-1.87	(0.13)	-0.86	(0.15)	-0.02	(0.22)	1.05	(0.16)	409	(8.0)	427	(8.6)	437	(10.2)	472	(15.7)	**1.64**	(0.29)
Puebla	-1.53	(0.11)	-3.01	(0.08)	-2.14	(0.09)	-1.30	(0.15)	0.35	(0.17)	379	(7.0)	406	(9.6)	429	(5.7)	449	(8.7)	**2.13**	(0.36)
Querétaro	-0.92	(0.18)	-2.50	(0.14)	-1.50	(0.21)	-0.50	(0.28)	0.85	(0.17)	399	(9.8)	433	(10.8)	440	(12.4)	467	(16.3)	**2.02**	(0.37)
Quintana Roo	-0.97	(0.09)	-2.43	(0.07)	-1.42	(0.11)	-0.55	(0.11)	0.51	(0.10)	379	(7.5)	405	(6.9)	422	(7.8)	438	(6.3)	**1.85**	(0.27)
San Luis Potosí	-1.27	(0.17)	-2.87	(0.14)	-1.90	(0.18)	-0.94	(0.22)	0.64	(0.25)	380	(9.8)	394	(11.8)	417	(6.7)	459	(17.6)	**1.92**	(0.36)
Sinaloa	-0.96	(0.07)	-2.37	(0.05)	-1.40	(0.08)	-0.58	(0.09)	0.52	(0.09)	389	(7.0)	406	(6.1)	417	(6.2)	432	(7.5)	**1.56**	(0.25)
Tabasco	-1.17	(0.09)	-2.63	(0.08)	-1.67	(0.09)	-0.86	(0.12)	0.50	(0.10)	357	(6.0)	372	(6.5)	377	(6.0)	408	(7.8)	**1.66**	(0.25)
Tamaulipas	-0.89	(0.09)	-2.25	(0.09)	-1.33	(0.09)	-0.53	(0.11)	0.57	(0.13)	390	(7.1)	402	(8.8)	414	(13.1)	437	(10.3)	**1.62**	(0.28)
Tlaxcala	-1.16	(0.08)	-2.50	(0.07)	-1.68	(0.06)	-0.93	(0.11)	0.48	(0.13)	395	(8.2)	401	(7.6)	417	(6.5)	433	(6.8)	**1.54**	(0.20)
Veracruz	-1.47	(0.10)	-3.07	(0.08)	-2.18	(0.12)	-1.10	(0.15)	0.48	(0.16)	375	(6.7)	399	(10.8)	400	(7.9)	436	(14.0)	**1.67**	(0.29)
Yucatán	-1.17	(0.15)	-2.72	(0.09)	-1.77	(0.17)	-0.78	(0.22)	0.61	(0.17)	383	(7.2)	404	(8.2)	401	(8.7)	453	(7.3)	**1.96**	(0.37)
Zacatecas	-1.17	(0.08)	-2.55	(0.06)	-1.78	(0.05)	-0.93	(0.11)	0.58	(0.13)	389	(7.2)	402	(6.8)	411	(6.7)	439	(7.0)	**1.54**	(0.29)

• PISA adjudicated region.

Notes: Values that are statistically significant are indicated in bold (see Annex A3).

See Table II.2.4a for national data.

1. ESCS refers to the *PISA index of economic, social and cultural status*.

StatLink http://dx.doi.org/10.1787/888932964965

[Part 2/2]
Students' socio-economic status and mathematics performance, by region
By national quarters of the PISA index of economic, social and cultural status; results based on students' self-reports

Table B2.II.2

	ESCS[1]					Performance on the mathematics scale, by national quarters of this index				Increased likelihood of students in the bottom quarter of the ESCS index scoring in the bottom quarter of the mathematics performance distribution	
	All students	Bottom quarter	Second quarter	Third quarter	Top quarter	Bottom quarter	Second quarter	Third quarter	Top quarter		
	Mean index S.E.	Mean index S.E.	Mean index S.E.	Mean index S.E.	Mean index S.E.	Mean score S.E.	Mean score S.E.	Mean score S.E.	Mean score S.E.	Ratio	S.E.
OECD											
Portugal											
Alentejo	-0.35 (0.14)	-1.72 (0.07)	-0.87 (0.15)	-0.05 (0.19)	1.25 (0.16)	439 (12.3)	479 (14.9)	497 (9.2)	542 (11.7)	**2.41**	(0.40)
Spain											
Andalusia•	-0.36 (0.07)	-1.65 (0.05)	-0.81 (0.08)	-0.04 (0.10)	1.06 (0.07)	435 (6.1)	456 (6.7)	478 (5.3)	521 (7.5)	**2.01**	(0.27)
Aragon•	-0.06 (0.06)	-1.34 (0.05)	-0.45 (0.05)	0.32 (0.10)	1.23 (0.06)	442 (7.6)	488 (10.1)	520 (6.1)	539 (7.2)	**2.80**	(0.35)
Asturias•	-0.02 (0.05)	-1.28 (0.04)	-0.44 (0.05)	0.34 (0.08)	1.28 (0.05)	455 (7.1)	484 (6.3)	509 (7.9)	550 (8.3)	**2.16**	(0.22)
Balearic Islands•	-0.15 (0.04)	-1.43 (0.04)	-0.53 (0.05)	0.20 (0.06)	1.16 (0.04)	432 (8.4)	473 (7.0)	487 (7.8)	513 (6.5)	**2.35**	(0.28)
Basque Country•	0.03 (0.03)	-1.21 (0.03)	-0.31 (0.03)	0.46 (0.04)	1.17 (0.02)	472 (3.2)	499 (4.0)	517 (3.9)	542 (3.3)	**1.89**	(0.13)
Cantabria•	-0.06 (0.04)	-1.28 (0.04)	-0.47 (0.04)	0.28 (0.07)	1.21 (0.05)	460 (4.9)	477 (4.9)	494 (5.8)	537 (7.3)	**1.76**	(0.20)
Castile and Leon•	-0.10 (0.05)	-1.35 (0.04)	-0.49 (0.05)	0.26 (0.07)	1.19 (0.05)	470 (7.6)	500 (4.9)	519 (6.8)	546 (6.1)	**2.18**	(0.31)
Catalonia•	-0.14 (0.08)	-1.44 (0.07)	-0.53 (0.09)	0.28 (0.12)	1.15 (0.06)	451 (7.2)	474 (7.0)	509 (8.6)	541 (7.0)	**2.17**	(0.28)
Extremadura•	-0.46 (0.05)	-1.72 (0.04)	-0.96 (0.05)	-0.20 (0.07)	1.03 (0.07)	422 (8.2)	446 (5.3)	466 (7.4)	514 (6.0)	**2.04**	(0.25)
Galicia•	-0.18 (0.05)	-1.43 (0.05)	-0.59 (0.05)	0.15 (0.08)	1.16 (0.04)	458 (5.3)	473 (6.2)	499 (5.2)	527 (6.1)	**1.84**	(0.18)
La Rioja•	-0.15 (0.02)	-1.42 (0.04)	-0.55 (0.03)	0.21 (0.04)	1.18 (0.03)	457 (6.1)	487 (6.4)	511 (5.3)	560 (5.1)	**2.16**	(0.25)
Madrid•	0.11 (0.07)	-1.22 (0.08)	-0.26 (0.08)	0.57 (0.11)	1.37 (0.06)	458 (6.0)	488 (5.7)	529 (8.0)	542 (5.8)	**2.41**	(0.29)
Murcia•	-0.48 (0.05)	-1.76 (0.04)	-0.87 (0.05)	-0.17 (0.07)	0.88 (0.07)	427 (6.6)	439 (6.4)	473 (7.1)	511 (6.3)	**1.90**	(0.19)
Navarre•	-0.11 (0.04)	-1.33 (0.04)	-0.51 (0.05)	0.23 (0.06)	1.17 (0.05)	481 (4.9)	503 (4.6)	527 (6.0)	559 (4.5)	**2.18**	(0.27)
United Kingdom											
England	0.29 (0.02)	-0.76 (0.03)	0.02 (0.04)	0.62 (0.03)	1.27 (0.02)	460 (5.0)	478 (5.4)	511 (4.6)	546 (4.5)	**1.88**	(0.14)
Northern Ireland	0.29 (0.02)	-0.76 (0.02)	-0.08 (0.03)	0.61 (0.04)	1.38 (0.02)	444 (4.6)	471 (5.4)	502 (4.6)	541 (5.4)	**2.17**	(0.17)
Scotland•	0.13 (0.02)	-0.96 (0.02)	-0.18 (0.03)	0.49 (0.03)	1.18 (0.02)	463 (4.0)	487 (4.2)	504 (3.5)	546 (4.6)	**1.95**	(0.14)
Wales	0.19 (0.02)	-0.82 (0.02)	-0.12 (0.03)	0.50 (0.02)	1.19 (0.02)	436 (3.5)	461 (3.0)	473 (3.7)	512 (3.4)	**1.80**	(0.13)
United States											
Connecticut•	0.49 (0.06)	-0.75 (0.08)	0.24 (0.08)	0.90 (0.06)	1.56 (0.05)	450 (6.4)	481 (8.5)	529 (9.1)	568 (6.9)	**2.55**	(0.27)
Florida•	0.20 (0.06)	-0.98 (0.06)	-0.07 (0.07)	0.58 (0.07)	1.27 (0.03)	429 (5.7)	456 (8.1)	465 (8.5)	520 (8.9)	**1.90**	(0.26)
Massachusetts•	0.44 (0.07)	-0.77 (0.07)	0.23 (0.09)	0.86 (0.07)	1.44 (0.06)	459 (6.2)	491 (6.6)	532 (11.9)	576 (10.6)	**2.40**	(0.33)
Partners											
Argentina											
Ciudad Autónoma de Buenos Aires•	-0.20 (0.09)	-1.82 (0.09)	-0.55 (0.12)	0.40 (0.11)	1.18 (0.06)	343 (15.1)	407 (9.8)	452 (10.3)	473 (7.7)	**3.69**	(0.59)
Brazil											
Acre	-1.36 (0.10)	-2.88 (0.08)	-1.85 (0.12)	-0.99 (0.13)	0.30 (0.12)	332 (7.8)	351 (6.7)	361 (7.8)	393 (17.9)	1.78	(0.39)
Alagoas	-1.70 (0.13)	-3.07 (0.09)	-2.35 (0.12)	-1.42 (0.22)	0.06 (0.16)	325 (5.5)	325 (8.4)	345 (10.0)	377 (15.5)	1.39	(0.31)
Amapá	-0.92 (0.12)	-2.29 (0.08)	-1.25 (0.12)	-0.54 (0.14)	0.41 (0.18)	335 (10.4)	355 (8.7)	364 (11.7)	391 (17.0)	1.91	(0.36)
Amazonas	-1.06 (0.06)	-2.41 (0.06)	-1.40 (0.06)	-0.74 (0.07)	0.31 (0.08)	335 (5.7)	354 (5.6)	353 (6.5)	382 (14.2)	1.44	(0.34)
Bahia	-1.52 (0.09)	-3.05 (0.08)	-2.14 (0.14)	-1.15 (0.15)	0.28 (0.09)	350 (7.8)	344 (14.8)	369 (20.4)	434 (10.1)	1.48	(0.40)
Ceará	-1.54 (0.10)	-3.06 (0.07)	-2.09 (0.13)	-1.21 (0.13)	0.21 (0.21)	354 (5.5)	366 (8.7)	374 (14.4)	423 (25.6)	1.46	(0.26)
Espírito Santo	-1.17 (0.10)	-2.73 (0.12)	-1.68 (0.11)	-0.78 (0.10)	0.51 (0.21)	388 (11.2)	380 (9.0)	411 (14.1)	482 (21.5)	1.38	(0.37)
Federal District	-0.68 (0.10)	-2.11 (0.06)	-1.18 (0.09)	-0.28 (0.14)	0.84 (0.18)	369 (7.7)	390 (12.9)	419 (16.4)	486 (18.3)	2.05	(0.31)
Goiás	-1.25 (0.09)	-2.60 (0.10)	-1.63 (0.09)	-0.95 (0.11)	0.17 (0.11)	346 (7.0)	368 (12.1)	383 (8.6)	422 (9.5)	1.93	(0.37)
Maranhão	-1.42 (0.19)	-2.93 (0.13)	-1.91 (0.20)	-1.02 (0.22)	0.19 (0.24)	317 (10.4)	324 (15.2)	350 (14.0)	386 (27.3)	1.68	(0.43)
Mato Grosso	-1.34 (0.08)	-2.72 (0.09)	-1.81 (0.05)	-1.05 (0.09)	0.24 (0.17)	348 (8.7)	356 (7.3)	367 (9.4)	410 (23.9)	1.56	(0.27)
Mato Grosso do Sul	-0.96 (0.10)	-2.50 (0.07)	-1.49 (0.12)	-0.48 (0.16)	0.66 (0.08)	370 (7.5)	394 (12.1)	413 (7.4)	462 (13.1)	2.24	(0.38)
Minas Gerais	-1.29 (0.08)	-2.75 (0.07)	-1.81 (0.11)	-0.96 (0.11)	0.38 (0.13)	377 (6.4)	391 (11.0)	403 (10.2)	443 (15.3)	1.70	(0.31)
Pará	-1.21 (0.17)	-2.63 (0.10)	-1.66 (0.18)	-0.85 (0.20)	0.29 (0.20)	333 (8.1)	344 (8.0)	372 (9.1)	392 (9.4)	1.78	(0.35)
Paraíba	-1.13 (0.09)	-2.86 (0.11)	-1.58 (0.19)	-0.56 (0.14)	0.46 (0.11)	344 (13.0)	377 (10.5)	415 (16.8)	449 (16.7)	2.64	(0.49)
Paraná	-1.09 (0.12)	-2.52 (0.09)	-1.52 (0.10)	-0.78 (0.13)	0.48 (0.27)	365 (6.5)	386 (7.8)	402 (8.2)	465 (44.8)	2.10	(0.45)
Pernambuco	-1.61 (0.12)	-3.00 (0.13)	-1.99 (0.17)	-1.24 (0.11)	-0.21 (0.11)	337 (10.5)	350 (8.0)	373 (9.6)	392 (12.8)	1.77	(0.37)
Piauí	-1.26 (0.09)	-2.86 (0.11)	-1.78 (0.12)	-0.89 (0.12)	0.51 (0.06)	345 (8.0)	367 (10.4)	378 (9.4)	451 (17.9)	2.27	(0.42)
Rio de Janeiro	-0.94 (0.07)	-2.18 (0.05)	-1.28 (0.04)	-0.66 (0.08)	0.36 (0.17)	365 (10.5)	380 (8.6)	386 (11.0)	428 (19.2)	1.67	(0.35)
Rio Grande do Norte	-1.32 (0.13)	-2.79 (0.11)	-1.84 (0.13)	-1.01 (0.18)	0.38 (0.20)	346 (6.6)	351 (4.9)	373 (13.8)	450 (26.8)	1.62	(0.32)
Rio Grande do Sul	-1.20 (0.08)	-2.54 (0.07)	-1.64 (0.09)	-0.86 (0.10)	0.26 (0.08)	382 (9.2)	401 (6.5)	416 (7.3)	427 (8.6)	1.86	(0.41)
Rondônia	-1.39 (0.16)	-2.88 (0.10)	-1.87 (0.20)	-1.00 (0.21)	0.20 (0.19)	366 (7.0)	371 (7.5)	383 (8.8)	410 (11.7)	1.50	(0.37)
Roraima	-1.04 (0.08)	-2.51 (0.08)	-1.48 (0.09)	-0.66 (0.12)	0.50 (0.09)	331 (6.3)	344 (7.3)	363 (8.1)	412 (15.5)	1.92	(0.37)
Santa Catarina	-1.19 (0.12)	-2.58 (0.08)	-1.61 (0.13)	-0.87 (0.14)	0.29 (0.16)	388 (10.9)	407 (11.8)	416 (9.1)	453 (17.0)	1.83	(0.37)
São Paulo	-0.94 (0.05)	-2.33 (0.05)	-1.37 (0.05)	-0.61 (0.07)	0.54 (0.06)	374 (3.4)	390 (4.2)	406 (6.0)	447 (12.0)	1.65	(0.18)
Sergipe	-1.25 (0.10)	-2.76 (0.08)	-1.63 (0.15)	-0.83 (0.11)	0.21 (0.08)	353 (7.4)	384 (11.3)	389 (11.2)	413 (18.7)	1.80	(0.41)
Tocantins	-1.31 (0.09)	-2.82 (0.07)	-1.75 (0.10)	-0.91 (0.13)	0.27 (0.10)	337 (6.2)	346 (9.3)	370 (8.1)	409 (12.9)	1.69	(0.35)
Colombia											
Bogotá	-1.09 (0.05)	-2.34 (0.04)	-1.42 (0.06)	-0.75 (0.06)	0.14 (0.07)	370 (3.4)	391 (4.7)	395 (4.1)	417 (8.0)	**1.86**	(0.19)
Cali	-0.81 (0.08)	-2.09 (0.07)	-1.12 (0.09)	-0.49 (0.08)	0.47 (0.10)	345 (7.4)	368 (6.5)	386 (9.8)	417 (7.3)	**2.09**	(0.33)
Manizales	-0.77 (0.07)	-2.25 (0.09)	-1.03 (0.09)	-0.36 (0.07)	0.57 (0.05)	362 (5.9)	393 (5.4)	416 (7.7)	446 (10.5)	**2.60**	(0.31)
Medellín	-0.94 (0.10)	-2.43 (0.10)	-1.31 (0.09)	-0.57 (0.11)	0.56 (0.15)	357 (5.4)	370 (6.2)	393 (9.2)	459 (22.3)	**1.96**	(0.31)
Russian Federation											
Perm Territory region•	-0.12 (0.03)	-1.13 (0.05)	-0.36 (0.04)	0.23 (0.04)	0.76 (0.02)	445 (6.8)	479 (6.6)	493 (7.7)	521 (9.0)	**2.11**	(0.25)
United Arab Emirates											
Abu Dhabi•	0.29 (0.03)	-0.91 (0.06)	0.14 (0.04)	0.65 (0.03)	1.28 (0.02)	384 (4.3)	413 (4.6)	439 (6.1)	453 (7.6)	**1.91**	(0.15)
Ajman	-0.09 (0.06)	-1.30 (0.12)	-0.26 (0.06)	0.25 (0.06)	0.96 (0.06)	379 (11.2)	389 (11.1)	414 (11.0)	431 (8.7)	1.71	(0.34)
Dubai•	0.50 (0.01)	-0.46 (0.02)	0.37 (0.01)	0.77 (0.01)	1.32 (0.01)	418 (3.1)	457 (3.2)	486 (3.2)	496 (2.7)	**2.27**	(0.14)
Fujairah	0.01 (0.03)	-1.16 (0.06)	-0.19 (0.04)	0.36 (0.04)	1.03 (0.03)	392 (6.1)	396 (10.1)	424 (9.9)	432 (21.5)	1.34	(0.31)
Ras al-Khaimah	0.06 (0.08)	-1.19 (0.14)	-0.12 (0.09)	0.43 (0.07)	1.11 (0.06)	394 (8.1)	394 (10.3)	434 (9.6)	441 (6.6)	1.50	(0.19)
Sharjah	0.44 (0.04)	-0.59 (0.05)	0.34 (0.05)	0.76 (0.03)	1.25 (0.03)	400 (11.1)	440 (7.9)	466 (12.4)	452 (13.7)	**2.02**	(0.40)
Umm al-Quwain	-0.10 (0.04)	-1.32 (0.09)	-0.25 (0.05)	0.27 (0.05)	0.93 (0.05)	377 (9.1)	393 (10.7)	393 (8.7)	432 (12.0)	1.47	(0.39)

• PISA adjudicated region.
Notes: Values that are statistically significant are indicated in bold (see Annex A3).
See Table II.2.4a for national data.
1. ESCS refers to the *PISA index of economic, social and cultural status*.
StatLink ᵃˢᵖ http://dx.doi.org/10.1787/888932964965

[Part 1/4]
Relationship between mathematics performance and elements of socio-economic status, by region

Table B2.II.3 *Results based on students' self-reports*

	Score-point difference in mathematics performance associated with each of the following factors, after accounting for the other factors												
	Intercept		Parents' highest occupational status		Parents' highest level of education		Index of cultural possessions		Index of home educational resources		Number of books at home		Wealth	
	Mean score	S.E.	Score dif.	S.E.	Score dif.	S.E.	Score dif.	S.E.	Score dif.	S.E.	Score dif.	S.E.	Score dif.	S.E.
Australia														
Australian Capital Territory	293	(29.4)	1	(0.2)	6	(2.3)	2	(4.3)	5	(4.5)	**21**	(2.8)	-10	(4.5)
New South Wales	342	(16.5)	1	(0.1)	6	(1.2)	2	(2.1)	**12**	(2.2)	**17**	(1.6)	-8	(2.5)
Northern Territory	381	(54.9)	1	(0.4)	-1	(3.9)	-1	(7.8)	15	(8.0)	**14**	(4.2)	14	(7.2)
Queensland	328	(16.7)	1	(0.1)	6	(1.2)	-2	(2.3)	9	(2.1)	**18**	(1.7)	0	(2.9)
South Australia	334	(23.1)	1	(0.1)	6	(1.6)	-3	(3.5)	9	(2.7)	**16**	(2.4)	-8	(2.2)
Tasmania	332	(19.8)	1	(0.1)	3	(1.5)	0	(3.3)	9	(2.7)	**18**	(2.2)	-10	(3.5)
Victoria	347	(13.9)	1	(0.1)	5	(1.2)	-1	(2.7)	7	(2.4)	**16**	(1.5)	-11	(2.7)
Western Australia	359	(20.1)	1	(0.1)	5	(1.6)	0	(3.3)	**13**	(2.3)	**16**	(2.0)	-4	(2.6)
Belgium														
Flemish Community•	375	(9.9)	1	(0.1)	3	(0.8)	-4	(1.8)	**12**	(2.3)	**16**	(1.2)	0	(2.3)
French Community	396	(11.8)	1	(0.1)	0	(0.7)	4	(2.6)	9	(2.5)	**16**	(1.8)	4	(2.2)
German-speaking Community	443	(19.4)	1	(0.2)	-2	(1.3)	-4	(4.5)	**13**	(4.0)	**18**	(3.0)	-10	(4.1)
Canada														
Alberta	408	(13.9)	1	(0.1)	0	(1.0)	-2	(2.9)	5	(2.7)	**18**	(2.3)	-3	(2.3)
British Columbia	415	(16.5)	1	(0.1)	2	(1.1)	2	(2.9)	5	(2.1)	**17**	(2.1)	-7	(1.9)
Manitoba	373	(18.1)	1	(0.1)	3	(1.2)	2	(3.1)	4	(2.2)	**16**	(1.9)	3	(2.5)
New Brunswick	388	(18.5)	1	(0.1)	2	(1.2)	-6	(3.0)	8	(2.5)	**16**	(2.1)	-9	(3.3)
Newfoundland and Labrador	373	(35.2)	1	(0.1)	1	(1.9)	4	(3.9)	0	(3.2)	**14**	(3.0)	-1	(2.9)
Nova Scotia	350	(19.7)	0	(0.1)	4	(1.6)	-5	(3.2)	8	(3.4)	**18**	(2.1)	-7	(3.0)
Ontario	397	(14.3)	1	(0.1)	2	(1.0)	4	(1.9)	0	(1.7)	**15**	(1.5)	-5	(2.3)
Prince Edward Island	380	(18.4)	1	(0.1)	1	(1.3)	2	(3.2)	5	(3.1)	**14**	(2.1)	-10	(3.1)
Quebec	397	(14.3)	1	(0.1)	3	(1.0)	0	(1.9)	3	(2.1)	**18**	(1.5)	-1	(2.2)
Saskatchewan	410	(17.7)	0	(0.1)	2	(1.2)	1	(3.3)	1	(2.3)	**15**	(2.1)	1	(2.5)
Italy														
Abruzzo	418	(15.2)	1	(0.2)	-2	(0.9)	8	(3.1)	9	(4.2)	**13**	(2.4)	-4	(4.6)
Basilicata	398	(10.7)	1	(0.1)	1	(1.1)	8	(2.9)	0	(3.6)	**10**	(2.3)	3	(5.1)
Bolzano	422	(11.6)	1	(0.1)	-1	(0.9)	-2	(2.7)	5	(2.6)	**18**	(1.6)	-8	(2.4)
Calabria	367	(13.7)	1	(0.2)	0	(0.9)	0	(3.2)	**12**	(2.9)	**12**	(2.0)	1	(3.8)
Campania	374	(16.1)	1	(0.2)	0	(1.1)	9	(4.1)	2	(3.5)	**15**	(3.3)	-3	(3.4)
Emilia Romagna	414	(16.1)	1	(0.2)	-1	(1.2)	**10**	(4.2)	5	(2.6)	**18**	(2.3)	-2	(2.7)
Friuli Venezia Giulia	456	(26.0)	1	(0.1)	-1	(1.5)	5	(3.9)	8	(3.2)	**15**	(2.6)	1	(3.1)
Lazio	394	(18.0)	1	(0.2)	0	(1.1)	**10**	(3.3)	-4	(2.9)	**17**	(2.7)	-2	(3.6)
Liguria	409	(13.9)	1	(0.2)	-2	(0.9)	6	(3.2)	7	(3.4)	**18**	(2.5)	-6	(3.0)
Lombardia	435	(11.6)	1	(0.2)	-1	(0.7)	8	(3.1)	1	(2.7)	**15**	(1.9)	1	(4.0)
Marche	456	(13.2)	1	(0.1)	-2	(1.0)	5	(3.6)	2	(3.2)	**11**	(2.2)	5	(3.7)
Molise	403	(12.9)	1	(0.2)	0	(1.1)	6	(3.3)	**13**	(3.5)	**11**	(2.2)	-1	(4.1)
Piemonte	424	(9.8)	1	(0.1)	-1	(0.7)	3	(2.9)	4	(2.5)	**17**	(2.5)	4	(4.4)
Puglia	410	(10.8)	1	(0.1)	0	(0.9)	4	(3.2)	9	(2.9)	**11**	(2.3)	1	(4.1)
Sardegna	389	(16.0)	1	(0.2)	-1	(1.1)	8	(2.9)	8	(4.0)	7	(2.8)	-7	(4.5)
Sicilia	393	(11.0)	1	(0.1)	-1	(0.9)	6	(3.2)	8	(3.2)	9	(2.7)	1	(3.6)
Toscana	422	(14.6)	1	(0.2)	-1	(0.9)	**14**	(4.0)	4	(3.1)	**14**	(2.5)	3	(4.3)
Trento	463	(15.8)	1	(0.2)	-2	(1.1)	5	(3.7)	1	(2.6)	**10**	(1.8)	-5	(3.1)
Umbria	446	(24.0)	0	(0.2)	-2	(1.2)	5	(3.8)	**10**	(3.9)	**17**	(2.9)	0	(3.8)
Valle d'Aosta	414	(14.2)	1	(0.2)	1	(1.1)	0	(4.0)	9	(3.7)	**15**	(2.7)	-7	(4.3)
Veneto	452	(14.0)	1	(0.2)	-2	(1.0)	4	(3.8)	8	(3.1)	**18**	(2.4)	1	(3.7)
Mexico														
Aguascalientes	404	(14.6)	0	(0.2)	2	(1.1)	5	(2.7)	4	(3.1)	4	(3.3)	5	(3.8)
Baja California	364	(12.0)	0	(0.2)	1	(1.8)	-1	(2.9)	-2	(3.5)	**15**	(3.7)	0	(2.6)
Baja California Sur	363	(15.8)	0	(0.2)	2	(1.1)	1	(3.0)	2	(3.0)	6	(2.5)	3	(2.7)
Campeche	344	(14.8)	1	(0.1)	3	(0.8)	-3	(3.3)	9	(3.3)	2	(3.1)	-5	(2.9)
Chiapas	358	(13.1)	1	(0.2)	0	(1.1)	-9	(3.4)	6	(4.3)	3	(3.3)	1	(2.7)
Chihuahua	376	(15.9)	1	(0.2)	2	(0.8)	1	(3.6)	1	(4.5)	9	(3.6)	4	(3.7)
Coahuila	378	(11.1)	1	(0.2)	1	(1.0)	3	(3.5)	6	(3.5)	**10**	(3.5)	4	(3.6)
Colima	406	(15.9)	0	(0.2)	1	(0.9)	1	(3.0)	5	(2.8)	6	(3.0)	7	(2.2)
Distrito Federal	384	(14.2)	0	(0.1)	1	(1.0)	5	(4.6)	5	(2.9)	7	(3.2)	2	(3.0)
Durango	380	(12.2)	1	(0.1)	1	(1.2)	5	(3.2)	5	(3.6)	6	(3.4)	-4	(4.5)
Guanajuato	379	(17.3)	1	(0.1)	2	(1.1)	1	(2.7)	6	(3.0)	3	(2.5)	2	(3.1)
Guerrero	350	(15.4)	0	(0.2)	2	(0.9)	-4	(3.7)	8	(3.3)	2	(2.7)	1	(3.0)
Hidalgo	380	(17.3)	0	(0.2)	3	(1.0)	-5	(3.5)	9	(2.2)	0	(2.7)	2	(2.8)
Jalisco	431	(12.3)	0	(0.2)	1	(1.0)	0	(3.0)	5	(3.6)	3	(3.1)	7	(4.1)
Mexico	393	(17.2)	0	(0.1)	2	(1.0)	-2	(2.6)	4	(3.7)	8	(3.3)	5	(4.3)
Morelos	386	(13.8)	0	(0.1)	2	(1.1)	1	(2.9)	0	(3.4)	9	(4.0)	11	(4.3)
Nayarit	394	(14.4)	0	(0.2)	3	(1.2)	-1	(3.7)	1	(4.1)	-6	(3.7)	8	(4.7)
Nuevo León	401	(11.8)	0	(0.2)	1	(0.7)	4	(2.8)	6	(3.0)	7	(2.3)	3	(2.9)
Puebla	389	(15.1)	0	(0.2)	5	(1.1)	-6	(3.3)	7	(3.9)	-3	(2.2)	5	(2.9)
Querétaro	411	(18.4)	0	(0.2)	1	(1.5)	-3	(3.6)	8	(3.1)	4	(2.9)	5	(3.3)
Quintana Roo	372	(13.2)	0	(0.1)	2	(0.8)	3	(2.7)	-1	(3.5)	8	(2.9)	8	(3.3)
San Luis Potosí	397	(15.7)	0	(0.1)	2	(1.1)	2	(3.1)	4	(3.5)	3	(3.5)	9	(3.3)
Sinaloa	372	(14.1)	0	(0.1)	2	(0.9)	0	(2.8)	-1	(3.2)	8	(2.3)	3	(3.8)
Tabasco	348	(13.5)	0	(0.2)	1	(1.0)	0	(4.8)	4	(3.2)	7	(3.2)	1	(3.0)
Tamaulipas	360	(21.1)	0	(0.1)	2	(1.3)	-2	(3.1)	4	(2.4)	**10**	(4.7)	0	(3.4)
Tlaxcala	375	(13.4)	0	(0.1)	2	(1.1)	-4	(3.6)	9	(2.5)	4	(2.8)	-3	(2.1)
Veracruz	375	(16.0)	0	(0.2)	2	(0.9)	-4	(2.9)	6	(3.6)	5	(2.6)	3	(3.8)
Yucatán	358	(9.4)	1	(0.2)	2	(1.4)	-7	(2.5)	**13**	(4.6)	6	(3.4)	-4	(3.1)
Zacatecas	375	(12.7)	0	(0.1)	2	(1.0)	-4	(3.9)	7	(2.7)	5	(2.6)	0	(2.8)

• PISA adjudicated region.
Notes: Values that are statistically significant are indicated in bold (see Annex A3).
See Table II.2.6 for national data.
1. Unique variation is the variation explained by each factor after taking into account the variation explained by the other factors in the model.
StatLink http://dx.doi.org/10.1787/888932964965

[Part 2/4]

Relationship between mathematics performance and elements of socio-economic status, by region

Table B2.II.3 *Results based on students' self-reports*

	Intercept		Parents' highest occupational status		Parents' highest level of education		Index of cultural possessions		Index of home educational resources		Number of books at home		Wealth	
	Mean score	S.E.	Score dif.	S.E.	Score dif.	S.E.	Score dif.	S.E.	Score dif.	S.E.	Score dif.	S.E.	Score dif.	S.E.
Portugal														
Alentejo	407	(14.2)	1	(0.3)	1	(1.2)	8	(5.3)	2	(3.7)	12	(2.7)	1	(3.6)
Spain														
Andalusia•	369	(8.2)	1	(0.1)	1	(0.8)	6	(2.5)	5	(3.0)	19	(2.1)		(3.0)
Aragon•	368	(13.4)	1	(0.2)	2	(0.8)	12	(3.1)	1	(3.4)	20	(2.2)		(2.8)
Asturias•	369	(12.3)	1	(0.2)	2	(1.1)	10	(3.2)	5	(3.6)	20	(2.0)		(3.7)
Balearic Islands•	385	(13.4)	1	(0.1)	-1	(0.8)	4	(3.6)	7	(2.3)	17	(2.1)		(3.2)
Basque Country•	398	(6.6)	1	(0.1)	1	(0.5)	3	(1.6)	5	(1.6)	16	(1.3)		(1.9)
Cantabria•	392	(12.1)	1	(0.2)	0	(1.0)	5	(3.2)	7	(3.4)	17	(2.6)	-1	(2.7)
Castile and Leon•	379	(11.4)	1	(0.1)	3	(0.7)	-1	(2.4)	5	(2.8)	19	(2.2)		(3.0)
Catalonia•	390	(14.8)	1	(0.2)	2	(1.0)	9	(2.4)	1	(2.4)	15	(2.1)		(3.6)
Extremadura•	361	(8.8)	1	(0.2)	0	(0.9)	8	(2.2)	12	(3.3)	16	(2.2)		(3.1)
Galicia•	393	(10.4)	1	(0.1)	0	(1.0)	1	(2.3)	7	(3.0)	18	(1.4)		(3.1)
La Rioja•	373	(11.1)	1	(0.1)	1	(0.8)	6	(3.5)	5	(3.0)	24	(2.1)		(3.8)
Madrid•	368	(10.4)	0	(0.1)	3	(0.7)	9	(3.6)	0	(2.8)	18	(2.4)		(3.4)
Murcia•	361	(10.0)	1	(0.1)	1	(0.7)	7	(3.0)	7	(2.7)	21	(2.1)		(3.1)
Navarre•	401	(10.3)	1	(0.1)	2	(0.8)	0	(3.0)	0	(2.8)	16	(1.9)		(3.5)
United Kingdom														
England	391	(15.6)	1	(0.1)	0	(0.9)	0	(1.8)	6	(1.7)	22	(1.3)		(1.9)
Northern Ireland	403	(20.6)	1	(0.1)	-1	(1.4)	3	(2.5)	6	(2.5)	20	(1.5)		(2.8)
Scotland•	410	(11.6)	1	(0.1)	0	(0.8)	2	(2.1)	9	(1.8)	19	(1.4)		(2.4)
Wales	402	(12.8)	1	(0.1)	-2	(0.8)	-3	(2.1)	11	(1.7)	21	(1.4)		(2.0)
United States														
Connecticut•	308	(18.2)	1	(0.1)	5	(1.2)	-1	(2.9)	4	(3.1)	23	(2.1)		(3.0)
Florida•	397	(13.8)	1	(0.2)	-1	(1.4)	0	(3.1)	3	(2.0)	17	(2.1)	1	(2.6)
Massachusetts•	349	(20.3)	1	(0.1)	3	(1.5)	3	(3.0)	0	(2.5)	23	(2.1)		(3.3)
Argentina														
Ciudad Autónoma de Buenos Aires•	288	(23.4)	1	(0.1)	5	(1.2)	2	(3.4)	1	(2.8)	12	(2.7)		(3.9)
Brazil														
Acre	338	(11.0)	1	(0.2)	2	(0.9)	-5	(3.2)	5	(2.9)	2	(2.7)		(4.5)
Alagoas	347	(10.1)	0	(0.2)	2	(0.9)	0	(4.7)	14	(5.8)	-1	(3.4)		(6.3)
Amapá	340	(19.6)	0	(0.2)	3	(0.9)	-4	(3.4)	11	(3.4)	-4	(2.7)		(6.3)
Amazonas	332	(14.1)	0	(0.2)	2	(0.7)	-5	(4.9)	13	(2.3)	1	(2.9)		(6.6)
Bahia	368	(27.2)	1	(0.3)	-1	(1.6)	2	(4.8)	13	(4.6)	2	(9.2)		(6.2)
Ceará	375	(12.6)	1	(0.2)	1	(0.9)	-5	(5.0)	8	(4.5)	3	(3.4)	1	(6.7)
Espírito Santo	382	(23.5)	1	(0.3)	1	(1.3)	-4	(2.8)	7	(3.5)	13	(3.4)	1	(6.4)
Federal District	334	(20.7)	1	(0.2)	3	(1.3)	-1	(5.5)	9	(4.7)	9	(3.6)	1	(3.6)
Goiás	338	(13.7)	0	(0.2)	3	(0.9)	-7	(4.9)	9	(4.5)	9	(3.7)		(3.9)
Maranhão	338	(13.1)	1	(0.3)	2	(1.4)	-4	(6.2)	13	(5.5)	-2	(4.3)	1	(5.6)
Mato Grosso	376	(16.1)	1	(0.3)	0	(1.1)	0	(4.4)	8	(3.6)	0	(3.8)	1	(6.4)
Mato Grosso do Sul	344	(16.9)	0	(0.2)	4	(1.1)	-2	(3.8)	8	(4.4)	7	(3.2)		(3.6)
Minas Gerais	365	(14.8)	0	(0.3)	2	(1.2)	-6	(3.8)	7	(3.9)	9	(2.9)		(4.1)
Pará	347	(11.3)	0	(0.1)	2	(0.7)	-6	(3.0)	8	(2.7)	-2	(2.9)		(3.5)
Paraíba	356	(13.6)	1	(0.3)	2	(0.8)	-2	(4.5)	7	(3.2)	3	(3.2)	1	(6.0)
Paraná	338	(13.2)	1	(0.3)	3	(1.4)	-4	(6.3)	1	(3.0)	13	(6.7)	1	(6.7)
Pernambuco	334	(10.6)	0	(0.3)	3	(1.2)	-8	(3.3)	0	(3.4)	3	(3.8)	1	(5.1)
Piauí	325	(19.7)	0	(0.3)	5	(0.8)	-8	(2.8)	8	(4.3)	12	(7.7)	1	(3.6)
Rio de Janeiro	344	(18.8)	1	(0.2)	1	(1.1)	-8	(2.9)	5	(3.5)	9	(3.2)	1	(5.6)
Rio Grande do Norte	342	(19.6)	1	(0.2)	2	(1.2)	-6	(3.5)	2	(3.8)	15	(6.2)	2	(3.8)
Rio Grande do Sul	377	(13.8)	0	(0.1)	1	(0.8)	-14	(4.8)	10	(3.4)	9	(5.4)		(3.9)
Rondônia	367	(11.3)	0	(0.2)	2	(0.8)	-6	(2.7)	7	(3.8)	-2	(3.3)		(3.4)
Roraima	341	(14.0)	1	(0.2)	2	(1.1)	-5	(2.5)	7	(4.7)	3	(4.3)	1	(3.6)
Santa Catarina	363	(16.9)	0	(0.2)	2	(0.9)	-9	(3.6)	8	(3.5)	13	(3.3)		(5.0)
São Paulo	347	(9.3)	1	(0.2)	2	(0.6)	2	(1.9)	6	(2.5)	8	(2.3)		(4.7)
Sergipe	353	(19.2)	1	(0.2)	2	(1.3)	-12	(4.0)	16	(4.4)	0	(4.1)		(6.0)
Tocantins	344	(13.5)	1	(0.2)	1	(1.0)	-8	(2.6)	11	(3.5)	4	(3.0)	1	(4.3)
Colombia														
Bogotá	368	(9.2)	0	(0.2)	2	(0.7)	-3	(2.0)	-1	(2.3)	7	(1.9)	1	(3.5)
Cali	317	(12.3)	0	(0.1)	3	(0.8)	0	(2.6)	2	(2.1)	7	(2.3)		(3.9)
Manizales	338	(11.2)	1	(0.2)	3	(0.7)	-2	(3.3)	-4	(3.2)	10	(2.8)	1	(3.8)
Medellín	365	(13.6)	1	(0.2)	1	(0.9)	-1	(2.7)	-4	(2.7)	11	(2.6)	2	(2.9)
Russian Federation														
Perm Territory region•	322	(32.0)	1	(0.2)	7	(2.1)	11	(2.7)	8	(2.7)	9	(2.6)		(2.9)
United Arab Emirates														
Abu Dhabi•	305	(13.0)	1	(0.1)	3	(0.9)	2	(2.1)	15	(1.8)	7	(1.6)		(1.6)
Ajman	356	(19.7)	0	(0.2)	3	(1.3)	8	(3.9)	7	(3.6)	2	(2.9)		(3.1)
Dubai•	308	(11.9)	1	(0.1)	5	(0.7)	3	(1.8)	19	(1.7)	11	(1.2)		(1.3)
Fujairah	339	(21.4)	1	(0.3)	2	(1.6)	3	(4.6)	10	(4.0)	4	(2.8)		(3.9)
Ras al-Khaimah	325	(23.2)	1	(0.2)	3	(1.1)	4	(3.9)	9	(3.6)	3	(3.1)		(2.4)
Sharjah	294	(27.7)	1	(0.3)	6	(1.4)	5	(4.0)	13	(5.1)	6	(3.6)		(5.1)
Umm al-Quwain	371	(30.4)	1	(0.4)	-1	(1.6)	11	(6.3)	14	(4.9)	5	(3.6)		(4.6)

• PISA adjudicated region.
Notes: Values that are statistically significant are indicated in bold (see Annex A3).
See Table II.2.6 for national data.
1. Unique variation is the variation explained by each factor after taking into account the variation explained by the other factors in the model.
StatLink http://dx.doi.org/10.1787/888932964965

EXCELLENCE THROUGH EQUITY: GIVING EVERY STUDENT THE CHANCE TO SUCCEED – VOLUME II

[Part 3/4]
Relationship between mathematics performance and elements of socio-economic status, by region
Table B2.II.3 *Results based on students' self-reports*

	Explained variation in student performance (unique[1], common and total)							
	Unique to:						Common explained variation (explained by more than one factor)	Total explained variation
	Parents' highest occupational status	Parents' highest level of education	Index of cultural possessions	Index home educational resources	Number of books at home	Wealth		
	%	%	%	%	%	%	%	%
Australia								
Australian Capital Territory	2.7	1.0	0.0	0.2	7.1	0.9	11.3	23.1
New South Wales	2.0	1.0	0.0	1.0	4.1	0.5	10.2	18.7
Northern Territory	3.0	0.1	0.0	1.8	2.9	1.1	14.3	23.2
Queensland	2.2	1.2	0.0	0.7	5.5	0.0	11.1	20.8
South Australia	1.7	1.1	0.1	0.8	4.5	0.5	7.2	15.8
Tasmania	5.7	0.3	0.0	0.9	5.9	0.8	12.2	25.9
Victoria	2.1	1.1	0.0	0.5	4.5	1.1	6.8	16.1
Western Australia	2.3	0.7	0.0	1.3	4.1	0.1	10.5	19.2
Belgium								
Flemish Community●	4.5	0.5	0.1	1.1	3.7	0.0	13.8	23.7
French Community	4.2	0.0	0.2	0.7	4.3	0.1	16.9	26.3
German-speaking Community	1.9	0.3	0.2	1.4	5.4	0.8	4.4	14.3
Canada								
Alberta	2.7	0.0	0.0	0.3	6.8	0.1	6.0	16.0
British Columbia	1.6	0.2	0.0	0.2	5.5	0.8	6.4	14.7
Manitoba	1.9	0.6	0.1	0.2	5.5	0.1	10.3	18.6
New Brunswick	2.8	0.2	0.4	0.9	5.3	0.8	4.9	15.2
Newfoundland and Labrador	7.7	0.0	0.1	0.0	3.8	0.0	12.9	24.5
Nova Scotia	1.3	1.1	0.2	0.9	6.5	0.4	7.8	18.4
Ontario	2.8	0.2	0.2	0.0	4.6	0.3	6.7	14.8
Prince Edward Island	3.4	0.1	0.1	0.3	3.8	0.9	7.8	16.4
Quebec	1.6	0.6	0.0	0.1	5.7	0.0	9.8	17.8
Saskatchewan	1.1	0.2	0.0	0.0	4.8	0.0	4.4	10.5
Italy								
Abruzzo	3.3	0.3	0.5	0.7	2.9	0.1	8.0	15.9
Basilicata	2.0	0.0	0.6	0.0	1.5	0.0	9.0	13.2
Bolzano	2.6	0.1	0.0	0.2	5.0	0.5	6.1	14.5
Calabria	1.4	0.0	0.0	1.2	2.5	0.0	7.5	12.6
Campania	2.8	0.0	0.7	0.0	3.2	0.1	11.0	17.8
Emilia Romagna	2.1	0.1	0.7	0.2	5.1	0.0	14.4	22.7
Friuli Venezia Giulia	1.4	0.1	0.2	0.5	4.2	0.0	8.3	14.7
Lazio	1.1	0.0	0.7	0.1	4.6	0.0	7.5	14.1
Liguria	3.0	0.4	0.3	0.4	5.2	0.3	10.3	19.9
Lombardia	2.1	0.0	0.5	0.0	3.9	0.0	11.1	17.8
Marche	1.4	0.4	0.2	0.1	2.4	0.2	5.0	9.7
Molise	2.5	0.0	0.4	1.6	2.3	0.0	8.5	15.3
Piemonte	1.5	0.1	0.1	0.1	5.3	0.1	8.9	16.2
Puglia	2.7	0.0	0.2	0.8	2.1	0.0	10.2	16.0
Sardegna	5.7	0.1	0.6	0.5	0.8	0.3	7.6	15.6
Sicilia	3.9	0.1	0.3	0.6	1.5	0.0	9.0	15.5
Toscana	3.1	0.2	1.3	0.1	3.2	0.1	13.6	21.6
Trento	3.9	0.2	0.2	0.0	2.2	0.2	6.1	12.8
Umbria	0.4	0.3	0.2	0.9	5.6	0.0	6.9	14.3
Valle d'Aosta	1.1	0.0	0.0	0.8	4.5	0.4	7.0	13.9
Veneto	2.6	0.4	0.1	0.5	5.0	0.0	10.5	19.2
Mexico								
Aguascalientes	0.5	0.6	0.3	0.2	0.3	0.5	9.1	11.4
Baja California	0.7	0.1	0.0	0.1	3.3	0.0	2.8	7.0
Baja California Sur	1.1	0.8	0.0	0.1	0.7	0.2	7.6	10.5
Campeche	1.4	1.4	0.2	1.0	0.1	0.6	5.4	10.0
Chiapas	2.9	0.0	1.0	0.3	0.1	0.0	2.0	6.4
Chihuahua	1.2	0.5	0.0	0.0	1.2	0.2	7.9	11.1
Coahuila	1.5	0.2	0.1	0.6	1.4	0.2	9.0	13.1
Colima	0.8	0.1	0.0	0.3	0.6	0.9	8.5	11.1
Distrito Federal	0.8	0.1	0.3	0.3	1.0	0.1	9.4	12.1
Durango	1.7	0.3	0.4	0.3	0.6	0.3	6.7	10.3
Guanajuato	1.2	0.7	0.0	0.3	0.1	0.1	9.6	12.1
Guerrero	0.7	0.7	0.2	0.8	0.1	0.0	5.0	7.5
Hidalgo	1.0	1.3	0.4	1.1	0.0	0.1	9.3	13.3
Jalisco	0.1	0.1	0.0	0.3	0.2	0.9	4.6	6.2
Mexico	0.0	0.4	0.1	0.2	1.3	0.4	4.1	6.6
Morelos	0.5	0.4	0.0	0.0	1.4	2.2	15.0	19.4
Nayarit	0.7	0.9	0.0	0.0	0.4	0.9	5.6	8.6
Nuevo León	0.9	0.1	0.2	0.5	1.0	0.2	9.0	11.8
Puebla	0.1	3.8	0.4	0.5	0.1	0.5	9.8	15.3
Querétaro	0.9	0.1	0.1	0.9	0.3	0.4	8.5	11.3
Quintana Roo	0.6	0.8	0.2	0.0	1.0	1.0	8.5	12.0
San Luis Potosí	0.6	0.5	0.0	0.2	0.2	2.2	15.4	19.1
Sinaloa	0.3	0.8	0.0	0.0	1.1	0.2	3.5	5.9
Tabasco	1.4	0.1	0.0	0.3	0.8	0.0	5.3	8.1
Tamaulipas	0.9	0.5	0.1	0.2	1.3	0.0	5.1	8.2
Tlaxcala	0.5	0.6	0.2	1.0	0.3	0.2	3.1	6.0
Veracruz	0.5	0.7	0.2	0.4	0.5	0.2	8.1	10.5
Yucatán	2.2	0.4	0.6	2.1	0.6	0.4	7.0	13.4
Zacatecas	0.8	0.7	0.2	0.7	0.4	0.0	6.7	9.5

● PISA adjudicated region.
Notes: Values that are statistically significant are indicated in bold (see Annex A3).
See Table II.2.6 for national data.
1. Unique variation is the variation explained by each factor after taking into account the variation explained by the other factors in the model.
StatLink ᕥᕦᖴ http://dx.doi.org/10.1787/888932964965

[Part 4/4]
Relationship between mathematics performance and elements of socio-economic status by region
Table B2.II.3   *Results based on students' self-reports*

	Explained variation in student performance (unique[1], common and total)							
	Unique to:						Common explained variation (explained by more than one factor)	Total explained variation
	Parents' highest occupational status	Parents' highest level of education	Index of cultural possessions	Index home educational resources	Number of books at home	Wealth		
	%	%	%	%	%	%	%	%
Portugal								
Alentejo	2.0	0.1	0.5	0.0	1.9	0.9	15.6	21.1
Spain								
Andalusia•	1.8	0.2	0.3	0.2	6.3	0.1	14.9	23.7
Aragon•	1.0	0.5	1.0	0.0	5.7	0.1	16.0	24.3
Asturias•	1.1	0.4	0.7	0.2	6.1	0.0	15.9	24.3
Balearic Islands•	3.1	0.1	0.2	0.4	6.2	0.1	11.3	21.4
Basque Country•	1.5	0.2	0.1	0.3	4.7	0.2	10.0	17.0
Cantabria•	2.8	0.0	0.2	0.4	5.4	0.7	10.9	20.5
Castile and Leon•	1.3	0.8	0.0	0.3	6.5	0.5	11.0	20.3
Catalonia•	1.8	0.3	0.8	0.0	4.4	0.3	15.8	23.5
Extremadura•	3.4	0.0	0.5	1.0	3.6	0.1	14.8	23.4
Galicia•	1.8	0.0	0.0	0.5	6.0	0.2	8.4	16.8
La Rioja•	2.2	0.0	0.3	0.1	8.4	0.1	14.6	25.8
Madrid•	0.7	1.0	0.7	0.0	5.5	0.0	15.2	23.1
Murcia•	1.9	0.1	0.5	0.4	6.8	0.1	15.6	25.3
Navarre•	1.7	0.5	0.0	0.0	4.7	0.1	10.7	17.8
United Kingdom								
England	2.9	0.0	0.0	0.3	9.0	0.1	10.2	22.6
Northern Ireland	3.1	0.0	0.1	0.4	7.5	0.1	13.7	24.9
Scotland•	2.7	0.0	0.0	0.9	7.1	0.2	12.2	23.2
Wales	2.4	0.2	0.1	1.3	8.8	0.1	9.3	22.2
United States								
Connecticut•	1.5	0.9	0.0	0.1	7.7	0.2	17.8	28.4
Florida•	2.5	0.1	0.0	0.1	5.5	1.4	10.7	20.3
Massachusetts•	2.2	0.3	0.1	0.0	7.6	0.2	16.1	26.5
Argentina								
Ciudad Autónoma de Buenos Aires•	2.2	2.7	0.0	0.0	2.1	0.5	19.8	27.3
Brazil								
Acre	1.8	0.6	0.3	0.4	0.1	0.9	10.3	14.3
Alagoas	0.4	1.1	0.0	2.6	0.0	0.2	10.0	14.3
Amapá	1.0	2.5	0.3	2.2	0.5	0.4	9.8	16.7
Amazonas	1.7	0.9	0.4	2.7	0.1	0.1	6.1	12.0
Bahia	6.6	0.2	0.1	1.6	0.1	0.6	17.6	26.8
Ceará	1.5	0.3	0.3	0.7	0.1	2.7	13.7	19.2
Espírito Santo	0.9	0.2	0.1	0.4	1.8	2.5	16.9	22.9
Federal District	3.3	1.1	0.0	0.9	1.2	1.6	22.1	30.3
Goiás	0.9	2.3	0.6	1.1	1.5	1.2	12.6	20.4
Maranhão	1.4	1.3	0.2	1.6	0.1	0.9	13.3	18.7
Mato Grosso	1.9	0.1	0.0	0.9	0.0	4.0	13.2	20.1
Mato Grosso do Sul	1.0	4.0	0.1	0.8	0.8	0.4	17.2	24.2
Minas Gerais	1.1	0.6	0.6	0.6	1.2	0.5	9.6	14.2
Pará	1.8	1.1	0.5	1.0	0.2	1.2	9.7	15.5
Paraíba	3.6	0.7	0.1	0.6	0.2	2.5	21.7	29.2
Paraná	2.5	1.2	0.2	0.0	2.1	2.7	19.4	28.1
Pernambuco	1.3	2.7	1.1	0.0	0.3	1.5	7.8	14.7
Piauí	0.4	3.7	0.6	0.6	2.2	1.7	21.8	31.0
Rio de Janeiro	3.6	0.1	0.9	0.3	1.8	2.2	9.2	18.3
Rio Grande do Norte	1.3	0.7	0.4	0.1	3.0	5.1	23.5	33.9
Rio Grande do Sul	0.8	0.2	2.8	1.5	1.5	0.8	3.9	11.5
Rondônia	0.8	0.9	0.6	1.0	0.1	0.1	4.4	7.9
Roraima	1.7	0.9	0.3	0.8	0.2	4.3	15.7	24.0
Santa Catarina	1.3	1.2	1.2	1.0	2.3	0.2	8.1	15.3
São Paulo	3.2	0.6	0.1	0.5	1.1	0.6	11.9	17.9
Sergipe	2.9	0.8	2.2	3.8	0.0	0.0	7.7	17.5
Tocantins	2.3	0.5	0.7	1.5	0.3	0.8	11.7	17.8
Colombia								
Bogotá	0.3	1.0	0.1	0.0	0.8	3.3	4.9	10.5
Cali	1.4	1.9	0.0	0.1	1.0	1.0	10.7	16.1
Manizales	1.6	1.9	0.1	0.3	1.5	3.2	13.9	22.4
Medellín	2.0	0.2	0.0	0.2	1.5	7.4	20.1	31.3
Russian Federation								
Perm Territory region•	1.6	0.9	1.0	0.6	1.7	0.3	8.0	14.1
United Arab Emirates								
Abu Dhabi•	3.2	0.8	0.1	2.5	1.1	2.4	7.7	17.7
Ajman	0.3	1.4	0.9	0.9	0.2	0.6	4.5	8.9
Dubai•	1.1	1.2	0.1	3.7	2.3	0.6	9.1	18.0
Fujairah	1.9	0.5	0.1	1.5	0.4	0.9	4.9	10.2
Ras al-Khaimah	3.3	0.9	0.2	1.3	0.3	0.5	5.6	12.0
Sharjah	1.1	2.0	0.3	2.2	0.8	3.6	6.9	16.9
Umm al-Quwain	1.8	0.1	1.5	3.5	0.8	0.4	8.0	16.0

• PISA adjudicated region.
Notes: Values that are statistically significant are indicated in bold (see Annex A3).
See Table II.2.6 for national data.
1. Unique variation is the variation explained by each factor after taking into account the variation explained by the other factors in the model.
StatLink ⟡ http://dx.doi.org/10.1787/888932964965

[Part 1/2]
Variation in mathematics performance, by region

Table B2.II.5   *Results based on students' self-reports*

	Mean performance[1]		Total variation in mathematics performance[2]		Variation in mathematics performance between schools[3]		Variation in mathematics performance within schools[4]		As a percentage of the average total variation in mathematics performance across OECD countries			Index of academic inclusion[5]	
	Mean score	S.E.	Mean	S.E.	Mean	S.E.	Mean	S.E.	Total variance	Between schools variance	Within schools variance	Index	S.E.
Australia													
Australian Capital Territory	518	(3.6)	9 327	(556)	1 925	(385)	7 385	(586)	110.0	22.7	87.1	79.3	(3.5)
New South Wales	509	(3.6)	10 396	(532)	3 646	(556)	6 796	(206)	122.6	43.0	80.1	65.1	(3.5)
Northern Territory	452	(10.4)	11 899	(1 314)	3 566	(1 855)	8 243	(915)	140.3	42.1	97.2	69.8	(11.2)
Queensland	503	(2.9)	8 783	(332)	1 851	(301)	6 953	(223)	103.6	21.8	82.0	79.0	(2.8)
South Australia	489	(3.3)	8 313	(362)	1 808	(304)	6 459	(258)	98.0	21.3	76.2	78.1	(3.0)
Tasmania	478	(3.4)	8 936	(455)	1 607	(396)	7 305	(365)	105.4	18.9	86.1	82.0	(3.7)
Victoria	501	(3.7)	8 281	(425)	2 083	(420)	6 241	(254)	97.7	24.6	73.6	75.0	(3.9)
Western Australia	516	(3.4)	8 843	(340)	2 162	(321)	6 768	(256)	104.3	25.5	79.8	75.8	(2.8)
Belgium													
Flemish Community•	531	(3.3)	10800	(429)	5651	(557)	5106	(181)	127.3	66.6	60.2	47.5	(2.8)
French Community	493	(2.9)	9 222	(385)	4 207	(547)	5 021	(184)	108.8	49.6	59.2	54.4	(3.4)
German-speaking Community	511	(2.1)	8 184	(359)	2 649	(1 129)	5 300	(505)	96.5	31.2	62.5	66.7	(9.7)
Canada													
Alberta	517	(4.6)	8 306	(325)	1 670	(375)	6 678	(270)	98.0	19.7	78.8	80.0	(3.6)
British Columbia	522	(4.4)	7 378	(339)	1 009	(207)	6 360	(285)	87.0	11.9	75.0	86.3	(2.5)
Manitoba	492	(2.9)	7 914	(373)	1 404	(348)	6 438	(293)	93.3	16.6	75.9	82.1	(3.7)
New Brunswick	502	(2.6)	6 793	(310)	625	(170)	6 184	(258)	80.1	7.4	72.9	90.8	(2.3)
Newfoundland and Labrador	490	(3.7)	7 466	(376)	1 401	(435)	6 240	(353)	88.0	16.5	73.6	81.7	(4.7)
Nova Scotia	497	(4.1)	6 624	(376)	477	(134)	6 152	(397)	78.1	5.6	72.6	92.8	(1.9)
Ontario	514	(4.1)	7 626	(315)	1 163	(209)	6 531	(238)	89.9	13.7	77.0	84.9	(2.4)
Prince Edward Island	479	(2.5)	7 068	(367)	382	(197)	6 648	(357)	83.4	4.5	78.4	94.6	(2.7)
Quebec	536	(3.4)	8 244	(315)	2 370	(340)	5 797	(196)	97.2	27.9	68.4	71.0	(3.0)
Saskatchewan	506	(3.0)	7 125	(331)	706	(202)	6 339	(244)	84.0	8.3	74.8	90.0	(2.6)
Italy													
Abruzzo	476	(6.4)	8 079	(754)	4 088	(1 007)	3 982	(191)	95.3	48.2	47.0	49.3	(6.3)
Basilicata	466	(4.3)	7 185	(339)	3 038	(551)	4 143	(223)	84.7	35.8	48.9	57.7	(4.6)
Bolzano	506	(2.1)	8 000	(239)	3 493	(671)	4 461	(177)	94.3	41.2	52.6	56.1	(4.8)
Calabria	430	(5.7)	7 764	(600)	3 634	(579)	4 148	(225)	91.6	42.9	48.9	53.3	(4.2)
Campania	453	(7.7)	7 988	(613)	3 714	(559)	4 198	(224)	94.2	43.8	49.5	53.1	(4.0)
Emilia Romagna	500	(6.4)	9 384	(768)	4 555	(779)	4 529	(238)	110.7	53.7	53.4	49.9	(4.5)
Friuli Venezia Giulia	523	(4.4)	7 712	(563)	3 476	(681)	4 204	(188)	90.9	41.0	49.6	54.7	(5.0)
Lazio	475	(6.8)	8 092	(524)	3 875	(512)	4 155	(182)	95.4	45.7	49.0	51.7	(3.5)
Liguria	488	(6.2)	8 285	(521)	3 768	(778)	4 432	(231)	97.7	44.4	52.3	54.1	(5.3)
Lombardia	517	(7.6)	7 478	(542)	3 366	(545)	4 019	(185)	88.2	39.7	47.4	54.4	(4.2)
Marche	496	(5.5)	7 298	(581)	2 811	(608)	4 351	(189)	86.1	33.2	51.3	60.7	(5.3)
Molise	466	(2.3)	7 217	(387)	3 088	(718)	4 127	(203)	85.1	36.4	48.7	57.2	(5.8)
Piemonte	499	(5.8)	7 706	(458)	2 894	(507)	4 681	(230)	90.9	34.1	55.2	61.8	(4.3)
Puglia	478	(6.1)	7 470	(561)	3 549	(553)	3 854	(197)	88.1	41.9	45.4	52.1	(4.1)
Sardegna	458	(5.3)	7 608	(423)	3 197	(519)	4 341	(216)	89.7	37.7	51.2	57.6	(4.1)
Sicilia	447	(5.1)	6 768	(483)	2 790	(495)	3 811	(175)	79.8	32.9	44.9	57.7	(4.5)
Toscana	495	(4.9)	8 663	(458)	4 557	(649)	4 082	(176)	102.2	53.7	48.1	47.2	(3.7)
Trento	524	(4.1)	6 802	(385)	2 893	(564)	3 833	(184)	80.2	34.1	45.2	57.0	(4.9)
Umbria	493	(6.8)	7 788	(675)	3 828	(753)	3 833	(212)	91.8	45.1	45.2	50.0	(5.1)
Valle d'Aosta	492	(2.2)	6 923	(352)	2 872	(909)	3 947	(215)	81.6	33.9	46.6	57.9	(7.8)
Veneto	523	(7.6)	8 265	(731)	4 214	(658)	3 872	(219)	97.5	49.7	45.7	47.9	(4.1)
Mexico													
Aguascalientes	437	(4.5)	5 331	(441)	1 860	(384)	3 443	(201)	62.9	21.9	40.6	64.9	(4.9)
Baja California	415	(5.8)	5 204	(381)	1 561	(379)	3 679	(213)	61.4	18.4	43.4	70.2	(5.2)
Baja California Sur	414	(5.4)	5 252	(326)	1 486	(355)	3 754	(208)	61.9	17.5	44.3	71.6	(5.0)
Campeche	396	(3.9)	4 999	(342)	1 368	(385)	3 661	(186)	59.0	16.1	43.2	72.8	(5.7)
Chiapas	373	(7.2)	5 551	(528)	2 260	(429)	3 392	(236)	65.5	26.6	40.0	60.0	(4.8)
Chihuahua	428	(7.8)	6 122	(438)	2 444	(626)	3 651	(200)	72.2	28.8	43.1	59.9	(6.3)
Coahuila	418	(8.1)	5 172	(522)	1 529	(430)	3 687	(226)	61.0	18.0	43.5	70.7	(6.0)
Colima	429	(4.5)	5 936	(398)	2 754	(728)	3 145	(257)	70.0	32.5	37.1	53.3	(6.9)
Distrito Federal	428	(5.0)	5 367	(398)	1 796	(403)	3 561	(298)	63.3	21.2	42.0	66.5	(5.3)
Durango	424	(5.7)	5 292	(341)	1 718	(376)	3 539	(200)	62.4	20.3	41.7	67.3	(5.0)
Guanajuato	412	(5.4)	5 661	(393)	1 944	(431)	3 819	(272)	66.8	22.9	45.0	66.3	(5.2)
Guerrero	367	(3.4)	4 431	(317)	1 248	(302)	3 283	(201)	52.3	14.7	38.7	72.5	(5.0)
Hidalgo	406	(5.8)	5 412	(386)	2 275	(462)	3 077	(206)	63.8	26.8	36.3	57.5	(5.2)
Jalisco	435	(5.9)	5 199	(321)	1 636	(379)	3 559	(189)	61.3	19.3	42.0	68.5	(5.1)
Mexico	417	(5.6)	4 467	(426)	1 240	(358)	3 092	(209)	52.7	14.6	36.5	71.4	(6.1)
Morelos	421	(8.5)	6 185	(989)	2 855	(949)	3 310	(209)	72.9	33.7	39.0	53.7	(8.4)
Nayarit	414	(5.9)	5 925	(470)	1 492	(438)	4 152	(242)	69.9	17.6	49.0	73.6	(5.8)
Nuevo León	436	(8.2)	5 450	(325)	1 663	(320)	3 861	(291)	64.3	19.6	45.5	69.9	(4.4)
Puebla	415	(4.9)	5 489	(473)	1 582	(472)	3 843	(231)	64.7	18.7	45.3	70.8	(6.3)
Querétaro	434	(6.4)	5 594	(474)	1 836	(456)	3 719	(211)	66.0	21.7	43.9	67.0	(5.6)
Quintana Roo	411	(5.4)	5 060	(284)	1 285	(321)	3 710	(222)	59.7	15.2	43.7	74.3	(4.9)
San Luis Potosí	412	(7.4)	5 637	(425)	1 941	(497)	3 724	(328)	66.5	22.9	43.9	65.7	(6.1)
Sinaloa	411	(4.2)	4 727	(256)	1 074	(266)	3 600	(194)	55.7	12.7	42.5	77.0	(4.5)
Tabasco	378	(3.8)	5 024	(434)	1 385	(385)	3 688	(215)	59.3	16.3	43.5	72.7	(5.6)
Tamaulipas	411	(7.4)	5 595	(489)	1 475	(383)	4 073	(367)	66.0	17.4	48.0	73.4	(5.4)
Tlaxcala	411	(5.0)	5 145	(281)	1 372	(327)	3 760	(207)	60.7	16.2	44.3	73.3	(4.8)
Veracruz	402	(6.3)	5 577	(414)	1 506	(381)	4 170	(315)	65.8	17.8	49.2	73.5	(5.1)
Yucatán	410	(4.6)	5 516	(316)	1 455	(429)	3 982	(216)	65.1	17.2	47.0	73.2	(5.9)
Zacatecas	408	(4.2)	5 193	(307)	1 044	(265)	4 152	(251)	61.2	12.3	49.0	79.9	(4.2)

• PISA adjudicated region.
Note: See Table II.2.8a for national data.
1. The statistics computed for this table were estimated for all students, whether they had data on socio-economic status or not.
2. The total variation in student performance is calculated from the square of the standard deviation for all students.
3. In some countries, sub-units within schools were sampled instead of schools; this may affect the estimation of between-school variance components (see Annex A3).
4. Due to the unbalanced clustered nature of the data, the sum of the between- and within-school variation components, as an estimate from a sample, does not necessarily add up to the total.
5. The *index of academic inclusion* is calculated as 100*(1-rho), where rho stands for the intra-class correlation of performance, i.e. the variation in student performance between schools, divided by the sum of the variation in student performance between schools and the variation in student performance within schools.

StatLink ⟐ http://dx.doi.org/10.1787/888932964965

[Part 2/2]
Variation in mathematics performance, by region
Table B2.II.5 *Results based on students' self-reports*

	Mean performance[1]		Total variation in mathematics performance[2]		Variation in mathematics performance between schools[3]		Variation in mathematics performance within schools[4]		As a percentage of the average total variation in mathematics performance across OECD countries			Index of academic inclusion[5]	
	Mean score	S.E.	Mean	S.E.	Mean	S.E.	Mean	S.E.	Total variance	Between schools variance	Within schools variance	Index	S.E.
Portugal													
Alentejo	489	(10.3)	8 062	(668)	2 504	(613)	5 628	(426)	95.1	29.5	66.4	64.2	(5.5)
Spain													
Andalusia•	472	(3.8)	7 245	(314)	868	(197)	6 406	(257)	85.4	10.2	75.6	84.1	(2.4)
Aragon•	496	(5.4)	8 600	(440)	1 324	(276)	7 212	(409)	101.4	15.6	85.1	84.5	(2.8)
Asturias•	500	(4.3)	8 702	(523)	1 137	(380)	7 217	(304)	102.6	13.4	85.1	84.4	(4.0)
Balearic Islands•	475	(4.8)	7 580	(380)	970	(229)	6 635	(305)	89.4	11.4	78.3	77.7	(2.6)
Basque Country•	505	(2.5)	7 061	(171)	1 420	(227)	5 567	(127)	83.3	16.7	65.7	77.7	(2.6)
Cantabria•	491	(3.5)	8 040	(357)	933	(322)	6 975	(294)	94.8	11.0	82.3	84.2	(3.6)
Castile and Leon•	509	(4.2)	7 011	(345)	998	(282)	5 957	(239)	82.7	11.8	70.2	84.7	(3.5)
Catalonia•	493	(5.2)	7 067	(329)	1 470	(292)	5 570	(230)	83.3	17.3	65.7	77.1	(3.4)
Extremadura•	461	(4.4)	8 608	(388)	1 260	(291)	7 386	(300)	101.5	14.9	87.1	84.4	(2.9)
Galicia•	489	(4.2)	7 395	(318)	902	(189)	6 582	(323)	87.2	10.6	77.6	84.0	(2.3)
La Rioja•	503	(1.9)	10 005	(465)	808	(254)	9 142	(556)	118.0	9.5	107.8	90.9	(2.4)
Madrid•	504	(3.5)	7 546	(375)	1 293	(319)	6 234	(278)	89.0	15.2	73.5	81.8	(3.6)
Murcia•	462	(4.7)	8 079	(487)	1 255	(368)	6 842	(289)	95.3	14.8	80.7	84.5	(3.9)
Navarre•	517	(3.1)	7 350	(367)	604	(185)	6 660	(297)	86.7	7.1	78.5	90.7	(2.4)
United Kingdom													
England	495	(3.9)	9 132	(389)	2 641	(341)	6 501	(192)	107.7	31.2	76.7	71.1	(2.7)
Northern Ireland	487	(3.1)	8 705	(378)	4 189	(387)	4 497	(170)	102.7	49.4	53.0	51.8	(2.5)
Scotland•	498	(2.6)	7 460	(282)	1 066	(197)	6 395	(197)	88.0	12.6	75.4	85.7	(2.3)
Wales	468	(2.2)	7 264	(214)	831	(151)	6 418	(194)	85.7	9.8	75.7	88.5	(1.9)
United States													
Connecticut•	506	(6.2)	9 818	(480)	2 296	(455)	7 453	(337)	115.8	27.1	87.9	76.4	(3.7)
Florida•	467	(5.8)	7 256	(400)	1 288	(365)	5 962	(235)	85.6	15.2	70.3	82.2	(4.2)
Massachusetts•	514	(6.2)	9 595	(569)	2 546	(627)	6 979	(319)	113.2	30.0	82.3	73.3	(4.9)
Argentina													
Ciudad Autónoma de Buenos Aires•	418	(7.3)	9 022	(1 340)	5 097	(1 477)	3 851	(201)	106.4	60.1	45.4	43.0	(7.2)
Brazil													
Acre	359	(5.6)	4 466	(467)	969	(489)	3 508	(214)	52.7	11.4	41.4	78.3	(8.6)
Alagoas	342	(6.0)	4 886	(748)	1 835	(635)	3 021	(271)	57.6	21.6	35.6	62.2	(8.4)
Amapá	360	(8.6)	4 185	(526)	1 249	(392)	2 994	(300)	49.4	14.7	35.3	70.6	(6.8)
Amazonas	356	(5.5)	4 212	(777)	1 227	(780)	3 004	(245)	49.7	14.5	35.4	71.0	(13.2)
Bahia	373	(8.7)	6 452	(1 030)	3 006	(1 215)	3 516	(408)	76.1	35.5	41.5	53.9	(10.4)
Ceará	378	(8.8)	6 324	(1 090)	2 798	(1 085)	3 538	(291)	74.6	33.0	41.7	55.8	(9.8)
Espírito Santo	414	(9.7)	7 433	(944)	4 015	(1 225)	3 437	(260)	87.7	47.4	40.5	46.6	(7.8)
Federal District	416	(9.1)	6 974	(1 171)	3 811	(1 111)	3 198	(237)	82.3	44.9	37.7	46.6	(7.5)
Goiás	379	(5.9)	5 125	(488)	1 855	(634)	3 354	(280)	60.4	21.9	39.6	64.4	(8.1)
Maranhão	343	(13.2)	5 960	(1 265)	2 880	(1 033)	3 131	(362)	70.3	34.0	36.9	52.1	(9.4)
Mato Grosso	370	(9.0)	5 387	(989)	2 182	(969)	3 081	(241)	63.5	25.7	36.3	58.5	(10.9)
Mato Grosso do Sul	408	(7.5)	5 457	(510)	2 263	(646)	3 199	(273)	64.4	26.7	37.7	58.8	(7.2)
Minas Gerais	403	(6.7)	5 172	(462)	1 556	(580)	3 593	(243)	61.0	18.3	42.4	68.8	(8.0)
Pará	360	(4.2)	4 558	(360)	1 728	(413)	2 875	(215)	53.8	20.4	33.9	62.5	(5.9)
Paraíba	395	(6.7)	6 203	(1 000)	2 870	(920)	3 455	(378)	73.1	33.8	40.7	54.6	(8.4)
Paraná	403	(11.6)	6 623	(1 772)	3 063	(1 825)	3 610	(242)	78.1	36.1	42.6	54.1	(14.9)
Pernambuco	363	(7.5)	4 479	(539)	1 326	(545)	3 121	(234)	52.8	15.6	36.8	70.2	(8.7)
Piauí	385	(7.4)	6 581	(1 168)	3 568	(1 570)	3 101	(253)	77.6	42.1	36.6	46.5	(11.1)
Rio de Janeiro	389	(6.7)	4 930	(566)	1 872	(568)	3 151	(225)	58.1	22.1	37.2	62.7	(7.3)
Rio Grande do Norte	380	(9.1)	7 021	(1 445)	4 005	(1 734)	3 149	(301)	82.8	47.2	37.1	44.0	(10.9)
Rio Grande do Sul	407	(5.5)	4 587	(356)	1 291	(349)	3 293	(219)	54.1	15.2	38.8	71.8	(5.6)
Rondônia	382	(5.3)	4 089	(307)	892	(265)	3 252	(306)	48.2	10.5	38.3	78.5	(5.3)
Roraima	362	(5.7)	5 247	(480)	2 182	(799)	3 078	(250)	61.9	25.7	36.3	58.5	(9.1)
Santa Catarina	415	(8.3)	5 599	(571)	1 877	(647)	3 777	(260)	66.0	22.1	44.5	66.8	(8.1)
São Paulo	404	(4.4)	6 147	(525)	2 454	(604)	3 686	(165)	72.5	28.9	43.5	60.0	(6.0)
Sergipe	384	(8.9)	4 978	(762)	1 577	(696)	3 532	(254)	58.7	18.6	41.7	69.1	(9.5)
Tocantins	366	(7.3)	5 888	(736)	2 066	(788)	3 860	(211)	69.4	24.4	45.5	65.1	(8.8)
Colombia													
Bogotá	393	(3.4)	4 379	(317)	700	(274)	3 656	(155)	51.6	8.3	43.1	83.9	(5.3)
Cali	379	(6.1)	4 965	(359)	1 765	(312)	3 154	(160)	58.6	20.8	37.2	64.1	(4.2)
Manizales	404	(4.1)	5 205	(582)	1 893	(568)	3 336	(170)	61.4	22.3	39.3	63.8	(7.0)
Medellín	393	(7.5)	6 875	(962)	3 342	(1 024)	3 520	(153)	81.1	39.4	41.5	51.3	(7.7)
Russian Federation													
Perm Territory region•	484	(5.5)	7 883	(775)	2 593	(783)	5 312	(283)	93.0	30.6	62.6	67.2	(6.8)
United Arab Emirates													
Abu Dhabi•	421	(4.0)	7 728	(401)	3 205	(498)	4 512	(150)	91.1	37.8	53.2	58.5	(3.9)
Ajman	403	(7.9)	5 571	(649)	1 443	(556)	4 143	(358)	65.7	17.0	48.9	74.2	(7.6)
Dubai•	464	(1.2)	8 882	(212)	4 135	(530)	4 708	(153)	104.8	48.8	55.5	53.2	(3.3)
Fujairah	411	(9.9)	6 801	(436)	2 546	(713)	4 254	(248)	80.2	30.0	50.2	62.6	(6.7)
Ras al-Khaimah	416	(6.7)	5 673	(465)	1 426	(539)	4 015	(232)	66.9	16.8	47.4	73.8	(7.4)
Sharjah	439	(9.0)	7 016	(628)	2 838	(655)	4 251	(340)	82.7	33.5	50.1	60.0	(5.9)
Umm al-Quwain	398	(4.0)	5 593	(608)	1 200	(433)	4 427	(364)	66.0	14.1	52.2	78.7	(6.2)

• PISA adjudicated region.
Note: See Table II.2.8a for national data.
1. The statistics computed for this table were estimated for all students, whether they had data on socio-economic status or not.
2. The total variation in student performance is calculated from the square of the standard deviation for all students.
3. In some countries, sub-units within schools were sampled instead of schools; this may affect the estimation of between-school variance components (see Annex A3).
4. Due to the unbalanced clustered nature of the data, the sum of the between- and within-school variation components, as an estimate from a sample, does not necessarily add up to the total.
5. The *index of academic inclusion* is calculated as 100*(1-rho), where rho stands for the intra-class correlation of performance, i.e. the variation in student performance between schools, divided by the sum of the variation in student performance between schools and the variation in student performance within schools.
StatLink ᵇᵐˢᴾ http://dx.doi.org/10.1787/888932964965

[Part 1/4]
Relationship between performance in mathematics and socio-economic status, between and within schools[1], by region

Table B2.II.6   *Results based on students' self-reports*

| | Within-school association of ESCS[2] and mathematics performance[3] | | Between-school association of ESCS and mathematics performance[4] | | Percentage of the overall variation in mathematics performance explained by students' ESCS | | Percentage of the overall variation in mathematics performance explained by students' and schools' ESCS | |
	Student-level score-point difference associated with one-unit increase in the student-level ESCS	S.E.	School-level score-point difference associated with one-unit increase in the school mean ESCS	S.E.	Between-school	Within-school	Between-school	Within-school
Australia								
Australian Capital Territory	**37**	(7.4)	**89**	(19.7)	32.6	13.1	59.9	13.2
New South Wales	**26**	(2.2)	**66**	(8.8)	26.8	6.9	47.8	7.0
Northern Territory	**40**	(5.5)	**86**	(28.0)	44.9	10.8	72.0	11.0
Queensland	**32**	(3.0)	**58**	(7.3)	46.2	7.6	70.3	7.7
South Australia	**22**	(3.9)	**58**	(9.8)	34.1	4.7	61.3	4.8
Tasmania	**29**	(3.8)	**57**	(8.3)	54.6	9.5	84.3	9.8
Victoria	**18**	(2.6)	**70**	(9.0)	25.1	3.4	55.5	3.6
Western Australia	**23**	(3.5)	**70**	(8.5)	39.8	4.5	74.6	4.7
Belgium								
Flemish Community•	**20**	(1.9)	**107**	(8.1)	22.0	5.2	71.2	5.2
French Community	**19**	(2.2)	**92**	(7.0)	28.3	4.5	79.3	4.5
German-speaking Community	**8**	(2.7)	**137**	(39.4)	-5.4	1.5	60.9	1.4
Canada								
Alberta	**21**	(2.5)	**74**	(13.2)	28.7	8.8	60.5	8.8
British Columbia	**19**	(2.4)	**35**	(10.5)	34.2	7.4	50.2	7.4
Manitoba	**27**	(2.9)	**38**	(8.6)	41.5	8.3	57.0	8.4
New Brunswick	**22**	(3.7)	**34**	(10.7)	35.5	7.1	52.6	7.1
Newfoundland and Labrador	**33**	(3.6)	**38**	(8.9)	51.1	16.3	67.8	16.3
Nova Scotia	**26**	(3.3)	**23**	(12.2)	35.8	10.1	45.6	10.1
Ontario	**24**	(2.5)	**30**	(8.7)	31.1	7.1	42.3	7.2
Prince Edward Island	**25**	(2.6)	**49**	(18.7)	43.8	7.9	74.5	7.8
Quebec	**21**	(2.0)	**64**	(8.5)	26.0	6.0	53.9	6.0
Saskatchewan	**24**	(2.8)	9	(10.1)	26.7	11.1	28.1	11.1
Italy								
Abruzzo	**7**	(2.3)	**106**	(19.5)	7.1	1.5	48.7	1.5
Basilicata	**8**	(2.4)	**78**	(10.8)	11.3	1.6	58.3	1.6
Bolzano	**6**	(3.1)	**101**	(13.0)	6.5	0.5	50.3	0.5
Calabria	**4**	(2.1)	**80**	(10.2)	7.4	0.5	52.3	0.5
Campania	**5**	(2.2)	**80**	(10.9)	7.2	2.1	60.8	2.1
Emilia Romagna	**10**	(2.9)	**102**	(11.4)	12.8	2.0	69.4	2.0
Friuli Venezia Giulia	**4**	(2.4)	**96**	(14.8)	7.3	0.2	56.6	0.2
Lazio	**4**	(2.5)	**98**	(11.5)	4.4	0.8	48.9	0.8
Liguria	**5**	(2.7)	**104**	(14.1)	7.6	0.4	63.1	0.5
Lombardia	**9**	(2.8)	**70**	(12.0)	11.9	2.2	50.0	2.2
Marche	**6**	(2.4)	**77**	(19.8)	7.2	1.5	42.4	1.4
Molise	**6**	(2.5)	**88**	(14.4)	9.1	0.7	59.6	0.7
Piemonte	**9**	(2.6)	**79**	(14.1)	9.7	3.0	51.8	3.0
Puglia	**8**	(2.5)	**78**	(9.5)	12.3	1.1	61.7	1.1
Sardegna	**10**	(2.1)	**77**	(9.4)	14.7	2.1	60.4	2.1
Sicilia	**9**	(2.1)	**74**	(10.2)	13.4	2.5	59.2	2.6
Toscana	**8**	(2.4)	**82**	(15.6)	9.4	2.5	50.9	2.5
Trento	**4**	(2.8)	**93**	(14.6)	6.0	0.2	55.8	0.1
Umbria	1	(2.0)	**92**	(17.9)	3.1	0.2	46.7	0.2
Valle d'Aosta	**8**	(3.1)	**61**	(19.0)	11.1	3.0	37.8	3.1
Veneto	**5**	(2.3)	**90**	(25.0)	6.1	1.3	49.8	1.3
Mexico								
Aguascalientes	**6**	(2.3)	**36**	(6.4)	14.5	1.1	46.6	1.2
Baja California	4	(2.7)	**32**	(11.5)	6.5	0.3	25.4	0.3
Baja California Sur	**8**	(2.4)	**40**	(9.2)	20.7	1.5	58.0	1.4
Campeche	**11**	(3.7)	13	(8.5)	19.8	3.2	27.7	3.1
Chiapas	0	(2.3)	**26**	(6.6)	0.8	0.4	19.2	0.4
Chihuahua	**6**	(1.8)	**54**	(10.0)	12.0	1.1	57.7	0.9
Coahuila	**6**	(3.0)	**39**	(9.3)	21.8	0.5	61.6	0.6
Colima	2	(1.7)	**51**	(8.0)	6.8	0.2	57.7	0.2
Distrito Federal	3	(2.1)	**36**	(5.7)	13.4	0.1	53.2	0.1
Durango	**6**	(2.5)	**32**	(8.3)	15.4	0.8	46.5	0.7
Guanajuato	**6**	(2.4)	**29**	(6.7)	20.0	1.0	49.4	1.1
Guerrero	**7**	(2.4)	**21**	(6.2)	14.7	1.6	31.1	1.7
Hidalgo	**7**	(2.2)	**31**	(6.2)	16.2	1.4	42.9	1.4
Jalisco	4	(2.5)	**26**	(8.6)	9.6	1.0	28.5	1.1
Mexico	5	(2.4)	**29**	(9.6)	9.6	2.3	31.8	2.4
Morelos	**7**	(2.3)	**38**	(8.2)	22.2	1.9	60.6	1.9
Nayarit	**6**	(2.2)	**25**	(7.2)	16.4	0.7	36.9	0.8
Nuevo León	-1	(2.5)	**46**	(4.9)	7.3	-0.5	73.0	-0.3
Puebla	**6**	(2.9)	**27**	(5.8)	30.5	0.6	61.4	0.8
Querétaro	4	(5.2)	**27**	(5.6)	17.4	0.8	47.8	0.8
Quintana Roo	**8**	(2.3)	**34**	(6.1)	26.1	1.7	60.3	1.9
San Luis Potosí	4	(2.5)	**34**	(4.0)	29.0	1.0	79.7	1.2
Sinaloa	5	(2.4)	**37**	(6.8)	11.4	1.3	51.0	1.3
Tabasco	**6**	(2.6)	**29**	(6.6)	18.2	0.9	48.0	0.9
Tamaulipas	**6**	(3.0)	**41**	(8.7)	15.7	0.8	53.3	0.7
Tlaxcala	4	(1.9)	**26**	(9.1)	10.8	1.0	33.1	1.0
Veracruz	**9**	(2.2)	**15**	(5.5)	28.7	1.6	41.5	1.6
Yucatán	**7**	(2.4)	**22**	(6.1)	28.9	0.8	51.1	1.0
Zacatecas	**7**	(2.7)	**24**	(6.4)	32.6	5.5	54.7	5.6

• PISA adjudicated region.
Notes: Values that are statistically significant are indicated in bold (see Annex A3).
See Table II.2.9a for national data.
1. In some countries, sub-units within schools were sampled instead of schools as administrative units; this may affect the estimation of school-level effects (see Annex A3).
2. ESCS refers to the *PISA index of economic, social and cultural status*.
3. Two-level regression of mathematics performance on student ESCS and school mean ESCS: within-school slope for ESCS and student-level variation explained by the model.
4. Two-level regression of mathematics performance on student ESCS and school mean ESCS: between-school slope for ESCS and school-level variation explained by the model.
5. Two-level regression of mathematics performance on student-level ESCS, student-level ESCS squared, school mean ESCS, and school mean ESCS squared. The within-school index of curvilinearity corresponds to the coefficient of student-level ESCS squared.
6. Two-level regression of mathematics performance on student ESCS, student ESCS squared, school mean ESCS and school mean ESCS squared: between-school index of curvilinearity corresponds to the coefficient of school mean ESCS squared.
StatLink 🔗 http://dx.doi.org/10.1787/888932964965

[Part 2/4]
Relationship between performance in mathematics and socio-economic status, between and within schools[1], by region

Table B2.II.6   *Results based on students' self-reports*

	Within-school association of ESCS[2] and mathematics performance[3]		Between-school association of ESCS and mathematics performance[4]		Percentage of the overall variation in mathematics performance explained by students' ESCS		Percentage of the overall variation in mathematics performance explained by students' and schools' ESCS	
	Student-level score-point difference associated with one-unit increase in the student-level ESCS	S.E.	School-level score-point difference associated with one-unit increase in the school mean ESCS	S.E.	Between-school	Within-school	Between-school	Within-school
Portugal								
Alentejo	19	(4.0)	55	(12.8)	36.4	6.2	75.3	6.2
Spain								
Andalusia•	29	(2.2)	13	(5.8)	52.7	12.0	57.5	12.0
Aragon•	27	(3.3)	32	(8.4)	51.7	8.2	67.8	8.3
Asturias•	28	(2.9)	27	(7.3)	56.5	8.4	69.1	8.6
Balearic Islands•	26	(2.8)	24	(8.4)	41.7	10.8	52.2	10.8
Basque Country•	19	(1.5)	39	(5.8)	38.1	6.0	58.7	6.1
Cantabria•	27	(2.8)	14	(9.6)	27.3	9.7	30.4	9.7
Castile and Leon•	25	(3.0)	19	(9.0)	29.4	8.7	35.6	8.7
Catalonia•	25	(2.3)	33	(7.4)	45.2	10.3	63.9	10.4
Extremadura•	29	(2.4)	25	(6.2)	46.4	11.3	57.8	11.4
Galicia•	21	(3.2)	24	(7.0)	42.2	6.9	56.0	6.9
La Rioja•	34	(3.3)	26	(10.5)	61.4	12.5	72.9	12.5
Madrid•	28	(3.2)	17	(7.1)	48.4	9.4	54.6	9.5
Murcia•	30	(2.3)	22	(12.0)	31.1	11.9	37.6	11.9
Navarre•	27	(2.9)	17	(5.7)	72.3	8.8	81.1	8.9
United Kingdom								
England	24	(2.0)	75	(7.6)	33.1	6.3	63.9	6.3
Northern Ireland	12	(2.2)	122	(6.5)	18.6	4.7	83.8	4.7
Scotland•	28	(2.1)	50	(7.0)	46.4	7.7	72.4	7.8
Wales	28	(2.1)	45	(7.0)	43.5	7.9	63.9	8.0
United States								
Connecticut•	34	(3.1)	54	(8.2)	57.8	9.9	85.0	10.1
Florida•	26	(2.6)	55	(10.7)	41.9	8.0	73.5	8.0
Massachusetts•	30	(4.1)	59	(10.4)	49.1	7.6	80.3	7.7
Argentina								
Ciudad Autónoma de Buenos Aires•	13	(2.4)	56	(9.2)	28.6	4.2	70.6	4.3
Brazil								
Acre	10	(2.7)	33	(7.3)	36.4	4.6	76.5	4.7
Alagoas	5	(2.5)	39	(9.2)	16.6	0.7	63.9	0.4
Amapá	10	(2.7)	43	(8.8)	23.6	4.8	63.3	4.8
Amazonas	6	(3.0)	51	(16.2)	14.1	0.7	61.3	0.7
Bahia	7	(2.9)	42	(9.3)	21.3	0.4	63.8	0.5
Ceará	3	(2.2)	48	(8.5)	11.7	1.1	70.3	1.0
Espírito Santo	10	(3.2)	42	(12.0)	19.2	2.6	50.3	2.7
Federal District	8	(3.8)	67	(8.4)	20.3	1.9	86.6	1.9
Goiás	7	(3.0)	59	(7.6)	25.1	2.6	93.8	2.4
Maranhão	5	(3.4)	54	(11.1)	13.0	1.1	60.1	1.0
Mato Grosso	7	(3.0)	46	(10.0)	15.5	1.3	54.6	1.3
Mato Grosso do Sul	11	(2.7)	44	(6.9)	36.7	3.4	83.6	3.4
Minas Gerais	11	(3.0)	30	(8.1)	32.3	3.4	62.7	3.3
Pará	11	(2.8)	36	(6.8)	21.6	4.1	48.3	4.0
Paraíba	14	(3.5)	38	(8.9)	40.4	5.6	77.3	5.7
Paraná	11	(2.8)	58	(8.5)	28.7	4.3	84.5	4.4
Pernambuco	14	(3.0)	26	(14.0)	27.3	5.1	43.7	5.1
Piauí	2	(3.3)	57	(8.6)	10.9	0.1	84.4	0.2
Rio de Janeiro	6	(4.3)	71	(8.4)	14.4	2.4	80.5	2.5
Rio Grande do Norte	2	(3.0)	64	(7.8)	10.6	-0.7	87.0	-0.7
Rio Grande do Sul	10	(2.7)	23	(9.6)	16.4	2.3	30.7	2.3
Rondônia	10	(2.6)	15	(7.8)	18.6	3.4	28.9	3.4
Roraima	9	(2.7)	56	(3.9)	27.0	2.1	88.5	2.0
Santa Catarina	13	(3.7)	32	(10.9)	20.4	3.2	40.4	3.3
São Paulo	7	(1.8)	54	(7.4)	18.4	1.2	70.2	1.2
Sergipe	6	(4.3)	39	(14.0)	17.8	1.0	55.5	1.1
Tocantins	11	(3.2)	46	(11.2)	21.6	3.2	61.5	3.1
Colombia								
Bogotá	11	(2.1)	44	(7.8)	32.3	2.4	74.6	2.5
Cali	12	(2.5)	41	(7.8)	25.7	3.0	58.9	3.0
Manizales	12	(2.4)	42	(7.7)	35.9	2.8	77.8	3.0
Medellín	10	(2.0)	56	(7.0)	27.3	2.0	79.7	2.1
Russian Federation								
Perm Territory region•	19	(2.7)	82	(18.9)	18.8	3.6	50.2	3.6
United Arab Emirates								
Abu Dhabi•	10	(2.3)	67	(11.1)	11.3	1.7	41.7	1.7
Ajman	14	(4.3)	43	(22.7)	14.2	2.8	31.5	2.8
Dubai•	13	(2.4)	96	(10.4)	11.6	1.3	47.4	1.3
Fujairah	10	(4.6)	60	(26.8)	6.7	1.3	25.3	1.3
Ras al-Khaimah	14	(3.7)	36	(12.9)	18.6	3.4	37.6	3.3
Sharjah	19	(4.1)	49	(28.0)	9.6	3.7	20.3	3.7
Umm al-Quwain	15	(5.8)	77	(13.5)	15.3	2.6	51.0	2.6

• PISA adjudicated region.
Notes: Values that are statistically significant are indicated in bold (see Annex A3).
See Table II.2.9a for national data.
1. In some countries, sub-units within schools were sampled instead of schools as administrative units; this may affect the estimation of school-level effects (see Annex A3).
2. ESCS refers to the *PISA index of economic, social and cultural status*.
3. Two-level regression of mathematics performance on student ESCS and school mean ESCS: within-school slope for ESCS and student-level variation explained by the model.
4. Two-level regression of mathematics performance on student ESCS and school mean ESCS: between-school slope for ESCS and school-level variation explained by the model.
5. Two-level regression of mathematics performance on student-level ESCS, student-level ESCS squared, school mean ESCS, and school mean ESCS squared. The within-school index of curvilinearity corresponds to the coefficient of student-level ESCS squared.
6. Two-level regression of mathematics performance on student ESCS, student ESCS squared, school mean ESCS and school mean ESCS squared: between-school index of curvilinearity corresponds to the coefficient of school mean ESCS squared.
StatLink ⟐ http://dx.doi.org/10.1787/888932964965

[Part 3/4]
Relationship between performance in mathematics and socio-economic status, between and within schools[1], by region

Table B2.II.6   *Results based on students' self-reports*

	Within-school index of curvilinearity of ESCS[5]		Between-school index of curvilinearity of ESCS[6]		Percentage of the overall variation in mathematics performance explained by students' study programmes		Percentage of the overall variation in mathematics performance explained by students' study programmes and students' and schools' ESCS	
	Student-level score-point difference associated with one-unit increase in the student-level ESCS	S.E.	School-level score-point difference associated with one-unit increase in the school mean ESCS	S.E.	Between-school	Within-school	Between-school	Within-school
Australia								
Australian Capital Territory	-8	(4.7)	59	(49.4)	7.3	7.2	59.9	14.0
New South Wales	0	(1.7)	6	(13.6)	6.8	4.4	51.5	9.0
Northern Territory	-7	(5.9)	-44	(27.2)	1.6	7.5	68.2	16.2
Queensland	4	(2.6)	1	(11.8)	13.9	8.0	73.1	14.0
South Australia	0	(3.2)	14	(11.3)	8.0	3.3	65.5	6.9
Tasmania	0	(3.2)	8	(13.9)	-2.7	4.4	82.5	10.4
Victoria	-4	(2.6)	26	(15.5)	6.3	2.2	57.3	4.6
Western Australia	1	(3.0)	10	(12.6)	9.4	6.2	74.8	9.3
Belgium								
Flemish Community*	0	(1.2)	11	(6.4)	76.6	24.7	83.9	26.1
French Community	2	(1.6)	-12	(10.4)	70.7	24.2	89.6	25.2
German-speaking Community	5	(3.7)	-250	(198.6)	75.7	25.5	78.9	25.7
Canada								
Alberta	-1	(2.4)	22	(32.0)	19.2	6.7	65.2	10.5
British Columbia	-1	(2.3)	**66**	(20.1)	8.5	4.3	50.9	7.8
Manitoba	2	(2.3)	8	(9.1)	8.2	3.1	57.0	9.6
New Brunswick	2	(3.3)	**50**	(24.6)	16.0	11.6	58.6	14.3
Newfoundland and Labrador	0	(3.6)	-18	(11.7)	0.0	0.0	67.8	16.3
Nova Scotia	2	(3.9)	-30	(28.5)	49.0	5.2	61.2	11.7
Ontario	3	(1.6)	-4	(13.3)	3.6	2.8	42.0	8.3
Prince Edward Island	**3**	(1.5)	-110	(81.6)	17.0	1.9	76.1	7.9
Quebec	-1	(1.7)	8	(13.5)	25.2	15.3	61.2	17.5
Saskatchewan	-1	(2.9)	-1	(22.0)	17.8	8.0	28.4	13.5
Italy								
Abruzzo	-2	(1.8)	**-108**	(47.0)	50.5	2.0	60.4	2.6
Basilicata	2	(2.5)	**-44**	(17.7)	55.7	0.0	63.6	1.6
Bolzano	**-6**	(2.3)	-37	(24.6)	53.2	0.1	65.0	0.5
Calabria	2	(1.6)	28	(15.5)	50.1	1.9	57.2	2.2
Campania	3	(1.9)	-21	(14.4)	59.4	1.7	69.6	2.1
Emilia Romagna	-3	(2.2)	**-34**	(13.5)	54.9	0.7	77.6	1.9
Friuli Venezia Giulia	**-4**	(1.8)	-1	(21.6)	51.9	-0.8	62.5	-0.1
Lazio	0	(1.6)	12	(20.7)	41.1	1.0	54.1	1.2
Liguria	-1	(1.9)	6	(20.4)	59.8	0.2	71.6	0.6
Lombardia	0	(1.8)	**-29**	(12.9)	33.7	0.4	57.8	2.0
Marche	-1	(1.7)	**-87**	(34.4)	53.9	0.8	57.2	1.5
Molise	0	(2.3)	-15	(21.4)	44.9	0.2	63.8	0.8
Piemonte	-1	(1.9)	**-64**	(20.7)	63.4	1.2	66.0	2.8
Puglia	0	(1.5)	**-35**	(15.8)	50.7	0.2	67.7	1.1
Sardegna	-2	(2.1)	**-28**	(13.7)	53.1	0.5	68.4	2.3
Sicilia	-1	(1.3)	-5	(17.2)	55.7	0.8	69.9	2.6
Toscana	-1	(1.8)	**-42**	(17.5)	70.9	2.0	72.0	2.9
Trento	**-5**	(2.3)	-25	(27.2)	45.8	0.1	58.2	0.2
Umbria	3	(2.0)	**-52**	(21.5)	48.2	0.2	58.0	0.2
Valle d'Aosta	-3	(3.0)	-21	(14.9)	34.7	3.4	44.9	4.2
Veneto	0	(1.8)	**-79**	(15.4)	69.8	0.7	70.7	1.4
Mexico								
Aguascalientes	-2	(1.7)	0	(7.0)	29.6	0.1	77.9	1.1
Baja California	-1	(1.8)	**25**	(11.3)	51.1	-0.2	67.3	0.0
Baja California Sur	0	(1.9)	7	(9.5)	46.5	0.0	80.0	1.3
Campeche	3	(1.6)	2	(6.8)	50.2	-0.3	56.3	3.1
Chiapas	3	(1.7)	9	(6.8)	31.9	0.3	45.4	0.2
Chihuahua	5	(2.2)	1	(11.7)	18.5	0.3	73.6	0.8
Coahuila	1	(2.2)	10	(7.9)	38.6	-0.1	73.1	0.5
Colima	2	(1.5)	4	(7.2)	53.2	0.1	72.2	0.2
Distrito Federal	0	(1.5)	**-19**	(7.6)	43.4	-0.2	84.8	-0.1
Durango	2	(1.9)	9	(5.3)	54.3	-0.2	65.3	0.5
Guanajuato	-1	(1.4)	-6	(4.6)	76.2	0.3	81.1	1.1
Guerrero	1	(1.3)	6	(4.5)	53.8	0.0	62.4	1.5
Hidalgo	1	(1.3)	-3	(3.7)	46.4	0.2	65.7	1.5
Jalisco	1	(1.4)	-7	(7.9)	48.7	0.3	53.4	1.0
Mexico	0	(1.9)	4	(7.8)	40.3	1.8	60.2	2.5
Morelos	1	(1.3)	-4	(7.9)	41.7	0.2	74.3	1.9
Nayarit	0	(1.2)	-2	(4.5)	31.1	-0.1	66.8	0.7
Nuevo León	0	(1.7)	2	(3.6)	47.7	-0.3	79.2	-0.3
Puebla	-2	(1.4)	-4	(3.5)	59.4	-0.4	85.9	0.6
Querétaro	-4	(2.2)	7	(4.6)	43.5	0.6	74.3	0.7
Quintana Roo	-1	(1.8)	5	(4.2)	68.6	0.4	82.7	1.8
San Luis Potosí	2	(1.3)	-1	(2.4)	35.0	0.8	89.5	1.1
Sinaloa	-1	(1.7)	**18**	(8.2)	35.0	0.7	66.7	1.2
Tabasco	1	(1.4)	4	(5.4)	66.8	0.0	78.8	1.0
Tamaulipas	2	(1.7)	0	(6.9)	34.4	0.0	74.8	0.7
Tlaxcala	1	(1.4)	-24	(5.8)	45.4	0.6	58.9	1.1
Veracruz	0	(1.0)	3	(4.3)	8.2	-0.1	47.6	1.6
Yucatán	0	(1.5)	2	(4.2)	64.0	0.0	85.6	0.9
Zacatecas	**3**	(1.3)	-4	(4.1)	48.0	4.3	74.2	5.5

* PISA adjudicated region.

Notes: Values that are statistically significant are indicated in bold (see Annex A3).

See Table II.2.9a for national data.

1. In some countries, sub-units within schools were sampled instead of schools as administrative units; this may affect the estimation of school-level effects (see Annex A3).

2. ESCS refers to the *PISA index of economic, social and cultural status*.

3. Two-level regression of mathematics performance on student ESCS and school mean ESCS: within-school slope for ESCS and student-level variation explained by the model.

4. Two-level regression of mathematics performance on student ESCS and school mean ESCS: between-school slope for ESCS and school-level variation explained by the model.

5. Two-level regression of mathematics performance on student-level ESCS, student-level ESCS squared, school mean ESCS, and school mean ESCS squared. The within-school index of curvilinearity corresponds to the coefficient of student-level ESCS squared.

6. Two-level regression of mathematics performance on student ESCS, student ESCS squared, school mean ESCS and school mean ESCS squared: between-school index of curvilinearity corresponds to the coefficient of school mean ESCS squared.

StatLink 🔗 http://dx.doi.org/10.1787/888932964965

[Part 4/4]
Relationship between performance in mathematics and socio-economic status, between and within schools[1], by region

Table B2.II.6 *Results based on students' self-reports*

	Within-school index of curvilinearity of ESCS[5]		Between-school index of curvilinearity of ESCS[6]		Percentage of the overall variation in mathematics performance explained by students' study programmes		Percentage of the overall variation in mathematics performance explained by students' study programmes and students' and schools' ESCS	
	Student-level score-point difference associated with one-unit increase in the student-level ESCS	S.E.	School-level score-point difference associated with one-unit increase in the school mean ESCS	S.E.	Between-school	Within-school	Between-school	Within-school
Portugal								
Alentejo	0	(2.1)	**-27**	(9.1)	83.2	15.1	89.3	18.3
Spain								
Andalusia•	2	(1.8)	2	(7.8)	0.0	0.0	57.5	12.0
Aragon•	-7	(1.9)	-22	(11.2)	0.0	0.0	67.8	8.3
Asturias•	-1	(2.7)	7	(12.0)	0.0	0.0	69.1	8.6
Balearic Islands•	-3	(1.8)	-16	(13.0)	0.0	0.0	52.2	10.8
Basque Country•	-2	(1.4)	**-24**	(6.9)	0.0	0.0	58.7	6.1
Cantabria•	4	(2.2)	31	(15.4)	0.0	0.0	30.4	9.7
Castile and Leon•	-2	(2.0)	2	(14.7)	0.0	0.0	35.6	8.7
Catalonia•	0	(1.9)	-6	(13.2)	0.0	0.0	63.9	10.4
Extremadura•	0	(2.0)	3	(9.8)	0.0	0.0	57.8	11.4
Galicia•	-1	(1.7)	2	(11.1)	0.0	0.0	56.0	6.9
La Rioja•	2	(3.1)	2	(18.3)	3.9	2.9	71.6	13.4
Madrid•	-8	(2.0)	-5	(12.1)	0.0	0.0	54.6	9.5
Murcia•	1	(2.0)	-7	(18.5)	0.0	0.0	37.6	11.9
Navarre•	-1	(2.3)	-5	(6.2)	0.0	0.0	81.1	8.9
United Kingdom								
England	2	(1.8)	6	(15.1)	7.2	2.4	63.9	6.6
Northern Ireland	-2	(2.3)	-10	(16.5)	2.8	3.4	83.8	5.1
Scotland•	**6**	(2.3)	-5	(13.7)	1.3	4.6	70.7	10.9
Wales	**6**	(2.3)	13	(14.9)	6.7	1.9	64.5	8.6
United States								
Connecticut•	**5**	(1.9)	-5	(11.6)	17.0	4.4	87.9	12.2
Florida•	**7**	(2.1)	32	(20.3)	20.0	12.5	74.3	17.0
Massachusetts•	**6**	(2.5)	8	(17.3)	0.0	0.0	80.3	7.7
Argentina								
Ciudad Autónoma de Buenos Aires•	-1	(1.6)	**-32**	(12.6)	29.0	8.3	75.5	10.7
Brazil								
Acre	3	(2.1)	6	(6.2)	25.4	4.7	73.6	7.4
Alagoas	-1	(1.6)	**31**	(13.7)	36.6	2.7	83.5	3.3
Amapá	0	(2.2)	8	(12.0)	21.3	3.7	73.2	6.3
Amazonas	-1	(1.6)	**24**	(7.6)	26.6	1.5	68.5	2.3
Bahia	1	(2.3)	13	(10.6)	14.9	3.8	77.0	4.9
Ceará	0	(2.1)	6	(8.3)	22.4	3.0	82.7	3.1
Espírito Santo	3	(1.9)	20	(10.5)	18.2	8.4	61.0	10.7
Federal District	0	(3.1)	-5	(9.7)	34.9	8.2	91.1	9.0
Goiás	-2	(1.8)	6	(6.6)	27.1	6.4	94.9	6.9
Maranhão	0	(1.6)	**25**	(9.6)	25.8	2.4	83.7	3.3
Mato Grosso	0	(2.2)	12	(7.3)	14.7	4.7	63.3	5.7
Mato Grosso do Sul	1	(1.6)	9	(11.2)	37.3	8.5	90.8	11.7
Minas Gerais	0	(2.2)	9	(7.2)	29.0	10.6	78.0	13.1
Pará	1	(1.3)	9	(16.8)	44.3	2.7	69.9	6.9
Paraíba	0	(2.7)	6	(7.3)	14.9	5.2	80.0	10.4
Paraná	0	(2.1)	**18**	(5.6)	17.2	9.4	87.7	12.0
Pernambuco	-2	(1.8)	**20**	(6.3)	32.3	5.3	58.2	11.0
Piauí	-2	(1.5)	**14**	(4.9)	19.6	8.6	87.9	8.7
Rio de Janeiro	-2	(2.2)	-24	(12.6)	22.8	7.4	86.1	8.3
Rio Grande do Norte	-2	(2.2)	**22**	(4.2)	14.0	4.4	89.0	4.4
Rio Grande do Sul	-2	(2.0)	6	(13.1)	31.4	6.1	49.3	8.4
Rondônia	2	(1.5)	1	(10.1)	47.7	12.5	68.3	14.5
Roraima	2	(2.5)	9	(5.2)	37.4	8.7	95.7	10.1
Santa Catarina	**4**	(1.8)	-1	(11.6)	55.6	7.1	67.8	10.1
São Paulo	-2	(1.2)	**20**	(6.8)	12.6	6.6	72.5	7.4
Sergipe	-2	(2.7)	18	(15.5)	46.0	5.9	68.3	7.3
Tocantins	3	(2.0)	17	(9.8)	11.0	8.2	68.1	10.3
Colombia								
Bogotá	-1	(1.6)	9	(5.2)	14.8	12.4	73.4	13.7
Cali	-2	(1.6)	**-19**	(7.3)	14.4	10.2	66.4	10.6
Manizales	-1	(1.2)	**23**	(7.0)	19.4	13.4	78.1	15.1
Medellín	1	(1.1)	**19**	(3.9)	11.1	13.0	78.3	14.1
Russian Federation								
Perm Territory region•	-4	(2.8)	66	(34.9)	2.0	2.0	54.9	4.7
United Arab Emirates								
Abu Dhabi•	-1	(1.2)	28	(15.7)	13.9	7.7	40.4	8.4
Ajman	4	(2.4)	-33	(44.1)	51.0	7.2	52.6	9.5
Dubai•	-1	(1.2)	9	(16.8)	5.2	3.2	45.9	4.0
Fujairah	1	(2.8)	49	(40.3)	18.5	7.6	38.1	8.8
Ras al-Khaimah	3	(1.9)	1	(19.2)	52.9	2.1	67.5	5.0
Sharjah	0	(2.6)	-5	(36.9)	8.3	7.2	20.9	9.9
Umm al-Quwain	**8**	(3.9)	-8	(34.2)	76.4	3.6	79.6	6.5

• PISA adjudicated region.
Notes: Values that are statistically significant are indicated in bold (see Annex A3).
See Table II.2.9a for national data.
1. In some countries, sub-units within schools were sampled instead of schools as administrative units; this may affect the estimation of school-level effects (see Annex A3).
2. ESCS refers to the *PISA index of economic, social and cultural status*.
3. Two-level regression of mathematics performance on student ESCS and school mean ESCS: within-school slope for ESCS and student-level variation explained by the model.
4. Two-level regression of mathematics performance on student ESCS and school mean ESCS: between-school slope for ESCS and school-level variation explained by the model.
5. Two-level regression of mathematics performance on student-level ESCS, student-level ESCS squared, school mean ESCS, and school mean ESCS squared. The within-school index of curvilinearity corresponds to the coefficient of student-level ESCS squared.
6. Two-level regression of mathematics performance on student ESCS, student ESCS squared, school mean ESCS and school mean ESCS squared: between-school index of curvilinearity corresponds to the coefficient of school mean ESCS squared.
StatLink ᵐˢ▶ http://dx.doi.org/10.1787/888932964965

[Part 1/4]
Students' socio-economic status, by region
Table B2.II.7   *Results based on students' self-reports*

	ESCS[1]		Variation in ESCS		Skewness of the distribution of ESCS		Percentage of students with low ESCS[2] (Approximated by the percentage of students with a value of ESCS lower than -1)	
	Mean index	S.E.	Variance	S.E.	Skewness	S.E.	%	S.E.
Australia								
Australian Capital Territory	0.6	(0.02)	0.6	(0.03)	-0.8	(0.20)	1.6	(0.4)
New South Wales	0.2	(0.02)	0.8	(0.01)	-0.5	(0.05)	7.3	(0.6)
Northern Territory	0.1	(0.06)	0.8	(0.03)	-0.5	(0.08)	10.4	(2.4)
Queensland	0.2	(0.02)	0.8	(0.01)	-0.3	(0.05)	7.4	(0.6)
South Australia	0.2	(0.02)	0.8	(0.03)	-0.6	(0.14)	7.9	(1.0)
Tasmania	0.0	(0.03)	0.8	(0.02)	-0.1	(0.07)	11.6	(0.9)
Victoria	0.3	(0.02)	0.8	(0.01)	-0.5	(0.07)	5.2	(0.5)
Western Australia	0.3	(0.03)	0.8	(0.01)	-0.4	(0.05)	6.7	(0.7)
Belgium								
Flemish Community●	0.2	(0.02)	0.9	(0.02)	-0.4	(0.15)	9.9	(0.6)
French Community	0.1	(0.03)	0.9	(0.02)	-0.2	(0.06)	11.4	(1.0)
German-speaking Community	0.3	(0.03)	0.8	(0.01)	-0.1	(0.07)	6.1	(0.9)
Canada								
Alberta	0.5	(0.03)	0.8	(0.01)	-0.3	(0.05)	3.0	(0.4)
British Columbia	0.5	(0.04)	0.9	(0.02)	-0.3	(0.06)	4.5	(0.6)
Manitoba	0.3	(0.03)	0.9	(0.02)	-0.3	(0.06)	8.5	(1.1)
New Brunswick	0.4	(0.02)	0.8	(0.02)	-0.2	(0.07)	4.8	(0.6)
Newfoundland and Labrador	0.3	(0.04)	0.9	(0.02)	-0.1	(0.05)	7.9	(1.5)
Nova Scotia	0.3	(0.03)	0.8	(0.01)	-0.1	(0.05)	5.7	(0.6)
Ontario	0.4	(0.04)	0.9	(0.02)	-0.5	(0.12)	6.2	(0.8)
Prince Edward Island	0.3	(0.02)	0.8	(0.02)	-0.4	(0.05)	6.1	(0.7)
Quebec	0.3	(0.03)	0.8	(0.01)	-0.4	(0.04)	6.3	(0.6)
Saskatchewan	0.4	(0.02)	0.8	(0.01)	0.0	(0.05)	3.5	(0.5)
Italy								
Abruzzo	0.0	(0.04)	0.9	(0.02)	0.1	(0.06)	13.5	(1.0)
Basilicata	-0.2	(0.03)	1.0	(0.02)	0.3	(0.05)	21.9	(1.2)
Bolzano	-0.1	(0.02)	0.8	(0.01)	0.1	(0.05)	12.5	(0.9)
Calabria	-0.2	(0.05)	1.0	(0.02)	0.2	(0.06)	25.3	(1.5)
Campania	-0.2	(0.06)	1.0	(0.02)	0.3	(0.06)	24.7	(1.9)
Emilia Romagna	0.0	(0.04)	0.9	(0.02)	0.0	(0.06)	14.8	(1.2)
Friuli Venezia Giulia	0.0	(0.04)	0.9	(0.02)	-0.1	(0.05)	12.2	(1.4)
Lazio	0.2	(0.05)	0.9	(0.02)	-0.2	(0.07)	11.0	(1.2)
Liguria	0.0	(0.04)	0.9	(0.02)	-0.1	(0.09)	13.1	(1.2)
Lombardia	0.1	(0.05)	1.0	(0.02)	0.0	(0.06)	15.7	(1.7)
Marche	0.0	(0.04)	0.9	(0.02)	0.1	(0.06)	16.5	(1.2)
Molise	-0.1	(0.03)	0.9	(0.02)	0.2	(0.05)	19.0	(1.2)
Piemonte	-0.1	(0.04)	0.9	(0.01)	0.1	(0.04)	17.4	(1.1)
Puglia	-0.3	(0.04)	1.0	(0.02)	0.3	(0.06)	28.6	(1.6)
Sardegna	-0.1	(0.05)	1.0	(0.02)	0.2	(0.06)	22.6	(1.5)
Sicilia	-0.1	(0.05)	1.0	(0.02)	0.1	(0.04)	22.2	(1.4)
Toscana	0.0	(0.06)	0.9	(0.02)	0.0	(0.08)	15.6	(1.3)
Trento	0.0	(0.03)	0.9	(0.02)	0.1	(0.06)	11.7	(1.1)
Umbria	0.1	(0.04)	0.9	(0.02)	0.1	(0.05)	11.1	(1.3)
Valle d'Aosta	-0.2	(0.03)	1.0	(0.02)	0.2	(0.05)	23.5	(1.4)
Veneto	-0.1	(0.04)	0.9	(0.02)	0.2	(0.06)	16.6	(1.5)
Mexico								
Aguascalientes	-0.8	(0.08)	1.2	(0.03)	0.2	(0.07)	46.6	(2.9)
Baja California	-0.7	(0.08)	1.0	(0.05)	0.0	(0.08)	42.1	(3.5)
Baja California Sur	-0.8	(0.09)	1.1	(0.03)	0.0	(0.12)	42.6	(4.2)
Campeche	-1.3	(0.09)	1.3	(0.04)	0.2	(0.09)	60.7	(2.9)
Chiapas	-1.7	(0.13)	1.2	(0.07)	0.5	(0.10)	72.7	(4.1)
Chihuahua	-0.8	(0.10)	1.1	(0.03)	0.0	(0.11)	44.6	(3.9)
Coahuila	-0.8	(0.12)	1.1	(0.04)	0.1	(0.13)	46.5	(5.4)
Colima	-0.8	(0.10)	1.2	(0.04)	0.0	(0.08)	43.9	(3.1)
Distrito Federal	-0.6	(0.12)	1.2	(0.05)	0.2	(0.06)	40.2	(3.5)
Durango	-1.0	(0.14)	1.2	(0.04)	0.2	(0.18)	52.9	(6.1)
Guanajuato	-1.3	(0.12)	1.2	(0.07)	0.5	(0.09)	63.3	(4.1)
Guerrero	-1.7	(0.09)	1.2	(0.04)	0.4	(0.08)	72.9	(2.3)
Hidalgo	-1.4	(0.10)	1.2	(0.06)	0.4	(0.09)	67.0	(3.1)
Jalisco	-1.1	(0.12)	1.2	(0.05)	0.3	(0.09)	54.8	(3.7)
Mexico	-1.1	(0.08)	1.1	(0.04)	0.3	(0.10)	56.3	(3.6)
Morelos	-0.9	(0.14)	1.3	(0.05)	0.1	(0.09)	51.1	(4.0)
Nayarit	-1.0	(0.11)	1.3	(0.04)	0.1	(0.09)	52.7	(3.4)
Nuevo León	-0.4	(0.16)	1.1	(0.05)	-0.1	(0.16)	33.0	(4.3)
Puebla	-1.5	(0.11)	1.3	(0.06)	0.6	(0.10)	69.4	(3.4)
Querétaro	-0.9	(0.18)	1.3	(0.06)	0.2	(0.17)	52.6	(6.3)
Quintana Roo	-1.0	(0.09)	1.1	(0.04)	0.0	(0.08)	49.5	(3.8)
San Luis Potosí	-1.3	(0.17)	1.4	(0.09)	0.4	(0.11)	61.9	(5.0)
Sinaloa	-1.0	(0.07)	1.1	(0.03)	0.1	(0.06)	49.5	(2.9)
Tabasco	-1.2	(0.09)	1.2	(0.03)	0.3	(0.07)	59.8	(3.3)
Tamaulipas	-0.9	(0.09)	1.1	(0.04)	0.1	(0.05)	47.8	(3.4)
Tlaxcala	-1.2	(0.08)	1.2	(0.05)	0.4	(0.06)	61.4	(2.9)
Veracruz	-1.5	(0.10)	1.4	(0.06)	0.4	(0.10)	64.2	(3.0)
Yucatán	-1.2	(0.15)	1.3	(0.05)	0.3	(0.14)	56.5	(5.3)
Zacatecas	-1.2	(0.08)	1.2	(0.04)	0.5	(0.08)	61.5	(2.7)

● PISA adjudicated region.
Note: See Table II.2.13a for national data.
1. ESCS refers to the *PISA index of economic, social and cultural status*.
2. Students with low ESCS are those with a value on the *PISA index of economic, social and cultural status* lower than -1.
3. Distribution of the school mean ESCS, percentiles calculated at the student level.
4. The *index of social inclusion* is calculated as 100*(1-rho), where rho stands for the intra-class correlation of socio-economic status, i.e. the between-school variation in the *PISA index of social, economic and cultural status* of students, divided by the sum of the between-school variation in students' socio-economic status and the within-school variation in students' socio-economic status.

StatLink ᴬᴿᴾ http://dx.doi.org/10.1787/888932964965

[Part 2/4]
Students' socio-economic status, by region
Table B2.II.7 *Results based on students' self-reports*

	ESCS[1]		Variation in ESCS		Skewness of the distribution of ESCS		Percentage of students with low ESCS[2] (Approximated by the percentage of students with a value of ESCS lower than -1)	
	Mean index	S.E.	Variance	S.E.	Skewness	S.E.	%	S.E.
Portugal								
Alentejo	-0.3	(0.14)	1.1	(0.03)	0.3	(0.14)	32.9	(4.5)
Spain								
Andalusia*	-0.4	(0.07)	1.0	(0.02)	0.2	(0.08)	31.1	(2.5)
Aragon*	-0.1	(0.06)	1.0	(0.02)	-0.1	(0.06)	18.9	(1.5)
Asturias*	0.0	(0.05)	1.0	(0.02)	0.0	(0.07)	17.7	(1.4)
Balearic Islands*	-0.2	(0.04)	1.0	(0.02)	0.0	(0.06)	22.1	(1.4)
Basque Country*	0.0	(0.03)	0.9	(0.01)	-0.3	(0.04)	14.6	(0.7)
Cantabria*	-0.1	(0.04)	1.0	(0.02)	0.1	(0.05)	18.1	(1.2)
Castile and Leon*	-0.1	(0.05)	1.0	(0.02)	0.0	(0.06)	19.4	(1.5)
Catalonia*	-0.1	(0.08)	1.0	(0.02)	-0.1	(0.09)	21.3	(2.2)
Extremadura*	-0.5	(0.05)	1.1	(0.02)	0.3	(0.05)	35.7	(1.8)
Galicia*	-0.2	(0.05)	1.0	(0.02)	0.0	(0.11)	21.7	(1.6)
La Rioja*	-0.1	(0.02)	1.0	(0.02)	0.0	(0.05)	21.4	(1.1)
Madrid*	0.1	(0.07)	1.0	(0.02)	-0.2	(0.08)	14.3	(1.4)
Murcia*	-0.5	(0.05)	1.0	(0.03)	0.1	(0.06)	32.2	(1.8)
Navarre*	-0.1	(0.04)	1.0	(0.02)	0.0	(0.05)	18.5	(1.3)
United Kingdom								
England	0.3	(0.02)	0.8	(0.01)	-0.2	(0.04)	5.2	(0.4)
Northern Ireland	0.3	(0.02)	0.8	(0.01)	0.1	(0.05)	4.0	(0.5)
Scotland*	0.1	(0.02)	0.8	(0.01)	-0.1	(0.04)	9.7	(0.6)
Wales	0.2	(0.02)	0.8	(0.01)	0.0	(0.04)	5.6	(0.5)
United States								
Connecticut*	0.5	(0.06)	0.9	(0.02)	-0.4	(0.06)	6.3	(1.1)
Florida*	0.2	(0.06)	0.9	(0.02)	-0.3	(0.09)	9.4	(1.2)
Massachusetts*	0.4	(0.07)	0.9	(0.03)	-0.5	(0.08)	6.4	(1.1)
Argentina								
Ciudad Autónoma de Buenos Aires*	-0.2	(0.09)	1.2	(0.03)	-0.5	(0.10)	26.4	(2.7)
Brazil								
Acre	-1.4	(0.10)	1.2	(0.04)	0.2	(0.10)	62.6	(3.4)
Alagoas	-1.7	(0.13)	1.2	(0.06)	0.5	(0.14)	71.5	(4.6)
Amapá	-0.9	(0.12)	1.0	(0.06)	-0.1	(0.11)	45.5	(4.5)
Amazonas	-1.1	(0.06)	1.1	(0.03)	0.1	(0.09)	52.3	(2.7)
Bahia	-1.5	(0.09)	1.3	(0.06)	0.3	(0.12)	66.3	(3.9)
Ceará	-1.5	(0.10)	1.3	(0.08)	0.4	(0.15)	69.0	(3.5)
Espírito Santo	-1.2	(0.10)	1.2	(0.09)	0.2	(0.09)	56.7	(2.2)
Federal District	-0.7	(0.10)	1.1	(0.07)	0.1	(0.08)	43.8	(3.0)
Goiás	-1.3	(0.09)	1.1	(0.04)	0.2	(0.07)	62.5	(3.7)
Maranhão	-1.4	(0.19)	1.2	(0.07)	0.1	(0.11)	63.4	(6.1)
Mato Grosso	-1.3	(0.08)	1.2	(0.07)	0.3	(0.12)	64.8	(2.6)
Mato Grosso do Sul	-1.0	(0.10)	1.2	(0.03)	0.1	(0.10)	51.3	(3.6)
Minas Gerais	-1.3	(0.08)	1.2	(0.06)	0.3	(0.14)	61.8	(3.1)
Pará	-1.2	(0.17)	1.1	(0.04)	0.1	(0.15)	57.4	(6.7)
Paraíba	-1.1	(0.09)	1.3	(0.07)	-0.1	(0.20)	53.4	(4.6)
Paraná	-1.1	(0.12)	1.2	(0.10)	0.2	(0.09)	56.9	(3.5)
Pernambuco	-1.6	(0.12)	1.1	(0.05)	0.2	(0.13)	70.4	(3.2)
Piauí	-1.3	(0.09)	1.3	(0.04)	0.2	(0.09)	61.5	(2.9)
Rio de Janeiro	-0.9	(0.07)	1.0	(0.06)	0.1	(0.07)	49.5	(2.0)
Rio Grande do Norte	-1.3	(0.13)	1.2	(0.08)	0.3	(0.12)	63.5	(4.4)
Rio Grande do Sul	-1.2	(0.08)	1.1	(0.03)	0.2	(0.10)	58.0	(3.3)
Rondônia	-1.4	(0.16)	1.2	(0.05)	0.2	(0.16)	62.9	(6.0)
Roraima	-1.0	(0.08)	1.2	(0.04)	0.0	(0.10)	52.5	(3.3)
Santa Catarina	-1.2	(0.12)	1.1	(0.05)	0.2	(0.09)	59.2	(4.4)
São Paulo	-0.9	(0.05)	1.1	(0.02)	0.1	(0.05)	51.1	(2.2)
Sergipe	-1.3	(0.10)	1.1	(0.02)	0.0	(0.11)	56.8	(3.9)
Tocantins	-1.3	(0.09)	1.2	(0.04)	0.1	(0.09)	60.3	(3.5)
Colombia								
Bogotá	-1.1	(0.05)	1.0	(0.02)	0.0	(0.07)	52.2	(2.3)
Cali	-0.8	(0.08)	1.0	(0.03)	-0.1	(0.08)	41.4	(3.3)
Manizales	-0.8	(0.07)	1.1	(0.03)	-0.3	(0.07)	37.8	(3.4)
Medellín	-0.9	(0.10)	1.2	(0.05)	0.0	(0.08)	46.5	(3.3)
Russian Federation								
Perm Territory region*	-0.1	(0.03)	0.8	(0.02)	-0.5	(0.06)	12.1	(1.2)
United Arab Emirates								
Abu Dhabi*	0.3	(0.03)	0.9	(0.02)	-0.7	(0.06)	8.7	(0.8)
Ajman	-0.1	(0.06)	0.9	(0.04)	-0.5	(0.09)	14.2	(2.0)
Dubai*	0.5	(0.01)	0.7	(0.01)	-0.7	(0.06)	3.6	(0.2)
Fujairah	0.0	(0.03)	0.9	(0.02)	-0.5	(0.08)	12.2	(1.2)
Ras al-Khaimah	0.1	(0.08)	0.9	(0.04)	-0.7	(0.13)	12.3	(2.3)
Sharjah	0.4	(0.04)	0.8	(0.04)	-1.1	(0.15)	4.3	(0.7)
Umm al-Quwain	-0.1	(0.04)	0.9	(0.03)	-0.5	(0.10)	15.5	(1.8)

* PISA adjudicated region.
Note: See Table II.2.13a for national data.
1. ESCS refers to the *PISA index of economic, social and cultural status*.
2. Students with low ESCS are those with a value on the *PISA index of economic, social and cultural status* lower than -1.
3. Distribution of the school mean ESCS, percentiles calculated at the student level.
4. The *index of social inclusion* is calculated as 100*(1-rho), where rho stands for the intra-class correlation of socio-economic status, i.e. the between-school variation in the *PISA index of social, economic and cultural status* of students, divided by the sum of the between-school variation in students' socio-economic status and the within-school variation in students' socio-economic status.
StatLink http://dx.doi.org/10.1787/888932964965

[Part 3/4]
Students' socio-economic status, by region

Table B2.II.7 *Results based on students' self-reports*

	Variation in distribution of students across ESCS						Variation in distribution of schools across ESCS[3]						Index of social inclusion[4]	
	25th percentile of ESCS		75th percentile of ESCS		Interquartile range of distribution of students across ESCS		25th percentile of school mean ESCS		75th percentile of school mean ESCS		Interquartile range of distribution of schools across ESCS			
	Index	S.E.	Index	S.E.	Range	S.E.	Index	S.E.	Index	S.E.	Range	S.E.	Index	S.E.
Australia														
Australian Capital Territory	0.3	(0.04)	1.0	(0.03)	0.8	(0.04)	0.4	(0.00)	0.8	(0.01)	0.3	(0.01)	86.9	3.9
New South Wales	-0.3	(0.03)	0.9	(0.02)	1.2	(0.03)	-0.1	(0.02)	0.6	(0.03)	0.6	(0.04)	74.5	2.2
Northern Territory	-0.4	(0.12)	0.8	(0.08)	1.1	(0.12)	-0.1	(0.09)	0.4	(0.07)	0.5	(0.11)	81.3	6.8
Queensland	-0.4	(0.04)	0.8	(0.02)	1.2	(0.03)	-0.1	(0.04)	0.5	(0.08)	0.6	(0.08)	78.6	2.4
South Australia	-0.4	(0.04)	0.8	(0.03)	1.1	(0.04)	-0.1	(0.03)	0.5	(0.03)	0.6	(0.04)	78.0	3.5
Tasmania	-0.6	(0.03)	0.6	(0.04)	1.2	(0.04)	-0.3	(0.03)	0.3	(0.01)	0.7	(0.02)	76.8	4.1
Victoria	-0.2	(0.05)	0.9	(0.01)	1.1	(0.05)	0.1	(0.04)	0.6	(0.04)	0.5	(0.05)	80.2	2.4
Western Australia	-0.3	(0.04)	0.9	(0.03)	1.2	(0.04)	-0.1	(0.07)	0.6	(0.03)	0.7	(0.07)	74.9	2.5
Belgium														
Flemish Community•	-0.6	(0.02)	0.9	(0.03)	1.5	(0.03)	-0.2	(0.02)	0.5	(0.04)	0.7	(0.04)	73.8	2.9
French Community	-0.6	(0.04)	0.9	(0.03)	1.4	(0.04)	-0.3	(0.06)	0.5	(0.07)	0.8	(0.08)	70.1	2.8
German-speaking Community	-0.4	(0.03)	1.0	(0.03)	1.4	(0.03)	0.0	(0.00)	0.6	(0.00)	0.6	(0.00)	90.6	2.2
Canada														
Alberta	-0.1	(0.04)	1.2	(0.03)	1.2	(0.03)	0.3	(0.03)	0.7	(0.08)	0.4	(0.08)	88.6	2.2
British Columbia	-0.1	(0.06)	1.1	(0.03)	1.2	(0.05)	0.2	(0.05)	0.8	(0.03)	0.7	(0.06)	83.3	2.2
Manitoba	-0.4	(0.05)	1.0	(0.03)	1.4	(0.05)	0.1	(0.04)	0.5	(0.02)	0.4	(0.04)	80.5	3.6
New Brunswick	-0.3	(0.04)	1.0	(0.02)	1.3	(0.04)	0.1	(0.04)	0.6	(0.02)	0.5	(0.04)	88.4	2.2
Newfoundland and Labrador	-0.4	(0.05)	1.0	(0.05)	1.4	(0.06)	0.0	(0.14)	0.7	(0.01)	0.6	(0.14)	81.2	4.6
Nova Scotia	-0.3	(0.04)	0.9	(0.06)	1.2	(0.07)	0.1	(0.03)	0.5	(0.05)	0.4	(0.06)	90.8	2.4
Ontario	-0.2	(0.05)	1.1	(0.03)	1.3	(0.04)	0.2	(0.05)	0.7	(0.04)	0.5	(0.06)	82.5	2.4
Prince Edward Island	-0.2	(0.02)	1.0	(0.02)	1.2	(0.03)	0.1	(0.00)	0.5	(0.00)	0.4	(0.00)	95.0	1.6
Quebec	-0.3	(0.03)	1.0	(0.03)	1.3	(0.03)	0.1	(0.03)	0.6	(0.05)	0.6	(0.06)	79.3	2.4
Saskatchewan	-0.2	(0.03)	1.0	(0.03)	1.2	(0.03)	0.2	(0.02)	0.6	(0.02)	0.4	(0.03)	92.6	1.6
Italy														
Abruzzo	-0.6	(0.04)	0.7	(0.05)	1.3	(0.05)	-0.2	(0.03)	0.3	(0.15)	0.5	(0.15)	84.6	2.6
Basilicata	-0.9	(0.05)	0.4	(0.07)	1.3	(0.06)	-0.6	(0.08)	0.2	(0.04)	0.7	(0.08)	77.0	3.3
Bolzano	-0.7	(0.03)	0.5	(0.02)	1.2	(0.03)	-0.3	(0.01)	0.2	(0.00)	0.5	(0.01)	81.3	2.7
Calabria	-1.0	(0.06)	0.5	(0.06)	1.5	(0.05)	-0.7	(0.09)	0.2	(0.07)	0.9	(0.11)	78.6	2.5
Campania	-1.0	(0.06)	0.5	(0.12)	1.5	(0.09)	-0.6	(0.08)	0.3	(0.11)	0.9	(0.12)	71.9	4.0
Emilia Romagna	-0.7	(0.06)	0.7	(0.06)	1.3	(0.06)	-0.4	(0.05)	0.4	(0.11)	0.8	(0.13)	75.2	3.6
Friuli Venezia Giulia	-0.6	(0.06)	0.7	(0.05)	1.2	(0.04)	-0.2	(0.09)	0.4	(0.06)	0.5	(0.12)	79.0	4.0
Lazio	-0.5	(0.06)	0.8	(0.07)	1.3	(0.05)	-0.2	(0.15)	0.5	(0.07)	0.7	(0.16)	81.5	2.9
Liguria	-0.6	(0.04)	0.7	(0.08)	1.3	(0.06)	-0.3	(0.08)	0.4	(0.08)	0.7	(0.11)	80.6	3.0
Lombardia	-0.7	(0.07)	0.8	(0.08)	1.4	(0.06)	-0.3	(0.12)	0.4	(0.07)	0.7	(0.14)	73.9	4.1
Marche	-0.7	(0.06)	0.6	(0.06)	1.3	(0.05)	-0.3	(0.08)	0.3	(0.07)	0.6	(0.09)	85.0	2.1
Molise	-0.8	(0.03)	0.5	(0.06)	1.3	(0.06)	-0.5	(0.02)	0.3	(0.02)	0.8	(0.02)	79.7	3.4
Piemonte	-0.7	(0.03)	0.6	(0.06)	1.3	(0.04)	-0.4	(0.14)	0.2	(0.08)	0.7	(0.16)	80.3	3.4
Puglia	-1.1	(0.05)	0.4	(0.07)	1.5	(0.06)	-0.8	(0.04)	0.1	(0.08)	0.9	(0.08)	75.8	3.2
Sardegna	-0.9	(0.05)	0.6	(0.11)	1.5	(0.11)	-0.4	(0.07)	0.1	(0.10)	0.6	(0.11)	80.1	3.5
Sicilia	-0.9	(0.06)	0.7	(0.09)	1.6	(0.08)	-0.5	(0.11)	0.3	(0.07)	0.8	(0.14)	81.6	3.3
Toscana	-0.7	(0.05)	0.7	(0.12)	1.4	(0.08)	-0.5	(0.06)	0.4	(0.08)	0.8	(0.09)	71.4	4.2
Trento	-0.6	(0.03)	0.6	(0.03)	1.2	(0.04)	-0.2	(0.13)	0.3	(0.07)	0.5	(0.14)	80.6	3.1
Umbria	-0.5	(0.04)	0.8	(0.05)	1.3	(0.05)	-0.2	(0.02)	0.4	(0.02)	0.6	(0.02)	80.7	3.8
Valle d'Aosta	-0.9	(0.06)	0.5	(0.06)	1.4	(0.08)	-0.5	(0.00)	0.1	(0.00)	0.6	(0.00)	81.2	6.4
Veneto	-0.7	(0.04)	0.6	(0.07)	1.3	(0.05)	-0.4	(0.05)	0.2	(0.14)	0.7	(0.14)	78.0	4.3
Mexico														
Aguascalientes	-1.7	(0.08)	0.2	(0.16)	1.8	(0.13)	-1.3	(0.11)	-0.3	(0.07)	1.0	(0.11)	66.6	5.4
Baja California	-1.5	(0.08)	0.1	(0.12)	1.5	(0.10)	-1.1	(0.14)	-0.5	(0.17)	0.6	(0.24)	76.3	5.1
Baja California Sur	-1.6	(0.08)	0.0	(0.08)	1.6	(0.06)	-1.3	(0.18)	-0.3	(0.06)	1.1	(0.19)	72.6	4.2
Campeche	-2.3	(0.12)	-0.3	(0.13)	2.0	(0.13)	-1.8	(0.35)	-1.0	(0.02)	0.8	(0.35)	63.2	6.2
Chiapas	-2.7	(0.06)	-0.9	(0.20)	1.8	(0.16)	-2.2	(0.06)	-1.4	(0.28)	0.9	(0.26)	63.4	7.1
Chihuahua	-1.6	(0.13)	0.0	(0.15)	1.6	(0.10)	-1.3	(0.20)	-0.4	(0.35)	0.9	(0.36)	72.5	4.2
Coahuila	-1.6	(0.11)	0.0	(0.21)	1.6	(0.14)	-1.3	(0.09)	-0.3	(0.12)	1.0	(0.11)	61.9	5.3
Colima	-1.7	(0.08)	0.2	(0.18)	1.9	(0.14)	-1.3	(0.13)	-0.1	(0.14)	1.1	(0.19)	65.6	5.5
Distrito Federal	-1.5	(0.13)	0.4	(0.25)	1.9	(0.17)	-1.0	(0.22)	-0.1	(0.42)	0.9	(0.30)	59.1	6.5
Durango	-1.9	(0.10)	-0.1	(0.27)	1.9	(0.19)	-1.5	(0.20)	-0.4	(0.35)	1.1	(0.29)	66.9	5.0
Guanajuato	-2.2	(0.08)	-0.5	(0.15)	1.7	(0.11)	-1.9	(0.03)	-0.7	(0.16)	1.2	(0.15)	50.5	6.0
Guerrero	-2.6	(0.11)	-0.9	(0.16)	1.6	(0.15)	-2.1	(0.17)	-1.3	(0.17)	0.8	(0.23)	71.1	5.7
Hidalgo	-2.4	(0.09)	-0.6	(0.14)	1.7	(0.11)	-1.8	(0.13)	-1.0	(0.12)	0.7	(0.12)	59.4	8.0
Jalisco	-2.0	(0.09)	-0.2	(0.20)	1.8	(0.16)	-1.6	(0.13)	-0.6	(0.18)	1.0	(0.20)	68.1	6.2
Mexico	-1.9	(0.10)	-0.3	(0.10)	1.6	(0.09)	-1.5	(0.15)	-0.8	(0.13)	0.7	(0.22)	74.7	6.4
Morelos	-1.9	(0.10)	0.3	(0.23)	2.2	(0.17)	-1.5	(0.13)	-0.2	(0.27)	1.3	(0.26)	57.0	5.8
Nayarit	-2.0	(0.16)	-0.1	(0.18)	1.9	(0.13)	-1.4	(0.23)	-0.6	(0.12)	0.9	(0.23)	68.9	5.7
Nuevo León	-1.3	(0.10)	0.5	(0.25)	1.8	(0.18)	-1.0	(0.25)	0.0	(0.23)	1.0	(0.27)	54.2	6.7
Puebla	-2.5	(0.09)	-0.7	(0.18)	1.8	(0.15)	-2.2	(0.13)	-0.9	(0.21)	1.4	(0.25)	53.2	5.3
Querétaro	-1.9	(0.17)	0.1	(0.29)	2.0	(0.17)	-1.7	(0.39)	-0.3	(0.13)	1.4	(0.38)	46.9	5.5
Quintana Roo	-1.9	(0.10)	-0.1	(0.10)	1.7	(0.09)	-1.5	(0.21)	-0.5	(0.06)	1.0	(0.18)	67.6	4.7
San Luis Potosí	-2.3	(0.19)	-0.3	(0.26)	2.1	(0.24)	-2.0	(0.45)	-0.7	(0.33)	1.3	(0.53)	46.1	6.3
Sinaloa	-1.8	(0.08)	-0.1	(0.11)	1.7	(0.08)	-1.3	(0.03)	-0.6	(0.11)	0.7	(0.10)	76.0	4.5
Tabasco	-2.1	(0.09)	-0.3	(0.14)	1.8	(0.11)	-1.6	(0.13)	-0.8	(0.08)	0.7	(0.15)	65.8	7.7
Tamaulipas	-1.7	(0.06)	-0.1	(0.13)	1.6	(0.10)	-1.3	(0.16)	-0.6	(0.09)	0.7	(0.18)	74.6	6.3
Tlaxcala	-2.0	(0.06)	-0.4	(0.14)	1.6	(0.12)	-1.6	(0.09)	-0.9	(0.27)	0.7	(0.27)	67.1	5.9
Veracruz	-2.6	(0.11)	-0.5	(0.22)	2.1	(0.20)	-2.3	(0.24)	-0.8	(0.17)	1.4	(0.30)	48.9	6.1
Yucatán	-2.2	(0.12)	-0.2	(0.23)	2.0	(0.17)	-1.9	(0.24)	-0.7	(0.37)	1.2	(0.35)	49.5	5.7
Zacatecas	-2.1	(0.06)	-0.4	(0.15)	1.7	(0.13)	-1.7	(0.12)	-0.8	(0.06)	0.9	(0.15)	70.5	6.3

• PISA adjudicated region.
Note: See Table II.2.13a for national data.
1. ESCS refers to the *PISA index of economic, social and cultural status*.
2. Students with low ESCS are those with a value on the *PISA index of economic, social and cultural status* lower than -1.
3. Distribution of the school mean ESCS, percentiles calculated at the student level.
4. The *index of social inclusion* is calculated as 100*(1-rho), where rho stands for the intra-class correlation of socio-economic status, i.e. the between-school variation in the *PISA index of social, economic and cultural status* of students, divided by the sum of the between-school variation in students' socio-economic status and the within-school variation in students' socio-economic status.

StatLink ⟐ http://dx.doi.org/10.1787/888932964965

[Part 4/4]
Students' socio-economic status, by region
Table B2.II.7 *Results based on students' self-reports*

	25th percentile of ESCS		75th percentile of ESCS		Interquartile range of distribution of students across ESCS		25th percentile of school mean ESCS		75th percentile of school mean ESCS		Interquartile range of distribution of schools across ESCS		Index of social inclusion[4]	
	Index	S.E.	Index	S.E.	Range	S.E.	Index	S.E.	Index	S.E.	Range	S.E.	Index	S.E.
Portugal														
Alentejo	-1.2	(0.12)	0.5	(0.29)	1.7	(0.19)	-0.9	(0.26)	0.1	(0.26)	1.0	(0.31)	7?.2	5.6
Spain														
Andalusia•	-1.2	(0.07)	0.5	(0.14)	1.7	(0.10)	-0.8	(0.06)	-0.1	(0.14)	0.7	(0.14)	7?.5	3.9
Aragon•	-0.8	(0.06)	0.8	(0.10)	1.6	(0.09)	-0.5	(0.06)	0.3	(0.16)	0.8	(0.16)	7?.1	3.7
Asturias•	-0.8	(0.04)	0.8	(0.09)	1.6	(0.07)	-0.4	(0.08)	0.3	(0.18)	0.7	(0.18)	7?.1	3.9
Balearic Islands•	-0.9	(0.04)	0.7	(0.07)	1.5	(0.05)	-0.5	(0.10)	0.1	(0.06)	0.5	(0.12)	8?.0	3.8
Basque Country•	-0.7	(0.03)	0.8	(0.03)	1.5	(0.02)	-0.2	(0.03)	0.3	(0.10)	0.5	(0.10)	7?.6	2.2
Cantabria•	-0.8	(0.03)	0.7	(0.07)	1.5	(0.06)	-0.3	(0.04)	0.1	(0.13)	0.4	(0.13)	8?.4	3.6
Castile and Leon•	-0.8	(0.05)	0.7	(0.07)	1.5	(0.05)	-0.4	(0.04)	0.3	(0.06)	0.7	(0.07)	8?.4	3.1
Catalonia•	-0.9	(0.09)	0.7	(0.13)	1.6	(0.08)	-0.5	(0.13)	0.3	(0.20)	0.8	(0.21)	7?.3	3.3
Extremadura•	-1.3	(0.03)	0.3	(0.10)	1.6	(0.09)	-0.9	(0.04)	-0.2	(0.09)	0.7	(0.09)	7?.0	3.8
Galicia•	-0.9	(0.05)	0.6	(0.08)	1.5	(0.06)	-0.6	(0.05)	0.2	(0.16)	0.8	(0.17)	7?.9	2.9
La Rioja•	-0.9	(0.04)	0.7	(0.05)	1.6	(0.06)	-0.5	(0.00)	0.1	(0.00)	0.6	(0.00)	8?.8	2.8
Madrid•	-0.7	(0.07)	1.0	(0.09)	1.6	(0.06)	-0.3	(0.08)	0.6	(0.14)	0.9	(0.12)	6?.8	3.7
Murcia•	-1.3	(0.06)	0.2	(0.07)	1.5	(0.06)	-0.8	(0.06)	-0.2	(0.06)	0.6	(0.08)	8?.7	2.9
Navarre•	-0.8	(0.03)	0.7	(0.07)	1.5	(0.06)	-0.5	(0.06)	0.2	(0.07)	0.6	(0.08)	7?.0	4.7
United Kingdom														
England	-0.3	(0.03)	0.9	(0.02)	1.2	(0.02)	0.0	(0.05)	0.5	(0.02)	0.5	(0.05)	7?.7	2.4
Northern Ireland	-0.4	(0.03)	1.0	(0.03)	1.4	(0.03)	-0.1	(0.03)	0.7	(0.03)	0.7	(0.04)	7?.9	2.5
Scotland•	-0.5	(0.02)	0.8	(0.03)	1.3	(0.02)	-0.1	(0.05)	0.3	(0.04)	0.4	(0.06)	8?.0	2.3
Wales	-0.4	(0.02)	0.8	(0.02)	1.2	(0.02)	0.0	(0.04)	0.4	(0.06)	0.4	(0.07)	8?.5	1.6
United States														
Connecticut•	-0.2	(0.08)	1.2	(0.05)	1.3	(0.05)	0.2	(0.11)	0.9	(0.07)	0.7	(0.12)	7?.4	3.7
Florida•	-0.4	(0.09)	0.9	(0.06)	1.3	(0.05)	-0.1	(0.12)	0.5	(0.09)	0.6	(0.10)	8?.2	2.6
Massachusetts•	-0.2	(0.09)	1.1	(0.05)	1.3	(0.06)	0.1	(0.18)	0.8	(0.09)	0.7	(0.19)	6?.9	4.0
Argentina														
Ciudad Autónoma de Buenos Aires•	-1.1	(0.12)	0.8	(0.09)	1.9	(0.08)	-1.0	(0.13)	0.5	(0.07)	1.6	(0.12)	4?.3	3.2
Brazil														
Acre	-2.4	(0.13)	-0.4	(0.15)	1.9	(0.12)	-1.8	(0.12)	-1.2	(0.27)	0.6	(0.21)	7?.7	7.8
Alagoas	-2.7	(0.09)	-0.8	(0.30)	1.9	(0.27)	-2.2	(0.09)	-1.6	(0.56)	0.6	(0.58)	6?.8	7.5
Amapá	-1.7	(0.11)	-0.2	(0.15)	1.5	(0.10)	-1.3	(0.02)	-0.7	(0.09)	0.6	(0.09)	7?.6	8.8
Amazonas	-1.7	(0.09)	-0.4	(0.09)	1.3	(0.11)	-1.3	(0.13)	-0.9	(0.23)	0.4	(0.25)	8?.7	7.9
Bahia	-2.6	(0.09)	-0.5	(0.22)	2.1	(0.22)	-2.2	(0.22)	-1.3	(0.33)	0.8	(0.39)	5?.6	11.4
Ceará	-2.5	(0.13)	-0.7	(0.17)	1.9	(0.16)	-2.1	(0.10)	-1.2	(0.17)	0.9	(0.17)	5?.3	9.8
Espírito Santo	-2.2	(0.13)	-0.2	(0.20)	2.0	(0.22)	-1.7	(0.10)	-1.1	(0.61)	0.6	(0.64)	5?.7	9.9
Federal District	-1.5	(0.05)	0.3	(0.23)	1.8	(0.21)	-1.3	(0.09)	-0.1	(0.11)	1.2	(0.12)	5?.8	7.8
Goiás	-2.0	(0.09)	-0.5	(0.15)	1.5	(0.13)	-1.7	(0.19)	-1.1	(0.21)	0.5	(0.21)	6?.1	7.9
Maranhão	-2.4	(0.18)	-0.5	(0.27)	1.9	(0.18)	-1.9	(0.26)	-1.1	(0.17)	0.8	(0.31)	6?.2	9.5
Mato Grosso	-2.2	(0.10)	-0.6	(0.12)	1.6	(0.12)	-1.7	(0.08)	-1.2	(0.14)	0.5	(0.16)	7?.9	12.3
Mato Grosso do Sul	-1.9	(0.09)	0.2	(0.15)	2.1	(0.11)	-1.6	(0.15)	-0.7	(0.61)	0.9	(0.53)	6?.7	6.1
Minas Gerais	-2.3	(0.13)	-0.4	(0.09)	1.9	(0.12)	-1.7	(0.21)	-1.0	(0.24)	0.7	(0.33)	6?.9	8.6
Pará	-2.1	(0.15)	-0.4	(0.31)	1.7	(0.19)	-1.6	(0.09)	-1.0	(1.15)	0.6	(1.11)	7?.6	8.0
Paraíba	-2.2	(0.20)	-0.1	(0.07)	2.0	(0.20)	-1.8	(0.14)	-0.3	(0.03)	1.6	(0.15)	5?.6	5.2
Paraná	-1.9	(0.13)	-0.3	(0.19)	1.6	(0.21)	-1.6	(0.18)	-1.0	(0.37)	0.6	(0.44)	6?.4	12.7
Pernambuco	-2.4	(0.23)	-0.9	(0.06)	1.5	(0.20)	-2.1	(0.20)	-1.2	(0.16)	0.9	(0.17)	7?.1	6.6
Piauí	-2.3	(0.16)	-0.3	(0.20)	2.0	(0.17)	-1.8	(0.07)	-1.2	(0.59)	0.6	(0.61)	5?.1	9.2
Rio de Janeiro	-1.6	(0.04)	-0.3	(0.18)	1.3	(0.18)	-1.2	(0.09)	-0.8	(0.15)	0.4	(0.19)	7?.2	9.5
Rio Grande do Norte	-2.2	(0.18)	-0.4	(0.22)	1.8	(0.19)	-1.8	(0.30)	-1.0	(0.24)	0.8	(0.36)	5?.6	9.2
Rio Grande do Sul	-2.0	(0.09)	-0.4	(0.09)	1.6	(0.09)	-1.6	(0.06)	-0.8	(0.13)	0.8	(0.13)	7?.7	6.3
Rondônia	-2.4	(0.16)	-0.6	(0.24)	1.8	(0.19)	-1.9	(0.04)	-1.1	(0.27)	0.8	(0.26)	7?.0	7.4
Roraima	-1.9	(0.08)	-0.1	(0.22)	1.8	(0.19)	-1.5	(0.14)	-1.0	(0.08)	0.5	(0.14)	6?.4	9.0
Santa Catarina	-2.1	(0.10)	-0.4	(0.23)	1.7	(0.17)	-1.6	(0.12)	-1.0	(0.14)	0.7	(0.14)	7?.0	7.5
São Paulo	-1.7	(0.07)	-0.2	(0.07)	1.6	(0.06)	-1.4	(0.04)	-0.6	(0.11)	0.8	(0.11)	6?.9	4.7
Sergipe	-2.2	(0.17)	-0.5	(0.08)	1.7	(0.13)	-1.7	(0.16)	-0.7	(0.55)	1.0	(0.54)	6?.9	5.5
Tocantins	-2.3	(0.15)	-0.4	(0.14)	1.9	(0.14)	-1.8	(0.15)	-0.9	(0.41)	0.9	(0.42)	7?.9	5.5
Colombia														
Bogotá	-1.8	(0.04)	-0.4	(0.06)	1.4	(0.05)	-1.3	(0.18)	-0.8	(0.05)	0.5	(0.17)	8?.9	4.5
Cali	-1.5	(0.08)	-0.2	(0.10)	1.3	(0.08)	-1.3	(0.06)	-0.5	(0.12)	0.8	(0.12)	6?.5	5.1
Manizales	-1.5	(0.14)	0.0	(0.08)	1.6	(0.10)	-1.2	(0.15)	-0.2	(0.37)	1.0	(0.38)	5?.5	4.9
Medellín	-1.7	(0.11)	-0.2	(0.17)	1.6	(0.15)	-1.5	(0.06)	-0.7	(0.21)	0.8	(0.19)	5?.0	5.9
Russian Federation														
Perm Territory region•	-0.7	(0.03)	0.5	(0.04)	1.1	(0.03)	-0.3	(0.05)	0.1	(0.05)	0.4	(0.07)	8?.7	3.5
United Arab Emirates														
Abu Dhabi•	-0.2	(0.04)	0.9	(0.03)	1.1	(0.04)	0.0	(0.04)	0.7	(0.04)	0.7	(0.05)	7?.5	3.0
Ajman	-0.5	(0.09)	0.5	(0.05)	1.0	(0.07)	-0.3	(0.24)	0.3	(0.18)	0.6	(0.29)	8?.8	3.5
Dubai•	0.1	(0.02)	1.0	(0.01)	0.8	(0.02)	0.3	(0.00)	0.8	(0.00)	0.6	(0.01)	7?.1	2.5
Fujairah	-0.5	(0.05)	0.6	(0.06)	1.1	(0.06)	-0.3	(0.00)	0.3	(0.09)	0.6	(0.08)	8?.8	4.0
Ras al-Khaimah	-0.4	(0.10)	0.7	(0.05)	1.1	(0.08)	-0.2	(0.15)	0.4	(0.16)	0.7	(0.20)	8?.8	4.8
Sharjah	0.1	(0.05)	0.9	(0.03)	0.9	(0.05)	0.2	(0.05)	0.7	(0.07)	0.5	(0.07)	8?.2	4.4
Umm al-Quwain	-0.6	(0.08)	0.5	(0.05)	1.1	(0.09)	-0.2	(0.00)	0.0	(0.00)	0.2	(0.00)	9?.5	4.0

• PISA adjudicated region.
Note: See Table II.2.13a for national data.
1. ESCS refers to the *PISA index of economic, social and cultural status.*
2. Students with low ESCS are those with a value on the *PISA index of economic, social and cultural status* lower than -1.
3. Distribution of the school mean ESCS, percentiles calculated at the student level.
4. The *index of social inclusion* is calculated as 100*(1-rho), where rho stands for the intra-class correlation of socio-economic status, i.e. the between-school variation in the *PISA index of social, economic and cultural status* of students, divided by the sum of the between-school variation in students' socio-economic status and the within-school variation in students' socio-economic status.

StatLink ⎯ http://dx.doi.org/10.1787/888932964965

[Part 1/4]
Mathematics performance and immigrant background, by region
Table B2.II.9   *Results based on students' self-reports*

| | Percentage of students | | | | ESCS[1] | | | | Mathematics performance | | | |
| | Non-immigrant | | Immigrant | | Non-immigrant | | Immigrant | | Non-immigrant | | Immigrant | |
	%	S.E.	%	S.E.	Mean index	S.E.	Mean index	S.E.	Mean score	S.E.	Mean score	S.E.
Australia												
Australian Capital Territory	83.8	(1.5)	16.2	(1.5)	0.61	(0.02)	0.68	(0.04)	521	(3.7)	542	(10.5)
New South Wales	73.3	(1.8)	26.7	(1.8)	0.29	(0.02)	0.19	(0.04)	504	(3.1)	547	(8.5)
Northern Territory	85.2	(1.6)	14.8	(1.6)	0.12	(0.05)	0.26	(0.15)	454	(9.7)	472	(19.5)
Queensland	80.7	(1.0)	19.3	(1.0)	0.21	(0.03)	0.12	(0.05)	505	(3.2)	511	(5.9)
South Australia	85.3	(1.3)	14.7	(1.3)	0.21	(0.02)	0.17	(0.11)	492	(3.6)	500	(7.6)
Tasmania	93.5	(0.9)	6.5	(0.9)	0.00	(0.03)	0.35	(0.11)	480	(3.7)	515	(13.4)
Victoria	78.0	(1.6)	22.0	(1.6)	0.36	(0.03)	0.21	(0.05)	500	(3.0)	521	(8.9)
Western Australia	70.5	(1.8)	29.5	(1.8)	0.23	(0.03)	0.30	(0.05)	517	(3.7)	524	(5.2)
Belgium												
Flemish Community*	89.5	(0.9)	10.5	(0.9)	0.24	(0.02)	-0.49	(0.09)	544	(3.2)	447	(7.8)
French Community	78.9	(1.9)	21.1	(1.9)	0.22	(0.03)	-0.18	(0.08)	508	(3.1)	459	(7.3)
German-speaking Community	77.0	(1.4)	23.0	(1.4)	0.24	(0.04)	0.43	(0.06)	520	(2.7)	490	(6.0)
Canada												
Alberta	74.9	(1.9)	25.1	(1.9)	0.55	(0.03)	0.41	(0.05)	521	(4.7)	526	(7.3)
British Columbia	64.1	(2.9)	35.9	(2.9)	0.48	(0.04)	0.43	(0.06)	521	(4.4)	534	(6.9)
Manitoba	76.8	(1.6)	23.2	(1.6)	0.34	(0.04)	0.00	(0.06)	500	(3.4)	488	(6.8)
New Brunswick	94.2	(1.1)	5.8	(1.1)	0.35	(0.03)	0.68	(0.07)	503	(2.6)	517	(14.5)
Newfoundland and Labrador	97.7	(0.8)	2.3	(0.8)	0.26	(0.04)	c	c	493	(3.7)	c	c
Nova Scotia	95.9	(0.8)	4.1	(0.8)	0.29	(0.03)	0.77	(0.12)	499	(4.4)	531	(13.1)
Ontario	56.5	(3.0)	43.5	(3.0)	0.55	(0.04)	0.30	(0.06)	515	(4.2)	519	(6.5)
Prince Edward Island	95.7	(0.7)	4.3	(0.7)	0.33	(0.02)	0.35	(0.11)	479	(2.6)	532	(12.6)
Quebec	84.8	(1.7)	15.2	(1.7)	0.36	(0.03)	0.23	(0.07)	544	(3.1)	510	(7.4)
Saskatchewan	92.5	(0.7)	7.5	(0.7)	0.42	(0.02)	0.24	(0.09)	512	(3.0)	492	(8.2)
Italy												
Abruzzo	94.2	(0.9)	5.8	(0.9)	0.07	(0.04)	-0.56	(0.09)	480	(6.4)	432	(7.9)
Basilicata	98.7	(0.3)	1.3	(0.3)	-0.21	(0.03)	c	c	467	(4.2)	c	c
Bolzano	94.2	(0.5)	5.8	(0.5)	-0.05	(0.02)	-0.26	(0.08)	512	(2.1)	447	(10.4)
Calabria	96.4	(0.6)	3.6	(0.6)	-0.21	(0.05)	-0.50	(0.14)	434	(5.6)	378	(16.2)
Campania	98.4	(0.4)	1.6	(0.4)	-0.18	(0.06)	c	c	454	(7.9)	c	c
Emilia Romagna	84.8	(1.3)	15.2	(1.3)	0.10	(0.04)	-0.65	(0.07)	516	(6.2)	423	(9.7)
Friuli Venezia Giulia	90.3	(1.1)	9.7	(1.1)	0.11	(0.04)	-0.51	(0.15)	530	(4.4)	471	(10.6)
Lazio	90.3	(1.2)	9.7	(1.2)	0.22	(0.05)	-0.38	(0.14)	479	(6.8)	444	(10.7)
Liguria	89.3	(1.1)	10.7	(1.1)	0.09	(0.04)	-0.53	(0.08)	497	(6.2)	419	(7.9)
Lombardia	90.6	(1.5)	9.4	(1.5)	0.11	(0.05)	-0.49	(0.07)	524	(7.3)	463	(10.6)
Marche	89.3	(1.4)	10.7	(1.4)	0.02	(0.05)	-0.50	(0.08)	502	(5.8)	456	(10.5)
Molise	97.1	(0.6)	2.9	(0.6)	-0.10	(0.03)	c	c	469	(2.3)	c	c
Piemonte	91.6	(0.8)	8.4	(0.8)	-0.02	(0.04)	-0.59	(0.09)	503	(7.1)	459	(7.9)
Puglia	97.4	(0.4)	2.6	(0.4)	-0.30	(0.04)	-0.47	(0.15)	481	(6.0)	435	(14.0)
Sardegna	96.9	(0.8)	3.1	(0.8)	-0.13	(0.05)	-0.48	(0.19)	461	(5.1)	390	(21.7)
Sicilia	97.3	(0.6)	2.7	(0.6)	-0.08	(0.05)	c	c	451	(4.7)	c	c
Toscana	88.9	(1.0)	11.1	(1.0)	0.08	(0.06)	-0.65	(0.12)	505	(5.0)	438	(7.4)
Trento	90.9	(1.0)	9.1	(1.0)	0.06	(0.03)	-0.50	(0.07)	529	(4.1)	474	(9.2)
Umbria	88.4	(1.1)	11.6	(1.1)	0.18	(0.04)	-0.39	(0.08)	501	(5.9)	447	(11.0)
Valle d'Aosta	93.6	(0.9)	6.4	(0.9)	-0.16	(0.03)	-0.68	(0.15)	496	(2.5)	465	(11.9)
Veneto	88.3	(1.5)	11.7	(1.5)	0.01	(0.04)	-0.63	(0.06)	534	(7.5)	456	(11.5)
Mexico												
Aguascalientes	99.1	(0.3)	0.9	(0.3)	-0.75	(0.08)	c	c	439	(4.5)	c	c
Baja California	97.5	(0.5)	2.5	(0.5)	-0.71	(0.08)	c	c	417	(6.0)	c	c
Baja California Sur	98.8	(0.3)	1.2	(0.3)	-0.76	(0.09)	c	c	416	(5.2)	c	c
Campeche	94.6	(2.1)	5.4	(2.1)	-1.23	(0.09)	-2.22	(0.20)	401	(3.6)	330	(12.5)
Chiapas	97.4	(0.7)	2.6	(0.7)	-1.75	(0.14)	c	c	378	(6.4)	c	c
Chihuahua	99.2	(0.4)	0.8	(0.4)	-0.80	(0.10)	c	c	430	(7.8)	c	c
Coahuila	99.3	(0.3)	0.7	(0.3)	-0.81	(0.12)	c	c	420	(8.1)	c	c
Colima	99.2	(0.2)	0.8	(0.2)	-0.75	(0.10)	c	c	431	(4.4)	c	c
Distrito Federal	97.9	(0.8)	2.1	(0.8)	-0.56	(0.11)	c	c	429	(4.8)	c	c
Durango	99.2	(0.4)	0.8	(0.4)	-0.98	(0.13)	c	c	427	(5.7)	c	c
Guanajuato	99.2	(0.2)	0.8	(0.2)	-1.26	(0.12)	c	c	414	(5.1)	c	c
Guerrero	97.5	(0.6)	2.5	(0.6)	-1.65	(0.09)	c	c	370	(3.2)	c	c
Hidalgo	98.8	(0.5)	1.2	(0.5)	-1.45	(0.10)	c	c	409	(5.5)	c	c
Jalisco	99.5	(0.2)	0.5	(0.2)	-1.07	(0.12)	c	c	436	(5.9)	c	c
Mexico	98.9	(0.4)	1.1	(0.4)	-1.06	(0.08)	c	c	419	(5.7)	c	c
Morelos	99.3	(0.3)	0.7	(0.3)	-0.86	(0.14)	c	c	423	(8.5)	c	c
Nayarit	98.9	(0.5)	1.1	(0.5)	-1.00	(0.10)	c	c	416	(5.5)	c	c
Nuevo León	98.9	(0.5)	1.1	(0.5)	-0.43	(0.15)	c	c	437	(8.3)	c	c
Puebla	98.7	(0.6)	1.3	(0.6)	-1.51	(0.11)	c	c	418	(4.4)	c	c
Querétaro	99.6	(0.2)	0.4	(0.2)	-0.91	(0.18)	c	c	436	(6.1)	c	c
Quintana Roo	97.2	(0.6)	2.8	(0.6)	-0.97	(0.09)	c	c	414	(4.8)	c	c
San Luis Potosí	99.3	(0.5)	0.7	(0.5)	-1.24	(0.17)	c	c	415	(6.9)	c	c
Sinaloa	99.2	(0.3)	0.8	(0.3)	-0.95	(0.07)	c	c	413	(4.2)	c	c
Tabasco	97.6	(0.7)	2.4	(0.7)	-1.15	(0.09)	c	c	383	(3.4)	c	c
Tamaulipas	98.0	(0.4)	2.0	(0.4)	-0.88	(0.09)	c	c	414	(7.3)	c	c
Tlaxcala	99.0	(0.3)	1.0	(0.3)	-1.13	(0.08)	c	c	414	(4.9)	c	c
Veracruz	99.0	(0.6)	1.0	(0.6)	-1.45	(0.11)	c	c	405	(6.1)	c	c
Yucatán	97.7	(0.6)	2.3	(0.6)	-1.15	(0.15)	c	c	414	(4.3)	c	c
Zacatecas	98.7	(0.3)	1.3	(0.3)	-1.16	(0.08)	c	c	413	(4.0)	c	c

* PISA adjudicated region.
Notes: This table was calculated considering only students with data on the *PISA index of economic, social and cultural status*. Values that are statistically significant are indicated in bold (see Annex A3).
Students with an immigrant background are students whose parents were born in a country other than the country of assessment.
See Table II.3.4a for national data.
1. ESCS refers to the *PISA index of economic, social and cultural status*.
StatLink ⟶ http://dx.doi.org/10.1787/888932964965

[Part 2/4]
Mathematics performance and immigrant background, by region
Table B2.II.9   *Results based on students' self-reports*

| | Percentage of students | | | | ESCS¹ | | | | Mathematics performance | | | |
| | Non-immigrant | | Immigrant | | Non-immigrant | | Immigrant | | Non-immigrant | | Immigrant | |
	%	S.E.	%	S.E.	Mean index	S.E.	Mean index	S.E.	Mean score	S.E.	Mean score	S.E.
Portugal												
Alentejo	94.8	(1.1)	5.2	(1.1)	-0.34	(0.14)	-0.66	(0.17)	490	(10.3)	48	(17.8)
Spain												
Andalusia•	96.6	(0.6)	3.4	(0.6)	-0.35	(0.07)	-0.49	(0.13)	475	(3.8)	43	(14.7)
Aragon•	86.8	(1.2)	13.2	(1.2)	0.05	(0.06)	-0.74	(0.08)	510	(5.3)	42	(9.4)
Asturias•	93.7	(0.8)	6.3	(0.8)	0.02	(0.05)	-0.68	(0.10)	505	(4.2)	43	(9.6)
Balearic Islands•	81.0	(1.9)	19.0	(1.9)	-0.05	(0.04)	-0.57	(0.07)	489	(4.6)	42	(6.6)
Basque Country•	91.3	(0.8)	8.7	(0.8)	0.11	(0.03)	-0.71	(0.05)	516	(2.3)	43	(5.7)
Cantabria•	90.7	(1.3)	9.3	(1.3)	-0.01	(0.05)	-0.59	(0.06)	497	(3.6)	448	(6.1)
Castile and Leon•	93.1	(1.1)	6.9	(1.1)	-0.04	(0.05)	-0.91	(0.09)	514	(4.1)	44	(10.0)
Catalonia•	86.2	(1.8)	13.8	(1.8)	-0.04	(0.08)	-0.64	(0.11)	505	(4.3)	43	(9.8)
Extremadura•	96.6	(0.6)	3.4	(0.6)	-0.45	(0.05)	-0.66	(0.16)	464	(4.8)	42	(14.7)
Galicia•	94.5	(0.7)	5.5	(0.7)	-0.16	(0.05)	-0.39	(0.08)	493	(4.0)	44	(10.3)
La Rioja•	82.0	(1.1)	18.0	(1.1)	0.01	(0.03)	-0.83	(0.06)	520	(2.4)	43	(6.7)
Madrid•	83.9	(2.0)	16.1	(2.0)	0.25	(0.07)	-0.59	(0.07)	515	(3.7)	45	(9.8)
Murcia•	84.6	(1.4)	15.4	(1.4)	-0.38	(0.05)	-1.05	(0.07)	473	(5.0)	41	(6.7)
Navarre•	84.6	(1.2)	15.4	(1.2)	0.03	(0.05)	-0.83	(0.06)	529	(3.2)	45	(4.8)
United Kingdom												
England	86.0	(1.3)	14.0	(1.3)	0.30	(0.02)	0.20	(0.06)	501	(3.3)	488	(8.9)
Northern Ireland	96.1	(0.5)	3.9	(0.5)	0.30	(0.02)	0.09	(0.12)	491	(3.0)	482	(11.6)
Scotland•	91.6	(0.8)	8.4	(0.8)	0.13	(0.02)	0.23	(0.07)	498	(2.5)	524	(7.4)
Wales	96.0	(0.7)	4.0	(0.7)	0.20	(0.02)	-0.05	(0.07)	472	(2.2)	461	(8.5)
United States												
Connecticut•	83.7	(1.7)	16.3	(1.7)	0.59	(0.06)	0.01	(0.09)	516	(5.9)	473	(10.0)
Florida•	76.1	(2.2)	23.9	(2.2)	0.30	(0.05)	-0.12	(0.07)	471	(6.3)	461	(5.9)
Massachusetts•	80.6	(2.5)	19.4	(2.5)	0.58	(0.07)	-0.13	(0.09)	522	(6.5)	490	(11.5)
Argentina												
Ciudad Autónoma de Buenos Aires•	83.8	(1.8)	16.2	(1.8)	0.01	(0.08)	-1.28	(0.10)	431	(6.9)	355	(10.4)
Brazil												
Acre	99.5	(0.4)	0.5	(0.4)	-1.35	(0.10)	c	c	361	(5.8)	c	c
Alagoas	100.0	c	c	c	-1.70	(0.13)	c	c	345	(6.2)	c	c
Amapá	99.8	(0.2)	0.2	(0.2)	-0.93	(0.12)	c	c	363	(8.7)	c	c
Amazonas	98.6	(0.4)	1.4	(0.4)	-1.07	(0.06)	c	c	359	(5.4)	c	c
Bahia	99.4	(0.4)	0.6	(0.4)	-1.51	(0.09)	c	c	376	(8.2)	c	c
Ceará	99.9	(0.1)	0.1	(0.1)	-1.55	(0.11)	c	c	380	(8.9)	c	c
Espírito Santo	100.0	c	c	c	-1.17	(0.10)	c	c	416	(10.4)	c	c
Federal District	97.1	(0.6)	2.9	(0.6)	-0.65	(0.10)	c	c	420	(8.9)	c	c
Goiás	99.0	(0.4)	1.0	(0.4)	-1.24	(0.09)	c	c	382	(5.6)	c	c
Maranhão	99.3	(0.4)	0.7	(0.4)	-1.40	(0.19)	c	c	349	(13.3)	c	c
Mato Grosso	99.2	(0.4)	0.8	(0.4)	-1.34	(0.08)	c	c	373	(8.9)	c	c
Mato Grosso do Sul	97.7	(1.0)	2.3	(1.0)	-0.92	(0.10)	c	c	413	(7.4)	c	c
Minas Gerais	99.5	(0.5)	0.5	(0.5)	-1.29	(0.08)	c	c	407	(6.5)	c	c
Pará	99.6	(0.3)	0.4	(0.3)	-1.20	(0.17)	c	c	362	(3.9)	c	c
Paraíba	99.9	(0.1)	0.1	(0.1)	-1.13	(0.09)	c	c	396	(6.3)	c	c
Paraná	99.0	(0.2)	1.0	(0.2)	-1.09	(0.12)	c	c	405	(11.4)	c	c
Pernambuco	99.6	(0.2)	0.4	(0.2)	-1.61	(0.12)	c	c	365	(7.6)	c	c
Piauí	99.8	(0.2)	0.2	(0.2)	-1.25	(0.09)	c	c	387	(7.5)	c	c
Rio de Janeiro	99.3	(0.3)	0.7	(0.3)	-0.94	(0.08)	c	c	391	(7.0)	c	c
Rio Grande do Norte	99.7	(0.2)	0.3	(0.2)	-1.30	(0.14)	c	c	383	(8.7)	c	c
Rio Grande do Sul	99.9	(0.1)	0.1	(0.1)	-1.18	(0.08)	c	c	408	(5.4)	c	c
Rondônia	98.7	(0.4)	1.3	(0.4)	-1.37	(0.17)	c	c	385	(5.3)	c	c
Roraima	96.8	(0.9)	3.2	(0.9)	-1.03	(0.08)	c	c	366	(5.5)	c	c
Santa Catarina	98.9	(0.5)	1.1	(0.5)	-1.18	(0.12)	c	c	419	(7.9)	c	c
São Paulo	99.0	(0.4)	1.0	(0.4)	-0.94	(0.05)	c	c	407	(4.4)	c	c
Sergipe	99.8	(0.2)	0.2	(0.2)	-1.23	(0.10)	c	c	387	(8.8)	c	c
Tocantins	99.4	(0.2)	0.6	(0.2)	-1.31	(0.09)	c	c	368	(7.5)	c	c
Colombia												
Bogotá	99.8	(0.1)	0.2	(0.1)	-1.09	(0.05)	c	c	394	(3.4)	c	c
Cali	99.0	(0.3)	1.0	(0.3)	-0.81	(0.08)	c	c	380	(6.2)	c	c
Manizales	100.0	(0.0)	0.0	(0.0)	-0.77	(0.07)	c	c	405	(4.2)	c	c
Medellín	99.6	(0.2)	0.4	(0.2)	-0.93	(0.10)	c	c	396	(7.6)	c	c
Russian Federation												
Perm Territory region•	92.6	(0.7)	7.4	(0.7)	-0.12	(0.03)	-0.15	(0.07)	488	(5.5)	450	(8.5)
United Arab Emirates												
Abu Dhabi•	48.4	(2.1)	51.6	(2.1)	0.33	(0.04)	0.25	(0.05)	395	(3.5)	452	(5.2)
Ajman	46.0	(2.9)	54.0	(2.9)	-0.01	(0.08)	-0.15	(0.07)	389	(10.5)	418	(7.3)
Dubai•	31.3	(0.3)	68.7	(0.3)	0.38	(0.02)	0.55	(0.01)	408	(2.1)	492	(1.8)
Fujairah	74.7	(2.3)	25.3	(2.3)	-0.09	(0.04)	0.30	(0.07)	397	(4.9)	463	(19.9)
Ras al-Khaimah	69.1	(4.0)	30.9	(4.0)	0.08	(0.07)	0.00	(0.14)	406	(6.3)	441	(9.0)
Sharjah	41.3	(5.6)	58.7	(5.6)	0.39	(0.11)	0.47	(0.05)	405	(10.0)	465	(7.8)
Umm al-Quwain	67.3	(2.5)	32.7	(2.5)	-0.10	(0.06)	-0.16	(0.08)	393	(5.7)	410	(6.4)

Column labels on the left margin: OECD (upper section), Partners (lower section).

• PISA adjudicated region.
Notes: This table was calculated considering only students with data on the *PISA index of economic, social and cultural status*. Values that are statistically significant are indicated in bold (see Annex A3).
Students with an immigrant background are students whose parents were born in a country other than the country of assessment.
See Table II.3.4a for national data.
1. ESCS refers to the *PISA index of economic, social and cultural status*.
StatLink ⟐🖳 http://dx.doi.org/10.1787/888932964965

[Part 3/4]
Mathematics performance and immigrant background, by region

Table B2.II.9 *Results based on students' self-reports*

	Difference in mathematics performance between non-immigrant and immigrant students		Difference in mathematics performance between non-immigrant and immigrant students AFTER accounting for ESCS		Increased likelihood of immigrant students scoring in the bottom quarter of the mathematics performance distribution		Population relevance of immigrant students scoring in the bottom quarter of the mathematics performance distribution		Effect size for immigrant background in mathematics performance (positive number implies an advantage for non-immigrant students)		Increased likelihood of non-immigrant students scoring in the bottom quarter of the mathematics performance distribution		Population relevance of non-immigrant students scoring in the bottom quarter of the mathematics performance distribution	
	Score dif.	S.E.	Score dif.	S.E.	Ratio	S.E.	%	S.E.	Effect size	S.E.	Ratio	S.E.	%	S.E.
Australia														
Australian Capital Territory	21	(11.3)	18	(11.0)	0.89	(0.18)	-1.9	(2.96)	0.22	(0.12)	1.13	(0.25)	9.7	(15.57)
New South Wales	**44**	(8.4)	**48**	(7.6)	0.64	(0.07)	-10.6	(2.45)	**0.44**	(0.08)	**1.56**	(0.16)	29.1	(6.50)
Northern Territory	18	(16.6)	9	(14.6)	1.13	(0.33)	1.9	(4.76)	0.17	(0.16)	0.89	(0.32)	-10.9	(27.74)
Queensland	6	(6.4)	10	(6.2)	1.02	(0.12)	0.3	(2.22)	0.06	(0.07)	0.98	(0.11)	-1.3	(9.30)
South Australia	7	(8.3)	9	(8.3)	0.96	(0.15)	-0.6	(2.27)	0.08	(0.09)	1.05	(0.17)	3.5	(13.11)
Tasmania	**35**	(14.2)	20	(12.8)	0.45	(0.20)	-3.7	(1.47)	**0.39**	(0.15)	**2.38**	(1.04)	53.4	(19.57)
Victoria	**21**	(8.4)	**26**	(7.9)	0.86	(0.11)	-3.2	(2.64)	**0.23**	(0.09)	1.17	(0.16)	11.5	(9.03)
Western Australia	7	(5.8)	4	(5.2)	0.92	(0.11)	-2.6	(3.44)	0.07	(0.06)	1.09	(0.14)	6.1	(8.12)
Belgium														
Flemish Community*	**-97**	(7.4)	**-65**	(5.3)	**2.75**	(0.19)	15.5	(1.92)	**-1.02**	(0.07)	0.36	(0.03)	-132.6	(12.43)
French Community	**-48**	(7.8)	**-31**	(6.2)	**1.94**	(0.23)	16.5	(3.84)	**-0.52**	(0.08)	0.52	(0.06)	-61.5	(11.76)
German-speaking Community	**-30**	(7.1)	**-35**	(6.8)	**1.53**	(0.21)	10.8	(3.94)	**-0.33**	(0.08)	0.65	(0.09)	-36.3	(12.94)
Canada														
Alberta	5	(7.1)	10	(6.1)	0.99	(0.15)	-0.3	(3.63)	0.06	(0.08)	1.02	(0.14)	0.9	(10.90)
British Columbia	13	(7.2)	**14**	(6.6)	0.86	(0.11)	-5.4	(4.73)	0.16	(0.09)	1.17	(0.17)	9.6	(8.30)
Manitoba	-12	(8.0)	1	(7.7)	1.25	(0.19)	5.5	(4.11)	-0.14	(0.09)	0.80	(0.13)	-18.1	(13.41)
New Brunswick	14	(14.9)	6	(14.7)	0.75	(0.37)	-1.5	(2.17)	0.18	(0.19)	1.40	(0.58)	24.0	(35.45)
Newfoundland and Labrador	c	c	c	c	c	c	c	c	c	c	c	c	c	c
Nova Scotia	**32**	(14.2)	19	(13.8)	0.67	(0.28)	-1.4	(1.18)	**0.39**	(0.17)	1.54	(0.66)	32.4	(27.34)
Ontario	4	(7.1)	12	(6.3)	1.03	(0.12)	1.2	(5.12)	0.04	(0.08)	0.97	(0.12)	-1.6	(6.64)
Prince Edward Island	**53**	(13.2)	**53**	(11.5)	0.33	(0.16)	-3.0	(0.90)	**0.63**	(0.17)	**3.03**	(1.53)	65.7	(16.59)
Quebec	**-34**	(7.4)	**-30**	(6.4)	**1.58**	(0.17)	8.1	(2.40)	**-0.38**	(0.08)	0.63	(0.07)	-45.4	(11.67)
Saskatchewan	**-19**	(8.8)	-15	(7.9)	1.29	(0.21)	2.1	(1.49)	**-0.24**	(0.11)	0.78	(0.12)	-25.9	(18.37)
Italy														
Abruzzo	**-48**	(8.2)	**-32**	(8.1)	**1.80**	(0.24)	4.4	(1.42)	**-0.57**	(0.11)	0.56	(0.08)	-72.0	(20.62)
Basilicata	c	c	c	c	c	c	c	c	c	c	c	c	c	c
Bolzano	**-64**	(10.8)	**-59**	(10.6)	**2.14**	(0.26)	6.2	(1.43)	**-0.69**	(0.11)	0.47	(0.06)	-101.0	(21.16)
Calabria	**-55**	(15.8)	**-48**	(16.6)	**2.05**	(0.42)	3.6	(1.49)	**-0.60**	(0.19)	0.49	(0.10)	-97.7	(37.33)
Campania	c	c	c	c	c	c	c	c	c	c	c	c	c	c
Emilia Romagna	**-93**	(9.7)	**-69**	(8.4)	**2.96**	(0.30)	22.9	(2.71)	**-0.97**	(0.09)	0.34	(0.03)	-128.1	(16.84)
Friuli Venezia Giulia	**-59**	(10.6)	**-44**	(10.8)	**2.12**	(0.31)	9.8	(2.40)	**-0.68**	(0.11)	0.47	(0.07)	-91.3	(23.47)
Lazio	**-35**	(9.2)	**-21**	(8.6)	**1.60**	(0.24)	5.5	(2.11)	**-0.39**	(0.11)	0.63	(0.10)	-50.9	(19.46)
Liguria	**-79**	(9.4)	**-62**	(8.7)	**2.42**	(0.38)	13.2	(3.19)	**-0.92**	(0.11)	0.42	(0.06)	-109.8	(25.85)
Lombardia	**-61**	(10.4)	**-44**	(9.0)	**2.20**	(0.31)	10.2	(2.29)	**-0.71**	(0.12)	0.46	(0.07)	-97.6	(23.73)
Marche	**-46**	(11.0)	**-37**	(10.9)	**1.92**	(0.25)	8.9	(2.84)	**-0.55**	(0.13)	0.52	(0.06)	-74.8	(17.81)
Molise	c	c	c	c	c	c	c	c	c	c	c	c	c	c
Piemonte	**-44**	(13.1)	**-30**	(12.7)	**1.94**	(0.35)	7.3	(2.70)	**-0.52**	(0.15)	0.52	(0.10)	-79.5	(27.25)
Puglia	**-46**	(13.5)	**-41**	(13.3)	**2.01**	(0.51)	2.5	(1.29)	**-0.57**	(0.19)	0.50	(0.11)	-95.4	(46.75)
Sardegna	**-71**	(20.2)	**-62**	(18.0)	**2.08**	(0.43)	3.2	(1.44)	**-0.83**	(0.20)	0.48	(0.08)	-101.5	(38.64)
Sicilia	c	c	c	c	c	c	c	c	c	c	c	c	c	c
Toscana	**-68**	(7.8)	**-44**	(8.6)	**2.38**	(0.30)	13.3	(2.57)	**-0.75**	(0.10)	0.42	(0.05)	-106.0	(19.81)
Trento	**-56**	(9.5)	**-43**	(10.4)	**1.94**	(0.30)	7.9	(2.52)	**-0.67**	(0.13)	0.52	(0.09)	-78.7	(23.31)
Umbria	**-54**	(8.9)	**-42**	(9.4)	**1.90**	(0.25)	9.4	(2.49)	**-0.63**	(0.11)	0.53	(0.07)	-72.2	(17.69)
Valle d'Aosta	**-31**	(12.6)	-19	(12.1)	**1.54**	(0.33)	3.3	(2.04)	**-0.40**	(0.16)	0.65	(0.15)	-48.6	(29.26)
Veneto	**-77**	(10.8)	**-61**	(10.6)	**2.84**	(0.42)	17.7	(3.95)	**-0.84**	(0.11)	0.35	(0.05)	-133.5	(25.08)
Mexico														
Aguascalientes	c	c	c	c	c	c	c	c	c	c	c	c	c	c
Baja California	c	c	c	c	c	c	c	c	c	c	c	c	c	c
Baja California Sur	c	c	c	c	c	c	c	c	c	c	c	c	c	c
Campeche	**-71**	(12.1)	**-59**	(13.8)	**2.87**	(0.43)	9.2	(2.90)	**-1.10**	(0.23)	0.35	(0.06)	-160.1	(36.92)
Chiapas	c	c	c	c	c	c	c	c	c	c	c	c	c	c
Chihuahua	c	c	c	c	c	c	c	c	c	c	c	c	c	c
Coahuila	c	c	c	c	c	c	c	c	c	c	c	c	c	c
Colima	c	c	c	c	c	c	c	c	c	c	c	c	c	c
Distrito Federal	c	c	c	c	c	c	c	c	c	c	c	c	c	c
Durango	c	c	c	c	c	c	c	c	c	c	c	c	c	c
Guanajuato	c	c	c	c	c	c	c	c	c	c	c	c	c	c
Guerrero	c	c	c	c	c	c	c	c	c	c	c	c	c	c
Hidalgo	c	c	c	c	c	c	c	c	c	c	c	c	c	c
Jalisco	c	c	c	c	c	c	c	c	c	c	c	c	c	c
Mexico	c	c	c	c	c	c	c	c	c	c	c	c	c	c
Morelos	c	c	c	c	c	c	c	c	c	c	c	c	c	c
Nayarit	c	c	c	c	c	c	c	c	c	c	c	c	c	c
Nuevo León	c	c	c	c	c	c	c	c	c	c	c	c	c	c
Puebla	c	c	c	c	c	c	c	c	c	c	c	c	c	c
Querétaro	c	c	c	c	c	c	c	c	c	c	c	c	c	c
Quintana Roo	c	c	c	c	c	c	c	c	c	c	c	c	c	c
San Luis Potosí	c	c	c	c	c	c	c	c	c	c	c	c	c	c
Sinaloa	c	c	c	c	c	c	c	c	c	c	c	c	c	c
Tabasco	c	c	c	c	c	c	c	c	c	c	c	c	c	c
Tamaulipas	c	c	c	c	c	c	c	c	c	c	c	c	c	c
Tlaxcala	c	c	c	c	c	c	c	c	c	c	c	c	c	c
Veracruz	c	c	c	c	c	c	c	c	c	c	c	c	c	c
Yucatán	c	c	c	c	c	c	c	c	c	c	c	c	c	c
Zacatecas	c	c	c	c	c	c	c	c	c	c	c	c	c	c

* PISA adjudicated region.
Notes: This table was calculated considering only students with data on the *PISA index of economic, social and cultural status*. Values that are statistically significant are indicated in bold (see Annex A3).
Students with an immigrant background are students whose parents were born in a country other than the country of assessment.
See Table II.3.4a for national data.
1. ESCS refers to the *PISA index of economic, social and cultural status*.
StatLink http://dx.doi.org/10.1787/888932964965

[Part 4/4]
Mathematics performance and immigrant background, by region
Table B2.II.9 *Results based on students' self-reports*

	Difference in mathematics performance between non-immigrant and immigrant students		Difference in mathematics performance between non-immigrant and immigrant students AFTER accounting for ESCS		Increased likelihood of immigrant students scoring in the bottom quarter of the mathematics performance distribution		Population relevance of immigrant students scoring in the bottom quarter of the mathematics performance distribution		Effect size for immigrant background in mathematics performance (positive number implies an advantage for non-immigrant students)		Increased likelihood of non-immigrant students scoring in the bottom quarter of the mathematics performance distribution		Population relevance of non-immigrant students scoring in the bottom quarter of the mathematics performance distribution	
	Score dif.	S.E.	Score dif.	S.E.	Ratio	S.E.	%	S.E.	Effect size	S.E.	Ratio	S.E.	%	S.E.
OECD														
Portugal														
Alentejo	-3	(15.4)	8	(14.4)	1.13	(0.38)	0.7	(1.82)	-0.03	(0.17)	0.91	(0.25)	-1.3	(34.98)
Spain														
Andalusia•	**-40**	(14.1)	**-35**	(15.8)	**1.77**	(0.43)	2.6	(1.48)	**-0.49**	(0.17)	0.57	(0.14)	-7.5	(39.77)
Aragon•	**-83**	(10.0)	**-60**	(8.3)	**2.77**	(0.30)	18.9	(3.07)	**-0.96**	(0.11)	0.36	(0.04)	-12.4	(17.20)
Asturias•	**-75**	(9.2)	**-50**	(8.3)	**2.34**	(0.28)	7.8	(2.03)	**-0.76**	(0.10)	0.43	(0.05)	-11.8	(21.36)
Balearic Islands•	**-60**	(6.6)	**-47**	(6.1)	**2.32**	(0.33)	20.1	(3.90)	**-0.73**	(0.08)	0.43	(0.06)	-8.2	(17.66)
Basque Country•	**-86**	(6.1)	**-67**	(5.4)	**2.87**	(0.21)	13.9	(1.74)	**-1.06**	(0.08)	0.35	(0.03)	-14.7	(14.52)
Cantabria•	**-49**	(6.7)	**-33**	(7.2)	**1.74**	(0.28)	6.5	(2.08)	**-0.63**	(0.09)	0.58	(0.08)	-6.0	(22.41)
Castile and Leon•	**-68**	(9.9)	**-44**	(9.1)	**2.31**	(0.35)	8.3	(2.02)	**-0.87**	(0.13)	0.43	(0.06)	-11.9	(28.42)
Catalonia•	**-70**	(9.0)	**-52**	(8.6)	**2.72**	(0.30)	19.2	(3.40)	**-0.89**	(0.13)	0.37	(0.04)	-11.6	(17.57)
Extremadura•	**-43**	(16.6)	**-36**	(14.5)	**1.82**	(0.39)	2.7	(1.49)	**-0.48**	(0.20)	0.55	(0.13)	-7.8	(35.38)
Galicia•	**-52**	(9.6)	**-46**	(9.6)	**1.97**	(0.31)	5.1	(1.46)	**-0.61**	(0.12)	0.51	(0.07)	-8.7	(26.43)
La Rioja•	**-85**	(7.5)	**-59**	(7.6)	**2.85**	(0.33)	24.9	(3.55)	**-0.92**	(0.09)	0.35	(0.04)	-11.5	(15.16)
Madrid•	**-60**	(11.0)	**-34**	(10.9)	**2.30**	(0.37)	17.3	(4.67)	**-0.69**	(0.13)	0.43	(0.07)	-9.4	(21.33)
Murcia•	**-59**	(7.6)	**-39**	(6.6)	**2.17**	(0.31)	15.2	(3.73)	**-0.70**	(0.09)	0.46	(0.06)	-8.7	(18.25)
Navarre•	**-73**	(4.8)	**-51**	(5.3)	**2.81**	(0.26)	21.8	(2.53)	**-0.93**	(0.07)	0.36	(0.03)	-11.6	(14.35)
United Kingdom														
England	-13	(8.6)	-9	(6.7)	**1.36**	(0.14)	4.8	(1.86)	-0.13	(0.09)	0.73	(0.07)	-2.6	(11.06)
Northern Ireland	-9	(11.4)	1	(11.3)	1.22	(0.24)	0.8	(0.87)	-0.09	(0.12)	0.82	(0.16)	-2.6	(22.54)
Scotland•	25	(7.0)	22	(6.2)	0.86	(0.14)	-1.2	(1.23)	**0.28**	(0.08)	1.18	(0.20)	1.2	(13.56)
Wales	-11	(8.9)	-2	(7.8)	1.29	(0.21)	1.2	(0.84)	-0.12	(0.10)	0.78	(0.13)	-2.9	(19.29)
United States														
Connecticut•	**-43**	(8.1)	-15	(8.4)	**1.81**	(0.16)	11.7	(1.99)	**-0.43**	(0.08)	0.55	(0.05)	-5.7	(11.45)
Florida•	-10	(5.9)	5	(4.4)	1.12	(0.13)	2.8	(2.84)	-0.12	(0.07)	0.89	(0.10)	-.0	(9.17)
Massachusetts•	**-32**	(11.4)	4	(9.5)	**1.64**	(0.22)	11.0	(3.32)	**-0.32**	(0.11)	0.61	(0.08)	-4.6	(14.69)
Partners														
Argentina														
Ciudad Autónoma de Buenos Aires•	**-76**	(8.7)	**-25**	(7.9)	**2.83**	(0.33)	22.8	(3.53)	**-0.85**	(0.07)	0.35	(0.04)	-11.1	(18.06)
Brazil														
Acre	c	c	c	c	c	c	c	c	c	c	c	c	c	c
Alagoas	c	c	c	c	c	c	c	c	c	c	c	c	c	c
Amapá	c	c	c	c	c	c	c	c	c	c	c	c	c	c
Amazonas	c	c	c	c	c	c	c	c	c	c	c	c	c	c
Bahia	c	c	c	c	c	c	c	c	c	c	c	c	c	c
Ceará	c	c	c	c	c	c	c	c	c	c	c	c	c	c
Espírito Santo	c	c	c	c	c	c	c	c	c	c	c	c	c	c
Federal District	c	c	c	c	c	c	c	c	c	c	c	c	c	c
Goiás	c	c	c	c	c	c	c	c	c	c	c	c	c	c
Maranhão	c	c	c	c	c	c	c	c	c	c	c	c	c	c
Mato Grosso	c	c	c	c	c	c	c	c	c	c	c	c	c	c
Mato Grosso do Sul	c	c	c	c	c	c	c	c	c	c	c	c	c	c
Minas Gerais	c	c	c	c	c	c	c	c	c	c	c	c	c	c
Pará	c	c	c	c	c	c	c	c	c	c	c	c	c	c
Paraíba	c	c	c	c	c	c	c	c	c	c	c	c	c	c
Paraná	c	c	c	c	c	c	c	c	c	c	c	c	c	c
Pernambuco	c	c	c	c	c	c	c	c	c	c	c	c	c	c
Piauí	c	c	c	c	c	c	c	c	c	c	c	c	c	c
Rio de Janeiro	c	c	c	c	c	c	c	c	c	c	c	c	c	c
Rio Grande do Norte	c	c	c	c	c	c	c	c	c	c	c	c	c	c
Rio Grande do Sul	c	c	c	c	c	c	c	c	c	c	c	c	c	c
Rondônia	c	c	c	c	c	c	c	c	c	c	c	c	c	c
Roraima	c	c	c	c	c	c	c	c	c	c	c	c	c	c
Santa Catarina	c	c	c	c	c	c	c	c	c	c	c	c	c	c
São Paulo	c	c	c	c	c	c	c	c	c	c	c	c	c	c
Sergipe	c	c	c	c	c	c	c	c	c	c	c	c	c	c
Tocantins	c	c	c	c	c	c	c	c	c	c	c	c	c	c
Colombia														
Bogotá	c	c	c	c	c	c	c	c	c	c	c	c	c	c
Cali	c	c	c	c	c	c	c	c	c	c	c	c	c	c
Manizales	c	c	c	c	c	c	c	c	c	c	c	c	c	c
Medellín	c	c	c	c	c	c	c	c	c	c	c	c	c	c
Russian Federation														
Perm Territory region•	-37	(8.2)	-37	(7.6)	1.67	(0.24)	4.8	(1.69)	-0.45	(0.10)	0.60	(0.10)	-59.0	(20.55)
United Arab Emirates														
Abu Dhabi•	**58**	(5.1)	**60**	(4.5)	0.47	(0.05)	-38.2	(5.81)	**0.71**	(0.06)	2.15	(0.24)	35.7	(4.27)
Ajman	**28**	(8.9)	**32**	(7.9)	0.60	(0.11)	-27.7	(9.60)	**0.39**	(0.13)	1.67	(0.35)	23.6	(9.30)
Dubai•	**84**	(3.0)	**77**	(3.0)	0.32	(0.02)	-88.6	(4.04)	**1.01**	(0.04)	3.16	(0.16)	40.4	(1.72)
Fujairah	**66**	(17.4)	**60**	(15.2)	0.29	(0.14)	-21.8	(7.13)	**0.86**	(0.26)	3.43	(1.63)	64.5	(14.82)
Ras al-Khaimah	**34**	(6.9)	**36**	(5.9)	0.73	(0.12)	-9.2	(4.40)	**0.45**	(0.09)	1.38	(0.19)	20.7	(9.35)
Sharjah	**59**	(12.0)	**57**	(12.2)	0.41	(0.10)	-52.7	(13.92)	**0.77**	(0.17)	2.44	(0.59)	37.0	(10.68)
Umm al-Quwain	16	(9.0)	18	(8.8)	0.83	(0.19)	-5.9	(6.90)	0.22	(0.12)	1.21	(0.25)	12.2	(13.97)

• PISA adjudicated region.
Notes: This table was calculated considering only students with data on the *PISA index of economic, social and cultural status*. Values that are statistically significant are indicated in bold (see Annex A3).
Students with an immigrant background are students whose parents were born in a country other than the country of assessment.
See Table II.3.4a for national data.
1. ESCS refers to the *PISA index of economic, social and cultural status*.
StatLink ⟐ http://dx.doi.org/10.1787/888932964965

[Part 1/8]

Table B2.II.15 Mathematics performance and student population, by schools' socio-economic profile and region
Results based on students' self-reports

	Percentage of students						Mean ESCS[1]						Mean mathematics performance					
	Socio-economically disadvantaged schools[2]		Socio-economically average schools[2]		Socio-economically advantaged schools[2]		Socio-economically disadvantaged schools[2]		Socio-economically average schools[2]		Socio-economically advantaged schools[2]		Socio-economically disadvantaged schools[2]		Socio-economically average schools[2]		Socio-economically advantaged schools[2]	
	%	S.E.	%	S.E.	%	S.E.	Mean index	S.E.	Mean index	S.E.	Mean index	S.E.	Mean score	S.E.	Mean score	S.E.	Mean score	S.E.
OECD																		
Australia																		
Australian Capital Territory	c	c	33.1	(0.9)	66.9	(0.9)	c	c	0.33	(0.04)	0.76	(0.03)	c	c	484	(5.1)	534	(4.2)
New South Wales	23.2	(2.3)	49.7	(3.4)	27.1	(2.9)	-0.33	(0.03)	0.22	(0.02)	0.79	(0.02)	455	(6.4)	503	(4.7)	566	(9.7)
Northern Territory	23.7	(2.3)	61.9	(9.6)	14.4	(10.0)	-0.42	(0.10)	0.23	(0.06)	c	c	401	(17.0)	452	(7.5)	c	c
Queensland	29.1	(3.3)	49.8	(4.3)	21.1	(3.0)	-0.27	(0.03)	0.24	(0.02)	0.75	(0.04)	459	(5.2)	508	(3.3)	557	(5.4)
South Australia	30.0	(3.3)	52.5	(4.2)	17.6	(2.6)	-0.29	(0.04)	0.26	(0.02)	0.77	(0.04)	458	(6.0)	488	(4.7)	543	(8.7)
Tasmania	41.3	(1.3)	42.2	(1.5)	16.6	(1.3)	-0.38	(0.03)	0.14	(0.04)	0.73	(0.05)	446	(3.7)	483	(5.7)	544	(6.8)
Victoria	15.7	(2.5)	61.1	(3.7)	23.3	(3.2)	-0.30	(0.03)	0.26	(0.02)	0.80	(0.03)	460	(6.5)	492	(4.2)	551	(8.2)
Western Australia	31.0	(3.4)	39.0	(4.6)	30.1	(3.9)	-0.23	(0.03)	0.25	(0.03)	0.76	(0.03)	473	(6.7)	514	(5.0)	566	(6.3)
Belgium																		
Flemish Community•	26.9	(2.6)	39.2	(3.5)	33.9	(2.6)	-0.45	(0.05)	0.12	(0.02)	0.67	(0.03)	453	(7.0)	521	(4.7)	605	(5.4)
French Community	32.1	(3.7)	34.6	(4.4)	33.4	(3.5)	-0.49	(0.04)	0.13	(0.03)	0.68	(0.04)	421	(6.1)	500	(5.4)	556	(5.6)
German-speaking Community	10.2	(0.0)	47.0	(0.3)	42.9	(0.3)	c	c	0.09	(0.05)	c	c	c	c	489	(3.5)	c	c
Canada																		
Alberta	7.6	(2.5)	64.9	(4.6)	27.5	(4.2)	-0.07	(0.04)	0.41	(0.02)	0.93	(0.04)	473	(18.6)	502	(4.2)	565	(6.7)
British Columbia	20.7	(4.0)	48.2	(6.1)	31.0	(4.6)	-0.06	(0.03)	0.39	(0.03)	0.91	(0.03)	500	(8.1)	514	(5.7)	550	(6.2)
Manitoba	28.4	(3.2)	55.3	(3.0)	16.3	(1.3)	-0.23	(0.06)	0.32	(0.03)	0.93	(0.04)	463	(6.9)	495	(3.5)	535	(7.8)
New Brunswick	27.6	(3.0)	48.0	(2.2)	24.4	(1.4)	0.00	(0.03)	0.36	(0.03)	0.81	(0.05)	486	(5.0)	495	(3.1)	537	(7.7)
Newfoundland and Labrador	26.5	(3.3)	52.1	(3.0)	21.4	(1.0)	-0.33	(0.05)	0.36	(0.04)	0.85	(0.07)	447	(6.7)	498	(3.3)	526	(6.2)
Nova Scotia	24.3	(5.3)	63.3	(6.6)	12.4	(1.8)	-0.02	(0.02)	0.34	(0.05)	0.85	(0.07)	487	(5.2)	498	(6.3)	514	(9.0)
Ontario	22.2	(4.1)	49.8	(5.8)	27.9	(4.5)	-0.12	(0.04)	0.42	(0.02)	0.91	(0.04)	486	(7.5)	509	(3.9)	546	(7.1)
Prince Edward Island	42.8	(0.4)	27.8	(0.4)	29.4	(0.4)	0.14	(0.04)	0.36	(0.04)	c	c	470	(4.0)	476	(4.3)	c	c
Quebec	25.4	(3.8)	50.0	(4.0)	24.7	(1.9)	-0.15	(0.04)	0.31	(0.02)	0.89	(0.03)	499	(6.7)	528	(4.4)	590	(6.7)
Saskatchewan	12.7	(2.8)	72.6	(3.2)	14.6	(1.4)	-0.09	(0.06)	0.40	(0.02)	0.85	(0.05)	490	(7.6)	506	(3.7)	521	(4.7)
Italy																		
Abruzzo	9.8	(4.7)	64.4	(6.2)	25.8	(4.0)	-0.45	(0.07)	-0.12	(0.03)	0.61	(0.05)	424	(15.8)	459	(9.9)	538	(10.2)
Basilicata	45.4	(4.8)	35.4	(5.4)	19.2	(1.7)	-0.63	(0.04)	-0.09	(0.05)	0.57	(0.06)	429	(6.7)	478	(9.3)	530	(7.1)
Bolzano	25.1	(0.7)	51.4	(0.7)	23.5	(0.6)	-0.53	(0.04)	-0.09	(0.02)	0.48	(0.05)	456	(3.6)	507	(3.2)	556	(4.1)
Calabria	42.7	(4.8)	37.4	(5.9)	19.9	(4.0)	-0.72	(0.04)	-0.02	(0.04)	0.51	(0.05)	392	(7.9)	440	(11.9)	494	(11.0)
Campania	43.7	(6.2)	29.7	(7.1)	26.6	(6.6)	-0.71	(0.05)	-0.06	(0.04)	0.53	(0.10)	404	(7.9)	463	(12.3)	521	(7.9)
Emilia Romagna	25.3	(5.4)	44.7	(7.0)	30.0	(4.5)	-0.58	(0.06)	-0.12	(0.04)	0.62	(0.04)	430	(11.5)	492	(7.0)	571	(9.3)
Friuli Venezia Giulia	20.4	(5.3)	36.2	(6.0)	43.5	(3.2)	-0.63	(0.08)	-0.04	(0.04)	0.44	(0.04)	458	(17.3)	512	(9.3)	563	(6.5)
Lazio	10.5	(4.5)	42.9	(5.7)	46.6	(5.3)	-0.59	(0.08)	-0.06	(0.05)	0.54	(0.04)	395	(7.4)	445	(8.6)	520	(10.8)
Liguria	13.8	(3.6)	51.3	(5.7)	34.9	(5.4)	-0.71	(0.08)	-0.10	(0.04)	0.50	(0.04)	413	(7.1)	473	(7.7)	540	(9.2)
Lombardia	22.3	(5.8)	41.7	(8.0)	36.0	(5.8)	-0.59	(0.04)	-0.08	(0.04)	0.61	(0.06)	468	(14.3)	499	(8.4)	568	(8.7)
Marche	21.1	(4.7)	48.7	(6.3)	30.2	(5.3)	-0.54	(0.04)	-0.14	(0.04)	0.48	(0.05)	433	(13.0)	498	(7.8)	537	(12.9)
Molise	36.6	(0.9)	35.7	(0.8)	27.6	(0.9)	-0.59	(0.04)	-0.10	(0.05)	0.49	(0.05)	426	(3.9)	460	(3.6)	529	(4.8)
Piemonte	26.2	(3.7)	48.2	(5.2)	25.6	(4.2)	-0.59	(0.04)	-0.09	(0.03)	0.53	(0.04)	447	(6.7)	499	(8.0)	550	(9.8)
Puglia	47.3	(3.8)	37.3	(4.9)	15.4	(3.9)	-0.78	(0.04)	-0.05	(0.05)	0.54	(0.06)	438	(7.4)	507	(10.0)	530	(8.0)
Sardegna	28.2	(5.4)	52.1	(6.4)	19.7	(3.9)	-0.66	(0.05)	-0.14	(0.04)	0.68	(0.08)	406	(11.3)	460	(8.5)	526	(5.5)
Sicilia	33.3	(5.2)	42.1	(7.1)	24.5	(5.1)	-0.62	(0.04)	-0.07	(0.04)	0.54	(0.08)	402	(7.0)	449	(9.0)	505	(8.6)
Toscana	30.3	(5.9)	30.4	(5.0)	39.3	(5.1)	-0.61	(0.05)	-0.10	(0.04)	0.56	(0.07)	429	(11.0)	498	(11.9)	545	(10.0)
Trento	20.5	(3.8)	50.8	(4.8)	28.7	(2.1)	-0.61	(0.03)	-0.02	(0.03)	0.48	(0.05)	457	(9.8)	529	(7.2)	563	(6.9)
Umbria	10.1	(4.3)	47.6	(4.9)	42.3	(2.8)	-0.66	(0.08)	-0.10	(0.04)	0.53	(0.03)	394	(15.1)	479	(10.0)	531	(6.1)
Valle d'Aosta	42.1	(0.9)	42.3	(0.9)	15.5	(0.5)	-0.60	(0.04)	-0.07	(0.05)	c	c	474	(3.3)	486	(4.1)	c	c
Veneto	30.4	(5.1)	43.2	(6.4)	26.4	(4.9)	-0.61	(0.04)	-0.04	(0.04)	0.53	(0.05)	455	(8.2)	535	(7.0)	581	(15.5)
Mexico																		
Aguascalientes	14.8	(5.6)	38.6	(6.1)	46.5	(4.2)	-1.71	(0.07)	-1.12	(0.05)	-0.16	(0.09)	389	(9.1)	430	(5.9)	458	(7.0)
Baja California	4.0	(2.4)	41.1	(8.2)	54.9	(8.7)	c	c	-1.11	(0.07)	-0.34	(0.08)	c	c	400	(10.1)	427	(11.5)
Baja California Sur	16.9	(6.0)	33.5	(7.8)	49.6	(9.0)	-1.62	(0.06)	-1.11	(0.07)	-0.27	(0.06)	372	(10.9)	401	(8.7)	438	(7.4)
Campeche	33.8	(8.6)	51.0	(8.9)	15.2	(3.9)	-2.19	(0.14)	-1.15	(0.05)	0.10	(0.10)	378	(8.0)	395	(6.1)	437	(15.5)
Chiapas	69.2	(7.9)	23.3	(7.2)	7.5	(4.5)	-2.16	(0.07)	-1.10	(0.10)	c	c	356	(7.9)	402	(8.8)	c	c
Chihuahua	18.0	(7.7)	43.9	(10.3)	38.1	(9.1)	-1.67	(0.13)	-1.00	(0.06)	-0.18	(0.10)	392	(15.1)	410	(9.0)	466	(11.5)
Coahuila	16.7	(7.3)	40.5	(8.9)	42.8	(9.4)	-1.73	(0.09)	-1.15	(0.04)	-0.15	(0.12)	384	(15.6)	401	(5.1)	448	(12.1)
Colima	16.1	(5.3)	37.3	(6.8)	46.6	(5.3)	-1.87	(0.07)	-1.08	(0.06)	-0.10	(0.12)	367	(4.5)	416	(9.3)	462	(7.4)
Distrito Federal	9.7	(6.0)	46.4	(7.6)	43.8	(6.6)	c	c	-1.00	(0.06)	0.14	(0.17)	c	c	410	(5.2)	459	(7.4)
Durango	23.3	(6.9)	41.6	(9.3)	35.1	(9.7)	-1.85	(0.09)	-1.20	(0.06)	-0.17	(0.10)	394	(7.4)	418	(9.7)	454	(9.8)
Guanajuato	52.4	(8.3)	21.2	(7.6)	26.3	(5.9)	-1.96	(0.07)	-1.07	(0.07)	-0.05	(0.16)	386	(7.6)	414	(8.6)	461	(5.1)
Guerrero	60.7	(7.8)	29.4	(8.0)	9.9	(3.7)	-2.08	(0.08)	-1.20	(0.05)	-0.37	(0.22)	353	(5.5)	384	(8.6)	402	(16.9)
Hidalgo	55.3	(7.2)	28.2	(7.2)	16.4	(4.0)	-1.98	(0.08)	-1.20	(0.06)	-0.08	(0.27)	387	(6.4)	412	(14.2)	463	(12.5)
Jalisco	32.0	(9.0)	35.2	(9.9)	32.8	(7.3)	-1.81	(0.09)	-1.20	(0.05)	-0.21	(0.10)	413	(8.6)	426	(11.0)	466	(6.4)
Mexico	23.3	(8.3)	51.5	(9.7)	25.2	(7.6)	-1.75	(0.07)	-1.14	(0.04)	-0.28	(0.18)	400	(11.6)	412	(6.3)	444	(14.9)
Morelos	20.5	(6.8)	43.9	(7.6)	35.6	(6.9)	-1.87	(0.10)	-1.26	(0.06)	0.19	(0.16)	364	(15.3)	409	(5.1)	471	(12.6)
Nayarit	19.9	(4.5)	52.0	(4.6)	28.1	(5.0)	-2.17	(0.11)	-1.05	(0.05)	-0.13	(0.12)	388	(16.3)	404	(7.7)	451	(7.2)
Nuevo León	1.9	(1.4)	30.7	(9.0)	67.3	(8.8)	c	c	-1.14	(0.07)	-0.05	(0.14)	c	c	398	(4.2)	455	(7.7)
Puebla	58.4	(7.5)	21.5	(6.9)	20.1	(5.2)	-2.18	(0.10)	-1.13	(0.07)	-0.08	(0.18)	394	(7.7)	434	(8.4)	456	(7.5)
Querétaro	28.4	(8.6)	30.6	(6.8)	41.0	(12.2)	-2.08	(0.10)	-1.12	(0.06)	0.04	(0.18)	404	(8.5)	427	(10.5)	461	(13.1)
Quintana Roo	22.8	(8.0)	42.1	(7.6)	35.1	(6.5)	-1.82	(0.09)	-1.17	(0.08)	-0.19	(0.08)	382	(7.9)	393	(7.3)	450	(4.7)
San Luis Potosí	45.4	(9.2)	27.9	(8.8)	26.7	(6.5)	-2.12	(0.11)	-1.20	(0.07)	0.10	(0.18)	380	(6.3)	411	(5.3)	468	(9.5)
Sinaloa	16.6	(5.2)	46.5	(6.5)	36.9	(5.3)	-1.77	(0.06)	-1.16	(0.05)	-0.33	(0.10)	399	(10.0)	388	(6.0)	445	(4.6)
Tabasco	41.2	(8.3)	35.4	(7.8)	23.3	(5.3)	-1.77	(0.08)	-1.16	(0.08)	-0.10	(0.15)	358	(7.1)	375	(9.1)	420	(8.9)
Tamaulipas	16.3	(7.3)	41.1	(10.2)	42.6	(10.9)	-1.78	(0.09)	-1.10	(0.06)	-0.35	(0.12)	382	(9.2)	393	(8.9)	439	(9.0)
Tlaxcala	36.2	(6.5)	42.4	(6.1)	21.4	(4.1)	-1.80	(0.07)	-1.17	(0.05)	-0.05	(0.15)	381	(6.4)	422	(4.7)	440	(6.0)
Veracruz	60.1	(7.3)	18.1	(7.1)	21.8	(3.4)	-2.16	(0.11)	-1.06	(0.10)	0.09	(0.19)	387	(7.1)	410	(14.3)	437	(17.3)
Yucatán	41.0	(9.0)	26.9	(7.4)	32.1	(8.9)	-2.01	(0.08)	-1.25	(0.05)	-0.04	(0.21)	388	(6.0)	407	(8.4)	441	(13.4)
Zacatecas	31.2	(7.0)	48.8	(7.9)	20.0	(3.5)	-1.92	(0.08)	-1.12	(0.07)	-0.09	(0.20)	379	(8.3)	412	(5.6)	447	(6.6)

• PISA adjudicated region.

Notes: Values that are statistically significant are indicated in bold (see Annex A3).

See Table II.4.2 for national data.

1. ESCS refers to the *PISA index of economic, social and cultural status*.

2. Advantaged (disadvantaged) schools are those where the typical student in the school, or the socio-economic profile of the school, is above (below) the ESCS of the typical student in the country, the country mean ESCS. In each school, a random sample of 35 students are to take part in PISA (for more details see the *PISA 2012 Technical Report* [OECD, forthcoming]). The socio-economic profile of the school is calculated using the information provided by these students. Therefore, the precision of the estimate depends on the number of students that actually take the test in the school and the diversity of their answers. This precision was taken into account when classifying schools as advantaged, disadvantaged or average. If the difference between the school socio-economic profile and the ESCS of the typical student in the country (the mean ESCS at the country level) was not statistically significant, the school was classified as a school with an average socio-economic profile. If the school profile was statistically significantly above the country mean, the school is classified as a socio-economically advantaged school. If the profile was below the country mean, the school is classified as a socio-economically disadvantaged school.

StatLink http://dx.doi.org/10.1787/888932964965

[Part 2/8]
Table B2.II.15 Mathematics performance and student population, by schools' socio-economic profile and region
Results based on students' self-reports

	Percentage of students						Mean ESCS[1]						Mean mathematics performance					
	Socio-economically disadvantaged schools[2]		Socio-economically average schools[2]		Socio-economically advantaged schools[2]		Socio-economically disadvantaged schools[2]		Socio-economically average schools[2]		Socio-economically advantaged schools[2]		Socio-economically disadvantaged schools[2]		Socio-economically average schools[2]		Socio-economically advantaged schools[2]	
	%	S.E.	%	S.E.	%	S.E.	Mean index	S.E.	Mean index	S.E.	Mean index	S.E.	Mean score	S.E.	Mean score	S.E.	Mean score	S.E.
OECD																		
Portugal																		
Alentejo	22.9	(9.0)	46.3	(13.9)	30.8	(12.6)	-1.14	(0.05)	-0.42	(0.05)	0.34	(0.13)	419	(14.1)	494	(9.7)	532	(10.2)
Spain																		
Andalusia•	44.0	(6.6)	36.2	(7.3)	19.7	(5.8)	-0.84	(0.04)	-0.23	(0.03)	0.49	(0.08)	448	(5.0)	484	(7.3)	503	(7.0)
Aragon•	24.4	(6.0)	41.4	(6.0)	34.3	(4.2)	-0.65	(0.04)	-0.22	(0.04)	0.55	(0.08)	454	(8.1)	493	(7.4)	531	(7.3)
Asturias•	17.0	(4.7)	50.0	(6.6)	33.0	(5.4)	-0.69	(0.03)	-0.18	(0.03)	0.57	(0.08)	463	(15.3)	489	(4.5)	536	(6.7)
Balearic Islands•	19.5	(5.0)	60.1	(6.9)	20.4	(4.7)	-0.72	(0.04)	-0.20	(0.03)	0.52	(0.08)	434	(10.1)	477	(4.2)	509	(8.4)
Basque Country•	10.6	(1.9)	49.5	(3.3)	39.9	(3.0)	-0.77	(0.04)	-0.17	(0.02)	0.48	(0.03)	443	(10.3)	500	(3.1)	528	(3.7)
Cantabria•	9.1	(3.1)	70.2	(5.4)	20.7	(5.1)	-0.66	(0.04)	-0.18	(0.03)	0.59	(0.08)	481	(8.8)	484	(3.8)	523	(8.0)
Castile and Leon•	14.7	(5.3)	49.8	(7.2)	35.5	(5.0)	-0.75	(0.09)	-0.26	(0.04)	0.39	(0.05)	491	(6.6)	498	(6.8)	532	(5.1)
Catalonia•	23.4	(6.3)	42.3	(6.8)	34.3	(6.7)	-0.82	(0.04)	-0.26	(0.04)	0.49	(0.06)	451	(7.4)	485	(6.0)	532	(7.1)
Extremadura•	52.8	(5.1)	32.5	(4.4)	14.7	(3.7)	-0.85	(0.03)	-0.28	(0.05)	0.52	(0.10)	444	(5.7)	461	(4.8)	524	(6.2)
Galicia•	30.1	(5.3)	42.8	(6.6)	27.1	(4.8)	-0.73	(0.04)	-0.23	(0.04)	0.51	(0.07)	468	(7.6)	483	(5.8)	521	(6.0)
La Rioja•	24.2	(0.5)	46.3	(0.6)	29.5	(0.3)	-0.61	(0.05)	-0.24	(0.04)	0.39	(0.04)	475	(4.6)	494	(3.3)	541	(3.6)
Madrid•	16.4	(4.2)	39.7	(6.2)	43.9	(6.1)	-0.68	(0.06)	-0.18	(0.04)	0.67	(0.08)	458	(11.7)	496	(5.7)	528	(5.6)
Murcia•	48.3	(6.6)	45.1	(7.5)	6.5	(3.8)	-0.82	(0.04)	-0.25	(0.05)	c	c	444	(6.5)	477	(8.5)	c	c
Navarre•	22.6	(3.9)	51.7	(5.7)	25.7	(4.2)	-0.70	(0.05)	-0.17	(0.03)	0.54	(0.08)	493	(4.4)	511	(4.5)	548	(4.5)
United Kingdom																		
England	23.4	(3.0)	51.5	(3.5)	25.1	(2.8)	-0.23	(0.04)	0.27	(0.02)	0.79	(0.03)	449	(9.7)	488	(4.2)	552	(6.2)
Northern Ireland	28.2	(3.7)	41.7	(4.4)	30.1	(2.6)	-0.20	(0.03)	0.21	(0.02)	0.84	(0.03)	419	(4.6)	475	(6.4)	566	(3.8)
Scotland•	31.4	(3.6)	56.0	(4.4)	12.7	(2.8)	-0.24	(0.03)	0.19	(0.02)	0.78	(0.04)	468	(5.4)	504	(2.8)	548	(7.5)
Wales	24.4	(2.8)	63.7	(3.6)	11.9	(2.3)	-0.21	(0.03)	0.24	(0.02)	0.68	(0.03)	439	(4.6)	472	(2.5)	507	(6.0)
United States																		
Connecticut•	25.1	(6.2)	42.8	(6.9)	32.1	(5.5)	-0.18	(0.06)	0.46	(0.03)	1.04	(0.04)	448	(11.2)	502	(5.2)	556	(7.8)
Florida•	24.2	(6.0)	50.6	(6.5)	25.2	(6.8)	-0.32	(0.03)	0.21	(0.03)	0.67	(0.05)	430	(6.2)	464	(5.2)	508	(10.6)
Massachusetts•	27.2	(6.0)	39.9	(7.4)	33.0	(6.5)	-0.19	(0.05)	0.40	(0.04)	1.00	(0.06)	464	(9.0)	504	(4.9)	566	(11.2)
Partners																		
Argentina																		
Ciudad Autónoma de Buenos Aires•	20.9	(5.7)	18.5	(5.2)	60.5	(4.3)	-1.39	(0.07)	-0.93	(0.05)	0.44	(0.06)	322	(19.9)	383	(16.1)	462	(6.5)
Brazil																		
Acre	46.5	(10.7)	35.3	(10.5)	18.2	(5.6)	-1.86	(0.07)	-1.25	(0.06)	-0.26	(0.17)	341	(6.7)	358	(6.2)	405	(16.0)
Alagoas	70.5	(8.1)	12.8	(6.6)	16.7	(6.3)	-2.12	(0.07)	c	c	c	c	328	(4.6)	c	c	c	c
Amapá	3.7	(4.0)	56.4	(10.3)	39.9	(9.5)	c	c	-1.23	(0.04)	-0.43	(0.22)	c	c	339	(6.8)	392	(10.6)
Amazonas	3.1	(3.2)	78.7	(9.2)	18.2	(8.4)	c	c	-1.19	(0.04)	-0.31	(0.18)	c	c	347	(5.5)	397	(22.7)
Bahia	73.7	(5.8)	9.9	(3.7)	16.4	(4.4)	-1.98	(0.09)	c	c	c	c	352	(12.2)	c	c	c	c
Ceará	68.7	(7.6)	15.8	(7.0)	15.5	(4.3)	-1.99	(0.04)	c	c	c	c	360	(4.5)	c	c	c	c
Espírito Santo	36.8	(8.9)	40.4	(11.4)	22.8	(3.7)	-1.89	(0.15)	-1.30	(0.05)	c	c	389	(10.0)	379	(9.2)	c	c
Federal District	1.2	(1.0)	53.5	(9.2)	45.2	(8.9)	c	c	-1.24	(0.05)	0.01	(0.22)	c	c	370	(10.5)	471	(16.3)
Goiás	29.0	(9.4)	57.0	(11.1)	14.0	(5.9)	-1.82	(0.11)	-1.30	(0.06)	c	c	348	(9.3)	374	(7.5)	c	c
Maranhão	43.5	(12.6)	42.0	(10.6)	14.5	(9.9)	-1.97	(0.11)	-1.32	(0.06)	c	c	322	(11.5)	328	(7.8)	c	c
Mato Grosso	48.4	(5.5)	41.3	(4.9)	10.3	(4.1)	-1.76	(0.08)	-1.23	(0.06)	c	c	358	(12.2)	359	(8.0)	c	c
Mato Grosso do Sul	30.3	(7.6)	32.8	(7.4)	36.9	(6.7)	-1.72	(0.05)	-1.19	(0.06)	-0.11	(0.08)	374	(11.1)	385	(7.6)	458	(8.7)
Minas Gerais	44.1	(9.0)	35.0	(8.5)	20.8	(6.6)	-1.83	(0.06)	-1.32	(0.07)	-0.07	(0.31)	383	(7.1)	394	(4.3)	462	(15.3)
Pará	32.4	(7.8)	48.4	(13.2)	19.3	(12.9)	-1.78	(0.06)	-1.26	(0.03)	c	c	331	(7.1)	356	(15.8)	c	c
Paraíba	43.7	(8.2)	18.5	(5.6)	37.8	(8.4)	-1.98	(0.08)	-1.21	(0.11)	-0.09	(0.19)	355	(14.3)	378	(6.6)	450	(16.7)
Paraná	25.4	(8.5)	51.1	(9.7)	23.5	(4.0)	-1.77	(0.04)	-1.25	(0.04)	0.02	(0.38)	366	(12.8)	387	(5.0)	479	(39.5)
Pernambuco	58.7	(13.2)	34.7	(14.2)	6.6	(4.1)	-1.99	(0.08)	-1.23	(0.06)	c	c	347	(10.0)	377	(6.0)	c	c
Piauí	47.0	(9.8)	29.8	(10.6)	23.2	(3.2)	-1.94	(0.09)	-1.31	(0.04)	c	c	353	(6.1)	367	(11.9)	c	c
Rio de Janeiro	c	c	81.4	(5.2)	18.6	(5.2)	c	c	-1.14	(0.04)	-0.08	(0.31)	c	c	374	(7.4)	456	(16.4)
Rio Grande do Norte	59.1	(8.9)	18.6	(7.9)	22.3	(4.6)	-1.89	(0.08)	-1.17	(0.08)	0.10	(0.23)	349	(5.4)	357	(6.9)	484	(26.1)
Rio Grande do Sul	39.8	(8.4)	32.9	(6.1)	27.3	(6.5)	-1.72	(0.04)	-1.20	(0.07)	-0.38	(0.12)	389	(11.7)	405	(12.0)	436	(8.7)
Rondônia	46.5	(11.7)	40.5	(12.7)	13.0	(8.6)	-1.96	(0.05)	-1.16	(0.07)	c	c	370	(7.0)	383	(9.3)	c	c
Roraima	24.3	(9.7)	54.3	(8.6)	21.5	(4.7)	-1.66	(0.10)	-1.21	(0.04)	0.07	(0.06)	331	(7.8)	346	(5.4)	437	(4.7)
Santa Catarina	30.2	(10.1)	52.6	(10.8)	17.2	(6.0)	-1.86	(0.08)	-1.16	(0.05)	c	c	387	(19.1)	416	(9.2)	c	c
São Paulo	18.4	(5.3)	46.1	(5.1)	35.6	(4.3)	-1.70	(0.04)	-1.22	(0.03)	-0.19	(0.07)	374	(6.7)	380	(3.9)	449	(11.6)
Sergipe	34.8	(8.5)	36.9	(10.9)	28.3	(8.7)	-1.91	(0.07)	-1.36	(0.06)	-0.33	(0.08)	357	(10.2)	375	(5.4)	429	(22.9)
Tocantins	42.2	(8.3)	36.8	(11.0)	21.0	(8.6)	-1.84	(0.06)	-1.26	(0.05)	-0.30	(0.13)	343	(9.5)	352	(9.1)	436	(11.8)
Colombia																		
Bogotá	9.3	(2.8)	54.6	(8.1)	36.1	(8.0)	-1.76	(0.06)	-1.24	(0.03)	-0.70	(0.08)	357	(7.3)	385	(3.5)	413	(6.6)
Cali	8.2	(4.2)	41.2	(7.0)	50.5	(7.7)	c	c	-1.22	(0.05)	-0.34	(0.09)	c	c	352	(6.0)	410	(7.0)
Manizales	15.0	(2.5)	23.8	(6.0)	61.2	(6.8)	-1.95	(0.10)	-1.21	(0.06)	-0.31	(0.07)	353	(3.9)	379	(4.0)	426	(7.6)
Medellín	16.1	(4.8)	41.5	(7.1)	42.4	(6.5)	-1.89	(0.10)	-1.32	(0.04)	-0.22	(0.13)	351	(6.9)	365	(5.0)	437	(12.8)
Russian Federation																		
Perm Territory region•	21.9	(5.2)	53.2	(6.2)	24.9	(4.3)	-0.62	(0.05)	-0.13	(0.02)	0.31	(0.03)	437	(9.5)	479	(5.0)	534	(13.8)
United Arab Emirates																		
Abu Dhabi•	29.9	(3.3)	40.5	(3.9)	29.6	(3.1)	-0.24	(0.05)	0.28	(0.03)	0.84	(0.03)	385	(5.4)	416	(6.4)	466	(8.2)
Ajman	55.9	(7.0)	44.1	(7.0)	c	c	-0.34	(0.07)	0.24	(0.06)	c	c	387	(11.2)	424	(7.4)	c	c
Dubai•	15.2	(0.1)	36.8	(0.3)	48.0	(0.2)	-0.19	(0.02)	0.35	(0.02)	0.83	(0.01)	388	(2.4)	450	(2.4)	498	(1.7)
Fujairah	60.6	(3.6)	29.3	(6.3)	10.1	(4.9)	-0.25	(0.04)	0.29	(0.06)	c	c	396	(4.6)	419	(18.6)	c	c
Ras al-Khaimah	39.7	(10.0)	47.5	(9.5)	12.8	(5.6)	-0.36	(0.09)	0.24	(0.04)	0.67	(0.06)	408	(10.6)	415	(7.9)	441	(6.9)
Sharjah	8.6	(2.2)	42.0	(8.7)	49.5	(8.4)	c	c	0.26	(0.05)	0.72	(0.04)	c	c	423	(13.5)	462	(16.4)
Umm al-Quwain	51.3	(0.2)	48.7	(0.2)	c	c	-0.28	(0.05)	0.08	(0.07)	c	c	378	(4.4)	418	(6.5)	c	c

• PISA adjudicated region.
Notes: Values that are statistically significant are indicated in bold (see Annex A3).
See Table II.4.2 for national data.
1. ESCS refers to the *PISA index of economic, social and cultural status*.
2. Advantaged (disadvantaged) schools are those where the typical student in the school, or the socio-economic profile of the school, is above (below) the ESCS of the typical student in the country, the country mean ESCS. In each school, a random sample of 35 students are to take part in PISA (for more details see the *PISA 2012 Technical Report* [OECD, forthcoming]). The socio-economic profile of the school is calculated using the information provided by these students. Therefore, the precision of the estimate depends on the number of students that actually take the test in the school and the diversity of their answers. This precision was taken into account when classifying schools as advantaged, disadvantaged or average. If the difference between the school socio-economic profile and the ESCS of the typical student in the country (the mean ESCS at the country level) was not statistically significant, the school was classified as a school with an average socio-economic profile. If the school profile was statistically significantly above the country mean, the school is classified as a socio-economically advantaged school. If the profile was below the country mean, the school is classified as a socio-economically disadvantaged school.
StatLink http://dx.doi.org/10.1787/888932964965

[Part 3/8]

Table B2.II.15 Mathematics performance and student population, by schools' socio-economic profile and region

Results based on students' self-reports

	Percentage of immigrant students						Percentage of immigrant students who do not speak the language of assessment at home						Percentage of students in rural schools (schools located in a village, hamlet or rural area; fewer than 3 000 people)					
	Socio-economically disadvantaged schools[2]		Socio-economically average schools[2]		Socio-economically advantaged schools[2]		Socio-economically disadvantaged schools[2]		Socio-economically average schools[2]		Socio-economically advantaged schools[2]		Socio-economically disadvantaged schools[2]		Socio-economically average schools[2]		Socio-economically advantaged schools[2]	
	%	S.E.	%	S.E.	%	S.E.	%	S.E.	%	S.E.	%	S.E.	%	S.E.	%	S.E.	%	S.E.
OECD **Australia**																		
Australian Capital Territory	c	c	6.2	(1.6)	17.4	(1.9)	c	c	6.2	(1.6)	5.5	(1.2)	c	c	c	c	c	c
New South Wales	31.1	(5.6)	8.6	(1.4)	30.6	(3.9)	14.3	(3.9)	8.6	(1.4)	12.1	(2.3)	63.6	(13.7)	36.4	(13.7)	c	c
Northern Territory	9.0	(3.7)	4.5	(1.4)	c	c	1.4	(0.7)	4.5	(1.4)	c	c	53.7	(6.7)	46.3	(6.7)	c	c
Queensland	17.5	(1.9)	4.1	(0.7)	20.8	(2.1)	3.6	(0.8)	4.1	(0.7)	5.6	(1.6)	88.2	(11.4)	11.8	(11.4)	c	c
South Australia	10.7	(2.4)	4.7	(1.0)	18.3	(2.7)	4.4	(1.9)	4.7	(1.0)	7.8	(2.0)	61.7	(14.7)	38.3	(14.7)	c	c
Tasmania	3.8	(1.0)	0.9	(0.6)	17.1	(3.7)	1.0	(0.5)	0.9	(0.6)	3.0	(1.5)	78.6	(1.2)	21.4	(1.2)	c	c
Victoria	22.6	(5.1)	7.2	(1.1)	21.7	(3.6)	10.9	(3.1)	7.2	(1.1)	6.5	(2.3)	41.3	(14.8)	45.7	(15.1)	13.0	(8.6)
Western Australia	26.4	(4.4)	5.6	(1.2)	34.0	(2.9)	4.9	(1.4)	5.6	(1.2)	5.3	(1.3)	100.0	c	c	c	c	c
Belgium																		
Flemish Community•	17.6	(2.5)	11.4	(1.6)	4.4	(0.8)	13.4	(2.3)	7.1	(1.0)	2.8	(0.6)	c	c	100.0	c	c	c
French Community	33.3	(5.2)	4.5	(0.7)	16.5	(2.4)	12.4	(2.2)	4.5	(0.7)	4.3	(1.1)	43.3	(21.0)	15.9	(15.1)	40.8	(21.2)
German-speaking Community	c	c	5.1	(1.2)	c	c	c	c	5.1	(1.2)	c	c	c	c	c	c	c	c
Canada																		
Alberta	40.1	(8.6)	10.8	(1.5)	29.2	(3.6)	22.8	(5.5)	10.8	(1.5)	13.2	(1.7)	10.9	(10.3)	70.9	(19.1)	18.2	(16.7)
British Columbia	36.0	(7.8)	16.4	(2.6)	38.7	(3.7)	21.8	(5.4)	16.4	(2.6)	23.6	(2.8)	c	c	100.0	c	c	c
Manitoba	34.1	(4.3)	10.7	(2.0)	17.4	(2.0)	19.0	(3.3)	10.7	(2.0)	11.7	(1.7)	56.2	(12.9)	41.6	(12.7)	2.2	(0.4)
New Brunswick	2.5	(0.7)	1.0	(0.5)	14.5	(3.9)	1.1	(0.5)	1.0	(0.5)	7.5	(2.7)	70.4	(10.3)	29.6	(10.3)	c	c
Newfoundland and Labrador	0.0	(0.0)	0.5	(0.2)	7.5	(3.4)	0.0	(0.0)	0.5	(0.2)	4.9	(3.4)	73.0	(9.7)	27.0	(9.7)	c	c
Nova Scotia	2.4	(1.2)	1.4	(0.4)	13.4	(3.1)	0.5	(0.4)	1.4	(0.4)	10.2	(2.4)	54.6	(11.5)	45.4	(11.5)	c	c
Ontario	63.1	(7.6)	13.4	(2.0)	51.9	(5.5)	28.3	(5.6)	13.4	(2.0)	22.3	(3.2)	0.3	(0.3)	83.4	(12.7)	16.3	(12.7)
Prince Edward Island	1.7	(0.6)	3.3	(1.0)	c	c	0.6	(0.3)	3.3	(1.0)	c	c	44.6	(0.6)	55.0	(0.6)	0.4	(0.0)
Quebec	19.0	(4.5)	7.7	(1.2)	14.2	(3.1)	10.2	(2.6)	7.7	(1.2)	6.3	(1.4)	52.0	(21.6)	30.5	(19.0)	17.5	(14.9)
Saskatchewan	4.4	(1.9)	3.7	(0.7)	14.3	(3.3)	3.6	(1.6)	3.7	(0.7)	9.2	(2.3)	16.5	(7.6)	78.5	(8.1)	4.9	(3.4)
Italy																		
Abruzzo	9.9	(4.3)	4.0	(1.0)	3.6	(1.3)	6.8	(4.0)	4.0	(1.0)	2.4	(1.0)	100.0	c	c	c	c	c
Basilicata	1.4	(0.5)	0.5	(0.3)	0.4	(0.3)	0.9	(0.4)	0.5	(0.3)	0.2	(0.2)	61.5	(34.4)	38.5	(34.4)	c	c
Bolzano	6.3	(1.1)	3.6	(0.5)	6.6	(1.4)	5.2	(1.1)	3.6	(0.5)	3.9	(1.1)	52.4	(2.2)	47.6	(2.2)	c	c
Calabria	4.3	(1.0)	0.6	(0.5)	2.3	(0.9)	2.6	(0.9)	0.6	(0.5)	1.3	(0.8)	75.0	(28.6)	25.0	(28.6)	c	c
Campania	2.1	(0.7)	0.7	(0.4)	0.4	(0.3)	1.1	(0.6)	0.7	(0.4)	0.2	(0.2)	100.0	c	c	c	c	c
Emilia Romagna	27.1	(4.0)	8.5	(1.3)	5.2	(0.8)	16.7	(3.5)	8.5	(1.3)	2.9	(0.5)	c	c	c	c	c	c
Friuli Venezia Giulia	19.8	(4.2)	4.1	(1.1)	6.2	(1.0)	15.6	(4.0)	4.1	(1.1)	3.3	(0.8)	100.0	c	c	c	c	c
Lazio	23.0	(5.0)	6.2	(1.8)	5.8	(1.2)	18.8	(5.4)	6.2	(1.8)	1.8	(0.6)	c	c	c	c	c	c
Liguria	26.3	(5.0)	6.0	(0.9)	5.0	(1.2)	17.5	(2.9)	6.0	(0.9)	2.5	(0.7)	c	c	c	c	c	c
Lombardia	14.0	(2.9)	6.3	(1.3)	5.1	(1.1)	9.1	(3.2)	6.3	(1.3)	1.9	(0.6)	c	c	100.0	c	c	c
Marche	16.4	(3.5)	7.1	(2.3)	5.0	(1.0)	13.5	(3.3)	7.1	(2.3)	2.3	(0.7)	c	c	100.0	c	c	c
Molise	3.7	(1.0)	2.9	(1.1)	0.0	(0.0)	1.8	(0.9)	2.9	(1.1)	0.0	(0.0)	34.3	(4.7)	65.7	(4.7)	c	c
Piemonte	11.7	(2.4)	5.5	(0.8)	3.4	(0.8)	7.3	(2.1)	5.5	(0.8)	2.6	(0.7)	c	c	100.0	c	c	c
Puglia	3.7	(0.7)	0.3	(0.2)	1.1	(0.8)	1.8	(0.5)	0.3	(0.2)	0.8	(0.5)	c	c	c	c	c	c
Sardegna	3.3	(1.5)	1.1	(0.5)	1.2	(0.7)	3.1	(1.9)	1.1	(0.5)	0.8	(0.6)	100.0	c	c	c	c	c
Sicilia	2.7	(1.1)	0.9	(0.3)	1.1	(0.4)	2.4	(1.3)	0.9	(0.3)	0.3	(0.3)	c	c	c	c	c	c
Toscana	21.5	(2.6)	6.8	(1.6)	4.6	(1.1)	16.0	(2.2)	6.8	(1.6)	2.5	(0.9)	c	c	100.0	c	c	c
Trento	13.6	(2.6)	5.7	(1.3)	8.2	(1.8)	9.1	(2.4)	5.7	(1.3)	4.2	(1.4)	41.7	(19.0)	48.6	(18.2)	9.6	(10.0)
Umbria	22.0	(8.4)	6.6	(1.3)	6.2	(1.0)	10.7	(5.8)	6.6	(1.3)	2.4	(0.6)	c	c	c	c	c	c
Valle d'Aosta	7.1	(1.4)	3.2	(0.8)	c	c	5.5	(1.3)	3.2	(0.8)	c	c	58.3	(2.9)	41.7	(2.9)	c	c
Veneto	25.5	(4.0)	3.8	(1.0)	4.9	(0.9)	20.2	(2.9)	3.8	(1.0)	3.1	(0.9)	74.8	(21.7)	25.2	(21.7)	c	c
Mexico																		
Aguascalientes	2.5	(0.7)	0.0	(0.0)	0.2	(0.2)	0.0	(0.0)	0.0	(0.0)	0.0	(0.0)	38.2	(20.1)	61.8	(20.1)	c	c
Baja California	c	c	0.0	(0.0)	1.5	(0.5)	c	c	0.0	(0.0)	0.0	(0.0)	32.0	(26.7)	68.0	(26.7)	c	c
Baja California Sur	3.9	(1.5)	0.0	(0.0)	0.8	(0.5)	0.0	(0.0)	0.0	(0.0)	0.0	(0.0)	44.4	(21.5)	44.5	(22.0)	11.1	(11.1)
Campeche	11.7	(5.7)	0.1	(0.1)	0.5	(0.4)	1.5	(1.3)	0.1	(0.1)	0.0	(0.0)	78.0	(13.1)	22.0	(13.1)	c	c
Chiapas	2.8	(0.8)	0.0	(0.0)	c	c	0.8	(0.5)	0.0	(0.0)	c	c	100.0	c	c	c	c	c
Chihuahua	2.6	(1.5)	0.0	(0.0)	0.0	(0.0)	0.0	(0.0)	0.0	(0.0)	0.0	(0.0)	52.1	(27.9)	47.9	(27.9)	c	c
Coahuila	2.2	(1.5)	0.0	(0.0)	0.4	(0.3)	0.0	(0.0)	0.0	(0.0)	0.0	(0.0)	50.3	(19.6)	49.7	(19.6)	c	c
Colima	2.5	(1.0)	0.0	(0.0)	0.2	(0.2)	0.0	(0.0)	0.0	(0.0)	0.0	(0.0)	48.6	(15.6)	51.4	(15.6)	c	c
Distrito Federal	c	c	0.0	(0.0)	3.3	(1.7)	c	c	0.0	(0.0)	0.6	(0.6)	c	c	c	c	c	c
Durango	2.8	(1.1)	0.0	(0.0)	0.2	(0.2)	0.0	(0.0)	0.0	(0.0)	0.0	(0.0)	74.2	(11.9)	25.8	(11.9)	c	c
Guanajuato	0.8	(0.3)	0.0	(0.0)	0.5	(0.4)	0.3	(0.3)	0.0	(0.0)	0.0	(0.0)	100.0	c	c	c	c	c
Guerrero	2.9	(0.9)	0.4	(0.4)	0.0	(0.0)	1.4	(0.7)	0.4	(0.4)	0.0	(0.0)	95.0	(4.4)	5.0	(4.4)	c	c
Hidalgo	1.2	(0.5)	0.0	(0.0)	0.0	(0.0)	0.0	(0.0)	0.0	(0.0)	0.0	(0.0)	88.4	(9.4)	11.6	(9.4)	c	c
Jalisco	0.8	(0.5)	0.0	(0.0)	0.7	(0.4)	0.4	(0.3)	0.0	(0.0)	0.0	(0.0)	100.0	c	c	c	c	c
Mexico	0.3	(0.3)	0.0	(0.0)	0.9	(0.6)	0.0	(0.0)	0.0	(0.0)	0.5	(0.5)	62.7	(22.4)	37.3	(22.4)	c	c
Morelos	0.8	(0.6)	0.0	(0.0)	1.0	(0.6)	0.0	(0.0)	0.0	(0.0)	0.3	(0.3)	42.4	(21.7)	57.6	(21.7)	c	c
Nayarit	0.2	(0.2)	0.6	(0.5)	0.9	(0.8)	0.0	(0.0)	0.6	(0.5)	0.0	(0.0)	72.1	(12.2)	27.9	(12.2)	c	c
Nuevo León	c	c	0.0	(0.0)	1.2	(0.6)	c	c	0.0	(0.0)	0.4	(0.3)	100.0	c	c	c	c	c
Puebla	2.0	(1.0)	0.0	(0.0)	0.0	(0.0)	1.2	(0.7)	0.0	(0.0)	0.0	(0.0)	94.6	(5.8)	c	c	5.4	(5.8)
Querétaro	0.7	(0.5)	0.0	(0.0)	0.3	(0.3)	0.0	(0.0)	0.0	(0.0)	0.0	(0.0)	88.3	(11.4)	c	c	11.7	(11.4)
Quintana Roo	2.9	(0.6)	0.0	(0.0)	3.0	(0.9)	1.3	(0.7)	0.0	(0.0)	0.6	(0.3)	81.7	(17.2)	18.3	(17.2)	c	c
San Luis Potosí	1.7	(1.0)	0.0	(0.0)	0.0	(0.0)	0.3	(0.2)	0.0	(0.0)	0.0	(0.0)	86.7	(7.4)	13.3	(7.4)	c	c
Sinaloa	0.6	(0.4)	0.0	(0.0)	0.0	(0.0)	0.0	(0.0)	0.0	(0.0)	0.0	(0.0)	86.3	(10.3)	13.7	(10.3)	c	c
Tabasco	2.3	(1.1)	0.0	(0.0)	0.2	(0.2)	0.0	(0.0)	0.0	(0.0)	0.0	(0.0)	59.2	(18.5)	40.8	(18.5)	c	c
Tamaulipas	2.9	(1.3)	0.0	(0.0)	1.2	(0.5)	0.0	(0.0)	0.0	(0.0)	0.0	(0.0)	72.4	(22.3)	27.6	(22.3)	c	c
Tlaxcala	1.8	(0.7)	0.0	(0.0)	0.0	(0.0)	0.0	(0.0)	0.0	(0.0)	0.0	(0.0)	89.5	(9.9)	c	c	10.5	(9.9)
Veracruz	1.4	(1.0)	0.0	(0.0)	0.2	(0.3)	0.2	(0.2)	0.0	(0.0)	0.0	(0.0)	100.0	c	c	c	c	c
Yucatán	3.2	(1.1)	0.2	(0.3)	0.9	(0.8)	0.9	(0.5)	0.2	(0.3)	0.0	(0.0)	86.5	(12.2)	13.5	(12.2)	c	c
Zacatecas	2.1	(0.6)	0.0	(0.0)	0.6	(0.4)	0.0	(0.0)	0.0	(0.0)	0.3	(0.3)	77.0	(8.4)	23.0	(8.4)	c	c

• PISA adjudicated region.

Notes: Values that are statistically significant are indicated in bold (see Annex A3).

See Table II.4.2 for national data.

1. ESCS refers to the *PISA index of economic, social and cultural status*.

2. Advantaged (disadvantaged) schools are those where the typical student in the school, or the socio-economic profile of the school, is above (below) the ESCS of the typical student in the country, the country mean ESCS. In each school, a random sample of 35 students are to take part in PISA (for more details see the *PISA 2012 Technical Report* [OECD, forthcoming]). The socio-economic profile of the school is calculated using the information provided by these students. Therefore, the precision of the estimate depends on the number of students that actually take the test in the school and the diversity of their answers. This precision was taken into account when classifying schools as advantaged, disadvantaged or average. If the difference between the school socio-economic profile and the ESCS of the typical student in the country (the mean ESCS at the country level) was not statistically significant, the school was classified as a school with an average socio-economic profile. If the school profile was statistically significantly above the country mean, the school is classified as a socio-economically advantaged school. If the profile was below the country mean, the school is classified as a socio-economically disadvantaged school.

StatLink http://dx.doi.org/10.1787/888932964965

[Part 4/8]

Mathematics performance and student population, by schools' socio-economic profile and region

Table B2.II.15 · *Results based on students' self-reports*

	Percentage of immigrant students						Percentage of immigrant students who do not speak the language of assessment at home						Percentage of students in rural schools (schools located in a village, hamlet or rural area; fewer than 3 000 people)					
	Socio-economically disadvantaged schools[2]		Socio-economically average schools[2]		Socio-economically advantaged schools[2]		Socio-economically disadvantaged schools[2]		Socio-economically average schools[2]		Socio-economically advantaged schools[2]		Socio-economically disadvantaged schools[2]		Socio-economically average schools[2]		Socio-economically advantaged schools[2]	
	%	S.E.	%	S.E.	%	S.E.	%	S.E.	%	S.E.	%	S.E.	%	S.E.	%	S.E.	%	S.E.
Portugal																		
Alentejo	6.8	(1.7)	3.2	(1.2)	2.0	(1.0)	3.4	(1.6)	3.2	(1.2)	1.5	(0.7)	16.7	(22.7)	83.3	(22.7)	c	c
Spain																		
Andalusia*	4.4	(1.2)	0.2	(0.2)	1.4	(1.0)	2.1	(0.6)	0.2	(0.2)	0.3	(0.3)	100.0	c	c	c	c	c
Aragon*	20.9	(3.1)	5.0	(0.8)	4.3	(1.2)	11.8	(3.0)	5.0	(0.8)	1.7	(0.7)	86.7	(14.3)	13.3	(14.3)	c	c
Asturias*	6.9	(1.9)	1.3	(0.4)	6.3	(1.3)	2.7	(0.9)	1.3	(0.4)	0.7	(0.3)	40.5	(34.3)	59.5	(34.3)	c	c
Balearic Islands*	36.7	(5.5)	12.2	(1.8)	8.6	(2.7)	22.7	(3.7)	12.2	(1.8)	5.3	(2.5)	c	c	c	c	c	c
Basque Country*	37.9	(6.5)	2.1	(0.4)	2.1	(0.4)	12.4	(3.6)	2.1	(0.4)	0.5	(0.2)	c	c	18.9	(18.7)	81.1	(18.7)
Cantabria*	9.3	(2.5)	3.0	(0.5)	6.0	(1.4)	2.1	(0.9)	3.0	(0.5)	0.9	(0.6)	18.0	(14.7)	82.0	(14.7)	c	c
Castile and Leon*	6.9	(2.0)	3.8	(1.0)	2.7	(1.1)	1.0	(0.7)	3.8	(1.0)	1.2	(0.6)	55.9	(26.4)	44.1	(26.4)	c	c
Catalonia*	26.2	(5.4)	10.7	(1.8)	7.5	(2.0)	25.2	(5.6)	10.7	(1.8)	7.3	(2.1)	c	c	100.0	c	c	c
Extremadura*	2.3	(0.7)	2.7	(1.2)	2.9	(0.7)	0.7	(0.3)	2.7	(1.2)	0.8	(0.5)	100.0	c	c	c	c	c
Galicia*	4.5	(1.5)	1.7	(0.4)	4.7	(1.1)	1.4	(0.7)	1.7	(0.4)	0.7	(0.2)	100.0	c	c	c	c	c
La Rioja*	23.3	(2.6)	7.3	(1.1)	8.1	(1.2)	8.4	(1.5)	7.3	(1.1)	2.5	(0.9)	7.5	(0.3)	92.5	(0.3)	c	c
Madrid*	33.3	(9.2)	6.1	(1.1)	6.7	(1.2)	8.2	(4.0)	6.1	(1.1)	1.2	(0.4)	c	c	c	c	c	c
Murcia*	18.0	(2.6)	3.5	(1.1)	c	c	6.5	(1.6)	3.5	(1.1)	c	c	100.0	c	c	c	c	c
Navarre*	23.5	(3.2)	2.2	(0.6)	6.7	(1.3)	5.8	(1.2)	2.2	(0.6)	1.0	(0.5)	60.0	(20.1)	40.0	(20.1)	c	c
United Kingdom							0.0	(0.0)										
England	24.1	(3.3)	3.5	(0.8)	15.5	(2.9)	11.9	(1.9)	3.5	(0.8)	7.5	(2.0)	8.8	(8.1)	46.3	(12.4)	44.9	(12.4)
Northern Ireland	4.4	(1.3)	2.2	(0.7)	4.1	(0.9)	3.5	(1.1)	2.2	(0.7)	2.1	(0.7)	41.4	(18.2)	44.1	(18.2)	14.5	(13.2)
Scotland*	8.3	(1.9)	1.8	(0.4)	12.5	(2.2)	2.7	(0.9)	1.8	(0.4)	3.0	(0.8)	19.9	(15.3)	51.1	(25.7)	29.1	(25.4)
Wales	5.1	(1.7)	2.1	(0.5)	2.2	(0.9)	2.9	(1.1)	2.1	(0.5)	0.9	(0.5)	23.9	(13.0)	61.1	(13.5)	15.0	(9.0)
United States							0.0	(0.0)										
Connecticut*	24.8	(3.2)	9.0	(1.5)	8.4	(1.7)	13.5	(2.4)	9.0	(1.5)	4.3	(1.5)	c	c	c	c	c	c
Florida*	36.6	(6.7)	10.0	(2.0)	15.7	(2.1)	19.4	(3.0)	10.0	(2.0)	7.1	(2.3)	c	c	100.0	c	c	c
Massachusetts*	45.1	(6.3)	5.6	(1.3)	8.0	(1.6)	24.9	(4.3)	5.6	(1.3)	2.4	(1.0)	c	c	c	c	c	c
Argentina																		
Ciudad Autónoma de Buenos Aires*	42.1	(5.1)	1.4	(0.7)	3.6	(0.7)	5.2	(1.9)	1.4	(0.7)	0.9	(0.4)	c	c	c	c	c	c
Brazil																		
Acre	0.8	(0.7)	0.0	(0.0)	0.0	(0.0)	0.0	(0.0)	0.0	(0.0)	0.0	(0.0)	c	c	c	c	c	c
Alagoas	0.0	(0.0)	c	c	c	c	0.0	(0.0)	c	c	c	c	100.0	c	c	c	c	c
Amapá	c	c	0.0	(0.0)	0.0	(0.0)	c	c	0.0	(0.0)	0.0	(0.0)	c	c	c	c	c	c
Amazonas	c	c	0.0	(0.0)	0.0	(0.0)	c	c	0.0	(0.0)	0.0	(0.0)	c	c	c	c	c	c
Bahia	0.8	(0.5)	c	c	c	c	0.0	(0.0)	c	c	c	c	c	c	c	c	c	c
Ceará	0.2	(0.2)	c	c	c	c	0.0	(0.0)	c	c	c	c	100.0	c	c	c	c	c
Espírito Santo	0.0	(0.0)	0.0	(0.0)	c	c	0.0	(0.0)	0.0	(0.0)	c	c	100.0	c	c	c	c	c
Federal District	c	c	0.0	(0.0)	0.6	(0.5)	c	c	0.0	(0.0)	0.0	(0.0)	100.0	c	c	c	c	c
Goiás	0.0	(0.0)	0.0	(0.0)	c	c	0.0	(0.0)	0.0	(0.0)	c	c	100.0	c	c	c	c	c
Maranhão	0.7	(0.7)	0.0	(0.0)	c	c	0.0	(0.0)	0.0	(0.0)	c	c	c	c	c	c	c	c
Mato Grosso	0.8	(0.5)	0.0	(0.0)	c	c	0.0	(0.0)	0.0	(0.0)	c	c	c	c	c	c	c	c
Mato Grosso do Sul	0.6	(0.5)	1.1	(0.9)	0.7	(1.2)	0.0	(0.0)	1.1	(0.9)	0.0	(0.0)	c	c	c	c	c	c
Minas Gerais	0.0	(0.0)	0.0	(0.0)	2.3	(2.8)	0.0	(0.0)	0.0	(0.0)	0.0	(0.0)	100.0	c	c	c	c	c
Pará	0.0	(0.0)	0.0	(0.0)	c	c	0.0	(0.0)	0.0	(0.0)	c	c	c	c	c	c	c	c
Paraíba	0.3	(0.3)	0.0	(0.0)	0.0	(0.0)	0.0	(0.0)	0.0	(0.0)	0.0	(0.0)	c	c	100.0	c	c	c
Paraná	0.5	(0.5)	0.2	(0.2)	2.5	(0.5)	0.0	(0.0)	0.2	(0.2)	1.7	(1.0)	c	c	c	c	c	c
Pernambuco	0.6	(0.4)	0.0	(0.0)	c	c	0.0	(0.0)	0.0	(0.0)	c	c	c	c	c	c	c	c
Piauí	0.0	(0.0)	0.0	(0.0)	c	c	0.0	(0.0)	0.0	(0.0)	c	c	100.0	c	c	c	c	c
Rio de Janeiro	c	c	0.0	(0.0)	0.9	(0.6)	c	c	0.0	(0.0)	0.9	(0.6)	c	c	c	c	c	c
Rio Grande do Norte	0.3	(0.4)	0.0	(0.0)	0.5	(0.5)	0.0	(0.0)	0.0	(0.0)	0.0	(0.0)	c	c	c	c	c	c
Rio Grande do Sul	0.3	(0.3)	0.0	(0.0)	0.0	(0.0)	0.3	(0.3)	0.0	(0.0)	0.0	(0.0)	c	c	100.0	c	c	c
Rondônia	2.3	(0.7)	0.0	(0.0)	c	c	0.0	(0.0)	0.0	(0.0)	c	c	100.0	c	c	c	c	c
Roraima	6.7	(2.5)	0.3	(0.2)	0.5	(0.6)	0.5	(0.5)	0.3	(0.2)	0.5	(0.6)	c	c	100.0	c	c	c
Santa Catarina	3.0	(1.8)	0.0	(0.0)	c	c	0.0	(0.0)	0.0	(0.0)	c	c	100.0	c	c	c	c	c
São Paulo	0.6	(0.4)	0.3	(0.2)	1.2	(0.9)	0.0	(0.0)	0.3	(0.2)	0.7	(0.6)	c	c	c	c	c	c
Sergipe	0.6	(0.6)	0.0	(0.0)	0.0	(0.0)	0.0	(0.0)	0.0	(0.0)	0.0	(0.0)	c	c	c	c	c	c
Tocantins	0.6	(0.4)	0.0	(0.0)	0.6	(0.8)	0.0	(0.0)	0.0	(0.0)	0.6	(0.8)	100.0	c	c	c	c	c
Colombia																		
Bogotá	1.0	(1.0)	0.0	(0.0)	0.2	(0.2)	0.0	(0.0)	0.0	(0.0)	0.0	(0.0)	c	c	100.0	c	c	c
Cali	c	c	0.0	(0.0)	0.1	(0.1)	c	c	0.0	(0.0)	0.0	(0.0)	c	c	c	c	c	c
Manizales	0.0	(0.0)	0.0	(0.0)	0.0	(0.0)	0.0	(0.0)	0.0	(0.0)	0.0	(0.0)	65.5	(20.5)	c	c	34.5	(20.5)
Medellín	1.2	(0.9)	0.0	(0.0)	0.2	(0.2)	0.0	(0.0)	0.0	(0.0)	0.2	(0.2)	c	c	100.0	c	c	c
Russian Federation																		
Perm Territory region*	8.5	(1.6)	0.4	(0.2)	5.2	(0.6)	0.2	(0.2)	0.4	(0.2)	0.4	(0.3)	65.5	(15.7)	34.5	(15.7)	c	c
United Arab Emirates																		
Abu Dhabi*	45.5	(3.4)	19.7	(3.8)	55.8	(5.5)	13.0	(3.7)	19.7	(3.8)	26.2	(4.5)	73.7	(11.7)	9.0	(9.5)	17.3	(4.9)
Ajman	55.0	(5.8)	5.4	(3.1)	c	c	13.4	(3.1)	5.4	(3.1)	c	c	58.7	(6.6)	41.3	(6.6)	c	c
Dubai*	50.0	(1.4)	40.9	(1.1)	76.9	(0.6)	29.7	(1.1)	40.9	(1.1)	37.2	(1.2)	14.2	(0.1)	68.1	(0.3)	17.7	(0.3)
Fujairah	10.4	(3.0)	29.6	(6.9)	c	c	4.3	(3.0)	29.6	(6.9)	c	c	66.1	(26.4)	c	c	33.9	(26.4)
Ras al-Khaimah	36.7	(7.6)	2.3	(0.9)	58.1	(12.5)	21.3	(5.6)	2.3	(0.9)	15.4	(7.7)	51.0	(24.7)	30.4	(20.6)	18.5	(18.7)
Sharjah	c	c	30.4	(7.9)	68.4	(10.6)	c	c	30.4	(7.9)	31.0	(8.3)	66.6	(29.9)	c	c	33.4	(29.9)
Umm al-Quwain	36.2	(2.8)	1.8	(1.0)	c	c	13.7	(2.0)	1.8	(1.0)	c	c	69.6	(0.8)	30.4	(0.8)	c	c

* PISA adjudicated region.

Notes: Values that are statistically significant are indicated in bold (see Annex A3).

See Table II.4.2 for national data.

1. ESCS refers to the *PISA index of economic, social and cultural status*.

2. Advantaged (disadvantaged) schools are those where the typical student in the school, or the socio-economic profile of the school, is above (below) the ESCS of the typical student in the country, the country mean ESCS. In each school, a random sample of 35 students are to take part in PISA (for more details see the *PISA 2012 Technical Report* [OECD, forthcoming]). The socio-economic profile of the school is calculated using the information provided by these students. Therefore, the precision of the estimate depends on the number of students that actually take the test in the school and the diversity of their answers. This precision was taken into account when classifying schools as advantaged, disadvantaged or average. If the difference between the school socio-economic profile and the ESCS of the typical student in the country (the mean ESCS at the country level) was not statistically significant, the school was classified as a school with an average socio-economic profile. If the school profile was statistically significantly above the country mean, the school is classified as a socio-economically advantaged school. If the profile was below the country mean, the school is classified as a socio-economically disadvantaged school.

StatLink ᴬᴹˢᴾ http://dx.doi.org/10.1787/888932964965

[Part 5/8]

Mathematics performance and student population, by schools' socio-economic profile and region

Table B2.II.15 — *Results based on students' self-reports*

| | Percentage of students in attending schools located in a city or large city (over 100 000 people) | | | | | | Difference in performance between students in socio-economically average versus disadvantaged schools | | | | Difference in performance between students in socio-economically advantaged versus average schools | | | |
| | Socio-economically disadvantaged schools[2] | | Socio-economically average schools[2] | | Socio-economically advantaged schools[2] | | Before accounting for student's ESCS[1] | | After accounting for student's ESCS[1] | | Before accounting for student's ESCS[1] | | After accounting for student's ESCS[1] | |
	%	S.E.	%	S.E.	%	S.E.	Score dif.	S.E.	Score dif.	S.E.	Score dif.	S.E.	Score dif.	S.E.
Australia														
Australian Capital Territory	c	c	31.5	(0.9)	68.5	(0.9)	c	c	c	c	50	(5.7)	27	(6.8)
New South Wales	17.4	(2.9)	47.0	(4.5)	35.5	(4.4)	48	(8.2)	28	(7.9)	63	(11.1)	44	(11.7)
Northern Territory	37.5	(7.4)	46.4	(8.9)	16.1	(15.3)	51	(18.0)	16	(15.2)	c	c	c	c
Queensland	21.0	(3.8)	49.7	(5.4)	29.2	(4.2)	49	(6.1)	32	(6.1)	49	(6.3)	34	(6.4)
South Australia	21.7	(3.9)	53.1	(5.0)	25.2	(3.5)	30	(7.2)	15	(8.0)	55	(10.4)	39	(9.9)
Tasmania	20.4	(1.7)	61.6	(2.0)	17.9	(1.2)	38	(6.4)	20	(7.1)	61	(8.3)	40	(8.7)
Victoria	12.6	(2.6)	57.9	(4.8)	29.6	(4.4)	32	(7.7)	18	(7.4)	59	(9.1)	46	(9.1)
Western Australia	25.6	(3.6)	36.7	(5.3)	37.7	(5.0)	42	(8.0)	29	(7.8)	52	(8.2)	35	(8.2)
Belgium														
Flemish Community•	33.8	(8.3)	26.6	(9.0)	39.6	(10.8)	68	(8.8)	51	(8.9)	84	(7.6)	70	(7.9)
French Community	37.1	(8.2)	22.6	(5.8)	40.3	(8.4)	79	(7.3)	65	(7.0)	56	(7.5)	41	(7.2)
German-speaking Community	c	c	c	c	c	c	c	c	c	c	c	c	c	c
Canada														
Alberta	11.2	(3.9)	52.2	(6.3)	36.6	(5.7)	29	(18.4)	20	(18.5)	63	(8.1)	49	(8.2)
British Columbia	17.4	(6.1)	44.5	(8.6)	38.1	(7.2)	15	(9.9)	4	(9.4)	35	(8.2)	22	(8.0)
Manitoba	24.8	(2.4)	52.3	(2.4)	22.9	(2.5)	32	(8.6)	16	(8.0)	40	(8.4)	20	(7.5)
New Brunswick	9.1	(0.9)	46.8	(1.7)	44.0	(1.8)	9	(5.6)	2	(5.4)	42	(8.6)	32	(8.5)
Newfoundland and Labrador	c	c	37.8	(2.7)	62.2	(2.7)	51	(8.0)	32	(6.2)	28	(6.7)	12	(6.2)
Nova Scotia	9.4	(1.4)	49.9	(5.0)	40.8	(4.1)	11	(8.3)	1	(6.9)	16	(11.5)	7	(11.3)
Ontario	25.3	(5.1)	41.2	(6.4)	33.6	(5.6)	22	(8.3)	6	(8.5)	37	(8.5)	24	(8.5)
Prince Edward Island	c	c	c	c	c	c	6	(5.6)	-1	(5.1)	c	c	c	c
Quebec	23.6	(5.1)	44.2	(5.6)	32.2	(5.1)	28	(8.0)	17	(7.3)	62	(8.0)	46	(7.9)
Saskatchewan	9.3	(2.1)	59.7	(2.9)	31.0	(3.0)	16	(8.9)	6	(9.2)	16	(5.7)	2	(5.6)
Italy														
Abruzzo	25.2	(13.0)	47.9	(12.4)	26.9	(5.0)	35	(20.8)	30	(20.1)	80	(13.9)	70	(14.5)
Basilicata	c	c	c	c	c	c	49	(9.6)	43	(10.1)	51	(11.2)	43	(10.3)
Bolzano	10.6	(0.8)	51.8	(1.1)	37.6	(1.2)	51	(4.8)	45	(4.5)	49	(5.4)	44	(6.0)
Calabria	16.9	(13.4)	49.5	(17.9)	33.6	(17.4)	49	(14.5)	40	(14.5)	53	(16.8)	47	(15.7)
Campania	23.5	(10.3)	38.7	(13.0)	37.8	(11.1)	59	(12.9)	53	(12.7)	58	(14.1)	54	(14.7)
Emilia Romagna	21.0	(8.7)	44.3	(11.4)	34.7	(7.6)	62	(13.1)	54	(12.7)	79	(12.3)	71	(12.7)
Friuli Venezia Giulia	23.6	(15.0)	18.2	(7.9)	58.2	(12.6)	53	(23.6)	47	(22.5)	51	(11.9)	47	(12.0)
Lazio	3.5	(1.1)	24.9	(9.1)	71.6	(9.0)	50	(11.8)	49	(11.7)	75	(13.0)	73	(13.8)
Liguria	16.5	(8.2)	33.9	(10.2)	49.6	(10.6)	60	(10.8)	51	(10.3)	67	(11.7)	59	(12.6)
Lombardia	15.4	(10.5)	52.9	(13.7)	31.7	(10.2)	31	(16.3)	25	(17.3)	69	(11.8)	62	(12.6)
Marche	35.9	(25.7)	24.5	(22.3)	39.6	(24.7)	65	(15.1)	62	(15.3)	39	(15.8)	33	(15.9)
Molise	c	c	c	c	c	c	34	(5.3)	28	(5.3)	70	(6.1)	67	(6.5)
Piemonte	c	c	61.1	(16.0)	38.9	(16.0)	52	(11.5)	47	(11.5)	51	(12.0)	44	(12.3)
Puglia	43.6	(11.6)	24.3	(11.6)	32.1	(7.4)	69	(12.3)	56	(11.6)	23	(12.1)	16	(12.0)
Sardegna	22.3	(11.1)	30.6	(13.0)	47.1	(13.5)	55	(16.6)	47	(16.2)	66	(10.9)	57	(12.0)
Sicilia	23.0	(9.6)	52.9	(13.5)	24.0	(11.0)	47	(12.0)	39	(12.5)	56	(12.4)	48	(11.9)
Toscana	10.7	(10.2)	34.0	(15.9)	55.3	(12.8)	68	(18.7)	62	(19.3)	47	(15.8)	40	(15.6)
Trento	7.0	(7.2)	44.7	(8.9)	48.3	(8.3)	73	(12.2)	66	(12.0)	33	(10.1)	30	(10.4)
Umbria	1.5	(1.4)	39.2	(8.6)	59.3	(8.4)	85	(14.8)	84	(15.5)	52	(11.4)	48	(11.3)
Valle d'Aosta	c	c	c	c	c	c	12	(5.7)	6	(6.3)	c	c	c	c
Veneto	20.8	(10.7)	45.4	(12.7)	33.8	(10.5)	80	(11.9)	73	(11.9)	46	(15.7)	46	(15.3)
Mexico														
Aguascalientes	5.7	(5.9)	34.0	(6.6)	60.3	(4.0)	41	(10.7)	36	(10.1)	28	(9.4)	13	(8.9)
Baja California	3.1	(2.3)	37.8	(8.7)	59.1	(9.2)	c	c	c	c	26	(18.9)	18	(17.8)
Baja California Sur	7.7	(5.7)	25.5	(10.8)	66.7	(11.1)	29	(13.9)	24	(13.8)	37	(13.8)	25	(12.9)
Campeche	c	c	63.7	(10.2)	36.3	(10.2)	17	(11.1)	7	(11.4)	42	(17.2)	28	(17.6)
Chiapas	34.4	(18.3)	38.9	(22.4)	26.7	(18.2)	46	(12.8)	51	(14.1)	c	c	c	c
Chihuahua	17.7	(10.0)	37.2	(11.8)	45.1	(10.4)	18	(21.0)	12	(20.0)	56	(14.8)	45	(14.1)
Coahuila	14.5	(10.2)	28.7	(10.6)	56.9	(12.7)	16	(16.4)	11	(17.7)	48	(12.5)	36	(11.1)
Colima	c	c	24.0	(5.6)	76.0	(5.6)	48	(10.5)	49	(10.9)	46	(14.0)	36	(12.3)
Distrito Federal	6.0	(4.7)	45.7	(8.3)	48.3	(6.4)	c	c	c	c	50	(8.7)	41	(9.2)
Durango	c	c	35.3	(13.2)	64.7	(13.2)	24	(14.3)	21	(13.9)	36	(15.4)	23	(15.6)
Guanajuato	18.8	(11.1)	32.7	(13.4)	48.5	(9.4)	29	(10.6)	21	(10.9)	47	(10.0)	42	(12.6)
Guerrero	17.5	(14.7)	66.0	(17.1)	16.5	(12.5)	32	(11.4)	26	(11.1)	18	(18.5)	15	(17.4)
Hidalgo	25.8	(21.6)	41.8	(24.3)	32.4	(20.8)	25	(17.0)	15	(17.5)	51	(18.4)	39	(16.3)
Jalisco	13.9	(12.9)	32.5	(7.2)	53.6	(12.4)	13	(13.8)	11	(15.0)	40	(11.3)	35	(10.1)
Mexico	c	c	39.2	(13.3)	60.8	(13.3)	12	(14.2)	8	(14.3)	32	(16.1)	25	(13.1)
Morelos	c	c	41.2	(14.8)	58.8	(14.8)	44	(15.8)	40	(16.8)	62	(12.6)	41	(9.4)
Nayarit	c	c	33.0	(11.9)	67.0	(11.9)	17	(18.4)	2	(18.0)	47	(10.3)	40	(10.7)
Nuevo León	1.3	(1.3)	33.6	(9.4)	65.1	(9.5)	c	c	c	c	57	(7.5)	45	(7.7)
Puebla	10.6	(11.3)	24.8	(16.6)	64.6	(13.6)	40	(13.6)	24	(13.7)	22	(10.9)	11	(11.6)
Querétaro	c	c	30.1	(14.1)	69.9	(14.1)	23	(13.4)	11	(13.9)	34	(16.9)	20	(13.5)
Quintana Roo	12.4	(5.7)	31.6	(13.0)	56.0	(12.9)	10	(11.4)	4	(10.6)	57	(8.8)	48	(8.7)
San Luis Potosí	22.1	(12.3)	27.7	(9.4)	50.2	(13.5)	30	(9.4)	23	(9.1)	57	(10.8)	40	(10.5)
Sinaloa	2.3	(2.4)	49.0	(8.6)	48.7	(8.2)	-11	(11.5)	-15	(11.5)	57	(7.7)	52	(7.6)
Tabasco	c	c	11.3	(10.3)	88.7	(10.3)	17	(11.3)	12	(10.9)	45	(12.6)	38	(11.5)
Tamaulipas	6.5	(5.0)	44.8	(12.3)	48.7	(11.1)	11	(15.4)	5	(18.1)	47	(13.0)	38	(11.7)
Tlaxcala	c	c	c	c	100.0	c	41	(6.9)	36	(6.5)	18	(7.7)	10	(8.6)
Veracruz	11.7	(10.6)	c	c	88.3	(10.6)	23	(16.6)	11	(17.5)	27	(22.5)	9	(18.3)
Yucatán	8.6	(8.4)	27.1	(12.1)	64.4	(13.6)	19	(10.8)	11	(11.0)	34	(15.7)	16	(16.9)
Zacatecas	c	c	36.7	(16.1)	63.3	(16.1)	33	(10.4)	22	(11.2)	35	(9.1)	27	(9.2)

• PISA adjudicated region.

Notes: Values that are statistically significant are indicated in bold (see Annex A3).

See Table II.4.2 for national data.

1. ESCS refers to the *PISA index of economic, social and cultural status*.

2. Advantaged (disadvantaged) schools are those where the typical student in the school, or the socio-economic profile of the school, is above (below) the ESCS of the typical student in the country, the country mean ESCS. In each school, a random sample of 35 students are to take part in PISA (for more details see the *PISA 2012 Technical Report* [OECD, forthcoming]). The socio-economic profile of the school is calculated using the information provided by these students. Therefore, the precision of the estimate depends on the number of students that actually take the test in the school and the diversity of their answers. This precision was taken into account when classifying schools as advantaged, disadvantaged or average. If the difference between the school socio-economic profile and the ESCS of the typical student in the country (the mean ESCS at the country level) was not statistically significant, the school was classified as a school with an average socio-economic profile. If the school profile was statistically significantly above the country mean, the school is classified as a socio-economically advantaged school. If the profile was below the country mean, the school is classified as a socio-economically disadvantaged school.

StatLink ᴴᴵᴸᴾ http://dx.doi.org/10.1787/888932964965

[Part 6/8]
Mathematics performance and student population, by schools' socio-economic profile and region
Table B2.II.15 *Results based on students' self-reports*

	Percentage of students in attending schools located in a city or large city (over 100 000 people)						Difference in performance between students in socio-economically average versus disadvantaged schools				Difference in performance between students in socio-economically advantaged versus average schools			
	Socio-economically disadvantaged schools[2]		Socio-economically average schools[2]		Socio-economically advantaged schools[2]		Before accounting for student's ESCS[1]		After accounting for student's ESCS		Before accounting for student's ESCS		After accounting for student's ESCS	
	%	S.E.	%	S.E.	%	S.E.	Score dif.	S.E.	Score dif.	S.E.	Score dif.	S.E.	Score dif.	S.E.
Portugal														
Alentejo	c	c	c	c	100.0	c	**75**	(16.9)	**58**	(16.9)	**38**	(13.2)	2	(14.5)
Spain														
Andalusia●	12.0	(8.5)	53.4	(14.1)	34.6	(12.7)	**36**	(8.8)	20	(9.1)	19	(10.1)		(8.2)
Aragon●	9.7	(5.4)	48.0	(8.6)	42.3	(7.6)	**39**	(10.8)	23	(10.2)	38	(10.1)	1	(8.7)
Asturias●	10.5	(5.9)	30.1	(8.5)	59.3	(9.6)	27	(16.0)	13	(15.9)	47	(8.0)	2	(5.8)
Balearic Islands●	23.3	(11.0)	33.9	(11.2)	42.8	(10.8)	**43**	(10.5)	27	(10.2)	33	(9.8)	1	(9.2)
Basque Country●	14.5	(2.3)	29.8	(4.9)	55.7	(5.4)	**57**	(11.2)	**42**	(10.4)	28	(4.7)	1	(4.4)
Cantabria●	c	c	63.0	(11.5)	37.0	(11.5)	2	(10.4)	-11	(10.1)	39	(8.2)	1	(7.2)
Castile and Leon●	4.0	(3.8)	22.3	(9.3)	73.7	(9.7)	6	(8.5)	-8	(7.7)	34	(8.8)	1	(9.2)
Catalonia●	29.7	(10.4)	27.1	(8.9)	43.2	(11.1)	**34**	(8.5)	20	(8.6)	47	(9.7)	2	(8.9)
Extremadura●	28.9	(20.4)	13.5	(12.6)	57.6	(21.9)	17	(8.0)	1	(8.7)	63	(8.1)	4	(7.3)
Galicia●	7.8	(7.3)	40.1	(10.5)	52.1	(11.3)	15	(9.3)	6	(9.2)	38	(8.1)	2	(8.8)
La Rioja●	9.8	(0.2)	37.8	(0.7)	52.4	(0.6)	19	(6.0)	6	(6.0)	47	(5.1)	2	(5.5)
Madrid●	14.8	(7.6)	49.4	(8.9)	35.9	(6.8)	**38**	(12.9)	21	(11.6)	31	(8.6)		(9.0)
Murcia●	10.8	(10.2)	67.4	(16.7)	21.8	(15.0)	33	(11.2)	15	(11.0)	c	c		c
Navarre●	11.1	(5.1)	61.0	(7.0)	27.9	(6.1)	18	(5.9)	3	(5.9)	37	(6.8)	1	(7.7)
United Kingdom														
England	28.0	(7.1)	43.5	(7.7)	28.6	(5.7)	**40**	(11.0)	24	(9.2)	64	(7.9)	4	(7.3)
Northern Ireland	34.8	(10.1)	35.6	(10.4)	29.6	(6.9)	**57**	(8.0)	**49**	(7.7)	91	(8.1)	7	(8.0)
Scotland●	39.9	(8.9)	30.7	(8.2)	29.3	(6.0)	**37**	(6.1)	24	(5.6)	44	(8.2)	2	(7.6)
Wales	35.9	(5.3)	47.7	(6.6)	16.4	(4.5)	**33**	(5.3)	19	(5.1)	35	(6.1)	2	(5.7)
United States														
Connecticut●	59.9	(16.2)	40.1	(16.2)	c	c	**55**	(12.5)	32	(10.8)	53	(9.4)	2	(9.4)
Florida●	26.0	(9.0)	39.9	(8.7)	34.1	(11.0)	**34**	(7.6)	20	(7.3)	45	(11.9)	3	(10.8)
Massachusetts●	77.4	(14.6)	22.6	(14.6)	c	c	**40**	(11.0)	22	(10.3)	62	(12.4)	3	(10.7)
Argentina														
Ciudad Autónoma de Buenos Aires●	21.2	(6.3)	20.0	(5.7)	58.7	(5.2)	**61**	(28.4)	54	(25.6)	79	(17.4)	5	(17.0)
Brazil														
Acre	27.6	(19.4)	37.8	(15.9)	34.6	(10.8)	16	(9.7)	9	(9.5)	47	(17.2)	3	(14.9)
Alagoas	4.4	(4.0)	32.0	(18.0)	63.6	(18.1)	c	c	c	c	c	c		c
Amapá	c	c	48.5	(10.6)	51.5	(10.6)	c	c	c	c	53	(12.2)	4	(9.0)
Amazonas	c	c	75.5	(13.8)	24.5	(13.8)	c	c	c	c	51	(22.5)	4	(18.9)
Bahia	c	c	51.3	(31.5)	48.7	(31.5)	c	c	c	c	c	c		c
Ceará	41.3	(10.1)	18.8	(12.4)	39.9	(10.9)	c	c	c	c	c	c		c
Espírito Santo	26.5	(13.2)	33.7	(14.8)	39.8	(7.3)	-10	(14.3)	-16	(14.2)	c	c		c
Federal District	0.6	(0.7)	45.4	(11.2)	54.0	(11.0)	c	c	c	c	100	(18.5)	7	(15.9)
Goiás	21.2	(14.1)	45.6	(16.6)	33.1	(12.6)	**26**	(11.5)	19	(10.5)	c	c		c
Maranhão	c	c	58.4	(19.6)	41.6	(19.6)	6	(16.2)	2	(16.9)	c	c		c
Mato Grosso	c	c	80.9	(4.6)	19.1	(4.6)	2	(16.1)	-2	(16.1)	c	c		c
Mato Grosso do Sul	23.1	(10.0)	8.4	(7.7)	68.5	(12.0)	12	(13.1)	8	(12.5)	73	(12.3)	4	(10.9)
Minas Gerais	20.4	(12.4)	34.6	(8.8)	45.0	(10.4)	11	(8.3)	6	(8.5)	69	(15.7)	5	(10.8)
Pará	1.1	(1.1)	58.3	(25.2)	40.6	(25.2)	26	(17.6)	21	(17.0)	c	c		c
Paraíba	10.0	(7.7)	20.3	(8.8)	69.7	(8.0)	23	(15.6)	10	(16.4)	72	(18.0)	5	(15.4)
Paraná	6.8	(6.4)	59.0	(15.4)	34.2	(14.9)	21	(12.0)	13	(11.1)	92	(39.8)	6	(24.4)
Pernambuco	44.2	(15.8)	49.1	(18.5)	6.8	(5.7)	**30**	(11.5)	20	(12.4)	c	c		c
Piauí	19.4	(13.5)	30.6	(12.7)	49.9	(14.8)	14	(13.9)	8	(13.1)	c	c		c
Rio de Janeiro	c	c	73.7	(6.8)	26.3	(6.8)	c	c	c	c	82	(15.6)	6	(12.2)
Rio Grande do Norte	15.1	(16.2)	40.1	(16.9)	44.8	(11.3)	8	(10.8)	3	(10.1)	127	(27.1)	10	(29.0)
Rio Grande do Sul	31.2	(14.7)	16.5	(13.1)	52.3	(14.5)	16	(16.9)	10	(16.9)	31	(15.2)	2	(17.3)
Rondônia	19.2	(16.0)	40.8	(24.5)	40.0	(25.7)	13	(13.2)	5	(12.3)	c	c		c
Roraima	21.8	(13.1)	47.6	(12.0)	30.6	(5.4)	15	(9.7)	11	(9.4)	91	(7.1)	7	(8.3)
Santa Catarina	c	c	60.2	(15.4)	39.8	(15.4)	29	(23.9)	20	(22.4)	c	c		c
São Paulo	9.1	(4.8)	45.2	(6.8)	45.7	(6.4)	6	(8.5)	3	(8.1)	68	(12.0)	5	(10.5)
Sergipe	8.6	(8.6)	48.5	(13.5)	42.9	(12.6)	19	(11.1)	16	(12.0)	53	(23.9)	4	(23.9)
Tocantins	18.8	(11.3)	21.5	(21.4)	59.6	(23.2)	9	(13.8)	3	(14.5)	84	(13.9)	7	(14.1)
Colombia														
Bogotá	9.8	(2.9)	52.6	(8.5)	37.7	(8.4)	**28**	(8.5)	22	(8.9)	29	(7.8)	20	(6.7)
Cali	8.2	(4.2)	41.2	(7.0)	50.5	(7.7)	c	c	c	c	57	(7.7)	4	(7.5)
Manizales	10.1	(2.3)	26.6	(6.6)	63.3	(7.1)	**26**	(5.3)	15	(6.4)	47	(8.4)	26	(6.9)
Medellín	13.6	(4.3)	40.0	(7.5)	46.4	(7.2)	14	(8.6)	9	(8.6)	72	(13.2)	39	(9.8)
Russian Federation														
Perm Territory region●	8.4	(5.7)	55.0	(10.0)	36.5	(8.8)	**42**	(11.2)	31	(11.6)	56	(14.8)	44	(14.3)
United Arab Emirates														
Abu Dhabi●	13.8	(4.2)	36.7	(4.9)	49.5	(4.7)	**31**	(9.3)	24	(8.6)	50	(11.3)	40	(10.9)
Ajman	49.4	(12.4)	50.6	(12.4)	c	c	**37**	(15.2)	27	(15.4)	c	c		c
Dubai●	10.4	(0.1)	35.0	(0.3)	54.7	(0.3)	**63**	(3.5)	**53**	(3.8)	48	(3.0)	37	(3.3)
Fujairah	32.7	(10.1)	67.3	(10.1)	c	c	23	(19.0)	17	(18.1)	c	c		c
Ras al-Khaimah	43.3	(13.0)	43.4	(10.8)	13.4	(3.0)	6	(12.0)	-7	(10.2)	26	(10.5)	18	(10.8)
Sharjah	5.6	(5.3)	44.5	(10.5)	49.9	(10.8)	c	c	c	c	39	(23.9)	29	(23.5)
Umm al-Quwain	c	c	c	c	c	c	**40**	(7.6)	35	(7.7)	c	c		c

● PISA adjudicated region.
Notes: Values that are statistically significant are indicated in bold (see Annex A3).
See Table II.4.2 for national data.
1. ESCS refers to the *PISA index of economic, social and cultural status*.
2. Advantaged (disadvantaged) schools are those where the typical student in the school, or the socio-economic profile of the school, is above (below) the ESCS of the typical student in the country, the country mean ESCS. In each school, a random sample of 35 students are to take part in PISA (for more details see the *PISA 2012 Technical Report* [OECD, forthcoming]). The socio-economic profile of the school is calculated using the information provided by these students. Therefore, the precision of the estimate depends on the number of students that actually take the test in the school and the diversity of their answers. This precision was taken into account when classifying schools as advantaged, disadvantaged or average. If the difference between the school socio-economic profile and the ESCS of the typical student in the country (the mean ESCS at the country level) was not statistically significant, the school was classified as a school with an average socio-economic profile. If the school profile was statistically significantly above the country mean, the school is classified as a socio-economically advantaged school. If the profile was below the country mean, the school is classified as a socio-economically disadvantaged school.
StatLink ━━◈━ http://dx.doi.org/10.1787/888932964965

[Part 7/8]

Table B2.II.15 Mathematics performance and student population, by schools' socio-economic profile and region

Results based on students' self-reports

OECD

	Relative risk and population relevance of scoring in the bottom quarter of the performance distribution												Effect size					
	Students in socio-economically disadvantaged schools[2]				Students in socio-economically average schools[2]				Students in socio-economically advantaged schools[2]				Mean among students in socio-economically disadvantaged schools[2]		Mean among students in socio-economically average schools[2]		Mean among students in socio-economically advantaged schools[2]	
	Relative risk	S.E.	Population relevance	S.E.	Relative risk	S.E.	Population relevance	S.E.	Relative risk	S.E.	Population relevance	S.E.	Effect size	S.E.	Effect size	S.E.	Effect size	S.E.
Australia																		
Australian Capital Territory	c	c	c	c	**2.0**	(0.3)	**25.5**	(5.2)	0.5	(0.1)	-51.4	(10.3)	c	c	**-0.54**	(0.06)	**0.54**	(0.06)
New South Wales	**2.3**	(0.2)	**23.3**	(4.0)	1.0	(0.1)	-1.6	(6.2)	0.3	(0.1)	-23.4	(4.0)	**-0.73**	(0.09)	-0.12	(0.09)	**0.82**	(0.12)
Northern Territory	**2.1**	(0.4)	**20.0**	(6.6)	0.9	(0.4)	-7.3	(24.9)	c	c	c	c	**-0.58**	(0.17)	0.01	(0.23)	c	c
Queensland	**2.3**	(0.3)	**27.1**	(5.1)	0.8	(0.1)	-12.0	(6.4)	0.3	(0.1)	-16.8	(3.1)	**-0.72**	(0.07)	0.08	(0.08)	**0.77**	(0.07)
South Australia	**1.9**	(0.2)	**21.2**	(4.7)	0.9	(0.1)	-5.4	(7.6)	0.3	(0.1)	-14.9	(3.5)	**-0.49**	(0.08)	-0.02	(0.09)	**0.77**	(0.11)
Tasmania	**2.4**	(0.4)	**36.5**	(5.4)	0.7	(0.1)	-13.5	(5.1)	0.2	(0.1)	-16.3	(2.6)	**-0.61**	(0.07)	0.10	(0.07)	**0.93**	(0.10)
Victoria	**1.8**	(0.2)	**11.3**	(2.0)	**1.3**	(0.2)	**14.7**	(6.6)	0.3	(0.1)	-19.9	(4.0)	**-0.54**	(0.08)	**-0.24**	(0.09)	**0.76**	(0.09)
Western Australia	**2.2**	(0.3)	**26.4**	(4.7)	1.0	(0.1)	-1.1	(5.1)	0.3	(0.1)	-25.1	(5.3)	**-0.72**	(0.09)	-0.05	(0.08)	**0.81**	(0.09)
Belgium																		
Flemish Community•	c	c	c	c	1.0	(0.1)	-1.2	(4.5)	0.1	(0.0)	-44.2	(4.9)	**-1.16**	(0.09)	**-0.17**	(0.08)	**1.30**	(0.10)
French Community	**4.6**	(0.6)	**53.5**	(5.5)	0.6	(0.1)	-14.5	(5.0)	0.1	(0.0)	-40.3	(5.4)	**-1.31**	(0.08)	0.11	(0.09)	**1.13**	(0.08)
German-speaking Community	c	c	c	c	c	c	c	c	c	c	c	c	c	c	c	c	c	c
Canada																		
Alberta	**2.0**	(0.4)	**7.0**	(3.4)	**1.5**	(0.3)	**25.9**	(11.0)	0.4	(0.1)	-21.4	(4.9)	**-0.52**	(0.21)	**-0.48**	(0.12)	**0.76**	(0.09)
British Columbia	**1.6**	(0.2)	**10.3**	(4.1)	1.2	(0.2)	**7.0**	(6.7)	0.5	(0.1)	-17.1	(5.1)	**-0.34**	(0.12)	-0.18	(0.10)	**0.48**	(0.09)
Manitoba	**1.7**	(0.2)	**16.3**	(4.9)	0.9	(0.1)	-7.7	(7.2)	0.4	(0.1)	-9.9	(1.6)	**-0.47**	(0.10)	0.07	(0.08)	**0.59**	(0.09)
New Brunswick	**1.4**	(0.2)	**10.5**	(3.7)	1.1	(0.2)	6.1	(6.9)	0.5	(0.2)	-14.3	(5.0)	**-0.28**	(0.07)	**-0.19**	(0.06)	**0.57**	(0.11)
Newfoundland and Labrador	**2.4**	(0.3)	**27.1**	(5.1)	0.7	(0.1)	-17.9	(6.7)	0.4	(0.1)	-14.4	(2.9)	**-0.73**	(0.09)	**0.19**	(0.09)	**0.54**	(0.08)
Nova Scotia	1.1	(0.2)	3.3	(4.5)	0.9	(0.1)	-3.7	(9.5)	0.9	(0.2)	-1.3	(2.9)	-0.17	(0.10)	0.02	(0.10)	0.22	(0.12)
Ontario	**1.6**	(0.2)	**12.6**	(3.9)	1.1	(0.1)	4.6	(5.9)	0.5	(0.1)	-16.8	(4.8)	**-0.42**	(0.10)	-0.13	(0.09)	**0.52**	(0.10)
Prince Edward Island	1.2	(0.1)	**9.0**	(4.5)	1.0	(0.1)	1.2	(3.4)	c	c	c	c	**-0.19**	(0.05)	-0.06	(0.06)	c	c
Quebec	**1.9**	(0.2)	**19.2**	(3.9)	1.1	(0.1)	**6.6**	(6.1)	0.2	(0.1)	-23.4	(3.5)	**-0.55**	(0.08)	**-0.18**	(0.08)	**0.87**	(0.10)
Saskatchewan	1.3	(0.2)	3.2	(2.7)	1.1	(0.1)	4.8	(9.5)	0.7	(0.1)	-4.8	(2.0)	**-0.23**	(0.10)	-0.01	(0.07)	**0.22**	(0.07)
Italy																		
Abruzzo	**2.1**	(0.6)	**9.8**	(7.2)	2.0	(0.9)	**38.6**	(21.6)	0.1	(0.0)	-30.5	(6.1)	**-0.70**	(0.26)	**-0.55**	(0.23)	**1.08**	(0.18)
Basilicata	**3.0**	(0.7)	**47.1**	(10.5)	0.6	(0.2)	-15.9	(7.0)	0.2	(0.1)	-19.1	(2.5)	**-0.87**	(0.12)	0.23	(0.13)	**1.00**	(0.10)
Bolzano	**2.5**	(0.2)	**26.8**	(2.9)	0.9	(0.1)	-7.8	(5.5)	0.3	(0.1)	-21.2	(2.6)	**-0.78**	(0.05)	0.03	(0.05)	**0.80**	(0.07)
Calabria	**2.8**	(0.8)	**43.0**	(11.0)	0.7	(0.2)	-12.8	(11.4)	0.1	(0.1)	-20.8	(5.2)	**-0.83**	(0.15)	0.19	(0.18)	**1.00**	(0.17)
Campania	**4.0**	(1.2)	**56.5**	(9.5)	0.6	(0.2)	-13.7	(7.6)	0.1	(0.1)	-30.2	(11.5)	**-1.11**	(0.16)	0.17	(0.17)	**1.21**	(0.15)
Emilia Romagna	**3.3**	(0.7)	**36.3**	(8.5)	0.8	(0.2)	-8.5	(9.3)	0.2	(0.1)	-32.1	(7.7)	**-1.08**	(0.16)	-0.15	(0.14)	**1.21**	(0.16)
Friuli Venezia Giulia	**2.9**	(0.7)	**27.5**	(10.3)	1.2	(0.4)	7.1	(11.7)	0.3	(0.1)	-46.7	(7.7)	**-1.01**	(0.26)	-0.21	(0.19)	**0.88**	(0.12)
Lazio	**2.6**	(0.5)	**14.7**	(6.8)	**1.7**	(0.5)	**23.9**	(11.4)	0.3	(0.1)	-50.2	(11.5)	**-1.14**	(0.13)	**-0.61**	(0.18)	**1.07**	(0.19)
Liguria	**2.9**	(0.5)	**20.6**	(5.5)	1.3	(0.3)	**12.7**	(11.0)	0.2	(0.1)	-36.7	(9.4)	**-1.10**	(0.13)	**-0.35**	(0.16)	**0.98**	(0.15)
Lombardia	**2.6**	(0.6)	**26.0**	(8.4)	1.3	(0.3)	**11.5**	(9.8)	0.2	(0.1)	-42.0	(11.1)	**-0.77**	(0.21)	**-0.36**	(0.15)	**1.04**	(0.16)
Marche	**3.1**	(0.6)	**30.4**	(7.9)	0.7	(0.2)	-14.3	(10.3)	0.4	(0.1)	-23.9	(6.3)	**-1.05**	(0.18)	0.04	(0.16)	**0.72**	(0.19)
Molise	**2.5**	(0.3)	**35.8**	(4.8)	1.0	(0.1)	-0.9	(4.2)	0.2	(0.1)	-30.5	(2.6)	**-0.81**	(0.07)	**-0.13**	(0.06)	**1.17**	(0.08)
Piemonte	**2.6**	(0.5)	**29.8**	(6.1)	0.9	(0.1)	-7.3	(7.3)	0.2	(0.1)	-24.5	(6.5)	**-0.86**	(0.14)	0.01	(0.11)	**0.85**	(0.13)
Puglia	**3.7**	(0.8)	**56.4**	(7.7)	0.4	(0.1)	-26.2	(8.4)	0.1	(0.0)	-15.7	(4.6)	**-0.97**	(0.14)	**0.55**	(0.16)	**0.80**	(0.11)
Sardegna	**3.1**	(0.8)	**37.6**	(8.9)	0.7	(0.2)	-20.4	(12.2)	0.1	(0.0)	-21.5	(5.5)	**-0.91**	(0.22)	0.06	(0.15)	**1.12**	(0.12)
Sicilia	**2.9**	(0.7)	**38.9**	(9.3)	0.8	(0.2)	-8.2	(9.7)	0.1	(0.1)	-28.1	(7.8)	**-0.91**	(0.15)	0.04	(0.17)	**1.05**	(0.15)
Toscana	**4.1**	(1.0)	**48.1**	(9.7)	0.8	(0.3)	-6.3	(8.8)	0.2	(0.1)	-48.0	(10.3)	**-1.15**	(0.20)	0.03	(0.19)	**0.98**	(0.17)
Trento	**3.5**	(0.7)	**33.8**	(8.5)	0.6	(0.2)	-22.1	(9.9)	0.4	(0.1)	-22.4	(4.8)	**-1.15**	(0.19)	0.13	(0.13)	**0.69**	(0.12)
Umbria	**3.4**	(0.6)	**19.5**	(9.2)	1.2	(0.4)	8.8	(16.0)	0.3	(0.1)	-38.4	(6.2)	**-1.41**	(0.21)	-0.30	(0.20)	**0.83**	(0.13)
Valle d'Aosta	**1.5**	(0.2)	**16.4**	(6.7)	1.1	(0.2)	4.9	(6.6)	c	c	c	c	**-0.39**	(0.06)	-0.12	(0.07)	c	c
Veneto	**4.7**	(1.3)	**53.1**	(10.7)	0.5	(0.1)	-30.1	(10.5)	0.2	(0.1)	-27.0	(8.2)	**-1.22**	(0.19)	0.24	(0.18)	**0.97**	(0.21)
Mexico																		
Aguascalientes	**2.4**	(0.4)	**17.1**	(7.6)	1.0	(0.2)	0.4	(7.6)	0.5	(0.1)	-27.7	(7.9)	**-0.86**	(0.16)	-0.15	(0.13)	**0.55**	(0.14)
Baja California	c	c	c	c	1.4	(0.6)	**15.2**	(18.4)	0.7	(0.3)	-17.3	(21.0)	c	c	-0.37	(0.26)	0.35	(0.26)
Baja California Sur	**2.3**	(0.5)	**17.8**	(8.1)	1.5	(0.3)	**13.8**	(9.1)	0.4	(0.1)	-47.5	(11.6)	**-0.75**	(0.19)	-0.29	(0.16)	**0.69**	(0.19)
Campeche	**1.7**	(0.4)	**18.6**	(10.0)	0.8	(0.2)	-9.1	(11.5)	0.4	(0.2)	-9.2	(2.5)	**-0.39**	(0.16)	-0.01	(0.16)	**0.68**	(0.24)
Chiapas	**4.0**	(1.2)	**66.9**	(11.4)	0.3	(0.1)	-19.0	(7.2)	c	c	c	c	**-0.81**	(0.19)	**0.55**	(0.21)	c	c
Chihuahua	1.8	(0.6)	**12.5**	(9.2)	1.6	(0.6)	**20.4**	(16.6)	0.3	(0.1)	-35.0	(16.5)	**-0.59**	(0.24)	-0.42	(0.24)	**0.84**	(0.19)
Coahuila	1.9	(0.6)	**13.2**	(8.3)	1.5	(0.4)	**17.1**	(11.8)	0.4	(0.1)	-37.1	(15.2)	**-0.58**	(0.28)	**-0.43**	(0.18)	**0.78**	(0.19)
Colima	**3.1**	(0.6)	**24.8**	(10.5)	1.3	(0.4)	10.0	(12.3)	0.3	(0.1)	-50.8	(12.6)	**-1.12**	(0.14)	-0.29	(0.21)	**0.85**	(0.18)
Distrito Federal	c	c	c	c	1.4	(0.4)	**14.6**	(15.1)	0.4	(0.1)	-34.3	(10.1)	c	c	**-0.47**	(0.22)	**0.82**	(0.12)
Durango	**2.0**	(0.5)	**19.3**	(9.3)	1.1	(0.3)	3.9	(13.5)	0.4	(0.2)	-26.3	(8.9)	**-0.59**	(0.18)	-0.17	(0.21)	**0.64**	(0.19)
Guanajuato	**3.1**	(0.8)	**52.4**	(10.6)	0.8	(0.2)	-4.2	(4.3)	0.1	(0.1)	-29.4	(8.4)	**-0.78**	(0.15)	0.05	(0.16)	**1.01**	(0.14)
Guerrero	**2.1**	(0.6)	**39.8**	(13.7)	0.5	(0.2)	-16.7	(8.2)	0.6	(0.4)	-4.2	(4.3)	**-0.56**	(0.16)	**0.38**	(0.19)	**0.55**	(0.25)
Hidalgo	2.0	(0.8)	**35.2**	(17.2)	0.9	(0.3)	-4.0	(10.1)	0.2	(0.1)	-15.3	(4.4)	**-0.62**	(0.22)	0.10	(0.23)	**0.99**	(0.23)
Jalisco	**1.7**	(0.3)	**18.2**	(8.0)	1.3	(0.4)	**10.2**	(10.3)	0.3	(0.1)	-28.2	(8.9)	**-0.47**	(0.13)	-0.19	(0.21)	**0.68**	(0.13)
Mexico	1.5	(0.4)	**10.9**	(9.0)	1.1	(0.3)	4.0	(13.7)	0.5	(0.2)	-13.7	(7.1)	-0.33	(0.21)	-0.17	(0.20)	**0.54**	(0.22)
Morelos	**2.8**	(0.6)	**27.4**	(11.0)	1.2	(0.4)	7.8	(14.6)	0.2	(0.1)	-40.5	(11.5)	**-1.03**	(0.20)	-0.30	(0.22)	**1.08**	(0.17)
Nayarit	**1.7**	(0.4)	**12.2**	(6.9)	1.4	(0.3)	**15.8**	(12.0)	0.3	(0.1)	-24.2	(6.8)	-0.42	(0.23)	-0.27	(0.16)	**0.72**	(0.15)
Nuevo León	c	c	c	c	**2.2**	(0.4)	**27.3**	(9.5)	0.4	(0.1)	-68.0	(20.4)	c	c	**-0.82**	(0.12)	**0.90**	(0.12)
Puebla	**3.2**	(0.8)	**55.9**	(10.5)	0.5	(0.2)	-11.1	(6.5)	0.2	(0.1)	-18.2	(6.1)	**-0.73**	(0.16)	0.34	(0.18)	**0.75**	(0.12)
Querétaro	**1.9**	(0.4)	**20.9**	(9.1)	1.0	(0.3)	0.8	(7.9)	0.5	(0.1)	-26.4	(9.3)	**-0.60**	(0.17)	-0.14	(0.16)	**0.62**	(0.22)
Quintana Roo	**1.8**	(0.4)	**14.9**	(9.6)	1.6	(0.6)	**20.5**	(15.1)	0.2	(0.1)	-36.0	(9.9)	**-0.53**	(0.15)	**-0.44**	(0.20)	**0.94**	(0.11)
San Luis Potosí	**2.8**	(0.9)	**44.7**	(14.5)	0.9	(0.2)	-4.2	(6.4)	0.2	(0.1)	-29.2	(9.4)	**-0.84**	(0.19)	-0.03	(0.18)	**1.13**	(0.17)
Sinaloa	1.2	(0.3)	3.3	(5.1)	**2.2**	(0.5)	**35.2**	(9.5)	0.3	(0.1)	-34.2	(8.8)	-0.21	(0.17)	**-0.66**	(0.13)	**0.85**	(0.12)
Tabasco	**2.0**	(0.5)	**29.7**	(12.3)	1.0	(0.3)	-1.0	(9.1)	0.2	(0.1)	-21.9	(6.4)	**-0.51**	(0.16)	-0.08	(0.17)	**0.81**	(0.13)
Tamaulipas	**1.7**	(0.4)	**10.6**	(7.5)	1.4	(0.4)	**13.3**	(13.4)	0.5	(0.2)	-29.2	(11.4)	**-0.49**	(0.18)	**-0.43**	(0.20)	**0.70**	(0.15)
Tlaxcala	**2.4**	(0.4)	**32.7**	(7.8)	0.7	(0.1)	-17.4	(6.3)	0.4	(0.1)	-13.9	(4.3)	**-0.68**	(0.10)	**0.27**	(0.11)	**0.53**	(0.12)
Veracruz	**2.1**	(0.6)	**39.4**	(16.8)	0.8	(0.3)	-4.7	(5.1)	0.4	(0.2)	-15.2	(5.5)	**-0.52**	(0.20)	0.13	(0.22)	**0.62**	(0.26)
Yucatán	**2.0**	(0.4)	**29.7**	(12.1)	0.9	(0.3)	-3.7	(7.4)	0.4	(0.2)	-21.8	(8.2)	**-0.53**	(0.15)	-0.06	(0.17)	**0.63**	(0.22)
Zacatecas	**2.2**	(0.4)	**27.2**	(9.4)	0.8	(0.2)	-11.9	(9.9)	0.3	(0.1)	-15.7	(4.4)	**-0.62**	(0.14)	0.09	(0.14)	**0.70**	(0.13)

• PISA adjudicated region.

Notes: Values that are statistically significant are indicated in bold (see Annex A3).

See Table II.4.2 for national data.

1. ESCS refers to the *PISA index of economic, social and cultural status*.

2. Advantaged (disadvantaged) schools are those where the typical student in the school, or the socio-economic profile of the school, is above (below) the ESCS of the typical student in the country, the country mean ESCS. In each school, a random sample of 35 students are to take part in PISA (for more details see the *PISA 2012 Technical Report* [OECD, forthcoming]). The socio-economic profile of the school is calculated using the information provided by these students. Therefore, the precision of the estimate depends on the number of students that actually take the test in the school and the diversity of their answers. This precision was taken into account when classifying schools as advantaged, disadvantaged or average. If the difference between the school socio-economic profile and the ESCS of the typical student in the country (the mean ESCS at the country level) was not statistically significant, the school was classified as a school with an average socio-economic profile. If the school profile was statistically significantly above the country mean, the school is classified as a socio-economically advantaged school. If the profile was below the country mean, the school is classified as a socio-economically disadvantaged school.

StatLink http://dx.doi.org/10.1787/888932964965

[Part 8/8]

Table B2.II.15 Mathematics performance and student population, by schools' socio-economic profile and region

Results based on students' self-reports

	Relative risk and population relevance of scoring in the bottom quarter of the performance distribution												Effect size					
	Students in socio-economically disadvantaged schools²				Students in socio-economically average schools²				Students in socio-economically advantaged schools²				Mean among students in socio-economically disadvantaged schools²		Mean among students in socio-economically average schools²		Mean among students in socio-economically advantaged schools²	
	Relative risk	S.E.	Population relevance	S.E.	Relative risk	S.E.	Population relevance	S.E.	Relative risk	S.E.	Population relevance	S.E.	Effect size	S.E.	Effect size	S.E.	Effect size	S.E.
OECD																		
Portugal																		
Alentejo	**3.7**	(1.1)	**37.8**	(11.8)	0.7	(0.2)	-16.1	(17.2)	0.3	(0.1)	-29.7	(17.7)	**-1.12**	(0.27)	0.11	(0.25)	**.75**	(0.18)
Spain																		
Andalusia•	**2.0**	(0.3)	**31.4**	(7.5)	0.7	(0.1)	-14.1	(6.4)	0.5	(0.1)	-10.7	(4.7)	**-0.52**	(0.09)	0.22	(0.12)	**.47**	(0.11)
Aragon•	**2.2**	(0.3)	**23.2**	(5.4)	1.0	(0.2)	-1.1	(7.1)	0.4	(0.1)	-25.7	(6.0)	**-0.61**	(0.10)	-0.06	(0.11)	**.60**	(0.11)
Asturias•	**1.7**	(0.3)	**11.2**	(5.3)	1.3	(0.2)	**13.3**	(8.8)	0.4	(0.1)	-23.8	(5.4)	**-0.48**	(0.15)	**-0.24**	(0.11)	**.61**	(0.09)
Balearic Islands•	**2.0**	(0.3)	**16.4**	(5.3)	1.0	(0.1)	-2.7	(9.1)	0.3	(0.1)	-15.3	(3.8)	**-0.58**	(0.13)	0.05	(0.11)	**.53**	(0.12)
Basque Country•	**2.4**	(0.3)	**13.0**	(2.0)	1.1	(0.1)	3.4	(4.3)	0.5	(0.0)	-22.2	(3.8)	**-0.82**	(0.13)	**-0.12**	(0.06)	**.47**	(0.06)
Cantabria•	1.1	(0.1)	0.8	(1.2)	**1.6**	(0.3)	**28.7**	(9.9)	0.5	(0.1)	-11.6	(4.6)	-0.12	(0.11)	**-0.30**	(0.09)	**.46**	(0.10)
Castile and Leon•	1.2	(0.2)	3.4	(3.1)	**1.6**	(0.3)	**22.3**	(8.2)	0.5	(0.1)	-21.9	(6.7)	**-0.25**	(0.10)	**-0.27**	(0.11)	**.44**	(0.10)
Catalonia•	**2.2**	(0.3)	**22.0**	(6.2)	1.1	(0.2)	3.5	(9.4)	0.4	(0.1)	-28.6	(7.9)	**-0.69**	(0.11)	-0.17	(0.13)	**.75**	(0.12)
Extremadura•	**1.7**	(0.2)	**27.4**	(6.6)	0.9	(0.2)	-2.9	(5.0)	0.2	(0.1)	-12.9	(4.1)	**-0.40**	(0.08)	-0.01	(0.09)	**.87**	(0.09)
Galicia•	**1.6**	(0.2)	**14.9**	(6.1)	1.1	(0.2)	4.7	(6.3)	0.4	(0.1)	-17.9	(5.0)	**-0.35**	(0.11)	-0.12	(0.09)	**.54**	(0.09)
La Rioja•	**1.5**	(0.1)	**10.6**	(2.6)	**1.3**	(0.1)	**10.4**	(4.5)	0.5	(0.1)	-19.3	(2.6)	**-0.37**	(0.05)	**-0.17**	(0.05)	**.56**	(0.05)
Madrid•	**2.1**	(0.3)	**15.5**	(4.7)	1.2	(0.2)	**6.6**	(6.2)	0.5	(0.1)	-30.2	(7.8)	**-0.62**	(0.13)	-0.15	(0.10)	**.51**	(0.09)
Murcia•	**1.6**	(0.2)	**23.0**	(8.0)	0.7	(0.1)	-16.6	(7.9)	c	c	c	c	**-0.40**	(0.12)	**0.31**	(0.13)	c	c
Navarre•	**1.4**	(0.1)	**8.8**	(2.9)	**1.3**	(0.1)	**12.4**	(5.9)	0.4	(0.1)	-17.2	(3.3)	**-0.36**	(0.06)	-0.13	(0.07)	**.52**	(0.08)
United Kingdom																		
England	**2.1**	(0.3)	**20.7**	(5.3)	1.1	(0.2)	3.0	(7.8)	0.3	(0.0)	-23.2	(3.3)	**-0.67**	(0.12)	-0.15	(0.11)	**.87**	(0.08)
Northern Ireland	**3.3**	(0.4)	**39.6**	(6.3)	1.0	(0.2)	-0.8	(7.4)	0.1	(0.0)	-40.0	(5.3)	**-1.19**	(0.09)	-0.22	(0.13)	**.52**	(0.11)
Scotland•	**1.9**	(0.2)	**21.8**	(4.6)	0.8	(0.1)	-15.8	(6.6)	0.3	(0.1)	-9.1	(2.5)	**-0.54**	(0.07)	**0.16**	(0.08)	**.68**	(0.10)
Wales	**1.7**	(0.2)	**15.2**	(3.4)	0.8	(0.1)	-13.7	(7.4)	0.4	(0.1)	-7.4	(1.8)	**-0.47**	(0.06)	0.13	(0.07)	**.53**	(0.07)
United States																		
Connecticut•	**2.7**	(0.4)	**29.4**	(7.0)	0.9	(0.2)	-2.7	(8.2)	0.3	(0.1)	-30.2	(7.5)	**-0.84**	(0.13)	-0.06	(0.13)	**.80**	(0.11)
Florida•	**2.0**	(0.3)	**18.9**	(6.4)	1.1	(0.2)	2.8	(11.9)	0.3	(0.2)	-21.0	(9.4)	**-0.60**	(0.10)	-0.07	(0.15)	**.69**	(0.15)
Massachusetts•	**2.1**	(0.4)	**23.2**	(7.0)	1.1	(0.2)	3.7	(7.3)	0.3	(0.1)	-28.5	(8.9)	**-0.75**	(0.14)	-0.17	(0.13)	**.86**	(0.13)
Partners																		
Argentina																		
Ciudad Autónoma de Buenos Aires•	**4.5**	(1.1)	**42.1**	(11.7)	1.6	(0.6)	**10.6**	(9.6)	0.1	(0.0)	-106.0	(19.2)	**-1.42**	(0.21)	-0.49	(0.26)	**.39**	(0.13)
Brazil																		
Acre	**1.8**	(0.5)	**27.7**	(11.3)	0.8	(0.2)	-5.9	(8.0)	0.4	(0.1)	-13.4	(5.9)	**-0.50**	(0.18)	-0.02	(0.16)	**.85**	(0.22)
Alagoas	1.6	(1.1)	**28.9**	(26.5)	c	c	c	c	c	c	c	c	**-0.63**	(0.29)	c	c	c	c
Amapá	c	c	c	c	**3.1**	(0.8)	**53.7**	(11.5)	0.3	(0.1)	-39.6	(14.3)	c	c	**-0.82**	(0.18)	**.88**	(0.19)
Amazonas	c	c	c	c	**2.5**	(1.0)	**52.4**	(22.0)	0.4	(0.2)	-12.8	(6.9)	c	c	**-0.62**	(0.21)	**.73**	(0.23)
Bahia	**4.2**	(1.9)	**68.8**	(18.1)	c	c	c	c	c	c	c	c	**-1.09**	(0.26)	c	c	c	c
Ceará	2.0	(0.9)	**40.3**	(15.1)	c	c	c	c	c	c	c	c	**-0.73**	(0.20)	c	c	c	c
Espírito Santo	1.3	(0.5)	10.8	(14.6)	1.8	(0.6)	**25.0**	(15.7)	c	c	c	c	-0.49	(0.27)	**-0.75**	(0.17)	c	c
Federal District	c	c	c	c	**8.1**	(4.7)	**77.5**	(10.9)	0.1	(0.1)	-67.1	(23.0)	c	c	**-1.44**	(0.24)	**.48**	(0.25)
Goiás	**1.9**	(0.5)	**20.8**	(10.5)	0.9	(0.3)	-6.6	(18.3)	c	c	c	c	**-0.68**	(0.17)	-0.17	(0.23)	c	c
Maranhão	1.5	(0.8)	**18.0**	(17.4)	1.2	(0.4)	7.1	(17.3)	c	c	c	c	-0.51	(0.31)	-0.34	(0.32)	c	c
Mato Grosso	1.3	(0.5)	**12.9**	(16.0)	1.1	(0.4)	3.4	(14.1)	c	c	c	c	-0.34	(0.26)	-0.26	(0.24)	c	c
Mato Grosso do Sul	**2.4**	(0.8)	**29.5**	(12.6)	1.4	(0.4)	**10.3**	(11.0)	0.2	(0.1)	-43.6	(12.5)	**-0.73**	(0.21)	**-0.50**	(0.18)	**.21**	(0.17)
Minas Gerais	**1.9**	(0.4)	**27.5**	(10.7)	1.0	(0.2)	-0.1	(8.0)	0.2	(0.2)	-19.3	(9.8)	**-0.53**	(0.15)	-0.21	(0.16)	**.11**	(0.26)
Pará	**1.9**	(0.4)	**22.0**	(8.1)	1.0	(0.4)	1.7	(18.7)	c	c	c	c	**-0.69**	(0.16)	-0.10	(0.46)	c	c
Paraíba	**3.1**	(1.0)	**47.5**	(12.5)	1.1	(0.3)	2.4	(5.7)	0.2	(0.1)	-46.2	(16.0)	**-1.02**	(0.21)	-0.29	(0.16)	**31**	(0.28)
Paraná	**1.9**	(0.4)	**19.0**	(10.1)	1.2	(0.3)	8.9	(14.0)	0.2	(0.1)	-24.2	(7.8)	**-0.67**	(0.20)	-0.42	(0.25)	**31**	(0.48)
Pernambuco	**2.2**	(0.6)	**41.0**	(14.0)	0.5	(0.2)	-20.1	(13.7)	c	c	c	c	**-0.61**	(0.20)	0.33	(0.19)	c	c
Piauí	**2.2**	(0.6)	**35.4**	(13.8)	1.0	(0.4)	0.2	(10.3)	c	c	c	c	**-0.81**	(0.20)	-0.35	(0.19)	c	c
Rio de Janeiro	c	c	c	c	**7.1**	(5.3)	**82.2**	(9.2)	0.2	(0.1)	-18.8	(5.6)	c	c	**-1.28**	(0.24)	**28**	(0.24)
Rio Grande do Norte	**2.7**	(1.1)	**49.4**	(15.3)	1.0	(0.4)	0.8	(6.5)	0.1	(0.0)	-26.8	(7.9)	**-0.99**	(0.23)	**-0.40**	(0.19)	**87**	(0.44)
Rio Grande do Sul	1.7	(0.5)	**21.8**	(12.0)	1.0	(0.2)	0.1	(7.6)	0.4	(0.2)	-18.1	(6.7)	-0.46	(0.24)	-0.05	(0.20)	**61**	(0.21)
Rondônia	1.5	(0.4)	**18.6**	(11.6)	0.9	(0.3)	-2.7	(12.5)	c	c	c	c	-0.35	(0.20)	0.04	(0.21)	c	c
Roraima	**2.0**	(0.5)	**19.7**	(11.3)	1.1	(0.4)	6.1	(18.2)	0.1	(0.1)	-22.6	(6.9)	**-0.61**	(0.18)	**-0.48**	(0.24)	**46**	(0.13)
Santa Catarina	2.2	(1.0)	**26.7**	(16.7)	0.8	(0.4)	-14.0	(24.5)	c	c	c	c	-0.55	(0.33)	0.02	(0.28)	c	c
São Paulo	**1.6**	(0.3)	**9.2**	(5.7)	**1.7**	(0.4)	**24.2**	(10.1)	0.3	(0.1)	-32.0	(5.5)	**-0.50**	(0.13)	**-0.58**	(0.13)	**96**	(0.15)
Sergipe	**2.0**	(0.7)	**25.6**	(12.6)	1.0	(0.2)	0.9	(9.4)	0.3	(0.2)	-24.1	(12.9)	**-0.64**	(0.23)	-0.20	(0.20)	**93**	(0.35)
Tocantins	1.7	(0.6)	**23.1**	(14.9)	1.3	(0.5)	9.3	(14.4)	0.1	(0.0)	-24.3	(13.2)	**-0.54**	(0.20)	-0.30	(0.24)	**27**	(0.17)
Colombia																		
Bogotá	**2.0**	(0.3)	**8.3**	(3.5)	1.3	(0.2)	**12.1**	(10.0)	0.5	(0.1)	-20.4	(8.0)	**-0.63**	(0.15)	**-0.26**	(0.12)	**50**	(0.11)
Cali	c	c	c	c	**2.2**	(0.5)	**33.2**	(9.7)	0.3	(0.1)	-59.5	(16.4)	c	c	**-0.69**	(0.15)	**99**	(0.13)
Manizales	**2.6**	(0.3)	**19.4**	(3.8)	**1.6**	(0.2)	**12.7**	(4.9)	0.3	(0.1)	-67.5	(13.0)	**-0.93**	(0.07)	**-0.49**	(0.09)	**88**	(0.10)
Medellín	**2.0**	(0.3)	**13.4**	(4.8)	**1.7**	(0.3)	**23.4**	(8.7)	0.3	(0.1)	-43.4	(11.6)	**-0.69**	(0.13)	**-0.62**	(0.13)	**00**	(0.15)
Russian Federation																		
Perm Territory region•	**2.2**	(0.4)	**20.3**	(7.0)	1.0	(0.2)	0.9	(11.2)	0.3	(0.1)	-21.7	(4.9)	**-0.71**	(0.14)	-0.11	(0.13)	**80**	(0.14)
United Arab Emirates																		
Abu Dhabi•	**1.9**	(0.3)	**21.9**	(5.7)	1.0	(0.2)	1.8	(6.7)	0.4	(0.1)	-23.3	(4.2)	**-0.64**	(0.10)	-0.10	(0.11)	**75**	(0.11)
Ajman	**2.4**	(1.0)	**43.9**	(16.6)	0.4	(0.1)	-34.7	(9.5)	c	c	c	c	**-0.51**	(0.21)	**0.51**	(0.21)	c	c
Dubai•	**2.8**	(0.1)	**21.5**	(1.4)	**1.2**	(0.1)	**7.2**	(1.9)	0.4	(0.0)	-43.9	(2.3)	**-1.07**	(0.04)	**-0.23**	(0.03)	**75**	(0.03)
Fujairah	1.5	(0.8)	**24.7**	(25.0)	0.9	(0.3)	-1.8	(8.4)	c	c	c	c	-0.46	(0.32)	0.13	(0.16)	c	c
Ras al-Khaimah	1.2	(0.3)	7.5	(10.7)	1.0	(0.3)	-1.2	(14.5)	0.7	(0.1)	-4.5	(3.0)	-0.16	(0.14)	-0.02	(0.15)	**37**	(0.14)
Sharjah	c	c	c	c	1.5	(0.5)	**16.4**	(13.0)	0.5	(0.2)	-32.9	(17.2)	c	c	-0.35	(0.28)	54	(0.28)
Umm al-Quwain	**3.0**	(0.8)	**50.6**	(10.3)	0.3	(0.1)	-48.0	(9.8)	c	c	c	c	**-0.55**	(0.10)	**0.55**	(0.10)	c	c

• PISA adjudicated region.

Notes: Values that are statistically significant are indicated in bold (see Annex A3).

See Table II.4.2 for national data.

1. ESCS refers to the *PISA index of economic, social and cultural status*.

2. Advantaged (disadvantaged) schools are those where the typical student in the school, or the socio-economic profile of the school, is above (below) the ESCS of the typical student in the country, the country mean ESCS. In each school, a random sample of 35 students are to take part in PISA (for more details see the *PISA 2012 Technical Report* [OECD, forthcoming]). The socio-economic profile of the school is calculated using the information provided by these students. Therefore, the precision of the estimate depends on the number of students that actually take the test in the school and the diversity of their answers. This precision was taken into account when classifying schools as advantaged, disadvantaged or average. If the difference between the school socio-economic profile and the ESCS of the typical student in the country (the mean ESCS at the country level) was not statistically significant, the school was classified as a school with an average socio-economic profile. If the school profile was statistically significantly above the country mean, the school is classified as a socio-economically advantaged school. If the profile was below the country mean, the school is classified as a socio-economically disadvantaged school.

StatLink http://dx.doi.org/10.1787/888932964965

[Part 1/4]

Table B2.II.16 Inequity in access to instructional content: Formal mathematics, by region

Results based on students' self-reports

	Formal mathematics: Percentage of the variation explained by student ESCS[1] (%)	S.E.	Percentage of the variation explained by student and school mean ESCS (%)	S.E.	Percentage of the variation explained by student and school mean and standard deviation of ESCS (%)	S.E.	Mean among students in socio-economically disadvantaged schools[2], relative to the country mean ESCS (Mean index)	S.E.	Mean among students in socio-economically average schools[2], relative to the country mean ESCS (Mean index)	S.E.	Mean among students in socio-economically advantaged schools[2], relative to the country mean ESCS (Mean index)	S.E.	Difference between students in disadvantaged and average schools (Dif.)	S.E.	Difference between students in average and advantaged schools (Dif.)	S.E.	Mean among non-immigrant students (Mean index)	S.E.	Mean among immigrant students (Mean index)	S.E.
OECD																				
Australia																				
Australian Capital Territory	11.2	(3.0)	13.1	(2.9)	13.2	(2.9)	c	c	1.52	(0.05)	1.80	(0.04)	c	c	**0.27**	(0.06)	1.67	(0.04)	2.01	(0.09)
New South Wales	11.0	(1.5)	13.1	(1.9)	14.0	(1.8)	1.46	(0.05)	1.72	(0.04)	2.07	(0.05)	**0.26**	(0.06)	**0.34**	(0.07)	1.64	(0.02)	2.09	(0.04)
Northern Territory	14.3	(4.7)	15.9	(4.7)	15.9	(4.7)	1.13	(0.11)	1.40	(0.07)	c	c	**0.27**	(0.13)	c	c	1.39	(0.06)	1.40	(0.19)
Queensland	14.4	(1.7)	16.8	(1.8)	16.8	(1.8)	1.42	(0.03)	1.68	(0.03)	2.04	(0.05)	**0.26**	(0.04)	**0.36**	(0.06)	1.65	(0.02)	1.80	(0.05)
South Australia	9.1	(2.2)	12.8	(3.0)	12.7	(3.0)	1.31	(0.05)	1.53	(0.04)	1.90	(0.08)	**0.22**	(0.06)	**0.37**	(0.09)	1.49	(0.03)	1.77	(0.07)
Tasmania	15.4	(2.4)	17.4	(2.4)	17.5	(2.4)	1.21	(0.04)	1.45	(0.04)	1.82	(0.06)	**0.24**	(0.05)	**0.37**	(0.08)	1.38	(0.03)	1.83	(0.13)
Victoria	6.6	(1.0)	9.3	(1.6)	10.3	(1.7)	1.45	(0.06)	1.60	(0.03)	1.91	(0.06)	**0.15**	(0.07)	**0.31**	(0.06)	1.57	(0.02)	1.92	(0.06)
Western Australia	12.0	(1.9)	16.9	(2.6)	17.0	(2.5)	1.54	(0.05)	1.83	(0.06)	2.17	(0.06)	**0.29**	(0.07)	**0.34**	(0.08)	1.81	(0.04)	1.92	(0.06)
Belgium																				
Flemish Community•	15.5	(1.5)	24.2	(2.2)	24.5	(2.2)	1.30	(0.05)	1.63	(0.03)	2.16	(0.04)	**0.33**	(0.06)	**0.52**	(0.05)	1.78	(0.02)	1.41	(0.05)
French Community	12.3	(1.9)	16.4	(2.1)	16.4	(2.1)	1.64	(0.04)	2.00	(0.03)	2.19	(0.03)	**0.36**	(0.05)	**0.19**	(0.04)	2.00	(0.02)	1.85	(0.05)
German-speaking Community	6.1	(1.9)	10.0	(2.3)	10.4	(2.4)	c	c	1.43	(0.04)	c	c	c	c	c	c	1.57	(0.03)	1.40	(0.07)
Canada																				
Alberta	7.0	(1.8)	10.3	(2.2)	10.9	(2.2)	1.68	(0.10)	1.86	(0.03)	2.15	(0.04)	0.18	(0.11)	**0.29**	(0.04)	1.88	(0.03)	2.08	(0.04)
British Columbia	4.0	(1.2)	4.7	(1.8)	4.7	(1.9)	1.88	(0.07)	1.88	(0.03)	2.06	(0.04)	0.00	(0.07)	**0.18**	(0.06)	1.85	(0.03)	2.08	(0.04)
Manitoba	9.5	(2.2)	9.7	(2.2)	10.9	(2.4)	1.73	(0.05)	1.79	(0.03)	1.99	(0.05)	0.05	(0.05)	**0.21**	(0.06)	1.78	(0.03)	1.91	(0.06)
New Brunswick	4.8	(1.6)	5.6	(2.0)	5.6	(1.9)	1.66	(0.03)	1.65	(0.03)	1.91	(0.06)	-0.01	(0.04)	**0.27**	(0.07)	1.70	(0.02)	1.87	(0.15)
Newfoundland and Labrador	9.9	(2.9)	10.3	(2.2)	10.3	(2.2)	1.74	(0.08)	2.01	(0.03)	2.12	(0.04)	**0.27**	(0.08)	**0.11**	(0.05)	1.96	(0.02)	c	c
Nova Scotia	6.3	(1.8)	6.6	(1.7)	8.3	(1.9)	1.95	(0.06)	2.09	(0.07)	2.10	(0.07)	0.15	(0.09)	0.01	(0.11)	2.05	(0.05)	2.24	(0.10)
Ontario	7.5	(1.4)	8.0	(1.5)	8.4	(1.6)	1.90	(0.05)	2.03	(0.03)	2.22	(0.03)	**0.12**	(0.05)	**0.19**	(0.04)	1.99	(0.03)	2.14	(0.03)
Prince Edward Island	8.8	(2.0)	9.3	(2.0)	9.3	(2.0)	1.66	(0.03)	1.66	(0.04)	c	c	0.00	(0.05)	c	c	1.71	(0.02)	1.90	(0.09)
Quebec	6.2	(1.3)	8.6	(1.6)	8.6	(1.5)	1.83	(0.04)	1.96	(0.02)	2.20	(0.03)	**0.14**	(0.04)	**0.24**	(0.03)	1.98	(0.02)	2.02	(0.04)
Saskatchewan	5.7	(1.6)	5.7	(1.6)	5.7	(1.6)	1.77	(0.06)	1.85	(0.03)	1.94	(0.05)	0.08	(0.07)	0.09	(0.05)	1.84	(0.02)	2.04	(0.08)
Italy																				
Abruzzo	4.5	(1.3)	12.2	(3.9)	12.1	(3.9)	1.50	(0.12)	1.76	(0.04)	2.11	(0.08)	0.26	(0.14)	**0.35**	(0.08)	1.84	(0.04)	1.58	(0.09)
Basilicata	6.2	(1.6)	11.8	(2.4)	12.2	(2.3)	1.67	(0.04)	1.99	(0.07)	2.11	(0.05)	**0.32**	(0.08)	0.12	(0.08)	1.88	(0.03)	c	c
Bolzano	8.0	(1.7)	14.5	(1.9)	14.6	(2.1)	1.18	(0.03)	1.43	(0.02)	1.69	(0.04)	**0.25**	(0.04)	**0.26**	(0.04)	1.44	(0.02)	1.35	(0.10)
Calabria	6.0	(2.1)	12.1	(3.8)	13.2	(3.6)	1.58	(0.05)	1.81	(0.07)	2.11	(0.09)	**0.23**	(0.08)	**0.30**	(0.13)	1.79	(0.04)	1.50	(0.12)
Campania	8.5	(2.4)	15.3	(4.3)	16.2	(3.9)	1.52	(0.06)	1.82	(0.07)	2.08	(0.13)	**0.30**	(0.08)	0.26	(0.15)	1.77	(0.04)	c	c
Emilia Romagna	12.8	(2.9)	21.7	(5.2)	21.8	(5.3)	1.49	(0.10)	1.77	(0.04)	2.19	(0.06)	**0.27**	(0.12)	**0.43**	(0.08)	1.89	(0.04)	1.53	(0.05)
Friuli Venezia Giulia	7.5	(2.6)	15.1	(5.3)	15.2	(5.5)	1.56	(0.14)	1.85	(0.06)	2.12	(0.04)	0.29	(0.16)	**0.27**	(0.07)	1.93	(0.03)	1.66	(0.10)
Lazio	7.0	(2.5)	16.8	(5.2)	17.7	(4.9)	1.36	(0.08)	1.67	(0.06)	2.10	(0.08)	**0.31**	(0.10)	**0.43**	(0.10)	1.85	(0.04)	1.66	(0.11)
Liguria	7.7	(1.9)	19.7	(4.0)	20.6	(4.3)	1.39	(0.05)	1.83	(0.03)	2.14	(0.08)	**0.44**	(0.06)	**0.31**	(0.09)	1.92	(0.04)	1.63	(0.07)
Lombardia	5.7	(1.6)	10.1	(2.6)	10.1	(2.6)	1.68	(0.06)	1.79	(0.06)	2.12	(0.05)	0.12	(0.10)	**0.33**	(0.08)	1.91	(0.04)	1.67	(0.05)
Marche	2.0	(0.6)	4.9	(1.9)	11.1	(2.9)	1.64	(0.09)	1.81	(0.05)	2.00	(0.06)	0.17	(0.11)	**0.19**	(0.09)	1.86	(0.03)	1.62	(0.07)
Molise	8.8	(2.0)	19.7	(2.8)	21.1	(2.9)	1.64	(0.04)	1.76	(0.04)	2.32	(0.03)	**0.12**	(0.06)	**0.56**	(0.05)	1.89	(0.03)	c	c
Piemonte	5.4	(1.8)	9.2	(3.8)	15.3	(4.5)	1.61	(0.06)	1.80	(0.08)	2.07	(0.09)	0.19	(0.10)	**0.27**	(0.12)	1.82	(0.06)	1.82	(0.07)
Puglia	5.2	(2.1)	19.5	(4.5)	20.0	(4.5)	1.66	(0.05)	2.09	(0.06)	2.15	(0.11)	**0.44**	(0.07)	0.06	(0.13)	1.90	(0.04)	c	c
Sardegna	5.7	(1.9)	10.9	(2.9)	11.0	(3.0)	1.48	(0.08)	1.67	(0.05)	2.02	(0.10)	**0.20**	(0.10)	**0.34**	(0.12)	1.69	(0.04)	c	c
Sicilia	5.3	(1.9)	15.1	(3.7)	15.5	(3.7)	1.50	(0.04)	1.72	(0.08)	2.11	(0.08)	**0.23**	(0.10)	**0.39**	(0.11)	1.75	(0.04)	c	c
Toscana	8.4	(2.5)	14.2	(5.3)	14.6	(5.3)	1.48	(0.08)	1.85	(0.06)	2.04	(0.07)	**0.37**	(0.12)	**0.20**	(0.10)	1.88	(0.04)	1.40	(0.06)
Trento	2.9	(1.7)	8.5	(3.4)	8.6	(3.2)	1.46	(0.08)	1.88	(0.05)	2.02	(0.05)	**0.41**	(0.10)	0.14	(0.07)	1.85	(0.03)	1.63	(0.09)
Umbria	9.2	(3.0)	14.1	(3.9)	14.7	(4.2)	1.52	(0.05)	1.76	(0.05)	2.06	(0.04)	**0.24**	(0.07)	**0.30**	(0.07)	1.90	(0.03)	1.69	(0.05)
Valle d'Aosta	7.1	(2.3)	9.3	(2.2)	9.6	(2.2)	1.58	(0.04)	1.67	(0.03)	c	c	0.09	(0.06)	c	c	1.71	(0.02)	1.57	(0.09)
Veneto	9.0	(1.9)	19.1	(6.2)	19.9	(5.6)	1.60	(0.06)	2.00	(0.06)	2.27	(0.11)	**0.40**	(0.10)	**0.27**	(0.12)	1.99	(0.05)	1.63	(0.08)
Mexico																				
Aguascalientes	7.2	(2.5)	12.4	(4.1)	13.0	(4.0)	1.52	(0.05)	1.76	(0.07)	1.98	(0.07)	**0.24**	(0.09)	**0.22**	(0.10)	1.84	(0.05)	c	c
Baja California	4.3	(1.5)	5.4	(2.1)	6.4	(2.9)	c	c	1.72	(0.09)	1.86	(0.05)	c	c	0.14	(0.08)	1.80	(0.05)	c	c
Baja California Sur	6.7	(3.1)	9.0	(4.8)	10.1	(4.7)	1.46	(0.13)	1.55	(0.07)	1.72	(0.09)	0.09	(0.14)	0.18	(0.15)	1.63	(0.04)	c	c
Campeche	3.4	(1.7)	4.7	(2.0)	5.9	(2.0)	1.65	(0.07)	1.66	(0.06)	2.16	(0.07)	0.01	(0.10)	**0.50**	(0.10)	1.78	(0.03)	1.32	(0.09)
Chiapas	2.1	(1.5)	5.2	(2.0)	6.7	(2.5)	1.43	(0.04)	1.78	(0.09)	c	c	**0.35**	(0.10)	c	c	1.57	(0.04)	c	c
Chihuahua	4.1	(2.2)	7.8	(3.2)	8.4	(3.4)	1.70	(0.09)	1.69	(0.07)	2.04	(0.06)	-0.01	(0.12)	**0.35**	(0.10)	1.83	(0.05)	c	c
Coahuila	5.8	(3.1)	8.9	(5.5)	10.9	(6.0)	1.55	(0.20)	1.57	(0.05)	1.91	(0.09)	0.03	(0.21)	**0.33**	(0.10)	1.71	(0.05)	c	c
Colima	7.2	(3.2)	11.2	(5.4)	11.4	(5.7)	1.36	(0.12)	1.77	(0.05)	1.98	(0.07)	**0.41**	(0.14)	**0.21**	(0.09)	1.81	(0.04)	c	c
Distrito Federal	2.6	(1.5)	3.4	(1.9)	4.1	(2.2)	c	c	1.78	(0.04)	2.08	(0.05)	c	c	**0.30**	(0.06)	1.91	(0.04)	c	c
Durango	6.4	(2.0)	8.9	(2.4)	11.2	(2.9)	1.56	(0.10)	1.63	(0.07)	1.91	(0.06)	0.07	(0.13)	**0.28**	(0.10)	1.73	(0.03)	c	c
Guanajuato	5.6	(2.3)	7.3	(2.8)	8.0	(3.4)	1.55	(0.07)	1.63	(0.08)	1.92	(0.07)	0.07	(0.09)	**0.29**	(0.11)	1.68	(0.05)	c	c
Guerrero	3.1	(1.6)	3.4	(2.1)	4.1	(2.5)	1.46	(0.08)	1.67	(0.03)	1.62	(0.13)	**0.22**	(0.09)	-0.05	(0.14)	1.54	(0.05)	c	c
Hidalgo	7.2	(2.6)	10.4	(3.1)	10.8	(3.1)	1.73	(0.05)	1.85	(0.07)	2.19	(0.09)	0.12	(0.10)	**0.34**	(0.11)	1.85	(0.04)	c	c
Jalisco	5.0	(2.1)	5.5	(2.1)	5.8	(2.2)	1.62	(0.07)	1.65	(0.06)	1.93	(0.05)	0.04	(0.08)	**0.28**	(0.07)	1.74	(0.04)	c	c
Mexico	2.3	(1.1)	3.0	(1.4)	3.4	(1.9)	1.78	(0.05)	1.82	(0.05)	2.05	(0.06)	0.04	(0.08)	**0.22**	(0.08)	1.88	(0.03)	c	c
Morelos	8.1	(2.6)	11.7	(4.0)	13.8	(4.8)	1.54	(0.07)	1.67	(0.07)	2.06	(0.07)	0.13	(0.11)	**0.39**	(0.09)	1.78	(0.05)	c	c
Nayarit	1.8	(1.7)	2.5	(2.5)	6.6	(3.4)	1.55	(0.12)	1.56	(0.04)	1.75	(0.06)	0.01	(0.14)	**0.19**	(0.08)	1.63	(0.04)	c	c
Nuevo León	7.8	(4.8)	12.7	(7.1)	13.3	(7.8)	c	c	1.59	(0.06)	2.10	(0.06)	c	c	**0.51**	(0.10)	1.94	(0.05)	c	c
Puebla	8.6	(2.9)	11.1	(3.8)	12.2	(3.8)	1.68	(0.07)	1.88	(0.06)	2.11	(0.06)	**0.20**	(0.10)	**0.22**	(0.08)	1.82	(0.05)	c	c
Querétaro	8.2	(3.2)	11.2	(3.5)	11.2	(3.5)	1.64	(0.07)	1.76	(0.03)	2.03	(0.05)	0.12	(0.08)	**0.28**	(0.06)	1.85	(0.05)	c	c
Quintana Roo	4.9	(2.6)	6.9	(3.5)	10.2	(4.0)	1.66	(0.08)	1.65	(0.07)	1.96	(0.09)	-0.01	(0.10)	**0.31**	(0.12)	1.77	(0.03)	c	c
San Luis Potosí	12.3	(4.0)	16.3	(4.8)	16.4	(4.8)	1.40	(0.06)	1.81	(0.06)	2.06	(0.06)	**0.40**	(0.11)	**0.26**	(0.08)	1.71	(0.06)	c	c
Sinaloa	4.1	(2.6)	6.4	(3.9)	8.5	(3.8)	1.69	(0.07)	1.58	(0.06)	1.96	(0.06)	-0.10	(0.09)	**0.38**	(0.08)	1.75	(0.04)	c	c
Tabasco	6.1	(2.5)	9.5	(2.6)	10.8	(3.1)	1.43	(0.06)	1.70	(0.06)	1.92	(0.08)	**0.27**	(0.10)	**0.22**	(0.10)	1.66	(0.04)	c	c
Tamaulipas	2.8	(1.4)	6.3	(2.4)	7.4	(2.1)	1.44	(0.08)	1.65	(0.08)	1.83	(0.07)	0.21	(0.13)	0.18	(0.12)	1.71	(0.04)	c	c
Tlaxcala	2.3	(1.1)	5.3	(2.2)	6.7	(3.8)	1.69	(0.08)	1.84	(0.05)	2.04	(0.06)	0.15	(0.09)	**0.20**	(0.08)	1.85	(0.04)	c	c
Veracruz	5.0	(3.0)	5.4	(3.6)	7.1	(4.0)	1.77	(0.05)	1.78	(0.04)	2.05	(0.11)	0.01	(0.07)	**0.27**	(0.12)	1.84	(0.04)	c	c
Yucatán	7.2	(2.1)	9.1	(2.7)	10.0	(2.5)	1.67	(0.06)	1.78	(0.12)	2.03	(0.09)	0.11	(0.14)	0.25	(0.15)	1.83	(0.04)	c	c
Zacatecas	5.4	(1.4)	7.0	(2.1)	7.3	(2.5)	1.47	(0.07)	1.64	(0.05)	1.95	(0.06)	0.17	(0.09)	**0.31**	(0.08)	1.65	(0.03)	c	c

• PISA adjudicated region.

Notes: Values that are statistically significant are indicated in bold (see Annex A3).

See Table II.4.3 for national data.

1. ESCS refers to the *PISA index of economic, social and cultural status*.

2. A socio-economically disadvantaged school is one whose students' mean ESCS is statistically significantly below the mean ESCS of the country; an average school is one where there is no difference between the students' and the country's mean ESCS; and an advantaged school is one whose students' mean ESCS is statistically significantly above the country mean.

StatLink http://dx.doi.org/10.1787/888932964965

[Part 2/4]

Table B2.II.16 Inequity in access to instructional content: Formal mathematics, by region

Results based on students' self-reports

		Formal mathematics																			
		Percentage of the variation explained by student ESCS[1]		Percentage of the variation explained by student and school mean ESCS		Percentage of the variation explained by student and school mean and standard deviation of ESCS		Mean among students in socio-economically disadvantaged schools[2], relative to the country mean ESCS		Mean among students in socio-economically average schools[2], relative to the country mean ESCS		Mean among students in socio-economically advantaged schools[2], relative to the country mean ESCS		Difference between students in disadvantaged and average schools		Difference between students in average and advantaged schools		Mean among non-immigrant students		Mean among immigrant students	
		%	S.E.	%	S.E.	%	S.E.	Mean index	S.E.	Mean index	S.E.	Mean index	S.E.	Dif.	S.E.	Dif.	S.E.	Mean index	S.E.	Mean index	S.E.
OECD	**Portugal**																				
	Alentejo	6.3	(2.2)	6.3	(2.3)	6.9	(2.9)	1.69	(0.05)	1.71	(0.06)	1.85	(0.06)	0.02	(0.08)	0.14	(0.10)	1.73	(0.04)	c	c
	Spain																				
	Andalusia•	15.3	(2.1)	15.4	(2.2)	15.6	(2.1)	1.72	(0.04)	1.87	(0.05)	2.07	(0.06)	**0.14**	(0.07)	**0.21**	(0.08)	1.86	(0.03)	c	c
	Aragon•	16.6	(2.8)	18.2	(3.1)	18.4	(3.2)	1.68	(0.05)	1.84	(0.03)	2.17	(0.05)	**0.16**	(0.05)	**0.32**	(0.06)	2.00	(0.03)	1.40	(0.08)
	Asturias•	9.6	(2.7)	10.5	(3.3)	10.6	(3.3)	1.86	(0.06)	1.90	(0.04)	2.16	(0.06)	0.05	(0.07)	**0.26**	(0.07)	2.01	(0.03)	1.56	(0.06)
	Balearic Islands•	15.9	(2.0)	16.4	(2.0)	16.4	(2.0)	1.54	(0.07)	1.71	(0.03)	1.98	(0.09)	**0.17**	(0.07)	**0.28**	(0.10)	1.81	(0.03)	1.43	(0.05)
	Basque Country•	9.1	(1.2)	11.0	(1.4)	11.0	(1.5)	1.58	(0.06)	1.83	(0.02)	2.01	(0.03)	**0.26**	(0.06)	**0.18**	(0.04)	1.91	(0.02)	1.56	(0.05)
	Cantabria•	11.6	(1.8)	12.8	(1.8)	13.0	(1.7)	1.65	(0.04)	1.87	(0.03)	2.19	(0.05)	**0.23**	(0.05)	**0.32**	(0.05)	1.94	(0.03)	1.68	(0.09)
	Castile and Leon•	10.7	(2.3)	11.3	(2.4)	12.0	(2.4)	1.90	(0.06)	1.88	(0.04)	2.17	(0.04)	-0.02	(0.06)	**0.29**	(0.05)	2.02	(0.03)	1.67	(0.08)
	Catalonia•	12.2	(2.3)	13.9	(2.8)	13.9	(2.8)	1.59	(0.07)	1.84	(0.05)	2.12	(0.04)	**0.25**	(0.09)	**0.29**	(0.07)	1.92	(0.03)	1.63	(0.08)
	Extremadura•	12.9	(2.3)	13.9	(2.3)	14.0	(2.4)	1.68	(0.03)	1.80	(0.04)	2.16	(0.07)	**0.11**	(0.06)	**0.36**	(0.08)	1.79	(0.03)	1.84	(0.08)
	Galicia•	7.9	(2.0)	9.3	(2.1)	9.5	(2.1)	1.61	(0.06)	1.81	(0.03)	1.98	(0.06)	**0.21**	(0.06)	**0.17**	(0.06)	1.80	(0.03)	1.61	(0.09)
	La Rioja•	11.3	(1.7)	12.0	(1.7)	11.9	(1.7)	1.86	(0.04)	1.98	(0.03)	2.19	(0.03)	**0.12**	(0.06)	**0.21**	(0.04)	2.12	(0.02)	1.60	(0.05)
	Madrid•	14.5	(2.6)	14.8	(2.5)	14.8	(2.5)	1.76	(0.09)	1.93	(0.04)	2.18	(0.04)	0.17	(0.09)	**0.25**	(0.05)	2.07	(0.03)	1.71	(0.07)
	Murcia•	14.2	(2.7)	16.6	(2.8)	17.4	(3.0)	1.65	(0.04)	1.98	(0.04)	c	c	**0.34**	(0.05)	c	c	1.90	(0.02)	1.47	(0.09)
	Navarre•	10.0	(2.1)	10.5	(2.2)	11.9	(2.4)	1.78	(0.05)	1.92	(0.03)	2.12	(0.05)	**0.15**	(0.06)	**0.20**	(0.06)	2.01	(0.03)	1.57	(0.05)
	United Kingdom																				
	England	8.7	(1.2)	10.7	(1.8)	10.7	(1.7)	1.50	(0.07)	1.64	(0.02)	1.91	(0.04)	0.14	(0.08)	**0.28**	(0.05)	1.65	(0.02)	1.82	(0.07)
	Northern Ireland	14.7	(2.4)	28.8	(2.5)	28.8	(2.5)	1.07	(0.04)	1.28	(0.05)	1.93	(0.02)	**0.21**	(0.06)	**0.65**	(0.06)	1.42	(0.02)	1.53	(0.11)
	Scotland•	12.2	(1.3)	13.2	(1.3)	13.3	(1.3)	1.24	(0.03)	1.38	(0.02)	1.74	(0.05)	**0.14**	(0.04)	**0.36**	(0.05)	1.37	(0.02)	1.56	(0.05)
	Wales	7.9	(1.1)	8.9	(1.4)	8.9	(1.3)	1.19	(0.03)	1.36	(0.02)	1.63	(0.06)	**0.17**	(0.04)	**0.28**	(0.06)	1.34	(0.02)	1.60	(0.08)
	United States																				
	Connecticut•	15.4	(2.2)	17.0	(2.4)	17.5	(2.5)	1.81	(0.06)	2.07	(0.03)	2.29	(0.05)	**0.27**	(0.07)	**0.22**	(0.06)	2.09	(0.04)	2.03	(0.06)
	Florida•	8.2	(1.9)	8.3	(2.0)	8.5	(2.1)	1.89	(0.05)	1.97	(0.02)	2.12	(0.06)	0.08	(0.06)	**0.15**	(0.06)	1.98	(0.03)	2.04	(0.03)
	Massachusetts•	9.8	(2.9)	10.5	(3.5)	10.8	(3.6)	1.94	(0.08)	1.97	(0.05)	2.30	(0.06)	0.03	(0.09)	**0.33**	(0.08)	2.07	(0.05)	2.09	(0.07)
Partners	**Argentina**																				
	Ciudad Autónoma de Buenos Aires•	13.1	(2.8)	16.1	(3.5)	16.4	(3.8)	1.19	(0.06)	1.32	(0.08)	1.83	(0.05)	0.13	(0.10)	**0.51**	(0.10)	1.68	(0.05)	1.30	(0.06)
	Brazil																				
	Acre	11.9	(5.3)	16.7	(7.9)	16.7	(8.0)	1.12	(0.04)	1.29	(0.09)	1.66	(0.19)	0.16	(0.10)	0.38	(0.22)	1.27	(0.06)	c	c
	Alagoas	14.4	(4.8)	21.0	(4.9)	21.8	(5.1)	1.06	(0.04)	c	c	c	c	c	c	c	c	1.25	(0.05)	c	c
	Amapá	10.8	(6.4)	14.3	(8.7)	14.4	(9.1)	c	c	1.18	(0.04)	1.60	(0.11)	c	c	**0.41**	(0.13)	1.34	(0.05)	c	c
	Amazonas	5.5	(2.8)	9.8	(6.1)	10.6	(6.3)	c	c	1.22	(0.06)	1.40	(0.16)	c	c	0.18	(0.16)	1.24	(0.05)	c	c
	Bahia	11.9	(3.2)	20.1	(4.9)	21.1	(4.9)	1.01	(0.08)	c	c	c	c	c	c	c	c	1.22	(0.07)	c	c
	Ceará	12.8	(4.2)	22.8	(5.3)	23.5	(5.2)	1.29	(0.06)	c	c	c	c	c	c	c	c	1.50	(0.07)	c	c
	Espírito Santo	18.0	(4.8)	22.1	(6.5)	22.5	(6.4)	1.40	(0.05)	1.28	(0.10)	c	c	-0.11	(0.10)	c	c	1.55	(0.07)	c	c
	Federal District	20.4	(6.6)	34.6	(5.2)	34.6	(5.2)	c	c	1.19	(0.05)	1.98	(0.10)	c	c	**0.79**	(0.10)	1.57	(0.05)	c	c
	Goiás	15.6	(5.2)	27.7	(7.1)	27.7	(7.2)	1.11	(0.10)	1.32	(0.07)	c	c	0.21	(0.11)	c	c	1.38	(0.06)	c	c
	Maranhão	11.2	(6.3)	15.7	(9.2)	15.7	(9.1)	1.19	(0.12)	1.22	(0.10)	c	c	0.03	(0.16)	c	c	1.33	(0.11)	c	c
	Mato Grosso	7.9	(4.3)	13.2	(6.4)	13.6	(6.4)	1.23	(0.11)	1.25	(0.12)	c	c	0.03	(0.18)	c	c	1.35	(0.08)	c	c
	Mato Grosso do Sul	14.9	(4.2)	22.6	(5.6)	23.5	(5.3)	1.23	(0.11)	1.56	(0.07)	1.85	(0.08)	**0.33**	(0.12)	**0.29**	(0.11)	1.58	(0.07)	c	c
	Minas Gerais	7.8	(3.5)	9.5	(4.8)	10.7	(5.8)	1.44	(0.06)	1.30	(0.07)	2.06	(0.10)	-0.14	(0.09)	**0.76**	(0.12)	1.55	(0.07)	c	c
	Pará	7.8	(5.4)	18.2	(10.2)	18.7	(11.0)	1.08	(0.06)	1.31	(0.15)	c	c	0.23	(0.16)	c	c	1.38	(0.05)	c	c
	Paraíba	21.9	(5.3)	25.9	(5.8)	26.9	(5.7)	1.26	(0.08)	1.38	(0.09)	1.99	(0.11)	0.12	(0.11)	**0.61**	(0.15)	1.57	(0.04)	c	c
	Paraná	15.4	(9.2)	24.9	(14.1)	25.1	(14.0)	1.24	(0.13)	1.26	(0.04)	1.95	(0.26)	0.02	(0.13)	**0.69**	(0.26)	1.42	(0.09)	c	c
	Pernambuco	9.5	(4.8)	10.0	(6.2)	11.6	(5.8)	1.29	(0.08)	1.33	(0.07)	c	c	0.04	(0.11)	c	c	1.36	(0.05)	c	c
	Piauí	17.1	(5.1)	30.5	(6.7)	30.5	(6.7)	1.31	(0.06)	1.52	(0.08)	c	c	**0.21**	(0.10)	c	c	1.60	(0.06)	c	c
	Rio de Janeiro	7.1	(3.9)	16.4	(4.9)	17.1	(5.1)	c	c	1.41	(0.07)	2.03	(0.10)	c	c	**0.63**	(0.13)	1.53	(0.06)	c	c
	Rio Grande do Norte	27.9	(7.1)	44.1	(7.8)	44.6	(7.7)	1.02	(0.06)	1.34	(0.12)	2.24	(0.12)	0.31	(0.17)	**0.90**	(0.17)	1.34	(0.08)	c	c
	Rio Grande do Sul	7.8	(4.8)	9.8	(6.0)	11.2	(6.5)	1.24	(0.09)	1.33	(0.08)	1.67	(0.15)	0.09	(0.12)	0.34	(0.18)	1.39	(0.04)	c	c
	Rondônia	8.6	(4.8)	10.3	(7.2)	10.3	(7.2)	1.13	(0.06)	1.21	(0.09)	c	c	0.08	(0.11)	c	c	1.25	(0.06)	c	c
	Roraima	15.0	(4.7)	23.6	(5.4)	23.7	(5.3)	1.12	(0.09)	1.27	(0.06)	1.91	(0.07)	0.15	(0.12)	**0.63**	(0.09)	1.40	(0.06)	c	c
	Santa Catarina	9.2	(5.1)	18.1	(8.4)	18.5	(8.3)	1.26	(0.12)	1.53	(0.07)	c	c	0.26	(0.17)	c	c	1.54	(0.07)	c	c
	São Paulo	13.5	(3.1)	23.4	(5.2)	24.8	(5.1)	1.16	(0.07)	1.23	(0.03)	1.84	(0.07)	0.07	(0.07)	**0.60**	(0.08)	1.44	(0.03)	c	c
	Sergipe	10.5	(5.6)	22.8	(11.0)	23.6	(11.6)	1.01	(0.10)	1.31	(0.08)	1.95	(0.19)	**0.30**	(0.12)	**0.63**	(0.21)	1.40	(0.10)	c	c
	Tocantins	8.9	(3.2)	12.0	(3.1)	12.9	(3.1)	1.32	(0.06)	1.34	(0.06)	1.88	(0.04)	0.02	(0.09)	**0.55**	(0.07)	1.46	(0.05)	c	c
	Colombia																				
	Bogotá	7.3	(1.9)	10.7	(2.4)	10.7	(2.5)	1.46	(0.15)	1.70	(0.05)	1.98	(0.05)	0.24	(0.16)	**0.28**	(0.08)	1.79	(0.03)	c	c
	Cali	8.0	(2.7)	10.7	(4.0)	11.3	(4.2)	c	c	1.55	(0.06)	1.96	(0.05)	c	c	**0.40**	(0.08)	1.76	(0.05)	c	c
	Manizales	12.5	(2.7)	15.0	(2.9)	15.1	(2.9)	1.54	(0.10)	1.53	(0.05)	1.99	(0.04)	-0.01	(0.11)	**0.46**	(0.06)	1.83	(0.04)	c	c
	Medellín	14.0	(4.3)	20.0	(5.0)	20.2	(4.9)	1.43	(0.05)	1.57	(0.05)	1.99	(0.06)	**0.14**	(0.07)	**0.42**	(0.07)	1.73	(0.05)	c	c
	Russian Federation																				
	Perm Territory region•	3.8	(1.4)	4.6	(1.7)	5.3	(1.4)	1.88	(0.04)	2.01	(0.02)	2.09	(0.03)	**0.12**	(0.04)	**0.08**	(0.03)	2.00	(0.02)	2.00	(0.06)
	United Arab Emirates																				
	Abu Dhabi•	2.7	(0.9)	5.3	(1.6)	5.8	(1.7)	2.01	(0.05)	2.07	(0.05)	2.29	(0.05)	0.06	(0.07)	**0.22**	(0.08)	2.00	(0.04)	.26	(0.03)
	Ajman	5.3	(2.2)	7.2	(3.7)	8.7	(4.5)	1.92	(0.09)	2.06	(0.04)	c	c	0.14	(0.10)	c	c	1.96	(0.08)	.02	(0.07)
	Dubai•	3.8	(0.8)	4.5	(0.8)	4.5	(0.8)	1.93	(0.03)	2.18	(0.02)	2.25	(0.02)	**0.25**	(0.03)	**0.07**	(0.03)	2.01	(0.02)	.26	(0.01)
	Fujairah	3.7	(1.7)	4.7	(3.3)	9.1	(4.5)	1.95	(0.05)	1.94	(0.09)	c	c	-0.01	(0.09)	c	c	1.91	(0.05)	.26	(0.14)
	Ras al-Khaimah	5.1	(2.7)	5.1	(2.7)	6.1	(2.4)	2.05	(0.09)	1.96	(0.06)	2.15	(0.08)	-0.09	(0.12)	0.19	(0.10)	1.96	(0.04)	.19	(0.10)
	Sharjah	2.7	(1.6)	3.7	(2.8)	6.4	(4.2)	c	c	2.14	(0.11)	2.26	(0.09)	c	c	0.12	(0.15)	2.01	(0.09)	.34	(0.06)
	Umm al-Quwain	8.6	(4.0)	8.7	(4.1)	14.9	(4.9)	1.86	(0.05)	1.86	(0.08)	c	c	0.00	(0.09)	c	c	1.80	(0.05)	.95	(0.10)

• PISA adjudicated region.

Notes: Values that are statistically significant are indicated in bold (see Annex A3).

See Table II.4.3 for national data.

1. ESCS refers to the *PISA index of economic, social and cultural status*.

2. A socio-economically disadvantaged school is one whose students' mean ESCS is statistically significantly below the mean ESCS of the country; an average school is one where there is no difference between the students' and the country's mean ESCS; and an advantaged school is one whose students' mean ESCS is statistically significantly above the country mean.

StatLink http://dx.doi.org/10.1787/888932964965

[Part 3/4]

Table B2.II.16 Inequity in access to instructional content: Formal mathematics, by region

Results based on students' self-reports

	Formal mathematics: Difference between non-immigrant and immigrant students		Mean among students who speak the language of assessment at home		Mean among students who do not speak the language of assessment at home		Difference between students who speak the language of assessment at home and those who do not		Mean among students in rural schools		Mean among students in town schools (small town and town)		Mean among students in urban schools (city and large city)		Difference between students in rural and town schools		Difference between students in town and urban schools		Difference between students in rural and urban schools	
	Dif.	S.E.	Mean index	S.E.	Mean index	S.E.	Dif.	S.E.	Mean index	S.E.	Mean index	S.E.	Mean index	S.E.	Dif.	S.E.	Dif.	S.E.	Dif.	S.E.
OECD																				
Australia																				
Australian Capital Territory	**0.35**	(0.10)	1.67	(0.03)	1.98	(0.14)	**-0.31**	(0.14)	c	c	c	c	1.70	(0.03)	c	c	c	c	c	c
New South Wales	**0.45**	(0.05)	1.64	(0.02)	2.14	(0.06)	**-0.51**	(0.06)	1.40	(0.07)	1.58	(0.03)	1.88	(0.04)	**-0.18**	(0.08)	**-0.30**	(0.05)	**0.48**	(0.07)
Northern Territory	0.01	(0.18)	1.42	(0.07)	c	c	c	c	1.08	(0.09)	1.44	(0.10)	1.48	(0.10)	**-0.36**	(0.14)	-0.04	(0.12)	**0.40**	(0.14)
Queensland	**0.15**	(0.06)	1.67	(0.02)	1.99	(0.11)	**-0.32**	(0.11)	1.39	(0.08)	1.54	(0.03)	1.77	(0.02)	-0.15	(0.08)	**-0.23**	(0.04)	**0.38**	(0.09)
South Australia	**0.27**	(0.07)	1.50	(0.03)	2.01	(0.09)	**-0.51**	(0.10)	1.37	(0.13)	1.36	(0.04)	1.62	(0.04)	0.01	(0.14)	**-0.26**	(0.06)	0.25	(0.14)
Tasmania	**0.44**	(0.13)	1.37	(0.03)	c	c	c	c	1.32	(0.05)	1.37	(0.04)	1.46	(0.04)	-0.05	(0.06)	-0.08	(0.06)	**0.14**	(0.06)
Victoria	**0.35**	(0.06)	1.58	(0.03)	1.99	(0.08)	**-0.41**	(0.08)	1.55	(0.06)	1.48	(0.04)	1.73	(0.03)	0.07	(0.07)	**-0.24**	(0.05)	**0.18**	(0.07)
Western Australia	0.11	(0.06)	1.80	(0.04)	2.18	(0.08)	**-0.38**	(0.09)	c	c	1.71	(0.11)	1.89	(0.04)	c	c	-0.18	(0.11)	c	c
Belgium																				
Flemish Community•	**-0.37**	(0.05)	1.82	(0.03)	1.42	(0.06)	**0.39**	(0.07)	c	c	1.74	(0.03)	1.74	(0.09)	c	c	-0.01	(0.11)	c	c
French Community	**-0.15**	(0.05)	2.02	(0.02)	1.79	(0.08)	**0.23**	(0.08)	c	c	1.95	(0.03)	1.97	(0.05)	c	c	-0.02	(0.06)	c	c
German-speaking Community	**-0.16**	(0.07)	1.51	(0.04)	c	c	c	c	c	c	1.53	(0.03)	c	c	c	c	c	c	c	c
Canada																				
Alberta	**0.20**	(0.05)	1.88	(0.03)	2.08	(0.07)	**-0.20**	(0.07)	1.79	(0.09)	1.84	(0.04)	2.01	(0.04)	-0.05	(0.10)	**-0.17**	(0.05)	**0.22**	(0.10)
British Columbia	**0.22**	(0.04)	1.85	(0.03)	2.14	(0.05)	**-0.29**	(0.05)	c	c	1.86	(0.03)	2.01	(0.04)	c	c	**-0.15**	(0.05)	c	c
Manitoba	0.13	(0.07)	1.80	(0.03)	1.91	(0.09)	-0.12	(0.09)	1.71	(0.08)	1.77	(0.05)	1.84	(0.03)	-0.06	(0.08)	-0.06	(0.06)	0.12	(0.08)
New Brunswick	0.17	(0.15)	1.71	(0.02)	c	c	c	c	1.66	(0.03)	1.71	(0.03)	1.74	(0.05)	-0.05	(0.05)	-0.02	(0.06)	0.08	(0.06)
Newfoundland and Labrador	c	c	1.96	(0.02)	c	c	c	c	1.82	(0.07)	1.97	(0.03)	2.12	(0.05)	**-0.15**	(0.07)	**-0.15**	(0.05)	**0.30**	(0.09)
Nova Scotia	0.20	(0.11)	2.05	(0.06)	c	c	c	c	2.08	(0.05)	2.00	(0.06)	2.22	(0.05)	0.08	(0.08)	**-0.22**	(0.08)	0.14	(0.07)
Ontario	**0.14**	(0.04)	2.00	(0.03)	2.16	(0.04)	**-0.15**	(0.05)	1.93	(0.04)	1.92	(0.03)	2.11	(0.03)	0.00	(0.05)	**-0.19**	(0.04)	**0.18**	(0.05)
Prince Edward Island	0.19	(0.10)	1.72	(0.02)	c	c	c	c	1.64	(0.03)	1.76	(0.03)	c	c	**-0.12**	(0.05)	c	c	c	c
Quebec	0.04	(0.04)	1.98	(0.02)	2.09	(0.06)	-0.11	(0.06)	1.88	(0.07)	1.97	(0.03)	2.03	(0.03)	-0.09	(0.07)	-0.06	(0.04)	0.15	(0.08)
Saskatchewan	**0.20**	(0.07)	1.85	(0.02)	1.93	(0.08)	-0.09	(0.08)	1.82	(0.03)	1.80	(0.03)	1.92	(0.04)	0.02	(0.05)	**-0.12**	(0.05)	**0.11**	(0.04)
Italy																				
Abruzzo	**-0.27**	(0.09)	1.87	(0.04)	c	c	c	c	c	c	1.84	(0.05)	1.75	(0.08)	c	c	0.09	(0.10)	c	c
Basilicata	c	c	1.92	(0.03)	c	c	c	c	c	c	1.85	(0.03)	c	c	c	c	c	c	c	c
Bolzano	-0.09	(0.10)	1.61	(0.06)	1.22	(0.08)	**0.39**	(0.11)	1.03	(0.05)	1.42	(0.02)	1.56	(0.03)	**-0.39**	(0.06)	**-0.14**	(0.04)	**0.53**	(0.07)
Calabria	**-0.29**	(0.14)	1.86	(0.04)	c	c	c	c	c	c	1.80	(0.05)	1.79	(0.12)	c	c	0.00	(0.14)	c	c
Campania	c	c	1.84	(0.05)	c	c	c	c	c	c	1.77	(0.05)	1.75	(0.08)	c	c	0.03	(0.11)	c	c
Emilia Romagna	**-0.36**	(0.06)	1.91	(0.04)	1.49	(0.09)	**0.42**	(0.10)	c	c	1.79	(0.06)	1.86	(0.06)	c	c	-0.08	(0.08)	c	c
Friuli Venezia Giulia	**-0.28**	(0.09)	2.00	(0.03)	1.61	(0.15)	**0.39**	(0.15)	c	c	1.89	(0.03)	1.91	(0.17)	c	c	-0.02	(0.18)	c	c
Lazio	-0.19	(0.10)	1.89	(0.04)	1.50	(0.18)	**0.39**	(0.19)	c	c	1.74	(0.08)	2.01	(0.08)	c	c	**-0.27**	(0.12)	c	c
Liguria	**-0.29**	(0.07)	1.92	(0.04)	1.59	(0.10)	**0.33**	(0.11)	c	c	1.86	(0.06)	1.89	(0.08)	c	c	-0.03	(0.11)	c	c
Lombardia	**-0.23**	(0.05)	1.93	(0.04)	1.57	(0.06)	**0.35**	(0.06)	c	c	1.91	(0.05)	1.89	(0.08)	c	c	0.03	(0.09)	c	c
Marche	**-0.23**	(0.07)	1.89	(0.04)	1.65	(0.10)	**0.25**	(0.11)	c	c	1.89	(0.03)	1.62	(0.14)	c	c	0.27	(0.16)	c	c
Molise	c	c	1.94	(0.03)	c	c	c	c	c	c	1.81	(0.03)	c	c	c	c	c	c	c	c
Piemonte	0.00	(0.08)	1.83	(0.06)	1.84	(0.08)	-0.01	(0.09)	c	c	1.84	(0.04)	2.04	(0.11)	c	c	**-0.20**	(0.10)	c	c
Puglia	c	c	1.95	(0.04)	c	c	c	c	c	c	1.89	(0.06)	1.98	(0.10)	c	c	-0.10	(0.12)	c	c
Sardegna	c	c	1.73	(0.04)	c	c	c	c	c	c	1.62	(0.05)	1.78	(0.08)	c	c	-0.16	(0.10)	c	c
Sicilia	c	c	1.80	(0.04)	c	c	c	c	c	c	1.73	(0.05)	1.78	(0.09)	c	c	-0.05	(0.11)	c	c
Toscana	**-0.48**	(0.07)	1.90	(0.04)	1.33	(0.07)	**0.57**	(0.07)	c	c	1.79	(0.06)	1.93	(0.08)	c	c	-0.14	(0.10)	c	c
Trento	**-0.22**	(0.08)	1.89	(0.04)	1.54	(0.14)	**0.34**	(0.13)	1.66	(0.14)	1.88	(0.04)	1.85	(0.09)	-0.22	(0.14)	0.03	(0.11)	0.19	(0.17)
Umbria	**-0.20**	(0.06)	1.92	(0.03)	1.61	(0.06)	**0.30**	(0.07)	c	c	1.83	(0.03)	1.92	(0.08)	c	c	-0.08	(0.10)	c	c
Valle d'Aosta	-0.14	(0.09)	1.71	(0.03)	c	c	c	c	1.57	(0.08)	1.76	(0.03)	c	c	**-0.19**	(0.09)	c	c	c	c
Veneto	**-0.36**	(0.08)	2.04	(0.05)	1.58	(0.07)	**0.47**	(0.08)	1.39	(0.07)	2.03	(0.08)	1.94	(0.08)	**-0.64**	(0.10)	0.09	(0.11)	**0.55**	(0.11)
Mexico																				
Aguascalientes	c	c	1.84	(0.05)	c	c	c	c	1.39	(0.05)	1.65	(0.06)	1.94	(0.07)	**-0.26**	(0.08)	**-0.29**	(0.09)	**0.55**	(0.08)
Baja California	c	c	1.79	(0.05)	c	c	c	c	c	c	c	c	1.80	(0.06)	c	c	c	c	c	c
Baja California Sur	c	c	1.63	(0.04)	c	c	c	c	1.50	(0.17)	1.60	(0.06)	1.68	(0.10)	-0.10	(0.17)	-0.08	(0.12)	0.18	(0.23)
Campeche	**-0.45**	(0.10)	1.78	(0.03)	c	c	c	c	1.79	(0.10)	1.70	(0.06)	1.78	(0.04)	0.10	(0.12)	-0.09	(0.07)	-0.01	(0.11)
Chiapas	c	c	1.59	(0.05)	c	c	c	c	1.35	(0.06)	1.65	(0.06)	1.64	(0.10)	**-0.30**	(0.09)	0.01	(0.12)	**0.29**	(0.11)
Chihuahua	c	c	1.86	(0.05)	c	c	c	c	1.27	(0.14)	1.90	(0.09)	1.86	(0.06)	**-0.63**	(0.17)	0.04	(0.09)	**0.59**	(0.14)
Coahuila	c	c	1.71	(0.05)	c	c	c	c	1.45	(0.10)	1.61	(0.07)	1.80	(0.06)	-0.16	(0.12)	-0.19	(0.09)	**0.35**	(0.12)
Colima	c	c	1.82	(0.04)	c	c	c	c	1.65	(0.12)	1.67	(0.07)	1.95	(0.06)	-0.02	(0.14)	**-0.27**	(0.10)	**0.30**	(0.13)
Distrito Federal	c	c	1.91	(0.04)	c	c	c	c	c	c	c	c	1.93	(0.04)	c	c	c	c	c	c
Durango	c	c	1.73	(0.03)	c	c	c	c	1.48	(0.10)	1.70	(0.05)	1.80	(0.08)	-0.22	(0.13)	-0.10	(0.11)	**0.32**	(0.13)
Guanajuato	c	c	1.67	(0.05)	c	c	c	c	1.55	(0.07)	1.54	(0.11)	1.79	(0.07)	0.01	(0.15)	-0.26	(0.13)	**0.24**	(0.09)
Guerrero	c	c	1.54	(0.06)	c	c	c	c	1.34	(0.06)	1.57	(0.08)	1.61	(0.06)	**-0.23**	(0.10)	-0.04	(0.10)	**0.27**	(0.08)
Hidalgo	c	c	1.88	(0.04)	c	c	c	c	1.54	(0.07)	1.95	(0.05)	1.92	(0.12)	**-0.41**	(0.09)	0.03	(0.13)	**0.38**	(0.15)
Jalisco	c	c	1.74	(0.04)	c	c	c	c	1.49	(0.14)	1.77	(0.05)	1.74	(0.07)	-0.27	(0.15)	0.02	(0.09)	0.25	(0.16)
Mexico	c	c	1.89	(0.03)	c	c	c	c	1.72	(0.11)	1.85	(0.04)	1.95	(0.05)	-0.13	(0.12)	-0.10	(0.06)	0.23	(0.12)
Morelos	c	c	1.79	(0.05)	c	c	c	c	1.60	(0.07)	1.76	(0.07)	1.86	(0.11)	-0.15	(0.10)	-0.10	(0.15)	**0.26**	(0.13)
Nayarit	c	c	1.65	(0.04)	c	c	c	c	1.57	(0.12)	1.60	(0.05)	1.67	(0.06)	-0.03	(0.13)	-0.07	(0.08)	0.10	(0.14)
Nuevo León	c	c	1.94	(0.05)	c	c	c	c	c	c	1.82	(0.11)	2.01	(0.07)	c	c	-0.19	(0.13)	c	c
Puebla	c	c	1.84	(0.05)	c	c	c	c	1.70	(0.08)	1.77	(0.07)	2.04	(0.05)	-0.07	(0.10)	**-0.27**	(0.09)	**0.34**	(0.09)
Querétaro	c	c	1.85	(0.05)	c	c	c	c	1.63	(0.12)	1.78	(0.04)	1.95	(0.05)	-0.16	(0.13)	**-0.16**	(0.06)	**0.32**	(0.13)
Quintana Roo	c	c	1.79	(0.03)	c	c	c	c	1.55	(0.11)	1.67	(0.07)	1.86	(0.04)	-0.12	(0.14)	-0.19	(0.10)	**0.31**	(0.12)
San Luis Potosí	c	c	1.74	(0.05)	c	c	c	c	1.42	(0.10)	1.77	(0.12)	1.86	(0.06)	**-0.35**	(0.16)	-0.09	(0.13)	**0.44**	(0.12)
Sinaloa	c	c	1.75	(0.04)	c	c	c	c	1.68	(0.11)	1.70	(0.05)	1.79	(0.06)	-0.02	(0.12)	-0.09	(0.08)	0.11	(0.14)
Tabasco	c	c	1.67	(0.04)	c	c	c	c	1.45	(0.05)	1.64	(0.05)	1.97	(0.07)	**-0.19**	(0.08)	**-0.33**	(0.08)	**0.52**	(0.08)
Tamaulipas	c	c	1.70	(0.04)	c	c	c	c	c	c	1.63	(0.08)	1.72	(0.04)	c	c	-0.09	(0.11)	c	c
Tlaxcala	c	c	1.86	(0.04)	c	c	c	c	1.67	(0.12)	1.88	(0.03)	c	c	-0.21	(0.13)	c	c	c	c
Veracruz	c	c	1.85	(0.03)	c	c	c	c	1.74	(0.09)	1.79	(0.02)	2.10	(0.09)	-0.04	(0.09)	**-0.32**	(0.10)	**0.36**	(0.13)
Yucatán	c	c	1.84	(0.04)	c	c	c	c	1.55	(0.10)	1.79	(0.07)	1.89	(0.08)	**-0.24**	(0.12)	-0.10	(0.11)	**0.35**	(0.12)
Zacatecas	c	c	1.65	(0.03)	c	c	c	c	1.54	(0.07)	1.65	(0.03)	1.79	(0.13)	-0.11	(0.08)	-0.15	(0.13)	0.25	(0.16)

• PISA adjudicated region.

Notes: Values that are statistically significant are indicated in bold (see Annex A3).

See Table II.4.3 for national data.

1. ESCS refers to the *PISA index of economic, social and cultural status*.

2. A socio-economically disadvantaged school is one whose students' mean ESCS is statistically significantly below the mean ESCS of the country; an average school is one where there is no difference between the students' and the country's mean ESCS; and an advantaged school is one whose students' mean ESCS is statistically significantly above the country mean.

StatLink http://dx.doi.org/10.1787/888932964965

[Part 4/4]
Inequity in access to instructional content: Formal mathematics, by region

Table B2.II.16 *Results based on students' self-reports*

	Formal mathematics																		
	Difference between non-immigrant and immigrant students		Mean among students who speak the language of assessment at home		Mean among students who do not speak the language of assessment at home		Difference between students who speak the language of assessment at home and those who do not		Mean among students in rural schools		Mean among students in town schools (small town and town)		Mean among students in urban schools (city and large city)		Difference between students in rural and town schools		Difference between students in town and urban schools		Difference between students in rural and urban schools	
	Dif.	S.E.	Mean index	S.E.	Mean index	S.E.	Dif.	S.E.	Mean index	S.E.	Mean index	S.E.	Mean index	S.E.	Dif.	S.E.	Dif.	S.E.	Dif.	S.E.
Portugal																				
Alentejo	c	c	1.73	(0.04)	c	c	c	c	c	c	1.77	(0.03)	c	c	c	c	c	c	c	c
Spain																				
Andalusia•	c	c	1.86	(0.03)	c	c	c	c	c	c	1.78	(0.04)	1.96	(0.06)	c	c	**-0.18**	(0.08)	c	c
Aragon•	**-0.60**	(0.09)	2.02	(0.03)	1.31	(0.16)	**0.71**	(0.17)	1.72	(0.06)	1.86	(0.06)	1.98	(0.04)	-0.13	(0.09)	-0.13	(0.07)	**0.26**	(0.07)
Asturias•	**-0.46**	(0.06)	2.02	(0.03)	c	c	c	c	c	c	1.93	(0.04)	2.04	(0.05)	c	c	-0.11	(0.06)	c	c
Balearic Islands•	**-0.39**	(0.06)	1.87	(0.04)	1.48	(0.06)	**0.39**	(0.08)	c	c	1.68	(0.04)	1.87	(0.08)	c	c	**-0.19**	(0.09)	c	c
Basque Country•	**-0.36**	(0.05)	1.92	(0.03)	1.59	(0.13)	**0.33**	(0.13)	1.91	(0.06)	1.85	(0.03)	1.91	(0.03)	0.06	(0.06)	-0.05	(0.04)	0.00	(0.07)
Cantabria•	**-0.27**	(0.09)	1.94	(0.03)	c	c	c	c	1.83	(0.14)	1.86	(0.04)	2.06	(0.05)	-0.03	(0.14)	**-0.20**	(0.07)	0.23	(0.14)
Castile and Leon•	**-0.35**	(0.05)	2.02	(0.03)	c	c	c	c	c	c	1.97	(0.04)	2.08	(0.05)	c	c	-0.11	(0.07)	c	c
Catalonia•	**-0.29**	(0.07)	2.05	(0.04)	1.64	(0.08)	**0.41**	(0.09)	c	c	1.88	(0.05)	1.87	(0.08)	c	c	0.01	(0.10)	c	c
Extremadura•	0.05	(0.04)	1.80	(0.03)	c	c	c	c	1.65	(0.06)	1.75	(0.03)	2.15	(0.07)	-0.11	(0.06)	**-0.39**	(0.07)	**0.50**	(0.09)
Galicia•	**-0.19**	(0.10)	1.85	(0.04)	c	c	c	c	1.60	(0.06)	1.81	(0.04)	1.83	(0.07)	**-0.21**	(0.07)	-0.02	(0.09)	**0.23**	(0.09)
La Rioja•	**-0.52**	(0.06)	2.12	(0.02)	1.63	(0.10)	**0.50**	(0.10)	1.75	(0.07)	1.92	(0.03)	2.12	(0.02)	**-0.17**	(0.08)	**-0.20**	(0.04)	**0.37**	(0.06)
Madrid•	**-0.37**	(0.08)	2.08	(0.03)	1.72	(0.10)	**0.36**	(0.10)	c	c	1.95	(0.04)	2.05	(0.05)	c	c	-0.10	(0.08)	c	c
Murcia•	**-0.43**	(0.10)	1.91	(0.04)	1.46	(0.14)	**0.45**	(0.14)	c	c	1.79	(0.04)	1.94	(0.07)	c	c	-0.16	(0.08)	c	c
Navarre•	**-0.44**	(0.05)	2.07	(0.03)	c	c	c	c	1.77	(0.06)	1.99	(0.03)	1.88	(0.05)	**-0.23**	(0.07)	**0.12**	(0.05)	0.11	(0.08)
United Kingdom																				
England	**0.16**	(0.07)	1.65	(0.02)	1.89	(0.08)	**-0.23**	(0.08)	1.75	(0.06)	1.62	(0.04)	1.76	(0.04)	0.13	(0.08)	**-0.14**	(0.06)	0.01	(0.06)
Northern Ireland	0.11	(0.10)	1.43	(0.02)	1.36	(0.14)	0.07	(0.14)	1.26	(0.15)	1.42	(0.05)	1.40	(0.06)	-0.16	(0.17)	0.03	(0.09)	0.13	(0.16)
Scotland•	**0.19**	(0.06)	1.37	(0.02)	1.35	(0.10)	0.02	(0.10)	1.56	(0.10)	1.37	(0.02)	1.38	(0.04)	**0.19**	(0.06)	-0.01	(0.05)	**-0.19**	(0.08)
Wales	**0.26**	(0.08)	1.35	(0.02)	1.62	(0.10)	**-0.28**	(0.10)	1.35	(0.08)	1.34	(0.02)	1.40	(0.03)	0.01	(0.08)	-0.05	(0.04)	0.05	(0.09)
United States																				
Connecticut•	-0.06	(0.05)	2.10	(0.03)	1.97	(0.09)	0.12	(0.08)	c	c	2.13	(0.04)	1.93	(0.06)	c	c	**0.20**	(0.08)	c	c
Florida•	0.06	(0.03)	1.99	(0.03)	2.00	(0.05)	-0.01	(0.04)	c	c	1.95	(0.05)	2.04	(0.03)	c	c	-0.09	(0.05)	c	c
Massachusetts•	0.02	(0.07)	2.08	(0.05)	2.03	(0.10)	0.05	(0.10)	c	c	2.09	(0.05)	2.00	(0.09)	c	c	0.09	(0.10)	c	c
Argentina																				
Ciudad Autónoma de Buenos Aires•	**-0.38**	(0.07)	1.68	(0.05)	c	c	c	c	c	c	c	c	1.59	(0.05)	c	c	c	c	c	c
Brazil																				
Acre	c	c	1.27	(0.06)	c	c	c	c	c	c	1.24	(0.09)	1.31	(0.09)	c	c	-0.07	(0.13)	c	c
Alagoas	c	c	1.26	(0.05)	c	c	c	c	c	c	1.10	(0.05)	1.63	(0.11)	c	c	**-0.53**	(0.12)	c	c
Amapá	c	c	1.32	(0.04)	c	c	c	c	c	c	1.10	(0.10)	1.42	(0.07)	c	c	**-0.32**	(0.13)	c	c
Amazonas	c	c	1.23	(0.05)	c	c	c	c	c	c	1.19	(0.08)	1.27	(0.05)	c	c	-0.08	(0.07)	c	c
Bahia	c	c	1.23	(0.08)	c	c	c	c	c	c	1.11	(0.12)	c	c	c	c	c	c	c	c
Ceará	c	c	1.51	(0.07)	c	c	c	c	c	c	1.38	(0.04)	1.68	(0.16)	c	c	-0.30	(0.16)	c	c
Espírito Santo	c	c	1.56	(0.07)	c	c	c	c	c	c	1.46	(0.11)	1.66	(0.12)	c	c	-0.20	(0.17)	c	c
Federal District	c	c	1.57	(0.05)	c	c	c	c	c	c	1.20	(0.09)	1.65	(0.09)	c	c	**-0.45**	(0.12)	c	c
Goiás	c	c	1.38	(0.06)	c	c	c	c	c	c	1.26	(0.09)	1.55	(0.15)	c	c	-0.29	(0.21)	c	c
Maranhão	c	c	1.33	(0.11)	c	c	c	c	c	c	1.18	(0.08)	1.53	(0.19)	c	c	-0.34	(0.21)	c	c
Mato Grosso	c	c	1.36	(0.08)	c	c	c	c	c	c	1.36	(0.09)	1.29	(0.13)	c	c	0.07	(0.16)	c	c
Mato Grosso do Sul	c	c	1.58	(0.07)	c	c	c	c	c	c	1.39	(0.12)	1.72	(0.07)	c	c	**-0.33**	(0.13)	c	c
Minas Gerais	c	c	1.55	(0.07)	c	c	c	c	c	c	1.52	(0.10)	1.56	(0.08)	c	c	-0.04	(0.13)	c	c
Pará	c	c	1.37	(0.05)	c	c	c	c	c	c	1.11	(0.06)	1.64	(0.07)	c	c	**-0.53**	(0.09)	c	c
Paraíba	c	c	1.58	(0.04)	c	c	c	c	c	c	1.34	(0.08)	1.80	(0.05)	c	c	**-0.46**	(0.09)	c	c
Paraná	c	c	1.42	(0.09)	c	c	c	c	c	c	1.34	(0.10)	1.50	(0.18)	c	c	-0.16	(0.24)	c	c
Pernambuco	c	c	1.37	(0.06)	c	c	c	c	c	c	1.29	(0.10)	1.40	(0.08)	c	c	-0.12	(0.14)	c	c
Piauí	c	c	1.62	(0.06)	c	c	c	c	c	c	1.44	(0.08)	1.94	(0.12)	c	c	**-0.49**	(0.18)	c	c
Rio de Janeiro	c	c	1.53	(0.06)	c	c	c	c	c	c	1.37	(0.09)	1.59	(0.07)	c	c	-0.22	(0.13)	c	c
Rio Grande do Norte	c	c	1.34	(0.08)	c	c	c	c	c	c	1.09	(0.07)	1.71	(0.15)	c	c	**-0.62**	(0.18)	c	c
Rio Grande do Sul	c	c	1.39	(0.04)	c	c	c	c	c	c	1.40	(0.03)	1.39	(0.14)	c	c	0.01	(0.15)	c	c
Rondônia	c	c	1.26	(0.06)	c	c	c	c	c	c	1.14	(0.05)	1.47	(0.15)	c	c	**-0.34**	(0.16)	c	c
Roraima	c	c	1.39	(0.05)	c	c	c	c	c	c	1.28	(0.11)	1.43	(0.07)	c	c	-0.16	(0.13)	c	c
Santa Catarina	c	c	1.54	(0.08)	c	c	c	c	c	c	1.43	(0.08)	1.67	(0.14)	c	c	-0.25	(0.16)	c	c
São Paulo	c	c	1.45	(0.02)	c	c	c	c	c	c	1.38	(0.08)	1.47	(0.05)	c	c	-0.09	(0.11)	c	c
Sergipe	c	c	1.41	(0.11)	c	c	c	c	c	c	1.26	(0.11)	1.56	(0.19)	c	c	-0.31	(0.22)	c	c
Tocantins	c	c	1.47	(0.05)	c	c	c	c	c	c	1.35	(0.04)	1.61	(0.13)	c	c	-0.25	(0.13)	c	c
Colombia																				
Bogotá	c	c	1.79	(0.03)	c	c	c	c	c	c	c	c	1.79	(0.04)	c	c	c	c	c	c
Cali	c	c	1.77	(0.05)	c	c	c	c	c	c	c	c	1.74	(0.05)	c	c	c	c	c	c
Manizales	c	c	1.82	(0.04)	c	c	c	c	1.78	(0.17)	c	c	1.82	(0.04)	c	c	c	c	0.04	(0.18)
Medellín	c	c	1.73	(0.05)	c	c	c	c	c	c	c	c	1.73	(0.05)	c	c	c	c	c	c
Russian Federation																				
Perm Territory region•	0.00	(0.05)	2.00	(0.02)	c	c	c	c	1.89	(0.05)	2.02	(0.02)	2.03	(0.03)	**-0.12**	(0.06)	-0.01	(0.04)	**0.14**	(0.06)
United Arab Emirates																				
Abu Dhabi•	**0.26**	(0.05)	1.98	(0.04)	2.34	(0.06)	**-0.36**	(0.07)	1.96	(0.10)	2.01	(0.05)	2.22	(0.04)	-0.06	(0.12)	**-0.21**	(0.07)	**0.27**	(0.10)
Ajman	0.06	(0.09)	1.98	(0.07)	1.72	(0.24)	0.27	(0.24)	c	c	2.03	(0.09)	1.86	(0.10)	c	c	0.17	(0.12)	c	c
Dubai•	**0.25**	(0.03)	1.99	(0.03)	2.24	(0.02)	**-0.25**	(0.04)	2.20	(0.04)	2.17	(0.06)	2.19	(0.01)	0.04	(0.05)	-0.02	(0.04)	0.02	(0.04)
Fujairah	**0.35**	(0.13)	1.92	(0.06)	2.30	(0.08)	**-0.38**	(0.09)	c	c	2.03	(0.06)	1.83	(0.10)	c	c	0.20	(0.13)	c	c
Ras al-Khaimah	**0.23**	(0.10)	1.98	(0.06)	2.22	(0.22)	-0.24	(0.22)	2.16	(0.04)	2.03	(0.08)	1.94	(0.06)	0.14	(0.13)	0.09	(0.10)	**0.23**	(0.12)
Sharjah	**0.33**	(0.09)	2.01	(0.12)	2.35	(0.08)	**-0.35**	(0.15)	c	c	2.22	(0.10)	2.19	(0.08)	c	c	0.03	(0.15)	c	c
Umm al-Quwain	0.15	(0.11)	1.83	(0.05)	c	c	c	c	2.04	(0.08)	1.80	(0.05)	c	c	**0.23**	(0.10)	c	c	c	c

• PISA adjudicated region.
Notes: Values that are statistically significant are indicated in bold (see Annex A3).
See Table II.4.3 for national data.
1. ESCS refers to the *PISA index of economic, social and cultural status*.
2. A socio-economically disadvantaged school is one whose students' mean ESCS is statistically significantly below the mean ESCS of the country; an average school is one where there is no difference between the students' and the country's mean ESCS; and an advantaged school is one whose students' mean ESCS is statistically significantly above the country mean.
StatLink http://dx.doi.org/10.1787/888932964965

[Part 1/6]

Table B2.II.24 Pre-primary school attendance, mathematics performance and students' socio-economic status, by region

Results based on students' self-reports

	Percentage of students with						Mean ESCS[1]						Average mathematics performance of students with					
	No pre-primary school attendance		Pre-primary school attendance for one year or less		Pre-primary school attendance for more than one year		No pre-primary school attendance		Pre-primary school attendance for one year or less		Pre-primary school attendance for more than one year		No pre-primary school attendance		Pre-primary school attendance for one year or less		Pre-primary school attendance for more than one year	
	%	S.E.	%	S.E.	%	S.E.	Mean index	S.E.	Mean index	S.E.	Mean index	S.E.	Mean score	S.E.	Mean score	S.E.	Mean score	S.E.
OECD																		
Australia																		
Australian Capital Territory	2.1	(0.6)	45.9	(1.5)	51.9	(1.7)	c	c	0.5	(0.0)	0.7	(0.0)	c	c	515	(4.7)	531	(4.9)
New South Wales	2.8	(0.4)	40.2	(1.1)	57.0	(1.2)	-0.3	(0.1)	0.2	(0.0)	0.3	(0.0)	452	(12.7)	501	(4.0)	523	(4.2)
Northern Territory	4.7	(1.2)	61.5	(3.3)	33.9	(3.4)	c	c	0.1	(0.1)	0.2	(0.1)	c	c	460	(11.8)	462	(13.2)
Queensland	5.0	(0.5)	54.6	(1.2)	40.4	(1.1)	0.0	(0.1)	0.1	(0.0)	0.3	(0.0)	466	(9.3)	504	(3.3)	513	(4.2)
South Australia	5.1	(0.6)	51.5	(1.7)	43.4	(1.7)	-0.1	(0.2)	0.2	(0.0)	0.3	(0.0)	452	(16.0)	496	(4.1)	491	(4.5)
Tasmania	4.7	(0.7)	60.0	(1.7)	35.3	(1.8)	0.0	(0.1)	0.0	(0.0)	0.1	(0.0)	475	(18.1)	482	(3.5)	479	(6.7)
Victoria	5.7	(0.5)	36.5	(1.3)	57.8	(1.4)	-0.2	(0.1)	0.2	(0.0)	0.4	(0.0)	461	(9.6)	496	(4.4)	511	(4.0)
Western Australia	5.8	(0.7)	39.6	(1.3)	54.6	(1.4)	0.0	(0.1)	0.2	(0.0)	0.3	(0.0)	492	(12.8)	508	(4.1)	529	(4.0)
Belgium																		
Flemish Community•	2.0	(0.3)	3.0	(0.3)	94.9	(0.5)	-0.4	(0.1)	-0.4	(0.2)	0.2	(0.0)	454	(14.3)	442	(14.1)	538	(3.1)
French Community	2.6	(0.3)	6.1	(0.5)	91.3	(0.6)	-0.5	(0.1)	-0.1	(0.1)	0.2	(0.0)	420	(10.8)	438	(8.2)	502	(3.1)
German-speaking Community	2.2	(0.5)	32.4	(1.9)	65.4	(2.0)	c	c	0.3	(0.1)	0.3	(0.0)	c	c	509	(6.0)	514	(3.3)
Canada																		
Alberta	4.6	(0.5)	57.2	(1.6)	38.3	(1.6)	0.4	(0.1)	0.4	(0.0)	0.7	(0.0)	507	(9.4)	508	(4.3)	544	(5.9)
British Columbia	4.6	(0.6)	50.0	(1.6)	45.4	(1.7)	0.3	(0.1)	0.3	(0.0)	0.7	(0.0)	497	(11.0)	507	(4.2)	549	(4.9)
Manitoba	6.0	(0.7)	52.9	(1.6)	41.1	(1.5)	-0.2	(0.1)	0.2	(0.0)	0.4	(0.0)	457	(10.6)	490	(3.7)	507	(4.4)
New Brunswick	7.8	(0.7)	58.8	(1.4)	33.3	(1.5)	0.0	(0.1)	0.3	(0.0)	0.5	(0.1)	470	(7.2)	500	(3.6)	521	(4.7)
Newfoundland and Labrador	2.8	(0.8)	56.3	(1.9)	41.0	(1.6)	c	c	0.2	(0.0)	0.4	(0.1)	c	c	486	(3.7)	505	(5.8)
Nova Scotia	17.9	(1.2)	43.0	(1.4)	39.1	(1.2)	-0.1	(0.1)	0.3	(0.1)	0.5	(0.0)	491	(5.9)	496	(4.4)	509	(6.7)
Ontario	5.8	(0.4)	25.7	(1.3)	68.5	(1.2)	0.2	(0.1)	0.4	(0.1)	0.5	(0.0)	488	(9.1)	503	(5.1)	525	(4.4)
Prince Edward Island	3.2	(0.5)	58.7	(1.5)	38.0	(1.4)	0.1	(0.1)	0.2	(0.0)	0.5	(0.0)	459	(14.6)	471	(3.6)	497	(3.8)
Quebec	19.7	(0.9)	45.2	(1.0)	35.2	(1.3)	0.1	(0.0)	0.3	(0.0)	0.5	(0.0)	512	(4.5)	539	(3.6)	553	(4.6)
Saskatchewan	5.3	(0.7)	54.6	(2.1)	40.1	(1.8)	0.3	(0.1)	0.3	(0.0)	0.5	(0.0)	490	(9.2)	501	(3.3)	523	(4.4)
Italy																		
Abruzzo	3.7	(0.5)	5.5	(0.8)	90.8	(1.1)	-0.3	(0.1)	-0.1	(0.1)	0.1	(0.0)	405	(12.4)	438	(10.4)	482	(6.5)
Basilicata	1.6	(0.3)	3.5	(0.5)	94.9	(0.6)	c	c	-0.3	(0.1)	-0.2	(0.0)	c	c	443	(12.0)	468	(4.3)
Bolzano	3.1	(0.4)	7.5	(0.6)	89.4	(0.7)	-0.6	(0.1)	-0.4	(0.1)	0.0	(0.0)	435	(14.2)	484	(8.4)	512	(2.0)
Calabria	4.2	(0.5)	6.7	(0.6)	89.1	(0.8)	-0.2	(0.1)	0.0	(0.1)	-0.2	(0.1)	393	(13.6)	414	(12.0)	434	(5.9)
Campania	3.1	(0.5)	9.0	(1.0)	87.9	(1.2)	-0.4	(0.2)	-0.3	(0.1)	-0.2	(0.1)	384	(14.7)	431	(9.4)	458	(7.9)
Emilia Romagna	5.8	(0.6)	8.8	(0.8)	85.4	(1.1)	-0.5	(0.1)	-0.4	(0.1)	0.1	(0.0)	423	(16.9)	474	(10.5)	509	(6.7)
Friuli Venezia Giulia	4.4	(0.7)	3.8	(0.5)	91.8	(0.8)	-0.4	(0.2)	0.1	(0.1)	0.1	(0.0)	452	(16.4)	491	(11.2)	529	(4.3)
Lazio	4.4	(0.6)	8.4	(0.8)	87.2	(0.9)	0.0	(0.1)	0.0	(0.2)	0.2	(0.1)	428	(15.7)	439	(11.7)	481	(6.5)
Liguria	6.6	(0.8)	10.4	(1.1)	83.0	(1.2)	-0.2	(0.1)	-0.2	(0.1)	0.1	(0.0)	439	(14.4)	454	(7.7)	497	(6.4)
Lombardia	3.9	(0.5)	6.9	(0.8)	89.3	(1.0)	-0.4	(0.2)	0.0	(0.1)	0.1	(0.1)	456	(12.4)	483	(9.8)	523	(7.7)
Marche	6.0	(0.9)	7.0	(0.9)	87.0	(1.1)	-0.4	(0.1)	0.0	(0.1)	0.0	(0.0)	432	(11.4)	458	(11.8)	505	(5.5)
Molise	3.2	(0.6)	3.6	(0.6)	93.2	(0.8)	-0.1	(0.2)	-0.4	(0.2)	-0.1	(0.0)	433	(18.7)	426	(21.5)	469	(2.5)
Piemonte	3.8	(0.7)	8.8	(0.7)	87.4	(1.1)	-0.4	(0.2)	-0.2	(0.1)	0.0	(0.0)	466	(12.7)	477	(7.0)	502	(6.8)
Puglia	2.8	(0.5)	6.9	(0.6)	90.3	(0.7)	-0.7	(0.1)	-0.2	(0.1)	-0.3	(0.0)	438	(14.1)	445	(11.5)	483	(6.2)
Sardegna	4.4	(0.8)	6.5	(0.8)	89.1	(1.1)	-0.4	(0.1)	-0.1	(0.1)	-0.1	(0.0)	413	(16.1)	443	(12.6)	462	(5.1)
Sicilia	5.0	(1.0)	13.2	(0.9)	81.8	(1.4)	-0.5	(0.1)	0.0	(0.1)	-0.1	(0.0)	389	(22.0)	436	(9.2)	453	(5.0)
Toscana	4.6	(0.7)	8.4	(0.8)	87.0	(0.9)	-0.6	(0.1)	-0.1	(0.1)	0.0	(0.1)	419	(11.6)	473	(8.2)	504	(5.2)
Trento	5.1	(0.9)	4.9	(0.6)	90.1	(1.1)	-0.2	(0.1)	-0.2	(0.1)	0.0	(0.0)	479	(16.3)	488	(11.6)	529	(4.1)
Umbria	3.9	(0.4)	8.0	(0.6)	88.1	(0.7)	-0.5	(0.1)	0.0	(0.1)	0.2	(0.0)	440	(10.3)	473	(14.5)	498	(6.6)
Valle d'Aosta	4.3	(0.8)	5.6	(0.8)	90.1	(1.0)	-0.2	(0.2)	-0.2	(0.1)	-0.2	(0.0)	458	(15.6)	457	(13.6)	497	(2.4)
Veneto	5.6	(1.0)	5.7	(0.7)	88.8	(1.2)	-0.5	(0.1)	-0.3	(0.2)	0.0	(0.0)	458	(15.8)	464	(8.8)	532	(7.6)
Mexico																		
Aguascalientes	4.9	(0.8)	20.8	(1.3)	74.3	(1.5)	-1.2	(0.1)	-1.1	(0.1)	-0.6	(0.1)	403	(10.4)	438	(7.4)	440	(4.6)
Baja California	7.8	(1.5)	26.1	(2.0)	66.1	(2.6)	-1.3	(0.2)	-0.9	(0.1)	-0.6	(0.1)	388	(12.8)	415	(6.3)	419	(7.1)
Baja California Sur	6.4	(1.1)	17.7	(1.8)	75.9	(2.5)	-1.7	(0.1)	-1.0	(0.1)	-0.7	(0.1)	382	(18.0)	392	(7.0)	423	(4.3)
Campeche	16.2	(1.3)	11.7	(1.2)	72.1	(1.6)	-1.9	(0.1)	-1.7	(0.2)	-1.1	(0.1)	360	(7.4)	385	(8.8)	407	(4.0)
Chiapas	21.8	(2.1)	12.3	(1.2)	65.8	(2.5)	-2.3	(0.1)	-1.8	(0.2)	-1.6	(0.1)	353	(8.9)	368	(13.0)	382	(7.1)
Chihuahua	13.9	(2.3)	28.4	(3.1)	57.7	(4.8)	-1.5	(0.1)	-1.0	(0.1)	-0.5	(0.1)	385	(7.5)	423	(6.4)	443	(9.3)
Coahuila	6.7	(1.0)	18.2	(1.6)	75.1	(2.1)	-1.2	(0.1)	-1.1	(0.1)	-0.7	(0.1)	381	(12.3)	424	(8.5)	421	(8.5)
Colima	8.3	(1.1)	14.1	(1.5)	77.7	(1.5)	-1.2	(0.2)	-0.9	(0.1)	-0.7	(0.1)	375	(10.1)	437	(8.9)	434	(4.7)
Distrito Federal	5.6	(0.9)	17.1	(1.1)	77.4	(1.6)	-0.9	(0.3)	-0.7	(0.2)	-0.5	(0.1)	402	(12.2)	421	(6.8)	432	(5.4)
Durango	7.1	(1.2)	18.5	(1.7)	74.4	(2.3)	-1.6	(0.2)	-1.3	(0.1)	-0.9	(0.1)	389	(15.8)	422	(7.7)	429	(6.5)
Guanajuato	7.9	(1.7)	14.2	(1.5)	77.9	(1.8)	-1.8	(0.2)	-1.5	(0.1)	-1.2	(0.1)	366	(11.0)	411	(11.2)	417	(5.5)
Guerrero	15.7	(1.8)	14.8	(1.4)	69.5	(2.5)	-2.2	(0.1)	-1.7	(0.1)	-1.5	(0.1)	345	(6.7)	361	(7.8)	374	(3.6)
Hidalgo	9.1	(1.3)	26.5	(2.1)	64.4	(2.5)	-2.1	(0.2)	-1.6	(0.1)	-1.3	(0.1)	379	(7.3)	406	(8.5)	412	(6.2)
Jalisco	7.3	(1.2)	12.7	(1.3)	80.0	(1.4)	-1.7	(0.2)	-1.3	(0.1)	-1.0	(0.1)	401	(12.6)	434	(13.1)	439	(5.6)
Mexico	8.5	(1.8)	23.7	(1.7)	67.8	(3.0)	-1.7	(0.2)	-1.4	(0.1)	-0.9	(0.1)	400	(11.8)	415	(5.5)	421	(6.4)
Morelos	8.0	(0.9)	21.2	(1.5)	70.8	(2.0)	-1.5	(0.2)	-1.3	(0.1)	-0.7	(0.1)	387	(12.0)	409	(7.2)	430	(9.1)
Nayarit	6.3	(1.0)	16.5	(1.3)	77.2	(1.8)	-1.7	(0.2)	-1.1	(0.1)	-0.9	(0.1)	374	(19.0)	412	(9.3)	418	(5.0)
Nuevo León	4.2	(0.9)	20.3	(1.5)	75.5	(1.4)	-0.6	(0.1)	-0.7	(0.1)	-0.4	(0.2)	413	(14.8)	434	(8.1)	438	(8.8)
Puebla	11.9	(1.8)	13.9	(1.6)	74.1	(2.6)	-2.3	(0.1)	-1.9	(0.1)	-1.3	(0.1)	371	(9.1)	412	(8.3)	424	(4.7)
Querétaro	5.0	(1.4)	19.4	(2.0)	75.6	(3.0)	-1.8	(0.2)	-1.4	(0.2)	-0.7	(0.2)	388	(9.5)	421	(9.5)	441	(5.9)
Quintana Roo	9.2	(1.4)	21.2	(1.5)	69.7	(1.6)	-1.6	(0.1)	-1.1	(0.1)	-0.8	(0.1)	369	(9.0)	400	(5.6)	420	(5.3)
San Luis Potosí	8.6	(2.3)	12.2	(1.3)	79.2	(3.4)	-2.1	(0.2)	-1.7	(0.2)	-1.1	(0.2)	365	(11.1)	404	(10.3)	419	(7.0)
Sinaloa	8.1	(1.2)	20.0	(1.8)	71.9	(1.7)	-1.6	(0.1)	-1.1	(0.1)	-0.9	(0.1)	387	(10.3)	412	(6.1)	414	(4.2)
Tabasco	13.9	(1.6)	11.3	(1.3)	74.8	(1.7)	-1.7	(0.1)	-1.4	(0.2)	-1.0	(0.1)	346	(7.1)	376	(7.6)	386	(4.2)
Tamaulipas	7.8	(2.6)	31.1	(2.7)	61.1	(3.0)	-1.6	(0.2)	-1.1	(0.1)	-0.7	(0.1)	381	(11.9)	409	(7.5)	416	(8.2)
Tlaxcala	5.7	(0.7)	23.7	(2.2)	70.6	(2.4)	-1.8	(0.2)	-1.5	(0.1)	-1.0	(0.1)	373	(11.4)	411	(7.2)	415	(5.0)
Veracruz	10.0	(1.6)	20.3	(1.5)	69.6	(1.7)	-2.0	(0.2)	-1.8	(0.1)	-1.3	(0.1)	379	(9.6)	398	(7.8)	408	(7.0)
Yucatán	10.8	(1.5)	11.7	(1.2)	77.5	(1.8)	-1.8	(0.2)	-1.2	(0.2)	-1.1	(0.1)	372	(8.2)	401	(9.8)	417	(4.6)
Zacatecas	9.0	(1.3)	13.9	(1.4)	77.1	(2.1)	-1.6	(0.1)	-1.4	(0.1)	-1.1	(0.1)	372	(9.7)	413	(7.1)	415	(3.9)

• PISA adjudicated region.

Notes: This table was calculated considering only students with data on the *PISA index of economic, social and cultural status*. Values that are statistically significant are indicated in bold (see Annex A3).

See Table II.4.12 for national data.

1. ESCS refers to the *PISA index of economic, social and cultural status*.

StatLink http://dx.doi.org/10.1787/888932964965

[Part 2/6]

Pre-primary school attendance, mathematics performance and students' socio-economic status, by region

Table B2.II.24   *Results based on students' self-reports*

	Percentage of students with						Mean ESCS[1]						Average mathematics performance of students with					
	No pre-primary school attendance		Pre-primary school attendance for one year or less		Pre-primary school attendance for more than one year		No pre-primary school attendance		Pre-primary school attendance for one year or less		Pre-primary school attendance for more than one year		No pre-primary school attendance		Pre-primary school attendance for one year or less		Pre-primary school attendance for more than one year	
	%	S.E.	%	S.E.	%	S.E.	Mean index	S.E.	Mean index	S.E.	Mean index	S.E.	Mean score	S.E.	Mean score	S.E.	Mean score	S.E.
Portugal																		
Alentejo	11.3	(1.6)	17.4	(1.3)	71.2	(2.1)	-0.6	(0.2)	-0.7	(0.2)	-0.2	(0.1)	442	(15.1)	458	(12.5)	505	(8.9)
Spain																		
Andalusia•	7.3	(1.2)	10.5	(0.9)	82.1	(1.6)	-0.8	(0.1)	-0.4	(0.1)	-0.3	(0.1)	427	(8.6)	464	(8.3)	478	(3.6)
Aragon•	6.1	(0.9)	7.0	(0.7)	87.0	(1.4)	-0.5	(0.1)	-0.3	(0.1)	0.0	(0.1)	426	(14.8)	446	(11.0)	508	(5.3)
Asturias•	2.5	(0.4)	6.0	(0.7)	91.5	(0.8)	-0.7	(0.1)	-0.5	(0.1)	0.0	(0.0)	405	(14.8)	420	(15.6)	509	(4.1)
Balearic Islands•	7.0	(0.9)	8.3	(1.0)	84.7	(1.5)	-0.7	(0.1)	-0.5	(0.1)	-0.1	(0.0)	407	(10.2)	435	(6.7)	487	(4.8)
Basque Country•	10.3	(0.8)	11.4	(0.6)	78.3	(1.1)	-0.2	(0.1)	-0.2	(0.0)	0.1	(0.0)	487	(5.5)	487	(4.1)	514	(2.6)
Cantabria•	3.8	(0.6)	7.3	(0.8)	88.8	(1.0)	-0.3	(0.1)	-0.4	(0.1)	0.0	(0.0)	443	(10.6)	444	(9.1)	499	(3.6)
Castile and Leon•	4.5	(0.6)	4.8	(0.7)	90.7	(1.0)	-0.7	(0.1)	-0.5	(0.1)	0.0	(0.1)	464	(15.4)	455	(12.5)	515	(4.0)
Catalonia•	6.0	(0.9)	5.2	(0.6)	88.9	(1.2)	-0.6	(0.2)	-0.5	(0.1)	-0.1	(0.1)	434	(8.5)	455	(9.3)	500	(5.0)
Extremadura•	3.6	(0.6)	7.4	(0.8)	88.9	(1.2)	-0.8	(0.2)	-0.6	(0.1)	-0.4	(0.1)	414	(17.8)	426	(8.3)	468	(4.2)
Galicia•	3.5	(0.5)	6.7	(0.7)	89.8	(0.8)	-0.7	(0.2)	-0.5	(0.1)	-0.1	(0.0)	440	(17.8)	443	(9.3)	495	(4.0)
La Rioja•	7.0	(0.7)	5.4	(0.7)	87.6	(0.9)	-0.9	(0.1)	-0.7	(0.1)	0.0	(0.0)	405	(13.7)	433	(11.0)	517	(2.4)
Madrid•	4.5	(0.7)	9.2	(1.0)	86.4	(1.3)	-0.6	(0.1)	-0.4	(0.1)	0.2	(0.1)	464	(12.4)	458	(9.0)	512	(3.5)
Murcia•	6.9	(1.2)	8.2	(0.7)	84.9	(1.5)	-0.9	(0.2)	-0.5	(0.1)	-0.4	(0.0)	396	(10.2)	439	(9.7)	471	(4.9)
Navarre•	9.4	(0.9)	9.9	(1.0)	80.7	(1.5)	-0.3	(0.1)	-0.4	(0.1)	0.0	(0.0)	488	(8.6)	484	(9.5)	525	(3.1)
United Kingdom																		
England	4.6	(0.4)	24.7	(0.6)	70.6	(0.8)	-0.1	(0.1)	0.2	(0.1)	0.4	(0.0)	447	(9.2)	481	(4.7)	509	(3.3)
Northern Ireland	7.7	(0.6)	49.6	(1.3)	42.8	(1.3)	0.0	(0.1)	0.3	(0.0)	0.4	(0.0)	459	(8.2)	489	(4.1)	496	(4.2)
Scotland•	3.0	(0.3)	29.5	(1.0)	67.5	(1.0)	-0.1	(0.1)	0.0	(0.0)	0.2	(0.0)	459	(10.8)	492	(3.8)	505	(2.8)
Wales	5.6	(0.4)	27.3	(0.8)	67.1	(0.9)	0.0	(0.1)	0.0	(0.0)	0.3	(0.0)	429	(6.4)	459	(3.5)	478	(2.3)
United States																		
Connecticut•	0.9	(0.3)	12.6	(0.9)	86.5	(1.1)	c	c	0.0	(0.1)	0.6	(0.1)	c	c	481	(7.2)	512	(6.2)
Florida•	1.6	(0.3)	20.8	(1.5)	77.6	(1.5)	-0.1	(0.2)	0.1	(0.1)	0.2	(0.1)	436	(13.5)	467	(5.3)	469	(6.2)
Massachusetts•	1.1	(0.3)	13.8	(1.1)	85.1	(1.1)	c	c	0.1	(0.1)	0.5	(0.1)	c	c	496	(7.2)	518	(6.5)
Argentina																		
Ciudad Autónoma de Buenos Aires•	3.7	(0.6)	9.3	(0.9)	87.0	(1.3)	-1.0	(0.2)	-0.9	(0.1)	-0.1	(0.1)	354	(18.5)	357	(8.8)	430	(6.8)
Brazil																		
Acre	27.3	(3.6)	34.9	(2.6)	37.7	(3.6)	-1.8	(0.1)	-1.3	(0.1)	-1.1	(0.1)	337	(5.8)	354	(5.7)	381	(7.7)
Alagoas	29.2	(2.0)	34.0	(2.3)	36.7	(1.9)	-2.1	(0.1)	-1.7	(0.2)	-1.3	(0.1)	325	(7.7)	340	(7.5)	363	(9.0)
Amapá	19.2	(2.9)	31.2	(2.1)	49.6	(3.1)	-1.3	(0.1)	-0.9	(0.2)	-0.8	(0.1)	341	(10.6)	357	(8.7)	373	(8.7)
Amazonas	32.6	(2.7)	28.4	(1.9)	39.0	(2.8)	-1.3	(0.1)	-1.0	(0.1)	-0.9	(0.1)	348	(6.0)	351	(6.2)	369	(9.5)
Bahia	28.0	(4.9)	29.1	(3.9)	42.9	(5.1)	-1.9	(0.2)	-1.5	(0.1)	-1.2	(0.1)	353	(10.7)	372	(12.6)	393	(11.2)
Ceará	25.7	(1.9)	25.5	(2.0)	48.7	(2.1)	-1.6	(0.1)	-1.7	(0.1)	-1.4	(0.1)	367	(10.8)	369	(8.4)	394	(11.8)
Espírito Santo	14.9	(1.1)	21.7	(1.9)	63.4	(2.4)	-1.5	(0.1)	-1.2	(0.2)	-1.1	(0.1)	392	(10.4)	414	(13.0)	423	(11.1)
Federal District	11.4	(0.7)	28.0	(2.0)	60.5	(2.0)	-1.3	(0.1)	-0.9	(0.1)	-0.4	(0.1)	388	(10.8)	396	(9.2)	434	(10.3)
Goiás	22.6	(1.2)	37.1	(2.3)	40.3	(2.1)	-1.6	(0.1)	-1.4	(0.1)	-1.0	(0.1)	369	(8.8)	373	(7.2)	395	(6.4)
Maranhão	20.8	(2.3)	26.2	(2.4)	53.0	(2.7)	-1.4	(0.2)	-1.4	(0.1)	-1.4	(0.2)	345	(14.6)	336	(12.1)	352	(15.1)
Mato Grosso	31.3	(2.5)	35.0	(2.6)	33.7	(3.1)	-1.6	(0.1)	-1.4	(0.1)	-0.9	(0.1)	356	(9.2)	365	(8.8)	392	(12.1)
Mato Grosso do Sul	22.7	(2.7)	34.0	(2.7)	43.3	(3.6)	-1.8	(0.1)	-1.0	(0.1)	-0.5	(0.1)	376	(8.5)	403	(5.8)	433	(10.5)
Minas Gerais	12.4	(1.8)	34.3	(2.3)	53.3	(2.6)	-1.6	(0.2)	-1.5	(0.1)	-1.1	(0.1)	404	(12.4)	385	(7.6)	416	(7.0)
Pará	23.8	(2.2)	27.1	(2.2)	49.1	(2.0)	-1.4	(0.1)	-1.2	(0.2)	-1.1	(0.1)	348	(5.5)	358	(5.7)	370	(5.6)
Paraíba	23.4	(2.7)	31.0	(2.7)	45.6	(4.4)	-1.5	(0.2)	-1.3	(0.1)	-0.8	(0.1)	372	(9.6)	388	(12.5)	417	(5.2)
Paraná	23.4	(2.4)	38.3	(3.3)	38.3	(3.8)	-1.6	(0.1)	-1.2	(0.1)	-0.7	(0.2)	370	(8.0)	399	(4.9)	434	(21.4)
Pernambuco	27.7	(3.1)	31.8	(2.0)	40.5	(3.5)	-1.9	(0.1)	-1.7	(0.1)	-1.4	(0.1)	353	(7.4)	355	(9.4)	378	(8.1)
Piauí	14.7	(2.2)	29.0	(1.7)	56.3	(2.1)	-1.8	(0.2)	-1.2	(0.2)	-1.1	(0.1)	355	(15.0)	374	(10.8)	402	(5.5)
Rio de Janeiro	21.5	(2.0)	28.1	(2.5)	50.4	(3.5)	-1.2	(0.1)	-1.0	(0.0)	-0.8	(0.1)	372	(8.4)	382	(8.8)	401	(7.6)
Rio Grande do Norte	19.5	(1.7)	30.6	(2.2)	49.9	(2.8)	-1.7	(0.2)	-1.5	(0.1)	-1.1	(0.1)	353	(8.7)	369	(9.4)	399	(13.6)
Rio Grande do Sul	22.0	(2.1)	44.8	(1.9)	33.2	(2.3)	-1.5	(0.1)	-1.3	(0.1)	-0.9	(0.1)	392	(7.5)	412	(5.1)	414	(7.5)
Rondônia	35.5	(3.5)	28.0	(1.9)	36.5	(3.0)	-2.0	(0.2)	-1.3	(0.2)	-0.9	(0.2)	372	(5.5)	377	(8.2)	397	(7.2)
Roraima	24.3	(1.9)	27.4	(1.6)	48.2	(2.2)	-1.4	(0.1)	-1.1	(0.1)	-0.8	(0.1)	338	(6.1)	357	(7.1)	380	(8.2)
Santa Catarina	18.0	(2.4)	38.9	(2.9)	43.2	(4.6)	-1.5	(0.1)	-1.4	(0.1)	-0.9	(0.2)	378	(9.9)	414	(6.1)	436	(9.7)
São Paulo	11.2	(0.9)	35.5	(1.8)	53.4	(1.9)	-1.5	(0.1)	-1.0	(0.0)	-0.8	(0.1)	368	(5.6)	395	(4.6)	419	(5.8)
Sergipe	12.4	(2.0)	37.1	(2.1)	50.5	(2.5)	-1.7	(0.1)	-1.3	(0.1)	-1.1	(0.1)	374	(8.4)	370	(10.6)	399	(9.7)
Tocantins	28.6	(2.5)	38.1	(2.2)	33.3	(2.5)	-1.6	(0.1)	-1.2	(0.1)	-1.1	(0.1)	355	(7.8)	360	(6.7)	381	(10.7)
Colombia																		
Bogotá	11.0	(1.0)	59.9	(1.7)	29.1	(1.7)	-1.3	(0.1)	-1.1	(0.1)	-1.0	(0.1)	382	(6.0)	393	(3.0)	398	(6.9)
Cali	16.3	(1.3)	47.3	(1.8)	36.5	(1.7)	-1.1	(0.1)	-0.8	(0.1)	-0.7	(0.1)	362	(8.5)	385	(6.7)	381	(7.5)
Manizales	8.4	(1.4)	53.0	(1.3)	38.6	(1.7)	-1.6	(0.1)	-0.8	(0.1)	-0.5	(0.1)	382	(7.7)	404	(5.5)	411	(5.4)
Medellín	8.6	(1.4)	59.5	(1.8)	32.0	(2.0)	-1.8	(0.1)	-1.0	(0.1)	-0.5	(0.1)	347	(7.9)	390	(5.5)	417	(14.3)
Russian Federation																		
Perm Territory region•	10.0	(1.1)	6.9	(0.7)	83.1	(1.4)	-0.6	(0.1)	-0.3	(0.1)	0.0	(0.0)	449	(7.6)	461	(12.5)	491	(5.4)
United Arab Emirates																		
Abu Dhabi•	27.1	(1.1)	25.6	(1.0)	47.3	(1.3)	-0.1	(0.0)	0.3	(0.0)	0.5	(0.0)	389	(4.7)	425	(5.9)	443	(4.1)
Ajman	40.8	(3.0)	25.9	(1.7)	33.3	(3.5)	-0.3	(0.1)	0.0	(0.1)	0.1	(0.1)	390	(8.9)	404	(9.5)	429	(7.8)
Dubai•	17.3	(0.7)	28.9	(0.8)	53.9	(0.8)	0.3	(0.0)	0.5	(0.0)	0.6	(0.0)	425	(4.0)	467	(2.8)	480	(1.8)
Fujairah	26.4	(2.9)	20.8	(1.8)	52.7	(2.6)	-0.3	(0.1)	0.1	(0.1)	0.1	(0.1)	388	(8.5)	404	(18.7)	431	(7.2)
Ras al-Khaimah	27.3	(3.6)	22.1	(2.2)	50.6	(3.4)	-0.3	(0.1)	0.1	(0.1)	0.2	(0.1)	399	(8.6)	414	(8.8)	428	(6.5)
Sharjah	18.8	(2.4)	29.2	(2.0)	52.1	(3.4)	0.2	(0.1)	0.4	(0.1)	0.5	(0.1)	406	(10.2)	440	(9.2)	456	(12.6)
Umm al-Quwain	32.2	(2.3)	20.0	(2.4)	47.8	(2.8)	-0.4	(0.1)	0.0	(0.1)	0.0	(0.1)	383	(6.0)	394	(9.0)	413	(7.4)

• PISA adjudicated region.
Notes: This table was calculated considering only students with data on the *PISA index of economic, social and cultural status*. Values that are statistically significant are indicated in bold (see Annex A3).
See Table II.4.12 for national data.
1. ESCS refers to the *PISA index of economic, social and cultural status*.
StatLink ⟨ms⟩ http://dx.doi.org/10.1787/888932964965

[Part 3/6]
Pre-primary school attendance, mathematics performance and students' socio-economic status, by region

Table B2.II.24 — *Results based on students' self-reports*

| | Difference in mathematics performance between students who reported having attended pre-primary school for one year or less and those who had not attended pre-primary school | | | | Difference in mathematics performance between students who reported having attended pre-primary school for more than one year and those who had not attended pre-primary school | | | | Increased likelihood of students who had not attended pre-primary school scoring in the bottom quarter of the national mathematics performance distribution | | Population relevance of students who had not attended pre-primary school scoring in the bottom quarter of the national mathematics performance distribution | |
| | Before accounting for student's ESCS[1] | | After accounting for student's ESCS[1] | | Before accounting for student's ESCS[1] | | After accounting for student's ESCS[1] | | | | | |
	Score dif.	S.E.	Score dif.	S.E.	Score dif.	S.E.	Score dif.	S.E.	Ratio	S.E.	%	S.E.
Australia												
Australian Capital Territory	c	c	c	c	c	c	c	c	c	c	c	c
New South Wales	49	(12.9)	32	(13.8)	71	(13.0)	41	(13.8)	2.03	(0.3)	3	(0.8)
Northern Territory	c	c	c	c	c	c	c	c	c	c	c	c
Queensland	39	(9.4)	31	(9.0)	47	(9.4)	30	(9.0)	1.76	(0.2)	4	(1.0)
South Australia	44	(15.6)	35	(13.4)	39	(15.9)	24	(13.4)	1.96	(0.3)	5	(1.5)
Tasmania	7	(18.6)	5	(17.3)	4	(20.1)	-3	(18.3)	1.30	(0.3)	1	(1.3)
Victoria	34	(8.5)	24	(8.7)	49	(9.2)	30	(9.1)	1.98	(0.2)	5	(1.3)
Western Australia	17	(12.6)	12	(11.0)	38	(12.5)	23	(10.5)	1.55	(0.2)	3	(1.4)
Belgium												
Flemish Community•	-12	(18.2)	-14	(16.1)	83	(13.6)	53	(12.9)	c	c	c	c
French Community	18	(12.8)	4	(10.6)	82	(10.6)	54	(9.1)	2.26	(0.3)	3	(0.9)
German-speaking Community	c	c	c	c	c	c	c	c	c	c	c	c
Canada												
Alberta	2	(9.2)	2	(9.2)	38	(9.7)	27	(10.0)	1.27	(0.2)	1	(1.0)
British Columbia	10	(10.9)	9	(11.0)	52	(11.8)	43	(11.7)	1.53	(0.3)	2	(1.2)
Manitoba	34	(11.0)	21	(9.6)	51	(12.1)	25	(9.9)	1.51	(0.3)	3	(1.7)
New Brunswick	29	(8.3)	21	(8.1)	50	(9.0)	42	(9.2)	1.72	(0.2)	5	(1.6)
Newfoundland and Labrador	c	c	c	c	c	c	c	c	c	c	c	c
Nova Scotia	4	(7.8)	-6	(7.2)	18	(8.9)	0	(9.6)	1.18	(0.2)	3	(3.2)
Ontario	16	(8.4)	10	(8.3)	37	(8.8)	27	(7.9)	1.34	(0.2)	2	(1.0)
Prince Edward Island	12	(15.5)	8	(14.9)	38	(15.2)	22	(15.1)	1.52	(0.4)	2	(1.2)
Quebec	27	(4.5)	21	(4.4)	41	(5.6)	24	(5.1)	1.53	(0.1)	9	(1.9)
Saskatchewan	11	(9.6)	10	(9.9)	33	(9.0)	26	(9.2)	1.34	(0.3)	2	(1.4)
Italy												
Abruzzo	33	(15.3)	29	(14.4)	76	(12.4)	69	(12.5)	2.14	(0.4)	4	(1.2)
Basilicata	c	c	c	c	c	c	c	c	c	c	c	c
Bolzano	49	(16.0)	46	(15.7)	77	(14.4)	61	(14.2)	2.20	(0.3)	4	(0.9)
Calabria	21	(17.6)	17	(16.9)	41	(15.0)	41	(14.6)	1.60	(0.4)	2	(1.3)
Campania	48	(12.2)	40	(12.0)	74	(14.5)	66	(12.3)	2.52	(0.4)	4	(1.2)
Emilia Romagna	51	(16.6)	43	(14.8)	86	(16.2)	66	(13.4)	2.03	(0.3)	6	(1.8)
Friuli Venezia Giulia	39	(19.6)	30	(17.3)	76	(16.2)	64	(14.7)	2.22	(0.5)	5	(2.2)
Lazio	11	(16.8)	11	(16.1)	53	(14.1)	49	(14.7)	2.05	(0.4)	4	(1.7)
Liguria	14	(14.7)	12	(12.8)	58	(13.1)	48	(10.9)	1.82	(0.3)	5	(2.2)
Lombardia	27	(14.0)	13	(14.2)	66	(13.0)	52	(12.9)	2.00	(0.4)	4	(1.2)
Marche	27	(18.1)	22	(21.0)	74	(10.5)	67	(10.7)	2.36	(0.4)	8	(2.5)
Molise	-7	(29.3)	3	(28.7)	36	(18.7)	36	(18.1)	2.07	(0.5)	3	(1.4)
Piemonte	11	(15.6)	10	(15.6)	36	(16.5)	27	(16.8)	1.66	(0.4)	2	(1.6)
Puglia	7	(17.0)	-6	(16.8)	44	(14.7)	31	(14.4)	1.83	(0.6)	2	(1.5)
Sardegna	30	(19.4)	20	(20.4)	49	(15.3)	42	(16.1)	1.61	(0.4)	3	(1.6)
Sicilia	47	(22.2)	35	(19.8)	64	(21.0)	55	(19.4)	2.06	(0.4)	5	(2.4)
Toscana	54	(12.4)	41	(12.7)	84	(12.6)	64	(11.2)	2.61	(0.3)	7	(1.4)
Trento	9	(18.6)	10	(18.9)	50	(16.6)	45	(16.5)	1.73	(0.4)	4	(1.8)
Umbria	33	(15.8)	22	(16.6)	58	(10.4)	45	(10.6)	1.51	(0.3)	2	(1.1)
Valle d'Aosta	-1	(23.4)	-2	(22.3)	39	(15.8)	39	(15.3)	1.66	(0.4)	3	(1.6)
Veneto	7	(15.4)	-1	(15.2)	74	(13.8)	61	(12.5)	2.53	(0.3)	8	(2.0)
Mexico												
Aguascalientes	35	(10.7)	33	(10.7)	37	(10.4)	24	(10.8)	1.66	(0.5)	3	(2.4)
Baja California	27	(10.3)	24	(9.1)	30	(14.5)	21	(12.7)	1.54	(0.4)	4	(2.6)
Baja California Sur	9	(14.7)	-2	(14.5)	40	(16.6)	21	(15.6)	1.99	(0.4)	6	(2.3)
Campeche	26	(10.7)	23	(11.2)	47	(7.1)	36	(7.4)	2.24	(0.4)	17	(4.0)
Chiapas	15	(12.5)	14	(11.7)	30	(8.5)	24	(8.4)	1.53	(0.3)	10	(4.6)
Chihuahua	38	(8.4)	32	(8.6)	58	(9.2)	38	(10.1)	2.42	(0.4)	16	(4.2)
Coahuila	43	(11.2)	40	(10.9)	39	(9.4)	26	(9.1)	1.87	(0.3)	5	(2.0)
Colima	62	(12.7)	58	(11.8)	59	(8.7)	47	(7.6)	2.39	(0.2)	10	(1.7)
Distrito Federal	19	(14.1)	16	(14.2)	30	(12.4)	21	(11.4)	1.66	(0.4)	4	(2.0)
Durango	33	(15.9)	30	(14.9)	40	(17.5)	26	(17.2)	1.83	(0.6)	6	(3.9)
Guanajuato	45	(14.3)	40	(13.6)	51	(10.2)	38	(9.1)	2.03	(0.4)	8	(3.7)
Guerrero	16	(8.6)	13	(8.7)	30	(6.7)	22	(6.8)	1.55	(0.2)	8	(3.6)
Hidalgo	27	(10.3)	20	(9.9)	33	(8.3)	16	(8.1)	1.44	(0.2)	4	(1.9)
Jalisco	32	(11.9)	29	(11.4)	37	(12.5)	29	(11.1)	1.75	(0.4)	5	(3.0)
Mexico	15	(12.0)	11	(11.8)	21	(11.5)	10	(11.2)	1.55	(0.3)	4	(3.5)
Morelos	22	(9.3)	18	(9.7)	43	(11.1)	20	(10.6)	1.79	(0.4)	6	(2.6)
Nayarit	38	(15.9)	30	(15.6)	44	(18.2)	33	(18.0)	1.95	(0.4)	6	(2.5)
Nuevo León	21	(13.4)	23	(12.9)	25	(14.5)	20	(13.7)	1.47	(0.5)	2	(2.1)
Puebla	42	(11.4)	36	(11.6)	53	(8.5)	35	(8.5)	2.02	(0.3)	11	(3.0)
Querétaro	33	(11.3)	27	(11.7)	54	(9.9)	35	(11.1)	2.02	(0.5)	5	(2.6)
Quintana Roo	31	(9.7)	27	(10.3)	51	(8.4)	37	(9.2)	2.02	(0.3)	9	(2.3)
San Luis Potosí	39	(12.1)	33	(10.4)	54	(11.6)	32	(8.3)	2.07	(0.4)	8	(4.5)
Sinaloa	25	(10.9)	20	(11.1)	27	(8.7)	16	(8.9)	1.65	(0.3)	5	(1.9)
Tabasco	31	(9.7)	29	(9.5)	40	(6.6)	31	(7.4)	1.80	(0.4)	10	(4.8)
Tamaulipas	28	(11.7)	24	(11.7)	35	(11.0)	16	(9.5)	1.55	(0.3)	4	(2.3)
Tlaxcala	38	(11.1)	35	(10.5)	42	(10.3)	31	(9.7)	2.11	(0.4)	6	(2.2)
Veracruz	19	(10.8)	16	(11.5)	29	(8.9)	17	(9.2)	1.47	(0.4)	5	(3.4)
Yucatán	29	(9.5)	20	(10.1)	45	(8.3)	32	(7.8)	1.93	(0.4)	9	(3.9)
Zacatecas	41	(11.9)	38	(11.2)	43	(9.2)	35	(8.8)	2.01	(0.3)	8	(2.7)

• PISA adjudicated region.
Notes: This table was calculated considering only students with data on the *PISA index of economic, social and cultural status*. Values that are statistically significant are indicated in bold (see Annex A3).
See Table II.4.12 for national data.
1. ESCS refers to the *PISA index of economic, social and cultural status*.
StatLink ᴍᴤᴘ http://dx.doi.org/10.1787/888932964965

[Part 4/6]

Pre-primary school attendance, mathematics performance and students' socio-economic status, by region

Table B2.II.24 — *Results based on students' self-reports*

| | Difference in mathematics performance between students who reported having attended pre-primary school for one year or less and those who had not attended pre-primary school | | | | Difference in mathematics performance between students who reported having attended pre-primary school for more than one year and those who had not attended pre-primary school | | | | Increased likelihood of students who had not attended pre-primary school scoring in the bottom quarter of the national mathematics performance distribution | | Population relevance of students who had not attended pre-primary school scoring in the bottom quarter of the national mathematics performance distribution | |
| | Before accounting for student's ESCS[1] | | After accounting for student's ESCS[1] | | Before accounting for student's ESCS[1] | | After accounting for student's ESCS[1] | | | | | |
	Score dif.	S.E.	Score dif.	S.E.	Score dif.	S.E.	Score dif.	S.E.	Ratio	S.E.	%	S.E.
Portugal												
Alentejo	16	(10.6)	18	(9.4)	**63**	(9.8)	**50**	(8.6)	**2.15**	(0.4)	12	(3.9)
Spain												
Andalusia*	**37**	(10.6)	**24**	(11.0)	**51**	(8.4)	**37**	(8.4)	**2.01**	(0.3)	7	(1.8)
Aragon*	21	(17.2)	11	(12.6)	**82**	(14.1)	**66**	(11.2)	**2.50**	(0.3)	8	(1.9)
Asturias*	15	(19.3)	8	(18.2)	**103**	(14.9)	**81**	(14.0)	**2.95**	(0.4)	5	(1.2)
Balearic Islands*	**29**	(10.8)	**25**	(9.6)	**80**	(9.2)	**63**	(8.5)	**2.50**	(0.3)	9	(1.9)
Basque Country*	0	(6.0)	-2	(5.8)	**27**	(5.5)	**19**	(5.3)	**1.38**	(0.1)	4	(1.2)
Cantabria*	1	(15.5)	2	(15.1)	**56**	(10.5)	**48**	(10.1)	**2.12**	(0.3)	4	(1.1)
Castile and Leon*	-8	(16.3)	-14	(12.7)	**51**	(14.6)	**34**	(12.5)	**1.90**	(0.3)	4	(1.4)
Catalonia*	21	(12.5)	13	(13.0)	**67**	(8.6)	**50**	(8.0)	**2.15**	(0.3)	6	(1.6)
Extremadura*	12	(17.8)	5	(14.6)	**54**	(16.1)	**42**	(13.8)	**1.74**	(0.3)	3	(1.1)
Galicia*	3	(21.5)	-3	(20.1)	**55**	(17.4)	**41**	(16.3)	**1.92**	(0.3)	3	(1.2)
La Rioja*	28	(16.5)	22	(16.0)	**113**	(14.1)	**84**	(13.9)	**2.95**	(0.3)	12	(2.1)
Madrid*	-6	(15.3)	-15	(13.0)	**47**	(11.9)	**21**	(10.3)	**1.64**	(0.3)	3	(1.2)
Murcia*	**43**	(12.4)	**33**	(13.2)	**76**	(10.3)	**60**	(9.4)	**2.45**	(0.3)	9	(2.4)
Navarre*	-4	(12.4)	-2	(12.3)	**37**	(8.3)	**29**	(8.3)	**1.57**	(0.2)	5	(1.6)
United Kingdom												
England	**33**	(8.4)	**24**	(8.1)	**62**	(8.8)	**43**	(8.5)	**1.89**	(0.2)	4	(0.7)
Northern Ireland	**30**	(7.9)	**20**	(7.8)	**37**	(9.0)	**20**	(8.6)	**1.58**	(0.2)	4	(1.4)
Scotland*	**32**	(10.6)	**28**	(10.2)	**46**	(10.8)	**35**	(10.5)	**1.84**	(0.3)	2	(0.9)
Wales	**31**	(7.1)	**30**	(6.7)	**49**	(6.9)	**41**	(6.4)	**1.75**	(0.2)	4	(0.9)
United States												
Connecticut*	c	c	c	c	c	c	c	c	c	c	c	c
Florida*	**30**	(14.2)	**26**	(12.9)	**33**	(13.8)	**20**	(12.4)	1.56	(0.4)	1	(0.6)
Massachusetts*	c	c	c	c	c	c	c	c	c	c	c	c
Argentina												
Ciudad Autónoma de Buenos Aires*	4	(19.2)	1	(15.5)	**76**	(18.3)	**40**	(13.5)	**2.34**	(0.5)	5	(1.8)
Brazil												
Acre	**16**	(5.1)	8	(5.9)	**44**	(7.7)	**30**	(7.5)	**1.64**	(0.3)	15	(6.0)
Alagoas	14	(8.8)	9	(8.9)	**38**	(9.8)	**22**	(9.1)	1.28	(0.2)	7	(5.6)
Amapá	**15**	(7.1)	6	(10.0)	**32**	(6.5)	**23**	(7.7)	**1.76**	(0.3)	13	(4.2)
Amazonas	3	(8.4)	1	(8.4)	21	(11.1)	15	(9.9)	1.22	(0.4)	6	(10.1)
Bahia	18	(15.6)	8	(12.7)	**39**	(17.1)	22	(14.7)	1.64	(0.6)	15	(12.4)
Ceará	2	(12.3)	4	(12.2)	**27**	(12.1)	21	(11.4)	1.30	(0.3)	7	(7.2)
Espírito Santo	**21**	(10.1)	14	(9.9)	**31**	(8.3)	**17**	(7.5)	1.25	(0.3)	3	(4.2)
Federal District	8	(10.5)	-5	(7.8)	**46**	(8.6)	12	(8.5)	1.48	(0.4)	5	(3.6)
Goiás	4	(8.8)	-1	(8.4)	**26**	(7.4)	7	(6.5)	1.32	(0.2)	7	(3.8)
Maranhão	-9	(9.9)	-9	(11.0)	8	(7.2)	8	(7.8)	1.00	(0.2)	0	(4.4)
Mato Grosso	9	(8.2)	6	(7.8)	**36**	(10.5)	**20**	(7.9)	1.33	(0.3)	9	(6.7)
Mato Grosso do Sul	**26**	(9.5)	14	(8.9)	**57**	(13.2)	19	(10.9)	**1.85**	(0.4)	16	(6.8)
Minas Gerais	**-19**	(9.3)	**-21**	(9.5)	11	(10.5)	-2	(10.0)	0.99	(0.2)	0	(2.8)
Pará	11	(7.5)	7	(7.0)	**22**	(6.4)	**14**	(7.0)	1.32	(0.2)	7	(4.8)
Paraíba	17	(13.7)	9	(9.1)	**46**	(8.0)	**24**	(8.1)	**1.80**	(0.3)	16	(5.3)
Paraná	**29**	(7.4)	**20**	(8.0)	**64**	(18.5)	**29**	(7.9)	**1.91**	(0.3)	17	(5.2)
Pernambuco	2	(8.0)	-1	(7.7)	**25**	(6.5)	**14**	(5.1)	1.08	(0.2)	2	(4.8)
Piauí	**19**	(9.8)	-1	(10.8)	**47**	(10.8)	25	(11.6)	**1.79**	(0.4)	10	(5.1)
Rio de Janeiro	10	(10.1)	6	(9.3)	**29**	(10.3)	**20**	(8.0)	1.35	(0.2)	7	(4.2)
Rio Grande do Norte	16	(10.3)	11	(9.9)	**46**	(15.4)	24	(10.5)	**1.59**	(0.4)	10	(6.0)
Rio Grande do Sul	**19**	(8.6)	16	(8.8)	**21**	(9.4)	12	(11.3)	1.54	(0.4)	11	(7.2)
Rondônia	6	(10.4)	0	(10.1)	**26**	(7.6)	15	(8.1)	1.39	(0.3)	12	(6.7)
Roraima	**19**	(7.8)	12	(8.1)	**42**	(11.1)	**25**	(9.3)	**1.71**	(0.3)	15	(6.0)
Santa Catarina	**36**	(8.3)	**33**	(8.1)	**58**	(10.9)	**46**	(9.9)	**2.14**	(0.4)	17	(4.5)
São Paulo	**27**	(6.8)	**21**	(6.1)	**51**	(7.6)	**30**	(6.2)	**1.79**	(0.2)	8	(1.7)
Sergipe	-5	(11.5)	-10	(10.0)	24	(10.5)	14	(8.1)	1.02	(0.3)	0	(3.6)
Tocantins	6	(6.9)	-2	(6.0)	**26**	(9.2)	13	(6.7)	1.34	(0.2)	9	(5.4)
Colombia												
Bogotá	11	(6.1)	8	(6.4)	15	(8.4)	7	(7.4)	1.20	(0.2)	2	(2.1)
Cali	23	(8.9)	15	(7.7)	19	(8.3)	7	(7.4)	**1.47**	(0.3)	7	(3.8)
Manizales	**22**	(10.1)	-3	(7.6)	**29**	(10.9)	-4	(10.2)	**1.75**	(0.3)	6	(2.6)
Medellín	**43**	(8.6)	**25**	(8.7)	**70**	(15.2)	14	(8.7)	**2.16**	(0.3)	9	(2.9)
Russian Federation												
Perm Territory region*	12	(13.2)	0	(11.9)	**42**	(8.1)	**22**	(7.5)	**1.66**	(0.2)	6	(2.0)
United Arab Emirates												
Abu Dhabi*	**37**	(6.0)	**29**	(5.3)	**54**	(5.6)	**43**	(5.8)	**1.99**	(0.2)	21	(2.6)
Ajman	14	(10.5)	8	(9.6)	**39**	(7.8)	**32**	(7.2)	**1.65**	(0.2)	21	(6.9)
Dubai*	**43**	(5.0)	**31**	(5.2)	**55**	(4.7)	**43**	(4.6)	**2.00**	(0.1)	15	(1.7)
Fujairah	16	(14.8)	10	(13.0)	**43**	(7.7)	**36**	(7.9)	**1.70**	(0.3)	16	(5.6)
Ras al-Khaimah	14	(8.0)	8	(7.9)	**29**	(9.0)	**20**	(9.1)	**1.42**	(0.2)	10	(4.9)
Sharjah	**34**	(10.1)	**29**	(9.4)	**50**	(14.8)	**42**	(13.8)	**1.82**	(0.4)	13	(5.5)
Umm al-Quwain	10	(11.5)	2	(12.0)	**30**	(9.8)	**20**	(9.9)	**1.69**	(0.3)	18	(6.7)

* PISA adjudicated region.
Notes: This table was calculated considering only students with data on the *PISA index of economic, social and cultural status*. Values that are statistically significant are indicated in bold (see Annex A3).
See Table II.4.12 for national data.
1. ESCS refers to the *PISA index of economic, social and cultural status*.
StatLink ⣿⣿🖼️ http://dx.doi.org/10.1787/888932964965

[Part 5/6]
Pre-primary school attendance, mathematics performance and students' socio-economic status, by region

Table B2.II.24 *Results based on students' self-reports*

	Effect size for students who had not attended pre-primary school		Effect size for students who had attended pre-primary school for one year or less		Effect size for students who had attended pre-primary school for more than one year		Proportion of the variation in student performance explained by having attended pre-primary school for less than one year	
	Effect size	S.E.	Effect size	S.E.	Effect size	S.E.	%	S.E.
Australia								
Australian Capital Territory	c	c	-0.1	(0.1)	0.2	(0.1)	2.0	(1.2)
New South Wales	-0.6	(0.1)	-0.2	(0.0)	0.2	(0.0)	2.1	(0.6)
Northern Territory	c	c	0.1	(0.1)	0.1	(0.1)	2.8	(1.7)
Queensland	-0.4	(0.1)	0.0	(0.0)	0.1	(0.0)	1.2	(0.5)
South Australia	-0.4	(0.2)	0.1	(0.1)	0.0	(0.1)	1.1	(0.8)
Tasmania	-0.1	(0.2)	0.0	(0.1)	0.0	(0.1)	0.1	(0.3)
Victoria	-0.4	(0.1)	-0.1	(0.0)	0.2	(0.0)	1.9	(0.7)
Western Australia	-0.3	(0.1)	-0.2	(0.1)	0.2	(0.1)	1.7	(0.7)
Belgium								
Flemish Community•	-0.8	(0.1)	-0.9	(0.1)	0.8	(0.1)	3.7	(0.9)
French Community	-0.8	(0.1)	-0.7	(0.1)	0.7	(0.1)	4.3	(0.9)
German-speaking Community	c	c	0.0	(0.1)	0.1	(0.1)	0.6	(0.6)
Canada								
Alberta	-0.2	(0.1)	-0.4	(0.1)	0.4	(0.1)	3.9	(1.0)
British Columbia	-0.4	(0.1)	-0.5	(0.1)	0.5	(0.1)	6.7	(1.5)
Manitoba	-0.5	(0.1)	-0.1	(0.1)	0.2	(0.1)	2.1	(0.9)
New Brunswick	-0.5	(0.1)	-0.1	(0.1)	0.3	(0.1)	2.9	(1.1)
Newfoundland and Labrador	c	c	-0.2	(0.1)	0.2	(0.1)	1.4	(0.8)
Nova Scotia	-0.1	(0.1)	-0.1	(0.1)	0.2	(0.1)	0.9	(0.7)
Ontario	-0.4	(0.1)	-0.2	(0.1)	0.3	(0.1)	1.9	(0.7)
Prince Edward Island	-0.3	(0.2)	-0.3	(0.1)	0.3	(0.1)	2.6	(1.0)
Quebec	-0.4	(0.0)	0.0	(0.0)	0.2	(0.0)	2.6	(0.7)
Saskatchewan	-0.2	(0.1)	-0.2	(0.1)	0.3	(0.1)	2.0	(0.8)
Italy								
Abruzzo	-0.9	(0.1)	-0.5	(0.1)	0.6	(0.1)	3.6	(1.1)
Basilicata	c	c	-0.3	(0.1)	0.3	(0.1)	0.5	(0.4)
Bolzano	-0.8	(0.1)	-0.3	(0.1)	0.4	(0.1)	2.7	(0.9)
Calabria	-0.4	(0.2)	-0.2	(0.1)	0.3	(0.1)	1.1	(0.8)
Campania	-0.8	(0.2)	-0.3	(0.1)	0.4	(0.1)	2.7	(1.1)
Emilia Romagna	-0.8	(0.1)	-0.3	(0.1)	0.6	(0.1)	5.1	(1.8)
Friuli Venezia Giulia	-0.9	(0.2)	-0.4	(0.1)	0.7	(0.1)	3.8	(1.5)
Lazio	-0.5	(0.2)	-0.4	(0.1)	0.5	(0.1)	3.0	(1.1)
Liguria	-0.6	(0.1)	-0.4	(0.1)	0.6	(0.1)	4.2	(1.4)
Lombardia	-0.7	(0.1)	-0.4	(0.1)	0.5	(0.1)	3.3	(1.0)
Marche	-0.9	(0.1)	-0.5	(0.2)	0.7	(0.1)	5.9	(1.4)
Molise	-0.4	(0.2)	-0.4	(0.3)	0.4	(0.2)	1.4	(1.1)
Piemonte	-0.4	(0.2)	-0.3	(0.1)	0.3	(0.1)	1.2	(0.8)
Puglia	-0.5	(0.2)	-0.4	(0.1)	0.5	(0.1)	1.9	(0.8)
Sardegna	-0.6	(0.2)	-0.2	(0.1)	0.3	(0.1)	1.5	(1.0)
Sicilia	-0.7	(0.2)	-0.2	(0.1)	0.4	(0.1)	3.2	(2.1)
Toscana	-0.8	(0.1)	-0.3	(0.1)	0.5	(0.1)	4.3	(1.2)
Trento	-0.5	(0.2)	-0.5	(0.2)	0.5	(0.1)	2.8	(1.4)
Umbria	-0.6	(0.1)	-0.2	(0.1)	0.4	(0.1)	2.1	(0.7)
Valle d'Aosta	-0.4	(0.2)	-0.4	(0.2)	0.5	(0.1)	2.1	(1.0)
Veneto	-0.7	(0.1)	-0.7	(0.1)	0.8	(0.1)	6.2	(1.6)
Mexico								
Aguascalientes	-0.6	(0.2)	0.0	(0.1)	0.1	(0.1)	1.2	(0.7)
Baja California	-0.4	(0.2)	0.0	(0.1)	0.1	(0.1)	1.3	(1.3)
Baja California Sur	-0.5	(0.2)	-0.4	(0.1)	0.5	(0.1)	3.9	(1.9)
Campeche	-0.6	(0.1)	-0.2	(0.1)	0.5	(0.1)	6.1	(1.7)
Chiapas	-0.4	(0.1)	-0.1	(0.1)	0.3	(0.1)	2.7	(1.4)
Chihuahua	-0.7	(0.1)	-0.1	(0.1)	0.4	(0.1)	6.5	(1.9)
Coahuila	-0.6	(0.1)	0.1	(0.1)	0.1	(0.1)	2.0	(1.0)
Colima	-0.8	(0.1)	0.1	(0.1)	0.3	(0.1)	4.5	(1.3)
Distrito Federal	-0.4	(0.2)	-0.1	(0.1)	0.2	(0.1)	1.1	(0.7)
Durango	-0.5	(0.2)	0.0	(0.1)	0.2	(0.1)	2.0	(1.8)
Guanajuato	-0.7	(0.1)	0.0	(0.1)	0.3	(0.1)	3.4	(1.7)
Guerrero	-0.4	(0.1)	-0.1	(0.1)	0.3	(0.1)	2.7	(1.2)
Hidalgo	-0.5	(0.1)	0.0	(0.1)	0.2	(0.1)	1.6	(0.8)
Jalisco	-0.5	(0.2)	0.0	(0.1)	0.2	(0.1)	1.8	(1.4)
Mexico	-0.3	(0.2)	-0.1	(0.1)	0.2	(0.1)	0.9	(1.1)
Morelos	-0.5	(0.1)	-0.2	(0.1)	0.4	(0.1)	2.9	(1.2)
Nayarit	-0.5	(0.2)	0.0	(0.1)	0.2	(0.1)	1.9	(1.6)
Nuevo León	-0.3	(0.2)	0.0	(0.1)	0.1	(0.1)	0.5	(0.6)
Puebla	-0.7	(0.1)	-0.1	(0.1)	0.4	(0.1)	5.3	(1.6)
Querétaro	-0.7	(0.1)	-0.2	(0.1)	0.4	(0.1)	3.2	(1.2)
Quintana Roo	-0.7	(0.1)	-0.2	(0.1)	0.4	(0.1)	4.9	(1.4)
San Luis Potosí	-0.8	(0.2)	-0.1	(0.1)	0.4	(0.1)	4.4	(2.1)
Sinaloa	-0.4	(0.1)	0.0	(0.1)	0.1	(0.1)	1.1	(0.8)
Tabasco	-0.6	(0.1)	0.0	(0.1)	0.4	(0.1)	3.8	(1.2)
Tamaulipas	-0.5	(0.2)	0.0	(0.1)	0.2	(0.1)	1.5	(1.2)
Tlaxcala	-0.6	(0.2)	0.0	(0.1)	0.2	(0.1)	1.8	(1.0)
Veracruz	-0.4	(0.1)	-0.1	(0.1)	0.2	(0.1)	1.4	(0.8)
Yucatán	-0.6	(0.1)	-0.1	(0.1)	0.4	(0.1)	3.7	(1.5)
Zacatecas	-0.6	(0.1)	0.0	(0.1)	0.3	(0.1)	3.0	(1.3)

• PISA adjudicated region.
Notes: This table was calculated considering only students with data on the *PISA index of economic, social and cultural status*. Values that are statistically significant are indicated in bold (see Annex A3).
See Table II.4.12 for national data.
1. ESCS refers to the *PISA index of economic, social and cultural status*.
StatLink ᴍᴤᴘ http://dx.doi.org/10.1787/888932964965

[Part 6/6]

Pre-primary school attendance, mathematics performance and students' socio-economic status, by region

Table B2.II.24   *Results based on students' self-reports*

	Effect size for students who had not attended pre-primary school		Effect size for students who had attended pre-primary school for one year or less		Effect size for students who had attended pre-primary school for more than one year		Proportion of the variation in student performance explained by having attended pre-primary school for less than one year	
	Effect size	S.E.	Effect size	S.E.	Effect size	S.E.	%	S.E.
Portugal								
Alentejo	**-0.6**	(0.1)	**-0.4**	(0.1)	**0.6**	(0.1)	7.4	(1.9)
Spain								
Andalusia*	**-0.6**	(0.1)	-0.1	(0.1)	**0.3**	(0.1)	2.6	(0.8)
Aragon*	**-0.8**	(0.1)	**-0.6**	(0.1)	**0.8**	(0.1)	7.0	(1.8)
Asturias*	**-1.2**	(0.2)	**-0.9**	(0.1)	**1.0**	(0.1)	7.9	(1.9)
Balearic Islands*	**-0.9**	(0.1)	**-0.5**	(0.1)	**0.8**	(0.1)	7.6	(1.6)
Basque Country*	**-0.3**	(0.1)	**-0.3**	(0.0)	**0.3**	(0.0)	1.9	(0.5)
Cantabria*	**-0.6**	(0.1)	**-0.6**	(0.1)	**0.6**	(0.1)	3.9	(1.0)
Castile and Leon*	**-0.6**	(0.2)	**-0.7**	(0.2)	**0.7**	(0.1)	3.7	(1.6)
Catalonia*	**-0.8**	(0.1)	**-0.5**	(0.1)	**0.7**	(0.1)	4.8	(1.2)
Extremadura*	**-0.5**	(0.2)	**-0.4**	(0.1)	**0.5**	(0.1)	2.5	(0.9)
Galicia*	**-0.5**	(0.2)	**-0.6**	(0.1)	**0.6**	(0.1)	3.6	(0.9)
La Rioja*	**-1.1**	(0.2)	**-0.8**	(0.1)	**1.0**	(0.1)	11.4	(2.3)
Madrid*	**-0.5**	(0.1)	**-0.6**	(0.1)	**0.6**	(0.1)	4.2	(1.2)
Murcia*	**-0.8**	(0.1)	**-0.3**	(0.1)	**0.6**	(0.1)	5.3	(1.6)
Navarre*	**-0.4**	(0.1)	**-0.4**	(0.1)	**0.5**	(0.1)	3.4	(1.1)
United Kingdom								
England	**-0.6**	(0.1)	**-0.3**	(0.0)	**0.4**	(0.0)	3.2	(0.7)
Northern Ireland	**-0.4**	(0.1)	0.0	(0.1)	0.1	(0.1)	1.1	(0.5)
Scotland*	**-0.5**	(0.1)	**-0.1**	(0.0)	**0.2**	(0.0)	1.2	(0.5)
Wales	**-0.5**	(0.1)	**-0.2**	(0.0)	**0.3**	(0.0)	2.4	(0.6)
United States								
Connecticut*	c	c	**-0.3**	(0.1)	**0.4**	(0.1)	1.6	(0.5)
Florida*	**-0.4**	(0.2)	0.0	(0.1)	0.1	(0.1)	0.2	(0.2)
Massachusetts*	c	c	**-0.2**	(0.1)	**0.3**	(0.1)	1.0	(0.8)
Argentina								
Ciudad Autónoma de Buenos Aires*	**-0.8**	(0.2)	**-0.8**	(0.1)	**0.8**	(0.1)	7.1	(1.6)
Brazil								
Acre	**-0.5**	(0.1)	-0.1	(0.1)	**0.5**	(0.1)	7.3	(2.3)
Alagoas	**-0.4**	(0.1)	-0.1	(0.1)	**0.4**	(0.1)	4.9	(2.1)
Amapá	**-0.4**	(0.1)	-0.1	(0.1)	**0.4**	(0.1)	3.8	(1.5)
Amazonas	-0.2	(0.1)	-0.1	(0.1)	**0.3**	(0.1)	2.2	(1.8)
Bahia	**-0.4**	(0.2)	-0.1	(0.1)	**0.4**	(0.1)	4.1	(3.2)
Ceará	-0.2	(0.1)	-0.2	(0.1)	**0.3**	(0.1)	2.7	(1.9)
Espírito Santo	**-0.4**	(0.1)	0.0	(0.1)	**0.2**	(0.1)	1.6	(0.8)
Federal District	**-0.5**	(0.1)	**-0.4**	(0.1)	**0.5**	(0.1)	5.8	(1.4)
Goiás	-0.2	(0.1)	-0.2	(0.1)	**0.3**	(0.1)	2.8	(1.4)
Maranhão	0.0	(0.1)	-0.2	(0.1)	**0.2**	(0.1)	0.8	(0.7)
Mato Grosso	-0.3	(0.1)	-0.1	(0.1)	**0.4**	(0.1)	4.4	(2.0)
Mato Grosso do Sul	**-0.6**	(0.2)	-0.2	(0.1)	**0.6**	(0.1)	9.5	(3.8)
Minas Gerais	0.0	(0.1)	**-0.4**	(0.1)	**0.4**	(0.1)	3.7	(1.7)
Pará	-0.3	(0.1)	-0.1	(0.1)	**0.2**	(0.1)	1.8	(1.0)
Paraíba	**-0.4**	(0.1)	-0.2	(0.2)	**0.5**	(0.1)	5.8	(2.0)
Paraná	**-0.6**	(0.1)	-0.1	(0.2)	**0.6**	(0.2)	9.4	(3.9)
Pernambuco	-0.2	(0.1)	-0.2	(0.1)	**0.4**	(0.1)	3.2	(1.3)
Piauí	**-0.5**	(0.2)	-0.2	(0.1)	**0.4**	(0.1)	5.0	(2.8)
Rio de Janeiro	-0.3	(0.1)	-0.1	(0.1)	**0.3**	(0.1)	3.1	(1.7)
Rio Grande do Norte	**-0.4**	(0.1)	-0.2	(0.1)	**0.4**	(0.2)	5.2	(3.0)
Rio Grande do Sul	-0.3	(0.1)	0.1	(0.1)	0.1	(0.1)	1.6	(1.4)
Rondônia	-0.3	(0.1)	-0.1	(0.1)	**0.4**	(0.1)	3.3	(1.7)
Roraima	**-0.5**	(0.1)	-0.1	(0.1)	**0.4**	(0.1)	5.7	(2.6)
Santa Catarina	**-0.7**	(0.1)	-0.1	(0.1)	**0.5**	(0.1)	7.7	(2.5)
São Paulo	**-0.6**	(0.1)	**-0.2**	(0.1)	**0.4**	(0.1)	4.6	(1.2)
Sergipe	-0.2	(0.2)	**-0.3**	(0.1)	**0.4**	(0.1)	3.9	(1.4)
Tocantins	-0.2	(0.1)	-0.1	(0.1)	**0.3**	(0.1)	2.1	(1.3)
Colombia								
Bogotá	-0.2	(0.1)	0.0	(0.1)	0.1	(0.1)	0.4	(0.5)
Cali	-0.3	(0.1)	0.1	(0.1)	0.0	(0.1)	1.3	(1.0)
Manizales	**-0.4**	(0.1)	0.0	(0.1)	0.1	(0.1)	1.1	(0.9)
Medellín	**-0.7**	(0.1)	-0.1	(0.1)	**0.4**	(0.1)	5.3	(2.2)
Russian Federation								
Perm Territory region*	**-0.5**	(0.1)	**-0.3**	(0.1)	**0.4**	(0.1)	2.7	(1.0)
United Arab Emirates								
Abu Dhabi*	**-0.6**	(0.1)	0.0	(0.1)	**0.4**	(0.1)	6.7	(1.2)
Ajman	**-0.4**	(0.1)	0.0	(0.1)	**0.5**	(0.1)	4.9	(2.0)
Dubai*	**-0.6**	(0.1)	0.0	(0.0)	**0.3**	(0.0)	4.5	(0.7)
Fujairah	**-0.5**	(0.1)	-0.2	(0.2)	**0.5**	(0.1)	5.3	(1.8)
Ras al-Khaimah	-0.3	(0.1)	-0.1	(0.1)	**0.3**	(0.1)	2.7	(1.7)
Sharjah	**-0.6**	(0.2)	0.0	(0.1)	**0.4**	(0.1)	5.1	(2.9)
Umm al-Quwain	-0.3	(0.1)	-0.1	(0.2)	**0.3**	(0.1)	3.2	(2.0)

* PISA adjudicated region.

Notes: This table was calculated considering only students with data on the *PISA index of economic, social and cultural status*. Values that are statistically significant are indicated in bold (see Annex A3).

See Table II.4.12 for national data.

1. ESCS refers to the *PISA index of economic, social and cultural status*.

StatLink ⫘ http://dx.doi.org/10.1787/888932964965

[Part 1/2]
Variation in mathematics performance across students, schools and regions
Table B2.II.25 *Results based on students' self-reports*

		Observed variance							
		Observed among all students				As a % of total variance in OECD countries			
		Total variation in mathematics performance	Variation in mathematics performance within schools	Variation in mathematics performance between schools within regions	Variation in mathematics performance between regions	Total variation in mathematics performance	Variation in mathematics performance within schools	Variation in mathematics performance between schools within regions	Variation in mathematics performance between regions
OECD	Australia	9 422	6 639	2 654	128	96.0	67.7	27.1	1.3
	Belgium	11 081	5 028	5 772	281	112.9	51.2	58.8	2.9
	Canada	7 998	6 285	1 552	161	81.5	64.1	15.8	1.6
	Italy	9 309	4 145	4 395	769	94.9	42.2	44.8	7.8
	Mexico	5 547	3 540	1 762	245	56.5	36.1	18.0	2.5
	Spain	7 707	6 233	1 270	204	78.5	63.5	12.9	2.1
	United Kingdom	9 009	6 395	2 593	20	91.8	65.2	26.4	0.2
	OECD countries	9 812	5 266	3 527	1 020	100.0	53.7	35.9	10.4
Partners	Brazil	6 139	3 379	2 467	293	62.6	34.4	25.1	3.0
	Colombia	5 589	3 537	1 941	112	57.0	36.0	19.8	1.1
	United Arab Emirates	8 187	4 430	3 553	204	83.4	45.1	36.2	2.1

Note: Three level models at the country level with available data for regions as described in the tables of Annex B2.
1. ESCS refers to the *PISA index of economic social and cultural status*.
2. Three level model for each country where ESCS enters in the model at the student level (level 1), the mean ESCS at the schools enters at the school level (level 2) and the mean ESCS at the region level enters at the regional level (level 3).
StatLink ⟮⟯ http://dx.doi.org/10.1787/888932964965

[Part 2/2]
Variation in mathematics performance across students, schools and regions
Table B2.II.25 *Results based on students' self-reports*

		Accounting for ESCS[1] at the individual, school and regional level											
		Observed among those with valid ESCS				Variance after accounting for ESCS differences[2]				% explained by ESCS at student, school and regional level			
		Total variation in mathematics performance	Variation in mathematics performance within schools	Variation in mathematics performance between schools within regions	Variation in mathematics performance between regions	Total variation in mathematics performance	Variation in mathematics performance within schools	Variation in mathematics performance between schools within regions	Variation in mathematics performance between regions	Total variation in mathematics performance	Variation in mathematics performance within schools	Variation in mathematics performance between schools within regions	Variation in mathematics performance between regions
OECD	Australia	9 201	6 538	2 531	131	7 483	6 253	1 132	98	18.7	4.4	55.3	25.5
	Belgium	11 004	5 008	5 717	279	6 473	4 817	1 572	84	41.2	3.8	72.5	70.0
	Canada	7 793	6 128	1 504	161	6 761	5 816	809	136	13.2	5.1	46.2	15.5
	Italy	9 299	4 109	4 425	764	6 483	4 083	1 995	405	30.3	0.7	54.9	47.0
	Mexico	5 542	3 532	1 763	247	4 618	3 514	1 001	104	16.7	0.5	43.2	57.9
	Spain	7 606	6 145	1 271	190	6 221	5 594	599	28	18.2	9.0	52.9	85.3
	United Kingdom	8 720	6 264	2 431	25	6 949	5 987	930	32	20.3	4.4	61.7	0.0
	OECD countries	7 149	5 000	1 600	549	7 149	5 000	1 600	549	23.0	3.4	47.8	47.6
Partners	Brazil	6 139	3 379	2 467	293	4 532	3 338	1 037	157	26.2	1.2	58.0	46.4
	Colombia	5 588	3 534	1 936	119	4 305	3 443	826	35	23.0	2.6	57.3	70.3
	United Arab Emirates	8 178	4 422	3 551	205	6 618	4 348	2 240	30	19.1	1.7	36.9	85.3

Note: Three level models at the country level with available data for regions as described in the tables of Annex B2.
1. ESCS refers to the *PISA index of economic social and cultural status*.
2. Three level model for each country where ESCS enters in the model at the student level (level 1), the mean ESCS at the schools enters at the school level (level 2) and the mean ESCS at the region level enters at the regional level (level 3).
StatLink ⟮⟯ http://dx.doi.org/10.1787/888932964965

ANNEX B3
LIST OF TABLES AVAILABLE ON LINE

The following tables are available in electronic form only.

Chapter 2 Equity in outcomes

http://dx.doi.org/10.1787/888932964908

| WEB | Table II.2.2 | Elements of socio-economic status, by quarters of socio-economic status within countries |
| WEB | Table II.2.3 | Elements of socio-economic status across countries |

Chapter 3 The challenge of diversity

http://dx.doi.org/10.1787/888932964927

| WEB | Table II.3.12 | Difference in mathematics performance, by immigrant background |
| WEB | Table II.3.13 | Relationship between student characteristics, socio-economic elements and mathematics performance |

Chapter 4 Equity in opportunities to learn and in resources

http://dx.doi.org/10.1787/888932964946

WEB	Table II.4.4	Correlation between student performance and selected student, school and parent characteristics
WEB	Table II.4.5	Correlation between student socio-economic status and selected student, school and parent characteristics
WEB	Table II.4.6	Correlation between school socio-economic profile and selected student, school and parent characteristics
WEB	Table II.4.7	Correlation of the variation of students' socio-economic status within a school and selected student, school and parent characteristics
WEB	Table II.4.11	Impact of socio-economic status after accounting for student characteristics and educational resources at school

Annex B2 Results for regions within countries

http://dx.doi.org/10.1787/888932964965

WEB	Table B2.II.4	Percentage of resilient students and low-achievers among disadvantaged students in PISA 2012, by gender and region
WEB	Table B2.II.8	Relationship between mathematics performance and school location, by region
WEB	Table B2.II.10	Mathematics performance, immigrant background and language spoken at home, by region
WEB	Table B2.II.11	Mathematics performance and immigrant background for first- and second-generation students, by region
WEB	Table B2.II.12	Proficiency levels in mathematics, by immigrant background for first- and second-generation students, by region
WEB	Table B2.II.13	Concentration of immigrant students in school, by region
WEB	Table B2.II.14	Concentration, in school, of students who do not speak the language of assessment at home, by region
WEB	Table B2.II.17	Correlation between student performance and selected student and school characteristics, by region
WEB	Table B2.II.18	Correlation between student socio-economic status and selected student and school characteristics, by region
WEB	Table B2.II.19	Correlation between school socio-economic profile and selected student and school characteristics, by region
WEB	Table B2.II.20	Correlation of the variation of students' socio-economic status within a school and selected student and school characteristics, by region
WEB	Table B2.II.21	Inequality in access to educational resources: Student-teacher ratio, by region
WEB	Table B2.II.22	Inequality in access to educational resources: Percentage of teachers with university-level qualifications, by region
WEB	Table B2.II.23	Inequality in access to educational resources: Disciplinary climate, by region

These tables, as well as additional material, may be found at: *www.pisa.oecd.org*.

Annex C

THE DEVELOPMENT AND IMPLEMENTATION OF PISA – A COLLABORATIVE EFFORT

PISA is a collaborative effort, bringing together experts from the participating countries, steered jointly by their governments on the basis of shared, policy-driven interests.

A PISA Governing Board, on which each country is represented, determines the policy priorities for PISA, in the context of OECD objectives, and oversees adherence to these priorities during the implementation of the programme. This includes setting priorities for the development of indicators, for establishing the assessment instruments, and for reporting the results.

Experts from participating countries also serve on working groups that are charged with linking policy objectives with the best internationally available technical expertise. By participating in these expert groups, countries ensure that the instruments are internationally valid and take into account the cultural and educational contexts in OECD member and partner countries and economies, that the assessment materials have strong measurement properties, and that the instruments place emphasise authenticity and educational validity.

Through National Project Managers, participating countries and economies implement PISA at the national level subject to the agreed administration procedures. National Project Managers play a vital role in ensuring that the implementation of the survey is of high quality, and verify and evaluate the survey results, analyses, reports and publications.

The design and implementation of the surveys, within the framework established by the PISA Governing Board, is the responsibility of external contractors. For PISA 2012, the development and implementation of the cognitive assessment and questionnaires, and of the international options, was carried out by a consortium led by the Australian Council for Educational Research (ACER). Other partners in this Consortium include cApStAn Linguistic Quality Control in Belgium, the Centre de Recherche Public Henri Tudor (CRP-HT) in Luxembourg, the Department of Teacher Education and School Research (ILS) at the University of Oslo in Norway, the Deutsches Institut für Internationale Pädagogische Forschung (DIPF) in Germany, the Educational Testing Service (ETS) in the United States, the Leibniz Institute for Science and Mathematics Education (IPN) in Germany, the National Institute for Educational Policy Research in Japan (NIER), the Unité d'analyse des systèmes et des pratiques d'enseignement (aSPe) at the University of Liège in Belgium, and WESTAT in the United States, as well as individual consultants from several countries. ACER also collaborated with Achieve Inc. in the United States to develop the mathematics framework for PISA 2012.

The OECD Secretariat has overall managerial responsibility for the programme, monitors its implementation daily, acts as the secretariat for the PISA Governing Board, builds consensus among countries and serves as the interlocutor between the PISA Governing Board and the international Consortium charged with implementing the activities. The OECD Secretariat also produces the indicators and analyses and prepares the international reports and publications in co-operation with the PISA Consortium and in close consultation with member and partner countries and economies both at the policy level (PISA Governing Board) and at the level of implementation (National Project Managers).

PISA Governing Board

Chair of the PISA Governing Board: Lorna Bertrand

OECD countries
Australia: Tony Zanderigo
Austria: Mark Német
Belgium: Christiane Blondin and Isabelle Erauw
Canada: Pierre Brochu, Patrick Bussiere and Tomasz Gluszynski
Chile: Leonor Cariola Huerta
Czech Republic: Jana Paleckova
Denmark: Tine Bak and Elsebeth Aller
Estonia: Maie Kitsing
Finland: Tommi Karjalainen
France: Bruno Trosseille
Germany: Elfriede Ohrnberger and Susanne von Below
Greece: Vassilia Hatzinikita and Chryssa Sofianopoulou
Hungary: Benõ Csapó
Iceland: Júlíus Björnsson
Ireland: Jude Cosgrove and Gerry Shiel
Israel: Michal Beller and Hagit Glickman
Italy: Paolo Sestito
Japan: Ryo Watanabe
Korea: Sungsook Kim and Keunwoo Lee
Luxembourg: Amina Kafai

Mexico: Francisco Ciscomani and Eduardo Backhoff Escudero
Netherlands: Paul van Oijen
New Zealand: Lynne Whitney
Norway : Anne-Berit Kavli and Alette Schreiner
Poland: Stanislaw Drzazdzewski and Hania Bouacid
Portugal: Luisa Canto and Castro Loura
Slovak Republic: Romana Kanovska and Paulina Korsnakova
Slovenia: Andreja Barle Lakota
Spain: Ismael Sanz Labrador
Sweden: Anita Wester
Switzerland: Vera Husfeldt and Claudia Zahner Rossier
Turkey: Nurcan Devici and Mustafa Nadir Çalis
United Kingdom: Lorna Bertrand and Jonathan Wright
United States: Jack Buckley, Dana Kelly and Daniel McGrath

Observers
Albania: Ermal Elezi
Argentina: Liliana Pascual
Brazil: Luiz Claudio Costa
Bulgaria: Neda Kristanova
Chinese Taipei: Gwo-Dong Chen and Chih-Wei Hue
Colombia: Adriana Molina
Costa Rica: Leonardo Garnier Rimolo
Croatia: Michelle Bras Roth

Hong Kong-China: Esther Sui-chu Ho

Indonesia: Khairil Anwar Notodiputro

Jordan: Khattab Mohammad Abulibdeh

Kazakhstan: Almagul Kultumanova

Latvia: Andris Kangro, Ennata Kivrina and Dita Traidas

Lithuania: Rita Dukynaite

Macao-China: Leong Lai

Montenegro: Zeljko Jacimovic

Panama: Arturo Rivera

Peru: Liliana Miranda Molina

Qatar: Hamda Al Sulaiti

Romania: Roxana Mihail

Russian Federation: Isak Froumin and Galina Kovaleva

Serbia: Dragica Pavlovic-Babic

Shanghai-China: Minxuan Zhang

Singapore: Khah Gek Low

Thailand: Precharn Dechsri

United Arab Emirates: Moza al Ghufly and Ayesha G. Khalfan Almerri

Uruguay: Andrés Peri and Maria Helvecia Sanchez Nunez

Viet Nam: Le Thi My Ha

PISA 2012 National Project Managers

Albania: Alfonso Harizaj

Argentina: Liliana Pascual

Australia: Sue Thomson

Austria: Ursula Schwantner

Belgium: Inge De Meyer and Ariane Baye

Brazil: João Galvão Bacchetto

Bulgaria: Svetla Petrova

Canada: Pierre Brochu and Tamara Knighton

Chile: Ema Lagos Campos

Colombia: Francisco Reyes

Costa Rica: Lilliam Mora

Croatia: Michelle Bras Roth

Czech Republic: Jana Paleckova

Denmark: Niels Egelund

Estonia: Gunda Tire

Finland: Jouni Välijärvi

France: Ginette Bourny

Germany: Christine Sälzer and Manfred Prenzel

Greece: Vassilia Hatzinikita

Hong Kong-China: Esther Sui-chu Ho

Hungary: Ildikó Balazsi

Iceland: Almar Midvik Halldorsson

Indonesia: Yulia Wardhani Nugaan and Hari Setiadi

Ireland: Gerry Shiel and Rachel Perkins

Israel: Joel Rapp and Inbal Ron-Kaplan

Italy: Carlo Di Chiacchio

Japan: Ryo Watanabe

Jordan: Khattab Mohammad Abulibdeh

Kazakhstan: Gulmira Berdibayeva and Zhannur Azmagambetova

Korea: Ji-Min Cho and Mi-Young Song

Latvia: Andris Kangro

Liechtenstein: Christian Nidegger

Lithuania: Mindaugas Stundza

Luxembourg: Bettina Boehm

Macao-China: Kwok Cheung Cheung

Malaysia: Ihsan Ismail and Muhamad Zaini Md Zain

Mexico: María Antonieta Díaz Gutierrez

Montenegro: Divna Paljevic Sturm

Netherlands: Jesse Koops

New Zealand: Kate Lang and Steven May

Norway: Marit Kjaernsli

Peru: Liliana Miranda Molina

Poland: Michal Federowicz

Portugal: Ana Sousa Ferreira

Qatar: Aysha Al-Hashemi and Assad Tounakti

Romania: Silviu Cristian Mirescu

Russian Federation: Galina Kovaleva

Scotland: Rebecca Wheater

Serbia: Dragica Pavlovic-Babic

Shanghai-China: Jing Lu and Minxuan Zhang

Singapore: Chew Leng Poon and Sean Tan

Slovak Republic: Julia Miklovicova and Jana Ferencova

Slovenia: Mojca Straus

Spain: Lis Cercadillo Pérez

Sweden: Magnus Oskarsson

Switzerland: Christian Nidegger

Chinese Taipei: Pi-Hsia Hung

Thailand: Sunee Klainin

Tunisia: Mohamed Kamel Essid

Turkey: Serdar Aztekin

United Arab Emirates: Moza al Ghufly

United Kingdom: Rebecca Wheater

United States: Dana Kelly and Holly Xie

Uruguay: Maria Helvecia Sánchez Nunez

Viet Nam: Thi My Ha Le

OECD Secretariat

Andreas Schleicher (Strategic development)

Marilyn Achiron (Editorial support)

Francesco Avvisati (Analytic services)

Brigitte Beyeler (Administrative support)

Simone Bloem (Analytic services)

Marika Boiron (Translation support)

Francesca Borgonovi (Analytic services)

Jenny Bradshaw (Project management)

Célia Braga-Schich (Production support)

Claire Chetcuti (Administrative support)

Michael Davidson (Project management and analytic services)

Cassandra Davis (Dissemination co-ordination)

Elizabeth Del Bourgo (Production support)

Juliet Evans (Administration and partner country/economy relations)

Tue Halgreen (Project management)

Miyako Ikeda (Analytic services)

Tadakazu Miki (Analytic services)

Guillermo Montt (Analytic services)

Giannina Rech (Analytic services)

Diana Tramontano (Administration)

Sophie Vayssettes (Analytic services)

Elisabeth Villoutreix (Production co-ordination)

Pablo Zoido (Analytic services)

PISA 2012 mathematics expert group

Kaye Stacey (Chair) (University of Melbourne, Australia)

Caroline Bardini (University of Melbourne, Australia)

Werner Blum (University of Kassel, Germany)

Joan Ferrini-Mundy (Michigan State University, United States)

Solomon Garfunkel (COMAP, United States)

Toshikazu Ikeda (Yokohama National University, Japan)

Zbigniew Marciniak (Warsaw University, Poland)

Mogens Niss (Roskilde University, Denmark)

Martin Ripley (World Class Arena Limited, United Kingdom)

William Schmidt (Michigan State University, United States)

PISA 2012 problem solving expert group

Joachim Funke (Chair) (University of Heidelberg, Germany)

Benő Csapó (University of Szeged, Hungary)

John Dossey (Illinois State University, United States)

Arthur Graesser (The University of Memphis United States)

Detlev Leutner (Duisburg-Essen University, Germany)

Romain Martin (Université de Luxembourg FLSHASE, Luxembourg)

Richard Mayer (University of California, United States)

Ming Ming Tan (Ministry of Education, Singapore)

PISA 2012 financial literacy expert group

Annamaria Lusardi (Chair) (The George Washington University School of Business, United States)

Jean-Pierre Boisivon (Université de Paris II Panthéon-Assas, France)

Diana Crossan (Commission for Financial Literacy and Retirement Income, New Zealand)

Peter Cuzner (Australian Securities and Investments Commission, Australia)

Jeanne Hogarth (Federal Reserve System, United States)

Dušan Hradil (Ministry of Finance, Czech Republic)

Stan Jones (Consultant, Canada)

Sue Lewis (Consultant, United Kingdom)

PISA 2012 questionnaire expert group

Eckhard Klieme (Chair) (Deutsches Institut für Internationale Pädagogische Forschung (DIPF), Germany)

Eduardo Backhoff (University of Baja California at the Institute of Educational Research and Development, Mexico)

Ying-yi Hong (Nanyang Business School of Nanyang Technological University, Singapore)

David Kaplan (University of Wisconsin – Madison, United States)

Henry Levin (Columbia University, United States)

Jaap Scheerens (University of Twente, Netherlands)

William Schmidt (Michigan State University, United States)

Fons van de Vijver (Tilburg University, Netherlands)

Technical advisory group

Keith Rust (Chair) (Westat, United States)

Ray Adams (ACER, Australia)

Cees Glas (University of Twente, Netherlands)

John de Jong (Language Testing Services, Netherlands)

David Kaplan (University of Wisconsin – Madison, United States)

Christian Monseur (University of Liège, Belgium)

Sophia Rabe-Hesketh (University of California – Berkeley, United States)

Thierry Rocher (Ministry of Education, France)

Norman Verhelst (CITO, Netherlands)

Kentaro Yamamoto (ETS, United States)

Rebecca Zwick (University of California, United States)

PISA 2012 Consortium

Australian Council for Educational Research

Ray Adams (International Project Director)

Susan Bates (Project administration)

Alla Berezner (Data management and analysis)

Yan Bibby (Data processing and analysis)

Phillipe Bickham (IT services)

Esther Brakey (Administrative support)

Robin Buckley (IT services)

Mark Butler (Financial literacy instruments and test development)

Wei Buttress (Project administration and quality monitoring)

Renee Chow (Data processing and analysis)

John Cresswell (Reporting and dissemination)

Alex Daraganov (Data processing and analysis)

Jorge Fallas (Data processing and analysis)

Kate Fitzgerald (Data processing and sampling)

Kim Fitzgerald (IT Services)

Paul Golden (IT and helpdesk support)

Jennifer Hong (Data processing and sampling)

Nora Kovarcikova (Survey operations)

Winson Lam (IT services)

Petra Lietz (Questionnaire development)

Tom Lumley (Reading instruments and test development)

Greg Macaskill (Data management and processing and sampling)

Ron Martin (Science instruments and test development)

Barry McCrae (Problem solving and science instrument and test development)

Louise McDonald (Graphic design)

Juliette Mendelovits (Reading and financial literacy instruments and test development)

Martin Murphy (Field operations and sampling)

Thoa Nguyen (Data processing and analysis)

Stephen Oakes (IT management and support)

Elizabeth O'Grady (Questionnaire development and project support)

Penny Pearson (Administrative support)

Ray Peck (Mathematics and financial literacy instruments and test development)

Fei Peng (Quality monitoring and project support)

Ray Philpot (Problem Solving instruments and test development)

Anna Plotka (Graphic design)

Dara Ramalingam (Reading instruments and test development)

Sima Rodrigues (Data processing and analysis)

Alla Routitsky (Data management and processing)

James Spithill (Mathematics instruments and test development)

Rachel Stanyon (Project support)

Naoko Tabata (Survey operations)

Stephanie Templeton (Project administration and support)

Mollie Tobin (Questionnaire development and project support)

David Tout (Mathematics instruments and test development)

Ross Turner (Management, mathematics instruments and test development)

Maryanne Van Grunsven (Project support)

Charlotte Waters (Project administration, data processing and analysis)

Maurice Walker (Management, computer-based assessment)

Louise Wenn (Data processing and analysis)

Yan Wiwecka (IT services)

cApStAn Linguistic Quality Control (BELGIUM)

Raphael Choppinet (Computer-based verification management)

Steve Dept (Translation and verification operations)

Andrea Ferrari (Linguistic quality assurance and quality control designs)

Musab Hayatli (Right-to-left scripts, cultural adaptations)

Elica Krajceva (Questionnaire verification co-ordinator)

Shinoh Lee (Cognitive test verification co-ordinator)

Irene Liberati (Manuals verification co-ordinator)

Laura Wayrynen (Verifier training and verification procedures)

Educational Testing Service (ETS)

Jonas Bertling (Questionnaire instruments and test development)

Irwin Kirsch (Reading Components)

Patricia Klag (Problem-solving instruments and test development)

Patrick Kyllonen (Questionnaire instruments and test development)

Marylou Lennon (Questionnaire instruments and test development)

Richard Roberts (Questionnaire instruments and test development)

Matthias von Davier (Questionnaire instruments and test development)

Kentaro Yamamoto (Member TAG, problem-solving instruments and test development)

Deutches Institut für Internationale Pädagogische Forschung (DIPF, GERMANY)

Frank Goldhammer (Test developer, problem solving)

Eckhard Klieme (Chair of Questionnaire Expert Group)

Silke Hertel (Questionnaire development)

Jean-Paul Reeff (International Consultant)

Heiko Rolke (Software Design & Software Development

Management [Delivery System, Translation System])

Brigitte Steinert (Questionnaire development)

Svenja Vieluf (Questionnaire development)

Institutt for Lærerutdanning Og Skoleutvikling (ILS, NORWAY)

Bjornar Alseth (Mathematics instruments and test development)

Ole Kristian Bergem (Mathematics instruments and test development)

Knut Skrindo (Mathematics instruments and test development)

Rolf V. Olsen (Mathematics instruments and test development)

Arne Hole (Mathematics instruments and test development)

Therese Hopfenbeck (Problem-solving instruments and test development)

Leibniz Institute for Science and Mathematics Education (IPN, GERMANY)

Christoph Duchhardt (Mathematics instruments and test development)

Aiso Heinze (Mathematics instruments and test development)

Eva Knopp (Mathematics instruments and test development)

Martin Senkbeil (Mathematics instruments and test development)

National Institute for Educational Policy Research (NIER, JAPAN)

Keiichi Nishimura (Mathematics instruments and test development)

Yuji Surata (Mathematics instruments and test development)

The TAO Initiative: Henry Tudor Public Research Centre, University of Luxembourg (LUXEMBOURG)

Joel Billard (Software Engineer, School Questionnaire)

Marilyn Binkley (Project Consultant, Assessment Expert)

Jerome Bogaerts (Software Engineer, TAO Platform)

Gilbert Busana (Electronic Instruments, Usability)

Christophe Henry (System Engineer, School Questionnaire and Hosting)

Raynald Jadoul (Technical Lead, School Questionnaire and Electronic Instruments)

Isabelle Jars (Project Manager)

Vincent Koenig (Electronic Instruments, Usability)

Thibaud Latour (Project Leader, TAO Platform)

Lionel Lecaque (Software Engineer, Quality)

Primael Lorbat (Software Engineer, Electronic Instruments)

Romain Martin (Problem Solving Expert Group Member)

Matteo Melis (Software Engineer, School Questionnaire)

Patrick Plichart (Software Architect, TAO Platform)

Vincent Porro (Software Engineer, Electronic Instruments)

Igor Ribassin (Software Engineer, Electronic Instruments)

Somsack Sipasseuth (Software Engineer, Electronic Instruments)

Unité d'analyse des Systèmes et des Pratiques d'enseignement (ASPE, BELGIUM)

Isabelle Demonty (Mathematics instruments and test development)

Annick Fagnant (Mathematics instruments and test development)

Anne Matoul (French source development)

Christian Monseur (Member of Technical Advisory Group)

WESTAT

Susan Fuss (Sampling and weighting)

Amita Gopinath (Weighting)

Jing Kang (Sampling and weighting)

Sheila Krawchuk (Sampling, weighting and quality monitoring)

Thanh Le (Sampling, weighting and quality monitoring)

John Lopdell (Sampling and weighting)

Keith Rust (Director of the PISA Consortium for sampling and weighting)

Erin Willey (Sampling and weighting)

Shawn Lu (Weighting)

Teresa Strickler (Weighting)

Yumiko Sugawara (Weighting)

Joel Wakesberg (Sampling and weighting)

Sergey Yagodin (Weighting)

Achieve Inc.

Michael Cohen (Mathematics framework development)

Kaye Forgione (Mathematics framework development)

Morgan Saxby (Mathematics framework development)

Laura Slover (Mathematics framework development)

Bonnie Verrico (Project support)

HallStat SPRL

Beatrice Halleux (Consultant, translation/verification referee, French source development)

University of Heidelberg

Joachim Funke (Chair, Problem Solving Expert Group)

Samuel Greiff (Problem-solving instruments and test development)

University of Melbourne

Caroline Bardini (Member Mathematics Expert Group)

John Dowsey (Mathematics instruments and test development)

Derek Holton (Mathematics instruments and test development)

Kaye Stacey (Chair Mathematics Expert Group)

Other experts

Michael Besser (Mathematics instruments and test development, University of Kassel, Germany)

Khurrem Jehangir (Data analysis for TAG, University of Twente, Netherlands)

Kees Lagerwaard (Mathematics instruments and test development, Institute for Educational Measurement of Netherlands, Netherlands)

Dominik Leiss (Mathematics instruments and test development, University of Kassel, Germany)

Anne-Laure Monnier (Consultant French source development, France)

Hanako Senuma (Mathematics instruments and test development, Tamagawa University, Japan)

Publication layout

Fung Kwan Tam

ORGANISATION FOR ECONOMIC CO-OPERATION AND DEVELOPMENT

The OECD is a unique forum where governments work together to address the economic, social and environmental challenges of globalisation. The OECD is also at the forefront of efforts to understand and to help governments respond to new developments and concerns, such as corporate governance, the information economy and the challenges of an ageing population. The Organisation provides a setting where governments can compare policy experiences, seek answers to common problems, identify good practice and work to co-ordinate domestic and international policies.

The OECD member countries are: Australia, Austria, Belgium, Canada, Chile, the Czech Republic, Denmark, Estonia, Finland, France, Germany, Greece, Hungary, Iceland, Ireland, Israel, Italy, Japan, Korea, Luxembourg, Mexico, the Netherlands, New Zealand, Norway, Poland, Portugal, the Slovak Republic, Slovenia, Spain, Sweden, Switzerland, Turkey, the United Kingdom and the United States. The European Union takes part in the work of the OECD.

OECD Publishing disseminates widely the results of the Organisation's statistics gathering and research on economic, social and environmental issues, as well as the conventions, guidelines and standards agreed by its members.

OECD PUBLISHING, 2, rue André-Pascal, 75775 PARIS CEDEX 16
(98 2013 05 1P) ISBN 978-92-64-20112-5 – No. 60967 2013-04